Caerphilly Castle (from a photograph by Collings).

GRIFFITHS AND WATSON.

Annals and Antiquities

OF

THE COUNTIES

AND

COUNTY FAMILIES OF WALES

CONTAINING

A RECORD OF ALL RANKS OF THE GENTRY, THEIR LINEAGE, ALLIANCES, APPOINTMENTS, ARMORIAL ENSIGNS, AND RESIDENCES;

Ancient Pedigrees and Memorials of Old and Extinct Families;

NOTICES OF THE HISTORY, ANTIQUITIES, PHYSICAL FEATURES, CHIEF ESTATES, GEOLOGY, AND INDUSTRY OF EACH COUNTY;

ROLLS OF HIGH SHERIFFS AND MEMBERS OF PARLIAMENT FOR THREE HUNDRED YEARS, ETC., ETC.

ALL COMPILED BY DIRECT VISITATION OF THE COUNTIES, AND FROM RELIABLE AND ORIGINAL SOURCES.

With numerous Illustrations on Wood from Photographs.

BY THOMAS NICHOLAS, M.A., PH.D, F.G.S., &c.

Author of " The Pedigree of the English People," &c.

SECOND ISSUE, REVISED AND MUCH ENLARGED.

IN TWO VOLUMES.

VOL II.

GENEALOGICAL PUBLISHING CO., INC.

First printing: London, 1872
Second printing, revised and enlarged: London, 1875

Reprinted by Genealogical Publishing Co., Inc.
Baltimore, Maryland, 1991, 2000, 2011

Library of Congress Catalogue Card Number 91-72170

ISBN, Volume II: 978-0-8063-1316-0
ISBN, the two-volume set: 978-0-8063-1314-6

Made in the United States of America

(*From the Beaufort Progress*, 1684.)

MARGAM ABBEY, AS IT WAS IN 1684.

 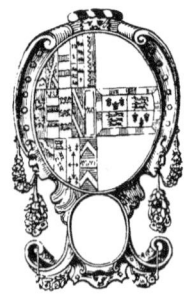

ARMS OF SIR RICE MANSELL.   MANSELL IMPALING SOMERSET.

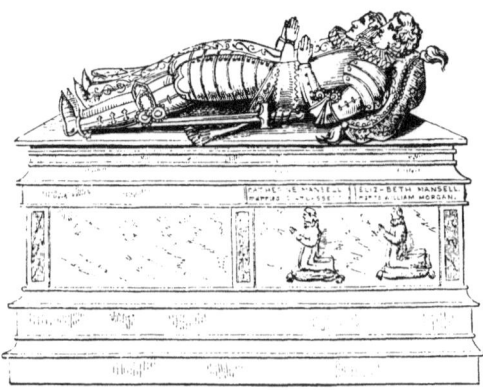

TOMB OF SIR RICE MANSELL, KT., OF MARGAM (*d.* 1589), AND DAME CECIL HIS WIFE.

"Caer wen y barwn . . .
Y sy gaer unvaint a llys Greinvil"
(To Grenville's palace is the baron's fair fortress equal).

Margam Abbey, the next antiquarian monument of importance as we move eastward, has a fame noted as that of Nêdd, albeit the sight of its desolation is not so impressive. It has the advantage of perishing amid scenes of unsurpassed quiet, the songs of birds, and the shelter of mighty forest trees; while the ruins of Neath Abbey and Castle are made to lie in deeper gloom by the grime and smoke, the stifling breath of furnaces, the din and turmoil on all sides surrounding them. The abbey of Margam stands in the extensive park of the demesne of Margam, the seat of C. R. Mansel Talbot, Esq., M.P., and formerly of his ancestors, the Mansels of Margam, Penrice, &c.; and was unquestionably the nucleus around which this great historic manor and its fame and influence grew. The date of its foundation, if we take Dugdale as our guide, was A.D. 1147. Its founder was Robert,

MARGAM ABBEY—THE CHAPTERHOUSE.

Earl of Gloucester, natural son of Henry I., who married the daughter of Fitzhamon, the Norman Lord of Glamorgan, and succeeded him in the lordship. Giraldus Cambrensis, who visited the place in 1188, says, "We pursued our journey by the little cell of Ewennith [the abbey of Ewenny not having been *seen*, perhaps] to the noble Cistercian monastery of Margan. This monastery, under the direction of Conan, a learned and prudent abbot, was at this time more celebrated for its charitable deeds than any other of that order in Wales. On this account it is an undoubted fact that, as a reward for that abundant charity which the monastery had always in times of need exercised towards strangers and poor persons in a season of approaching famine, their corn and provisions were perceptibly, by divine assistance, increased, like the widow's cruse of oil by the means of the prophet Elijah." Then come a series of strange prodigies, the relation of which, in Giraldus's estimation, enhanced the glory of this celebrated abbey and its monks.

After the dissolution of the monasteries by Henry VIII., the abbey of Margam, with its wide domain, whose revenues were valued at £181 7s. 4d., was sold to Sir Rice Mansel, of Oxwich Castle, who fitted up part of the building, with extensive additions, as a family residence of no mean splendour, and this for several generations continued to be the chief abode of the Mansels. In the *Beaufort Progress* the following account is given of this magnificent abbey residence, as it stood in 1684:—

"Margam or Margan was anciently an abbey, one of whose abbots, John Delaware, became the thirty-ninth Bishop of Landaff, and died June 30, 1256. The arms in the margin [of the Book] of Gwrgan ap Ithell, King of Glamorgan, viz., *Mars*, three chevronels, *Luna*, are often repeated in the old stone worke of Margham."

"Margham is a very noble seat, first purchased by Sir Rice Mansell, Knight, who, with his lady, ly buried in Little St. Bartholomew's, neer Smithfield, London. It appears, from some noble ruines about it, to have been formed out of an ancient religious house; the modern additions are very stately, of which the stables are of freestone, . . . the roof being ceiled, and adorned with cornishes and fretwork of goodly artifice."

"The ancient gate-house, before the court of the house, remaines unaltered, because of an old prophesie among the bards thus concerning it and this ffamily, namely, 'That as soon as this porch or gate-house shall be pulled down this family shall decline and go to decay; *ideo quære*.'"

"Its scituation is among excellent springs, furnishing all y$_e$ offices thereof with excellent water, att the foot of prodigious high hilles of woods, shelter for the deer, about a mile

MARGAM ABBEY—THE CRYPT.

distant from an arm of the sea, parting this shore and the county of Cornwall in England, below which, and washed almost round with the salt water, is a marsh, whereto the deer, the tide being low, resort much by swimming, and thrive to such an extraordinary weight and fatness as I never saw or heard the like."

The Duke of Beaufort, as the Lord President of Wales, was welcomed on this stately

(*From the Beaufort Progress,* 1684.)

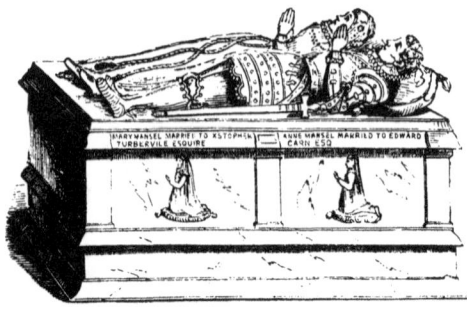

Tomb of Sir Edward Mansel, Kt., of Margam, (*d* 1585), and Jane Somerset his Wife.

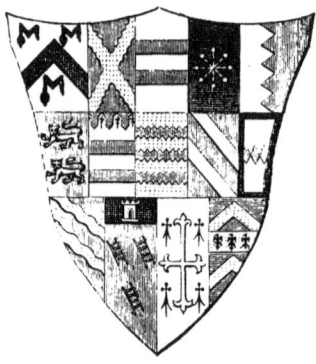

Arms of Sir Rice Mansel, of Margam, with 14 Quarterings.

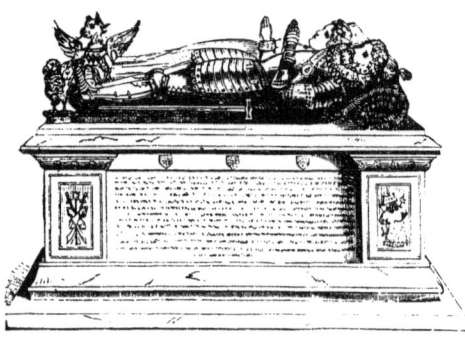

Tomb of Sir Lewis Mansel, Bart., of Margam, and Elizabeth his Wife.

occasion at Margam, as indeed everywhere, with the greatest "loyalty" and respect. He was "conducted to the summer banqueting-house, built after the Italian, where regular simitrie, excellent sculpture, delicate graving, and an infinity of good Dutch and other painting, make a lustre not to be imagined. Its pavements are of marbles, black, red, mixt, and white, chiefly the product of his own quarries in lands in the county. Here nothing was spared that the noble place could afford of diversion ; hence his Grace was enterteined with the pastime of seeing a brace of bucks run down by three footmen, which were afterwards led into Margham anti-court alive, and there judged fit for the table, before ye huntsman gave the fatall stroke with his semiter." The house was thrown open to all, "where as many as came, eat and drank as their appetites led them." The customs of the seventeenth century gave full licence, and we may well imagine the consequence !

It is strange how little notice the Duke, or his secretary and reporter, T. Dineley, took of the abbey buildings which still in great part survived. One of the objects of the *Progress*, judging from the result, was to collect *monumental inscriptions*, and several of these, with neat cuts of the massive altar-tombs of the Mansels, with effigies in full armour, are given. They are described as being "in a small neat chapell on ye south side of the chancell." An "honorary monument in white marble, carrying a representation of Sir Rice Mansell, Knight, dame Cecill, his lady, at length lying on cusheons" (died A.D. 1589, but buried in London) ; others " to Sir Edward Mansell and the Right Hon. dame Jane, his lady, youngest daughter of Henry Somerset, Lord Herbert, seconde Earle of Worcester of that name ; Sir Lewys Mansell, Kt. and Bart.," and " dilectissima ejus conjux Elizabetha," &c., are given. There they lay, and there perhaps they still lie, effigies and all, a peaceful and distinguished line—once the lords of many acres, the holders of great entertainments, warriors and statesmen :—

> " The knights are dust,
> And their good swords are rust,
> Their souls are with the saints, we trust."

The *Progress* is not unmindful of heraldry. " The paternall coat of the Mansells is—*Argent, a chevron between three maunches or, sleeves sable.* This word maunche is French, and hath its derivation from the Latin word *manica*, signifying the sleeve of a garment."

The male line of the Mansels of Margam became extinct in 1750 ; some years after this, about 1780, the house was pulled down, and its contents removed to Penrice Castle. The abbey chapterhouse was still nearly perfect in 1774, when Mr. Wyndham visited the place ; but the ruins were left uncared for, and went into rapid decay.

The modern mansion of Margam is a superb structure. (See further *Talbot of Margam*.)

But what of the earlier tombs of Margam Abbey ? of the long succession of abbots and of holy monks, whose crosiers and crosses, with their names, once marked many a stone of the place, and had been viewed with reverence by the eyes of many generations? In the duke's progress no mention is made of them ! They had given place to a new generation of tombs, more splendid and more interesting, which themselves have now become "relics of antiquity." Still, in some obscure corners of chapel or crypt some of them must have lain. The lords of Avan, large contributors to the abbey, and buried there, must have had some durable memorials. A fragment of an effigy, in chain mail, supposed to be one of them, still exists, but without name or other sign ; and two elegantly sculptured stones, one bearing a foliated pastoral staff of the twelfth century with imperfect inscriptions. The inscription on one of these is legible :—

"Constans et certus, jacet hic Ryewallis opertus,
Abbas Robertus, cujus Deus esto misertus."

Camden notices a stone with a crosier, a memorial of "Abbot Henry," as in his time covering a drain. The duke commemorates in his progress only the family who entertained him The old abbey belonged to a corrupter phase of religion. The reformed church now set up —though at the date of the progress, the days of the Rye House Plot, and Charles II.'s sorry exit from the stage of life, in a tottering state—must at least on the surface be respected; and prudence might counsel silence about abbots and monks, even though belonging only to the dead past.

Kenfig town and Castle, both alike mere fragments left on the strand, not far from Margam, supply to that splendid demesne the most striking contrast. The early records say that Kenfig was a princely British residence, retained by Fitzhamon as part of his own acquisitions in Glamorgan. The town, once large, and still recognised in the formalities of county business as a contributory borough, was partly destroyed in the sixteenth century by a fearful storm and inundation of the sea, which left the place and adjacent lands covered by a wilderness of sand.

The *Ogham stone* of Kenfig, on the road-side between Kenfig and Margam, was, if we remember rightly, the first monument with true "Ogham" characters discovered in Wales. Since that time six others have been made out. (See on other Ogham stones, p. 155.) The stone itself was long known, and mentioned by Camden as bearing the inscription PUNPEIUS CARANTORIUS, probably in memory of some man, Briton or Roman, of Roman or post-Roman times; but the marginal indentations it bears had not been thought worthy of attention until made out by Mr. Westwood as characters of the Ogham alphabet. This monument is an undressed monolith, standing about 4 ft. 6 in. above ground. The Ogham does not correspond with the Roman inscription, and Camden is not quite correct in his rendering of the latter. (See *Archæol. Cambr.*, i., 182.)

Coity Castle, near Bridgend, marks a spot of historic note more than coeval with the Norman subjugation of Glamorgan. The name, *Coed-ty*, "wood-house," intimates that at the time it received that designation it was surrounded by woodland, as indeed from the nature of the country it is easy to believe; but of the time of its first settlement by a British lord, or the extent of the demesne, we have no certain information. At the time of the Norman invasion the hereditary lord of Coity was Morgan ap Meurig, of the line of Iestyn ap Gwrgant (*pace* Mr. E. A. Freeman, who stoutly disbelieves pedigrees unless they happen to be of Saxon or Norman birth); and in the old account by Sir Edward Mansel, quoted in all histories of Coity, and upon whose fidelity no doubt has been cast, Morgan's daughter and heir is said to have been married to Paganus Turbervill, one of Robert Fitzhamon's knights, who thenceforward became lord of the place. The romantic story is as follows :—

"After eleven of the knights had been endowed with lands for their services, Pain Turbervill asked Sir Robert where was his share ; to which Sir Robert answered, ' Here are men, and here are arms ; go, get it where you can.' So Pain Turbervill with the men went to Coity, and sent to Morgan, the Welsh lord, to ask if he would yield up the castle; whereupon Morgan brought out his daughter Sara [otherwise called "Sar" and "Assar"] by the hand, and passing through the army with his sword in his right hand, came to Pain Turbervill, and told him if he would marry his daughter, and so come like an honest man into his castle, that he would yield it to him quickly; 'and if not,' said he, 'let not the blood of any of our men be lost, but let this sword and arm of mine, and those of yours, decide who shall call this castle his own.' Upon this, Pain Turbervill drew his sword and

COITY CASTLE.

took it by the blade in his left hand, and gave it to Morgan, and with his right hand embraced the daughter; and after settling every matter to the liking of both sides, he went with her to church and married her, and so came to the lordship by true right of possession, and being so counselled by Morgan, kept in his castle two thousand of the best of his Welsh soldiers."

The account further states that Turbervill, having thus without aid of Fitzhamon's men and by lawful and peaceful process become owner of Coity, was unwilling to acknowledge his obligation " to pay the *noble* that was due to the chief lord every year to Sir Robert, but chose to pay it to Caradoc ap Iestyn, as the person he owned as chief lord of Glamorgan,"— thus siding visibly with the native race. " This caused hot disputes, but Pain, with the help of his wife's brother, got the better [see p. 497], till in some years after that it was settled that all the lords should hold of the seigniory, which was made up of the whole number of lords in junction together."

In the " Iolo MSS." it is recorded that Pain Turbervill was succeeded at Coity by eleven generations of his descendants, ending in the male line with Sir Richard Turbervill, who, leaving no legitimate son, settled his property upon his nephew, Sir Laurence Berkrolles, son of his sister Catherine and her husband, Sir Roger Berkrolles, Lord of St. Athan's. Sir Laurence married Matilda, daughter of Sir Thomas Despencer, then of Caerphili Castle. These records give her a character and end not out of keeping with those of her kindred, for she is said to have "poisoned her husband, so that he died," whereupon "she was buried alive, agreeably to the sentence pronounced upon her by the country and the lord, Sir Richard Begam, Lord of Glamorgan."

The demesne of Coity now passed to a member of another of the great houses of Glamorgan, also of Norman descent, Sir William Gamage, "son of Gilbert, the son of Sir William Gamage by Assar [Sarah], the fourth daughter of Sir Pain Turbervill, the third " of that name. Then comes this curious piece of information from the same MS.: " And now, as the possessions had thrice descended by distaff, that is, by the right of a daughter, the royal lordship of Coetty became alienated, and went as an escheat of Sir Richard Begam, as the law required. But although property may, prerogative cannot descend beyond three times successively by distaff, hence the king is now lord of the Court of Coetty, and is supreme governor of the county halls of justice; but the Gamages are the lords of the land, and to them appertain the possessions and manorial supremacy of the estates." The line of *Gamage of Coity* terminated in an heiress, Barbara, daughter of John Gamage of Coity Castle, who, *circa* 1584, became wife of Sir Robert Sydney (brother of Sir Philip Sydney), of Penshurst, afterwards Earl of Leicester. (See further *Gamage of Coity Castle.*)

The other side of Bridgend from Coity is *Ogmore Castle*, another of those spots in Glamorgan made memorable by the Norman settlement. It stands at the junction or *aber* of the Wenny stream with the Ogwr, and was called by the Welsh *Castell Aberogwr*. By some freak of pronunciation, since the days of Leland, the " Ogwr," as he properly calls it, has come to be called Ogmore. There must have been here a British settlement and estate, if not a stronghold, for the *Brut* informs us that Fitzhamon gave to William de Londres (William de Lwndwn) "the lordship of *Aber-ogwr*, and the lands thereto belonging." William is credited with having strengthened the place, and built the " keep," still standing, and said to be in the early Norman style. But his stay here was not long, for, as noticed elsewhere, he pushed his way onward to Carmarthenshire (although some accounts say that this was done by his son, Maurice de Londres), where he built Cydweli Castle, possibly ambitious of escaping the position of a retainer to the conqueror of Morganwg, and becoming owner of an independent lordship held directly from the king. But he also held lands in

England, as did most of the inferior lords of Glamorgan,—Humfreville, Fleming, St. Quentin, and Sully; like them he considered the other side of the Severn Channel as his home, and there he, like them, was buried.

At *Newton Nottage*, nigh to the harbour of Porthcawl, we find a neighbourhood possessing a good deal of antiquarian interest, which has had the advantage of careful illustration from an antiquary on the spot, the Rev. H. H. Knight, B.D. (see *Account of Newton Nottage*, reprinted from "Arch. Cambr.," 1853). The chief antiquities consist of British circles, barrows, and Celtic and Roman remains, a Medusa face, coins, &c., which prove either that the *Via Julia* passed that way (an improbable thing judging from the position), or perhaps that "some officer from the cohorts quartered in the Roman camp about Pyle was tempted by the sheltered aspect and pleasant sea view to fix his residence here; or some British chief, unmolested while he paid taxes to the Roman authorities, resided in this part of the extensive tract called *Tir y Brenhin*," as Mr. Knight conjectures. Some of these antiquities were found near Danygraig House. Mr. Knight's brochure throws a good deal of light also upon the old manor lands, estates, and families of this primitive district, and is a model of what ought to be attempted in every part of the country.

At *Marcross* are the remains of a *cromlech*, unless recently destroyed. The "spirit of improvement," now abroad, is so fatal to pre-historic monuments that nothing respecting them is certain except that they are in daily peril of destruction, and therefore there may no longer be a cromlech at Marcross, called the *Old Church*. The ruins of either a castle or a monastic building, also pointed out here, may be safely considered to be the latter, both from the name Marcross (Mary-cross), and the monastic *barn* near at hand. (See further *Van of Marcross*, and *Marcross of Marcross*.)

Ewenny Abbey falls behind none of the ecclesiastical and monastic ruins of Glamorgan either in the bold and impressive character of its architecture, its age, or the perfect preservation of many of its parts. Though the monastery is a ruin, the nave of the priory church is still used for worship—the aisles and north transept having disappeared. The style is pure Norman, the plan of the church a Greek cross; the stone of which it is built —perhaps the lias of the locality—has stood so well that the angularities are still sharp, and the joints close and regular. The whole of the buildings, church, convent, offices, gardens, &c., were surrounded by lofty walls and powerful tower defences, indicating that the inmates lived in times of danger, and in a country unsettled if not unfriendly. The chief entrance is by a magnificent gateway, defended by towers and portcullis, still remaining in tolerably good preservation; and these, with the terrace walls, partly existing, are picturesquely mantled with ivy. Under the tower of the south gate there was a deep dungeon, only six feet in diameter, the entrance covered by a strong iron grating, through which prisoners were let down. The great central tower is exceedingly massive—too much so to be graceful, but is a picture of strength and durability, sustained by buttresses of such dimensions as almost to defy time. On the whole, this great monument, in the early Norman style, is one of the most interesting architectural studies in the country.

This priory was founded for the Benedictines soon after the conquest of Glamorgan, by William de Londres, Lord of Ogmore (Ogwr), and made by Maurice de Londres, in 1141, a cell to St. Peter's Abbey at Gloucester. It contains some interesting monuments, among which is one to the memory of Maurice de Londres, having an ornamental cross in relief extending from one end to the other, with the following inscription deeply engraved round the border:—

"Ici gist Morice de Londres le fondeur,
Dieu lui rend son labeur."

The living of Ewenny is a donation in the patronage of Thomas Picton Turbervill, Esq., whose mansion, built about the beginning of the present century, on the site of the old priory, stands within the fortifications of the monastic edifice. (See further, *Turbervill of Ewenny Abbey*.)

It would be a mistake to suppose that these religious foundations at Ewenny, Margam, and Neath, were any proofs of extraordinary piety on the part of their Norman donors. These lords only yielded to the demands put upon them by the times. The Welsh princes of the same age were doing the same work north and south. Madoc, Lord of Dinas Brân, was building *Valle Crucis Abbey;* the Lord Rhys, of Dinefawr, was building those of *Ystrad Fflur* and *Talley*, and Rhys ap Tewdwr probably had long ago set up the great abbey of *Whitland.*

Dunraven Castle, a modern structure, the seat of the Earl of Dunraven, stands on the site of an ancient British castle of great fame and antiquity on a lofty promontory near the sea, where a little stream joins the tide. Its early name is said to have been *Dindryfan*, and tradition has clothed it with the dignity of chief palace of the kings of Wales from times so remote as those of Brân ap Llyr and his more renowned son, the brave Caractacus. It is enough to say that of this we have no evidence beyond tradition; but as Caractacus is allowed by all, even critics of Mr. Freeman's school—who reject the British accounts in order apparently to have more room to swallow "English,"—to have existed, he must have resided somewhere, and, during his leadership of the Silures, *Dindryfan* may well be supposed to have been one of his castles; and who will say that Caerleon or Caerwent was not another?

Dunraven, on the parting of Morganwg between Fitzhamon's knights, fell, along with Ogmore, to the share of William de Londres; and either he or his son Maurice gave it and the lands or lordship thereto belonging to Sir Arnold Butler. This family continued at Dunraven for ten generations (see *Butler of Dunraven*), till it terminated in an heiress, Eva, who married Sir Richard Vaughan, of the Vaughans of Bredwardine, Tre'rtwr, &c.; and the manor remained in his descendants till the time of his great-grandson, Sir George Vaughan, son of Sir Walter, grandson of Sir Richard, who, losing his three sons by an untimely death by drowning, "sold the lordship and estate of Dunraven in 1642 to Humphrey Wyndham, Esq." (See *Vaughan of Dunraven, Wyndham of Dunraven*, and *Dunraven of Dunraven*.)

St. Donat's Castle, already partly described (see *engraving*, p. 466), derives its name from the little parish church in its grounds dedicated to *St. Dunawd*, an early Welsh Christian,—perhaps that staunch abbot of Bangor Iscoed, who withstood the assumption of the monk Augustine. (See Williams' *Eccles. Antiq. of the Cymry*, 141.) Fitzhamon gave William le Esterling, one of his knights, "the lordship of *Llanwerydd*" (*Brut y Tywysog.*), the Welsh name of St. Donat's, who founded here a family which in course of time became known under the altered form *Stradling*, and continued in possession of the estate for a period of more than six hundred years. William le Esterling built here a castle, but whether in substitution for another belonging to a Welsh chieftain or on a virgin site it is hard to say; but that there was a lordship of Llanddunwyd or Llanwerydd before the Fitzhamon conquest, and that the land was taken from its rightful owner and given to Le Esterling, is clearly taught us in the Stradling pedigree (Jenkins' 4to. MS., p. 223), for it is there stated that in the fourth generation " Sir Robert Stradling married Hawisia, daughter of Sir Hugh Brin, Kt., whose mother was the lawful Welsh heiress, on failure of male issue, to the castle and manor of St. Donat's (in Welsh, Llanddunwyd)," and that "by this marriage the Stradlings acquired a rightful title by just heirship to the estate," and ever since "successively continued to enrol their names as Welshmen" and "warm patrons of Welsh literature." The last of the Stradlings of St. Donat's was Sir Thomas, who died *s. p.* 1738, at the age of twenty-eight, when the extensive estates were divided, St. Donat's falling, by virtue of a deed made by Sir Thomas, to the share of Sir John de la Fountain Tyrwhit, Sheriff of Glamorganshire 1750. (See further *Stradling of St. Donat's*, in "Old and Extinct Families.") The estate afterwards passed to the Drake family, and is now, by purchase, the property of Dr. J. Nicholl-Carne. What portion, if any, of Le Esterling's first castle remains in the present venerable structure it is difficult to determine, but it is quite certain that the bulk of St. Donat's Castle as it now stands is of a comparatively recent age.

The castle of St. Donat's is unquestionably one of the most perfect of the ancient baronial halls of Wales, and highly interesting as having never been left uninhabited through the changes of several centuries since it was founded. Several parts of the venerable pile clearly belong to an earlier structure, but the great bulk of the building is said to be of the age of Henry VIII. In the MS. above quoted it is said, pp. 223—226, that Sir John Stradling, created a baronet by James I., " made the new park and planted it with trees; he planted also many trees in the old park, and rebuilt in a great measure the old tower which was blown down by a tremendous storm in the reign of Queen Elizabeth, when many of the old trees in the park were thrown down "; that Sir Edward Stradling, *temp.* Henry VI., who in 1412 inherited the estates of Berkrolles, returning from Jerusalem, where he was made Knight of the Sepulchre, " brought with him from Italy a man skilful in carving, who made the ornamental columns to be seen in St. Donat's Castle." We have no account at hand of the erection of the main part of the present structure. Since its purchase by Dr. Nicholl-Carne it has been subject to careful and extensive restoration, its antique features scrupulously spared as far as possible, and the new work done, under the guidance of the learned proprietor, in keeping with the character of the whole.

The church of *Lantwit Major* and its precincts, indeed the whole site of the village and surrounding spaces, offers to the antiquarian a field of research of the greatest interest. The earlier name was *Caer Wrgan*. The later and present Welsh name, *Llanilltyd-fawr*, of which "Lantwit-major" is partly a corruption and partly a translation, commemorates St. Illtyd (Iltutus), the celebrated monk-professor of the fifth century, who here either originated or resuscitated a school which with growing strength and reputation continued to flourish for 700 years. It was, of course, a monastic seminary, and both depended upon and fed what in process of time became an imposing monastery. The institution became the resort of youths noble, ignoble, and royal, and ecclesiastics high and low from all parts of Britain and the Continent; the college sent forth learned men as teachers and bishops to many distant parts, among them St. David, Paulinus, Bishop of Leon, Samson, Archbishop of Dôl, in Brittany, &c. The Norman conquest of Glamorgan gave a blow to the establishment of Llanilltyd-fawr. Robert Fitzhâmon transferred the property it had accumulated to Tewkesbury Abbey; but the college and monastery still retained a portion of their income till the time of Henry VIII., whose Act for dissolving the monasteries included this place, and bestowed its revenues upon the new chapter of Gloucester Cathedral. The ancient *tithe-barn*, in ruins, still survives; the monastery, halls, and other buildings, which have wholly disappeared, " stood on a place called Hill-head, on the north side of the tythe-barn." The ruins of the schools are in a garden on the north side of the churchyard. Strewn far and near, in garden walls, field fences, jambs of cottage doorways and windows, and in the furrows of the paddocks around, are fragments of hewn and carved stone—relics of what at one time was a town of no inconsiderable dimensions, suggestive of wholesome reflections on the change which ages make in human things, and calling up unavailing regrets at the little we really know of the men and the doings which once distinguished so remarkable a spot. And yet the past seems to rise with something like distinctness, constructed by the imagination from the few authentic facts we know,—

"Visions of the days departed, shadowy phantoms fill the brain;
They who live in history only, seem to walk the earth again."

Lantwit-major, by long and holy tenure consecrated to education and religion, is on the estate of Dr. Nicholl-Carne of St. Donat's Castle, and that gentleman a few years ago gave proof of the estimation in which he held this feature of the place, as well as his concern for the advancement of education in modern Wales. When the editor of this work inaugurated the movement for university education for Wales, and visited Glamorganshire to advance the scheme, Dr. Nicholl-Carne offered as a free gift six acres of land on this spot, including the very site of the ancient buildings, for the erection of a university college for South Wales. It was then proposed to erect a corresponding college for the North near Menai Bridge, where a site of seven acres had also been tendered gratis. The decision, however, to establish one central college, and the purchase of the noble Castle House premises at Aberystwyth, prevented the final acceptance of the Lantwit-major site,—in many respects, and especially in the history of Welsh culture, the most interesting in all Wales. The projected institution at our date of writing is still unopened; but a large sum of money remains funded, and a building of ample capacity and unrivalled architectural excellence has been purchased since 1867; while a college such as that proposed, free from sectarian narrowness, and superior in the quality of its teaching, now that elementary and middle-class education is so happily progressing, is more than ever demanded in the Principality.

The church of Lantwit-major is itself a huge and complex monument of antiquity. It seems a thing almost entirely of the past. The date accorded to its first foundation is A.D. 408; but the building now standing consists of several parts of unequal age. The lady chapel and the old church to which it is attached are very ancient, the former measuring forty feet long, decorated with statues of saints, &c. ; the latter sixty-four feet long, displaying great rudeness in the arches, and an imperfect clerestory, but with a reredos of some beauty. Then continues what has been usually considered a more modern structure of three aisles, of the age, it is said, of Henry I., and erected by Henry Neville, Lord of Glamorgan. This extends to a length of ninety-eight feet, by fifty-three feet in width, and supports a tower " containing six bells of exquisite tone."

The church and churchyard abound in antiquities. The chief object of interest in the latter is the *Cross of St. Iltutus*, erected in the sixth century by Archbishop Samson of Dôl, in Brittany, and a pupil of the Llanilltyd College. Its height is now about six feet above the surface; its breadth at the base about two feet six inches, diminishing upwards to one foot ten inches. The carving on its face is well done ; and a border divided into sections runs along the side, with an inscription yielding the words CRUX ILTUTI . . . SAMSON POSUIT HANC CRUCEM PRO ANIMA EJUS. The head of the cross has been broken off—of course, as all the guide-books say, by the " Puritans,"—for as Cromwell destroyed all castles, so the " Puritans " alone did all the mischief to ecclesiastical monuments !

Another cross shaft, of almost equal interest, and of more curious history, stands against the church wall. A tradition floated among the old people that a huge stone monument had fallen into a new grave and been left there. In 1789, *Iolo Morganwg*—whose vocation seemed to be to bring out the hidden things of darkness, whether of stone or parchment—felt a desire to search for the missing object. He lived at Flimstone, a few miles away ; and being a mason by trade, had perhaps a cunning art with stones. At all events, remembering the tradition, he began digging, and, strange to say, soon came upon the ancient cross, and placed it in its supposed original position against the church wall, where it now stands. It is a ponderous stone, slightly pyramidal in form, six feet nine inches high, one foot three inches across the centre, seventeen inches at the top, and eighteen inches thick. An inscription on the side, judged to be of the same era as that of the *Crux Iltuti*, partly illegible, shows that it is a monument to a king or kings of Glamorgan.

A third cross, discovered in 1730, of similar date with that of the first mentioned, seems to be a monument set up by Howel, Prince of South Wales, on his penance and absolution for the murder of his brother, Prince Rhys.

Llantrisant Castle, whose remains occupy the craggy heights on which this historic little town is planted, was a place of great strength under the lords of Glamorgan. From its towers its master could view a wide extent of fertile country lying at his mercy. On the division of the lands by Fitzhamon, Llantrisant, centre of the hundred of Miskin, fell to the share of Einion ap Collwyn, along with Senghenydd (Caerphilly). In A.D. 1247 it had come under the power of the line of Iestyn ap Gwrgant, in the person of Howel ap Meredydd, who was expelled therefrom by Gilbert de Clare, then the supreme lord of Glamorgan ; but the Norman was foiled in his attempt to possess Miskin and Llantrisant by Cadwgan Fawr. From hence, after leaving Neath Abbey and Caerphilly Castle, Despencer, the favourite of Edward II., was taken to Hereford for execution. Edward le Despencer confirmed the charter of Llantrisant, *temp.* Edward III. Thomas le Despencer did the same. Leland says,

"Llantrissant Castelle, longing to the king, as principal house of Miskin, lyith half a mile from the est ripe of Lay (Ely). . . . The castelle stondeth on the toppe of a hille, and is in ruine. It hath been a fair castelle and had two wardes, and the inner diked, having among other toures one great and high caulled 'Gigvran' [W., *cigfran*, a raven], and at this castelle is the prison of Miskin and Glyn Rodney. There were 2 faire parkes by South Llantrissent, now onpalid, and without deere."

Near Cowbridge, which has no castle or other important object of antiquity to boast of except a tumulus and part of a cromlech, is *Llanblethian Castle*, otherwise called *St. Quintin's Castle*, whose entrance gateway, ivy-covered, would indicate a place at one time of great extent and strength. This castle had its origin in the Norman conquest of Glamorgan, when the lordship of Llanblethian fell to the share of Sir Robert St. Quintin, one of Fitzhamon's companions. "To Robert de Sancwintin," says the *Brut*, "was given the lordship of Llanfleiddian-fawr and the royal burg of *Pontfaen*" (Cowbridge). The castle, which was probably first built as a Norman stronghold by De St. Quintin, on a site which is said to have been previously occupied by a British place of defence and centre of a lordship, stands on high ground on the western bank of the little river *Daw*.

The St. Quintin family are said to have continued to enjoy the castle and lordship until the time of Henry III. The property afterwards came into the hands of the Herberts of Swansea, and thence to the Marquess of Bute. (See *De St. Quintin of Llanbleiddian*.)

In the same immediate neighbourhood, commanding views of exquisite richness and beauty, is the *castle of Llandough*, with its contiguous little parish church, already partly noticed. Llandough or *Llandocha* lordship came to Sir William Herbert from his great-grandmother, daughter and heir of Sir Matthew Cradock, Kt., who had here one of his principal residences. The castle of Llandough was not a military stronghold, but a castellated mansion. It is now inhabited by the Rev. T. Stacey.

Penlline Castle (now the seat of John Homfray, Esq.) has been a place of note from the twelfth century, when it became the property of a Norman settler named Sir Robert Norris, *vice-comes*, or sheriff of the lordship under Robert of Gloucester, successor and son-in-law of Fitzhamon. The Norris family continued at Penlline for several generations; were in possession at the time of Spencer's survey; and ceased in the male descent with Sir John Norris, Kt.

Beaupre Castle, also near Cowbridge, is a complete and picturesque ruin standing in a field between St. Hilary and St. Mary Church. Tradition relates that prior to the Norman subjugation of Glamorgan, a British fortress existed on the spot, and the early Welsh name of the place is said to have been *Maes Essyllt*, which some have considered as the proper original of *Beau-pré* (Fair-meadow). *Maes* certainly means a field, but how *essyllt* can be the original of the French *pré* or the English "meadow" we know not. D. Jenkin's MS. has it (p. 457) that this Maes-Essyllt was the ancient and "favourite abode of the *Sissyllt* family, from whom are descended the noble family of Cecil, Marquises of Exeter and Salisbury," and that "Llewelyn ap Sissyllt [Prince of North Wales], who inherited the principality of South Wales in right of his wife [d. circa 1020], frequently held his court at this place." In this princely line the lordship is reported to have continued until it was purchased (*temp.* Henry II.) by Sir Philip Bassett, Lord Chief Justice of England, a near descendant of John Bassett, chancellor or *vice-comes* to Robert Fitzhamon. We believe the lands of Beaupre have

THE COUNTY FAMILIES OF WALES.

The Porch of Beaupre Castle. (See p. 528.)

THE COUNTY FAMILIES OF WALES.

DYFFRYN—THE SEAT OF HOWEL GWYN, ESQ. (*See further, p.* 629).

ever since continued in the family of Bassett, although the place of residence has been removed to a little distance, and the original seat allowed to fall to ruin. (See *Basset of Beaupre.*)

The entrance-porch of this ruin is at once an extremely beautiful specimen and a peculiar medley of architecture containing Italian features, held by some to be the earliest of that order introduced into England. The age, as shown by a date over the entrance, is 1586, and the work was done by a native of the neighbourhood, Richard Twrch by name, who acted in the double capacity of architect and working builder. The story is that this man and his brother William were stonecutters (*temp.* Edward VI.), and worked the Sutton freestone quarries; that, a disagreement arising between them, Richard left the country, and for many years worked at his trade in London, and afterwards in Italy, where he attained "great proficiency in the science of architecture and the arts of masonry and sculpture." At last, returning to his native neighbourhood, he re-entered upon his former business at Sutton quarries, and executed work in a manner so superior as soon to command admiration and large employment. He was engaged by the Bassetts to build at Beaupre Castle first the chapel in the year 1586, and afterwards the porch in 1600. This porch is in the three Greek orders, the Doric, Ionic, and Corinthian, wrought with an elegance and delicacy not often to be seen in structures of much later date and by the most celebrated architects. It is remarkable, however, that the doorway arches in the porch and chapel are in pointed Gothic, while all besides is in the composite Grecian. See a paper on this subject by *Iolo Morganwg, Cambr. Journ.*, v., 138.

Fonmon Castle, Penmark Castle, and *Wenvoe Castle,* all of Norman origin, and noticed elsewhere, lie in the south-eastern part of the county, not far from the sea. (See *Jones of Fonmon Castle, Thomas of Wenvoe,* and *Jenner of Wenvoe.*)

Llancarfan, in this same district, is a place of antiquarian and historic interest, chiefly as the site of an early monastery, and as the birthplace of the celebrated chronicler, *Caradoc* of Llancarfan. Caradoc lived in the twelfth century, but of the details of his life little is known. His memorial is in his work, *Brut y Tywysogion,*—"Chronicle of the Princes of Wales," several copies of which in MS. have come down to our time, varying considerably in dialect, and in the copiousness of their narrative, but substantially agreeing in their *facts,* as copies of the same original work, modified by different transcribing editors of different ages and provinces, might be expected to do. For the *Brut,* in four different recensions, see *Myvyrian Archæol. of Wales,* vol. ii.

The *monastery* of Llancarfan, called also Llanfeithin, is said to have been founded by Germanus. Dubricius (*Dyfrig*) has the credit of having been its first head, or abbot, before his appointment to the see of Llandaff. This college sent forth six missionaries to convert "the Scots of Ireland." The monastery of Llancarfan is believed to have been destroyed about 1400, by the Normans, since which time we find no mention of its affairs.

The celebrated *cromlech* of St. Nicholas, known by the name of *Llech y Filast,* is the largest in *superficial* measurement in Britain, being in length twenty-four feet, in greatest breadth seventeen feet, by about two and a half feet in thickness. The cubic measurement of this magnificent flag is three hundred and twenty-four feet. A crack runs across at about six feet from the narrower end. The supporting stones, five in number, prop it up at a height of some six feet, and enclose, on three sides, an apartment not less than sixteen feet by fifteen. One of the supporters forms a wall sixteen feet in length. Truly a stupendous tomb! A companion *cromlech* at Dyffryn, at a short distance from the former, measures fourteen feet by thirteen feet in the widest part, supported by three stones above seven feet high. These, and *Arthur's Stone*, in Gower, already described, are the chief *pre-historic* remains in Glamorganshire.

In passing from *Lantwit-major* and *Llancarfan*, by *St. Fagan's*, to *Llandaff*, it is impossible not to feel that we are treading at every foot on ground possessing peculiar interest in the history of the Christian Church in Britain. These were all early settlements of the faith. Dyfrig, Catwg, Illtyd, and Dewi, and considerably earlier, Fagan, are foremost names in the ecclesiastical antiquities of Wales, and all of them were intimately connected with the Vale of Glamorgan.

ANCIENT CROSS AT LLANDAFF.

The cathedral church of *Llandaff*, whose more recent history has already been noticed, is said to have been invested with the dignity of a chief church, whose head pastor was an overseer of neighbouring pastors, in other words a bishop, as early as the fifth century. *Dyfrig* (Dubricius), already named as first abbot of the monastery of Llancarfan, was its first bishop, and next to him was *Teilo*. By the liberality of Meurig, King of Glamorgan, all the lands between the rivers Taff and Elwy were conferred upon this church. The early structure, on the same spot as the present cathedral (see engravings, pp. 468-9), was repeatedly destroyed and rebuilt during the incursions of the Saxons, Danes, and Normans, and the contentions of the British princes among themselves. The cathedral, out of the dilapidations of which the beautiful pile now standing forth in its renovated glory has arisen, was a work of the time of Henry I., and the year given for its foundation is A.D. 1120,

Urban being then the bishop. The conquest of Glamorgan by the Normans, and the barbarities therein practised, had reduced the former sanctuary to ruins, and the work was now to be done from the foundations. It took about sixty years to complete the nave, and eighty more to complete the choir, or "eastern chapel."

It was during the progress of this work (A.D. 1188) that Giraldus Cambrensis, in company with Archbishop Baldwin of Canterbury, on their tour through Wales preaching the *Crusades*, visited Llandaff. He says little about the cathedral, and makes no allusion to its building; but from what he incidentally mentions we are given to understand that the church had then a "high altar,"—an essential part, of course, in a church of the twelfth century, but a part which here might be only substitutionary and temporary. "On the following morning," he says (*Itin.*, 7), "the business of the cross being publicly proclaimed at Llandaf, *the English standing on one side*, and *the Welsh on the other* [showing a sharp line of race distinction !], many persons of each nation took the cross ; and we remained there that night with William [de Salso Marisco], bishop of that place, a discreet and honourable man. The word Llandaf signifies the church situated upon the river *Taf*, and is now called the church of St. *Teileau* [*Teilo* is spelt by Giraldus to suit the Norman-French pronunciation], formerly bishop of that see. The archbishop having celebrated mass early in the morning before the high altar of the cathedral, we immediately pursued our journey by the little cell of Ewenith [we must suppose that Giraldus, pursuing a too northerly route, had not *seen* Maurice de Londres' great monastery of Ewenny, which by this date was building, if not complete,—see p. 523] to the noble Cistercian monastery of Margan."

The cathedral which was in process of building in the twelfth century had become a crumbling pile by the eighteenth. Browne Willis, writing of it in 1715, says, "The glorious structure has fallen into a most deplorable state of decay within these few years." The southern tower at last fell. The authorities now collected a sum of money, and set to work to "deface" what remained, and to add to it incongruous deformities by way of supposed restoration and improvement. It was now that those objectionable features were introduced, already referred to at p. 471. The nave, however, "was left roofless, and St. Mary's Chapel deserted." Thus it continued until the modern restoration, which has ended in so much majesty and beauty. (See pp. 467—471.)

"The western façade of our cathedral," says Dean Conybeare, in a paper in the *Archæol. Cambrensis*, "is a very beautiful and characteristic specimen of the transition between the later Norman and early pointed styles contemporaneously with the age of our Richard Cœur de Lion. It appears to rest on the clearest evidence that the principal features of this new style—its pointed arches with its multifoil or cuspidated mouldings—were borrowed from Saracenic architecture, and first introduced by the influence of the Crusades; and we therefore naturally associate the style so derived with the name of a monarch so identified with these military adventures."

"Our western façade presents a specimen of this style, exquisitely beautiful, and nearly unrivalled for the elegance and simplicity of its composition and execution, and, from the great predominance of its pointed over its Norman features, seems to be a late example of the transition style. It is composed of three stories, besides the extreme angle forming the upper termination of the pediment. Of these three stories, the lowest exhibits the great western doorway, which is Norman just so far as its rounded arch can entitle it to that denomination ;

but this is supported by triple clustered columns with slender shafts, surmounted by capitals with long thin necks, overhung by protruding foliage, intermingled with birds, apes, and human figures, all marked characters of the confirmed pointed style."

"The second story of the western façade presents three narrow and lofty lancet windows, which, with their two intermediate piers, are faced by an arcade of five lancet arches, alternately broader and more narrow, the former corresponding with the windows, the latter with the dividing piers. The third, or sub-pedimentary story, exhibits a central window with an arch very nearly, if not exactly round. This is flanked on either side by an arcade gradually lowering, which is formed by a series of three arches. . . . All the shafts and capitals of this arcade are still of the early pointed style."

CASTELL COCH, ON THE TAFF.

Following the Taff a few miles to the interior, we come in view of *Castell Coch* (the Red Castle; so called by reason of the colour of its stones, taken probably from the durable red dolomite of the Radir beds). This picturesque ruin stands boldly on a craggy declivity facing the Taff, high enough to command a view of the Channel beyond Cardiff, and of the mountain gorges and passes inland,—a most important post to watch and guard against incursions from the Vale of Glamorgan into the hilly parts, and the contrary. The age of the structure is not known, but the spot is believed to be the site of the castle of *Ivor Bach*, the chieftain of short stature but puissant spirit mentioned by Giraldus (see p. 501), who broke into Cardiff Castle, carried off William, Earl of Gloucester, his wife and son into the woods, and declined their release until his demands were fully satisfied. The present castle is thought to be a Norman work of later date than Ivor's time; but of its builder and its subsequent history next to nothing is known. Ivor Bach, at the very time of the above exploit, was holding his lands in fee from the Lord of Glamorgan, whom he imprisoned, and it was inevitable that sooner or later a post so important as Castell Coch should become a mere outpost of Cardiff Castle, and in connection with Caerphilly, Llantrisant, and Coity Castles, serve in checking the Welsh and cutting off their retreat when ravaging the Vale of Glamorgan.

Caerphilly Castle is the grandest and most wonderful ruin in Wales or England. We have already given a large engraving showing the vastness of its extent from one of its sides (see *frontispiece*), and here supply two others, the one giving its general position among the bleak hills of Senghenydd, the other a view of its main entrance and leaning tower. A strange obscurity rests upon the *name* of this fortress. The earlier British name, *Senghenydd* (a corruption of St. Cenydd, who is said in the *Brut* to have founded a monastery on the spot), is both familiar and intelligible, but the modern *Caerphilly*, or, more correctly, if the components are Welsh, *Caerphili*, is a perfect puzzle. How it arose, and what its reason, no man can tell. Conjecture, therefore, has been rife; and the most far-fetched and strained derivations have been proposed. It were beneath the dignity of scholars not to search for a

CAERPHILLY CASTLE—GENERAL VIEW.

key among the archives of Greek or Latin, and we have been accordingly offered *Cara-filia*, on the assumption that some one's "beloved daughter" had held some relation to the place. The wise in the legendary lore of Britain would fetch the word from *Beli Mawr*, and supply *Caer-Beli*—forgetting that the name to be explained is in reality of comparatively modern manufacture. Edward Lhwyd makes it to be *Caer-vyli*, "the king's stronghold or city," from *vol*, a king. But did the Welsh contain such a word for "king" in the thirteenth century? And was Caerphilly the city of a king at any time, except in one or two instances as a place of temporary lodgment? Others have an idea that the name may be from *Philip*. We know of no "Philip" who called this castle his own. Philip ap Meredydd, of Cilsant, once held the castle for a time, and entertained there 500 horsemen, and it has been ingeniously suggested that the name might have arisen from that circumstance. But Philip ap Meredydd, it is to be remembered, lived in the fifteenth century, for his son, Sir Thomas Philips, received the honour of knighthood, according to the late Sir Thomas Phillipps, of Middlehill —a branch of the Cilsant stock—in 1511, and we have ground for believing and showing hereafter that this castle went by the name Caerphilly long before his age.

On the partition of Morganwg by Fitzhamon, *circa* A.D. 1092—1094, this lordship, under the British name *Sainghenydd*, fell to the share of Einion ap Cadifor ap Collwyn (*Brut y Tywysog.*). A.D. 1217, Llewelyn the Great, during one of his victorious marches through the south, gave the castle, called by the same chronicle *Seinhenyd*, to his son-in-law, Reginald de Breos, after Rhys Fychan had attacked it, and the garrison, out of fear, had set fire to both castle and town. In 1221 John de Breos repaired the castle of *Sang Henyd*. In 1270, *for the first time*, we meet in the *Brut* a form of the new name *Caerphilly*. "In that year Llewelyn ap Gruffydd took the castle of Caer-Filu." At this time the castle and lordship of Caerphilly were held by Gilbert de Clare, Earl of Gloucester, Lord of Glamorgan. The reason of the change of name in the *Brut*, from *Senghenyd* to *Caer-Filu*, is the one thing to be found out. The time when these entries were actually made in the Brut of Caradoc is

CAERPHILLY CASTLE—MAIN ENTRANCE AND LEANING TOWER.

not of much importance; for whenever made they must be presumed to give the castle its proper name for the time being—"Senghenyd" when it was called Senghenyd, and "Caerfilu" when it came to be called Caerfilu. Neither in person, place, nor event can we discover a plausible reason for the new and ever since persistent designation.

The first of the De Clares who possessed this lordship was Gilbert above named, surnamed "the red;" but how he obtained it is not quite clear. Some say it was by purchase. Like most of the Lords of Glamorgan he held immense estates in England, and was a man of foremost influence and activity under Henry III. and Edward I., and married Joan of Acre, daughter of the latter. The repulse he met when attempting to arrest the lordship of Miskin and castle of Llantrisant from the line of Iestyn has already been mentioned. How much of the castle, now in ruins, existed in his time it is impossible to say. Dying in 1295, he left his vast possessions, including Caerphilly Castle, to Gilbert, his son by Joan, a boy only five years of age. He grew up a strong partisan of Edward II., and in defence of his failing cause fell in the battle of Bannockburn, A.D. 1314, in the twenty-third year of his age, leaving no issue, when his manor and castle devolved upon his three sisters, the eldest of whom, Eleanor, married Hugh le Despencer the younger, who in her right became, as Lord of Glamorgan, seised of Caerphilly Castle.

Hugh Despencer was at once the most splendid and most unfortunate of the lords of Caerphilly. He so far enlarged, strengthened, and decorated the fortress that the fallen and crumbling masses which now open such a field of desolation to the beholder may be said to be the ruins of Despencer's castle. He, like De Clare, was devoted to the feeble Edward. In 1326 the king fled to Bristol, pursued by the queen and barons of the kingdom, but encouraged to persist by the two Despencers, father and son. The elder Despencer was executed at Bristol; and the younger, with the king, fled. There is confusion in the accounts of subsequent events and their sequence—the embarking for Ireland, or Lundy Island; the refuge at Neath Abbey; the defence of Caerphilly Castle; the escape thence, and the subsequent capture of Despencer and the king near or at Llantrisant; and the execution of the former at Hereford, &c.: but it is certain that in 1326 the younger Hugh Despencer, after his father's execution, and after the concealment at Neath Abbey, had the king with him at Caerphilly Castle, and that they were here hotly besieged by the queen's forces, under command of Roger Mortimer, who, besides serving her Majesty, claimed the castle as his inheritance by a right preceding that of Despencer, viz., the will of Joan of Acre, his mother by her second husband, Ralph de Mortimer.

The investing army on this occasion is said by some to have numbered 10,000 men, but the same number is assigned as the investing army under the Glamorgan insurgent, *Llewelyn Bren*, who is said to have reduced the castle in 1315; and it is just possible that the two sieges are confounded. Although Despencer and his master seem to have thrown themselves into the castle precipitately, they must have contemplated such a step long before, and Despencer had counted the cost of defending his stronghold against a formidable attack. Improving upon the work of De Clare, he had built a castle second to none in the kingdom; he felt that he and the king, with a few partisans, had to confront the popular cause supported by the queen and the barons of England, and that the estimation in which he and his family were held presaged no good if he failed in the conflict. He had therefore entrenched himself strongly, gathered the largest force available, stocked his fields and his barns, and laid in provisions on an immense scale.

The castle being of vast extent, there has been no end of exaggeration respecting the number of live animals and other provisions laid up within the walls preparatory to the siege. We hear of "2,000 fat oxen, 12,000 cows, 25,000 calves, 30,000 fat sheep, 600 draught-horses, and a sufficient number of carts for them, 2,000 fat hogs; of salt provisions 200 beeves, 600 muttons, 1,000 hogs; 200 tuns of French wine, 40 tuns of cider and wine the produce of Despencer's own estates, with wheat enough to make bread for 2,000 men for four years, and salt filling the great round tower (now 'the leaning tower'), being laid up within the castle. But the extravagance of this account is patent. The truth probably is that Despencer had provided food to this extent on his estates, partly within and partly without his castle; but that he had driven within his walls, even if the walls were sufficiently capacious to admit, such a multitude of live cattle, hogs, horses, and sheep, which would require for their daily sustenance such an amount of provision, is totally incredible on any other supposition than that of his suicidal folly. We believe the story has arisen from the confounding of preparations for this siege with other and later accounts we have of the great wealth of the Despencers in cattle as well as in money. Another Despencer, Thomas (the last of his race), Lord of Glamorgan, and, by restoration, of Caerphilly, on petitioning Parliament for the reversal of the sentence of banishment pronounced against his forefather, Hugh Despencer, delivered an inventory of the said Hugh's territories and property at the time of his impeachment. From this we find (see *Collins' Peerage*) that this Hugh Despencer was lord of not less than fifty-nine lordships in various counties in England and Wales, was possessed of 28,000 sheep, 1,000 oxen and steers, 1,200 kine with their calves, forty mares with their colts of two years, 160 drawing horses, 2,000 hogs, 3,000 bullocks, 40 tuns of wine, 600 bacons, fourscore carcasses of Martinmas beef, 600 muttons in his larder, ten tuns of cider; armour, plate, jewels, and ready money better than £10,000, thirty-six sacks of wool, and a library of books."

All this bustle at Caerphilly, we may remember, took place after the conquest of Wales by Edward I. But that conquest had nothing or little to do with Glamorgan—this Lordship Marcher, since the time of Rufus, being a fee under the English king. And this Edward II., who was now being hunted about by his own queen and subjects, and hiding his head at Caerphilly, was a son of that conqueror of Wales, as well as father of an equally puissant soldier, Edward the Black Prince. Queen Isabella's forces succeeded in reducing this great fortress, whose defence was, at least in part, conducted for Despencer by John de Felton. It took a great deal of arrow-throwing, stone-throwing with the *ballista*, and battering with ponderous *rams*, before a breach was effected. This was made, it is said, near the "leaning tower," which was thrown out of its perpendicular, if report be true, by an explosion, but far more likely by undermining, either at that time or subsequently. As the castle was long inhabited after this attack, such a leaning tower would scarcely have been allowed to continue to mar the structure and record the disaster, so that the fracture is more likely to be the result of later attacks, either by Owen Glyndwr (A.D. 1400) or during the Civil War.

For four generations the Despencer family suffered degradation, until another Hugh, mentioned above, succeeded, *temp.* Edward III., in recovering a vast amount of his forefathers' landed estates, but had scarcely completed this success when death overcame him. He left a widow, but no issue. He was followed by his brother Edward, by his brother's son Edward (who went with the Black Prince to France, fought at Poictiers, and is styled by Froissart "a great baron and good knight," died at Cardiff 1365), and by the same Edward's son, Thomas, who died on the scaffold at Bristol for treason A.D. 1400, when all his estates were confiscated. His daughter and heiress, Isabel, married as her second husband Richard de Beauchamp, Earl of Warwick. (See *The Despencers.*)

The Beauchamps and the Nevilles, Earls of Warwick, next Lords of Glamorgan by marriage alliance, were men of great note and splendour, and passed away in rapid succession, their line ending in heiresses who married princes and kings. During their brief day of stately magnificence we hear little of Caerphilly Castle, or whether it always continued in the same succession, but have much reason to believe that soon after the extinction of the Despencer glory it was allowed to fall into neglect. It was at last used as a prison, and finally dismantled after the Civil War. Leland, *circa* 1540, describes " Cairfilly Castelle " as " sette among marisches, where be ruinous walles of wonderfull thicknesse, and a toure kept up for prisoners." It is the property of the Marquis of Bute. After lying long in silent desolation, visited only by the curious tourist and antiquarian, its repose was broken in July, 1871, by a great gathering of archæologists, for whose reception the great hall of the castle had been fitted up with considerable magnificence. The noble owner, who presided, invited his guests to a sumptuous luncheon in the ancient banqueting-hall of the Despencers, roofed in for the occasion, and the entertainment was continued by a discourse on the castle from G. T. Clark, Esq., of Dowlais, and by inspection of the plan and chief features of the fortress, and the wilderness of ruins lying about. Will there ever be another great event at Caerphilly Castle?

The *extent* of this fortress when in its glory it is now hard to ascertain; but it is believed that the walled castle, with its projecting earthworks and redoubts, covered not less than thirty acres of ground. Lewis has described the castle as follows :—" The buildings in the several courts, together with a spacious area, were enclosed within a lofty outer wall of great thickness, defended by square towers at intervals, between which a communication was kept up by an embattled corridor. In the outer court were the barrack for the garrison, and from it was an entrance through a magnificent gateway flanked by two massive hexagonal towers, leading by a drawbridge over the moat into an inner ward, from which was an eastern entrance into the extensive court that contained the state apartments, by a massive gateway, strongly defended with portcullises, of which the grooves are still remaining: the western entrance to this court was also over a drawbridge, through a splendid arched gateway, defended by two circular bastions of vast dimensions. The court in which were the superb ranges of state apartments is seventy yards in length and forty in width, enclosed on the north side by a lofty wall strengthened with buttresses, and in the intervals pierced with loopholes for the discharge of missiles, and on the other sides by the buildings and the towers which guarded the entrances. The *great hall*, on the south side of the quadrangle, is in a state of tolerable preservation, and retains several vestiges of its ancient grandeur. This noble apartment was seventy feet in length, thirty feet wide, and seventeen feet high, and was lighted by four lofty windows of beautiful design, on which the ogee-headed arches, richly ornamented with fruit and foliage, are finely wrought in the Decorated style. Between the two central windows are the remains of a large fireplace, of which the mantel is highly embellished in beautiful and elegant detail: on the walls are clusters of triple circular pilasters, resting upon ornamented corbels at the height of twelve feet from the floor, and rising to the height of four feet, for the support of the roof, which appears to have been vaulted. The suite comprises various other apartments of different dimensions, and of corresponding elegance, in a greater or less degree of preservation. Near the south-east angle of the central building is the armory, a circular tower of no great elevation; and almost adjoining is the 'leaning tower.' This tower, already referred to above, and pictured in the engraving, is eleven feet out of the perpendicular, and is seventy feet in height. Near the armory is a spacious corridor, above one hundred feet in length, in the wall of the inner enclosure, communicating with the several apartments, and with the guards who were stationed in the embattled towers which protected the walls." The position of the stables, and yards for horse exercise, &c., is ascertainable; showing provision for men-at-arms and garrison forces, storing places for material, &c., on a scale unequalled, it is believed, in any feudal castle in the kingdom.

As might be expected, Caerphilly Castle at one time occupied a large space in the popular imagination; tales respecting the exploits of its besiegers and defenders were numerous; even to this day it is doubtful whether the apparitions of the mailed and fierce De Clares and Despencers are not occasionally seen flitting among its broken and gloomy ramparts. The wholesale spoliation and cruelty practised by the latter family towards the inhabitants burnt deep into the native mind. Whenever a man's lands were cleared of cattle, or his house of goods. it was known that Despencer had been at work. Hence arose the popular saying (which to this day plays on the lips of the peasantry), when anything was hopelessly lost, "It's gone to Caerphilly;" and when an excited temper bade its object depart to the worst and hottest of places, the volition went forth in the energetic words, " Go to Caerphilly!" This saying is old, for we find it in the works of the bard *Dafydd ap Gwilym*, circa A.D. 1380, the period cf the later Despencers,—

A gên y gwr gan ei gi, a'i gorff el i Gaerffili!
"Let his soul pass into his dog, and his body go to Caerphilly!"

When Caerphilly Castle was in its prime, and Castell Coch and Llantrisant co-operating with it to protect the lordship of Glamorgan, and its heart the castle of Caerdyf against the free children of the mountains, there existed in the Valley of Rhondda Fâch, not far off, an important monkish establishment, of which, at present, not a single trace is discoverable— the *Monastery of Penrhys*. Dugdale says nothing of it; Bishop Tanner does not name it; but here and there in the Welsh records, in the songs of the bards, and allusive expressions of annalists, it often occurs. The " Holy Well," near its site, still pours forth its pellucid waters,—full of virtue, it used to be believed, to cure the ailments of pilgrims. According to Mr. Llewelin, who personally inspected the place (*Cambrian Journal*, 1862), "the spring, which is entered by stone steps, is arched over, and at the back, above the spring, there stands a niche, in which it is evident that there stood originally an image of the Virgin, to whom the monastery was dedicated." He adds, "When I visited Pen Rhys about twenty years ago, some portions of the monastery existed, though incorporated with modern erections, and difficult to identify. The present farmhouse of Pen Rhys has been erected on the site of the ancient monastery. . . . The barn, which stands in a field near the house, called to this day 'Y Fynwant,' or the churchyard, was formed, to a considerable extent, out of portions of the ancient monastic buildings; one of the windows, and parts of the old walls of which were, at that period, very clearly discernible."

Since that time, however, a new spirit has entered the Rhondda Valley, which cannot afford room for other rubbish than its own. Deep pits, tall chimneys, whistling engines, long-drawn-out villages, with teeming multitudes of men, women, and children, white by nature but black from coal, are now the visible objects; and it is hard to believe that this vale was once the gem of Glamorgan for its lovely scenery, and the calm and silent home of drowsy, bead-counting monks—who, however, for the times, were not without their use.

The monastery of Pen Rhys is supposed to have been founded by Robert, Earl of Gloucester, the successor of Fitzhamon as Lord of Glamorgan, and grandson, on his mother's side, of Rhys ap Tewdwr; and tradition says that it was built as a memorial of that celebrated prince, who is held by many to have fallen in this neighbourhood, and not, as is more probable, near Brecon (see p. 67). In the "Iolo MSS." it is said that on the spot where Prince Rhys was beheaded, "at a place called Pen Rhys, was afterwards erected the great monastery of that name in the parish of Ystrad-dyfodwg;" and over his grave "was raised a large tumulus near the monastery, which is called Bryn y Beddau, *i.e.*, the hill (or tumulus) of graves." The same allusion to the monastery is found in Rees Meyrick's *Morganiæ Archæographie*, 1578. In the Iolo MSS. it is recorded, "After the insurrection of Owain Glyndwr had come to an end, the monastery of Pen Rhys was suppressed, and its possessions sold by Henry V., about the year of Christ 1415, for the favour it had shown to Owain and his party." This partisanship had been discovered in the fact that a meeting of bards, held at the monastery, had been presided over by Owain Glyndwr during his raid into Glamorgan (A.D. 1402). That this meeting had taken place is a fact borne out by other evidence, for in Dr. John David Rhys's learned grammar, *Cambro-Brit. Cymrææve Ling. Inst.*, 1592, we find an ode to *Wyrif Fair Wenn o Ben Rhys* (Mary, the Fair Virgin of Pen Rhys), which was delivered at the congress by the bard *Gwylim Tew*.

Morlais Castle, near Merthyr Tydfil, is a ruin of whose history very little is really known. Planted on an eminence above the lesser Taff, it was evidently intended to guard the narrow valley against the enemy. But whether the enemy first provided against was Briton or Norman it is hard to say. On two sides it is made proof against assault by the deep escarpment of the valley, and on the remaining sides by a deep excavation in the rocks. In form it is an irregular pentagon. Part of the ruins are Gothic, which would suggest a Norman, or at least not pre-Norman origin.

Cardiff Castle, which comes last in our way to describe, was the cynosure of all the other strongholds of Norman Glamorganshire, as, through the development of new circumstances and industries, it has come to be a centre of mighty influence of a different kind in our own day. At the mouth of the river *Dyf*, now called Taff (from the same Celtic root with Tâf, Teivi, Dovey, Tafwys, *Thames*), the British princes of Morganwg had long planted their chief residence. Its site appears to have been the very mound on which the ancient keep of Cardiff Castle now stands (see p. 462). Morgan, and Gwrgant, and Iestyn, the son of Gwrgant, had here their castle; and Robert Fitzhamon, when he crushed the last-named ruler, appropriated the residence as well as the territory to his own use. The castle lies conveniently in the mid-distance between the champaign country stretching westward as far as Margam, and eastward as far as and beyond the Usk. It has never been doubted that on this spot the Norman pitched his tent, and that on this spot his successors continued their state and riot for four hundred years.

The Britons, even after the Roman occupation, had not developed that type of civilization which creates large towns, a circumstance which scarcely of itself speaks to their disadvantage;

for it is hard to see any great superiority in the "civilization" of such modern creations as the Seven Dials, or the crowded districts of the "Black Country." At Caer-dyf, when Iestyn ruled, and when the Normans conquered Glamorgan, there was no "town." The "Caer" first, the castle afterwards, was the only paramount interest existing, all the other atoms of mill, church, monastery, smithy, armory, gathered around it to draw for themselves succour and life. After several generations of Norman settlement, the dues payable to the Lord of Glamorgan from the town ("burgus") of Cardiff were not half the amount payable by the "mill." This is shown by the *Extenta de Kairdiif* returned, *temp.* Henry III., or about A.D. 1262, already partly quoted (see p. 498, &c.). Of course the lord of the land at the *castellum* paid himself no taxes; he felt it hard enough to have the trouble to receive, and to receive so little. He was responsible in life and service to his "sovereign lord, the King" (souzerain, souverain; Lat., *superus*), and for the land he was to no other power responsible—a state of things to which the whole "land question" in England must by and by refer itself in order to encompass itself with light. The dues from "Kairdiif" in 1262 were as follows, as testified on oath by Robertus Upedyke, Stephanus Bagedrip, Richardus Lude, and nine other jurors :—

Redditus burgi est [town return]	xx^{li.} iiij^{s.}	viij^{d.}	
Et Molendina valent [mills, do.]	xlvi	o	o
Et de prisa cervisie [prisage on beer--*Cwrw*] . . .	xiiij	o	o
Et de piscaria [fishing]	viii	o	o
Et de theloneo mercati [market toll]	iiij	o	o

Other miscellaneous but trifling charges follow, making a total of fourteen times twenty, and sixteen pounds sixteen pence, or £96 1s. 4d., which only slightly more than doubles the mill dues alone. Where the "mills" were situated, or how many existed, it is of course impossible to say. There were more than one, and probably they were all on the river side.

The earlier castle of *Caer-dyf* was doubtless strengthened and enlarged, if not entirely rebuilt, by Robert Fitzhamon, for it is not conceivable that the requirements of a Norman feudal fortress could be met by the simple *Llys*, or fortified palace, and *Caer* of a British chief. Fitzhamon also surrounded the town with walls. He died 1102, and was buried at Tewkesbury. The castle whose remains still partially continue in the "ancient keep," is believed to have been chiefly if not wholly built by his successor and son-in-law, Robert of Gloucester, natural son of Henry I. He died 1147, and was succeeded as Earl of Gloucester and Lord of Glamorgan by his son William. The surprise and capture of the castle by Ivor Bach, the Lord of Castell Coch, related by Giraldus, who visited Caerdyf in 1188, took place in his time (see p. 501). The castle was then "surrounded with high walls, guarded by one hundred and twenty men-at-arms, a numerous body of archers, and a strong watch, and the city contained many stipendiary soldiers." (*Itin.*, 6.) The name of the town at this early time was "Caer-*dyf*," of which the modern English Car*diff* is a better representative than the modern Welsh Caer*dydd*. So was the Norm.-Latin Kair-*diif* of the *Extenta* above quoted. In fact Caer-*dydd* is nothing better than a *lapsus pennæ* which crept into the *Brut;* and its derivation from Aulus *Did*ius, the Roman general, is a pedantic makeshift. The name is taken from the river on which the "Caer" stood.

For several generations, as the De Clares, Despencers, Beauchamps, and Nevilles succeeded each other as Lords of Glamorgan—taking, however, a far more prominent part in English than in Welsh affairs, and ruling with a sway more cruel than facile over Glamorgan,—we hear little of the castle of Cardiff as such. The estates which, after many changes, confiscations, restorations, and sales, remained to the lords of this castle, came at last by purchase from Edward VI. to the Herberts, and by marriage, in 1766, of John Stuart, Earl, and afterwards Marquess of Bute, with the heiress of the Herberts, to the line of Bute. (See *Bute, Marquess of.*)

The present residential castle of Cardiff was built by the first Marquess of Bute on part of the site of the ancient fortress. Of the latter scarcely anything remains except the "keep" illustrated on p. 462, and the *Curthose Tower*, sometimes called the " Black Tower," standing on the left, close to the chief entrance from the town, and celebrated chiefly for having been the place of confinement, for the space of twenty-six or twenty-eight years, of Robert Curthose, Duke of Normandy, detained here by his brother, Henry I.

THE CURTHOSE TOWER, CARDIFF CASTLE.

Robert had doubtless given both Rufus and Henry a good deal of trouble both in Normandy and England, but no small part of their anxiety concerning him arose from the fact that as eldest son of the Conqueror he, by right of succession, was entitled to the throne of England. He fell into Henry's hands while drawing the sword to do battle for that throne. That his confinement, however, in Cardiff Castle until death, A.D. 1134, released him, was of the severe and cruel character generally represented, and that he had been deprived of his eyesight by command of Henry, are things by no means worthy of implicit credit. The story of the blinding by means of "a hot brass basin being held so near his face that the humours of the eyes thereby dried up," though related by Matthew Paris and in Caradoc's *Brut*, implies a brutality not quite in keeping with the indulgence generally granted him. William of Malmesbury, usually accurate, tells us that his imprisonment was made as easy as possible, and that he was supplied with an elegant table, buffoons to divert him, &c. True, indulgences of this kind might be granted to a blind man; but there is a strange silence about this blinding where it might be expected to be mentioned. After

Robert had been confined about thirteen years, Lewis of France, suzerain of Normandy, brought a complaint before the Pope, A.D. 1119, respecting Henry's imprisonment and hard treatment of Robert, stating that he "treated him contrary to all right and reason," and "in a most scandalous manner made him prisoner and detained him in a long captivity;" but of putting out his eyes nothing is said. (See *Ord. Vitalis*, xii., 21.)

In the same year Henry, in a conference with Calixtus, defends himself thus :—" I laid siege to Tinchebrai [in Normandy], the real cavern of demons, where William, Count de Mortain, brought my brother against me with a great army, and I fought against it on the Starved Field in the name of the Lord and for the defence of my country; there by the aid of God, who knew the purity of my intentions, I conquered my enemies, making prisoners of both the count my brother, and his cousin, with many traitors, and I have detained them in close custody to the present day for fear of their causing some disturbance to me and my kingdom. As for my brother, I have not caused him to be bound in fetters like a captive enemy, but treating him like a noble pilgrim worn with long sufferings, I have placed him in a royal castle, and supplied his table and wardrobe with all kinds of luxuries and delicacies in great abundance.' (*Ibid.*, 24.) Could he thus ignore the cruel act of blinding if it had been done? It is true that Robert, after this, continued nearly fourteen years a prisoner, and might in that space of time be subjected to worse treatment; and Henry's affectation of leniency, like his affectation of piety, may reasonably be taken with distrust; but Robert's age at this time—for he was nearly eighty years old when he died in 1134—would both have made him a quiet prisoner, and inclined his brother to refrain from wreaking upon him unnecessary barbarities. But that Robert of Normandy was a prisoner in the Curthose Tower until he died is as well substantiated as any other historical fact.

In A.D. 1402, "the irregular and wild Glyndwr" came with fire and sword to Glamorganshire, burnt the bishop's palace, and the archdeacon's residence at Llandaff, then attacked and burnt Cardiff, with its castle and "religious houses," and proceeded to deal the same measure to the castle of Humfreville at *Penmark*, which he finally cast to the ground. He also in this incursion devastated the castles of Penlline, Landough, Flemingston, Dunraven, Talyvan, Llanblethian, Malefant, &c.

In the Civil War, Cardiff, like many other towns in Wales, zealously espoused the cause of Charles I., and Cromwell was brought upon the scene. The castle was "bombarded from an entrenchment about a quarter of a mile to the west of the town, and a cannonade was kept up for three days; the castle offered a stubborn resistance, but was afterwards taken through the treachery of a deserter, who in the night conducted a party of the besiegers through a subterranean passage under the Taafe into the castle." (*Cardiff Guide*, 1829.) Of course, Cromwell profited from the deed and took the castle; but, *suo more*, immediately commanded the traitor to be hanged. In 1642 the Marquis of Hertford surprised the castle, "having crossed over from Minehead with a few royalists; but it was shortly afterwards retaken by the Cromwellians" (*ibid.*). In 1647, Colonel Prichard, the governor, refused to surrender the castle to Major-General Henry Stradling, the commander of the Royalists.

In the Duke of Beaufort's *Progress* (1684) we find the following notes on the castle :— " The castle of Cardiff hath in it the coat armors of the twelve knights belonging to Robert

Fitz Hamon, who gained the dominion of the shire of Glamorgan from Justin ap Gwrgan in the reign of William Rufus, where he kept his court monthly, and used therein *jura regalia*, having his twelve knights to attend him, . . . they having their severall lodgings and apartments given them, and their heires for ever within the castle."

"*Castle Hall.* The chimney-piece is formed of the shields and coat armour of the said Robert Fitz Hamon and of his twelve knights about it."

"The Black Tower thereof is famous for the imprisonment of Robert *of Gloucester* [?], who remained there for the space of twenty-eight years, and had his eyes put out."

Seal of the Corporation of Cardiff. "I have scratched off the Common Seal of Cardiff, which was affixed to a Deed of Surrender of the Ancient Charter of this town to his Majesty, and which this community most humbly desired his Grace, the Duke of Beaufort, to deliver up accordingly. The form of which seal, as it appears to me (and I have exhibited [in engraving on margin] from a bare impression in soft wax received from the hands of Mr. Thomas Jeyne since the Progress), is, as to the circumscription,—S. COMMUNE DE KERDIF. As arms, I guess it to be—The field . . . [not filled] two lyoncels rampand combatant, ...; upon a rock in base . . .; a chief, . . . with an Inescocheon of the ensigns armorial of . . . ."

Caerdiff Church is fair. "Adjoining to the north wall of the east end of the north aisle is seen the chiefest monument (almost gone to decay by the injury of time, and by neglect) of two brothers, Herbert. *John Herbert,* who was principall secretary to Queen Elizabeth and King James, having had the honour of being employed in severall foreign embassies, viz., to Denmark, Poland, Holland, and France, &c. *Sir William Herbert* of Swansey, Knight, at whose quondam house there his Grace was enterteined in his Progress."

The Priories of Cardiff.—In olden Cardiff there were "severall religious houses," which met with severe treatment from "the rude hands of that Welshman," as Shakspeare has it, Owen Glyndwr. Bishop Tanner (*Not. Mon.*) describes them as "[1] a goodly priory, founded by Robert, first Earl of Gloucester; [2] a priory of black monks, or Benedictines; [3] a house of black friars in Crockerton Street; [4] a house of *grey friars,* dedicated to *Saint Francis,* under the custody or wardship of Bristol; and also [5] a house of white friars." None of these orders experienced any favour from our hero except the *Franciscans* in "Crockerton Street." They, being firm adherents to the late King Richard, Owain's friend, were carefully protected, and Crockerton Street (now "Crockherbtown") was not burnt. Leland says that Owain Glyndwr "spared the Friars Minors, on account of the love he bare them," but he "afterwards took the castle and destroyed it, carrying away a large quantity of treasure which he found therein; and when the Friars Minors besought him to return them their books and chalices which they had lodged in the castle, he replied, 'Wherefore did you place your goods in the castle? If you had kept them in your convent, they would have been safe'" (*Collect.*, i., 389). There still remains on the side of Crockherbtown towards the castle ground a portion of this old priory of the Franciscans, carefully protected by the friendly ivy; and this is probably the only visible memorial existing of all these "religious houses."

The *Roman camp* on "Bryn y Gynnen," near Neath, is remarkable more for the memorial contained in the *name* than for the remains surviving—*Bryn y Gynnen* meaning "the hill of contention." But as the camp was probably used during disturbances long subsequent to the Roman age, it is quite possible that the designation is comparatively recent.

The stone called *Maen Llythyrog*, on the hill near Margam, contained, as mentioned in *Camden*, a rather doubtful inscription, but conjectured to read, BODVOCUS HIC JACIT FILIUS CATOTIS, IRNI PRONESSOS, ETERNALIVE DOMAN (*i. e.*, "eternali in domo").

The age of the stone in the parish of Cadoxton, near Neath, considered by Edward Lhwyd as remarkable, is not known. Its name of *Maen dau lygad yr Ych* is from two cavities in its surface once serving as mortices to hold upright pillars, one of which, not long removed, was found at a gate by the road-side. It bore the inscription, MARCI (or *Memoriæ*) CARITINI, FILII BERICI (*or Bericii*). See *Gough's Camden*.

The cross on Mynydd Gelli-Onnen, Llangyfelach, described by Edward Lhwyd in *Camden*, is probably early. It was a flat stone, three inches thick, two feet broad at bottom, and about five feet high, with rounded top, "formed round like a wheel," and adorned with "a kind of flourish or knotted work," with a man's face and hands on each side further down, and at the bottom "two feet as rude and ill-proportioned as the hands and face."

We must probably consider as *pre-historic* or "Druidic" the *circle*, mentioned also by Lhwyd in Camden on "*Carn Llechart*" hill. It is described as "above seventeen or eighteen yards in diameter, the highest stone then standing not above one yard high." In the centre of the area was a *Kistvaen* about five feet long by four wide, the top stone fallen.

Modern Cardiff—with which this work has little concern, except as it regards some of its chief families—may be summed under three heads,—the castle, the port, and an energetic municipal government. The increase of the town has been remarkably rapid (see p. 461); but it has too many of the features of a place marred morally by a seafaring and foreign intrusion and a rank licentiousness. In the suddenness of its rise it has been subject to a disproportionate growth, but the law of a healthy community is asserting itself; intelligence and Christian culture are nourishing the youthful blood of a vigorous and orderly city, by and by to appear as distinguished for its moral tone as for its trade, wealth, and populousness.

SECTION V.—INDUSTRY, CONDITION OF SOCIETY, AND CRIME IN GLAMORGANSHIRE.

Glamorganshire, beyond all other counties in the United Kingdom, Lancashire itself not excepted, is distinguished for the fewness and at the same time stupendousness of its staple industries. They are three or four only in number, and all relate to minerals and metals. The *copper* mart for all the world is at Swansea; Merthyr, Dowlais, and surrounding places dig, melt, and work *iron* for all lands; as for *coal*, it has been already shown that nearly 600 square miles of the county belong to the coal measures, and these are being drawn upon as fast as home and foreign requirements and the capabilities of miners permit. It is not the province of such a work as the present to enter into the statistics or the methods of metallurgy and mining, otherwise in Glamorganshire a tempting field would be found open; general references have been made to the development of the vast iron and coal trade of the county (see section *Physical Description*), and it only remains here to touch upon the *copper-smelting*, which, being nearly peculiar to this county, possesses a more distinctive character.

That mystery of trade—its tendency to group and concentrate its various branches—which has made Manchester the centre of cotton, and Sheffield the workshop of cutlery, has made Swansea the home of copper-smelting. The local supply of coal had something to do with the matter in all these cases, but it was not the only reason in any of them, for the coal of Glamorganshire might have told for cotton-mills as well as for copper-working, and the coal of Lancashire might have made Liverpool the emporium and furnace for copper. If people knew as much two centuries ago as is known at present, Milford Haven had been made the port for cotton, and the country from Pembroke to Glamorgan would have by this time become the land of chimney-stacks and spindles.

Copper-smelting.

Copper-smelting in Swansea and Neath had its origin in the nearness of the ports to the mines of Cornwall, and to the coal supply of their own locality. The trade, although largely developed within the present century, is by no means of recent beginning. In fact, it is entitled to be considered of some antiquity. Col. Grant-Francis, F.S.A., has industriously searched out the "rise and growth" of the trade, and has embodied the account in an interesting work (privately printed 1867) called *The Smelting of Copper in the Swansea District*, from whose reliable pages we gather our information. The real cradle of the trade was Neath. Copper ore was worked at Treworth, "near Perin Sandes," in Cornwall, in 1583 by a company whose head-quarters were at Fenchurch Street, London, and who in that year erected a "meltinge-house at Neath in Wales." To Neath was sent in 1584, from "Keswicke," one of the company's "copper makers with an under melter and ye Douch [Dutch] carpenter for a time to serve and ready him in these causes." The skilled workmen first employed seem to have been Dutch or German, the overlooker at the first melting-place at Neath being named Ulricke Frosse, having first been "a lovinge servaunt and ov'seer of ye minerall woorkes at Trewoorth."

In July, 1585, after things had long gone on very slowly, with much anxiety and many pious committals of the enterprise to the care of Almighty God, Ulricke Frosse reports some progress. "We have founde out a waye to melte 24 c. of owre everye daye with one furnas, the Lord be thanked, and if we have owre anoughe from yo'r side [Cornwall] we maye with God's helpe melte w'th tow [two] furnases in 40 weekes 560 tons of owre." October 4th following "came John Bwaple, one of Wales, with his bark for a frayght of copper owre, and [we] did delyver hem the 21 of October 15 ton and 8 hundred of copp' owre for Wales. The 15 October came one Thom's Roberts from Wales from the company, with a fraight of tymber and necessaryes for the workes." Still in 1586 not much progress had been made in the "meltinge," for Frosse writes to his superiors in London, "We looke dayly for the copper refiner from Keswicke, and have in readines as much copper roste and blake copper as will make a 20 tonne of good fine copper. We have done nothing all this winter for lake of ewre. We are able to melte w'th two furnises in the space of 40 weekes the quantitie of 560 tonne of ewre if wee might have it, and if the ewre be clean and well sorted the mor copper it will yield. . . . If lake of ewre hath not been [poor Frosse's English is not yet perfect] wee might have hath by this time about 40 tonne of copper, which must be for seene hereafter, o'r els it wilbe long befor they parteners will com to their owne againe." Thus slowly we feel our way at first, dealing out expenses rather cautiously, and bearing with honest Dutch Ulricke's remonstrances about " lake of ewre," &c. One of our chief men, Mr. Carnsewe, knows the value of "frynde Ulryke," and believes Cornish miners as good as Dutch any day. " Mr. Weston's p'vydence in bryngynge hys Dutche myners hether to aplye such busynys in this countrye ys more to be comended than his ignorance of o'r countrymen's actyvytyes in such matters, who owte of all p'adventure to be skylfull in mynynge, as harde and dylygent laborers and as good chepe workmen in that kynde of travell as are to be founde in Europe ; whereof to make yow good p'ffe lett the same Mr. Weston's Germans have some myn assignyd only to them, and lett yo'r Ulryke take suche as he is now acquayntyd w'th of our countrymen, . . . and let it be consyderyd w'che of them for on hole somer's space shall put yow to moste charges, and gayne yow moste, and soo of them that doo lesse yow shall make yo'r estymacyon by p'ffe." Our Ulricke Frosse has already made a discovery in melting, and he is afraid " of no ewre soever," but he will " overcom it." Bad, hard " ewre from St. Youste [Just] has come to hand," and " put us to harteshifte for melting it, but a metchen wee have found out· by change " has helped us, and " I thank God," says our Ulricke, " wee are able to master it well innough. God send us anough of it, for the metchen we have for it doth not only healp to melt it easye, but also to melt it speedelye and with small fewle, and bringes out all that is in it. . . . God send the mynes to prosper and to mak good greement amongst the parteners in setting the work forward, whereby they may have p'fitt, and the comon wealt may be maintained to God's honner." Our " lovinge servaunt Ulricke " has also found, or has learnt, that a variety of ores mixed together will melt more easily than one by itself. " Send such owre as you have—*sende of all sorts;* the better it will melte, and w'th more profit." This practice is still found the best.

Our Company, " The Mines Royal Society," had obtained its charter from Queen Elizabeth in 1581, and consisted of several noblemen and others, such as the Lord Treasurer, the Earl of Pembroke, the Earl of Leicester, the Lord Montjoy, Alderman Ducket, Customer Smyth, Alderman Gamage, George Needham, &c. ; and extended their operations from Cornwall to Cumberland and Wales. The first patent had been granted as early as 1564 to " Thomas Thurland, Master of the Savoy, and Daniell Hogstetter, a Germain, and too their heyrs and assignees,"—an instrument of some length, fully set forth by Col. Francis, with others that followed in its train. The first works opened at Neath (1684) are believed to have been built on the spot now occupied by the " Mines Royal Works," near the Neath Abbey railway station. Here it was that our " lovinge frynde Ulricke Frosse " first lit up his furnace, and fought with scanty funds and " harte owres " [hard ores].

Next followed the operations of the " Mine Adventurers " and " The Governor and Company of Copper Miners in England," the former headed by Sir Humphrey Mackworth, and now extinct, the latter still surviving. Both began their work in the last decade of the seventeenth century. Sir Humphrey Mackworth's works were set up at Melincrethyn, a mile from Neath.

The copper-smelting trade began near *Swansea* several years later. Col. Francis's subsequent researches have made out that in a case of law, in 1734, the town clerk of

Swansea set forth that in the year 1717 *works were first erected* upon the river of Swansea for smelting copper and lead ores, and that the works were situated above the town and about two miles beyond the corporation boundary. In 1720 another work was erected upon Swansea river within the limits of the corporation. The works erected in 1717 were promoted by Dr. Lane, and their site was near Glandwr, now corrupted into "Landore," a word belonging to no language. This gentleman, therefore, was the pioneer of copper-smelting at Swansea; and the stability and growth of the trade in that neighbourhood is said to be greatly due to the intelligent and firm management of Gabriel Powell, agent of the then Duke of Beaufort, owner of the land.

Thus commenced the great copper-works in the neighbourhood of Swansea, a neighbourhood which, for miles round, they and their adjuncts have since swallowed up. The Aberavan or Taibach Works followed in 1727; Forest Works—Lockwood, Morris, and Co., 1827, by removal from Llangyfelach; Penclawdd, by John Vivian, in 1800; Loughor—Morris and Rees, 1809; the great Havod Works—R. H. & J. H. Vivian, 1810; Morfa Works—Williams, Foster, and Co., 1834; Llansamlet Works, 1866. The amount of copper ore brought into Swansea, smelted and wrought into various forms and for various purposes, and then shipped off to different parts of the world, even at the present time, despite the fluctuations in the trade, must be enormous.

The bad reputation which "copper smoke" has earned from its effect upon vegetation is well known, although its effects on animal life, judging from the constant aggregation of that life in Swansea and its district, would seem to be highly favourable. Dr. Percy, in his *Metallurgy*, confirms the general opinion that "the sulphurous and choking exhalations of the copper-works are an unmistakable nuisance," and it is hard to believe that they can be conducive to health in man, or tree, or grass. They have had some hand in transforming the district of Havod, "the summer dwelling," which a poet of 1737 apostrophized thus:—

> "Delightful Havod, most serene abode!
> Thou sweet retreat, fit mansion for a god!
> Dame Nature lavish of her gifts we see,
> And paradise again restored in thee!"

into a region at least several degrees removed from a paradise, a region by which *Sketty* and the *Forest* do not, as then, "own themselves outdone," and to which "Swansea virgins" do not—

> "Every morn repair
> To range the fields and breathe the purer air."

But chemical science, although it cannot grow trees and flowers amid the fires, smoke, dust, and rust of the modern Havod, has shown how the deleterious exhalation of the copper-roasting furnace may be made beneficial to vegetation. Gerstenhöfer, the German chemist, recently discovered a method for condensing this sulphurous smoke into an acid used in making phosphate manures. The marketable value of the article thus producible from the smoke which was escaping a few years ago from the Swansea copper-works has been estimated at £200,000 yearly! The Messrs. Vivian immediately availed themselves of the invention and applied it to their works, and probably other proprietors have since followed their example. Mr. Hussey Vivian, in a speech he delivered on the subject in 1866, said he "believed that that district was destined to become the fertilizer of a very large portion of

England." From the appliances which they had then by way of experiment set up, he thought that "they would produce manure enough for something like 40,000 acres of turnip every year." Superphosphates have now become an important article for the agriculturist, and we would fain hope that no more "beautiful white smoke is seen rolling away over Kilvey Hill."

The Nationality of Crime in Glamorgan.

So peculiar is the composition of the population of this county that its social and moral phenomena may be expected to have some features of their own. Drawn together from all parts of the kingdom by the prospect of employment and high wages, and in many cases by the hope of shelter and prey, the crowded denizens of Merthyr, Aberdare, and Pontypridd, as well as of Swansea, Neath, and Cardiff, are not to be looked upon as belonging to the Welsh nation except in a qualified sense, and that nation cannot be properly credited with their good or bad qualities as citizens. It is established beyond question that Wales is distinguished for its comparative freedom from crime; it is equally clear that the populous county of Glamorgan has more than the Welsh average of misdemeanants, and much more than the average of heinous crimes. These facts suggest unavoidably the questions, Is the prevalence of breaches of the law in Glamorganshire traceable to the mixed character of the inhabitants? and, What, among cases of conviction, is the proportion of Welsh persons to persons of other nationalities?

We are supplied with the following valuable observations on the general subject from the pen of J. C. Fowler, Esq., stipendiary magistrate for the Merthyr district, who beyond most others is qualified to speak upon it with authority :—

"To a student of social characteristics nothing can be more interesting than the tracing of crime to its birthplaces. An investigation of this kind throws much valuable light upon the moral condition and social virtues and vices of any distinct populations, and on the incidents and circumstances which may be supposed to affect their conduct. The immediate object of the following remarks is to discover and disclose how far the population of the Principality yield to the temptation to crime, and what are the influences and circumstances which may be supposed to restrain them from yielding more than they do.

"The Principality comprises twelve counties, of which the entire population is about 1,250,000. Of this number more than 400,000 souls are found in the single county of Glamorgan; that is, one-third of the entire population of Wales. This county contains within its boundaries three very large parliamentary boroughs (of which two are great seaports), and also very extensive works of various kinds. All these commercial enterprises are carried on by the aid of large masses of Irish and English labourers and artificers. If any one will take the trouble to follow the accounts in the newspapers of the circuits of the judges of assize in Wales, he will perceive that their charges to the grand juries are almost always couched in complimentary terms in every county except Glamorgan. For example, on the 18th of July, 1871, the judge of assize at Carmarthen is reported to have 'congratulated the Grand Jury on the fact that the calendar contained so few cases for trial.' The number of prisoners was five. But the same judge is reported to have said in his charge to the Grand Jury of Glamorganshire on the 21st of the same month that 'he could not congratulate them on the appearance of the calendar,' which contained the formidable number of thirty-six prisoners, and disclosed many serious offences. The calendars of prisoners for trial at the Quarter Sessions for this county are also exceptionally long,—far longer than the great majority of English counties produce. It therefore becomes important and interesting to discover how far these unpleasant phenomena are attributable to native vice, and how much is due to the immigrant population. For this purpose we take a return which has been supplied by the governors of the county prisons of the birthplaces of all the prisoners who have been in their custody for the last five years. The total number of prisoners in the county gaol at Cardiff during the last five years was 8,226. Of this number no less than 2,133 were English, 129 Scotch, 555 foreigners, and 2,228 Irish, leaving a balance of only 3.181 Welsh prisoners out of the total of 8,226.

"Again, the total number of prisoners who have been in the custody of the governor of the county gaol at Swansea during the last *ten* years was 7,857. Of these, 1,570 were English, 82 Scotch, 1,461 Irish, 191 foreigners, 14 natives of colonies, and 74 unknown, leaving a balance of 4,471 Welsh prisoners out of the total 7,857. Again, if the calendar of one Quarter Sessions is taken at random as a sample, it will be found that in October, 1869, ninety prisoners were committed for trial. It appears that only about fifty of this number were natives of Wales, and still fewer natives of the county of Glamorgan. And at the sessions of June, 1870, out of 74 prisoners for trial 37 were not natives of Wales. These local indications are entirely corroborated by the general return of the birthplace of persons committed for trial in England and Wales. If the commitments for the year 1865 are examined, it appears that out of 98,656 commitments only 3,435 related to natives of Wales, while 18,569 were Irish cases. These facts and figures seem to establish the conclusion that though a dark shade of criminality has fallen upon the county of Glamorgan from the statistical returns supplied to the Legislature, it would be a grievous error to attribute it to the vicious tendencies of the native population. The fact is that whenever masses of persons are transferred from their native counties and parishes to distant localities, many powerful and restraining influences are withdrawn from them. Ireland is remarkably free from *ordinary* crime, but when the Irish are transplanted to England and Wales, they figure very darkly in the criminal statistics. The Welsh at home have the benefit of many restraining influences. The population is in general sparse, and consequently that natural police exists which consists in everybody knowing everybody and their pursuits. Then the Welsh people have a strong sense of the importance of religion, and almost every family is connected with one denomination of Christians or another. The result of these and other corrective circumstances is the happy and creditable fact that probably very few families resident in the rural districts of Wales, not excepting Glamorgan, would feel any apprehension in retiring to rest without taking any precautions whatever against nocturnal violence or intrusion."

The question thus temperately and judiciously presented is worthy of the consideration of the county authorities, and administrators of justice. Our judges of assize, coming as comparative strangers, are struck with the contrast between the calendar of Glamorganshire and Monmouthshire and those of other counties of Wales (for Monmouthshire is in reality in Wales), and too readily ascribe the difference to density of population. The cause is a much more complex one—the admixture of foreign nationalities, and not always the best materials of those nationalities. These parts are also sadly blighted by "the curse of intemperance," the prolific breeder of crime. That ingenious contrivance of modern legislation whereby revenue is made by multiplying temptations to intemperance, and spent in providing police and prisons to curb and punish the resulting disorder and crime, displays its working in Glamorganshire with most deplorable effect.

SECTION VI.—OLD AND EXTINCT FAMILIES OF GLAMORGANSHIRE.

The two classes of families belonging to this section—those that are totally *extinct*, and those that are *old*, but in some cases in the collateral and female descents not quite extinct—are unusually numerous in Glamorganshire. And it is noteworthy that in the former class is included a large proportion of foreign households introduced by the conquest of Glamorgan by the Normans. Glamorgan, in a far more marked degree than Brecknockshire, became a Normanized region, as the latter county was more Normanized than any of the remaining counties of Wales. The disappearance of the Norman families has been total and most remarkable. No favour of fortune has been able to prolong their race. To some extent, no doubt, this is attributable to the fact that notwithstanding their possession of large estates in this country, their homes were properly the other side the Severn; there they had their widest domains, their family sepulchres, their alliances, and in most cases there their descendants continued longest to flourish. This applies to the De Breoses, Despencers, De Londres, De Clares, Humfrevilles, Bronvilles, Flemings, &c. But even there, for long ages, the effigies that repose upon their tombs, and the names inscribed in the annals of old England, are the only memorials left of the pride and renown of many of them. It is not retribution, but the stern operation of natural law, before whose measured march all things human are made subject to incessant change, which has borne them away to oblivion. In Wales, of course, they were interlopers and unconscionable plunderers, but were not a whit worse than others of their time who had equal opportunities. Might was the patent to right in those days of violence, not only as taught by the gigantic trespass made by William the Bastard on the liberties and rights of Englishmen, but by the semi-barbarous sentiments of the age in all European lands.

By reason of the dominance of the Normans in this county, and the entire change they effected, we shall give them precedence in the memorials here introduced. On the ground of antiquity of origin most of them are not entitled to much consideration as compared with the households they overthrew; for they were, in the literal sense of the term, adventurers, obtained property and founded families by one stroke of pillage. Drawn from the "free companies" which traversed France, selling their lance and battle-axe to the highest bidder, hosts of William's knights had left no homes in that land, and had come in his train merely from a hope of bettering their fortune. And they are entitled to be called "Normans" only by a sort of courtesy—assuming that there is something honourable in the name beyond the halo which our cowardly nature ever paints around the head of success. We have no proof that of the twelve knights who became lords in Glamorgan, and the dozens of others less distinguished who under their shadow settled on the lands of the Welsh, there were half a dozen men of Norman blood. William himself, as we have already shown, was but in small part of Scandinavian origin. Not a seventh part of his subjects in the duchy of Normandy were anything else but Celts—the old race, somewhat mixed, of ancient Gaul. But in drawing together his great army of invasion he had gone out to all the neighbouring provinces of France, and notably into Brittany—that country of a purely Celtic race, next relations to the Cymry of Wales; and who will now say that most of the "Normans" who became Lords of Morganwg under Fitzhamon were not of near consanguinity with the people whose lands they appropriated? This is doubtless novel doctrine, but it necessarily follows from a candid scrutiny of historical facts.

1 —EXTINCT FAMILIES OF "NORMAN" DESCENT.

Robert Fitzhamon.

It has already been noted that Fitzhamon himself founded no family. Of four daughters he had, two embraced a religious life, and he was succeeded in his vast estates by his daughter Mabelia, or "Mabel," wife of his successor, Robert of Gloucester. Fitzhamon's name therefore disappeared with himself. But although a conqueror—and often after the Norman fashion disposed to rule with a strong hand,—and in spite of the fact that his rule extended only over a period of some dozen years, and left little space therefore to soften down the asperities of conquest, Fitzhamon left behind him a character not entirely hateful to the Welsh. He had qualities which tended, had the age been of a milder temper, to cause the burden of oppression to lie lightly upon his vassals. Of his antecedents we know little, except that he was nearly related to William the Conqueror, succeeded his father, Hamon Dentatus, as Lord of Astremeville in Normandy, came to England as a knight in the service of the Conqueror, had assigned him the possessions of Brictric the Saxon, Lord of Gloucester, of which he was seised when commissioned by Rufus to push on his fortunes among the South Welsh. Holding Gloucester and Glamorgan, he had also the care of his lands in Normandy, and while employed in a warlike expedition in that duchy was wounded with a spear at the siege of Falaise, of which wound he died A.D. 1102. He was brought to be buried at the abbey of Tewkesbury, which, as Lord of Gloucester, he had founded. He is said to have borne—"*Sa., a lion rampant guardant or, incensed gu.*"

Robert of Gloucester.

The second lord paramount of Glamorgan was Robert, natural son of Henry I. by Nest, daughter of Rhys ap Tewdwr, Prince of South Wales. Robert, by his wife Mabel, dau. of Fitzhamon, had four sons,—William, his successor as Lord of Glamorgan; Roger, Bishop of Worcester, who died at Tours in France, A.D. 1179; Hamon, who died at the siege of Toulouse, A.D. 1159; and Philip. Robert of Gloucester was the founder of Margam Abbey and Keynsham Abbey. To him was committed by Henry I. the custody of Robert, Duke of Normandy, whose long imprisonment in the Curthose Tower of Cardiff

Castle we have noticed. William was that Lord of Glamorgan (as well as of Gloucester) who was captured by Ivor Bach, Welsh Lord of Castell Coch, in his castle of Cardiff, and, with his wife and son, carried away to the hills, and there detained until he had restored to Ivor "everything unjustly taken from him," and given "compensation of additional property" (Giraldus, *Itin.*, 6). He *m.* Hawise, dau. of the Earl of Leicester (the lady thus unceremoniously dealt with by Ivor), and dying A.D. 1173, was buried at Keynsham Abbey, which his father had founded. Leaving no son his line ceased with himself, and he was ultimately succeeded by his younger daughter, Amicia, whose husband, Richard de Clare, Earl of Hertford, became, in his wife's right, Lord of Gloucester and Glamorgan.

The De Clares.

The De Clares, next to Fitzhamon and Robert of Gloucester, were the greatest of the Lords of Glamorgan. The first of their line in that lordship was the Richard just mentioned, who married Amicia, dau. of William, Lord of Glamorgan, son of Robert of Gloucester, and through her became Lord of Gloucester and Glamorgan. His son, Gilbert de Clare, his successor, active among the barons who brought King John to grant Magna Charta, *m.* Isabel, dau. of William Marshall (Mareschal), Earl of Pembroke, and had with other issue an eldest son, Richard, who, upon his death in Brittany A.D. 1229, inherited his lordships as a minor, under the guardianship of the famous Hugh de Burgh, Earl of Kent. Hugh de Burgh had a dau., Margaret, whom young Richard de Clare had a liking for and married, much, it is said, to the displeasure of the king—the king in those days being considered entitled to advise, and at times even more than advise his barons in the matter of marriage,— but from whom he afterwards was divorced. His second wife was Maude, dau. of John de Lacy, Earl of Lincoln, by whom he had issue. His eldest son,—

Gilbert de Clare, surnamed by the Welsh, Gilbert *Gôch*, "the red," *m.* Alice de March, dau. of Guy, Count of Angoulême. She was niece of the French king, who bestowed upon her a portion of 5,000 marks. He was the first Lord of Glamorgan who obtained possession of Caerphilly Castle (p. 534). Gilbert de Clare, like his father and grandfather, was zealous for the cause of the barons as against King Henry III. On the death of the king, A.D. 1272, he was one of the barons who met at the New Temple, London, to proclaim King Edward I.; and on Edward's return from the Holy Land, where he was pursuing his knightly duties at the time of his accession, was the first to welcome and entertain him at his castle of Tonbridge. Having divorced his first wife, he *m.*, after the lapse of some years, Joan of Acre, dau. of King Edward I., who, in her turn, *m.*, as her second husband; Ralph de Mortimer (see *Caerphilly Castle*). Gilbert de Clare *d.* at Monmouth Castle A.D. 1295, and was buried at Tewkesbury Abbey. He left by his second wife, Joan, a son and successor,—

Gilbert de Clare, Earl of Gloucester, and Lord of Glamorgan, who at the time of his accession was only five years of age. He grew up to manhood, and was guardian of the kingdom during Edward II.'s absence in the Scottish wars. He fell in the battle of Bannockburn, A.D. 1314, in his twenty-third year, and was buried at Tewkesbury Abbey with his ancestors. Dying unmarried A.D. 1313, and leaving no issue, he left his great possessions to his three sisters, co-heiresses, and the earldom of Gloucester as well as the line of the De Clares became extinct. The arms of the De Clares were—*Or, three chevrons gu.*

The Despencers.

Hugh le Despencer, *temp.* Edward II., had a son Hugh, who *m.* Eleanor, eldest sister of the last Gilbert de Clare above named, and in her right became Lord of Glamorgan. Too ambitious of extending his territory, and favoured by the king, he came into conflict with De Breos, Lord of Gower, and other barons, among whom were De Bohun, Mortimer, Audley, Mowbray, Berkley, Seys, and Talbot, who took up arms, ravaged his lands in Morganwg, formed so large a confederacy among the barons of England and the Marches as to overpower the king, Despencer's protector, and obtain a sentence of deprivation and banishment against the obnoxious Despencer family. The Earl of Leicester, however, who was at their head, was defeated in the field, and the Despencers' prospects once more brightened. The young Hugh Despencer is said now to have procured from the king, in addition to his former lordship of Glamorgan (see *Dugdale*), the manors and castles of Swansea, Oystermouth, Pennard, and Loughor, in Gower, which he exchanged with Eleanor, wife of John de Burgh, for the manors and castles of Usk, Tre-grug, Caerleon, &c., in Monmouthshire. The ruins of his magnificence are still seen at Caerphilly (see *Caerphilly Castle*). Adversity, however, in time overcame both king and favourite, and (his father having already perished) Despencer lost his life on the scaffold, having been impeached before Parliament at Hereford A.D. 1326. His sentence was, "to be drawn upon a hurdle, with trumps and trumpets, throughout all the city of Hereford, and then to be hanged and quartered."

He left two sons, Hugh and Edward. The former became Lord of Glamorgan, having been received into favour by the new sovereign, Edward III., who bestowed upon him an extensive share of the possessions of his late father, which upon his impeachment had escheated to the Crown. In the 17th Edward III. he is styled Lord of Glamorgan, and on his death, six years subsequently, he was seised of the several manors and castles which had belonged to his father in Glamorganshire. He had *m.* Elizabeth, dau. of William Montacute, Earl of Salisbury, who afterwards married Guy de Breos, taking with her as her dower among other of their late husband's possessions in Glamorganshire, "the castle, town, and manor of Neath, the hamlets of Cilybebyll and Britton, the whole territory of Nedd, on both sides the river, the castle, lordship, and town of Kenfig, the castle and manor of Llanblethian, and the castle, town, and manor of Talyvan." This Hugh Despencer dying without issue A.D. 1349, his other possessions passed to his brother Edward, who in turn was followed by his son,—

Edward Despencer, Lord of Glamorgan, whose wife was Elizabeth, dau. and heiress of Baron Burgherst. This was the Despencer who accompanied the Black Prince to France and fought at Poictiers (see p. 536). He died at Cardiff (Caerphilly Castle being probably no longer one of the family residences) A.D. 1375, and was buried at Tewkesbury Abbey, leaving his son Thomas as his successor in the lordship of Glamorgan.

Thomas Despencer *m.* Constance, dau. of Edmund de Langley, Duke of York, fifth son of King Edward III. He it was who petitioned Parliament for a reversal of the sentence of banishment still recorded against his great-grandfather, though now, as regarded his family, practically a dead letter. In this he succeeded, as well as in obtaining the favour of Richard II., and for a time with great zeal and devotion espoused the king's cause against the House of Lancaster. But in this case neither liege lord nor feoffee was a person long to be depended upon. Despencer basely deserted a base master, and assisted in his deposition; but the next king, Henry IV., showed little appreciation of his services: as soon as he had seated himself on the throne, Despencer was deprived of all his estates, apprehended at Bristol in his attempt to fly the kingdom, condemned by the House of Commons, and executed in the market-place of Bristol A.D. 1400. He left a son, Richard, who *d. s. p.* 1414, and one surviving dau., Isabel. His estates in Glamorganshire, which had escheated to the Crown on his impeachment, were restored to his widow, and descended to the dau. and her heirs. (See *Beauchamps* below.) Thus ended the proud, grasping, and unfortunate family of Despencer, who had been oppressors of the weak, and flatterers and traitors towards the strong. Their arms were—*Quarterly, arg. and gu., in the second and third quarters a fret or; over all a bend sa.*

The Beauchamps.

Richard Beauchamp, Baron Abergavenny, afterwards cr. Earl (*comes*) of Worcester by his marriage with Isabel Despencer above named, succeeded to the lordship of Glamorgan, and held his court at Cardiff Castle. On his death (A.D. 1431) his widow *m.*, by special dispensation from the Pope, his relative, Richard Beauchamp, Earl of Warwick, one of the most distinguished knights of the age. He visited the Holy Land, and signalized his strength and prowess in many tournaments and feats of arms. Upon his death, which took place at Rouen in Normandy, A.D. 1439, his earldom and lordship vested in his son Henry. This young earl in his nineteenth year tendered his services for the defence of the duchy of Aquitaine, was created, A.D. 1444, Premier Earl of England, advanced to the dignity of Duke of Warwick, with next precedency, along with the Duke of Buckingham, to the Duke of Norfolk. His territorial influence under grants and charters from the king was largely increased in the Channel Islands, the Isle of Wight, Somersetshire, and Wales. He obtained the Forest of Dean, with its castles and manors, for a rental of £100 a year. He is said to have been married, when only ten years of age, to Cicely, dau. of Richard Neville, Earl of Salisbury, by whom he left an only dau., Anne, born at Cardiff Castle, upon whose death in 1449 the lordship of Glamorgan, and her other estates and honours, devolved upon her aunt, Anne, sister of the late Duke of Warwick. She was at this time married to Richard Neville, Earl of Salisbury, who was shortly after cr. Earl of Warwick. Here ended the name of Beauchamps, Lords of Glamorgan. The Beauchamps bore—*Gu., a fesse between three cross cresslets, or.*

The Nevilles.

Richard Neville, Earl of Salisbury of that day, born about 1420, became the husband of Anne, sister and heiress of Henry Beauchamp, Lord of Glamorgan, and in her right became Earl of Warwick and Lord of Glamorgan. He is well known in English history as "the king-maker," and his influence in public affairs, like that of the Beauchamps and Despencers, was much greater through his English than through his Welsh territories. The lordship of Glamorgan had by this time fallen into some obscurity, and the great castle of Caerphilly was scarcely used as one of the lord's castles. His vast power in the state was owing to an unusual combination of circumstances and personal qualities. His two uncles, William and Edward, were at the same time, through marriage, Barons Fauconberg and Abergavenny, and another uncle, George Neville, also through marriage, was Baron Latimer. Still more important was his relation to Richard, Duke of York, who had married Cecily, dau. of Warwick's grandfather, the Earl of Westmoreland, and who, as representative of Lionel, Earl of Clarence, third son of Edward III., was the lineal heir to the throne now occupied by the House of Lancaster, descended from Edward IV.'s son, John of Gaunt. In this way Richard Neville, Earl of Warwick, and King Edward IV., son of Richard, Duke of York, were first cousins. He was slain 1471, and his estates were forfeited.

It has been said that at this time the Nevilles were the most extensively and influentially connected family that has ever existed among the nobility of England. All these advantages, however, would have proved of little value to an inferior or indiscreet man. Richard Neville was neither. Of good intellectual capacity and ready eloquence, he was courteous and affable in behaviour, brave, prompt, and enduring as a soldier, and boundless as well as magnificent in hospitality. Stow says of him (*Chronicle*), "When he came to London he held such an house that six oxen were eaten of a breakfast, and every tavern was full of his meat; for who [ever] had any acquaintance in that house, should have as much sodden and roast as he might carry upon a long dagger." Wherever he resided he kept open house; the number of people welcomed to his tables at his various mansions was so great that they have been computed, perhaps with some exaggeration, at not less than thirty thousand.

The whole history of the struggle between the Yorkists and the Lancastrians is the history of this remarkable man. From the first armed rising against Henry VI., A.D. 1455, to the settlement upon the throne of Edward IV., after the defeat of the Lancastrians at the battle of Barnet, his genius and energy were felt.

The Earl of Warwick leaving no son, in him the line of the Nevilles became extinct, and virtually also that of Lords of Glamorgan. His eldest dau., Isabel Neville (*d.* 1477), *m.* George Plantagenet, Duke of Clarence, brother of Edward IV., and left by him (who was put to death in 1478) a son, Edward, styled Earl of Warwick, beheaded on Tower Hill in 1499; and a dau., Margaret, cr. Countess of Salisbury, also executed on Tower Hill, at the age of seventy, in 1541. The Earl of Warwick's second dau., Anne Neville, *m.* first Edward, Prince of Wales, son of Henry VI., who was murdered in 1471, by whom she had no issue; and secondly, Richard, Duke of Gloucester, afterwards King Richard III., who kept the lordships of Glamorgan and Abergavenny in his own hands during his lifetime, after which they fell to Henry VII., his uncle. Thus ended the house of Neville.

The arms of the Nevilles were—*Gu., a saltier arg.*

The lordship of Glamorgan (with that of Abergavenny), now held by the first Tudor king, was conferred by him upon his uncle, Jasper, Earl of Pembroke (younger son of Owen Tudor, of *Penmynydd Môn*), upon whose death it again reverted to the Crown, and was held by Henry VIII. and his son, Edward VI. This young king sold the lordship to William Herbert, Earl of Pembroke, from whom it has descended to the present noble owner. (See further under *Bute, Marquis of.*)

Here cease those great baronial families, the Lords of Glamorgan proper; and we have next to notice another powerful but less magnificent family who held a lordship in Gower, not under obligation of service to the Lord Paramount of Glamorgan, but directly under the king.

The De Breos Family.

After the Lords of Glamorgan above enumerated, the most important family of Norman descent which bore rule in this county was that of *De Breos*, whose lordship in Gower was a Lordship Marcher. Their principal territories in Wales, however, were the lordships of Brecknock and Abergavenny. Philip de Breos, whose father, William de Breos, came to England with the Conqueror, in right of his wife, dau. of Fitz-Walter, Earl of Hereford, became seised of the lordships of Brecknock, Abergavenny, and Gower, and held besides the barony of Brembre in Sussex, with some fifty-six other lordships in that and other counties (*Doomsday*). He *d.* in the reign of Henry II. This great house continued through eight successions—the last of the Gower line being William de Breos, who in the 22nd of Edward I., A.D. 1294, was one of the lords summoned to a *parliament* on the affairs of the nation, and in the 29th year of the same king received a like summons in the rank of barons. Edward also granted him *jura regalia* in Gower of equal extent and dignity with those enjoyed by Gilbert de Clare, Lord of Glamorgan. Being, however, as Walsingham has it, a person of "large patrimony but great unthrift," he deemed it convenient to dispose by sale his territory of Gower to the Earl of Hereford, who was deprived of it by force by Hugh Despencer the younger, King Edward II.'s favourite. This led to the insurrection of the barons under the leadership of Thomas, Earl of Lancaster. William de Breos, Lord of Gower, *d.* A.D. 1322, leaving no male issue. See further *De Breos*, p. 69, &c., and Nicolas, *Synop. of Peerage*, i., 82.

Two of the De Breoses, Reginald (*d.* 1221) and his son William (*d.* 1229), came into intimate relationship with Llewelyn ap Iorwerth, Prince of North Wales. The former married Gwladys, the prince's daughter; the latter became his prisoner at Aber palace, and abusing the indulgence shown him, exposed himself to the righteous vengeance which cut short his life on the gallows (p. 69). We have already shown that Caerphilly Castle came first to the De Breos family by grant of it to this Reginald by his father-in-law Llewelyn.

The De Breos arms were—*Az., semée of cross crosslets gu., a lion rampant or, armed and langued gu.* The De Breoses, Lords of Brecknock, are also said (see Jones's *Hist. of Breck.*) to have borne *Barry of six vair of ermine and gu.*

The above were *Barones Majores*, holding from the sovereign: the following were *Barones Minores*, holding from, and under obligation of service to the great Barons, and not, like them, entitled to be summoned to the king's council.

De Granville.

The line of Granville is traced to Rollo, the first Scandinavian conqueror of Normandy, and from Rollo Richard Granvyl, Granvyld, or Granville, who came over with his relative, William the Conqueror, was sixth in descent. He was brother of Robert Fitzhamon, whom he assisted in the conquest of Glamorgan, and received for his services the lordship of Neath (see *Neath Abbey* and *Castle*). Though Richard himself is said to have returned to Normandy, and afterwards to have taken the cross and died on a journey to Palestine, he left a son and successor to his estates in Wales. The line, however, did not continue long in Wales, but much longer in Cornwall (see *Grenfell, Maesteg House*), where Richard's grandson, also named Richard, *m.* a dau. of James Trewynt, of Trewynt, or Treint. (See *Pedigree of Lady Llanover.*) The Granvilles bore—*Gu., three clarions or.*

De Londres.

William de Londres (or Londinensis), supposed to have been born in London, a soldier under Fitzhamon in compassing the conquest of Glamorgan, and thereafter Lord of Ogmore, or Aberogwr, had a son, Maurice de Londres, who divides with his father the honour of founding Ewenny Abbey (see *Ewenny Abbey*). Maurice, otherwise called Meyrick, left a son, William de Londres, who succeeded him as Lord of Ogmore. Both father and son are highly extolled also for their grants of land to Neath Abbey and monastery, and for their personal valour and general excellence. The line soon lost its prominence in Glamorganshire, its chief possessions and place of burial being in England, where also its political influence mainly lay.

The De Londres arms were—*Gu., three trefoils slipped in bend arg., in chief a lion passant or.*

De Turberville of Coity.

The Turbervilles at one time were a numerous family with several branches in Glamorganshire, as at Tythegston, Penlline, and Llanilltyd, or Lantwit; but were in all cases sprung from the Turbervilles of Coity Castle, the first of whose line, as already shown (see *Coity Castle*), was Sir Pain de Turberville. This "Norman" was probably, as his name would indicate, derived from the Celts of Brittany or Normandy, a probability made all the stronger by his choosing to wife the dau. of Morgan ap Meurig, the Welsh lord of Coity. He was the first of the foreign race to set this example, and was not readily imitated. He is said to have been followed at Coity Castle in regular succession by ten or eleven of his descendants, eight of whom were from father to son direct,—Gilbert, Pain, Pain, Gilbert, Richard, Pain, Gilbert, which last Gilbert was succeeded by his brother Richard, with whom issue male failed, and who devised the Coity lordship to his nephew, Sir Laurence Berkrolles, who *d.* A.D. 1412. (See *Berkrolles of St. Athan's*, and *Gamage of Coity Castle.*)

The arms of De Turberville are said to have been—*Checky, or and gu., a chief ermine.*

De Berkrolles of St. Athan's.

This family was settled at East Orchard, St. Athan's, for nearly 300 years, the first founder of the house being Sir Roger Berkrolles, who received the lordship as a reward for his knightly service under Robert Fitzhamon. The last of the line male, Sir Laurence Berkrolles, whose fortune, as seen under *Turberville of Coity Castle*, was increasing when his name was about to pass into oblivion, by his wife, a dau. of the Despencers, had no issue (see p. 522), and his inheritance passed to Sir Edward Stradling, who was maternally descended from the Berkrolles. The Berkrolles arms were—*Az., a chevron between three crescents or.*

De Humfreville of Penmark.

Gilbert de Humfreville was founder of this house. Having assisted Fitzhamon in the subjugation of Morganwg, he was presented with the lands of Penmark, or Penmarch Howell, and his heirs male enjoyed the same until the reign of Edward III., when the line ceased, and the lordship of Penmark descended to Sir John St. John, of Fonmon Castle. Sir Henry de Humfreville, Kt., was living near the end of the reign of Edward II. (*circa* 1327), as shown by his signature to a deed to which are also attached the names of Sir Philip Fleming, Sir William Berkrolles, &c. The Humfreville arms were—*Arg., a fesse between six cinquefoils gu.*

St. John of Fonmon Castle.

One of the "twelve knights," Sir *Oliver* St. John (to whom, however, Burke gives the name *John*), received as his share of the lands of Glamorgan the lordship of Fonmon. This was about A.D. 1094-5, and his descendants are said to have continued to possess, if not always to reside at Fonmon Castle, for 400 years or more, when Sir Oliver St. John of that place, an adventurous soldier in Ireland under Elizabeth, was raised to the peerage of England A.D. 1559, under the title of Baron St. John of Bletsoe, Viscount Grandison, and Baron Trégoze, being descended through a remote maternal ancestor from the Beauchamps, Lords of Bletsoe, in Northamptonshire (comp. D. Jenkin's MS., p. 221). His son, also called Oliver, 3rd Baron, was advanced in 1624 to the dignity of Earl of Bolingbroke, a title which became extinct, and was renewed in the same family in favour of Henry St. John, the celebrated politician and writer of the time of Queen Anne and George I., cr. Baron Tregoze and Viscount Bolingbroke A.D. 1712. Oliver St. John, first Earl Bolingbroke, sold the Fonmon estate about the middle of the seventeenth century to Col. Philip Jones, M.P., one of Cromwell's privy council, ancestor of the present proprietor (see *Jones, Fonmon Castle*). The title, Baron St. John of Bletsoe, still survives.

Fonmon in the Norman-French took the form *Faumont*, but does not seem to have been a name imposed by the Normans, who are more likely to have corrupted in this as in many other cases an earlier native designation. Close by runs a stream called *Cen-fon*, and both names are related.

The St. Johns bore—*Arg., on a chief gu., two mullets pierced or.*

Le Esterling (Stradling) of St. Donat's Castle.

We have no better account of the first entrance of this family upon Welsh territory than that given in Caradoc's *Brut*, to the effect that when Robert Fitzhamon took upon himself the rule and chieftainship of the whole district of Glamorgan, " to *William Desterlin* was allotted the lordship of *Llanwerydd*"—the earlier designation of St. Donat's. Of a family which in after times occupied a place almost vying in importance with that of the major barons, we have little information until this William de Esterling, or le Esterling—a name which gradually resolved itself in the popular articulation, and even in written record, into the form *Stradling*—took his share of the lands which Fitzhamon did homage for to Rufus, A.D. 1092 or 1094. It has been said by Collins that William le Esterling derived originally from the "eastern people called *Easterlings*, who dwelt near the Baltic Sea;" but whether this is anything better than a conjecture suggested by the form of the name we cannot say.

The sixth in descent after Sir William was Sir Peter Stradling, Knt., who *m.* Joan, sole heir of Thomas Hawey, of Cwmhawey, in Somerset, now called Comb-hay. He was succeeded by his son, Sir Edward, who *m.* Eleanor, dau. of Sir Gilbert Strongbow. To him and his wife and children, William de *Sancto Donato*, Abbot of Neath (probably a relative), in consideration of certain concessions, gave, in 1341, "a general participation of the spiritual good things of his abbey, and founded an obit after their death, annually for ever" (see Clark's *Castle of St. Donat's*, 1871). In the deed executed on the occasion Sir Edward is denominated "Dominus de Sancto Donato *Anglicanus*"—a description which seems to imply either a preceding or a contemporary *Wallicanus* Lord of St. Donat's.

The next Sir Edward, Knight of the Sepulchre, son of the last, was sent to Parliament by the co. of Somerset in the 17th Edward III., or 1344, and was Sheriff of Glamorgan in 1367. Through his wife, Gwenllian, dau. and eventually h. of Sir Roger Berkrolles, he became possessor of East Orchard and Merthyr Mawr.

The Stradlings had a vein of piety and a taste for pilgrim adventure. The last-mentioned Sir Edward, and his son Sir William, both visited Jerusalem, and obtained the dignity—much coveted in those days—of Knight of the Sepulchre. Sir William's son and successor, Sir Edward Stradling, also made a pilgrimage to the Holy Land, and found a grave at Jerusalem about A.D. 1478. He *m.* Jane, dau. of Henry Beaufort, son of John of Gaunt, and in addition to a number of illegitimate children, he had by his wife a son and successor, *Sir Harry Stradling*, whose story acquired a tinge of romance from his capture, while crossing the Severn estuary, by the Breton pirate, Colin Dolphin. His captor demanding a ransom price of 2,200 marks, or about £1,400, Sir Harry to meet the exaction had to sell his manor of Sutton in Glamorganshire, and those of Bassaleg, Rogerston, and Tregwilym, in Monmouthshire, besides two manors in the co. of Oxford—a transaction which throws some light on the value of land and money, as well as on the state of society in those days. Sir Harry, like his forefathers, paid a visit to Jerusalem, and died on his way home in the island of Cyprus, being at the time only about thirty years of age. A letter he wrote from Rome to his wife (Elizabeth, dau. of Sir William ap Thomas Herbert, Lord of Raglan) is worth quoting, in illustration of the customs and sentiments of the times, as well as of the English used by Sir Harry Stradling.

"Ryght herteley belowyd wyfe, I grete wele a thowsande tymes, lettynge yowe wete [know] that at the makyng of this lett^r I was in gode hele, eblessyd be God, and that is grete wond^r, for there was nev^r meñ that had so pelowse [perilous] a wey as we hadde, save only eworschep be God we were not let [hindered] in no place, nor tangled: the pilgremys that were goyng to Cales [Calais] were iij tymes cast alonde w^t storme; and assone as I come, eblessyde be God, we were over w^{t}yn iiij owres, and taried there till the furst Sonday o^f Clene Lent, and a Sonday aft^r mas we toke our jorne, and wente owte of the towne vij schore p'sones, and went so till we come to the londe of Luke [Lucca], and there euery mañ dyd wex wery of othur. Notw^{t}stonding I met at Londoñ iij of my sonne Mile is neyperes [neighbours] aprest [ready] and ij othur. Also, Joh^n Wach^n [Vychan] and Joh^n Lewis Gont^{er}, yor cosyñ, and iiij w^t them; and so we were xij p'sons, and n^{er} nev^{er} dep'tyd [separated] till we come to Rome, . . . and a gode Fryday in the mornyng we come to Rome; the nyght tafore we lay in a forest und^r a tre, evell at ese by cause we wolde overtake the . . . and see the vernicle [a relic of St. Veronica]. And so we saw hit Friday, Sat'day a Sonday to fore masse—the pope he assoyled [absolved] vs of plena remyssio, & afte^r he hadde songe his masse he come ageyñ and assoyled them as fre as that day theye were borñ, and for to say that there was pepull, there was w^{t}oute nom^r, and for se othur plac^{es} of Remission w^{t}out eny mo nom^r. And also as tochyng yor absolucioñ I hadde grete labo^r and cost to gete hit vnd^r ledde, and therefore lett eny mañ or womañ bewar howe he makythe a vow, hit is akowven^{n}t must be kept. Also I hope to God to remove towarde Wenys [Venice] by litell est^{er} day, and I have gete my licens of the Pope and iiij Englische meñ more w^t me; and yef I kan go in savete, I will go. yef no I will be at home by Mydsomr, and yef I go h^t will be alhalowyn tyde or I come home. And also Richard Rethe [Rees] is in gode hele blessyd be God, save he was a litell crasid in his legge a fortenygt w^t a senewe spronge, and nowe he is hole. Notw'stondyng Tom Gethyn offeryd to go in his place, but he will not by no mene. Also I pray yowe to se my dayes kept at Barry, for ye dayes must nede be kept or ellse I must be schamyd. Also I requere yowe to thynke ou^{er} my last will, as my trust is in yowe abowe all pepull. Also astochyng the westment at Londoñ there is apoñ hit iij li [pounds] whereof I payed a nobull in ernyst; Joh^{n}n de Bole kañ tell, he was at the bargeñ makyng & William Jenkyñ. Also the Kyng of Hungery hathe hadde a grete distress aponne Turk^{es} to the nomer of xl thowsande and his sonne takyñ and is w^t Cristen meñ, and therefore I trust to God ow^r wey will be the bett^{er}. Also as for yor absolucion Tom Gethyñ bryngethe hit home, by cause ye porer y^t a man goythe the bet^{er} hit is, but hit costithe grete gode [a large sum], and nere hit were [were it no:] for yor sowle his helthe hit schulde nev^r be boght for me; I hadde neuer so grete travayle forno thyng. Als^o that ye be gode maystres to Res De [Rhys Du—"the black"]; he was gode to me cc myle in my feleschepe, and boed [remained] behynde at the last and meght not go. And when I come to Rome I met w^t Thom Gethyñ and there he went not fro me, but went all the staciones w^t me bett^r then he y^t hadde be here vij yere to fore, for he knewe evy place as well w^{t}oute ye towne as w^{t}yn, and bode here iiij dayes apoñ his cost to have you^r bull [of absolution]. Right hertely belowyd wyfe, almyhty IHU have yowe in his kepynge; and loke that ye be agode chere and prey for me, as I trust to God to pray for yowe; for I trust to God at this ow^r I am clene to God and to the worlde, as clene as ye day I was borne.

"Wretyn at Rome the last day of Marche. Yo^r husbonde, HARRE STRADLYNG.
(Addressed) "To my Right hertely belowyd wyfe, Elyzabethe Stradlyng."

The above letter was printed in the *Archæologia*, from the autograph still in possession of Col. G. G. Francis, F.S.A. It shows how completely the magnates of that day were subject to the power of the priesthood, and to ceremonial conceptions of religion. Of Sir Harry's morals we have little account beyond what is favourably implied in the tenor of this letter; but some of his immediate predecessors, equally zealous with himself as pilgrims to Rome, were not always "as clean to God and to the world as the day they were born." Sir Harry left a son, named Thomas, who *m*. Janet, dau. of Thomas Mathew, Esq., of Radir (who *m*. as her second husband Sir Rhys ap Thomas, of Dinefawr), and dying young, left two sons, Edward and Harry. The former succeeded, and *m*. Elizabeth, dau. of Sir Thomas Arundel, Knt., of Laneyron, in Cornwall, and had by her four sons and two daus. (besides a number of illegitimate children), the heir being Thomas, who succeeded on the death of his father in 1535; was Sheriff of Glamorgan 1547-8; knighted by Edward VI. 1549; Commissioner for the Marches of Wales; M.P. for East Grinstead; Commissioner for the Suppression of Heretics, under Elizabeth, 1558. He m. Catherine, dau. of Sir Thomas Gamage, of Coity. The building of the Stradling Chapel in St. Donat's Church is ascribed to him.

It was this same Sir Thomas Stradling (*State Papers*, Eliz., Vol. XVII.) who was committed to the Tower by command of Elizabeth, for the pretended "invention" or discovery of the form of a *cross*, "rather longer than a man's foot," in the interior substance of a tree on his estate blown down in a storm. Sir Edward, believing in the miracle, gets the cross "copied;" our Lords of the Council, and her dread Majesty, hear of the scandal, and Sir Thomas, as a lesson in Protestantism, is "sent to the Tower"! From this durance, he, the proud Lord of St. Donat's, as a beseeching "orator" sends his humble petition to the Queen's most excellent Majesty, and explains that, "wher as abowte Est' 1559 certein trees were cast down by the wynde in a park of your orator's in Wales amongest the whych ther was one tree cloven in the myddes from the top downe hard to the grownde . . . in the very sape or hert whereof was a picture of a crosse of xiiij. inches longe, apparent, and pleyn to be seen, . . . of which crosse your orator made a patron [pattern] conteyning the length, brede, and facion thereof, and bryngeng the same wth hym to London caused iiij pictures thereof to be painted. . . . Yo'r orator is very sorye that he had not fyrst fownde meanes to have made yo'r Grace prevy therof; . . . for yf he had knowen or thought that yo'r Highnes or yo'r counsell wolde have ben offendyd there wth or taken it in yll parte, he wolde not for any thing have done it. And for as moche as that he dyd therein was not don upon any sediciouse purpose or yll entent, but only of ignorance, for the which he have all redy susteyned above v. weykes imp'sonme't, yo'r orator most humbly besecheth yo'r mostte excellent ma^e of yo'r accostomed clemencie to bere wth hys ignorance therin," &c. Cecil, the minister, who thought it salutary "to punish massmongers, for the rebating of their humours," sees from these words that his method is succeeding. But there is yet much questioning and careful inquiry. A commission is appointed to examine the "tree," and the part of the tree is cut out and sent up to London! In the end, Sir Thomas Stradling is allowed, on his giving a bond to forfeit 1,000 marks, should he fail to appear if called upon before the Privy Council, to return to his home (see Clark's *St. Donat's Castle*, p. 22). His son and heir was—

Sir Edward Stradling, the ablest and most eminent of his house, a man of refined tastes, a patron of Welsh literature, and an author. Anthony a' Wood (*Athenæ Oxon.*) says of him that having been educated in the University of Oxford, he travelled "in various countries, spent some time at Rome, returned an accomplished gentleman, and retiring to his inheritance, which was large, built a firm structure on that foundation of literature he had laid at Oxford and elsewhere, . . . was at the charge of such herculean works for the public good that no man in his time went beyond him for his singular knowledge in the British language and antiquities, for his eminent encouragement of learning and learned men, and for his great expense and indefatigable industry in collecting together several ancient manuscripts of learning and antiquity, all which, with other books, were reduced into a well-ordered library at St. Donat's, to the great credit and renown of the family. He writ a Welsh

Grammar mostly in Latin. He wrote also the conquest of the lordship of Glamorgan by Morganwg, with other pieces, and having *m.* Agnes, dau. to Sir Edward Gage, of Firle, in Sussex, paid his last debt to nature 15th May, 1609." He was sheriff three times, and was builder of the sea wall at St. Donat's. A collection of letters addressed to him was published by the late antiquary, the Rev. J. M. Traherne. Dying *s. p.* in 1609 in his eightieth year, he was succeeded by his kinsman,—

Sir John Stradling, 1st Bart., son of Francis, son of Henry, grandson of the Sir Harry who was captured by the pirates, and wrote the interesting letter to his "right hertely belowyd wyfe" which we have given. Sir John was also a man of some literary tastes. He graduated at Oxford 1583, "being then accounted a miracle for his forwardness in learning and pregnancy of parts" (Wood). He travelled abroad, was cr. a baronet 1611, and settled at St. Donat's. He published a volume of Latin epigrams, *Beati Pacifici*, 1623; and "*Divine Poems*" in seven several classes, "written to King Charles I." He *m.* Elizabeth, dau. of Edward, son of Sir Edward Gage of Firle (and niece of Agnes, the last Sir Edward's wife), and had a numerous family. His death took place 1637, when his eldest son,—

Sir Edward Stradling, Kt., and 2nd Bart. of St. Donat's, succeeded to the estates. He was a colonel in the army of Charles I., for whom he and his brothers fought with entire devotion. At Edgehill he was taken prisoner. His wife was Mary, dau. of Sir Thomas Mansel of Margam. Sir Edward *d.* 1644, and was buried at Oxford in the chapel of Jesus College. His eldest son,—

Sir Edward Stradling, 3rd Bart., was a staunch and active soldier in the army of Charles I. He brought a troop of horse of his own to aid the king at Newbury, and after the disaster of that day retired to Oxford (as his father had done after the battle of Edgehill), and there died of consumption, it is said before his father. He had *m.* Catherine, dau. of Sir Hugh Perry, and wife afterwards of Bussey Mansel of Breton Ferry. Their eldest son,—

Sir Edward Stradling, 4th Bart., M.P. for Cardiff 1698, *m.* Elizabeth, dau. of Anthony Hungerford, Esq., and had several sons, of whom the eldest, Edward, inherited the title and estates as 6th Bart.; was Sheriff of Glamorgan 1710, M.P. for Cardiff 1714—1722; *m.* Elizabeth, dau. of Sir Edward Mansel of Margam, by whom he had issue several children, who all died young. The property and title descended to his brother,—

Sir Thomas Stradling, 6th Earl, who *d.* unmarried 1738, in his twenty-eighth year, when the title and line of Stradling became extinct. His estates passed to Bussy, Lord Mansel, for the term of his life, and thereafter became the subject of prolonged litigation, which ended in ample benefit to the lawyers, and a settlement by authority of Parliament by which they were divided into four portions: (1) St. Donat's and Sully, which fell to the share of Sir John Tyrwhit, Bart., "by virtue of a deed entered into between Sir Thomas and Sir John during their travels in foreign countries" (Jenkin's MS.). (2) Merthyr Mawr and Monknash were allotted to Hugh Bowen of Kittle Hill, grandson, on the mother's side, of Sir Edward Stradling. This portion was divided between him and his eldest son, George. (3) Penlline, Llamphey, and Cwmhawey in Somerset fell to Louisa Barbara Mansel, dau. and h. of Bussy Mansel of Briton Ferry, "by virtue of a deed made by Sir Thomas Stradling to his first cousin, the said Bussy Mansel, afterwards Lord Mansel." She *m.* George Venables Vernon, cr. Lord Vernon. (4) St. Athan's estate was sold to pay the lawyers.

The arms of the Stradlings were—*Paly of eight arg. and az., on a bend gu. three cinquefoils or.* The ancient crest—*A pelican rising or;* the modern crest—*A stag courant, collared arg., attired and unguled or.*

The present owner, by purchase, of St. Donat's Castle, claims to be the nearest representative living of this eminent family. (See *Nicholl-Carne of St. Donat's Castle.*)

Le Fleming of St. George and Flemingston.

The first of this family in Glamorgan was Sir John le Fleming, on whom Fitzhamon is said to have bestowed the manors of St. George, Wenvoe, Flemingston, Llanmaes, &c. His wife was Amicia, dau. of Baldwin Magnus, Lord of Whitney. He had a younger son, called by the Welsh Fleming *melyn,* "the yellow," to whom he gave the manors of Flemingston and Constantine Walles, "which continued in his descendants until, on failure of issue male, William Fleming sold the estate to Lewis Thomas, Esq., of Bettws."

Sir John Fleming's eldest son, Sir William Fleming, succeeded him in the lordships of St. George, Wenvoe, and Llanmaes. In the reign of Edward II., under the younger Hugh Despencer, a Sir William Fleming was in possession of these lands. He was executed at Cardiff, because, as some say, he had, as sheriff of the lordship of Glamorgan, unjustly condemned *Llewelyn Bren,* of Senghenydd, to death. He was buried in the cemetery of Grey Friars, "outside the north gate of the town of Cardiff."

After the time of this Sir William, the inheritance, in the absence of issue male, descended to his dau., who *m.* Edmund Malifant, of Pembrokeshire, whose descendants enjoyed it till the time of Henry VII., when Edmond Malifant, who had *m.* a dau. of Sir Matthew Cradock, *d.* without issue, and the estate fell to John Butler, Esq., of Dunraven, who had *m.* Elizabeth, dau. of William Fleming, and after the death, *s. p.*, of their descendant, John Butler, Esq., both estates fell to Walter Vaughan, Esq., who had *m.* Joan, dau. and h. of the said John Butler (see *Vaughan of Dunraven*).

The Fleming escutcheon bore—*Az., three crescents inter seven crosses or.*

Fleming of Monkton.

This branch of the family sprung from Thomas Fleming (second son of Richard Fleming, of Flemingston), and Catherine his wife, dau. of James Turberville, of Tythegston. James Fleming, Esq., of Monkton, their son, *m.* Ann, dau. of Howel Carne, jun., of Nash, whose son, Rees Fleming, Esq., of Monkton, *m.* Mary, dau. of Richard Lougher, of Tythegston, and had a son, also called Rees Fleming, of Monkton, whose wife was Mary, dau. of Rees Williams of Sully. The family continued at Monkton for several generations further.

Fleming of Penlline and Swansea.

This family sprung from Richard, a younger son of Sir William Fleming, of St. George, who was himself the heir of the first Le Fleming of the Conquest. A son or grandson of Richard, Thomas Fleming is the first we have found as "of Penlline." He *m.* Angharad, dau. of Jenkin ap Richard ap Jenkin ap Richard Fawr; and his son, John Fleming, of Penlline, *m.* Mayzod, dau. of Walter ap William ap Hopkin ap David ap David Ddu, said in one MS. to be "a conjuror." His son,—

William Fleming, is called, not of Penlline, but of Swansea. By his wife, Sage, dau. and co-h. of Hugh David ap Meredith, of Nicholaston Hall, he had a son and successor, Henry, "of Wimlod, Recorder," &c., who *m.* Alice, dau. and co-h. of Jenkin Dawkin, of Gellihir. Their son, William, *m.* a dau. and h. of Nicholas Evans, of Llangenech, and was succeeded by his son, Evan Fleming, whose wife was a dau. of the celebrated Thomas Evans of Peterwell, Card. (living 1661), and had issue; but we have no means of further tracing the succession. In the list of *Portreeves and Mayors* of Swansea the name of William Fleminge occurs for 1601, Henry Fleminge for 1613, and the same for 1624. These were in all likelihood the above-named William and Henry.

De St. Quintin of Llanblethian (Llanbleiddian).

Sir Robert de St. Quintin, who became possessed of the lordship of Llanblethian under Fitzhamon, is said to have been grandson of the knight Sir Herbert de St. Quintin, who came in the train of William to the conquest of England, and whose name occurs in the *Roll of Battle Abbey.* He was of the province of Picardy, after the chief town of which, St. Quintin, he was called. Sir Robert erected the castle at Llanblethian (Bleiddian) which in after times went by his name. His gr. grandson,—

Sir Herbert St. Quintin, was summoned as a baron to a *parlement* held by Edward I. A.D. 1294, "but never afterwards; and for the reason that that writ cannot be considered as a regular summons to parliament, and consequently that there never was such a barony, although the Earls of Pembroke, whose ancestors married the heir general of this Herbert de St. Quintin, styled themselves barons of St. Quintin" (Nicolas, *Synop. of Peerage*). With this Herbert, who left no son, the name of St. Quintin ceased, and his estates fell to his two daus., one of whom, Elizabeth, *d. s. p.;* the other, Laura, by her third husband, Sir Robert Grey, of Rotherfield, had an only dau. and heiress, Elizabeth, whose son William (by Lord Fitzhugh) *m.* Margery, dau. of William, Lord Willoughby d'Eresby, and left a son, Henry, whose wife was Alice Neville, dau. of Richard, Earl of Salisbury, by whom he left with other issue Elizabeth, who *m.* Sir William Parr, Knt., and had (besides an elder son, Lord Parr) Sir Thomas Parr, who left a son William, Marquis of Northampton, Katherine Parr, sixth wife of Henry VIII., and Anne Parr, who *m.* William Herbert, Earl of Pembroke. Anne, being co-h. with her brother, brought to the Earl of Pembroke the lordship of Llanblethian, which from that time has formed part of the estates of the Lords of Glamorgan.

The St. Quintin arms were—*Or, three chevrons gu. on a chief arg., a fesse wavy.*

De Syward of Talyfan.

Sir Richard Syward, who on the partition of Glamorgan between the knights received as his share the lordship of Talyfan, is not known to have been a "Norman," but bore a name which betrays rather a Saxon origin—*Se-weard* (sea-watchman). It may well be believed that Fitzhamon had many English in his train, for we know that he had even many Welsh, led by such chieftains as Einion ap Cadivor ap Collwyn.

The lordship of Talyfan lay contiguous to that of Miskin, and De Syward is said in some of the earlier books to have been given, along with Talyfan, "the ancient burgh of *Pontfaen* (Cowbridge). The word Tal-y-fan is almost tautological, conveying strongly the meaning of an elevated place or land, which was perhaps the character of the region. *Tal* is an ancient Welsh vocable signifying "head," and *ban* expresses prominence, height, so that *Tal-y-fan* would mean the top of the high place or land.

It is believed that the issue male of Richard de Syward continued in possession of this lordship until the time of Edward III., when the heir then in possession, according to Sir Edward Stradling's account, sold it to Despencer, the then Lord of Glamorgan, and went to reside upon property which the family had in Somerset.

The arms ascribed to the Sywards were—*Arg., a cross flory, fitchée, sa.*

Le Sore of Peterston and St. Fagan's.

This family was founded by Sir *Peter* le Sore, after whom the lordship of Peterston, given him by Fitzhamon, was named. His descendants in the male line are said to have continued to enjoy it until the time of Henry IV., when the line ceased, and the inheritance fell to several relatives. The lordship of St. Fagan's went to the Veales, and remained in that family "until Alice Veale, the heiress, married David Mathew, who had four daughters, between whom the lordships of St. Fagan's and Llysworney were divided" (Jenkin's MS.).

Alexander le Sore and Henry le Sore "were witnesses to old deeds to the effect that Peter le Veal was Lord of St. Fagan's. This was at a time when no dates were used" (*ib.*). Sir Mayo, Morys, or Matthew Sore, was contemporary with Ifor Hael and Dafydd ap Gwilym (fourteenth century). It is said that Sir Mayo came into collision with Owen Glyndwr when that chieftain overran Glamorgan (A.D. 1402), and that Owen "cut off his head;" and tradition has reported that a skull long preserved in Peterston Church was the skull of Sir Mayo le Sore. The property was now divided between co-heiresses.

The arms ascribed to the Le Sores were—*Quarterly: or and gu., in the first canton, a lion passant az.*

De Sully of Sully.

Sir Reginald de Sully received the lordship of Sully as his share of the lands of Glamorgan when conquered by Robert Fitzhamon. The Sullys, however, were not of long continuance, the male line having become extinct in the time of Edward I., when the heiress of the estate became wife of Sir Thomas de Avan, Lord of Avan, a descendant of Iestyn ap Gwrgant. His grandson, Sir Thomas de Avan, left an only daughter, Jane, who *m.* Sir William Blunt, who exchanged the lordships of Avan and Sully with Gilbert de Clare for lands in England. From him the Blunts of Shropshire were descended.

In the "Neath Register," according to D. Jenkin's MS. (p. 217), the names occur of Sir Walter de Sully, Kt., Rumund de Sully, and Meyrick de Sully; but no intimation is conveyed whether this register had belonged to Neath *Abbey*, or of the place where it was deposited.

The Sullys are said to have borne—*Ermine, three chevrons gu.*

Such is the account available of the *Barones Minores* who are held to have shared under Robert Fitzhamon the lands of Glamorgan. Some of them continued long and flourished, identifying themselves by degrees more fully with the people whom they had overthrown, intermarrying with them, learning their language, adopting their customs, and forming at last an undistinguishable part of their body. The *Turbervilles* began this wise and far-seeing policy. The *Stradlings* continued it longest, and won thereby such commanding influence that their fame and power in the county even eclipsed those of some of the lords in chief of Glamorgan. The day of others was short, their power small. In most cases their line ceased and their estates were dissipated. In others they felt themselves as strangers among a people whose sense of wrong recoiled from them, and sought home and rest on the other side the Severn. But in our day not a trace of any of them remains! The *name* of Turbervill still survives at Ewenny, representing not a direct but a circuitous maternal descent; and similarly the blood of the Stradlings is still represented at St. Donat's. The *race* of the vanquished, according to an indefeasible law, has in the long run proved victorious, and the intrusive race has virtually vanished from the soil.

There remain to be mentioned other families, not strictly numbered among the minor lords of Glamorgan, but of greater power, and equally of the so-called "Norman" type. Among these the Gamages of Coity Castle hold distinguished prominence.

Gamage of Coity Castle.

In the section on "Antiquities," under *Coity Castle,* some account has already been given of this important family and their entrance upon that estate. The Gamages, before their settlement by marriage at Coity, were seated at Rogiad, or Roggiatt, in Monmouthshire. They were of Norman descent, but of later introduction into Wales than the age of Fitzhamon's conquest of Glamorgan. Godfrey de Gamaches, of the ville or castle of Gamaches, in Viscin, near Rouen, Normandy, received from Henry II., A.D. 1159, a grant of lands in Hottesdon, co. Salop, and from Richard I. land in Marnshall in the same county. He inherited also two knights' fees in the county of Hereford under the Lacys. He *d.* before 1176. His eldest son, Matthew, settled in Normandy, and his second son, William de Gamage, inherited the English estates of Mansel Gamage, county Hereford, Gamage Hall in Dimock, and other lands in the county of Gloucester. He was keeper of Ludlow Castle, and *d.* before A.D. 1240. From William descended Sir Pain de Gamage, Lord of Rogiad, Mon., and Sir Robert Gamage of the same place, whose eldest son was—

William Gamage, of Rogiad, who, as already shown, *m.* Sara, or Assar, dau. and co-h. of Pain de Turberville of that place, whose ancestor had *m.*, in the time of Fitzhamon, the dau. and h. of Morgan ap Meurig, of the line of Iestyn ap Gwrgant. William Gamage was Sheriff of Gloucestershire A.D. 1325.

Gilbert Gamage, son of William, was succeeded by his son, Sir William Gamage, who on the death of his kinsman, Sir Laurence Berkerolles of St. Athan's, succeeded to the lordship of Coity (see *Coity Castle*). He *m.* Mary, dau. of Sir Thomas Rodburgh, and had issue—

Thomas Gamage, of Coity and Rogiad, who *m.* Matilda, dau. of Sir John Dennis; and a dau., Margaret, who *m.* Sir Richard de la Bere, of Weobly and Molton, in Gower, who received for services on the field of Cressy a crest, "five ostrich feathers issuing from a ducal coronet." Thomas Gamage was succeeded by his son—

John Gamage, of Coity, who *m.* Margaret, dau. and co-h. of Morgan Llewellyn ap Evan ap Llewellyn, of Radir, and had a son and heir named Morgan, who by his wife Elinor, dau. of Sir Roger Vaughan, of Tretower (*Tre'rtwr*), Brec., half-brother to William, Earl of Pembroke, had, besides his son and successor Thomas, six daus.,—Elizabeth, who *m.* first John Stradling, and afterwards John Price of Glyn Nèdd; Margaret, *m.* first Jenkin Thomas of Llanfihangel, and secondly James Turberville of Llantwit Major; Jane, *m.* Sir William Bawdrip of Penmark; Ann, *m.* Robert Raglan of Llantwit; Catherine, *m.* first Reginald Powell of Perth-hir, co. Monmouth; secondly William Stanton of Horningham, Wilts, by whom she had a son William and three daus.; Gwenllian, *m.* Thomas ap Meurig.

Sir Thomas Gamage, son of Morgan, *m.*, first, Margaret, dau. of Sir John St. John of Fonmon Castle, Glam., and Bletsoe Park, by a dau. of Morgan Jenkin Philip of Pencoed Castle, Mon., paternally descended from Gruffydd ap Bleddyn, Lord of Cilsant; secondly, Joyce, dau. of Sir Richard Croft. By Margaret St. John, Sir Thomas had issue Robert; John; Edward; Catherine, *m.* Sir Thomas Stradling of St. Donat's Castle; Mary, *m.* Matthew Herbert of Swansea and Cogan Pill; Margaret, *m.* William Howard, Lord Howard of Effingham, and had issue Charles, Earl of Nottingham, commander against the Spanish Armada, Sir William Howard, of Lingfield, and others (Dugd., 11, 278). She *d.* 19th May, 1581. Lord Wm. Howard *d.* 11th January, 1572-3. Elizabeth *m.* Richard Wogan, Esq., of Wiston and Boulston, co. Pembroke; secondly, Jenkin Gwyn. Sir Thomas's eldest son,—

Robert Gamage, *m.* Joan, dau. of Philip Champernon, of Darlington, and had issue (besides his eldest son, John) Thomas, *m.* Joan, dau. of William ap Thomas Vaughan; Margaret, *m.* Miles Mathew of Llandaff,—secondly, Thomas Lewis of Van, living 1583,—thirdly, Captain Herbert of Cardiff; Elinor, *m.* William Lewis of St. Pierre, co. Monmouth, 1583; Elizabeth (Ann or Catherine), *m.* Watkin Lougher of Tythegston, Sheriff for Glamorgan in 1635 (see *Sheriffs*); Joyce, *m.* John Gwyn, Llandilo, co. Carmarthen; and Joan.

John Gamage *m.* Gwenllian, dau. and h. of Sir Thomas ap Jenkin Powell of Glyn-Ogwr, and had issue *Barbara*, sole heiress, *b.* 1562, *m.*, in or before 1584, Sir Robert Sydney, second son of Sir Henry Sydney of Penshurst, Kent, and next brother to the accomplished Sir Philip Sydney; he was nephew to the Earls of Leicester and Warwick, and was the first

Earl of Leicester of the Sydney line (*cr.* 1618). Barbara Gamage, the last of this line (Countess of Leicester), was grandmother of the celebrated Algernon Sydney, son of Sir Robert Sydney of Coity, second Earl of Leicester (*succ.* 1626), who was beheaded in the reign of Charles II. The title in the Sydney line became extinct on the death of Jocelyne, seventh earl, A.D. 1743. (See further *Coity Castle*.)

The Gamage arms, as given by Sir Robert Atkyns, are—*Arg., five fusils in bend gu., on a chief az. three escallops or.*

Gamage of Abergarw.

Edward Gamage, son of John Gamage, parson of St. Bride's Minor, was parson of Llanharry, and the fourth in lineal descent from Sir Thomas Gamage of Coity Castle, being grandson of Thomas, the second son of Robert and Joan Champernon, his wife. He *m.* Mary, dau. of John Jenkin Turberville of Abergarw, and had issue John; Mary, *m.* Morgan ap Llewellyn of Derllwyn.

John Gamage *m.* Martha, dau. of Thomas Lougher of Cornelau, and had John, a vicar, *m.* in co. Derby; Edward, *m.* Mary, dau. of Benjamin Watkins, Court Colman; Thomas, *m.* Ruth, dau. of Thomas Mathew, Cefn Gorwydd, in Gower; Ann, *m.* John James, St. Bride's; Sarah, married—

John *Thomas*, parson of Coity; whence descend the *Thomases of Caldicot*, co. Monmouth. John Thomas, and Sarah Gamage, his wife, had issue John and Edward.

John Thomas was incumbent of South Petherton and Ilminster, co. Somerset. He *m.* the widow of — Prouse, Esq., barrister-at-law, but left no issue.

Edward Thomas was Rector of St. Bride's Minor, co. Glamorgan, and Vicar of Caldicot, co. Monmouth; had issue by his wife, Ann Lloyd, Theresa; Edward, Vicar of Llangwm; James, of Mount St. Alban's; Samuel, brought up to the law; John, *d.* young in London; Ann, and William.

The Gamage Family in America.

A branch of the Gamage family settled in Northamptonshire traced their descent lineally from Sir Thomas Gamage of Coity. From this branch descended the Rev. Smith Percy Gamage, LL.D., and his brother, Henry Gamage. The former was, during the American war, a chaplain in the U.S. army.

Some of the family had also migrated to the New World at an early period in company with their kinsman, Lord Effingham, when he was Governor of Virginia; others joined the famous Duke of Marlborough, and under him held high positions both in the army and navy. Joseph or John Gamage received a grant of land from the Crown at Brixworth, Northamptonshire, for distinguished service in the army: his descendants are still living in New England, some of whom held high positions in the army and navy during the War of Independence, and were in the great battle of Bunker's Hill. Samuel Gamage was lieutenant on board the *Dunn* frigate. He was a man of enduring courage, of acknowledged worth and virtue, unflinching in his adherence to the cause of civil and religious liberty. His brother, Dr. William Gamage, born at Cambridge, New England, 1748, was an eminent physician in his native town, and secured both fame and fortune.

Capt. John Gamage, "a self-made, noble-minded man, trusting in Providence, constructed his own fortune, and engaged heartily and courageously in the great struggle for American independence." He was taken prisoner in the revolution on board the *Yankee Hero* by H.M.S. *Milford*, and imprisoned for twelve months on board H.M.S. *Renown*, Capt. Banks commander. "He died in 1824, laden with years and honours. It is only recently that his two aged sons and a daughter, all verging on ninety, followed their eminent parent to the land of rest—'the land o' the leal.'"

Several members of the Gamage family graduated at Harvard College. The house in which the family lived at Cambridge is still called "Gamage House."

Butler of Dunraven.

That this family, which resided for some ten generations at Dunraven, *i.e.*, from the eleventh to the fourteenth century, was of Norman origin is probable both from the name (Botteler) and from their relation to De Londres, the preceding lord of the place. The lordship was a part of the lands acquired by William de Londres on the conquest of Glamorgan by Fitzhamon and his companion knights. The Caradoc *Brut* informs us that "William de Londres, Lord of Ogmore (*Ogwr*), won the lordships of Cydweli and Carnwyllion from the Welsh, and gave the castle and manor of Dunraven to his *servant*, Sir Arnold Butler." A lord's "servant" in those days was a knight, and the origin of Butler may have been quite as good, though his fortune was not quite so prosperous, as that o De Londres. The Butlers married well, and extended in their alliances as far as Pembrokeshire.

Sir Arnold Butler was succeeded (*temp.* Henry I.) by his son Pierce, and he by his son,—

Sir John Butler, Kt., of Dunraven, who *m.* Isabel, dau. and co-h. of Sir Robert de Cantelupe, "Lord of Cantleston, in Glamorgan." He had a son, John, not styled a knight, who *m.* a dau. of Sir David de la Bere, Kt., and left a son,—

John Butler, Esq., of Dunraven, who *m.* Isabel, dau. of Sir William Fleming (see *Fleming of St. George*), and had issue John Butler, his heir, who *m.* Gwenllian, dau. of Tomkin (Thomas) Turberville, Esq. His son,—

John Butler, Esq., of Dunraven, *m.* a dau. of Sir John Wogan, Kt., of Wiston, Pembrokeshire, and had two sons, Thomas and John. The latter (*circa* 1550) *m.* Elizabeth, dau. and h. of Philip Percival, Esq., of Coedgantlas (now Coedcenlas), Pemb., where he afterwards resided; and the former and elder son and h. (see *Butler of Coedganlas*),—

Thomas Butler, Esq., of Dunraven, *m.* a dau. of David Mathew, Esq., of Radir. His son and successor, John Butler, Esq., of Dunraven, *m.* Jane, dau. of John Bassett, Esq., of Beaupre, and had a son, *Arnold Butler*, who *m.* Sibylla, dau. of Sir John Monnington, Kt., and had issue, but all *d. vit. pat.* (see *Note*), and a dau.,—

Joan, or as some say, *Ann* Butler, heiress of Dunraven, who *m.* Sir Richard Vaughan, Kt., of Bredwardine, and had issue. (See *Vaughan of Dunraven.*) The senior line of Butler of Dunraven was now extinct, but the junior branch continued some short time longer in Pembrokeshire.

Arms of Butler of Dunraven,—*Az., three cups or, with three covers over them.*

Note.—In the valuable MS. volume of pedigrees in the possession of Joseph Joseph, Esq., F.S.A., drawn up by "J. H." about A.D. 1720 (as determined by internal evidence, p. 11 *et pass.*), the following *mem.* occurs respecting the last Arnold Butler's household:—"The sons and daughter of this Arnold Butler of Dunraven, with other young men, went in a boat to the Skut Sker, near Ogmoore, for pleasure, but being careless in fastening the boat it ran adrift, so that they were all drowned; and after the death of the said Arnold, the estate of Butler of Dunraven, &c. (and Fleming's lordship of St. George, which fell to John Butler), descended all to Walter Vaughan of Bradwardine, Esq., as next heir to his uncle, A. B.; all which happened about the time of Queen Mary."

"As for the Buttlers of Southerdown, and others of the same family in St. Bride's and elsewhere, they say they came of the younger sons of the above said Jenkin Butler, but their pedigree as well as some others have been neglected."

Carne of Nash; Carne of Ewenny.

For the genealogy of the Carnes see *Nicholl-Carne of St. Donat's.*

Mansel of Margam.

The family of Mansel is not extinct. The Mansels of Carmarthenshire will be found under that county. For the Mansels of Margam and Penrice see *Margam Abbey*, *Penrice Castle*, and *Mansel-Talbot of Margam.*

The Herberts.

For this important and numerous family, see, among the Lords of Glamorgan, *Herbert, Earl of Pembroke; Bute, Marquis of.* The Herberts are also found in *Powis Castle, Montgomery, Rhaglan, Colebrook, Crickhowel, Havod Ychtryd, Cogan, Swansea,* &c.

The Bassetts.

This family, although of early introduction into Glamorgan, is not extinct. Its origin and history will be found under *Beaupre Castle* and *Basset of Beaupre.*

Other families of Norman origin in the county of Glamorgan, almost all long ago extinct, were the following (compare Meyrick, *Morganiæ Archæogr.; Golden Grove MS.; Glamorgan Pedigrees*, from MS. of Sir Isaac Heard, Kt., ed. by Sir Thos. Phillipps, Bart., 1845; D. Jenkin's MS. ; Lewys Dwnn's *Herald. Visit. of Wales*, &c.) :—

De Cantelupe of Cantleston.—This was a Norman family which came early, probably under the reign of Rufus, into Glamorgan, and had lands and a residence at a place afterwards called after their name, *Cantleston*, and in W. *Tregantlo*. They had a succession of four or five generations—William de Cantelupe, the first; Richard; Elias; his brother William, and Robert, named under "Butler of Dunraven."

Scurlage of Scurlage Castle, Gower.—Sir Herbert Scurlage is the first we hear of at this place. His settlement was earlier than the name of his manor, said to have been called after himself. The Welsh name of the stronghold, adopted as is likely after his time, was *Trecastell*, and it was inherited by the *Gibbon* family. Sir Herbert Scurlage, believed to have been of Norman origin, obtained this manor from Sir Richard de Clare about A.D. 1250, the object of his being stationed here being to "curb the natives." According to the custom of the age, and the more effectually to overawe the Welsh, he built a castle, small portions of which still remain, near Llanddewi, in Gowerland ; and for a brief period pursued no doubt the usual methods of "curbing the natives." We hear nothing of his descendants. The place comes next before us as the habitation of a Welsh family, descendants of Einion ap Collwyn (see *Gibbon of Trecastell*). Nothing more is known of the Scurlages.

Button of Dyffryn (Worlton).—About the name *Button*, by which this Norman family continued to be called for some twelve or fourteen generations, there is some obscurity. The more proper appellation was Le Grant. This was the name by which the first settler was known. From Gwion le Grant, Duke of Seville, who *m.* Mabel, dau. of Richard de Clare, it is said, was descended in the fifth generation *Thomas le Grant*, the first who assumed or submitted to the surname *Button*. Some say it was a nickname, with playful reference to the smallness of his stature. He *m.* Grisly, or Grissyl, the Welsh heiress of Dyffryn, probably late in the thirteenth century. His son was Howel Button, who *m.* Gwenllian, dau. of Tomkin Turberville, of Tythegston, her mother being Lucy, dau. and co-h. of Sir John Norris, Knt., of Penlline Castle. His descendants intermarried with the families of Gethin of Llandaff, Thomas of Llanfihangel, Kemeys of Newport, Richard of Wallas, Lewis of Van, Aubrey of Llantrithyd, &c. We find the Buttons of Dyffryn filling the office of Sheriff of Glamorgan in 1556, 1564, 1588, 1641, 1666, 1709, 1727. Not long after this date, when Martin Button, Esq., had been sheriff, the male line became extinct, and the family of *Pryce* entered Dyffryn by the marriage of Thomas Pryce with the heiress of that place.

The arms of the Buttons were—*Az., three bats or.*

Voss of Boverton (the Roman *Bovium*).—This family must have settled at Boverton in the latter part of the fourteenth century. The earlier form of the name we meet is *Vaulx*, but it gradually softened into Vaus and Voss. Richard Vaulx had a son William, whose wife was Elizabeth, a dau. of Thomas Fleming of Monkton. He had a son,— Griffith Vaus, Esq., who *m.* Joan, dau. and co-h. of Gruffydd Gôch, of the line of Gwaethfoed, the well-known Lord of Cardigan, and had issue a dau. Elizabeth, who became maid of honour to Queen Elizabeth, and married Roger Sais, Esq. (see *Sais,* or *Seys, of Boverton*). The Voss name does not again occur at Boverton, but it continued in the neighbourhood for several generations, probably in the descendants of a younger son of Richard Vaulx, the first above named. In the church of Llantwit Major, "on the north side of the belfry," there is or was a monument to Matthew Voss (*b.* 1405, *d.* 1534, " after having lived to the very advanced age of 129 years "), who is supposed to have been a younger son of the said Richard Vaulx, and ancestor of those bearing the name of Voss after the failure of male issue at Boverton. Another monument, of freestone, fixed in the wall of the same church, once "defaced and turned inside," contained inscriptions to the memory of the Voss family.

There were Vosses residing at Llantwit and neighbourhood, at Nicholaston, &c., in the seventeenth and eighteenth centuries. John, a son of John Voss of Nicholaston, went to reside at Swansea, and was ancestor to the Vosses, bankers of Swansea. This family it is believed is not quite extinct, but has recently left Swansea.

The Voss arms were—*Or, three lions rampant arg., upon a bend sa.* Crest—*Two wings adorsed or, upon a ducal coronet.*

Raglan of Carnllwyd.—This ancient family, traceable through fifteen generations in Glamorgan, is in strictness to be considered of Norman descent, as were all the Herberts, from whose stock it issued. In the only pedigree available of the Raglans, found in the valuable MS. from the collection of Sir Isaac Heard, Clarencieux, printed by the late Sir Thomas Phillipps, Bart., no *dates* are given, and the age of the family must be determined by internal evidence. Thus Robert Raglan, the third of the line, marries Elinor, dau. of Sir Roger Vaughan, of Tre'rtwr, Brec., who fell at Agincourt A.D. 1415.

Robert, youngest son of Evan Thomas ap Gwilym Herbert, was the first progenitor of the Raglans of Carnllwyd. His son John was surnamed "Raglan" because "his father had been brought up with his uncle, Sir William Thomas Herbert, at Raglan." Now Sir William was a contemporary with Sir Roger Vaughan, and like him was knighted on the field of Agincourt by Henry V. John "Raglan" *m.* a dau. and h. of Robert Mathew, of Carnllwyd, and settled at that place, where his descendants lived for many generations. The last was Thomas Raglan, who left only daughters, and the name became extinct.

The arms of this family would probably be those of *Herbert,* quartering *Mathew.*

De Cardiff of Cardiff.—Sir Richard de Cardiff received of William, Earl of Gloucester, third Lord of Glamorgan, "thirty *libratæ* of land" to hold by the fourth part of a knight's fee at Newton Nottage. (Meyrick, *Morganiæ Arch.*) He held the office of *Dapifer,* or steward to the earl. His dau. and h. *m.* Sir Thomas de Sanford, whose heirs for two generations, and probably not longer, enjoyed the property. Their name is still commemorated in

"Sanford's Well," near Newton Nottage Church. The arms of De Cardiff according to the *Golden Grove MS.* were—"*Az., three piles in point or.*"

De Rayle of Wrinston.—Sir Simon de Rayle was lord of the mesne manor of Wrinston, and Michaelston. Part of the walls of his house remained till comparatively recent times, at a place called *Court y Rayle* (now Courtyrala). John de Rayle was Lord of Wrinston in the Despencers' time.

Marcross of Marcross.—Sir Philip Marcross, lord of the mesne manor of Marcross, left no son. His dau. and h. *m.* William de Pincerna, son of Simon de Halweia (Halwey), who succeeded to the inheritance. Sir Richard de Pincerna, Kt., probably his son, obtained the fee of Gelligarn on terms of a knight's service, for which he did homage to Le Sore, Lord of St. Fagan's (see *Le Sore*). After his death, Samson de Halweia, the heir, "being annoyed and oppressed by his neighbours at Ruthyn, and brought to extreme poverty, exchanged his inheritance with the House of Neath for Littleham in Devonshire. This exchange was successively ratified by Sir John le Sore and his son, Robert le Sore, by deeds recorded in the *Registrum de Nith.*

Norris of Penlline.—Sir Robert Norris, *vice-comes* or sheriff under Robert of Gloucester, second Lord of Glamorgan, appears to have been the first of this line that settled in Glamorgan. He received the mesne manor of Penlline (upon which he built his castle) from William, third Lord of Glamorgan. This and other similar facts show that the lands had not been all appropriated at the first conquest. In the time of Despencer's survey the lordship of Penlline was held by Sir John Norris, Kt., whose estates fell to his four daughters, co-heiresses, three of whom *m.* respectively into the families of Walsh of Llandough (Llandocha), Morgan of Pencoed (of the Morgans of Tredegar), and Turberville of Coity.

Jeol of Gileston.—In the time of Despencer's survey Thomas Jeol, or Jule, held from the heir of Hugh Despencer ("de hærede Hugonis le Despencer man. de Jeoliston, cum advocatione ecclesiæ ejusdem") the manor of Jeoliston (Gileston), with the advowson of its church, for one knight's service. It was rated of the value per annum of £4 12s. 2d. John Thomas's heir at the time is also said to have been of the age of thirteen. This was in A D. 1350.

Bonville of Bonvilston.—Simon Bonville was, at an early stage of the Norman dominion in Glamorgan, mesne lord of a piece of land which was subsequently called after his name, and which the Welsh, disregarding his surname, called *Tre Simon.* His stronghold, according to Jenkin's MS., "was built in a wood south of Bolston (now called Court yr Abad), and was surrounded by a great moat; parts of the walls were carried away to build other houses, and part converted into lime for manuring the land." We know little of the after history of this family; but it is said that a descendant of one of their branches settled in Carmarthenshire, through whom Mr. Bonville, now living near Carmarthen, claims his lineage.

Bennet of Laleston.—This ancient Glamorganshire family has only very recently disappeared. Their first and long-continued seat was in Gower. By marriage of John Bennet (living 1699) into the family of Jones of Laleston, near Bridgend, they settled at that place, and there remained through six generations, till the death *s. p.* a few years ago of John Wick Bennet, Esq., of Laleston. They several times supplied sheriffs for the county of Glamorgan (see *Sheriffs*, &c.). Their first founder in Gower is said to have been Sir Gervase Benet de Penclawdd, contemporary with the Conqueror, and a knight in his service. The Bennet arms were—*Arg., three goats' heads erased sa., barbed or, langued gu.*

Note.—Our careful genealogist, "J. H.," has this note:—"As for the Bennets of Penrees, in Gower, they were ever reputed to come from Loughor, for it is certain that there were Bennets in Bringwyn and Travele, and other places in Loughor, for many generations till the time of Charles the Second: yet it may be that they came from Kilfigin " [near Usk].

Dawkin of Kilvrough.—Another Gower house of long continuance, but now extinct, is that of Dawkin of Kilvrough, tracing descent from Sir William de Langton, Kt., lord of the manors of Langrove and Henllisk, in Gower, *temp.* Edward II., whose ancestor is said to have "entered England soon after the Conqueror." Rowland Dawkin, in lineal descent from *Dawkin* Langton, son of the said Sir William, in the year 1585 built the house at *Kilvrough*. His grandson, Rowland Dawkin, was a zealous supporter in these parts of Cromwell's government, a colonel in his army, and in 1654—1658 M.P. for Carmarthen. He was also "Governor of Carmarthen in the time of Cromwell;" he *d*. 1691, and "was buried at Pennard Church, in the north side of the chancel" (J. H.'s MS., *circa* 1720). The last male possessor of Kilvrough and builder of the mansion now standing was William Dawkin, Esq., fourth in descent from the said Rowland, and Sheriff of Glamorgan 1773. He left by his wife Mayzod a dau. and h., Mary, who *m*. a French gentleman assuming the title of Marquis de Choiseul, by whom she had no issue, and from whom she separated. She sold in 1820 the mansion and demesne of Kilvrough to the late Thomas Penrice, Esq. (see *Penrice of Kilvrough House*). The Dawkin arms were—*Gu., a chevron arg. between three lions rampant or.*

Malefant of St. George's, &c.—The Malefants, or Malifants, were a Pembrokeshire family of Norman origin, but some of their members married and settled in Glamorgan; and we find in the Iolo MSS., p. 493, one of the castles destroyed or ravaged by Owen Glyndwr in this county named "Malefant's" Castle. Where this castle was situated it is not easy to say. William Malifant, of Pembrokeshire, at an early period is said to have *m*. "Elizabeth, dau. and h. of John de Londres, by whom he had Landawke" (or Llandough); and later, Edmond Malifant, of the same line, marries the dau. and h. of Sir William Fleming, Kt., and is called "of St. George's." As Llandough is expressly mentioned in the castles destroyed by Owen on this incursion into Glamorgan, it is almost certain that the Malifant castle he is said to have destroyed was the residence of this Malifant of St. George, who had not long before obtained it by this marriage with the dau. of Fleming, owner of the lordship. (See *Fleming of St. George and Wenvoe*.) Richard Maliphant, Esq., of Cydweli, traces to this family. The Malifant arms were—*Gu., a fret arg.*

Tomb of Sir Matthew Cradock, Kt., and his Wife Katherine, Swansea Church.
(*Beaufort Progress.*)

Arms of Cradock.

Arms of Stradling.

Arms of Sir Hugh Johnys, Kt.

Swansea Corp. Seal,
Temp. King John.

Cardiff Common Seal,
1684.

Monumental Brass of Sir Hugh Johnys, Kt., and Dame Maude his Wife, Swansea Church. (*Beaufort Progress.*)

2.—FAMILIES OF BRITISH DESCENT.

When we speak of a family which has descended through many generations being of a particular race or nationality, the statement must be taken as subject to qualification. Above, families have been described as *Norman*, although in some cases the very origin was doubtful, and in almost all, through the intermarriages of many successions, the prevailing blood had become that of the native race. And now that we speak of families of *British* descent, it is not to be forgotten that in many cases the Celtic blood, at first somewhat pure, had through frequent union with English and Anglo-Norman become considerably mixed. Thus the Mathews of Llandaff intermarry with the Gamage and Stradling houses; the Cradocks with the Mansels and Walshes, &c. But the well-known physiological law of the prevalence of the stronger or less intermittent race would secure in the British families a nearer adherence to the original type than would occur with the Anglo-Norman houses, excepting those originally of the Celtic race.

But in both cases a fact of interest is suggested respecting the ethnological character of the Glamorgan population, especially the better class families, viz., that they are of mixed derivation in an unusual degree. This fact, obvious from the simple records of alliances, is testified by the frequent occurrence of that Scandinavian light complexion which gave *Rufus* the name of "red," and which prevails in the Scottish highlands and islands settled upon by the Danes. That this colour is not more abundant in Glamorgan is owing to the neutralizing power of the Silurian and Celtic swarthiness, which, if foreign intrusion through modern immigration did not favour its rival, would in course of time regain the hold it had in the age of Tacitus (*Vit. Agric.*, xi.), and raise anew in some minds the conjecture that the people of Gwent and Glamorgan were of Iberian origin, relations of the Spanish race.

Cradock of Swansea and Cardiff.

Sir Matthew Cradock, Kt., of Swansea, the first and last of his line bearing that surname, was a man of great mark in Glamorgan under the first two Tudor kings. As shown on his beautiful tomb, still surviving in Swansea Church, he held the offices of Deputy to the Earl of Worcester in Glamorgan, Chancellor of the same, and Steward of Gower and Kilvey. He was lineally descended in the eighth degree from Einion ap Collwyn (who was of the sept of *Caradoc* Freichfras), in whose descendants the name *Caradoc* frequently recurred, but was adopted as a surname for the first time in this family (surnames being as yet but partially used by the Welsh) by this *Matthew*, son of Richard ap Gwilim ap Evan, from Caradoc Freichfras. He *m.*, first, Alice, daughter of Philip Mansel, of Oxwich Castle; secondly, Lady Katherine Gordon, widow of the notorious *Perkin Warbeck*. Lady Katherine, by whom he had no issue, survived him, and twice afterwards married, her last husband being Christopher Asshton, Esq., of Fyfield, Berks; and although she is said on the Swansea monument to lie in that tomb—as Sir Matthew, who built the tomb in his lifetime, had probably fondly expected,—she is known to have died and to have been buried at Fyfield (1537).

By his first wife, Alice Mansel, Sir Matthew Cradock had an only dau., Margaret, who *m.* Richard Herbert, Esq., of Ewias, father of Sir William Herbert, created Earl of Pembroke 1551 (see *Herberts, Earls of Pembroke; Bute, Marquis of; Herbert of Llanarth*, &c.), and of Sir George Herbert of Swansea, ancestor of the Herberts of Cogan, White Friars, Cardiff, Swansea, Cilybebyll, &c.; and of the Llewelyns of Ynysygerwn; Trahernes of Castellau, &c. (See further, *Traherne of St. Hilary.*)

Sir Matthew Cradock resided at the "Place House," Swansea, the ruins of which, in course of removal, are pictured in the Rev. J. M. Traherne's *Historical Notices* of Sir Matthew, from which we have taken these particulars; but, as there intimated, "it is impossible to say how much of the building" then pulled down "was the work of Sir Matthew." He *d.* A.D. 1531. By his will, recently discovered in the Prerogative Court of Canterbury, he refers to his house as "my new place at Swainsey," leaves the farm of *Corners Well* (which lies to the south of Cogan Pill House), and twenty-six kine and one bull to William Herbert, second son of his grandson, Sir George Herbert; and to his daughter Margaret estates in reversion during her life, with the injunction "upon" his "blessing" not in anything to break this his "last will;" provides for his widow, the Lady Katherine, whom he appoints his sole executrix; charges his lands with "the sum of xx nobles per ann." for the maintaining and repairing of "the chapel of St. Anne, in Swansea Church" (afterwards called "Cradock's Chapel," and now "Herbert's Chapel,") which he says was built "time out of mind" by his ancestor, John Horton, where his tomb was erected during his lifetime), "and to find a priest to sing there for evermore for my soul, my wife's soul, my ancestors' souls, and [good, generous man!] for *all* Christian souls." The lands still produce "nobles," but the priest and his singing have long ago gone their way—without loss, we trust, to Sir Matthew Cradock or any of the other "Christian souls."

The Cradock arms were—*Az., semée of cross crosslets, three boars' heads couped arg.*

Cradock of Cheriton.

The Cradocks of Cheriton were a junior line, proceeding, it is said, from *Robert* ap Evan, deriving from Einion ap Collwyn, while Sir Mathew Cradock of Swansea was descended from *Gwilim* ap Evan, an elder brother. These Cradocks settled at Cheriton about the time of Henry VII., by mar. of David Cradock with the heiress of Philip Delabere of that place, and maintained their surname in the male line for several generations. They intermarried with Mansells, Flemings, Popkins, and Bassetts. Philip Cradock, the fifth possessor of Cheriton, sold that place "about 1657 to Thomas Philip of Swansey" (J. H.'s MS.). His great-gr. son, Philip Cradock, is described as of Tir-Coch, and living in 1699, having *m.* Susan, dau. of Harry Mansel, Esq., by whom he had a son, Morgan, "a priest." The writer of the MS. just cited has this note respecting the arms of the Cradocks:—"Memdm. That the above-named Evan ap Caradock killed a monstrous wild boar in Clyné Forrest, in the parish of Oystermouth, upon which occasion the arms were altered."

Lougher of Tythegston.

This family, which will be hereafter noticed in the lineage of *Knight of Newton Nottage*, was of Cymric origin, and had representatives in the male line till A.D. 1701, when the last Richard Lougher, Esq., of Tythegston, died, and his estate passed to his daughters. In Knight's *Account of Newton Nottage* it is said, " There seems to be no reason to doubt that one of the descendants of Leyson of Avan (the great-gr. son of Morgan, the son of Caradoc ap Iestyn) residing at Loughor [in Gower] took his name from that ancient town, and transmitted it to his posterity. By a receipt of Lady Lucy Bassett, called 'Lucy Verch Griffith Nicholas,' dated Oct. 10, 1472 (12th Edward IV.), it appears that Richard Lougher farmed from her a moiety of Weobley Castle in Gower. Three years later his name is mentioned in a singular kind of marriage compact; Richard Lougher covenants with John ap Griffith Howell to give his daughter Ann to David son of John ap Griffith; if Ann did not live to fulfil the contract, that then David should marry some other daughter of Richard Lougher, and interchangeably, in case of David's premature death, a son of Lougher should marry a daughter of John ap Griffith, with proviso that the marriage portion of fifty marks [£33 6s. 8d.] then covenanted to be paid under special conditions should be still payable between the parties under any of these contemplated contingencies."

Watkin Lougher was succeeded in 1608 by his eldest son, Richard, who spent much of his life and fortune in legal contests with Sir Thomas Mansel of Margam, Moris Mathew of Glyn Ogwr, and Sir Edward Stradling of St. Donat's. His son and successor, Watkin Lougher, was Sheriff of Glamorgan 1635, " when Charles I. was making his fatal experiment of ruling without a parliament." The maritime counties of Wales were required to provide £2,204, second assessment of "*ship-money*." To the instrument issued for this purpose were attached the well-known names of Humphrey Chetham (founder of the Chetham Library, Manchester); William Glyn (of Elernion,) High Sheriff of Carnarvon; John Scourfield, Sheriff of Pembrokeshire; &c. Watkin Lougher, sheriff, had much trouble, of course, in raising his portion of this oppressive tax, and his deputy at Cardiff, Arthur Lloyd by name, had also trouble, annoyance, and loss, and bitterly chafes against his hard lot, the commands of our sovereign and dread lord the king notwithstanding. " My labour," he says, "and the labour of my cousin Roberts, in wearing out our bodies and clothes, hindarance and loss of time at home, and the spoiling of my gelding for ever, which stood me in £8; God send you and me well to do in this troublesome office, *and to go out of it in* safety!" It is a strange thing at present to hear that Carmarthen, Cardiff, and *Liverpool* were rated at the same amount for this royal " ship-money " business, viz., £15. The county of Glamorgan was to contribute £200.

Richard Lougher, Watkin's son, the last of that name at Tythegston, succeeded in 1651, was Sheriff of Glamorgan 1655 and 1696; *m.* Cecil, dau. of Judge Jenkins, surnamed " Heart of Oak," and " Pillar of the Law," of Hensol Castle. He left no son, but three daughters, the eldest being Cecil, who *m.* Edward Turberville, of Sutton, and left a dau., Cecil, who *m.* Robert, son of Sir John Knight, Kt., of Redleape, Mayor of Bristol 1670, M.P. for Bristol, &c., from whom the family of Knight of Tythegston is descended (see *Knight of Tythegston; Knight of Newton Nottage*).

Mathew of Llandaff, Radir, &c.

This very ancient and long-continuing family derived from Gwilym, son of Gwaethfoed, Lord of Cardigan, by Morfydd, dau. of Ynyr, King of Gwent, through Gruffydd Gethin, ranked as tenth from Gwaethfoed, and Ivan ap Gruffyd Gethin, who *m.* Cecil, dau. and heiress of Watkin Llewelyn of Llandaff, of the lineage of Iestyn ap Gwrgant. He settled at Llandaff. His son, Matthew Ivan Gruffydd, and his grandson, David Mathew, introduced the surname, which never ceased for twelve generations. They intermarried with the Flemings of Flemingston, Morgans of Tredegar, Gamages of Coity, Stradlings of St. Donat's, &c., and branched off at early periods into the vigorous families of Mathew of Castell Menych (Monk's Castle) and Mathew of Radir, Mathew of Aberaman, and Mathew of Sweldon and Llancaiach, all of whom are now extinct. The House of Llandaff supplied sheriffs for Glamorgan in the years 1546, 1769, and member of Parliament in the person of Thomas Mathew, father and son, in 1744, 1756. This same Thomas Mathew, sen., of Llandaff, was Rear-Admiral and Admiral of the White; and Thomas the son was a major in the army. In his election he polled 954 votes against 212 given for his "opponent," Charles Van, Esq. By his wife, Anne, dau. of Robert Knight, Esq., of Sutturm, he had, besides several other children, a son, also named Thomas Mathew, Esq., of Llandaff, the sheriff of 1769, who *d.* 1771, *s. p.*

The Mathews of Llandaff bore the arms of Gwaethfoed—*Or, a lion rampant regardant sa., crowned gu.*

Mathew of Radir.

The same in descent with the foregoing, and branching off from Llandaff with *Thomas*, third son of David, who has been described as first settling the surname of *Mathew*. Thomas *m.* Cate, dau. and co-h. of Morgan Llewelyn ap Ivan. Their eldest son was William, who became Sir William Mathew, Kt., of Radir. He was succeeded by his son Sir George Mathew, Kt. This family supplied several sheriffs for the co. of Glamorgan; *ex. gr.*, William Matthew, 1567; do., 1579; Henry Mathew, 1589; Thomas Mathew, 1613.

Edmund Mathew, Esq., of Radir, a younger brother, succeeded his two elder brothers, who *d. s. p.*, as possessor of the estates, and was himself succeeded by his eldest son, George Mathew, who *m.* a dau. of Sir John Pornes, Kt., who was the widow of the Earl of Ormond, and had a son, Theobald Mathew, Esq., who is called in "J. H.'s" MS. "Lord of Bishopstown and Llandaffe," not of Radir. He *m.* three times, and had George, two other sons, and daus., but we discover no traces of their further history. Theobald Mathew *d.* A.D. 1700. No little confusion exists in the MSS. respecting the marriages and successions of these later Mathews of Radir; but about the high position and influence of the family in this co. there cannot be a doubt.

Mathew of Castell Menych (Monk's Castle).

Robert Mathew, second son of Ivan ap Gruffydd Gethin (see *Mathew of Llandaff*), was the first of this branch family of the Mathews. He *m.* Gwladys, dau. of Llewelyn Powel Fychan, of Brecon, and had two sons, William, his successor at Castell Menych, and Morgan, from whom descended the Mathews of Roos, Aberaman, and Brynwhith. William's wife was Margaret, dau. of John Gamage, Esq., Lord of Coity, and his son Robert, of Castell Menych, *m.* Alice, dau. of John Thomas, Esq., of Pantygored, of the lineage of Madoc ap Iestyn ap Gwrgant. Eight more generations from father to son succeed at Castell Menych. They intermarry with the Raglans of Carnllwyd, Lewises of Vann, Morgans of Bedwellty, and Jenkins of Hensol; the last-mentioned marriage, being followed by no issue male, terminated the name at Castell Menych, *circa* A.D. 1700. Cecil, the heiress, *m.* Charles Talbot, cr. Baron Talbot of Hensol and Lord Chancellor 1733. He *d.* 1737 (see *Talbot of Hensol Castle*). The Castell Menych estate henceforth vested in the Talbots.

Thomas Mathew of Castell Menych was Sheriff of Glamorgan 1613, and his son of the same name was sheriff 1668.

For the arms of Mathew of Castell Menych see *Mathew of Llandaff*. The Talbot arms were—*Gu., a lion rampant within a border engrailed or, a crescent for difference*—the arms still borne by the Talbots, Earls of Shrewsbury, Talbots of Margam, &c.

Sir Hugh Johnys of Swansea.

This remarkable man may be said in a sense to form his own family : the space his life occupied, and the disguise under which his descendants (not bearing his name, since he left no son) passed down the stream of time, which is ever engulfing families and their memorials, necessarily centre all our attention upon himself. And yet Hugh ap John, *al.* Jones and Jonys, was of a good and noble stock, for he was descended from no less renowned forefathers than the *Vychans* (Vaughans) *of Tre'rtwr*, Brec., and maternally from *Sir David Gam*. Sir Roger Vaughan of Tre'rtwr (Tretower), who was knighted and died on the field of Agincourt, Oct. 23, A.D. 1415, was his gr. grandfather, and Sir Roger's wife, his gr. grandmother, was Gwladys, dau. of the testy but brave Sir David Gam, who also was knighted and died on that fatal day.

Sir Roger Vaughan, Kt., left a son, Watkin, and he a natural son, *John* Watkin Vaughan, or, as the Welsh of those times would say, John ap Watkin ap Roger Vychan, who was father of Hugh, afterwards Sir Hugh Johnys. The origin of this surname is plain,—Hugh was *John's*, or *John-his* (*sc.*, son), euphonically expressed *Jones*, or *Jonys*. Sir Hugh's wife was Mawde, dau. of Rees Cradock, Esq., uncle of Sir Mathew Cradock (see *Cradock of Swansea*). As we have said, he left no son to survive him, but two daus., Gwenllian and Jeannette, co-heiresses: the former *m.* David Rees ap Ievan of Ynyspenllwch; the latter, John David Morgan of Cadley and Cefngorwedd. The interesting monograph on Sir Hugh Johnys, by Col. Grant-Francis, F.S.A., from which these particulars are obtained, contains no further account of his descendants, nor is the year of his birth or death precisely known. We find it stated, however, in the Beaufort *Progress*, p. 170, referring to a later time, that "of this family of Jones was Hugh Jones, Lord Bishop of Llandaff, consecrated 1566, being the first Welshman that was bishop of his church in almost three hundred years before." For this link of relationship we find no further authority.

Of the tenor of his active life as a soldier we can judge from the ample epitaph on the monumental *brass* still in the chancel of St. Mary's, Swansea. He was, it is clear, "a knight clad in mail, sniffing from afar the smell of adventure," whose language meetly was,—

> " Therefore, friends,
> As far as to the Sepulchre of Christ,
> Whose soldier now—under whose blessed Cross
> We are impressed and engaged to fight."

The antique spelling has been corrected into modern, but no word omitted or added :—

"Pray for the soul of Sir Hugh Johnys, Knight, and Dame Maude, his wife, which Sir Hugh was made a knight at the Holy Sepulchre of our Lord Jesu Christ in the city of Jerusalem, the 14th day of August, the year of our Lord God 1441. And the said Sir Hugh had continued in the wars there a long time before, by the space of five years, that is to say, against the Turks and Saracens, in the parts of Troy, Greece, and Turkey, under John, that time Emperor of Constantinople, and after that was Knight Marshal of France, under John, Duke of Somerset, by the space of five years, and in like wise, after that, was Knight Marshal of England under the good John, Duke of Norfolk, which John gave unto him the manor of Landimore, to him, and to his heirs for evermore, upon whose souls, Jesu, have mercy."

Sir Hugh Johnys, though a hardy soldier, was not proof against the soft blandishments of the sex. When as yet a bachelor, but after his knighthood and foreign service, he "fell in love" with Elizabeth, the beautiful dau. of Sir Richard Woodville, and afterwards as widow of Sir Thomas Gray, married to King Edward IV. Miss Strickland in her "Lives" refers to this affair thus:—" While yet in attendance on Queen Margaret, she [Elizabeth Woodville] captured the heart of a brave knight, Sir Hugh Johns, a great favourite of Richard, Duke of York. He had nothing in the world wherewithal to endow the fair Woodville but a sword whose temper had been proved in many a battle in France ; he was, however, a timid wooer, and very impolitically deputed others to make to the beautiful maid of honour the declaration of love which he wanted courage to speak himself."

From this trouble of the affections, although aided by the direct and strong recommendations of the Duke of York and the great Earl of Warwick, the "king-maker," Sir Hugh did not emerge with success. He was looked coldly upon by the young beauty, and took to the wise course of marrying Maude Cradock, who probably made him a better wife than a maid of honour would have made.

Sir Hugh Johnys was not so destitute of means to endow a wife as Miss Strickland suggests. His patrimony may have been small, but he had received from the Duke of Norfolk, as stated on his monument, the lordship of Landimor, whose castle he is said to have repaired and beautified ; and Col. Francis, who visited the spot and has investigated the changes of ownership of this manor, although the subject is surrounded with some difficulty, does not see reason to doubt the statement on the *brass*. There are other properties mentioned as belonging to Sir Hugh Johnys; but it is quite likely that his means, when measured against the demands which a lady from court would make upon them, were too inadequate.

About the *arms* of Sir Hugh Johnys there seems to hang a good deal of obscurity. In the Beaufort *Progress* (1684) it is said that when the Duke of Beaufort, or rather Mr. Dineley, his recorder, inspected the church of St. Mary, the arms had disappeared, "having been stolen away" like the scroll issuing out of Sir Hugh's mouth, but they were "also discernible among some broken glass"—whether in a window is not stated,—" and said by others of the town to be the arms of Sir Hugh Jones and his lady." They are then figured on the margin of the *Progress* thus:—*Arg., a fesse gu. between three cocks of the second, armed, crested, and jelloped of the same*—"by the name of JONES." It is added, "These armes were very worthily borne by this *bold Britan*, Sir Hugh Johyns (now Jones), Lord of *Landimore*. The second "brass escocheon (*sic*) robbed from the tomb," and which was understood to bear arms of the lady, is blazoned thus:—*Quarterly: 1st and 4th, sa., a chevron arg. between three boys' heads couped at the shoulders, around the neck a snake entwined, proper; 2nd and 3rd, sa., a chevron arg. between three spear-heads of the same, guttés de sang.*

This entire shield would appear to be suitable rather for Sir Hugh Johnys himself; for he, being descended from the Vaughans of Tre'rtwr, might adopt the boys' heads of the first and fourth quarters, the arms of that family (the illegitimacy of the father would not in those days prevent this), as descended from Moreiddig Warwyn (*circa* 1200), grandson of Bleddyn ap Maenarch. Moreiddig is fabled to have been born with a snake around his neck—the "reason" why he adopted these arms instead of those of his ancestor Bleddyn. The spear-heads of the second and third-quarters were the proper arms of Bleddyn. But about the "three cocks" said by Mr. Dineley to have been "worthily borne by this *bold Britan*, Sir Hugh," there is room for much doubt. As he found them not on the tombstone, but "among some broken glass," and received only some verbal accounts in support of his conjecture, we cannot positively say that Sir Hugh Johnys, Kt., bore these arms in addition to those belonging to his lineage. At the same time Sir Hugh, being a knight with a *penchant* for fighting, may have adopted as his appropriate symbol a bird so famous both for his contentiousness and courage, especially as the tincture was *gules*.

Seys of Boverton.

This family, which continued at Boverton for four generations, claimed derivation from Bleddyn ap Maenarch, Lord of Brecknock in the eleventh century, and quartered his arms. Boverton was the property of the Voss family, which ended here in an heiress, Elizabeth Voss, Maid of Honour to Queen Elizabeth, who *m.* Roger Seys, Esq. (son of Ievan *Sais*, Esq., of Cowbridge), Attorney-General of all Wales. Roger Seys died 1599, and was buried at Llantwit Major. His son, Richard Seys, of Boverton "and Swansea," had to wife Margaret, dau. of Leyshon Evans, Esq., of the Gnoll, by a dau. of Matthew Herbert, Esq., of Swansea, and had a large family. The eldest son, Evan, of Boverton, a serjeant-at-law, besides a son Richard, had a dau. Margaret, who *d.* single in London, 1696, leaving her cousin, William Seys of Swansea, sole executor,—and Elizabeth, who also *d.* single, leaving her nephew Peter, Lord King, sole executor.

Richard Seys, Esq., of Boverton, *m.* and had a family; but his two sons, Evan and William, *d. s. p.*, the latter in 1710. The eldest dau., Anne, *m.* Peter King, afterwards Lord Chancellor of England, nephew of John Locke, and father, by Anne Seys, of four succeeding Lords King, from whom are descended the present Earls of Lovelace, who still quarter the arms (three spear-heads) of Bleddyn ap Maenarch. The male line at Boverton was now extinct, and the Seyses henceforth existed at Swansea, Caerleon, Reeding, &c.—all extinct.

The arms of Seys of Boverton were—*Quarterly: 1st and 4th, az., 6 plates, on a chief or, a demi-lion rampant gu.; 2nd and 3rd, sa., a chevron arg. between three spear-heads of the same, with their points imbrued.* Crest—*A demi-lion rampant, gu.* Motto—*Crescit sub pondere virtus.*

Van of Marcross.

This ancient British family went, by Norman-French rendering, by the name De Anne, or perhaps more properly *De Avan*. They were traditionally said to have settled at first in Cornwall, and to have come over to Marcross, near St. Donat's, in the reign of Edward III. Here they remained for at least ten generations. But junior branches continued longer elsewhere. We have seen under Mathew of Llandaff, that Charles Van, Esq., contested the co. of Glamorgan in 1756 against Major Thomas Mathew of Llandaff. The residence of Charles Van is not mentioned; but it may be conjectured with great probability to have been Llanwern, Monmouthshire. No *Van* is found among the sheriffs of Glamorgan, except in 1618, when Edward Van, Esq., of Marcross, held the office.

John de Anne, who *m.* the heiress of Marcross, held this lordship of the heirs of Hugh Despencer at one knight's service, valued per annum at 37s. 6d., and his son, John, at the time of the survey was forty years of age—" et Johēs de Anne est fils et hæres ejus 40, annorum ætat." This John, we presume, was father of Paganus de Anne, or Payn Van, who was lord of the manor of Marcross 7th Henry VI., 1429, and sold the lordship of Llandough and St. Mary Church, 22nd Henry VI., 1444, to Sir William Thomas, Kt., of Raglan, his son William, and their heirs for ever. " Testibus hiis, Ludovicus Matthew, David Matthew, William Bawtrip, William Jeule, et Johannes Fleming [all well-known names], Armigeri, die lunæ post fest. assumpt. beatæ Mariæ virginis," &c.

Payn Van *m.* Anne, dau. of Gruffydd ap Ivan (Bevan) ap Leyson, Esq., Lord of Baglan, and had a son William, after whom came in succession John, Edmond, William, George, Edward, the last, Sheriff of Glamorgan 1618, *m.* Grace, dau. of Francis Stradling, Esq., and sister of Sir George Stradling, of St. Donat's Castle. Edward Van had one son and one dau. The latter, named Elizabeth, *m.*, first, William Matthew, jun., of Aberaman. Secondly, Sir Richard Bassett of Beaupre, Kt. John Van, Esq., of Marcross, was the last of the line we have account of at that place. He *m.*, 1678, Mary, dau. of William Thomas of Llanfihangel, and had issue; but of the issue no record is at hand. (See *Van of Llanwern.*)

The arms of the Vans of Marcross were—*Sa., a chevron between three butterflies* (some say bees) *displayed arg.*

Thomas of Llanfihangel and Brigan.

The old mansion of Llanfihangel Manor, near Llantwit Major, with its picturesque gables and finely mullioned windows, now a comfortable farmhouse, presents to the passer by an object of unfailing interest. Here the family of Thomas resided. Under *Lougher of Tythegston* it has been shown that that family took its name from Loughor, the place of its abode. The father was priest of Loughor (Castell-llwchwr), Richard by name, son of Gronw, sixth son of Ivan ap Leyson, Lord of Baglan, near Aberavon; and one of his brothers was named *Thomas* ap Gronw, who received the surname *Ddu* — "the black," by reason of the colour of his hair. They were of the lineage of Iestyn ap Gwrgant. The maternal ancestors of this family were, however, of mixed blood, beginning with the Bassons, who, became Lords of Brigan by grant of Gilbert de Clare, A.D. 1257. Stephen Basson, or Bauson, the first lord, was the man sent by Henry III. with a great force to encounter Prince Llewelyn ap Gruffydd, A.D. 1257, but was repulsed with great loss near Llandeilofawr (*Annal. Cambr.*, *sub ann.* 1257). The line of Basson ceased with his son; his granddau., Beatrice, *m.* the Welshman, Aaron ap Howel Fychan ap Cadwgan ap Bleddyn ap Maenarch. This British line continued at Brigan for twelve generations (assuming the name *Thomas* on mar. of the heiress with Thomas, fifth son of Ivan ap Leyson, and brother of *Gronw*, ancestor of the Llanfihangel line), till Anthony Thomas, Esq., who *m.* Elinor, dau. of William Bassett, clerk, of Bonvilleston and Newton Nottage, *d. s. p.* about the end of the eighteenth century.

Thomas Ddu, named above, *m.* the heiress of Llanfihangel, as his father's brother had *m.* the heiress of Brigan. His descendants intermarried with the Vans of Marcross, Flemings of Flimstone, Carnes of Ewenny, Mathews of Llandaff, &c. Edward Thomas of Llanfihangel was Sheriff of Glamorgan in 1633, and created a baronet 1640. He *m.* Susan, dau. of Sir Thomas Morgan of Rhiwpera, Knt., and had a son,—

Sir Robert Thomas, Bart., of Llanfihangel and Bettws, whose wife was Mary, dau. of David Jenkins, sen., Esq., of Hensol. He had no son; his only dau., Susannah, who *m.* Robert Savours, Esq., of Breach, Llanblethian, had no issue, and *d.* in the lifetime of her father. Sir Robert sold his estate of Llanfihangel about 1650 to Humphrey Edwin, Esq.

The *arms* of Thomas of Llanfihangel are not known to us, but as the lineage was that of Iestyn ap Gwrgant, it may be presumed the arms would follow, with quarterings for alliances.

Gibbon of Trecastle (Gower).

Tracing to Einion ap Collwyn, the opponent of Iestyn ap Gwrgant, *Gibbon* ap Llewelyn, eighth in descent, had a son Richard ap *Gibbon* of Trecastell—a place previously known under a foreign name (see *Scurlage of Scurlage Castle*). How Richard Gibbon became possessed of the favour of the De Breoses so as to obtain this property we have no means at hand of knowing. A Welshman himself, he also *m.* a Welsh wife, Catherine, dau. of Howel ap Ivan, of the line of Bleddyn ap **Maenarch**.

Seventh in descent from Richard, Thomas Gibbon, Esq., of Trecastle, son of George, was Sheriff of Glamorgan in 1679; and his son, Grant Gibbon, Esq., of Trecastle (*d.* 1771), served the same office in 1735. The grandson of Grant, William Gibbon, son of William (*d.* 1764) by Alice, dau. of Rees Powell, Esq., of Llanharan, was also of Trecastle, and *m.*, 1784, his second cousin, dau. of Samuel Price, Esq., of Park.

The *arms* of Gibbon of Trecastle were those of Einion ap Collwyn—*Sa.*, *a chevron arg. between three fleurs-de-lis of the same.*

There were also *Gibbons of Cefntreban,* or *Pentrebean,* St. Fagan's, one of whom, " Dr. Gibbon, built the great house at St. Fagan's;"; but they were not, as far as is known, of the same stock with the Gibbons of Trecastle in Gower.

Popkin of Ynys-Tawe and Forest.

There were Popkins of Ynys-Tawe and Forest, both of the same lineage, the former the senior line, and both now extinct. They claimed descent from Rhodri Mawr, King of Wales, through his eldest son, Prince Anarawd (*succ.* A.D. 877). Gruffydd Gethin, the first named in the pedigrees as of Ynys-Tawe, ninth in descent, had a son Hopkin ap Gruffydd, and he a son David *ap Hopkin* of Ynys-Tawe, who *m.* Eva, dau. of Jenkin ap Leyson of Avan, of the race of Iestyn ap Gwrgant. Hopkin ap David ap Hopkin followed, and had a son David ap Hopkin, whose son, *Hopkin David* of Ynys-Tawe, had an elder son,—

David *Popkin,* who finally fixed the patronymic as a surname. He *m.* Jennet, dau. of Robert William, Esq., of Court Rhyd-hir, and, with other children, had a son and successor, John [*sc.,* son of] David Popkin, of Ynys-Tawe, who, adhering to the favourite family name, called his eldest son Hopkin [*sc.,* son of] John David Popkin, who was also of Ynys-Tawe. By his wife Luce, dau. of Harry Rees ap Gruffydd, he left an elder son, his successor, David Popkin, who *m.* Jane, dau. of Thomas Morgan Cadwgan, Esq., and was succeeded by his son, Hopkin David Popkin, living 1678, whose wife was a`dau. of John David Rosser of Trewyddfa. The account of this elder branch here ceases in our MSS.

The Forest *junior* line begins with Hopkin, second son of the above Hopkin David of Ynys-Tawe, and continues at Forest, near Neath, for ten generations. This line seems to have held a higher position in the county than the senior. Thomas Popkin of Forest was Sheriff of Glamorgan in 1718, and his grandson Thomas held the same office in 1755. They intermarried with the families of Dawkins of Ynystawlog, Evans of Peterwell, Card.; and the last-mentioned Thomas *m.* Justina Maria, dau. of Sir John Stepney of Llanelly. The last male representative was Bennet Popkin, Esq., of Forest, " who went to reside at Kittlehill in pursuance of a limitation in the will of his aunt, Mrs. Bennet." He *m.* Mary, dau. and co-h. of David White, Esq., of Miskin, and *d. s. p.* (See *Bath of Ffynone.*)

The arms of the Popkins were—*Or, a stag passant gu., attired and hoofed sa. ; a bordure engrailed gu.*

Price of Penllē'rgaer and Nydfywch.

Of the sept of Bleddyn ap Maenarch, Lord of Brecknock when the Normans under

Newmarch attacked that country, A.D. 1091 or thereabouts, was David Evan *Fwya* (the "greater," or perhaps "senior"), whose father was Gwilym *Ddu*. A junior gr. grandson of his, William ap David, founded the family of *Nydfywch;* and a senior gr. grandson, brother of the former, named Evan ap David, was of *Penlle'rgaer*.

To Evan ap David succeeded at Penlle'rgaer his son Griffith, his grandson Rees, and gr. grandson John *ap Rees*, with whom originated the surname *Price*. He lived in the time of Elizabeth; *m*. Elizabeth, dau. of Roger Seys, Esq., of Boverton, Attorney-General for South Wales, by Elizabeth Voss, heiress of Boverton (see *Seys of Boverton*, and *Voss of do.*). His son Griffith Price succeeded at Penlle'rgaer, and was followed by four generations of his descendants (Thomas Price was Sheriff of Glamorganshire 1739), under the last of whom, Griffith Price, Esq., barrister-at-law, issue male failed. He *m*. Jane, dau. and h. of Henry Matthew of Nydfywch (thus reuniting the two families, the latter having adopted the surname *Matthew* from Matthew ap John ap William of that place), and had a dau. Mary, who *d. s. p.* He *m*. a second time, but had no issue. By his will he devised the Penlle'rgaer estate to his cousin John Llewelyn, Esq., of Ynysygerwn, near Neath (Sheriff of Glamorgan in 1790), in whose family it still continues. (See *Llewelyn of Penllè'rgaer and Ynysygerwn*.)

Evans of Gnoll.

This important family, which ended in the marriage of the heiress with Sir Humphrey Mackworth, a lawyer and a celebrated mine proprietor (began his mining operations at Neath, 1695), resided at Gnoll, near Neath, for six or seven generations. They derived from Iestyn ap Gwrgant, through Morgan Fychan Leyson, the second son of Evan ap Leyson, who *m*. a dau. of Jenkyn ap Rhys ap Llewelyn, of Glŷn Nêdd.

In the fourth generation, *Evan* ap David ap Evan is said to be "of Neath or Gnoll." His son, David *Evans*, who began the surname, was Sheriff of Glamorgan in 1562; David Evans, his grandson, held the same office in 1632. This last David *m*. Elinor, dau. of Sir Walter Rice, of Newton—the absurd name attempted for a time to be given to the venerable *Dinefawr* (Carm.). He had an eldest son, Edward Evans, Esq., of Gnoll, who *m*. Frances, dau. of Sir William Button, Knt., and had issue, besides Mary, who *m*. Walter Evans, Esq., of *Llwyn-eryr*, the original of "Eaglesbush," a son (see *Evans of Eaglesbush*),—

Herbert, afterwards Sir Herbert Evans, Knt., Sheriff of Glamorgan in 1661, who *m*. Anne, dau. and co-h. of William Morgan, Esq., of Pencryg. He had issue five daughters, who all *d. s. p.* except one, who, eventually sole heiress, *m*. Humphrey Mackworth, knighted 1682.

The arms of Evans of The Gnoll were *Iestyn ap Gwrgant's—Gu.*, three chevrons arg.

The *Mackworths* were originally from Mackworth, in Derbyshire; there was a Humphrey Mackworth of Betton, in Salop; but Sir Humphrey Mackworth came to Wales from Bentley, parish of Tardely, Worcestershire. He was created a knight only, but the family, an ancient one, had had a baronetcy in it, cr. in 1619, in the person of Thomas Mackworth, of Normanton; and this title was revived in 1776 in the person of Sir Humphrey of the

Gnoll's grandson, Sir Herbert Mackworth, Bart., M.P. for Cardiff 1768, 1774, 1780, and 1784, *d.* 1792.

Sir Robert Mackworth, his son, *m.* 1792, but *d.* 1794, *s. p.*, when the title devolved upon his brother, Sir Digby; but the estate had been devised to his widow, who *m.* Capel Hanbury Leigh, Esq., of Pontypool Park, Lord Lieutenant of Mon. Gnoll Castle was afterwards sold to the late Henry John Grant, and since his death has been again sold. Sir Digby Mackworth was of Glen-Usk, in Mon., where his descendants still are seated.

Cradock of Long Ash.—This family are only supposed to be of kindred origin with the Cradocks of Cheriton. " J. H." could not " find their line exactly;" but they "were at Long Ash very long, for I saw a deed," he says, " dated in the time of King Edward IV., that John Cradock of Long Ash, yeoman, purchased a close called the Hams, part of the tenement of Harry ap Owen." This family continued for eight or nine generations from Philip Cradock, who lived at Long Ash *temp.* Henry VIII., but whether all the time at the same place we have no means of knowing. They seem to have disappeared with Elizabeth Cradock, who *m.* " Owen Evan, clerk." A note by " J. H." says, "And it is further to be remembered that the said William Cradock, sen., upon the account of disinheriting his daughter, Katherine, was very much troubled in conscience, as he said ; then he settled other lands on her and her heirs, which they still enjoy [*circa* 1720], viz., the two new parks, Northways, Blindwell, and other lands in Bishopston, and the Field : the deeds and writings touching the same I have seen."

Thomas of Llanbradach.—Thomas Bevan of Llanbradach (*d. circa* 1500), son of Evan Llewelyn David (see MS. of Sir Isaac Heard, Clarencieux, ed. by Sir T. Phillipps, Bart., and D. Jenkin's MS.), brother of Gwilym David of Rhiwperra, Esq., *m.* Ann, dau. of Lewis Richard Gwyn, Esq., " of Upper Senghenydd, that is, Morlais Castle." His son, Rhys Thomas, *m.* Elizabeth, dau. of Richard Carne, Esq., of Nash. His gr. grandson, Thomas Thomas, *m.* Dorothy, dau. of Sir John Carew, Knt., Sheriff of Pembr. 1622.

William Thomas, Esq., of Llanbradach, his son, Sheriff of Glamorgan 1675, had as wife a dau. of Thomas Morgan of Machen (the *Tredegar* house). His son Thomas was Sheriff of Glamorgan in 1705, and his gr. grandson James in 1728, on whose death without issue the estate of Llanbradach fell to his kinsman (father's brother), William Thomas, Esq., of Tredommen. William's line terminated through the failure of issue in his gr. grandson, Thomas Thomas, Esq. The present Mrs. Thomas of Llwyn Madoc in Breconshire is of this family.

Jenkins of Hensol.—This family is principally known through one of its members, " Judge Jenkins of Hensol," and the noble house into which it finally merged. Of the line of Einion Sais and Bleddyn ap Maenarch, Lord of Brecon, *Jenkin* ap Richard *m.* Jennet, dau. of Evan ap William Sir Howel ap William ap Hopkin ap Evan ap Leyson, grandson of Morgan, Lord of Avan (after whom it is supposed Morga*n* or Marga*m* Abbey was called). Jenkin's son was *David Jenkins*, barrister-at-law, ultimately judge of the Western Circuit of Wales under Charles I.,—a man of great force of character and some eccentricity, named " Heart of Oak " and " Pillar of the Law." Being a staunch royalist, he took an active part against the Parliament during the civil war; was made prisoner at Hereford 1645; sent to the Tower; refused to kneel at the bar of the House of Commons, and was fined for his contempt £1,000, was impeached for high treason, and when an Act was passed for his trial, he met it with the declaration that he would "die with the Bible under one arm and Magna Charta under another!"—a virtuous declaration, but one somewhat inconsistent for an adherent of the Stuarts. Being, however, liberated in 1656, on the restoration of Charles II., he returned to his estate in Glamorganshire, where he ended his days, and was buried at Cowbridge. He *m.* Cecil, dau. of Sir Thomas Aubrey, Kt., of Llantrithyd, by whom, besides other children, he had a son David Jenkins, Esq., of Hensol, Sheriff of Glamorgan 1685, who *m.* Mary, dau. and co-h. of Edward Pritchard, Esq., of Llancayach, and left a son Richard, who *d. s. p.*, and a dau. Cecil, whose husband was Charles Mathew, Esq., of Castell Menych (Monk's Castle). She had one dau., Cecil, who, as heiress of Hensol, brought that property, as well as Castell Menych, to her husband, Charles Talbot, 1717, Solicitor-General to the Prince of Wales 1733, Lord High Chancellor of England by the title Baron Hensol of Hensol, co. of Glamorgan. (See further *Hensol Castle.*)

Thomas of Danygraig.—Members of this family married with Mansels of Briton-Ferry, Middletons of Middleton Hall, Carm.; but they were of short continuation at Danygraig, having become extinct early in the 18th century. They traced their lineage, according to "J. H.'s" MS., from Einion ap Collwyn through *Owen Philip*, Portreeve of Swansea, 1600, eldest son of Philip John ap Rhys of Glyn-Nedd. In the fourth generation from Owen, Walter *Thomas m.* Catherine, dau. of Hopkin David Edward of *Danygraig*, and had issue William, his successor, who *m.* Catherine, dau. of Arthur Mansel, Esq., of Briton-Ferry. William had several daus. and two sons, Walter and William, both of whom *d. s. p.*, but the younger, the survivor, "gave all his estate, except the customary lands in the parish of Oystermouth, to his uncle, Bussy Mansel, Esq., of Briton-Ferry, his mother's brother." It seems that William Thomas, sen., son-in-law of Arthur Mansel, was, like many of the Mansels, of strong royalist sentiments, and "suffered much for his loyalty to King Charles I. He was obliged to sell part of his estate at Llandilo-Talybont, which consisted of fee-farms, in order to prevent its being sequestered in those troublesome times, and retired to Carmarthen, where he lived some years, and then returned to Swansea. He lies buried in the south aisle of the church there, and has a handsome large monument [now gone] erected to his memory.—J. H."

The arms borne by Thomas of Danygraig, according to "J. H.'s" MS., were—*Sa., a chevron between three fleurs de lis arg.* If so, the arms of *Collwyn* ap Tangno, of North Wales, must have been adopted by mistake for Einion ap *Collwyn*, the real ancestor.

Thomas of Wenvoe Castle.—A family of Welsh origin, and known by the name Thomas, lived on their inheritance at Wenvoe in the latter part of the fifteenth century, when the heiress of Thomas ap Thomas *m.* Ievan Harpway of Tre Simon, descended from an old family in Herefordshire, who thereupon assumed the surname *Thomas* and dwelt at Wenvoe. His son Thomas *m.* first a Basset, secondly a Carne; and his grandson John Thomas of Wenvoe *m.* Anne, dau. of Rees Meyrick of Cottrel (the author of *Morganiæ Archæographia*). A later descendant, Edmund Thomas of Wenvoe Castle, was Sheriff of Glamorgan in 1626; his grandson Edmund filled the same office in 1665; and his gr. grandson, created a baronet in 1694, was sheriff in 1700. His title, on his death *s. p.* in 1703, devolved upon his brother, Sir Edmund Thomas, who *m.* Mary, dau. of the Right Hon. John Howe of Stowell, co. of Gloucester. His son, Sir Edmund Thomas, Bart., of Wenvoe Castle, M.P. for Wilts 1759, was succeeded in 1767 by his eldest son Edmund, who *d. unm.* 1789, having previously sold the Wenvoe Castle estate to Peter Birt, Esq., while the title descended to his brother, Sir John Thomas, who resided in England, whose representative at the present time is Sir George Vignoles Thomas, ninth baronet (*b.* 1856), of the Plâs, Chingford, Essex, who bears the ancient arms of Thomas of Wenvoe—*Sa., a chevron and canton ermine.*

Meyrick of Cottrel.—The name of this family, long extinct, has become familiar to our age through *Rees Meyrick*, author of a valuable historical work entitled *Morganiæ Archæographia.* It was written A.D. 1578, and first printed a few years ago by the late Sir Thomas Phillipps, Bart. Rees Meyrick, or, as he seems to have written it, *Mireke*, was of Cottrel, near Cardiff, where his ancestor, Meurig ap Hywel, ninth in descent from Cynfyn Fychan, of the line of Einion ap Collwyn, was the first to settle. We know little of the successors of Rees Meyrick of Cottrel, except that one of them, Morgan Meyrick, probably son of Rees, was Sheriff of Glamorgan in 1609. We have seen above that John Thomas, Esq., of Wenvoe, *m.* Anne, a dau. of Rees Meyrick of Cottrel.

The arms of Meyrick of Cottrel were those of Einion ap Collwyn—*Sa., a chevron arg. between three fleurs-de-lis of the same.*

Prichard of Collene, or Collenau.—This family sprung from that of Gibbon of Trecastle in Gower, of the sept of Einion ap Collwyn. (See *Gibbon of Trecastle.*) Evan *ap Richard*, second son of Richard Gibbon, was the first of this branch line. He *m.* Gwenllian, heiress of William Thomas of Collene, and settled at that place about the year 1500. For several generations the names of the representatives continued to vary from Evan ap Richard (Prichard) and Richard ap Evan (Bevan) until about the ninth, when with Evan *Prichard*, Esq., of Collene, this surname obtained dominance, and continued for three or four generations. From this family issued the *Prichards* of Tylcha, descendants of Thomas Prichard, fourth son of Richard Bevan (ap Evan), the sixth of Collene; and maternally the *Bevans* of Trevarryg in Llantrisant. Trecastle was before called *Scurlage Castle.*

All these used the arms of Einion ap Collwyn. (See *Meyrick of Cottrel.*)

Powell of Llanharan and Maesteg.—From Einion ap Collwyn through the old family of Powells of Llangynwyd, or Llwydiarth, and Coytrehên (Thomas Powell of Coytrehên was Sheriff for Glamorgan 1673), was descended Rees *Powell* of Maesteg, son of John Gwyn ap Howell, a younger son of Llwydiarth. His third successor at Maesteg, Gervase Powell, Esq., *m.* "Catherine Oliver, heiress of St. John the Baptist Chapel, parish of Llantrisant, commonly called 'Capel Ievan Bedyddiwr.'" His son was Rees Powell, Esq., of Llanharan, who was father of *Rees Powell*, Esq., of Llanharan,—"one of the most worthy gentlemen ever brought up in Glamorgan in learning, piety, and charity to the poor." He *d.* unmarried 1738, aged about twenty-five. His brother William, heir of Llanharan, *d.* also *unm.* in 1770, whereupon his brother, the Rev. Gervase Powell, LL.B., rector of Llanfigan and Merthyr Tydfil, succeeded. He *m.* Elizabeth, dau. of Charles Vaughan, Esq., of Scethrog, Brec., and had issue three daus., co-heiresses, who all married and divided the estate. Llanharan mansion and demesne were afterwards purchased by Richard Hoare Jenkins, Esq.

The arms of Powell of Llanharan were those of Einion ap Collwyn,—*Sa.*, *a chevron arg. between three fleurs-de lis of the same.*

Note.—Chief Men of the Cromwellian Period.

The cause of the Parliament and nation, as against the despotic tendencies of Charles I., found in Glamorgan a number of heroic supporters. For the most part men in the prime of life, in some instances only entering upon the stage of mature manhood, earnest, conscientious, energetic, their service to the popular interest was immense, although their number was but small. Chief among these men were Bussy Mansel, of Briton Ferry; Rowland Dawkin, of Kilvrough; John Price, of Gellihir, in Gower; and Col. Philip Jones, of Swansea. Except John Price, they all rose to high command in the army; became members of Cromwell's parliament; and the last-named, Philip Jones, a man of remarkable ability and high integrity, became comptroller of the Lord Protector's household, and was elevated in 1658 to the House of Lords. Having purchased the estate of Fonmon Castle, after the Restoration he was permitted to retire to his home, where he spent the remainder of his days in comparative ease and quiet. (See further, *Jones of Fonmon Castle.*) Arms: *A chevron arg. between three spear-heads of the same embrued.*

THE CROMWELL FAMILY.

The county of Glamorgan nurtured the Welsh forefathers of Oliver Cromwell. That man, whose thought was action, whose measures so materially influenced the fortunes of this country, and who on more than one occasion betrayed a leaning in favour of Wales, was well aware, when battering the castle of Cardiff, that he was then in the near vicinity of the cradle whence his family had sprung. Noble, in his laborious *Memoirs of the Protectoral House of Cromwell*, has carefully investigated the Welsh descent of the Protector, tracing the paternal lineage from son to father in direct line to *Morgan Williams* of Whitchurch (*Eglwys Newydd*), near Llandaff, descended from the lords of the ancient Comot of *Cibwr* (Kibbor), of the line of Bleddyn ap Cynfyn, Prince of Powys. Maternally, he was of the family of Thomas Cromwell, Earl of Essex, whose surname was assumed. An ancestor of Morgan Williams, William Morgan ap John of Whitchurch, was of the privy council of Henry VII. A.D. 1495. Morgan Williams of Whitchurch *m.* ——, dau. of Walter Cromwell of Putney, Middlesex, and sister of Lord Thomas Cromwell, " blacksmith or ironmaster's son, the *Malleus Monachorum*, or, as old Fuller renders it, ' Mauler of Monasteries.' "—(*Carlyle.*) He had issue a son, Richard, who adopted his mother's maiden surname, now become celebrated in the person of his uncle, the great minister of Henry VIII. and friend of Cardinal Wolsey. Richard (gr. gr. grandfather of Oliver, Protector) became Sir Richard Cromwell, Kt., " a righthand man of the Mauler of Monasteries," was made one of the Privy Chamber of Henry VIII., 1527, and was given the lordship of *Neath*, with the suppression of the abbey of which place he had probably something to do. In two MS. letters in the British Museum, addressed (1536) to Lord Cromwell, he expressly signs himself " your most bounden nephew,"—which establishes the truth of the pedigree (*Cotton MSS.*, Cleop. E. iv., 204). Carlyle has shown that this Sir Richard "has signed himself in various law deeds and notarial papers, still extant, 'Richard Cromwell, *alias* Williams;' also that his sons and grandsons continued to sign 'Cromwell, *alias* Williams,' and even that our Oliver himself, in his youth, has been known to sign so." (*Letters, &c., of Cromwell*, i., 24.) Sir Richard's son, Sir Henry Cromwell, Kt., of Hinchinbrook, Hunts, *m.* Joan, dau. and h. of Sir Philip Warren, and had three sons :—1, Sir Oliver Cromwell, Kt. of the Bath at the coronation of James I., 1603, who *m.* Lady Anne, widow of Sir Horatio Palavicini ; 2, Robert ; 3, Henry. The second son, Robert, living at Huntingdon, *m.*, about 1591, Elizabeth Steward, the young widow of William Lynne, Esq., of Bassingbourne, Cambr., and dau. of William Steward, Esq., of Ely, said by the genealogists to have "indubitably descended from the royal Stuart family of Scotland." He had ten children, of whom *Oliver* was the fifth. Of the ten, seven survived to manhood, but the only son who so survived was Oliver. The spot where Oliver was born is still familiar to all who know Huntingdon, but the house has been twice rebuilt, and has lost every trace whatever of the home of Oliver's youth. Robert Oliver was a considerable owner of land around Huntingdon, and his eldest brother, Sir Henry Cromwell, lived in the great house of Hinchinbrook close by. The little brook Hinchin ran through Robert's lands and courtyard of his house, where it is believed a brewer had once carried on his business—a circumstance which was easily converted by his detractors into proof that Cromwell's father was himself a "*brewer*"! As Carlyle remarks, "the splenetic credulity and incredulity, the calumnious opacity, the exaggerative ill-nature, and general flunkeyism and stupidity of mankind, are ever to be largely allowed for in such circumstances." Robert Cromwell sat once in Parliament in his younger days (1593); is found on various public Commissions for draining the fens ; served as magistrate at Quarter Sessions, &c., and was generally a man of energy and mark.

Oliver Cromwell, his fifth child, student of the law, afterwards a gentleman farmer at St. Ives, officer in the army, and finally Lord Protector of England, was born 25th April, 1599 ; *m.*, Aug., 1620, in London, Elizabeth Bourchier, dau. of Sir James Bourchier, Knt., of London, and Felstead, Essex. He was then in his twenty-first year, and had taken up his residence with his mother at St. Ives, Hunts. His dwelling was Slepe Hall House : the great barn where he treasured his corn, and by and by drilled his soldiers, still stands; but nearly all other memorials of him at St. Ives have vanished. Troublous times arose, and Oliver was not a man to loiter when he thought duty called. He was therefore soon in the active public world—in Parliament, in the field, in the thick of battle. His life henceforth is known to all men. He became the foremost man, as well as the "best abused" man in all England.

SECTION VII.—THE MANORS OF GLAMORGAN IN THE SEVENTEENTH CENTURY.

The following succinct description of the ancient manorial demesnes of Glamorgan as they stood about 200 years ago is so full of topographical and personal fact and allusion, that its insertion here cannot fail to be of interest to the historical and antiquarian reader. It is extracted from the valuable MS. of *Glamorganshire Pedigrees*, once in the possession of Sir Isaac Heard, Kt., Clarencieux King-at-Arms, printed by the late Sir Thomas Phillipps, Bart., 1845. The original MS. of which this was a copy certified by Sir Isaac Heard had evidently been written at different times, and by different persons, but completed about 1771, its latest and concluding date. Internal evidence clearly suggests that the more recent portion of it was the work of a member of the family of Truman, of Pant-y-Llwydd, whose pedigree is fully given, with the date 1770 several times repeated. Other parts are about a century earlier, doubtless brought together from the productions of different hands by the last compiler. Thus, in the pedigree of Mansel of Briton Ferry, Bussy Mansel is described as "*now* of Brytonfery, 1678;" Sir Edward Mansel, Knt. and Bart., as "now of Muddlescum, 1678;" "William Herbert, now of Kilybebyll, 1678;" and "Rowland Harys, now of Bryn Coch, 1678."

The age of that portion of the MS. here extracted cannot be determined with like precision; but from fair inference it appears to be generally contemporaneous with the dates last mentioned. Thus, manors are given as then "belonging to Sir John Aubrey, Knt., of Llantrithyd;" and we know that Sir John flourished both before and after the end of the seventeenth century. "Richard Lychwr" is one of three described as persons who "do present a minister to the church of Newton Nottage." The last Richard Lougher *d.* in 1701. Then we have "Manors belonging to Sir Edward Mansel, Knt., Bart." Sir Edward was sheriff of this co. in 1688; M.P. 1660, 1680, and 1685, &c.; and entertained at Margam the Duke of Beaufort, on his lordly progress through Wales in 1684. Of *Avan Wallia* it is said that it had "two courts and three parishes," and "Mr. Bushi Mansel is patron of these three churches." Mr. Bussy Mansel was Sheriff of Glamorgan in 1678. These allusions are conclusive of the age of this important document, while its own contents make it manifest that the writer was competent from local knowledge and skill in grouping relevant information for the task of writing on the subject. It requires similar local knowledge to determine how far these manors continue in our time to belong to lineal representatives, where existing, of the former possessors. The greater part of the manors of the "Earl of Pembroke" are still vested in the Marquis of Bute.

THE MANORS OF THE EARL OF PENBROCK IN THE COUNTY OF GLAMORGAN.

The said earl hath the Castle of Cardiffe (which stands in the manor of Roath); the manor of Llys-Talybout; the manor of Leck [Llech] with that of Cayre [*q.* Caerau?]; St. George's—which are free, copyhold, and demesne lands. Michelston-super-Ely is of like tenure. The lord is patron of the church there, and of the church of St. George's.

St. Nicholas is divided between the said earl, Martin Button, Esq., and the heir of Cottrel, and the patronage of that church belongs to them by turns. Walterston, within the parish of Llancarvan; Llanvaes, that was sometime two parts, one belonging to the Duke of Bedford, then Lord of Glamorgan, and the other part belonging to Malefant, that married the heiress of Fleming, but the Earl of Penbrock hath it entire, and is patron of the church there.

Boverton and *Llantwit-Major* was kept by Sir Robert Fitzhamon in his own hand, which he kept in husbandry for provision of corn towards his house at Cardiffe. It is a spacious lordship, in circuit about four miles, having about 900 acres of land in demesne, free, and customary lands, and every tenant upon his death or alienation of his customary lands payeth the best beast, and for want of a beast 5s. in the name of a heriot [*heriot*—a fine due in copyhold estates to the lord of the manor, on death of holder]. The Dean of Gloucester hath the tithe corn there. Basset hath the advowson there. There are four wells of wholesome water in this manor, and none of them drieth in summer. They call them Odnants, Odnais, Sigin Well, and Six Wells. They run in one stream into Severn, at Colehugh. Six Wells springeth in the south, and runneth northward into Severn ; Sigin Well runneth towards the south, thither, and yet there is neither mountain nor hill to urge the two springs thus contrary.

Lantwit Rawleigh is in the west part of Lantwit parish, and was purchased by William, the eldest brother of Philip, Earl of Penbrock, of Sir Thomas Baglan, Knt. *Llanbleithian* is a large manor ; it came by marrying Quintin's heiress to Seward, Lord of Talyvan, and when the male issue of the Sewards failed, an heiress of the last of them married William Par, after Marquis of Northampton; and now the Earl of Penbrock is lord of it. *Eglwys Brewis*, or a great part of it, belongeth to Evan Saies, Esq. It is a fine little lordship.

Ruthyn containeth Lanharan, and part of Lanhilid, and part of Saint Mary's Hill. This lordship was given by Fitz Hamon to [Madoc] the second son 'of Justyn, and is large and spacious ; the forest of Garth Maylwg is in it, but the wood thereof was sold to the Iron Men [the miners of Merthyr].

Newton Nottage contains 1,200 acres of land, and is divided between the Earl of Penbrock and Richard Lychwr [Lougher], Esq., and the heir of Sir William Herbert, Knt. It was given by William, Earl of Gloster (then Lord of Glamorgan), unto one Sir Richard Cardiffe, who had one only daughter, that married one Sir Thomas Sanford, Knt., and had issue Sir Richard Sanford, Knt., Lord of Newton ; but how the Sanfords went from the same I could not find as yet. There are three wells in this lordship, which flow and ebb twice in twenty-four hours, and at every time contrary to the sea, whereupon Sir John Stradling, Knt., Baronet, moralized.

The borough of *Kynfigge* [*Kenfig*] Sir Robert Fitz Hamon kept in his own hands, and builded a castle there, and used the same as one of his dwelling-houses. Howbeit, in a short time both the town and castle were drowned by the sand of the sea, and there remaineth but out cottages, bearing the name of the borough of Kynfigge, which hath the whole liberties yet remaining, as the said town formerly had ; saving that the weekly markets and annual faires are lost. The King's Majesty is patron of the church there. Kynfigg river springeth in Ceven Cribwr, and runneth to Pile, and so under Kynfygge Castle to the sea of Severn.

The borough of *Avan*, together with the lordship of *Avan Walia*, was given by Fitz Hamon to Cradock ap Justyn, which, after many ages, fell to a daughter that married one of the Blunts, that exchanged the same with the Lord of Glamorgan for lands in England.

Neath Burgus, with the castle, was given in the division by Sir Robert Fitz Hamon to Sir Richard Greenfield, Knt. [see De Granville], whose heir founded an abbey and gave the lands there towards the maintenance thereof, and went to an estate that they had in Devonshire, near Bedeford, to dwell. The lord is patron of the church there, and the valuation is 5. (*Sic MS.*) There is in the lordship of Neath four Courts Baron, viz. : Neath Manerium, Neath Citra, Neath Ultra, and Kil-y-Bebyll. Avan Walia hath two courts and three parishes, viz. : Avan Burgus, Baglan, and Michelston-super-Avan (otherwise called Ynys Avan). Mr. Bushi Mansel is patron of those three churches.

The borough of *Cowbridge* was kept by Robert Fitz Hamon in his own hands, and the bailiffs thereof do still yield their yearly accompts at the Earl of Penbrock's audits, for the profits and perquisitts of their court there. Mr. Basset is patron of the church. The fishing of Taff, Rumney, Ely, Ogmor, Avan, and Neath, do belong to the Earl of Penbrock. The Wardsilver, paid by the several Gentlemen of Ward that held their manors in knight service of the said earl, as under the Castle of Cardiffe, amounts to £7 9s. ob.

Saint Henydd Subtus [Lower Senghenydd], wherein the Red Castle is, once the chief house of Ivor Pettite, Lord of Saint Henydd. Also Carffili Castle and Gurles [Morlais] Castle, in Upper Saint Henydd, belongs to the said earl, and the patronage of Celligar and Merthyr Churches.

The castle and borough of *Lantrissent*, with the lordships of Clun, Pentyrch, and Trewern, was given to Einion ap Collwyn ; but Sir Robert Fitz Hamon kept *Glynrondde* in his own hands. There are in the lordships of Miskin and Glynrondde seven parish churches, viz. : Lantrissent, Lantwit Vairdre, Ystradtvodwg, Lanwnno, Aberdâr, Pentyrch, and Radyr. The Dean of Gloster and his lessees hath the tithe sheaf there. Basset is patron of the vicarage of Lantrissent.

The lordship of Glynrondde butteth upon the south part of Brecknockshire, and hath in it a good and large common of pasture given by Justyn's father to the tenants, and still called, after his name, *Hir Wayn Wrgan*. Both Ronddes spring in that lordship.

Tir Iarll was kept by Fitz Hamon in his own hands, and hath two parish churches, viz. : Langynwyd and Bettws ; and hath in it two tenures, freehold and lease, or patent lands. *Note.*—That William and Philip,

Earls of Penbrock, were the greatest lords that had lands in Glamorgan either before or after Justyn's time. [See *Pembroke, Earls of; Bute, Marquess of.*]

The Manors belonging to the Right Hon. H. Marquis of Worcester.

The castle and borough of *Swansey*, the castles of Ostermouth and Caslychwr; Kilvai, Sub-boscos, and Super-boscos; Penarth, Hamon, Kittle, and Trewyddva; Penmanor, part thereof; Ilston; Michelston-le-Pit, Wrinston, West Orchard, and Lancarvan, four small lordships. West Orchard hath no court but at Michaelmas. The lord is patron of the church of Michelston-le-Pit.

Manors belonging to Sir Edward Mansel, Knt., Baronet.

Margam, Havod y Porth, Laleston, Pile, Horgro, Aber Kynfigg, Langewyd, holden in chief of the king, Porth Inon, Nicholaston, Scurla (or Horton), and Penrees. These four lordships in Gower contain three parishes, and the lord is patron of the three churches of Pile and Kynfigg, being both but one vicarage.

Manors of the Earl of Lester [Leicester].

The several lordships of Coyty Anglia, Coyty Walia, Newcastell, Court Colman, Lan Hary, and Newland, wherein are demesne lands, customary, free, and copyhold. The lord is patron of Coyty Church, Coe-Church, Saint Bride's Minor, and Lanhary. Jo. Gamadge, Esq., bought Court Colman of Thomas Lyson, Doctor of Physick.

Manors that do or did belong to St. John, Earl of Bullingbrock [Bolingbroke].

The castle of *Penmark*, with the lordship, came to the Saint Johns by marrying an heiress to one of the Humphrevills; it hath free and copyhold lands. The castle and lordship of *Fonmun* butteth upon the river Thawe: it hath copy and free lands; both manors are in the parish of Penmark, and the Dean had once the tythe sheaf and the presentation of a vicar to the church.

The manor of *Lancadle* butteth upon the eastern part of the river Thawe, within the parish of Lancarvan. It hath free and copyhold lands. It is (or was) holden in soccage under the Earl of Penbrock, as they of his manor at Saint Nicholas. *Cum Kidi* joineth with the manor of Penmark, and is within the said parish, and hath free and copyhold lands. It hath been part of Humphrevill's lands. [See *De Humfreville.*]

For the manor of *Barry* I find no record to whom it was given in the division. Camden saith that it had that name from one Barricus, a holy man, born and bred there. It hath in it the like tenures and two parish churches, viz.: Barry and Port Kery; the lord is patron of both.

Manors once belonging to Carn [of Ewenny].

Wenny, sometime a priory, purchased (after the suppression) by Sir Edward Carn, Knt. It is holden in Capite. The lord is patron of the church of Wenny. *Saint Mary*, by Cowbridge, and *Landoch* are two manors holden under the Castle of Cardiffe by knight service. *Colwynston* manor stands upon the river Alem. It was sometime the Stradling's land. It owes knight service to Ogmor Castle: also part of Saint Bride's Major the like tenure.

Manors belonging once to Sir John Stradling, Knt., Baronet.

Saint Donat's was given in the division to Sir William le Esterling, Knt.: the lord is patron of the church there. *Monke Ash* (or Nash Major) was the Greenfields' [Grenvilles'], and given by them to the Abbey of Neath, and after the suppression purchased from Sir Richard Cro[m]well, Knt., by Sir Thomas Stradling, of Saint Donat's, Knt.

Lanphe came to the Stradlings by the marriage of Sir Edward Stradling, Knt., with the heiress of Berkrolles. Lanphe is holden by knight service under the Dutchie of Lancaster, and Merthyr Mawr by knight service under Lanbleithan. He had also a fourth part of Penlline, under Cardiffe Castle.

Merthyr Mawr was once the land of the Sewards, and came to Berkrolls by marrying an heiress of Seward; and from Barkrolls to Stradling, by the above-said marriage. Thomas [?], Lord Bishop of Landaffe, is patron of the church there. *Llanmaes*, in Saint Fagan's, situate on both sides of Ely, being antient lands belonging to the Stradlings.

Sully, given in the division to Sir Reynold Sully, Knt., whose great-granddaughter being an heiress, married Sir Lyson de Avan, and conveyed the said lordship to that name [see *De Sully*]. Again, a daughter and heiress to Sir Thomas de Avan, Lord of Sully, married one Blunt, an English Knt., who exchanged her lands in Wales with the then Lord of Glamorgan for lands in England. It fell by escheat to the Crown, and was purchased from Queen Mary by Sir Thomas Stradling, Knt., (holden) de Rege.

East Orchard was given in the division to Sir Roger Barkrolls, Knt., where stood his chief dwelling-house [see *De Berkrolles*]. It is situate upon the river Thawe, and came to the Stradlings by the aforesaid marriage. It is holden under Cardiffe Castle.

Castleton and *West Orchard* are both in the parish of Saint Athan, and holden by knight service under the castle of Cardiffe. The lord is patron of the church there. *Gileston* is holden by Mr. Giles from Sir John Stradling, Knt., by lease for 1,000 years at £2 per annum. Knight service under Castleton. The lessee is patron of the church there during the time.

Manors that belonged to Sir William Herbert, Knt., and after his death, sans issue, divided between Sir William Dorington, Knt., Mr. Herbert of Cogan Pill, and William Herbert of Swansey, Esq.

Roath Tewkesbury (so called after the Lord of Glamorgan had given it to the abbey of Tewkesbury), after the suppression of the abbeys was purchased by Sir George Herbert, Knt., the grandfather of Sir William Herbert, Knt.; and therein Sir William builded the fair house, called the Fryers, by Cardiffe: holden de Rege.

Landoch came to Sir William Herbert from his great-grandmother, daughter and heiress to Sir Matthew Cradock, Knt., which, after the death of Richard Herbert, Esq., married Sir William Bawdrip, Knt. In this lordship was the chief dwelling-house of Sir Matthew Cradock, Knt. [see *Llandough Castle*]. The lord is patron of the church there. It is holden under the castle of Cardiffe. He had also part of St. Andrews and Denys Powis of the King.

Cantlostown, once the Cantelupes Land, and it came first to Sir William Horton, Knt., by marrying the daughter and heiress of Thomas Cantlo, Esq., and from his granddaughter, Jonet, daughter and heiress to his son, Jenkin Horton, to Sir Matthew Cradock, her son and heir by Richard Cradock, Esq., to whom she married; and from the heiress of Sir Matthew Cradock, to her son and heir, Sir George Herbert, Knt. It is within the parish of Merthyr Mawr, and is holden under the castle of Lanbleithian. Cornely was some-time the Lovells' Lands, after, the Cradocks', and now the Herberts', holden in Soccage under Kynfigg Castle.

A third part of *Newton Nottage* belonged to Sir William Herbert. The three lords, viz., the Earl of Penbrock, the heir of Sir William Herbert, and Richard Lychwr [Lougher], Esq., do present a minister to the church by turns. Also at Swansey Sir William had a fair dwelling-house and much land thereunto belonging, and the tithe sheafe of Cadoxton by Neath. He had also a part of Penmaen, and a third part of Langenith, in Lower Gower.

Manors belonging to Sir John Awbrey, of Lantrithyd, Knt.

The lordship of *Talyvan*, which was sometime the Sewards', purchased by John Thomas Basset, Esq., of King Edward the Sixth, where are free, customary, lease, and copyhold lands. Welsh Saint Donat's is the parish church. A great part of Saint Mary Hill, and the manor of Lan Madock, in Lower Gower, belong to the Knt.

Lands of Edward Van, of Marcross, Esq.

Edward Van, Esq., had a moiety of Marcross, and a fair house at Lantwit, and much good land there-unto belonging, (held) under the Castle of Cardiffe.

Manors belonging to Sir Edward Lewis, sen., Knt., of Van.

Van, where [are] his chief dwelling-house and goodly demesne thereunto belonging. The manor of St. Fagan's, wherein is a fair house, builded by Dr. Gibbon, with much demesne lands and rent belonging there-unto. The manor of *Adensfield, Penmark,* and *Splot,* part of the lordship of Peterston *super* Ely. The manor of *Carn-Llwyd.* The manor of *Roath Kensam* [Keynsham] being part of Roath, given by the Lord of Glamorgan to the abbey of Kensam, and after the suppression purchased by Edward Lewis, Esq., father to Thomas Lewis.

The manor of *Cornton*, situate in Ogmor Lands in the duchy of Lancaster, and is holden in knight service under the castle of Ogmor. Sir Edward Lewis, Knt., had also the manor-house of *Radyr*, and the park and demesne lands thereunto belonging.

Sir Francis Popham, Knt., had the manor of *Cadoxton*, wherein are three tenures, viz., demesne, free, and copyhold lands. There are two churches in it, whereof the lord is patron.

Manors of Sir Richard Basset of Bewper.

Sir Richard Basset, Knt., had the manor of *St. Hilary*, wherein standeth Bewper, his chief dwelling-house, and very goodly and faire demesnes thereunto belonging. He had also one moiety of *Marcross*, and goodly demesne lands there. He had also *Viswere*, wherein standeth a faire house, and goodly demesne lands thereunto belonging.

The Ancient Divisions of Glamorgan.

The boundaries and divisions of Glamorgan and Monmouthshire before the Norman conquest are not clearly ascertainable. But there seems to be no reason for doubting that from the end of the Roman period (fifth century), when the Severn washed the western side of *Britannia Prima*, and the consolidation of the Saxon states under Egbert (ninth century), when the Wye rather than the Severn was the western boundary of the Anglo-Saxon dominion, the country between the Severn and the Wye had belonged more to Wales than to England, and had a population almost entirely British. Here Elystan Glodrudd is said to have ruled a territory known by the various names, Fferyllwg, Ferleg, Ferlex. From the Wye westward, however, the country was always considered as belonging purely and simply to the Welsh, as it has continued to this day part of Wales. Monmouth and Glamorgan—the former popularly considered, and in some enactments named as in England—were before the Norman age and formation of the Lordship Marcher of Glamorgan generally associated together under the title of Gwent and Morganwg, and doubtless (along with surrounding districts) inhabited by a clan or division of the Britons which recognised a bond of common origin or interest—the *Silures*, although the land was partitioned under two or more rulers.

This region maintained, also, a kind of separateness from South Wales. It was not a portion at any time (except when force prevailed) of the wider country known as the "south part" of Wales, or *Deheubarth;* it was not included in either of the three provinces or kingdoms into which Rhodri the Great (ninth century), King of Wales, divided his dominions between his sons. Howel Dda, King of South Wales, was considered an interloper when attempting to obtain rule in Glamorgan, and was checked by Edgar, the English king.

But not even the conquest of this region by the Normans, and their long and powerful rule over it, in the slightest degree obliterated the public sense that the country of Morgan and the Gwenta of the Silures still belonged to and formed an essential part of Wales. The ancient British division into *cantrefs* and *comots*, made perhaps in the time of Howel Dda, or possibly first originated and fully systematized by Prince Llewelyn ap Gruffydd (thirteenth century)—they were certainly formally defined and established by that prince—extended to Glamorgan and Gwent as well as to any other part of Wales, and remain more or less in force to this day ;—*ex. gr.*, Cardiff is in the hundred of *Cibwr* (now spelt "Kibbor"), and Llantrisant in that of Miskin, the chief difference being that the ancient *comots* are now termed *hundreds*, and the ancient *cantrefs* fallen into abeyance. And it is to be noticed that the old British topography placed Gwent and Morganwg (Monmouth and Glamorgan) under one system of six *cantrefs*, including twenty-four *comots*, a division from the influence of which it is not yet altogether practicable to relieve the popular mind. A part of the co. of Monmouth especially—that lying between the Usk and the Taff, forming the *cantref* of Gwaunllwg, or Gwentllwg—is often popularly considered as in Glamorgan, and it requires an effort of the memory respecting the actual county boundary to dispel the illusion. The old British division of Glamorgan proper (which excluded Gower [Gwyr], classing it with Carmarthen as a part of Deheubarth, but included a part of Monmouthshire) was into six cantrefs and twenty-four comots, as before stated.

GLAMORGANSHIRE.

Cantrefs.	Comots.
Gro Nedd, or Gorfynydd. [This cantref, which formed the extreme *western* part of Glamorgan, had its western limit on the river Neath (*Nêdd*), though some say it extended to the Tawe.]	Rhwng Nêdd ac Afan ["between Nedd and Avan"]. Tir yr Hwndrwd ["the hundred land"]. Tir Iarll ["the Earl's land." Its centre was Coity. It included the site of Bridgend, and part of Bettws]. Glyn Ogwr ["the Vale of Ogwr," now Ogmore. To the interior from Coity to the hills—parishes of Llangeinor and Llandyfodwg].
Penychen, also called Pen y Nen.	Talyfan [see manor of *Talyfan*, in "Manors of Glamorgan"]. Miskin [included Llantrisant, &c.]. Rhuthyn [the territory given by Fitzhamon to Madoc, son of Iestyn. Its etymology implies a *red* soil— W., *rhuäd*, red. Included Llanharan, &c.]. Glyn Rhoddni ["Vale of Rhondda," parish of Ystradyfodwg, &c.].
Cantref Breiniawl ["the Royal Hundred," so termed because it included the lord's castle of Cardiff, and primarily the seat of British rule].	Cibwr [now "Kibbor." Cardiff, Roath, Whitchurch, Llanishen, Llysfaen, Llanedern. The district between Lower Rhymney and Taff]. Senghenydd [Caerphilly, Castell Coch, &c.]. Uwch Cayach ["Upper Cayach"—Merthyr Tydfil, Aberdare, Llanwonno, &c.]. Is Cayach ["Lower Cayach"—Gelligaer, Llanfabon, Eglwys-ilan].
Gwaunllwg [otherwise "Gwentllwg." This cantref is now included in *Monmouthshire*. It comprises the marshy and level parts between Cardiff and Newport, and generally the lower lands between the lower Rhymney and Usk].	Yr Haidd. Y Dref Berfedd, or Canol ["the central part"]. Edelygion Eithaf [some divide this into two comots]. Y Mynydd ["the Mountain"].

Other cantrefs, named "Gwent Uwch Coed" and "Is Coed," containing eight or nine comots, were situated in the remaining part of Monmouthshire, and, together with the above, constituted "Gwent and Morganwg." (See in *Myvyr. Arch. of Wales*, vol. ii.: "*Parthau Cymru.*")

It is notable that these cantrefs by no means include the whole of modern *Glamorgan*. Apparently all the undulating district usually called "the Vale of Glamorgan," by the Welsh *Bro Morganwg*, is omitted; and the parts embraced appear to correspond with the region called "Morgannok," as distinguished from "Glamorgan" (see p. 503),—in other words, the northern and hilly parts of the county. Whether this indicates that the Welsh princes in settling the geographical divisions of Wales in the thirteenth century refrained from intermeddling with the Vale of Glamorgan as being in too exclusive a sense the domain of the Norman lords and their mesne fief-holders, is worth inquiring into. The fact itself is remarkable, but seems to have strangely escaped the notice of antiquarians. Almost all the *Barones minores* we have noticed, as well as the Lord Paramount of Glamorgan himself, had their manors in the parts not included in the *cantrefs* of the Welsh partition, while these cantrefs correspond with some considerable exactitude with the lands said by tradition and the *Bruts* to have been granted by Fitzhamon to the sons of Iestyn, to Einion ap Collwyn, to Robert ap Seissyllt, and other Welshmen. These included Senghenydd, Miskin, Avan, Aberavan, the district between Nêdd and Tawe, Maes Essyllt, &c.; in fact, the hilly as distinguished from the champaign country. In the latter some thirty parishes, forming the modern "hundreds" of Dinas Powys, Cowbridge, and Ogmore, are not perceptibly included in the *comots* enumerated in the survey of Prince Llewelyn. Did that prince confine his survey to lands held by Welshmen only? Is this another indication of that proud and contemptuous temper which, when England was lost, would see in the word "Britain" nothing but Wales, and in the word "Britons" nothing but the Cymry—thus endeavouring, by ignoring, to annihilate misfortune? This were indeed after a new mode—

"To take arms against a sea of troubles,
And by opposing end them;"

but if excusable in any, such hallucination might be excusable in Prince Llewelyn, the man who, beyond most heroic men, not even excepting Alfred, had battled long and bravely with "outrageous fortune," not generally, although finally, without the success his genius and marvellous self-devotion merited.

Section VIII.—Sheriffs and Under-Sheriffs of Glamorgan, A.D. 1541—1872.

Sheriffs, in the modern sense of the term, were first appointed for Glamorgan by 27th Henry VIII. (A.D. 1536), which constituted that Lordship Marcher, with Gower, a County, and formally united this part as well as Monmouthshire and all the remainder of Wales with England. Up to this time the office of sheriff had vested in the lord of the lordship, who, by the nature of his tenure, governed in the absence of the king's writ, administering justice in his own court, and even enacting laws, under certain limitations, on his own responsibility; although upon this point it is necessary to keep in mind the important fact that the Norman conquest of Glamorgan, like the Norman conquest of England, allowed the laws and customs of the conquered in great part to remain in force. Such new enactments and modes of administration as were necessary for the planting of the feudal system among the people the Normans did their best to harmonize with the native laws, but, where perfect accord was impossible, supplied the lack on the rough and ready principle of, *sic volo*, &c.

The first Sheriff named for Glamorgan is Sir George Herbert, Knt., of Swansea, A.D. 1541. The following tabular arrangement is deemed to be as far as possible correct, and is taken, with slight alteration, from that published by Rev. H. H. Knight (1850), which up to the year 1792 was from the MS. of Evan Simmons, of Nottage, thence to 1850 from a MS. of Howel Gwyn, Esq. It has been completed from further additions by the last-named gentleman, and collated with a copy of a MS. by Thomas Morgan, of Cardiff.

It will be observed that the under-sheriffs in the early times were men of about the same standing as the sheriffs, and very often members of their family.

GLAMORGANSHIRE.

HIGH SHERIFFS.	UNDER-SHERIFFS.	A.D.

HENRY VIII.

1	Sir George Herbert, of Swansea .	Jenkin Franklin, Gent.	1541
2	Sir Rice Mansel, Knt., of Margam	William Bassett, Gent., of Beaupre	1542
3	Sir Edward Carne, Knt., of Ewenny	James Button, of Worlton	1543
4	William Bassett, Esq., of Beaupre	John Turbervill, of Llanblethian	1544
5	Sir George Mathew, of Radir	Thomas Lewis	1545
6	John Thomas Bassett, Esq., of Llantrithyd	William Meyrick	1546

EDWARD VI.

7	Miles Mathew, Esq., of Llandaff	William Jones, Gent.	1547
8	Sir Thomas Stradling, Knt., of St. Donat's	Robert Stradling, his brother	1548
9	Edward Lewis, Esq., of Vann	John Smith, of Cardiff	1549
10	Christopher Turbervill, Esq., of Penlline	Thomas Powell, of Llangynwyd	1550
11	James Thomas, Esq., of Llanfihangel	James Thomas, his son	1551
12	William Herbert, Esq., of Cogan Pill	Henry Lewis, of Cardiff	1552

MARY.

13	Sir George Herbert, Knt., of Swansea	David John Vaughan	1553

PHILIP AND MARY.

14	Sir Rice Mansel, Knt., of Margam	Thomas Powell, of Llangynwyd	1554
15	Sir Edward Carne, Knt., of Ewenny	Miles Button, Esq.	1555
16	Edward Lewis, Esq., of Vann	Thomas Griffith	1556
17	James Button, Esq., of Worlton	Miles Button, Esq.	1557
18	William Bassett, Esq., of Beaupre	Jenkin Williams, of Cowbridge	1558

ELIZABETH.

19	Sir Richard Walwyn, Knt., of Llantrithyd	John Unett	1559
20	Edward Lewis, Esq., of Vann	John Smith	1560
21	John Carne and Thomas Lewis, Esqs., of Vann	Thomas Griffith	1561
22	Thomas Carne, Esq., of Ewenny	John Kemeys, Kefn-mably	1562
23	David Evans, Esq., of Neath	Richard Thomas	1563
24	Sir William Herbert, Knt., of Swansea	William Herbert, Cardiff	1564
25	Miles Button, Esq., of Worlton	Robert Button	1565
26	William Jenkins, Esq., of Tythegston	Edward Holland	1566
27	William Herbert, Esq., of Cogan Pill	John Smith	1567
28	William Mathew, Esq., of Radir	Walter Williams	1568
29	Christopher Turbervill, Esq., of Penlline	Henry Matthew	1569
30	Thomas Lewis, Esq., of Vann	Roger Seys, Gent.	1570
31	Miles Button, Esq , of Worlton	David Robert, of Cardiff	1571
32	Thomas Carne, Esq., of Ewenny	John Smith	1572
33	Richard Gwynn, Esq., of Llansannor	Jenkin Williams	1573
34	Sir Edward Stradling, Knt., of St. Donat's	Leyson Lewis	1574
35	Edward Kemeys, Esq., of Keven-mably	Walter Williams, of Gelligaer	1575
36	Sir Edward Mansel, Knt., of Margam	Thomas Powell	1576
37	Nicholas Herbert, Esq., of Cardiff	Reynold David	1577
38	Sir William Herbert, Knt., of Swansea	William Herbert, of Cardiff	1578
39	John Thomas, Esq., of Llanfihangel	Lewis Griffith	1579
40	William Mathew, Esq., of Radir	Henry Mathew, his brother	1580
41	Thomas Carne, Esq., of Ewenny	William David	1581
42	Sir William Herbert, Knt., of Swansea	Lewis Griffith	1582
43	Sir Edward Stradling, Knt., of St. Donat's	Lambrook Stradling, of Cardiff	1583
44	George Herbert, Esq., of Nash	Rees Lewis	1584
45	Edward Kemeys, Esq., of Keven-mably	John Andrew	1585
46	Nicholas Herbert, Esq., of Cardiff	John Gamage	1586
47	Thomas Lewis, Esq., of Vann	Gabriel Lewis, Esq., of Llanishen	1587
48	John Carne, Esq., of Ewenny	George Kemeys, Llanblethian	1588

SHERIFFS AND UNDER-SHERIFFS OF GLAMORGAN.

			A.D.
49	Miles Button, Esq., Worlton	Edward Button, his son	1589
50	Henry Mathew, Esq., of Radir	Morgan Gibbon, of St. Fagan's	1590
51	Anthony Mansel, Esq., of Llantrithyd	Thomas Pranch	1591
52	Sir William Herbert, Knt., of Swansea	Lewis Griffith, of Cilybebill	1592
53	Edmund Mathew, Esq., of Radir	Marmaduke Mathew	1593
54	Sir Thomas Mansel, Knt., of Margam	Anthony Powell	1594
55	Edward Kemeys, Esq., of Keven-mably	William St. John	1595
56	Sir Edward Stradling, Knt., of St. Donat's	John Stradling, Gent.	1596
57	Richard Bassett, Esq., of Beaupre	Thomas Bassett, his son	1597
58	John Gwyn, Esq. (died); Rowland Morgan, Esq.	William Powell	1598
59	Thomas Lewis, Esq., of Ruperra [Rhiw-peri]	Thomas Lewis Reynold	1599
60	Edward Prichard, Esq., of Llancayach	William Williams	1600
61	John Carne, Esq., of Ewenny	Hopkin Evans, Gent.	1601
62	Edward Lewis, Esq., of Vann	Gabriel Lewis, Esq.	1602

JAMES I.

63	Thomas Aubrey, Esq., of Llantrithyd	Thomas Bassett, Gent.	1603
64	Sir Thomas Mansel, Bart., of Margam	Anthony Powell, Gent.	1604
65	Edward Kemeys, Esq., of Keven-mably	Morgan Cradock, Gent.	1605
66	Sir William Herbert, Knt., of Swansea	Hopkin David Edward	1606
67	Sir Rowland Morgan, Knt., of Llandaff	Philip Williams	1607
68	John Stradling, Esq., of St. Donat's	William Stradling	1608
69	Richard Bassett, Esq., of Beaupre	Thomas Bassett, his son	1609
70	Morgan Meyrick, Esq., of Cottrel	W. Meyrick, his brother	1610
71	George Lewis, Esq., of Llystalybont	David Lloyd, of Cardiff	1611
72	Lewis Thomas ap William, Esq., of Bettws	Philip William Eglwysilan	1612
73	Sir Edward Lewis, Knt., of Vann	William Robert, of St. Andrew's	1613
74	Thomas Mathew, Esq., of Castlemenych	Miles Mathew, his brother	1614
75	Gabriel Lewis, Esq., of Llanishen	Evan Thomas ap Evan	1615
76	Christopher Turbervill, Esq., of Penlline	Rees Knapp	1616
77	David Kemeys, Esq., of Keven-mably	Henry Penry, Gent.	1617
78	William Mathew, Esq., of Aberaman	Robert Mathew, his brother	1618
79	Edward Van, Esq., of Marcross	Owen Price, Gent.	1619
80	Sir John Stradling, Knt. and Bart., St. Donat's	George Williams	1620
81	John Carne, Esq., of Ewenny	William Roberts	1621
82	William Bassett, Esq., of Beaupre	Jenkin Cradock, Gent., of Llancarvan	1622
83	Sir Thomas Mansel, Knt. and Bart., of Margam	John Rowe, of Gower	1623
84	Lewis Thomas ap William, Esq., of Bettws	John Powell	1624

CHARLES I.

85	Anthony Gwynn, Esq., of Lansannor	Rees Howard, of Llantrithyd	1625
86	William Bawdrip, Esq., of Splott	Owen Price, succ. by William Price	1626
87	Edmund Thomas, Esq., of Wenvoe	James Thomas, his brother	1627
88	Henry Mansel, Esq., of Gower	Watkin Lougher, of Nottage	1628
89	Sir Thomas Lewis, Knt., of Penmark	Jenkin Cradock, Llancarvan	1629
90	Thomas Lewis, Esq., of Llanishen	Lewis Thomas Richard	1630
91	Sir Anthony Mansel, Knt., of Briton-ferry	Lewis Thomas, Gent.	1631
92	David Evans, Esq., of Neath	George Williams	1632
93	Edward Thomas, Esq., of Llanfihangel	Morgan Griffith	1633
94	John Aubrey, Esq., of Llantrithyd	Henry Penry, ditto	1634
95	Watkin Lougher, Esq., of Tythegston	Lewis Thomas Griffith	1635
96	Sir Lewis Mansel, Knt. and Bart., of Margam	Jenkin Cradock, of Llancarvan	1636
97	Edward Prichard, Esq., of Llancayach	Thomas Powell	1637
98	Nicholas Kemeys, Esq., of Keven-mably	Morgan Howard	1638
99	John Carne, Esq., of Ewenny	Morgan Griffith	1639
100	Robert Button, Esq., of Duffryn	Henry Penry, of Llantrithyd	1640
101	William Bassett, Esq., of Miskin	Richard Bevan	1641
102	Richard Bassett, Esq., of Fishward	Robert William, of St. Hilary	1642
103	Sir Charles Kemeys, of Keven-mably, and William Thomas, Esq., of Swansea, for 2 years	Morgan Howard	1643 / 1644

600   GLAMORGANSHIRE.

A.D.

104	Edward Carne, Esq., of Ewenny, and	}	
	Bussey Mansel, Esq., of Briton-ferry, pricked	Richard ap Evan	1645
	by Parliament		
105	Richard Jones, Esq., of Michaelston	Evan Prichard, of Diwedid	1646
106	John Price, Esq., of Gellihir	William Morgan, of Neath	1647
107	Walter Thomas, Esq., of Swansea	William Williams	1648

COMMONWEALTH AND PROTECTORATE.

108	John Herbert, Esq., of Roath	John Griffith	1649
109	George Bowen, Esq., of Kittle Hill	John Bowen, his son	1650
110	Rees Powell, Esq., of Coytrehên	Robert Thomas	1651
111	Edward Stradling, Esq., of Roath	Lewis William	1652
112	William Bassett, Esq., of Miskin	Richard ap Evan	1653

OLIVER CROMWELL, LORD PROTECTOR.

113	Humphrey Wyndham, Esq., of Dunraven	Humphrey Wyndham, his son	1654
114	Richard Lougher, Esq., of Tythegston	Watkin Jones, Gent., of Monkton	1655
115	William Herbert, Esq., of Swansea	Thomas David, Gent.	1656
116	Stephen Edwards, Esq., of Stembridge	George Thomas	1657
117	Richard Davies, Esq., of Penmaen	Leyson Davies, his brother	1658

RICHARD CROMWELL, PROTECTOR.

118	Richard Davies, Esq., the same	John Morgan	1659

CHARLES II.

119	Herbert Evans, Esq., of Eaglesbush	David Evans, of Neath Abbey	1660
120	Gabriel Lewis, Esq., of Llanishen	William Morgan, of Rubiné	1661
121	Edmund Gamage, Esq., of Newcastle	John Powell	1662
122	John Gronow de Bedwas, Esq.	William Morgan	1663
123	Edmund Thomas, Esq., of Wenvoe	Edmund Perkins	1664
124	Martin Button, Esq., of Dyffryn	Moor Perkins	1665
125	Edward Mathew, Esq., of Aberaman	John Richard, of Henllan	1666
126	Thomas Mathew, Esq., of Castle-menych	Miles Mathew, of Cardiff	1667
127	Thomas Button, Esq., of Cottrel	David Thomas, of Llyswomey	1668
128	Philip Hoby, Esq., of Neath Abbey	John Llewelin, of Ynis-y-Gerwn	1669
129	Edmund Thomas, Esq., of Orchard	John Powell	1670
130	Philip Jones, Esq., of Fonmon Castle	David Evans	1671
131	Thomas Powell, Esq, of Coytrehên	Edward Williams, of St. Mary Church	1672
132	Thomas Lewis, Esq., of Penmark	Moor Perkins	1673
133	William Thomas, Esq., of Llanbradach	John Thomas, of Llancarvan	1674
134	Richard Seys, Esq., of Rhyddings	Rowland Harris	1675
135	Miles Mathew, Esq., of Llancayach	Edward Williams, of St Mary Church	1676
136	Bussey Mansel, Esq., of Briton-ferry	Jervis Powell	1677
137	Thomas Gibbon, Esq., of Trecastle	Charles Evans, of Llanwit Fairdre	1678
138	George Bowen, Esq., of Kittle Hill	John Powell	1679
139	Thomas Morgan, Esq., of Llanrumney	William Morgan, of Coedygoras	1680
140	Oliver Jones, Esq., of Fonmon	John Watkins, of Gower Land	1681
141	Reynold Deere, Esq., of Wenvoe	Thomas Morgan, of Coedygoras	1682
142	Thomas Lewis, Esq., of Llanishen	William Morgan, of Coedygoras	1683
143	David Jenkins, Esq., of Hensol	Jervis Powell	1684

JAMES II.

144	Sir John Aubrey, Bart., of Llantrithyd	Evan Edwards	1685
145	William Aubrey, Esq., of Pencoed	Charles Evans	1686
146	Sir Edward Mansel, Bart., of Margam	Edward Williams, of St. Mary Church	1687
147	Sir Edward Mansel, the same	The same	1688

WILLIAM III. AND MARY.

148	Thomas Lewis, Esq., of Penmark	Robert Powell, of Llysworney	1689

SHERIFFS AND UNDER-SHERIFFS OF GLAMORGAN. 601

			A.D.
149 Thomas Carne, Esq., of Nash	. . .	David Thomas, of Lysworney . .	1690
150 John Price, Esq., of Gellihir	. . .	John Wilkins, of the same . . .	1691
151 William Seys, Esq., of Rhyddings	. .	John Deere, Esq., of Llantwit . .	1692
152 William Mathew, Esq., of Aberaman .	. .	Charles Evans, of Llantwit Fairdre .	1693
153 Richard Herbert, Esq., of Cilybebyll .	. .	Griffith Evans, of Gelligron. . . .	1694
154 John Bennett, Esq., of Kittle Hill	. .	Evans Evans	1695
155 Richard Lougher, of Tythegston .	. .	Edward Thomas, of Pwllywrach . .	1696
156 Richard Morgan, Esq., of St. George's	. .	Jervis Powell, of Llantrisant . .	1697
157 George Howells, Esq., of Bovill .	. . .	Richard Bassett, of St. Andrew's .	1698
158 John Whitwick, Esq. (died in office)	. .	Robert Powell, of Llysworney . .	1699
159 Sir John Thomas, Bart., of Wenvoe .	. .	Charles Evans, of Llantwit Fairdre .	1700
160 Thomas Mansel, Esq., of Penrhys Castle	. .	Evan Evans	1701

ANNE.

161 Daniel Morris, Esq., of Glyncastle	. .	Jervis Powell	1702
162 William Bassett, Esq., of Cowbridge .	. .	William Llewelyn, of Monkton . .	1703
163 Robert Jones, Esq., of Fonmon .	. .	Thomas Wilkins, of Llanblethian .	1704
164 Thomas Thomas, Esq., of Llanbradach	.	Roger Wilkins, of Cowbridge . .	1705
165 William Stanley, Esq., of Neath Abbey	.	Thomas Hawkins	1706
166 Roger Powell, Esq., of Energlyn	. .	Michael Richards, of Cardiff . .	1707
167 Richard Carne, Esq., of Ewenny	. .	Edward Jenkins, of Landough . .	1708
168 Thomas Button, Esq., of Cottrel	. .	Wat. Morgan (clerk to Edward Jenkins)	1709
169 Sir Edward Stradling, Bart., of St. Donat's .		Robert Powell, of Wilton . . .	1710
170 Sir John Aubrey, Bart., of Llantrithyd	.	Edward Jenkins, of Landough . .	1711
171 John Carne, Esq., of Clementston	. .	Thomas Wilkins, of Llanblethian .	1712
172 Sir Charles Kemeys, Bart., of Keven-mably	.	Evans Evans (clerk to T. Wilkins) .	1713

GEORGE I.

173 Hoby Compton, Esq., of Neath Abbey	. .	Thomas Cory, of Margam . . .	1714
174 Gabriel Lewis, Esq., of Llanishen	. .	Gabriel Powell, of Swansea . .	1715
175 John Jones, Esq., of Dyffryn .	. .	John Jones (his son)	1716
176 Edward Thomas, Esq., of Ogmore	. .	Thomas Cory, of Margam . . .	1717
177 Thomas Popkin, Esq., of Forest .	. .	W. Frampton (clerk to Gabriel Powell)	1718
178 Michael Williams, Esq., of Bridgend .	.	Anthony Maddocks	1719
179 William Dawkin, Esq., of Kilvrough .	.	William Phillips, of Swansea . .	1720
180 William Richards, Esq., of Cardiff	. .	Michael Richards, of ditto . . .	1721
181 William Morgan, Esq., of Coedygoras	.	Henry Morgan (his brother) . .	1722
182 Edward Evans, Esq., of Eaglesbush	. .	Thomas Cradock, of Margam . .	1723
183 James Williams, Esq., of Cardiff	. .	Henry Llewellyn, of ditto . . .	1724
184 Abraham Barbour, Esq., of St. George's	.	Edward Herbert, of Cardiff . .	1725
185 Morgan Morgans, Esq., of Lanrumney	.	Canon Wilkins, of Lanblethian . .	1726

GEORGE II.

186 Martin Button, Esq., of Dyffryn .	. .	Edward Powell, of Brynhill . .	1727
187 James Thomas, Esq., of Llanbradach .	.	Henry Llewellyn, of Cardiff . .	1728
188 Robert Jones, Esq., of Fonmon .	. .	Richard Powell, of Landough . .	1729
189 John Llewellin, Esq., of Ynis-y-gerwn	.	Gabriel Powell, of Swansea . .	1730
190 John Carne, Esq., of Nash .	. .	Richard Leyson, of Prisk . . .	1731
191 Reynold Deere, Esq., of Penlline	. .	Edward Thomas (his nephew) . .	1732
192 Herbert Mackworth, Esq., of Gnoll	. .	William Powell, of Swansea . .	1733
193 William Bassett, Esq., of Miskin .	. .	Thomas Leyson, of Prisk . . .	1734
194 Grant Gibbon, of Trecastle	. .	Richard Leyson, of Prisk . . .	1735
195 Hopkin Rees, Esq., of St. Mary Hill .	.	David Lewis, of Penkyrn, for Richard Leyson	1736
196 Robert Knight, Esq., of Tythegston	. .	Richard Powell, of Landough . .	1737
197 Edmund Lloyd, Esq., of Cardiff	. .	William Powell, of Llanharan . .	1738
198 Thomas Price, Esq., of Penlle'rgaer	. .	Hugh Powell, of Swansea . . .	1739
199 Richard Turbervill, Esq., of Ewenny .	.	Richard Powell, of Neath . . .	1740
200 Rowland Dawkins, Esq., of Kilvrough	.	Richard Dawkins, of Hendrewen .	1741
201 Robert Morris, Esq., of Ynysarwad	. .	John Jeffreys, of Swansea . . .	1742
202 Matthew Deere, Esq., of Ash Hall	. .	Anthony Maddocks, of Cefnidfa . .	1743

GLAMORGANSHIRE.

			A.D.
203	Henry Lucas, Esq., of Stouthall, in Gower	Edward Hancorn, Gent	1744
204	Thomas Lewis, Esq., of Llanishen	Richard Powell, of Neath	1745
205	Whitelock Nicholl, Esq., of Ham	Edward Lewis, of Penlline	1746
206	Thomas Powell, Esq., of Tondû	Edward Savours, of Coedycynllan	1747
207	John Mathews, Esq., of Brynwith	John Thomas, of Cowbridge	1748
208	Joseph Price, Esq., of Gellihir	John Morgan, of Swansea	1749
209	Richard Jenkins, Esq., of Marlas	Anthony Maddocks, of Cefnidfa	1750
210	William Evans, Esq., of Eaglesbush	Hugh Powell. of Swansea	1751
211	Rowland Bevan, Esq., of Oxwich	Edward Hancorn	1752
212	Thomas Rous, Esq. (Under Sheriff acted)	Thomas Edmonds, of Cowbridge	1753
213	Edward Walters, Esq., of Pittcott	Nathaniel Taynton, of Cowbridge	1754
214	Thomas Popkin, Esq., of Forest	Edward Hancorn	1755
215	William Bruce, Esq., of Llanllethian	John Thomas, of Cowbridge	1756
216	Thomas Lewis, Esq., of Newhouse	Richard Thomas	1757
217	Edward Mathews, Esq., of Aberaman	John Thomas, of Cowbridge	1758
218	Thomas Pryce, Esq., of Dyffryn Golych	Mansel Williams, of Neath	1759
219	Sir John de la Fountain Tyrwhit, Bart., of St. Donat's	(Office done by his deputy, William Rees, of St. Mary Hill, his steward)	1760

GEORGE III.

220	Samuel Price, Esq., of Coity	William Prothero (for William Rees)	1761
221	Philip Williams, Esq., of Dyffryn	Mansel Williams, of Neath	1762
222	Robert Morris, Esq., of Swansea	Elias Jenkins	1763
223	Abraham Williams, Esq., of Cathays	Thomas Williams, of Cowbridge	1764
224	Calvert Richard Jones, Esq., of Swansea	William Jenkins, of Neath	1765
225	William Curre, Esq., of Clementston	Edward Lewis, of Penlline	1766
226	Edward Powell, Esq., of Tondû	William Jenkins, of Neath	1767
227	Thomas Bennet, Esq., of Laleston	Iltid Thomas, of Swansea	1768
228	Thomas Mathews, Esq., of Llandaff	Thomas Williams, of Cowbridge	1769
229	Richard Gordon, Esq., of Burry's Green, Gower	Elias Jenkins, of Swansea	1770
230	William Thomas, Esq., of Llanblethian	Thomas Williams, Cowbridge	1771
231	Edward Thomas, Esq., of Tregroes	William Rees, Esq., St. Mary Hill	1772
232	William Dawkin, Esq., of Kilvrough	Iltid Thomas, of Swansea	1773
233	John Edmondes, Esq., of Cowbridge	Thomas Thomas, of Cardiff	1774
234	Daniel Jones, Esq., of Glanbrân	Iltid Thomas, of Swansea	1775
235	William Hurst, Esq., of Gabalva	Thomas Thomas, of Cardiff	1776
236	David Thomas, Esq, of Pwllywrach	William Rees, Esq., of St. Mary Hill	1777
237	John Lucas, Esq., of Stouthall	Iltid Thomas, of Swansea	1778
238	Bartholomew Greenwood, Esq., of Cardiff (excused, being bailiff of Cardiff); Christopher Bassett, Esq., of Llanelay	William Rees, Esq., of St. Mary Hill	1779
239	Peter Birt, Esq., of Wenvoe Castle	Thomas Thomas, of Cardiff	1780
240	Charles Bowen, Esq., of Merthyr-mawr	Thomas Thomas	1781
241	Thomas Mansel Talbot, Esq., of Margam	Hopkin Llewelyn, of Margam	1782
242	William Kemeys, Esq., of Ynysarwad	William Rees, Esq., of St. Mary Hill	1783
243	John Richard, Esq., of Energlyn	Thomas Thomas, of Cardiff	1784
244	Stephen White, Esq., of Miskin	William Rees, Esq., of Court Colman	1785
245	Thomas Drake Tyrwhit, Esq., of St. Donat's Castle	Watkin Morgan, of Llandough	1786
246	John Price, Esq., of Llandaff Court	John Wood, of Cardiff	1787
247	Richard Jenkins, Esq., of Pantynawel	Thomas Williams, of Cowbridge	1788
248	John Llewelin, Esq., of Welsh St. Donat's	John Wood, of Cardiff	1789
249	William Lewis, Esq, of Pentyrch	Hopkin Llewellyn, Gent.	1790
250	John Richards, Esq., Corner House, Cardiff	John Wood, Cardiff	1791
251	John Llewelyn, Esq., of Ynis-y-gerwn	Mr. Hopkin Llewelyn	1792
252	John Lucas, Esq., of Stouthall	Rees Davies, Swansea	1793
253	Henry Knight, Esq., of Tythegston	John Thomas, Cowbridge	1794
254	Wyndham Lewis, Esq., of Llanishen	John Wood, of Cardiff	1795
255	Herbert Hurst, Esq., of Gabalva	Ditto	1796
256	Robert Rous, Esq., of Cwrtyrala	Ditto	1797
257	Samuel Richardson, Esq., Hensol Castle	J. Williams, Cardiff	1798
258	John Goodrich, Esq., of Energlyn	John Wood	1799

SHERIFFS AND UNDER-SHERIFFS OF GLAMORGAN.

No.	Sheriff	Under-Sheriff	A.D.
259	Robert Jenner, Esq., Wenvoe Castle	John Wood	1800
260	Robert Jones, Esq., Fonmon Castle	William Vaughan	1801
261	Richard Mansel Phillips, Esq., Sketty	John Jeffreys, Swansea	1802
262	John Morris, Esq., of Clasemont	William Vaughan	1803
263	Richard T. Picton, Esq., of Ewenny	William Vaughan	1804
264	Thomas Markham, Esq., of Nash	Edward Powell, Llantwit	1805
265	Anthony Bacon, Esq., of Cyfarthfa	John Wood, Cardiff	1806
266	George Wynch, Esq., of Clementston	Edward Powell	1807
267	John N. Miers, Esq., Cadoxton Lodge	G. Llewelyn	1808
268	Jeremiah Homfray, Esq., of Llandaff	Wyndham Lewis	1809
269	Thomas Lockwood, Esq., Danygraig	John Jeffreys, Swansea	1810
270	Sir Robert Lynch Blosse, Bart., Gabalfa	Thomas Bassett	1811
271	Morgan Popkin Traherne, Esq., Coytrehên	W. Vaughan	1812
272	William Jones, Esq., Corntown Lodge	Thomas Bassett	1813
273	The Hon. William Booth Grey	John Wood	1814
274	William Tait, Esq., Cardiff	E. P. Richards	1815
275	Richard John Hill, Esq., Plymouth Lodge	John Powell, Brecon	1816
276	Thomas Bates Rous, Esq., of Cwrtyrala	E. P. Richards	1817
277	Lewis Weston Dillwyn, Esq., Penlle'rgaer	Lewis Thomas, Swansea	1818
278	Josiah John Guest, Esq., Dowlais	John Jones	1819

GEORGE IV.

No.	Sheriff	Under-Sheriff	A.D.
279	Richard Blakemore, Esq., Velindre	E. P. Richards	1820
280	William Forman, Esq., Penydarran	William Meyrick	1821
281	Sir John Morris, Bart., Sketty Park	John James	1822
282	John Edwards, Esq., Rheola	William Meyrick	1823
283	John Bassett, Esq., Bonvilston House	Thomas Basset	1824
284	John Bennet, Esq., Laleston	John Jackson Price	1825
285	Thomas Edward Thomas, Esq., Swansea	John Jackson Price	1826
286	John Henry Vivian, Esq., Marino	John Jackson Price	1827
287	Robert F. Jenner, Esq., Wenvoe Castle	E. P. Richards	1828
288	William Crawshay, Esq., Cyfarthfa Castle	William Meyrick	1829

WILLIAM IV.

No.	Sheriff	Under-Sheriff	A.D.
289	William Williams, Esq., Aberpergwm	David Powell	1830
290	Richard H. Jenkins, Esq., Lanharan House	Alexander Cuthbertson	1831
291	Frederick Fredricks, Esq., Dyffryn	Alexander Cuthbertson	1832
292	Richard T. Turbervill, Esq., Ewenny	William Lewis	1833
293	Henry J. Grant, Esq., The Gnoll	David Powell	1834
294	John Dillwyn Llewelyn, Esq., Penlle'rgaer	Thomas Thomas	1835
295	Thomas Penrice, Esq., Kilvrough House	John Jenkins	1836

VICTORIA.

No.	Sheriff	Under-Sheriff	A.D.
296	Howel Gwyn, Esq., Alltwen	John Gwyn Jeffreys	1837
297	Howel Gwyn, Esq.—R. O. Jones, Esq., Fonmon Castle	John G. Jeffreys	1838
298	Charles H. Smith, Gwernllwynwith	Charles Basil Mansfield	1839
299	Michael Williams, Esq., Morfa	C. B. Mansfield	1840
300	Joseph Martin, Esq., Ynystawe	C. B. Mansfield	1841
301	Henry Lucas, Esq., Uplands	J. G. Jeffreys	1842
302	John Homfray, Esq., Llandaff Court	J. G. Jeffreys	1843
303	John Bruce Pryce, Esq., Dyffryn	William Davies	1844
304	Robert Savours, Esq., Trecastle	William Lewis	1845
305	Richard Franklin, Esq., Clementson	William Lewis	1846
306	Nash V. Edwards Vaughan, Esq., Rheola	Alexander Cuthbertson	1847
307	Thomas W. Booker, Esq., Velindre	Thomas Evans	1848
308	Richard Boteler, Esq., Landough Castle	Thomas Evans	1849
309	Rowland Fothergill, Esq., Hensol Castle	E. G. Smith	1850

		A.D.
310	Gervase Turbervill, Esq., Ewenny	1851
311	Griffith Llewellyn, Esq., of Baglan Hall	1852
312	Richard Hill Miers, Esq., of Ynyspenllwch	1853
313	William Llewelyn, Esq., of Court Colman	1854
314	Wyndham W. Lewis, Esq., of The Heath	1855
315	John Samuel, Esq., Cowbridge	1856
316	Evan Williams, Esq., of Dyffryn Ffrwd	1857
317	Henry Lewis, Esq., Green Meadow	1858
318	Charles Williams, Esq., Roath	1859
319	George Grey Rous, Esq., Court-y-Rala	1860
320	Edward Robert Wood, Esq., Stouthall	1861
321	Sir Ivor B. Guest, Bart., Dowlais	1862
322	John P. Traherne, Esq., Coytrehên	1863
323	Robert F. L. Jenner, Esq., Wenvoe Castle	1864
324	Thomas William Booker, Esq., Velindre	1865
325	William Graham Vivian, Esq., Singleton	1866
326	Thomas Penrice, Esq., Kilvrough House	1867
327	George Thomas Clark, Esq., Dowlais House	1868
328	Edward Romilly, Esq., Porthkerry	1869
329	E. W. J. Thomas, Esq., Coedriglan	1870
330	Vaughan H. Lee, Esq., Rheola	1871
331	Charles Henry Williams, Esq., Roath Court	1872

Section IX.—PARLIAMENTARY ANNALS OF GLAMORGAN.

The powers of the Lords Marchers, who alone were entitled to appear as barons in the king's council, were abolished by the eighth Henry, by the Act of the twenty-seventh year of his reign (A.D. 1536-7), whereby he formally and finally united Wales to England; and for that year a knight of the shire was doubtless summoned to represent the interests and wishes of the population in Parliament.

Before the conquest of Wales, and its nominal union with England under Edward I., no parliamentary representation, properly speaking, existed among the Welsh, but a kind of autocracy of the princes, tempered by the voice of popular assembly, prevailed. After Edward's conquest an occasional summons for delegates from Wales to the suzerain's council was issued. Edward II., A.D. 1322, sent forth a writ directing that twenty-four persons from South Wales, and an equal number from North Wales, "with full and sufficient power on behalf of the whole community of their parts," should attend a *parliamentum* which he was about to hold at York. Of the result of such summons among a nation by no means forward at that time to comply with any "direction" from the English king, we have no record. Glamorgan, however, for *legislative* purposes, did not yet form part of either England or Wales—although territorially and ethnically of course belonging to the latter,—but lay under that exceptional species of government known as the regal authority (*Jura Regalia*) of the Lords Marchers—an authority, it is true, not wholly tantamount to a free *imperium in imperio*, but still sufficiently independent to exclude all voice of the people in their own representation. Henry put an abrupt end to this feudal rule, made the Glamorgan and Gower Lordships Marcher a County, and gave the inhabitants of the county and of the royal burgh of Cardiff the privilege of choosing and sending each a delegate to the national Parliament.

Upon what principle of *suffrage* the selection of a representative was then made is not quite plain; but it is probable that the franchise settled under Edward III., which extended in counties to small holders, and in boroughs to house tenants, had remained unaltered in England, and was now applied to Wales.

The names of the *first* Members sent from Glamorgan and Cardiff (1537), like many others of the same date, have been lost. The representative for the next parliament was George Herbert, Esq., of Swansea, for the co., and John Bassett, Esq., of the Inner Temple (*Interioris Templi*), for the boroughs. In 1654 and 1656, under Cromwell and the Commonwealth, the county returned *two* members; and in the year preceding (1683), when specific constituencies in Wales were not represented, but the whole Principality, including Monmouthshire, was represented by 7 *members*, one of these was a prominent Glamorgan gentleman, Bussy Mansel, Esq., of Briton Ferry. In 1658-9 (Cromwell) *Swansea*, which had never before been granted the parliamentary franchise, returned a member, William Foxwist, Esq. With this exception the borough delegation from this county was confined to Cardiff, not on account of its population, for in that respect its inferiority was obvious, but on account of its ancient *status* as a princely and lordly seat. It is for men of local and antiquarian knowledge, such as Col. Francis, to find out why Swansea, although at the head of the later Lordship Marcher of Gower, did not claim, or failed to secure, the privilege of parliamentary representation until Cromwell gave it the boon, as well as to find whence came and whither went William Foxwist, Esq.—of whom, however, more hereafter (p. 610).

By the Reform Bill of 1832, Swansea (with Neath, Aberavon, and Kenfig), with all its importance as a port and centre of mining and manufacturing wealth and population, for the first time obtained the permanent privilege of returning a member to the Commons Merthyr Tydfil, which now, with Aberdare, &c., contains a population nearly equal to Cardiff and Swansea together, despite their recent increase, was at the same time made a Parliamentary District of boroughs.

1.—*Members of Parliament for the County of Glamorgan, from* A.D. 1542—1872.

HENRY VIII.

	A.D.
George Herbert, Esq., of Swansea. [Second son of Richard Herbert of Ewias; was knighted; *d.* 1570; bro. of William Herbert, 1st Earl of Pembroke; cr. 1551, (from whom descend the Earls of Pembroke and Carnarvon); and father of Matthew Herbert, Esq., of Swansea, and William Herbert, Esq., of Cogan, who built the house at *Cogan Pill*]	1542

EDWARD VI.

	A.D.
George Mathew, Esq. [of Radir; was knighted; third of the line of Radir, and son of Sir William Matthew, Knt.; Sheriff for Glam., 1544]	1547

MARY.

	A.D.
Sir George Mathew, Knt., of Radir [the same]	1553
Anthony Mansel, Esq. [second son of Sir Rice Mansel, Kt. of Oxwich, the first of Margam Abbey; brother of Sir Edward Mansel, of Margam]	1553
[Sir] Edward Mansel [Knt., of Margam, above named. On his tomb it is said that he had fifteen sons and four daus. by his wife Jane, dau. of Henry Somerset, Earl of Worcester. See *Margam Abbey*]	1554

PHILIP AND MARY.

	A.D.
Sir Edward Carne, Knt. [of Ewenny; Sheriff 1554]	1554
Sir Edward Carne, Knt., the same	1555
William Herbert de Cogan, Esq. [Sheriff 1551, 1556; son of Sir George Herbert of Swansea; built Cogan House, near Cardiff; *m.* Alice, dau. of Sir Thomas (or John) Raglan, Knt., widow of William Mathew, of Castle Menych. From his eldest bro. Matthew descended the Herberts of Cogan,	

GLAMORGANSHIRE.

	A.D.
four generations, Herberts of White Friars, Cardiff, and of Swansea]	1557

ELIZABETH.

William Morgan, Esq. [of Llantarnam?].	1558-9
Willi m Bassett, Esq. [of Beaupre; Sheriff in 1558]	1563
William Bassett, Esq., the same	1571
William Herbert, sen., Esq. [of Cogan; his nephew, "William Herbert, *jun.*," became Sir William, Knt.]	1572
Robert Sydney, Esq. [afterwards (1586) Sir Robert Sydney; 2nd son of Sir Henry Sydney, K G., of Penshurst; *m.*, about 1584, Barbara Gamage, heiress of Coity; was made Governor of Flushing, &c.; cr. Baron Sydney and Viscount Lisle, and in 1618 Earl of Leicester. See further *Gamage of Coity Castle*]	1585
Thomas Carne, Esq. [of Ewenny; Sheriff in 1571 and 1580; *m.* a dau. of Sir John Wyndham, of Orchard Wyndham, Somerset; father of Sir John Carne, Knt., of Ewenny]	1586
Thomas Carne, Esq., the same	1588
Sir Robert Sydney, Knt. [see under A.D. 1585]	1592
Sir Thomas Mansel, Knt. [afterwards Bart., of Margam; Sheriff 1593 and 1603. See *Mansel of Margam*]	1597
Sir John Herbert, Knt. [of Neath Abbey; 2nd son of Matthew Herbert, Esq., of Swansea; Sheriff in 1605; *d.* 1617, *æt.* 67]	1601

JAMES I.

Philip Herbert, Esq., in his place, raised to the peerage, Sir Thomas Mansel, Knt.	1603
[Philip Herbert was 2nd son of Henry, 2nd Earl of Pembroke; cr. Baron Herbert of Shurland, Kent, and Earl of Montgomery, 1605; succ.. as 4th Earl of Pembroke on death of his b. William 1630, *d.* 1650. Nicolas, *Synop. Peerage*.]	
Sir Thomas Mansel, Knt. [of Margam (see A.D. 1597); cr. a bart., 1611, on the first institution of the order by James I]	1614
William Price, Esq.	1620
Sir Robert Mansel, Knt. [Vice-Admiral; 10th son of Sir Edward Mansel of Margam, by Lady Jane Somerset, dau. of Henry, 2nd Earl of Worcester. See *Margam Abbey*. He was knighted by the Earl of Essex for his valour in taking the city of Cadiz, 1596; made Vice-Admiral by James I.; *m.* Elizabeth, dau. of Sir Nicholas Bacon, Knt., Keeper of the Great Seal, and sister of the celebrated Lord Chancellor Bacon]	1623

CHARLES I.

	A.D.
Sir Robert Mansel, Knt. (the same)	1625
Sir John Stradling, Knt. and Bart. [of St. Donat's]	1626
Sir Robert Mansel, Knt. (as before)	1628
Sir Edward Stradling, Knt. and Bart. [of St. Donat's]. 1st session	1640
Philip Lord Herbert. [Earl of Montgomery; son and successor in 1650 of Philip Herbert, 4th Earl of Pembroke. See 1603] 2nd session	1640

THE COMMONWEALTH AND CROMWELL.

The "Little" or "Barebones" Parliament is called. Six members are summoned for all Wales, without special constituencies:—Bussy Mansel, Hugh Courtenay, James Philips, Richard Pryse, John Williams, John Bowen and Philip Jones for Mon.	1653
[Bussy Mansel is well known as of Briton Ferry, Glam.; James Philips was of Cardigan; Richard Pryse, of Gogerddan; and if Hugh Courtenay was the otherwise known hot "royalist officer," he must have been summoned as a compromise.]	

OLIVER CROMWELL, LORD PROTECTOR.

Col. Philip Jones [of Swansea, afterwards of Fonmon Castle; founder of the family of Jones of Fonmon; an officer of distinguished merit; Governor of Swansea and Cardiff under Cromwell; became one of His Highness's Council; Comptroller of the Household; was elevated to the House of Lords. See *Jones of Fonmon Castle*, and Col. Francis's *Life of Col. Philip Jones*, in his *Charters of Swansea*]. William Thomas, Esq., of Wenvoe.	1654
Col. Philip Jones, of Fonmon (the same) Edmund Thomas, Esq., of Wenvoe [son of William, one of the members for 1654].	1656

RICHARD CROMWELL, LORD PROTECTOR.

Evan Seys, Esq. [of Boverton, Serjeant-at-law. See *Seys of Boverton*. This parliament, after a few short and interrupted sittings, dissolved itself, and by its own authority called another parliament to meet on April 25, 1660].	1658-9

CHARLES II.—"THE RESTORATION."

Sir Edward Mansel, Bart., of Margam [Sheriff in 1688; son of Sir Lewis Mansel, Bart.; *m.* Martha, dau. and co-h. of Edward Carne, Esq., of Ewenny;

PARLIAMENTARY ANNALS OF GLAMORGAN.

	A.D.
was succ. by his son, Sir Thomas, afterwards Lord Mansel] . . .	1660
Sir Edward Mansel (the same) . .	1661
Bussy Mansel, Esq. [of Briton-Ferry; the friend of Cromwell, and zealous promoter of his cause in the co. of Glamorgan]	1678
Bussy Mansel, Esq. (the same) . .	1680
Sir Edward Mansel, Bart. [same as for 1660, &c.]	1680-1

JAMES II.

Sir Edward Mansel, Bart., of Margam (the same)	1685
Bussy Mansel, Esq , of Briton Ferry .	1688

WILLIAM AND MARY—THE REVOLUTION.

Bussy Mansel, Esq., of Briton Ferry .	1689
Bussy Mansel, Esq. (the same) .	1695
Bussy Mansel, Esq. (the same) . .	1598
Sir Thomas Mansel, Bart. [of Margam; Sheriff in 1701; was made Comptroller of the Household under Queen Anne, a member of the Privy Council, Vice-Admiral of South Wales, Governor of Milford Haven; cr. Baron Mansel of Margam 1712; d. 1723. See *Margam Abbey*]. . . .	1700
Sir Thomas Mansel, Bart., of Margam (the same)	1701

ANNE.

Sir Thomas Mansel, Bart., of Margam (the same)	1702
Sir Thomas Mansel, Bart., of Margam (the same)	1705
Sir Thomas Mansel, Bart. (the same) .	1707
Sir Thomas Mansel. Bart. (the same) .	1708
Robert Jones, Esq. [of Fonmon Castle, son of the late Col. Philip Jones of Fonmon	1710
Robert Jones, Esq. (the same) . .	1713
Robert Jones, Esq. (the same) . .	1714

GEORGE I. (HOUSE OF HANOVER).

Robert Jones, Esq., of Fonmon Castle (the same)	1714
Robert Jones, Esq. (the same) . .	1715
Sir Charles Kemeys, Bart., *vice* Jones, deceased	1715
Sir Charles Kemeys, Bart., of Keven-Mably	1722

GEORGE II.

Sir Charles Kemeys, Bart. (the same) .	1727
Hon. William Talbot [son of Charles, Baron Talbot of Hensol] . .	1734
[*Bussy Mansel, Esq.*, of Margam, contested, the poll continuing for ten days. 1501 voted—for Mansel, 823; for Talbot, 678; but 247 were struck off from Mansel, and only 21 from	

	A.D.
Talbot. The sheriff, William Basset of Miskin, accused of great partiality].	
Bussy Mansel, Esq. [of Margam, afterwards Lord Mansel, elected *vice* Talbot, succ. to the peerage on death of his father, Lord Chancellor Talbot, Baron Hensol]	1737
Bussy Mansel. Esq., of Margam (the same)	1741
Thomas Mathew, Admiral [of Llandaff; son of Brig.-Gen. Edward Mathew of Llandaff; father of Major Thomas Mathew of Llandaff, by Henrietta Burgess, an Antigua lady. He was chosen *vice* Bussy Mansel, who succ. to the peerage on death of his brother Christopher, 3rd Lord Mansel of Margam, 1750, *s. p. m.*, when the title became extinct. The four successions from the first lord, Thomas, of Margam, in 1711, to death of Bussy, fourth Lord Mansel, only lasted thirty-nine years. The revival of this title in the person of the present C. R. Mansel Talbot, M.P., has recently been declined] . . .	1744
Charles Edwin, Esq. [of Llanfihangel? The election took place at Bridgend. The name Edwin came to Glamorgan, it is believed, with Humphrey Edwin, Esq., who in or about 1650 purchased Llanfihangel from Sir Robert Thomas, 2nd Bart., the last of his line. See *Thomas of Llanfihangel*] . . .	1747
Charles Edwin, Esq. (the same) . .	1754
Dec. 29th. Major Thomas Matthew [of Llandaff], *vice* Edwin, deceased. [A contest took place between Matthew and Charles Van—see *Van of Marcross,*—who was probably of Llanwern, Mon. Votes for Matthew, 954; for Van, 212. The election was held at Cardiff]	1756

GEORGE III.

Sir Edmund Thomas, Bart. [of Wenvoe Castle]	1761
Sir Edmund Thomas, Bart. [re-elected 11th May, upon his appointment as Commissioner of Woods and Forests]	1763
Richard Turbervill, Esq. [of Ewenny, Dec., 1767, *vice* Thomas, deceased. Election at Bridgend] . . .	1767
Hon. George Venables Vernon [of Briton Ferry; son and h. of George Venables, 1st Lord Vernon, Baron of Kinderton, co. Chester; *m.* Louisa Barbara (by whom he had no surviving issue), dau. and h. of Bussy, last Lord Mansel of Margam, who had Briton Ferry by will of Thomas Mansel of that place, who *d. s. p.*; succ. as 2nd	

608   GLAMORGANSHIRE.

	A.D.
Lord Vernon 1780. This title is not extinct]	1768
Hon. George Venables Vernon (the same) [" Mr. Thomas Price of Dyffryn offered himself in case Lord Vernon was dead"]	1774
Charles Edwin, Esq. [was a *Wyndham* of Dunraven, assumed his mother's surname, an *Edwin* of Llanfihangel, see A.D. 1747 ; *vice* Vernon who *s.* to the peerage on death of his father, Lord Vernon]	1780
Thomas Wyndham, Esq [of Dunraven Castle ; elected at Bridgend, Sept., 1789, *vice* Charles Edwin, resigned. Mr. Traherne (*List of Knights of the Shire*) says "*vice* his father, Charles Wyndham, who took the Chiltern Hundreds"]	1789
Thomas Wyndham, Esq., of Dunraven (the same). [The Wyndhams came to Dunraven in 1642, when Thomas Wyndham bought the estate from Sir George Vaughan, Knt. See *Vaughan of Dunraven*. Thomas Wyndham, Esq., was the last of his line, leaving an only dau., who *m.*, 1810, Wyndham Quin Lord Adare, afterwards 2nd Earl *of Dunraven*] . . .	1790—1812
Benjamin Hall, Esq., *vice* Wyndham deceased [of Hensol Castle. See *Llanover, Baron, of Llanover ;* also *Hensol Castle*]	1814
Sir Christopher Cole, K.C.B. ; *Feb. vice* Hall deceased. [Son of Humphrey Cole, Esq., of Childown, Surrey ; was a Post-Capt. R.N., Col. of Royal Marines ; *m.* Mary, dau. of Henry, 2nd Earl of Ilchester, and widow of T. M. Talbot, Esq., of Margam ; resided at Penrice Castle ; *d. s. p.* 1836]	1818
John Edwards, Esq. [Rheola and Llanelay	

	A.D.
—no further account is found of this brief interruption in the representation]	1818
GEORGE IV.	
Sir Christopher Cole, K.C.B. [same as for 1818 : a contest occurred between Cole, Edwards, and Grey ; the first polling 791 votes, the second 656, the third 151—total votes 1,598. Polling lasted twelve days]	1820
Sir Christopher Cole, K.C.B. (the same)	1826
WILLIAM IV.	
C. R. Mansel Talbot, Esq., of Margam, [present senior Member ; has continuously represented the co. up to the present time. See *Talbot of Margam*]	1830
Do. [General Election under *Reform Act*, when he was chosen as a second member for the co.]	
Lewis Weston Dillwyn, Esq., F.R.S., of Penlle'rgaer	1832
C. R. Mansel Talbot, Esq., of Margam . ⎫ Lewis Weston Dillwyn, Esq., of Penlle'rgaer . . . . . ⎬	1835
VICTORIA.	
C. R. Mansel Talbot, Esq., of Margam . ⎫ Richard Wyndham Quin Viscount Adare ⎬ [afterwards 3rd Earl of Dunraven] ⎭	1837
C. R. Mansel Talbot, Esq., of Margam . ⎫ Sir George Tyler, K.H. [of Cottrel, *vice* Viscount Adare resigned ; eldest son of Admiral Sir Charles Tyler, G.C.B. ; became Rear-Admiral 1852; continued Mr. Talbot's colleague till 1857] ⎬	1851
C. R. Mansel Talbot, Esq., of Margam and Penrice Castle . . . . ⎫ Henry Hussey Vivian, Esq., of Parkwern, Swansea . . . . . ⎬	1857
The sitting Members, 1872.	

2.—*Members of Parliament for Cardiff and Contributory Boroughs*, A.D. 1542—A.D. 1872.

HENRY VIII.

John Bassett, Esq., of the Inner Temple .	1542

EDWARD VI.

John Cokk, Esq. [the name otherwise unknown]	1547

MARY.

David Edwards [*Browne Willis* gives David Evans]	1553
David Evans, Gent., 2nd Parl. . .	1553
Edward Herbert, Esq. [place unknown ; probably son of Richard, son of Howel Thomas Herbert of Berth-hir, and	

grandson of Thomas William Jenkin of Raglan]	1554

PHILIP AND MARY.

William Colchester [place unknown] .	1554
Willis gives no return	1555
Lysanno *ap Ryse*, Esq. [This was doubtless Leyson Piice of Briton Ferry, son of Rhys ap Evan, of the line of Iestyn, through Evan ap Leyson, Lord of Baglan. He *m.* Maud, dau. of David Evans, Esq., of Gnoll, Sheriff in 1562]	1557

ELIZABETH.

Willis gives no return	1558-9

PARLIAMENTARY ANNALS OF GLAMORGAN.

	A.D.
Henry Lewis, Esq. [of Cardiff; Under-Sheriff 1552]	1563
Henry Morgan, Esq. [no place given—probably Glanrumney] . . .	1571
David Roberts, Gent. [Under-Sheriff 1571]	1572
Nicholas Herbert, Esq. [of Cogan; Sheriff 1578 and 1587; 3rd son of Matthew Herbert, Esq., of Swansea] . .	1585
George Lewis, Esq. [of Llys-Talybont; 2nd son of Thomas Lewis, Esq., of Van; Sheriff 1569; *m.* Catherine, dau. of Miles Mathew, Esq., of Castle Menych]	1586
David Roberts, Gent. [probably same as for 1572]	1592
Nicholas Hawkins [place unknown] .	1597
William Lewis, Gent. [place unknown] .	1601

JAMES I.

Matthew Davies, Gent. [place unknown].	1603
William Thomas, Gent. [place unknown]	1614
William Herbert, Esq. [There were three of this name living at this time at or near Cardiff, William of Cogan Pill, son of Nicholas Herbert (see 1585); William of White Friars, Cardiff; and William, jun., who was slain at the battle of Edge Hill, 1642. But this last could scarcely be the member for Cardiff] . . .	1620
William Price, Esq. [the Under-Sheriff for 1626 was of this name] . .	1623

CHARLES I.

William Price, Esq. (the same) . .	1625
William Price, Esq. (the same) . .	1626
Lewis Morgan, Esq. [place not given, probably Glanrumney; grandson of member for 1563; his mother was dau. of Nicholas Herbert, of Cogan]	1628
William Herbert, Esq. [probably of Cogan. See next Parl.], 1st session	
William Herbert, Esq. [probably of Cogan; father of William Herbert of Swansea, Cogan, and White Friars; was slain at the battle of Edge Hill, 1642], 2nd Session	1640
Algernon Sidney, *vice* Herbert . . [This Algernon Sidney, or Sydney, was son of Robert Sydney, Earl of Leicester, and was doubtless brought to Cardiff through the Coity connection (see *Coity Castle*). As Col. Sydney he became celebrated under Cromwell, was a strong republican, but against Cromwell's "usurpation." This Parl., known as the "Long Parliament," continued to sit at intervals, until, in 1648, Col. Pride's "Purge" put a stop to its "further debate." Sydney had continued all this time a member.	1642

	A.D.
In 1645 Cromwell thought highly of him as an officer in the Parliament army. "I am confident," he says to Fairfax, "he will serve you faithfully;" but in 1653, in dismissing the "Long" or "Rump" Parl., or, as he called the act, "putting an end to their prating," Cromwell, pointing to the Speaker, said to Harrison, "Fetch him down!" and seeing Algernon Sydney sitting next to the Speaker, he exclaimed, "Put *him* out!" then pointing to the mace, said, "Take away that bauble." Sydney, however, continued a staunch Commonwealth and anti-royalty man; opposed the Restoration; survived Cromwell; concerted with Shaftesbury, Hampden, and Russell in 1681; was arrested as concerned in the "Rye House Plot," was tried by the miscreant Jeffreys, Charles II.'s instrument, condemned, and executed on Tower Hill 1683.]	

THE COMMONWEALTH AND CROMWELL.

The "Little" Parliament. No return for the boroughs. See under *County* .	1653

OLIVER CROMWELL, LORD PROTECTOR.

John Price, Esq. [prob. "John Price, Esq,," of Gellihir, in Gower, an active man in the Protector's cause] . . .	1654
John Price, Esq. (the same) . . .	1656

RICHARD CROMWELL, LORD PROTECTOR.

John Price, Esq. [the same. This parliament was interrupted sitting Oct. 13, reassembled Dec. 26, and continued sitting till March 16, when it passed a vote not only dissolving itself, but the parliament of Nov. 3, 1640, and summoning a new parliament for April 25th, 1660]	1658-9

CHARLES II.

Bussy Mansel, Esq., of Briton Ferry .	1660-1
Sir Robert Thomas, Bart., of Llanfihangel	1678-80
Bussy Mansel, Esq. [for *County* in 1680]	1681

JAMES II.

Francis Gwyn, Esq, of Llansannor . .	1685
Thomas Mansel, Esq., of Margam [afterwards a Bart.]	1688-9
Sir Edward Stradling, Bart., of St. Donat's	1695—1700
Thomas Mansel, Esq. [of Briton Ferry] .	1701

ANNE.

Thomas Mansel, Esq. (the same) . .	1702-5

	A.D.
Sir John Aubrey, Bart. [of Llantrithyd]	1707-8
Sir Edward Stradling, Bart., of St. Donat's	1710-14

GEORGE I. (HOUSE OF HANOVER).

Sir Edward Stradling, Bart. (the same)	1714
Sir Edward Stradling, 4th Bart. of St. Donat's ; *m.* Elizabeth, dau. of Anthony Hungerford	1722

GEORGE II.

Sir Edward Stradling, Bart. (the same)	⎫
Hon. Bussy Mansel [of Margam, afterwards Lord Mansel of Margam, M.P. for the co. 1737, 1741], *vice* Stradling, deceased	⎬ 1727
Hon. Herbert Windsor [afterwards Baron Mountjoy, &c., peerage of Ireland]	1734
Herbert Mackworth, Esq. [*vice* Windsor, who succ. to the peerage as Baron Mountjoy]	1739
Herbert Mackworth, Esq. [the same ; son of Sir Humphrey Mackworth, Knt., of Gnoll]	1741
Thomas Edmonds, Esq. [no place specified—probably of Cowbridge—the same with the Under-Sheriff of 1753. Of this family possibly is the Rev. Thomas Edmondes, M.A., at present Vicar of Llanblethian-cum-Cowbridge]	1747
Herbert Mackworth, Esq. [the same as for 1741 and 1761]	1754

GEORGE III.

Herbert Mackworth, Esq., of Gnoll	1761
Herbert Mackworth, Esq. [of Gnoll ; son of the member last given ; was member also in 1774, 1780, and 1784 ; cr. a baronet 1776 ; *d.* 1792]	1768—84
Hon. John Stuart [Lord Mount-Stuart, eldest son of John, 4th Earl of Bute, and 1st Marquess of Bute ; *m.* Elizabeth, dau. and sole h. of Patrick Crichton, Earl of Dumfries]	1790
Lord Evelyn James Stuart, *vice* Stuart deceased [3rd son of 1st Marquess of Bute ; *b.* in 1773 ; Col. in the army ; *d.* 1842]	1794—6
Lord William Stuart [Capt. R.N. ; brother of the member for 1794—1796]	1801—18
Lord Evelyn James Stuart [*vice* Stuart deceased ; same as member for 1794—6]	1814
Lord P. James H. C. Stuart [brother of Evelyn James, last member; contested with Frederick Wood ; for Stuart, 45 ; Wood, 17]	1818

GEORGE IV.

Wyndham Lewis, Esq. *vice* Lord James Stuart, retired [of Green Meadow, was opposed by E. Ludlow, but after six days' contest was returned by a considerable majority; was afterwards member successively for Aldburgh and Maidstone ; he *d.* 1838, and his widow, Mary Anne, dau. of John Evans, Esq., of Brampford Speke, Devon, *m.,* 1839, Benjamin Disraeli, Esq., M.P. (now Right Hon.), colleague with Mr. Lewis, in 1837, in the representation of Maidstone]	1820
Lord P. James H. Crichton-Stuart [same as member for 1818]	1826—32
John Nicholl, Esq. [gained election against Lord James H. C. Stuart ; votes for Nicholl, 342 ; for Stuart, 191]	1832
John Nicholl, Esq. [on appointment to be Judge Advocate-General]	1841
Rt. Hon. John Nicholl	1847
Walter Coffin, Esq., of Llandaff [son of late Walter Coffin, Esq., of Bridgend ; had a contest with Rt. Hon. John Nicholl, D.C.L. ; obtained a majority of 26]	1852
Col. James Frederick Dudley Crichton-Stuart [eldest son of the late Lord Patrick James Herbert Stuart, brother of the late John, 2nd Marquess of Bute ; is cousin of the present marquess]	1857

Is the present sitting member, 1872.

3.—*Members of Parliament for Swansea and Contributory Boroughs down to* 1872.

Swansea, notwithstanding its great population and importance as the largest corporate town and port in the county, had not the privilege of sending a representative to Parliament till 1832, when the Reform Bill conceded to it this justice.

Once, indeed, before—during that brief period of exceptional administration inaugurated by the Commonwealth and by Cromwell—Swansea had sent a delegate to Parliament. That delegate was *William Foxwist,* a member of a Cheshire family residing at Carnarvon (Dwnn, *Herald. Visit.* 11, 286), and a Judge of Great Sessions in Wales. We find some few other facts of his history previous to the year of his membership for "Swansea." His name is given in *Browne Willis* (*Not. Parl.*) as serving for *Carnarvon Town* in 1640, the first year of the "Long Parliament" of Charles I., "in the room" of "William Thomas, Esq.," of Aber, who had either been "deceased or displaced" between 1640 and 1653, the latter being the date of Cromwell's "Little" Parliament. He also served for the co. *of Anglesey*, as colleague of George Twistleton, another Cromwellite, in the "Barebones" Parliament of 1654. In 1658-9 he appears at Swansea. That he was a political Republican, and an Independent in ecclesiastical polity—two things which by no means go together as a rule—is likely enough, and that he was a staunch friend of the Cromwellian cause is morally certain, for he was a commissioner for Carnarvon in 1657 to raise money for the Protectorate, and in a place of honour in the grand funeral procession of Cromwell, along with *Walter Cradock*, and *Serjeant Seys* (of Boverton), *Edmund, Lord Thomas* (of Llanfihangel), and *Philip, Lord Jones* (of Fonmon). See Francis's *Charters of Swansea*. His arms were: *Arg., on a chevron sa. a mullet pierced of the field betw.* 3 *crosslets fitchées sa.*

RICHARD CROMWELL, LORD PROTECTOR.

	A.D.
William Foxwist, Esq. [of what place not stated	1658-9]

WILLIAM IV.

	A.D.
John Henry Vivian, Esq. [First enfranchisement of the borough under the *Reform Act*. Registered voters, 1, 307. Mr. Vivian chosen without a contest]	1832
John Henry Vivian, Esq.[registered voters, 1,322]	1835

VICTORIA.

	A.D.
John Henry Vivian, Esq.[registered voters, 1,349]	1837
John Henry Vivian, Esq. [reg. voters, 1,447]	1841
John Henry Vivian, Esq. [reg. voters, 1,563]	1847
John Henry Vivian, Esq. [reg. voters, 1,694]	1854
Lewis Llewelyn Dillwyn, Esq. . . [*vice* Mr. Vivian, *deceased*. Mr. Dillwyn has continued without interruption to represent Swansea to the present time. Thus the constituency has escaped a contest, and has only had two members since its creation as a parliamentary borough by the Reform Act of 1832]	1855
The sitting member, 1872.	

4.—Members of Parliament for Merthr Tydfil District.

The District of Merthyr, the great centre of iron and coal operations, having rapidly grown in wealth and population, was conceded by the Reform Bill of 1832 the parliamentary franchise. In 1831 the population of Merthyr was 22,083. In 1861 the population of the Parliamentary District, including Aberdare, was 83,875. In 1871 it had risen so high as 96,891.

	A.D.		A.D.
Josiah John Guest, Esq., of Dowlais [registered votes, 502] . . .	1832	Sir Josiah John Guest, Bart [reg. voters, 822]	1847
Josiah John Guest, Esq. [reg. votes, 564]	1835	Henry Austin Bruce, Esq. [*vice* Guest, *dec.*, now (1872) the Right Hon. H. A. Bruce, Secretary of State for the Home Department. See *Bruce of Dyffryn*].	1852
Josiah John Guest, Esq. [reg. votes, 582. Contest between Guest and J. B. Bruce. Voted for Guest, 309; for Bruce, 135]	1837		
Sir Josiah John Guest, [cr. Baronet 1838. On the register this year, 760] . .	1841		

Merthyr Tydfil having by census of 1861 a population of 83,875, is empowered to send to Parliament henceforth two representatives. The representation was contested in 1868 with the following result:—Richard Fothergill, Esq. (local ironmaster), 7,439 votes; Henry Richard, Esq., of London (Secretary of Peace Society), 11,683 votes; Rt. Hon. H. A. Bruce, 5,776 votes. Mr. Bruce was eventually elected for Renfrewshire.

Richard Fothergill, Esq., of Abernant House . . . . } A.D. 1868
Henry Richard, Esq., of London . . . . }

The sitting Members, 1872.

SECTION X.—THE LORD LIEUTENANTS OF GLAMORGAN,
A.D. 1660—A.D. 1872.

The office of Lord Lieutenant—the sovereign's representative in counties in matters pertaining to their military arrangements—was brought into full maturity at the Restoration In the time of Elizabeth, a class of magistrates, invested in crises of danger with extraordinary powers, did the work of calling forth and arraying the military forces of their county. In still earlier times " Commissions of Array " were issued to muster and arm the different districts. The right of the Crown to issue such commissions was denied by the Parliament, and constituted one of the great questions in debate between the Commons and Charles I. But with his assumption of power at the Restoration, Charles II. was allowed to exercise this right to the full (14 Car. II., cap. 3). The duties of Lord Lieutenants and their Deputy Lieutenants have been defined in the various *Militia Acts*, but the functions of their office have been in a great degree curtailed by the Army Regulations of 1872.

Lord Lieutenant.	Date of Appointment.
	A.D.
Carbery, Richard Vaughan, 2nd Earl of, of Golden Grove, Carm.	18th Sept., 1660.
Carbery, Richard Vaughan, Earl of, (the same) reappointed	22nd Dec., 1660.
Carbery, Richard Vaughan, Earl of,(the same) do.	19th July, 1662.
Worcester, Henry Somerset, 3rd Marquess and 7th Earl of,	20th July, 1673.
Beaufort, Henry Somerset (the same), cr. Duke of, 1682. He was styled "Lord President of Wales" (d. 1699)	28th March, 1685.
Macclesfield, Charles Gerard, 1st Earl of (d. 1694)	22nd March, 1689.
Pembroke and Montgomery, Thomas Herbert, 8th Earl of, (d. 1733)	11th May, 1694.
Bolton, Charles Paulet, 3rd Duke of, (d. 1754)	22nd March, 1728.
Plymouth, Other Lewis Windsor, 4th Earl of, (d. 1771)	6th Nov., 1754.
Mount-Stuart, John, Lord, afterwards 1st Marquess of Bute	22nd March, 1772.
Bute, John Stuart, 4th Earl of .	19th Dec. 1794.
Bute, John Crichton Stuart, 2nd Marquess of, and Custos Rotul., (d. 1848)	2nd June, 1815.
Talbot, Christopher Rice Mansel, Esq., M.P., (and Custos Rotul.)	5th May, 1848.

Present Lord Lieutenant, 1872.

SECTION XI.—BISHOPS OF LLANDAFF FROM THE CONQUEST TO 1872.
[*The See had already existed about 600 years.*]

Appointment.
A.D.
1059 Herewald (a Saxon); d. 1103; consec. 1059;
[The see vacant four years.]
1108 Urban, Archdeacon of Llandaff; consecrated 10th August, 1108; d. 1133.
[The see vacant six years.]
1139 Uhtred; consecrated 1139; d. 1148.

Appointment.
A.D.
1148 Galfrid, followed Uhtred 1148; d. 1153.
1153 Nicholas ap Gwrgant; (a Welshman); d. 1183.
1185 William de Salso Marisco; d. circa 1191. was bishop when Giraldus Cambr. visited Llandaff (see p. 531).

BISHOPS OF LLANDAFF.

Appointment.

A.D.	
1196	Henry, Prior of Abergavenny; *d.* 1218.
1219	William, Prior of Godcliffe; *d.* 1240. [See was now vacant about four years.]
1244	William de Burgh, Chaplain to the King (Henry III.); consecrated 1244; *d.* 1253.
1253	John de la Warr; elected 26th July, 1253; *d.* 1256.
1256	William de Radnor; el. 30th July; *d.* 1265.
1266	William de Breos, Prebendary of Llandaff; elected March, 1266; *d.* 19th March, 1287.

[It is believed that no bishop was appointed between 1287 and 1296, but Le Neve on the Authority of Prynne states that Philip de Staunton succ. in September.—1287, Nicolas, *Peerage.*]

1296	John de Monmouth; nominated March, 1295; consecrated February, 1296; *d.* 1323.
1323	John de Eglescliffe; translated from Connor, Ireland, September, 1323; *d.* 2nd January, 1346. To succeed him, John Coventre was elected by the clergy, but rejected by the Pope.
1347	John Paschall; appointed 3rd June; *d.* 11th October, 1361.
1361	Roger Cradock; translated from Waterford, Ireland, 15th December, 1361; *d.* 1382.
1383	Thomas Rushooke, Confessor to the King (Richard II.); translated to the see of Chichester in 1386.
1386	William de Bottlesham, titular Bishop of Bethlehem; translated to Rochester in 1389.
1389	Edmund de Brumfeld; appointed 17th Dec.; *d.* 1391.
1393	Tideman de Winchcomb, Abbot of Beauly; appointed 5th July, 1393; translated to Worcester in 1395.
1395	Andrew Barret; appointed 25th August, 1395; *d.* 1396.
1396	John Burghill, *alias* Bruchilla, Confessor to King Richard II.; appointed 15th June; translated to Lichfield and Coventry 1398.
1398	Thomas Peverel; translated from Ossory, in Ireland, 1398, and to Worcester in 1407.
1408	John la Zouche; appointed 7th June.
1425	John Wells; app. 9th July, 1425; *d.* 1440.
1441	Nicholas Ashby, Prior of Westminster; *d.* 1458.
1458	John Hunden, Prior of King's Langley, Herts; resigned some time before his death.
1476	John Smith; appointed July, 1476; *d.* 1478.
1478	John Marshal; appointed 18th September.
1496	John Ingleby, Prior of Shene; *d.* 1500.
1500	Miles Salley, or Sawley; *d.* 1516.
1516	George Athequa, de Attica, or Attien, a Spaniard; was chaplain to Queen Katherine of Arragon.
1537	Robert Holgate, Prior of Watton; translated to York 10th January, 1545.

Appointment.

A.D.	
1545	Anthony Kitchin, or Dunstan; *d.* Oct., 1566.
1567	Hugh Jones, "first Welshman appointed bishop of his church in almost 300 years." (See p. 580.)
1575	William Blethyn, Prebendary of York; *d.* 1590.
1591	Gervase Babington, Prebendary of Hereford; translated to Exeter in 1595.
1595	William Morgan [*the Translator of the Bible into Welsh;* a native of Penmachno, Carn.]; translated to St. Asaph 1601.
1601	Francis Godwin, Canon of Wells; translated to Hereford 1617.
1617	George Carleton, translated to Chichester 1619.
1619	Theophilus Field; translated to St. David's 1627.
1627	William Murray; translated from Kilfenora, Ireland.
1639	Morgan Owen; elected March, 1639; *d.* 1645. [*The see is vacant about* 16 *years.*]
1660	Hugh Lloyd, Archdeacon of St. David's; *d.* 1667.
1667	Francis Davies, Archdeacon of Llandaff; elected 29th July, 1667; *d.* 15th March, 1674.
1675	William Lloyd, Prebendary of St. Paul's; elected 6th April; translated to Peterborough 1679.
1679	William Beaw; consecr. 22nd June; *d.* 1707.
1707	John Tyler, Dean of Hereford; *d.* 1724.
1724	Robert Clavering, Canon of Christ Church, Oxford; elected 1724; translated to Peterborough 1728.
1728	John Harris, Prebendary of Canterbury; *d.* 1738.
1738	Matthias Mawson; transl. to Chichester 1740.
1740	John Gilbert, Dean of Exeter; translated to Salisbury 1748.
1748	Edward Cresset, Dean of Hereford; *d.* 1755.
1755	Richard Newcome, Canon of Windsor; translated to St. Asaph in 1761.
1761	John Ewer, Canon of Windsor; translated to Bangor 1769.
1769	Hon. Shute Barrington, Canon of St. Paul's; translated to Salisbury 1782.
1782	Richard Watson (the eminent theologian), Archdeacon of Ely; elected 1782; *d.* 1816.
1816	Herbert Marsh (the eminent Biblical scholar); translated to Peterborough 1819; *d.* 1839.
1819	William Van Mildert; translated to Durham 1826.
1826	Charles Richard Sumner; translated to Winchester 1827.
1827	Edward Copleston; appointed 1827; *d.* 1849.
1849	Alfred Ollivant; appointed 1849. *Present bishop.*

SECTION XII.—THE MAGISTRACY OF THE COUNTY AND BOROUGHS OF GLAMORGAN, 1872.

1.—COUNTY MAGISTRATES.

Bassett, Richard, Esq., Bonvilston.
Batchelor, Sydney James, Esq., Penarth.
Bath, Charles, Esq., Ffynone.
Bath, Henry James, Esq., Swansea.
Benson, Henry Roxby, Esq., Tyrllandwr.
Benson, Starling, Esq., Fairy Hill.
Berrington, Arthur V. D., Esq., Cefngola.
Berrington, Jenkin Davies, Esq., of Pantygoitre.
Biddulph, John, Esq., Swansea.
Blosse, Ven. Archdeacon Henry Lynch, Bridgend.
Booker, Thomas William, Esq., Velindre.
Brogden, James, Esq., Tondu.
Bruce, Alan Cameron, Esq., London.
Bruce, Rt. Hon. Henry Austin, M.P., Duffryn.
Bruce, Lewis Knight, Esq., St. Nicholas.
Bruce, Rev. William, St. Nicholas.
Budd, James Palmer, Esq., Ystalyfera.
Bute, John Patrick, Marquess of, Cardiff Castle.

Calland, John Forbes, Esq., Gnoll.
Cameron, Nathaniel Pryce, Esq., Swansea.
Carne, J. W. Nicholl-, Esq., D.C.L., St. Donat's.
Cartwright, William Sheward, Esq., Newport.
Clark, George Thomas, Esq., Dowlais.
Corbett, John Stuart, Esq., Cogan.
Crawshay, Robert Thompson, Esq., Cyfarthfa.

David, Charles Williams, Esq., Cardiff.
David, Evan Williams, Esq., Fairwater.
Davies, Evan Jones, Esq., Merthyr.
Davies, Joseph, Esq., Bedwas.
Davies, Rees Edward, Esq., Mardy.
Davis, David, Esq., Cwm.
Davis, David, Esq., Maesyffynon.
Dillwyn, Henry de la Beche, Esq., London.
Dillwyn, Lewis Llewelyn, Esq., M.P., Hendrefoilan.

Eaton, Robert, Esq., Bryn-y-mor.
Edmond, William, Esq., Blaen-y-maes.
Edmondes, Rev. Thomas, Cowbridge.
Edwardes, Rev. Frederick Francis E., Gileston.
Elliott, George, Esq., Aberaman.
Evans, Henry Jones, Esq., Cardiff.
Evans, Herbert Edward, Esq., Eaglesbush.
Evans, Thomas John, Esq., Merthyr.

Falconer, Thomas, Esq., Co. Court Judge, Usk.
Fisher, Samuel Sharpe Horman, Esq., Llwynderw.
Fothergill, George, Esq., Treforest.
Fothergill, Richard, Esq., M.P., Aberdare.
Fowler, J. C., Esq. (*Stipendiary for Merthyr*), Gnoll.
Francis, George Grant, Esq., Cae Bailey.
Franklin, Richard, Esq., Clementston.

Gibbon, John Samuel, Esq., Newton.
Gilbertson, William, Esq., Pontardawe.
Gough, Richard Douglas, Esq., Ynyscedwyn.
Gould, Hubert Churchill, Esq., Ash Hall.
Grenfell, Pascoe St. Leger, Esq., Maesteg House.
Griffith, Rev. David Hanmer, Cadoxton.
Griffith, Rev. John, Merthyr.
Griffiths, Rev. Walter, Dylais.
Guest, Arthur Edward, Esq., Tynygraig.
Gwyn, Howel, Esq., Duffryn.
Gwynne, Frederick Finines, Esq., New House.

Hall, Richard, Esq., Baglan.
Herbert, John Maurice, Esq., *Co. Court Judge*.
Homfray, John, Esq., Penlline Castle.
Homfray, John Richard, Esq., Penlline Castle.
Hutchins, Edward John, Esq., Dowlais.

Insole, James Harvey, Esq., Llandaff.

James, David W., Esq., Porth.
James, John Williams, Esq., Swansea.
Jeffreys, John Gwyn, Esq., Gellygron.
Jenkin, John Trevillian, Esq., Swansea.
Jenkins, George Henry, Esq., Penlline.
Jenkins, John Blandy, Esq., Llanharry.
Jenner, Hugh, Esq., Wenvoe.
Jenner, Robert F. Lascelles, Esq., Wenvoe.
Johnes, John, Esq., *Co. Court Judge*, Dolaucothi.
Jones, Robert Oliver, Esq. (*Stipendiary*), Fonmon Castle.

Knight, Rev. Charles Rumsey, Tythegston Court.

Lee, Rev. Henry Thomas, Dinaspowis.
Lee, Vaughan Hanning, Esq., Lanelay.
Lewis, Henry, Esq., Green Meadow.
Lewis, James, Esq., Tydraw.
Llewellyn, Edward Turberville, Esq., Hendrescythan.
Llewellyn, Griffith, Esq., Baglan.
Llewellyn, William, Esq., Court Colman.
Llewelyn, John Dillwyn, Esq., Penlle'rgaer.
Llewelyn, John Talbot Dillwyn, Esq., Ynysygerwn.
Lloyd, Herbert, Esq., Killybebyll.

Martin, William, Esq., Ynystawe.
Mayberry, Rev. Charles, Penderyn.
Moggridge, Matthew, Esq., Swansea.
Morgan, Evan, Esq., St. Helen's.
Morgan, Hon. Frederick Courtenay, Ruperra.
Morgan, Hon. Godfrey Charles, Tredegar.
Morris, George Byng, Esq., Danygraig.
Morris, Sir John Armine, Bart., Sketty Park.
Morris, Robert Armine, Esq., Oystermouth.
Morse, Thomas Robert, Esq., Glanogwr.

THE MAGISTRACY OF GLAMORGAN.

Nicholl, George Whitlock, Esq., Ham.
Nicholl, John Cole, Esq., Merthyr-mawr.

Page, Charles Harrison, Esq., Llandaff.
Penrice, Thomas, Esq., Kilvrough.
Phillips, Griffith, Esq., Whitchurch.
Prichard, William, Esq., Crofta.
Pryce, John Bruce, Esq., Duffryn.

Randall, John, Esq., Neath.
Randall, John Henry, Esq., Bridgend.
Rhys, Rees Hopkin, Esq., Aberdare.
Richards, Evan Matthew, Esq., M.P., Brooklands.
Richards, Richard, Esq., Bellevue.
Richardson, James Coxon, Esq., Glanyrafon.
Richardson, John Crow, Esq., Pantygwydir.
Rickards, Rev. Hely Hutchinson Keating, Landough.
Rickards, Robert Hillier, Esq., Clifton.
Roberts, Richard Thomas, Esq., Aberdare.
Romilly, Edward, Esq., Porthkerry.
Romilly, Frederick, Esq., Porthkerry.
Rous, George Grey, Esq., Courtyralla.
Rowland, John Henry, Esq., Froodvale.

Salmon, Thomas Deere, Esq., London.
Salmon, William, Esq., Penlline Court.
Smith, Charles Henry, Esq., Gwernllwynwith.
Stacey, Francis Edmond, Esq., Landough.
Strick, George Burden, Esq., West Cross.
Struve, William Price, Esq., Bridgend.
Stuart, James F. Dudley Crichton, Esq., M.P., Cardiff.

Talbot, Christopher Rice Mansel, Esq., M.P., *Lord Lieutenant*, Margam Park.
Talbot, Theodore Mansel, Esq., Margam Park.
Thomas, Charles Evan, Esq., London.
Thomas, George Williams G., Esq., Coedriglan.
Thomas, Hubert de Burgh, Esq., Llanblethian.
Thomas, Iltid, Esq., Glanmor.
Thomas, John B. D., Esq., Tregroes.
Traherne, Anthony Powell, Esq., Broadlands.
Traherne, George Montgomery, Esq., St. Hilary.
Traherne, John Popkin, Esq., Coytrehên.
Tredegar, Rt. Hon. the Lord, Tredegar Park.
Turbervill, Thomas Picton, Esq., Ewenny Abbey.
Tyler, Rev. Roper Trevor, Llantrithyd.
Tynte, Charles Kemeys Kemeys, Esq., Cefn-Mably.

Vachell, Frederick Charles, Esq., Highmead.
Vivian, Arthur Pendarvis, Esq., M.P., Craigavon.
Vivian, Henry Hussey, Esq., M.P., Parkwern.
Vivian, William Graham, Esq., Singleton.

Walter, James, Esq., Ffynone, Swansea.
Williams, Charles Henry, Esq., Roath.
Williams, David Evan, Esq., Hirwain.
Williams, Rev. David Watkin, Fairfield.
Williams, Evan, Esq., Duffryn Ffrwd.
Williams, Evan Thomas, Esq., Duffryn.
Williams, George Croft, Esq., Llanrumney.
Williams, Gwilym, Esq. (*Stipendiary*), Miskin Manor.
Williams, Morgan Stuart, Esq., Aberpergwm.
Wilson, Charles Thomas, Esq., Brynnewydd.
Wood, Edward Robert, Esq., Stouthall.

Clerk of the Peace, Thomas Dalton, Esq.

2.—BOROUGH MAGISTRATES.

Justices of the Peace for the Borough of Cardiff, 1872.

Charles Williams David, Esq., *Mayor*.
Robert Oliver Jones, Esq., *Stipendiary Magistrate*.
William Thomas Edwards, Esq., M.D.
William Done Bushell, Esq.
Thomas Edward Heath, Esq.
James Harvey Insole, Esq.
George Bird, Esq.
James Pride, Esq.

William Alexander, Esq.
Griffith Phillips, Esq.
William Bradley Watkins, Esq.
Edward Stock Hill, Esq.
George Johnson, Capt. R.N., Esq.
Henry James Paine, Esq., M D.
Samuel Nash, Esq.
Alexander Bassett, Esq.

Justices of the Peace for the Borough of Swansea, 1872.

	A.D.		A.D.
The Mayor and Ex-mayor for the time being.		John Crow Richardson, Esq., of Uplands	1859
Starling Benson, Esq., of Swansea	1836	John Oakshot, Esq., of Swansea	1859
George Grant Francis, Esq., of Cae Bailey	1855	William Henry Michael, Esq., of Swansea	1860
James Walters, Esq., of Fynone	1855	Jeremiah Clarke Richardson, Esq., of Swansea	1868
Evan Mathew Richards, Esq., of Swansea	1855	William Henry Forester, Esq., of Swansea	1868
John Williams James, Esq., of Swansea	1855	Sydney Hall, Esq., of Swansea	1868
Michael Martin Williams, Esq., of Swansea	1855	George Browne Brock, Esq., of Swansea	1868
John Biddulph, Esq., of Dderwenfawr	1857	Thomas Phillips, Esq., of Swansea	1868
Trevor Addams Williams, Esq., of Clyncollen	1859	John Trevillian Jenkin, Esq., of Swansea	1868
Silvanus Padley, the younger, Esq., of Swansea	1859	Mr. George Bowen, Attorney-at-Law, *Clerk*	1866

GLAMORGANSHIRE.

Section XIII.—PORTREEVES AND MAYORS OF SWANSEA, A.D. 1600—A.D. 1872.

Portreeves.

Name	A.D.	Name	A.D.	Name	A.D.
Owen Phillippe	1600	Thomas Williams	1652	David Thomas, Gent.	1708
William Fleminge	1601	John Daniel	1653	Griffith Phillips, Gent.	1709
William John Harry	1602	William Bayly	1654	John Rice	1710
Jenkin Franklin }	1603	Lewis Jones, *Mayor*	1655	Joseph Ayres, Gent.	1711
William John Harry, *Deputy* }		John Daniel, *Mayor*	1656	Jenkin Jones, Gent.	1712
John Thomas Bevan	1604	William Bayly, *Mayor*	1657	Gabriel Powell, Gent.	1713
John David Edwards	1605	Thomas Williams, *Mayor*	1658	Walter Hughes, Gent.	1714
William Watkins	1606	William Jones	1659	Ditto	1715
John Daniel }	1607	Leyson Seys	1660	Abraham Ayres, Gent.	1716
John David Edwards, *Deputy* }		Ditto	1661	Anthony Cupitt, Gent.	1717
George Herbert, Esq.	1608	Isaac Affter	1662	Richard Parry, Gent.	1718
John Robartes	1609	Ditto	1663	Griffith Phillips, Gent.	1719
William John Harry	1610	William Vaughan	1664	John Mansell, Gent.	1720
John David	1611	William Bayly	1665	Walter Hughes, jun., Gent.	1721
John David	1612	Lewis Jones	1666	Walter Hughes, Gent.	1722
Henry Fleminge	1613	Isaac Affter	1667	Robert Rogers, Gent.	1723
John Daniel	1614	Robert Jones	1668	David Thomas, Gent.	1724
Walter Thomas	1615	Gamaliel Hughes	1669	William Phillips, Gent.	1725
William John Harry	1616	William Thomas	1670	Gabriel Powell, Gent.	1726
John David	1617	David Bevan	1671	Walter Hughes, Gent.	1727
Owen Price	1618	Lewis Jones	1672	Robert Hughes, Gent.	1728
Mathew Franklin	1619	Isaac Affter	1673	Abraham Ayres, *died* }	1729
John Daniel	1620	William Herbert, Esq.	1674	Walter Vaughan, Gent. }	
Harry Vaughan	1621	Robert Jones	1675	Walter Vaughan, Gent.	1730
John William John	1622	Gamaliel Hughes	1676	John Mansell, Gent.	1731
Owen Price	1623	William Thomas	1677	William Watkins, Gent.	1732
Henry Fleminge	1624	Thomas Phillips	1678	John Powell, Esq.	1733
Walter Thomas	1625	Ditto	1679	Walter Hughes, Gent.	1734
Rice David	1626	Ditto	1680	Walter Vaughan, Gent.	1735
Patrick Jones	1627	Ditto	1681	John France, Gent.	1736
Mathew Franklin	1628	Ditto	1682	John Morgan, Gent.	1737
John Bennett	1629	Ditto	1683	Walter Vaughan, Gent.	1738
John Williams	1630	Ditto	1684	Hugh Powell, Gen.,	1739
Rice David	1631	Ditto	1685	Gabriel Powell, Gent.	1740
Francis Affter	1632	Ditto	1686	John Mansell, Gent.	1741
David Jones	1633	Ditto	1687	John Collins, Gent.	1742
Patrick Jones	1634	Gamaliel Hughes	1689	John Powell, Gent.	1743
Mathew Franklin	1635	Owen Rogers	1690	John France, Gent.	1744
John Williams	1636	Ditto	1691	Richard Powell, Gent.	1745
Patrick Jones	1637	Jenkin Jones	1692	John Powell, Gent.	1746
Mathew Franklin	1638	William Seys	1693	John Whitney, Gent.	1747
Lewis Jones	1639	Edward Mansell, Esq.	1694	Edward Phillips, Gent.	1748
John Williams	1640	Ditto	1695	John Morgan, Gent.	1749
Patrick Jones	1641	John Franklin	1696	Hugh Powell, Gent.	1750
Mathew Franklin	1642	William Seys, Esq.	1697	Walter Vaughan, Gent.	1751
Lewis Jones	1643	George Rice	1698	John Collins, Gent.	1752
John Williams	1644	Owen Rogers	1699	John Jenkins, Gent.	1753
Patrick Jones	1645	John Reece	1700	Hopkin Walter, Gent.	1754
John Daniel	1646	David Jones	1701	Christopher Rogers, Gent.	1755
John Bowen	1647	Jenkin Jones	1702	John France, Gent.	1756
William Bayly	1648	Lewis Thomas	1703	James Thomas, Gent.	1757
Mathew Franklin	1649	Walter Hughes	1704	Walter Vaughan, Gent.	1758
Lewis Jones	1650	Gabriel Powell	1705	John Collins, Gent.	1759
Mathew Davies	1651	Christopher Rogers	1706	John Jenkins, Gent.	1760
		Griffith Phillips	1707	Hopkin Walter, Gent.	1761

PORTREEVES AND MAYORS OF SWANSEA.

	A.D.		A.D.		A.D.
Phillip Rogers, Gent. .	1761	Thomas Maddocks, Gent. .	1785	John Morris, Esq. . .	1811
Christopher Rogers, Gent. .	⎱	Gabriel Jeffreys, Gent.	1786	Charles Collins, Esq. . .	1812
John Gwyther, Gent. . .	⎰ 1762	Ditto	1787	William Jeffreys, Esq. . .	1813
James Thomas, Gent. . .	⎱	John Roberts, Gent. .	1788	John Jeffreys, Esq. . .	1814
James Thomas, Gent. . .	1763	Griffith Jenkin, Gent. . .	1789	John Grove, Esq. . .	1815
David Vaughan, Gent.	1764	William Grove, Gent. . .	1790	Rob. Nelson Thomas, Esq.	1816
Robert Ball, Gent. . .	1765	Thomas Morgan, Esq. . .	1791	Thomas Edw. Thomas, Esq.	1817
William Davies, Gent. .	1766	William Jeffreys, Gent.	1792	William Grove, Esq. . .	1818
Thomas Maddocks, Gent. .	1767	Rowland Pritchard, Esq. .	1793	Griffith Jenkin, Esq. . .	1819
Williams Powell, Gent. .	1768	William Jones, Esq. . .	1794	John Jones, Esq. . . .	1820
William Jeffreys, Gent. .	1769	Gabriel Powell, Gent. . .	1795	John Charles Collins, M D.	1821
Iltid Thomas, Gent. . .	1770	Gabriel Jeffreys, Gent. .	1796	William Grove, Esq. . .	1822
Phillip Rogers, Gent. . .	1771	Thomas Powell, clerk . .	1797	Calvert Rich. Jones, Esq. .	1823
James Thomas, Gent. . .	1772	Thomas Maddocks, Esq. .	1798	Richard Jeffreys, Esq. . .	1824
William Davies, Gent. .	1773	Griffith Jenkin, Esq. . .	1799	Lewis Thomas, Esq. . .	1825
Thomas Maddocks, Gent. .	1774	William Grove, Esq. .	1800	Gabriel Powell, Esq. . .	1826
Gabriel Jeffreys, Gent. .	1775	Thomas Morgan, Esq. .	1801	Sir John Morris, Bart. . .	1827
Gabriel Powell, jun., Gent. .	1776	Charles Collins, Esq. . .	1802	John Grove, Esq. . .	1828
William Jeffreys, Gent. .	1777	John Jeffreys, Esq. . .	1803	Thomas Thomas, Esq. .	1829
Thomas Powell, clerk . .	1778	William Jeffreys, Esq. . .	1804	Charles Collins, Esq. . .	1830
Iltid Thomas, Gent. . .	1779	Rowland Pritchard, Esq. .	1805	Thomas Grove, Esq. . .	1831
William Powell, Gent. .	1780	William Jones, Esq. . .	1806	Thomas Edw. Thomas, Esq.	1832
Philip Rogers, Gent. . .	1781	Gabriel Jeffreys, Esq. . .	1807	Silvanus Padley, Esq. . .	1833
Prichard Rowland, Esq. .	1782	Griffith Jenkin, Esq. . .	1808	Calvert Rich. Jones, Esq. .	1834
Ditto	1783	Sir John Morris, Bart. .	1809	Ditto, re-elected till Nov.	1835
Thomas Maddocks, Gent. .	1784	William Grove, Esq. . .	1810		

(MAYORS *hereafter take the place of Portreeves.*)

Nathaniel Cameron, Esq. .	1835	Michael J. Michael, Esq. .	1848	J. Trevillian Jenkin, Esq. .	1861
Ditto	1836	Christopher James, Esq. .	1849	Evan M. Richards, Esq. .	1862
Richard Mansel P., Esq. .	1837	Owen Gething W., Esq. .	1850	Charles Bath, Esq. . .	1863
John Grove, Esq. . .	1838	Thomas Edward T., Esq. .	1851	J. Clarke Richardson, Esq. .	1864
Lewis Weston Dillwyn, Esq.	1839	John J. Strick, Esq. . .	1852	George B. Strick, Esq. .	1865
Mathew Moggridge, Esq. .	1840	George Grant Francis, Esq.	1853	Thomas Phillips, Esq. . .	1866
Richard Aubrey, Esq. .	1841	J. Trevillian Jenkin, Esq. .	1854	George B. Brock, Esq. .	1867
Geo. Gwynne Bird, Esq. .	1842	Evan M. Richards, Esq. .	1855	Charles T. Wilson, Esq. .	1868
Starling Benson, Esq. . .	1843	John Oakshot, Esq. . .	1856	John Jones Jenkins, Esq. .	1869
John Richardson, Esq. .	1844	William H. Michael, Esq. .	1857	Washington Brown, Esq. .	1870
Charles H. Smith, Esq. .	1845	J. Trevillian Jenkin, Esq. .	1858	John Glasbrook, Esq. . .	1871-72
Timothy B. Essery, Esq. .	1846	Thomas Ed. Thomas, Esq. .	1859		
L. Llewelyn Dillwyn, Esq. .	1847	John Crow Richardson, Esq.	1860		

Note on Cromwell's Charter, 1655.

Under the years 1655-8 in the above list it is noticeable that the title "Portreeve" was changed into "Mayor." This was in virtue of the charter granted by Cromwell in 1655, which in its preamble says :—"Whereas our town of Swanzey, in our co. of Glamorgan, within our dominion of Wales, is an ancient port town, and populous, situate on the sea-coast towards France, convenient for shipping and resisting foreign invasions, and time out of mind hath been a town corporate," &c., &c. It then ordains that "the town shall be for ever hereafter adjudged a free town and borough, and that "the people therein dwelling, and hitherto called and known by the name of *Portreeve*, Aldermen, and Burgesses, &c., shall from henceforth and for ever be, continue, and remain one Body Politique and corporate in deed and in name, by the name of *Mayor*, Aldermen, and Burgesses of the 'town of Swanzey.'" The Protector then nominates "our well-beloved *Lewis Jones*, now Portreeve, to be the first and present Mayor ;" "our right trusty and well-beloved Councillor, *Philip Jones*, to be first and present *High Steward*; our well-beloved *Rowland Dawkins*, Lewis Jones, John Bowen, Henry Fleming, John Bennett, John Daniel, William Bayley, Mathew David, Thomas Williams, William Vaughan, William Jones, and Robert Jones, to be the first and present twelve *Aldermen ;*" "our beloved *John Price*, Esq., Evan Evan Lewis, John Matthew, David Griffiths, Jenkin Phillip, Thomas Phillip, David Bayley, John Williams, John Daniel, John Simond, John Richard, and Thomas Dollin, to be first and present twelve Capital *Burgesses ;*" and "our well-beloved *John Gibbs*, Esquire, to be first and present *Recorder*."

Common Seal of Swansea, *Temp.* King John.

THE COUNTY FAMILIES OF GLAMORGANSHIRE.

BUTE, John Patrick Crichton-Stuart, 3rd Marquess of, Cardiff Castle.

Cr. Marquess of Bute and Earl of Windsor (Gt. Brit.) 1796; Earl of Dumfries (Scot.) 1633; Lord Crichton (Scot.) 1488; Viscount Kingarth and Earl of Bute (Scot.) 1703; Lord Mount-Stuart (Scot.) 1761; Baron Cardiff of Cardiff Castle (Gt. Brit.) 1776; a baronet 1627. Knight of the Holy Sepulchre, and Grd. Cross of the Roman Order of St. Gregory; hereditary keeper of Rothesay Castle, which belongs to the Crown; hereditary Sheriff of Buteshire; only son of John, 2nd Marquess (*d.* March 18, 1848), and his second wife, Sophia Frederica Christina, dau. of 1st Marquess of Hastings; *b.* at Mountstuart, Isle of Bute, 12th Sept., 1847; *ed.* at Harrow and Ch. Ch., Oxon.; *s.* on the demise of the 2nd Marquess, 18th March, 1848; *m.*, April 16, 1872, to the Hon. Gwendaline Mary Anne (*b.* 1854), eldest dau. of Edward George Fitzalan, 1st Baron Howard of Glossop, Derbyshire, by Augusta, only dau. and h. of the Hon. George Henry Talbot, and niece of the 17th Earl of Shrewsbury.

Lord Howard, cr. Baron Howard of Glossop 1869, is 2nd son of Henry Charles, 13th Duke of Norfolk; Premier Duke and Hereditary Earl Marshal of England, by Lady Charlotte Sophia Leveson-Gower, eldest dau. of George, 1st Duke of Sutherland. The Howards are held to be of Saxon rather than of Norman origin; but first came into prominent notice *temp.* Edward I., when William Howard (see *Dugdale*) was Chief Justice of the Common Pleas, and held large possessions in the co. of Norfolk.

Heir presumptive: Lieut.-Col. Crichton-Stuart, M.P. for Cardiff, his 1st cousin.
Residences: Cardiff Castle, Glamorgan; Mountstuart, N.B.; Dumfries House, N.B.
Town Address: Carlton Club.
Arms: Quarterly, quartered: 1st and 4th grand quarters; 1st and 4th, or, a fesse, checky arg. and az., within a double tressure flory counter-flory gu.—STUART; 2nd and 3rd, arg., a lion rampant az.—CRICHTON: 2nd grand quarter, the arms of *Windsor*: 3rd grand quarter, per pale az. and gu., three lions rampant arg.—HERBERT, Earl of Pembroke.
Crests: 1st, a demi-lion rampant gu., over it the motto, *Nobilis est ira leonis—Stuart;* 2nd, a dragon vert, flames issuing from the mouth—*Crichton*; 3rd, a wyvern vert. holding in the mouth a sinister hand couped at the wrist—*Herbert*.
Supporters: *Dexter*, a horse arg. bridled gu.; *sinister*, a stag ppr. attired or.
Motto: Avito viret honore.

LINEAGE.

This noble family, in the male line, derives its descent from John, Sheriff of Bute 1400, nat. son of Robert II. of Scotland. Its entrance into Wales is of recent date, through marriage into the line of Herberts, Lords of Glamorgan. For a history of the Lords and lordship of Glamorgan, see, *ant'*, *Robert Fitzhamon, Earl of Gloucester; The De Clares; The Despencers; The Beauchamps; The Nevilles,* &c. For the *Herberts*, see *Earl of Pembroke and Powis, Herbert of Llanarth,* &c.

Lady Charlotte Herbert, dau. and heiress of Philip, 7th Earl of Pembroke, married Thomas, Viscount Windsor (Irel.), brother to the 1st Earl of Plymouth. Charlotte, dau. and heiress of the 2nd and last Visct. Windsor, and as such heiress of Cardiff Castle and estates, married, Nov. 12, 1766, John, 4th Earl of Bute, afterwards 1st Marquess of Bute.

William Herbert, son of Sir Richard Herbert, Kt., of Ewyas, by Margaret, dau. and heiress of Sir Matthew Cradock, Kt., of Swansea (see *Cradock of Swansea*), *m.* Anne, dau. of Thomas, Lord Parr, sister of Catherine Parr, Henry VIII.'s last wife, and was created by that king, 1551, Baron Herbert of Cardiff, and Earl of Pembroke. He obtained from the same king, and from Edward VI., the lordship of Glamorgan. Sixth in descent after William was Philip, 7th Earl, above named.

The issue of the marriage of his granddau. Charlotte with John, 1st Earl of Bute, was—

1. JOHN, the heir, *b.* 1767, but *d.* 1794, during the lifetime of his father; *m.*, 1792, Elizabeth, dau. and h. of Patrick Crichton, Earl of Dumfries, and left by her—

(1) JOHN, who became 2nd Marquess of Bute.
(2) Patrick James Herbert, whose son, Col. James Frederick Dudley Crichton, is present M.P. for Cardiff, and heir presumptive to the title.

2. Herbert Windsor, *b.* 1770, *d.* 1825.
3. Evelyn James, *b.* 1773, M.P. for Cardiff in several parlts. (*d.* 1842), usually called "Lord James Stuart."
4. Charles, served in the navy; lost at sea 1756.
5. Henry, *b.* 1777, *m* Gertrude Amelia, dau. and h. of George Villiers, Earl Grandison, and had issue; *d.* 1809.
6. William, *b.* 1778, Capt. R.N.; *m.*, and had issue a dau., who *d.* unm.
7. George, *b.* 1780; entered the navy, became Rear-Admiral and C.B.; *m.*, and had issue.
8. Maria Alicia Charles, *m.* to Charles Pinfold Esq.; *d.* 1841.
9. Charlotte, *m.* to Sir W. J. Homan, Bart.

By a second marriage 1800 (with Frances, dau. of Thomas Coutts, Esq., Lord Bute had additional issue:—
1. Dudley Coutts, who *m.* Christ. Alexandrine Egypta, dau. of Prince Lucien Bonaparte, of Canino.
2. Frances, *m.* to Dudley, Viscount Sandon.
JOHN, 2ND MARQUESS OF BUTE, K.T., F.R.S., &c., *s.*, 1803, to the Earldom of Dumfries, and in 1814, on the death of his grandfather, to the Marquisate of Bute; *m.* 1st, 1818, Lady Maria North, dau. of George, 3rd Earl of Guilford (she *d.* 1841, *s.p.*); 2nd, April 10th, 1845, Lady Sophia Christina Hastings, as above, and had issue an only child,—
JOHN PATRICK CRICHTON-STUART, the present Marquess, as above.

Note.—For a sketch of the history of *Cardiff Castle*, see pp. 461, 539, &c.; and for *Caerphilly Castle*, see p. 533, *et passim.* It is believed that the ancient "keep" of Cardiff Castle is a remain of the first erection by Fitzhamon. Great part of the present residential castle was built by Beauchamp, Earl of Warwick, *temp.* Henry VI. (see *The Beauchamps*); but it has been added to at different periods, and largely remodelled and renovated by the late Marquis of Bute. It has recently received and is in process of receiving extensive additions from the present noble owner—notably a campanile of great height and beauty, and its precincts are made more roomy and convenient.

The great docks of Cardiff, called the "Bute Docks," were commenced by the enterprise of the late Marquess, carried on by his trustees, and are still in course of augmentation under direction of the present Marquess, to whom they entirely belong.

BASSET, Richard, Esq., of Bonvilston House, Glamorgan.

J. P. and D. L. for the co. of Glamorgan; Major 1st Glam. R. V.; son of the late T. M. Basset, Esq. (*d.* 1840), of Bonvilston House; *b.* 1820; *m.*, 1843, Ann Maria, dau. of John Homfray, Esq., of Pennline Castle, co. of Glam., and has issue.

Heir: John Richard, *b.* 1839.
Residence: Bonvilston House, near Cowbridge.
Arms: Arg., a chevron between three bugle-horns stringed sa.

LINEAGE.

This family is a branch of the Basset house of Beaupré, originating in *Thomas Bassett*, youngest son of Jenkin, and brother of William Basset (Sheriff for Glamorgan A.D. 1557) above named. Thomas Bassett *m.* the heiress of Llantrithyd, and the family for two or three generations resided there. The present Richard Basset, Esq., of Bonvilston House, is 11th in descent from *Thomas Bassett* above named.

BASSET, William West James, Esq., of Beaupré, Glamorganshire.

A Major in the army; was Capt. 74th Highlanders; son of the late Col. William Bruce, K.H., of the 79th Highlanders, by Isabella, 3rd dau. of Col. Thomas Basset, by Elizabeth, dau. of Alexander Cruikshanks, Esq., of Aberdeen; *b.* 1830; *m.*, 1862, Eliza, dau. of Richard Weekes, Esq., Barrister-at-law, and has issue; succ. to the Beaupré estate, entailed upon him, on the death, 1865, of his aunt, Mrs. Basset, widow of Capt. Richard Basset, of Beaupré, his mother's brother, and thereupon assumed the surname *Basset* instead of Bruce.

Heir: William Richard, *b.* 1863.
Residence: Beaupré, near Cowbridge.
Arms: The Basset arms are —Arg., a chevron between three bugle-horns stringed sa.
Crest: A stag's head cabossed.
Motto: Gwell angau na chywilydd, "Better death than shame."

LINEAGE.

The Bassets have been in Glamorganshire in all probability since the time of the conquest of the lordship by the Normans, when Sir John Basset was vice-comes to Fitzhamon, and received, as is believed, the mesne lordship of *Maes-Essyllt*, or St. Hilary, which then or soon after received the N.-French name of *Beau-pré*, "fair meadow." The name Basset is found in the various rolls of *Battle Abbey* as that of one of the Conqueror's knights at the battle of Hastings; and although the Beaupré Basset cannot be distinctly traced to this man, he was at no great distance from him, and from the post of honour he filled under Fitzhamon may reasonably be conjectured to be of his family. (See *Beaupré Castle.*)

The first Bassets of Beaupré of whom we have historic certainty (probably son and grandson of the vice-comes just mentioned) were Ralph and his son, Richard de Basset, *temp.* Henry II., both successively Lords Justiciaries of England. Of the former of these, *Ordericus Vitalis* rather severely remarks that he was one of those "persons of low origin" whom for their obsequious services the king raised to the rank of nobles, taking them so to speak from the dust, exalting them above earls and distinguished lords of castles," &c. (*Lib.* XI., *cap.* ii.). At the same time, if his father or near relative was vice-comes under Fitzhamon, this account is scarcely faithful.

William Basset, Esq., of Beaupré, about ninth in lineal descent from Sir Ralph, was Shenff of Glamorgan A.D. 1557 (see *Sheriffs*). His grandson Richard filled the same office 1590 and 1608; and Richard's grandson William in 1621. William's eldest son,—

Sir Richard Basset, Kt., of Beaupré, Sheriff of Glam. 1641, *m.*, 1st, Mary, dau. of Edmund Thomas of Wenvoe, by whom he had a son, William, who *m.* and *d. s. p.*; 2ndly, Elizabeth, dau. of Edward Van, Esq., of Marcross, and had a son,—

Sir Richard Basset, Knt., of Beaupré, who, by his wife Priscilla, dau. of Philip Jones, Esq., of Fonmon (see *Jones of Fonmon*), had with other issue two sons, Philip and *Richard*, and three daus., who were all married. The line of Basset of Beaupré is continued through the grandson of Richard Thomas Basset, Esq., an officer in the army, who *m.*, 1790, Mary, dau. of Alexander Cruikshanks,

THE COUNTY FAMILIES OF GLAMORGANSHIRE. 621

Esq., of Aberdeen, and had, with other issue. a son, *Richard Basset*, Esq., late of Beaupré, and a dau., *Isabella*, *m.* to Major William Bruce, K.H., whose son William, on inheriting after the demise of his uncle Richard, who *d.* 1842, and of his aunt, Richard's widow, who *d.* 1856, assumed the name Basset, and is the present—
WILLIAM WEST JAMES BASSET, of Beaupré, as above.

BATH, Charles, Esq., Ffynone House, Glamorganshire.

J. P. for the co. of Glamorgan ; Capt. 4th Glam. Rifle Volunteers ; Mayor of Swansea 1864 ; Knight of the Sardinian Order of SS. Maurice and Lazarus ; member of Swansea School Board, &c. ; younger son of the late Henry Bath, Esq., of Swansea ; (see also *Bath of Alltyferin*, co. Carm.,) *b.* at Swansea, January 15, 1832 ; *ed.* at private schools, Swansea and Falmouth ; *m.*, August 12, 1856, Emily Elizabeth, youngest daughter and *co-heiress* of John Lucas Popkin, Esq.

The *Popkins* were an ancient Glamorganshire family of Ynystawe and Forest, on which patrimonies they continued for many generations (see *Popkin of Ynystawe*, &c.). In junior branches they were also of Danygraig and Llysnewydd, but all gradually became extinct. (See "J. H.'s" MS., pp. 40—43; and D. Jenkin's MS., *apud* Col. Francis, pp. 149—152.) *John Popkin*, about the end of the 18th cent., *m.* Sophia *Laugharn*, gr. granddau. of Arthur Laugharn, Esq., who was descended paternally from the Laugharns of St. Bride's, Pembr., and *m.* Elizabeth, dau. of David Owen, Esq., of Henllys, Pembr. (see *Laugharn of St. Bride's*, and *Owen of Henllys*). Arthur Laugharn bore on his shield the arms of Laugharn (gu., 3 wolves' heads erased or, in a bordure), impaling those of Owen of Henllys (a boar arg. chained to a holly tree proper). See ancient *pedigree* of Laugharns, &c., in the possession of Charles Bath, Esq. John, son of John Popkin and Sophia Laugharn, *m.* Barbara Ann Lucas; and his son, John Lucas Laugharn, by his wife, Livia Wozencraft, had three daus., Mary Ann (*m.* Rev. Lewis Morgan), Sophia (*m.* J. C. Richardson, Esq.), and EMILY ELIZABETH, as above.

Residence: Ffynone House, Swansea.
Arms: Gu., a chevron paly of six arg. and or, between three plates, on a chief or three wolves' heads erased sa.
Crest: A wolf's head erased, gorged with a collar vair, holding in the mouth a rose slipped proper.
Motto: Habere et dispertire.

BEAUFORT, Duke of, Henry Charles Fitzroy Somerset.

(See *Beaufort, Duke of, Troy House, co. of Monmouth.*)

BEVAN, Robert Cooper Lee, Esq., of Fosbury, Berks, and Trent Park, Enfield.

Justice of the Peace for Middlesex; a banker, city of London ; eldest son of the late David Bevan, Esq., of Fosbury, Wilts, and Belmont, Herts, who *d.* 1846 (see *Lineage*); *b.* Feb. 8, 1809, at Walthamstow, Essex ; *ed.* at Harrow and Trinity Coll., Oxon. ; *m.*, 1st, Feb. 28, 1836, Lady Agneta Elizabeth Yorke, only dau. of Admiral Sir Joseph Sydney York, K.C.B., and sister of Charles Philip, 4th Earl of Hardwicke ; she had precedence as an earl's daughter granted her by royal warrant, dated 10th Feb., 1836 (*b.* 9th Dec., 1811; *d.* July 8, 1851); and was buried at Trent Park, Enfield ; 2ndly, Emma Frances Shuttleworth, eldest daughter of the late Bishop of Chichester; *s.* 1846 ; has issue 7 sons and 6 daughters by both wives.

Heir: Sydney Bevan, *b.* 6th Oct., 1838, in York Terrace, Regent's Park ; baptized 21st April following, at Trent Church, Enfield.
Residences: Fosbury, Hungerford, Berkshire ; Trent Park, Enfield, Mid.
Town House: 25, Princes Gate, Kensington, S.W.
Arms: Quarterly : 1st and 4th, ermine, a bull passant gu. between three annulets of the same, two in chief, one in base—BEVAN ; 2nd and 3rd, az., three bars engrailed or, over all a bend lozengy arg. and gu.—LEE.
Crest: A wyvern or, semée of annulets, holding in its claws two annulets gu.
Mottoes: Non sine industriâ ; Deus praesidium.

LINEAGE.

This ancient family derives its descent from Iestyn ap Gwrgant, the last Prince of Glamorgan, son of Gwrgant ap Ithel, Prince of Glamorgan, who lived in Cardiff Castle *circa* A.D. 1030, and Gwladus, daughter of Ednowen Bendew, Lord of Tegeingl (part of the present Flintshire), founder of one of the fifteen tribes of North Wales, 11th century. (See *Ednowain Bendew*, p. 438.)

PATERNAL DESCENT.

Iestyn ap Gwrgant, Prince of Glamorgan, *m.* Denis, dau. of Bleddyn ap Cynfyn, Prince of Powys ; 2ndly, Angharad, dau. of Elystan Glodrudd, Prince of Ferlex, by whom he had—
Caradog ap Iestyn, Lord of Avan, who *m.* Gwladus, dau. of Gruffydd ap Rhys ap Tewdwr, Prince of South Wales. His son,—
Morgan ap Caradog, Lord of Avan, *m.* Gwenllian, dau. of Ifor *Bach*, Lord of Caerphili (see *Ivor Bach*), and had issue Morgan Gam ap Morgan ap Caradog, Lord of Avan, whose son,—
Morgan Fychan ap Morgan, Lord of Blaenbaglan (near Aberavon, Glam.), *m.* Elen, dau. of Howell Fychan, Lord of Cilfai, and had a son,—
Rhys ap Morgan Fychan, of Blaenbaglan, who *m.* the dau. of Griffith ap Ivor, and had issue—
Leyson ap Rhys of Blaenbaglan. He *m.* Gwladus,

dau. of Howell ap Griffith Fychan ap Griffith-Gwyr, Lord of Gower. The issue of this marriage was the well-known—

Evan ap Leyson of Blaenbaglan, who *m*. Jennet, dau. of Gwilym ap Howel Fychan ap Howel Melyn. Hopkin ap Evan ap Leyson of Blaenbaglan. *m*. Gwladus, dau. of Jenkin ap Rhys Fychan. Their son, William ap Hopkin of Blaenbaglan, *m*. Lucy, dau. of Hopkin Lewellyn Lloyd of Llangynwyd. Their son,—

Hopkin ap William of Blaenbaglan, *m*. Gwyrfil, dau. of Jenkin Rhys ap Jenkin of Glyn-nêdd (Vale of Neath), and left a son,—

David ap Hopkin of Blaenbaglan, after of Cwrt-y-Bettws, who *m*. Elen, dau. of Henry Fychan. Their son,—

Jenkin ap David of Cwrt-y-Bettws, or Bettws Court, in the hamlet of Penisa'r-coed ("lower woodland"), in the parish of Cadoxton, near Neath, *m*. Mary, dau. of Jenkin ap Rhys, and left a son,—

Thomas ap Jenkin, who by his wife, Gwladus, dau. of Lleyson ap Rhys, had a son,—

Hopkin ap Thomas, who *m*. Angharad, dau. of Thomas ap Llewelyn. Their son,—

David ap Hopkin, *m*. Mary, dau. of Evan ap Llewelyn. Their son, Hopkin ap Davydd, *m*. Siwan, dau. of Rhys Gethin ; and their son,—

Thomas ap Hopkin, *m*. Sarah, dau. of Meredydd Ddu ("the black"). Their son, William ap Thomas, *m*. Elizabeth, dau. of Davydd Llwyd, whose son, Owen ap William of Cwrt-y-Bettws, *m*. Gwenllian, dau. of Rhys ap Evan. Their 2nd son, Evan ap Owen, *m*. Jennet Morgan, and left a son,—

Jenkin *ap* Evan, otherwise Jenkin *Bevan*.

Jenkin Bevan, of Rhosilly, in Gower, co. of Glamorgan (who first settled this surname *Bevan*), *m*. Elizabeth, dau. of Rev. Peter ———, afterwards Rector of Rhosilly. His 3rd son,—

William Bevan, of the town of Swansea, co. of Glamorgan, became a Quaker (*d*. 5th Dec., 1702, æt. 75 ; buried in the Friends' Burial-ground, Swansea. Will is dated 7th Jan., 1700 ; codicil, 6th June, 1701. Proved 24th Feb. following at Carmarthen). His wife was named Priscilla, and she was buried with her husband. His son,—

Silvanus Bevan, Esq., of the town of Swansea, was 4th but 2nd surviving son ; *b*. 9th Aug., 1661; proved his father's will as above in 1701 (*d*. 4th Dec., 1725 ; buried at Swansea ;) *m*. 14th Feb., 1685, Jane, dau. of William Phillips of Swansea ; *d*. 14th Nov., 1727. His 4th son,—

Timothy Bevan, Esq., of Hackney, co. Middlesex (*b*. 2nd July, 1704 ; *d*. 12th June, 1786); *m*., 8th Sept., 1735 at the "Bull and Mouth," Elizabeth, dau. of David Barclay, Esq., of London ; *d*. 30th August, 1745, æt. 32, at Hackney. His son,—

Silvanus Bevan, Esq., of Fosbury House, co. Wilts, 3rd but eldest surviving son and heir (*b*. 3rd Oct., 1743 ; *d*. 25th Jan., 1830, æt. 87 ; buried at St. Nicholas, Brighton), by his second wife, Louisa Kendall (*b*. 1749 ; *m*., 23rd Sept., 1773, at St. Giles's ; *d*. 1838 ; buried at St. Nicholas, Brighton), had, with other issue,—

David Bevan, Esq., of Fosbury House, co. Wilts, of Trent Park, Enfield, Middlesex, and of Belmont, Herts, his eldest son and heir ; *b*. 6th Nov., 1774 (*d*. at Belmont, 24th Dec., 1846, æt. 72 ; buried at Trent Church). He *m*., 30th April, 1798, at St. Marylebone, Favell Bourke, only dau. and only child that left issue of Robert Cooper Lee, Esq., sometime of the island of Jamaica, and afterwards of Bedford Square, St. Pancras, co. of Middlesex. She *d*. 25th August, 1841, æt. 60, and was buried in Trent Church, Enfield. His eldest son and heir is—

ROBERT COOPER LEE BEVAN, Esq., of Fosbury House, co. Wilts, and of Trent Park, Enfield, co. Middlesex, as above.

There is also another branch of the BEVAN family through the common ancestors, Silvanus Bevan of Swansea, and Jane, dau. of William Phillips, of the same place.

Paul Bevan, of the town of Swansea, 5th and youngest son of the above Silvanus Bevan (*b*. 19th Dec., 1705 ; *d*. 9th Jan., 1767, æt. 61); *m*., 9th May, 1754, Elizabeth, eldest dau. of Richard and Esther Phillips of Swansea (*d*. 15th May, 1771, æt. 47). He left a son,—

Silvanus Bevan, co. Glamorgan (*b*. 13th Sept., 1758 ; *d*. 15th July, 1783 ; buried at Swansea), who *m*., 17th Nov., 1780 Mary, dau. of Edward and Anna Fox, of Wadebridge, co. Cornwall (*d*. 1787 ; buried in Cornwall). By her he left a second and only surviving son,—

Paul Bevan, Esq., of Tottenham. Middlesex (*b*. 30th Aug., 1783 ; *d*. 12th June, 1868), who *m*., 1st, 24th Oct., 1804, Rebecca, dau. of Jasper and Anne Capper, of London, who *d*. 9th Nov., 1817 ; 2ndly, May, 1831, Judith Nicholls Dillwyn, who *d*. 27th June, 1868. He left issue surviving by the 1st wife,—

1. WILLIAM BEVAN, Esq., of the Old Jewry, city of London, and St. Stephen's Square, Bayswater, solicitor, now living.

2. *Samuel Bevan*, Esq., of Rosewood, Pangbourne, Berks, now living.

3. Mary, only dau., *m*. to Alfred Waterhouse, Esq., of Whiteknights Park, Reading, Berks.

BIDDULPH, John, Esq., of Swansea, Glamorgan.

J. P. and D. L. for the co. of Glamorgan ; 2nd son of the late John Biddulph, Esq., of Ledbury, and brother of the late Robert Biddulph, Esq., of Ledbury, M.P. for the city of Hereford ; *b*. 1804 ; *m*. the only dau. of the late William Chambers, Esq., of Llanelly ; was formerly of Dderwen, near Swansea.

Note.—The Biddulphs of Ledbury have been resident upon their estate there from the time of Anthony Biddulph, who was Sheriff for the co. of Hereford in 1694. They were descended from the Biddulphs of Elmhurst, *circa* 1550. (See further, *Myddelton Biddulph of Chirk Castle*.)

BLOSSE, Ven. Archd. Henry Lynch, Newcastle House, Glamorganshire.

Archdeacon of Llandaff ; M.A. ; Preb. of Caerau in Llandaff Cathedral 1859 ; Vicar of Newcastle, Dio. of Llandaff, 1839 ; Surrogate and Rural Dean ; J. P. for the co. of Glamorgan ; is patron of the livings of Bishton, Kilgwrrwg, Llanvihangel Tor y Mynydd, St. Lythan's ; son of the late Sir Robert Lynch Blosse, Bart., of Castle Carra, co. Mayo, and brother of the present Sir

Robert of the same place; *b.* 1814, at Gabalva, near Cardiff; *ed.* at Trinity College, Dublin; *gr.* A.B. 1835, M.A. 1860; *m.*, in 1843, to Charlotte Fanny, daughter of Rev. Robert Knight, Tythegston Court, Glam.; has issue 4 sons, 5 daughters.

Heir: Robert Charles Lynch Blosse, *b.* 1848.
Residences: Newcastle House, Bridgend; the Canonry, Llandaff.
Motto: Nec temere nec timide.

BOOKER, Thomas William, Esq., of Velindre, Glamorganshire.

J. P. and D. L. for the co. of Glamorgan; son of the late Thomas William Booker Blackmore, Esq., M.P. for Herefordshire, who assumed the surname Booker in place of his own of Blackmore; *b.* at Velindre, 1830; *m.*, 1861, Caroline Emily, daughter of the late Robert Lindsay, Esq., of Glanafon; has issue six daughters.

Residence: Velindre, Cardiff, Glamorganshire.
Arms: Per pale, or and vert, an eagle displayed within a bordure charged with four roundels and four fleurs-de-lis all counterchanged.
Crest: On a wreath of the colours, a demi-eagle displayed or, in the beak a fleur-de-lis vert.
Motto: Ad cœlum tendit.

Note.—*Velindre* is a local name whose etymology is clear and significant, but whose form has been slightly marred by a provincial more than by an English pronunciation. The name, signifying the "mill-house," or "mill-residence" (W., *melin*—hill, *tre*—abode), should of course terminate with an *e*, but it is usually spelled Velindra.

BROGDEN, Alexander, Esq., of Coytrehen, Glamorganshire.

M.P. for Wednesbury (elected 1868); a magistrate for the county of Lancaster; eldest son of the late John Brogden, Esq., of Sale, near Manchester, by Sarah Hannah, daughter of Alexander McWilliams, Esq.; *b.* at Sale, 1825; *ed.* at King's College, London; *m.*, 1848, Anne, daughter of the late James Garstang, Esq., of Manchester, and has issue one son and one daughter.

Heir: James Garstang Brogden, *b.* 1850.
Residences: Coytrehên House, Bridgend; Lightburne House, Ulverston; Holm Island, Grange, Lancashire.
Town Address: 6, Belgrave Mansions, S.W.; Reform Club, S.W.
Arms: Quarterly: 1st and 4th, gu., fretty arg., a chief or—BROGDEN; 2nd and 3rd, az., three lozenges or pierced, a chief arg. within a bordure engrailed—GARSTANG.
Crest: From a ducal crown a hand and arm holding a rose proper.
Motto: Constans et fidelis.

Note.—*Coytrehên* (*Coed-tre-hên*), "the ancient wood-house," like *Tondû*, belonged in the 17th and 18th centuries to the influential family of the Powells. The modern spelling is marred especially by a terminal *e*, which disguises the etymological significancy of the word. The W. *hên*, with the vowel lengthened, and sounded like *a* in mane, gives the meaning of "old" or "ancient." As a matter of linguistic accuracy it is of use that local names should be preserved as far as possible in their integrity.

BROGDEN, James, Esq., of Tondû, Glamorganshire.

Justice of the Peace for the County of Glamorgan; F.G.S.; fourth son of the late John Brogden, Esq., of Sale, near Manchester, by Sarah Hannah, dau. of Alexander McWilliams; *b.* at Manchester, 1832; *ed.* at King's College, London; *m.*, 1859, Helen Milne, daughter of the late Captain Milne, of Aden; and has issue.

Heir: Duncan Dunbar, *b.* 1861.
Residence: Tondû House, Bridgend, Glamorgan.
Town Address: 4, Queen's Square, Westminster.
Arms: Per pale: *dexter*, gu., fretty arg., a chief or—BROGDEN; *sinister*, quarterly,—1st and 4th, per bend arg. and gu., 3 roses counterchanged; 2nd and 3rd, gu., a lion rampant or, on a chief or embattled, two Cornish choughs ppr.
Crest: Out of a ducal crown, a dexter hand and arm holding a rose-bud ppr.
Motto: Constans et fidelis.

Note.—*Tondû* was well known in the 17th and 18th centuries as the residence of the Powell family of the lineage of Powell of *Llwydiarth* and *Coetre-hên*, from whom also came the Powells of *Enê'rglyn*. The Powells, of Tondû supplied several sheriffs for the co. of Glamorgan. They were of the sept of Einion ap Collwyn. (See also *Powell of Maesteg and Llanharan.*)

BRUCE, Right Hon. Henry Austin, of Dyffryn, Glamorganshire.

Called to the Bar at Lincoln's Inn 1843; was appointed Police Magistrate at Merthyr Tydfil; J. P. and D. L. for the co. of Glamorgan; M.P. for Merthyr 1852—1868; became Under Secretary for the Home Department 1862; Vice-President of the Committee of Council 1864; Charity Commissioner, and Member of the Privy Council, 1864; M.P. for Renfrewshire 1868—1872; Secretary for the Home Department 1869; second son of John Bruce *Pryce*, Esq., of Dyffryn, St. Nicholas, co. of Glamorgan (son of John Knight, Esq., of Llanblethian), who, instead of his own surname, assumed that of *Bruce*, his mother's maiden surname (as did also his brother, James Lewis Knight, afterwards Lord Justice Sir J. L. Knight Bruce, *d.* 1867); and subsequently, on inheriting under the will of Thomas Pryce,

Esq., of Dyffryn-Goluwch, that of *Pryce;* but was not herein followed by his sons, who have retained the surname *Bruce;* b. 1815; *m.*, 1st, 1846, Annabella, dau. of Richard Beadon, Esq., of Clifton (she *d.* 1852); 2ndly, 1854, Norah, dau. of the late Lieut.-Gen. Sir William Napier, K.C.B., and has issue.

Heir: Henry Campbell Bruce, *b.* 1851.
Residence: Dyffryn, near Aberdare.
Town House: 1, Queen's Gate, W.
Arms: 1st, gu. 3 chevrons arg. a crescent for difference—PRYCE; 2nd, or, a saltire gu. on a chief of the last a martlet or—BRUCE.

LINEAGE.

For lineage, see hereafter, *Bruce Pryce of Dyffryn.*

CARNE, John Whitlock Nicholl-, Esq., of Dimlands and St. Donat's Castle, Glamorganshire.

D.C.L., M.A.; J. P. and D. L. for the co. of Glamorgan; Barrister-at-law (called to the Bar by the Society of the Inner Temple, 1840), was on the Oxford and South Wales Circuits; Chairman of P. Sessions; late Commissioner in Bankruptcy; Patron of St. Donat's Vicarage, co. Glamorgan; author of an "Essay on the Improvement of Time," and "The Art of Poetry;" son of the late Rev. Robert Nicholl and Elizabeth Carne, his wife, dau. and h. of Captain Charles Loder Carne, R.N., of Nash Manor; *b.* at Dimlands (Glamorganshire), 17th April, 1816; *ed.* at Jesus College, Oxford; *grad.* B.A. 1837, M.A. 1839, D.C.L. 1843; became F.S.A. 1848; *m.*, 10th April, 1844, Mary Jane, only dau. of Peter Whitfield Brancker, Esq., of Field House, Wavertree, Liverpool; *s.* to Llantwit estates 1849, Park Newydd, Llanwonno, in 1854, St. Donat's estate 1861, Nash 1869; has issue 2 sons and 4 daus. living (1 son and 2 daus. dead). Eldest son was Edward Stradling Nicholl, *b.* 8th Sept., 1849; *d.* 1st July, 1862.

Heir: John Devereux Vann Loder, *b.* 1854.
Residences: Dimlands, Cowbridge; St. Donat's Castle, Bridgend.
Arms: Sa., 3 pheons arg., for NICHOLL; gu., pelican in her piety or, for CARNE.
Crest: On a tower, a Cornish chough, wings expanded ppr.—*Nicholl;* out of ducal coronet a pelican displayed with 2 heads —*Carne.*
Mottoes: En toute loyale. Heb Dduw heb ddim; Duw a digon.

LINEAGE.

This family derives its descent from Ynyr, King of Gwent (9th cent.), whose grandson *Dyfrig,* or Devereux, who lived at the time of the Conquest, first assumed the name of *Carne,* from a place called *Pen Carne,* in Monmouthshire, where he was nurtured. It intermarried in early times with the families of Herbert, Mansel, Stradling, Berkrolles, Loder, St. Maur, Gamage, De Lacy, Giles, Fleming, Whitlock, Poyntz, &c.; and among its distinguished members in past time may be named Sir Edward Carne, of Ewenny (fifth in the Ewenny line, which began with Sir Edward, second son of Howel Carne, of Nash), Commissioner for the Suppression of the Monasteries, *temp.* Henry VIII., and purchased Ewenny Abbey at its dissolution; Sir Edward Carne, of Nash, Teller of the Exchequer and Receiver-General for S. Wales; Sir Augustine Nicholl, Chief Justice; Sir Bulstrode Whitlock, Judge of Common Pleas under the Commonwealth; &c.

Sir Edward Carne, Kt., of Nash, just named (fifteenth in descent in the Nash senior line), *m.* Anne, fourth dau. of Sir Edward Mansel of Margam, and left a son and successor, William Carne, Esq., who by his wife Jane, dau. and h. of William Thomas, Esq., of Llanfihangel (see *Thomas of Llanfihangel*), left with other issue a son,—

Thomas Carne, Esq., of Nash, who *m.* Jane, dau. of Sir Edward Stradling, Bart., of St. Donat's. He was Sheriff of Glamorgan in 1690 (see *Sheriffs,* where it will be seen that Carnes of Ewenny were sheriffs in 1543, 1555, 1562, 1572, 1581, 1588, 1601, 1620, &c.). His grandson,—

Edward Carne, Esq., of Nash, *m.* Grace, dau. of Edward Mathew, Esq., of Aberaman, Sheriff of Glam. 1693 (see *Mathew of Llandaff, Radir, Aberaman,* &c.), and had a large family. His eldest son and heir was—

John Carne, Esq., of Nash, Sheriff of Glam. 1731; *m.*, July 8, 1728, Elizabeth, dau. and co-h. of Charles Loder, Esq., of Hinton.

John Carne Clerk, his eldest son (his second son, Rev. Edward Carne, B.D., Rector of St. Athan's, *d. unm.;* but his third son, *Capt. Charles Loder Carne, R.N., m.*, and had issue *Elizabeth,* of whom again), *m.* Eleanor his first cousin (dau. of Richard Carne, Esq., fifth son of Edward Carne, of Nash, and Grace his wife above named), and had issue a dau. and only surviving child, Eleanor. He *d.* at Nash, 1798, *æt.* 66.

Eleanor Carne, of Nash, *b.* Nov. 18, 1769; *m.*, Aug. 29th, 1798, Thomas Markham, Esq., of Cheltenham, and *d. s. p.* 1842, when the estates fell to *Elizabeth* Carne above named, who *m.* as her second husband—

The Rev. Robert Nicholl of Dimlands, son of Whitlock Nicholl, Esq., of the Ham, co. Glamorgan (of the family of Nicholl of Llantwit Major, descended from the Turbervilles—see *Turberville of Coity*), who inherited in right of his wife, and assumed her surname of *Carne* in addition to his own. He had, besides four daus.—Emma Anne, Anna Maria, Ellen Louisa, and Frances Susan,— two sons,—

1. ROBERT CHARLES NICHOLL-CARNE, Esq., of Nash, J. P. and D. L. of co. Glamorgan; called to the Bar; *m.*, 1838, Sarah Jane, dau. and co-h. of Rev. N. Poyntz, M.A., of Alvescot House, Oxfordshire (she *d. s. p.* 1861). Mr. Nicholl-Carne *d. s. p.* 1869.

2. JOHN WHITLOCK NICHOLL-CARNE, Esq., now of Dimlands, St. Donat's Castle, Nash, &c., as above.

*Note.—*For a notice of *St. Donat's Castle,* see under that title *ante. Dimlands* was altered and improved 1850-1. The restoration of St. Donat's Castle, commenced in 1861, is not yet quite completed. On the estate is *Gwrgant's-town*, once the seat of Iestyn ap Gwrgant, and several Roman and Danish encampments. There was a monastery of Black Benedictines at Nash.

CLARK, George Thomas, Esq., of Dowlais House, Glamorganshire.

J. P. and D. L. for the co. of Glamorgan; High Sheriff of Glamorgan in 1868; Chairman of Merthyr Board of Guardians; Hon. Col. of 2nd Adm. Bat. of Glamorgan Rifle Volunteers; author of various papers, chiefly in antiquarian journals, History of Castle of St. Donat's, &c.; son of the Rev. Geo. Clark, A.M., of Trin. Coll., Camb., by Clara, dau. of Thomas Dicey, Esq.; *b.* at Chelsea, 1809; *ed.* at the Charterhouse; *m.*, in 1850, Ann Price, 2nd dau. of the late Henry Lewis, Esq., of Park, co. Glamorgan, and sister to Henry Lewis, Esq., of Greenmeadow, co. Glamorgan; has issue 1 son and 1 dau.

Residences: Dowlais House, Merthyr Tydfil; Talygarn, Cardiff.
Arms: Gu., a fleur-de-lis or, in chief a canton ermine.
Crest: A lion rampant or.
Mottoes: " Non major alio non minor ; " over crest, " Try and tryst."

LINEAGE.

This family is of Staffordshire origin, descended from Joseph Clark, who was of Burton in 1500. Among its members have been various authors of more or less distinction, chiefly divines bearing the name of Samuel, of whom were the martyrologist; the editor of an early and learned Harmony of the Gospels; and Dr. S. Clark, of St. Alban's, author of the well-known "Promises of Scripture." For the Lewis lineage see *Lewis of Greenmeadow, Lewis of Van,* &c.

CORBETT, John Stuart, Esq., Cogan Pill, Glamorganshire.

J. P. for the co. of Glamorgan; son of the late Ven. Archdeacon Stuart Corbett, of York; *b.* 1816, at Wortley, near Sheffield; *m.*, 1844, Miss Elizabeth Evan, of the Gothic, Radnorshire; has issue three sons and one daughter.

Heir: John Stuart.
Residence: Cogan Pill, near Cardiff.

Note.—*Cogan Pill* is an ancient mansion (recently restored and altered) which was built and for several generations inhabited by the Herberts. We have account that William Herbert, Esq., was Sheriff of co. Glam. 1551—1556, son of Sir George Herbert, Kt., of Swansea, who was of Cogan Pill, and built the house there. This early structure appears to have been on an extensive scale, of superior construction, and in the Gothic style. During recent alterations a fine Gothic arch, long filled up and plastered over, was brought to view, and has been carefully preserved. The mansion of Cogan Pill has descended, with the other estates of the Herberts in Glamorganshire, to the Marquess of Bute.

CRAWSHAY, Robert Thompson, Esq., of Cyfarthfa Castle, Glamorganshire.

Son of the late William Crawshay, Esq., of Caversham Park, Berks, and Cyfarthfa Castle, Sheriff of Glamorganshire 1828-9, well known as the great ironmaster in South Wales; *b.* at Cyfarthfa, 1817; *m.*, 1846, dau. of N. N. Yeates, Esq., and has issue three sons and two daughters.

Residences: Cyfarthfa Castle, Glam.; Cathedine, Brec.
Arms: A plough and dog, upon cannon balls.
Motto: Perseverance.

LINEAGE.

This family derives its descent from the Crawshays of Normanton, Yorkshire. See further *Cyfarthfa Castle.*

DAVIES, Rees Edward, Esq., of Gwaelod-y-Garth, Glamorganshire.

A Barrister-at-law; called at the Inner Temple 1864; J. P. for the co. of Glamorgan; son of William Davies, Esq., of The Mardy, co. Glamorgan, by Mary, dau. and co-heir of Rees Davies, Esq., of Mirlanga; *b.* at Gwaelod-y-Garth, Oct. 25, 1841; *ed.* at Christ Church, Oxford; *grad.* B.A. and B.C.L.; 1st class in Law and Modern History; *m.*, April 8, 1869, Florence, only dau. of the Rev. Robert Gandall, M.A., Laudian Professor of Arabic in the University of Oxford, by Louisa, eldest dau. of Thomas Pearse, Esq., of Warnborough, Hants, and granddau. of the late Lord Charles Kerr; *s.* on the death of his elder brother, 1859; had issue a dau., Gwendoline, *d.* June 12, 1870.

Heir presumptive: His brother, Augustus Richard, Lieut. 22nd Foot.
Residence: Gwaelod-y-Garth, Merthyr Tydfil, Glamorganshire.
Town Addresses: 4, King's Bench Walk, Inner Temple; and New University Club, St. James's.

LINEAGE AND HISTORY.

The family continues in possession of the old estate upon which their ancestors resided for generations. Of the two old houses, however, belonging to it, Mirlanga was abandoned in a ruinous state about 1780; and The Mardy, built at a very early date, had not of late years been occupied by the family except at intervals, and in 1869 the

remaining fragment was taken down. The estate, by gifts and devises, with their attendant litigation, has at different times been greatly curtailed. One of these devises was as early as 1558 the subject of a suit in chancery. No addition to this property has been made since 1727, when some neighbouring farms were purchased by Thomas Lewis ap Richard, of The Mardy. It was with his eldest son and heir, DAVID ap Thomas, that the old Welsh intermittent system of name-giving ended, and the present surname of Davies (ap David) originated. From father to son the Mirlanga property descended in the male line until the death of Rees Davies in 1816. He by his wife Jane, dau. and subsequently heiress of Samuel Rees, Esq., left two daughters, co-heirs. The elder, Margaret, m., 1st, D. W. Meyrick, Esq , of The Gaer ; and 2nd, E. L. Richards, Esq., for many years Chairman of Quarter Sessions for Flintshire. By her death *s. p.* in 1845 her moiety of the estate passed to her sister Mary, owner and co-heiress of the other moiety. She in 1836 m. William Davies, Esq. (see above), younger son of William Davies, Esq., of Pentremawr, and by him, who d. in 1848, and whom she survived but a fortnight, left issue surviving—
1. William Rees D. Davies, d. unm. 1859.
2. REES EDWARD (as above).
3. Arthur Rowland, of Christ Church, Oxford, d. unm. 1868.
4. Augustus Richard, Lieut. 22nd Foot.

DAVIS, David, Esq., Maes-y-Ffynon, Glamorganshire.

J. P. for the co. of Glamorgan ; son of the late David Davis, Esq., of Blaen-gwawr, Aberdare ; (a younger brother is Lewis Davis, Esq., of Preswylfa, Cardiff, and Brynderwen, Pontypridd ;) b. Sept. 13, 1821 ; m., Nov. 3, 1846, to Caroline Jones, dau. of John Jones, Esq., Dowlais ; has issue 1 son and 3 daus.

Residence: Maes-y-ffynon, Aberdare.

DILLWYN, Lewis Llewelyn, Esq., of Hendrefoilan, Glamorganshire.

M.P. for the Borough of Swansea since 1855 ; F.G.S. ; J. P. and D. L. for co. of Glamorgan ; Major Commandant 3rd Glamorgan Volunteer Rifles ; Director of the Great Western Railway Co. ; Chairman of the Directors of the Glamorganshire Banking Co. ; son of the late Lewis Weston Dillwyn, Esq., J. P. and D. L. for the co. of Glam., Sheriff for the same 1818, and M.P. 1835-7, by Mary, dau. of the late John Llewelyn, Esq., of Penlle'rgaer ; b. May 19, 1814, at Swansea ; ed. at Bath ; m., 1838, Elizabeth, daughter and heiress of Sir H. de la Beche, C.B., the eminent geologist ; has issue one son and three daughters.

Heir: His son, Henry de la Beche Dillwyn, b. 1843.

Residence: Hendrefoilan, near Swansea.
Town Address: 10, Princes Terrace, S.W.
Arms: Gu., on a chevron arg., three trefoils slipped of the first.
Crest: A stag's head couped proper.
Motto: Craignez honte.

LINEAGE.

This family derives its descent from Sir John Dilwyn, of Dilwyn, co. Hereford. The family afterwards settled at Langorse, Breconshire, and in 1699 William Dillwyn, the great-great-grandfather of the present representative, emigrated from Breconshire to Philadelphia ; his grandson, William Dillwyn, returned to England, and settled at Higham Lodge, near Walthamstow.

DUNRAVEN, Windham Thomas, 4th Earl of, Dunraven Castle, Glamorganshire.

Baron Adare (*cr.* 1800) ; Viscount Mount-Earl (*cr.* 1816) ; Viscount Adare and Earl of Dunraven (*cr.* 1822),—all in the peerage Ireland ; Baron Kenry, of Kenry, in the Peerage of Great Britain (*cr.* 1866) ; a Baronet (*cr.* 1781).
Was a Lieut. in the 1st Life Guards, and Aide-de-camp to Lord Kimberley, Lord Lieut. of Ireland 1866 ; Lieut. in 4th Oxford R. V. ; son of the late Edwin Richard Windham Wyndham Quin, 3rd Earl of Dunraven (*d.* 1872), M.P. for the co. of Glamorgan 1837—51, by his wife, Augusta, dau. of Thomas Goold, Esq., a Master in the Irish Chancery (she *d.* 1866) ; *b.* 1841 ; *ed.* at Chr. Ch., Oxon. ; *m.*, 1869, Florence, dau. of Lord Charles Lennox Kerr, son of 6th Marquess of Lothian, by Emma Charlotte, sister of Sir John Hanmer, Bart., of Bettisfield, M.P. ; *s.* to the title, Dunraven estates, &c., on the demise of his father, 1872.

Residences: Dunraven Castle, near Bridgend ; Adare Manor, near Limerick.
Town House: 5, Buckingham Gate.
Arms: Quarterly, quartered : gr. quarters, 1st and 4th, vert, a pegasus passant ermine, a chief or – QUIN ; 2nd and 3rd, gu., a hand couped at the wrist, holding a dagger ppr., in chief two crescents arg.—O'QUIN OF MUNSTER ; 2nd and 3rd, az., a chevron between 3 lions' heads erased or—WYNDHAM.
Crests: 1. A wolf's head, couped arg.—*Quin* ; 2. A lion's head erased within a fetterlock or—*Wyndham.*
Supporters: Two ravens ppr., collared and lined or.

LINEAGE.

This family in the male descent is of Irish lineage. Its connection with Glamorgan originated in the purchase of Dunraven from Sir George Vaughan (see *Vaughan of Dunraven*), 1642, by Humphrey Wyndham, Esq. (Sheriff of Glamorgan 1654), and the marriage of that gentleman with a

THE COUNTY FAMILIES OF GLAMORGANSHIRE.

Welsh lady of an ancient Cymric family, viz., Jane Carne, of Ewenny (see *Carne of St. Donat's*, &c.), in 1656. His son, John Wyndham (*d.* 1697), was *s.* by his son Francis, who left an only dau ,— Joan Wyndham, heiress of his estate, who *m.* Francis Wyndham, Esq., of Clearwell ; he *m.* secondly Catherine, dau. and h. of Sir Humphry Edwin, Kt., of Llanfihangel, near Cowbridge (see *Thomas of Llanfihangel*). His son from the second marriage, Charles Wyndham, assumed his mother's maiden name of Edwin (see *Parl. Annals for co., ann.* 1780—89), and was *s.* by his son,— Thomas Wyndham, Esq., of Dunraven, M.P. for many years for the co. of Glam. (see *Parl. Annals*, 1789–1812). He left an only dau. and h.,— Caroline Wyndham, who *m.*, Dec., 1810, Windham Henry (Wyndham) Quin, Lord Adare, 2nd Earl of Dunraven (*d.* 1850). He assumed thereupon the surname *Wyndham* prefixed to that of *Quin*, and quartered the Wyndham arms. His son and succ.,— Edwin Richard Wyndham, Viscount Adare, *b.* 1812, became 3rd Earl Dunraven, and left, with other issue,— WYNDHAM THOMAS, 4th Earl, as above.

FISHER, Samuel Sharpe Horman-, Esq., of Llwyn Derw, Glamorganshire.

J. P. for the co. of Glamorgan ; second son of the late Roger Staples Horman-Fisher, Esq., of Bentworth Hall, Hants, and James Street, Buckingham Gate, London, by Elizabeth, his wife, dau. and h. of John Horman, Esq., of Finchley ; *b.* 1823 ; *m.* Jane, second dau. of Robert Eaton, Esq., of Bryn-y-Mor, co. Glamorgan, and by her has issue 1 dau.,—
Margaret Jane.

Residence: Llwyn Derw, near Swansea.
Arms: Quarterly, 1st and 4th, on a chevron, engrailed with plain cotises, between 3 demi-lions guardant gu., each supporting between the paws a dexter gauntlet ppr., three bezants ; 2nd and 3rd, bendy of eight, or and az., per bend sinister, counterchanged, on a chief gu., a lion passant or : impaling in right of his wife, quarterly, 1st and 4th arg., in chief 3 escallop shells, a fesse az. ; 2nd and 3rd, arg., a lion rampant.
Crest: 1st, issuant from a crown pallisado, or, a demi-lion guardant supporting a gauntlet, as in the arms ; 2nd, in front of a cross crosslet, gu.., two Roman fasces, with the battle-axe in saltire, ppr.
Mottoes: Sustento justitiam—HORMAN ; Virtutem extendere factis—FISHER.

LINEAGE.

This family traces to an ancestor bearing the name *Piscator*, holding lands at the time of the *Domesday* survey in a district since included in the county of Bedford. A branch settled at Alderways, in Staffordshire ; and from them were descended Sir John *Fisher*, a Justice of the Common Pleas *temp.* Henry VIII., Sir Robert Fisher, Bart., of Packington, Warwickshire, and Sir Thomas Fisher, Bart., of St. Giles's, Middlesex, both of which titles became extinct.

The branch from which Mr. Fisher of Llwyn Derw traces in direct line settled in the north of England. Joseph Fisher, son of Joseph Fisher of Cockermouth, Cumberland, had a son,— Robert Fisher, Esq., of Mitcham, Surrey, called to the Bar at the Inner Temple, and *s.* his elder brother, Josiah, 1806. By a first wife he had three sons, one of whom, *Robert*, became of Chetwynd, Salop ; and by a second wife, Mary, dau. and h. of Baron Butz, a noble of Germany, he had three other sons, one of whom was— Roger Staples Fisher, Esq., of Bentworth Hall, Hants, who *m.*, 1819, Elizabeth, dau. and h. of John Horman, Esq., of Finchley, and by her had several sons, the second being—
SAMUEL SHARPE HORMAN-FISHER, as above.

FOTHERGILL, Richard, Esq., of Abernant House, Glamorganshire.

M.P. for Merthyr Tydfil (1868) ; J. P. and D. L. for the co. of Glamorgan ; is a large ironmaster at Aberdare, Penydarran, &c. ; eldest son of the late Rowland Fothergill, Esq.; *b.* 1822 ; *m.*, 1st, 1847, Miss Elizabeth Lewis ; 2ndly, 1850, Mary, dau. of W. Roden, Esq.. A brother of Mr. Fothergill was the late Rowland Fothergill, Esq., of Hensol Castle, J. P. and D. L., Sheriff for the co. of Glamorgan 1850 (see *Hensol Castle*), who *d.* 1871 ; and a sister is Miss Fothergill, now residing at the same place.

Residence: Abernant House, Aberdare.
Town Address: 1, Hyde Park Gardens.

FOWLER, John Coke, Esq., of Gnoll, Glamorganshire.

Deputy Chairman of the Glamorganshire Quarter Sessions ; Stipendiary Magistrate for the Merthyr district ; called to the Bar at the Inner Temple ; Author of "Church Pews, their Origin and Legal Incidents," "Collieries and Colliers," "Essay on Milford Haven," &c. ; son of William Tancred Fowler, Esq. ; *b.* at Derby, 1815 ; *ed.* at Rugby and Pembroke College, Oxford ; *grad.* B A. 1837 ; *m.*, 1st, 1844, Augusta, dau. of John Bacon, Esq. ; 2ndly, 1850, Anna, dau. of Evan Thomas, Esq., of Sully and Llwyn Madoc ; has issue three sons and four daus.

Heir: John Bacon Fowler.
Residences: West Gnoll, near Neath ; and St. David's Cottage, Merthyr Tydfil.
Arms: Azure, a chevron arg. charged with three crosses formée, sa., between three lions passant guardant or ; quartering three crescents and cross fleury.
Crest: A cubit arm and hand, with a falconer's lure.

LINEAGE.

This family derives its descent from the Fowlers of St. Thomas's, in the county of Stafford, and through the grandmother of the above-named J. Coke Fowler from the Cokes of Trusley, the Wardes of Gyndale, in Yorkshire, the Fowlers of Harnage Grange, in the parish of Cound, Salop, and the Fowlers of Abbey Cwm-hir, Radnorshire.

FRANCIS, George Grant, Esq., of Cae Bailey, Glamorganshire.

F.S.A. of London and Scotland, and member of many learned societies at home and abroad; Col. Commanding 1st Glamorgan Artillery Volunteers; J. P. for the co. of Glamorgan 1865, and for the borough of Swansea 1855; Vice-President of the Royal Institution of South Wales; Mayor of Swansea 1853-54; Author of *The History of Neath and its Abbey*, 8vo., 1845; *Hist. of the Swansea Grammar School*, 8vo., 1849; *Hist. of Copper-Smelting in Glamorganshire*, 8vo., 1867; *Charters granted to Swansea*, with illustrations and notes, folio, 1867; *Memoir of Sir Hugh Johnys, Kt.*, 8vo., 1645; *Lordship of Gower*, 1870; and monographs on Welsh History and Topography; eld. son of Mr. John Francis; *b.* at Swansea, January, 1814; *ed.* at the High School, Swansea; *m.*, 1840, Sarah, eldest dau. of John Richardson, Esq., J. P., Mayor of Swansea, 1844 (see *Richardson of Pantygwydir*); has issue three sons, John Richardson, George Grant, and Attwell.

Heir: John Richardson, *m.* to Lucy Margaret, younger dau. of John Edwards, Esq., of Brampton Bryan, Hereford (formerly High Sheriff of co. of Radnor), and has issue Walter and Reginald.
Residence: Cae Bailey, Swansea.
Town Address: Pall Mall Club, Waterloo Place.
Arms: As given by Papworth's ordinary of arms: Gu., on a bend or, 3 lions' heads erased ppr., between two bezants; for FRANCIS (quartering therewith *Attwell, Grant,* and *Stuart*).
Crests: A lion statant ppr. for *Francis*; a burning mountain for *Grant.*
Mottoes: Spes mea in Deo; Stand sure.

LINEAGE.

This family derives its descent from the Francises of Castle Cary, co. of Somerset, and the Grants of that ilk on the banks of Spey, Inverness-shire.

Note.—The 1st Glam. Artill. Volunteers—raised through Col. Francis's exertions in 1859—presented him with a sword of honour, "as a mark of its esteem and regard." He has brought together at the Royal Institution of South Wales, of which he is founder, large collections of local fossils, antiquities, coins, and seals (once forming his own private collection at Cae Bailey, and which he presented to thetown), and one of the best collections of Works on Wales extant, of which he compiled and printed a catalogue. The Town Council entrusted him with the restoration and methodizing of their muniments, a work performed so satisfactorily as to call forth a warm eulogium from Lord Chief Justice Campbell in the Court of Queen's Bench. He was active in restoring to public use the ancient Grammar School of Bishop Gore (of which he was many years chairman, and is still one of the trustees); in promoting railway and dock accommodation for his native town; and in erecting the fort at the Mumbles for the protection of the shipping. The preservation and restoration of Oystermouth Castle, one of the many ancient ruins pertaining to the noble House of Beaufort, Lords of Gower and Kilvey, are owing to his exertions, for which he was presented with a piece of plate. In the year 1851 he was selected to represent the Swansea District as Local Commissioner at the Great Exhibition, and he filled a like office in connection with the National Crimean Fund.

For many years Colonel Grant-Francis has been Hon. Sec. for South Wales to the Society of Antiquaries of London. He took part in the formation of the Cambrian Archæological Society, and has frequently contributed to its journal, the *Archæologia Cambrensis*. Mr. L. W. Dillwyn's "Contributions towards a History of Swansea," 1840, show that he was a coadjutor at that interesting piece of topography. The British Association appointed him Secretary to its department of Ethnology, when it held its meeting at Swansea in 1851. The benefit of his local and antiquarian knowledge has been most readily extended to the present work.

FRANKLEN, Richard, Esq., of Clementston, Glamorganshire.

Is J. P. and D. L. for the co. of Glamorgan; was Sheriff for same co. 1846.

(*Further particulars not received.*)

GRENFELL, Pascoe St. Leger, Esq., of Maesteg House, Glamorganshire.

J. P. and D. L. for the co. of Glamorgan; son of the late Pascoe Grenfell, Esq. (*d.* 1837), of Taplow House, Bucks, M.P. for Great Marlow, by the Hon. Georgiana St. Leger, dau. of St. Leger Aldworth, first Viscount Doneraile in the peerage of Ireland (she *d.* 1818); *m.* Catherine, dau. of James Du Pré, Esq., and has issue several sons and daus.

Heir: Pascoe Du Pré Grenfell.
Residence: Maesteg House, near Swansea.
Arms: Gu., three organ-rests [or clarions] or.
Crest: A dragon on a chapeau.

LINEAGE.

The Grenfells were originally of Cornwall, their seat being at Penzance in that co. Descent has been claimed on their behalf from the Norman stock of De Granville or Granvyl, whose representative, Richard de Granville, obtained under Fitzhamon the lordship of Neath, co. of Glamorgan. Some of his descendants settled in Devon and Cornwall (see *De Granville*, and the *Ped. of Lady Llanover*).

GRIFFITH, The Rev. John, of Merthyr Tydfil, Glamorganshire.

Rector of Merthyr Tydfil; Rural Dean and Surrogate; formerly Vicar of Aberdare; J. P. for the co. of Glamorgan; patron, as Rector of Merthyr, of Penydarran District Church; author of various pamphlets and sermons on the *Church*, and *Education in Wales;* son of the late Thomas Griffith, Esq.; *b.* at Aberystwyth; *ed.* at the Grammar School, Swansea, and Queen's Coll., Cambridge; *grad.* B.A. 1841, M.A. 1844; *m.*, 1st, 1847, Sarah Frances King, daughter of William King, Esq., West India merchant, London; 2ndly, 1863, Louisa Stuart, daughter of Alexander Stuart, Esq., Isle of Bute; *s.* to Braichycelyn estate, near Aberdovey, in 1850; has issue 2 sons, 3 daughters.

Heir : John Griffith.
Residences: Rectory, Merthyr Tydfil; and Braichycelyn, near Aberdovey.

GRIFFITHS, The Rev. John, of Neath, Glamorganshire.

Was Pres. of the Council of the National Eisteddfod from the year 1860; elected F.G.H.S. in 1868; Head Master of Cardigan Grammar School 1839; P.C. Nantyglo 1844; Rector of Llansannor 1846; Vicar of St. Mary Hill, Glam., 1847; Rector of Neath and Llantwit 1855; Surrogate of Llandaff 1855; Author of Sermons and Addresses on various occasions; eldest son of Thomas Griffiths, Esq., Dolygwartheg, Cardiganshire; *b.* at Parknoyadd, Aberayron, May 11, 1820; *ed.* at Tyglyn and Cardigan Grammar School; *grad.* at Lampeter College 1837, " Harford Scholar," 1st class; *m.*, Dec. 18, 1844, Mary, dau. of Caleb Lewis, Esq., of Cardigan; *s.* 1869.

Heir: His brother Arthur, Rector of Llanelly, Breconshire.
Residences: The Rectory, Neath; Dolygwartheg, near Aberayron.
Town Address: Thomas's Hotel, Charles Street, Haymarket.
Arms: Gu., a lion rampant or, in a true lover's knot arg., between four fleurs-de-lis, their stalks bending to the centre of the escutcheon (quartering the Llangolman arms).
Crest: A horse's head couped ppr.
Motto: "A gadwo Duw, cadwedig yw."

LINEAGE.

This family derives its descent from Rhys Griffith ab Einion. Its long and ancient home was Penybenglog, in the county of Pembroke. That estate was sold at the death of Robert Griffith, who was *m.* to Elizabeth, eldest dau. of George Lloyd, Esq , of Cwmgloyn, his cousin-german, A.D. 1738. He died without issue, leaving his estate between his three sisters, co-heiresses. One of these, *Janet*, married her cousin, Arthur Griffiths, Esq., of Llangolman and Clynderwen. Eldest son, Thoma, Griffith; next in descent, John Griffith, eldest son, who *m.* Mary, dau. of Jacob Picton, Esq., of Pencnwc. The next in descent was Thomas Griffiths (eldest son), father of the present representative of the family, JOHN GRIFFITHS, Dolygwartheg, co. of Cardigan, and Rector of Neath, as above.

Among distinguished members of this family in past time may be named "*Howel Gawr,*" so surnamed for defeating the French king's champion, when he got for his arms—*gules*, a lion rampant *or*, in a "'true lover's knot," *argent*, between four "fleurs-de-lis," their stalks tending to the centre of the escutcheon; *Rees ap Rhydderch,* who accompanied James de Audeley, then Lord of Cemaes, as his Esquire, to France, in the time of Edward the Third. He was grandson of Howel Gawr. For his gallant services he got an augmentation to his arms, viz., his own, counter-flowered of France.

GWYN, Howel, Esq., of Dyffryn, Glamorganshire.

J. P. and D. L. for the co. of Glamorgan; J. P. for the co. of Brecon; High Sheriff for the co. of Glam. 1837-8; was M.P. for Brecon 1866—69, and previously M.P. for Penrhyn and Falmouth 1847—57; eldest son of the late William Gwyn, Esq., of Abercrave, co. Glam. (who *d.* 1830, by his wife, Mary Anne Roberts, of Barnstaple, Devon; *ed.* at the Univ. of Oxford; *m.*, 1831, Ellen, only dau. of John Moore, Esq., of Plymouth.

Residence: Dyffryn, near Neath.
Arms: Sa., a fesse, or, in chief a sword, point upwards, in base, a sword, point downwards, both in pale, arg. pommelled and hilted or.
[These are also the arms of the co. of Brecon]
Crest: A dagger, arg., erect, in hand prop., passed through a boar's head couped, or.
Motto: Vim vi repellere licet.

LINEAGE.

This family is derived from a common ancestor with that of Gwynne, formerly of Glanbrân, Carm., and *Gwynne-Holford* of *Buckland*, Brec., which comp. It is traced in the pedigrees to Brychan Brycheiniog, through Trahaearn ap Einion, Lord of Cwmmwd, near Talgarth, who lived in the 12th cent. From him was descended in direct line through Rhys ap Philip ap David of Llwynhowel,—

Rhydderch ap Rhys, who lived early in the 15th cent., and *m.* Gwenllian, or, as *Dwnn* says, Owen. dau. and h. of Howel ap Gryffydd of Trecastle, They had three sons, Thomas Gwyn ap Rhydderch, David Coch Gwyn, of Glanbrân, and Howel Gwyn, of Ystrad-Walltter. The second became founder of the Glanbrân branch; the first that of the branch now represented by Howel Gwyn, Esq., of

Dyffryn, of whom we here treat. The name *Gwyn* also is said first to have appeared in the family with these sons, who being of light complexion were called Gwyn, which means "white," or "light in colour," to indicate the peculiarity, and in the case of David, who was red-haired, the epithet *coch*, "red," was added—David Coch-Gwyn.

Thomas Gwyn, of Trecastell, *m.* Elen, dau. of Roger Vychan, of Talgarth,—(we now follow a MS. in possession of Howel Gwyn, Esq., at Dyffryn, with a few additions from a copy of a MS. in St. Mark's Coll., Chelsea), and had issue Howel Gwyn of Trecastell, whose wife was a dau. of Gwiliam Llewelyn. Their son was—

Thomas ap Howel, of Trecastell, who *m.* Margaret, dau. and h. of Edward Games, Esq., of Newton, Brec. (or, a lion passant gu.).

Howel Gwyn, Esq., their son, *m.* Mary, dau. and co-h. of James Boyle, Esq.. of the Hay, who was a descendant of Sir John Boyle, Kt., of the order of St. Michael, of Glyntawe, and *m.* a dau. of Sir Peers Trevanion, of Cornwall, Kt. (He bore—arg., on a fesse az., inter 2 chevronels gu., 3 escallops). Their son,—

Edward Gwyn, Esq., of Glyntawe, *m.* a dau. and h. of John Llewelyn. (He bore—Quarterly, 1st and 4th sa., a fesse or, between 2 daggers, "their points in chief and base," or, the hilts and pommels of the second ; 2nd and 3rd, or, "three vespertillios or bats " displayed, az., armed, eyed, and crused gu. We have here, in 1 and 4, the elements of the modern Gwyn arms.) They left a son,—

John Gwyn, Esq., of Glyntawe ("now living" —St. Mark's Coll. MS.), who *m.* Anne, dau. and h. of Capt. Thomas Price (or Prees), of Defynog. St. Mark's MS. adds, "Arg., bulls' head cabossed, sable, armed or ;" meaning, probably, Prees's arms. John Gwyn was succeeded by his son,—

James Gwyn, A.M., who *m.* Elizabeth, dau. of William Brewster, Esq., of Burton Court, Hereford, and had a son named William, Attorney at Law, of Neath, whose wife was Eliza, only dau. of Hugh Edward, of Blaensawdde, whose son, John Gwyn, was also Attorney at Law at Neath, and *m.* Priscilla, dau. of Matthew Roach, Esq., of Barnstaple, Devon, Merchant, leaving two sons, Matthew and William, and a dau., Elizabeth. The second son,—

William Gwyn, of Abercrave, *m.*, 1799, Mary Anne, dau. of Edward Roberts, Esq., of Barnstaple, and had, with other issue, HOWEL GWYN, as above.

Note.—The Llanelwedd branch of the Gwyns terminated in Sir Rowland Gwynne, Kt., of that place. One dau. married into the Penpont family (see *Williams Penpont*), another into that of Castell-Madog. (See *Price, Castle-Madoc.*)

HILL, Edward Stock, Esq., of Rookwood, Llandaff, Glamorganshire.

Lieut.-Colonel 1st Ad. Brigade, Glam. Art. Volunteers ; J. P. for co. Glamorgan, and bor. of Cardiff ; son of Charles Hill, Esq., late of Druid's Stoke, co. of Gloucester ; *b.* at Bristol, 14th January, 1834; *ed.* at Bishop's College, Clifton ; *m.*, 26th April, 1866, Fanny Ellen, daughter of the late Lieut.-General Tickell, C.B., Royal Engineers ; has issue 2 daughters and 2 sons.

Residence: Rookwood, Llandaff.
Town Address: Junior Carlton Club.
Arms: Arg., two chevronels gu. between two water-bougets sa. in chief and a mullet of the second in base, a crescent for difference
Crest: A dove ppr., collared sa., one foot resting on a mullet arg., and holding in the mouth an olive branch vert.
Motto: Perseverantia omnia vincit.

Note.—The mansion of *Rookwood* was erected in 1866.

HOMFRAY, John, Esq., of Penlline Castle, Glamorganshire.

J. P. and D. L. for the co. of Glamorgan ; Sheriff for same co. 1843 (see *Sheriffs*); son of the late Sir Jer. Homfray, Kt. (*d.* 1833), of Llandaff (Sheriff of co. Glam. 1809), by Mary (*d.* 1830), dau. and h. of John Richards, Esq , of Cardiff, and has, with other issue,—

JOHN RICHARDS HOMFRAY, Esq.,of Pwllywrach, co. of Glam. ; J. P. and D. L. for the same co. ; *m.*, 1824, Mary Elizabeth, eldest surviving dau. of Sir Glynne Earle Welby, Bart., of Denton Hall, Lincolnshire, and has issue.

Mr. Homfray *s.* to the estates on the demise of his father, 1833.

Heir: John Richards.
Residence: Penlline Castle, near Cowbridge.

LINEAGE.

The Homfray family is of considerable antiquity, having been long seated in Yorkshire before branching off into Wales and the east of England. Their origin is said to be Norman. Their advent into Glamorganshire was through the marriage of Francis Homfray, Esq., of Wollaston Hall, Worcestershire, with Miss Hannah Popkin, of Coytrehên, near Bridgend, and that of his son Jeremiah (afterwards "Sir Jeremiah" above named) with Mary Richards of Llandaff. For a notice of *Penlline Castle* see p. 528 *ante*.

JEFFREYS, John Gwyn, Esq., of Gelligron, Glamorganshire.

J. P. for the cos. of Glamorgan and Brecon ; F.R.S. ; F.G.S. ; F.L.S. ; was *ed.* for the law and called to the bar at Lincoln's Inn ; Recorder of Swansea ; son of the late John Jeffreys, Esq., of Swansea ; *b.* 1809 ; *m.*, 1840, Anne, dau. of the late Richard Janion Nevill, Esq., of Llanelly, co. of Carm., and sister of Charles W. Nevill, Esq., of Westfa, co. of Carm., and has issue.

THE COUNTY FAMILIES OF GLAMORGANSHIRE.

Heir: Howel Gwyn.
Residences: Gelligron, near Swansea; 25, Devonshire Place, W.

LINEAGE.

This branch of the family of *Jeffreys* of Breconshire has been established in Swansea and neighbourhood for several generations, and has taken a prominent part in local affairs. The name often occurs among the Portreeves of Swansea. They originated with John Jeffreys of Abercynrig, Brec., Sheriff of his co. 1631, and were afterwards seated at the Priory, Brecon, of which place was Jeffrey Jeffreys, Esq., Sheriff o his co. in 1741. (See *Sheriffs of Breconshire.*)

JENKIN, John Trevillian, Esq., of Swansea, Glamorganshire.

J. P. for the co. of Glamorgan; was Mayor of the borough of Swansea 1854, 1858, 1861; son of David Jenkin, of Swansea, gentleman; *b.* at Swansea on the 12th October, 1809; *ed.* at Swansea; *m.*, on the 23rd October, 1838, to Annetta, daughter of David Sanders, Esq., and Alderman of Swansea.

Residence: The Mirador, Swansea.
Crest: A lion rampant.
Motto: Sic modo.

LINEAGE.

This family descends on the mother's side from the Holditches of Devonshire.

JENKINS, George Henry, Esq., of Walterston House, Glamorganshire.

M.D., M.R.C.S., and L.A.C., formerly in practice; J. P. for the co. of Glamorgan; 5th son of the late Richard Jenkins, Esq., Newport, Monmouthshire; *b.* at Newport, December 11th, 1817; *grad.* M.D., Univ. Aberdeen, 1854; *m.*, 1847, Mary Ann, eldest dau. of the late John Thomas, Esq., Surgeon R.N., and co-heiress of the late John Jenkins Thomas, Esq., Caercady House, Lieut. 5th Dragoon Guards, and has issue; succ. his uncle, William Jenkins, Esq., of Walterston, 1851; has issue a son and heir, William Richard.

Heir: William Richard Jenkins.
Residence: Walterston House, Glamorgan (built by Walter de Mapes, Chaplain to Henry I. in the twelfth century).
Arms: Arg., three gamecocks gu.
Crest: A gamecock, as in arms.
Motto: Fe dâl am daro.

LINEAGE.

This family is descended from Richard Jenkins, Esq., of Pantynawel, co. Glamorgan, who *m.* Ann, dau. of John Carne, Esq., and granddau. of Sir John Carne, Knt. The Jenkinses of Pantynawel, members of which family in the sixteenth century and subsequently held the office of High Sheriff of Glamorgan, were descended from Trim ap Maenarch, who *m.* Ellen, dau. to Iestyn ap Gwrgant, the last Prince of Glamorgan, and were of the same stock with the Vaughans of Bredwardine, Hergest, Tretower, and Clyro.

JENKINS, Rev. John David, B.D., Aberdare, Glamorganshire.

Fellow of Jesus College, Oxford; Canon of Pieter Maritzburg; Vicar of Aberdare; formerly C. of St. Paul's, Oxford; author of "The Age of the Martyrs;" son of William David Jenkins, Esq., of Castellau Fach, Llantrisant, co. of Glamorgan; *b.* at Merthyr Tydfil; *ed.* at Sir Edward Stradling's Grammar School, Cowbridge, and Jesus Coll., Oxon.; *grad.* B A. 1850, M.A. 1852, B D., 1859; *s.* to Castellau Fach 1837.

Residence: The Vicarage, Aberdare.
Arms: Gules, three chevrons argent.

LINEAGE.

This family traces its descent from Iestyn ap Gwrgant, and bears his arms.

JONES, Robert Oliver, Esq., of Fonmon Castle, Glamorganshire.

Stipendiary Magistrate for the borough of Cardiff; J. P. and D. L. for co. Glamorgan; Sheriff for same co. 1838, in succession of Howel Gwyn, Esq.; elder son of the late Major-Gen. Oliver Thomas Jones, who commanded in the Peninsular war; *b.* 1811; *m.*, first, 1843, Alicia (*d.* 1851), dau. of Evan Thomas, Esq. (see *Thomas of Llwynmadoc*); secondly, 1853, Sarah Elizabeth, dau. of John Bruce Pryce, Esq., of Dyffryn; has by first wife issue surviving one son and one dau., Edith Alicia. Mr. Jones has also a brother, Captain Oliver John Jones, R.N., *b.* 1813.

Heir: Oliver Henry.
Residence: Fonmon Castle, near Cardiff.
Arms: Quarterly: 1st, sa., a chevron arg. between three spear-heads ppr., the points embrued—*Bleddyn ap Maenarch;* 2nd, a wyvern's head erased vert., in the mouth a dexter hand gu.— *King Pelinor;* 3rd, gu. a chevron ermine—*Philip Gwys,* Lord of Wiston; 4th, arg., a stag couchant gu. attired and unguled or, in its mouth a branch vert—*Matilda of Gower* (an heiress).
Crest: A dexter cubit arm in armour grasping a spear, all ppr.

These were the arms of Col. Philip Jones (see lineage), granted him by *George Owen,* York Herald.

LINEAGE.

The founder of this family was COL. PHILIP JONES, a distinguished officer in Oliver Cromwell's army, and zealous promoter of the republican cause against the Stuarts. By the large wealth he accumulated through the liberality of the Protector, he purchased the Fonmon estate, and laid a solid basis for a permanent and influential family. The details of his life have been brought to light more fully by a recent memoir drawn up from authentic sources by Col. Grant-Francis, F.S.A., in his *Charters of Swansea*, from which it appears that Col. Philip Jones was not merely a political partisan and successful soldier, but a man of the highest character for probity and piety.

Col. Philip Jones was *b.* at Swansea, 1618, the son of David Johnes, who was son of Philip *John's*, grandson of *John* ap Rhys, of the line of Bleddyn ap Maenarch, Lord of Brecknock. He *m.* Jane, dau. of William Price, Esq., of Gellihir, in Gower; joined the Parliament forces; was made Governor of Swansea, 1645, the year in which Bussey Mansel of Briton Ferry was made Commander-in-Chief of the forces of Glamorgan under General Fairfax; obtained from Cromwell in 1849 Forest Issa on the Tawe at a rental of £30; was the second on the list of "Commissioners for the Better Propagation of the Gospel in Wales;" was sent several times to Parliament; in 1653, though not one of the "six" summoned from Wales, was in the "Little Parliament;" in 1854 represented Monmouthshire; in 1665 had a double return for Breconshire and Glamorganshire, but chose the latter. He was then raised to Cromwell's House of Peers, and made Comptroller of the Household. At the Restoration he settled down quietly, was allowed to remain on his estate of Fonmon, and was confirmed as *Custos Rot.* of his co. Attempts were made to prove him guilty of peculation, but these signally failed. He served as High Sheriff under Charles II. (1671, see *Sheriffs*). He *d.* 1674 at Fonmon, and was buried at the adjoining church of Penmark. By his wife, Jane Price, he left a son and heir (called after the Protector)

OLIVER JONES, Esq., of Fonmon Castle, Sheriff for Glam. 1681, whose son,—

Robert Jones, Esq., of Fonmon Castle, was M.P. for co. of Glamorgan 1713—1715, when he *d.* By his wife Mary, dau. of Humphrey Edwin, Esq, of Llanfihangel (see *Thomas of Llanfihangel*), he left a son,—

Robert Jones, Esq., of Fonmon Castle; Sheriff of Glam. 1729; *m.* Mary Forrest, of Minehead, Somerset, and with other issue left by her a son,—

Robert Jones, Esq., of Fonmon Castle. By his second wife, Joanna, dau. of Edmund Lloyd, Esq, of Cardiff, he had, with other issue—

1. Robert Jones, Esq., of Fonmon Castle, *b.* 1773, *d.* 1834. *unm.*, and was succeeded by his nephew (as below).
2. Oliver Thomas Jones, *b.* 1776, entered the army, and became Lieut.-Gen. under Sir John Moore in the Peninsular war (*d.* 1815). By his second wife, Maria Antonia Swinburne, he left, with one dau., Rosa Antonia, two sons,—
ROBERT OLIVER, now of Fonmon Castle (as above), and—
Oliver John, Capt. R.N.

KNIGHT, Rev., Charles Rumsey, of Tythegston Court, Glamorganshire.

Clerk; Vicar of Merthyr Mawr, Glam., 1871; formerly Vicar of St. Bride's Major, 1843 to 1863; Incumbent of Donative of Ewenny 1863 to 1871; Rural Dean; Proctor in Convocation for the clergy of the diocese of Llandaff; J. P. for the co. of Glamorgan; eldest son of the late Rev. Robert Knight, of Tythegston Court, Rector of Newton Nottage (see *Knight of Newton Court*); *b.* at Lechlade, Gloucestershire, 1817; *ed.* at Wadham Coll., Oxford; *grad.* B.A. 1839, M.A. 1841; *m.*, 1st, 1843, Mary, dau. of Thomas Bassett, Esq., of Bonvilston House, Glamorganshire (she *d.* in 1848); 2ndly, 1854, Mary Ann Elizabeth, dau. of the late Rev. Thomas Stacey, M.A., Precentor of Llandaff Cathedral; and has issue 3 sons and 3 daughters; succ. 1854.

Heir: Robert Lougher, *b.* 1858.
Residence: Tythegston Court, near Bridgend.
Town Address: Oxford and Cambridge Club, Pall Mall.
Arms: Arg., 3 pallets gu., within a bordure engrailed sa.; on a canton of the second a spur with rowel downwards, or.
Crest: On a ducal coronet an eagle displayed proper.
Motto: Gloria calcar habet.

LINEAGE.

This family traces its lineage from *Francis Knight* (of the sept of *Iestyn ap Gwrgant*, last Prince of Glamorgan), Alderman and afterwards Mayor of the city of Bristol, to whom a grant was made from Queen Elizabeth in 1562 of an estate at Congresbury, in the county of Somerset; his descendant, George Knight was also Mayor of Bristol in 1639. Another descendant, Sir John Knight, Kt., also mayor in 1663 and 1670, was Member of Parliament for the city of Bristol, and gave great offence to the court party after the Revolution by his speech against naturalizing foreigners, or "Froglanders," as he called them (see Macaulay's *History of England*). He was knighted on the occasion of a royal visit to Bristol; and laid the foundation of the Hotwells. His son, *Robert Knight*, Esq., *m.*, 1708, Cecil *Turbervill* of Sutton, granddaughter and heiress of Richard Lougher, Esq. (see *Lougher of Tythegston*). His son,—

Robert Knight, Esq., of Tythegston, succ. in 1732; High Sheriff of Glamorgan in 1737; *m.* Lydia, daughter of John Rogers, D.D., Dean of Wells;—her mother was the eldest sister of Henry Hare, last Lord Coleraine of that family, whose will, on his dying without legitimate issue in 1749, became the subject of litigation for fourteen years between the representatives of his natural daughter, Rose Duplessis, and the co-heiresses at law, Mrs. Knight, and Ann, wife of William Bassett of Miskin. At length, by a compromise, the real estates passed to the former, and the personalities to the latter.

Henry Knight, Esq., sole heir of Robert, *m.* Catherine, daughter of John Lynch, D.D., Dean of Canterbury, and granddaughter of Archbishop Wake, by whom he had two sons,—

Henry Knight, Esq., who was High Sheriff in

THE COUNTY FAMILIES OF GLAMORGANSHIRE. 633

1794, Colonel of the Glamorgan Militia, and Vice-Lieutenant of the county in 1808; and *Robert*, Rector of Tewkesbury. Henry died without issue in 1825, and was succeeded at Tythegston Court by his eldest nephew,—
Rev. Robert Knight, M.A., Rector of Newton Nottage. He *m.* Emma, dau. of Thomas Eagle, Esq., of Pilston, Mon., and had, with other issue,—
REV. CHARLES RUMSEY KNIGHT, the present representative of the family, as above.

Note.—Tythegston Court, which was altered from an old Gothic mansion to its present form in 1769, had been the seat of a long line of *Loughers* and *Turbervills* in continuous succession. The estate having descended nearly 300 years in the same blood, no title appears to have been ever made of it. It probably vested originally in the Turbervills by conquest. No record is to be found among the family papers more ancient than a copy of the will of Richard Turberville, bearing date 27th April, 1501. He was succeeded by his son John, upon whose death in 1533 a long strife—mentioned by Leland—arose in reference to his numerous estates between his daughter Gwenllian, *m.* to Watkin Lougher, and Christopher, son of his brother Jenkin, which ended in 1546 in an arbitration by which certain other manors were awarded to Christopher Turbervill, and to Gwenllian and her son Richard (the father Watkin being dead) the manor of Tythegston and its appurtenances. Thus the Loughers, who had for many generations been settled at Sker and Baglan, and the borough of Loughor, and were in direct descent from Iestyn ap Gwrgant, Lord of Glamorgan, became settled at Tythegston.—There is a *cromlech* near the mansion, the lower part covered by a mound of stones and earth, the large upper slab being alone visible.

KNIGHT, Rev. Edward Doddridge, of Nottage Court, Glamorganshire.

Rector of Newton Nottage, and Lord of the "Pembroke Manor;" Rural Dean; formerly P.C. of Tredegar (1838—1846); Rector of Llandough (1816—1858); is patron of Newton Nottage 2 turns out of 3; son of the late Rev. Robert Knight, M.A., formerly Vicar of Tewkesbury, Gloucestershire; *b.* at Tewkesbury, Dec., 1806; *ed.* at Exeter Coll., Oxford; *grad.* B.A. 1829; *m.*, 1837, Mary, dau. of Thomas Place, Esq., of Ffrood Vale, Neath; and has issue five daughters; succ. his brother, Rev. H. H. Knight, B.D., 1857.

Residence: Nottage Court, Bridgend.
Arms: Arg., three pallets gu. within a bordure engrailed sa.; on a canton of the second, a spur with rowel downwards or.
Crest: On a ducal coronet an eagle displayed ppr.

LINEAGE.

This family traces its descent from Iestyn ap Gwrgant on father's side, and the celebrated divine Dr. Doddridge on the mother's side. For lineage, see further *Knight of Tythegston*, and *Lougher of Tythegston*.

Note.—Nottage Court—a venerable mansion in the Elizabethan style—has been in the family ever since its erection, excepting an interval of forty years. It was restored by the Rev. H. H. Knight (the present proprietor's brother) in 1841-6.

LEE, Vaughan Hanning, Esq., of Rheola, Glamorganshire.

Was a Major in the army; J. P. for the co. of Glamorgan; son of John Lee, Esq, of Dillington Park, Somerset, by Jessie, dau. and co-h. with her brother, the late Nash V. Edwards Vaughan, Esq., of Rheola (*d.* 1871), of John Edwards, Esq., of Llanelay, Llantrisant, Glam., who, on inheriting by the will of William Vaughan, Esq., assumed the surname Vaughan in addition to his own; *b.* 1836; *s.* to the Rheola property 1871.

Residences: Rheola, near Neath; Llanelay, Llantrisant.
Arms: The arms of *Vaughan*,—Sa., a chevron arg. between three boys' heads couped ppr., a snake vert enwrapping the neck (quartering the arms of *Lee*).

LEWIS, Henry, Esq., of Greenmeadow, Glamorganshire.

J. P. and D. L. for the co. of Glamorgan; High Sheriff of the same 1858; eldest son of the late Henry Lewis, Esq., of Park, Glamorganshire (*d.* 1838), by his wife Mary, dau. of George Emerson, Esq. (she *d.* 1841); *b.* 1815; *s.* 1838; *m.*, first, Ann Morgan, dau. of Walter Morgan, Esq., Merthyr, and had issue by her, who *d.* 1857,—
1. Mary Price.
2. Blanche Eliza.
3. HENRY.
Secondly, Sophia Antoinette Ximenes Gwynne, dau. of Colonel Gwynne, Glanbrane Park, Carmarthenshire, by whom he had issue—
1. Thomas Wyndham.
2. Roderick Gwynne.
3. Catherine Fanny.
4. Gwendoline.
5. Wyndham Gwynne.

Heir: Henry Lewis, *b.* 1847.
Residence: Green Meadow, near Cardiff.
Arms: Quarterly: 1st, sa., a lion rampant arg.—LEWIS; 2nd, sa., a chevron between three spear-heads az. embrued—PRICE; 3rd, sa., a chevron between three fleurs-de-lis or; 4th, or, on a canton gu. 2 lions passant guardant—LEWIS.
Crests: A lion sejant arg.—*Lewis;* a lamb or, bearing a pennon of St George.—*Price*.
Mottoes: "Patriæ fidus;" "Ofner na ofno angau."

LINEAGE.

The ancient family of *Lewis*, of Van, Llanishen, Newhouse, and Green Meadow, trace direct and authentic descent from *Gwaethfoed*, Lord of Cardigan and Cibwyr (tenth century), who (according to the *Iolo MSS.*), though acknowledging himself a regulus under Edgar the English king, when summoned to meet that king at Chester and row the royal barge, curtly refused any answer, and when pressed for some word of reply, uttered the memorable saying which his numerous descendants in several of their lines have adopted as their *motto*,— "*Fear him who fears not death*,"—the independence and courage of which answer struck the king with wonder, and led to personal acquaintance and friendship. *Ivor Bach*, Lord of *Castell Coch*, to whom frequent reference has been made in the preceding sketch of Glamorgan *Annals*, was fourth in descent from Gwaethfoed ; and Madoc ap Howel Velyn, Lord of St. Fagan's (as successor of his mother, Sarah, dau. of Sir Mayo le Soer, the Norman lord of that district), was sixth from Ivor Bach.

Edward Lewis, Esq., of *Van*, Sheriff of Glamorgan 1549, 1556, and 1560 (see *Sheriffs*), the first of the family to adopt the surname LEWIS, *m.* Anne, dau. of Sir William Morgan, Kt., of Pencoed, and was succeeded by his eldest son, *Thomas Lewis*, Esq., sheriff for the years 1570 and 1587, who by his first wife, Margaret, dau. of Robert Gamage, Esq., of Coity Castle (his second wife being Catherine, dau. of Sir George Mathew, Kt., of Radir— see *Mathew of Radir*), left a son and heir,—

Sir Edward Lewis, Kt., of *Van*, Sheriff of Glamorgan 1602 and 1613 ; knighted 1603; bought, 1616, the mansion of St. Fagan's of William Herbert, Esq., and was Lord of Penmark, Carnllwyd in Llancarvan, &c.; *m.* Blanche, dau. of Thomas Morgan, Esq., of Machen (see *Morgan*, and *Lord Tredegar*), and had four sons, *Edward*, William, Nicholas, *Thomas*. The first Sir Edward Lewis, Kt., of Van, *m.* Anne, dau. of Robert, Earl of Dorset, and widow of Lord Beauchamp, and founded the family of Lewis of Burstal, of Edington, Wilts, and of Van, Glam. The fourth son,—

Sir Thomas Lewis, of Penmark, knighted 1628 ; Sheriff of Glam. 1629 (*d.* 1669), *m.* a dau. of Edmund Thomas, Esq., of Wenvoe (see *Thomas of Wenvoe*), and left—besides his eldest son, Thomas, who *m.* but *d. s. p.*, and other issue—a second son,—

Gabriel Lewis, Esq., who became of *Llanishen*, deputy-sheriff under his father, Sir Thomas Lewis, 1587, and Sheriff of Glamorgan 1615 ; *m.* Elizabeth, dau. of William Carne, Esq., of Nash, and was succeeded by his son,—

Thomas Lewis, Esq., of Llanishen, Sheriff of Glamorgan 1630, who by his wife Eleanor, dau. of Thomas Johns, Esq., of Abergavenny, had a son,—

Gabriel Lewis, Esq., his successor at Llanishen, Sheriff of Glam. 1663. He *m.* Grace, dau. of Humphrey *Wyndham*, Esq., of Dunraven Castle, Glam., and had a son and heir,—

Thomas Lewis, Esq., of Llanishen, Sheriff of Glam. 1673 and 1683 ; *m.*, first, Elizabeth Van, by whom he had issue Thomas, Sheriff of Glam. 1745, who had a son Wyndham and two daus., who all *d. s. p.*

[*Note.*—There was a Gabriel Lewis of Llanishen, who was Sheriff of Glamorgan 1715 (see *Sheriffs*), who could not be the same with Gabriel Lewis, Sheriff for 1663, and yet we find in the pedigrees no other account of him.]

Thomas Lewis, Esq., of Llanishen, *m.*, secondly Elizabeth, dau. of Henry Morgan, Esq., of Pen llwyn, Mon., and had a second son,—

Thomas Lewis, Esq., of Newhouse, Sheriff of Glamorgan 1757; *m.* Elizabeth, dau. of Morgan Thomas, Esq.; and besides a second son, *William*, of Green Meadow, or Pentyrch, Sheriff of Glam. 1790, who *d. s. p.*, left an eldest son and heir,—

Rev. Wyndham Lewis, M.A., of Newhouse, who *m.* Mary, dau. of Samuel Price, Esq., of Park and Coity, co. of Glam., and left issue, besides *Henry*, second son,—

Thomas, eldest son, who *m.*, and left one son, John, *d. s. p.*, and two daus.—

Wyndham, third son, of Green Meadow, M.P. for Cardiff 1820 (see *Parl. Annals*) ; *m.*, 1815, Mary Anne, dau. of John Evans, Esq., of Bramford Speke Devon ; *d. s. p.* 1838 ; she afterwards *m.* Benjamin Disraeli, Esq., M.P. (now "Right Hon."), and has recently been cr. "Viscountess Beaconsfield."

Henry Lewis, Esq. (second son), of Park and Green Meadow, *m.* Mary, dau. of George Emerton, Esq., and had issue,—

HENRY LEWIS, Esq., now of Green Meadow (as above).

Wyndham W. Lewis, Esq., of The Heath, near Cardiff, J. P. and D. L. for co. of Glam. ; *m.*, first, Annie. dau. of George Overton, Esq. ; secondly, Elizabeth, dau. of the late William Williams, Esq., of Aberpergwm.

Mary Jane, *m.* to Henry A. Vaughan, Esq

Anne Price, *m.* to George Thomas Clark, Esq. (see *Clark of Dowlais House*).

Catherine Price, *m.* to George Collins Jackson, Esq., an officer in the army.

LLANDAFF, The Right Rev. Alfred Ollivant, D.D., Bishop of.

Son of the late William Ollivant, Esq., of Manchester ; *b.* 1798 ; *ed.* at St. Paul's School and Trin. Coll., Camb. ; 6th Wrangler, B.A., and Senior Chancellor's Medallist, 1821 ; M.A. 1824, B.D. and D.D. 1836 ; *m.*, 1828, Alicia, dau. of Lieut.-Gen. William Spencer, and has issue ; was Vice-Prin. of St. David's Coll., Lampeter, 1827—1843; Reg. Prof. of Divinity, Camb., 1843—1849; consecrated Bishop of Llandaff (reputed the ninety-second in succession— see *Bishops of Llandaff*) in room of Copleston deceased, 1849. The See of Llandaff has jurisdiction over the cos. of Monmouth and Glamorgan, excepting the deanery of Gower in the latter, which is under the see of St. David's. The Bishop of Llandaff is patron of sixty-five livings, of the deanery of Llandaff, the Archdeaconries of Llandaff and Monmouth, the Chancellorship and Precentorship of the Cathedral, and the Prebends. Income of see, £4,200.

Dr. Ollivant is author of various *Sermons*, *Lectures*, and *Charges*, and some *Pamphlets* on ecclesiastical and ecclesiastico-political subjects.

Residence: Bishop's Court, Llandaff.
Town Address: Athenæum Club, S.W.
Arms of the See: Sa, two crosiers in saltire, one or, the other arg ; on a chief az. three mitres with labels of the second.

Note.—For a notice of the cathedral of this see, and its recent restoration, see *Llandaff Cathedral*. The episcopal see of Llandaff which now contains 215 benefices, had its origin in a place for Christian worship built at a very early period on the bank of the river Tâf—most likely on the spot where the cathedral now stands—and called Llandâ, "the church on the Tâf;" but the congregation here gathered, and its bishop, or minister obtained superintending power over the surrounding congregations gathered by degrees during the Roman civil domination only in the fifth century. *Dyfrig* (Dubricius) is said to have been the first bishop. Meurig, King of Glamorgan, has the reputation of having founded the see and endowed it with lands between the rivers Tâf and Ely. For a time *Caerleon*, the great Roman city, was considered, as well as Llandaff, as the home of the see, and probably through its civic importance obtained the pre-eminence and had the character, at least in after times, of primacy of the British Church. It lost this standing when *Dewi* (St. David), who had become its bishop, removed, or rather returned to St. David's. (See *St. David's, Bishop of;* and *Llanddewi-brefi*.)
The *Bishops of Llandaff*, since the conquest of Glamorgan by the Normans, are given elsewhere.

LLEWELYN, John Dillwyn, Esq., of Penlle'rgaer, Glamorganshire.

J. P. and D. L. for the co. of Glamorgan : High Sheriff for the same 1835 ; eldest son of the late Lewis Weston Dillwyn, Esq., F.R.S., of Penlle'rgaer, sometime M.P. for the co. of Glam. (see *Parl. Annals of co. Glam.*), and Sheriff for the same 1818 ; *b.* 1810 ; *m.*, 1833, Emma Thomasina, dau. of Thomas Mansel Talbot, Esq., of Margam Abbey, co. of Glam., and has, with other issue,—
John Talbot Dillwyn Llewelyn, Esq., now of Ynysygerwn (which see). See also *Dillwyn of Hendrefoilan.*

Residence: Penlle'rgaer, near Swansea.
Arms: Gu., on a chevron arg. three trefoils slipped of the first.

LINEAGE.

This family, which had its early seat in Herefordshire, is of the old Cymric stock of that part, as the name clearly indicates. They had also representatives seated in Breconshire, whence they emigrated to the United States. A further notice is found under *Dillwyn of Hendrefoilan*. See also *Price of Penlle'rgaer*, under "Old and Extinct Families."

LLEWELLYN, Griffith, Esq., of Baglan Hall, Glamorganshire.

J. P. and D. L. for the county of Glamorgan; was High Sheriff for the same 1852 ; is patron of the living of Aberavon-cum-Baglan, Glamorganshire; son of the late Griffith Llewellyn, Esq., of the same place, by Catherine, dau. and h. of the late J. Jones, Esq., of Baglan Hall ; *b.* Aug., 1806 ; *ed.* at Rugby School; *m.*, Oct, 1850, Madelina, eldest daughter of Pascoe St. Leger Grenfell, Esq., of Maesteg House, Swansea, J. P. and D. L. of co. Glamorgan; *s.* to his mother's estate 1840.

Residence: Baglan Hall, Aberavon.
Town Address: Union Club, Trafalgar Square.
Arms: 3 crosslets azure.
Crest: Boar's head.
Motto: Unus et idem.

Note.—The inheritors of this estate have been settled at Baglan for about 200 years ; but the date of erection of the present mansion is not precisely known. It has been restored and altered in recent times.

LLEWELLYN, William, Esq., of Court Colman, Glamorganshire.

J. P. and D. L. for the co. of Glamorgan ; Sheriff for the same co. 1854 (see *Sheriffs*); Capt. 1st. Glam. R. V. ; son of the late William Llewellyn, Esq., M.D., nephew of late Griffith Llewellyn, Esq., of Baglan Hall ; *b.* 1820 ; *m.*, 1844, Eleanor Emma, dau. of the late Rev. Robert Knight, A.M., of Tythegston Court, Rector of Newton Nottage (see *Knight of Tythegston Court*), by Emma, dau. of Thomas Eagles, Esq., of Pilston, Mon., and has issue.

Residence: Court Colman, near Bridgend.

LLEWELYN, John Talbot Dillwyn, Esq., Ynysy-gerwn, Glamorganshire.

J. P. and D. L. for the county of Glamorgan ; son of John Dillwyn Llewelyn, Esq., of Penlle'rgaer, J. P. and D. L. for Glamorganshire, and Sheriff for the same 1835 (see *Dillwyn Llewelyn of Penlle'rgaer);* *b.* at Penlle'rgaer, May 26, 1836 ; *ed.* at Eton and Christ Church, Oxford ; *grad.* M.A. 1859 ; *m.*, May 7th, 1861, to Caroline Julia Hicks Beach, eldest daughter of the late Sir Michael Hicks Beach, Bart., M.P., of Williamstrip Park, Gloucestershire ; has issue three sons and two daughters.

Residence: Ynysygerwn, near Neath.
Arms: Gu., on a chevron arg. three trefoils slipped of the first.
Crest: A stag's head couped ppr.
Motto: Craignez honte.

LLOYD, Herbert, Esq., of Cilybebyll, Glamorganshire.

J. P. for the co. of Glamorgan ; son of the

late Francis E. Lloyd, Esq., of Cilybebyll (who assumed the surname Lloyd on inheriting at the death of his mother), son of Henry Leach, Esq., of Milford and Cilybebyll, and his wife, Mary Brand, dau. of John Jones, Esq., of Brawdy, in the co. of Pembroke, in whose right Cilybebyll came to the Leach family; b. 1838; m., 1864, Frances Harriet, dau. of S. G. Pardon, Esq., of Tinerara, Ireland, and has issue.

Residence: Cilybebyll, near Neath.

MORGAN, Evan, Esq., St. Helen's, Glamorganshire.

J. P. and D. L. for the co. of Glamorgan; was Capt. in the R. Artillery, and served under Wellington in the Peninsular war; was Lieut. Col. of the Royal Glam. Artillery Militia, and is still Hon. Colonel of the same; was Chairman of the first Swansea Dock Company; son of the late John Morgan, Esq.; *s.* on the death of his elder brother John, *unm.*, a General in the Indian Army; a younger brother, Thomas Morgan, was Capt. R.N.; *m.*, first, a dau. of Admiral Cheshyre, by whom he had issue three sons (all officers in the army) and two daus.; secondly, Miss Winthrop, eldest dau. of Admiral Winthrop. Col. Morgan's eldest son, Jeffrey, served in the Abyssinian war, was in command of the Engineers at the storming of King Theodore's stronghold, and was spoken of in warm terms for his bravery in the general orders. He lies buried in African soil, but a monument has been erected to his memory in St Mary's Church, Swansea.

Residence: St. Helen's, Swansea.
Town Address: Junior United Service Club.
Arms: Sa., a chevron arg. between three spear-heads imbrued—BLEDDYN AP MAENARCH.

LINEAGE.

The arms borne by the Morgans indicate descent from Bleddyn ap Maenarch, Lord of Brecknock in the twelfth century.

MORGAN, Hon. Godfrey Charles, Ruperra Castle, Glamorganshire.

J. P. and D. L. for the co. of Monmouth, and J. P. for cos. of Glamorgan and Brecon; M. P. for Breconshire since 1858; was Capt. 17th Lancers, served in Crimean war, and received Crimean medal and clasps and Turkish war medal; is Major of Royal Gloucestershire Yeomanry Hussars; eldest surviving son of Charles Morgan, first Baron Tredegar, of Tredegar Park, Mon., and Ruperra Castle, Glam., by Rosamond, dau. of Gen. Godfrey Basil Mundy; *b.* 1830; *ed.* at Eton; is *unm.*

Residences: Ruperra Castle, near Cardiff; and Tredegar Park, near Newport, Mon.
Town Address: Carlton Club; Army and Navy Club.
Arms: See *Lord Tredegar.*

LINEAGE.

For the descent of this ancient Cymric family see *Tredegar, Baron, of Tredegar Park.*

MORRIS, George Byng, Esq., of Sketty, Glamorganshire.

Is J. P. and D. L. for the co. of Glamorgan; second son of the late Sir John Morris, Bart, of Sketty Park, and Hon. Lucy Juliana, dau. of John, 5th Viscount Torrington; *b.* 25th March, 1816, at Bryn, Swansea; *m.*, 23rd October, 1852, Emily Matilda, sole dau. of C. H. Smith, Esq., of Gwernllwynwith and Derwen-Fawr, Glamorganshire, and has issue 6 sons and 4 daughters, the eldest son being Robert, *b.* 1853.

Residence: Danygraig, Bridgend.
Arms: Sa., on a saltire engrailed, ermine, a bezant charged with a cross couped gu.
Crest: A lion rampant or, charged on the shoulder with a cross couped gu., within a chain in form of an arch, or.
Motto: Scuto fidei.

LINEAGE.

For the genealogy of this family see under *Sir John Armine Morris, Bart.*, of Sketty Park.

Note.—The co. of Glamorgan has two places of considerable note and antiquity, called *Danygraig* ("under the rock"), and both in the vicinity of rocky eminences—the residence of Byng Morris being one, and Danygraig, situated between Neath and Swansea, near the Shore, the home of a branch of the Popkins and the Thomases, in the 17th and 18th centuries, being the other. At Danygraig, Bridgend, some interesting Roman or Romano-British antiquities were a few years ago discovered. "In removing a bank in order to improve the grounds in the year 1850, a coin of a Roman empress, much worn, but distinguishable by the head-dress, was dug up. Pieces of stucco with signs of a diamond pattern, &c., were also found. Tradition speaks of the site of an old house near the Ridge, under the large elm under which these things were discovered. It was on the left, or north side of the occupation road, which continued from the main road towards the foot of the *Graig*, and then joined Bistil Lane, long since taken into the fields. The *Rhwsted*, or 'house-stead,' was the name of the old barn close at hand" (Knight's *Newton Nottage*). See also p. 523, *ante.*

MORRIS, Sir John Armine, Bart., of Sketty Park, Glamorganshire.

A baronet of the United Kingdom, cr. 1806 ; J. P. and D. L. of the co. of Glamorgan ; sometime an Officer in the 60th Rifles ; is patron of the living of Morriston, near Swansea ; eldest son of the late Sir John Morris, Bart., and the Hon. Lady Morris, dau. of 5th Viscount Torrington ; *b.* at Bryn House, near Swansea, July 13, 1813 ; *ed.* at Westminster School, and Sandhurst College ; *m.*, December, 1847, Catherine Ann, dau. of Ronald Macdonald, Esq. ; *s.* to title as 3rd baronet, and to the estates, February, 1855 ; has issue—
1. ROBERT ARMINE, *b.* 1848.
2. John, *b.* 1850.
3. George Cecil, *b.* 1852.
4. Arthur Ronald, *b.* 1855.
5. Herbert, *b.* 1858.
And four daughters.

Heir: Robert Armine Morris.
Residences: Sketty Park, and Havod, near Swansea ; Marina Villa, Mumbles.
Town Address: Carlton Club.
Arms: Sable, on a saltier engrailed ermine, a bezant charged with a cross couped gu.
Crest: Within a chain in the form of an arch a lion rampant or, charged on the shoulder with a cross couped as in the arms.
Motto: Scuto fidei.

LINEAGE.

This family traces its descent maternally from *Owain Gwynedd*, Prince of North Wales (12th cent.), through Cadwgan Fawr, and the Parrys of Neuadd Trefawr, co. of Cardigan, one of whom was Stephen Parry, Esq., M.P. for Cardigan A.D. 1714—1727 (see *Members of Parl. for Cardigan*), and paternally from the Morrises of Bishop's Castle, Salop. It has intermarried with the Musgraves of Cumberland, and the Byngs, Viscounts Torrington. Sir John Morris, Kt., *temp.* Henry VII., was of this stock.

JOHN MORRIS, Esq., of Clasemont, near Swansea ; *b.* 1745 ; cr. a baronet 1806 ; *m.* Henrietta, dau. of Sir Philip Musgrave, Bart., of Eden Hall, Cumberland, by whom he had, with several daus., a son and heir,—

Sir John Morris, 2nd Bart. of Clasemont ; *b.* 1775 ; *m.*, 1809, Lucy Juliana, dau. of John Byng, 5th Viscount Torrington, and had issue, besides several daus.,—
1. JOHN ARMINE, the present and 3rd Baronet of Sketty Park (as above).
2. *George Byng* (see *Byng Morris of Danygraig*).
3. Frederick, an officer in the R.N.
4. Charles Henry, C.B., *b.* 1824, a Col. in the Royal Artillery.

Note.—Sketty Park, formerly belonging to Lord Broke, descendant of Earl Warwick, conqueror of the kingdom of Glamorgan, was enclosed with a wall by the grandfather of the present baronet. Several of the ruined castles in Gower were built by the above-mentioned *Earl of Warwick*. Sketty Park was built about 1820—partially with the Bath and Portland stone, the remains of the former Mansion House at Clasemont, in the same county, erected in 1770 by the grandfather of the present baronet, whose father was the first of the family who removed from North to South Wales, and first resided at Tredegar, Mon. The etymology of "*Sketty*" is probably *is-Ketty*, "lower Ketty."

NICHOLL, Iltyd, Esq., of the Ham, Glamorganshire.

J. P. for Monmouthshire and Glamorganshire ; Sheriff of Monmouthshire 1831 ; eldest son of the late Rev. Iltyd Nicholl, D.D., Rector of Treddington, Worcestershire ; *b.* at Treddington 19th July, 1785 ; *ed.* at St. Paul's School, London ; *m.*, 11th August, 1807, Eleanor, only child of George Bond, Esq. ; of Newland, Gloucestershire, and Court Blethin, Monmouthshire (she *d.* 1850), and had issue three sons and two daughters.

Heir: George Whitlock Nicholl, Esq., of Court Blethin, co. of Mon., J. P. for the co. of Mon.
Residences: The Ham, Glamorganshire ; Court Blethin, Monmouthshire.
Arms: Sable, three pheons argent.
Crest: A battlemented tower surmounted by a Cornish chough proper.
Motto: Duw a digon.

LINEAGE.

The family of *Nicholl* have been seated at The Ham nearly 300 years, and were found even earlier than that period (as well as later) at Llantwit Major, where resided John Nicholl, whose will was proved 1599, and who bore the arms still borne by the family, viz., Sa., 3 *pheons arg.* His son was called Iltyd—a name which has been continued at frequent intervals ever since. From Iltyd Nicholl, of The Ham, 3rd son of Iltyd, gr. grandson of the above John Nicholl, has descended the long line of the Ham family. His mother was Cecil, dau. of Edmond Turbervill, Esq., of Llantwit Major. He left a son,—

Iltyd Nicholl, Esq., of The Ham, *b.* 1635, who *m.* Mary, dau. of Morgan Jones, Esq., of Frampton, and had issue—

Iltyd Nicholl, of The Ham, Clerk, Rector of Llanmaes, who by his wife, Susannah, dau. and co-h. of John Whitlock, Esq., of Bingham, Somerset, had, besides John, 3rd son, founder of the Merthyr Mawr branch (see *Nicholl of Merthyr Mawr*), an eldest son and heir.—

Whitlock Nicholl, Esq., of The Ham ; J. P. and D. L. for the co. of Glam. ; Sheriff of same co. 1746. He *m.*, 1741, Anne, dau. and co-h. of John Lewis, Esq., of Penlline, "by whom he had 14 children, 6 sons and 8 daus, of whom eight only survived their parents, and three sons and one dau. only had issue." (D Jenkin's MS.) The eldest son was—

Rev. Iltyd Nicholl, D.D., Rector of Treddington, who was the progenitor of a large family. His eldest son and h. being—
1. ILTYD NICHOLL, Esq., now of The Ham (as above) and his sixth son being—
6. Rev. Robert Nicholl, M.A., late of Dimlands (see *Nicholl-Carne of Dimlands and St. Donat's Castle*).

NICHOLL, John Cole, Esq., of Merthyr Mawr, Glamorganshire.

J. P. for the co. of Glamorgan; eldest son of the late Right Hon. John Nicholl, D.C.L., M.P. for Cardiff Boroughs 1832—1852, and Judge Advocate-General, 1841 (see *Parl. Annals, Glam.*); *b.* 1823; *ed.* at Ch. Ch., Oxford; *m.*, 1860, Mary De la Beche, dau. of L. Ll. Dillwyn, Esq., M.P. of Hendrefoilan, co. of Glamorgan, and has issue.

Residence: Merthyr Mawr, near Bridgend.
Town Address: Carlton Club.
Arms: Sa., three pheons arg.
Crest: On a tower, a Cornish chough, wings expanded, ppr.

LINEAGE.

This family is a junior branch of that of Nicholl of Ham, in the same co. (see *Nicholl of Ham*, and *Nicholl-Carne of St. Donat's Castle*). John Nicholl, Esq., of Llanmaes, third son of the Rev. Iltyd Nicholl, of Ham, Rector of Llanmaes, was grandfather of Sir John Nicholl, Kt., of Merthyr Mawr, whose son, Sir John Nicholl, Kt. (above named), M.P. for Cardiff; *m.* Jane Harriet, dau. of the late Thomas Mansel Talbot, Esq., of Margam Abbey, and had, with other issue,—
JOHN COLE NICHOLL, now of Merthyr Mawr.

PEARSON, John Richard, Esq., of Craig yr Haul, Glamorganshire.

Late Captain Royal Artillery; J. P. for co. of Monmouth; son of Rev. J. Pearson, of Herongate, Brentwood, Essex, Rector of Little Warley and East Horndon, Essex, Rural Dean, &c.; *b.* at Bognor, Sussex, 16th April, 1833; *ed.* at Rugby; *m.*, 1st, 1854, Charlotte, dau. of Col. Crommelin, (she *d.* 1856); 2nd, 1861, Cecile, dau. of the late George Charles Holford, Esq., of New Park, Wilts, and granddaughter of the late Josiah Holford, Esq., of Cilgwyn, Carmarthenshire.

Residence: Craig yr Haul, Castleton, Cardiff.
Town Address: Junior United-Service Club.
Arms: Arg., semée of billets, on a pile az. three horses' heads ppr.
Crest: A horse's head couped ppr., semée of billets and murally gorged.
Motto: In Deo spes.

PENRICE, Thomas, Esq., of Kilvrough, Glamorganshire.

J. P. for the co. of Glamorgan; served the office of High Sheriff for same co. in 1867; is patron of the livings of Ilston, Pennard, and Langennith, in the co. of Glamorgan; 2nd son of the late John Penrice, Esq., of Great Yarmouth, in the co. of Norfolk; *b.* 6th April, 1820, at Hopland Hall, near Gt. Yarmouth; *ed.* at Eton; *m.*, 10th June, 1852, Louisa, the 2nd daughter of the Rev. George Ernest Howman, M A., of Barnesley Rectory, Gloucestershire; succ. his uncle, Thomas Penrice, Esq., of Kilvrough (Sheriff for Glam. 1836; Capt. in 16th Lancers, and served under Wellington), in the year 1846; has issue two daughters.

Residence: Kilvrough, near Swansea.
Arms: Per pale indented arg. and gu., in canton a wolf's head couped at the neck sa.
Crest: Two wings elevated, charged with two mullets of six points in pale gu.
Motto: Tuto et celeriter (above crest); Justus et propositi tenax (under shield).

LINEAGE.

Mr. Penrice of Kilvrough traces from an ancient family of the same name which has been for many generations located in the county of Worcester, the eldest branch of which family was seated at *Penrice Castle*, near Swansea, in the lordship of Gower and county of Glamorgan, a lordship which passed into the hands of the Mansels of Margam through the marriage of Isabella Penrice with a member of that family. See *Mansel of Margam, Penrice Castle,* &c.

Note.—Kilvrough—one of the many places of note in the historic district of Gower - is well known as the old abode of the Dawkin family, the most celebrated of whose members was Col. Rowland Dawkin, M.P., a distinguished officer in the Cromwellian army. See *ante Dawkin of Kilvrough*, and *Memoir*, by Col. Francis, F.S.A.

PRICHARD, William, Esq., of Crofta House, Glamorganshire.

J. P. for co. of Glamorgan; son of the late William Prichard, Shipowner of Cardiff; *b.* 1811; *m.* Miss Bradley of Cardiff; has issue three daughters, co-heiresses.

Residence: Crofta House, near Llantrisant.

PRYCE, John Bruce, Esq., of Dyffryn, Glamorganshire.

J. P. and D. L. for the co. of Glamorgan; eldest son of the late John Knight, Esq., of Llanblethian, in the same co., by Margaret, dau. of William Bruce, Esq., of that place, whose surname, and subsequently that of Pryce, he adopted (see *Lineage*); *b.* 23rd July, 1784; *m.*, 1st, 1807, Sarah (*d.* 1842), dau. of Rev. Hugh Williams Austin, a resident of Barbadoes; 2ndly, 1844, Alicia Grant, dau. of William Bushly, Esq., of London; had issue by first wife five sons and seven daus. The sons are—

THE COUNTY FAMILIES OF GLAMORGANSHIRE. 639

1. *John Wyndham*, barrister-at-law, *m.*, and had issue ; 2. Henry Austin, barrister-at-law, now of the Privy Council and Secretary of the Home Department (see *Bruce of Dyffryn*); 3. Rev. William Bruce, M.A., Canon of Llandaff, and Rector of St. Nicholas; 4. Robert, a col. in the army; 5. Lewis Knight.

Residence: *Dyffryn*, St. Nicholas, near Cardiff.

LINEAGE.

The family of Bruce Pryce of Dyffryn traces maternally to an ancient Glamorgan stock, the Lewises of Van and Llanishen, of the lineage of Ivor Bach of Castell Coch, living in the twelfth century, of whom Giraldus Cambrensis (*Itin.*, *VI.*) gives account (see *Ivor Bach*). Sir Thomas Lewis, Knt., of Llanishen, had a son, Gabriel Lewis, Esq., of the same place, Sheriff of Glamorgan 1615 (see *Lewis of Green Meadow*), whose dau. Jane *m.*—William *Bruce*, Esq., of Llanblethian, co. of Glam., and had issue a dau. and only surviving child, Margaret Bruce, who *m.*—John *Knight*, Esq., of Llanblethian, and had issue besides 3 daus.—

1. JOHN, now of Dyffryn as above, who, instead of his own surname of Knight, adopted his mother's maiden surname, *Bruce*, and subsequently, on inheriting Dyffryn under the will of Thomas Pryce, Esq., who made him heir in case of the death without issue of his own daughter, Mrs. Grey, (*d.* 1837,) wife of the Hon. W. Booth Grey, that of *Pryce.*
2. William Bruce Knight, Chancellor, and afterwards Dean of Llandaff, *d.* 1845.
3. James Lewis, Knight, afterwards Lord Justice Sir J. L. Knight Bruce, *d.* 1867.

RICHARDS, Evan Matthew, Esq., of Brooklands, Glamorganshire.

J. P. and D. L. for the co. of Glamorgan ; M.P. for Cardiganshire, elected 1868 ; was Mayor of Swansea 1856 and 1863 ; son of the late Mr. R. Richards, of Swansea ; *b.* at Swansea, January, 1821 ; *m.* Maria, daughter of James Sloane, Esq. ; has issue six sons and one daughter.

Heir: William Frederic.
Residence: Brooklands, Swansea.
Town Address: 3, Kensington Gate; Reform Club.

RICHARDSON, James Coxon, Esq., of Glan'rafon, Glamorganshire.

J. P. for the co. of Glamorgan; F.G.S., &c., &c. ; fourth son of John Richardson, Esq., J. P. of Swansea, and brother of J. Crow Richardson, Esq., of Pantygwydir, Glam., and Glanbrydan Park, Carm. ; *b.* at South Shields, co. of Durham, 1817 ; *ed.* at Myrtle Hall School, Gloucestershire ; *m.*, first, Hannah Mary, second dau. of Thomas Barker, Esq., J. P., &c., of Rosella Hall, Northumberland ; secondly, Elizabeth, dau. of John Nichol, Esq., of London, the adopted child of the Rt. Hon. Sir John Pirie, Bart. ; thirdly, Georgiana Skirrow, second dau. of John Nelson, Esq., of Doctors' Commons and of Seymour Street, Hyde Park, London ; has issue—
By second mar, John Pirie, *b.* 1848.
By third mar., three sons and two daus. :—
Nelson Moore, *b.* 1855.
Ida Caroline Frances, *b.* 1856.
Horace Grant, *b.* 1858.
Evelyn Georgina, *b.* 1860.
Lionel James, *b.* 1862.

Residence: Glan'rafon, near Swansea.
Arms: Sa., on a chief arg. three lions' heads erased, ermines, langued gu.
Crest: On a mural crown or, a lion's head erased of the arms.
Motto: Pretio prudentia præstat.

RICHARDSON, John Crow, Esq., of Pantygwydir, Glam., and Glanbrydan Park, Carm.

J. P. for the co. of Glamorgan and for the bor. of Swansea; was Mayor of Swansea 1860-1, and for several years Captain and Acting Commandant of the 3rd Glamorgan Rifle Volunteers; eldest son of John Richardson, Esq., J. P., of Swansea, and of Whitby Lodge, Northumberland ; *b.* at Leith, Jan. 30, 1810 ; *m.*, first, 6th Nov., 1837, Elizabeth, eldest dau. of Mr. Thomas Walters, of Swansea ; secondly, Aug. 23, 1848, Eliza Fletcher, youngest dau. of the Rev. John Ross, of Crawford, Lanarkshire ; purchased the Pantygwydir estate 1860 ; has issue by first marriage—
John Crow, only son, *b.* 26th Feb., 1842 ; *m.* Theresa Eden Pearce Serocold, and has issue Alfred John and Ernald Edward.
Amy, *b.* 17th Sept., 1840, *m.*, June 1, 1864, George Pearce Serocold, Esq., of Rodborough Lodge, Gloucestershire, whose father was Dean of Ely and Principal of Jesus Coll., Cambridge.

Heir: John Crow Richardson.
Residences: Pantygwydir, near Swansea ; Glanbrydan Park, Carmarthenshire.
Arms (granted 1615) : Sa., on a chief arg. three lions' heads, erased, ermines, langued gu.
Crest: On a mural crown or, a lion's head of the arms.
Motto: Pretio prudentia præstat.

LINEAGE.

This family is of common origin with that from which Sir Thomas Richardson, Kt., one of the judges of the Exchequer, was descended, and which is extensively seated in the cos. of Durham and Northumberland.

ROMILLY, Edward, Esq., of Porth Kerry, Glamorganshire.

J. P. and D. L. for the co. of Glamorgan; Sheriff for same co. 1869; younger son of the late Sir Samuel Romilly, Kt., by Anne, dau. of Francis Garbett, Esq., of Knill Court, co. of Radnor, and brother of Lord Romilly, Master of the Rolls; *b.* 1804; *ed.* at Trinity Hall, Cambr.; *m.*, 1830, Sophia, dau. of Alexander Marcet, Esq., M.D.; was M.P. for Ludlow 1833-4; was Chairman of Audit Board of Public Accounts.

Residence: Porth Kerry, near Cowbridge.
Town Address: 14, Stratton Street, W.
Arms: Arg., in base a rock with nine projections, from each of which issuant a lily, all ppr.; on a chief az., a crescent between two mullets of the first.
Crest: On a wreath a crescent arg.

ROUS, Col. George Grey, of Courtyrala, Glamorganshire.

Entered the army and became Lieut.-Col. of Grenadier Guards; J. P. and D. L. for the co. of Glamorgan; Sheriff for same co. 1860; eldest son of the late Thomas Bates Rous of Courtyrala, J. P., D. L., and Sheriff (in 1817) of the co. of Glamorgan, by his wife Charlotte Gwendoline, dau. of Sir Robert Salusbury, Bart., of Llanwern, Mon.; *b.* 1818; is *unm.*

Residence: Courtyrala, near Cardiff.
Town Address: Guards' Club.
Arms: Or, an eagle displayed az., pruning the wing, foot and beak gu.
Crest: A dove arg.
Motto: Vescitur Christo.

LINEAGE.

The Roll of Battle Abbey contains the name *Rous*, and the name takes in some records the form *Rufus*. This family is said to descend from this knight in the Conqueror's train, whose full designation was Ranalphus le Rufus. Before the settlement of the family in Wales, through the purchase of Piercefield (Mon.) by Thomas Rous, Esq. (*d.* 1737), they had been successively seated at Edmerstone and Halton in Devonshire. Of their number was the celebrated *Francis Rouse*, translator of the Psalms (still used by the Scotch Kirk), Member for Truro, or Devonshire, of the Little Parliament, Provost of Eton, and Speaker of Cromwell's Parliament (*Carlyle;* and *Roll of Battle Abbey,* p. 94).
Thomas Rous, Esq., of Piercefield, son of Thomas Thomas Rous just named, sold that estate to the Morris family. He *m.* Mary, dau. of Thomas Bates, Esq., and had, besides his eldest son William, who *d. unm.*, Thomas Bates, George, and Robert.
Thomas Bates Rous, Esq., who resided in England, and was sometime M.P. for Worcester, *d. s. p.* in 1800, and was *s.* by his brother,—
George Rous, Esq., of London, Barrister-at-law, M.P. for Shaftesbury, &c. His eldest son,—
Thomas Bates Rous, the first of Courtyrala, Sheriff of co. of Glamorgan 1817; *m.*, 1811, a dau. of Sir Robert Salusbury, Bart., and had with several daus. a son and heir,—
George Grey Rous, now of Courtyrala (as above).

Note.—*Courtyrala* is a manor of considerable antiquity, having its name from Sir Simon de *Rayle*, Lord of the Manor of Wrinston and Michaelston, Glam., whose place of residence and feudal rule was subsequently called *Court-y-Rayle,* corrupted into "Courtyrala." See *ante, De Rayle of Wrinston.*

SALMON, William, Esq., of Penlline Court, Glamorganshire.

J. P. and D. L. for the co. of Glamorgan; only son of the late W. Salmon, Esq., of Petistree House, Suffolk, by Sarah, dau. of Denny Cole, Esq., of Sudbury Priory, Suffolk; *b.* 1790; *m.*, 1816, Hester, elder dau. and co-h. of Reynold Thomas Deere, Esq., J. P. and D. L., of Penlline Court, and has issue—
Thomas Deere, *b.* 1820; *ed.* at Eton and Exeter Coll., Oxford, where he *grad.* M.A.; is a barrister of Lincoln's Inn.

Heir: Thomas Deere Salmon.
Residence: Penlline Court, near Cowbridge.
Crest: A dexter arm, embowed, in armour, holding a scimitar proper.
Motto: Dum spiro spero.

LINEAGE.

Mr. Salmon is lineally descended from Sir Thomas Salmon, Kt., *temp.* Richard I., and collaterally from John Salmon, Lord High Chancellor of England, *temp.* Edward II. Hester, his wife, was of a very ancient Glamorganshire family, which traced its descent from Edwin, fourth son of Howel Dda, or Howel the Good, King of South Wales and Powys 907, and of all Wales 940,—and from Herbert, natural son of King Henry I.

SMITH, Charles Henry, Esq., of Gwernllwyn-with, Glamorganshire.

J. P. for the co. of Glamorgan; High Sheriff of the same county in 1839; son of the late Charles Smith, Esq., of Gwernllwynwith; *b.* 25th Dec., 1804; *m.*, 1831, Emily, dau. of Sir George Leeds, Bart., of Croxton Park, Camb.; has surviving issue one daughter, Emily Matilda. (See *Byng Morris, Danygraig.*)

Residence: Gwernllwynwith, near Swansea.
Arms: Or and az, indented sinisterwise, two crosses counterchanged.
Crest: Out of coronet, a dove volant.

THE COUNTY FAMILIES OF GLAMORGANSHIRE.

SQUIRE, Rev. Edward Burnard, Swansea, Glamorganshire.

Rural Dean; Vicar of Swansea 1846; Chaplain of 1st Glamorganshire Artillery Volunteers; formerly in Convocation; was Lieut. Indian Navy and Paymaster in the Burmese war 1827—1829; Author of a "Series of Sermons on Special Occasions," "British Sovereignty in India," &c.; *b.* at Taunton 1804; *ed.* at St. Bee's College; *m.*, first, Eliza Anne, dau. of Capt. William Bruce, Indian Navy, and British resident of Bushire in Persia; secondly, Caroline Herschel, dau. of George Harvey, F.R.S.; thirdly, 26th Oct., 1852, dau. of Thomas Bowen, Esq., of Johnstone Hall, Pembrokeshire, sister of the late Bishop Bowen, of Sierra Leone; has issue 3 sons and 3 daus. living.

Residence: The Vicarage, Swansea.
Crest: Tiger's paw holding a fleur-de-lis.
Motto: Tiens ferme.

STERRY, Alfred, Esq., of Danycoed, Glamorganshire.

Son of Richard Sterry, Esq, Oakfield Lodge, Croydon; *b.* 1823; *m.*, 1864, Alice Rosina, daughter of Henry Crawshay, Esq., of Langland, near Swansea, and Oaklands, Gloucestershire; has issue 1 son, 2 daus.

Residence: Dan y Coed, near Swansea.
Arms: (not received).

STUART, James Frederick Crichton-, M.P, Cardiff, Glamorganshire.

Lieut.-Col. in the army (retired); served in the Grenadier Guards 1842—1861; Lord Lieutenant of Buteshire; M.P. for united boroughs of Cardiff, Cowbridge, and Llantrisant since first elected in 1857; son of late Lord James Stuart, M.P., brother to 2nd Marquess of Bute (see *Bute, Marquess of*); *b.* Feb. 17, 1824; *ed.* at Eton, and Trinity Coll., Cambridge; *m.* Gertrude Frances, dau. of the Rt. Hon. Sir G. H. Seymour, G.C.B.; has issue 1 son and 2 daughters.

Town Residence: 25, Wilton Crescent.
Arms: 1st and 4th, or, a fesse checky arg. and az. within a double tressure flory counterflory gu. —STUART; 2nd and 3rd, arg., a lion ramp. az.— CRICHTON; over all a crescent for difference.
Crests: 1. A demi-lion ramp. gu., and over it the motto "Nobilis est ira leonis"—*Stuart.* 2. A dragon vert, flames issuing from the mouth, ppr.—*Crichton.*
Motto: Avito viret honore.

LINEAGE.

For *Lineage*, see *Bute, Marquess of*, Cardiff Castle, of whose family Col. Stuart is a cadet.

TALBOT, Christopher Rice Mansel-, Esq., of Margam Park, Glamorganshire.

Lord Lieut. of Glamorganshire since 1848; M.P. for Glamorganshire since 1830; is patron of five livings, Reynoldston, Oxwich-cum-Nicholaston, Langeinor, Llandough-cum-St. Mary Church, and Margam Vicarage; eldest son of the late Thomas Mansel Talbot, Esq., of Margam Park, J. P. and D. L. for the co. of Glamorgan, and Sheriff for same co. 1781, by the Lady Mary Lucy, dau. of Henry Thomas, 2nd Earl of Ilchester; *b.* at Penrice Castle, near Swansea, May 10, 1803; *ed.* at Harrow, and Oriel Coll., Oxford; *grad.* B.A. in 1824, First Class in Mathematics; succ. 1824; *m.*, 1835, to Lady Charlotte Butler, sister to the Earl of Glengall (she *d.* 1846), and has issue one son, three daughters.

Heir: Theodore Mansel, *b.* 1837; *ed.* at Christ Church, Oxford; J. P. for co. of Glam.
Residences: Margam Park, and Penrice Castle, Glamorganshire.
Town House: 3, Cavendish Square.
Arms: Gu., a lion rampant or, armed and langued az., within a bordure engrailed of the second.
Crest: A lion or, with tail extended.
Motto: Prest d'accomplir.

LINEAGE.

This branch of the *Talbot* family, of common origin with Talbots, Earls of Shrewsbury, Lord Chancellor Talbot of Hensol Castle, Talbots of Castle Talbot, Ireland, &c., came into Glamorgan through the marriage of John Ivory Talbot, Esq., of Lacock Abbey, with Mary, dau. and h. of Thomas Mansel, Lord Mansel of Margam. The *Mansel* family had for many ages held a position of prime influence in Glamorgan, seated successively at Oxwich Castle, Penrice Castle, and Margam Abbey (which see), from about A.D. 1400, when Sir Hugh Mansel *m.* Isabel, dau. of Sir John Penrhys, Lord of Oxwich and Penrhys (Penrice), to A.D. 1750, when Bussy, the last Lord Mansel of Margam and Penrice, died, and the estate passed by the marriage just mentioned to the Mansel-Talbot line.

From Sir Hugh Mansel, Kt., *Sir Rhys* (Rice) *Mansel*, Kt., Lord of Oxwich, and builder of Oxwich Castle, Chamberlain of Chester, Sheriff of Glamorgan in 1542, was fifth in descent; from Henry Mansel, Esq., the first who settled in Gower (*temp.* Edward I.), tenth; and from Philip Mansel, or Maunchel, who is said to have "come in with the Conqueror," about eighteenth. At the dissolution of the monasteries he purchased Margam Abbey from the commissioners of Henry VIII., and partly by adaptation of the structure of the abbey, partly by new buildings constructed there (1552), formed a large and sumptuous mansion, which became the chief residence of the Mansel family.

Sir *Edward Mansel*, Kt., his son, *m*. Lady Jane, 4th dau. of Henry, 2nd Earl of Worcester, by whom he had 15 sons and 4 daus. He was Sheriff of Glamorgan 1576. His second son, Francis, was made a baronet by James I., and by his wife Catherine, dau., and h. of Henry Morgan, Esq., of Muddlescombe was progenitor of the Mansels of *Iscoed* and *Trimsaran*, Carm. From his third son, Philip, were descended the Mansels of *Swansea*. Robert, fourth son, knighted by the Earl of Essex for his valour in taking Cadiz, 1596, made Vice-Admiral by James I., *m*. Elizabeth, sister of the celebrated Lord Bacon. On the death of Sir Edward in 1585 (see *Margam Abbey*)—
Sir Thomas Mansel, Kt. and Bart., of Margam, succeeded. He was Sheriff of Glamorgan 1594, 1604, and 1623; M.P. for same co. 1597, &c. (see *Parl. Annals of Glam.*). By Mary, his first wife, dau. of Lewis Lord Mordaunt, he had four sons (by a 2nd wife he had daus.), the heir being—
Sir Lewis Mansel, Bart., of Margam. Was Sheriff of Glam. 1636; in conjunction with Edward Viscount Mandeville, and William Carne, Esq., of Nash, he obtained from Charles I. the office of Chamberlain and Chancellor of South Wales during their respective lives and the survivor of them. By his third wife, Elizabeth, dau. of Henry, Earl of Manchester, Lord Privy Seal, he had two sons, Henry and Edward, and was succ. by the younger and surviving of them,—
Sir Edward Mansel, Bart., of Margam, one of the most distinguished of his race. He was Sheriff for the co. of Glam. 1688; M.P. for same co. 1660, 1680, and 1685; entertained at Margam the Duke of Beaufort on his progress as Lord President of Wales in 1684 (see *Margam Abbey*); *m*. Martha, dau. and co-h. of Edward Carne, Esq., of Ewenny, and was succ. by his 2nd but eldest surviving son,—
Sir Thomas Mansel, Bart., afterwards Lord Mansel of Margam, M.P. for co. of Glamorgan 1700—1710; cr. Baron Mansel of Margam by Queen Anne in 1712; Comptroller of the Household under Queen Anne, and Member of Privy Council (see further *Parl. Annals*). He *m*. Martha, dau. and h. of Francis Millington, Esq., and by her, besides four daus., had three sons, *Robert*, *Christopher*, and *Bussy*. The first *m*., had issue one son, *Thomas*, and dying in his father's lifetime, left the succession in that son.
Thomas, 2nd Lord Mansel of Margam, succ. as a minor at his grandfather's death, and *d. unm.*, æt. 25.
Christopher, 3rd Lord Mansel of Margam, dwelt at Newick Place, Sussex, and was never married. He settled Margam estate, after the death of his brother Bussy, upon Thomas Mansel, eldest son of his sister Mary, wife of John Ivory Talbot, Esq., above-mentioned; *d*. 1744, and was buried at Newick.
Bussy, 4th and last Lord Mansel of Margam, now succ. He was before his elevation to the peerage M.P. for Cardiff 1727, and afterwards for Glamorgan 1737. (See *Parl. Annals.*) He *d. s. p.* in London 1750, and was buried at St James's, Westminster.
Thomas Talbot, Clerk, in right of his mother now inherited Margam and Penrice Castle estates. He *m*. Jane, dau. of Thomas Beach, Esq., of Keevil, Wilts, and had two sons, Thomas and Christopher; the eldest,—
Thomas Mansel Talbot, Esq., of Penrice Castle and Margam, *m*., 1794, Lady Mary Lucy Fox Strangways, dau. of Henry Thomas, 2nd Earl of Ilchester (she *m*. 2ndly, 1815, Sir Christopher Cole, K.C.B. [see *Parl. Annals*, p. 608]), and had with other issue (see *Traherne, Mrs., St. Hilary; Llewelyn, Penllergaer, &c.*)—
CHRISTOPHER MANSEL-TALBOT, now of Margam and Penrice Castle (as above).

THOMAS, Hubert de Burgh, Esq., of Pwllywrach, Glamorganshire.

Is one of the co-heirs to the Barony of Burgh or Borough of Gainsborough, now in abeyance; J. P. for county of Glamorgan; late Captain of the 18th Glamorgan Rifle Corps; is patron of Colwinston Vicarage; *b*. at Pwllywrach, Sept. 6th, 1842; *ed*. at Cheltenham College, and Trin. Coll., Oxford; *s*. to estates 1853.

Heir: His brother, Robert Curre.
Residence: Pwllywrach.
Arms: Gu., three chevrons arg.
Crest: A paschal lamb.
Mottoes: Nil desperandum; Christo duce.

THOMAS, John Blackwell Dawson, Esq., of Tregroes, Glamorganshire.

J. P. for the co. of Glamorgan; *b*. 3rd March, 1840, at Fulham, Middlesex; *m*., 17th June, 1868, Louisa, second daughter of Charles Dawson, Esq., of Exmouth, Devon; *s*. to estates 1863; has issue one son, Edward Dawson.

Heir: Edward Dawson.
Residences: Tregroes, near Bridgend; Withycombe, near Exmouth.
Motto: Nil desperandum.

THOMAS, Richard Robert Rees, Esq., Court House, Glamorganshire.

Son of the late William Thomas, Esq; *b*. Nov. 12th, 1823; *ed*. at the Swansea Grammar School; *m*, 1st, Feb., 1857, Janet Jane, eldest dau. of Thomas Thomas, Esq., of Lechwan, Lanfabon; 2ndly, September, 1864, Anna Mary, daughter of Christopher Williams, Esq., of Llantwit Major; *s*. June, 1858; has issue two sons and one daughter.

Residence: Court House, Merthyr.
Arms: A lion rampant, holding a laurel branch in the paw.
Crest: A demi-lion as in arms.
Motto: Floreat laurus.

TRAHERNE, Anthony Powell, Esq., of Broadlands, Glamorganshire.

Entered the army 17th Foot 29th July,

1853; Lieut. 6th June, 1854; Captain 4th December, 1857; served in the Crimean war from December, 1854, to end of the war; present at the assault of Redan 18th June, bombardment and surrender of Kinbourn, medals and clasp; appointed adjutant of 1st ad. Batt. Glamorgan Rifle Volunteers in August, 1863; J. P. for the co. of Glamorgan; 3rd surviving son of Morgan Popkin Traherne, Esq., and Elizabeth Margaret, his wife (*née* Rickards); *b.* at Coytrehen, near Bridgend, 4th January, 1834; *ed.* at Woolwich and Sherborne; *m.*, February 9, 1865, Lucy Lockwood, dau. of the late Thomas Onslow, Esq.; has issue one son, Onslow Powell.

Heir: Onslow Powell.
Residence: Broadlands, near Bridgend.
Town Address: Naval and Military Club, Piccadilly.
Motto: Ofna Dduw a'r Brenhin: "Fear God and the King."

TRAHERNE, Mrs., of St. Hilary, Glamorganshire.

Charlotte Louisa Traherne, of St. Hilary and Coedriglan, widow of the Rev. John Montgomery Traherne, M.A., of Coedriglan, F.R.S, F.S.A.; Chancellor of Llandaff; J.P. and D. L. for the co. of Glamorgan (*d. s. p.* 1860); 3rd dau. of the late Thomas Mansel Talbot, Esq, of Margam and Penrice Castle, co. Glam., by Lady Mary Lucy, dau. of Henry Thomas, 2nd Earl of Ilchester; is sister of C. R. Mansel Talbot, Esq., M.P. of Margam and Penrice Castle, Lord Lieut. of Glamorganshire since 1848 (see *Mansel Talbot of Margam*); *b.* at Penrice Castle, Feb. 5th, 1800; *m.*, 1830, to Rev. John Montgomery Traherne (see for lineage, under *George Montgomery Traherne of St. Hilary*); *s.* her husband 1860; is patron of the livings of St. George-super-Ely, St. Bride's-super-Ely cum Michaelston-super-Ely.

Heir: To *Coedriglan*, George Montgomery Traherne, Esq., nephew of Rev. John M. Traherne; and to St. Hilary, Llewelyn Basset Saunderson, Esq., a cousin.
Residence: St. Hilary, near Cowbridge.
Arms: Az., a chevron sable inter 3 choughs proper, on a canton barry of six arg. and az., a lion rampant gules.
Motto: Dives qui contentus.

LINEAGE.

For the Talbot lineage see *Mansel-Talbot of Margam*; and for the Traherne lineage, which traces directly in the female line through the Herberts of Swansea, progenitors of the Earls of Pembroke, Powis, &c., see the next succeeding article, and also *pedigree* in Traherne's *Hist. Notice of Sir Matthew Cradock, Kt.*

Note.—The family mansions at Coedriglan and St. Hilary are modern structures. On the estate is *St. George's Castle* in ruins, the manor belonging to which was given by Fitzhamon to Sir John Fleming (see *Le Fleming of St. George's and Flemingston*). An interesting specimen of the ancient Pigeon-house is found at Cadoxton-juxta-Barry.

TRAHERNE, George Montgomery, Esq., of St. Hilary, Glamorganshire.

J. P. for the co. of Glamorgan; son of the late Rev. George Traherne, M.A., Univ. Coll., Oxford, Vicar of St. Hilary and Rector of St. George's, co. Glamorgan, by Ellin, dau. of the late John Gilbert Royds, Esq.; *b.* at St. Hilary, July 30, 1826; *ed.* at Brasenose Coll., Oxford; *grad.* B.A. 1849, M.A. 1853; *m.*, in 1860, Harriet, dau. of the late Jonathan Beever, Esq., of Cefn Coch, in the co. of Denbigh. Mr. Traherne, as representing the eldest branch of the family, is heir to the Coedriglan estates. (See also *Mrs. Traherne of St. Hilary.*)

Heir Presumptive: His brother, Llewellyn Edmund Traherne, Esq., late 60th Royal Rifles.
Residence: St. Hilary, near Cowbridge.
Arms: Arg., a chevron sa. between three choughs proper, 2 and 1; on a canton barry of six, arg. and az., a lion rampant gu.
Crest: A goat's head erased surmounting a wreath.
Motto: Ofna Dduw a'r Brenhin; "Fear God and the king."

LINEAGE.

The Trahernes resided for many centuries at *Castellau*, near Llantrisant, which estate was sold in 1808, and at *Coedriglan*, near Cardiff, which still continues in their possession. They are descended through Sir George Herbert of Swansea from the sept of *Einion ap Collwyn* (*temp.* William Rufus), Lord of Senghenydd and Miskin after the conquest of Glamorgan by the Normans (see p. 495, and *Einion ap Collwyn*, *passim*).

William Edmund Traherne, Esq., of Castellau, *m.*, 16th Aug., 1630, Margaret Williams, dau. of William ap Jenkin ap William, of Aberpergwm, by Elizabeth Evans, dau. of Leyshon Evans, Esq., of Neath, by his wife Margaret Herbert, dau. of Mathew Herbert, Esq., of Swansea (see p. 585), of the line of *Iestyn ap Gwrgant*, and had a son,—
Edmund Traherne, Esq., of Castellau (*d.* 1697), whose wife was Prudence Llewelyn, dau. of John Llewelyn of Ynysygerwn, of the same ancient lineage. He left by her—
Llewellyn Traherne, Esq., of Castellau (*d.* 1766, æt. 80), who *m.* Anstance Wells, and had by her one son, Edmund (of whom again), and three daus., who all *d. s. p.*; the youngest, Mary, *m.* John Llewellin, Esq., of *Coedriglan*.

Edmund Traherne, Esq., of Castellau (d. 1795), m. twice, first to Mary, dau. of Thomas Llewelyn, Esq., of Welsh St. Donat's, and had issue— Llewelyn Traherne, Esq. (b. 1766, d. 1841), who by his first wife, Charlotte, dau. of John Edmondes, Esq., had a son, *John Montgomery Traherne* (see *Mrs. Traherne of St. Hilary*); and by his second wife, Barbara Maria Manning, had a son,— George Traherne, Clerk, M.A., Vicar of St. Hilary, &c. (d. 1852), who by his wife Ellin, dau. of the late John Gilbert Royds, Esq,, of Greenhill, co. of Lancaster, had— GEORGE MONTGOMERY TRAHERNE, now of St. Hilary (as above).

TREDEGAR, Charles Morgan Robinson Morgan, Baron, Ruperra Castle, Glamorganshire.

(See *Tredegar, Baron, Tredegar Park,* Monmouthshire.)

TURBERVILL, Thomas Picton, Esq., of Ewenny Abbey, Glamorganshire.

B.-Major h. p. Royal Artillery; J. P. for the co. of Glamorgan; patron of the Donative of Ewenny, St. Bride's Major, and Llandyfodwg; son of Captain Thomas Warlow, Bengal Engineers, eldest son of Thomas Warlow, Esq., of Castle Hall, co. of Pembr., a nephew of Gen. Sir Thomas Picton; b. 8th December, 1827; ed. at private school, and Royal Military Academy; m. Lucy Eliza Connop, only dau. of Lt.-Col. Henry Connop, Birdhurst, Croydon; s. to the Ewenny estates in 1867, when he assumed the surname Turbervill.

Heir Presumptive: His brother, John Picton Warlow, Esq.
Residence: Ewenny Abbey, near Bridgend.
Town Address: Jun. United Service Club.
Arms: Quarterly: 1st and 4th, checky or and sable, a fesse erminois—TURBERVILL; 2nd and 3rd, per chevron or and gules, three escutcheons, each charged with a tower counterchanged —WARLOW.
Crests: An eagle displayed sa., armed and wings tipped or, a crossbow erect in front of two swords in saltire ppr., pommels and hilts or.
Motto: "Avi numerantur avorum."

LINEAGE.

The *Carnes*, possessors of Ewenny Abbey, by purchase at the dissolution, passed into the Turbervills by m. of the heiress with Edward *Turbervill*, Esq., of Sutturn, whose son, Richard *Turbervill*, Esq., Sheriff of Glam. 1740, and M.P. for same co. 1767, d. s. p., and settled his estates upon his 2nd wife (née Herbert, heiress of Cilybebylly) during her lifetime, and afterwards upon—
Richard Turbervill Picton, Esq. (eldest brother of General Sir Thomas Picton), son of his sister's dau. (that sister being a dau. of Edward Turbervill by the heiress of Watkin Lougher, Esq., of Tythegston; and that daughter being her only surviving child by her second husband, Edward Powell, Esq., of Llandough), wife of Thomas Picton, Esq., of Poyston, co. of Pembroke. Mr. Picton now assumed the surname Turbervill; High Sheriff of the co. of Glam. 1804; m. Margaret, dau. and co.-h. of the Rev. Gervase Powell, LL.B., of Llanharan (see *Powell of Llanharan*), by whom he had Richard, his heir, Gervase, and Elizabeth.
Richard Turbervill, Esq., of Ewenny Abbey; Capt. in Glam. Militia; Sheriff of the co. of Glam. 1833; J. P. and D. L. of the same co.; d. s. p., and was s. by his brother,—
Gervase P. Turbervill, Lieut.-Col. in the army; J. P. and D. L., and Sheriff (1851), for the co. of Glamorgan; he married twice, his 2nd wife being Sarah Anne, dau. of George Warry, Esq. He d. s. p. 1861, and his estates went partly to his widow, and partly to his sister, Miss Elizabeth Turbervill of Corntown Court, near Bridgend.
THOMAS PICTON TURBERVILL, Esq.,(as above), s. in 1867.

Note.—For the history of Ewenny Abbey and Priory see *Ewenny Abbey*, and for further genealogical details see *Turbervill of Tythegston; Turbervill of Coity Castle; Carne of Ewenny; Nicholl-Carne of St. Donat's*, &c.

TYLER, Colonel George Henry, of Cottrell, Glamorganshire.

Lieut.-Colonel in the army, and served in the Crimean war and in India; eldest son of the late Sir George Tyler, Kt. and Vice-Admiral, of Cottrell (J. P. and D. L. of co. of Glamorgan, M.P. for the same co. 1851-7), by Harriet Margaret, dau. of the Rt. Hon. John Sullivan, of Richings, Berks. Lady Tyler now resides at Cottrell. Col. Tyler was b. 1824, and s. 1862; has brothers in the army; his second surviving brother is Gwinnett Tyler, Esq., of Gernos, in the co. of Cardigan, J. P. and D. L. for that co.; m., 1852, Judith, dau. and h. of the late Major Parry of Gernos, and has issue.

Residence: Cottrell, near Cardiff.
Arms: Sa., on a fesse wavy or, between three tigers passant guardant, a cross pattée of the first between two crescents gu.; in centre chief a *medal* or (presented to Sir Charles Tyler for service at Trafalgar).
Crest: A tiger salient guardant, navally crowned or, holding in dexter paw the French tricolor depressed and reversed.

Note.—*Cottrell*, beautifully situated on rising ground near the high road from Cardiff to Cowbridge is locally celebrated as the home of *Rees Meyrick*, author of the *Morganiæ Archæographia* (1578). See *Meyrick of Cottrell*.

TYLER, Rev. Roper Trevor, of Llantrithyd, Glamorganshire.

M.A., Rector of Llantrithyd, Glamorgan, and Vicar of Monachlog-ddu, Pembrokeshire; has been Rural Dean 34 years; formerly Domestic Chaplain to King William IV., when Duke of Clarence; J. P. for the co. of Glamorgan; second son of the late Admiral Sir Charles Tyler, G.C.B., of Cottrell, Glamorganshire; *b.* at Pembroke, 1801; *ed.* at Westminster School, and University College, Oxford; *grad.* B.A. 1823, M.A. 1827; *m.*, August 9, 1838, Isabel, 4th daughter of John Bruce Pryce, Esq., of Dyffryn, Glam.; *s.* to the Mount Alyn estate, Denbighshire, 1846; has issue 3 sons and 6 daughters.

Heir: Eldest son, Trevor Bruce Tyler, of the Royal Horse Artillery, *b.* 1841.
Residence: Llantrithyd, near Cowbridge.
Arms: Sa., on a fesse wavy or, between 3 tigers passant guardant, a cross pattée of the first betw. two crescents gu., in centre chief a medal inscribed "Trafalgar." (See *Tyler of Cottrell.*)
Crest: A tiger salient guardant navally crowned or, holding in dexter paw a French tricolor depressed and reversed.
Motto: "My king and country."

LINEAGE.

The Tylers derive paternally from the Dacre and Teynham families, maternally from the Leaches of Corston and Allens of Creselly, Pembrokeshire.

TYNTE, Charles John Kemeys-, Esq., of Keven Mably, Glamorganshire.

J. P. and D. L. for cos. of Glamorgan, Monmouth, and Somerset; F.R.S.; was M.P. for West Somerset 1832—1837, and for Bridgewater 1847—1865; only son of the late Colonel Charles Kemeys Kemeys Tynte, of Keven Mably, and of Halsewell, Somerset, J. P. and D. L., F.A.S.; *b.* 1800; *m.*, first, 1821, Elizabeth, dau. and co-h. with her sisters, Mrs. Bagot and Lady Pilkington, of the late Thomas Swinnerton, Esq., of Butterton Hall, co. of Stafford, and by her, who *d.* 1838, had issue surviving—
Charles Kemeys Tynte, Esq., *b.* 1822.
Secondly, 1841, Vincentia, dau. of the late W. Brabazon, Esq., of Rath House, co. Louth, and has had issue 6 sons and 1 dau., Vincentia Margaret Anne Kemeys.

Heir: Charles Kemeys.
Residences: Keven Mably, near Cardiff; Halsewell House, Somerset.
Town Address: United Service Club.
Arms: The arms of Sir Charles Kemeys, of Keven Mably, figured and described in the *Progress* of the Duke of Beaufort (who visited the place in 1684), and "often repeated in Keven Mably" (we presume in the windows, on the mantelpieces, &c.), were—"*Vert, on a chevron arg. three barbed arrow-heads (pheons) sa.*", im-paling those of his wife, dau. of Lord Wharton,—*Sa., a maunch arg. on a bordure or, an orle of lions' paws erased in saltire gu.*" These still continue in the *Kemeys Tynte* coat, having quartered with them the Tynte of Halsewell insignia, viz., *Gu., a lion couchant between six cross crosslets arg.*; adding in a second grand quarter, "*az., two bars wavy arg., over all a bend gu.,*" and in a fourth the arms of Lupus, Earl of Chester.

LINEAGE.

The two families of *Kemeys* and *Tynte* were united by the marriage, at the beginning of the eighteenth century, of Sir John Tynte, second Bart. of Halsewell, Somerset, with Jane, dau. and h. of Sir Charles Kemeys, second Bart. of Keven Mably, who *d.* 1702.

Of the early period of the Kemeys family the accounts are somewhat confused, but it is generally agreed that their origin was Norman. They rose to prominence at the period of the conquest of Gwent and Glamorgan. The original form of the name is uncertain, although it is said to be Camois or Camys, identical with Camois in the Roll of Battle Abbey. That a branch settled in Pembrokeshire, and gave the name to the lordship of *Cemmes* in that county, is a mistake (see *Barony of Cemmaes*). They were known as "Kemeys of Began" as early as the thirteenth century. David, grandson of *Jenkin Kemeys* of Began, settled at Keven Mably *circa* 1450, by marriage with the heiress Sibyl, dau. of Evan ap Llewelyn. His successors at Keven Mably intermarried with chief Welsh families of Gwent and Glamorgan, such as Gwyn of Senghenydd, Morgan of Machen (the Tredegar sept). His gr. gr. grandson,—
Edward Kemeys, Esq., of Keven Mably, was Sheriff of co. Glamorgan in 1575; and the fourth possessor after him,—
Sir Nicholas Kemeys, Sheriff of Glamorgan in 1638, was cr. a baronet by Charles I. in 1642. His son was—
Sir Charles Kemeys, second Bart. above mentioned, whose dau. Jane, sole heiress after the death *s. p.* of her brother, Sir Charles, third Bart., *m.*—
Sir John Tynte, Bart., of Halsewell, Somerset, who *d.* 1710, and was succeeded by his son,—
Sir Charles Kemeys Tynte, who *d. s. p.*, and was succeeded by a son of his sister Jane, who had *m.* Colonel Johnstone the Foot Guards, Comptroller of the Household to George, Prince of Wales (George IV.). He assumed the name Kemeys Tynte, and was succeeded by his son,—
Charles Kemeys Kemeys-Tynte, Esq., of Halsewell and Keven Mably, *b.* 1779; *m.* Anne, dau. of Rev. T. Leyson, and had with other issue one son,—
CHARLES JOHN KEMEYS-TYNTE, now of Keven Mably (as above).

VIVIAN, Arthur Pendarves, Esq., of Glanafon, Glamorganshire.

M.P. for the western division of the co. of Cornwall; Deputy Warden of the Stannaries of Devon and Cornwall; J. P. and D. L. for the co. of Glamorgan; and Lt.-Col. 1st Adm. Batt. Glamorgan Rifle

Volunteers; 3rd son of late John Henry Vivian, Esq., F.R.S., many years M.P. for Swansea, and brother of the first Baron Vivian; *b.* in London, 4th of June, 1834; *ed.* at Eton, the Mining Academy of Freiburg in Saxony, and Trin. Coll., Cambridge; *m.*, 4th March, 1867, Lady Augusta Emily, dau. of the 3rd Earl of Dunraven; has issue two sons,—
1. Henry Windham.
2. Gerald William.

Heir: Henry Windham, *b.* 3rd Feb., 1868.
Residence: Glanafon, Taibach, South Wales.
Town Address: 19, James Street, Buckingham Gate, S.W.
Arms: Or, on a chevron azure, between three lions' heads erased ppr., three annulets or, &c. (*Vide Baron Vivian,* and *Vivian, Park Wern.*)
Motto: Vive revicturus.

LINEAGE.

See *Vivian of Singleton; Vivian of Park Wern;* and *Baron Vivian of Glynn.*

VIVIAN, Henry Hussey, Esq., of Park Wern, Glamorganshire.

J. P. and D. L. for the co. of Glamorgan; Lieut.-Col. of 4th Glamorganshire Rifle Volunteers; was M.P. for Truro 1852—1857, and has been M.P. for Glamorganshire from 1857 to the present time; eldest son of the late John Henry Vivian, Esq., M.P., F.R.S., of Singleton, Swansea, by Sarah, dau. of Arthur Jones, Esq.; *b.* at Singleton, Swansea, July 6, 1821; *ed.* at Eton, and Trinity College, Cambridge; *m.*, 1st 1847, Jessie Dalrymple, *d.* Feb., 1848, dau. of Ambrose Goddard, Esq., of The Lawn, Swindon; 2ndly, 1852, Caroline Elizabeth, only dau. of Sir Montague J. Cholmely, Bart., M.P., of Easton Hall, Grantham, *d.* 25th Jan., 1868; 3rdly, Nov. 3, 1870, Averil, dau. of Capt. Richard Beaumont, R.N.; *s.* on death of his father in 1855; has issue one son, Ernest Ambrose, by first marriage; one son, John Aubrey, by second marriage; a dau., Violet Averil Margaret, *b.* 3rd Dec., 1871, by third marriage; patron of the living of Sketty.

Residence: Park Wern, Swansea.
Town Address: 7, Belgrave Square.
Arms: Or, on a chevron azure, between three lions' heads erased proper, as many annulets of the field; on a chief embattled, gules, a wreath of oak between two martlets.
Crest: Issuant from an arch between two towers, a demi-hussar, holding in left hand a pennon, in right a sabre.
Motto: Vive revicturus (see *Lord Vivian,* in Peerage of England).

LINEAGE.

This family is of the same descent as that of Baron Vivian of Glynn, Cornwall. The late J. H. Vivian, F.R.S., of Singleton, was brother of Sir Richard Hussey Vivian, Bart., of Glynn, created Baron of Glynn, near Truro, Cornwall, 1841, a Baronet 1828; who served with great distinction under Wellington in the actions of Orthez, Waterloo, &c.

Note.—Parkwern is a modern elegant mansion in the beautiful neighbourhood of Sketty, near Swansea. *Singleton* (in the same neighbourhood), to which Mr. H. H. Vivian is heir, erected about forty years ago, stands in an extensive park.

VIVIAN, William Graham, Esq., of Clyne Castle, Glamorganshire.

J. P. and D. L. for the co. of Glamorgan; High Sheriff in 1866; second son of the late J. H. Vivian, Esq., F.R.S., of Singleton, who was the first, and continued for twenty-three years, M.P. for Swansea; and nephew of the late Lord Vivian, of Glynn, Cornwall (*d.* 1855), by Sarah, dau. of Arthur Jones, Esq.; *b.* November 25, 1827; *ed.* at Eton College.

Residence: Clyne Castle, near Swansea.
Town Address: 7, Belgrave Square.
Arms: Or, on a chevron azure, between three lions' heads erased ppr., three annulets. (*Vid. Baron Vivian,* and *Vivian of Park Wern.*)
Motto: Vive revicturus.

LINEAGE.

For lineage see *Vivian of Park Wern.*

Note.—Clyne Castle is an old stone castellated house, recently much added to, containing a fine hall and extensive reception-rooms, situated on a hill-side, and commanding a magnificent sea view, with Clyne Wood, 250 acres, immediately adjoining the house.

WALTER, James, Esq., of Ffynone, Glamorganshire.

J. P. of the borough of Swansea and of the co. of Glamorgan; son of the late Thomas Walters, Esq., of Swansea; *b.* at Swansea; was owner of iron-works and collieries; proprietor of the Ffynone estate, Swansea; is *unm.*

Residence: Penlan, near Swansea.
Arms: Or, a lion rampant sa., thrust through the body with two swords in saltire ppr.
Crest: A dove with an olive branch ppr.

Note.—The ancestors of this family, as may be seen from notices of them in Francis's *Gower,* had been long settled in that part of Glamorgan.

WILLIAMS, Charles Henry, Esq., of Roath Court, Glamorganshire.

J. P. of the co. of Glamorgan; Capt. 1st Glam. Light Horse Volunteers; son of the late Charles Crofts Williams, Esq., of Roath Court; *b*. 1837; *ed*. at Rugby School, and Magd. Coll., Cambridge; *m*., 1865, Millicent Frances, dau. of Robert Herring, Esq., of Cromer, Norfolk; has issue 2 sons and 2 daus.

Residence: Roath Court, Cardiff.
Town Address: Wyndham Club.
Arms: Quarterly, per fesse indented : 1st and 4th, arg., a lion passant guardant ; 2nd and 3rd, az., a fleur-de-lis arg.
Crest: An embowed arm in armour grasping a sword.
Motto: Esse quam videri.

WILLIAMS, Evan, Esq., of Dyffryn Ffrwd, Glamorganshire.

J. P. and D. L. for the co. of Glamorgan ; Sheriff for the same co. 1857 (see *Sheriffs*); eldest son of the late Henry Williams, Esq., of Dyffryn Ffrwd ; *b*. 1800; *m*., 1834, Charlotte, dau. of William Thomas, Esq., of Cefnllogell, Mon., and has issue a son, Evan Thomas.

Heir: Evan Thomas, *b*. 1841; J. P. for co. of Glamorgan ; is *m*.
Residence: Dyffryn Ffrwd, near Cardiff.
Arms: Quarterly : 1st and 4th, vert, a chevron between three cockatrices' heads erased or— WILLIAMS ; 2nd and 3rd, sa., a lion rampant arg. —LEWIS.
Crest: A cockatrice's head, as in arms.

LINEAGE.

Thomas ap Evan of Eglwysilan, who *d*. 1612, son of Evan ap Meuric (*d*. 1752), had a son,—
Evan ap Thomas (*b*. 1581, *d*. 1666), who *m*. Catherine, dau. of Edward Lewis, Esq., of Llanishen, and had with other children—
Thomas ap Evan of Eglwysilan, *b*. 1615; *m*. Eleanor, dau. of Morgan Jones, D.D., of Frampton, co. of Glamorgan. He was succeeded by his eldest son,—
Thomas Thomas (or Thomas, *son of* Thomas), *b*. 1636; *m*. Catherine, eldest dau. of Edward Watkin, and had a son,—
Evan Thomas, Esq., of Dyffryn Ffrwd, in Eglwysilan, the first named as of Dyffryn Ffrwd ; *m*. Jane, dau. of Philip ap Edward Herbert, by whom, with other issue, he had—
Evan Thomas, Esq., *m*. Ann, dau. of William Gibbon, of Pen-Craig-vatha, *b*. 1702. They had no surviving male issue, and only one dau.,—
Mary Thomas, h. of Dyffryn Ffrwd (*b*. 1721, *d*. 1814); *m*. Morgan Williams, Esq., of Pendwylon (*d*. 1785); had issue Morgan, Thomas, and Henry. The survivor,—
Henry Williams, Esq., *s*. to Dyffryn Ffrwd, and had a son,—
EVAN WILLIAMS, Esq., the present owner, as above.

WILLIAMS, Gwilym, Esq., of Miskin Manor, Glamorganshire.

Stipendiary Magistrate for the Pontypridd District 1872; for several years J. P.

for the co. of Glamorgan.; a Barrister called to the Bar at the Middle Temple 186– ; eldest and only surviving son of the late David Williams, Esq., of Ynyscynon, co. of Glamorgan; *b*. 183–; *m*. Emily Williams, dau. of the late William Williams, Esq., of Aberpergwm, a wellknown and ancient Welsh family, seated at Aberpergwm about 300 years (see *Williams of Aberpergwm*), and has issue ; *s*. to the estate of Miskin, &c., obtained by purchase, on the demise of his father, 1856. (See *Miskin, Lordship of*.)

Residence: Miskin Manor, near Pontypridd.
Town Address: The Middle Temple.

WILLIAMS, Morgan Stuart, Esq., of Aberpergwm, Glamorganshire.

J. P. for the co. of Glamorgan ; eldest surviving son of the late William Williams, Esq., of Aberpergwm (*d*. 1855); J. P. for the co. of Glamorgan, and Sheriff for same co. in 1830, by Matilda, dau. and h. of Thomas Smith, Esq., of Castellau, co. of Glamorgan ; *b*. 1846 ; is *unm*.

Residence: Aberpergwm, near Neath.
Arms: Quarterly : 1st and 4th, sa., three fleursde-lis arg.—EINION AP COLLWYN ; 2nd and 3rd, or, three chevrons arg.—IESTYN AP GWRGANT.
Crest: The holy lamb and flag.
Motto: Y ddioddefws i orfu : "Suffered that he might conquer."

LINEAGE.

The family of Aberpergwm is as well known in Wales for its honourable and ancient standing as for its warm and unaffected patriotism. Aberpergwm, in the Vale of Neath, has been its seat for seven or eight generations, *i.e.*, since Jenkin ap William ap Jenkin ap Hopkin of Blaen-Baglan, a descendant in direct line (through Evan ap Leyson, Lord of Baglan) of Iestyn ap Gwrgant, by Caradoc, his eldest son, settled at that place *circa* 1560.
Jenkin ap William, of Blaen-Baglan, *m*. Angharad, dau. of Llewelyn ap Gwilym of Garreg-fawr, and granddau. of John ap Rhys of Glyn Nedd (of whom see note below), and was succeeded by his eldest son,—
William ap Jenkin, of Glyn Nêdd or *Aberpergwm*, *m*. to his second wife, Mary, dau. of Leyson Price (or Ap Rhys), Esq., of Briton Ferry, being widow of Matthew Penry, gent., of Llanedi, and by her had with other issue—
Leyson Williams, Esq., his successor at Aberpergwm (living 1638). He *m*., first, Anne, dau. of Thomas Bassett, Esq., of Miskin, and widow of John Llewelyn Williams, Esq., of Ynysygerwn, who *d. s. p.*; secondly, Mary, dau. of William Bassett, Esq., of Beaupre, by whom he had a son,—
George Williams, Esq., of Aberpergwm (living 1665). From him descended—
Rees Williams, Esq., of Aberpergwm, who had three sons, William, Rees, and Thomas, clerk.

William Williams, Esq., late of Aberpergwm, whose zealous culture of the Cymric tongue and attachment to the history and traditions of his country are known to all, spent seventeen years of his earlier manhood in foreign travel, and during that time attained a considerable knowledge of Continental languages. After his return he *m*., 1837, Matilda, dau. and h. of Col. Thomas Smith, of Castellau, near Pontypridd, and had issue four sons and two daus. The sons were Rhys, Lleision, *Morgan* Stuart, and George, all old family names. Mr. Williams *d.* in 1855, and was buried at the church of Aberpergwm. The two elder sons having *d. s. p.*, the third son,—
MORGAN STUART WILLIAMS, has succeeded to Aberpergwm (as above).

Note.—For a view of *Aberpergwm* see p. 475. *John ap Rhys*, of Glyn-nêdd—the older name of the place,—through mar. with whose granddau. (see *Lineage* above) Jenkin ap William came to Aberpergwm, was a man of mark in his day, kept a hospitable house, and was a friend of the "bards." We know this from a poem addressed to him, in the usual bardic style of boundless eulogy, by the best historic poet Wales possesses—*Lewis Glyn Cothi* (fifteenth century). He gives the festive board of Aberpergwm the next place to that of Arthur's palace; the language spoken there was the ancient speech of the Britons ("heniaith y Brytaniaid"); John ap Rhys was chief of the gentry from Gower to Mary's church and to North Wales; the bard wished for himself cold and sickness if John ap Rhys was not the dearest of the sons of Japhet ("os oes ei hoffach o waed Siaphedd"); his fame equalled that of Seth, of three quarters of the globe, even of the land of Israel, and of "the three bountiful ones," &c.; *he* is not excelled in peace, *she* (his wife, "of the seed of Watkin Llwyd," of Brecon) in the bottomless abundance of her mead ("eigion medd"); he knew not their like; the succour of Mary (and several saints) be to Elizabeth, and that of the angels to Non of Glyn Nedd, &c. The annotator of the poem remarks, "The same language which was spoken at Aberpergwm in the middle of the fifteenth century is still (1857) not only spoken there, but cultivated."

The country between the rivers Neath (Nêdd) and Avan, the stream which joins the sea at Aberavon, belonged to the lordship of Avan, which was possessed after the Fitzhamon conquest by Caradoc, eldest son of Iestyn ap Gwrgant, and his successors, in whose lineage, as already shown, was the house of Aberpergwm, whose patrimony extended along both banks of the river Nêdd.

WILLIAMS, The Very Rev. Thomas, the Deanery, Llandaff, Glamorganshire.

Dean of Llandaff 1857; Archdeacon of Llandaff 1843—1857; Examining Chaplain to late and present Bishop of Llandaff; Author of "Letter to the Bishop of Llandaff on the Condition and Wants of the Diocese," various Sermons and Charges, &c.; eldest son of the late Robert Williams, Esq., of Aberbran, Breconshire; is Patron of the Priory Church of St. John's, Brecon; *b.* at Monmouth, August 10, 1801; *ed.* at Shrewsbury School, and Oriel Coll., Oxford; *grad.* 1st class Lit. Hum. B A. 1822, M.A. 1825; *m.*, 1828, Elizabeth, dau. of Archdeacon Davies, M.A., of Brecon; has issue 4 sons and 3 daus. living.

Heir: Rev. Garnons Williams, of Abercamlais, Brecon.
Residence: The Deanery, Llandaff.
Arms: Arg., a chevron gu. between three bulls' heads sa. (quartering *Penry* of Llwyncyntefin, *Garnons*, and *Davies*).
Crest: A bull's head.
Motto: Fide et amore.

LINEAGE.

This family derives its descent from Sir Thomas Bullen, one of Bernard Newmarch's knights. The pedigree and descent of Aberbrân, without alienation, from the time of Edward III., may be seen in Jones's *Hist. of Breconshire*, ii., 701. See also *Williams of Abercamlais*.

WOOD, Edward Robert, Esq., of Stouthall, Glamorganshire.

J. P. and D. L. for the co. of Glamorgan; Sheriff for same co. 1861; Lieut.-Col. of Royal Glam. Inf. Militia, and formerly an officer in the army; son of the late John Wood, Esq., of Cardiff; *m.* Mary, dau. and h. of the late Col. J. Nicholas Lucas, of Stouthall.

Residence: Stouthall, near Swansea.
Arms: An oak tree fructed ppr.

Note.—John Lucas of Stouthall *m.* Catherine, dau. of William Powell, Esq., of Glanareth, Llangadock, Carm., by his wife Catherine, dau. of John Bowen, Esq., of Gurrey, Carm. W. Powell was murdered in his own house, and thereupon followed a celebrated trial at Hereford which resulted in the execution of Walter Evan and David Llewelyn, 30th March, 1770. William Williams, the principal, had successfully made his escape to France.

Arms of Glamorgan.

ANNALS, &c., OF WALES.

MERIONETHSHIRE
(MEIRIONYDD).

THE name *Merioneth*—a near approach to the Cymric form, although, in its present application to a *county*, of a date only contemporary with the *Statute of Rhuddlan* (A.D. 1284)—is to be ranked as one of the ancient territorial designations of Wales. *Meirion*, lineal in descent from Cunedda, and brother of Meurig, King of South Wales, whose daughter married Rhodri the Great, and therefore flourishing in the early part of the ninth century, was Lord of *Meirionydd*, and gave the district over which he ruled his name. That district, however, was by no means co-extensive with the present "county," but formed the tract on the sea-coast between the rivers Dyfi and Maw, and inland as far as Cader Idris, which, in the topographical division of Wales into *cantrefs* and *comots*, about the time of the last Prince Llewelyn or earlier, was distinguished as the *cantref* of *Meirion*. To this and the other cantrefs reference will again be made. The terminating *ydd*, or *eth*, is one of common occurrence in ancient Welsh names of districts, as in Maelien*ydd*, Gwinion*ydd*, Eivion*ydd*, Mefen*ydd;* and seems to have had the meaning of a *tract* or *extent* of country belonging to the person whose name formed the preceding part of the word. Merioneth, in ancient Cymric and Latin records, takes the various forms, Meirionnith, Meyronnith, Meironit, Meronnyth, &c.

SECTION I.—PHYSICAL DESCRIPTION OF MERIONETH.

This county, beyond question the wildest and most picturesque in Wales, may be described as a series of mountains with just sufficient breaks in valleys, gullies, and chasms to separate them. Its nearest approach to a plain is the celebrated Vale of Edeirnion, on the Dee, beyond Bala. The mountains are too abrupt and craggy to admit of an elevated table-land of any size.

The county takes the general form of a triangle, nearly equilateral. The side lying on the Cardigan Bay, extending from Aberdyfi (corruptly "Aberdovey") to Beddgelert, is about thirty-seven miles in a straight line; the other sides proceeding from these points, and after various deviations from a direct course meeting on the river Dee in the Vale of Llangollen, are between forty and fifty miles each. The entire triangle has an area of 666 square miles, or 385,291 acres. How much of this surface is arable land it would be perilous to say: a much larger proportion would be desolate moorland, or bare and craggy rock; but in narrow intervals between the hills, where the cataracts leap, and the small rivers pursue their lively and noisy courses, there are found scenes of smiling fertility and beauty, abysmal steeps and tangled primitive forest, the charms of which it is impossible for any effort of imagination to surpass. No part of Britain more bewitchingly invites the artist, or more sweetly regales the intelligent tourist.

The population of Merioneth has been less affected by the stimulus of growing trade than that of several other counties of the Principality. The great slate quarries of Festiniog, however, and the port of Portmadoc, an auxiliary to the trade they have developed, have drawn a large accession to the north-western corner of the county; while the formation of railways along the coast connecting Cardiganshire with Carnarvonshire, and through the heart of the county from Llangollen to Barmouth, in obedience to the modern spirit of travel and the behests of this county's physical attractions, have operated in the same way at various other points. In 1801 the population of Merioneth was 27,506. Through the last five decades it stood as follows:—

Total population of Merioneth in	1831	...	35,609
,,	,,	1841	39,332
,,	,,	1851	38,843
,,	,,	1861	38,963
,,	,,	1871	47,369

These census results show only a trifling increase in the thirty years preceding 1861; but in the ten years following the increase is more than a fifth of the sum-total of the inhabitants.

The great physical outlines of the county, traced by its mountains and valleys, rivers and estuaries, are well defined. Cader Idris, 2,914 feet above the sea level, is not in fact the loftiest elevation in the county, although it enjoys a wider fame than any other, for Aran Mowddwy, or Mawddwy, a less precipitous and therefore less interesting mass, some fifteen miles to the north-east of it, attains a height of 2,955 feet. These mountains are the boldest heights, terminating in the south-west of the great *Berwyn* range running nearly the whole length of the county on its southerly side, and dividing it generally by various spurs and windings from Montgomeryshire and Denbighshire. The third great elevation in this range is Cader Fronwen, some seven miles south of Corwen, and measuring 2,563 feet. West of Bala, and near the centre of the county, is a group of mountains called the *Arenig*, of which the Arenig Fawr, 2,809 feet, is the highest point. The *Harlech* range, stretching nearly due north, parallel with the coast from Barmouth to Festiniog, and in apparent relation with the royal heights of Snowdon, is the third system of mountains in this rugged county, but its highest points fall considerably short of the other elevations. We have already said that no extensive table-lands exist; but in the central parts between the triangularly situated points of Bala, Dolgelley, and Festiniog, there is a general elevation of the mountain bases, which causes this part to be the great watershed of Merionethshire. Here the chief streams and their tributaries have their birth. Here is situated that ridge, scarcely perceptible to the eye even when the spectator stands upon it, which makes the tiny rivulet, the beginning of the *Dee*, to run in one way in search of the Bala lake, and the equally diminutive *Wnion* to turn in another in search of Dolgelley and a confluence with

PHYSICAL DESCRIPTION OF MERIONETH.

the Mawddach. In this high region spring the Cain and the Eden, which, with other streams, form the *Maw*, and, along with the Wnion, which they join below Dolgelley, pursue their widening course to the estuary of Barmouth, environed by scenes of picturesque beauty which the banks of the Rhine can only approximately rival. Here also, from the bosom of the high Arenig (2,809 feet), the Lliw and the Trywerin, both contributing to the Dee, and the stream of Cwm Prysor, which travels by Trawsfynydd to join the Dwyryd and Traeth Bach in the Cardigan Bay, take their rise. This is a region of mist, bogs, and lakes, of wild fowl and diminutive sheep, of humble cottages, turf fires, simple and shy manners, and withal nearly unmixed Celtic blood. No coach-road has yet traversed it, and no railway ever will invade it,—unless, indeed, some treasures of gold, copper, or slate, as yet undiscovered, should tempt the enterprise of the ages coming to form one. On the heights of Festiniog to the north, multitudes have gathered to work the cleavage rocks; in the contrary direction the fair valley of the Dee, Bala Lake, and the delightful ravine of the Wnion, Dolgelley, and Cader Idris, are thronged in summer by sight-devouring tourists from all lands; but as yet the moors, heaths, and craigs of *Craig y Dinas*, *Llech Idris*, *Bedd Porus*, and *Mynydd yr Wden*, are left in their undisturbed quietude, and the Cymry here have it all their own way.

The *Dysynni* river, which ends its course at Towyn, has its proper head in the *Llyn*, or lake, "Meingul," but receives additions to its volume from the various streamlets which issue from the sides of Tal-y-llyn ("the lake eminence") and Cader Idris, and traverses the region of

Cantref Meirion,

ruled in ancient times by the chieftain whose name is now impressed upon the whole county, and which included the three *comots* of—

Talybont, Ystumaner, Pennal.

In the last-named comot (which has sometimes been considered as part only of Ystumaner), and near the modern village of Pennal, was fought a great battle in the fifteenth century between the Yorkists, under William, Earl of Pembroke, and the Lancastrians, led by Thomas ap Gruffydd ap Nicholas (of Dinefawr, father of the celebrated Sir Rhys ap Thomas), who won the day. These York and Lancaster conflicts (the *Wars of the Roses*) led eventually to the placing of the Welshman, Henry VII., on the English throne, greatly through the aid of the said Sir Rhys ap Thomas. (See p. 240.) This whole district is wild and romantic. Aberdyfi is a little town growing into prominence; and so is Towyn; the situation of both being inviting to the passing visitor, through the unsurpassed salubrity of the climate, magnificence of the sands, and charms of the inland scenery. Near Pennal are the mansions of *Esgair* and *Pantlludw* (see *Ruck of Pantlludw*); *Talgarth Hall* (see *Thruston of Talgarth Hall*); *Pennal Tower* (see *Thruston of Pennal Tower*); *Llugwy* (see *Anwyl of Llugwy*); *Bryn-awel* (see *Pughe of Bryn-awel*); and *Ynys-y-maengwyn* (see *Corbet of Ynys-y-maengwyn*). Across the Dysynni we are in the ancient comot of *Talybont*, rich in memories and grand in aspect. Here we immediately encounter the mansion and demesne of *Peniarth*, famous in modern times as containing the most valuable collection of Welsh MSS. extant, and certainly one of the most interesting in its bearing upon Celtic literature and Cymric history in Europe—the British Museum alone excepted.

PENIARTH: THE SEAT OF W. W. E. WYNNE, ESQ. (*from a photo. by Mr. J. Owen*).

This ancient seat of the Wynne family is situated in the parish of Llanegryn, and on the north bank of the Dysynni. The present house is a large, square, substantial building, partly built in 1700, partly in 1812. To the north is a wing of large dimensions, erected some time after the older part of the house. It contains the billiard-room, some offices, and bedrooms. The more ancient part of Peniarth was pulled down when the house was altered, in 1812. It is said to have been of great antiquity, but had no architectural features to denote its age. It came into possession of Griffith ap Aron, an ancestor of the present owner, by a mortgage dated in 1416, which was never redeemed.

Peniarth is especially remarkable for its library of printed books, and manuscripts of very great value. The collection of books here was a very valuable one prior to the bequest by the late Sir Robert Williames Vaughan, Bart., of the celebrated "Hengwrt MSS." to his friend and kinsman, Mr. Wynne. Amongst the printed books we may mention *Cranmer's Bible*, printed on vellum in 1539, and beautifully illuminated, of which *three* copies only issued from the press; a probably unique copy of the *Speculum vitæ Christi, printed by Caxton;* a beautiful copy of the very rare *Welsh Testament* of 1567, edited by Salusbury. Amongst the MSS. is the celebrated *Sanct Greal;* the still more celebrated *Black Book of Carmarthen*, part of which was written about the year 1190, and is believed to be in the handwriting of *Cynddelw Brydydd Mawr* (Cynddelw the great poet); and the *Book of Taliesin*, written soon after the year 1200.

Talybont, somewhat more than two miles from Peniarth, near the road to Towyn, gives its name to the extensive *comot*, now "hundred," in which it stands, and is the manor-house of the ancient manor of *Talybont*. It was in the possession of Prince Llewelyn, and afterwards of the sovereigns of England till the reign of James I., when it became the property of the Owens of Peniarth from whom it descended to the Wynnes. (See *Wynne of Peniarth*.)

Prince Llewelyn, in 1275, dates his letters to the Archbishops of Canterbury and York, and their suffragans in council, in London, from this place. (See hereafter *History of Merionethshire*.) In 1295 King Edward I. dates a charter from hence.

There are no vestiges of the residence which Llewelyn owned here; but it is probable that the large artificial mound, close to the bank of the Dysynni, formed part of its defences.

On a rock in the comot of Talybont, upon the bank of the little river Llaethnant ("the milk stream"), was situated, says Vaughan the antiquary, of Hengwrt, a strong castle called *Castell y Biri*, built, he thinks, by the Earl of Chester, when Gruffydd ap Cynan, Prince of North Wales, was his prisoner. In the parish of Llangelynin, close by the shore, are the ruins, according to the same eminent antiquary, of *Caer Bradwen*, the stronghold of the chieftain Bradwen, father of Ednowain, founder of one of the fifteen noble tribes of North Wales.

To the east of Talybont, in the ancient British—

Cantref of *Cedewain* and *Comot* of *Mawddwy*,

lies *Mallwyd*, a parish "delightfully situated between the salient angles of three abrupt mountains," and rendered popular to the Welsh people by the residence there in the middle of the seventeenth century of Dr. John Davies (*d.* 1644), author of a Welsh and Latin Lexicon (*Antiquæ Linguæ Brit. Rudimenta*, 1621), and assistant of Bishop Parry of St. Asaph in the translation of the Bible into Welsh (or rather, in the re-editing of Dr. Morgan's translation), the son of a "poor weaver of Llanferres," but withal of a good family, for he was entitled to call "Vaughan of Hengwrt" his "cousin" (Yorke's *Royal Tribes;* and Dr. Davies' *Letter* to Sir John Wynne of Gwydir, *Cambr.* Reg., ii., 470). He was a man of extensive attainments and great worth, and "out of his own means built three public bridges for his parish." Penetrating two or three miles farther into the Berwyn Hills we come upon Dinas Mawddwy and Llan-yn-Mawddwy, which with Mallwyd formed the comot of Mawddwy, in the ancient division of Wales, belonging to the princedom of *Powys Wenwynwyn*. This is pre-eminently, even in Merionethshire, a region of hills, the piled-up outskirts of a stormy sea of mountains stretching across Bwlch-y-groes as far as Bala Lake northwards, and as far as Cader Idris westwards, with scarcely room for the rivulets and the high-roads to pass side by side between. Llan-yn-Mawddwy is noted in more modern times for its succession of learned rectors; but the whole region around has recently felt a powerful and beneficial impulse from the formation of the new demesne of *Plâs Dinas Mawddwy*, the property of Sir Edmund Buckley, Bart. (See *Buckley of Plâs Dinas Mawddwy*.)

After some years ago becoming possessed of the Dinas Mawddwy estate, the proprietor added thereto, by purchase and exchange, large tracts of surrounding lands, and has consolidated a wide and compact estate. By the addition of Eunant and Rhiwargo in the co. of Montgomery, and Aberhirnant in Merioneth, his domain now extends from below Mallwyd to near the town of Bala. This magnificent chaotic district contains spots of the most exquisite beauty, as well as extensive tracts where Nature disports herself in her most abandoned and uncultured wildness. The formation is of the Cambrian series, and contains lead mines and slate. The enterprising proprietor opened up the district in 1867 by the construction at his own expense of a public railway, seven miles long, called the Mawddwy line, traversing the fair valley of Dyfi, and joining the Cambrian Railway at Cemmaes Road station.

The old house of the Myttons has been replaced by the sumptuous mansion of Plas Dinas Mawddwy, now (1872) nearly completed. It is situated at the foot of the rugged "Moel y Dinas" ("the stronghold eminence"), on a small plateau, just sufficiently large for the ornamental grounds and gardens of such an establishment, near the fall of the little river Cerest into the Dyfi (Dovey).

The scenery around, in boldness all that mountains can make it, is enlivened by tiny well-wooded valleys, frequent cascades rushing over precipitous rocks, and tastefully laid-out plantations; the lofty rocks of Cowarch are nigh, and the bold peak of Aran Fawddwy, about five miles off, visible from great distances, is on the estate.

Among the few antiquities of this neighbourhood is the old oratory or religious house of *Cae Abatty*, of which a rude arch in one of the farm buildings, and a part of a massive refectory table, are the only vestiges remaining. There is a *well* in the grounds of the *Plâs* formerly held in esteem for its sanitary virtues, or "miraculous cures," and the bridge over the Clywedog near Mallwyd, called *Pontrhyd-y-Cleifion* ("the invalids' bridge"), is thought to bear allusion to it. The name *Cwm yr Eglwys* ("the church vale") seems to intimate the existence at one time of a church at Ffridd Gilcwm, but no signs of it now remain.

The hill of "Moel y Dinas," above the mansion, is supposed to have been the natural stronghold of the district, and for this purpose it was well suited, both by its form, and the springs of water which issue from its spacious summit.

Plâs Dinas Mawddwy: the Seat of Sir Edmund Buckley, Bart., M.P.
(*from a photo. by Mr. J. Owen*).

656   MERIONETHSHIRE.

Sir Edmund Buckley is Lord of the Manor of Mawddwy, a manor having peculiar privileges descending from its first lord, William de la Pale, or *Will Coch o Fawddwy* ("red Will of Mawddwy"), who in 1289 had a grant of the district from his brother, Owen ap Gruffydd, son of Gwenwynwyn, Prince of Powys Wenwynwyn, who preserved his territories by becoming a tributary to King John, and holding them *in capite*. The lord of the manor appoints the mayor of the ancient borough of Dinas Mawddwy, who has magisterial authority, fallen, however, into desuetude beyond the committal of offenders to the stocks or iron fetters, called " Y neg fawr." This, together with the town " mace," is kept at the Plâs as the only insignia of the former municipal government. The mayor is selected from amongst the burgesses, and half-yearly leet-courts are regularly held, and well attended.

The old town of Dinas is rapidly disappearing, as its houses are taken down one after another to make room for the improvement and enlargement of the grounds about the Plâs;

PLÂS DINAS MAWDDWY—FRONT VIEW.

while, to the advantage of its inhabitants, a new town is rising near the Mawddwy railway station and the Minllyn slate and slab works, which bids fair to surpass in importance the ancient " city," and will be considerably nearer the parish church of Mallwyd.

One portion of Sir Edmund's estate, that of *Dugoed* ("Blackwood"), near *Llidiart y Barwn* ("the Baron's Gate"), on the road from Mallwyd to Welshpool, is well known as the scene of an atrocious murder, committed by a party of bandits called *Gwilliaid Cochion Mawddwy* (" the red vagabonds of Mawddwy "), the following account of which was written by the celebrated Robert Vaughan, Esq., of Hengwrt, who was great-grandson of the unfortunate Baron Owen :—

" Lewis Owen [of Llwyn, near Dolgellau], Esq., vicechamberlaine & Baron of ye Excheq.

of North Wales, lived in great credit and authoritie, in ye tyme of King Henry 8, Edw. 6, and Queen Mary, as it appeareth by their letters under sign Manuell directed to him and John Wynne ap Meredith of Gwedir, Esq^{re,} touching matters that concerned the peace and quiet governm^{nt} of the country, as the apprehending of and punishing of felons and outlaweys (which from the civille warres betweene Yorke and Lancaster abounded in y_e countrey, and never left robbing, burning of houses, and murthering of people, in soe much that being very numerous they did often drive great droves of cattell sometymes to y^e number of a hundred & more from one countrey to another at middle day, as in the tyme of warre with out feare, shame, pittie or punishm^t, to the utter undoin of the poorer sorte); And they in y^e performance of the dutie required by some of those letters (being authorized to call to theyr ayde the power of the counties, and alsoe to keep sessions of goal delivery when

PLÂS DINAS MAWDDWY—SIDE VIEW.

occasion required) raysed a great company of talle and lustie men; and on a Christmas eave tooke above 80 felons and outlawes, whome they punished according to the nature of theire delinquencies; as the noble S^r Jo. Wynn of Gwedir, Knt. and Baronet [author of the *History of the Gwydir Family, d.* 1st of March, 1626-7], grandchild of the former John Wynn, often tould me. The letters aforesaid I have seen and read, and are yet extant in the house of Gwedir. Afterwards the said Lewis Owen, being High Sheriffe of ye county of Merioneth, and having occasion to goe to Montgomeryshire assizes, to treat with ye Lord of Mouthewy, about a marriage to be had betweene Jo^h Owen, his sonne & heire, & ye daughter of ye sayd Lord of Mouthewy, was in his returne met by a damned crew of thieves & outlawes, who in the thick woods of Mouthewy lay in wayt for his coming, and had cutt downe long trees to crosse ye way and hinder his passage, & being come to the place, they let flie att him a shower of arrowes, whereof one lighted in his face, the which he took out with his hand & brake it; then they all fell upon him with theire bills and javelings & killed him. His men upon the first assault fledd, & left him onely accompanied with his son in law, John Llwyd of Keiswyn, Esqre, who defended him till he fell down to the ground as dead, where he was found having above 30 bloody wounds in his body. This cruell murther was committed about Alhallowtide in ye yeare of our Lord 1555. And the murtherers soone after were for ye most parte taken & executed, some few fledd the land & never returned. And soe with the losse of his life he purchased peace & quietnes to his countrey, the wch God be praised we enjoy even to o^r dayes."

Baron Owen was murdered on the 11th of October (1555), not far from a place still called *Llidiart y Barwn* ("the Baron's Gate"). There is a tradition extant which relates that the mother of a young man who was executed when the first batch of the outlaws were apprehended, earnestly besought Baron Owen to spare his life; but her entreaties were refused. "Then," exclaimed the enraged mother, baring her bosom, "these breasts have nourished those who will avenge my son and wash their hands in the blood of their kinsman's murderers!"

The first Gwilliaid or their captains are said to have been at one time persons of property, masters of "eighty hearths," and rendered desperate by some acts of oppression. The site of their chief mansion is still shown in the upper part of the farm of Dugoed Mawr. These having become outlaws, rallied round them all the turbulent spirits of the neighbourhood. The whole property belonging to several branches of the family was forfeited, excepting one farm, Dugoed Issa, the owner of which, though a relation, was endowed with more prudence or honesty than his fellows. This farm was sold to the late Sir Watkin W. Wynn above 100 years ago. These men fixed scythes in the chimneys of Dugoed Mawr, to prevent the robbers from entering the house, but they were removed, as is known to persons living, some sixty years since. The Dugoed estate was sold by Sir Watkin W. Wynn to the late Mr. Buckley, senior, of Ardwick.

The marriage alluded to in the foregoing account between John, son and heir of Baron Owen, and Ursula, daughter of Richard Mytton, of Plâs y Dinas, Lord of Mawddwy, took place, and they had several children, who became by marriage allied with some of the principal families of the county.

Quitting the romantic defiles of Dinas Mawddwy,—

> "Once for freemen hiding-places,
> Lurking-places for the robber band,"

the road to Bala, in one direction, mounts the lofty pass of *Bwlch-y-groes*, and looks straight on to the basin of the Dee; in another direction it makes for Dolgelley over the pass of *Bwlch-Oer-ddrws* ("the cold doorway pass"), a name which is not inappropriate. Immediately around is a bleak and dismal waste, but as the eye traverses the distance and surveys the heights of Cader Idris, the wooded basin of the Maw, and the deep depression through which the Wnion rushes down to Dolgelley, the environment of the estuary of Barmouth, and the range of the Harlech Mountains, the prospect becomes grand and enchanting.

These bleak heights of "Oer-ddrws" were often the rendezvous of patriotic bands during the wars of the Edwardian period, and notably one of the places of council, where chief men of the surrounding districts met, after the death of Owen Glyndwr, to concert measures for the safety and good government of the country.

The summits of Aran Fawddwy and Aran Benllyn to the north of this pass were occupied as stations by the Trigonometrical Survey. From the former, 2,955 feet high, the panorama of mountain and valley, crumbling steeps and dismal chasms, is truly magnificent. To the north-east is seen the largest lake in Wales—*Llyn Tegid*, mirroring in its pellucid depths the mountains hanging on its margin, and the Vale of *Edeirnion* stretching beyond, conducting the ample flow of the Dee into the Vale of Llangollen. Nearly due east extends the devious range of the Berwyn Hills, separating the basin of the Dee from the basin of the Severn, the county of Merioneth from the county of Montgomery, and in ancient times the kingdom of *Gwynedd* from that of *Powys*. From a lake in the eastern side of Aran the Dyfi begins its course, first through a gloomy chasm or *cwm*, and then through a narrow and tortuous valley, which gradually grows in breadth and beauty as it passes Dinas Mawddwy and Mallwyd for Machynlleth and the sea.

On the way from Bwlch-Oer-ddrws to Dolgelley there is a gradual stony descent into a genial and cultivated district. *Caerynwch*, the ancient seat of the Vaughans and Richards (see *Richards of Caerynwch*), is passed on the right, embosomed in trees on the banks of the *Clywedog*. In the beautiful country around Dolgelley are situated several of the most venerable mansions in North Wales. On the high ground, three miles to the north, is the famous *Nannau*, for many ages the home of the Nanneys and the Vaughans (see *Vaughan of Nannau*), remarkable now for the extent of its park, its elevated situation (being 700 feet above the sea), and the fine forest trees which, notwithstanding its height, enrich it. Near the house stood till 1813 the celebrated hollow oak called *Ceubren yr Ellyll* ("the demon's hollow tree") measuring in girth 27½ feet. It was and still is a tradition that Owain Glyndwr, having slain his cousin Howel Selé, the owner of Nannau, who, instead of joining in the insurrection, had treacherously attempted his life, cast the body into this hollow tree, where it remained for forty years. This tradition gave birth to the visions of goblins which long made the spot the dread of the peasantry, and which for many ages to come will invest it with a degree of superstitious interest. Above Nannau is a lofty precipitous rock called *Mael Offrwm* (the hill of sacrifice), or, as some have named it, *Moel Orthrwm* (the hill of oppression); but nothing is certainly known of its past history. The last Sir Robert Vaughan, Bart., of Nannau, *d*. 1859, leaving no issue, divided his extensive estates between his relations and friends. The Nannau property he left to the Hon. Thomas Pryce Lloyd (see *Lloyd of Pengwern*) for life, with remainder to John Vaughan, Esq., now residing at Nannau; the *Hengwrt* estate was given to his wife's three sisters (Hon. Miss Lloyds), also for life; and the Rhug estate he bestowed upon the Hon. C. H. Wynn, younger son of Lord Newborough (see *Wynn of Rhûg*).

In the valley nearer the town of Dolgelley is the mansion of *Hengwrt*, just named, a place in some respects of greater celebrity even than Nannau. It was the home of the same house of Vaughan, and obtained distinction mainly through its eminent owner, Robert Vaughan, Esq., the antiquary, a contemporary with *Camden*, and an extensive collector of valuable MSS., and other works on Welsh history and literature, which are now part of the unique library of *Peniarth*, and under the pious care of their present owner likely to be turned to permanent public use. Mr. Vaughan died 1667.

In the new neighbourhood of Dolgelley are *Dolserau*, the seat of Charles Edwards, Esq.; *Vronwnion*, the seat of Lewis Williams, Esq.; *Bryn-y-gwin*, the seat of Hugh John Reveley, Esq.; *Abergwynant*, the seat of Col. Henry W. St. Pierre Bunbury, C.B.; and *Hengwrtucha*, the seat of Howel Morgan, Esq. All these are situated in the ancient comot of *Talybont*, which included the site of the town of Dolgelley, and extended from Llanfachreth in the north-east to Llanegryn on the Cardigan Bay in the south-west, taking in the whole Cader Idris region between the estuary of Mawddach and the Dyssynni river. To the north of Dolgelley, at the distance of two miles, and near the junction of the Maw and the Wnion, are the remains of *Cymmer Abbey*, presenting upon the whole a sadly neglected ruin, but still retaining a few of the finer features of window, interior arch, and pillar, which formed part in the thirteenth century of a magnificent pile. The abbey was Cistercian, and it is believed to have been erected under the auspices of Prince Gruffydd ap Cynan in the twelfth century. Llewelyn the Great gave it a charter in 1209. Elizabeth granted it to Robert, Earl of Leicester. It became afterwards the property of the Vaughans. *Dolmelynllyn*, the seat of Charles R. Williams, Esq., lies further up the vale.

The estuary of the Mawddach from Dolgelley to Barmouth yields scenes of physical beauty and grandeur which are seldom equalled. When the tide is in, the estuary is a splendid lake, whose margins are deeply indented by projections of the hills and by retiring creeks kept open by the mountain streams, and almost everywhere wooded to the water's edge. On the south rise the abrupt eminences of Cader Idris; on either side in the nearer approaches to the water the country is craggy, deeply gullied, and sweetly clad in groves of fir, ash, and oak. The railway runs parallel with the high road on the southern side, and on the northern is about the most charming coach drive in the kingdom. The banks of the Rhine are tame compared with the banks of the Mawddach, and Switzerland itself, though doubtless abounding in scenes of different type and of more colossal grandeur, possesses nothing of similar scale and character to surpass this exquisite district. When the beetling summits of Cader Idris are tipped with snow, the sublime words of Byron come instinctively to the beholder's mind :—

> "Above me are the Alps,
> The palaces of nature, whose vast walls
> Have pinnacled in clouds their snowy scalps,
> And throned eternity in icy halls
> Of cold sublimity. . . .
> All that expands the spirit, yet appals,
> Gathers around the summits, as to show
> How earth may soar to heaven, yet leave vain man below."

And at many a quiet nook and dell along this estuary Henry Vaughan's lines respecting the patriarch are equally obedient to the memory :—

> "I ask not why he did remove
> To happy Mamre's holy grove,
> Leaving the cities of the plain
> To Lot and his successful train;

> For rural shades have the sweet sense
> Of piety and innocence."

On this northern road is *Caer-deon*, the charming residence of the Rev. W. E. Jelf, B.D.; nearer Barmouth, *Glandwr*, the residence of William Jones, Esq.; and *Coesfaen*, the residence of Charles Jones, Esq.

The town of *Bar-mouth*, prettily situated, has a name which is a curious distortion of the native *Aber-maw* (the confluence with the sea of the *Maw* river). From this point northward as far as *Traeth-bach*, and inland to the valley of the Maw and the line of SARN HELEN, extended the ancient—

Comot of Ardudwy (now a "hundred"), in the *Cantref of Dunodig*,

forming then, along with the comot of *Eivionydd* beyond the estuary of Portmadoc, a part of *Arfon*, and not of *Meirionydd*. The first place we meet and requiring notice here is the very interesting mansion and demesne of *Corsygedol* (see *Coulson of Corsygedol*), the ancient seat of the Vaughans, and subsequently of the Mostyns, who obtained it through marriage (see *Vaughan of Corsygedol*). When much of the Mostyn estates was sold, Corsygedol was purchased by the predecessor of the present owner, who greatly improved both the residence and estate. This venerable mansion now contains the finest collection of paintings—works of the old and modern masters—known to exist in the Principality, and it has been the liberal practice of Mr. Coulson to allow the collection to be freely seen by visitors, who obtain tickets for the purpose, at certain times of the year. The mansion retains most of its features as an Elizabethan structure. A MS. history of the place preserved at Mostyn, and written by William Vaughan, Esq., of Corsygedol, states that the fine old gatehouse, leading into the quadrangle, fronting the principal entrance, was designed by the writer's countryman, "*Ynyr Shôn*" (Inigo Jones). The site of Corsygedol is elevated, commanding a noble view of the Cardigan Bay, the promontory of Lleyn with the peaks of the Rivel (*Yr Eifl*), and Bardsey Island. It looks on the swelling tide which is charged in the legend with drowning *Cantref y Gwaelod* ("the lowland hundred")—an evil which probably it never committed except in some poet's imagination, and the popular belief of recent ages. In the near vicinity are several remarkably fine *cromlechs*, one near the house, *Coeten Arthur*, near the church of Llanddwywe, and two in the fields above the village of Dyffryn. There are also *menhirs* (meini hirion) below Dyffryn, near the shore. This strange assemblage of pre-historic monuments, all within two miles distance, and doubtless only a residue of what once existed, argues for this locality in primitive times some very specific, and probably sacred character, such as belonged to the south-western part of Anglesey. The whole country of Ardudwy is also famous in historic associations of the most stirring kind, some of which must be touched upon in our historic section. (See *History and Antiquities of Merionethshire.*)

Near the beautiful and romantic *Artro* is *Cwmbychan*, the old home of the Lloyds; *Taltreiddyn* (Dr. Griffith); *Pen'rallt* (J. Humphrey Jones, Esq.); *Llanfair* (Misses Richards); and *Cae-Nest*, the residence of Capt. Wayne. This is also a district thickly studded with memorials of a hoary antiquity, and of historic deeds. The vale or plain of *Dyffryn* was a field where often the wage of battle was tried in times both of British civil strife, and of contest with English and Norman invaders; the ravines and crags of the Artro and its tributaries gave refuge and concealment to many a band of retreating patriots, and the celebrated pass of *Drws Ardudwy* was repeatedly a real Thermopylæ.

HARLECH CASTLE (*from a photograph by Bedford*).

> "Chiefless towers!
> There they stand, as stands a lofty mind,
>   Worn, but unstooping to the baser crowd,
>   All tenantless, save to the crannying wind,
>   Or holding dark communion with the cloud.
> There was a day when they were young and proud,
>   Banners on high, and battles passed below;
> But they who fought are in a bloody shroud,
>   And those which waved are shredless dust ere now,
> And the bleak battlements shall bear no future blow."

On the lofty cliffs overlooking the Bay of Cardigan and the estuary of Traethbach, and guarding this entrance from the sea into Gwynedd and the marching-ground from north to south, was planted the powerful fortress of *Harlech Castle*, one of the most colossal in the kingdom. This was a position of strength during the rule of the native princes. Welsh records say that a tower was built here by Maelgwyn Gwynedd, who *d.* A.D. 547 ("Mortalitas magna fuit in Britannia in qua pausat Maelcun rex Guenedotæ."—*Annal. Cambriæ*). *Twr Bronwen*, "the Tower of Bronwen,"—its name in still earlier times, was changed in the eleventh century into *Caer Collwyn*, when Collwyn ap Tangno, founder of one of the noble tribes of North Wales (see p. 337), had here his residence. Edward I., the conqueror of Wales, saw the importance of the position, and nearly all the structure, whose ruins are now the admiration of the beholder, was built by him about 1286, soon after the erection of Conway Castle, and while Carnarvon Castle was still in process of building. Though Llewelyn, the last Prince of Wales, had now been four years in his grave (at an obscure rural spot still left unmarked by Welsh "patriotism"), the country continued turbulent and defiant, and these great garrison fortresses were part of the stupendous machinery of "pacification." Once more Harlech Castle became the scene of stirring events when *Owain Glyndwr* in 1404 attacked and took it. Henry IV. recovered the place in 1408. Margaret of Anjou, the heroic queen of Henry VI., after her defeat at Northampton, found in Harlech Castle a temporary refuge. When Edward IV. had succeeded in making the House of York triumphant, he yet found three castles in the kingdom holding out for the Lancastrian party, and one of these was Harlech, under command of the intrepid Welshman *Dafydd ap Jevan ap Einion*. By order of the king, William Herbert, Earl of Pembroke, led a powerful army to Harlech, and demanded the surrender of the place; but Sir Richard Herbert, the earl's brother, received from the stout defender this answer,—" I held a tower in France till all the old women in Wales heard of it, and now the old women of France shall hear how I defend this castle." Famine, however, at length succeeded, and Dafydd ap Jevan made an honourable capitulation.

During the civil wars in 1647 the redoubtable Parliamentarian General Mytton took this fortress from Major Hugh Pennant, who held it for the king. It was the last fortress in Wales that stood out for Charles I.

Further on towards Talsarnau lie *Glynn Hall*, the ancient seat of the Wynns, now the property by marriage of the Gore family (see *Ormesby-Gore of Brogyntyn*, Porkington), and occupied by John Edward Parry, Esq., J. P.; *Maesyneuadd*, formerly the seat of the Wynnes, and more recently of the Nanneys; and *Cae'rffynon*, the recently erected residence of L. N. Thomas, Esq.

In following the main road from Barmouth through Dyffryn Ardudwy we have left to the interior a region of mountains and vales, streams and lakes, as picturesque and beautiful in aspect, and as primitive and unconscious of the invading force of the life and customs of modern times, as any in Wales. From the higher points of the Harlech mountains is viewed a panorama of wonderful extent and grandeur, including the whole sweep of the Bay of Cardigan, the rugged region of *Snowdonia*, nearly the whole of the promontory of Lleyn, the interior country to the east as far as the Arenig and Berwyn ranges, and to the south bounded by Cader Idris. Everywhere from the crests and passes the spectator looks down on spots of excessive wildness intermixed with others of equal comeliness—as from the *Foel-ddu*, above the pretty little vale of Cwmbychan; from the pass of Bwlch-*Tyddiad*, commanding on both sides the mountain numerous ravines and green cwms and bottoms, mostly wooded with oak or fir, interspersed with grey projections of rock, and all conducting streamlets either to the Vale of Artro towards the sea, or the vale of the Eden towards the east. In this district are the small but pretty lakes of *Llyn Morwynion*, famous for the legend of the men of Ardudwy who had stolen for wives the maidens of the Vale of Clwyd, and being overtaken and slain in this pass, had their deaths avenged by the maidens drowning themselves in the lake, thenceforward called *Llyn Morwynion* (" The Maidens' Lake"); *Llyn Dwr-glas; Llyn Eiddew*, and *Llyn Dywarchen*. From the *Foel Wen*, which overshadows *Maesygarnedd*, an old house of some historic interest as once the residence of Colonel Jones, one of the Parliamentary leaders who signed the death-warrant of Charles I., the prospect is enchanting; but as the traveller mounts the pass of *Drws Ardudwy*, looking down the diminutive lakes of *Llyn Perfeddau, Llyn Howel*, &c., and surrounded by rocky hill-sides polished as by the hand of man, and a wilderness of moraine *débris*—both plain indications that this district at some remote period was subject to powerful glacier action,—the scene becomes overwhelmingly grand and impressive; and every inch withal is sacred ground in the annals and traditions of Ardudwy. Through the basin of the Eden, leading from Dolgelly to Festiniog, the Roman conqueror made his military road, *Sarn Helen;* on the shore side the enemy could march and deploy at pleasure; but the crags and passes of *Drws Ardudwy*, and the general range of the Harlech hills, were inviolable retreats of the Britons, whence on many an occasion they defied alike the heavily armed legions of Rome and the mailed men-at-arms of the Plantagenets.

On the promontory of *Penrhyn-deudraeth*, situated, as its name indicates, between two sands ("the two sands headland"), we find the remains of the ancient mansion of *Parc*, for many generations the home of the Anwyls (see *Anwyl of Llugwy*); and near at hand the castellated residence of Mrs. Williams of Deudraeth Castle, delightfully planted on a slope facing the estuary of Traethbach.

DEUDRAETH CASTLE: THE RESIDENCE OF MRS. WILLIAMS.

In the same locality is *Plâs yn Penrhyn* (W. Casson, Esq.); and near Portmadoc, but in Carnarvonshire, *Morfa Lodge* (Edward Breese, Esq.). Portmadoc, a creation of art and commerce, worthily perpetuates the name of the late Mr. Madock, M.P., of *Tanyrallt*, in the near vicinity, whose far-seeing enterprise brought about the construction of the great embankment, which has taken from the tide several thousand acres of what is now productive land, as well as formed a safe harbour for shipping. On the way to the well-known *Pontaberglaslyn*, passing *Aberdunant* (Mrs. Jones-Parry) on the left, situated on the Carnarvonshire side of the Glaslyn river; and *Ynysfawr* (John Jones, Esq.) on the right, situated on the Merionethshire side, we have before us, looking north, those towering "palaces of nature," the Snowdonian range. Occasionally when his cloudy vestments are blown aside, the venerable head of Snowdon himself comes in sight, when it is plainly seen, as far as Wales is concerned (putting Snowdon instead of "Mont Blanc" in the poet's verse), that—

PHYSICAL DESCRIPTION OF MERIONETHSHIRE. 665

DOLFRIOG: THE RESIDENCE OF DR. FARRE, F.R.S. (*from a photograph*).

> "Snowdon is the monarch of mountains,
> They crowned him long ago,
> On a throne of rocks, in a robe of clouds,
> With a diadem of snow."

Under the shelter of the craggy and barren *Arddu*, a spur of the Snowdonian system, which on the eastern side of the vale seems to keep watch at the portal of the hills, with his companion *Moel Hebog* on the west, and resting in a little vale as sweet and sunny as if it lay on the Italian side of Monte Rosa, is *Dolfriog*, the residence in Wales of Dr. Arthur Farre, F.R.S., known to all as one of the Court Physicians.

Anything more barren than the rocky mountains around—rugged masses, greatly disturbed, of the Llandeilo group, interspersed with igneous dykes bearing copper and other ores—it would be hard to see; and a spot more pleasant and richly clad in verdure than the site of Dolfriog, nestling on the brink of a mountain stream, a tributary of the Glaslyn, and near Pont-aber-Glaslyn, it would be equally a task to discover. Our *illustrations* are correctly engraved from excellent photographs, and give a perfectly faithful representation of the scene.

The pass of Aberglaslyn, where the counties of Merioneth and Carnarvon meet, is a yawning gulf, the result of a convulsion which separated the mountain mass, leaving on either side almost perpendicular walls,—

> "Heights which appear as lovers who have parted."

From whichever direction the traveller approaches the pass, the surprise awaiting him is the same. He is caught, as it were, in the jaws of the mountain monster, and the awe of impending destruction almost overpowers him. But it is only for a few moments; the fair vale again opens, the rush and echoing of the waters die away, and he feels the agreeable relief of a return of his old sensations, without, however, losing the impression of mystery and sublimity he has just received. This pass, on a small scale, reminds one of that of Tête Noir, or Pfeffer's Bad, and has the advantage in the comparison of not being too overwhelming in its sublimity, while those are utterly immense and bewildering in their grandeur. The quiet and homely beauty of the vale and village of Beddgelert above, and the wider and more varied view that opens towards the estuary below Aberglaslyn, are universally admired. To the *geological* aspects of this part of Merioneth more specific reference will again be made.

In passing from the basin of the Glaslyn to *Festiniog*, we can enter, in imagination or by painful pedestrian labour (for there is no high road), a pass between *Moelwyn* and Moel-bach mountains, coming out into view of the delightful Vale of Festiniog about Tan-y-grisiau, and enjoy a scene of great magnificence. A combination of bleak and barren eminences (apparently provided to supply half the world of present and future times with *slate*), of grassy and sheltered valleys with yawning chasms, noisy waterfalls, and rugged wooded steeps, alternately enveloped in mist and lit up by blinking sunshine, gives to this picturesque region a character and charm all its own. The atmosphere of Festiniog is, in spite of its humidity, peculiarly salubrious and refreshing. Lord Lyttelton has said of the place, "With a woman one loves, with the friend of one's heart, and a good library of books, one may pass an age here and think it a day. If one has a mind to live long and renew his youth,

Dolfriog: Near View.

let him come and settle at Festiniog." Here are the "falls of the Cynfael," and the "pulpit of Hugh Llwyd." In this favoured neighbourhood is *Tanybwlch*, the seat of William Edward Oakeley, Esq.; *Glanwilliam*, the seat of Samuel Holland, Esq., M.P.; *Plas-newydd* (John Whitehead Greaves, Esq.), &c.

We are still in the ancient comot of *Ardudwy*, and in making our journey eastward, across the central wastes and moorlands, for the fairer scenes of the Bala Lake and the Dee Valley, have to cross *Sarn Helen*, see suddenly, in the region of wild hills and heaths, the comeliness of *Cwm Prysor*, pass under the shadows of the Arenigs, then enter the ancient—

Cantref of *Penllyn*, and *Comot* of *Uwch-meloch*,

and along a fast descending and pretty valley come to Pont Llafar, on the Bala Lake (*Llyn Tegid*). In this immediate neighbourhood is *Glan-y-Llyn* (" the lake margin "), the hunting and fishing seat of Sir Watkin Williams Wynn, Bart., of Wynnstay, owner of a large tract of the surrounding country, and of the fishery of the lake. Three or four mountain streams join the Dyfrdwy ("the waters of two"), the infant Dee, a little distance from its entrance into the lake at the upper end, where the aspect of the land is cold and uninviting, while on either side the lake, which is about four miles long, the margin is prettily wooded, and provided with a good coach road. To the south-east the great ramparts of the Berwyn range rise in gloomy and barren grandeur; but at the lower extremity of the lake, where the stream of the Dee, carrying in its ample bosom the waters of all the streamlets which the watersheds of the Arenigs, the Arans, and the Berwyns send down into the lake, pours forth, to traverse the beautiful and historic vale of Edeirnion, the face of nature assumes a new and softened appearance, and crowding beauties such as those of the Clwyd or the Towy greet the spectator.

In the neighbourhood of Bala we find *Fron-Dderw* (John Jones, Esq.); *Rhiwlas* (R. J. Ll. Price, Esq.); *Bodweni* (W. Pryse Jones, Esq.); *Cil-Talgarth* (Francis Jones, Esq.); *Fronheulog* (Mrs. Davies); *Aberhirnant* (late H. T. Richardson, Esq.); and the more ancient and celebrated *Rhiwaedog* (see *Lloyd of Rhiwaedog*, in "Old and Extinct Families"). Further down the vale is *Crogen*, the beautiful new mansion of Henry Robertson, Esq., replacing and standing nearly on the site of the ancient *Palé* (see *Lloyd of Crogen*, in "Old and Extinct Families"); and *Llandrillo* (Rev. John Wynne).

We are now in the middle of *Edeirnion*, equally celebrated as a vale and as the ancient territory ruled by *Owen Brogyntyn*—of whom hereafter. Owen's descendants were numerous, and for many generations held manors in Edeirnion at such well-known places as *Crogen*, *Rhûg*, *Hendwr*, *Dol-y-Glesyn* (Dolau-gleisiou), and *Maesmawr* (see Dwnn, *Herald. Visit.*, ii., 125). As we approach Corwen we quit the comot of Edeirnion, and enter that of—

Glyn-Dyfrdwy, in *Cantref y Barwn*,

a cantref which contained also the comot of *Dinmael*, corresponding with that part of Merioneth here projecting northward into Denbighshire. This is the last of the ancient Welsh divisions now contained in Merioneth, since the cantref of Arwystli in the basin of the upper Severn was classed by Henry VIII. as part of Montgomeryshire. In the beautiful neighbourhood of Corwen, which gives the beginning of fairer scenes in the *Vale of*

Llangollen, are *Rhûg*, the celebrated seat in past times of the Salusburys and Vaughans (see *Wynn of Rhûg*); *Rhagatt* (see *Mrs. Lloyd of Rhagatt*); *Plas Issa* (John Lloyd, Esq.); *Bryntirion* (Mrs. Price); *Tynllwyn* (Capt. Robert Taylor), &c. The old mansion of *Maesmawr* is across the boundary in Denbighshire; and so is *Plâs yn Yâle* (see *Yale of Plâs yn Yâle*). Below Corwen, in the most picturesque part of the vale of the Dee, and just within the Merionethshire border, is the interesting spot where stood the castle of *Owain Glyndwr*, of which scarcely a trace now remains. All the lands around on either side of the river, and partly lying in the two subsequently formed counties of Merioneth and Denbigh, belonged to his domain, and formed the subject of that dispute (see p. 386) which

RHÛG: THE SEAT OF THE HON. CHARLES HENRY WYNN.

led to the long and disastrous insurrection, which he headed with a wrathful energy foreshadowed, as the poet makes him think, by signs and portents at his birth :—

"I say the earth did shake when I was born—
The heavens were all on fire—the earth did tremble."—"*Henry IV.*"

SECTION II.—HISTORY AND ANTIQUITIES OF MERIONETH.

1.—*History*.

The general history of this district is identical with that of the kingdom of *Gwynedd*, or North Wales, as separate from *Powys*, and has already in the main been indicated in our notices of Anglesey and Carnarvonshire, to which, to avoid repetition, we must refer.

The people which now inhabit this county represent with an unusual degree of purity the original inhabitants, who were of the *Cymric* branch of the Celtic race. This purity has been favoured by the secluded and mountainous character of the country, and its freedom from those disturbing political and industrial forces which have so powerfully affected Pembrokeshire and Glamorganshire, and the gradual effects of intercourse which have considerably changed the racial complexion of the counties of Flint and Montgomery. The study of *races* and their *antiquities*, so zealously and beneficially promoted in the present age, has not hitherto shaken the old belief, based on the testimony of Greek and Roman writers as well as on the traditions and history of the Britons, that this island of Britain was first possessed by a people who came from Gaul, who were Celts, who crossed over at different times, forming successive waves of colonization, the one pushing the other before it, and that the *Cymry* (carrying in their name the name of the ancient *Cimbri*) are substantially represented by the people of Merioneth and generally of Wales at the present time.

That the Romans had taken Merioneth under their care and placed it under tribute is evident from the great military road of *Sarn Helen* (Helen's Causeway—so called by the Britons perhaps after Helen, mother of Constantine the Great), which, after the conquest of Anglesey (see p. 9), they formed from *Maridunum* (Carmarthen) to *Segontium* (Carnarvon), as a means of rapid transit of troops and *matériel*, and exaction of tribute ; but beyond these objects it is quite improbable that the Roman conquest of Merioneth contemplated anything.

During the Saxon period we have no notices of this part of Wales. Nor did any known events of importance transpire here under the earlier Norman kings. The Lord Marcher conquests on the borders, however, by degrees began to influence these interior and not easily accessible parts, drawn now into conflict with the foreign foe under the leadership of the puissant *Owain Gwynedd*, Prince of North Wales, and his sons. Owain put an effectual stop to Henry II. and the English army by the victory of Corwen in 1165. The post occupied by the Welsh prince on this memorable occasion is believed to have been *Caer-Drewyn*, a circular fortress of loose stones on the summit of a steep hill between Corwen and Rhagatt, while Henry was encamped on the opposite side of the valley.

The Henrys, however, went on gaining power in North Wales. Henry III., in the exercise of a kind of feudal superiority, in 1240 "grants" lands in Merioneth to Howel and Meredydd, sons of Cynan, and grandsons of Owain Gwynedd ; but already Cynan himself was Lord of *Eifionydd* (in the same county), and we have no lack of proof that the territory given to the sons of Cynan was none else than *Meirionydd* itself—that great cantref between the Barmouth and Dyfi estuaries which ultimately gave its name to the county. The territory ruled by Cynan and his sons extended from the southern part of the promontory of Lleyn and the base of Snowdon to the Dyfi. When *Giraldus Cambrensis* passed this way, A.D. 1188, stopping "for the night at the church of Llanfair, that is, St. Mary's Church in the province [*comot*] of Ardudwy," the ruler of the country was Cynan, as the crusading archdeacon, in his graphic description of the region, incidentally mentions. How Cynan had got into possession is known from other sources. The *Annales Cambriæ*, A.D. 1148, have this record :—" Cynan and Howel, sons of Owain [Gwynedd], by force snatched Meironit from Cadwalader [brother of Owain]."

"This territory of Conan," says Giraldus, " and particularly *Merionyth* [the *cantref* already named], is the rudest and roughest district in all Wales ; the ridges of the mountains are very high, terminating in sharp peaks, and so irregularly jumbled together that if the shepherds conversing or disputing with each other from their summits should agree to meet, they could scarcely effect their purpose in the course of the whole day. The lances of this country are very long; for as South Wales excels in the use of the bow, so North Wales is distinguished for its skill with the lance, insomuch that an iron coat of mail will not resist the stroke of a lance thrown at a small distance. The next morning the youngest son of Conan, named Meredyth, met us at the passage of a bridge, attended by his people, where many persons were signed with the cross [embarking in a crusade to the Holy Land], amongst whom was a fine young man of his suite, and one of his intimate friends; and Meredyth, observing that the cloak, on which the cross was to be sewed, appeared of too thin and common a texture, with tears flowing threw him down his own" (*Itin.*, v.).

This same Meredydd and his brother Hywel eventually succeeded their father in the lordship of Meirionydd. But even already, as appears from Giraldus, they were empowered to rule over a part of the territory in their own right, for as the archdeacon and the archbishop proceed on their journey "over Traeth-mawr and Traeth-bychan, that is, the greater and the smaller arm of the sea" (as his imperfect knowledge of Welsh inclined him to translate), "they come to parts where two stone castles have newly been erected, one called *Deudraeth*, belonging *to the sons of Conan*, situated in Evionyth, towards the northern mountains, the other named *Carn Madryn*, the property of the sons of Owen, built on the other side of the river [Dulas], towards the sea, on the promontory of Lhyn."

Little more is heard of Meirionydd proper, and its immediately adjacent lands of Eifionydd, &c., until the year 1221, when Llewelyn the Great (ap Iorwerth), who, it would seem, had placed his son Gruffydd in the seat of power in that district, compelled him, owing to a dispute, to relinquish his rule, and took the territory of Meirionydd (including Ardudwy) into his own hands, strengthening his position by building a castle there (*Llwyd*).

In 1256 the last Llewelyn (son of Gruffydd just mentioned), having anew revolted against Henry (see p. 324, &c.), and foiled the opposition raised against him by his brothers Owain and Dafydd, on his way to the south, occupied Meirionydd (*Annal. Cambr.*). The territory was then in the occupation of the son of Meredydd ap Cynan, who, according to the same authority, in 1241 had been reinstated in his patrimony by the English king. Henry at the same time had restored to Gruffydd, son of Gwen-wynwyn, his princedom of southern Powys.

In the year 1275, when the struggle between Llewelyn and Edward I. was about to reach its hottest (see p. 325, &c.), it was from his castle at Talybont, in Meirionydd, that Llewelyn addressed his letters of complaint and expostulation to the Archbishops of Canterbury and York, in council in London, seeking relief, and proposing new terms of peace. "See, reverend father," he pleads, "the Lord Edward, now noble King of England, after the said peace, taketh into his hands certain barons' lands in Wales, of which they and their ancestors have been long possessed, and keepeth a barony which should be ours by the form of peace. Other barons of our country, . . . running to him, he helps and maintains; although they have robbed within our land, committed slaughter, . . . and do still daily commit the like ; and although we have often sent our griefs and complaints by solemn embassies to the said noble Lord Edward as well before he was king as since, yet unto this day he never did any redress therein. . . . We therefore earnestly beseech your fatherhoods to consider what danger would happen both to the people of England and of Wales by reason of the breach of the covenants of peace aforesaid, if new wars and discord follow (which may God forbid), mindful of the prohibition of the holy father the Pope, lately in council at Lyons, that no war should be moved among Christians, lest thereby the affairs of the Holy Land should be neglected; and that it may also please you to help with your council with the lord the King that he would use and order us according to the peace agreed upon, &c. Dated at *Talybont*, the 6th day of Oct., ann. 1275."

Small comfort came of beseeching their "reverend fatherhoods." To the epistle above partly quoted, and the long list of "griefs" accompanying it, the Archbishop of Canterbury, having come to Wales, sends answer, assuring the prince that he "had come for the spiritual and temporal health of them whom he loved well; that he could not tarry long; besought them to come to an unity with the English people and peace with our lord the king; if they should contemn this advice, he would forthwith signify their stubbornness to 'the high Bishop and court of Rome:' the king's power was daily increasing, and if war ensued they had nothing to expect but disaster; the realm of England was under the special protection of Rome, which loved it better than any other kingdom; he 'much bewailed that the Welshmen were more cruel than the Saracens;' they had been accustomed to 'reverence God and ecclesiastical persons,' but now revolted from that devotion, committed slaughter and burnt 'in the holy time,' which was 'great injury to God;' if they had been injured—which is doubtful, for 'we in no wise know it,' the judges in the cause would have signified the king's majesty; and, in fine, to leave no doubt—'unless they now come to peace they shall be resisted by decree and censure of the Church, as well as by war of the people.'"

Llewelyn, smarting under a sense of injury, and disgusted by the wily and heartless policy of the Church dignitaries, unfurling the banner of revolt, embarks upon that troublous sea which never permits him any more a quiet haven. For seven years he struggles with the power of England, aided by defection and treachery among his own people; and in 1782, when he and the independence of his country fell together, *Meirionydd* and adjacent cantrefs are constituted a "county" under the new regulations of the *Statute of Rhuddlan*.

While *Meirionydd* was the central and most prominent district in these parts, and as such most frequently mentioned, the cantref of *Penllyn*, about the Bala Lake, now forming parts of Merionethshire, was also an important lordship, always or mostly under separate government; and the comots of *Edeirnion* and *Mawddwy*, already described, belonged to the princedom or kingdom of *Powys*. Penllyn was the patrimony of *Rhirid Flaidd, temp.* Henry II., and continued in his son Madoc, and grandson Rhirid *Fychan* (corrupted "Vaughan"), from whom several of the chief old families of Merionethshire bearing that name are traced, such as Vaughan of Rhûg, Nannau, &c. *Edeirnion*, although a part of Powys, was at times ruled as a separate lordship, as in the time of Owen Brogyntyn, natural son of Madoc, last Prince of Powys, son of Bleddyn ap Cynfyn.

Among other events which connect the name of Owain Brogyntyn with the territory now included in Merionethshire is the battle of Crogen, which he won against the forces of Henry II. in 1165. But as the dwelling-place of Owain was at *Brogyntyn* (Porkington), in *Powys*, now in Salop, and his lands in Edeirnion and Dinmael were properly a part of *Powys Fadoc*, further reference to him must be sought under Montgomery. All these lordships were held as fiefs under the English crown from the time when feudal superiority was first established under the Norman and Plantagenet sovereigns (see *Powys*).

2.—*Antiquities of Merionethshire.*

Among the more important *pre-historic* antiquities must be mentioned the five great *cromlechs* of Ardudwy—two on the demesne of Corsygedol, two near the village of Dyffryn, and one at Gwern Einion, near the church of Llanbedr, in the Vale of Artro. All these are located, as seems to be the rule with respect to cromlechs, near the sea. Burial-places of the great, they were fitly erected on the margin of that symbol of immensity, whose moaning would also be a fitting and lasting dirge. Those mysterious monuments of the same class in Anglesey, Carnarvonshire, Pembrokeshire, and Glamorgan, and the still more wonderful erections in Brittany, like many others in different parts of the world, are instances to the same effect, assisting the pre-historic archæologist towards a sound induction as to the real reason of the choice of such a position. Near Llanbedr and Harlech are also *menhirs* (maen-hir) of considerable size. *Llech Idris*, in the valley of the Cain; *Maen-llwyd*, near Bryn-teg, in the valley north of the Eden; a stone in the valley above Pont-llafar, north of the Bala Lake, are marked in the Ordnance Survey maps, and have been identified.

An important class of ancient remains exists abundantly in this county, concerning whose character as *historic* or *pre-historic* there is always a difficulty in deciding, viz., the primitive British *camps* and *caers*. No part of Wales possesses so many of these, in a state almost unchanged since the ages of ancient warfare, as doth Merioneth,—a circumstance easily explained if we only call to mind the warlike character of the district, and the extremely hilly and broken surface, which not only supplied at every point fitting positions for defence, but has since precluded their invasion by the growth of agriculture and "improvement." The banks of the Artro bear to this day a primeval aspect. On many of its abrupt knolls and precipitous and sheltering rocks, enveloped in gnarled oak and brushwood, small circular British camps, built of loose unmortared stones, often of prodigious size, remain in their integrity; but it is useless to speculate as to their age—when they were first built or last used. Their simple construction suggests a pre-historic origin; but their advantageous positions would not be despised in the later conflicts of the country. Ardudwy still retains the descendants of the people who built these rude strongholds, and maintains much of the wild aspect which it presented to the Roman and the Norman, albeit that a new spirit, under the culture of religion and modern manners, has passed into its inhabitants.

The chief and most interesting *caer* of the Vale of Artro is that of *Craig y Ddinas*, standing up abruptly in the middle of the little valley, and partly connected by an elongation of one side with the left bank. It has all the features of an ancient British fortress, of formidable strength, although, owing to the narrow limits of the crown of the rock, of small dimensions. From the grounds of Aber-Artro the rock, with the deep and romantic glen beneath, forms a most conspicuous and striking object. The crest is surrounded by a rampart; some of the walls are of great thickness, suggesting the existence here of a castle of unusual strength. In addition to the accustomed signs of a military post, it has some features of a very peculiar and mysterious nature, some of which perhaps had relation to religious rites. A tumulus, or *carnedd*, which Mr. Lines, who examined the place in 1870, thought was still unopened (*letter* to Capt. Wayne, of Cae-nest), stands on the summit, and between the carnedd and the thick walls already mentioned there stands an isolated rock, seven feet high, at the back of which are "indications of structural arrangements of a semicircular form, as though for seats. These are overgrown by brushwood, which should be cleared off. The seven-feet stone may have been a stone of adoration. Altogether there seems to have been a singular combination of purpose in the remains of this rock. The great block which hangs on the edge of the precipice at the west has evidently been used for some mysterious proceedings. It possesses some singular geometric incisions two inches deep on its end next to the carnedd. Is it impossible that this was a stone of sacrifice, and the victims allowed to glide from its surface into the abyss below?"

Mr. Lines hazards the conjecture that this might be the place of confinement of Elfin, son of Gwyddno Garanhir (the somewhat legendary Lord of Ceredigion and *Cantre'r Gwaelod*), and that Taliesin's lines in reference to Elfin's deliverance have reference to it,—

"It is I who am a diviner, and a leading bard,
Who know every passage of the cave of silence,
And shall set Elphin free,—Elphin, the son of Gwyddno,
Is in the land of Arthro," &c.—*Myvyr. Archæol.*

Whether Mr. Lines' conjectures thus communicated to Capt. Wayne are accurate or not, this great rock and the ancient human works which crown it are full of interest; and the country around contains many *caers* and *barrows*, camps and entrenched positions, equally unknown as yet even to archæologists and their journals, which it would be well to inspect and describe. A British *caer* stands on the estate of Mr. Humphrey Jones of *Penrallt*, near the Artro vale. On the farm of Llwyn-Griffri, Talybont, at the back of the house, is an old *fort* of considerable size, and probably of comparatively modern date, which has been examined and measured by Dr. Griffith, but the results have not yet been published. The *caer* of another *Craig y Ddinas*, overlooking the Vale of Isgethin, above Llanddwywe, is on a bold and imposing position; and near it is a large *cairn*, where the ashes of fallen heroes are probably reposing. *Castell y Beri*, on a hill above Llanfihangel y Pennant, was more likely an early as well as a later place of strength; *Caerau Crwyni*, and the neighbouring post called *Y Gaer*, between Mynydd Mynyllod and Rhug, and *Caer Drewyn* in the same neighbourhood, north of Corwen, are other examples of British *caers* of early origin, but probably used by foe as well as friend in later times, as advantage and exigency counselled.

Beddau Gwyr Ardudwy ("the graves of the men of Ardudwy"), connected with the legend of Llyn Morwynion, already mentioned, near Festiniog; and *tumuli*, such as *Tommen y Mur*, near Festiniog; *Carneddi Pengwm*, by Llanaber, and the huge *carn* near Talybont, Llanddwywe; the two tumuli, each called *Carneddwen*, near Pont Calettwr, below Bala; a *carn* at the north-eastern base of Mynydd Mynyllod, and *Tommen y Castell*, north of Corwen, are well known, and must be considered pre-historic in the sense that they are of a kind common in a period anterior to history, and are themselves devoid of record, although it is not to be doubted that the practice of erecting tumuli over the graves of great men and their families descended far into historic times. Many of the tumuli of Merioneth remain undisturbed, and promise useful revelations to skilful archæologists.

The earliest *historic* remains of importance in this county are the *Roman roads* which traverse it. These are traceable a considerable distance through parts now the least frequented, and following a route which involved many engineering difficulties. The great trunk of *Sarn Helen*, as called by the natives, but *Via Maritima* by the Romans, entered this county from the south near Llugwy and Talgarth Hall on the river Dyfi; had a station at *Penrallt;* made its devious way,—

"Per varios casus, per tot discrimina rerum,"

to Dolgelley; passing the spot where Cymmer Abbey, now itself an ancient ruin, was built many hundred years afterwards, it proceeded directly north along the valley of the Maw to the great station near Trawsfynydd (*Tommen-y-Mur*, the *Heriri Mons*), where it met another coming from Bala, and, as is highly probable, a third coming from Meifod (*Mediolanum*), by Dinas Mawddwy and Drws-y-Nant: from Tommen-y-Mur these roads divided themselves into two branches, one proceeding to Carnarvon (*Segontium*) by Beddgelert, the other by Caerhun (*Conov-ium*—the station on the *Conwy*) to Bangor.

Of monuments of the *historic* period in this county, *Harlech Castle*, already noticed (see p. 662), is the most celebrated and imposing, although in point of age not the earliest. The princely seat at *Talybont* has left nothing visible to the eyes of the searcher but the *mound* which has grown out of its ruins. *Cymmer Abbey*, near Dolgelley, comes next after Harlech Castle as to the importance of its remains. *Egryn Abbey* stood on the margin of a mountain stream joining the sea three miles north of Barmouth, and near the present high road; the traces of it remaining are very obscure, but the district all around is redolent of antiquity— a land of barrows, caers, and cromlechs, of traditions and legends, sharply cut Celtic features, tall frames, and "long heads"—monuments all alike of the brave folk who in the far distant past possessed these regions, worshipped God and showed reverence to their dead according to the varying behests of the descending ages,—making one feel as he witnesses them that he is truly in an ancient land and among an ancient people, who are still speaking the language which sounded at the hearth, in the shepherd's cry from the hill-tops, and in the warrior's shout in the charge of battle, two and three thousand years ago. This language is itself an interesting remain of antiquity, and yet, in a sense, is not old. Taking the English as its companion in the transactions of commerce, higher literature, and culture of the schools, it seems to claim a right of perpetual rule in those more sacred places—the homes of the common people, and the shrines of their faith.

The Cadvan stone in Towyn Churchyard is ancient, but the inscription, excepting the one word CATVANIANUS, is illegible. The characters are an approach to the old Welsh alphabet, and the stone, which is not a pillar proper, is said by Nicholson to have been for many years removed to the woods of Bodtalog, and restored to its place by Mr. Edward Scott. In its original state the monument was supported by other stones. Cadvan, the Breton saint, who came to Wales in the sixth century, and to whom the church is dedicated, is commemorated by this stone.

The legend of the *Grave of Gelert* is universally known, but as it is a conceded privilege in our day to doubt everything except one's own existence and merits, we have been advised to doubt whether there ever existed a Gelert or a Gelert's Grave. The tale, we are told, has its counterpart in many lands—in France, in Persia, in Ireland; and is best treated by being relegated to that mysterious land, at once the prolific fountain of all wisdom and of all superstition—the EAST. But how came the spot now called Gelert's Grave to be so called at all? And could not the story pass from Wales to the East as well as from the East into Wales, as the whole train of the Arthurian romances is known to have done? The hypothesis, at least, is as dependent for belief upon credulity as is the legend or story itself.

Prince Llewelyn ap Iorwerth—so runs the legend—had a celebrated greyhound named Gelert, "a lamb at home, a lion in the chase," given him by his father-in-law, King John of England. While out for sport among the Snowdon hills, his child had been left in a hunting lodge he had at this place. Gelert was absent this day from the chase, but on his master's return met him at the door covered with blood. The prince, alarmed, ran into the nursery, and found his child's cradle overturned, and the ground flowing with blood. Concluding too hastily that the dog had killed the child,—

> "'Hell-hound! my child's by thee devoured!'
> The frantic father cried;
> And to the hilt the vengeful sword
> He plunged in Gelert's side.
>
> "Aroused by Gelert's dying yell,
> Some slumberer wakened nigh:
> What words the parent's joy could tell
> To hear his infant's cry!
>
> "Concealed beneath a mangled heap,
> His hurried search had missed;
> All glowing from his rosy sleep,
> The cherub boy he kissed.
>
> "Nor scath had he, nor harm nor dread,
> But the same couch beneath
> Lay a gaunt wolf all torn and dead,
> Tremendous still in death.
>
> "Ah! what was then Llewelyn's pain!
> For now the truth was clear,
> His gallant hound the wolf had slain,
> To save Llewelyn's heir."

The ancient bards, who must have had the power of long vision into the invisible, could see under the waves of Cardigan Bay the tops of the submerged houses of *Cantref y Gwaelod!* This legend relates that under Gwyddno Garanhir (*circa* A.D. 500), ruler of Ceredigion (Cardigan), a lowland tract belonging to his dominion extended far out into what is now sea, opposite to the estuary of Barmouth and the whole hundred of Ardudwy. Some, to increase the wonder, enlarged it into the whole of the bay, enclosed by a line drawn from Towyn to the south-western point of Lleyn. From overflowing many of the "cities" said to exist here, the sea was kept in check by dykes and gates; but "Seithenyn the drunkard" forgot the sea, and the mischief was done. Of the "three arrant drunkards of the Isle of Britain," according to the *Triads*, "Seithenyn, the son of Seithyn Saidi, King of Dyfed," was one, and he, having charge of the floodgates, "in his drink let the sea over Cantref y Gwaelod, so that there were lost of houses and land the whole that were there, where formerly were found sixteen fortified cities [dinas-dref], superior to all the towns and cities of Cymru, excepting only Caerllion ar Wysg [Caerleon on Usk], . . . and the men that escaped that inundation landed in Ardudwy, the country of Arfon, and the mountains of Eryri, and other places not heretofore inhabited."

This is all the evidence of the alleged inundation we possess. That a lowland tract existed here is rendered probable enough by the still remaining Marsh of Harlech, which is of considerable extent, and of low level, stretching some four miles in length by two or three in the widest part, between Harlech and Traeth-bach. But that a region containing "sixteen fortified cities" was here submerged so late as the fifth or sixth century, when intercourse with the world was so wide, without some further record of it having been left is scarcely credible, while the allegation that the ridge of *Sarn Badrig*, visible at low water, is a remain of the "dykes" is utterly absurd. An examination of this ridge proves that it is a natural rock, and a little study of the geological features of the adjacent country will show that it corresponds with the lines of the mountains, and of the Lleyn promontory. The "great blocks" of which it is alleged to have been built (as if the Cymry had for once become Cyclopean builders), only follow the analogy of the interior hills, a fact very strikingly illustrated in the bold rock north of Talsarnau, just where the railway enters upon the Traeth-bach viaduct,—

"In sooth, O bard, these stones are ancient stones!
Laid by an Ancient Hand."

Section III.—THE GEOLOGY OF MERIONETHSHIRE.

In every individual feature the structure of the rocks of this county is the same with that of the rocks of Carnarvonshire (see *Geology of Carnarvonshire*). It consists of three great groups, the lower Silurian Llandeilo, the Cambrian, and the stratified igneous rocks, with some dykes and beds of greenstone, felspathic porphyry, and lavas. The whole country between Barmouth and Festiniog, bounded by the sea, by Traeth-bach, and the upper valley of the Maw, is of the *Cambrian* formation. The region of igneous stratified rocks embraces the ranges of Cader Idris, Aran Mawddwy, the Arenigs, and the heights of Festiniog. Between the Dyfi and the Dysynni the Llandeilo rocks alone prevail. Of these the hills of Dinas Mawddwy and Talyllyn are composed, as well as the country around Bala, the vale of Edeirnion, the shores of the estuary of Mawddach, Penrhyn-deudraeth, &c. Caradoc rocks constitute the greater part of Bwlchygroes and the Berwyn hills on towards Llandrillo. At Pont-aber-Glaslyn the river cuts through the Llandeilo mass, into which metalliferous igneous dykes have protruded. Slate is worked at Festiniog, Dinas Mawddwy, Machynlleth, and Pennal, in the Llandeilo beds; at Diphwys in the Harlech hills, in the Cambrian, but of a quality greatly inferior to that of the Bethesda and Llanberis slate of the same beds. From end to end the county of Merioneth is included in the *lower Silurian* series. The rocks throughout have been subject to violent convulsions, and in places to volcanic action.

Section IV.—NOBLE TRIBE OF MERIONETHSHIRE.

The only founder of a noble tribe ascribed to this county is *Ednowain ap Bradwen*, who flourished in the twelfth century. He has sometimes been styled "Lord of Merioneth," but in the MS. published in the *Cambrian Register*, i. 153, which contains the best account of him extant, this is questioned, since the Welsh princes and their issue were always Lords of Merioneth; but it is conjectured that he might have held Merioneth in fee from the princes, and thus have received the title of lord of it. It is held as certain that he was possessed of all the comot of *Talybont*, except Nannau, and for the most part of *Estumaner*. His castle, called *Llys Bradwen*, was situated below Dolgelley, between Cader Idris and the estuary. Not a stone of it remains upon another at present, although the foundations can be traced; but at the time of the writing of the MS. referred to, the ruins are said to have consisted of "large stones, as usually laid to form the foundations of a building, and marked the form as well as the simplicity of the habitations of the ancient *reguli* of Wales, agreeing exactly with the account given of them by Whitaker in his *History of Manchester*, who says that they were commonly placed in the hollow of a valley, and either upon the margin of a stream, or at the confluence of two, for the conveniency of water, and security from winds. And the followers lived immediately about the person of their chief, or in little bodies along the windings of the valley, to be within reach of the usual signals of the lord—the striking of the shield or the blowing of the horn." The ground plan of Llys Bradwen is said to have been oblong, but having at the front a circular apartment, which served as the hall of audience and court of justice. The oblong building behind contained the chieftain's own apartments. Around this principal building were the traces of several others of various forms and dimensions.

His great great grandson's son, Llewelyn ap Tudur, is said to have done homage, along with other lords and gentlemen of Wales, to Edward I. His grandson, Aron ap Ednyfed ap Llewelyn, we are further informed, "had two sons, more eminent than the rest of his children, Ednyfed and Gruffydd," from one of whom, "William David Lloyd, of Peniarth, Esq., lately deceased, was descended, whose inheritance is come to Margaret, the mother of Lewis Owen, Esq. of Peniarth, deceased." The will of David Lloyd, father of the said William, is dated 11th July, 1570. (Note, *Herald. Visit. of Wales*, ii. 238.) When Owain Glyndwr was hard pressed by Henry IV., Ednyfed ap Aron is said to have given him refuge in a cave by the sea-side, in the parish of Celynin, which cave was afterwards called *Ogof Owain*. Several of the old gentry of Merioneth traced to Ednowain ap Bradwen. Some also of the families of Carmarthenshire and Cardiganshire, such as the Lewises of Abernant-bychan (now extinct), and Leweses of Llysnewydd and Llanllyr (see *Lewes of Llysnewydd*), claim the same descent. Maternally, W. W. E. Wynne, Esq., of Peniarth, is of Ednowain's lineage.

Ednowain ap Bradwen bore: *Gu. three snakes nowed, arg.*

Note on Rhirid Flaidd.

This distinguished man, Lord of Penllyn (a cantref containing five parishes north of the Bala Lake), Eifionydd, Pennant, Melangell, and Glyn in Powys, and as some say, of eleven towns or *trefs* in the hundred of Oswestry, has occasionally been described, but erroneously, as founder of one of the fifteen noble tribes of North Wales (see *Noble Tribes*). At the same time his territories were larger and his influence much more extensive than those of several of the founders of noble tribes. He flourished at the time of Henry II., and his son, Richard I. Paternally his descent was from Cynedda Wledig, but maternally it is alleged that his lineage was Norman, his mother being a descendant of Richard, Earl of Avranches, by his son William, whose brother was Hugh *Lupus*, Earl of Chester. Whether Rhirid was called *Flaidd* (the wolf) from a cognomen of his maternal ancestors, or from his possession of a hungry and savage nature, it is not easy to say. His eldest son, Madoc, had a son, Rhirid *Fychan* (the younger, or the little), who married into the family of Fychan (*Vaughan*) of Nannau, and from him were descended the subsequent *Vaughans* of Nannau and Rhug. From his son David Pothon, who married Cicely, daughter of Sir Alexander Myddelton, Lord of Myddelton, in Shropshire, the Myddeltons of Chirk Castle, &c., were descended, retaining the maternal surname.

Note on Owain Brogyntyn.

Owain Brogyntyn, Lord of Edeirnion, a district (as already shown) now in Merioneth, but then in the princedom of Powys, was a man of great note and influence, of princely blood though of illegitimate birth, and left a numerous posterity in that lordship. But he is properly classed under Montgomeryshire, on the borders of which his seat of *Brogyntyn*, corrupted into "Porkington," was situated. (See *Ormsby-Gore of Brogyntyn.*)

Section V.—OLD AND EXTINCT FAMILIES OF MERIONETHSHIRE.

The ancient houses of this county, almost without exception of purely Cymric lineage, and by no means few in number, considering the wild and mountainous character of the district, have shown a vitality truly remarkable. Even to this day several of the chief families of the fourteenth and fifteenth centuries have their representatives on the ground, holding the same domains, and bearing in some instances, the same names. The old blood has departed from *Corsygedol*, *Rhiwaedog*, *Dolgelley* (Owen); at *Nannau*, *Ynysymaengwyn*, *Hengwrt*, *Maesypandy*, and *Gwerclas*, it has been intermittent and evanishing; but at *Nannau* the more recent name of *Vaughan*, at least, still continues, and the ancient sept of *Wynn of Glyn*, in more than one direction endures, represented in blood in its present owner (see *Ormsby-Gore of Brogyntyn*), and by name as well as in blood in the person of the owner of *Peniarth* (see *Wynne of Peniarth*). Edeirnion and Mawddwy, contrasting with each other in the type of their landscape, have been subject to a like fate in the disappearance of a large proportion of their venerable households, as they had once enjoyed a like distinction in the possession of a goodly number of them. The land has got into fewer hands. The comparatively small but compact manor where the plain country gentleman lived familiarly among his neighbours, and kept hospitable board for friend, for stranger, and for poor, has, in many an instance, dwindled down to the common farmhouse, or left on its site but the greensward or the forest. It may be all for the better. The old division of population into gentry and poor is replaced by another, in which, even in Merioneth, a stout and numerous *middle class* of industrious farmers and tradesmen occupies a prominent position, and gives to society a breadth and vigour unknown to the olden times.

Vaughan of Corsygedol.

The Vaughans of Corsygedol, who became so distinguished under that name in Merioneth, were the progeny of a younger son of Einion ap Gruffydd, of Corsygedol, who was of the sept of Osborn Wyddel, represented in the eldest branch by the Wynns of Glyn, and now by Wynne of Peniarth (see *Wynne of Peniarth*). The surname *Vaughan* began with Gruffydd *Fychan,* probably so called to distinguish him as son or *junior* from his father Gruffydd ap Einion, woodwarden of the comot of Estimaner A.D. 1382—1385, and captain of forty archers from Merioneth for King Richard II. Gruffydd ap Einion's mother was Tangwystl, dau. of Rhydderch ap Ievan Llwyd, of Gogerddan, the distinguished bard (see *Pryse of Gogerddan*). The Vaughans of Corsygedol continued at that place and under that name from the end of the fourteenth to the end of the eighteenth century, intermarrying, in this long interval, among others, with the families of Griffith of Penrhyn, Carn.; Lloyds of Dolgelynin, Mont.; Wogans of Stonehall, Pemb.; Nanneys of Nannau; Owens of Clenenney, &c. They frequently supplied sheriffs for Merioneth. (See *Sheriffs*.)

Gruffydd Vaughan, of Corsygedol, was one of the defenders of Harlech Castle under the brave Dafydd ap Ievan ap Einion, his cousin (see *Harlech Castle*). In an account of him by Vaughan of Hengwrt, the antiquary, he is said to have been "in great credit with Jasper, Earle of Pembrok [son of Owen Tudor, and uncle of Henry VII.], who lay in his house at Corsygedol, when he fled to France in the tyme of Edward IV., and as some report, Harry, the Earle of Richmond with him, who afterwards was King of England." Lowry, his wife, was niece of the celebrated *Owain Glyndwr*. Gruffydd Vaughan, Esq., was Lord of Corsygedol when *Lewys Dwnn* in 1588 visited the place, and wrought out the pedigree of the family.

Upon the death, in 1791, of Evan Lloyd Vaughan, Esq., M.P. for Merioneth, the last representative in the male line of this ancient family, Corsygedol and the rest of his ample estates passed to his niece, Margaret, wife of Sir Roger Mostyn, of Mostyn, Bart. (Note on *Dwnn*, ii., 220.) Corsygedol continued in the Mostyn family until it was purchased by the predecessor of the present owner (see *Coulson of Corsygedol*).

The Vaughans of Corsygedol bore—*Ermine, on a saltire gu., a crescent or* (with sixteen quarterings).

Nanney of Nannau.

" From Cadwgan, the second son of the founder of the tribe, descend the Nanneys of Nannau."— *Yorke*. The founder referred to was Bleddyn ap Cynfyn, Prince of Powys from whom the third royal tribe of Wales was descended. *Howel Selyf*, or *Selê*, possessor of Nannau in the time of Owain Glyndwr (see *Nannau*), was ninth from Bleddyn ap Cynfyn. His grandfather, Ynyr Fychan (*junior*), son of Ynyr ap Meurig, in the 33rd of Edward I., presented a petition to the Prince of Wales, stating that the king had made him Rhaglor (W., *Rhaglaw*) of the comot of Talybont for his service in taking Madoc ap Llywelyn, who in the last war had made himself Prince of Wales. The petition was not granted, inasmuch as Ynyr could show no charter or title to the office. (See Notes on *Heraldic Visit. of Wales*, ii., 226.) When Dwnn visited Nannau in 1588 he was head of the family, and signed the pedigree. His grandson, the head of the family, was Hugh Nanney, Esq., whose name is found in the list of sheriffs of his county in 1627 and 1638, and who died 1647. His grandson, Col. Hugh Nanney, M.P., Col. of the Militia of his co., and Vice-Admiral of North Wales in the last year of William III. (*mon.* in Llanfachreth Ch.), was the last of the line of Nanney; he married Catherine, dau. of William Vaughan, Esq., of Corsygedol, but by her left only daughters; the third of whom, Catherine, married Robert Vaughan, Esq., the celebrated antiquary, of Hengwrt, by whom she had several children, the eldest of whom, Hugh Vaughan, eventually succeeded to the Nanney estates, but *d. unm.* His next brother, Robert Howel Vaughan, of Nanney and Hengwrt, was in 1792 made a baronet, and was succeeded by his son, the popular Sir Robert Vaughan, Bart., M.P., of Nannau, who represented his county in Parliament for the long period of forty-four years. He was also father of Griffith ap Howel Vaughan, Esq., of Rhug and Hengwrt, and Col. Edward William Vaughan, who, on inheriting the Rhug estates, assumed by licence the additional surname of Salesbury, and *d.* in 1807. (Note *Herald. Visit. of Wales*, ii., 228.) Sir Robert Williams Vaughan, 3rd Bart. of Nannau, *d. s. p.* 1859, when the title became extinct, and the estates were divided. Nannau was left to the Hon. Thomas Pryce Lloyd (see *Lloyd of Pengwern*) for life, and then to John Vaughan, Esq. (see *Vaughan of Nannau*); Hengwrt was given during life to his late wife's three sisters, with remainder likewise to John Vaughan, Esq., and the great collection of the *Hengwrt MSS.* was bequeathed to his kinsman, W. W. E. Wynne, Esq., of Peniarth. The Rhûg estates were given to the Hon. C. H. Wynn, second son of Lord Newborough (see *Wynn of Rhûg*).

The *Nanneys* of Nannau bore—*Or, a lion rampant az.* The coat of the Vaughans of Nannau was—*Or and gu., four lions rampant counterchanged of the field;* on the centre of the shield the Nanney escutcheon.

Owen of Dolgelley.

The Owens of Dolgelley, whose most celebrated member was Lewis ap Owen, Esq., usually called "the Baron," sheriff for the co. of Merioneth 1546, 1555; M.P. for the same co. 1547, 1552 (see *Parl. Annals*), Chamberlain and Baron of the Exchequer of North Wales, whose murder by "Gwylliaid Mawddwy" has already been noticed, were for some generations a very prominent house. Their paternal lineage was drawn from Gwrgant ap Ithel, Prince of Glamorgan (11th cent.). They intermarried with the Pulestons of Emral, the Myttons of Mawddwy, and the Bodvels of Bodvel. Lewis Owen, grandson of the Baron, was sheriff of Merioneth 1598; married, but *d. s. p.* Junior branches of the family, however, continued to a late period at Caerberllan and Garthyngharad, and may not even now be quite extinct.

The arms of the Owens were those of Iestyn ap Gwrgant, Prince of Glamorgan,—*Gu.*, *three chevrons arg.*

Lloyd of Rhiwaedog.

Rhiwaedog, near Bala, a spot of historic interest by reason of the great battle which tradition relates was fought here between the Welsh under *Llywarch Hên*, the prince-bard, and the Saxons, when the aged bard lost Cynddelw, the last survivor of twenty-four sons, whose sanguinary character gave its name to the place (*rhiw*, a declivity; and *gwaedog*, bloody). It is situated in the narrow and *long* valley of *Hir*-nant, nearly two miles from the Dee, and an equal distance from the mansion of *Aberhirnant*. Rhirid Flaidd is said by Yorke (*Royal Tribes*) to have dwelt at Rhiwaedog.

The Lloyds of Rhiwaedog were a family of distinction, and of great antiquity. They traced their lineage to Owain Gwynedd, in the same branch as the Maurices of Clenenney, and Anwyls of Park (see *Anwyl of Llugwy*). They intermarried with the Pulestons, Vaughans of Llwydiarth, the Nanneys, Kynastons, and other chief houses. In Mr. Wynne's notes on *Dwnn* (ii., 226) we find that in the eighteenth century Rhiwaedog and its large possessions passed· to the Dolbens; the mansion and a remnant of the estate became eventually by descent vested in two ladies of the name of Iles, by the survivor of whom they were bequeathed to Mrs. Price, of Rhiwlas. The old mansion of Rhiwaedog presents a sad picture of dilapidation and neglect, uttering a loud complaint against the ignorance or indifference of the proprietor.

There are still descendants of this ancient family at Bala; the elder male branch was represented by George Price Lloyd, Esq., of Plas-yn-y-dre. The arms borne by the Lloyds were those of Owain Gwynedd,—*Vert, three eagles displayed in fesse or.*

Hughes of Gwerclas.

This family, which is not yet quite extinct, traced from Gwaethfoed of Ceredigion, through Bleddyn ap Cynfyn, Prince of Powys, and his descendant, Owain Brogyntyn, Lord of Edeirnion and Dinmael (see *Owain Brogyntyn*). Huw ap William, living A.D. 1546, and described by Lewys Dwnn (*Heraldic Visit. of Wales*) as one of the barons of Edeirnion, and Lord of all Cymmer, removed from Cymmer, in Edeirnion, so long the residence of his ancestors, to the adjoining mansion of *Gwerclas,* within the barony. He *d.* in 1600. His son Humphrey ap Huw, or *Hughes,* Sheriff of Merioneth in 1618, was head of the family at the visitation by Lewys Dwnn. He *d. s. p.,* and was succeeded by his brother, Richard Hughes, as tenth baron of Cymmer, in Edeirnion.

This senior and a junior branch of this ancient family were not long since united by the marriage of John Hughes, Esq., barrister-at-law of the Inner Temple, with his kinswoman, Dorothea, eldest surviving daughter of Richard Hughes Lloyd, Esq., of Plymog, Gwerclas,

Cymmer, and Bashall, of which marriage there is issue a son, Talbot de Bashall Hughes, b. 1836.

The armorial bearings of this house are those of the Princes of Powys,—*Arg., a lion rampant sa.*

Hughes and Nanney of Maesypandy and Maesyneuadd.

Maesypandy, in the parish of Talyllyn, now reduced to a farmstead, was for many ages the seat of a family of note. Rhys Hughes, Esq., Sheriff of the co. of Merioneth in 1582, was representative of his house at the visitation of Lewys Dwnn in 1588, paying *ten shillings* to the Deputy Herald for his labour in making out the family pedigree. They traced their lineage from *Einion Sais* (see *Games of Newton*), who is said in the pedigrees to have been a descendant of *Caradoc Freichfras*, and they bore the arms ascribed by the heraldic bards to that redoubtable knight.

The heiress of the Hughes family married Lewis Nanney, Esq., a grandson by a younger son of Hugh Nanney, Esq., of Nannau. He was Sheriff of Merioneth in 1634. She was married, secondly, to John Lloyd, Esq., of Ceiswyn, Sheriff of Merioneth in 1652 and 1667. The Maesypandy estates, after being vested for several generations in his family, passed into that of Wynn of Maesyneuadd, Talsarnau, through the marriage of William Wynn, Esq., to Lowry, eldest sister of John Nanney, Esq. Their only son, William Wynn, Esq., Sheriff for Merioneth in 1758, assumed the surname of Nanney. He *d.* 1795, and his grandson, John Nanney, in 1838 became owner of Maesyneuadd and Maesypandy (see Notes *Herald. Visit. of Wales*, ii., 238). He, the last of this line, *d.* in 1868. (See *Mrs. Nanney of Bronwylfa.*)

The Nanneys bore on their coat—Quarterly, 1st and 4th, *or, a lion rampant az.*—for NANNEY; 2nd and 3rd, *ermine, on a saltire gu. a crescent or*—for WYNN.

Wynn of Glyn.

This ancient family, whose name is no longer associated with Glyn, is nevertheless not extinct. (See *Wynn of Peniarth* and *Ormsby-Gore of Brogyntyn.*)

David ap Morgan of Crogen.—This gentleman, who was seated at the ancient "Plas-yng-Nghrogen," when Dwnn in 1594 had the family lineage attested by him, is usually said to have been a descendant of Owen Brogyntyn. His grandson, David Morgan, living in the early part of the seventeenth century, was also seated at Crogen; but we have no means of ascertaining the time when the family became extinct. They bore the arms of Owen Brogyntyn.

Pyrs of Maesmawr ("Maesmore") was another powerful branch of the Owen Brogyntyn sept. The time when Maesmawr (*maes*, a plain, a field; and *mawr*, large, wide) became their home is uncertain. It was part of the lordship of their ancestor Owen. It continued in their possession long after the pedigree was drawn up by Dwnn (*Heraldic Visit. of Wales*, ii., 122) when "Cadwaladr Pyrs, Esq.," was chief of the house. The name of "Peirs Maesmore" appears in the subsidy rolls for the co. of Merioneth 1636. From him were several descents, until in 1775, or soon after, the heiress of Maesmawr married Edward Lloyd, Esq., of Trefnant, Mont., in which family the estate thereafter continued (*ib.*, note, 123). Maesmawr, once in Powys, on the creation of Denbighshire by Henry VIII. was placed within the boundary line of that county.

Meyrick of Ucheldref.—Of the same descent with *Meyrick of Bodorgan*, Anglesey (which see), through *Einion Sais* of Bodorgan. Ucheldref, an estate of several farms, in the parish of Gwyddelwern, near Corwen, was at the end of the sixteenth century possessed by "Edmund Meirig, Dr. of the Civill Law" (as Dwnn has it), Archdeacon of Bangor, and Canon of Lichfield, who married, first, a Conwy of Bodrhyddan, and secondly, a Williams of Cochwillan. The estate continued in the Meyrick family till about the middle of the eighteenth century, "when it became, as is supposed by bequest, the property of the Kyffins of Maenan, in Denbighshire. From them it passed by marriage to the Kenricks of Nantclwyd." (*Ib.*, ii., 127.)

Vaughan of Dolmelynllyn.—This was a branch of the ancient family of Hengwrt and Nannau (see *Nanney* and *Vaughan of Nannau*), not of early or of long settlement at this now venerable place. Griffith Vaughan, Esq., the first of the house, fourth son of Robert Vaughan, Esq., the antiquary of Hengwrt, settled at Dolmelynllyn, having married Jane, dau. of John ap John ap Robert, of Glyn Malden. He *d*. in 1700. His great-great-grandson, Robert Vaughan, Esq., an officer in the army, sold the estate of Dolmelynllyn and Glyn Malden, and *d*. unmarried about the end of the eighteenth century. This estate is now the property of Charles Reynolds Williams, Esq. (See *Williams of Dolmelynllyn.*)

Vaughan of Llanuwchllyn.—This family of Vaughan, of the sept of *Rhirid Flaidd*, Lord of Penllyn, were long settled in the parish of Llanuwchllyn, probably at *Glan-llyn*, on the margin of the Bala Lake, a property inherited by the present Sir Watkin W. Wynn, Bart., of Wynnstay, through marriage of the first Sir Watkin with Anna Josephina, dau. and co-heiress of the last Vaughan (Edward) of Llanuwchllyn and Llwydiarth, Mont. (See *Vaughan of Llwydiarth.*) The surname *Vaughan* originated at Llanuwchllyn with Ieuan *Fychan* ("the younger," the "*little*"), son of Ieuan ap Gruffydd (*d*. 1370), whose tomb is extant in the church of Llanuwchllyn. (Note, *Heraldic Visit. of Wales*, ii., 229.) The head of this house in 1588 was Robert Vaughan, Esq. His arms, according to *Dwnn*, were—*Vert, a chevron between three wolves' heads erased arg.*—the insignia of Rhirid Flaidd.

Edwards of Prysg.—John Edwards of Prysg, near Llanuwchllyn, living in 1588, was of the lineage of *Rhirid Flaidd*, Lord of Penllyn, in the same line, through *Ieuan Fychan* ap Ieuan ap Gruffydd, with the Vaughans of Llanuwchllyn mentioned above. This last Ieuan (ap Gruffydd) is stated in an autograph MS. of the eminent antiquary, Robert Vaughan, of

Hengwrt, to have "lived in great credit and esteeme in the days of King Edward III., who allowed him an annuall stipend for guarding and conducting of ye Justice of North Wales with a companie of archers, whilest he should sociourne and stay in ye countie of Merioneth." (Note, *Heraldic Visit. of Wales*, ii. 232.) This intimates a state of unsettledness in the country somewhat parallel to what we see in Ireland now, when Justice Keogh has to be escorted by a company of soldiers by railway. The Prysg estate, together with Caergai, is believed to have been sold in 1740 by the Rev. Henry Mainwaring and Mary Elizabeth, his wife, dau., and at length heiress of John Vaughan, Esq. (Sheriff of Merioneth in 1709) to Sir Watkin W. Wynn, and is in the possession of the present Sir Watkin. The arms of Edwards of Prysg were those of Rhirid Flaidd,—*Vert, a chevron between three wolves' heads erased arg.*

Lloyd of Rhiw-gôch.—The Lloyds of Rhiw-gôch, in the parish of Trawsfynydd, were for several generations people of good position in their county, and derived their lineage from *Llywarch ap Bran* (twelfth century) of Anglesey, founder of the second Noble Tribe of North Wales. Robert Lloyd, Esq., representative of the family at the end of the sixteenth century, and later, was M.P. for Merioneth 1586 and 1614; Sheriff in 1596, 1602, 1615, and 1625, and was living in 1636. His eldest son, Ellis Lloyd, Esq., living *temp.* Charles II., was the last heir male of the estate, which eventually passed with his daughter, Jane, to her husband, Henry Wynn, Esq., a younger son of Sir John Wynn, Bart., of Gwydir. The estate was ultimately bequeathed by the last Sir John Wynn (son of the said Henry, and Jane Lloyd), to his kinsman, Watkin Williams, Esq.; by whose representative, Sir Watkin Williams Wynn, Bart., of Wynnstay, they are at present possessed.

The arms of Lloyd of Rhiw-gôch were those of Llywarch ap Brân,—*Arg., a chevron, sa. between three Cornish choughs (or crows) proper.*

Powys of Cymmer.—This was a family of good and ancient lineage, tracing from Brochwel Ysgythrog, Prince of Powys; but its settlement at Cymmer, near Dolgelley, is not known to be earlier than the dissolution of the monasteries, *temp.* Henry VIII. *John Powys*, a Serjeant-at-Arms to Henry VIII., and living also in the 1st and 2nd of Philip and Mary, Sheriff of Merioneth in 1543, had, A.D. 1550, granted to him in perpetuity, or on lease, the Abbey of Cymmer, with the greater portion of its possessions. He is styled in a charter of Edward VI., "John Powes *de hospitio suo*," *i. e.*, of the king's household. Among his descendants, who for several generations continued at "Vaner Cymer," as *Dwnn* has it, —doubtless meaning thereby the *Manor* of Cymmer, *John Powys*, his grandson, represented the family in 1588, and paid the Deputy Herold "five shillings" for putting the imprimatur of the College of Arms on his pedigree.

Nanney of Cefn-deuddwr.—The house of Cefn-deuddwr was in the parish of Trawsfynydd, and the Nanneys of that place were an offshoot of the great house of *Nannau*, and bare the same arms with a martlet for difference of the *third* son. This branch of the Nanneys has become extinct in the present century, when the lineal representative, Rev. Richard Nanney (*d.* 1812), devised the estate to his sister's son, David Ellis, Esq., of *Gwynfryn*, co. of Carn., who, soon dying *s. p.*, left the united estates of Gwynfryn and Cefn-deuddwr to his sister's son, Owen Jones, Esq., of Brynkir, who took after his own surname those of Ellis and Nanney. He *d.* 1870. (See further *Ellis Nanney of Gwynfryn*.)

Griffith of Tanybwlch.—The early name of Tanybwlch (now Plas Tanybwlch) was Bwlch-Coed-dyffryn—the home of a much respected family, whose lineage was derived from Collwyn, founder of the fifth Noble Tribe of North Wales, and whose surname, when surnames came into use among the Welsh, was first *Evans*, then *Gryffydd*. Ivan Evans was head of the house in 1588. Margaret, the heiress of his grandson, Ivan Evans (Sheriff for Merioneth in 1635), by Elizabeth Wynn of Glyn, married Robert Gryffydd of Bach-y-Saint, co. of Carn., who was living in 1723. (Note, *Herald. Visit. of Wales*, ii., 224.) Their descendant, Margaret, only child of Evan Gryffydd, Esq , conveyed the Tanybwlch estate, by marriage, to William *Oakeley*, Esq., of an ancient family in Shropshire, and elder brother of the late Sir Charles Oakeley, Bart. (See further, *Oakeley of Plas Tanybwlch*.)

Price of Esgairweddan.—The earlier name of Esgairweddan, near Towyn, was "Plas yn y Rofft"—so it is called by Lewys Dwnn (1588). The family, eventually using the surname *Price* (ap Rhys), claimed direct descent from *Owain Gwynedd*, Prince of North Wales, through his eldest son, Ierwerth, who, on account of a personal deformity, was not allowed to succeed his father. The time of their first residence at this place is not known. Edward Prys, who represented the family in 1588, had only daughters, but he had several married brothers who had issue. The line of Price of Esgairweddan became extinct with Robert Price, Esq. (*d.* 1702), who left two daughters, Mary the survivor, and Anne, who *d.* in 1750. The estates, at the demise of the former, passed to the Edwardses of Talgarth, and are now vested in Capt. Thruston of Talgarth Hall. (Note on *Dwnn*, ii., 240.) See further, *Thruston of Talgarth Hall.*

Lloyd of Dol-y-gelynen.—Near Pennal is situated the old homestead of Dol-y-gelynen ("Holly-dale") where dwelt for many ages a family of some note in their day, but now long extinct. They traced their descent from Einion ap Seissyllt, Lord of Meirionydd, and thence to *Gwyddno Garanhir* (Goron Aur?—See *Dwnn*), and eventually adopted the surname Lloyd (*Llwyd*)—but from what circumstance is not now apparent. Rhys Lloyd, Esq., of Dol-y-gelynen, living in 1609, was fourth in descent from the eminent poet, *Dafydd Llwyd ap L'ywelyn*, of Mathavarn, near Machynlleth (*fl.* 1470—1520), who is said to have greatly aided by his writings the cause of the Earl of Richmond (Henry VII.) in Wales, and is believed to have entertained the Earl at Mathavarn on his way to Bosworth Field. (Note on *Dwnn*, ii., 241.) Dol-y-gelynen continued long in the possession of the Lloyds, for in 1698 David Lloyd of that place was one of the commissioners for collecting a subsidy voted by Parliament.

Lewis and Wynn of Pengwern.—The mansion of Pengwern, near Festiniog, bears in its age and decrepitude many traces of former notability. For a long series of years it was the patrimony of a family of influence and wealth, deriving from the same venerable stock with the Wynns of Glyn and Peniarth, Vaughans of Corsygedol, &c., viz., Osborn Wyddel. (See *Wynn of Peniarth; Vaughan of Corsygedol.*) Their lineage came through the celebrated *Dafydd ap Ieuan ap Einion*, the defender of Harlech Castle during the War of the Roses, whereas the Corsygedol line came through *Gruffydd* ap Einion. The first to adopt the surname *Lewis*, was John, son of Lewis, grandson of Dafydd ap Ieuan ap Einion, aforesaid. Morys Lewis was Sheriff of Merioneth in 1596. The line of *Lewis* ended in an heiress, Anne (dau. of Morys Lewis), who in 1689 married *Owen Wynne*, Esq., of Llwyn, Denbighshire, a younger branch of the great house of Gwydir. Their lineal descendant Maurice Wynn, LL.D., of Llwyn and Pengwern, Rector of Bangor Iscoed, dying unmarried, bequeathed the estates to his nephew, the Rev. Lloyd Fletcher, a younger son of his sister Ellinor, by Phillips Lloyd Fletcher, Esq., of Gwernhayled, co. of Flint.), who assumed the surname of Wynne. The Pengwern estate is now lineally inherited by Phillips Lloyd Fletcher, Esq. (See *Fletcher of Nerquis Hall, Flintshire.*)

The arms of the Lewis family were,—*Ermine, on a saltire gu., a crescent or,*—the arms of the Wynnes.

Lloyd of Nant-y-mynach.—Near Mallwyd was the old place, *Nant-y-mynach* (whose name seems to embody an allusion to some monastic institution once existing in the neighbourhood), the home in the olden time of the *Lloyds*, a family of the sept of *Ednowain ap Bradwen*, founder of one of the Fifteen Noble Tribes, of Llys Bradwen, near Dolgelley. The head of this old family in 1594 was Richard Lloyd; but how far his descendants, beyond his sons John, Samuel, and Lodwig, continued the line, we are not able to ascertain. The arms of Richard Lloyd were, first, those of Ednowain ap Bradwen,—*Gu., three snakes enowed, arg.;* secondly, those of Gruffydd ap Adda of Dolgôch,—*Or, a lion rampant regardant sa.*

Price of Corsygarnedd Llahfachreth.—The Prices of Corsygarnedd, were a family of some importance and respectability at least as far back as the beginning of the seventeenth century. The surname Price appears to have been first adopted by Griffith *Price* (*ap Rhys*), Esq. (*b.* August 4, 1693), son of *Rhys* Gruffydd of Corsygarnedd, by his wife Anne, one of the Meiricks of Berth-lwyd. Griffith, the eldest son (*b.* April 8, 1718; *d.* 1804), *m.* Jonnet (*d.* 1788), only dau. and h. of David Lloyd, Esq., of Braich-y-Ceunant (as shown by the inscription on a tablet in Llanfachreth Church), and left an only child and h., Laura, who became the wife of Edward Edwards, Esq., of *Cerrig-llwydion*, Denb. This marriage also ultimately issued in an heiress, Anne, who married John Edwards, Esq., 2nd son, of Dolserau—a family different from her own, being the Edwards of Ness Strange, Salop (see *Edwards of Dolserau*), by whom she had an only son, Edward Lloyd Edwards, Esq., of Dolserau, owner through his mother of Cerrig-llwydion, &c. His only child, Louisa Janette Anne, the present Mrs. Richards of Caernwch, succeeded to his estates, and is senior representative of the Prices of Corsygarnedd, Lloyds of Braich-Ceunant, as well as Edwardses of Cerrig-llwydion. (See, further, *Richards of Caerynwch.*) One of the cadet branches of the Price family of Corsygarnedd is now represented by J. Pryce Jones, Esq., of the Groves, Wrexham, who is maternally descended from Richard, son of the first Griffith Price of Corysgarnedd.

The arms as shewn on the memorial tablet, are those of Llywarch ap Brân,—*Arg.*, a *chevron between three Cornish choughs, sa.*, with which the second Griffith Price quartered those of his wife,—*Per pale, a cross patoncé between four Cornish choughs, ppr.; sa. a chevron arg. between three boars' heads of the second, erased, langued gu.*

Wynn and Vaughan of Bod-talog.—Bod-talog, near Towyn, was long the possession of the Wynns, a branch of the Gwydir stock. Dwnn says: "Ieuan Gwyn had Bod-talog, and his wife was Catherine, dau. of David ap Howel ap Owen of Llanbrynmair." Ieuan *Fychan* was a grand juror for co. Merioneth, A.D. 1453. The pedigree is brought down to 1623 by Vincent, 136, 1001, (Coll. of Arms) Sir John Wynn, of Gwydir, being then living. In the invaluable notes to Dwnn's *Herald. Visit. of Wales* (which, though anonymous, are known to be from the competent hand of Mr. W. W. E. Wynne of Peniarth, and from which we have frequently quoted), we are informed that the late John Vaughan, Esq., of *Penmaen-Dyfi*, was representative of this ancient house of Bod-talog.

Among the other numerous families of Merioneth were those of *Philips of Hendrefechan* (near Harlech, in Ardudwy), remarkable for having produced a long succession of poets of note, such as "Siôn Phylip," d. 1620, "Gwilyn Phylip," Gruffydd Phylip (1658), and Philip John Philip (1674); *Morgan of Taltreuddyn* (originating in Ieuan ap Jenkin ap Meredydd ap Alo, but who called himself Ieuan Collier), whose arms were—*Or, three lions' heads erased, gu., within a bordure engrailed az.*,—the insignia of Alo, and the arms of Ednyfed Fychan, and which about the middle of the eighteenth century merged, by marriage of the heiress, into the family of Griffith of Llanfair, co. of Carn.; *Gwyn of Llwyn-Griffri*, of the same line, and bearing the same arms as the last mentioned family, excepting those of Ednyfed; *Edwards of Llwyn-du*, (Llanaber), also of the same sept, but using other arms, viz., *sa. a lion rampant arg.; Owen of Talybont* (Llanegryn), of the line of Lewis Owen, "the baron," of Dolgelley, obtained Talybont with extensive privileges attached to it, by purchase, from the crown, *temp.* James I. (one of their number, Hugh Owen, was founder of the Free School at Llanegryn, and father of the celebrated Dr. John Owen, the great Nonconformist Dean of Christ Church, Vice-Chancellor of Oxford University, and Chaplain to Oliver Cromwell); *Jones of Maesygarnedd* (near Llanbedr), one of whose line was Col. John Jones, M.P. for Merioneth, who became brother-in-law of Oliver Cromwell, and was one of those who signed the death-warrant of Charles I.; *Lloyd of Plas yn 'Ddôl* (Edeirnion), of the sept of Marchudd ap Cynan, founder of the Eighth Noble Tribe, and bore his arms,—*Gu., a saracen's head erased ppr.*, and continued at Plas yn 'Ddôl till near the end of the seventeenth century, when it was sold to the Joneses, whose representative, the late Richard Parry, sold it to Col. Vaughan of Rhug, of which estate it now forms part.

In the vale of Dyfi and the hilly Mawddwy there were many old families of high respectability, who have left no representatives—such as the *Broughs* and *Myttons of Dinas Mawddwy*, two names located on the Lordship of Mawddwy through marriage in succession with heiresses, the former, through the marriage of Hugh Brough with the granddaughter of William Willcock (*Will Gôch*—"red Will"), called "de la Pole," because he came from Pool, Mont., Lord of Mawddwy, of the line of Owain Cyfeiliog; the latter through the marriage of Thomas Mytton, Esq., with a daughter of Sir John Brough, Lord of Mawddwy, whose mansion stood on the site of the newly erected Plas Dinas Mawddwy (see *Buckley of Plas Dinas Mawddwy); David ap Howel of Llan-y-Mawddwy* (of the same line of Owain Cyfeiliog), whose family intermarried with that of Nannau, &c., and continued at Llan-y-Mawddwy for some time; *Lloyd of Plas yn Ngheiswyn* (Talyllyn), of the line of Gwaethfoed, Lord of Cardigan, one of whose members, John Lloyd, Esq., was Sheriff of Merioneth in 1550, 1558, and 1562. There were several others of less note and short continuance.

Prys of Tyddyn-du, Maentwrog.

Edmund Prys of Tyddyn-du, Maentwrog, merits especial notice, not merely as a man of good family and high standing in the Church, but as author of an early translation of the *Psalms* into Welsh, which continues in use to the present day, and the writer of other less important works. He was born at Gerddi Bluog, Llandecwyn, near Maentwrog, *circa* 1541; of the race of *Hedd Molwynog;* educated at Jesus Coll., Cambridge; became Vicar of Maentwrog 1572; of Llanddwywe 1580; was made Archdeacon of Merioneth 1576, and obtained a Canonry in St. Asaph 1602. He *d.* 1621, *æt.* 80, and was buried at Maentwrog, but no stone shows the place of his rest. He left a family, but of the history of them and their issue little is known. Edmund Prys being a bard, wrote "poetry" in the *twenty-four* regular metres, and many of his productions, especially his friendly tournament in verse with *William Cynwal,* display a vein of pleasantry and much genuine humour. He wrote also some Latin poetry. We may imagine the state of ignorance into which the people had been plunged at this period when we say that for nearly sixty years after Edmund Prys's Psalms and Dr. Morgan's Bible were printed in London (1588), not a single book in the Welsh language was printed in Wales. The political wisdom of the time displayed itself in the systematic discouragement of the Welsh language, and attained the result of popular ignorance and depravity. The first Welsh book issued from the press in Wales yet discovered was "The Whole Duty of Man," printed at Wrexham in 1718, more than 270 years after the invention of printing!

SECTION V.—HIGH SHERIFFS OF MERIONETHSHIRE, A.D. 1284—1872.

Sheriffs of counties under the Plantagenets and up to Henry VIII. were usually appointed for life, or during pleasure, and the persons so appointed were not always residents, or even natives of the Principality. Under Henry VIII. it was ordered that three persons should be nominated by "the President, Council, and Justices of Wales," as suitable for the office of sheriff, and certified by the same to the Privy Council, "to the end that the king maight appoint one of them in every of the said shires to be sheriff for that year, like as is used in England." The following list of Merioneth sheriffs in its earlier part up to A.D. 1541 is the fruit of the research of W. W. E. Wynne, Esq., of Peniarth, and the succeeding part, up to 1847 (see *Archæol. Cambr.*, 1847, p. 120), has also passed under his careful scrutiny and correction. The *Gwiliedydd* for 1828 published a list of the Sheriffs of Merioneth from A.D. 1538, and of Montgomery from the year 1540, but those lists were in many instances incorrect, both as to the name of sheriff and year of office. This is especially the case in the earlier dates. Recent Sheriffs have been supplied by E. Breese, Esq All notes in brackets are by the author.

EDWARD I.

Robert de Staundon [he probably held the office till 1304] 1284-94
Robert de Eccleshale 1304

EDWARD II.

Ievan ap Howel [of what place it is impossible to determine] the name being common . 1309
Robert de Eccleshale, again . . . 1311-13
Robert ap Rees ["quamdiu nobis placuerit"] 1314-16
John Cam, Sheriff; Thomas de Peulesdon, Deputy 1319-20
Griffith ap Rees, again 1321-23
Griffith ap Rees, ' *Knight*" (the same) . . 1327

EDWARD III.

Griffith ap Rees (the same) 1327
Edmund Hakelut 1329-30
Griffith, [son of William de la Pole, Lord of Mawddwy, or "Will Goch"] . . 1331
Richard de Holond 1332
Robert de Middleton, "valletus regis," later in the year 1332
Walter de Manny [appointed for life] . . 1332
Howel ap Grono [prob. *deputy* to De Manny] . 1343
John de Housum, or Hosum [also *deputy* under De Manny] 1345
Meurig Maelan [prob. *deputy* to De Manny] 1347-8
Einion ap Gr. (Griffith) [Mr. Wynne considers him the same person with Einion ap Griffith, Sheriff of Carn. 25 Edw. III.] 1352
Rañ del Hope [sub-sheriff to Walter de Manny] 1353
Griffith ap Llewelyn ap Kenric of Corsygedol 1372
John de Baildon [not *deputy*, De Manny being now dead] 1376

RICHARD II.

Richard Bailden 1387
Vivian Colier, the younger, of Harlech. [See *Morgan of Taltreuddynn* and *Gwyn of Llwyn-griffri*] 1391
John Banham 1396

HENRY IV.

Einion ap Ithel of Rhiwaedog died, being sheriff of this co. [Vaughan of Hengwrt says that "after" the death, not "upon" the death of De Manny, Einion ap Ithel was appointed for life] . . . 1400

HENRY, PRINCE OF WALES, *postea* HENRY V.

Thomas Strange 1412

HENRY V.

Thomas Strange (the same) 1421

HENRY VI.

Robert de Orelle 1423-6
Thomas Burneby (appointed for life) . . 1432
John Hampton [*deputy* for Burneby] . 1437-8
Thomas Burneby was sheriff 1448
Thomas Burneby and Thomas Parker . . 1452
Thomas Burneby 1455-7
Vivian Palgus. [See *Philips of Hendrefechan*. The curious name "Palgus" was assumed by the descendants of the *Colliers* of Harlech, who themselves had assumed the latter name in place of the Welsh patronymic, "ab Alo." See Dwnn, *Her. Visit.*, ii., 220] 1457

EDWARD IV.

Roger Kynaston, Esq., of Hordley, Salop [afterwards Sir Roger Kynaston, Kt.] . 1461
Thomas Croft, Esq. (appointed for life) . . 1464
Sir Roger Kynaston, Kt. (reappointed for life) 1473

HENRY VII.

Piers Stanley, Esq. [prob. of *Harlech*] . . }
Richard Pole [another instance of two sheriffs } 1485
appointed for the same year] . . . }
Piers Stanley, Esq. 1515

HENRY VIII.

Ellis ap Maurice, Esq., of Clenenney [*deputy* to Piers Stanley] 1517
John Scudamor, sheriff and escheator . . 1520
Humphrey ap Howel ap Jenkin of Ynys-y-Maengwyn [*deputy* to John Scudamor] . 1521
William Brereton, sheriff; Hugh Lewis, *deputy* 1528
John Puleston, *deputy* to Brereton . . . 1530
William Brereton and John Puleston ["the longer liver of them," or "conjunctum et divisum"] 1533-5
John Puleston, made sheriff "for life" . . 1536
John Puleston; Lewis ap Owen, *deputy* [see *Lewis ap Owen of Dolgelley*] . . 1537-38
Ellis ap Maurice, Esq., of Clenenney, *Carn*. [he was owner of property in Beddgelert, Llanfrothen, &c., co. of Mer.] . . 1541
[From this time, with the single exception of the year of "Restoration," *i.e.*, the coming of Charles II. to the throne, the office was not held for more than one year.]
Jenkin Vaughan, Esq., of Caethlé . . . 1542
John Powys, Esq., of Vaner 1543
Robert Salesbury, Esq., of Rhûg [see *Salusburv, &c., of Rhûg*] 1544
Edward Stanley, Esq., of Harlech [of the

HIGH SHERIFFS OF MERIONETHSHIRE. 691

Stanleys of Hooton, Cheshire, son of Peers Stanley of Ewloe, Flint; Gov. of Harlech Castle. See also *Ann.* 1485] . . 1545
Lewis Owen, Esq., of Dolgelley [Vice-chamb. of N. Wales, and Baron of the Exchequer of Carn. See *Lewis Owen of Dolgelley ; Dinas Mawddwy*, &c.] 1546

EDWARD VI.

Richard Mytton, Esq., Lord of Mawddwy [see *Mytton of Dinas Mawddwy*] . . 1547
Rice Vaughan, Esq., of Corsygedol . . 1548
Robert Salesbury, Esq., of Rhûg . . . 1549
Ieuan ap David Lloyd, Esq., of Ceiswyn. [See *Lloyd of Plas yn Ngheiswyn*] . . . 1550
John ap Hugh ap Evan, Esq., of Mathafarn, *Mont*. 1551
Ellis Price, Esq., LL.D., of Plas Iolyn, *Denb.* 1552
Edward Stanley, Esq, of Harlech . . . 1553

MARY.

Edward Mytton, Esq., Lord of Mawddwy . 1554
Lewis Owen, Esq., of Dolgelley [same as for 1546. His murder took place this year.] 1555
Ellis Price, Esq., LL.D., of Plas Iolyn, *Denb.* See *Ellis Price of Plas Iolyn*.] . . 1556
Rice Vaughan, Esq., of Corsygedol . . 1557
Ieuan ap David Lloyd, Esq., of Ceiswyn . 1551

ELIZABETH.

John Salesbury, Esq., of Rhûg . . . 1559
Edward Stanley, Esq., of Harlech . . 1560
Hugh Puleston, Esq. [of the Emral stock] . 1561
Ieuan ap David Lloyd, Esq., of Ceiswyn . 1562
Griffith Glynne, Esq. [of Pwllheli?] . . 1563
Ellis Price, Esq., LL.D., of Plas Iolyn, *Denb.* 1564
Ellis ap William Lloyd, Esq., of Rhiwaedog . 1565
John Lewis Owen, Esq., of Dolgelley [afterwards of Llwyn, near that town ; son of "Baron Owen"] 1566
Griffith Glynne, Esq. [of Pwllheli ; Sheriff of co. Carn. 1564] 1567
Ellis Price, Esq., LL.D., of Plas Iolyn . . 1568
Piers Salesbury, Esq. 1569
Owen Wynne, Esq. 1570
John Yerwerth, Esq. [supp. to be of Prysg. See *Edwards of Prysg*] 1571
John Gwynne ap Ellis, Esq. 1572
John Lewis Owen, Esq., of Dolgelley (same as for 1566) 1573
Ellis Price, Esq., LL.D., of Plas Iolyn . 1574
Rowland Pughe, Esq., the elder, of Mathafarn, *Mont.* 1575
Evan Lloyd David ap John, Esq., of Nantmynach [see *Lloyd of Nant-mynach*] . . 1576
John Wynne ap Cadwalader, Esq., of Rhiwlas 1577
John Salesbury, Esq., of Rhûg . . . 1578
Ellis Price, Esq., LL.D., of Plas Iolyn . . 1579

John Pryse, Esq., of Gogerthan, *Card.* . . 1580
Evan Lloyd, Esq., of Yale, *Denb.* . . 1581
Rees Hughes, Esq., of Maes-y-pandy . . 1582
Richard ap Hugh ap Evan, Esq. . . . 1583
Ellis Price, Esq., LL.D., of Plas Ioyln . . 1584
Piers Salesbury, Esq. 1585
John Wynn ap Cadwalader, Esq., of Rhiwlas . 1586
Hugh Nanney, Esq., the elder, of Nannau . 1587
Griffith Vaughan, Esq., of Corsygedol . . 1588
John Wynn, Esq., of Gwydir, *Carn.* [owner of property in the hundred of Ardudwy. See *Wynn of Gwydir*] 1589
John Lewis Owen, Esq., of Llwyn . . 1590
William Maurice, Esq., of Clenenney [afterwards Sir William] 1591
Griffith Wynne Esq., of Berth ddu, *Carn.* . 1592
Cadwaladr ap Rhys, Esq. [Maesmawr?] . 1593
John Vaughan, Esq., of Glanllyn [see *Vaughan of Llanuwchllyn*] 1594
Morris Lewis, Esq., of Festiniog . . . 1595
Robert Lloyd, Esq., of Rhiwgôch [see *Lloyd of Rhiwgôch*] 1596
John Conwy, Esq. [of Bodrhyddan ?] . . 1597
Lewis Owen, Esq., of Llwyn . . . 1598
Matthew Herbert, Esq., of Dolguog, *Mont.* . 1599
Piers Salesbury, Esq. 1600
John Wynn, Esq., of Gwydir [*cr.* a baronet 1611, *d.* 1626] 1601
Robert Lloyd, Esq., of Rhiwgôch [same as for 1596] 1602

JAMES I.

Griffith Vaughan, Esq., of Corsygedol . . 1603
Thomas Vaughan, Esq., of Pant-glas, *Carn.* . 1604
Thomas Needham, Esq. [See *Sher. Denb.* 1617]. 1605
Sir William Maurice, Kt., of Clenenney . 1606
Sir James Pryse, Kt., of Ynys-y-Maengwyn . 1607
Ednyfed Griffith, Esq., of Gwydd-gwion . 1608
John Price, Esq., of Rhiwlas . . . 1609
Matthew Herbert, Esq., of Dolguog, *Mont.* . 1610
William Lewis Anwyl, Esq., of Park [see *Anwyl of Llugwy*] 1611
Sir John Wynn, Knt., the younger, of Gwydir 1612
John Lloyd, Esq., of Vaynol, *Flint.* . . 1613
John Vaughan, Esq., of Caergai . . 1614
Robert Lloyd, Esq., of Rhiwgôch . . . 1615
John Lloyd, Esq., of Rhiwaedog [see *Lloyd of Rhiwaedog*] 1616
Lewis Gwyn, Esq., of Dolau-gwyn . . 1617
William Wynne, Esq., of Glyn . . . 1618
Humphrey Hughes. Esq., of Gwerclas . . 1619
Sir James Pryse, Kt., of Ynys-y-Maengwyn . 1620
John Vaughan, Esq., of Caergai . . . 1621
John Vaughan, Esq., of Caethlé . . . 1622
Thomas Lloyd, Esq., of Nantfreyr . . 1623
William Lewis Anwyl, Esq, of Park . . 1624

CHARLES I.

Robert Lloyd, Esq., of Rhiwgôch . . 1625
William Vaughan, Esq., of Corsygedol . 1626

MERIONETHSHIRE.

	A.D.
Hugh Nanney, Esq., of Nannau	1627
Peerce, Lloyd, Esq., of Dôl	1628
William Oxwicke, Esq., of Coventry. [In the Gwiliedydd list he is called "Oxwiste of Cefn-yr-Onen." Was he the same with William Foxwist, the republican M.P. for Carnarvon, 1640, and for Swansea 1658-92? See William Foxwist, M.P., under co. Glamorgan, p. 610].	1629
Henry Pryce, Esq., of Taltreuddyn	1630
Rowland Pugh, Esq., of Mathafarn, Mont.	1631
John Owen, Esq., of Clenenney [afterwards knighted]	1632
Edmund Meyrick, Esq., of Garthlwyd	1633
Lewis Nanney, Esq., of Maes-y-pandy. [See Nanney of Maes-y-pandy]	1634
Evan Evans, Esq., of Tanybwlch. [See Griffith of Tanybwlch]	1635
Richard Vaughan, Esq., of Cors-y-gedol, died John Lloyd, Esq., of Rhiwaedog, served remainder of year	1636
William Wynne, Esq., of Glyn	1637
Hugh Nanney, Esq., of Nannau	1638
Griffith Lloyd, Esq., of Maes-y-neuadd	1639
Thomas Phillips, Esq., of the co. of Salop	1640
Lewis Anwyl, Esq., of Cemmaes, died Griffith Nanney, Esq., of Dolaugwyn, served remainder of year	1641
John Lloyd, Esq., of Rhiwaedog	1642
Rowland Vaughan, Esq., of Caergai	1643
John Morgan, Esq., of Celli-Iorwerth	1644
William Owen, Esq. [of Brogyntyn, Constable of Harlech Castle. "Noe sessions kept this yeare; he held out his castle for ye king for halfe a yeare siedge."—Old list of Sheriffs at Porkington, ending 1673]	1645
No sheriff appointed	1646
Lewis Owen, Esq., of Peniarth	1647
Owen Salesbury, Esq., of Rhûg. [He was "made by the Parliament. Noe sessions kept this yeare."—Old List, quoted by Mr. Wynne]	1648

THE COMMONWEALTH.

Maurice Williams, Esq., of Nanmor. ["In the beginning of his time, upon the 30th of Jan., 1648, was our soueraigne lord ye king beheaded, and a new patent seal to all sheriffes, and monarchy altered to the state government."—Ib.].	1649
Robert Anwyl, Esq., of Park	1650
Maurice Wynn, Esq., of Crogen	1651
John Lloyd, Esq., of Maes-y-pandy	1652
Lewis Lloyd, Esq., of Rhiwaedog	1653

OLIVER CROMWELL, LORD PROTECTOR.

Maurice Lewis, Esq., of Pengwern, Festiniog	1654
John Anwyl, Esq., of Llanfendigaid	1655
William Vaughan, Esq., of Caethlé	1656

	A.D.
Robert Wynn, Esq., of Sylfaen	1657
Howel Vaughan, Esq., of Glanllyn	1658

RICHARD CROMWELL, LORD PROTECTOR.

Richard Anwyl, Esq. ["The youngest son of William Lewis Anwyl, Esq."—Old List]	1659

CHARLES II.—"THE RESTORATION."

Richard Anwyl, Esq. (the same)	1660
Humphrey Hughes, Esq., of Gwerclas	1661
William Salesbury, Esq., of Rhûg	1662
Roger Mostyn, Esq., of Dôl-y-corslwyn	1663
John Wynne, Esq., of Cwm-mine	1664
Maurice Williams, Esq., of Nanmor	1665
Lewis Lloyd, Esq., of Rhiwaedog	1666
John Lloyd, Esq., of Maes-y-pandy	1667
Richard Wynn, Esq., of Branas	1668
Robert Wynne, Esq., of Glyn	1669
John Vaughan, Esq.	1670
Maurice Wynn, Esq., of Llandanwg	1671
Howel Vaughan, Esq., of Vaner [Cymmer Abbey—of the Nannau house]	1672
Nathaniel Jones, Esq., of Hendwr	1673
Owen Wynne, Esq., of Glyn	1674
Hugh Tudor, Esq., of Egryn [son of William ap Tudyr, of the tribe of Marchudd ap Cynan, m. Gwen, dau. of Richard Vaughan of Cors-y-gedol]	1675
Sir John Wynn, Bart. [of Gwydir and Rhiwgoch. Henry Wynn m. Jane, dau. and h., of the latter place. See Lloyd of Rhiwgoch].	1676
Griffith Vaughan, Esq., of Cors-y-gedol	1677
John Nanney, Esq., of Llanfendigaid	1678
Robert Wynne, Esq., of Maes-y-neuadd	1679
Richard Nanney, Esq., of Cefn-deuddwr	1680
Edmund Meyrick, Esq., of Ucheldre	1681
William Vaughan, Esq., of Caergai	1682
Vincent Corbet, Esq, of Ynys-y-maengwyn	1683
Anthony Thomas, Esq., of Hendre	1684

JAMES II.

Lewis Lewis, Esq., of Penmaen	1685
Richard Poole, Esq., of Caenest	1686
Richard Mytton, Esq., of Dinas Mawddwy. [See Brougn and Mytton of Dinas Mawddwy].	1687
Sir Robert Owen, Kt., of Glyn	1688

WILLIAM AND MARY.

Charles Hughes, Esq., of Gwerclas	1689
John Jones, Esq., of Uwchlaw'rcoed	1690
John Grosvenor, Esq.; died, and was succ. by Hugh Nanney, Esq., of Nannau	1691
Thomas Owen, Esq., of Llynlloedd, Mont.	1692
Owen Wynne, Esq., of Pengwern	1693
William Anwyl, Esq., of Deleiniog	1694
Richard Owen, Esq., of Peniarth	1695
John Lloyd, Esq., of Aberllefeni	1696
Howel Vaughan, Esq., of Vaner [Cymmer]	1697

HIGH SHERIFFS OF MERIONETHSHIRE.

	A.D.
Richard Vaughan, Esq., of Cors-y-gedol	1698
William Lewis Anwyl, Esq., of Park	1699
Evan Wynne, Esq., of Cwm-mine	1700
John Nanney, Esq., of Llanfendigaid	1701

ANNE.

Edward Holland, Esq., of Pentre	1702
David Lloyd, Esq., of Hendwr	1703
Morris Williams, Esq., of Havod-garegog	1704
John Lloyd, Esq., of Rhwiwaedog	1705
Sir William Williams, Bart., of Llanvorda	1706
Sir Griffith Williams, of Marle	1707
John Wynne, Esq., of Garthmeilio	1708
John Vaughan, Esq., of Caergai	1709
Roger Price, Esq., of Rhiwlas	1710
Thomas Meyrick, Esq., of Berth-lwyd	1711
Hugh Owen, Esq., of Cae'rberllan	1712
William Owen, Esq., of Glyn	1713

GEORGE I.

William Wynn, Esq., of Maes-y-neuadd	1714
Lewis Owen, Esq., of Peniarth	1715
John Evans, Esq., of Cyffty	1716
Richard Weaver, Esq., of Corwen	1717
Griffith Wynne, Esq., of Taltreuddyn	1718
Ellis Jones, Esq., of Nant-bydyr	1719
Hugh Hughes, Esq., of Gwerclas	1720
Richard Mytton, Esq., of Dinas Mawddwy	1721
Thomas Price, Esq., of Glyn	1722
David Lloyd, Esq., of Bodnant	1723
Owen Lloyd, Esq., of Hendwr	1724
Robert Lloyd, Esq., of Dôlglessyn	1725
Athelstan Owen, Esq., of Rhiwaedog	1726

GEORGE II.

William Wynn, Esq., of Taltreuddyn	1727
John Nanney, Esq., of Maes-y-pandy	1728
Griffith Roberts, Esq., of Blaen-y-ddôl	1729
Ffoulk Lloyd, Esq., of Cilau	1730
William Price, Esq., of Rhiwlas	1731
Edward Lloyd, Esq., of Gwerclas	1732
Hugh Thomas, Esq., of Hendre	1733
Robert Wynne, Esq., of Maes-y-neuadd	1734
Robert Vaughan, Esq., of Hengwrt [the Antiquary]	1735
John Mytton, Esq., of Dinas Mawddwy	1736
Robert Meyrick, Esq., of Ucheldré	1737
John Lloyd, Esq., of Rhiwaedog	1738
Richard Anwyl, Esq., of Dolfeiniog	1739
Thomas Price, Esq., of Rhûg	1740
Robert Wynne, Esq., of Cwm-mine	1741
Robert Griffith, Esq., of Tan-y-bwlch	1742
Maurice Jones, Esq., of Ddôl	1743
William Lewis Anwyl, Esq., of Bod-talog	1744
Edward Williams, Esq., of Peniarth	1745
Robert Parry, Esq., of Goppa	1746
Hugh Lloyd, Esq., of Gwerclas	1747
Owen Wynne, Esq., of Pengwern, Festiniog	1748
Owen Holland, Esq., of Pentre-mawr	1749

	A.D.
William Wynne, Esq., of Park, and Wern, Carn.	1750
Maysmore Maurice, Esq., of Rhagatt	1751
Hugh Vaughan, Esq., of Hengwrt	1752
Robert Price, Esq., of Cae-côch	1753
John Mostyn, Esq., of Clegyr	1754
William Humphreys, Esq., of Maerdy	1755
Richard Owen, Esq., of Caethlé	1756
Peter Price, Esq., of Dol-garnedd	1757
William Wynne, Esq., of Maes-y-neuadd	1758
Humphrey Edwards, Esq., of Talgarth	1759

GEORGE III.

Robert Vaughan Humphreys, Esq., of Caerynwch	1760
Lewis Owen, Esq., of Cae'rberllan	1761
Robert Wynne, Esq., of Cwm-mine	1762
John Mytton, Esq., of Dinas Mawddwy	1763
William Lloyd, Esq., of Rhiwaedog	1764
John Pugh, Esq., of Garthmaelan	1765
Edward Vaughan Pugh, Esq., of Ty-gwyn	1766
Thomas Kyffin, Esq., of Bryn-yr-odyn	1767
Robert Godolphe Owen, Esq., of Glyn	1768
Rice James, Esq., of Dol-y-gelynen	1769
Evan Griffith, Esq., of Plas Tan-y-bwlch	1770
Richard Parry, Esq., of Goppa	1771
William Wynne, Esq., of Peniarth and Park	1772
Lewis Edwards, Esq., of Talgarth. [See *Price of Esgair-weddan*]	1773
Thomas Powel, Esq., of Bron-biban	1774
Lewis Nanney, Esq., of Llwyn	1775
William Williams, Esq., of Peniarth-uchaf	1776
John Vaughan, Esq., of Dol-melynllyn	1777
Richard Price, Esq., of Rhiwlas	1778
Henry Arthur Corbet, Esq., of Ynys-y-maengwyn	1779
Thomas Roberts, Esq., of Tan-y-gaer	1780
Edward Lloyd, Esq., of Maes-mawr, Corwen	1781
William Humphreys, Esq., of Maer-dy	1782
Robert Evan, Esq., of Bodweni, Bala	1783
Robert Howel Vaughan, Esq., of Hafod Owen	1784
John Jones, Esq., of Cyff-dy	1785
Griffith Price, Esq., of Braich-y-Ceunant. [See *Price of Cors-y-garnedd*]	1786
John Jones, Esq., of Rhyd-y-fen	1787
Griffith Evans, Esq., of Cwm-yr-afon	1788
Edward Lloyd, Esq., of Palé	1789
John Wynne Pugh, Esq., of Garth-maelan	1790
Griffith Roberts, Esq., of Bodunlliw	1791
Edward Corbet, Esq., of Ynys-y-maengwyn	1792
William John Lenthall, Esq., of Uchel-dré	1793
Owen Ormsby, Esq., of Glyn. [See *Ormsby-Gore of Glyn*, &c.]	1794
Robert Lloyd, Esq., of Cefn Coed	1795
Sir Edward Pryce Lloyd, Bart., of Park, appointed, but in his place— Thomas Lloyd, Esq., of Cwmheision, appeared in the *Gazette*, 19th March	1796
Bell Lloyd, Esq., of Tyddyn Llan. [See *Mostyn of Mostyn*]	1797

694   MERIONETHSHIRE.

	A.D.
Robert Watkin Wynne, Esq., of Cwm-mine	1798
Sir Thomas Mostyn, Bart., of Cors-y-gedol. [See *Vaughan of Cors-y-gedol*].	1799
Buckley Hatchett, Esq., of Ty'ny-pwll	1800
J. Passingham, Esq., of Hendwr	1801
John Meredydd Mostyn, Esq., of Clegyr	1802
John Forbes, Esq., of Cefn-bodiog	1803
Sir Edward Price Lloyd, Bart., of Park, and Pengwern, *Flint*	1804
John Edwards, Esq., of Penrhyn, and Greenfields, Machynlleth	1805
Hugh Jones, the elder, Esq., of Hengwrt-uchaf, was excused, and— Thomas Jones, Esq., of Ynys-faig, appointed R. H. Kenrick, Esq., of Ucheldré. [See *Meyrick of Ucheldre*]	1806
	1807
Pryce Edwards, Esq., of Talgarth	1808
William Davis, Esq., of Ty-uchaf	1809
John Davies, Esq., of Aberllefeni	1810
Hugh Reveley, Esq., of Bryn-y-gwin	1811
William Wynn, Esq., of Peniarth	1812
Thomas Edwards, Esq., of Ty-issaf	1813
William Gryffydd Oakeley, Esq., of Plas Tan-y-bwlch	1814
Lewis Vaughan, Esq., of Penmaen-Dyfi	1815
John Davies, Esq., of Fron-heulog	1816
Sir John Evans, Kt., of Hendre-forfydd	1817
John Edwards, Esq., of Coed-y-bedw	1818
Edward Owen, Esq., of Garth-yngharad	1819

GEORGE IV.

Thomas Fitzhugh, Esq., of Cwm-heision	1820
John Mytton, Esq., of Dinas Mawddwy	1821
James Gill, Esq., of Pant-glâs	1822
John Wynn, Esq., of Meyerth [W., *Buarth?*]	1823
Athelstan Corbet, Esq., of Ynys-y-maengwyn	1824
Francis Roberts, Esq., of Gerddi-bluog	1825
William Casson, Esq., of Cynfel	1826
Thomas Hartley, Esq., of Llwyn	1827
Thomas Casson, Esq., of Blaen-y-ddôl	1828
William John Bankes, Esq., of Dôl-y-moch	1829

WILLIAM IV.

Jones Panton, Esq., of Llwyn-Gwern	1830
Hugh Lloyd, Esq., of Cefn-bodiog	1831
William Turner, Esq., of Croesor	1832
George Jonathan Scott, Esq., of Peniarth-uchaf	1833
Charles Gray Harford, Esq., of Bryntirion	1834

	A.D.
John Henry Lewis, Esq., of Dolgun	1835
John Ellerker Boulcott, Esq., of Hendreissaf	1836

VICTORIA.

Sir Robert Williams Vaughan, Bart., of Nannau	1837
John Manners Kerr, Esq., of Plas Issaf	1838
The Hon. Edward Lloyd Mostyn, of Plas-hên	1839
George Price Lloyd, Esq., of Plas-yn-dre	1840
John Williams, Esq., of Bron Eryri	1841
The Hon. Thomas Price Lloyd, of Mochras	1842
Owen Jones Ellis Nanney, Esq., of Cefn-ddeudwr	1843
David White Griffith, Esq., of Sugyn	1844
Richard Watkin Price, Esq., of Rhiwlas	1845
Sir Robert Williames Vaughan, Bart., of Nannau	1846
John Griffith Griffith, Esq., of Taltreuddyn-fawr	1847
Hugh Jones, Esq., of Gwernddelwa [Hengwrt-ucha	1848
Robert Davies Jones, Esq., of Aberllefeni	1849
Edward Humphrey Griffith, Esq., of Gwastad-fryn	1850
Henry Richardson, Esq., of Aberhirnant	1851
George Casson, Esq., of Blaen-y-ddôl	1852
Thomas Arthur Bertie Mostyn, Esq., of Cilau	1853
George Augustus Huddart, Esq., of Plas-yn-Penrhyn	1854
Charles John Tottenham, Esq., of Plâs-Berwyn, Llangollen	1855
John Priestley, Esq., of Hafod-garegog	1856
John Nanney, Esq., of Maesyneuadd	1857
Edmund Buckley, Esq., of Plas Dinas	1858
Hugh John Reveley, Esq., of Bryn-y-gwin	1859
David Williams, Esq., of Deudraeth Castle [appointed 23rd Jan.] Charles Frederick Thruston, Esq., of Talgarth Hall [appointed 22nd Feb.]	1860
David Williams, Esq., of Deudraeth Castle	1861
Samuel Holland, Esq., of Plas-yn-Penrhyn	1862
Howel Morgan, Esq., of Hengwrt-uchaf	1863
Lewis Williams, Esq., of Vronwnion	1864
Richard Meredyth Richards, Esq., of Caerynwch	1865
John Corbet, Esq., of Ynys-y-maengwyn	1866
William Watkin Edward Wynne, Esq., of Peniarth	1867
Richard John Lloyd Price, Esq., of Rhiwlas	1868
Henry Robertson, Esq., of Crogen	1869
Clement Arthur Thruston, Esq., of Pennal Tower	1870
Charles Edwards, Esq., of Dolserau	1871
Edward Foster Coulson, Esq., of Cors-y-gedol	1872

SECTION VII.—LORD LIEUTENANTS AND CUSTODES ROTULORUM OF MERIONETHSHIRE.

The functions of the *Lord Lieutenant* of a county have been noticed at p. 612. The *Custos Rotulorum* (Keeper of the Rolls) has charge of the county records,—those being the most important which pertain to the administration of justice. Not unfrequently the two

LORD LIEUTENANTS AND CUSTODES ROTULORUM.

offices are held by one and the same person. Up to the year 1689 the functions afterwards performed by the lieutenants of counties generally belonged to the "Lord President" of the Court of the Marchers, or "Lord President of Wales" as otherwise termed.

The following list has been drawn from the Docket Books at the Crown Office, Westminster, and collated with a shorter list made by W. W. E. Wynne, Esq., of Peniarth (see *Archæol. Cambr.*, 1846):—

Lord Lieutenants, &c.	Date of Appointment.
Eure, Ralph Eure (or Evre), Baron, of Wilton, Durham, appointed the King's Lieutenant in the Principality of Wales	19th July, 1607.
Compton, William Compton, Baron (cr. Earl of Northampton 1618)	24th Nov., 1617.
Bridgwater, John Egerton, Earl of (cr. 1617), appointed Lord President of Wales	12th May, 1633.
Pembroke and Montgomery, Philip Herbert, Earl of, nominated by the House of Commons Lord Lieutenant of Wilts, *Merioneth*, and Carnarvon	11th Feb., 1642.
Strange, James Stanley, Lord, afterwards 7th Earl of Derby, part of one year only	1642.

[*Note.*—The Parliament now disputed the right of the king (Charles I.) to appoint lieutenants, and no further appointment was made till Charles II. assumed power in 1660.]

Carbery, Richard Vaughan, Earl of, appointed Lord Lieutenant for cos. Anglesey, Carnarvon, Denbigh, Flint, Montgomery, and *Merioneth* [had already been appointed for the cos. of South Wales. See p. 108]	22nd Sept., 1660.
Carbery, Richard Vaughan, Earl of, reappointed	19th July, 1662.
Owen, Sir John, Kt., appointed Custos Rotulorum of Merioneth	1663.
Owen, William, Esq., appointed Custos Rotulorum of Merioneth	1666.
Wynn, John, Esq., Custos Rotulorum	1675.
Beaufort, Henry Somerset, 1st Duke of, appointed Lord President of North and South Wales	28th March, 1685.
Powis, William Herbert, Marquess of (cr. Viscount Montgomery and Marquess of Powis 1687), appointed Custos Rotulorum for Merioneth	14th April, 1688
Macclesfield, Charles Gerard, Earl of, Lord Lieutenant of the cos. of North and South Wales. (See p. 108)	22nd March, 1689.
Williams, Sir William, Kt. and Bart., one of his Majesty's learned Counsel, Custos Rotulorum for co. Merioneth	8th Oct., 1689.
Wynn, Sir John, Kt. and Bart., Custos Rotulorum for the co. of Merioneth	19th March, 1690.
Macclesfield, Charles Gerard, Earl of, reappointed Lord Lieutenant of the cos. of Montgomery, Denbigh, Flint, Carnarvon, *Merioneth*, and Anglesey, their several boroughs, &c.	10th March, 1695.
Derby, William Stanley, Earl of, Lieutenant of the cos. of North Wales last named, and of the co. of Lancaster. (He *d.* before the end of the year)	18th Jan., 1702.
Cholmondeley, Hugh, Lord, Lord Lieutenant of North Wales in the room of the Earl of Derby, dec.	2nd Dec., 1702.
Wynn, Sir John, Bart, of Rhiw-goch and Wattstay, Custos Rotulorum for the co. of Merioneth	1707.
Vaughan, Edward, Esq., Custos Rotulorum for same	7th Jan., 1710.
Cholmondeley, Hugh, Earl of, reappointed Lord Lieutenant of North Wales	21st Oct., 1714.
Owen, Lewis, Esq., of Peniarth, Custos Rotulorum for the co. of Merioneth	10th Dec., 1722.
Cholmondeley, George, 2nd Earl of, succ. his brother as Lord Lieutenant of North Wales and Cheshire	7th April, 1725.
Cholmondeley, George, 3rd Earl of, Lord Lieutenant and Custos Rotulorum of North Wales, in place of his father, dec.	14th June, 1733.
Vaughan, William, Esq., of Cors-y-gedol, Cust. Rot. and M.P., app. Lord Lieutenant for co. Merioneth, with a revocation of a former commission to George, Earl of Cholmondeley, as respects the co. of Merioneth	26th April, 1762.
Wynn, Sir Watkin Williams, Bart., of Wynnstay, Lord Lieutenant and Custos Rot. for the co. of Merioneth	1775.
Williams, Watkin, Esq., of Penbedw, *Denb.*, Lord Lieutenant (31st August) and Custos Rot. (4th Sept.) for the co. of Merioneth	1789.
Wynn, Sir Watkin Williams, 4th Bart., of Wynnstay, Lord Lieutenant (10th June) and Custos Rot. (28th Nov.) for the co. of Merioneth	1793.

Wynn, Sir Watkin Williams, 5th Bart., of Wynnstay, Lord Lieutenant and Custos Rot.
of cos. Merioneth and Denbigh . . . . . . , . . . 29th Dec., 1830.
Mostyn, Hon. Edward Mostyn Lloyd (now Lord Mostyn), Lord Lieutenant of Merioneth
(still holding the office) . . . . 25th June, 1840.

Section VIII.—PARLIAMENTARY ANNALS OF MERIONETHSHIRE, A.D. 1542—1872.

Merioneth being one of the early counties, formed by Edward I. (A.D. 1283) immediately upon his conquest of Wales, it probably enjoyed some kind of parliamentary representation before the Act of Union of Henry VIII. conceded that right to all the counties of the Principality without distinction. Representatives are known to have been summoned from Wales in the fifteenth of Edward II. In the twentieth year of the same king, *twenty-four* representatives were summoned from North Wales. And these delegates appear to have been of a station more nearly allied to the people than the great barons who had the right to attend the king's council. The Act of the fifteenth Edward II. (A.D. 1321) ordains " that for ever thereafter the matters to be established for the estate of the king, and for the estate of the realm and of the people, should be treated, accorded, and established in Parliament by the king, and with the assent of the prelates, earls, and barons, and *the commonalty of the realm*, according *as had been before the custom*." This seems to be the earliest statute extant which plainly recognises popular representation on a basis much wider than that conceded by the charter of King John.

The Commons had properly no existence in England before the reign of Edward I. In Wales there was an established code of laws in each princedom; but their administration lay greatly in the hands of the prince, whose power was in all ages checked by assemblies of the people. Nothing coming up to the idea of a *parliament*, however, and no electoral franchise, existed. In England, the Plantaganet Parliament, reflecting still earlier times, was a council of prelates more than of lay barons. In most summonses during the reigns of Henry IV., V., and VI., the "spiritual lords" (bishops and abbots) were nearly double the number of the temporal lords, in consequence of the absence of the latter in actual service, in war, or from other causes; but sometimes their numbers were nearly equal.

The Act 27th Henry VIII., sect. 29, enacted that "one knight should be chosen and elected for every of the shires of Brecknock, Radnor, Montgomery, and Denbigh—the newly constituted counties,—and for every other shire within the said country or dominion of Wales; and for every borough being a *shire town* within the said county except the shire town of the county of *Merioneth*, one burgess; and the election to be in like manner, form, and order, as knights and burgesses be elected and chosen in other shires of this realm."

The qualification for county and borough voters alike between Edward I. and Henry VI. was the *holding of a house*. By the 1st of Henry V., both members and electors were to be *resident* within the shire or borough at the date of the writ of summons. By the 8th of Henry VI., the *county* franchise was limited to those who held lands or tenements of the yearly value of *forty shillings* at the least, within the county concerned—a qualification which continued to very recent times.

PARLIAMENTARY ANNALS OF MERIONETHSHIRE. 697

HENRY VIII.

	A.D.
Edward Stanley, Esq. [see *Sheriffs*, 1545]	1524

EDWARD VI.

Lewis Owen, Esq. ["Baron Owen," see *Owen of Dolgelley*]	1547
Lewis Owen, Esq. (the same)	1552

MARY.

John Salesbury, Esq. [of Rhûg, Sheriff 1559]	1553
Lewis Owen, Esq. (same as for 1547, session April 22—May 5)	1554

PHILIP AND MARY.

Lewis Owen, Esq., of Dolgelley (the same)	1554
[No name preserved in the records]	1555
Elizeus [Ellis?] Price, Esq. [of Rhiwlas?]	1557

ELIZABETH.

Ellis Price, Esq.	1558
Ellis Price, Esq. (the same)	1563
Hugh Owen, Esq. [of Cae'rberllan, son of "Baron Owen"]	1571
John Lewis Owen Esq. [brother of last]	1572
Cadwalader Price, Esq. ["Cad. *ap Rhys*," of Rhiwlas]	1585
Robert Lloyd, Esq. [of Rhiwgôch]	1586
Robert Salesbury, Esq. [of Rhûg]	1588
Gruffydd Nanney, Esq. [son of Hugh, of Nannau]	1592
Thomas Middleton, Esq.	1597
Robert Lloyd, Esq. [of Rhiwgôch]	1601

JAMES I.

Edward Herbert, Esq. [of Dolguog?]	1603
Robert Lloyd, Esq. [of Rhiwgôch]	1614
William Salesbury, Esq.	1620
Henry Wynn, Esq. [prob. of Rhiwgoch]	1623

CHARLES I.

Henry Wynn, Esq. (the same)	1625
Edward Vaughan, Esq. [of Llwydiarth?]	1628
Henry Wynn, Esq. . . . 1st session ⎫	
William Price, Esq., succ. by— ⎬	1640
John Jones . . . 2nd session ⎭	

THE COMMONWEALTH AND CROMWELL.

Six members summoned for all Wales after Cromwell had dismissed the "Long Parliament"	1653
The "Little Parliament"	1653

OLIVER CROMWELL, LORD PROTECTOR.

John Vaughan, Esq. [of Cefnbodiog]	1654
Col. John Jones [prob. of Maes-y-garnedd, one of the signataries of the death-warrant of Charles I.]	1656

RICHARD CROMWELL, LORD PROTECTOR.

Lewis Owen, Esq.	1658-9

CHARLES II.—THE RESTORATION.

	A.D.
Henry Wynne, Esq. [of the Gwydir family?]	1660
[Writ issued to elect a Knight of the Shire in the place of Henry Wynne, Esq., deceased (*Docket Book*, 1672), but who was elected has not been discovered]	1672

WILLIAM AND MARY.

[*Prob.* Hugh Nanney, Esq., of Nannau]	1689
Hugh Nanney, Esq., of Nannau	1700
[Writ to elect a Knight of the Shire in room of Hugh Nanney, Esq., dec.—*Docket Bk.*]	1701

ANNE.

Richard Vaughan, Esq. (?)	1702
Richard Vaughan, Esq.	1707

GEORGE I.

Richard Vaughan, Esq. (the same)	1715

GEORGE II.

Richard Vaughan, Esq. (the same)	1727
William Vaughan, Esq. [of Cors-y-gedol]	1734
William Vaughan, Esq. (the same)	1747-64

GEORGE III.

William Vaughan, Esq. (the same)	1760-8
John Pugh Pryse, Esq. [of Gogerddan]	1768-74
Evan Lloyd Vaughan, Esq. [of Cors-y-gedol]	1774
Evan Lloyd Vaughan, Esq. [the same; *d.* 1792]; the last male representative of the Vaughans of Cors-y-gedol	1790-2
Robert Williams Vaughan, Esq. [afterwards Bart., of Hengwrt]	1792
Sir Robert Williams Vaughan, Bart. [of Hengwrt; represented the co. till 1836]	1796

GEORGE IV.

Sir Robert Williams Vaughan, Bart. (the same)	1820

WILLIAM IV.

Sir Robert Williams Vaughan, Bart. (the same)	1830-6
Richard Richards, Esq. [of Caerynwch, *vice* Vaughan resigned. Seat contested; voted for Richards 501; for Sir W. Williams Wynn 150]	1836

VICTORIA.

Richard Richards, Esq. [the same, and continuously till the general election of 1852]	1837-52
William Watkin Edward Wynne, Esq., of Peniarth	1852
The same, and continuously till 1865, when he resigned	1857-65
William Robert Maurice Wynne, Esq. [of Peniarth; eldest son of the last member]	1865
David Williams, Esq., of Deudraeth Castle	1868
Samuel Holland, Esq., of Glanwilliam [*vice* Williams, *dec.*]	1870

Section IX.—COUNTY MAGISTRATES OF MERIONETHSHIRE, 1872.

Mostyn, Right Hon. Lord, of Mostyn Hall, *Lord Lieutenant.*
Ansell, Charles, Esq.
Buckley, Sir Edmund, Bart., M.P., of Plas Dinas Mawddwy.
Bunbury, Henry W. St. Pierre, Esq., of Abergwynant.
Casson, John, Esq.
Casson, William, Esq.
Corbet, Athelstane John Soden, Esq., of Ynys-y-Maengwyn.
Davies, Edward Morris, Esq.
Davies, Frederick, Esq.
Davis, David, Esq.
Davis, Lewis, Esq.
Edwards, Charles, Esq., of Dolserau.
Ellis, John Williams (Clerk), of Glas-fryn, *Carn.*
Ford, John Ranate Minshull, Esq., of Llwyn-gwern.
Foulkes, John, Esq., of Aberdyfi.
Greaves, John Whitehead, Esq., of Plas-weunydd.
Green, Thomas, Esq.
Holland, Samuel, Esq., M.P., of Glan-william.
Huddart, George A., Esq., of Bryn-kir.
Jones, Charles, Esq., of Coes-faen.
Jones, John (Clerk), of Barmouth.
Jones, John, Esq., of Fron-dderw.
Jones, John, Esq., of Ynys-fawr.
Jones, John, Esq., of Ynysgain.
Jones, William, Esq , of Glandwr.
Jones, William Pryse, Esq., of Bodweni.
Kettle, Rupert, Esq., of Towyn.
Lloyd, John, Esq., of Plas Issaf, Corwen.
Lloyd, Morgan, Esq., of Cefn-gellgwm.
Mathew, Edward Windus, Esq., of Wern, *Carn.*
Morgan, Howel, Esq., of Hengwrt-uchaf.
Nanney, Hugh Ellis, Esq., of Gwynfryn.
Oakeley, William Edward, Esq., of Plas Tanybwlch.
Parry, John Edward, Esq., of Glyn-Hall.
Parry, Robert Sorton, Esq., of Aberia.
Price, Richard J. Lloyd, Esq., of Rhiwlas.
Pryse, Robert Davies, Esq.
Pugh, William T., Esq., of Cefn-amberth.
Pughe, John, Esq., of Bryn-awel, Aberdyfi.
Reveley, Hugh John, Esq., of Bryn-y-gwin.
Richards, Owen, Esq., of Bala.
Richards, Richard Meredyth, Esq., of Caerynwch, *Chairman of Quarter Sessions.*
Richardson, Henry Thomas, Esq.
Roberts, Hugh Beaver, Esq.
Robertson, Henry, Esq., of Crogen.
Taylor, Robert Mascie, Esq.
Thruston, Charles Frederick, Esq., of Talgarth Hall.
Thruston, Clement Arthur, Esq., of Pennal Tower.
Tottenham, Charles John, Esq., of Plas Berwyn.
Tottenham, Charles Robert Worsley, Esq.
Vane, Right Hon. the Earl, Plas Machynlleth.
Vaughan, John, Esq., of Nannau.
Whalley, George Hammond, Esq., M.P., of Plas Madoc, *Denb.*
Williams, Abram Jones, Esq., of Gellewig, *Carn.*
Williams, Arthur Osmond, Esq., of Deudraeth Castle.
Williams, David (Clerk), Trawsfynydd.
Williams, Lewis, Esq., of Vron-wnion.
Wingfield, Richard Robert, Esq.
Wynn, John (Clerk), of Llandrillo.
Wynn, Sir Watkin Williams, Bart., of Wynnstay, *Denb.*
Wynn, The Hon. Charles Henry, of Rhûg.
Wynne, William Robert Maurice, Esq., of Peniarth.
Wynne, William Watkin Edward, Esq., of Peniarth.
Yale, William Corbet, Esq., of Plas yn Yale.

THE COUNTY FAMILIES OF MERIONETHSHIRE.

ANWYL, Robert Charles, Esq., of Llugwy, Merionethshire,

Fourth but only surviving son of the late Evan Anwyl, Esq., of Llugwy, by his wife, Jemima Morgan (see *Lineage*); *b.* 12th July, 1849; *ed.* at Shrewsbury School, and is pursuing his studies for the law in London; succ. on the demise of his father, 1872; has six sisters living. (See *Lineage*.)

Residence: Llugwy, near Machynlleth.
Arms: 1. Vert, three eagles displayed in fesse or—OWAIN GWYNEDD,—a fleur-de-lis or for difference 6th son.
2. Sa., a chevron between three fleurs-de-lis arg.—COLLWYN AP TANGNO.
3. Vert, a chevron between 3 wolves' heads erased arg.—RHIRID FLAIDD.
4. Per pale az. and gu., 3 lions rampant arg.—HERBERT OF CEMMAES.
5. Arg., an eagle displayed with 2 necks sa.—MEURIG LLWYD OF LLWYN Y MAEN.
6. Arg., a lion passant sa. between 3 fleurs-de-lis gu.—EINION AP SEISSYLLT.
Crest: An eagle displayed or.
Motto: Eryr eryrod Eryri, "The eagle of the eagles of Snowdon."

LINEAGE.

The ancient family of *Anwyl* have resided at Llugwy from the time when Maurice Anwyl (*circa* 1695) *m.* Joan, the heiress of that place, but previously for many ages at Park, in the parish of Llanfrothen, in the same co. of Merioneth. There *Lewys Dwnn*, Deputy Herald, found them, in 1611, when pursuing his *Heraldic Visitation of Wales;* and there they had then been seated for several generations. Their lineage is from *Owain Gwynedd*, the illustrious Prince of North Wales (12th cent.), son of Prince Gruffydd ap Cynan, of the direct line (through the eldest son, Anarawd) of *Rhodri Mawr*, King, first of N. Wales, then of all Wales (9th cent.). The grandson of Owain Gwynedd,—

Thomas (ap Rhodri ap Owain), Lord of Rhiwllwyd, *m.* Agnes, dau. of Einion ap Seissyllt, Lord of Mathafarn, widow of Owain Brogyntyn, Lord of Edeirnion (see *Arms*, 6). His descendants, Lords of Rhiwllwyd, were successively Cardog, Gruffydd, Dafydd, and—

Howel, who *m.* Efa, dau. of Ifan ap Howel ap Meredydd of Ystumcegid, of the line of *Collwyn ap Tungno*, founder of the fourth noble tribe of N. Wales (see p. 337). The son of Howel,—

Meredydd of Ystumcegid, living 26th Edward III. (1352), *m.* Morfydd, dau. of Ieuan ap Dafydd ap Trahaern Goch of Graianog, in Lleyn, and left two sons—the younger Robert, of Cesail-gyfarch, whose grandson Meredydd purchased and settled at *Gwydir*, the ancestor of the Wynns of Gwydir and Wynnstay, the Lord Willoughby D'Eresby, &c. (see p. 313, and *Wynn of Gwydir*); the elder,—

Ieuan, or Ifan, of Ystumcegid, *m.* Lucy, dau. of Hywel Selé, Lord of Nannau, and had a son,—

Meredydd, of Ystumcegid, esquire of the body to John of Gaunt (see *Arms*, 3), who *m.* Angharad, dau. and h. of Einion ap Ithel of Rhiwaedog, Mer. His son John, frequently mentioned in Sir John Wynn's *Hist. of the Gwydir Family*, living and signing a deed A.D. 1484, was succeeded by his eldest son,—

Maurice, or Morys, of Clenenney (see p. 343), and Rhiwaedog, who *m.* Angharad, dau. of Ellis ap Gruffydd ap Einion. By a deed dated 18th August, 1511, he conveys "Plas Clenenney to feoffees, for himself for life, with remainder to his son Ellis (note to *Dwnn*, ii., 70). His eldest son, William *Llwyd*, was of *Rhiwaedog* (which see); and his 3rd son,—

Robert ap Morys, was of *Parc* (Park), Llanfrothen, near Penrhyn-deudraeth, Mer. By his wife Lowry, dau. of Lewis ap Ifan ap Dafydd, he left a large family, but the eldest and the only one of whose issue we have account was—

Lewis, surnamed *Anwyl*, of Parc, the first of the long line of *Anwyls* (1602). John, 2nd son of Robert ap Morys, assumed the surname Roberts (Robert's, *sc.* "son"=ap Robert), and resided at Vaner (Cymmer Abbey), Dolgelley. Lewis Anwyl, Esq., of Parc, *m.* twice, his first wife, by whom alone he had issue, being Elizabeth, dau. of Morys ap Ifan ap Sion of Brynkir, Carn., who was also of the race of O.vain Gwynedd. He was *s.* by his only son,—

William Lewis Anwyl, Esq., of Parc, Sheriff of Merioneth 1611, 1624, who *m.* Elizabeth, dau. and co-h. of Edward Herbert, Esq., of Cemmaes, in Cyfeiliog, grandson of Sir Richard Herbert, Kt. (see *Herbert of Montgomery*, &c.), whose arms are the arms of the Earls of Powis,—"Per pale az. and gu., 3 lions ramp. arg." By her he left a numerous offspring of 8 sons and 4 daus. Catherine *m.* William Wynne, Esq., of Glyn, Sheriff of Mer. 1618, 1637, *d.* 1658, whose present direct male representative is W. W. E. Wynne, Esq., of Peniarth. The eldest son,—

Lewis Anwyl (*d.* 1638), *m.* Frances, dau. of Sir William Jones of Castellmarch, Carn. (see p. 342), and had issue an only dau., who *m.* William Owen, Esq., of Clenenney; Robert, 2nd son, Sheriff of Mer. 1650 (*d.* 1653), inherited Parc, and by his wife, Catherine, dau. of Sir John Owen of Clenenney (see p. 343), had two sons, Richard of Parc, who *d. s. p.*, and Owen of Penrhyn deudraeth, who had no issue male, and whose only dau., Catherine, *m.* Sir Griffith Williams, Bart., of Marle (see under *Williams-Bulkeley*, p. 364), whose dau. Anne, heiress of Parc, & wife of Sir Thomas Prendergast, sold that place in 1748 to W. Wynne, Esq., of Wern. (Comp. up to

this point *Dwnn's Herald. Visit. of Wales,* ii., 70.) William Lewis Anwyl's 6th son was—
Evan Anwyl, Esq., who *m.* Catherine, dau. of Morys Williams, Esq., of Hafod-garegog [henceforth the lineage is derived from the College of Arms, and from registers], and left a son,—
Maurice Anwyl, Esq., who *m.* Joan, the heiress of *Llugwy,* and settled at that place. (See *Arms,* 6.) He had a son, Evan Anwyl, Esq., of Llugwy (*d.* 1721), who had also a son, Maurice Anwyl of Llugwy, and he a son and h., Evan Anwyl, Esq., of Llugwy, who *m.* and had issue, who all *d. s. p.;* and a 2nd son,—
Maurice Anwyl, of Llugwy, Clerk, B.A. of Oxford, who *m.* Anne, dau. of —— Lloyd, Esq., of Shrewsbury, and had issue—1. Maurice, *d. s. p.;* 2. Robert, *d. s. p.;* 3. *Evan,* of whom hereafter; 4. Elizabeth; 5. Catherine; 6. Charles; 7. Anne, who all *d. s. p.*
Evan Anwyl, Esq., of Llugwy (*d.* Jan. 18, 1872), *m.* Jemima, dau. of William Morgan, Esq., of Brynllys, co. of Montgomery, and had issue, besides, 1, Maurice; 2, Evan; 3, William, who all *d. s. p.,* a fourth son,—
ROBERT CHARLES ANWYL, now of Llugwy (as above), and five daughters,—
1. Anne; 2. Jemima; 3. Elizabeth Louisa; 4. Catherine Winifred; 5. Maria Florence.

Note.—The mansion of *Llugwy,* pleasantly situated on the banks of the Dovey (Dyfi), is very ancient, but of date unknown. The older abode of the Anwyls, Parc, near Penrhyn-deudraeth, although long neglected, has not altogether disappeared. It is approached by a drive of more than a mile in length. In front of the site of the house are four terraces, 150 feet long by 50 wide, supported by walls 12 feet high. The part of the house still standing, built in 1671, is said to have been the ball-room. On the gable are curious large round chimneys. On either side of the front door are pieces of beautifully carved stone, formerly gilded, from the chimney-piece in the dining-hall; and one sees here and there, sometimes even in the walls of the present sheepfolds, mullions from the windows in freestone. At the back of the old mansion there are the ruins of a stone bath with seats round it and steps to descend. The "gate-house" (lodge) is still standing, but much dilapidated. Parc is now the property of H. J. Reveley, Esq., of Brynygwin.

BREESE, Edward, Esq., of Dolfriog, Merionethshire.

(See *Breese of Morfa Lodge,* Carnarvonshire.)

BUCKLEY, Sir Edmund, Bart., of Plas Dinas Mawddwy, Merionethshire.

Baronetcy cr. 1868. J. P. and D. L. for the co. of Merioneth; M.P. for Newcastle-under-Lyme since 1865; Lord of the Manor of Hoylandswaine, Yorkshire; *b.* 1834; *m.,* 1860, Sarah, eldest dau. of William Rees, Esq., of Tonn, Llandovery, J. P. for the co. of Brecon (see *Rees of Tonn);* assumed in 1864 by royal licence the name and arms of Buckley for himself and his issue; succ. to the estates of Gratton Hall, Yorkshire, and Ardwick, Lancashire, on the death of Edmund Buckley, Esq., J. P. for the co. of Lancaster, and to the estate and lordship of Dinas Mawddwy during the lifetime of the latter, who in 1856 had purchased it from the Mytton family, in whose possession it had been since the time of King John; has had issue two sons and one dau.:—

1. Edmund, *b.* 1861.
2. William, *b.* 1863.
3. Sarah, *b.* 1864.

Heir: Edmund Buckley.
Residences: Plas Dinas Mawddwy, Mer.; Grotton Hall, Yorkshire.
Town Address: Carlton Club.
Arms: Sa., a chevron indented arg. between three escutcheons of the second, each bearing a bull's head caboshed of the field; a bordure wavy or.
Crest: On a wreath out of a fern brake ppr., a bull's head sa., the whole debruised by a bendlet sinister or.
Motto: Nec temere nec timide.

LINEAGE.

The Buckleys were long settled and possessed lands in the district of Saddleworth, Yorkshire. For Lady Buckley's descent see under *Rees of Tonn,* Carmarthenshire.

Note.—The mansion of *Plas Dinas Mawddwy* is of quite recent erection, its precincts and grounds being scarcely yet (1872) completed. The sumptuous character of this Plâs among the mountains may be judged of from the three engravings on pp. 655-7, where an account is also given of the ancient lordship of Mawddwy.

BUNBURY, Col. Henry William St. Pierre, of Aber-gwynant, Merionethshire.

Colonel, retired from the army; C.B.; served in India as Aide-de-camp to Sir Charles Napier, 1850, and in the Crimean War, at Inkermann and siege of Sebastopol; made a C.B. 1855; received the Crimean Medal and Order of the Medjidie; is a Knight of the Legion of Honour; Justice of the Peace for Merioneth; son of Lieut.-General Sir Henry Edward Bunbury, Bart., K.C.B., some years M.P. for Suffolk, by his first wife, Louisa Emilia, daughter of

General the Honourable Henry E. Fox, and brother of the present Sir Charles James Fox Bunbury, Bart., of Barton Hall, Suffolk ; *b.* at Brompton, 2nd September, 1812 ; *ed.* at home ; *m.*, 30th Nov., 1852, to Cecilia Caroline, daughter of General Sir George Napier, K.C.B. ; and has issue 3 sons and 1 daughter ; *s.* 1863.

Heir: Henry C. J. Bunbury.
Residence: Abergwynant, near Dolgelley.
Arms : Arg., on a bend sa. three chess rooks of the field.
Crest: Two swords saltierwise through the mouth of a leopard's face or, the blades ppr., hilted and pommelled or.
Motto : Firmum in vitâ nihil.

LINEAGE.

The Bunburys, Baronets, of Barton Hall, Suffolk, and earlier of Cheshire, of which Col. Bunbury is a younger branch, are of Norman origin, their first founder in England being a *St. Pierre*, a follower of Lupus, Earl of Chester, a nephew of William the Conqueror. The Bunburys were seated at Stanney Hall, Cheshire, till the beginning of the present century. Sir Thomas Bunbury, the first Baronet, received that dignity in 1681. Sir Charles, now living, is 8th Baronet.

CORBET, Athelstan John Soden, Esq., of Ynys-y-maengwyn, Merionethshire.

Son of the late John Soden, Esq., by his wife Henrietta, dau. of Charles Decimus Williames, Esq., of Berth-ddu, Mont., and Anne Maurice, of Lloran, Denb. (maternally descended from the Corbets), who, under the will of Mrs. Owen, of Rhiwsaeson (of the ancient line of Corbet of Ynys-y-maengwyn), assumed the surname Corbet in order that their issue might inherit the Ynys-y-maengwyn estate (see *Lineage*); *b.* 1849 ; *s.* on the death of his mother, 1868 ; is *unm.*

Residence: Ynys-y-maengwyn, Towyn, Mer.

LINEAGE.

The ancient line of Wynn of Ynys-y-maengwyn, according to Dwnn (*Herald. Visit. of Wales*), terminated in two daus., co-heiresses, Elizabeth and Catherine. The former (*d.* 1642) *m.* Sir James Pryse, Kt. (Sheriff of Merioneth 1608), son of Sir John Pryse, of Gogerddan, Card., and had issue one dau. only, Bridget Pryse, heiress to Ynys-y-maengwyn, who took for her first husband—
Robert *Corbet*, Esq., 3rd son of Sir Vincent Corbet, Kt., of Morton Corbet, Salop, and had issue. (She *m.*, 2ndly, Walter Lloyd, Esq., of Llanfair-clydogau.)
For several generations the Ynys-y-maengwyn estates continued in the Corbets, descendants of the above Bridget Pryse, until the Corbets ended in a sole heiress, Anne Corbet (dau. of Vincent Corbet), who *m.* Athelstan Owen, Esq., of *Rhiwsaeson*, Mont. Mrs. Owen *d.* 1760, *æt.* seventy-six, having created an entail, settling Ynys-y-maengwyn upon the descendants of her youngest dau. (her two sons having died *s. p.*), Anne, wife of *Pryse Maurice*, Esq., of *Lloran*, Denb., on condition of their assuming the name of *Corbet*.
Under this entail the estates were eventually vested in the late Athelstan Corbet, Esq. (previously Maurice), who *d.* 1835, and were subsequently held in trust for the benefit of his niece, eldest child of his sister Anne by her mar. with Charles Decimus Williames, Esq. (See *Note* on *Dwnn*, ii., 231.) That niece was Henrietta Soden (above named), and her issue was—
ATHELSTAN JOHN SODEN, now of Ynys-y-maengwyn (as above).

COULSON, Edward Foster, Esq., of Cors-y-gedol, Merionethshire, and Bellaport Hall, Salop.

J. P. for the cos. of Merioneth and Salop ; Sheriff for the former co. 1872 ; Lord of the manor of Norton in Hales, Salop; was formerly Captain East York Militia ; son of George Coulson, Esq., of Cottingham Castle, co. of York, by Jane, daughter of Hugh Ker, Esq., of Newfield, co. Ayr, N.B.; *m.*, 1853, his maternal cousin, Elizabeth, widow of Thomas Colville, Esq., and eldest daughter of Robert Kerr, Esq., Captain 33rd Regiment, of Annfield, co. Stirling, by Elizabeth, daughter of Hugh Ker, Esq., of Newfield, co. Ayr; *s.*, 1866, his maternal uncle, Rev. Hugh Ker, who by royal licence had assumed the name of Cokburne.

Heir presumptive: Hugh Ker Colville, *b.* 1847.
Residences : Cors-y-gedol, Dyffryn, Merioneth ; Bellaport Hall, Market Drayton, Salop.
Town Address: Union Club, Trafalgar Square.
Arms: Arg., an anchor in pale between two dolphins haurient, all ppr.
Crest: A dolphin embowed ppr.

LINEAGE.

Mr. Coulson is paternally descended from Robert de Colston, of Colston Hall, co. Lincoln, a family of consequence at the time of the Norman Conquest, and maternally from the Kers of Kersland, an ancient branch of the noble house of Fernihirst. He bears the Coulston arms (as above), as do also the Colstons of Roundway Park, Wilts.

Note.—There is an ancient British fortress a short distance from Cors-y-gedol, several cromlechs (see *Pre-historic Antiquities, ante*), and, on the sea-shore, some curious "kitchen-middens."

Cors-y gedol is of considerable interest to the lovers of history and antiquity. It had long been a residence of note when, between 1240 and 1243, the heiress of Cors-y-gedol, being a royal ward, was bestowed by Llewellyn the Great on Osborn Fitzgerald, called by the Welsh heralds *Osborn Wyddel*, son of John Fitz Thomas Fitz Gerald de Windsor, of the line of the Earl of Desmond—a subsequent creation. (See further the pedigree of *Wynne of Peniarth*.) In 1401 the owner of Cors-y-gedol married Lawra, daughter and heiress of Tudor Vaughan, own brother to Owen Glyndwr, who, it is said, was frequently concealed at Cors-y-gedol. In 1483 Jasper Tudor, Earl of Pembroke, left Cors-y-gedol to bring from France his nephew, Henry, Earl of Richmond, afterwards Henry VII. It is said—with what truth it is hard to determine—that Charles II. was at Cors-y-gedol during his wanderings, and slept in the state bed still preserved there. The date 1575 is over the chimney in the hall of the present house, which is thought, however, to be of rather earlier date; it was probably built in the time of Henry VIII.

The gate-house is after a design by Inigo Jones—a kinsman of the Vaughans. The modern additions to the house were made by the late Hugh Ker Cokburne, already mentioned, who also placed there the fine collection of paintings of the Italian, Spanish, Flemish, English, and French schools, and the rare ancient and modern china collections which give to Cors-y-gedol an artistic interest unrivalled in Wales.

EDWARDS, Charles, Esq., of Dolserau Hall, Merionethshire.

J. P. and D. L. for the counties of Merioneth and Cardigan; High Sheriff for Merioneth 1871; was M.P. for the borough of New Windsor from 1865 to 1868; son of the late Edward Edwards, Esq., of Dolserau; *b.* in London; *ed.* at Chatham House, Ramsgate; *m.* Mary Elizabeth, only child and heiress of the late William Tate, Esq., of Frognel House, Hampstead, and Kilbruchs, Peeblesshire, N.B.; succ. to Dolserau estate in 1858; has issue three sons and three daughters.

Heir: Charles Edward Munro.
Residences: Dolserau Hall, near Dolgelley; Bodtalog, near Towyn.

Town Address: 57, Great Cumberland Place, Hyde Park.
Crest: A lion rampant within a twisted rope.
Motto: Fidelis.

LINEAGE.

This family derives its descent from the Edwards of *Ness Strange* in the county of Salop (of the line of *Einion Efell*, Lord of Cynllaeth, in Powys, 12th cent.), who intermarried into the family of "Baron Owen," of Dolgelley (see *Lewis Owen of Dolgelley*). The third son of this marriage, Robert Owen, resided at Dolserau in the year 1510. It is regretted that a full genealogy of this ancient family has not been supplied. See some further notice under *Price of Cors-y-garnedd.*

Note.—The mansion of *Dolserau* was rebuilt by the present owner in 1864, and the old house was pulled down in 1865. The situation is sheltered and pleasant, in the vale of the Wnion, above Dolgelley, over which river a picturesque bridge leads from the high-road to the entrance gates. To the north are the heights of Nannau, and to the south those of Caerynwch.

ELLIS, Rev. John Williams, of Brondanw, Merionethshire.

(See further *Rev. John Williams Ellis of Glas-fryn, Carnarvonshire.*)

Note.—Brondanw (not Bronderw, see p. 353), Llanfrothen, Mer., long possessed by the family of Williams, was inherited by the present owner under the will of the late Miss Williams, whose surname he then assumed in addition to his own of Ellis. The Williamses intermarried, *temp.* Charles I., with the Madryns of Madryn, co. Carn., the Vaughans of Aberhin, co. Mer., now represented by the Wynnes of Peniarth. Mr. Williams of Brondauw was the first to move for the embanking of the Traeth-mawr Estuary, Portmadoc (since carried out on an extensive scale by the late Mr. Madocks), and failing to secure further co-operation, actually embanked his own lands.

Motto: Gweithred a ddengys: "The deed supplies the proof."

FARRE, Arthur, Esq., of Dolfriog, Merionethshire.

M.D. Cantab. Caius Coll.; Fell. Roy. Coll. Phys.; F.R.S.; Fell. Roy. Med. Chir. Soc.; Fell., and formerly President Roy. Micros. Soc.; Memb. Council King's Coll., Lond.; Examiner in Midwifery Roy. Coll. Surg.; Consulting Physician King's Coll. Hospital; Phys.-Accoucheur to H.R.H. the Princess of Wales; H.R.H. Princess Louis of Hesse, 1863; H.R.H.

Princess Christian of Schleswig Holstein 1868; H.R.H. Princess Mary Adelaide, Duchess of Teck; late Professor of Obstetric Med., King's Coll., Lond., and Physician-Accoucheur and Phys.-Diseases of Women and Children, King's Coll. Hospital; formerly Lecturer on Comp. Anat. and Forensic Med., St. Bartholomew's Hospital; Examiner in Midwifery Roy. Coll. Phys. 1861-4; Councillor 1857-9; Censor 1861-5; Harveian Orator 1872; author of contrib. to Trans. Roy. Soc. and Royal Microscopical Society; article "Uterus," Cyclopædia of Anatomy and Physiology; son of John Richard Farre, Esq., M.D., and Anne Elizabeth Crawley; *ed.* at Charterhouse, and Caius Coll., Cambridge; *grad.* M.D. 1841; *m.* Jessie Bethune Macdonald, dau. of late Lt.-Col. Macdonald, C.B., of H.M.'s 1st Reg. of Foot, Royal Scots, who served through Peninsula, led forlorn hope at St. Sebastian, was severely wounded at Waterloo, created Knight of St. Anne of Russia by Emperor of Russia. Dr. Farre is a D. L. for the co. of Merioneth.

Residence: Dolfriog, near Portmadoc, North Wales.
Town House: 12, Hertford Street, May Fair.
Arms: Gu., a saltire or cotised arg. between four fleurs-de-lis of the second.
Crest: A fleur-de-lis as in the arms.
Motto: Fidelis.

Note.—This family derives its descent from the *Farres* of Gillingham. Walter Farre died April 30, 1590. (See Morant's *History of Essex*, vol. i.) On maternal side Mrs. Farre is descended from the old family of Munros of Foulis.

GORE, John Ralph Ormsby-, Esq., of Glyn Hall, Merionethshire.

J. P. and D. L. for the cos. of Carnarvon and Salop; was M.P. for Carnarvonshire from 1837 to 1841; has been M.P. for North Shropshire since 1859; is patron of one living; eldest son of the late William Ormsby-Gore, Esq., J. P. and D. L. of Porkington (see *Lineage*); *b.* 1816; *m.*, 1844, Sarah, youngest dau. of Sir John Tyssen Tyrell, Bart., of Boreham House, Essex, by Elizabeth Anne, dau. of Sir T. Pilkington, and has issue a dau.,—
Fanny Mary Catherine, *m.*, 1863, the Hon. Lloyd Kenyon, eldest son of Lloyd, 3rd Lord Kenyon (who *d.* 1865), and has issue a son, LLOYD, *b.* 1864, now *Baron Kenyon.*

Residences: Porkington, Salop; Glyn Hall, Merioneth.

Town Address: Junior Carlton Club.
Arms: Quarterly: 1st and 4th, gu., a fesse between three cross crosslets fitchées or—GORE; 2nd and 3rd, gu., a bend between six cross crosslets fitchées or—ORMSBY.
Crests: 1. An heraldic tiger rampant ducally gorged or—*Gore;* 2. A dexter armed arm embowed ppr., holding in the hand a man's leg armed couped at the thigh—*Ormsby.*
Motto: In hoc signo vinces.

LINEAGE.

The Welsh descent of this family is from the *Wynns of Glyn,* in the co. of Merioneth, and the Owens of Clenenney, in the co. of Carnarvon. The surname of Wynn began with Robert *Wynn,* or Wynne, ap John ap Ievan, of Glyn, Talsarnau (probably called *Wynn* by reason of a light complexion), who *m.*, *circa* 1544, Catherine, dau. of Ellis ap Maurice (the family afterwards became *Owen*), of Clenenney. (See the further descent of the Wynns of Glyn in the full *pedigree* of *Wynne of Peniarth.*)

Margaret, eldest dau. and heiress of Owen Wynne, Esq., of Glyn, and *Sylfaen,* grandson of William Wynne (Sheriff of Mer. 1637), *m.* Sir Robert Owen, Kt., of Porkington, or Brogyntyn, Salop (the ancient seat of *Owen Brogyntyn,* a local name of great historic interest recently restored to its original form of Brogyntyn by the present owner), and of Clenenney in Carnarvonshire. (See *Morys* and *Owen of Clenenney.*)

Margaret, heiress of these united families, eldest dau. of William Owen, Esq., became wife of Owen Ormsby, Esq., of Willow-brook, co. Sligo, and by him had an only dau.,—

Mary Jane Ormsby, heiress to Porkington, Clenenney, Glyn, and Sylfaen, with other extensive possessions of her paternal and maternal ancestors. She *m.* in 1815—

William (Ormsby) Gore, Esq. (son of William Gore, Esq., M.P. for co. Leitrim), who assumed the surname Ormsby before his own of Gore. The eldest son of this marriage is—

JOHN RALPH ORMSBY-GORE, now of Porkington, Glyn, Clenenney, &c. (as above).

HOLLAND, Samuel, Esq., of Glan-William, Merionethshire.

M.P. for the co. of Merioneth since 7th January, 1870; J. P. and D. L. for counties of Merioneth and Carnarvon; was High Sheriff of Merioneth in 1862; Chairman of the Board of Guardians, and Chairman of two Insurance Societies for over twenty years; son of the late Samuel Holland, merchant, of Liverpool, by Catherine, dau. of John Menzies, Esq., of the same town; *b.* at Liverpool, 17th October, 1803; *m.*, 17th January, 1850, Ann, daughter of late Josiah Robins, Esq., of Aston, Birmingham.

Residence: Glan-William, Tan-y-bwlch, Merioneth.

Town Address: Reform Club.
Arms: Az., a lion rampant arg. within an orle of fleurs-de-lis or, over all a bend gu.
Crest: Out of a ducal crown or, a demi-lion ppr. holding in dexter paw a fleur-de-lis.

LINEAGE.

This family derives its descent from the Hollands of Denton, Lancashire.

JONES, John, Esq., of Fron-dderw, Merionethshire.

J. P. and D. L. for the co. of Merioneth; son of the late Thomas Jones, Esq., of Cae'rpant; *b.* 1807; *m.*, 1831, to Emma, daughter of John Gilliat, Esq., of Clapham, Surrey; has issue four sons and two daughters.

Residence: Fron-dderw, near Bala.
Motto: Gwna gyfiawnder, ac nac ofna: "Be just, and fear not."

Note.—Fron-dderw is beautifully situated on a slope above the town of Bala, commanding extensive views of the fair country of the Vale of Dee, and of the Berwyn mountains. *Ty-gwyn,* an estate belonging to Mr. Jones, is situated in the co. of Denbigh.

JONES, John, Esq., of Ynysfawr, Merionethshire.

J. P. for the co. of Merioneth; son of Evan Jones, Esq., by Jane, only dau. of Rev. Richard Pugh, Rector of Llanfrothen, Mer.; *b.* 24th March, 1829; *ed.* at Beaumaris Grammar School; *m.*, 1866, Lydia, dau. and co-h. of John Jones, Esq., of Oaklands, co. of Denbigh; has issue 1 son and 1 dau.

Heir: Evan Bowen, *b.* 13th Feb., 1869.
Residence: Ynysfawr, near Portmadoc.
Arms: Gu., three lions rampant regardant or.
Crest: A boar's head couped ppr.

LINEAGE.

Thomas Jones, Esq., of Holt Hall, co. of Denbigh, and Pentre, co. of Flint, *m.* in 1711 Mary Lloyd of Downing Uchaf, and had issue Thomas, afterwards Rector of Trawsfynydd, who *m.* Jane Williams of Brondauw, in the parish of Llanfrothen, co. of Merioneth, and had John, afterwards of Jesus College, Oxford, B.A. He *m.* Mary Ellis, and had issue—
Evan Jones, who by his wife, Jane Pugh, had a son,—
JOHN JONES, now of Ynysfor (as above).

Note.—*Ynys-fawr,* "the large Island," improperly "Ynysfor," is situated on a slight rise in the valley of the Glaslyn, and is surrounded with extensive tracts of land rescued from the recurring tide by the great embankment of *Traeth-mawr,* already noticed. It was just high enough to escape the overflow of the tide, and being more spacious than some other "islands" in the marsh, acquired probably on this account the distinctive name of Ynys-*fawr,* "the large island." The approaches to Ynysfawr give sufficient proof that the land is a new creation.

JONES, Rev. John, Barmouth, Merionethshire.

Rector of Llanaber 1843; Magistrate for the co. of Merioneth; M.A., Oxon; son of Griffith Jones, Esq., of Bryntirion, Dolgelley; *b.* at Dolgelley, 4th September, 1816; *ed.* at Beaumaris and Ruthin Schools, and Jesus College, Oxford; *grad.* B.A. 1839, M.A. 1842; *m.*, April 19, 1854, Adelaide, dau. of Edmund Abbey, Esq., M.D.; appointed to the rectory of Llanaber 1843; has issue two sons, Charles Griffith Glynne, and Edmund Osborne Jones.

Residence: Glanydon, Barmouth.

Note.—Llanaber Church, a beautiful example of Early English architecture, was restored in 1859. Barmouth Church built 1830; National Schools built 1843.

JONES, William, Esq., of Glandwr, Merionethshire.

A Member of the Court of Lieutenancy of the City of London, also of the Corporation, and Deputy of the ward of Bishopsgate; J. P. and D. L. for the co. of Merioneth; brought up to the law, and practised for many years as a solicitor in Crosby Square, and Vestry Clerk of the parish of St. Helen's, Bishopsgate, London; *b.* at Dolgelley, on the 20th September, 1792; *ed.* at Shrewsbury School; *m.* Harriet, youngest daughter of Thomas Cartwrigth, Esq., a member of the Corporation of London and Deputy of the Ward of Bridge; has issue three sons and three daughters.

THE COUNTY FAMILIES OF MERIONETHSHIRE. 705

Heir: William Halse Gatty Jones.
Residence: Glandwr, Llanaber, near Dolgelley, Merionethshire.
Town Address: Crosby Square, London.
Crest: On a rock a goat passant.
Motto: Un a wasnaethav, "One I serve."

LLOYD, John, Esq., of Plas-issaf, Merionethshire.

J. P. for Merionethshire; son of the late John Lloyd, Esq.; *b.* in London, 15th December, 1797; *m.* 17th June, 1828; *s.* to estates 27th Nov., 1821; has issue 3 sons and 3 daughters.

Residences: Plas-issaf, Corwen; Hendre Arddwyfaen, Denbighshire.
Town Address: 50, Brunswick Square, Brighton, Sussex.
Arms: Vert, a chevron inter three wolves' heads erased argent.
Crest: A wolf's head erased.
Motto: Y blaidd yn y blaen, "The wolf in the van."

LINEAGE.

This family derives its descent from *Rhirid Flaidd* (see *Rhirid Flaidd*) of Rhiwaedog, Lord of Penllyn, from whom are descended the Lloyds of Rhiwaedog and *Ddwyfaen*, the Myddeltons of Chirk Castle, Gwaenynog, &c., &c.

LLOYD, Morgan, Esq., of Cefn-gellgwm, Merionethshire.

Barrister-at-law; called by the Society of the Middle Temple 1847; J. P. for the co. of Merioneth; Author of "The Law and Practice of the County Courts," a treatise on "Prohibition," &c.; contested the Anglesey boroughs in the General Election of 1868 against the Honourable W. O. Stanley, but was unsuccessful; son of Mr. Morris Lloyd of Cefn-gellgwm, in the parish of Trawsfynydd; *b.* 14th July, 1822; *ed.* at Edinburgh University; *m.*, in August, 1848, Mary, the daughter of the late Honourable Admiral Elphinstone Fleming, and sister of the 14th Lord Elphinstone,—she *d.* in March, 1859; has issue two sons and one daughter.

Heir: Clement Elphinstone Lloyd.
Residence: Cefn-gellgwm, Merionethshire.
Town Address: 43, Chester Square, London.

LINEAGE.

This family derives its descent from Hugh Llwyd of Cynval, in the parish of Maentwrog, in the county of Merioneth, a well-known bard, who lived in the reigns of Elizabeth and James I. (See "Hugh Llwyd" and "Morgan Llwyd" in Williams' *Celebrated Welshmen*.)

LLOYD, Mrs., of Rhagatt, Merionethshire.

Gertrude Jane Mary Lloyd is widow of John Lloyd, Esq., of Rhagatt. Mr. Lloyd was J. P. for cos. Merioneth and Denbigh; High Sheriff for Denbighshire in 1863; D. L. for Merioneth; son of Edward Lloyd, Esq., of Rhagatt, and his wife, Frances, dau. of John Maddock, Esq., of Fron-iw, Denbighshire; *b.* at Rhagatt, 1812; *ed.* at Westminster and Chr. Ch., Oxon., where he graduated B.A. in 1833; *d. s. p.* 1865. Mrs. Lloyd is dau. of the late Philip Lake Godsal, Esq., of Iscoed Park, Flintshire, by the Hon. Grace Ann, dau. of William, 1st Lord Wynford; was *m.* to Mr. Lloyd in 1847.

Heir: Edward Owen Vaughan, son of Edward Lloyd, Esq., and nephew of the late John Lloyd, Esq.
Residence: Rhagatt, near Corwen.

LINEAGE.

The Lloyds of Rhagatt trace from *Tudor Trevor*, founder of the tribe of Marches, and as such are entitled to bear—*Per bend sinister ermine and ermines, a lion rampant or;* but the arms have not been supplied to us.

Note.—Rhagatt is probably a modification of *Rhagarth*, a place, according to Leland, situated on the north bank of the Dee in Yale, and belonging to Owain Glyndwr. It is a very pleasant spot a little below Corwen, in the Vale of the Dee. The mansion contains a number of valuable paintings, many from the hand of the late Mr. Lloyd himself, who was an accomplished artist; and a collection of pre-historic remains—fossil bones, flint and other implements, not long since discovered in the clefts of the limestone rock on the estate, and carefully preserved and arranged under the superintendence of Mrs. Lloyd.

MORGAN, Howel, Esq., of Hengwrt-uchaf, Merionethshire.

F.R.C.S.; D. L. for the cos. of Merioneth and Brecknock; in the Commission of the Peace for the cos. of Merioneth, Montgomery, and Brecknock; High Sheriff for Merioneth 1863; second son of John Morgan, Esq., of Dyfynog, Brecknockshire; *b.* 1820; *m.*, 13th September, 1860, Anne, second daughter and co-heiress of Hugh Jones, Esq., of Hengwrt-uchaf and Plas Hên (her eldest sister, Mary, *m.* Major Owen J. Ellis-Nanney, of Gwynfryn, co. Carnarvon; her youngest sister *m.* Rev. Charles Owen).

Residence: Hengwrt-uchaf, near Dolgelley.
Town Address: Union Club.
Arms: Quarterly: 1st and 4th, sa., a chevron arg. between 3 spears' heads imbrued—MORGAN. 2nd, quartered, 1st and 4th, sa., a fesse cotised or between two daggers arg., hilts and pommels or; that in chief pointing upwards, that in base downwards; 2nd and 3rd, or, 3 bats az., membered gu.—BRYCHAN. 3rd, arg., a bull's head caboshed gu. between three mullets of the 2nd— HAVARD.
Crest: A spear's head imbrued.
Motto: Gwell angau na chywilydd.

Note.—For lineage see *Morgan of Defynog,* Brecknockshire.

OAKELEY, William Edward, Esq., of Plas Tanybwlch, Merionethshire.

J. P. and D. L. for co. of Merioneth; late Captain in Staffordshire Yeomanry; son of William Oakeley, Esq., of Glanwilliam, Tanybwlch, Merioneth (4th son of Sir Charles Oakeley, 1st Bart., who rendered distinguished service in India under Lord Cornwallis), and Mary Maria Miles, dau. of Col. Sir Edward Miles, K.C.B.; *b.* Aug. 1, 1828; *ed.* at Eton and Corpus Christi, Oxon.; *m.*, 10th April, 1860, the Hon. Mary Russell, 2nd dau. of the Baroness de Clifford, of Clifford Castle, Herefordshire, by Com. John Russell, R.N., a cadet of the House of Bedford; succ. to estates in 1867; has issue one son and one daughter.

Heir: Edward de Clifford William.
Residences: Plas Tanybwlch, Merioneth; Cliff House, Alverstone, Leicester.
Town Address: Arthur's Club.
Arms: The arms of *Oakeley,* impaling *De Clifford.*
Motto: Paterni nominis patrimonium.

LINEAGE.

This family traces its lineage from the *Oakeleys of Oakeley,* Salop.

Note.—The mansion of *Plas Tan-y-Bwlch,* newly renovated and almost entirely rebuilt (1872), is delightfully situated on a slope overlooking the vale of Maentwrog, so much admired for its scenery. The estate contains slate quarries of a superior kind, let out on royalty. The ancient mansion of *Dol-y-Moch,* now a farmhouse, added by purchase, is on the estate.

PRICE, Richard Jones Lloyd, Esq., of Rhiwlas, Merionethshire.

J. P. of the co. of Merioneth; Sheriff of same co. 1868; son of the late Richard Watkin Price, Esq., of Rhiwlas; *b.* 1844; *m.*, 1869, a dau. of Capt. Hopwood, a Lancashire gentleman, and has issue.

Residence: Rhiwlas, near Bala.
Town Address: Carlton Club.
Arms: A lion rampant arg.

LINEAGE.

This family is of considerable antiquity, and in past times produced some distinguished men; but we have not been supplied with a full genealogy of Mr. Price's predecessors. The possessor of Rhiwlas, when the first Duke of Beaufort, in 1684, made his lordly progress through Wales as Lord President, and stopped a night at Rhiwlas on his way from "Gwidder" (Gwydir) to "Lloydyarth" (Llwydiarth, Mont.), was Col. Wm. Price, and a picture of the place as it then stood is engraved in the *Progress* (privately printed 1864).

PUGHE, John, Esq., of Bryn awel, Merionethshire.

F.R.C.S.E.; J. P. for the co. of Merioneth, translator of *Meddygon Myddfai;* author of "Eben Fardd," and other minor productions; son of David Roberts Pughe, Esq., of Bron-dirion Villa, Clynnog, Carnarvonshire; *b.* Sept. 8, 1814; *ed.* at Pwllheli and Carnarvon; *grad.* a Member Royal College of Surgeons in 1837, and Fellow of the same in 1853; *m.*, 1st, Feb. 20, 1839, Catherine, dau. of Samuel Samuel, Esq., of Carnarvon; 2ndly, Feb. 15, 1865, Maria Wilcox, dau. of Edwin Wilcox, Esq., of Bristol; *s.* to estates of Erwfaethlon, Towyn, Merioneth, Coch-y-Big, Clynnog, and Cwmarion, in 1862; has issue five sons and five daughters.

Heir: David Roberts Pughe, M.R.C.S., Machynlleth, Coroner of the Machynlleth district of the co. of Montgomery.
Residences: Bron-dirion Villa, Clynnog; and Bryn-awel, Aberdyfi.
Crest: A demi-wyvern rampant.
Motto: Goraf araeth gwaith: "The best speech, action."

LINEAGE.

This family derives its descent from Marchudd ap Cynan, founder of one of the fifteen tribes of

Gwynedd, and Gamel, Falconer to William the Conqueror. Prominent men in the line of descent have been Sir Thomas Scriven, *temp.* Charles I., and Ednyfed Fychan, of a much earlier date.

Rees Hughes, Clerk, Vicar of Wern, Shrewsbury, *m.* Mary Scriven, dau. of Sir Thomas Scriven, Kt., of Frodesley Hall, in direct descent from John Scriven, Lord of the Manor of Frodesley, *temp.* Henry V., who himself traced his lineage uninterruptedly to Gamel the Falconer, just named.

Scriven Hughes, the son, of Dyffryn Gwyn, near Towyn, Mer., had a dau., Catherine, and she by her husband, John ap Rhinallt *ap Hugh*, or Pugh, of Erw Faethlon, Towyn, had a dau., also named Catherine, who *m.*—

David Roberts, Esq., of Aberdyfi, who by his said wife Catherine had a son,—

John Pugh, Esq. (as he chose to be called), of Lleuar Bach, Clynnog, Carn. His son by Jane Prichard was—

David Roberts Pughe, Esq., of Coch-y-big, or Bron-dirion (*d.* 1862). He *m.* Elizabeth, dau. of William Owen, Esq., of Clwaen Wen, Anglesey, and had, besides a dau. who died young, two sons, viz.,—

JOHN PUGHE, Esq., now of Bryn-awel, &c. (as above).

David William Pughe, Esq., M.R.C.S., of Brondirion, Clynnog, *d.* 22nd Nov., 1862. (See further *Cyff Beuno*, by "Eben Fardd," p. 92.)

REVELEY, Hugh John, Esq., of Bryn-y-gwin, Merionethshire.

J. P. and D. L. for the co. of Merioneth; Sheriff for the same co. in 1859; son of the late Hugh Reveley, Esq., J. P. and D. L. for his co. (*d.* 1851), and Jane, his wife, dau. of Robert H. Owen, Esq., of Bryn-y-gwin (she *d.* 1846); *b.* at Bryn-y-gwin, 15th March, 1812; *ed.* at Wadham College, Oxford; *m.*, 13th July, 1850, to his cousin Jane, dau. of Algernon Reveley, Esq., of Bengal Civil Service; *s.* in 1851; has issue 6 daus.

Heir: Fanny Jane Reveley.
Residence: Bryn-y-gwin, near Dolgelley.
Arms: Quarterly: 1st and 4th, arg., a chevron engrailed gu. between three estoiles with twelve points az.—REVELEY,—2nd and 3rd, quarterly: 1st and 4th, az., a chevron between three cocks arg. (for *Aleth, Prince of Dimetia*); 2nd and 3rd, gu., three snakes ennowed arg. (*Ednowen ap Bradwen, Lord of Merioneth*)—OWEN.
Crests: An estoile as in the arms; a cock crowing arg. on a cap of maintenance.
Motto: Optima revelatio stella—for *Reveley;* Canaf tra byddaf—for *Owen.*

LINEAGE.

This family derives its descent from some of the best blood of Northumberland, the Greys of Chillingham, the Selbys of Branxton, the Ordes, the Lords Bertram of Mitford, &c., &c., and by marriage is connected with the Percys, Dukes of Northumberland, the first duke's mother having been Philadelphia Reveley. Another Philadelphia carried the old Reveley estates in Northumberland and Yorkshire into the Mitford family.

The pedigree of the Reveleys dates from the time of King Edward II. They were Lords of the Manor of Ancroft, in Northumberland, and in James I.'s time possessed the manors of Newton Underwood, Newton Park, and Throphill, when the family seat was removed from the Cheviots to Yorkshire, and the *Hall House* of Newby-Wiske built. In this house Hugh, the first Duke of Northumberland, was born.

The present representative through his grandmother is descended from the old Norman family of Champion de Crespigny, which took refuge in England at the time of the revocation of the edict of Nantes. She was *m.* to Henry Reveley, Esq., who began life as gentleman usher to Queen Charlotte; afterwards became Purveyor to the King, and a Commissioner of Excise. The issue of that marriage was Hugh Reveley, Esq., late of Bryn-y-gwin above mentioned, another son, and two daus.

Note.—The north side of "Tyrau-mawr," "the great towers," which is the west point of Cader Idris, nearest the sea, belongs to the Bryn-y-gwin estate, and has upon it a "Roman zigzag," which within memory was very distinct from all parts of the country. It formed part of the road which crossed over to Llanfihangel y Pennant and *Castell-y-Beri*, or Cae'r Berllan.

The *new* house at *Bryn-y-gwin* was built by the late Mr. Reveley immediately after his marriage in 1802, and commands a fine view, containing also a good library and some pictures, especially a Canalotti, the "Marriage of the Doge with the Adriatic." It has also a large and choice collection of old masters' drawings and etchings, many of them from Sir Joshua Reynolds' and Sir Peter Lely's collections, as well as coins, medals, &c. These collections were chiefly made by the present proprietor's grandfather, who was the author of a book upon the subject called "Notices Illustrative of the Drawings and Sketches of some of the most Distinguished Masters." He was offered a baronetcy by Mr. Pitt in the latter years of his life. His son, Hugh Reveley, Esq., was called to the bar, and appointed Speaker's secretary, by Sir John Mitford, his cousin, and afterwards followed him to Ireland as Purse-bearer when Sir John became Lord Redesdale and Lord Chancellor of Ireland. He served the office of Sheriff for Merioneth in 1811.

In the chancel of Mitford Church is a curious monument—mentioned by Boswell in his "Antiquities"—to the memory of Bertram Reveley, the same probably who married Rosamond Wentworth, of Wentworth Woodhouse, the niece of the great Lord Strafford. His son raised a body of horse in support of the king against the parliament, and was in the battle of Marston Moor. In the words of Mitford the historian, "Reveley held on with the defeated army under the Prince, and was afterwards killed at the decisive battle of Naseby."

RICHARDS, Richard Meredyth, Esq., of Caerynwch, Merionethshire.

J. P. and D. L. for the co. of Merioneth; High Sheriff for same co. in 1865; J. P. for the co. of Denbigh; Chairman of Quarter Sessions in the co. of Mer. since 1857; son of the late Richard Richards, Esq., J. P., D. L., sometime M.P. for the co. of Merioneth, and a Master in Chancery, by his wife, Harriet, dau. and co-h. of Jonathan Dennett, Esq.; *b.* 1821; called to the bar 1845; *m.*, 1st, 1845, Elizabeth Emma, dau. of William Bennett, Esq., of Farringdon House, Berks (she *d.* 1852); 2ndly, 1863, Louisa Janette Anne, only child and h. of the late Edward Lloyd Edwards, Esq., of Cerrig-Llwydion, Denbighshire; and has issue.

Heir: Richard Edward Lloyd, *b.* 1865.
Residence: Caerynwch, near Dolgelley.
Town Address: Carlton Club.
Arms: Quarterly: 1st, arg., a cross patencé engrailed sa. between four Cornish choughs ppr.; 2nd, ermine, on a saltire gu. an escallop arg.; 3rd, or, a lion ramp. gu.; 4th, vert, three eagles displayed in fesse arg.; and in right of his present wife, heiress of Cerrig-Llwydion, an escutcheon of pretence—gu. and az. a chevron ermine cotised or, between three Saxons' heads couped gutté de sang ppr.
Crest: A dexter arm naked, the hand grasping a scimitar, all ppr.
Motto: Ffyddlawn i'r gwirionedd.

LINEAGE.

Tudyr Vychan was possessor of Caerynwch in 1588, when Dwnn, Deputy Herald, visited the place (*Heraldic Visit. of Wales*, ii., 235). Third in descent from Tudyr *Vychan* was—
Robert *Vaughan*, Esq., of Caerynwch (*d.* 1693), who *m.* Margaret, dau. of Robert Vaughan, Esq., the "antiquary," of Hengwrt, and widow of William Pryce, B.D., Rector of Dolgelley, and had issue a dau. Grace, who *m.*—
John Humphreys, Esq., son of Capt. William Humphreys, of Maer-dy, Gwyddelwern. There were two or three generations of Humphreys at Caerynwch, ending in an heiress, Catherine, who *m*, 1785,—
Richard Richards, Esq. (son of Thomas Richards, Esq.), who was a talented barrister, and became Sir Richard Richards, chief Baron of the Court of Exchequer (*d.* 1823). By this mar. he left an eldest son,—
Richard Richards, Esq., of Caerynwch, who became a Master in Chancery, and represented the co. of Merioneth in Parliament from the death of Sir Robert W. Vaughan, Bart., of Nannau, in 1836, to 1852. By his wife, Harriet Dennett, he left, with other issue, a son,—
RICHARD MEREDYTH, now of Caerynwch (as above).

Note.—The mansion of *Caerynwch*, surrounded by a well-wooded and picturesque country, is a well-designed modern structure. The old residence at a short distance, now used as a farm-building, is curious as a specimen of the abodes of the Welsh gentry in former days. "It covers a considerable extent of ground, but down-stairs has only one sitting-room, square, and about eight feet high, adjoining to which is a hall, apparently of the same size. Over this is what appears to have been a drawing-room, handsomely wainscoted with oak, but open to the "valley" of the roof, the rafters coming so low at the sides of the room as not to admit of a person standing upright. The rest of the house consists of a few bedrooms and the offices. The whole building is very irregular, and seems to have been erected without any plan, and probably at different times."—(*Note* on Dwnn, ii., 236.)

RICHARDSON, The Rev. William, of Corwen, Merionethshire.

Rector of Corwen 1866; late Scholar of Jesus College, Oxford; Curate of Bala, March, 1854; Chaplain of Rhûg Chapel, August, 1854; Incumbent of St. Mary's, Llwydiarth, 1859—Patron, Sir W. W. Wynn, Bart., M.P.; son of Rev. P. D. Richardson, Vicar of St. Dogwell's *cum* Little Newcastle, Pembrokeshire; *b.* at St. Dogwell's, March, 1830; *ed.* at the Collegiate School, St. David's, Cowbridge School, Glamorganshire, and at Jesus Coll., Oxford; *grad.* B.A. 1853.

Residence: The Rectory, Corwen.

Note.—National Schools were built 1868; St. Julian's Church is in course of restoration (1872).

ROBERTSON, Henry, Esq., of Plas Crogen, Merionethshire.

J. P. for the co. of Merioneth; High Sheriff for same co. 1869; was M.P. for Shrewsbury 1862-3; *b.* 1816; *m.*, 1846, Elizabeth, dau. of W. Dean, Esq., of Shrewsbury, and has issue.

Residence: Plas Crogen.

Note.—The newly erected mansion of *Crogen* stands nearly on the site of the ancient mansion of *Palé*, and is surrounded by many of the fine old trees and other remains of the park of that well-known estate. The scenery of the Vale of Edeirnion in front is celebrated for its beauty, and the country is full of spots of historic interest. (See further *Crogen*, *Owen Brogyntyn*, *Rhirid Flaidd*, *Edeirnion*, &c.)

RUCK, Laurence, Esq., of Pantlludw, Merionethshire, and Newington Manor House, Kent.

Mr. Ruck is descended from an old Kentish family, one of whom, by name Laurence Ruck, in the time of Henry VIII. was bow-bearer to the king; *b.* 1820; *ed.* at Magdalen College, Oxford; *m.*, 1841, Mary Anne, dau. of Richard Matthews, Esq., of Esgair Lleferin, Merionethshire; and has issue 4 sons—Arthur, Richard, Ithel, Edward; and 2 daughters—Mary and Amy.

Residence: Pantlludw, Machynlleth, Merionethshire.
Arms: The arms of *Ruck*, impaling those of *Morris* of Esgair Lleferin, and *Jones* of Esgair Evan.

THE COUNTY FAMILIES OF MERIONETHSHIRE.

LINEAGE.

Mrs. Ruck, as shown in an extensive pedigree in possession of the family, is descended both on the paternal and maternal side from a long line of Welsh ancestry. Her father, Richard Matthews of Esgair Lleferin (who was of the old family of Matthews of Trenannau), was an officer in the 23rd Reg. Welsh Fusiliers. His father, Richard Matthews, *m.* Ann Morris, heiress of Esgair Lleferin, from whom Mrs. Ruck has inherited that property. Her mother was Mary, dau. of John Jones, Esq., of Esgair Evan, by Mary Morgan, of the Morgans of Fronfraith, Cardiganshire, claiming a pedigree from *Gwaethfoed*, Prince of Ceredigion in the 11th cent.

Note.—The residence of Pantlludw, erected about fifty years ago, is delightfully situated on an elevation commanding a view of the valley of the Dyfi above and below Machynlleth, and the spurs of Penllyman (Plinlimmon) to the east. In the tastefully arranged grounds is a remarkable yew of enormous size, one of the branches of which was some years ago blown down, and converted into elegant pieces of furniture. The age of this tree is calculated at nearly a thousand years. The mansion of *Esgair*, occupied by Col. Stewart, is a pretty place, boldly planted in the midst of highly picturesque scenery.

THRUSTON, Charles Frederick, Esq., of Talgarth Hall, Merionethshire.

Lord of the manor of Pennal; D. L. and J. P. for Merionethshire, and J. P. for Montgomeryshire; High Sheriff for Merionethshire in 1860; was in the 96th Light Infantry; eldest son of the late Captain Thomas Thruston, R.N., of Pennal Tower, Mer., by his first wife, Frances, dau. and heiress of Lewis Edwards, Esq., of Talgarth Hall; *b.* at Talgarth Hall, January 4th, 1824; *ed.* at Rugby; *m.*, 1848, Mary, daughter of the late Josiah Nisbet, Capt. R.N., and gr. dau. of Lady Nelson (widow of Lord Nelson), and has issue—

1. Mary Frances, *b.* 1850; *m.*, 1870, W. Edw. Allen, Esq., M.R.C.S., Bengal Medical Service.
2. Blanche Eliza, *b.* 19th July, 1851.
3. *Charles Nisbet*, *b.* 3rd Nov., 1853, F.R.C.S., Medical Service; *m.* 15th Sept., 1870.
4. Rose Emily, *b.* 17th June, 1855.
5. John Walter, *b.* 10th Feb., 1857.
6. Herbert Edwards, *b.* 29th April, 1859.
7. Lewis Arthur, *b.* 4th April, 1861.

Heir: Charles Nisbet, *b.* 1853.
Residence: Talgarth Hall, near Machynlleth.
Arms: "In a shield of sable, three bugle-horns with laces and tassells goulde, garnished azure."
Crest: "A white storke with blew legges standinge on a wreathe of yellowe and black, sett upon a helmet of steele with mantles and tassells of argent and gules." (Extract from a deed written by Wm. Dethick, Garter Principall Kinge of Arms, 1586.)
Mottoes: Esse quam videri; Thrust on.

LINEAGE.

The Thruston family were of Suffolk origin. The Welsh descent of the Thrustons of Talgarth Hall and Pennal Tower is traced maternally through the Edwards of Esgair-weddan from a very ancient stock, as shown in the following genealogy, revised and completed from Dwnn's *Herald. Visit. of Wales*, by the competent hand of W. W. E. Wynne, Esq., of Peniarth. (See also *Price of Esgairweddan, ante.*)

Ithel ap David ap Llowarch Vychan ap Llowarch ap Ievan ap David ap *Llewelyn ap Iorwerth*, Prince of North Wales, *m.* Gwen, dau. of Meredydd ap Madoc ap Meredith, descended from *Elystan Glodrudd*, Lord of Ferlys, a district between the Wye and Severn.

David ap Ithel, living probably 32nd Henry VI., 1454 (see *Notes of Inquisitions*, co. Mer:onei h, by Robert Vaughan, the antiquary of Hengwrt), *m.* Gwervil, dau. of Ithel Vychan ap Ithel Goch, of Ystrad Towy.

Griffith ap David, living probably in the township of Maesllangedris, parish of Talyllyn, 1453 *m.* Eva, dau. and heiress of Llewelyn ap Ievan, of the *Rofft* (Escairweddan).

David ap Griffith *m.* Alswn, dau. of Howel Gethin, and had a son,—

Ievan ap David, who *m.* Gwenllian, sole heiress of Llewelyn ap Owen ap Griffith ap Madoc ap Ievan, Caereinion.

Rees, eldest son (party to a deed on 19th July, 1595), *m.* Margaret, dau. of Thomas ap Rees ap David Lloyd, and from them were descended the Pryces of Escairweddan, who left their property to the Edwardses of Talgarth.

Richard, 2nd son of Ievan, *m.* Gwen, co-heir of Lewis ap Rees ap Morris ap Llewelyn, of Talgarth.

Lewis *Prichard* (ap Richard) of Talgarth, Gent., owner of Talgarth 19th Nov., 9th Charles I., *m.* Jane, youngest dau. of Humphrey Pughe, of Aberffrydlan, Gent., living, a widow, 22nd July, 18th Charles I.

Edward Lewis (*i. e.*, son of Lewis), of Tonfane and Talgarth, Gent., *b.* about 1598, *m.* Elizabeth, dau. of William Vaughan, son of Robert, one of the sons of Rees Vaughan, Esq., of Cors-y-gedol.

Lewis Edward (*i. e.*, son of Edward), of Tonfane and Talgarth, Gent. (buried at Llangelynin 1st May, 1688), had a son,—

Edward Lewis, Gent., of Talgarth (party to a deed 13th July, 1708, owner also of Tonfane), *m.* Lowry, living 13th July, 1708.

Lewis *Edwards*, Gent. (here the surname becomes settled), of Talgarth and Tonfane (settlement after his marriage dated 13th July, 1708), *m.* Mary, dau. of John Davies, Gent., of Machynlleth (and through this marriage property in the townships of Glyntrefnant and Eshireth, in and in the town of Machynlleth, passed into the Edwards family).

Humphrey Edwards, Esq., of Talgarth, *d.* 11th June, 1772, Sheriff of Merionethshire 1759, *m.* Mary, dau. and heiress of James Turner, Esq., of Oldport, co. Salop.

Humphrey's second brother, John, of Machynlleth, married Miss Owen, heiress of considerable property near Llanidloes, and by her had several children. Her eldest son was the late Sir John Edwards, Bart., M.P., whose only child is Mary Cornelia, now Countess Vane.

3 A

MERIONETHSHIRE.

Lewis Edwards, Esq., of Talgarth and Tonfane, died 17th Jan., 1797, aged forty-nine; Sheriff of co. Mer. 1773; *m.* Ann, dau. of Salusbury Pryce, D.D., Vicar of Meifod, and left one son, Pryce, who *d. s. p.*, and several daus., two only of whom were *m.*, and had issue—
Mary, co-heiress, *m.*, 16th March, 1796, to the Hon. Thomas Parker, afterwards Earl of Macclesfield, and *d.* at Holton Park, co. Oxford, 10th April, 1803, in her twenty-fourth year, leaving issue.
Frances, co-heiress, inherited Talgarth and Tonfane (*d.* 2nd December, 1828, aged thirty-eight), *m.* Charles Thomas Thruston, Captain in the Royal Navy, a member of the ancient family of Thruston, of Hoxne, co. Suffolk. He *m.*, 2ndly, Eliza, dau. of Admiral Sotheby, who *d.* in May, 1840, leaving a son, *Clement* (see *Thruston of Pennal Tower*). Capt. Thruston *d.* in London in 1858, and was buried at Pennal. Besides Parker, *d. unm.* 1844, aged about eighteen; Blanche, *d. unm.* in 1851; Emily, *d. unm.*, he left by first mar. his eldest son,—
CHARLES FREDERICK THRUSTON, Esq., now of Talgarth Hall (as above).

THRUSTON, Clement Arthur, Esq., of Penna Tower, Merionethshire.

J. P. for the co. of Merioneth; High Sheriff for the same co. 1870; Capt. Montgomeryshire Yeomanry Cavalry; contested Hastings in 1868; son of Charles Thomas Thruston, Captain Royal Navy, of Pennal Tower, late of Talgarth Hall, by his 2nd wife, Eliza, dau. of the late Admiral Sotheby; *b.* at Talgarth, near Machynlleth, June 12, 1837; *ed.* at Rugby and University College, Oxford; *grad.* B.A. 1860; called to the bar at Lincoln's Inn 1869, but does not practise; *m.*, 1861, Constance Sophia, dau. of the late Major-General Lechmere-Coore Russell, C.B., of Ashford Hall, Salop, and has issue two sons, one dau.; *s.* to estate 1858.

Heir: Edmund Heathcote, *b.* 1863.
Residence: Pennal Tower, near Machynlleth, North Wales.
Town Address: Boodle's Club.
Arms: " In a shield of sables three bugle-horns with lace and tassells of goulde, garnished azure."
Crest: " A white storke with blew legges standinge on a wreathe of yellowe and black sett upon a helmet of steele, with mantles and tassells of argent and gules " (arms thus made out by William Dethick, Garter King of Arms 1586).
Motto: Thrust on.

LINEAGE.

The family of Thruston is of considerable antiquity in the county of Suffolk, recently seated at Market Weston Hall, near Bury St. Edmund's, and formerly at Hoxon, co. Suffolk. (See further *Thruston, Talgarth*

Hall.) Mr. Thruston's great-uncle, Mr. Sotheby, was distinguished as one of the first poets of his day, and as an eminent literary man.

VAUGHAN, John, Esq., of Nannau, Merionethshire.

J. P. and D. L. for the co. of Merioneth; son of the late John Vaughan, Esq., of the Civil Service, and grandson of John Vaughan, Esq., of the Vaughans of Dolmelynllyn and Nannau, Merioneth, to whose estate he succeeded in 1842; he has also the inheritance in reversion of the Nannau and Hengwrt estates under the will of the late Sir R. Williams Vaughan, Bart., of Nannau and Hengwrt, who *d. s. p.* 1859, devising the Rhug part of the estates to the Hon. C. H. Wynn (see *Wynn of Rhug*), Hengwrt to the Hon. Misses Lloyd for life, and Nannau to the Hon. T. Pryce Lloyd during life (see *Pryce Lloyd of Pengwern*, Flint), after which they revert to Mr. Vaughan; *m.*, 1863, Eleanor, dau. of the late Edward Owen, Esq., of Garthyngharad (of the sept of "Baron Owen" of Dolgelley).

Residence: Nannau, near Dolgelley.
Arms: Quarterly, or and gu., four lions rampant counterchanged—VAUGHAN; on the centre of the shield a lion rampant az.—NANNEY.
Crest: A lion rampant az.

LINEAGE.

In past times the *Vaughans of Nannau* and *Hengwrt* were distinguished families in North Wales. Their lineage is derived from *Bleddyn ap Cynfyn*, Prince of Powys and North Wales 11th century. (See *Nanney* and *Vaughan of Nannau*.)

WAYNE, Herman, Esq., of Cae-Nest, Merionethshire.

Late Capt. 10th Regt.; son of Rev. W. H. Wayne, M.A., Vicar of Much Wenlock and patron of two livings, by his wife Jane, dau. of Samuel F. Milford, Esq., of Exeter; *b.* 1838, at Parwick Hall, Derbyshire; *m.*, 1862, Theresa Louisa, third dau. of the late Sir William Rouse Boughton, Bart., F.R.S., of Downton Hall, Shropshire, and late M.P. for Evesham. (His eldest brother, William Henry Wayne, Clerk, *b.* 1832, *m.*, 1856, Eliza, dau. of the late Capt. Henry Foskett, 15th Light Dragoons, and resides occasionally at Aber-Artro, Merionethshire.) Has issue 1 son and 2 daus.

Heir: Francis H. Milford.
Residence: Cae-Nest, near Harlech, Mer.
Arms: The Wayne arms are—Gu., a chevron ermine between three dexter gauntlets or.
Motto: Tempus et casus accidit omnibus.

THE COUNTY FAMILIES OF MERIONETHSHIRE.

LINEAGE.

This family derives from the Waynes of High Sheen, Staffordshire, seated at that place *temp.* Charles II. Col. Waine, Royalist, killed at Nantwich, was of this family; so was General Wayne, one of the Duke of Marlborough's leading officers.

Note.—Cae-Nest, a property which has long been in the family of the Pooles, lies in the picturesque and interesting Vale of Artro, a part teeming with antiquarian remains and historic associations. The fort, supposed to be British, situated on the river Artro, which runs close by the house, has been already noticed (see section on *Antiquities, ante*), as well as several other historic and pre-historic monuments scattered about the district.

WILLIAMS, Charles Reynolds, Esq., of Dolmelynllyn, Merionethshire.

Second son of Col. Monier Williams, Surveyor-General of Bombay; *b.* at Baroche, in the Bombay Presidency, on the 25th of Dec., 1815; *m.* Margaret, only daughter of John Romer, Esq., Member of Council of Bombay, and subsequently Acting Governor of that presidency; has issue one son and two daughters.

Residence: Dolmelynllyn, near Dolgelley.
Town Address: 48, Gloucester Square, Hyde Park.
Arms: Gu., a chevron ermine between three Saxons' heads couped ppr.
Crest: A stag's head.

GENEALOGICAL NOTE.

Colonel Monier Williams was a distinguished officer in the then East India Company's service, and was one of those who originated the survey on which the present revenue settlement was made. His elder brother (both sons of George Williams, formerly Chief Justice of Newfoundland) was Colonel George Williams, who represented Ashton-under-Lyne in the first reformed Parliament, and as a youth of twelve years of age, in company with his uncle, Major Griffith Williams of the Royal Artillery, joined General Burgoyne's army in North America, and carried the flag of truce to the enemy's camp on the surrender at Saratoga. From Major Griffith Williams was descended Lieut.-General Griffith Lewis, C.B., the late Colonel Commandant of the Royal Engineers.

Note.—*Dolmelynllyn*, situate in the romantic vale of the Maw, one of the most ancient residences in the county, formerly belonging to the Vaughans (see *Vaughan of Dolmelynllyn*), has been considerably enlarged within the last few years. Within the grounds is the well-known waterfall called "Rhaiadr Du"—"the black cascade."

WILLIAMS, Lewis, Esq., of Vronwnion, Merionethshire.

J. P. and D. L. for the co. of Merioneth; served the office of High Sheriff for the same county in 1864-5; son of the late Ellis Williams, Esq., of Dolgelley, merchant; *b.* at Dolgelly, in July, 1791; *ed.* at Shrewsbury School; *m.*, 1825, Margaret, eldest daughter of Griffith Jones, Esq., of Bryntirion, Dolgelley; has issue 5 sons (one dead) and 5 daughters (one dead).

Heir: The Rev. Ellis Osborne Williams, M.A., Vicar of Pwllheli.
Residence: Vronwnion, Dolgelley.
Arms: (Not sent).
Motto: Gwell gwerth na gwawd.

LINEAGE.

This family traces its lineage from the Owens of Pantffylip, in the county of Merioneth.

Note.—The present mansion of Vronwnion, modern Gothic, was built in 1824.

WILLIAMS, Mrs., of Deudraeth Castle, Merionethshire.

Annie Louisa Loveday, widow of the late David Williams, Esq., who was in 1868 elected M.P. for the co. of Merioneth, was a J. P. and D. L. for the two cos. of Merioneth and Carnarvon, and had served the office of Sheriff for both counties (1861-2), and *d.* 1869; is dau. of the late William Williams, Esq., of Peniarthucha, in the co. of Merioneth, Barrister-at-law; was *m.* to the late Mr. Williams, 1841; *s.* at his decease, 15th Dec., 1869; has issue 5 sons and 7 daus.; eld. dau. Angharad, *m.* 1872.

Heir (of entailed estates): Arthur Osmond, second son.
Residence: Deudraeth Castle.
Arms: (Not sent).

LINEAGE.

This family derives its descent from the *Saethons* of Saethon, in Lleyn. The last owner descended from the Saethons was David Williams, Esq., father of the late D. Williams, Esq., M.P. For upwards of a century after the civil wars the Saethons and Devereuxs held the property jointly, and were connected by intermarriages. Two of the latter served the office of Sheriff for Carnarvonshire in the eighteenth century. They were descended from Trahaiarn Gôch, Lord of Lleyn, and were an important family in the seventeenth century. (See further *Saethons of Saethon*, p. 342, *ante.*)

Note.—Near the site of the present house was the old castle of Castell Deudraeth (mentioned by Giraldus Cambrensis and Sir John Wynn of Gwydir), which was the residence of some of the sons of Owen Gwynedd, Prince of North Wales. The foundations of the old walls were in existence early in this century, and within the recollection of some old people in the neighbourhood. The present castle (see *engraving*, p. 664) was rebuilt by the late Mr. Williams in 1850. On the property, and near Castell Deudraeth, is the fine old Elizabethan mansion of Plasnewydd (now used as a farmhouse), and on an adjoining farm (Hendre), part of the same estate, is the house where Bishop Humphreys was born.

MERIONETHSHIRE.

WYNN, Hon. Charles Henry, of Rhûg, Merionethshire.

Second son of the Rt. Hon. Lord Newborough of Glynllivon Park, J. P. and D. L. for the co. of Carnarvon, by Frances Mary (*d.* 1857), dau. of the Rev. Walter de Winton, of Hay Castle, co. of Brecon; *b.* April 22nd, 1847, at Glynllivon Park; *ed.* privately; succ. to the Rhûg estate 1859, by the will of Sir Robert Williams Vaughan Bart., of Rhûg and Nannau; is *unm.*

Residence: Rhûg, near Corwen.
Town Address: Junior Carlton Club, Pall Mall.
Crests: A boar's head, couped ppr.; a dexter arm embowed armoured, holding a fleur-de-lis or.
Motto: Suaviter in modo, fortiter in re.

LINEAGE.

For the genealogy of the ancient family of which Mr. Wynn of Rhûg is a member, see *Newborough, Lord, of Glynllifon,* Carn.

WYNNE, William Watkin Edward, Esq., of Peniarth, Merionethshire.

J. P. and D. L. for the co. of Merioneth; M.P. for that co. from 1852 to 1865, and Sheriff 1867; son of the late William Wynne, Esq. (see *Lineage*); *b.* 23rd Dec., 1801; *ed.* at Westminster School and Oxford; *m.*, 8th May, 1839, Mary, 2nd of the three daus. and co-heiresses of the late Robert Aglionby Slaney, Esq., of Walford Manor and Hatton Grange, co. of Salop, M.P. for Shrewsbury, and by her has issue—
WILLIAM ROBERT MAURICE, *b.* 15th February, 1840; M.P. for the co. of Merioneth from 1865 to 1868; J. P. and D. L. for the co. of Mer.
Owen Slaney, *b.* 17th October, 1842, A.M. of Ch. Ch., Oxford.

Heir: WILLIAM ROBERT MAURICE WYNNE.
Residence: Peniarth, Merionethshire.
Town Address: Carlton and University Clubs.
Arms: Ermine, on a saltire gu., a crescent or.
Crest: On a chapeau, a boar passant arg.
Mottoes: Virtus unica nobilitas; and over the crest, "Tylwyth Eignion."

LINEAGE.

The Wynnes of Peniarth are cadets of the Wynnes of Glyn, who derived, with the Vaughans of Cors-y-gedol, Yales of Plas-yn-Yale, and Rogers Wynns of Bryn-tangor, from DOMINUS OTHO, supposed to have been of the family of the Gherhardini of Florence, who, proceeding to Normandy, and thence in 1057 to England, acquired, through the favour of EDWARD THE CONFESSOR, immense possessions in the latter country. These devolved on his son, WALTER FITZ OTHO, castellan of Windsor Castle, who *m.* Gwladys, dau. of Rhiwallon, brother of Bleddyn ap Cynfyn, King of Powys; and his son, GERALD FITZ WALTER DE WINDSOR, constable of the castle of Pembroke, living in 1108, *m.* Nesta, dau. of Rhys ap Tudor, Prince of South Wales, by whom he had issue three sons,—
1. MAURICE, his heir.
2. William, ancestor of the families of Carew, Grace, Fitzmaurices, Marquesses of Lansdowne, and Gerard.
3. David, Bishop of St. David's, from 14 Cal. Jan., 1147, to about May, 1176.
4. Angharad, who *m.* William de Barry, father, by her, of the celebrated Giraldus de Barry, styled *Cambrensis.*

The eldest son,—
MAURICE FITZGERALD, patriarch of the Irish Geraldines, accompanied Richard Strongbow, Earl of Striguil, near Chepstow, to Ireland in 1168; *d.* in 1177, buried in the abbey of Grey Friars, Wexford. By Alice, his wife, dau. of Arnulph, 4th son of Roger de Montgomery, he had issue—
1. Gerald FitzMaurice, Lord Justiciary of Ireland, who was summoned to parliament as Baron Offaly in 1205, and *d.* the same year, progenitor of the DUKES OF LEINSTER.
2. Thomas FITZMAURICE, of whom presently.
3. Alexander.
4. Maurice.
5. Nesta, *m.* Hervy de Marisco, Constable of Ireland.

The second son,—
THOMAS FITZMAURICE, surnamed *the Great,* who was a grantee by King JOHN of an estate of ten knights' fees, and *d.* in or before 1215, *m.* Elinor, dau. of Jordan de Marisco, a niece of Hervy de Marisco, Constable of Ireland. Their son was—
JOHN FITZTHOMAS, whose wardship was granted, 17 King JOHN, to Thomas FitzAnthony, the king's seneschal of Leinster. He was of full age in 1229; grantee of Decies and Desmond in 1259; and slain at Callan in 1260. This nobleman, who was founder of the abbey of Tralee, *m.* twice: 1st, Margery, dau. and sole h. of Thomas FitzAnthony, Lord of Decies and Desmond; and 2ndly, Honora, dau. of Phelim O'Connor, Kerry, by the latter of whom he had three sons: 1. Gilbert, ancestor of THE WHITE KNIGHT; 2. John, ancestor of THE KNIGHT OF GLYN; 3. Maurice, ancestor of THE KNIGHT OF KERRY. By his first wife John FitzThomas was father of—
Maurice FitzJohn, 2nd Lord of Decies and Desmond (slain with his father in 1260), father by Joan, dau. of John, Lord Cogan, of Thomas Fitz-Maurice, 3rd Lord Decies and Desmond, who *m.* Margaret, dau. of Walter de Burgo, son of Walter, Earl of Ulster, and was father of Maurice Fitz-Thomas, 4th Lord of Decies and Desmond, created by patent, dated 27th August, 1329, Earl of Desmond, and Lord of the Palatine Regalities of the co. of Kerry.

John FitzThomas is presumed to have been also father, by his 1st wife, of—

THE COUNTY FAMILIES OF MERIONETHSHIRE. 713

OSBORN, frequently denominated FitzGerald, but more commonly called by the Welsh heralds *Wyddel* (the Irishman), who emigrated from Ireland, his native country, about the middle of the thirteenth century, and obtained, by grant, marriage, or both, extensive possessions in Merionethshire, including the site of the present mansion of Cors-y-gedol. Osborn's first place of settlement in Wales, it is said, was Berllys, said to be a contraction of Osber-llys, the palace of Osborn, where traces of fortifications may yet be seen, and which is about a mile from the former place. This patriarch of the Geraldines of the Northern Cambrian Principality was assessed in the parish of Llanaber, co. of Merioneth, towards a tax of a fifteenth in 1294. He had an elder son,—

CYNRIC AP OSBORN, who, on the division of his father's lands, according to the custom of gavelkind, then prevalent in Wales, inherited Cors-y-gedol as a portion of his share. He was father of—

LLEWELYN AP CYNRIC, who *m.* Nest, or Nesta, dau. and co-h. of Griffith ap Adda, of Dolgoch, in the parish of Towyn, and of Ynys-y-Maengwyn, co. of Merioneth, a collector of the fifteenth in 1294, raglot (governor) of the comote of Estimaner, 3 and 7 EDWARD III.; living 17 EDWARD III.; derived from Madoc, son of Cadivor ap Gwaethvoed, Lord of Cardigan. By this lady Llewelyn had an eldest son,—

GRIFFITH AP LLEWELYN, of Cors-y-gedol, farmer of the office of Sheriff of Merioneth, 46 Edward III.; sheriff 15 Richard II.; woodwarden of the comote of Estimaner at some period between 7th July, 1382, and 12th October, 1385; *d.* probably between 29th September, 20 Richard II., and same day, 1 Henry IV. Griffith ap Llewelyn *m.* Efa, dau. of Madoc ap Ellis, of Cryniarth, in that co., and sister and co-h. of Llewelyn ap Madoc, Bishop of St. Asaph 1357—1375, derived from Owain Brogyntyn, Lord of Edeirnion, seised of Porkington (Brogyntyn), co. Salop, living 1161 —1166, youngest son of Madoc ap Meredith, last Prince of Powys. By this lady he had (with a dau., Angharad, wife of David ap Grono, of Burton, Flintshire, who with two daus., Efa and Angharad, were living 7th October, 4 HENRY VI.) a son and successor,—

EINION AP GRIFFITH, Esq., of Cors-y-gedol, woodwarden of the comote of Estimaner at one time between 7th July, 1382, and 12th Oct., 1385; captain of forty archers for the king from the co. of Merioneth, 10 Richard II.; living at Michaelmas, 20 Richard II. Einion *m.* Tangwystl, dau. of Rydderch ap Ievan Lloyd, of Gogerddan, co. of Cardigan, a distinguished Welsh bard, and had issue—

1. Iorwerth ap Einion, of Ynys-y-Maengwyn, co. Merioneth, farmer of the Ville of Towyn (lessee of the Crown dues or revenues in that district) at Michaelmas, 1415.
2. IEVAN AP EINION, of whom presently.
3. Griffith ap Einion, who, upon the division of his father's lands, under the law of gavelkind, *s.* to Cors-y-gedol. He held the office of woodward of the comote of Ardudwy, in Merioneth, at Michaelmas, 1400, and also in 2 and 3 HENRY V. Griffith was progenitor of, 1st, the Vaughans of Cors-y-gedol; 2nd, Yales of Plas-yn-Yale; Rogers Wynn, of Bryntangor (refer to YALE OF PLAS-YN-YALE).

1. Mali, *m.* 1st to Howel Sêle, of Nanney, now Nannau; and 2nd, to Owen ap Meredith ap Griffith Vychan, of Neuadd-wen, in Powysland.

2. Tibod, *m.*, 1st, Howel ap Ievan ap Iorwerth, of Cynllaeth; 2nd, Ievan Vychan ap Ievan Gethin, of Abertanat; and 3rd, Howel ap Tudur ap Grono. The 2nd son,—

IEVAN AP EINION, one of the Barons of Edeirnion, co. Merioneth, appears as one of the jurors in an inquisition held at Bala, 6th October, 1427. He *m.* Angharad, dau. and co-h. of David ap y Gwyn Llwyd, Baron of Hendwr-yn-Edeirnion in that shire, and had issue—

1. DAVID AP IEVAN AP EINION, "gentilman," who was appointed, during the ascendency of the house of Lancaster, Constable of the castle of Harlech. He *m.* Margaret, dau. of John Puleston, of Emral, in Flintshire, and left issue.
2. RHYS, of whom presently.
3. Griffith, of Hendwr, living in 1461, *m.* Isabel, dau. of Ievan ap Adda, of Pengwern, in Denbighshire, and from this marriage derived the house of Hendwr.
4. Thomas, living in 1461, *m.*, and had issue.
5. John, living in 1461.

1. Margaret, *m.*, 1st, Madoc ap Howel; and 2nd, John ap David Lloyd ap Howel, who held in farm the extent lands of the Crown in Penllyn in 1481.
2. Mali, *m.* David ap Rhys, 5th Baron of Kymmer-yn-Edeirnion, co. of Merioneth, of the royal line of Powys, one of the jurors in an inquisition held at Bala in October, 1427; he was dead 25th October, 23 HENRY VI., 1444, as appears by his inquisition, *post mortem*, taken 8 HENRY VII. (1492-93), which was returned into the Exchequer of Caernarvon.

The 2nd son,—

RHYS AP IEVAN, whose name occurs upon juries impanelled in Merionethshire, 27 and 31 HENRY VI., in the former of which years he was foreman, *m.* Gwenhwyvar, only dau. and h. of Howel Vaughan, of Fronoleu, co. Carnarvon, lineally descended from Owen Gwynedd, Sovereign Prince of North Wales, and had two sons, IEVAN and Rhydderch. The elder,—

IEVAN AP RHYS, living 4th March, 1513. *m.* Laurea, dau. and h. of Richard Bamville, and had (with two daus., one the wife of Morgan ap Robert, the other *m.* to John ap Madoc Vychan) a son and successor,—

JOHN AP IEVAN, Gent., of Glyn, living in October, 1545. He *m.* Gwenever, dau. and at length co-h. of Griffith ap Edneved, of Sylvaen, in Merionethshire, by whom (who was afterwards wife of Thomas ap Humfrey, Gent., of Berriew, co. Montgomery, and was living 4th June, 1578) he had, with two daus., one son,—

ROBERT WYNNE AP JOHN, Gent., of Glyn, who *m.*, about the year 1544, Katherine, dau. of Ellis ap Maurice, Esq., of Clenenney, Carnarvonshire, Sheriff of Merionethshire 1541,. and had two sons and three daus. Robert Wynne ap John was living 23rd April, 1592. His elder son and successor,—

MAURICE AP ROBERT WYNNE, Esq., of Glyn, *m.*, 1st, about the year 1588, Marselie, dau. of Cadwalader, one of the younger sons of Meredith ap Evan ap Robert, Esq., of Gwydir, and had one son, Cadwalader, who *d.* before his father, *s. p.*; he *m.*, 2ndly, Agnes, dau. of Robert ap Richard, Gent., of Llecheiddior, in Carnarvonshire, by whom (who was *b.* 1557, and *d.* 1623) he had two sons and three daus. Mr. Wynn was living 9th February, 1609-10, but *d.* 16th April, 1611. He was succ. by his eldest surviving son,—

WILLIAM WYNNE, Esq., of Glyn, High Sheriff for Merionethshire in 1618 and 1637, who d. December, 1658. He m. Katherine, eldest child of William Lewis Anwyl, Esq., of Park, co. Merioneth, by whom (who d. 23rd February, 1638-9) he had issue, with six younger sons and four daus., an eldest and a 2nd son, viz.,—

1. ROBERT.
2. Maurice, of Moel-y-Glo, Sheriff for Merionethshire in 1671, who m. Jane, dau. and h. of Griffith Lloyd, Esq., of Maesyneuadd, ancestor by her of the WYNNES, by change of name NANNEYS OF MAESYNEUADD.

The eldest son,—

ROBERT WYNNE, Esq., of Glyn, High Sheriff of Merionethshire 1657 and in 1669, m. in 1625, when he was a mere child, Katherine, eldest dau. and h. of Robert Owen, Esq., of Ystymkegid, co. Carnarvon, by whom (who d. 1675) he had issue—

1. OWEN WYNNE, Esq., of Glyn and Ystymkegid, Sheriff of Merionethshire 1674, of Flintshire 1675, and of Carnarvonshire 1676, who m. Elizabeth, dau. and co-h. of Robert Mostyn, Esq., of Nant, in Flintshire, 5th son of Sir Roger Mostyn, Knt., of Mostyn, and had two daus.—

(1) Margaret Wynne, h. of Glyn, Ystymkegid, and the other estates of her family, b. 7th June, 1663; m., in 1683, Sir Robert Owen, Knt., of Porkington, in Shropshire, and Clenenney, Carnarvonshire, M.P. for the co. of Merioneth (see ORMSBY GORE).

(2) Catherine, b. 13th August, 1664; m. to Peter Pennant, Esq., of Bichton, co. Flint, and d. in December, 1700.

2. Ellis, d. unm. 28th January, 1691, aged 52.
3. Robert, d. s. p.
4. WILLIAM, of whom presently.
1. Jane, b. in 1643; m. Ellis Brynkir, Gent., of Brynkir, co. Carnarvon.
2. Anne, m. to Rees Wynne, Esq., of Cynon, co. Montgomery, who d. in 1688.
3. Frances, d. unm. 29th October, 1675.

The 4th son,—

WILLIAM WYNNE, Esq., m. his cousin, Elizabeth, only child and h. of Maurice Jones, of Wern, and Frances Wynne, his wife, by whom (who d. 1715) he had—

WILLIAM, his heir.
Catherine m., 1st, Owen Owens, Esq., of Cefn, co. Carnarvon, who d. in 1712; 2ndly, Griffith Jones; and 3rdly, Edward Nanney.
Frances d. unm. in March, 1700.

Mr. Wynne, High Sheriff of Carnarvonshire 1686, was s. at his decease, January, 1701 or 1702, by his only son,—

WILLIAM WYNNE, Esq., of Wern, b. about the year 1685, who m., 1706, Catherine Goodman, h. of Elernion, co. Carnarvon, only dau. of Gabriel Goodman, of Beaumaris, merchant, by Elizabeth his wife, one of the daus. of William Glynne, Esq., of Eleirnion. By her (who d. 1743) he had—

WILLIAM.
Elizabeth, m., 27th October, 1732, the Rev. Richard Nanney, of Cefndeuddwr, in Merionethshire.
Catherine, m., 6th November, 1738, Francis Lloyd, of Monachdy, Anglesey, Sheriff for that co. in 1761.

Mr. Wynne, High Sheriff for Carnarvonshire in 1718, d. 1721, and was succ. by his only son,—

WILLIAM WYNNE, Esq., of Wern, b. 1708, High Sheriff for Carnarvonshire in 1735, and of Merionethshire in 1750, who m., June, 1744, Ellinor, dau. and at length heiress of the Rev. Griffith Williams, of Llandegwning and Aberkin, in Carnarvonshire. By her (who m., 2ndly, Evan Evans, Esq., of Penbryn, in the same co., and d. 1804) he had an only son, and successor at his decease, 13th April, 1766, viz.,—

WILLIAM WYNNE, Esq., of Wern, b. 1745, who m., December, 1771, Jane, eldest dau. and sole h. of Edward Williams, Esq. (a younger son of John Williams, Esq., of Bodelwyddan, Flintshire, one of the sons of the Right Hon. Sir William Williams, Bart., Speaker of the House of Commons in the reign of King CHARLES II.), of Peniarth, in Merionethshire, by Jane, Viscountess Dowager Bulkeley, his wife, and had issue—

WILLIAM, his heir.
Richard-Owen, m. Miss Sarah Pearce, by whom he had an only dau., who d. young. He d. in 1821.
Jane, m., in 1798, John Hornby, Esq., of The Hook, in Hampshire.
Elizabeth, m. Charles-James Apperley, Esq., and d. 1834.

Mr. Wynne, High Sheriff for Merionethshire 1772, and of Montgomeryshire in the following year, d. 20th July, 1796, and was succ. by his eldest son,—

WILLIAM WYNNE, Esq., of Peniarth, b. 19th September, 1774; m., 30th November, 1800, Elizabeth, youngest dau. and co-h. of the Rev. Philip Puleston, D.D., of Pickhill Hall, in Denbighshire, by Annabella his wife, eldest dau. of Richard Williams, Esq., of Penbedw, in the same co., youngest brother of the 1st Sir Watkin-Williams-Wynne, Bart. By this lady (who d. 16th June, 1822) Mr. Wynne had issue—

WILLIAM-WATKIN-EDWARD, the present representative.
Philip-Puleston, b. March, 1803; d. 15th Aug., 1838, unm.
Richard-Owen, b. March, 1804; d. 1st January, 1832, unm.
Thomas-Arthur, b. 1812; d. 1821.
Elizabeth-Annabella, m., 1823, William-Pierrepont Gardiner, Esq., son of the Rev. Frederick Gardiner, of Combe Hay, co. Somerset, and d. 1826.
Ellinor, m., 1823, Richard Burton-Phillipson, Esq., 2nd son of the Rev. Richard Burton-Phillipson, of Herringswell, in Suffolk.
Emma-Charlotte, d. 13th September, 1819.
Jane-Sydney (twin with Emma-Charlotte), m., 3rd November, 1840, Joseph Gill, Esq., of Baildon, co. York.
Harriet-Anne, m., in 1828, Richard-Owen Powell, Esq., only brother of William-Edward Powell, Esq., of Nanteos, co. Cardigan.
Augusta-Frances, m., 28th April, 1840, George-Jonathan Scott, Esq., of Betton Strange, in Shropshire, and Peniarth-ucha, Merionethshire.

Mr. Wynne was Sheriff for Merionethshire in 1812, and d. 8th February, 1834.

Note.—The mansion of *Peniarth* (see *engraving*, p. 652) is a large and substantial erection of brick and stone, the oldest part remaining having been built in 1700. On the estate is the manor-house of the ancient manor of Tal-y-bont, giving its name to the hundred of Talybont, in which it is situated. Prince Llewelyn ap Gruffydd (see pp. 653—671) and King Edward I. each dates a letter from this manor-house, which was the property of the Prince of North Wales.

ANNALS, &c., OF WALES.

MONMOUTHSHIRE.

(MYNWY.)

FROM *Myn-wy*, the ancient Cymric name of the "Monnow" river, and *Aber-Mynwy*, the name of the confluence of that stream with the Wye, we have got by translation the English name of *Mon-mouth*, the mouth, or aber, of the Monnow, as first the name of the site, then of the town, and next of the county. Some have conjectured that the root *Mon* is the same as *mawn*, turf or "peat," while *wy* is known to mean water, and that the original compound expresses, therefore, the character of a stream beginning its course in a peaty region.

SECTION I.—PHYSICAL DESCRIPTION OF MONMOUTHSHIRE.

This county takes the general form of a nearly equilateral parallelogram, one side being on the Severn estuary, the eastern side on the Wye and Monnow, the northern on the Monnow and part of Breconshire, and the western on Glamorganshire. It is included in the ancient *cantrefs* of *Gwent Uwch-Coed*, *Gwent Is-coed*, and *Gwent-llwg*, but does not contain the whole of those cantrefs. Its greatest length from a point in the Black Mountains on the north to the Goldcliff headland on the south is thirty-one miles; its greatest breadth from the point where the Wye enters the county, near Monmouth, to the banks of the Rhymney, near Tredegar, is twenty-eight miles. The superficial measurement is 496 square miles, or 368,399 acres, three-fourths of which may be considered under cultivation, or covered with rich woodland. The population of late years, through the increase in mining and manufacture, and the frequent settlement of families of position, attracted by the scenery of the Wye and the Usk valleys, has exhibited a rapid advance.

Total population of Monmouthshire in	1801	...	...	45,582.
,,	,,	1831	...	...	98,200.
,,	,,	1841	...	...	134,355.
,,	,,	1851	...	...	184,449.
,,	,,	1861	...	...	174,633.
,,	,,	1871	...	...	195,391.

In 1861 the county contained 33,077 inhabited houses, 2,021 uninhabited, and 226 in course of erection; in 1871, 35,488 inhabited, 1,668 uninhabited, and 201 in course of erection. It will be observed that in the present century the population has increased more than fourfold. In the two decenniads between 1831 and 1851 the stimulus given to population by the growth of the coal and iron industries was very marked, and increasingly progressive; between 1851 and 1861 a considerable relapse occurred, but the decenniad 1861—1871 more than recovered the loss.

Monmouthshire is invested with every natural feature which can render a district rich and beautiful. It has mountains and rivers which, if not on the largest scale, are eclipsed by none in their attractiveness. One of its sides lies on an estuary which has much of the appearance of a great inland lake, fringed on the opposite shore with the woodlands of Gloucestershire and Somerset, and subject to the remarkable spring tides which rush up the Severn from the Bristol Channel, rising at Newport to forty feet, and at Chepstow sometimes to sixty feet—the highest tidal altitude observed in Britain. The eastern side, along the Wye and Monnow, is bordered with landscapes unsurpassed in richness of form and colouring; through the centre, from south to north, runs the rapid Usk (*Wysg*), hung on either side with garlands of luxuriant vegetation; and followed beyond Abergavenny, where the river makes a *détour* in coming from Brecknockshire, we are met by the bolder magnificence of the Sugar-loaf and Skyrrid Fawr.

LLANOVER: THE SEAT OF THE RIGHT HON. LADY LLANOVER.

On the Usk, near Abergavenny, is *Llanover*, the chief country seat of the Right Hon. Lady Llanover, and a place which, through its association with her ladyship's name as a patron of the literature and supporter of the lore and traditions of her country, as well as with the name of the late Lord Llanover, has acquired not only a charm for the Welshman's ear, but a fame far wider than the boundaries of Wales.

In connection with the genealogical account of the Llanover family (see *Llanover, The Right Hon. Lady, of Llanover*) will be found copious notices of the mansion and its precincts. The interior is fitted up in the style of the most sumptuous residences; it contains a library of great extent and value, comprising choice works in various languages, with rare manuscripts; and large collections of precious works in painting and statuary. The hospitality of Llanover is known to all. At times the noble owner throws open her mansion to regale her guests with the choicest music of Wales, performed by persons dressed in the proper costume of the country, and using no language save the ancient speech of the Cymry. The late illustrious Baron Bunsen, who married the sister of Lady Llanover, was frequently a guest at this notable house, and was known, like most cultured Germans, to hold in high esteem the Cymric tongue, as a branch of the Celtic family of languages.

Not far from Llanover, in the fertile champagne country between Abergavenny and Monmouth, is *Llanarth*, the principal seat of John Arthur Edward Herbert, Esq. (see *Herbert of Llanarth*), representative of the elder branch of the ancient *Herbert* family. Llanarth was a very ancient Elizabethan mansion, with terraced gardens, at the bottom of which flowed the river or rivulet of the Clawr. The old fabric was unfortunately taken down by the grandfather of the present possessor, and its loss, as a monument of antiquity, is to be regretted. The present mansion is a striking specimen of modern architecture, and contains a magnificent suite of apartments filled with interesting family pictures and objects of *vertu*. The cellars are the only remaining portion of the ancient building, the walls of which are of such remarkable strength and thickness that a castle is believed to have originally stood upon the spot. The church, of a very early date, was formerly in the gift of the family; but was disposed of to the dean and chapter of Llandaff many years ago. The living of Llansantffraed still belongs to Mr. Herbert of Llanarth.

Llanarth commands a splendid view of *Pen y Val* and other mountains near Abergavenny; and its park is distinguished by some of the oldest and finest timber in a county famed for its forest trees. We have already alluded to its collection of family portraits, amongst which may here be particularized a portrait of Mr. Morgan of Penllwyn, whose only daughter, Florence, married the heir of Llanarth, and brought the Penllwyn estate into that family.

Mr. Morgan's portrait is a whole-length figure in a buff jacket, with a sword pendent from a sash across his shoulders, and a spear in his right hand; his head is bare, with hair flowing as in the costume of the time of Charles I. At his side stands a beautiful boy (his son) in a red dress, who is handing his helmet to him; both have large boots and gilt spurs. The companion picture is that of Mrs. Morgan, his wife, dressed in a black hood and gown with slashed sleeves; sitting near her is a figure of the same boy, holding in one hand a spear, and in the other a pair of lady's gloves. These curious portraits were formerly on panels in the fine hall at Penllwyn, and were brought from thence to Llanarth by the present possessor.

There are portraits of Sir Philip Jones, the gallant defender of Rhaglan Castle during the siege by Fairfax, and of Lady Jones, his wife. Another interesting portrait is that of Lady Arabella Fermor, the heroine of Pope's "Rape of the Lock." She is painted with the cross to which the well-known lines allude,—

> "High on her breast a radiant cross she wore,
> Which Jews might kiss, and infidels adore."

Another portrait is that of Lady Rachel, daughter of William, second Duke of Devonshire, and his wife Rachel, dau. of William, Lord Russell, and sister of Wriothesley, Duke of Bedford, who married Sir William Morgan of Tredegar. The inscription upon the ground of the portrait is "Lady Rachel Cavendish, a noted beauty."

Tre-Owain, the ancient and historic mansion of the Herberts, now of Llanarth, was built by the Welshman *Inigo Jones*, and was originally a large and splendid residence; but a considerable part has been taken down since Llanarth became the chief residence. The number, size, height, decorations of the apartments, the grand staircase of solid oak, and a fine screen, give striking evidence of the taste and magnificence of the beginning of the sixteenth century. The front of the house, faced with hewn stone, is distinguished by a beautiful porch. Over the entrance is a shield bearing the arms of the family, containing nine quarterings, of which the first are the three lions rampant of the Herberts.

Penllwyn Sarph is the old seat of a collateral branch of the Morgan family, whose last male heir was Henry Morgan. He died without issue in 1757, and left the estate to his sister Florence (or Florens), who married John Jones, Esq., of Llanarth. The place, which stands on a height and commands a magnificent view, is now used as a farmhouse, the venerable appearance of which is much heightened by great wide-spreading sycamores, in appearance coeval with the building. Though very ancient, it is quite capable of restoration to its original beauty. The name is supposed to be Druidical, and signifies "the chief grove of the serpent." The site was formerly surrounded with wood, but this was cut down before it was inherited by the present possessor.

Llansantffraed, also the property of Mr. Herbert, is more especially interesting as the ancient seat of *Tomas ap Gwilym*, from whom the Earls of Pembroke, Powis, and Carnarvon are descended, and the Dukes of Beaufort by the female line. Tomas ap Gwilym acquired Llansantffraed in the reign of Richard II., by his marriage with Maud, daughter of Sir John Morley, Knt., Lord of Raglan Castle. Tomas ab Gwilym died in 1438, and was buried in the church of Llansantffraed. This church contains a curious sepulchral inscription recording his death and that of his successors to the year 1624. Llansantffraed is still kept up, and is now the residence of Major Herbert, younger brother of Mr. Herbert of Llanarth.

Of former residences of the Herbert family, Perth-hîr, which vied for antiquity with *Gwernddû*, was one of the residences of Gwylim ap Siencyn, Lord of Gwerndd first who adopted a surname in conformity with the English law, and the fine patronymic of *ap Hywel* became corrupted into *Powel*, by which name that branch has been since known. He was killed at the battle of Banbury.

His lineal descendant, John Powel, Esq., dying without issue male, the estate passed into the family of Lorimer, one of whose ancestors had married a Powel of Perth-hîr. The mansion was formerly surrounded by a moat, provided with two drawbridges. It is now considerably reduced from its former size, and is used as a farmhouse. The ancient estates of the Herberts were once so large that they stretched from Perth-hîr to near Ross.

Troy, near Monmouth, now the residence of the Duke of Beaufort in this county, was another of the seats belonging to the family of Herbert. Tomas Herbert, son of Sir Gwylim ap Tomas, and brother of the first Earl of Pembroke, resided at Troy and died there. The Earl of Pembroke's natural son was called "Sir William Herbert of Troy." Elizabeth, daughter and heiress of William, second Earl of Pembroke, of the first creation, married

PHYSICAL DESCRIPTION OF MONMOUTHSHIRE.

Charles Somerset, first Earl of Worcester, by which marriage Troy came into the possession of the Somerset family. (See *Troy House;* and *Raglan Castle.*)

Clytha House, the seat of W. R. J. F. Herbert, Esq., also in this part of the fertile vale of the Usk, and on one of the high roads from Abergavenny to Monmouth, is a substantial mansion in an extensive park having many fine trees, and entered by an elegant Gothic archway. Although the surface in these parts is only diversified by undulations, these are often sufficiently lofty to command prospects of considerable extent; from the natural richness of the soil, superior husbandry, and tasteful ornamentation, the landscape is everywhere beautiful, while at no great distance the eye rests on a grand amphitheatre of hills.

Pantygoetre House (J. D. Berrington, Esq.) is in the same vicinity; and nearer Pontypool is *Nantyderry House,* situated on a gentle rising, surrounded by a fertile and richly wooded country.

NANTYDERRY HOUSE: THE SEAT OF THE REV. THOMAS EVANS (*from a photograph*).

Goitre House, now the residence of Col. Byrde, is nearer Abergavenny; and within a mile of that town is *Coldbrook Park* (now occupied by Capt. Standish Jackson), once celebrated as the home of the Herberts, and still presenting tokens of its former greatness in an ample park, magnificent trees, and large decorated apartments. On the west of the town lies *Llanfoist House,* one of the residences of the late Crawshay Bailey, Esq.; *Llanwenarth House* (James Humfrey, Esq.); *The Brooks,* the elegant new mansion of Charles J. Hill, Esq., J. P., which lies in that most delightful part of the Usk valley looking towards Crickhowel. *The Pentre* (Mrs. Wheeley) and *Pentre Court* (Rev. Mr. Wood) are prettily situated in the same locality.

Abergavenny is favoured with an investiture of magnificent scenery combining every element of beauty which inland landscape can produce. It stands on a sharp bend of the rapid Usk. North and west the country becomes highly mountainous. In different directions the bold but graceful forms of the Sugar-loaf (1,760 ft.), the rugged Skirrid, or "Holy

Mountain," and the Blorenge (1,720 ft.), present themselves. From the top of the Sugar-loaf, a position easily attainable by the pedestrian, the eye sweeps the rich and diversified rolling plains of Monmouthshire, the vale of the Usk, interspersed with plantations, and the woody hills on its right bank as far as Pontypool; and to the north traverses a sublime wilderness of mountains, from the heights above Llanthony Abbey to the Brecknockshire Beacons, and the distant *Fan* of Carmarthenshire. Taking a wider range, the counties of Salop, Radnor, Hereford, Worcester, Gloucester, Somerset, and Wilts come into view, with the broad estuary of the Severn, and the meandering line of the Wye. The Wrekin in Shropshire, the Malvern and the Mendip Hills, are distinctly visible. Seldom is so little labour as is required to mount the Skirrid and the Sugar-loaf rewarded with a spectacle so sublime and enchanting.

The most northern part of the county consists of a long narrow projection, bearing

TRILEY COURT: THE RESIDENCE OF MRS. FIELDER (*from a pencil sketch*).

slightly westwards by north, and plunging into the wildest parts of ancient *Brycheiniog*, the rugged spurs of the "Black Mountains," and the deep and secluded glens of Gronwy Fawr and Honddu, in the latter of which is *Llanthony* (prop. *Llan-Honddu*) *Abbey*. The defile of Gronwy is memorable for the murder, in 1135, of Richard de Clare (see p. 74). The "Vale of *Ewias*," eight miles long, is universally admired. On the left bank of the Honddu is the church of Cwmyoy; and near the right bank of the Monnow, the remains of *Old Castle*, once the abode of Sir John Oldcastle (Lord Cobham).

The neighbourhood of Abergavenny being so rich in physical beauty, and redolent with traditions and reminiscences—with the names of Vaughan, Herbert, Gam, and De Clare,—it is not to be wondered at that it abounds so much in the residences of persons of taste and leisure. The Vale of Crickhowel, as well as that of the Usk below Abergavenny, is studded with them; the road towards the vale of the *Honddu*, northwards, also brings to view several superior modern mansions, besides the older *White House*, and, notably, the ancient and most interesting baronial hall of *Llanfihangel Court*, the seat of the Hon. W. Powell Rodney, which deserves mention as one of the most venerable of the mansions of Monmouthshire, with grounds, terraces, and interior quite characteristic, an avenue of firs among the finest in the kingdom, and noble oak and chestnut trees. Of its first building there remains no account, but it is certain that the south-eastern part was erected in the year 1559, by Rhys Morgan, the then proprietor of the estate, who in 1576 sold the property to Nicholas Arnold, owner of Llanthony Abbey and its dependencies by grant from Henry VIII. (See further, *Rodney of Llanfihangel Court*.)

On a slope overlooking the valley, and not far from Llanfihangel Court, is *Triley Court*, the beautiful residence of Mrs. Fielder.

In the quiet and fair region between Abergavenny and Monmouth, and midway between the valley of the Usk and the scarcely less beautiful valley of the Monnow, is *Llantilio*

MALPAS COURT: THE RESIDENCE OF MRS. PROTHERO (*from a photograph*).

Court, the residence of the Hon. J. F. Clifford-Butler (see *Clifford-Butler of Llantilio Court*); and not far from the same neighbourhood is *Llanfair Grange* (Mrs. Little).

Returning to the valley of the Usk, and following the downward course of the stream, we find in the fair domains of Pontypool and Usk a number of seats of the county gentry, located amid scenes as luxuriant and delightful as any the eye wishes to dwell upon. Pontypool (a local name, said to be a corruption of *Pont ap Hywel*) is acquiring the reputation of a grimy place, but *Pontypool Park*, the seat of Mrs. Leigh, and John Capel Hanbury-Leigh, Esq. (see *Hanbury-Leigh of Pontypool Park*), surrounded by fine timber and an extensive demesne, is part of a very different world. *Bertholeu House*, Llangibby (Robert Bateman, Esq.); *Blaenavon House* (Edward Kennard, Esq.); *Abersychan* (Josiah Richards, Esq.); *Llangibby Castle*, the old home of the Williams, Baronets (Col. Thomas Wickham); *Beech Hill* (G. R. Greenhow-Relph, Esq.); *Llantarnam Abbey* (formerly the seat of the Bluetts), and several other mansions of note, are in this productive and well-cultivated locality.

Nearer the favoured neighbourhood of Usk we find *Cefn-tilla House*, the seat of Lord Raglan; *Plas-newydd* (Major McDonnell); *Court Blethin* (G. W. Nicholl, Esq.); *The Cottage*, Usk (the Dowager Lady Blake); *Ty-Brith* (Col. R. B. Roden); *Cefn-Ila* (Edward Lister, Esq.); *Scyborwen* (J. Jefferies Stone, Esq.), and others.

As the road approaches Newport, the mansion of *Malpas Court* is passed, standing on a gentle slope, and embowered in a fine plantation. (See *Prothero of Malpas Court.*)

In the immediate vicinity of Newport are several principal seats of the nobility and gentry, among which, by reason both of antiquity and standing, the leading place must be assigned to *Tredegar Park* (see *Tredegar, Baron, of Tredegar Park*). The present mansion, of the time of Charles II., is built of brick, in dimensions and arrangement according to a magnificent scale. The building standing here in the time of Leland (*circa* 1540) is described by that faithful topographer as "a very faire place of *stone*." The park, which contains noble specimens of timber, is in parts uninteresting, almost desolate in expression, but on the side nearest to the Vale of *Ebbwy* is picturesque and luxuriant. The house contains some noble suites of apartments, with paintings and statuary of great value, especially pictures of past members of this ancient family.

CAERLEON, MON.

Machen, near the Rhymney, the western boundary of Monmouthshire, is another mansion belonging to the Morgan family, usually occupied by one of its cadets. Beyond the stream, but in Glamorgan, is *Ruperra*, another of their old abodes. (See *Morgan of Ruperra Castle.*) *The Friars*, adjoining the town of Newport, is the residence of the Hon. C. Octavius S. Morgan, M.P., fourth son of the late Sir Charles Morgan (see *Morgan of The Friars*). *Stow Hill* (W. S. Cartwright, Esq.); *Bassaleg*—prop. *Maes-aleg* (Rev. Chancellor Williams); *Woodlands* (A. Homfray, Esq.); *Bryn-Glas* (Thomas Cordes, Esq.); *Holly House* (W. Treharne Rees, Esq.); *Llanfrechfa Grange* (F. J. Mitchell, Esq.); and *Waun Fawr* (Lawrence Heyworth, Esq.), are also in the near neighbourhood of Newport; while *Tynewydd* (James G. James, Esq.), *Crumlin Hall* (H. M. Kennard, Esq.), and *Farmwood* (Thomas Gratrex, Esq.), lie at various distances.

The wide lowland tract lying between Newport and the sea, stretching east and west from the New Passage to the mouth of the Rhymney, and known as the Caldecot and "Went-loog" levels, forms part of the ancient district of *Gwentllwg* (see *Hist. and Antiq. of Mon.*). In this district, on the banks of the Usk, before *New*port (Castell-*newydd*) had had its birth (see *Newport*), was situated the greatest Roman city in Wales, *Isca Silurum*, now Caerleon, of whose importance little now remains but the indestructible grandeur of the natural scenery around, and fragments of walls, pottery, and altars. (See *Caerleon* under *Hist. and Antiq. of Mon.*) *The Priory* (John Edward Lee, Esq.); *Llanwern House* (late Sir Charles J. Salusbury, Bart.); *The Garth* (Trevor S. Addams-Williams, Esq.); *Glen-Usk* (Samuel Homfray, Esq.); *Spring Grove* (Miss Thomas); *Llansoar* (John James, Esq.), and several other genteel residences, are situated in this eminently historic locality.

When we approach Chepstow and the banks of the Wye, perhaps it can be said with truth that we come to the most beautiful side of this universally admired county. It is the part best known both to natives and tourists, and needs not to be here described. These are now quiet scenes, though in the darker ages of the Church and the State so prominent and stirring. (See *Chepstow Castle, Tintern Abbey*, &c.) *Piercefield Park*, the seat of Henry Clay, Esq.; *Itton Court* (Mrs. Curre; see *Curre of Itton Court*); *St. Pierre* (C. E. Lewis, Esq.); *Crick* (John Laurence, Esq.); and *Sedbury Park* (George Ormerod, Esq.), are found in this charming neighbourhood. From the height of the Wind-cliff, or of Lancaut on the Gloucestershire side of the Wye, the grandeur of the prospect is unsurpassable. Mr. Coxe, the historian of Monmouthshire, mounted the latter eminence, and says, "As I stood on the brow of this precipice, I looked down upon the fertile peninsula of Lancaut, surrounded with rocks and forests, contemplated the hanging woods, rich lawns, and romantic cliffs of Piercefield, the castle and town of Chepstow, and traced the Wye sweeping in true line of beauty from the Bannagor Crags to its junction with the Severn. A boundless extent of country is seen in every direction from this commanding eminence, comprehending not less than *nine counties*. I traced with pleasing satisfaction, not unmixed with regret, the luxuriant valleys and romantic hills of this interesting county; but I dwelt with peculiar admiration on the majestic rampart [the Blorenge range] which forms its boundary to the west, and extends in one grand and broken outline from the banks of the Severn to the Black Mountains,"—

"Where the broken landscape, by degrees
Ascending, roughens into rigid hills,
O'er which the Cambrian mountains, like far clouds
That skirt the blue horizon, dusky rise."—*Thomson*.

The dwellers around *Monmouth* claim for their part not only the respect due to an historic county town, but pre-eminence in point of physical beauty. Many things conspire to justify the claim. The Wye and the Monnow here join; the larger river flows through spacious and fertile meads, while these are terminated in all directions by hills clad in the richest luxuriance and ever-changing hues. *Troy House*, the residence in this county of his Grace the Duke of Beaufort (see *Beaufort, Duke of, Troy House*), is about a mile from Monmouth, and on the little stream *Trothy*—whose name has been corrupted into the more euphonic Troy. We are indebted to his Grace the Duke of Beaufort for several of the heraldic and antiquarian illustrations of this work, copied from the *Progress* of his ancestor, the first Duke of Beaufort, through Wales in 1684, and only recently printed *privately*. To the mode in which the Beaufort family became possessed of this valuable estate, allusion has already been made under the article *Llanarth*. The mansion, surrounded by the richest and sweetest scenery, is said to have been designed by Inigo Jones, but its magnificence is

TROY HOUSE: THE SEAT OF HIS GRACE THE DUKE OF BEAUFORT.

due, not to its architectural design, but to its interior appointments. The elegance and spaciousness of the chief apartments, largely embellished with rare and costly paintings and statuary, and a variety of curiosities of an antiquarian kind, are greatly admired. The cradle of Henry V., who was born at Monmouth, and the armour he wore on the field of Agincourt,

THE BEAUFORT ESCUTCHEON (*from the Beaufort* PROGRESS).

when Fluellen, referring to Cressy, reminds the king of the valour of his countrymen,—" If your Majestie is remembered of it, the Welshmen did goot service in a garden where leeks did grow, wearing leeks in their Monmouth caps," are here preserved.

It may be said that the portion of the Wye bordering Monmouthshire, and a few miles above the town of Monmouth, is that which is most sought after by admirers of the picturesque. The portion of that river bounding Brecknockshire is confessedly fine, and its course through Herefordshire passes through spots of much beauty; but its glories grow and become more and more impressive as it approaches the end of its journey. From Goodrich Court by "Symond's Yat" and the "Doward Rocks" to Monmouth, and all the way thence to Chepstow, its banks are crowded with alternate scenes of bold picturesqueness and softly clad comeliness not often equalled in our island.

The productiveness of this part of Monmouthshire, owing to the rich red sandstone soil, aided by the advanced agriculture introduced of late years by the leading owners and occupiers of the land, is very great. Green crops are all but universal. The yield of

HENDRE—FRONT VIEW: THE SEAT OF JOHN ALLAN ROLLS, ESQ. (*from a photograph*).

wheat, as in Herefordshire, is heavy. The elm and the oak find here their congenial home, and grow to noble proportions. In old times this was doubtless a region for the Welsh to be proud of possessing, a region which nothing but sturdy defence could have prevented the Anglo-Saxons from snatching from their grasp; and it had been no wonder if Henry VIII. had more formally united it to England than he did. As the case stands the noble county of Monmouth remains in all respects (except as it regards the administration of justice, a mistaken popular notion, and the ill-informed practice of map-makers), a part and parcel of the principality of Wales. We shall see further into this point in our historical and antiquarian section.

In the district of Monmouth are located also *Dingestow Court* (see *Bosanquet of Dingestow Court*); *Croft-y-Bwla* (Major A. Rolls); *Hilston House* (P. B. Hamilton, Esq.); *The Hill*

(Capt. George G. Tyler); *The Garth* (Capt. James Davies); and *The Hendre* (John Allan Rolls, Esq.), a mansion of much architectural taste, and of recent renovation. Of this beautiful house we present two views,—the principal front from a photograph, and the courtyard from a lithograph.

We have briefly described the eastern and central drainage of the county by the rivers Wye and Usk and their tributaries; it only remains to mention in few words the western drainage by the Rhymney, Ebbwy, and Sirhowy, the first of which also forms the western boundary between this county and Glamorgan. It is remarkable that almost all these streams, pursuing courses so diverse, and flowing ultimately into the same estuary of the Severn, take their rise in the mountain system of Brecknockshire and its outlying spurs. The Monnow, the Usk, the Gronwy, the Ebbwy, the Sirhowy (the two last-named running together into the Usk below Newport), and the Rhymney, all set out on their beneficent

HENDRE—THE COURTYARD (*reduced from a lithograph*).

journey to water Monmouthshire, and, as it turns out, to convey much of the filth and blackness of the Tartarean region of "the hills" into the all-absorbing sea, from the north-western highlands lying beyond the limits of the county of Monmouth. Rhymney has the task of fertilizing the least productive parts of this county, for it runs through the coldest tracts of the carboniferous field; whereas the Usk and the Monnow lave almost everywhere fat banks of the old red sandstone—a fact rendered conspicuous during heavy rains by the colour of the stream.

All the rivers of Monmouthshire, not altogether excepting the proud and majestic Wye, have in the end to drag their volume into the sea through muddy and slimy channels, quite unworthy of the glory of their previous career. The flats of Caldecot and Went-loog, in great measure the creations, doubtless, of the streams themselves (like the Deltas of the Nile and the Rhone), not only by an almost dead level detain the river, but for the same reason detain the mud thrown into the channels by the tide. Nothing therefore but the scouring action of the powerful Severn tides prevents the increase of delta land along the coast of Monmouthshire.

Section II.—GEOLOGY AND MINERALOGY OF MONMOUTHSHIRE.

In almost every respect the geological formation of this county is the same with that of Glamorgan. The two great systems which divide between them almost the whole area of the county are the Old Red Sandstone and the Carboniferous; the former being by far the more extensive, the latter equally preponderating in point of mineral value. The two are sharply separated from each other by the limestone range of hills commencing with the Blorenge Mountain, west of Abergavenny, and continuing thence in a wavy line generally bearing south, leaving Pontypool on its western skirt, then taking a direction south-west by Machen, and crossing the Rhymney into Glamorganshire. It forms the dividing line between the red sandstone lowland between Cardiff and Whitchurch and the coal district of Caerphilly. That part of Monmouthshire which lies between this limestone line of hills and the Rhymney, enclosing the valleys of the Ebbwy, Sirhowy, &c., contains the whole of the coal and iron works of the county. Here lie Tredegar, Sirhowy, Ebbw Vale, Victoria, Beaufort, Blaenafon, Blaenau, Nantyglo, Abersychan, Pontypool, Risca, and other great works, the mineral products of which, owing to the conformation of the valleys and the consequent concentration of railways, are almost entirely shipped at Newport.

East of the mineral field thus marked off to the west, *i.e.*, east of the mouth of the Rhymney, Pontypool, and Abergavenny, the whole of Monmouthshire, with two or three small and curious exceptions, is taken up by the old red sandstone group, which also monopolizes nearly the whole of Breconshire and Herefordshire. In one place between Usk and Pontypool the power of the old red is broken by a band of the Ludlow and Wenlock rocks of some two miles in breadth, and not less than five miles in length, or from near Llangibby Castle to within a mile of Clytha House, including a good part of the bed of the Usk. These earlier rocks have been forced up by subterranean pressure, and the once superincumbent sandstone carried away to the general level of the country. A second instance of interference with the monopoly of the old red sandstone is found in the neighbourhood of Chepstow, where a tongue of the carboniferous limestone from the coal basin of the Forest of Dean crosses the Wye into Monmouthshire, forming in its course the precipitous rocks which, from the Wind-Cliff to the estuary of Severn, present such bold and picturesque fronts. This limestone bed passes Caldecot and Caerwent, and reaches westward as far as Magor. A fringe of *new* red sandstone, corresponding with the Gloucestershire rocks opposite, passes between this limestone and the Severn margin.

Section III.—HISTORY AND ANTIQUITIES OF MONMOUTHSHIRE.

The district now included in the county of Monmouth was in pre-Roman times part of the dominiom of the *Silures;* and it is next to certain that the principal seat of that people, when the brave Prince Caractacus proved so formidable an opponent of the Romans, was at *Caerwent* (Venta Silurum), in this county. Whatever the importance of the Silurian metropolis at that period, few signs of it now survive beyond crumbling walls, an occasional fragment of pottery, a carved stone, or inequalities of the ground, faintly indicating foundations of buildings, or their mouldering remains:—

> "All to the searching eyes of many an age
> Have offered but a blurred and wordless page;"

and these are the remains of the subsequent *Roman* rather than of the early British city. Although the central seat of the Silures may at this particular time, or generally, have been at Caerwent, the dominion of that distinguished British tribe extended to considerable distances east, west, and north, comprising nearly all Glamorgan, Brecknock, Hereford, Radnor, and parts of other modern counties. Its exact limits it is impossible to determine. The Roman *Silures* is probably a Latin modification of the British *Essyllwyr*, "the men of Essyllt;" but the precise origin of that name is not known. *Gwent* was doubtless an early British name applied to these parts, and is imitated by the Romans in "*Venta* Silurum." (See further, p. 483, &c.)

It was about a hundred years after the first establishment of the Roman power in the south of Britain before the country of the Silures was subdued. Caractacus had been in command against the legions under Aulus Plautius from the beginning of that general's operations against the southern Trinobantes. In A.D. 50, Plautius was succeeded by the great commander, Publius *Ostorius* Scapula, who with great energy pushed on the conquest of the southern and central parts of the island, penetrating as far as Yorkshire, but there was arrested in his progress by the news of the revolt of the Silures under Caractacus.

Of all the tribes of Britain, the Silures proved the most fierce and formidable foes of the Romans, and much of their power and success unquestionably arose from the sublime genius of their great commander. Caractacus for nine long and harassing years kept in check the best legions of Rome, numbering under Plautius 30,000 men; fought with them between *thirty* and *forty* battles, many of which ended in favour of the patriots; and was only overcome in the last struggle as by a hair-breadth of advantage. *Caer-Caradoc*, in Shropshire, is supposed to have been the scene of this disastrous conflict. Tacitus, whose portraiture of the British chief is that of a man of the loftiest character and most commanding ability, tells us (*Annal.*, xii., 34) that Caractacus, before the battle, harangued his soldiers in these memorable words:—"This day must decide the fate of Britain. The era of liberty or eternal bondage begins from this hour! Remember your brave ancestors, who drove the great Cæsar himself from these shores, and preserved their freedom, their property, and the persons and honour of their wives and children." The Britons were ardent for the conflict. Ostorius was dubious of the result, so strong was the position occupied by the patriot chief, and so numerous and disciplined were his troops. The signal for attack, however, after some hesitation was given, and the day decided for the Romans. Caractacus was sent in chains to Rome, where his name was already celebrated as the greatest general opposed to the imperial troops in Britain. "Curiosity was eager," says Tacitus, "to behold the heroic chieftain who for such a length of time made head against a great and powerful empire." Nor were they disappointed in the bearing of the man, now no longer a commander, but a prisoner in chains. His words when brought before the Emperor Claudius were royal words: "If to the nobility of my birth and the splendour of exalted station I had united the virtues of moderation [careful self-direction], Rome had beheld me, not a captive, but a royal visitor and a friend. The alliance of a prince descended from an illustrious line of ancestors, a prince whose sway extended over many regions, would not have been unworthy of your choice. A reverse of fortune is now the lot of Caractacus. The event to you is glorious—to me is humiliating. . . . The ambition of Rome aspires to universal conquest. I stood at bay for years; had I done otherwise, where on your part had been the glory of conquest, and where on mine the honour of a brave resistance? The bloody scene will soon be over, and the name of Caractacus will sink into oblivion. Preserve my life, and I shall be to late posterity a monument of Roman clemency." The noble prince was set at liberty; but whether he ever returned to Britain is not known.

At Caerwent the conquerors planned and built a Roman city with powerful walls and defences, whose outline is still traceable, and, imitating the British name *Gwent*, called it "*Venta* Silurum." The situation was inviting, being on a gentle rise in the midst of a plain, terminating at a small distance north and south in ranges of low hills. The city bounded by the walls appears to have been in the form of a parellelogram, about 500 yards long by 400 wide. The *Via Julia* from Gloucester to South Wales ran through the site, as does now the turnpike road. Leland, about the year 1540, visited the place, and says, "There yet appeare pavements of old streates, and in digginge they finde foundations of great brykes." As might be supposed, many Roman remains, as coins, tesselated pavement, fragments of altars, stamped bricks, &c., have been discovered. To this day many parts of the walls stand high above ground. According to Richard of Cirencester, Caerwent was a British city proper, but recent investigation proves at least its occupation by the Romans.

Some nine miles west of Caerwent, and on the margin of the Usk, stood a still more important city of Roman Britain, *Isca Silurum*, now *Caer-leon* (Caer-legionis). It went often by the designation "Isca [legionis] secundæ Augustæ," because here was stationed the second imperial legion which kept in check the country west of the Wye (*Vaga*). Richard of Cirencester calls it "Isca Coloniæ," because it was a city "possessed by a Roman colony," and invested with the rank of a *colonia*—the only one of that dignity in *Britannia Secunda*, or Wales. This spot competes with Caerwent for the honour of being the seat of Caractacus, and doubtless outshone the glory of that city in the later Roman period. It is now a neat but inconsiderable hamlet, to the casual observer giving no tokens of ancient glory or eventful history, but to all persons of knowledge and reading a spot of surpassing interest. You cross a common bridge and look around on luxuriant meads and hills clad in richest verdure, but witness no colossal ruins, no Corinthian columns with broken entablature, no strong and bastioned walls defying the hands of time. And yet this is the veritable spot where, sixteen hundred years ago, the pomp and splendour of Rome itself were imitated.

It was for two or three hundred years the fiscal, military, and commercial depôt for all the country to the west. It was furnished with all those appliances of luxury and tokens of power and wealth in which, in the degenerate days of the empire, the Romans so much delighted. And we have only to dig beneath the surface, as the local antiquaries have done, to discover substantial proofs of the matter. Altars once smoking with sacrifice to the Roman deities have been disinterred; fragments of columns and friezes, of tesselated pavement, of baths and marble statuary; articles of personal ornament, and of domestic use; weapons of offence and implements of handicraft, sepulchral memorials with the actual names of the dead, have all been discovered, as witnesses, silent but eloquent, to the people, the religion, the industry, the power, which Caerleon knew so many ages ago! The mound of a "great tower" still remains, and there are clear traces of the *amphitheatre* in a meadow adjoining the village.

CAERLEON—THE ROMAN AMPHITHEATRE (*now called "Arthur's Round Table"*).

How impressive are the words of Giraldus Cambrensis, who visited the place in the twelfth century, when many of the great buildings and portions of the fortifications were still standing!—"The city was of undoubted antiquity, and handsomely built of masonry with courses of bricks by the Romans. Many vestiges of its former splendour may yet be seen [this was nearly 700 years after the Roman sway had terminated in Britain], immense palaces, formerly ornamented with gilded roofs in imitation of Roman magnificence, raised by the Roman princes and embellished with beautiful erections; a tower of prodigious size; remarkable hot baths; remains of temples and theatres, all enclosed within noble walls, parts of which remain standing. You will find on all sides, both within and without the circuit of the walls, subterranean buildings, aqueducts, underground passages, and what I think worthy of notice, stones contrived with wonderful art to transmit the heat insensibly through narrow tubes passing up the side walls. . . . The city is well situated on the river Usk, navigable to the sea, adorned with woods and meadows. The Roman ambassadors here received their audience [referring to a post-Roman period] at the court of the great King Arthur, and here also the Archbishop Dubricius [Dyfrig] ceded his honours to David of Menevia."

In the great and solid city thus pictured to us in the dim twilight midway between us and the Roman era, it is believed the renowned King *Arthur* ruled, and the time he flourished is placed a few generations only after the Romans deserted it. This sentiment the Poet Laureate embodies in his song, for according to the "Idylls of the King," Arthur—

"Held court at old Caerleon upon Usk;"

and there, of course, had his *Round Table* and his *Knights*. There, moreover, we are made to see flitting the shadowy forms of Enid, Vivien, and Guinevere, nor is the sage but baffled "Merlin" absent.

How the glory of Caerleon departed, without a syllable in history to tell the tale, it is strange to contemplate. Certain it is that great and many events transpired here after the Britons had recovered their independence. Certain it is that the country was inhabited by a numerous and now cultured race; and there can be no doubt that they had established a kind of government. But of all periods in the history of Britain, whether as bearing upon the fortunes of Wales or England, this is the darkest and most perplexing. Whatever we may think of the romance of Geoffrey of Monmouth, and the tales of bards inferior as poets to Geoffrey, nothing is more probable than that Caerleon continued for ages a theatre of stirring events, and nothing contrary to authentic record lies in the doctrine that such a hero-king as *Arthur*, son of Uther Pendragon, flourished in the fifth century, and that Caerleon was his seat. The fact, which is beyond question, that a mighty and beauteous city, in an inhabited land, the seat of a bishop, the mart of nations, has within the period of history perished out of sight, without a memorial left of it, except what can be extracted from its dust, is far more astounding and incredible than that such a king as Arthur should have lived, and that he should have performed many of the exploits ascribed to him.

The history of Monmouthshire between the age ascribed to Arthur and the conquest by the Normans is involved in much obscurity. We hear occasionally of the existence of *Gwent* as a separate princedom from *Glamorgan*, or *Glewysig;* but sometimes the distinction is lost, and the two districts appear under one rule. We hear of "Ynyr, King of Gwent," in the ninth century, and he appears to have been an authentic person whose lineage descends to leading living families in Gwent and Glamorgan. During the so-called "Saxon Heptarchy" the kings of Saxon and Anglian blood who ruled over the kingdoms set up in England by the subjugation of the Britons of those parts and their incorporation with the conquering race, were in constant war either with each other or with the still unsubdued Britons of Wales, *i.e.*, all the inhabitants to the west of the Severn. Wales became divided at the death of Rhodri the Great (after a temporary union) into the three sovereignties of *Gwynedd* (North Wales), *Powys*, and *Deheubarth* (South Wales), but the last never contained the counties of Monmouth and Glamorgan, which always, either united or separate, maintained a rule of their own. *Asser* (9th cent.) mentions two kings of Gwent,

Brochmael and Fernail, as seeking the protection of King Alfred. Morgan Mwynfawr, after whose name Glamorgan was called (see pp. 459, 485, &c.), at times appears to hold sway over Gwent as well as Glamorgan, and the latter princedom seems to have exercised a kind of superiority over Gwent even when a separate rule existed. At this time, however, the English kings had come to claim a seigniory over the Welsh princes, as we have seen in the case of the quarrel between Howel the Good and Morgan Hên, Prince of Glamorgan, respecting the possession of *Ystrad Yw*, *Ewias*, and *Erging* (now Archenfield), when King Edgar interfered, and forbade Howel to seize those territories.

The Danes, when devastating and ultimately conquering England, were not sparing of their unwelcome visits to Gwent and Glamorgan. They frequently swept away the produce of the

Newport Castle.

Vale of Usk, coming thither only for plunder, and apparently never with a view of settlement. In the year 893, according to the *Brut*, " the Black Pagans " crossed the sea of Severn, and committed great havoc in Gwent, Glamorgan, and Brycheiniog; but Morgan on this occasion repulsed them with great slaughter. The *Annales Cambriæ* call them "Normanni," and give the date 895. Canute himself, in the year 1034, made a descent upon Gwent, and obtained a victory over Rhydderch ap Iestyn, the usurping prince of South Wales; but no further result followed.

The frequent Saxon incursions into the country west of the Wye issued in no conquest, the Gwentians always holding their own with various success. Under Edward the Confessor, Harold the Saxon, afterwards King of England, obtained considerable advantages, and appears to have temporarily occupied the strongholds of Chepstow, Caerwent, Caerleon, and Monmouth, and is said to have erected a palace fortress at Porth-is-coed (now " Portskewet "), where he gave a magnificent entertainment to the king; but the place was soon after rased to the ground by the Welsh, and not a trace of it remains.

The Norman conquest of Gwent and Glamorgan (*circa* A.D. 1092-4), one of the greatest events in the history of Wales, has already been in great measure detailed. (See *Glamorganshire—Norman Period.*) With this conquest the rule of the native princes of the district finally disappears. We do not find that Fitzhamon partitioned much of the country of *Gwent*—a term generally applying to the country between the rivers Wye and Usk—between his followers, as he did Glamorgan; but it is clear that his conquest included the greater part of what is now called Monmouthshire; and that he retained as part of his own lordship the whole of the level district between the Taff and the Usk, including the site of

PENCOED CASTLE.

the present *Newport*, and, presumably, the famous city of *Caerleon*. His successors, the Earls of Gloucester, were lords also of this district. On the decadence of Caerleon the Welsh had erected a fortress nearer the sea, which they called *Castell-Newydd* (the New Castle), referred to by Giraldus Cambrensis (A.D. 1188) under the name *Novus-burgus*, a literal rendering of the Welsh; but the loosely translated name "Newport" is of much more recent birth.

At this place, already a post of strength, the Normans erected a castle—one of that wonderful series of twenty or thirty fortresses in this county which rose under the wand of the Lords Marchers, and to this day, in their very desolation, attest the terribleness of the struggle which for 300 years the Normans maintained against the people of Gwent.

The building of the castle whose ruins still survive at Newport—a relic of antiquity clinging to life amid the devouring operations of the growing trade and commerce of that thriving place—is attributed to Robert, Earl of Gloucester, natural son of Henry I., and son-in-law and successor of Fitzhamon, conqueror and first Lord of Glamorgan. In right of his wife, Maude, Robert had acquired the lordship of Monmouth as well as Glamorgan— a fact which shows that Fitzhamon's lordship included great part of Gwent. This castle passed in succession, along with that of Cardiff, through the hands of the great Lords of Glamorgan—the De Clares, Le Despencers, Beauchamps, Nevilles, and Herberts.

Memorials of the same system of martial and irresponsible rule now established in Gwent are the castles of *Pencoed*, near Magor; of *Penhow*, *Llanfair*, and *Stirguil*, in the hilly district of Went-wood, with which sometimes is confounded the castle of Chepstow. The ruin of Pencoed Castle is very picturesque : its history is almost a blank,—even the name of its first builder being unknown.

On the little stream which laves the foot of ancient *Caerwent* and joins the sea at

CALDECOT CASTLE.

" Portskewet," and at the distance of a mile from the latter, is the extensive ruin of *Caldecot Castle*.

The great forest of Went-wood probably spreads itself as far as the margin of Caldecot level, and the little inlet at " Portskewet "—a name which is in all likelihood a corruption of *Porth-Is-coed* (" the Iscoed inlet," *Iscoed* being the name of the comot containing it)— would need a stout fortress to guard the interior possessions of the Lords Marchers against the sudden inroads of the incensed and unappeasable Welsh from the Severn sea. Hence in the defile at " Caldecot "—a corruption perhaps of *Cil-y-coed* (" the wood or forest defile ")—was erected the powerful stronghold of that name. Its actual origin is not known, nor can its architectural features be made to pronounce decisively as to its age or nationality. Several styles seem to combine to give it a perplexing variety of expression, as if Welsh, Saxons, and Normans had all had a hand through successive possessions in its rearing ; but the prevailing style is Norman, and the truth is likely to be that its age is later than the 11th century, and that strength rather than beauty or graceful symmetry was contemplated in its erection. The great family of De Bohun, Earls of Hereford and Constables of England, for a long time were its possessors, and they, possibly, were its builders. Not unfrequently, however, it fell to other masters, as the will of the sovereign determined; for the lease of the liege was the will of his suzerain. The first De Bohun, Humphrey, came to England with the Conqueror; his grandson, also named Humphrey, married the daughter and heiress of Milo, Earl of Hereford, and thus came into possession of the lordship. They were created Earls of Hereford in 1199, the second of that title being one of the barons who enforced Magna Charta, and the first of his line to hold the office of " High Constable of England." The De Bohuns became extinct in 1372.

ABERGAVENNY CASTLE (*from a drawing by Birket Foster.*)

A lordship of great power during the Norman feudal period in Monmouthshire was that of *Abergavenny*, the lord of which is usually styled in later ancient documents " De Bergavenny." This interesting town, surrounded by a display of landscape beauty seldom surpassed, was once strongly walled, and defended by a powerful castle—the whole having their origin in the Lord Marcher conquest. This lordship seems entitled to priority of date over either Brecknock or Glamorgan, its captor having lost no time in acting upon the royal licence to plunder. Hameline de Baalun, or Baladun, recorded as one of the adventurers who came to the conquest of England with William the Bastard, was, amongst others, commissioned to try his fortune on the Welsh borders. He subdued the district of Over-Went (the Welsh cantref of *Gwent Uwch-Coed*), and established his head-quarters at Abergavenny, where, like a hawk building his nest, he planted his warlike fortress. But he died almost immediately (1090), and without issue, when his nephew, Brian de Wallingford, clutched the prey. All these robber chiefs, to compensate, as they thought, for their cruelty and injustice, founded priories and churches, and endowed masses to be said for their souls. Hameline de Baladun founded a priory at Abergavenny, and there he was buried. As peace amongst the robbers was never of long continuance, the Lords Marchers maintained among themselves almost incessant feuds and wars; and so it happened that one man's lordship to-day became another's to-morrow. This was also partly the result of the arbitrary decisions of the sovereign, from whom all these unlawfully gotten lands were held *in capite*.

The castle of Abergavenny was held in succession by Walter of Gloucester, Philip de Breos, William de Breos, the Cantelupes, the Hastings, Beauchamps. Philip and William de Breos, father and son, lived under the reigns of Henry II. and Richard I. The Cantelupes got in by marriage with Eva, the heiress of de Breos, and the first of their line, William, is said to have been summoned to Parliament by Henry III. as Baron de 'Bergavenny, though no record of the fact appears to be extant, and to have been the first who assumed this title. The Hastings began as inheritors of the lordship with John, nephew of the last Cantelupe, A.D. 1272. The Beauchamps inherited by maternal descent from the Hastings, William Beauchamp being the first, A.D. 1392. Then came the Nevilles, in the last of which the title, Baron of Abergavenny, has continued uninterrupted since the year 1450, when Edward Nevill, son of Ralph, 1st Earl of Westmoreland, was summoned to Parliament as a baron by writ. He inherited the barony of Abergavenny by marriage with Elizabeth, heiress of Robert Beauchamp, the last baron of that line.

The name of William de Breos, Lord of Abergavenny, stands prominently in the darkest page of history as a man of boundless cruelty and duplicity. We learn from Matthew Paris and Hollingshed that, A.D. 1176, "William de Breause, having got a great number of Welshmen together into his castle," under pretence of friendly consultation, "proposed this ordinance to be received of them with a corporall oth," that "no traveller by the waie amongst them should beare any bow or other unlawful weapon;" "which oth when they refused to take because they would not stand to that ordinance, he condemned them all to death. This deceit he used towards them in revenge of the death of his uncle, Henry of Hereford, whom, upon Easter Even before, they had through treason murthered, and were now acquitted with the like againe."—*Hollingshed*, ii., 95. An incident of the time of Brian de Wallingford, the second Lord of Abergavenny, is given at p. 74. These were times of violence, unscrupulous lawlessness, and mad revenge in Upper Gwent, as, indeed, through the whole of the Marches of Wales.

The fortresses of *Grosmont, Skenfrith, White Castle,* were also defences of the Norman conquest of Upper Gwent—the first and second standing on the river Monnow, the third at half-distance between that river and Abergavenny. Grosmont Castle is an imposing and picturesque ruin, little known by reason of its distant situation, but in itself, and by reason of the fair scenes by which it is surrounded, worthy of inspection and admiration. It is regretted that a photograph of it could not be obtained for our pages. The position is high and commanding, overhanging the Monnow. The castle, which is in the Gothic style, built on the site of an earlier one, is thought to be of the thirteenth century. It was attacked by Llewelyn, Prince of Wales, but not taken; continued prominent during the wars of the Marchers; and was a favourite residence of the Earls of Lancaster.

White Castle (Castell Gwyn, said to be so called from Gwyn ap Gwaethfoed) is a great ruin, on the crown of a moderately high ridge. It had six irregular towers—one between 50 and 60 feet high. The entrance is guarded by two advanced massive towers, with portcullis and drawbridge, on the usual plan of a Norman fortress. The moat has been estimated at 14 feet deep by between 40 and 70 feet wide. The age of this great stronghold is unquestionably early—coeval with the first conquest of Upper Gwent. It probably originated with Brian de Wallingford, or his successor, but it is surprising how little is known of its history.

Llantony Abbey (properly *Llan-Honddu* Abbey), situated in the sequestered and beautiful mountain valley of the Honddu, north of Abergavenny, is a ruin of considerable extent. Giraldus, who visited the place in 1188, when its glory as a religious house was at its highest, has bestowed upon it a long and extravagant panegyric. "The situation was truly celebrated for religion, and more adapted to canonical discipline than all the monasteries of the British isle. The monks sitting in their cloisters, enjoying the fresh air, when they happen to look up towards the horizon behold the tops of the mountains [the Hatterel Hills], as it were, touching the heavens, and herds of wild deer feeding on their summits." Unintentionally, the picture he draws of the internal life of a monastery, even in so favoured a spot, is not inviting. There had been disputing and division and malversation in past times, and recently part of the monks had schismatically set up a priory at Gloucester, which seemed to trouble the spirit of Giraldus; but he sees their reward. "All the priors of this establishment, who were its enemies, died by divine visitation. William, who first despoiled the place of its herds and storehouses, being deposed by the fraternity, forfeited his right of sepulture among the priors. Clement seemed to like this place of study and prayer; yet, after the example of Heli the priest, as he neither reproved nor restrained his brethren from plunder and other offences, he died by a paralytic stroke. And Roger, who was more an enemy to this place than either of his predecessors, and openly carried away everything which they had left behind, wholly robbing the church of its books, &c., was also struck with paralysis long before his death."

"A rival daughter sprang up at Gloucester, under the protection of Milo, Earl of Hereford; as if by Divine Providence [Giraldus had singular notions of Providence], and the merits of the saints and prayers of those holy men (of whom two lie buried before the high altar), it were destined that the daughter church should be founded in superfluities, whilst the mother continued in that laudable state of mediocrity which she had always affected and coveted." Then we have a passage whose rhetoric is better than its Christianity. "Let the active therefore reside there, the contemplative here; there the pursuit of terrestrial riches, here the love of the celestial; there let them enjoy the concourse of men, here the presence of angels; there let the powerful of this world be entertained, here let the poor of Christ be relieved; there, I say, let human actions and declamations be heard, but here let reading and prayers be heard only in whispers; there let opulence, the parent and nurse of vice, increase with cares, here let the virtuous and golden mean be all-sufficient," &c., &c.

The abbey was of the Cistercian order, and was founded by William de Lacy, a Norman knight, in 1103, and afterwards largely endowed by Hugh de Lacy. It is considered one of the earliest structures in England in the Pointed style. It was suppressed at the dissolution. Mr. Lyne, under the name of "Father Ignatius," has of late been attempting to resuscitate monastic practices at this place in connection with the Church of England, but with less than moderate success.

Monmouth, the *Blestium* of Antoninus's *Itinerary*, became in Saxon times one of the posts of occupation of that people after their conquest of the parts between the Severn and the Wye—the ancient princedom of *Feryllwg*, or Ferlex. But there exists no evidence that the Welsh did not regain possession of this district, and retain it till the descent of the Normans. The conquest of Glamorgan and Gwent, under Rufus, by the venture of Fitzhamon and other knights, involved the district of Monmouth, and now, in all probability, were erected the fortifications, whose remains in part still continue, and whose outlines were

MONMOUTH BRIDGE, OVER THE MONNOW, WITH AN ANCIENT CITY GATE.

almost perfect when Leland visited the town in the sixteenth century. It then had four gates remaining,—Monk's Gate, Eastern Gate, Wye Gate, and Monnow Gate. The Monnow Gate, shown in our engraving, is the most perfect one, and the only gate now existing. *Monmouth Castle*, occupying an eminence, is now represented by a mere fraction of the powerful fortress once proudly cresting the hill, and for several generations the abode of royal possessors. Monmouth, as appears from *Domesday*, was made part of the king's demesne, and "De Monmouth" was afterwards added to the royal titles. Under Henry II. the renowned *John de Monmouth* was the lord of the place, and ceded his rights to Prince Edward, afterwards Edward I., to whom many of the castles of Wales were given. (See *Tomb of John of Monmouth*, p. 738.)

Monmouth continued in the Plantagenet line till it came to John of Gaunt, who married Blanche, daughter and heiress of Henry, Duke of Lancaster. Henry of Bolingbroke, afterwards Henry IV., son of John of Gaunt, was next owner; and here was born his distinguished son, Henry V., the hero of Agincourt, called "Harry of Monmouth," and who

HISTORY AND ANTIQUITIES: MONMOUTH IN 1684.

was proud, if Shakspeare be true, after the victory of that field, gained mainly by the aid of Welshmen, to respond to the impetuous Fluellin,—

"I am Welsh, you know, good countryman."

It afterwards came by inheritance, as part of the Duchy of Lancaster, to Henry VI., on whose attainder it fell to Edward IV. William Herbert, afterwards Earl of Pembroke, received it for a time, but on his death at Banbury it reverted once more to the king, and was part of the Duchy of Lancaster which fell to the share of Henry VII. In 1646 the castle was garrisoned for Charles I., but was attacked and taken by the Parliament, since which time it has gradually fallen into decay.

His Grace Henry, first Duke of Beaufort, ended his lordly *progress* through Wales in 1684 at Monmouth, and his own residence of Troy (see *Troy House*). Some interesting notes are found in the *Progress*, bearing upon the Monmouth of that day. Even then "the castle of Monmouth had nothing to show but the ruine of its ruines." "The bells of the church are said to have been brought out of France by order of Henry of Monmouth in his conquests, and say'd to be lettere'd about thus:—𝔐𝔦𝔰𝔰𝔞 𝔡𝔢 𝔠𝔬𝔢𝔩𝔦𝔰 𝔠𝔞𝔪𝔭𝔞𝔫𝔞 𝔰𝔲𝔪 𝔊𝔞𝔟𝔯𝔦𝔢𝔩𝔦𝔰." Respecting the tomb of John of Monmouth it is noted, "On the right hand entering the great south door is seen the monument of marble, anciently gilt and painted, and small figures on the sides and ends, obscured by the injury of the usurper's soldiers, and now

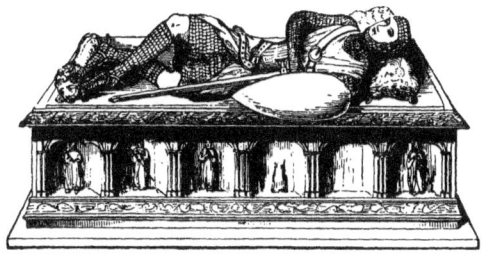

TOMB OF JOHN OF MONMOUTH—(*Beaufort Progress* 1684).

preserved by church pews and seats erected near it. The townsmen say it represents *John of Monmouth*. They show you also, in an old coffer near the chancell, his coate of maile and gauntlett, there being neither inscription nor arms on the shield discernible to give other light" (p. 231).

The Duke with his cavalcade, having lodged the night before at Ruperra Castle, arrived at Monmouth on the 19th August (1684), "where the regiment of foot of this county were then drawn into lines, making a guard from that town even to the walls of *Troy*, another magnificent place belonging to the Earle of Worcester [son of the Duke, himself afterwards second Duke of Beaufort], commander of this regiment, and were not onely all that accompanied his Grace through the Progress, the Deputy Lieutenants of the Militia here, but a numerous traine of Militia officers and gentry out of other neighbouring English counties were splendidly enterteined by the sayd noble Earle. The next day, company encreasing, to wait upon the Duke of Beaufort [Lord President of Wales and the Marchers, we must remember, and representing the authority of Charles II.], ample enterteinments were repeated by the Right Hon. Charles, Earle of Worcester, upon the same place, such as anticipate all enconium, &c. His Grace, accompanied with the Earle of Worcester, Sir John Talbot, — Aubery, Esq., and several of the deputy lieutenants of the adjoining counties, took a view of the Militia Regiment of this county of Monmouth, when the Earle of Worcester at the head of it on foot, as Colonell, with his leading staff, saluted his Grace, severall of the principal gentry, as Sir John Talbot, &c., placing themselves in front of the stand of pikes, doublings, countermarches, wheelings, variety of exercise, and good and close firings, were made; whence the Mayor and ye rest of the Magistracy of Monmouth Town, in their formalities, invited his grace to accept of the freedom of the place, &c."

"That done, his grace with all the gentleman that accompanied him to Monmouth Town Hall, were collationed there with a cold treat, during which the Militia Horse, then led by Sir Charles Kemis, gave severall vollies; and the troopers were treated as they were mounted with syder and ye noted Monmouth ale, drums beating, trumpets sounding, and bells ringing, so that each horse—

' Motus clangore turbarum,
Saxa quatit pulsa, rigidos vexantia frenos
Ora tenens, spargitque jubas et surrigit aures,' &c. ;

and from thence he was reconducted by the Mayor, his brether'n of Monmouth, and county troop, to *Troy*."

SEAL OF THE TOWN OF MONMOUTH—1684 (*Beaufort Progress*.)

So ended the memorable *Progress* of the 1st Duke of Beaufort through Wales and the Marches, begun on the 12th of July. He had started from Chelsea, through Chipping Norton and Worcester city, and thence through the counties of Salop, Montgomery, Denbigh, Flint, Carnarvon, Anglesey, Merioneth, Brecon, Carmarthen, Pembroke, Glamorgan, and Monmouth. He rode in a chariot of state, and was followed by a considerable retinue on horseback. The progress was rapid, although, through the badness of the roads, laborious, and the company were royally entertained at chief mansions in the respective counties,—such as Powis Castle; Chirke Castle; Mostyn; Baron Hill (called then Beaumaris); Gwydir; Rhiwlas; Llwydiarth; The Priory, Brecon; Golden Grove; Margam; Keven-Mably; Ruperra Castle. The object of the progress was doubtless to inspect the military forces of the counties, which in every case were brought out and paraded before the Lord President. His Grace was accompanied by a scholarly, rather pedantic gentleman, T. Dineley, Esq., who took notes of places and things, interspersing the whole with learned and often long quotations from the classical authors, and various curious and quaint remarks, and notices of churches, monuments, castles, &c. Clever sketches also were taken of buildings, arms, seals, and monuments, but whether these were by Mr. Dinely or another hand is not stated. This valuable account had lain in MS. in the archives of the Dukes of Beaufort up to the year 1864, when his Grace the present Duke resolved to have it printed. It has, however, not been published, and only a very limited number of copies were struck off. The editing was done by Charles Baker, Esq., F.S.A., and the printing and illustrations are in the most artistic and tasteful style. The Duke of Beaufort has most liberally and obligingly allowed the transference of many of the illustrations of arms, monuments, seals, and buildings (which are unique, and could not otherwise be recovered), from the *Progress* to the present work.

Henry, 1st Duke of Beaufort, was a man of great talent, the son of a man of world-wide celebrity—that Marquess of Worcester known as the author of *A Century of Inventions*, and the grandson of that venerable soldier who made himself memorable by his defence, at the age of eighty-four, of his castle of Raglan in 1646. (See *Beaufort, Duke of, of Troy House*.) The family of Somerset has been foremost in the service of the country at home and abroad, and in the patronage of letters, art, and general culture for many ages. In fact, the roll of the nobility of England contains no more illustrious names.

The magnificent ruin of *Raglan Castle*, in an undulating and fertile part of the county between Monmouth and Usk, in many respects stands foremost among the ancient remains of Britain, as Heidelberg Castle stands among the castles of the Neckar and the Rhine. It is not of the extent of Caerphilly or Carnarvon, nor of the antiquity of Harlech, Rhuddlan, or Chepstow; but it is of an age sufficient to make it venerable, and so decked with manifold beauty of design and execution as to awaken a sense of boundless admiration, mixed with unavoidable regret that a human work so grand and mighty should be lying ingloriously in the dust. It is a satisfaction, as the spectator wanders among the ruins, to observe the care bestowed by the noble owner upon the preservation from further decay of this "storied" place, and the admirable intelligence, the gentle sense of sympathy with glory in ruin, and the skill which maintains permanence without any appearance of busy "restoration," everywhere so visible. The Duke of Beaufort deserves the thanks of all men, of antiquarians especially, for the manner in which not only the ruins of Raglan, but the many relics of antiquity on his estates, are kept.

The first founding of Raglan Castle is not noted in history; but the spot on which it stands is known to have been occupied by a fortress some centuries before the present castle in its main parts was built. In the thirteenth century the De Clares were owners of Raglan. It passed from them to the Berkeleys, who possessed it only for a brief period. Next after them, and in the time of Henry V., we find it in the hands of Sir William ap Thomas, son of Sir Thomas ap Gwilym ap Jenkin (see *Herbert of Llanarth; Llanarth; Llansantffraed* &c.). His son, Lord William *Herbert*, of Raglan, afterwards Earl of Pembroke, had the custody for some time at his castle of Raglan of the Earl of Richmond, afterwards Henry VII. The last William Herbert of Raglan died without issue male, and his estates passed with his daughter and heiress, Elizabeth, to her husband, Sir Charles Somerset, created afterwards Earl of Worcester, who *d.* 1526. The property has ever since continued in this noble family.

The castle is said to exhibit a variety of styles, indicating progressive erection, some parts being apparently as early as the reign of Henry V., when the possessor was the above-named Sir William ap Thomas, some as late as Charles I., and believed to have been the

RAGLAN CASTLE – THE GREAT GATEWAY.

work of its last occupant, the gallant Marquess of Worcester, who, after a most heroic

RAGLAN CASTLE—ROYAL APARTMENTS.

defence, yielded it up on honourable terms to the army of the Parliament in 1646, and died in the same year.

The plan of the castle includes two great quadrangles, the first entered by the grand portcullised gateway shown in our first engraving, the second communicated with from the first

WINDOW OF DRAWING-ROOM.

In the range of buildings running between these courtyards were the great state apartments, the groined ceilings, carved bosses and corbels, mullioned windows, and elaborate fireplaces of

RAGLAN CASTLE, FROM THE MOAT.

which, even now in their desolation, tell of the elegance and splendour which surrounded the Lords of Raglan Castle in the sixteenth and seventeenth centuries. The keep, or citadel of this castle was as remarkable for its massive proportions as the more ornate interior was for delicacy of design and artistic execution. It stood separate from the main building on the south side, and was of later date than the greater portion of it; the form was that of a hexagon, each of the six sides measuring 32 feet; the walls were 10 feet thick and five stories high, built of solid square stones of the red sandstone strata of the country, the colour of which is said to have occasioned the name by which this enormous structure was known— *Twr Melyn Gwent*, "the Yellow Tower of Gwent." Some, however, have conjectured that the meaning is *Twr Melin Gwynt*, "the Windmill Tower." So powerfully constructed was the citadel that the artillery of the Parliamentary army, which only carried shot of twenty pounds, failed to do much damage except to its elegantly finished battlements; these, being of less thickness and solidity, were demolished. Time has since largely supplemented the work of Fairfax's siege. The citadel was connected with the castle by a bridge, powerfully

RAGLAN CASTLE—THE KITCHEN.

defended by lateral walls, turrets, and battlements, and spanning a moat 30 feet broad, and of great depth, which ran all round the citadel. But even such a place as this, intended as the last refuge in time of siege, and so mightily planned and protected, was not able to shelter the aged marquess, and his garrison of 800 men supported at his own cost, in defence of a failing cause. The army of the Parliament, commanded by the renowned Fairfax, whose head-quarters were at *Cefn-tilla*, night and day hailed its missiles upon the devoted fabric, all supplies were cut off, a breach was effected in the eastern curtain, drawbridge, ponderous gate, and portcullis were demolished; but at the last moment honourable terms were accepted, and the noble-hearted owner was allowed to quit his castle with colours flying and honour untarnished, but with a sense that he had but too faithfully served a weak and faithless king, now to receive as reward the confiscation of his splendid estates, and final ruin of his princely halls. He was taken prisoner to London, where he died in the same year, receiving thus a friendly riddance of all his troubles. His estates, valued at £20,000 per annum, were recovered by the family at the Restoration, but shorn of much of their beauty, and greatly reduced in value. Raglan Castle, in the fourteen years which had elapsed, had been dismantled; the great park, "planted with fine maiden oaks and large birch trees, richly stocked with all kinds of deer," and stretching away to great distances across woodland, plain, and river, had been converted into a barren wilderness. The Stuart dynasty and the popular vengeance it awakened had writ their names on the fair demesne of Raglan in characters many of which are not to this day obliterated.

The *castle of Usk* (*Wysc*), was once of large dimensions. From the magnificence of the scenery around, it is no cause of wonder that Richard Duke of York delighted to reside here. It is said that this was the birthplace of his two sons, Edward IV. and Richard III. When it is remembered that Henry V. was born at Monmouth, where his cradle is still exhibited (see *Troy House*), Monmouthshire will appear to have enjoyed sufficient honour of this kind. The fact is that as a land of castles it offered a safer asylum in those troublous times than even most parts of England.

The Castle of Usk, after belonging to Richard III. and Henry VII., became the property of William, first Earl of Pembroke, the second branch of the Herbert family. Philip, his fourth descendant, dying in 1683 without issue male, his only daughter and heiress, Charlotte conveyed it (by marriage) to Thomas, Viscount Windsor.

The estates in Gwent, possessed by this second branch, were scarcely inferior to those of the first Earl of Pembroke of the Herbert blood. Philip, the last proprietor of Usk Castle, could have passed almost the whole way through his own manors from the vicinity of Monmouth to Newton Down beyond Cowbridge (*Pen-y-Bont*) in Glamorgan, a distance of nearly sixty miles. The trustees of his daughter, in their annual circuit, were not unfrequently escorted by more than fifteen hundred of her tenants and dependents from Chepstow to the castle at Cardiff, where the accounts were audited and the rents received.

Charlotte, the heiress of Usk Castle, by her husband, Thomas, Viscount Windsor and Lord Montjoy, had a son, Herbert, who sold Usk Castle (now possessed by the Duke of Beaufort); and died in 1758, leaving two daughters—Charlotte Jane, married, 1766, to John, Lord Mountstuart (see *Marquess of Bute*), and Alice-Elizabeth, first wife of Francis, second Marquess of Hertford.

On our way to glance at that age of monkish religion and architectural magnificence in Gwent which is commemorated by *Tintern Abbey*, on the Wye, we pass the only large monument of the so-named *Druidic* religion and age now surviving in the county of Monmouth—the *stones*, or *cromlech* of *Tre-lech* (*tri*, three; and *llech*, a stone), which consist of three great stones set on end. The fine ruin of *St. Briavel's Castle*, built by Milo Fitzwalter, Earl of Hereford, *temp.* Henry I., is opposite, on the Gloucestershire side of the Wye but in the feudal ages was part of that system of the Marches which was not bounded by the

Wye, but extended from Gloucester to Brecknock, and from Chester to Cardiff. This was the Milo, Earl of Hereford and Lord of Brecknock, who held the jest with earnest Gruffydd ap Rhys on the margin of *Llyn Savathan* related at p. 56. The object of this castle was to check the Welsh in their incursions across the boundary into the Forest of Dean; but it is scarcely probable that the walls now remaining were built so early as the reign of the first Henry.

The situation of the abbey of *Tintern*—(*Din*, a high place of strength; *teyrn*, king) the name probably of an adjacent hill,—almost as much as the marvellous beauty of the architecture, contributes to the powerful effect produced by the spectacle of this majestic ruin.

TINTERN ABBEY—GENERAL VIEW, FROM THE WYE.

It has been pronounced "the most beautiful and picturesque of all our Gothic monuments." And the situation is one of the finest the old monks ever chose for the site of an abbey. It is enough to say that this spot is superior even to the site of Llantony. The abbey is planted on a meadow lying in a bend of the river, flanked at the back by an abrupt swelling of craggy hills clad in oak, ash, and hazel; in front, up stream, below, and everywhere the bold hills, the retiring glades, the rocks, and their green investment of timber and brushwood, vie with each other in offering to the eye the most graceful outline, the most varied and harmonious detail of light and shade. The noble Wye in its windings seems to flow out of a hill-side above, and into a hill-side below. Every nook and dell, every crag and mountain-top, the trim cottage, the white-sailed pleasure-boat, the leaping salmon, and the deep-designing angler on the brink, seem all brought together on purpose to give this glorious ruin a framework worthy of itself and of the broad page of Gwentian history it aids to fill.

Tintern Abbey has had a longer age as a ruin than it had of active service. "Man purposeth," &c. Its builders in planning those massive clustered pillars, those aspiring arches, buttressed to bear a "lanthorn tower" of mountain weight, those slenderly mullioned, richly traceried windows, as high again as the gables of many churches, the solidly vaulted roofs which once spanned cloister, chapterhouse, and hospitium, were in their own minds erecting a structure to compete with the hills in durability—and whose very dismantled and dishonoured shell seems now to defy time and elements in its demolition. But that vast labour and cost, thought, skill, and loving interest only issue in a pile of magnificence whose

TINTERN ABBEY, LOOKING UP THE NAVE TO THE EAST WINDOW.

topstone is scarcely set, and its matin and vesper bell scarcely begin their regular silvery notes before its knell is sounded and destruction sends down its storm of hail. It was, in fact, but the splendid efflorescence of a decaying body, which England found it on the whole, though with much regret and pain, necessary to remove. And so the "lanthorn tower" is gone long ago to mend the roads and fill up gaps in rustic fences; the beautiful tracery, the carved work in foliated boss and moulding, faces of saints and angels, the very effigies of mailed knights and gentle dames, founders and benefactors, have been cast out as rubbish, and ground into dust!

In the year 1130, some eight or nine and twenty years after the Norman had laid his iron hand on the Cymry of Gwent and Glamorgan, Walter de Clare, son of Gilbert de Clare, whose family had obtained certain territory in Wales, founded here a small priory for monks of the Cistercian order;—

> "A little lonely hermitage it was,
> Down in a dale, hard by a forest's side,
> Far from resort of people."—*Faëry Queen.*

THE WEST WINDOW, FROM THE CHANCEL.

Under the thrifty hands of the monks and frequent donations of the lords, who revelled in wealth gotten by robbery of the now prostrate inhabitants, it grew apace into importance. It had not, however, risen into note, and the building, now in ruins, had not been erected when Giraldus Cambrensis in 1188 passed through Gwent. Gilbert de Strongbow, Earl of Pembroke, the builder of Aberystwyth Castle, son of Richard de Clare, and owner then of the neighbouring castle of Striguil, largely endowed it, and his example was followed by the Earls of Pembroke, his successors. But it was Roger Bigod, Earl of Norfolk (son of Maud, sister and co-heiress of Anselme, last Earl of Pembroke of the Marshal line), who built Tintern Abbey, in 1268. This was the year in which it was so far finished that the monks for the first time celebrated mass within it; but the building had doubtless been proceeding for many years, and probably continued long after. If we calculate the completion of the abbey to be about A.D. 1300, it will be seen that the period of its survival was 236 years, for in 1536 Henry VIII. issued the mandate for the dissolution of the monasteries. Tintern Abbey and its lands, valued at no more than £132 1s. 4d., and having only thirteen monks, were granted to Henry Somerset, second Earl of Worcester, in whose family they still remain. The present Duke of Beaufort bestows great care upon the *preservation* of these beautiful remains, while avoiding all unsightly and ill-placed "restoration."

The plan of the abbey is cruciform; and the subsidiary buildings, such as the cloisters, chapterhouse, refectory, hospitium, or guest-chamber (where "open house" was kept for the pilgrim and the stranger in need), the kitchen, &c., were ranged on the northern side flanking the abbey as far as the eastern side of the transept. The length of the abbey was 228 feet; the nave and choir were only 37 feet wide, and the extreme width at the transepts was 150 feet.

The east window, shown in our second view, with its single mullion remaining, is 64 feet high, and occupies the whole width of the choir. The great central arches supporting the tower (when the tower was there) are 70 feet high. Through these the spectator looks at the eastern and western windows in the respective engravings. The western window, with almost all its mullions and tracery still complete, is 42 feet high. This window, as shown in the engraving, is in great part covered with ivy. The tops of the walls, along which are convenient pathways, are covered with turf, and here and there ornamented with spontaneous growth of shrubs and trees. Along the pillars, arches, and windows, the friendly ivy is allowed to twine and hang in garlands, and the floor, once shining in encaustic tiles, is covered with a carpet of greensward, through which the bases of the northern pillars of the nave crop up. (See *Engraving*, p. 747).

From Tintern Abbey to *Chepstow Castle* is but a small distance in space, but, with all the defects of the monastic system, the transition is like descending from a world of civilization to a world of barbarism. The monastic and the Lord Marcher systems lived contemporaneously, agreed in holding man in bondage, were mutually supporting, and died by the same hand; but taken and analyzed separately they are seen to have been animated by a different life, and lived with different aims. As Macaulay has eloquently written, "A system which, however deformed by superstitions, introduced strong moral restraints into communities previously governed only by vigour of muscle and audacity of spirit; a system which taught even the fiercest and mightiest ruler that he was, like his meanest bondsman, a responsible being, might have seemed to deserve a more respectful mention from philosophers and philanthropists. Had not such retreats been scattered here and there among the huts of a miserable peasantry and the castles of a ferocious aristocracy, European society would have consisted merely of beasts of burden and beasts of prey."

The town of Chepstow, as its name indicates, was a place of barter between the Saxons and Welsh (A.-Sax., *ceap.*, price, or bargain, *ceapian*, to bargain, sell; and *stoc*, euphonized *stow*, a stockaded or defended place), after the former had taken possession of the country between the Severn and the Wye. From the importance of the position in all times of war we may conclude that the Britons had here a place of strength, although it was not then a custom to erect castles. The Welsh name of Chepstow, *Casgwent*, *i. e.*, Castell Gwent, probably originated after the building of the present castle. The Anglo-Saxons, as they are called, or, more correctly, the governments set up in South-west and Central England after the amalgamation of the old Britons of the parts and their Germanic conquerors into one people—on taking possession of the British princedom of *Feryllwg* (Ferlex), which embraced the lands between the Wye and the Severn, would as soon as possible seize and strengthen this post, making it a place of trysting and negotiation with the independent Britons of the west. It is said that parts of the castle of Chepstow contain indications of "Saxon" work—a thing, however unlikely, not quite so incredible as the statement made by some others to the effect that some of its walls were built by "Julius Cæsar," who, it is well known, never penetrated halfway to Chepstow.

The stupendous ruins of Chepstow Castle are beyond question the remains of Norman work. It is quite improbable that the whole was built by the same owner or in the same age, for there are varieties of style and irregularities of plan showing the contrary. No castle in Britain stands on a grander site. It occupies along the margin of the Wye an almost perpendicular limestone cliff (part of the carboniferous system of the Forest of Dean), through which the river has excavated a passage. It is so closely built to the edge that its huge walls and the native rock appear all as one. Its building is ascribed to William Fitz-Osberne, Earl of Hereford, who is stated to have been a relation of the Conqueror and one of his companion knights in the invasion of England (although we find not his name in the *Roll of Battle Abbey*), and who had lands assigned him on the borders of Wales, including the basin of the lower Wye. This was the Fitz-Osberne who before the expedition started from Normandy, and when many chieftains were opposed to William's enterprise, cried out, " Why dispute ye thus ? He is your lord ; he has need of you. It were better your duty to make your offers, and not to await his requests. If you fail him now, and he gain his end, by heaven, he will remember it" (*Chronique de Normandie*). Fitz-Osberne prevailed, and was well rewarded. His life, however, was cut short by violence in Flanders, where he was involved in a love affair, and it is improbable that he had leisure after settling upon his possessions in Wales to build to completeness such a giant fortress as Chepstow Castle. His younger son, Roger Fitz-Osberne, succeeded to his vast estates in this county, his eldest son William to his estates in Normandy—for Fitz-Osberne was a man of note and seneschal of the duchy in his own country, and not a mere hungry military adventurer like most of William's companions. Roger Fitz-Osberne was a man of deep designs, and likely for his own purposes to build a fortress such as Chepstow Castle. While William was gone to Normandy to quell an insurrection, another was brewing for him in England and in Wales. Roger Fitz-Osberne had arranged and carried out without William's permission a marriage between his own sister Emma and the great Breton *Ralf de Gael*, Earl of Norfolk. It led to a rupture with the Conqueror and a terrible insurrection, in which the Welsh, who saw in Ralf the Breton a man of their own kin, heartily joined, and in which Chepstow Castle was fitted to play an important part. During the marriage rejoicings the conspiracy against the Conqueror was formed. Several bishops and abbots, many Norman barons and Saxon warriors, bound themselves by oath against King William (*Will. of Malmesb.*). But William's good fortune prevailed. Ralf was obliged to fly to his own land of Brittany, and Roger Fitz-Osberne was made a prisoner for life. " The race of William Fitz-Osberne," says Ordericus Vitalis, " has been uprooted from England, so that now there is not a corner in which it can set its foot."

The earldom of Hereford and the castle and lands of Chepstow passed to the Earls of Pembroke of the De Clare line, then to the Marshals and Herberts, and lastly to the Somersets, in which (now represented by his Grace, Henry, Duke of Beaufort) they still remain.

HISTORY AND ANTIQUITIES: CHEPSTOW CASTLE.

The ground-plan of the castle is long and narrow, stretching along the dizzy steep of the rock in massive walls and towers of various heights, and enclosing four separate courts, as if added by degrees as necessity required. The great entrance is from the side towards the town. The noble gateway is defended by two circular towers of great strength, portcullis, &c. Around the first court were arranged the grand hall, principal apartments, kitchen, &c.

A TOWER IN CHEPSTOW CASTLE.

On the side next the river the curtain between the first and second courts is pierced by a gateway. Another gateway enters the third court, in which was situated the chapel, a building of remarkable elegance, 90 feet long by 30 in width, with walls 40 feet high. The fourth court had its own entrance by a drawbridge and portcullis across the castle ditch, flanked by two square towers.

In the grand court first mentioned is the *keep*, a structure of large dimensions and wonderful solidity and beauty. It contained, amongst other parts, the tower, made celebrated through the confinement within it for twenty years of the republican Henry Marten, member of the "Rump" parliament (probably for some place in Berks.), once a friend of Cromwell, and one of those who signed the death warrant of Charles I. The parliament made a gift of

Chepstow Castle to Oliver Cromwell, but on the accession of Charles II. it reverted to the Marquess of Worcester, and Henry Marten became one of its involuntary occupants.

> "For thirty years, secluded from mankind,
> Here Marten lingered. Often have these walls
> Echoed his footsteps, as with even tread
> He paced around his prison."—*Southey*.

CHEPSTOW CASTLE—MARTEN'S TOWER, IN THE KEEP.

Marten's "tread" and temper may have become "even" after years of schooling within thick prison walls, but by nature he was of a choleric and impetuous turn, and of a loose and ill-governed life. When Cromwell entered with his guards to send the "Rump" about its business, this is the description (perhaps not unfaithful) we have of this man :—" Henry Marten is a tight little fellow, though of somewhat loose life; his witty words pierce yet, as light arrows through the thick oblivious torpor of the generations, testifying to us very clearly, Here was a right hard-headed, stout-hearted little man, full of sharp fire and cheerful light, sworn foe of cant in all its figures, an indomitable little pagan if no better. 'You call yourselves a Parliament, continues my Lord General in clear blaze of conflagration; 'you are no Parliament, some of you are drunkards, some of you are—' and he glares at Harry Marten and the poor Sir Peter [Wentworth], who rose to order, lewd livers both— 'living in open contempt of God's commandments.'"—*Carlyle*. After the Restoration, Marten was tried as a regicide at the Old Bailey, when he put in the plea that in concurring in the king's death and signing the warrant he only yielded obedience to the existing government. Perhaps his " lewd living " told in his favour with the court of Charles II.; at all events though found guilty, his life was spared. He was sent to the Tower for a time, and thence transferred to the keep of Chepstow Castle for the rest of his life. The term of his imprisonment here was twenty, not thirty years, as stated by Southey; he was allowed to retain his property, to have the company of his wife, to walk abroad under guard, and to pay visits to the gentry of the neighbourhood. He died in 1680, at the good age of seventy-eight, and was buried in the chancel of Chepstow Church. Over him was placed an acrostic epitaph, rather long, of his " own composition," and containing these lines :—

> "A true Englishman,
> Who in Berkshire was well known
> To love his country's freedom, 'bove his own. . . .
> Examples preach to th' eye ; care then, mine says,
> Not how you end, but how you spend your days."

CHEPSTOW CASTLE—THE ORATORY IN THE KEEP.

Among other fine apartments in the keep, most of which are believed to have been at the service of Henry Marten, was a beautiful "oratory," which it may be hoped, from the last line of his epitaph, he had learnt how to use.

As in other cases when Norman lords plundered and built castles, so at Chepstow, religious houses were founded, partly by the robber as a condonation of his crimes, partly by the monks as a means of counteracting the barbaric violence of the times. Some of the remains of the *Priory* of St. Kynemark are still traceable near the entrance to *Piercefield*. Remains of several "chapels" and other "religious" edifices are found in the town near the principal hotel, and in Bridge Street. A *Benedictine priory* of large dimensions stood on the site of the churchyard, and the present parish church embodies many portions of that building in good preservation, although disfigured by injudicious "restoration." This church contains a fine early monument to Henry, second Earl of Worcester (*d*. in 1549), great grandfather of the intrepid Henry, first Marquess of Worcester, owner and defender to the last extremity of Raglan Castle against the victorious Fairfax. (See *Raglan Castle*.)

The *walls* of Chepstow in part still remain. Their age is uncertain, but Norman features prevail in them; and it cannot be doubted that the building of the castle would be accompanied by the fortification of the town. But proof is wanting that the present walls are the first erected.

This magnificent castle and military post had upon the whole a quiet history. Its most stormy crisis was its last, when the wrath of the Parliament and the flaming zeal of the Welsh for Church and King met and fought here. It was in 1648. Charles was prisoner at Carisbrook. The Scotch in the north send an army of 40,000 to the field. The Welsh rush headlong into the fray. Chepstow is garrisoned under command of Sir Nicholas Kemeys. Pembroke is held fast by "drunken Col. Poyer," and Cardiff is strong under Col. Pritchard: the gentry are all for the King; the common people understand nothing, and follow the gentry. The Parliament's cause is in peril. Cromwell must march, or all will be lost; and Cromwell accordingly marches, 3rd March, 1648. In good time, while the general is hotly marching for Chepstow, the battle of St. Fagan's, under Horton, (8th May), ends in victory for the Parliament, and General Laugharn, with Stradlings, Kemeyses, &c., are broken in pieces. Cromwell breaks the walls of Chepstow; but tough Sir Nicholas, with his small remnant of a garrison of forty men within the castle, though sorely pressed, refuses to surrender, secretly planning escape by the river; but the scheme failing, the castle is stormed by Ewer (left in command by Cromwell, who has gone on to Pembroke), and Kemeys and his men are cut down without mercy.

From Pembroke, 7th June, Oliver writes to Major Thomas Saunders: "I have sent to have you removed out of Brecknockshire; indeed, into that part of Glamorganshire which lieth next Monmouthshire. For this end:—We have plain discoveries that Sir Trevor Williams of Llangibby, about two miles from Usk, in the co. of Monmouth, was very deep in the plot of betraying Chepstow Castle, so that we are out of doubt of his guiltiness thereof. I do hereby authorize you to seize him; as also the High Sheriff of Monmouth, Mr. Morgan [see *Sheriffs*], who was in the same plot. But because Sir Trevor Williams is the more dangerous man by far, I would have you seize him first. He is a man, I am informed, full of craft and subtlety, very bold and resolute, hath a house at Llangibby well stored with arms and very strong." . . . If you should march directly into that country and near him, it's odds he either fortify his house or give you the slip. . . . Wherefore you have a fair pretence to go out of Brecknockshire to quarter about Newport and Caerleon, which is not above four or five miles from his house. You may send to Col. Herbert, whose house lieth in Monmouthshire, who will certainly acquaint you where he is. You are also to send to Capt. Nicholas, who is at Chepstow, to require him to assist you, if he [Williams] should get into his house and stand upon his guard. Samuel Jones, who is quartermaster to Col. Herbert's troop, will be very assisting to you." In a "P.S." it is added, "If Captain Nicholas should light on him at Chepstow, do you strengthen him with a strong guard to bring him. If you seize his person, disarm his house, but let not his arms be embezzled."

SECTION IV.—MONMOUTHSHIRE A PART OF WALES.

The custom has become almost settled to consider the county of Monmouth a part of England, and to assign to Wales the even number of twelve counties, six south and six north. Maps of Wales are now constructed which make the Usk the eastern boundary; children at school are almost invariably taught that Monmouthshire is " in England; " and the erroneous notion is somewhat encouraged by a certain tone of " national " feeling which willingly winks at history and gives vantage to prejudice. Even the Registrar-General, (Census, 1871), although he admits it to be "essentially Cambrian," and puts it in the " Welsh Division," still ranks it among the " Counties of England. In a work on the annals of the counties of Wales it is proper that the groundlessness of this notion should be made known, and the county legitimately settled in its proper place as one of the thirteen counties of Wales.

There can be no question about the *ethnology* of the county of Monmouth. It *may* be true that even the blood of England is more *Cymric* than *Saxon*, and that we have reason herein to moderate, and even forget all national antipathy as between Welsh and English.* The people of Monmouthshire, to say the least of it, are as much Cymric as are the people of Glamorgan or Brecknock ; and, barring the change brought into the counties of Monmouth and Glamorgan within living memory by the influx of English-speaking persons, the *language* spoken by the natives still continues to testify to their race. In these respects, therefore, Monmouthshire is now, as in past times, a part and parcel of Wales.

In point of *government*, the relation of *Gwent* (*i.e.*, Monmouthshire and part of Glamorgan, &c.) to Wales always, even before the Norman Conquest, was that of a somewhat distinct and independent sovereignty. This has been repeatedly noticed in the course of our discussions. But nothing to affect the common bond of national unity arose out of this circumstance.

The earliest *geographical* recognition of Gwent in its relation to Wales, subsequently to the period when the distinction between England and Wales was made broad and prominent by the English conquest, is found in the ancient document called " *Parthau Cymru*," in the *Myvyrian Archaiology of Wales*. This purports to be a survey of Wales, North and South, made in the time of the last Llewelyn (13th century). There the cantrefs and comots of all Wales are marked. The district now mainly included in Monmouthshire is divided into three *cantrefs* and thirteen *comots* (see p. 596, " *Gwaunllwg*," " *Gwent Uwch-Coed*," " *Gwent Is-Coed*"). But about the relation of Gwent to Wales at this period there is no question, and therefore no need of evidence.

The Norman conquest of these parts had no tendency to unite them to England. The Lord Marcher system created independent lordships. If it be true that they had the effect of alienating the conquered districts from Wales, it must be remembered that they alienated

---

* This whole question is argued at length, and for the first time, in " *The Pedigree of the English People: an Argument, Historical and Scientific, on English Ethnology, shew the Progress of Race-Amamalgamation in Britain from the Earliest Times, with Especial Reference to the Incorporation of the Celtic Aborigines.*" By Thomas Nicholas, M.A., Ph.D., F.G.S., &c. Longmans & Co. Third Edition. 1872.

Denbighshire (or the "four cantrefs"), Montgomery, Brecknock, and Glamorgan as much as Monmouthshire. But they had in reality no such effect. Henry VIII., when he incorporated Wales with England by the "Act of Union," took the whole Principality with its inhabitants as a recognised unity, a country or "dominion," just as Scotland at a subsequent time was taken, as then recognised, as a separate nationality, with distinct character and limits. The effect of the Union was not to dismember Scotland. In like manner the effect of the Union was not to dismember Wales.

But it will be said that Henry's Act of Union made a difference as it respects *Monmouthshire*. Here comes therefore the point to be tested, and it must be examined with care. What then was the difference made by Henry with respect to Monmouthshire? In other words, in what respect did the junction of this county with England differ from the junction of the other counties of Wales with England? There *was* a point of difference—a very small but very distinct one, in no wise affecting the geographical classification or provincial relations of the county, yet large enough to have introduced the error now sought to be exposed and removed. It had to do simply with the circuit of the judges and the administration of the law, and had no reference whatever to the distribution of counties. Up to this time the Marches had not been subject to visitation by the king's judges. The King's Writ did not run in them, the power of *jura regalia*, conceded to the lords, entitling them to hold courts of their own, and even enact, within limits, laws of their own. Henry VIII. put a stop to this part of the rule of the Marchers, created the county of Monmouth, and placed it under the jurisdiction of Westminster. This seems to be all that was done; and on this slender basis has been built the whole of the notion that Monmouthshire is an English county. In a matter of so much speciality, where, out of a region subject to exceptional feudal rule, a regular county is created, and when created transferred, as the hypothesis goes, from one recognised nationality and "dominion" to another, we have a right to expect very definite and express language, and we know that Henry VIII. was never wanting in definiteness and point when putting forth a command or enactment. It was a characteristic, indeed, of all the Tudor sovereigns to make their will known beyond all possibility of doubt. We must therefore go to Henry's own act, and cite his own language.

The simple truth is, though many will be surprised to hear it, that the 27th Henry VIII. (the "Act of Union") itself expressly speaks of Monmouthshire as a part of the country or dominion of Wales, and says not a syllable about its junction with England except in the sense in which it speaks of the junction with England of Brecknock, Glamorgan, Carmarthen, Montgomery, and others. This is the part of the statute which concerns the case:—

"And forasmuch as there be many and divers Lordships Marchers within the said Countrey or Dominion of Wales, lyinge betwene the Shyres of Englande and the said Countrey or Dominion of Wales, and beying no parcell of any other Shires where the lawes and due correction is used and had; by reason whereof hath ensued and hath benne practised, perpetrated, committed and done within and amonge the sayde Lordshippes and Countreys to them adjoyning manifold and divers detestable murders, brennyng [burning] of houses, robberies, theftes, trespasses, rowtes, ryottes, unlawful assembles, embraceries, maintenaunces, recevinge of felons, oppressions, ruptures of the peace, and manifolde other malefactes contrary to all lawes and justice. And the sayde offenders thereupon makynge their refuge from Lordeshippes to Lordeship were and continued without punishment or

MONMOUTHSHIRE A PART OF WALES. 757

correction; for due reformacion whereof, and for as muche as divers and many of the said Lordeshippes Marches be now in the handes and possession of our Soveraine Lord the King, and the smallest number of them in the possession of other Lordes:—*It is therefore enacted* by thauctoritee aforesaid that divers of the said Lordshipes Marchers shall be united, annexed, and joined *to divers of the Shires of England;* and divers of the said Lordships Marchers shall be united, annexed, and joyned to divers of *the Shyres of the saide Country or Dominion of Wales,* in manner and forme hereafter following. And that all the *residue* of the said Lordeships Marchers *within the saide Countrey or Dominion of Wales* shall be served and divided into certaine particular Counties or Shires, that is to say: *The Countie or Shire of Mommouth,* the Countie or Shire of Brekenoke, the Countie or Shire of Radnor, the Countie or Shire of Mountgomery, the Countie or Shire of Denbigh. And that the Lordships, townships, parishes, commotes, and cantredes of Monmouth, Chepstow, Matherne, Llamnihangel, Magour, Goldecliffe, Newport, Wenllouge, Llanwerne, Caerlion, Uske, Trelecke, Tinterne, Skynfreth, Grousmont, Witecastell, Reglan, Calicote, Biston, Abergevenny, Penrose, Grenefeld, Maghen, and Hochvyslade, in the Countrey of Wales; and all and singular honours, lordships, castels, manours, landes, tenementes, and hereditamentes lying or being within the compas or precint of the lordships, towneships, hamlets, parishes, commotes, and cantredes, and every of them, in whose possession soever they be or shal be, and every parte therof, shall stand and be from and after the said feast of all sainctes, guildable, and shall be reputed, accepted, named, and taken as part and membres of the sayde shire of *Mommouth;* and that the saed Towne of Mommouth shall be named, accepted, reputed, used, had, and taken head and shire towne of the said countie or shire of Mommouth. And that the shiriffes, countie, and shire courte of and for the said shire or Countie of Mommouth shall be holden and kept one time at the saide towne of Mommouth, and the nexte time at the Towne of Newporte in the same countie or shire, and so to be kepte in the same two townes *alternis vicibus,* and accordynge to the lawes of this realme of Englande for ever and in none other places.

"And it is further enacted by thauchoritee aforesaide that all actions realles hereafter shall be conveied, pepetrated, or sued for any landes, tenementes, or heriditamentes, or any other thinge within the saide Countie or shire of Mommouth, and all actions personal within the same shire or countie of the summe of 40/- or above, and all actions mixte, shall be sued by originall writte out of the King's High Court of Chauncerie in Englande, and harde, determined, and tried before the Kinge's Justices in Englande by assize or *Nisi Prius* within the saide Countie of Mommouth, in suchelyke maner, fourme, and wise as all other actions realles, personalles, and actions mixte be sued, hard, determined, and tried in or for any shire of this realme of Englande. And that the King's Justices of his Benche or of his Common Benche of Westminster shall have full power and auctoritie to directe all maner processe to the shireffe and all other officers of the saide Countie of Mommouth, and also to directe writtes of *venire facias* to the same shireffe for the triall of every issue joined before them, and also to awarde Commissions of *Nisi Prius* into the said Countie of Mommouth for the triall of suche issues joyned before them in like maner and fourme as they do into every shire of this realme of Englande. And all and every the Kinge's subjectes and inhabitantes within the said Countie of Mommouth shall be for ever from and after the saide feaste of all sainctes obliged and bounden to be obedient and attendant to the Lord

3 D

Chauncellor of England, the Kinge's Justices, and other of the Kinge's most honourable Counsel, and unto all lawes, customs, ordinances, and statutes of this realme of Englande, in like maner, fourme, and wise as all other the Kinge's subjectes within every shire of this realme of Englande be obliged and bounden, any acte, statute, usage, custom, libertie, privilege, or any other thinge to the contrarie in any wise not withstanding." (*Public General Acts:* 27th HENRY VIII., *cap.* 26.)

We have quoted the statute *verbatim et literatim* that all may see that it contains nothing to justify the popular belief that Monmouthshire was made an English county, and Wales made to consist of twelve counties only, by the eighth Henry. The Act expressly recognises the shire of Monmouth as in a category different from those portions of the Marches which were to be joined to England, as carved out of a "residue" of the Marches "within the said country or dominion of Wales," and constituted a county of the same order and provincial character as the other then created counties of "Brekenoke, Radnor, Mountgomery," &c. No allusion is made to any distinction or difference except in the single matter of the substitution in Monmouth of the *jurisdiction of the Judges* of the King's Court at Westminster for that of the irresponsible and now displaced Lords Marchers. If a mere circuit arrangement took Monmouthshire from Wales then all the other twelve counties have now been taken from Wales, and no "Wales" further remains. The theory that Monmouthshire is an English county, first conceived by error, received without examination, and settled at last by an indolent consent, has thus in truth no historic or legal foundation, and must be pronounced a geographical blunder.

This conclusion appears still more clear and forcible when we look into our old topographical and legal writers. Authors of eminence who lived later than the age of Henry VIII. seem never to have heard of the limitation of Wales to the balanced number of six northern and six southern counties, and the handing over of fertile Gwent to the English side. *Camden, temp.* James I., writing systematically on the "Divisions of Britain," says that besides the counties belonging to England there were "THIRTEEN *more in Wales*, six whereof were in Edward the First's time, and the rest Henry VIII. settled by Act of Parliament;" and among the thirteen he in a subsequent part of his great work (*Britannia*) includes Monmouthshire. Is it conceivable that a man so well-informed as Camden, generally so painstaking and accurate, and certainly swayed by no partiality towards Wales, should so write, if by an Act of Henry VIII. the counties of Wales had been settled at *twelve*, and Monmouthshire made an English county?

Humphrey Llwyd, an equally accurate writer, living at the very time when Henry's Act of Union was passed, and writing his *Historie of Cambria* in 1568, only twenty-one years after Henry's death, describes South Wales as containing "*seven* counties," of which one was *Gwent* or *Monmouth* ("Gwenta, quae et Monumethensis," &c.), and says that these seven counties were ascribed to South Wales by the English ("ab Anglis tribuuntur").

Sir John Dodridge, in his *Historical Account of the Principality of Wales*, published in 1714, in giving at p. 2 the divisions of Wales, says, "The whole country is now allotted into shires, which are *thirteen* in number;" and among the thirteen he places *Monmouth*. Sir John Dodridge was an eminent lawyer, and would certainly have been aware of any statute, had such existed, which made the number of Welsh counties to be *twelve* and not thirteen. He was well aware of the statute 27 Henry VIII., and mentions that it ordained that Monmouthshire "should be governed from henceforth in like manner and by the same judges as other the shires of England" (p. 41).

The "vulgar error" of classifying this county with England, and not with "the countrey or dominion of Wales," as the statute of Henry VIII. denominates it, is not only "vulgar" (*i. e.*, diffused among the people), but is also comparatively recent. Not, indeed, that instances of it do not occur in authors of the eighteenth century,—*ex. gr.*, Browne Willis, in his *Notitia Parl.*, makes Monmouth an English county. But it has become a general and settled opinion only within the present century, and, as will be seen from the above facts, for no better reason than that some one made a mistake or perpetrated an imposture, and that others received and passed on what had been coined.

SECTION V.—HIGH SHERIFFS OF MONMOUTHSHIRE, A.D. 1541—1872.

Sheriffs were first appointed for Wales by Edward I., but as his conquests did not properly include the country now covered by Monmouthshire, which was a part of the Marches, where criminal law was administered under *jura regalia* in each lordship by its own lord, sheriffs in the modern sense of the term were not here appointed. The office in its functions was in fact administered by the lord (see further p. 597). By the Act 27th Henry VIII., c. 26, Monmouthshire was made a county, and the office of Sheriff of the County instituted. This was in A.D. 1535, but some delay in the actual appointment of a person to the office seems to have occurred, or the record of it has been lost, for the first sheriff known to have received the king's writ was Charles Herbert, Esq., in the year 1541. The following list is based upon the researches of the late industrious Thomas Wakeman, Esq. The prominence of the two great families of Herbert and Morgan in the earlier periods of the shrievalty is very remarkable. As to the *Herberts*, for a considerable space in the sixteenth and seventeenth centuries their number and authority in several of the counties of Wales, South and North, greatly surpass those of any other clan.

HENRY VIII.

	A.D.
Charles Herbert, Esq., of Troy [subs. knighted]	1541
Walter Herbert, Esq., of St. Julian's	1542
Walter ap Robert, Esq., of Pant-glâs. [Arms, *per pale az. and sa., three fleurs-de-lis or—* YNYR-GWENT]	1543
Henry Lewis, Esq., of St. Pierre. [*Arg., a lion rampant guardant sa.*]	1544
Reynold ap Howel, Esq., of Perth-hir. [See under *Herbert of Llanarth*]	1545
John Henry Lewis, Esq., of Mathern	1546

EDWARD VI.

	A.D.
Anthony Welsh, Llanwern. [*Ermine, a bend sa.*]	1547
Thomas Morgan, Esq., of Pencoed [afterwards knighted]	1548
Sir Charles Herbert, Kt., of Troy. [See 1541; was M.P. for co. under Mary, 1553]	1549
William Morgan, Esq., of Tredegar. [*Or, a griffin segreant sa.*]	1550

	A.D.
William Herbert, Esq., of Coldbrook	1551
Walter Herbert, Esq., of Skenfrith [nat. son of Sir Charles Herbert of Troy]	1552

MARY.

	A.D.
William Herbert, Esq., of St. Julian's	1553
Anthony Welsh, Esq., of Llanwern	1554
Walter ap Robert, Esq., of Pant-glâs [see 1543]	1555
William ap John ap Thomas, Esq., of Tre-Owen. [See *Llanarth lineage*]	1556
Rowland Morgan, Esq., of Machen	1557
Henry Lewis, Esq., of Mathern	1558

ELIZABETH.

	A.D.
Sir Thomas Morgan, Kt., of Pencoed	1559
Thomas Herbert, Esq., of Wonastow	1560
George James, Esq., of Llanddewi Rhydderch. [*Or, a wyvern's head erased vert, bloody hand in mouth erased at wrist*].	1561

MONMOUTHSHIRE.

	A.D.
Roger Williams, Esq., of Llangibby. [*Gyronny of eight ermine and sa., a lion rampant or*]	1562
William Herbert, Esq. [place not certain]	1563
William Herbert, Esq., of St. Julian's	1564
William Morgan, Esq. [place not certain]	1565
John Henry Kemeys, Esq., of Newport. [*Vert, on a chevron arg., three pheons sa.*]	1566
William John ap Roger, Esq., of Abergavenny. [*Herbert arms*]	1567
William Morgan, Esq., of Llantarnam. [Arms of *Morgan*. See 1550]	1568
Christopher Welsh, Esq., of Llanwern	1569
Rowland Morgan, Esq., of Llan-fedw	1570
William Herbert, Esq., of Coldbrook	1571
Thomas Herbert, Esq., of Wonastow	1572
William Morgan, Esq., of Wern-gochan? [*Three wolves passant in pale arg.*]	1573
Miles Morgan, Esq., of Tredegar. [Morgan arms as under 1550]	1574
Rowland Kemeys, Esq., of Faendre. [Arms as under 1566]	1575
Christopher Welsh, Esq., of Llanwern	1576
Richard Morgan, Esq. [place uncertain]	1577
William John ap Roger, Esq., of Abergavenny [see 1567]	1578
William Lewis, Esq., of St. Pierre	1579
Sir William Herbert, Kt., of St. Julian's	1580
Thomas Morgan, Esq., of Machen	1581
Edward Morgan, Esq., of Pencarn. [*Arg., three bulls' heads caboshed sa.*]	1582
Edward Morgan, Esq., of Llantarnam. [Arms of *Morgan*. See 1550]	1583
Matthew Herbert, Esq., of Coldbrook	1584
William Lewis, Esq., of Llanddewi Rhydderch. [*Checky or and az., on a fesse gu., three leopards' heads jessant, fleur-de-lis or*]	1585
Richard Morgan, Esq. [place not certain]	1586
John Jones, Esq., of Tre-Owen. [See *Herbert of Llanarth*]	1587
Henry Morgan, Esq., of Pen-llwyn. [*Arg., a lion rampant guardant sa.*]	1588
Henry Herbert, Esq., of Wonastow	1589
Nicholas Herbert, Esq. [place not given]	1590
Edward Lewis, Esq., of Fan [Glamorgan]	1591
Walter Vaughan, Esq., of Caldecot. [*Ermine, a saltier gu.*]	1592
Rowland Morgan, Esq., of Bedwellty. [*Arms as 1579*]	1593
Walter Jones, Esq., of Magor	1594
Matthew Herbert, Esq., of Coldbrook	1595
Matthew Prichard, Esq., of Llanover. [*Arms as 1561*]	1596
Andrew Morgan, Esq., of Llanfihangel. [Tredegar *arms*. See 1550]	1597
Henry Herbert, Esq., of Wonastow; died, and *succ.* by— William Morgan, Esq., of the Friars. [*Arms as 1550*]	1598
Henry Billingsley, Esq., of Penhow	1599
Richard Kemeys, Esq. [place not given]	1600

	A.D.
Edward Kemeys [Keven-Mabley? See Glam. *Sheriffs*, 1605]	1601
Edward Morgan, Esq. [place not given]	1602

JAMES I.

	A.D.
Henry Morgan, Esq., of Penllwyn. [*Arms as* 1568]	1603
John Gaynsford, Esq. [place, and name otherwise, not known]	1604
Rowland Williams, Esq., Llangibby. [*Arms as in* 1562]	1605
Valentine Prichard, Esq. [of Llanover?]	1606
William Price, Esq., of Llanfoist. [Arms of *Ynyr-Gwent*. See 1543]	1607
Sir Walter Montague, Kt., of Pen-coed. [*Arg., three fusils in fesse gu.*]	1608
Charles Jones, Esq., of Dingestow, afterwards knighted. [*Az., 'three talbots' heads erased arg.*]	1609
Henry Lewis, Esq., of St. Pierre	1610
William Rawlins, Esq., of Tre-gaer	1611
Sir William Morgan, Kt., of Tredegar	1612
Roger Bathern, Esq., of Penhow	1613
Giles Morgan, Esq., of Pen-crûg. [*Arms as in* 1561]	1614
William Jones, Esq., of Trewern. [*Herbert arms*]	1615
Thomas Van, Esq., of Coldra [*Coel-dre; arms, Sa., a chevron between 3 bees or*]	1616
Thomas Morgan, Esq., of Rhiw-pera. [Afterwards knighted. Arms, *Arg., three bulls' heads caboshed sa., a mullet for diff.*]	1617
George Milbourne, Esq., of Wonastow. [*Arg., a cross moline sa.*]	1618
William Hughes, Esq., of Cil-Uwch. [*Herbert arms*]	1619
Thomas Cocks, Esq. [place not given. Or, three bars az. on a canton arg., a lion's head erased gu., langued az.]	1620
Walter Aldey, Esq., of Chepstow Hardwick	1621
Robert Jones, Esq., of Grondre	1622
William Walter, Esq., of Persfield. [*Vert, a squirrel segreant or*]	1623
David Lewis, Esq., of Llanddewi Rhydderch. [*Arms as in* 1585]	1624

CHARLES I.

	A.D.
Edward Morgan, Esq. [place not given]	1625
Sir Charles Somerset, Kt., of Troy. [Sixth son of Edward, fourth Earl of Worcester; made Knight of the Bath 1610,—*Collins*]	1626
Sir Charles Williams, Kt., of Llangibby.	1627
William Kemeys, Esq., of "Kemeys"	1628
William Thomas, Esq., of Perth-oleu. [*Sa., three pheons arg., the two in chief point to point, that in base the point downwards*]	1629
John Walter, Esq., of Persfield	1630
William Baker, Esq., of Abergavenny. [*Arg., two chevronels sa.*]	1631
Nicholas Kemeys, Esq., of Llanfair	1632

HIGH SHERIFFS OF MONMOUTHSHIRE.

	A.D.
Nicholas Arnold, Esq., of Llanfihangel Crûg-Corneu	1633
Lewis Van, Esq., of Coel-dre	1634
George Milbourne, Esq., of Wonastow. [*Arms* as in 1618]	1635
Henry Probert, Esq., of Pant-glâs	1636
William Morgan, Esq., of Ty-mawr. [*Arms* as in 1550]	1637
William Herbert, Esq., of Coldbrook	1638
Nicholas Moor, Esq., of Crick. [*Arg.*, *three bars sa.*]	1639
No name	1640
No name	1641
Thomas Morgan, Esq., of Llan-soar. [*Arms* as 1582]	1642
Philip Jones, of Tre-Owain. [Lt.-Col., afterwards knighted; one of the defenders of Raglan Castle against Fairfax. See *Herbert of Llanarth, lineage*]	1643
Thomas Price, Esq., of Llanfoist. [*Arms* as under 1543]	1644
Sir Edward Morgan, Kt., of Pen-coed	1645
No name	1646
William Morgan, Esq. [of Pentridge? Arms, *Gu., three chevronels arg.*]	1647
Henry Vaughan, Esq., of Caldecot	1648

THE COMMONWEALTH AND CROMWELL.

No name given	1649
Roger Williams, Esq., of Newport	1650
No name given	1651
No name given	1652
Edward Kemeys, Esq., of Perth-oleu	1653

OLIVER CROMWELL, LORD PROTECTOR.

No name given	1654
No name given	1655
John Price [no place given; query of Gelli-hir? See *Parl. Ann. of Glam.*, 1654—8]	1656
Charles Herbert, Esq., of Hadnock?	1657

RICHARD CROMWELL, LORD PROTECTOR.

Roger Bates, Esq., of Cefn-tilla. [*Vert, a chevron between three garbs or*]	1658
Charles Van, Esq., of Coldra [Coel-dre]	1659

CHARLES II.

Charles Van, Esq., the same	1660
Thomas Morgan, Esq., of Machen. [*Arms, Or, a griffin segreant sa.*]	1661
William Jones, Esq., of Llanishen	1662
George Gwyn, Esq., of Itton. [*Sa., a fesse or between two swords in pale arg., hilted or, &c.* See *Gwyn of Dyffryn*]	1663
Roger Williams, Esq., of Cefn-tilla. [Llangibby arms]	1664
Philip Cecil, Esq., of Dyffryn. [Arms of Cecil, Marquess of Exeter]	1665
Walter Morgan, Esq., of Llantilio, Perth-oleu	1666

	A.D.
Christopher Perkins, Esq., of Pilston. [*Arg., a fesse dancette between six billets sa.*]	1667
William Herbert, Esq., of Coldbrook	1668
John Arnold, Esq., of Llanfihangel, Crûg-corneu	1669
Sir John Scudamore, Kt., of Ballingham. [*Gu., three stirrups leathered and buckled or*]	1670
Roger Bates, Esq., of Cefn-tilla	1671
Col. Philip Jones, of Llanarth	1672
Thomas Herbert, Esq., of Usk	1673
John Walter, Esq., of Persfield	1674
John Gwyn, Esq., of Ty-verie. [*Or, on a chevron couched sinister between three birds sa., five mullets arg.* "These very curious arms are from his seal to a deed, *penes* J. A. Herbert, Esq."]	1675
Rowland Prichard, Esq. [no place given]	1676
John Loof, Esq. [no place given]	1677
William Kemeys, Esq., of Kemeys	1678
James Herbert, Esq., of Coldbrook	1679
Thomas Morgan, Esq., of Penrhôs. [Tredegar arms. See 1550]	1680
William Jones, Esq., of Abergavenny. [*Gu., three lions rampant arg. on a canton sa., a fret or*]	1681
Edward Nicholas, Esq., of Tre-llech	1682
John Gabb, Esq., of Grosmont	1683
Walter Evans, Esq. [no place given]	1684

JAMES II.

Robert Gunter, Esq., Abergavenny	1685
Nicholas Jones, Esq., of Magor	1686
Richard Roberts, Esq. [no place given]	1687
Philip Jones, Esq., of Llanarth. [See *Herbert of Llanarth*]	1688

WILLIAM AND MARY.

Thomas Morgan, Esq., of Tredegar	1689
Charles Price, Esq., of Llanfoist	1690
David Evans, Esq. [no place given]	1691
Edward Fielding, Esq., of Tintern Parva [an alderman of Bristol]	1692
John Floyer, Esq., of Llantilio Perth-oleu	1693
Thomas Jones, Esq. [no place given]	1694
George Kemeys, Esq., of Kemeys	1695

WILLIAM III.

Edward Perkyns, Esq., of Pilston. [Arms as under 1667]	1696
John Morgan, Esq., of Machen	1697
George Lewis, Esq., of Pen-how	1698
George Kemeys, Esq., of Kemeys	1699
Edmund Morgan, Esq., of Pen-llwyn	1700
Thomas Morgan, Esq., of Llanrumney	1701

ANNE.

William Lewis, Esq., of Tre-worgen and Llanddewi Rhydderch. [Arms as under 1585]	1702
David Lloyd, Esq., of Hendre	1703

MONMOUTHSHIRE.

	A.D.
Lewis Morgan, Esq., of Penylan. [Tredegar arms. See 1550]	1704
Thomas Evans, Esq., of Llangattwg Vibonavel. [*Herbert arms within a bordure compony arg. and gu.*]	1705
John Curre, Esq., of Rogerston Grange. [*Arg., on a fesse between three cross crosslets sa., three martlets or*]	1706
Vere Herbert, Esq., of Caldecot. [Herbert arms]	1707
John Springet, Esq., of Grosmont	1708
David Lewis, Esq. [no place given]	1709
Christopher Perkyns, Esq., of Pilstone	1710
Thomas Price, Esq., of Llanfoist	1711
Walter [qy. Walwyn?] Cecil, Esq., of Dyffryn. [Arms as before]	1712
Giles Meredith, Esq., of Llanelen	1713
John Walter, Esq., of Persfield	1714

GEORGE I.

Christopher Price, Esq., of Llanfoist	1715
William Jones, Esq., of Usk Priory. [*Arg.*, a chevron gu. between three spear-heads imbrued sa.]	1716
James Hughes, Esq., of Gelli-wig. [*Gu.*, a chevron between three rams' heads caboshed or]	1717
Charles Van, Esq., of Llanwern	1718
Lawrence Lord, Esq., of Kemeys [a stranger who purchased the manor of Kemeys]	1719
Edward Thomas, Esq. [no place given]	1720
Charles Probert, Esq., of Tre-llech	1721
Henry Morgan, Esq., of Bedwellty. [*Arg.*, a lion rampant guardant sa.]	1722
John Jones, Esq., of Pant-y-goetre	1723
Matthew Powell, Esq., of Llantilio Crossenny. [*Quart.*: 1 and 4, *or, three lions couchant gu.*; 2 and 3, *per chevron embattled or and gu., three cinquefoils pierced counterchanged*]	1724
Morgan Morgan, Esq., of Llanrumney. [Arms as under 1550]	1725
Richard Lewis, Esq., of Court-y-gollen	1726

GEORGE II.

Henry Gore, Esq., of Langston. [*Gu.*, a fesse between three cross crosslets fitchée or]	1727
David Miles, Esq., of Llandderfel	1728
Robert Jones, Esq., of Grondre	1729
John Gwynne, Esq., of Ty-verie. [Arms as under 1675]	1730
Henry Nash. Esq., of Nash	1731
Edmund Bradbury, Esq., of Crick (*Crûg*). [*Sa.*, a chevron ermine betw. 3 buckles arg.]	1732
William Rees, Esq., of St. Bride's	1733
Henry Morgan, Esq., of Bedwellty. [Arms as under 1722]	1734
Richard Lewis, Esq., of Court-y-gollen. [Arms as under 1561, 1596]	1735
William Bonner, Esq. [place not known]	1736

	A.D.
Anthony Morgan, Esq., of Llanddewi Skyrrid. [*Gu.*, three chevronels arg.]	1737
William Seys, Esq., of Gaer. [*Sa.*, a chevron between three spear-heads imbrued arg. These arms were quartered by Seys of Boverton, Glam.]	1738
Paul Morgan, Esq., of Chepstow. [*Ermine*, a lion rampant sa.]	1739
Thomas Evans, Esq., of Llangattwg Vibonavel. [*Herbert, in a bordure compony arg. and gu.*]	1740
Francis Jenkins, Esq., of Caerau	1741
Richard Clerk, Esq., of The Hill	1742
Edward Perkyns, Esq., of Pillston. [Arms as under 1667]	1743
James Tudor Morgan, Esq., of Llangattwg Llyngoed. [*Per pale, arg. and sa.*, two lions rampant regardant counterchanged]	1744
William Aldey, Esq., of Chepstow Hardwick	1745
Thomas Jenkins, Esq., of Glascoed. [*Arg.*, a chevron gu. between three fleurs-de-lis sa.]	1746
John Day, Esq., of Dinham [qy. *Dinam?*]	1747
Aubrey Barnes, Esq., of Monmouth	1748
Sydenham Shipway, Esq., of Caldecot	1749
Philip Fisher, Esq., of Monmouth	1750
Evan Jones, Esq. [place not given]	1751
Thomas Parry, Esq. [place not given]	1752
William Jenkins, Esq., of Glascoed. [Arms as under 1746]	1753
John Chambers, Esq., of Llanfoist. [*Az.*, a right arm in armour embowed or, holding a red rose slipped, leaved ppr.]	1754
John Jones, Esq., of Graig-with [*Craig-gwydd?*]	1755
David Tregoze, Esq., of Tre-girog	1756
John Lewis, Esq., of Llantilio Crossenny	1757
Rowland Pytt, Esq., of Raglan	1758
William Morgan, Esq., of Bryn-gwyn. [Tredegar arms. See 1550]	1759
William Curre, Esq., of Itton. [Arms as under 1706]	1760

GEORGE III.

William Phillips, Esq., of Whitson. [*Gu.*, three boars' heads erased or]	1761
John Roberts, Esq., of Abergavenny	1762
Allan Lord, Esq., of Kemeys	1763
William Lloyd, Esq., The Hill, Abergavenny. [*Or, a lion rampant sa.*]	1764
Solomon Jones, Esq., of Llantilio Pertholeu	1765
William Winsmore, Esq., of Pant-y-goetre	1766
Thomas John Medlicott, Esq., of Monmouth [agent to Duke of Beaufort]	1767
Richard Lucas, Esq., of Llangattwg *juxta* Usk. [*Arg.*, on a canton sa. a ducal coronet or]	1768
George Duberley, Esq., of Dingestow	1769
Charles Milborne, Esq., of Wonastow. [*Arg.*, a cross moline sa.]	1770
Thomas Fletcher, Esq., of Monmouth	1771
Thomas Fydale, Esq., of Chepstow, merchant	1772
Morgan Lewis, Esq., of St. Pierre. [Arms as under 1544]	1773

HIGH SHERIFFS OF MONMOUTHSHIRE.

	A.D.
James Davis, Esq., of Chepstow	1774
William Nicholl, Esq., of Caerleon. [*Sa.*, three pheons arg.*]	1775
Philip Meakins, Esq., of Hardwick, Monmouth	1776
Edmund Probyn, Esq., of Newland. [*Ermine, on a fesse gu., a lion passant or*]	1777
Charles Price, Esq., of Llanfoist. [Arms under 1543]	1778
William Addams Williams, Esq., of Llangibby	1779
Thomas Hooper, Esq., of Pant-y-goetre	1780
William Jones, Esq., of Nash, Gloucestershire	1781
Edward Thomas, Esq. [place not given]	1782
Elisha Briscoe, Esq., of Dixton	1783
Christopher Chambre, Esq., of Llanfoist	1784
William Rees, Esq., of St. Bride's	1785
Robert Salusbury, Esq., of Llanwern. [*Gu., a lion rampant arg., ducally crowned or, between three crescents of the last*]	1786
Thomas Lewis, Esq., of Chepstow	1787
George Smith, Esq., of Persfield	1788
Thomas Lewis, Esq., of St. Pierre. [Arms under 1544]	1789
William Dinwoody, Esq., of Abergavenny	1790
William Harrison, Esq., of Ton, Raglan. [The inventor of the timepiece for finding the longitude]	1791
David Tanner, Esq., of Monmouth	1792
John Hanbury Williams, Esq., of Coldbrook. [*Or, a bend engrailed vert plain cotised sa.*]	1793
John Rolls, Esq., of Dyffryn. [For arms, see *Rolls of Hendre*]	1794
Richard Morgan, Esq., of Argoed	1795
Henry Barnes, Esq., of Monmouth	1796
Thomas Stoughton, Esq., of Pontypool	1797
Robert Morgan Kinsey, Esq., of Abergavenny	1798
Capel Hanbury Leigh, Esq., of Pontypool. [*Or, a bend engrailed vert plain cotised sa.*]	1799
Benjamin Waddington, Esq., of Llanover. [See *Lady Llanover of Llanover*]	1800
Thomas Williams, Esq., of Tidenham. [*Or, a griffin passant vert*]	1801
Thomas Morgan, Esq., The Hill, Abergavenny	1802
George Jones, Esq., of Salisbury in Magor. [*Sa., a stag at gaze arg. attired and unguled or*]	1803
William Addams Williams, Esq., of Llangibby	1804
Joseph Price, Esq., of Monmouth	1805
William Phillips, Esq., of Whitson. [Arms under 1761]	1806
William Partridge, Esq., of Monmouth	1807
William Morgan, Esq., of Mamhilod. [*Arg., a lion rampant guardant sa.*]	1808
John K. G. Kemeys, Esq., of Perth-oleu	1809
William Pilkington, Esq., of Hilston. [*Arg., a cross flory patoncé voided gu.*]	1810
Hugh Powell, Esq., of Llanfihangel. [See *Powell-Rodney*]	1811
Charles Lewis, Esq., of St. Pierre. [Arms under 1544]	1812

	A.D.
Samuel Homfray, Esq., of Pendarren. [*Quart. : 1 and 4, gu., a cross batonnée ermine ; 2nd quart., arg. and sa.; 3rd, sa. 4 pallets ermine*]	1813
Samuel Bosanquet, Esq., of Dingestow. [See *Bosanquet of Dingestow Court*]	1814
Sir Samuel B. Fludyer, Bart., of Trostré. [*Sa., a cross patoncé between four escallops arg., each charged with a cross patoncé of the field*]	1815
Sir Henry Prothero, Kt., of Llanternam. [*Arg., a lion rampant guardant sa.*]	1816
Robert Thompson, Esq., of Tintern Abbey	1817
Nathaniel Wells, Esq., of Persfield [Piercefield]	1818
George Buckle, Esq., of Chepstow	1819

GEORGE IV.

	A.D.
Sir Robert J. A. Kemeys, Kt., of Malpas	1820
Charles M. P. Morgan, Esq., of Tredegar	1821
James Jenkins, Esq., of Chepstow	1822
Joseph Bailey, Esq., of Nant-y-glo	1823
John Partridge, Esq., of Monmouth	1824
James Proctor, Esq., of Chepstow	1825
Benjamin Hall, Esq., of Llanover [afterw. cr. a Bart. and a Baron. See *Lady Llanover*]	1826
William Addams Williams, Esq., of Llangibby	1827
William Morgan, Esq., of Pant-y-goetre	1828
Thomas Fothergill, Esq., of Caerleon. [*Vert, a buck's head couped with a bordure engrailed or*]	1829

WILLIAM IV.

	A.D.
Iltyd Nicholl, Esq., of Usk. [*Sa., three pheons arg.*]	1830
William Hollis, Esq., of Shire-Newton. [*Sa., a bend between two talbots passant arg.*]	1831
Sir Mark Wood, Bart., of Rhymney	1832
William Vaughan, Esq., of Courtfield	1833
Charles Marriott, Esq., of Dixton	1834
John Buckle, Esq., of Wye-lands	1835
George Rooke, Esq., of Llandogo	1836

VICTORIA.

	A.D.
Philip Jones, Esq., of Llanarth. [See *Herbert of Llanarth*]	1837
John Jenkins, Esq., of Caerleon	1838
Colethurst Bateman, Esq., of Berth-oleu	1839
Summers Harford, Esq., of Sirhowy. [*Sa., two bends arg. on a canton az. a bend or*]	1840
Samuel Homfray, Esq., of Bedwellty	1841
John E. W. Rolls, Esq., of Hendre. [See *Rolls of Hendre*]	1842
Sir Digby Mackworth, Bart., of Glan-Usk. [*Per pale indented, sa. and ermine, a chevron gu., fretty or*]	1843
William Jones, Esq., of Clytha. [See *Herbert of Clytha*]	1844
William Phillips, Esq., of Whitson	1845

	A.D.		A.D.
Thomas Prothero, Esq., of Malpas Court	1846	James Proctor Carruthers, Esq., of Grondre	1861
William Mark Wood, Esq., of Rhymney	1847	John Best Snead, Esq., of Chepstow	1862
C. J. Kemeys-Tynte, Esq., of Cefn-Mabley, Glam.	1848	Henry Martyn Kennard, Esq., of Crumlin Hall	1863
		Lt.-Col. Henry C. Byrde, of Goetre House	1864
Edward Phillips, Esq., of Pontypool	1849	Arthur Davies Berrington, Esq., of Pant-y-Goetre	1865
John Arthur Herbert, Esq., of Llanarth	1850		
Crawshaw Bailey, Esq., of Nant-y-glo	1851	Henry Cotton Finch, Esq., of Blaenavon	1866
John Russell, Esq., of Wye-lands	1855	George R. Greenhow-Relph, Esq., of Beech Hill	1867
Edward Bagnall Dimmock, Esq., of Pontypool	1856	Frank Johnstone Mitchell, Esq., Llanvrechva Grange	1868
Thomas Gratrex, Esq., of Court St. Lawrence	1857		
Hon. Godfrey Charles Morgan, of Tredegar	1858	John Lawrence, Esq., of Crick House	1869
Edward Matthew Curre, Esq., of Itton	1859	Edward Lister, Esq., of Cefn Ila	1870
Hon. William Powell-Rodney, of Llanfihangel Court. [*Or, three eagles displayed purpure*]	1860	Thomas Cordes, Esq., of Bryn Glâs	1871
		James Charles Hill, Esq., The Brooks	1872

Section VI.—PARLIAMENTARY ANNALS OF MONMOUTHSHIRE, A.D. 1542—1872.

The Act which put an end to the government of the Lords Marchers gave the inhabitants the right to send delegates to represent their wishes at the English Parliament. But, as in the case of sheriffs, we do not discover that the Act became at once operative in procuring an election of members. The first election discovered was in the first year of Edward VI. (1547), which was twelve years after the passing of the 27th Henry VIII.—the Act which created the county of Monmouth, and gave that county the privilege of sending two knights to expound its opinions and needs at Westminster, and to the borough of Monmouth, as a "shire town," the right of sending one burgess. The members for the county and for the borough of Monmouth are here given together for each year. By the Reform Act Newport and Usk were made Contributory Boroughs along with Monmouth.

EDWARD VI.

Sir William Morgan, Kt. [of Tredegar; was sheriff in 1550] .
William Herbert, Esq., of Coldbrook [sheriff in 1551] .
Giles Morgan, Esq. [see son of Sir William above], for the *Bor.* } for the *Co.* 1547

Sir William Herbert, Kt., for the *Co.*
None named in Browne Willis for the *Bor.* } 1553

MARY.

Sir Charles Herbert, Kt., of Troy, sheriff 1549
Thomas Somerset, Esq. [2nd son of Henry, 2nd Earl of Worcester, *d.* 1587], for *Co.* } 1553
John Philip Morgan, Esq.[of Pencoed ?],for *Bor.*

Thomas Herbert, Esq. [of Wonastow, sheriff for 1560]
James Gunter, Esq.
John Philip Morgan, Esq., as above, for *Bor.* } for the *Co.* } 1554

PHILIP AND MARY.

John Somerset, Esq. .
David Lewes, Esq., LL.D. } for the *Co.*
John Philip Morgan (as before) for the *Bor.* } 1554

William Herbert, Esq. [of Coldbrook ?]
William Morgan, Esq. [of Llanternam] } for the *Co.* 1555

Thomas Lewes, Esq., for the *Bor.*

Francis Somerset, Esq.
William Morgan, Esq. (as before) } for the *Co.*
Matthew Herbert, Esq. [of Coldbrook] .
Rees Lewis, Esq., *vice* Herbert *dec.* } for the *Bor.* } 1557

ELIZABETH.

David Lewes, Esq., LL.D. .
Rowland Arnold (?) . } for the *Co.* 1558
Morys ap Howel for the *Bor.*

Matthew Herbert, Esq. (as above) } for the *Co.* 1563
George Herbert, Esq.

PARLIAMENTARY ANNALS OF MONMOUTHSHIRE.

	A.D.
Walter Horton, Gent. } for the *Bor.*	1563
John Cook, Esq., *vice* Horton	
Charles Somerset, Esq. [of Troy, knighted 1610] } for the *Co.*	1571
William Morgan, Esq., of Llanternam	
Charles Herbert, Esq., for the *Bor.*	
Charles Somerset, Esq. [of Troy, as above] } for the *Co.*	1572
Henry Herbert, Esq. [of Wonastow]	
More ap Howel, Esq., *died*, and in his place — } for the *Bor.*	
William Morgan, Esq.	
Sir William Herbert, Kt. [of St. Julian's] } for the *Co.*	1586
Edward Morgan, Esq. [of Llanternam]	
Morys Guilym, Gent., for the *Bor.*	
William Morgan, Esq., of Tredegar } for the *Co.*	1588
William Prodgers [*ap Roger*]	
Philip Jones, Esq. [qy. of Llanarth? afterw. Lieut.-Col. and Kt.]} for the *Bor.*	
Sir William Herbert, Kt., of St. Julian's } for the *Co.*	1592
Edward Kemmys, Esq., of Kemmes	
Edward Hubbard, Esq., for the *Bor.*	
Henry Herbert, Esq. [of Wonastow?] } for the *Co.*	1597
John Arnold, Esq. [of Llanfihangel?]	
Robert Johnson, Gent., for the *Bor.*	
Thomas Somerset [knighted 1604; 3rd son of Edward, fourth Earl of Worcester] } for the *Co.*	1601
Henry Morgan [of Penllwyn?]	
Robert Johnson (as above) for the *Bor.*	

JAMES I.

John Somerset, Esq.	
Sir John Herbert, Kt. [qy. of Neath Abbey?] } for the *Co.*	1603
Robert Johnson (the same) for the *Bor.*	
Sir Edward Morgan, Kt., for the *Co.* }	1614
Sir Robert Johnson, Kt., for the *Bor.*	
Sir Edward Morgan, Kt. (the same) } for the *Co.*	
Charles Williams, Esq., of Llangibby	
Thomas Ravenscroft, Esq., for the *Bor.* [This is a name unknown in Wales except here and in Flintshire, where William Ravenscroft was member for the county for several years. The family lived at Bretton, Hawarden (see pp. 440, 443), and intermarried with the *Salusburys* of Lleweni, Denb., one of whose descendants became resident at Llanwern, Mon.,— a branch only recently extinct. Did this connection lead to the relation of Thomas Ravenscroft to the borough of Mon.?]	1620

	A.D.
Robert Sydney, Viscount Lisle, of Penshurst. [See the connection of the Sydney family with cos. Mon. and Glam., under *Gamage of Coity Castle*. He was cr. Earl of Leicester 1618 ; title extinct with Jocelyn, 7th Earl, 1743,—see pp. 566—8] } for the *Co.*	1623
Sir William Morgan, Kt. [of Tredegar]	
Walter Steward, Esq., for the *Bor.*	
The same as for 1623 . . 1st session	1625

CHARLES I.

William Herbert, Esq. [of Coldbrook, *sheriff* 1638] } for the *Co.*	2nd session 1625
Nicholas Arnold, Esq., of Llanfihangel [*sheriff* 1633]	
William Fortescue, Gent., for the *Bor.*	
Nicholas Kemeys, Esq. [of Llanfair, *sheriff* 1632] } for the *Co.*	1628
Nicholas Arnold, Esq., of Llanfihangel (as above)	
William Morgan, Esq., for the *Bor.*	
William Morgan, Esq. [of Tymawr?] } for the *Co*	1st session 1640
Walter Rumsey, Esq.	
Charles Jones, Esq., *Recorder*, for the *Bor.*	
William Herbert, Esq. (the same) } for the *Co.*	2nd session 1640
John Herbert, Esq.	
Henry Herbert, Esq., *vice* John Herbert } for the *Bor.*	
Thomas Trevor, Esq.	
Thomas Pury, jun., *vice* Trevor	

THE COMMONWEALTH AND CROMWELL.

[The "Rump" or "Little" Parliament being dismissed, the "Barebones" Parliament is now called (see p. 403). For all the other cos. of Wales six members without specific constituencies are summoned. For their names see p. 606.]

Philip Jones, Esq., for the *Co.* [This was not one of several of that name of Llanarth and Tre-Owain, but the distinguished Cromwellite officer in Glamorganshire, Comptroller of the Household to the Lord Protector, raised to the House of Peers, &c. See *Jones of Fonmon Castle*.]	1653
No name given for the *Bor.*	

OLIVER CROMWELL, LORD PROTECTOR.

Richard, Lord Cromwell [son of the Protector] Col. Philip Jones [the same as above; he was also M.P. for *Glam.* same year. See *Parl. Ann. of Glam.* 1654] } for the *Co.*	1654
No name given for the *Bor.*	

MONMOUTHSHIRE.

Major-Gen. James Berry . . . . } [A Cromwellite officer; on the commission of Generals, acting for Hereford, Salop and North Wales; distinguished himself at Preston fight; a friend of Richard Baxter.] John Nicholas, Esq. [of Llan-melan?] . . } for the Co. 1656
None for the *Bor.*

RICHARD CROMWELL, LORD PROTECTOR.

William Morgan, Esq., of Machen
John Nicholas, Esq., of Llan-melan . . . . } for the Co.
Nathaniel Waterhouse, Esq., " of the City of Westminster," for the *Bor.* . . . } 1658-9

CHARLES II.

Edward, Marquess of Worcester . . 1660-7
[2nd Marquess 1646; Lord Lieutenant of North Wales; received in 1644 from Charles I. an extraordinary commission as Generalissimo of home, Irish, and foreign armies, and admiral of fleet, giving power to contract for moneys, to confer patents of nobility "from a marquis to a baronet," promising the king's "dear daughter Elizabeth" to his son in marriage, "with £300,000 in dower or portion, most part whereof" the marquess and his father are acknowledged to have "spent and disburst" in the king's "service," with "the title of Duke of Somerset" to him and his "heirs male for ever." The House of Lords, 1660, procured the revocation of the patent, and the marquess delivered it up. He was the celebrated author of *A Century of Inventions; d.* 1667. In the *Docket-Book*, Crown Office, he is by error named *Thomas*, where a writ is recorded as issued to appoint his successor to Parliament.]

[The following records are found in the Crown Office *Docket-Books :—*]

Writ issued to elect a burgess for the *borough* of Monmouth in the place of *Sir* George Probert, *Kt.* [His year of election has not been found] 1676
Writ issued to elect a Knight of the Shire for the co. of Monmouth in the room of William Morgan, *Esq.*, deceased. [The year of his election has not been found] . 1680

JAMES II.

Writ issued to elect a burgess for the borough of Monmouth in the room of Charles, *Marquess of Worcester.* [Year of his election not given] 1685

ANNE.

Writ to elect a Knight of the Shire in the room of Thomas, *Lord Viscount Windsor, who had succ.* as Lord Mountjoy . . . 1711
Writ to elect a Knight of the Shire *vice* James Gunter, *Esq., dec.* 1713

GEORGE I.

John Morgan, Esq. [prob. of Machen] . . . . . } for the Co.
Thomas Lewis, Esq. . . . } 1715
William Bray, Gent., for the *Bor.* . . }
John Hanbury, Esq., of Pontypool, *vice* Morgan, for the *Co.* 1719
Hon. A. Windsor, *vice* Bray, *dec.*, for the *Bor.* 1720
Sir William Morgan, K.B., of Tredegar . . . . } for the Co.
John Hanbury, Esq., of Pontypool } 1722
Edward Kemeys, Esq., for the *Bor.* . . }

GEORGE II.

Lord Charles Noel Somerset [*s.* 1745 as fourth Duke of Beaufort], *vice* Morgan, *dec.*, for the *Co.* 1731
John Hanbury, Esq., of Pontypool } for the Co.
Thomas Morgan, Esq. . . . } 1734
Lord Charles Noel Somerset for the *Bor.* . }
Charles Hanbury Williams, Esq. [afterwards Sir Charles], of Coldbrook, *vice* Hanbury, *dec.*, for the *Co.* 1735
Thomas Morgan, Esq. . . . }
Charles Hanbury Williams (as above) . . . . . } for the Co. 1741
Sir Charles Kemeys Tynte, *vice* Somerset, *s.* as fourth Duke of Beaufort . . . } for the *Bor.* 1745
William Morgan, Esq. . . . }
Capel Hanbury, Esq., of Pontypool Park . . . . } for the Co. 1747
Fulke Greville, Esq., for the *Bor.* . . . }
Benjamin Bathurst, Esq., *vice* Greville, for the *Bor.* 1754

GEORGE III.

Thomas Morgan, Esq., jun., *vice* Morgan, *dec.*, for the *Co.* 1763
John Hanbury, Esq., *vice* Hanbury, *dec.*, for the *Co.* 1765
John Stepney, Esq. [son of Sir Thomas Stepney of Prendergast, Pemb., *s.* as 7th Bart. 1774], *vice* Bathurst, *dec.* . } for the *Bor.* 1767
Sir John Stepney, Bart. (the same), for the *Bor.* 1774
Henry, Viscount Nevill, *vice* Hanbury, *dec.*, for the *Co.* 1784
Col. James Rook [*vice* Nevill, *s.* to peerage as second Earl of Abergavenny] for the *Co.* 1786
Henry Charles, Marquess of Worcester, *vice* Stepney, resigned [seventh Marquess; *s.* as sixth Duke of Beaufort 1803] . } for the *Bor.* 1788

	A.D.
John Morgan, Esq. . . . } for the *Co.*	
Col. James Rook . . .	
Charles Bragge, Esq. [*vice* Worcester, elected for the city of } for the *Bor.* Bristol]	1790
Robert Salusbury, Esq. [of Llanwern; Sheriff in 1786; was of Cotton Hall, Denb., and of the clan of *Lleweni* (see *Salusbury of Lleweni*); *m.*, 1780, Catherine, dau. and h. of Charles Van, Esq., of Llanwern, Mon.], *vice* Morgan, *dec.*, for the *Co.*	1792
Col. James Rook . . . } for the *Co.* Charles Morgan, Esq., afterwards a Bart.	1796
Sir Charles Thompson, Bart., for the *Bor.*	
General Lord R. E. H. Somerset [fourth son of Henry, fifth Duke of Beaufort], *vice* Thompson, *dec.*, for the *Bor.* . .	1799
Lieut.-Col. Lord Charles H. Somerset [elder brother of last member] for the *Bor.*	1802
Sir Charles Morgan, Bart., of Tredegar . . . . } for the *Co.* Lord A. John H. Somerset [fifth son of fifth Duke of Beaufort]	1806
Henry, Marquess of Worcester [*s.* as seventh Duke of Beaufort, *vice* Somerset, app. Govnr. Cape of Good Hope], for *Bor.* .	1813
Lord G. C. H. Somerset [second son of sixth Duke of Beaufort, *vice* Lord A. J. H. Somerset, *dec.*, for the *Co.* . . .	1816
Sir Charles Morgan, Bart. . . } for *Co.* Lord G. C. H. Somerset (as above)	1818

GEORGE IV.

Sir Charles Morgan, Bart. (the same) . . . . } for the *Co.* Lord G. C. H. Somerset (the same)	
Henry, Marquess of Worcester [see 1813, opposed by *John Hodder Moggridge*, Esq.; } for the *Bor.* votes for Worcester 90, for Moggridge 40] . . .	1820

	A.D.
WILLIAM IV.	
Lord G. C. H. Somerset (the same) } for the *Co.* William Addams Williams, Esq.	
Benjamin Hall, Esq. [afterwards Bart., and Baron Llanover; contested the seat with the *Marquess of Worcester*; votes—Hall, 168; Worcester, 149], for the *Bor.*	1831
Benjamin Hall, Esq. [seat contested by the *Marquess of Worcester*; votes—Hall, 393; } Worcester, 355], for the *Bor.* . .	1832
Benjamin Hall, Esq. [seat contested by Joseph Bailey, Esq., jun.; votes—Hall, 428; } Bailey, 424], for the *Bor.* . . .	1835

VICTORIA.

Reginald James Blewitt, Esq. [contested election; votes for Blewitt 440, for *Joseph* } Bailey, jun., 386], for the *Bor.* . .	1837
Lord Granville Charles Henry Somerset [the same as for 1831] . . . . . } for the *Co.* Hon. Charles O. S. Morgan, *vice* Williams, resigned .	1841 to 1852
Reginald James Blewitt, Esq. [contest; votes for Blewitt } for the *Bor.* 330, for Edwards none] .	
Hon. Charles O. S. Morgan (the same) . . . . } for the *Co.* Edward Arthur Somerset, Esq.	1852
Crawshay Bailey, Esq., for the *Bor.* . .	
The same, for *Co.* and *Bor.*	1857
The same, for *Co.* and *Bor.*	1859
Hon. Charles O. S. Morgan } for the *Co.* Lt.-Col. Poulett G. H. Somerset	1868
Crawshay Bailey, Esq. (the same), for the *Bor.*	
Hon. Charles O. S. Morgan (the same) . . . . Lt.-Col. Paulett G. H. Somerset, } for the *Co.* C.B. (the same) . . . Sir John Ramsden, Bart. [seat contested by *S. Homfray*, } for the *Bor.* Esq.; votes for Ramsden 1,641, for Homfray 1,449] .	1868

[*The present sitting Members*, 1872.]

SECTION VII.—THE COUNTY MAGISTRATES OF MONMOUTHSHIRE, 1872.

[Those marked thus * are Visiting Justices of the Monmouth County Prison, and those marked thus † of the Usk County Prison. The two bodies of Visiting Justices form the Finance Committee.]

His Grace the Duke of Beaufort, K.G., *Lord Lieutenant and Custos Rotulorum*, Badminton, Chippenham.
* † Samuel Richard Bosanquet, Esq., *Chairman of Quarter Sessions*, Dingestow Court, Monmouth.
† Granville Robert Henry Somerset, Esq., Q.C., *Deputy Chairman of Q. Sess.*, 6, Park Street, Westminster.

The Marquess of Worcester, Troy House, Monmouth.
Lord Raglan, Cefn Tilla, Usk.
Lord Tredegar, Tredegar Park, Newport.
The Honourable James Fitzwalter Clifford Butler, Llantillio Court, Abergavenny.
The Honourable William Powell Rodney, Llanvihangel Court, Abergavenny.

The Honourable Godfrey Charles Morgan, Tredegar Park, Newport.
Sir George Ferdinand Radzivil Walker, Bart., Castle town, Cardiff.
Amiel, Capt. J. T., The Chapel, Newport.
Bailey, Crawshay, Esq., Maindiff Court, Abergavenny.

MONMOUTHSHIRE.

Bannerman, James M., Esq., Wyaston Leys, Mon.
Bateman, Robert, Esq., Bertholeu House, Llangibby.
Berrington, Arthur Davis, Esq., Pantygoitre House.
Blewitt, Reginald James, Esq. (abroad).
* Bosanquet, Samuel Courthope, Esq., Dingestow Ct.
* † Bosanquet, S. Richard, Esq., Dingestow Court.
Brewer, John Edwin, Esq., Gorelands, Abergavenny.
Brewer, Tom Llewelyn, Esq., Dan-y-Graig, Newport.
Brown, Thomas, Esq., Chepstow.
† Byrde, Col. Henry Charles, Goytre House.

Carlisle, Richard, Esq., Llanvapley Court.
Cartwright, William Sheward, Esq., Stow Hill.
* Cave, George, Esq., Burfield, Westbury-on-Trim.
Clay, Henry, jun., Esq., The Mount, Chepstow.
† Clifford, Col. Henry Morgan, Llantillio Court.
Coates, Nathaniel, Esq., Sirhowy, Tredegar.
Cordes, Thomas, Esq., Brynglas, Newport.
Crawley, W., *Archdeacon*, Bryngwyn, Raglan.
Crompton-Roberts, C., Esq., Drybridge, Monmouth.

Darby, Abraham, Esq., Ebbw Vale, Newport.
* † Davies, Capt. James, The Garth, Mon.
Davies, Joseph, Esq., Bedwas, Newport.
Davies, Richard, *Clerk*, Court-y-Gollen, Abergavenny.
Dimmack, Edward Bagnall, Esq.

Eastham, James, Esq., Coed Cefn, Tregaer, Mon.
Evans, Thomas, *Clerk*, Nantyderry House, Pontypl.

Farquhar, James, *Clerk*, Llanddewi Skirrid.
Franks, John, Esq., Mount Ballan, Chepstow.

Gething, G. B., Esq., Springfield, Newport.
Gratrex, Thomas, Esq., Farmwood, Newport.
† Greenhow-Relph, George Relph, Esq., Beech Hill.
Griffiths, William, Esq., 7, Lower Berkeley Street.

Hamilton, Pryce Bowman, Esq., Hilston House.
Harford, Charles Lloyd, Esq.
Harford, Summers, Esq.
Herbert, John Arthur, Esq., Llanarth Court, Mon.
Hickman, Capt. Robert John, Monmouth.
Hill, James Charles, Esq., The Brooks, Abergavenny.
Homfray, Lorenzo Augustus, Esq., Woodlands.
† Homfray, Samuel, Esq., Glen Usk, Caerleon.
Homfray, Samuel George, Esq., Neuaddfach, Pontardulais, Carmarthenshire.
Hort, Fenton, Esq., Cheltenham.
Hubbuck, George Parker, Esq.
Humfrey, James, Esq., Llanwenarth, Abergavenny.

* Jackson, Robert, *Clerk*, Wonastow, Monmouth.
James, James George, Esq., Ty Newydd, Blackwood.
† James, John, Esq., Llansoar, Caerleon.
James, John Davies, Esq., Blackwood, Newport.
Jayne, Basil, Esq., Parade, Monmouth.
Jenkins, Alexander Howell, Esq., Bell Hall, Stourbdg.

Kennard, Edward, Esq., Blaenavon House, Pontypl.
Kennard, Henry Martin, Esq., Crumlin Hall.
King, Major, Clydach House, Abergavenny.

Lawrence, John, Esq., Crick House, Chepstow.
Levick, Frederick, Esq., Blaenau, Newport.
Lewis, Charles Edward, Esq., St. Pierre, Chepstow.
Lister, Edward, Esq., Cefn Ila, Usk.
Llewellin, John Cleeves, *Clerk*, Trevethin Vicarage.
Logan, John, Esq., Bath.

Manning, William Woodward, Esq.
Marsh, Capt. Henry Godfrey.
Marsh, Thomas Palmer Parr, Esq.
Master, Thomas W. Chester, Esq., Stratton House.
Maund, John, Esq., Windham Club, St. James's Sq.
† McDonnell, Major Francis, Plâs Newydd.
Mitchell, Frank Johnstone, Esq., Llanvrechva Grange.
Moggridge, Francis, Esq., Avon Lwyd, Caerleon.
Moggridge, Matthew, Esq., The Hove, Plymouth.
Morgan, Charles Octavius Swinnerton, Esq., M.P., The Friars, Newport.
Morgan, Hon. Arthur John, Tredegar Park.
Morgan, David, *Clerk*, Blaenau, Newport.

Needham, William, Esq., 34, Montpelier Square.
† Nicholl, George Whitlock, Esq., The Ham.
† Nicholl, Hume, Esq.
Nicholson, Charles, Esq., Llwyn-y-Celyn, Newport.

Ormerod, George, Esq., Sedbury Park, Chepstow.

Parkes, Charles James, Esq., Wentsland, Pontypool.
Payne, Lieut.-Col. John Selwyn, 8, Richmond Terrace, Clifton.
Pearson, Capt. J. R., Craig yr Haul, Castletown.
† Phillips, Edward Harris, Pulteney Street, Bath.
Phillips, Edward James, Esq., Drayton Villa, Maendy, Newport.
Phillips, William, Esq., Salisbury Lodge, Clifton.
Phillips, William Williams, Esq., The Grange.
Pope, Thomas. *Clerk*, Christchurch. Newport.
Potter, Richard, Esq., Argoed, Monmouth.
Powell, Henry St. John, Esq.
Powell, William, *Clerk*, Llanhennock, Caerleon.
Price, Thomas Phillips, Esq., Llanarth, Raglan.
Price, William, *Canon*, Llanarth, Raglan.

Rees, Richard, Esq., Abergavenny.
Rees, W. Treharne, Esq., Holly House, Newport.
Rhodes, Thomas William, Esq., Risca, Newport.
Richards, Josiah, Esq., Abersychan, Pontypool.
Roberts, Martyn John, Esq., Penydarren House.
Roden, Lieut.-Col. Richard Brown, Ty Brith.
Rolls, Major Alexander, Croft-y-Bulla, Mon.
Rolls, John Allan, Esq., The Hendre, Monmouth.
* Rooke, Lieut.-Col. Willoughby Sandilands, The Florence, Coleford.
Russell, John, Esq., Cheltenham.
Russell, Capt. John Richard.

Savery, Almericus Blakeney, Esq.
Scudamore, John Lucy, Esq., Kentchurch, Heref.
Seymour, Edward William, Esq., Porthmawr.
Seys, William Æneas, Esq., Tutshill House.
† Smith, Michael Parker, Esq.

COUNTY MAGISTRATES OF MONMOUTHSHIRE.

Somerset, Col. E. Arthur, Stoke House, Bristol.
Somerset, Col. Poulett, C.B.
Somerset, Granville Robert Henry, Esq., Q.C., 6, Park Street, Westminster, S.W.
Somerset, The Lord Henry, Esq., M.P., 19, Hill Street, Berkeley Square, London.
Somerset, William, *Clerk,* Wollaston Rectory.
Steward, W. James, Esq., Croft-y-Bwla, Monmouth.
Stone, John Jefferies, Esq., Scyborwen, Llantrisant.
Style, William Henry Marsham, Esq.

Thompson, John, Esq., Glyn Abbey, Cydweli, Carm.
Trumper, Thomas, Esq., The Lawns, Grosmont.
* Tyler, Capt. George Griffin, The Hill, Mon.
Tynte, C. Kemeys Kemeys, Esq., Cefn Mabley.
Tynte, Col. C. John Kemeys, Cefn Mabley.

* Vaughan, Col. John Francis, Courtfield.

Wheeley, Capt. W. Henry, of Pentre.
Wheeley, John Griffiths, Esq., of Pentre.
Wickham, Lieut.-Col. Thomas, Llangibby Castle, Newport.
Williams, Charles Henry, Esq.
Williams, Edmund Davies, Esq., Maesyruddud, Blackwood, Newport.
Williams, Ferdinand Capel Hanbury, Esq., Nant Oer.
Williams, Ferdinand Hanbury, Esq., Coldbrook Pk.
Williams, George Crofts, Esq., Llanrumney Hall.
Williams, Hugh, *Chancellor,* Bassaleg, Newport.
Williams, Philip, Esq., Aberbaiden, Abergavenny.
Williams, Philip Alfred, Esq., Abertillery, Newport.
Williams, Richard, *Clerk,* Ightfield House, Chepstow.
Williams, Thomas, *Dean of Llandaff,* The Deanery.
† Williams, William Addams, Esq., Boyd Villa, Pembroke Road, Clifton.
Willis, George, Esq., M.D., Monmouth.
Wyatt, Osmond Arthur, Esq., Troy House, Mon.

In the Commission of the Peace, but have not yet qualified.

The Honourable Frederic Courtenay Morgan, Tredegar Park, Newport.
Sir Samuel Fludyer, Bart.
Blackwell, Samuel Holden, Esq.

Carruthers, James Proctor, Esq., The Grondre.

Dorin, Joseph Alexander, Esq.

Falconer, Thomas, Esq., *Judge of C. C.,* Usk.

Gore, George, *Clerk,* Bath.

Herbert, John Maurice, Esq., Springfields, Ross.
Herbert, William, Esq., Clytha House, Raglan.
Herbert, William Reginald, Esq., Clytha House.
Heyworth, Capt. Lawrence, Waun Fawr.
Hooper, Thomas Clarence, Esq.
Hutchins, Edward John, Esq., Dowlais.

James, Jane, *Clerk.*
Jane, Warren Hurdman, Esq., Chepstow.
Jones, Philip, Esq.

Lee, John Edward, Esq., The Priory, Caerleon.

Lewis, Edward Freke, *Clerk,* Llanvair, Abergavenny.
Lewis, Thomas Freke, Esq., Abbey Dore, Hereford.

Machen, Edward, Esq.
Milman, Henry Salusbury, Esq., 1, Cranley Place, Onslow Gardens, London.
Morgan, Charles Augustus Samuel, *Clerk,* Machen.
Morgan, William Lee, *Clerk,* Cardiff.

Partridge, John, Esq., Bishop's Wood, Ross.
Price, Joseph Thomas, Esq., Monmouth.

Reed, James, Esq., Tredegar Iron Works, Tredegar.
Roden, William Serjeant, Esq.

Upton, John, Esq.

Vaughan, William, Esq., Courtfield, Ross.

Wienholt, William, Esq., Llanwern, Newport.
Williams, Thomas Lewis, *Clerk,* Portskewitt.
Williams, Trevor Samuel Addams, Esq., The Garth.
Wood, Major-General William Mark, Bishop's Hall, Romford, Essex.

Prothero, Charles, Esq., *Clerk of the Peace and County Treasurer,* Newport.

THE COUNTY FAMILIES OF MONMOUTHSHIRE.

BAILEY, Crawshay, Esq., of Maindiff Court, Monmouthshire.

J. P. and D. L. of the co. of Monmouth; was Capt. of the Royal Brecknock Militia; son of the late Crawshay Bailey, Esq., of Llanfoist House, co. of Monmouth (who d. 1871), J. P. and D. L. for the cos. of Glamorgan and Brecon, High Sheriff for co. of Monmouth 1851, and for several years M.P. for the Monmouth district of boroughs; and nephew of the late Sir Joseph Bailey, Bart., of Glanusk Park (see *Bailey of Glanusk Park*); *b.* at Nantyglo, 1821; *m.*, 1863, Mary, dau. of the Count Metaxa, of Cheltenham; *s.* 1871; has issue.

Residence: Maindiff Court, near Abergavenny.
Town Address: Carlton Club.
Arms: Arg., betw. two bars three annulets in fesse gu. between as many martlets of the last.
Crest: A griffin sejant arg. semée of annulets gu.

BATEMAN, Robert, Esq., of Bertholey, Monmouthshire.

J. P. and D. L. for the co. of Monmouth; fourth but eldest surviving son of the late Colthurst Bateman, Esq., of the same place, J. P. of the co. of Monmouth, and Sheriff of the same co. in 1839, by his wife Jane Sarah, dau. and sole h. of John Kemeys Gardner Kemeys, Esq., of Bertholey; *b.* 1819; *s.* on the decease of his brother John; is *m.* and has issue.

Residence: Bertholey House, near Usk.
Arms: Or, on a chevron between three escallops gu. an ostrich feather arg.
Crest: A pheasant ppr.

LINEAGE.

The *Batemans* are a family of long standing in co. Kerry, Ireland, where several of its members have been High Sheriffs and representatives in Parliament.

BEAUFORT, Duke of, Henry Charles Fitzroy Somerset, of Troy House, Monmouthshire, and Badminton, Glouc.

Creations—Baron Bottetcourt 1308; Baron Herbert 1461; Baron Herbert of Raglan, Chepstow, and Gower, 1506; Earl of Worcester 1514; Marquess of Worcester 1642; Earl of Glamorgan, Viscount Grosmont, and Baron Beaufort, 1644; Duke of Beaufort 1682.

Eighth Duke of Beaufort; K.G., P.C.; late Master of the Horse; Lord Lieutenant of the co. of Monmouth; Capt. 7th Hussars 1847; Lieut.-Col. in the army, retired 1861; Lieut.-Col. Commandant of the Gloucestershire Yeomanry Hussars; was M.P. for East Gloucestershire 1846—1853. *Born* Feb. 1, 1824; *ed.* at Eton; *m.*, July 3, 1845, Lady Georgiana Charlotte Curzon, eldest dau. of Richard, 1st Earl Howe, P.C., G.C.H.; *s.* on the death of his father, the seventh Duke of Beaufort, 1853; has issue living—

1. HENRY ADELBERT WELLINGTON FITZROY, Marquess of Worcester; *b.* 1847; *ed.* at Eton; Capt. in Royal Horse Guards, and Capt. Royal Glouc. Yeomanry Hussars; J. P. and D. L. for the cos. of Monmouth and Gloucester.
2. Henry Richard Charles (Lord), *b.* 1849.
3. Henry Arthur George (Lord), *b.* 1851.
4. Henry Edward Brudenell (Lord), *b.* 1853.
5. Henry Fitzroy Francis (Lord), *b.* 1855.
6. Lady Blanche Elizabeth Adelaide, *b.* 1856.

Residences: Troy House, Monmouth; Badminton, and Stoke Gifford, Gloucestershire.
Town Address: Carlton Club; White's Club.
Arms: The arms of France and England quarterly, viz., 1st and 4th, az., three fleurs-de-lis arg.—*France;* 2nd and 3rd, gu., three lions passant guardant in pale or—*England;* within a bordure compony arg. and az.
Crest: A portcullis or, nailed az., chains pendent gold.
Supporters: Dexter, a panther arg., flames issuing from the mouth and ears, ppr., plain collared and chained or, and semée of torteaux, &c.; *sinister,* a wyvern vert, in the mouth holding a sinister hand coupé at the wrist, gu.

LINEAGE.

The descent of this noble house is from the royal line of *Plantagenet* through John of Gaunt (son of

Edward III. of England), whose natural children, begotten by Catherine Swinford (whom he afterwards married`, were all legitimatized, and were caused by their father to be called by the name of Beaufort, after the castle of Beaufort, in Anjou, where they were born. But about the "exception," excluding all claim to the throne, there seems to be a doubt. The words "excepta dignitate regali" appear on the parliament rolls as an *interlineation*, added, as is supposed, at the time when Henry IV. exemplified the same grant in 1407, and in which exemplification the words are inserted (Nicolas's *Peerage* by Courthope 1858). John of Gaunt's eldest son was—

JOHN, of whom hereafter.

Henry, the second son, was made Bishop of Winchester, a Cardinal, and Lord Chancellor for England. His natural dau. Joan became wife of Sir Edward Stradling (see *Stradling of St. Donat's*).

Thomas, the youngest son, was created Earl of Dorset 1412, and Duke of Exeter 1416. He *d. s. p.* 1427.

JOHN BEAUFORT, the eldest son, created Earl of Somerset by Richard II., 1396, *m.* Margaret, sister and co-h. to Edmund Holland, Earl of Kent, and had by her four sons and two daus. The elder dau., Joan, *m.* James I. of Scotland, and after his death Sir James Stuart, son to Lord Lorne; the younger, Margaret, *m.* Thomas Courtenay, who was sixth Earl of Devonshire. The eldest son, Henry, *d. unm.*, and left his inheritance to his next brother,—

JOHN, third Earl of Somerset, created Duke of Somerset 1443. He *m.* Margaret, dau. of Sir John Beauchamp, of Bletshoe, Beds., and left an only dau., *Margaret*, who *m. Edmund Tudor*, Earl of Richmond, eldest son of Owen Tudor of Penmynydd, Môn., and Catherine of France, Queen of England, widow of Henry V., and had issue Henry, Earl of Richmond, afterwards King of England. John, first Duke of Som., *d.* 1444, leaving no male issue, and was succ. by his next brother,—

EDMUND, cr. Duke of Somerset 26th Henry VI., slain at battle of St. Alban's, 1455. His wife was Eleanor, second dau. and co-h. to Richard Beauchamp, Earl of Warwick. He was succ. by his eldest son,—

HENRY, third Duke of Somerset, K.G., who was renowned for his valour in the French wars; was Lieutenant of the Isle of Wight, Governor of Carisbrook Castle, and Governor of Calais; was taken prisoner when commanding Henry the Sixth's forces at the battle of Hexham, and beheaded by the Yorkists, leaving an only natural son,—

CHARLES SOMERSET, a man of extraordinary energy and ability, who rose to the highest pitch of fame and fortune. Henry VII., his kinsman, made him in 1485 one of his Privy Council, in 1488 Admiral of the Fleet, in 1490 Ambassador to the Emperor Maximilian; was also made Knight of the Garter, and Captain of the Guards. Having obtained such high distinction he won the hand of the wealthy heiress, Elizabeth, dau. and h. of William *Herbert*, Lord Herbert of Raglan, Chepstow, and Gower, and in her right inherited the title of Lord Herbert, by which name he was summoned to Parliament by Henry VIII. This king, recognising his near kinship, being maternally descended from Owen Tudor, constituted him Lord Chamberlain for life, and in 1514 advanced him to the dignity of Earl of Worcester. He *d.* 1526, when his title and estates devolved upon his eldest son,—

HENRY, second Earl of Worcester, who *m.*

Elizabeth, dau. of Sir Anthony Browne, Kt., by whom he left an eldest son and heir,—

WILLIAM, third Earl of Worcester, Knight of the Garter, &c. He *m.* Christian, dau. of Lord North, by whom he had an only son,—

EDWARD, fourth Earl of Worcester, Master of the Horse to Queen Elizabeth and James I., Lord Privy Seal, &c. He died at his house in the Strand 1628. His eldest surviving son, by Elizabeth, dau. of Francis, Earl of Huntingdon, was—

HENRY, fifth Earl of Worcester, the celebrated Royalist who defended Raglan Castle against Fairfax in 1646. The castle was surrendered and his estates sequestrated (see *Raglan Castle*). He was raised to the dignity of Marquess of Worcester 1642. By his wife, Anne, dau. and h. of John, Lord Russell, son of Francis, Earl of Bedford, he had issue nine sons and four daus. He was succ. by his eldest son,—

EDWARD, second Marquess of Worcester, Lord Lieutenant of North Wales, author of *A Century of Inventions*, 1663, in which the principle of the steam engine is plainly unfolded. By his first wife, Elizabeth, dau. of Sir Henry Dormer, Kt., he left with other issue a son,—

HENRY, third Marquess of Worcester, who was made Lord President of Wales and the Marches, and created Duke of Beaufort 1682. He made a *progress* through Wales in 1684. Opposed the Duke of Monmouth in 1685, and refused to take the oath of allegiance to William III. By Mary, his wife, dau. of Lord Capel and widow of Henry, Lord Beauchamp, he had several children, his second but eldest surviving son being—

CHARLES, styled Marquess of Worcester, who, dying in the lifetime of his father, left by his wife Rebecca, dau. of Sir Josiah Child, Kt. and Bart., an eldest son,—

HENRY, who at the death of his grandfather, Henry, first Duke of Beaufort, succeeded as second Duke. By his second wife, Rachel. second dau. and co-h. of Wriothesley Baptist Noel, Earl of Gainsborough, he left at his decease in 1714 an eldest son,—

HENRY, third Duke of Beaufort, who *m.* Frances, only child and h. of Sir James Scudamore, Bart., of Home Lacy, Heref., by whom he had no issue, and from whom he obtained a divorce in 1744. He *d.* 1746, and was succ. by his brother,—

CHARLES NOEL, fourth Duke of Beaufort, M.P. for the co. of Monmouth, who *m.* Elizabeth, dau. of John Berkeley, Esq., of Stoke Gifford, co. of Gloucester, by whom he had issue, besides five daus., one son, his successor,—

HENRY, fifth Duke of Beaufort and seventh Marquess of Worcester, K.G., who *m.*, 1776, Elizabeth, dau. of Edward Boscawen, Admiral of the Fleet, and had a numerous offspring. He was succ. by his eldest son,—

HENRY CHARLES, sixth Duke of Beaufort, *b.* 1766; *m.*, 1791, Charlotte Sophia, dau. of Granville, first Marquess of Stafford, by whom he had issue two sons and eight daus. His Grace *d.* 1835, when the titles and estates devolved upon his elder son,—

HENRY, seventh Duke of Beaufort, K.G., &c., *b.* 1792; *m.*, 1st, 1814, Georgiana Frederica, dau. of the Hon. Frederick Fitzroy, son of the second Lord Southampton, by whom (who *d.* 1821) he had issue two daus. (one surviving); 2ndly, 1822, Emily Frances, dau. of Charles Culling Smith, Esq., by whom he left issue a son and six daus. His Grace *d.* 1853, leaving issue as follows:—

i. HENRY CHARLES, now eighth Duke of Beaufort (as above).

ii. Georgiana Charlotte Anne (by first marriage), *b*. 1817; *m*., 1836, Sir C. W. Codrington, Bart.
iii. Emily Blanche Charlotte, *b*. 1828; *m*., 1848, George Hay, eleventh Earl of Kinnoull.
iv. Rose Caroline Mary, *b*. 1829; *m*., 1846, F. F. Lovell, Esq.
v. Henrietta Louisa Priscilla, *b*. 1831; *m*., 1855, John Morant, Esq., of Brockenhurst House, Hants; *d*. 1863.
vi. Geraldine Harriet Anne, Lady in Waiting to H.R.H. the Duchess of Cambridge, *b*. 1832.
vii. Catherine Emily Mary, *b*. 1834; *m*., 1858, the Hon. Arthur Walsh, M.P., eldest son of Lord Ormathwaite.
viii. Edith Frances Wilhelmine, *b*. 1838; *m*, 1863, William Henry, Baron Londesborough.

Note.—For engraving of *Troy House* see p. 724, and for an account of *Raglan Castle* see pp. 741—745.

BERRINGTON, Jenkin Davies-, Esq., of Pant-y-goetre, Monmouthshire.

J. P. for cos. Glamorgan and Carmarthen, and D. L. for Glamorgan; son of Jenkin Davies-Berrington Esq,. of Swansea; *b*. at Swansea, April 17, 1801; *ed*. at Harrow, and Trin. Coll., Camb.; *m*., February 3rd, 1827, Charlotte, dau. of Benjamin Hall, Esq., of Hensol Castle, co. Glamorgan, M.P. for Glamorgan, and sister of the late Lord Llanover, and has issue an only surviving son,—
ARTHUR DAVIES-BERRINGTON, Esq., of Pant-y-goetre, co. Monmouth, and Cefngolé, co. Glamorgan; J. P. and D. L. for cos. Monmouth and Glamorgan; High Sheriff for Monmouthshire 1866; *b*. March 30, 1833; *ed*. at Eton and at Exeter Coll., Oxford; *m*., first, Frances Lennox Heneage, dau. of Rev. Charles Lane, Rector of Wrotham, Kent, by whom he has issue *Arthur Tewdyr Davies-Berrington, b.* Sept. 7th, 1854, and two other sons, and a dau.; secondly, Ada Barbara, dau. of John Lane, Esq., of Leyton Grange, Essex, by whom he has issue a son and four daus.

Residence: Pant-y-goetre, Abergavenny.
Arms: Sable, three greyhounds courant arg.
—BERRINGTON; az., a wolf salient arg.—DAVIES.
Crests: A star of six points wavy, gu.; a wolf salient, arg.
Motto: Solem fero.

LINEAGE.

This family derives its descent in the male line from Tydwal Glôff, fifth son of Rhodri Mawr, the last British "King of all Wales," A.D. 820, whose cognizance, a wolf salient, is still borne in the arms; and in the female line represents the elder branch of the Awbrey family (see *Awbrey of Abercynrig, ante*, and Jones's "Brecknockshire"). The name and arms of Berrington were assumed at the close of the last century.

BOSANQUET, Samuel Richard, Esq., of Dingestow Court, Monmouthshire.

J. P. and D. L. for co. Monmouth; Chairman of Quarter Sessions for same co.; Author of "*A New System of Logic*," "*Principia*," "*First and Fourth Seals*," "*Excelsior*," "*Eirenicon*," "*The Successive Visions of the Cherubim*," and other works; eldest son of Samuel Bosanquet, Esq., of Forest House, Essex, and Dingestow Court, Monmouthshire, J. P. for the co. of Mon., and Sheriff for same co. 1814 (see *Sheriffs); b*. in London, April 1st, 1800; *ed*. at Eton, and Christ Church, Oxon.; *grad*. M.A. 1823; *m*., February 3rd, 1830, Emily, eldest dau. of George Courthope, Esq., of Whiligh, Sussex, and has issue 8 sons and 2 daus. (see *Lineage); s.* to estates 1843.

Heir: Samuel Courthope.
Residences: Forest House, Epping Forest, Essex; and Dingestow Court, Monmouth.
Arms: Or, a tree vert; in chief, gules, a crescent between two stars arg. Quartering arms of *Dunster* and *Gardiner*. The family being noble in France, the arms have supporters, viz., two lions rampant.
Crest: A demi-lion rampant.
Motto: Per damna, per cædes.

LINEAGE.

The Bosanquets trace their origin to the hilly district of the Cevennes (a Celtic word meaning a ridge, which has its cognate in the Welsh *cefn*, a back, a long extended eminence) in the south of France, approaching the north-west base of the Pyrenees. The old Celtic race was here comparatively undisturbed, and the free spirit of the mountains, revolting against the dominance of the priesthood, embraced Protestantism, and was only crushed, after the revocation of the edict of Nantes, by the "dragonnades" of Louis XIV. and the terrible persecutions which forced some 400,000 of the Huguenots, the cream of the population of France, to seek as exiles homes in other lands. The Bosanquets were among the many families who settled in England and never returned.
From Roubs Bosanquet de Colognac en Cevennes descended—
Pierre Bosanquet, hab. de Colognac en Cevennes, who *m*. Demoiselle Catherine Perrane, hab. de Colognac in Cevennes.
Their son, Fulcrand Bosanquet, hab. de Colognac, "et qui fut assassiné au dit lieu." His name occurs in a list of soldiers under M. le Baron de Vaillac, 1583 (parchment at Rock). He *m*. Bonne Boisse de Montpellier.
In 1623 Pierre Bosanquét, their son, *m*. Antoinette Mainville, called Demoiselle Catherine Mainvilla de Lunel in the *Gaussen* MS.
Pierre Bosanquet, their son, "dec. à Lunel, le

Dimanche à midi, septième Nov. 1700 N.S. (see David Bosanquet's MS. at Dingestow), *m.*, 1653, Gaillarde de Barbut, "hab. de Lunel, niece de la Demlle. Catherine Devaux de Colard, de suivant le testament de la dite Dem. C. Devaux, spouse du St. Jean Colard, et celui de la Demlle. Colard, leur fille."

It was the son of Pierre and Gaillarde de Barbut, David Bosanquet, that brought this family name to Wales. He was *b.* on Monday, Oct. 31, 1661, at Lunel; came to London at the Revocation of the Edict of Nantes; had the rights of a denizen granted him by warrant under the Great Seal, Dec. 16, 1687; was summoned before the Heralds' College to have his arms and pedigree recorded, 1687; *d.* July 5, 1732, æt. 70; buried in St. Stephen's, Coleman Street, where his monument remained in 1867. He *m.* Elizabeth, dau. of Claude Hays, Esq., by Eleanor, dau. of — Conyers, Esq , *b.* Saturday, Sept. 23, 1676; *d.* Sept. 30, 1737; buried in St. Stephen's, Coleman Street, London.

David Bosanquet had eleven children, one of whom, second son, named Samuel, was of Forest House, and also of Dingestow Court ; *b.* Sept. 4, 1700; *d.* Jan. 14, 1765, æt. 64. He *m.*, 1732, Mary, dau. and sole h. of William Dunster, Esq., of Leyton, Essex, *d.* Sept. 4, 1765, æt. 53.

Their eldest son, Samuel Bosanquet, the second of that name, of Forest House and Dingestow Court (*b.* 1744 ; *d.* July 4, 1806), *m.*, 1767, Eleanor, younger dau. of H. Lannoy Hunter, Esq., of Beech Hill, *d.* Jan. 7, 1819.

Samuel Bosanquet, their son, and the third of the name, of Forest House and Dingestow Court, (*b.* Aug. 26, 1768; *d.* June 3, 1843), *m.*, 1798, Letitia Philippa, dau. of James Whatman, Esq., of Vinters, baptized March 1, 1774; *d.* Dec. 8, 1855. Their eldest son is—

SAMUEL BOSANQUET, Esq., the fourth of that name, now of Forest House and Dingestow Court, representative of the eldest branch of the Bosanquet family, as above. Mr. Bosanquet has issue as under:—

1. Samuel Courthope.
2. Claude.
3. G. Stanley.
4. Albert.
5. Walter Henry.
6. Edmund Fletcher.
7. William David.
8. Richard Arthur.
9. Amy, *m.* Rev. J. Lloyd, and has issue.
10. Fanny Elizabeth.

From Charles Bosanquet, Esq., brother of Samuel Bosanquet the third, are descended the Bosanquets of Rock, Northumberland. James W. Bosanquet, Esq., of Claysmore, Mid.; W. H. F. Bosanquet, Esq., of Knockane Lodge, co. Waterford; and Admiral Bosanquet, are brothers of Samuel Bosanquet, of Dingestow Court. The Rt. Hon. Sir John Bernard Bosanquet, app. Judge of the Common Pleas 1830, and sometime a Lord Commissioner of the Great Seal, was a distinguished member of this honourable family.

Bosanquets, the bankers, of London, are of a junior branch of the family, from William, fourth son of David Bosanquet, the Huguenot exile.

The family became extinct in France in the present century.

Note.—The site of old Dingestow Castle is near the church. This stronghold was twice taken by the Welsh; and Simon de Poer, Sheriff of Herefordshire, was killed there. The masonry has been entirely destroyed. Forest House was a brick Tudor mansion, erected A.D. 1622. Of late years it has been modernized and stuccoed. The Earl of Norwich, one of the Parliamentary generals, lived and died there. Dingestow Court was built in 1623 ; it was enlarged, and the south front was rebuilt in stone in the Elizabethan style in 1846.

BUTLER, The Hon. James Fitzwalter Clifford-, of Llantilio Court, Monmouthshire.

Lieut.-Col. 2nd Administrative Battalion Monmouthshire Rifle Volunteers ; J. P. and D. L. for co. Monmouth ; son of Theobald Fitzwalter Butler, Lord Dunboyne, in the Peerage of Ireland, fourteenth Baron, cr. 1541 ; *b.* in Dublin, 20th May, 1839 ; *ed.* at Winchester School ; *m.*, 12th June, 1860, Marion, only child of Colonel Henry Morgan Clifford, of Llantilio, Abergavenny, and has issue 1 dau.,— Rosalinda Catherine Sophia.

Residence: Llantilio Court, near Abergavenny.
Arms : The *Dunboyne* arms, quartering *Clifford*.
Motto : Timor Domini fons vitæ.

LINEAGE.

For the genealogy of this family see *Dunboyne, Baron of*, in the Peerage of Ireland.

Note.—The fine old ruin of *White Castle* is in Llantilio parish, and the site of the moated residence of Sir David Gam is near Llantilio Court. There is an ancient British encampment on this estate in the adjoining parish of Penrhôs.

BYRDE, Lieut.-Col. Henry Charles, of Goetre House, Monmouthshire.

Lieut.-Col. in the Army; served in India; J. P. for the co. of Monmouth ; Sheriff for same co. 1864; is *m.* and has issue. (Col. Byrde being absent abroad in 1871, further information not obtained.)

Residence: Goetre House, near Abergavenny.

CLAY, Henry, Esq., of Piercefield Park, Monmouthshire.

J. P. for Staffordshire and Derbyshire ; son of the late Joseph Clay, Esq., banker, of Burton-on-Trent, *d.* 1824, by Sarah his wife ; *b.* at Burton-on-Trent, in 1797 ; *m.*, in 1824, Elizabeth, second dau. of J. Leigh, Esq, of Sandhills and Upton, Lancashire; *s.* to estates in 1824 ; has issue 3 sons, Henry, Joseph Spender, and Charles John; and 2 daus., Caroline Elizabeth and Emily Jane.

Heir : Henry Clay, jun., *b.* 1825 ; M.A. of Trinity Coll., Camb. ; J. P. for Monmouthshire ; *m.*, 1863, Mary Louisa, dau. of the late Henry Boden, Esq., and has issue ; *residence*, The Mount, Chepstow.

Residence: Piercefield Park, near Chepstow.
Arms: Arg., a chevron engrailed sa. between three trefoils of the second.
Crest: Two wings displayed arg.
Motto: Clarior virtus honoribus.

CORDES, Thomas, Esq., of Bryn Glas, Monmouthshire.

J. P. for Monmouthshire, and for the bor. of Newport; Sheriff for the co. of Monmouth 1871. (Further information not received.)

CURRE, William Edward Carne, Esq., of Itton Court, Monmouthshire.

A minor; son of the late Edward Mathew Curre, Esq., of Itton Court, J. P. and D. L. for Mon., and High Sheriff 1859 (*d.* Feb. 15th, 1868), by his wife Annie, second dau. of Thomas King, Esq., of Chepstow; *b.* June 26th, 1855; *ed.* at Harrow School; is Patron of the Rectory of Itton, Monmouthshire, a church, dedicated to St. Deiniol, of Early English architecture, and recently restored in memory of the late E. M. Curre, Esq.

Residence: Itton Court, near Chepstow.
Arms: Arg., on a fesse between three cross crosslets sa., three martlets or (see *Sheriffs*, 1706), quartering Turbeville, Lewis, Mathew, &c.
Crest: An eagle displayed or.
Motto: Gratus si amicus.

LINEAGE.

The late Edward Mathew Curre, Esq., of Itton Court, the only surviving son of William Curre, Esq. (*d.* 1855), by Mary Alexaphina (*d.* 1823), dau. of John Bushby, Esq., of Tinwald Downs, co. Dumfries, was *b.* March 8th, 1809; *s.* in 1855; *d.* February 15th, 1868. He *m.*, in 1854, Annie, second dau. of Thomas King, Esq., of Chepstow (as above), and granddau. of Elizabeth Pendrill, a lineal descendant of John Pendrill (see *Archæologia Cambrensis*, 1859, pp. 114 and 229), and had issue,—
1. WILLIAM EDWARD CARNE, now of Itton (as above).
2. John-Mathew, *b.* April 8th, 1859.
3. Constance-Rebecca.

This family, formerly of Stubwood, near Hungerford, Berkshire, has been seated in Monmouthshire from the time of Charles II., and co-represents the Glamorganshire families of Turbeville of Clementstone (for some time the seat of the Curres), Lewis of Pennline, and Mathew of Aberaman. For sheriffs of this family, see *Sheriffs*, 1706, 1760, and under co. Glam. 1765.

Note.—The ancient mansion of *Itton* has been from time to time restored; but certain parts of it, and especially the tower, are believed to be of the fourteenth century.

EVANS, The Rev. Thomas, of Nantyderry, Monmouthshire.

Represents in Monmouthshire the Evans family of Llangeler, co. of Carm., who trace from an ancient and distinguished ancestry; *b.* at Pensingrig, Llangeler—a property which at one time formed a part of the extensive estate of the Havards of Dolhaidd and "Goytre in Emlyn;" *ed.* at private and public schools, and Trin. Coll., Dublin; ordained in 1841 on the curacy of Goytre, Mon., and in the same year presented to the rectory by the Right Hon. the Earl of Abergavenny; is Surrogate for the diocese of Llandaff; author of several articles, editor of Rev. Daniel Rees' "Sermons;" J. P. for the co. of Mon.; *m.*, March 4th, 1862, Anne, only child and heiress of the late James Corfe, Esq., of Goodwood Villa, Clifton (from Corfe Castle, Dorset); and has issue 3 daus.,—
1. Charlotte Mary.
2. Catherine Anne.
3. Mabel Gladys.

Residence: Nantyderry, near Abergavenny.
Crest: A bull's head.
Motto: In Deo spes est.

LINEAGE.

The family pedigree, drawn from MSS. in the Heralds' College, Hugh Thomas's MSS., Dwnn's *Visitations*, and the Dale Castle MSS., edited by the late Sir Thomas Phillipps, Bart., was published in the *Cambrian Journal*, 1864, and serves as a reliable basis for the following particulars.

Sir Walter *Havard* (contracted from *Havre de Grace*, the seaport in Normandy whence he came) was one of the companion knights of Bernard de Neuf Marché, or Newmarch, when, in the time of William Rufus, he made his successful descent upon the country of Brycheiniog, the greater part of which in later times has been called Brecknockshire. For his services Walter Havard was presented with a tract of country called the manor or lordship of Pontwilym, in the immediate neighbourhood of Brecon.

The Havards continued Lords of Pontwilym for sixteen generations. In 1543, 1549, and 1555, Thomas Havard of Pontwilym served as high sheriff of his county. But for some unknown reason they now quitted their ancient home, and we next find them in the person of Harry Havard, the grandson of Thomas Havard aforesaid, at Dolhaidd, in Carmarthenshire. The dignity of this elder branch of the house seems still to be kept up, for, according to Edwards' MS. in the Her. Coll., Harry Havard of Dolhaidd *m.* Elen, dau. of Sir Rhys ap Thomas of Dinefawr. His grandson was—

Harry Havard " of Goytre in Emlyn," who *m.* Mary, dau. of the Rev. Morris (more correctly *Morys;* writers of old Welsh pedigrees distort names as by rule) Williams, Vicar of Llangeler *circa* 1613.

The Havards continued to reside on their ancestral estate at Goytre for five generations further.

THE COUNTY FAMILIES OF MONMOUTHSHIRE. 775

Morys, son of Harry aforesaid, was lineally represented by his gr. gr. son, John Havard of Penlone and Goytre, the last resident owner of the Havard estate. Harry, son of John, removed to Milford, and at length the name became extinct (see *Evans, Crickhowel*). Mary, only dau. of aforesaid John Havard, *m.*—

Luther Evans, Esq., of Llangeler, a man of ardent piety, son of Josiah Evans of Llangeler, tracing his lineage, according to the *Lewes MSS.*, from Hoedliw, Lord of Iscerdin in Llandysul, ap Llawr ap Assur ap Morudd, King of Cardigan, &c. Luther Evans, by his wife, Mary Havard, had issue—

Methusalem Evans, of Llangeler, who *m.*, 1st, Mary, eldest child of William Jones, Esq., son of Richard Jones of Penwernfawr, Llandygwydd, co. Cardigan, and had issue as follows:—

John Evans, Rector of Crickhowel (see *Evans, Crickhowel*), who is eldest son.

William Evans, B.D., Vicar of Usk, and J. P. for Mon. (deceased), *m.* Louisa Caroline, eldest dau. of the late W. A. Williams, Esq., of Llangibby Castle, M.P. for Mon., and has issue three sons and two daus.

Samuel Evans, Vicar of Marshfield, *m.* Emma, dau. of Griffith Davies Bowen, Esq., of Maeseglwys, and has issue two sons and two daus., eldest son in holy orders.

Hannah *m.* John James of Dolybryn, and has issue; eldest son in holy orders.

THOMAS EVANS (as above), Rector of Goytre, Mon.

Methusalem Evans *m.*, 2ndly, Hannah, dau. of Thomas Howell, Esq., of Pen'rallt Fadog, Llangeler, and had issue Howell Howell Evans, and George Evans, who died young.

Through his mother, Anne, only dau. of the aforesaid Josiah Evans, descended also from Hoedliw, Lord of Iscerdin, the late Rev. Daniel Rees of Gilvachlas, Llangeler, who for thirty-five years was Rector of Aberystruth, co. Mon., J. P. and D. L. for that county. He was eminent for his high attainments and usefulness as a minister of the church, was the author of a collection of hymns in English and Welsh, and of a volume of forty excellent sermons in English, published after his death. He is represented by his only surviving child, Susan Maria, who is *m.* to J. G. French, Esq., Wells, Somerset.

On the mother's side the Rev. Thomas Evans is descended, according to the same authorities, through Catherine, heiress of Thomas Lloyd, Esq., of Pantcilgane, Llangeler, Carm., from Meredydd ap Rhydderch, Lord of Derllysc Castle and "the half of Dyfed," grandson of Tewdwr Mawr (Tudor the Great), gr. gr. son of Howel Dda, King of Wales, who himself was grandson of Rhodri Mawr.

The first Lloyd (from the Forest), according to the *Lewes MSS.*, settled at Pantcilgane towards the end of the reign of Elizabeth, where the family possessed estates of considerable extent, and intermarried with several of the most ancient houses in the counties of Carmarthen and Cardigan.

FALCONER, Thomas, Esq., of Usk, Monmouthshire.

Judge of County Courts in Glamorgan, Breconshire, and part of Radnorshire since 1851; J. P. for the cos. of Monmouth, Glamorgan, and Brecknock (see *Magistrates*); was employed by Government in 1850 in a case of arbitration on the boundaries of Canada and New Brunswick; Author of *pamphlets* on Educational Endowments, &c.; son of the late Rev. Thomas Falconer, M.A.; *b.* 1805; called to the Bar at Lincoln's Inn 1830. Among brothers living are Dr. R. W. Falconer, M.D., of Bath; Rev. William Falconer, M.A, Rector of Bushey, Herts.

Residence: Usk, Monmouthshire.
Town Address: Lincoln's Inn.
Arms: Or, a falcon's head issuing from a heart gu. between three mullets az.
Crest: A falcon ppr.

GRATREX, Thomas, Esq., of Farmwood, Monmouthshire.

J. P. and D. L. for the co. of Monmouth, and J. P. for the bor. of Newport; Sheriff for the co. of Monmouth 1857. (Further particulars not received.)

GREENHOW-RELPH, George Relph, Esq., of Beech Hill, Monmouthshire.

J. P. for the co. of Monmouth; High Sheriff for the same co. in 1867.

(*Further information not received.*)

Residence: Beech Hill, near Usk.

HAMILTON, Price Bowman, Esq., of Hilston Park, Monmouthshire.

Late Lieut. 13th Hussars, formerly Major-commanding 7th L.A.V.; J. P. for Monmouthshire; son of the late John Hamilton, Esq., J. P. of Hilston Park (*d.* 1868), by Anne, dau. of the late Pryce Jones, Esq., of Cyfronydd, Mont.; *b.* at Bellefield, Cheshire, April 11th, 1844; *ed.* at Harrow; *s.* Dec. 20, 1868.

Heiresses: Sisters: 1. Alice Mary Sinclair, Countess of Mar; 2. Laura Jane Campbell Hamilton.
Residence: Hilston Park, Monmouth.
Town Address: Boodle's Club, St. James's Street; Windham Club, St. James's Square.
Arms: The arms of *Hamilton of Coats*, co. Lanark.
Crest: The same.
Motto: Through.

LINEAGE.

This family derives its descent from Robert II. of Scotland, through Paul Hamilton of Coats (1600), from whom John Hamilton, Esq., of the Deer Park, Greenock, gr. grandfather of the present representative, traced in direct line. The family has intermarried with several houses of distinguished rank, such as the Bute and Mar families.

MONMOUTHSHIRE.

HANBURY, John Capel, Esq., of Pontypool Park, Monmouthshire.

Son of the late Capel Hanbury Leigh, Esq., of Pontypool Park (who had adopted the surname Leigh in addition to his own of Hanbury), by his second wife, Emma Elizabeth (who survives), dau. of the late Thomas Bates Rous, Esq., of Courtyrala, co. Glamorgan; *b.* 1853; *s.*, on the death of his father, 1861, and resumed the designation Hanbury only, the original surname of his family.

Residence: Pontypool Park, Mon.
Arms: The arms of *Hanbury* and *Leigh*.

HERBERT, John Arthur Edward, Esq., of Llanarth, Monmouthshire.

J. P. and D. L. for co. of Monmouth; High Sheriff in 1858; was formerly in the Diplomatic Service; eldest son of the late John Jones, Esq., of Llanarth, J. P. and D. L. for co. of Monmouth, by the Hon. Lady Harriet, only dau. of Arthur James, 8th Earl of Fingall, K.P.; *b.* at Llanarth Court, 1818; *ed.* at Prior Park College, Bath; assumed in 1848 the name of Herbert, being lineally descended from the ancient family of *Herberts* (see *Lineage*), in lieu of that of Jones; *m.*, 1846, the Hon. Augusta Charlotte Elizabeth, only surviving child of the Right Hon. Baron Llanover, of Llanover and Abercarn, co. of Monmouth (see *Llanover, Lady, of Llanover,* &c.), and has issue as in *Lineage* below.

Heir: Ivor John Caradoc, *b.* 1851.
Residence: Llanarth, Monmouthshire.
Arms: Per pale az. and gu., three lions rampant arg. (with numerous quarterings).
Crest: A Saracen woman's head affrontée ppr., hair sa., wearing a wreath or and gu.
Motto: Asgre lan diogel ei pherchen: "Secure is he who has a pure conscience."

LINEAGE.

This very ancient family derive from HERBERT (great-grandson of Herbert, Count of Vermandois, lineal descendant of Charlemagne) who came to England with William the Conqueror.

His son HERBERT, called of Winchester, was Chamberlain and Treasurer to Henry I.

His son, HERBERT, obtained from Henry II. a confirmation of his father's landed possessions, and likewise the office of Chamberlain. He *m.* Lucie (or Lwsi), dau. and co-h. of Milo Fitzwalter, Earl of Hereford, and by her acquired the Forest of Dean, and large possessions in the county of Gloucester and in Brycheiniog, the district now known as the co. of Brecon, and *d.* in 1205.

PETER Fitz (or son of) Herbert, was one of the barons who signed Magna Charta. He *m.*, 1st, Alice, or Alis, dau. of Robert Fitz Roger Lord of Warkworth and Clavering, and had a son and h.; and 2ndly, Isabel, dau. and co-h. of William de Braos, and widow of Dafydd ab Llewelyn, Prince of North Wales, and thus acquired the lordships and castles of Blaen Llyfni, and Talgarth in Brycheiniog, with other possessions in Wales. He *d.* in 1235, and was succeeded by his son,

REGINALD, son of Peter, Lord of Blaen Llyfni, a feudal chief of great rank in the reign of Henry III. He *m.* Joan de Vivonia, dau. and co-h. of William de Vivonia, Lord of Chewton. Their third son,

PETER, son of Reginald, *b.* in 1275, *m.* Alice, dau. and h. of Bleiddian (or Bleddyn) Broadspear, Lord of Llanllywel, near Usk (*Wysg*), in Gwent. He died in 1323.

HERBERT, son of Peter, *m.* Margaret, dau. of Sir John Walsh, Kt., and left a son and h.,

ADAM, son of Herbert, lord of Llanllywel and of Betesley, or Beachly, on the Severn, who *m.* Christian, dau. and h. of Gwaryn Ddû (*the dark*), lord of Llandeilo, whose residence, Gweir Ddû, was situated near Abergavenny, where the remains and name still exist, with a once celebrated well—and in the church of that town is a stone figure representing a female, with the arms of Gwaryn Ddû upon it, believed to have been part of the tomb of Christian. Their son,

JOHN HERBERT AB (son of) ADAM, *alias* Siencyn (misspelt and miscalled Jenkin), Lord of Gwern Ddû, *m.* Gwenllian, dau. of Sir Aron ab Bledri, Kt., and left a son and h.,

GWILYM AB SIENCYN (misspelt William ap Jenkin), otherwise HERBERT, Lord of Gwern Ddû, living at the very ancient residence of Perth Hîr, near Monmouth, from 20th to 50th (1337) of Edward III., *m.* Gwenllian, dau. of Hywel Vychan (misspelt Howell Vaughan), and had four sons.

The *eldest* son, Siencyn ab Gwilym, was the ancestor of the Ab Rogers (Progers) of Gwern Ddû (*corruptly called Werndû*), which branch of the family is now extinct.

The *second* son, Dafydd ab Gwilym, was ancestor of the Morgans of Arxton, which branch became extinct in the male line in the 17th century.

The *third* son, Hywel ab Gwilym, ancestor of the Herberts of Llanarth.

The *fourth* son, Tomas ab Gwilym ab Siencyn (otherwise Herbert), Kt., ancestor of the Earls of Pembroke, Powis, and Carnarvon, Lord Herbert of Cherbury, &c. (See pedigree below.)

HYWEL AB GWILYM (the third son of Gwilym ab Siencyn Herbert), *m.* Maud, dau. of Hywel ab Rhys, and left a son,

SIENCYN (Jenkin) AB HYWEL, who *m.* Constance, dau. of Roger Fychan ab Walter Sais. Their son,

DAFYDD AB SIENCYN, fell at Banbury, fighting under the standard of his cousin, the Earl of Pembroke. He *m.* Margaret, dau. and co-h. of Thomas Huntley, of Tre-owain, Esq.

Their son, TOMAS AB DAFYDD AB SIENCYN, of Tre-Owain, &c., &c., *m.* Margaret, dau. of Morgan Cemaes, corruptly spelt Kemeys.

Their son, JOHN AB TOMAS, of Tre-Owain, &c., &c., *m.*, in 1481, Ann, dau. of Dafydd ab Gwilym Morgan, (refer to second son of Gwilym ab Siencyn), of Arxton, in the co. of Hereford, Esquire.

THE COUNTY FAMILIES OF MONMOUTHSHIRE. 777

Their issue were compelled by law to adopt the English custom of surnames; thus, *Gwilym ap John* (son of John) became corrupted into the name of—
WILLIAM JONES [but see *Sheriffs*, 1556], of Tre-Owain and Llanarth, lord of the manors of Hendref-Obaith, Castell Arnold, Llanarth, and Cefn-Dû-glawdd. He *m.* three times. His first wife was Constance, dau. of Thomas Morgan, and sister of Rowland Morgan, of Machen, Esquire. Their eldest son, JOHN JONES, of Tre-Owain, &c., &c., was living in 1563, but *d.* before 1609. He *m.* Ann, dau. of Giles Doddington, Esq.
Their son, WILLIAM JONES, of Tre-Owain, Llanarth, and Hendref-Obaith, *m.* Jane, only dau. and h. of Moor Gwilym, Esq., of Monmouth; and their son was
SIR PHILIP JONES, Kt., of Tre-Owain, Llanarth, &c., &c., Lieut.-Col. of the troops raised in the co. of Monmouth for Charles I., and one of the gallant defenders of Rhaglan Castle during the siege by Fairfax. Sir Philip Jones *m.* Elizabeth, dau. of Sir Edward Morgan, Bart., of Llantarnam Abbey, and *d.* in 1660.
Their son, WILLIAM JONES, of Llanarth and Tre-owain, *m.* Mary, dau. of Christopher Anderton, Esq., of Lostoch, co. Lancaster, and *d.* in 1667. Tre-Owain having been greatly damaged by Cromwell's army, Llanarth has since continued to be the chief residence of the family; but Tre-Owain still retains a magnificent staircase, and other remains of ancient grandeur.
Their son, PHILIP JONES, of Llanarth and Tre-Owain, *m.* Anne, dau. and h. of Anthony Bassett, Esq., of Cae Maen, in the co. of Glamorgan; and their son,
JOHN JONES, of Llanarth, Tre-Owain, and Pen-Llwyn, *m.* Florence, sister and h. of Henry Morgan, of Pen-Llwyn Sarph, Esquire (a branch of the Morgans of Tredegar): He *d.* in March, 1775, aged 88, leaving a son,—
PHILIP JONES, of Llanarth, Tre-Owain, and Penllwyn, *b.* in 1723, *m.* Catherine, youngest sister and co-h. of John Wyborne, Esq., of Hawkwell Place, in Kent. He died in 1782.
Their son, JOHN JONES, of Llanarth, Tre-Owain and Penllwyn, also of Upton Court, Berkshire, *m.*, in 1789, his cousin Mary, eldest dau. and co-h. of Richard Lee, Esq., of Llanffoist, near Abergavenny, and *d.* in June, 1828.
Their eldest son, JOHN JONES, of Llanarth, Tre-Owain and Penllwyn, *b.* 1790, *m.*, September, 1817, the Lady Harriet Plunkett, only dau. of Arthur James, 8th Earl of Fingall, and *d.* 22nd April, 1848, leaving, with other issue,
JOHN ARTHUR EDWARD JONES, now of Llanarth, Tre-Owain, and Pen-Llwyn (as above).
This gentleman (with his brothers and only surviving sister, viz.,—
Arthur James, C.B., Colonel in the army, and Assistant Adjutant-General;
Edmund Philip, late Major in the Royal Monmouth Militia, and now Chief Constable for the co. of Monmouth; and
Mary Louisa, since *m.* to John H. Tozer, Esq.),
was especially and alone authorized by royal licence and sign-manual, September 20, 1848, to adopt the surname of his illustrious ancestors (HERBERT), being *the representative of the elder branch* of the Herbert family in direct male descent for more than 800 years. Mr. Herbert of Llanarth being also descended from Ann, dau. of Dafydd ab Gwilym ab Morgan ab Dafydd ab Gwilym ab Siencyn of Gwern Ddû, represents in the female line the Arxton branch of the Herbert family.

Mr. Herbert of Llanarth has issue—
1. Ivor-John-Caradoc, *b.* 15th July, 1851, a Lieut. in the Grenadier Guards.
2. Arthur-James, *b.* August, 1854.
3. Edward-Bleiddian, *b.* January, 1858.
4. Stephan-Sulien-Carolus, *b.* 18th Dec., 1864, *d.* April 6th, 1869; and two daus.,—
1. Henrietta-Maria-Arianwen, and—
2. Florence Catherine-Mary.

Note.—For a notice of the mansion and estate of Llanarth, see p. 717, *ante*.

DESCENDANTS OF THE FOURTH SON OF *Gwilym ab Siencyn*, OTHERWISE HERBERT.

Note.—The fourth son, TOMAS AB GWILYM AB SIENCYN (otherwise HERBERT), Kt., of Perth-Hîr, near Monmouth, *m.* Maud, dau. and co-h. of Sir John Morley, Kt., and acquired thereby Llansantffraed, now the property of Mr. Herbert, of Llanarth.
Their youngest son, SIR WILLIAM AB TOMAS, Kt. (otherwise HERBERT), of Raglan Castle, was knighted by Henry V. at Agincourt. He *m.* Gwladys, dau. of Sir Dafydd Gam [who was widow of Sir Roger Vaughan, of Tretower (*Tre'rtwr*), who fell at Agincourt], by whom he had three sons.
The second son, Thomas, of Troy, *d. s. p.*

The *eldest* son, SIR WILLIAM HERBERT, K.G., created Earl of Pembroke by Edward IV., was beheaded by the Lancastrians after the battle of Banbury, July, 1469. He *m.* Anne, dau. of Sir Walter d'Evereux, Kt., and was *s.* in the Earldom by his eldest son *William*, who exchanged the dignity for that of *Huntingdon*, and left an only dau. and h., Elizabeth, who *m.* Charles Somerset, 1st Earl of Worcester, who assumed in his wife's right the title of Lord Herbert, of Raglan, Chepstow, and Gower. (See Beaufort.)
WILLIAM, 1st Earl of Pembroke, left also two natural sons; the *second* was Sir William Herbert, of Troy, from whom descended the AP HYWELS (Powell) of Troy, and HERBERTS, of Wonastow, whose h. conveyed that estate to the Milborne family, together with the old Priory House and estates near Abergavenny, now inherited by Col. C. Kemys (Cemaes) Tynte of Cefn Mably.
The Earl of Pembroke's eldest natural son was
SIR RICHARD HERBERT, Kt., of Ewias, whose eldest son, SIR WILLIAM HERBERT, K.G., was created Baron Herbert of Caerdiff, 10th October, 1551, and on the morrow, Earl of Pembroke. He was *s.* by his eldest son,
HENRY, 2nd Earl, K.G., who *d.* 1601, and was *s.* by his eldest son,
WILLIAM, who *d. s. p.*, whose brother,
PHILIP, 4th Earl of Pembroke, had in the lifetime of his brother been created Earl of Montgomery. He was *s.* in 1655 by his son
PHILIP, 5th Earl of Pembroke and 2nd of Montgomery, who *d.* 1669.
The 6th Earl, William, *d.* unmarried, and was *s.* by his only brother,
PHILIP, who left no male issue, and the honours devolved upon THOMAS, 8th Earl of Pembroke and 5th of Montgomery, who was *s.* in his titles by his eldest son,
HENRY, 9th Earl of Pembroke, whilst his fifth son,
WILLIAM, was the ancestor of the Earls of Carnarvon. (See below.)
HENRY, 10th Earl of Pembroke, *d.* 1794, and was *s.* by his son,
GEORGE AUGUSTUS, 11th Earl of Pembroke. By his 1st marriage this nobleman had a son,
ROBERT HENRY, 12th Earl, and by his 2nd marriage he was the father of
SIDNEY, created Lord Herbert of Lea, whose son,
GEORGE-ROBERT-CHARLES, 2nd Lord Herbert of Lea, *s.* on the death of his uncle, in 1862, to the Earldoms of Pembroke and Montgomery.
The Earls of Carnarvon (*Caer'narvon*) are also descended from this branch, as stated above.
The Hon. William Herbert, 5th son of Thomas, 8th Earl of Pembroke, was *s.* by his eldest son,
HENRY HERBERT, Esq., created, 1780, Lord Porchester, and 1793, Earl of Carnarvon. He was *s.* by his eldest son,
HENRY GEORGE, 2nd Earl, *d.* April, 1833, and was *s.* by his son,
HENRY-JOHN-GEORGE, 3rd Earl, who dying in 1849, was *s.* by his son,
HENRY HOWARD-MOLYNEUX-Herbert, the present Earl Carnarvon (1872).

The *third* son, SIR Richard (*Risiart*) HERBERT, of Montgomery, was slain at Banbury. His eldest son was ancestor of the Coldbrook family.
SIR RICHARD, his second son, was father of
EDWARD HERBERT, Esq., who left three sons,—
RICHARD, father of Edward, 1st Lord Herbert of Cherbury.
MATTHEW, M.P. for Monmouth in 1564, and Charles, whose grandson, Sir Arthur, a famous admiral, was created Earl of Torrington in 1689, but *d. s.p.* in 1716.
MATTHEW HERBERT, M.P., was the father of
FRANCIS HERBERT, of Oakley Park, whose son,
RICHARD, *m.* Florence, sole h. to the Lords Herbert of Cherbury, and that dignity was revived in 1743 for his son, HENRY ARTHUR HERBERT, who thus became 7th Lord Herbert of Cherbury, and on the death of William, 3rd Marquis of Powis, in 1745, the Earldom of Powis was conferred on Lord Herbert as his nearest male h. and the husband of his niece.
He died in 1772, and his only son,
GEORGE, 2nd Earl, dying unmarried in 1801, the titles became extinct and his sister, Henrietta-Antonia, became the representative of the Herberts of Powis (*properly Powys*) and Cherbury. She *m.*, in 1784,
EDWARD, 2nd Lord Clive, who in 1804 was created Lord Herbert of Cherbury and Earl of Powis. Their son,
EDWARD, 2nd Earl of Powis, *d.* in 1848, leaving, with other issue, Edward-James-Herbert, the present Earl (1872), *b.* 1818.

HERBERT, William, Esq., of Clytha House, Monmouthshire.

J. P. and D. L. for the co. of Monmouth; High Sheriff for same co. 1844 (see *Sheriffs*); third son of the late John Jones, Esq., of Llanarth, co. of Monmouth; *b.* 1798; assumed in 1862 the name of *Herbert*, the ancient surname of his family, in lieu of the more recently introduced surname of Jones; *m.*, 1833, Frances, dau. of Edward Huddleston, Esq., of Sawston Hall, Cambridgeshire, and has issue 2 sons and 2 daus.

Heir: William Reginald Joseph Fitzherbert, J. P. for the co. of Mon., *b.* 1841; *m.*, 1866, Charlotte, dau. of T. W. Giffard, Esq., and has issue.
Residence: Clytha House, Abergavenny.
Arms: For arms see *Herbert of Llanarth*.

LINEAGE.

This is a junior branch of that ancient family of which that of Llanarth, in the same co., is the senior. The full lineage is to be found under *Herbert of Llanarth*.

HILL, James Charles, Esq., of The Brooks, Monmouthshire.

J. P. and D. L. for the co. of Monmouth; Sheriff for the same co. 1872. (Further information not received.)

HOMFRAY, Samuel, Esq., of Glen-usk, Monmouthshire.

J. P. for the co. of Monmouth and for the bor. of Newport; Sheriff for the co. of Monmouth 1841; son of the late Samuel Homfray, Esq., sometime M.P. for Stafford, by Jane, his wife, dau. of the late Sir Charles Morgan, Bart., of Tredegar Park; *b.* 1795; *m.*, 1822, Miss Stabb, and has with other issue an eldest son,—
SAMUEL GEORGE HOMFRAY, Esq., of Neuaddfach, co. Carmarthen, J. P. for the co. of Mon.

Residence: Glen-usk, near Caerleon.
Town Address: Carlton Club.

HUMFREY, James, Esq., of Llanwenarth, Monmouthshire.

J. P. for the co. of Monmouth; eldest son of the late Richard Humfrey, Esq., of Dorset, by Lucy, dau. of James Morgan, merchant, of Bristol (mayor of that city in 1793), and senior surviving descendant of the Morgans of Llanwenarth (*vide Hist. of Brecknockshire*, vol. ii., page 479); *b.* July 29, 1817; *ed.* at Trinity College, Oxford; *grad.* B.A. 1840, M.A. 1843; *m.*, 1851, Marianne Dumaresq, dau. of the late Thomas Bath, Esq., of Brecon; *s.* in 1862, on the death of his mother; has issue a son and dau.

Heir: Frederic Morgan Humfrey.
Residence: Llanwenarth House, near Abergavenny.
Arms: Gules, a cross botonée, with three escallop shells on each end.
Crest: A harpy displayed.
Motto: L'homme vrai aime son pays.

LINEAGE.

This family is of Norman origin, and the earls progenitors were distinguished among the soldiery of the cross; there is a portrait of John Humfray, living in 1390, a gallant warrior of that day, still preserved in the British Museum. William Humfrey, the lineal descendant, resided in 1594 at Rotherham, in Yorkshire.

Note.—Exact date of erection of mansion is not known, but there are title-deeds bearing date 1602.

JAMES, James George, Esq., of Tynewydd, Monmouthshire.

In the Commission of the Peace for the co. of Monmouth; eldest son of the late Mr. Edmund James, of Tynewydd, parish of Bedwellty; *b.* at Tynewydd, December 6th, 1831; is *unm.*

Residence: Tynewydd, Blackwood, near Newport.

JAMES, John Davies, Esq., of Myrtle Grove, Monmouthshire.

In the Commission of the Peace for the

THE COUNTY FAMILIES OF MONMOUTHSHIRE. 779

co. of Monmouth; 2nd son of the late Mr. Edmund James; *b.* at Tynewydd, December 30th, 1833; is *unm.*

Residence: Myrtle Grove, Blackwood, near Newport.

KENNARD, Henry Martyn, Esq., of Crumlin Hall, Monmouthshire.

J. P. for the co. of Monmouth; High Sheriff for same co. in 1863 (see *Sheriffs*); younger son of Robert William Kennard, Esq., of Gatcombe Park, Isle of Wight, an ironmaster at Blaenavon, Monmouthshire, and sometime M.P. for the Isle of Wight; *b.* 1833; *m.* Catherine, dau. of the late Rev. George Thomas, M.A., of Ystrad-Mynach, and has issue.

Residence: Crumlin Hall, near Newport.

LAWRENCE, John, Esq., of Crick House, Monmouthshire.

Lord of the Manor of Langstone; J. P. for the co. of Monmouth; High Sheriff for the same co. in 1869; son of the late John Lawrence, Esq., and Anne his wife; *b.* at Maesyrhew House, co. of Monmouth, in 1807; *m.*, 1838, Adelaide Lucy, dau. of Thomas Edwards, Esq., of Pontypool, and his wife Catherine Ferrers, dau. of Edward Ferrers, Esq., of Badesley Clinton, Warwickshire; has issue 4 sons and 2 daus.

Heir: John Lawrence, Captain in the 4th Hussars, deceased.
Residences: Crick House, Chepstow, and The Graig, Cumbran.
Crest: A stag's head.
Motto: Deus omnia ducit.

LEWIS, Charles Edward, Esq., of St. Pierre, Monmouthshire.

J. P. and D. L. for the co. of Monmouth; son of Rev. Francis Lewis, M.A., B.D., of St. Pierre, by Mary, his first wife, dau. of George Emerson, Esq.; *b.* 26th April, 1830, at Portskewett, co. of Monmouth; *ed.* at Rugby; *m.*, 2nd Oct., 1858, Sarah Elizabeth, dau. of James Staunton Lambert, Esq., of Waterdale, co. Galway, Ireland, and the Hon. Camden Elizabeth, his wife; *s.* 1872; is Patron of the livings of St. Pierre w. Portskewett, and Mounton, co. of Monmouth.

Heir Presumptive: His brother, Thomas Freke Lewis, Esq., of Dorecourt, co. Hereford.
Residence: St. Pierre, near Chepstow.

Arms: Or, a lion rampant guardant sa.
Crest: A griffin segreant sable.
Motto: Ha persa la fede, Ha perso l'onóre.

LINEAGE.

This family derives its descent from Cadivor Prince of Dyved, which comprised Pembrokeshire, and part of Cardiganshire and Carmarthenshire. Cadivor flourished about the period of the Norman Conquest. The family of Lewis has resided and held prominent position for many ages in the co. of Monmouth, as will be seen by reference to the list of *Sheriffs, ante.*

Note.—On this estate are Caldicott Castle, Southbrook Camp (a Roman camp of some interest), the houses of Moyne's Court and of St. Pierre, both of which are of great antiquity—dates unknown. St. Pierre has a tower, and two courtyards supposed to have been used for protecting cattle in perilous times. Moyne's Court has a gateway with two towers, and an enclosed courtyard.

LLANOVER, The Right Hon. Augusta, Baroness Llanover, of Llanover and Abercarn, co. of Monmouth, South Wales.

Widow of the Right. Hon. Benjamin, Baron Llanover, Lord Lieutenant of the co. of Monmouth, who was born Nov. 8, 1802; *ed.* at Westminster school; entered as a Gentleman Commoner of Christ Church, Oxford; was created a baronet, July, 1838; Baron Llanover of Llanover and Abercarn, 1859; a Privy Councillor, 1854; held the office of President of the Board of Health, 1854-5, and that of First Commissioner of Works, 1855-8; was M.P. for the united boroughs of Monmouth, Newport, and Usk, 1832-7, and for the borough of Marylebone from 1837 until he was called to the House of Lords as Baron Llanover of Llanover and Abercarn.

Lord Llanover was the eldest son of Benjamin Hall, of Abercarn and Hensol Castle, in the cos. of Monmouth and Glamorgan, South Wales, Esq., M.P. for the co. of Glamorgan, by Charlotte, dau. of W. Crawshay, of Cyfarthfa Castle, Glamorgan, Esq. His grandfather, Benjamin Hall, D.D., Chancellor of the Diocese of Llandaff, who died Feb. 25, 1825, aged 82, a man of extensive learning and an erudite Welsh scholar, was descended from an ancient family in the co. of Pembroke, South Wales.

He *m.*, Dec. 4, 1823, Augusta (the present Lady Llanover), dau. and co-h. of Benjamin Waddington, of Llanover, Esq. (*vide* Pedigree *infra*), and had issue two sons, B. Hanbury Stuart, *b.* Jan. 19, 1826; *d.* 11th Feb., 1845; and B. Caradoc Trevor

Francis Zacchia, *b.* in Rome 23rd May, 1830; *d.* June 8, 1835; and one dau. surviving, the Hon. Augusta Charlotte Elizabeth; *m.* Nov. 12, 1846, to John Arthur Herbert, of Llanarth, Esq. *Vide Herbert of Llanarth.*

Lord Llanover *d.* at his house in Great Stanhope Street, London, April 27, 1867, leaving his estates to his widow, Lady Llanover.

Her ladyship is known throughout Wales by her bardic name of *Gwenynen Gwent;* is a patroness of Welsh literature, and besides several published productions, has edited, in six vols., the Correspondence of her distinguished relative, Mary Granville, Mrs. Delany, who died in the year 1788.

Residences: Llanover and Abercarn, Co. of Monmouth, South Wales; *Town House,* 9, Great Stanhope Street, May Fair, London.

Arms: Party per pale, argent and or, betw. three talbots' heads erased sa., two and one, their necks severally encircled with a mural crown or, a chevron sa. charged with three hawks' lures proper. In chief, a canton argent, charged with a sinister hand erect, couped at the wrist gu. On an escutcheon of pretence, argent, between three fleurs-de-lis azure, two and one, a fesse sable, charged with a lion passant guardant or.

Crest: A griffin's head or, with a hawk's lure proper in its mouth, and a palm branch vert behind. Supporters: Dexter, a dragon gules, gorged with a collar or, thereon a hawk's lure sa., chained gold; sinister, a goat argent, gorged with a collar vert, thereon a hawk's lure of the first, chained or.

Motto: "Ni ddaw Da o hir arofyn,"—*No good comes of long intending.*

PEDIGREE OF LADY LLANOVER.

Rollo, the conqueror of Normandy (formerly Neustria) and its 1st duke, *m.*, after his conquest of that country, Popeia, dau. of the Count of Senlis and Valois, whose elder brother *Herbert* (Count of Vermandois) is the ancestor of the Herberts of Llanarth (see pedigree). This was a mar. *more Danico,* but afterwards, having professed Christianity, and after the death of his wife Gisella, daughter of Charles the Simple, he *m.* Popeia *more Christiano.*

By Popeia he had one son and one dau. The son, William, became his successor as 2nd Duke of Normandy, and is usually designated William Longsword, whose first wife was Espriota, or Sprota, by whom he had one son, Richard, his successor.

Richard, 3rd Duke of Normandy, *m.*, 1st, Emma, dau. of Hugh, Earl of Paris, and sister of Hugh Capet, who *d. s. p.*; 2nd, Gunnora, sister (or dau.) of Herfast, a Danish noble, and had issue three sons, of whom the third,

Malger, or Mauger, was 1st Count of Corbeil. (His eldest brother Richard was 4th Duke of Normandy, and was father of Robert le Diable, who succeeded his brother Richard as 6th Duke, and was himself succeeded by his illegitimate son William, 7th Duke, who became the *Conqueror* of England.)

Malger's son, Hamon Dentatus, 2nd Count of Corbeil, Lord of Granville, Thorigny, Brely, and Creuly, *m.* Hadwise (or Hadwina), sister to the Emperor Otho, and widow of Hugh the Great.

The name of Granville has been variously spelt in former times. One of the earliest modes was Granvyl, or Granvyld, the present form being a corruption of the ancient Scandinavian name.

Their son, Richard, was called, after a part of his patrimony, Granvil (probably their chief residence in Normandy), containing the town of that name, over the gateway of which, as well as of Caen, the Granvil arms (*the three horsemen's rests*) still remain. He came with William the Conqueror to England, and at the death of his elder brother, Robert Fitzhamon, became Count of Corbeil, inherited all his Norman titles and estates, and the lordship of Bideford, and also founded the abbey of Neath, or, properly, *Nêdd*, in Glamorgan, in consequence, it is said, of a dream, in which he was warned to restore to the Cymry all the property remaining in his own power, of which they had been unjustly dispossessed. He returned home, and tried to fulfil the injunction; with the residue he founded the abbey of *Nêdd,* the ruins of which, and tesselated pavement therein found, with the Granville arms (the three horsemen's rests), still exist. Richard of Granville *m.*, 1st, Isabel, dau. of Walter Giffard, Earl of Bucks and Longueville; 2nd, Meiven, dau. of Caradoc ap Arthen, Lord of Glyn Nêdd, and thereby his family became naturalized as Welsh.

Richard of Granville, eldest son of the above, by his first wife, Isabel, *m.* Gundrea, or Gundreda, and had issue a son, Richard de Granville (*d. circ.* 1217), who *m.* Adeline, widow of Hugh Montfort, dau. of Thomas Fitz-Nicholas, of Middleton.

Richard de Granville, their son (*d.* 1248, qy. 1261?), *m.* Jane, dau. of William of Trevint, or Trewynt, in the parish of Blisland, in Cornwall (where they had great possessions), of which house nothing but the Gothic arch now remains.

Bartholomew de Granville, their son (*d.* 1325), *m.* Amy, dau. of Sir Vyel Vyvian, of Trevidren, co. Cornwall. His brother was William de Granville, Abp. of York, and Lord Chancellor of England (*d.* 1315).

The eldest son of Bartholomew, Henry de Granville (*d.* 1327), *m.* Ann, dau. and heiress of the family of Wortham.

Sir Theobald de Granville, their son, *m.* Joyce, dau. of Thomas Beaumont, Earl of Millent.

Their son, Sir Theobald de Granville, *m.* Margaret, dau. of Sir Hugh Courtenay, of Haccombe, by Maud, dau. of Sir John Beaumont, of Sherwell.

William de Granville, their second son, *m.* Philippa, dau. of William Lord Bonvil, of Chuton, as his second wife. Their hatchment, in stucco, is in Kilkhampton Church, Cornwall, which was built by the Granvilles.

Their son, Sir Thomas Granville (*d.* 1484), *m.*, as his second wife, Elizabeth, sister of Sir Theobald Georges. Here the Norman-French *de* seems to have been discontinued by this illustrious Danish, or rather Scandinavian family.

Sir Thomas Granville, their son, was Knight of the Bath at the mar. of Prince Arthur. He *d.* 1513. To his memory a magnificent monument, with his effigy in armour, still stands in Bideford Church. He *m.*, first, Isabella, dau. of Otho

Gilbert, of Compton. They had six daus. and two sons. The eldest son, Sir Roger Granville, "the great housekeeper" (d. 1524), m. Margaret, dau. of Richard Whitleigh, of Efford. Their son, Sir Richard Granville (d. March, 1551,) Marshal of Calais, m. Matilda, dau. and co-h. of John Bevil, of Gwarnoc, in Cornwall (d. April, 1551). Their second son (the eldest, John, having died young), Sir Roger Granville, m. Thomasin, dau. of Thomas Cole, of Slade, Devon. He was drowned in his father's lifetime, on board the *Mary Rose*, which ship went down with 700 men before the eyes of King Henry VIII., 1545, and left, with other issue,

A son, Sir Richard Granville, vice-admiral, who was killed in an action at sea, at Terceira, Aug., 1591. His wife was Mary, dau. and co-h. of Sir John St. Leger, of Annery (d. 1623).

Sir Bernard Granville, their son, who d. June 16th, 1636, m. Elizabeth, only dau. and h. of Philip Bevil, of Bryn and Killygarth, co. Cornwall.

Their son, Sir Bevil Granville, bapt. March 25, 1595, was slain at Lansdown fight, July 5, 1643, and buried in a vault at Kilkhampton Church, July 26. His younger brother, Sir Richard Granville, the "king's general in the west," was a Knight Banneret (d. at Ghent, 1658). Sir Bevil Granville m. Grace, dau. and co-h. of Sir George Smythe, of Matford (Maydford) par. of Heavitree, nr. Exeter. They had a family of thirteen children, and from them have descended in the *female* line the Earls Granville and Spencer of the present time (1871).

Their son, Bernard, messenger to Charles II. from the Duke of Albemarle, groom of the bedchamber at the Restoration, d. 14th June, 1701, and was buried in Lambeth Church, where a fine monument exists *out of sight, and partly dismantled*. He m. Anne, only dau. and heiress of the Hon. Cuthbert Morley, of Haunby, in Cleveland.

Sir Bevil Granville, their eldest son, knighted by James II., 1686, was governor of Barbadoes, and d. s. p., Sept 15, 1706. The second son, George, was created Baron Lansdown of Bideford, 1711, Sec. of War and Compt. of Household to Queen Anne (d. 1735). Bernard, their third son, Lieut.-Gov. of Hull, M.P. for Camelford and Fowey, d. Dec. 8, 1723. He m. Mary, dau. of Sir Martin Westcomb, Bart. d. 1747. Their eldest son, Bernard, of Calwich Abbey, h. at law to his uncle, George Granville, Lord Lansdown, was the last of the male line of Granville, d. s. p., 1775. The admired and revered *Mary Granville* was their eldest dau. She m., first, Alexander Pendarves, of Roscrow, Cornwall; second, Patrick Delany, D.D., Dean of Down, d. s. p., 1788. See the *Life and Correspondence of Mary Granville, Mrs. Delany*, by the Right. Hon. Lady Llanover.

Their other and youngest dau., Ann, b. 1707, d. 1761, m., 1740, John D'Ewes, of Welsbourn, Esquire, co. Warwick, second son of Court D'Ewes, Esq., of Maplebury, in the same co. The D'Ewes family were long established in Warwickshire, and first came to England from Kessel, temp. Henry VIII. Their first known ancestor, Geerardt D'Ewes, was lord of Kessel, duchy of Guelderland circ. 1400, and m. Ann, only dau. and h. of the Prince or Count of Horn.

From this mar. of John d'Ewes, Esq., and Ann Granville (with three sons), there was an only dau., Mary, who m. John Port, Esq., of Ilam, whose former name was Sparrow, but who took the name of Port on becoming heir to that ancient property. (The Sparrows were originally Welsh, of Allt yr Ynys, in North Wales, see *Angl. Sheriffs*, 1689, &c.) Born Feb. 22nd, 1746, d. 1814, leaving issue Georgina Mary Ann, and others.

Georgina Mary Ann m. Benjamin Waddington, of Llanover, Esq., and had two surviving daus., co-heiresses, Frances and *Augusta*.

[The family of Waddington is of very ancient origin. Walter de Waddington was Lord of Waddington, and had a daughter and heiress, who married in the 13th century (*temp. Edward I.*) Sir Roger Tempest, knight, of Bracewell. The town of Waddington is in Lincolnshire. In the 18th century there are records of intermarriages with the families of Beckwith of Aldborough, Tyrwhitt of Stainfield, and Cradock of Hartforth, co. York, and in 1740 the Rev. Joshua Waddington, Vicar of Harworth and Walkeringham, co. of Notts, married Ann, daughter of the Rev. Thomas Ferrand, Vicar of Bingley. Ann Ferrand was ultimately heiress to the property of her family of Towes in Lincolnshire, which devolved through her to their son Thomas. Their son Benjamin was of Llanover, as above.]

Frances m. Christian Carl Josias, the late Baron von Bunsen, for twenty years minister plenipotentiary from Prussia to Rome, and afterwards minister plenipotentiary for many years to the Court of St. James's.

AUGUSTA (now *Lady Llanover*) m., Dec. 4, 1823, Benjamin, the late Baron Llanover, of Llanover and Abercarn, South Wales, and has surviving issue the Hon. Aug. Charlotte Elizabeth, wife of John Arthur Herbert of Llanarth, Tre-Owain, and Penllwyn, Esquire. See *Herbert of Llanarth*.

Note.—The mansion in which Lady Llanover resides (see *engraving*, p. 716) is a fine specimen of Tudor architecture, and possesses one of the most perfect halls in the kingdom for beauty of design. The building was commenced by the late Lord Llanover in 1828, from designs by Hopper, and occupied eleven years in completion. There are two other residences on the Llanover estate, one of which is within a quarter of a mile of the last mentioned (the grounds and gardens of both being united), and was the birthplace of Lady Llanover, and the residence of her father, Benj. Waddington, Esq., who became its possessor in the last century. The house and grounds are well kept up in every respect. This house is very ancient in part, but was enlarged and modernized by the above-named gentleman.

The third mansion in the park of Llanover is very ancient, the precise date unknown. It is now occupied as a farmhouse, but still possesses a handsome and spacious panelled room, with an old oak staircase, two picturesque porches, and clustered chimneys; and there are the remains of buildings and foundations to a very considerable extent. This ancient edifice and contiguous land belonged in the time of Queen Elizabeth to the family of Ab Risiart, in later years commonly called "Prichard," of whom Matthew and William were buried in the ancient church of Llanover. The old name of the last-mentioned residence is Porth Hir, the meaning of which referred to a fine gateway and covered passage leading from one entrance to the other, large enough for carriages to drive under, but no longer existing. It is now commonly known as the "Cwrt," and recorded in old documents as Cwrt y Porth Hir, probably in consequence of the court leets of the manor having been held there.

The church of Llanover is one of the most ancient in South Wales, and when under restoration by the late Lord Llanover, the masonry of some of the old walls was remarked as being exactly similar to that of the ruins at Neath Abbey. The word "Llanover," by which the church and two of the mansions are known, means the consecrated spot or church of Gover, who with Henwg and Gwarreg were the three primitive saints of Gwent. Gover is believed to have been buried under a ponderous tombstone, on which is carved an ancient British cross, laid in the doorway of the church of his name within the front porch. There is also a very ancient font of stone, the tracery on the outside of which has been considered to be of the Druidic period, as well as the stones which form the remains of the ancient cross in the churchyard. The churchyard also contains a very beautiful tomb in stone, to the memory of the late Lord Llanover, designed by his own direction during life, and also modelled by Mr. W. Meredyth Thomas, brother of Mr. Evan Thomas, the well-known Welsh sculptor, and executed on the spot by Mr. W. M. Thomas, and by native workmen under his personal direction.

Among the objects worthy of special notice in the grounds at Llanover is the Ffynnon Over, or the Well of Gover, and its eight surrounding wells, all flowing different ways, but uniting in a bath. Numerous fine specimens of timber and rare trees and shrubs abound in the grounds at Llanover, among which is a Chichester elm near the lake in the gardens, planted by the late Lord Llanover, about thirty-eight years ago, and considered a marvel of rapid growth, having already reached a height of seventy-nine feet and measuring at six feet from the ground twelve feet in girth, and a rhododendron planted by the mother of Lady Llanover about seventy years ago, which is now (1871) more than one hundred *yards* in circumference, the plant consisting of one *single centre stem*. With regard to the elm above named, and the rhododendron, the late well-known authority, Sir William Hooker, who visited Llanover, said that the former was the most extraordinary instance of rapid growth he had ever seen in Great Britain, and that the rhododendron was, as far as his knowledge went, "*the largest in the world.*"

The mansion at Abercarn is situated in the midst of that extensive property, in the parish of Mynyddislwyn, and is also a very old and capacious house, but was partially modernized and reduced in size many years ago. It was a favourite residence of the late Lord Llanover, and of his father, who, however, principally lived at Hensol Castle in Glamorgan, which county he represented till the time of his death, and where the late Lord had considerable property at Pont y Pridd.

MACKWORTH, Sir Arthur William, Bart., of Glenusk, Monmouthshire.

Creation 1776. Is 6th Baronet; Adj. in Royal Engineers; son of the late Sir Digby Francis Mackworth, 5th Bart. (*d.* 1857) of Glenusk, by his wife, Mathilde Eleanor Eliza, dau. of Lieut.-Col. Peddie, K.H.; *b.* 1842; *s.* 1857; *m.*, 1865, Alice Kate, dau. of Joseph Cubitt, Esq., and has issue.

Heir: His son, DIGBY, *b.* 1868.
Residence: Glenusk, near Caerleon.
Town Address: Junior United Service Club.
Arms: Per pale indented sa. and ermine, on a chevron gu. five crosses pattées or (formerly quartered *Evans*).
Crest: A cock ppr.

LINEAGE.

For the lineage and history of this family in Wales, see *Evans* and *Mackworth, of Gnoll Castle,* co. of Glamorgan.

McDONNELL, Francis, Esq., of Plas Newydd, Monmouthshire.

J. P. for the co. of Monmouth; Major in the Royal Monmouth Militia; was formerly in the 71st Highlanders. (Further information not received.)

MITCHELL, Frank Johnstone, Esq., of Llanfrechfa Grange, Monmouthshire.

J. P. for the co. of Monmouth; Sheriff for the same co. 1868; son of F. H. Mitchell, Esq., of London; *b.* 1824; *m.*, 1860, Elizabeth, dau. of J. E. W. Rollo, Esq., of Hendre, co. of Mon., and has issue.

Residence: Llanfrechfa Grange, near Newport.
Arms: Sa., a chevron between three escallops or.

MORGAN, Hon. Charles Octavius Swinnerton, of The Friars, Monmouthshire.

M.P. for the co. of Monmouth since 1841 (see *Parl. Annals*, p. 767, *ante*); J. P. and D. L. for the same co.; F.R.S., F.S.A., V.P.S.A.; fourth son of the late Sir Charles Morgan, Bart., of Tredegar Park, and brother of the present Lord Tredegar (see *Tredegar, Baron*); *b.* 1803; *ed.* at Westminster School and Christ Church, Oxford; *grad.* B.A. 1825, M.A. 1832; is author of numerous *memoirs* on antiquarian and scientific subjects in journals of learned societies.

Residence: The Friars, Newport, Mon.
Town Address: 10, Charles Street, St. James's.
Clubs: Carlton; United University.
Arms: For Arms and Lineage, see *Tredegar, Baron, of Tredegar Park.*

PROTHERO, Mrs. Georgiana Mary, of Malpas Court, Monmouthshire.

Is widow of the Rev. Thomas Prothero, M.A., Chaplain in ordinary to the Queen;

J. P. and D. L. for the co. of Monmouth ; eldest son of the late Thomas Prothero, Esq., J. P. of Malpas Court, by his wife May Collins, of Ingatestone, Herefordshire. The late Mr. Prothero was *b.* August 17, 1811 ; *ed.* at the Charterhouse and at Brasenose Coll., Oxford ; *grad.* B.A. 1834, M.A. 1837. Mrs. Prothero, who is dau. of the late Rev. Math. Marsh, M.A., Canon of the Cathedral, and Chancellor of the Diocese of Salisbury, was *m.* 1837, and had issue 3 sons and 1 dau. Mr. Prothero *d.* June 11, 1870, leaving his estates to his widow for her life.

Heir: Francis Thomas Egerton Prothero, *b.* 1837 ; *ed.* at Eton, and Bras. Coll., Oxford ; *m.*, August, 1864, Mary, only dau. of Rev. Francis Lewis, of St. Pierre, Monmouthshire, and has issue 2 sons and 2 daus. ; *heir, Freke, b.* July, 1868 ; *residence,* Richmond, Surrey.
Residence: Malpas Court, Newport, Mon.
Arms: Argent, a chevron between 3 ravens sa.
Crest: A raven sa.
Motto: Deus pascit corvos.

Note.—This family has intermarried with the Douglasses (Earls of Merton), Macdonalds of Gordon Island, Money Kyrles of Herefordshire, Winningtons of Stanford Court, Worcestershire, &c.
Malpas Court (see *engraving,* p. 721) is a stone gabled mansion, erected in 1836, from designs by T. Wyatt, Esq., architect. The situation is commanding, and the extensive grounds are tastefully planted and laid out.

RAGLAN, Richard Henry Fitzroy Somerset, Baron of Cefn-tilla, Monmouthshire.

Creation 1852. 2nd Baron Raglan of Raglan ; J. P. and D. L. for the co. of Monmouth ; Capt. of Royal Gloucestershire Yeomanry Hussars ; was Lord in Waiting to the Queen ; second but only surviving son of the late Field-marshal, 1st Lord Raglan, son of the 5th Duke of Beaufort, Commander of the English army in the Crimea, where he died 28th June, 1855, by Lady Emily Harriet Wellesley, dau. of the Earl of Mornington ; *b.* 1817 ; *s.* 1855 ; *m.*, 1856, Lady Georgiana Lygon, 3rd and only surviving dau. of Henry, 4th Earl Beauchamp, and has issue 4 sons :—
1. GEORGE FITZROY HENRY, *b.* 1857, page of honour to the Queen.
2. Arthur Charles Edward, *b.* 1859.
3. Granville William Richard, *b.* 1862.
4. Richard Fitzroy, *b.* 1865.

Residence: Cefn-tilla, near Usk.
Town Address: Carlton Club.
Arms: The arms of France and England quarterly (see *Beaufort, Duke of*).

LINEAGE.

The lineage of Lord Raglan is that of the noble and ancient house of *Somerset.* See *Beaufort, Duke of, Troy House and Badminton.*

RODNEY, The Hon. William Powell, of Llanvihangel Court, Monmouthshire.

J. P. and D. L. for co. of Monmouth (High Sheriff 1860), and a Magistrate for co. Hereford ; entered the Civil Service of the East India Company in 1811 on the Bengal establishment, and on his return to England was appointed Secretary to the Comptrollers of Army Accounts, which situation he held until 1835 on the amalgamation of that department with the Audit Office ; son of George, second Lord Rodney, by Anne, dau. of the Rt. Hon. Thomas Harley (son of Edward, third Earl of Oxford and Mortimer) ; *b.* in the parish of St. George's, Hanover Square, 1794 ; *ed.* at Eton, and Haileybury College ; *m.,* 1824, Eliza Ann, youngest dau. of the late Thomas Brown, Esq., Member of the Supreme Council in India, and had, with other issue, an only son,—
William Powell, *b.* 1829 ; *m.*, 1856, Diana Hotham, second dau. of the late Sir J. W. Lubbock, Bart., and *d.* 1868, leaving with other issue a son,—
Harley, *b.* 1858.

Residence: Llanvihangel Court, near Abergavenny.
Arms: The arms of the noble house of *Rodney* are—Or, three eagles, wings inverted and displayed, purpure.
Crest: On a ducal coronet, an eagle, as in the arms.

LINEAGE.

For the genealogy of this family, see in the Peerages *Baron Rodney of Berrington.*

Notes.—Llanfihangel Court is considered to be one of the oldest mansions in the co. of Monmouth. It is uncertain when the original building was erected, but the south-eastern front is known to have been rebuilt in the year 1559 by Rhys Morgan, the then proprietor of the estate, who in 1576 sold the property to Nicholas Arnold, the proprietor of Llanthony Abbey and its dependencies, who held the same under grant from Henry VIII.
The property remained in the Arnold family till the year 1726, when it, together with that of Llanthony, was sold to the Hon. Edward Harley, Auditor of Impost to Queen Anne, brother to Robert, first Earl of Oxford and Mortimer (maternal ancestor of the Hon. W. P. Rodney, the present owner). The Hon. Edward Harley was the second son of Sir Edward Harley, K.B., of Brampton Brian, co. of Hereford ; he *m.* Sarah, third dau. of Thomas Foley, Esq., of Whitley, by whom he had Edward, third Earl of

Oxford and Mortimer, and two other sons, and one dau., who *m.* the Hon. J. Verney (Master of the Rolls, father of the thirteenth Lord Willoughby de Broke). He represented the borough of Leominster for thirty years. His skill in the law, great application to business, extensive knowledge, and unbiassed adherence to the constitution, were universally acknowledged. He purchased Llanvihangel Court and Llanthony Abbey of Nicholas Arnold, Esq., and other property in Monmouthshire and Herefordshire.

The chief features of Llanvihangel Court are the *avenues*, one consisting of Spanish chestnuts, and the other of Scotch fir. The chestnut avenue is about a quarter of a mile in length; the trees average twenty feet in circumference; the largest measures twenty-nine feet in circumference at six feet from the base. The fir avenue is about half a mile in length, and the trees average twelve feet; the largest measures seventeen and a half feet in circumference.

The *Holy* or *Skyrrid Mountain* (see p. 719) is a great feature in the neighbourhood, and forms a portion of the Llanvihangel property. It rises 1,498 feet above the level of the sea. From a distance it presents a strange and wild appearance, which is rendered the more striking by the immense fissure in the mountain's side, splitting it, as it were, into two parts, caused by a landslip, favoured by the inclination of the strata and slipperiness of the intervening clay. To a geologist there is little mystery though much of grandeur in the phenomenon; but an old legend declares that it occurred at the time of the crucifixion of our Saviour, when the "rocks were rent." On the top of the "Holy Mountain" (as it is called by some) may be plainly traced the site of a chapel, which was dedicated to St. Michael. It has long been a practice with Roman Catholics to repair thither on Michaelmas Eve for devotional purposes. The earth is still by some persons of that persuasion considered sacred, and is placed in the coffins and thrown into the graves of the deceased.

The distance from the mansion-house of Llanvihangel to the top of the mountain is one mile and three quarters.

Llanthony Abbey, though at one time part of the property of the Harley family, never came into the possession of the Hon. W. P. Rodney, but was sold in 1802 by Edward, fourth Earl of Oxford and Mortimer, to the late Sir Mark Wood, Bart., who afterwards sold it to the late Walter Savage Landor, Esq., the poet, and is now the property of his heir.

ROLLS, John Allan, Esq., of The Hendre, Monmouthshire.

J. P. and D. L. for the co. of Monmouth; F.S.A.; Captain Royal Gloucestershire Hussars; is Patron of Llangattock-Vibon-Avel, and St. Maughan's, Mon.; son of John Etherington-Welch Rolls, Esq., of The Hendre, J. P. and D. L. for the co. of Mon. (see *Lineage* below); *b.* at The Hendre, 19th Feb., 1837; *ed.* at Eton and Christ Church, Oxford; *m.*, 20th Oct., 1868, Georgiana Marcia, dau. of Sir Charles Maclean, Bart., of Morvaren, N.B., and has issue a son, *s.* to estates in May, 1870,—

JOHN MACLEAN, *b.* 25th April, 1870.

Heir : John Maclean Rolls.
Residence: The Hendre, near Monmouth.
Arms: Or, on a fesse dancettée, with plain cotises, between three billets sa., each charged with a lion rampant of the field, as many bezants.
Crest: Out of a wreath of oak, a dexter cubit arm, vested or, cuff sa., the arm charged with a fesse dancette, double cotised of the 2nd, charged with three bezants, in the hand, ppr., a roll of parchment arg.
Motto: Celeritas et veritas.

LINEAGE.

The original Hendre estate belonged to the Allen family. Mr. Henry Allen, *b.* 1691, *d.* 1767, to whose memory a monument is erected in the chancel of St. Mary's Church, Monmouth, devised it by his will to his nieces, the Misses Elizabeth and Sarah Coysh, the latter of whom was married to John Rolls, Esq., of The Grange, Bermondsey, on the 20th of October, 1767.

John Rolls, Esq., of The Grange, co. Surrey, J. P., *b.* 1735, High Sheriff of Monmouthshire 1794, *m.*, 21st Oct., 1767, Sarah, second dau. of Thomas Coysh, Esq,, and by her had issue. He *d.* 8th Sept., 1801, and was succeeded by his only surviving son,—

John Rolls, Esq., of Bryanston Square, London, of The Grange, Surrey, and of The Hendre, co. Monmouth, J. P., *b.* 20th Oct., 1776, *m.*, 27th Jan., 1803, Martha, only dau. and heiress of Jacob Barnett, Esq., and by her had issue—

1. JOHN ETHERINGTON-WELCH, of The Hendre, of whom presently.
2. *Alexander*, of Croft-y-Bwla, co. Monmouth, J. P., D. L., *b.* 18th July, 1818. (See further *Rolls of Croft-y-Bwla*.)
3. *Martha-Sarah*, *m.*, 1st Aug., 1840, to Major Macready, late 30th Regiment; he *d.* 1848.
4. *Jessy*, *m.*, 24th June, 1833, to George Simon Harcourt, Esq., M.P., of Ankerwycke House, co. Bucks, and had issue; she *d.* in Paris, 1842.
5. *Louisa Elizabeth*, *m.*, 12th July, 1830, to John Francis, eldest son of William Vaughan, Esq., of Courtfield, co. Hereford, and had issue; she *d.* 1853.

Mr. Rolls *d.* 1837, and was *s.* by his eldest son,—

John Etherington-Welch Rolls, Esq., of The Hendre, J. P. and D. L., High Sheriff 1842, *b.* 4th May, 1807, *m.*, 26th Feb., 1833, Elizabeth Mary, third dau. of Walter Long, Esq., of Preshaw House, co. Hants, by the Lady Mary, his wife, eldest dau. of the late Earl of Northesk, and had issue—

1. JOHN ALLAN ROLLS, Esq., his only son, now of The Hendre (as above), by whom at his decease, 27th May, 1870, he was succeeded.
2. Elizabeth Harcourt, *m.*, 19th Jan, 1860, to Frank Johnstone Mitchell, Esq., of Llanfrechfa Grange, co. Monmouth, eldest son of Francis H. Mitchell, Esq., of 12, Upper Wimpole Street, and has issue.
3. Patty, *m.*, 25th June, 1857, to the Rev. J. T. Harding, of Pentwyn, co. Monmouth, eldest son of the late John Harding, Esq., of Henbury, co. Somerset, and has issue.
4. Mary Octavia.
5. Anne Katherine, *m.*, 24th Jan., 1861, to Cornwallis Wykeham Martin, Lieutenant R.N., third son of Charles Wykeham Martin, Esq., of Leeds Castle, Kent, and has issue.

6. Georgina Emily, *m.*, Oct., 1866, to Thomas William Chester Master, Esq., eldest son of T. W. C. Master, Esq., of The Abbey, Cirencester, and Knole Park, Almondsbury, and has issue.
7. Ellen, *m.*, Nov., 1865, to the Rev. Richard Shard Gubbins, eldest son of the late Lieut.-Col. Gubbins, C.B., and has issue.

Note.—The *Hendre* (see *engravings*, p.   ) was originally built as a shooting-lodge, about 1828, by the grandfather of the present proprietor. It was subsequently considerably enlarged by the late Mr. John E. W. Rolls; a large open-roofed hall was added on the entrance front, from the designs of Mr. T. H. Wyatt, communicating with the drawing-room and conservatory. The present owner, Mr. John Allan Rolls, has also made some extensive alterations and additions to the house, including new dining-room, billiard-room, &c., and has entirely rebuilt the stables on an enlarged scale. These works are also from the designs of Mr. T. H. Wyatt, and form three sides of an extensive and picturesque quadrangle, harmonizing in style and date with the open-roofed hall.

ROLLS, Major Alexander, of Croft-y-bwla, Monmouthshire.

J. P. and D. L. of the co. of Monmouth; formerly of the 4th Regiment of Irish Dragoon Guards; 2nd son of the late John Rolls, Esq., J. P. of the Hendre, co. Monmouth, and of the Grange, Surrey, by his wife, Martha, only dau. and h. of the late Jacob Barnet, Esq.; *b.* 18th July, 1818; *m.*, 18th May, 1839, Kate, 3rd dau. of the late Ambrose Steward, Esq., of Stoke Park, Suffolk.

Residence: Croft-y-bwla, near Monmouth.
Arms: For arms and lineage, see *Rolls of the Hendre.*

TREDEGAR, Charles Morgan Robinson Morgan, Baron, of Tredegar Park, Monmouthshire.

Creations: Baron Tredegar 1859; baronet 1792. Is 1st Baron Tredegar and a baronet; Lord Lieutenant of Brecknockshire; J. P. and D. L. for the cos. of Monmouth and Brecknock; High Sheriff of co. of Monmouth 1821, for co. of Brecknock 1850; was M.P. for Brecon 1830-2, and 1835-7; eldest son of the late Sir Charles Gould Morgan, 3rd Bart. of Tredegar (see *Lineage*); *b.* 1793; *ed.* at Chr. Ch., Oxford; *m.*, 1827, Rosamond, dau. of General Godfrey Mundy, and has issue surviving—
1. GODFREY CHARLES, M.P., *b.* 1830 (see *Morgan of Ruperra Castle, Glam., and Tredegar Park*).
2. Frederic Courtenay, *b.* 1835; *m.* 1858, and has issue.

3. Arthur John, *b.* 1840.
4. George Gould, *b.* 1845.
5. Rosamond Marion, *m.*, 1848, N. H. Marsham Style, Esq., of Bicester House, Oxfordshire.
6. Selina Maria, *m.*, 1854, D. Robertson Williamson, Esq.
7. Fanny Henrietta, *m.*, 1854, Sir Geo. F. R. Walker, Bart.
8. Ellen Sarah, *m.*, 1856, Capt. H. Gore Lindsay.
9. Georgiana Charlotte, *m.*, 1857, Lord Francis N. Conyngham.
10. Mary Anna, *b.* 1843; *m.*, 1863, the Lord Viscount Hereford. (See *Hereford, Viscount, of Tregoyd.*)

Residences: Tredegar Park, near Newport; Ruperra Castle, near Cardiff.
Town House: 39, Portman Square.
Arms: Quarterly: 1st and 4th, or, a griffin segreant sa.—MORGAN; 2nd and 3rd, or, on a chevron between three roses az. as many thistles slipped of the field—GOULD.
Crest: A reindeer's head couped or attired gu.
Supporters: Dexter, a lion sa. charged on the shoulder with a thistle slipped or; *sinister,* a griffin sa. charged in same manner.

LINEAGE.

The descent of this noble family is from a junction of the ancient Welsh house of MORGAN, of Machen, Tredegar, Pencoed, and Ruperra, with the family of *Gould.* The Morgans have been prominent in Monmouthshire, Glamorganshire, and Carmarthenshire since the time of the Tudors, and derived their lineage paternally from *Cadivor Fawr,* Lord of Cilsant, through Llewelyn ap Ivor, Lord of St. Clears and Gwynfe, Carmarthenshire, and maternally from his wife, Angharad, dau. of Morgan Meredith, Lord of Tredegar. Llewelyn ap Ivor was succeeded in the second generation by—
Llewelyn ap Morgan, and he in the second generation by—
Sir John *Morgan,* Kt., of Tredegar who *m.* Janet, dau. of John David Mathew, of Radir, co. of Glam. (See *Mathew of Radir.*)
For several generations they intermarried with the Vaughans, the Stradlings, the Herberts, the Somersets, &c., until the line of Morgan ended in an heiress, Jane Morgan, eldest dau. of Thomas Morgan, Esq., of Ruperra, and niece of Sir William Morgan of Tredegar. She *m.* the eminent civilian,—
Dr. Charles Gould, judge advocate and member of the Privy Council, knighted in 1779, and made a baronet in 1792, who assumed the surname of Morgan. With other issue he had an eldest son,—
Sir Charles, 2nd Baronet, *b.* 1760, *m.* Mary Margaret, dau. of Capt. George Stoney, R.N. They had issue—
1. CHARLES MORGAN ROBINSON, now *Baron Tredegar* (as above).
2. George, who *m.* and had issue; *d.* 1845.
3. Rev Charles Augustus Samuel, M.A., *b.* 1800; Rector of Machen and Chancellor of Llandaff Cathedral, Chaplain in Ordinary to the Queen.
4. Charles Octavius Swinnerton, M.P., *b.* 1803. (See *Morgan of the Friars.*)

5. Maria Margaretta, *m.*, 1817, Lieut.-Gen. F. Miles Milman.
6. Charlotte Georgiana, *m.*, 1839, the 3rd Lord Rodney.

Note.—For a notice of *Tredegar Park,* see p. 722, *ante.*

WALKER, Sir George Ferdinand Radzivill, Bart., of Castleton, Monmouthshire.

Creation, Feb. 1835: first creation in Charles II.'s reigns. Is second Baronet; J. P. and D. L. for Monmouthshire; eldest son of the late Gen. Sir George Townsend Walker, first Bart., G.C.B., K.C.T.S., Lieutenant-Governor of Chelsea Hospital, Colonel of 50th Foot, and late Commander-in-chief of the Forces at Madras, East Indies, Groom of the Chamber to H.R.H. the Duke of Sussex; *b.* in London, May 24, 1825; *ed.* at Sandhurst; *m.*, Oct. 9th, 1854, the Hon. Fanny Henrietta, third dau. of Sir Charles Robinson Morgan, Bart., first Lord Tredegar (see *Tredegar, Lord*); *s.* 14th November, 1842; has issue 6 sons.

Heir: George Ferdinand, *b.* 1855.
Residence: Castleton, near Cardiff.
Arms: Erminois, on a pile embattled az., a mural crown charged with "Badajos," between two galtraps in pale or.
Crest: On a mural crown or, encircled by a wreath of laurel, an ostrich ppr.
Motto: Nil desperandum.

LINEAGE.

This family derives its descent from William Walker, Esq., second son of Sir Walter Walker, LL.D., of Bushey Hall, Herts, Judge Advocate to Catherine, Queen Consort of Charles II., and mother of Sir George Walker, Bart., of the first creation, of Bushey Hall. Sir Edward Walker, Secretary of War to King Charles I., was another distinguished member of this family.

Note.—The castle of Wentloog (W., *Gwentllwg*) stood nearly on the site of the present mansion, the lordship of Wentloog extending the whole distance between Newport, Monmouthshire, and Cardiff, Glamorganshire, on the shores of the British Channel (see *Gwentllwg, passim*). The date of erection of the mansion is unknown, but some portion is very old, probably part of the old castle of Wentloog.

WILLIAMS, Ferdinand Capel Hanbury, Esq., of Nant-oer, Monmouthshire.

J. P. and D. L. of the co. of Monmouth; late Lieut. 16th Lancers; son of F. Hanbury Williams, Esq., J. P. and D. L. of Coldbrook Park, co. of Monmouth; *b.* at Coldbrook Park, 27th June, 1834; *ed.* at Rugby; *m.*, 19th February, 1857, Lucy Anne, eldest dau. of Robert Wheeley, Esq., of The Pentre, near Abergavenny. Has issue 2 sons and 2 daus.

Heir: Ferdinand Pakington John Hanbury, *b.* 1858.
Residence: Nant-oer, near Abergavenny.
Arms: Or, a bend engrailed vert, plain cotised sa.
Crest: A demi-lion rampant out of a mural crown, holding a battle-axe sa.
Motto: Si non datur ultra.

LINEAGE.

This family derives its descent from Hambruach of Hambruach, co. Worcester, *temp.* Edward the Confessor; ancestor also of the Hanburys of Pontypool Park, co. Monmouth.

WILLIAMS, The Rev. Chancellor Hugh, of Bassaleg, Monmouthshire.

Chancellor of the Diocese of Llandaff, and Welsh Examining Chaplain to the Bishop of Llandaff, 1845; Vicar of Radir, Glamorgan, 1837; Vicar of Bassaleg 1838; J. P. of the co. of Monmouth; Patron of the Vicarages of Henllys and Risca, co. of Monmouth; Author of a Welsh translation of short *Addresses to Children,* by W. Brooke, S.P.C.K., 1826, a translation of a Letter on *Infant Baptism* by the late Dean Knight, 1830, also of translations into Welsh of *Prayers* and *Fast and Thanksgiving Services* 1831-33; eldest son of George Williams, Esq., by Mary his wife, dau. of George Williams, Esq., of Daisyback, Gumfreston, co. of Pembroke, and niece of Rev. Benjamin Hall, D.D., Chancellor of Llandaff, grandfather of the late Lord Llanover; *b.* at Daisyback, April 3, 1795; *ed.* at Ystradmeurig Grammar School, co. Cardigan, and Jesus Coll., Oxon.; *grad.* B.A. 1816, M.A. 1819, Deacon 1818, Priest 1819; *m.*, 25th May, 1825, Mary, dau. of the late Rev. W. J. Thomas, Vicar of Caerau, co. of Glamorgan; has issue 2 sons and 2 daus.

Heir: Hugh, LL.B., Curate of Woodkirk, Yorkshire, *b.* 1833.
Residence: Bassaleg Vicarage, near Newport.
Arms: Quarterly: 1st and 4th, or, a cross gu. between two doves ppr.; 2nd and 3rd, two serpents nowed, ppr. (borne by him as Chancellor of Llandaff).
Crest: A dove rising, a Calvary cross in one talon, and a serpent in beak, twined round the neck.
Motto: Duw a digon.

Note.—Bassaleg is a corruption, destitute of any excuse, of the Welsh *Maes-aleg,* "the field of Aleg," —a name commemorative of a battle. The country around contains several important entrenched posts, as *Maes-y-gaer,* in Tredegar Park, and *Craig-y-Saeson.*

WILLIAMS, William Addams, Esq., of Llangibby Castle, Monmouthshire.

J. P. for the co. of Monmouth; son of the late William Addams Williams, Esq., of Llangibby Castle, J. P. and D. L.; High Sheriff in 1827, and M.P. 1831-40 for the co. of Monmouth, by his wife, Anna Louisa, eldest dau. of the late Rev. Illtyd Nicholl, D.D., of The Ham, co. Glam. (see *Nicholl of Ham*); b. 1820; s. 1861, on the death of his father; m., 1850, Catherine, dau. of Thomas Cooke, Esq., and has issue 7 sons and 3 daus.; eldest son, ROWLAND, b. 1851.

Residence: Boyd Villa, Clifton.
Arms: Quarterly: 1st and 4th, gyronny of eight ermine and sa., a lion rampant or—WILLIAMS; 2nd and 3rd, ermine a chevron vaire or and az. between three roses ppr.—ADDAMS.
Crests: A talbot passant in pale ermine and or—*Williams;* a griffin's head erased ermine, beaked gu., over it a chevron as in arms—*Addams.*
Motto: En suivant la vérité.

LINEAGE.

This family is of ancient descent, and has frequently supplied sheriffs for the co. of Monmouth since 1562, when Roger Williams filled that office and bore the arms now quartered for Williams (see *Sheriffs of Mon.*). The line of Williams terminated in an heiress, Ellen Williams, dau. of Sir John Williams, Bart., of Llangibby, who m., 1748, William Addams, Esq., of Monmouth.

WORCESTER, Henry Adelbert Wellington Fitzroy, Marquess of, of Troy House, Monmouthshire.

(See *Beaufort, Duke of, Troy House and Badminton.*)

Note.—The ARMS OF BEAUFORT. Anciently, according to Collins, the Beaufort Arms were: "*Or, on a fesse bordered compony arg. and az. France and England Quarterly:*" and the ancient *Crest* was, "A *panther arg. diversely spotted and gorged with a ducal coronet or:*" but neither the reason nor time of the change is mentioned. The bordure, azure charged with six fleurs-de-lis and an equal number of martlets (or doves) alternately, as given in the Beaufort *Progress*, seems to be a mistake on the part of the artist. The history of the Beaufort Escutcheon gives no clue to such a bordure.

ANNALS, &c., OF WALES.

MONTGOMERYSHIRE

(SIR DRE-FALDWYN).

THE name, whether Welsh or English, borne by the burg of Montgomery, is a memorial of the conquest of this district by the Normans. On the high rock overshadowing the town—probably then a mere village—*Baldwyn*, appointed by the Conqueror Lieutenant of the March lands taken on this side of Wales, about 1092 built his castle and planned a town, ever since which time the Welsh have called it *Tre-faldwyn*—" Baldwyn's abode, or settlement." The natives soon seized his castle and his town, but in the very next year, 1093, were deprived of them by the redoubtable Roger *de Montgomery*—a Norman who had brought his name with him from his native home, and had been created by the Conqueror Earl of Shrewsbury and Arundel in 1066, the year of the conquest of England. Among the foreign settlers, and in the French, English, and Latin languages the place received its designation from his name—*Montgomery*. This part of the ancient *Powys* continued from the Norman Conquest to the reign of Henry VIII. under the feudal rule of the Lords Marchers, when, by the 27th of that king, it was constituted a regular *county*, called after Montgomery, its "shire town."

SECTION I.—DESCRIPTIVE AND HISTORICAL ACCOUNT OF MONTGOMERYSHIRE.

This county is oblong in form, bounded N. by Denbighshire, E. and S.E. by Shropshire, S. by Radnor, S.W. by Cardiganshire, and W.N.W. by Merioneth. In mean length from N.E. to S.W. it measures about 33 miles, and in mean breadth about 25 miles. Its superficial measurement is 839 square miles, or 483,323 statute acres, of which some 90,000 only are said to be under tillage. The population during the last five decades has been as follows:—

Total population of Montgomeryshire in 1831	...	...	...	65,700
,,	,,	1841	...	...	... 69,219
,,	,,	1851	...	...	... 67,335
,,	,,	1861	...	...	.. 66,919
,,	,,	1871	...	...	... 67,789

These figures exhibit a more stationary state of the population, unaffected either by increase or decline in trade, than is to be witnessed in most other parts of the Principality. The county has few mining operations; the staple woollen manufacture in the towns, though greatly improved in the style and finish of its products, has not been extensively developed; and even the formation of railways has hitherto brought no material accession to the population.

The great *surface features* of this county, although wanting in the lofty mountains and general ruggedness which give such character to Merioneth and Carnarvonshire, are especially interesting. The county, bounded on all sides by rising lands forming watersheds, may be said to lie compactly in the basin of the Severn and its tributaries. The fertile Severn valley, which has naturally determined the situation of the chief towns—Welshpool, Newtown, and Llanidloes—is the chief feature of the county. Into the Severn, whose direction in these parts is from S.W. to N.E., and which flows throughout near the south-eastern margin of the county, nearly all the streams of Montgomeryshire run. With the exception of the Dyfi (cor. " Dovey ") and its few small affluents on the western corner, the whole of the drainage of the county on either side is gathered into this noble river; and it is quite remarkable that three-fourths of the surface of the county show so regular a declivity in the same general direction that the streams which have their sources in the mountainous heights of the Berwyn and Aran ranges, or in the uplands of the county itself, run in nearly parallel courses. From the confines of Cardiganshire, where the Penllyman (cor. " Plinlimmon ") range forms the watershed, to the Denbighshire boundary, this is the case. The part of the Wye which traverses this county pursues a direction nearly N.W. and S.E. ; so does the Severn itself from its source to Llanidloes. Then follow the Clywedog, Taranon, Rhiw, Banw, Bechan, Tanat, and Rhaiadr, all generally parallel streams, showing that the county of Montgomery, with all its undulations and counter depressions, takes a general fall from the Merioneth side towards the Severn. The few small streams coming from the direction of the English border show a corresponding declivity, carrying the drainage into the same Severn trough. This stream accordingly, in passing into Shropshire just after receiving the united volumes of the Vyrnwy and the Tanat, carries with it nearly all the waters which the thirsty land of Montgomeryshire and the evaporating power of the sun have been able to spare.

With the exception of this noble and beautiful valley of the Severn, the county of Montgomery, though abounding in delightful vales and dingles, contains no broad and extensive low-lying level lands. The surface is generally broken and sharply undulating, pleasant in aspect, often well planted and cultivated, and sometimes, as on the Rhiw, Vyrnwy, and Tanat, extremely comely and picturesque. But a large proportion of the county towards the centre and on the side adjoining Merioneth is a region given up to heath and gorse, peat and morass, grouse and diminutive sheep. The population of these parts is still sparse. The roads are of the primitive kind—much what they were when in 1684 the Duke of Beaufort on his celebrated " Progress " made his way through great dangers from Bala to pass the night at Llwydiarth, then the princely mansion of the Vaughans.

EARLY INHABITANTS: ROMAN CONQUEST.

Ancient Inhabitants and Divisions.

The region now called Montgomeryshire was in the earliest historic times possessed by that division of the *Cymry* called by the Romans *Ordovices*, and was included, under the ancient Welsh nomenclature, in the political division called *Gwynedd*, or North Wales, but in later times, and through the Middle Ages, after the subdivision of Wales by Rhodri the Great into the three sovereignties of *Gwynedd*, *Powys*, and *Debeubarth*, was included in the second; and when Powys itself was parted into two it belonged to and formed the greater portion of *Powys Wenwynwyn*, sometimes called, from its situation higher up the Severn, "Upper Powys." To this parting of Powys reference will again be made.

That the *Romans* took general possession of these, like other parts of Wales, is clear from the evidences still existing in their great military roads and stations. No unsettlement of the native population took place under this conquest, nor were the native laws and customs, language, and religion made subject to any but the slightest alteration. But as Anglesey had been conquered at much cost (see p. 9), and must be held in subjection, in addition to the chief military highway—the Via Devana by Chester, Badfari, and Conovium, they made other roads through the interior, both for the purpose of quelling popular insurrection and raising revenue. One of these roads passed from Penkridge (Lat. *Penno-cruceum*)—W. *pen*, and *crug*, a cairn—by Wroxeter (*Uriconium*), across the Severn to a station called by Antoninus, *Mediolanum*, which is believed by many to be *Meifod*, or at least some spot near that place, such as *Clawdd Coch*, or *Caer-degfan* in this county. It then proceeded through the heart of the mountains to join the SARN HELEN for *Segontium*, near Carnarvon (see p. 675). Another Roman road skirted the western angle of the county at Machynlleth (*Maglona*). An important station seems to have existed at *Caersws*, and a road probably connecting Meifod and Machynlleth ran this way. The fewness of Roman remains found in Montgomeryshire, however, those at Caersws being the principal found,—suggests the idea that the Romans established here no permanent military camps, and built no town or powerful fortress; but, as necessity required, turned to use such British camps and strongholds as came in their way—as the remarkable camp near Dolarddyn, west of Welshpool, the Breidden camp, Caereinion, &c.

After the Roman dominion in Britain ceased (fifth century) we know nothing of the state of things which came into existence in these particular parts. A veil of mystery hangs over all the affairs of Wales for long ages. None but intermittent light, sufficient only to reveal incessant agitation and conflict with Mercia and the Danes, falls on Montgomeryshire till the reign of Rhodri the Great, who managed, in face of the perils brought by the "black pagans" (the Danes), to unite his country under his own sole rule, and at his death (A.D. 876, see p. 11), yielding to the custom of *gavelkind*, which in the main worked disastrously for Wales, divided his dominions between his three sons, assigning *Gwynedd* to Anarawd, the eldest, *Debeubarth*, or S. Wales, to Cadell, and *Powys* to Merfyn.

The limits of ancient Powys had long been curtailed by Offa of Mercia (*d.* 796), whose *Dyke*, traversing the eastern side of Montgomeryshire by Brompton, Nantcribba, Buttington,

Four Crosses, and Llanymynach, is his most lasting memorial. He had forced back the tide of Powysian patriotism by main and bloody force westward of this wonderful entrenchment—whose stupendousness surpasses any other ancient work in Britain,—and the seat of government had been removed from Pengwern (Shrewsbury) to *Mathrafal*. Here probably Merfyn had his court. An humble farmstead now alone marks the spot.

After a few generations of turmoil and division the line of Merfyn terminated in an heiress, whose son, *Bleddyn ap Cynfyn*, became a puissant prince worthy of his illustrious ancestors, Rhodri the Great, Cynan Tindaethwy—the hardy opponent of Offa, and Rodri Molwynawg, the scourge of the Mercians. He not only consolidated Powys, but succeeded in bringing under his rule the whole of North Wales, and, nominally at least, South Wales, and established a Powysian dynasty which lasted till the conquest of Wales by Edward I.

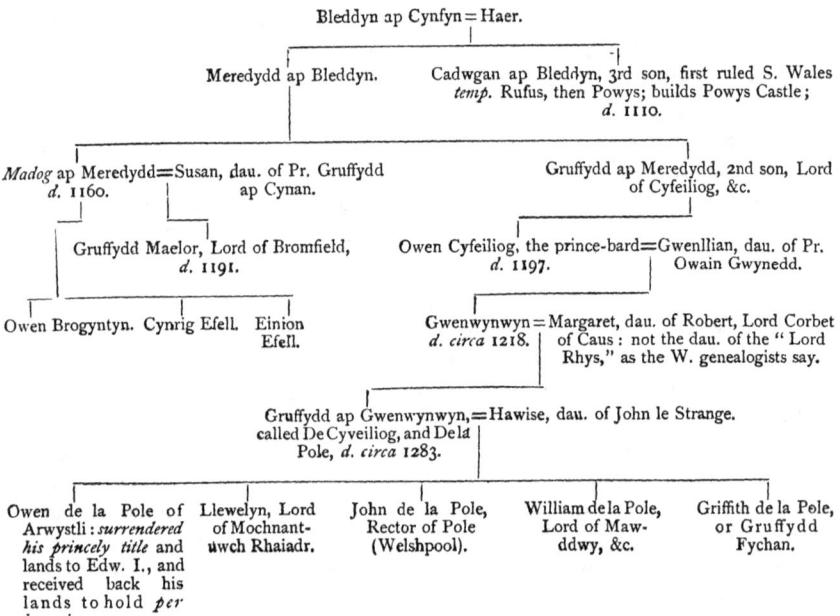

Powys was divided on the death of Meredydd, son of Bleddyn ap Cynfyn, between his son *Madog*, whose territory was afterwards called "Powys Fadog," otherwise "Lower Powys," and his grandson *Owen Cyfeiliog*, whose son *Gwenwynwyn* gave his name to the territory he ruled; and this is the region which, as already said, comprehended the present county of Montgomery, and, occasionally, much besides. Owen Cyfeiliog and his son Gwenwynwyn must have been men of high character as well as intelligence, for despite their leanings in favour of the English kings, they are always spoken of with respect, though without enthusiasm, in the annals of Wales.

In this brief survey we have already passed the point of time when the venerable *Powis Castle*, the centre and heart of Powys Wenwynwyn, was first founded. This place, first called, in Norman-French and English Pool, or Pole, then Welsh-pool, a name taken from the deep pool or lake still existing in the castle park, and by the Welsh Tre-llyn, altered into Tra-llwng (*tre*, a home, or settlement; and *llyn*, a pool, lake), received in later times from the Welsh the name *Castell Coch*, "the Red Castle," from the colour of the stone of which it was built (a name not yet extinct among the peasantry), and at last was designated Powis Castle. A more interesting castle does not exist in Wales. It connects the life of the present day with the whole history of the Marches, the darkest feudal times, and that exciting and perilous age when the princes of Wales were waging an unequal battle with the power of England, and their sceptres and diadems were one by one dropping into dust.

In the above pedigree of the Powysian princes we see the name of *Cadwgan*, 3rd son of Bleddyn ap Cynfyn. He is the reputed founder of the Red Castle, and the time when he had regained this territory by favour of King Henry I. and began erecting his castle, is generally agreed to be about the year 1108, two years before he met with a violent death at

Powis Castle—The Terraces (*from a photograph by Mr. Owen.*)

the hand of his nephew, Madog ap Rhirid (not Madog ap Meredydd, another nephew, who gave his name to Powys Fadog). The Powysian princes now abandoned *Mathrafael*, where a Norman chieftain, Robert de Vieux-pont, or Vipont, built himself a castle, and purloined a part of their territory. Powys Castle became henceforth the seat of the rulers of "Upper Powys;" its building, commenced as stated, by Cadwgan, was carried on by Gwenwynwyn, son and successor of Owen Cyfeiliog, grandson of Cadwgan's elder brother Meredydd. The chain of Norman oppression was being drawn closer and closer around the native princes, and the mighty efforts of the two Llewelyns to effect the deliverance of their country only plunged Powys into greater straits. Prince Llewelyn ap Iorwerth drove Gwenwynwyn from his princedom, and annexed it to his own extended dominions. Prince Llewelyn ap Gruffydd likewise took possession of Powys, by concession from the English king (Henry III.),—see p. 325. Gruffydd, son of Gwenwynwyn, nominal Prince of Upper Powys often called De Cyveiliog and De la Pole, died in 1283; and his son, Owen de la Pole, or Owen ap Gruffydd, the conquest of Wales having now been effected, was obliged to complete the downfall of his dynasty by surrendering his title of prince and his lands to Edward I., and receiving the latter back in fee from the king. (See a valuable paper on the "Feudal Barons of Powys," by Morris C. Jones, Esq., in *Montgomeryshire Collections*, 1868.) It may here be remarked that many of the papers in this collection (still in progress) are among the most elaborate and useful contributions to local topography, biography, and history published in any part of the kingdom.

Powys Castle was now a proper feudal castle. The last-named Owen de la Pole, its owner called also Owen of Arwystli and ap Gruffydd, died about 1293, leaving an infant son, Gruffydd, who died before his majority, and a daughter, *Hawyse*, who at her brother's demise became sole heiress of Upper Powys as well as of its chief fortress, Powys Castle. But as her father had permission to hold his lands only "sub nomine et tenura liberi

Powis Castle—West Front (*from a photo. by Mr. Owen*).

baronagii Angliæ," on condition of resigning to his lord the king the title and crown of his princedom, Hawyse, like her lands, by feudal custom, was at the disposal of the English king, and he gave her in marriage to one of his great soldiers, *John de Cherleton*, who thus became the first alien owner of Castell Coch. He was summoned to Parliament as "Johannes de Cherleton" from 7 Edward II. (1313) to 27 Edward III. (1353), in which last year he died. Four De Cherletons held the lordship of Pool, when the barony passed by marriage, *temp.* Henry V., to the Greys. From the Greys it was purchased, *temp.* Elizabeth, by Sir Edward *Herbert*, younger son of William Herbert, Earl of Pembroke. His son, Sir William Herbert, K.B., was in 1629 created by Charles I. Baron Powis of Powis Castle; his grandson, William Herbert, was in 1674 created Earl of Powis, and in 1687 Marquess of Powis. This branch of the Herberts became extinct in the line male in 1748 on the death of the third Earl and Marquess, William Herbert, when Powis Castle passed by the marriage of his niece Barbara to Henry Arthur Herbert, first Baron Herbert of Chirbury, descended from a common ancestry, who was now created Baron and Earl of Powis. His son, George Edward, dying without issue, Powis Castle passed (A.D. 1804) with his sister and heiress Henrietta Antonia, to her husband, Edward *Clive*, first Baron Clive, who was created Baron and Earl of Powis, in whose descendants it has ever since vested. (See *Powis, Earl of, Powis Castle.*)

The Duke of Beaufort, in his "*Progress*" through Wales and the Marches in 1684, was entertained over Sunday at Powis Castle, and has left on record the following account of the castle as it then stood. Many of the paintings here described are still in the castle, but in the course of nearly two hundred years many changes have taken place; the castle has undergone extensive repairs and some alterations; and its art treasures have been largely augmented by its present noble owner and his immediate predecessors. A museum of curiosities, in great part brought from India, was added by the celebrated Lord Clive.

POWIS CASTLE—EAST FRONT (*from a photo. by Mr. Owen.*)

After stating that Llewelyn the Great (ap Iorwerth), on his return from a raid into South Wales, *temp.* Henry III., overthrew this castle and burned the town of Oswestry, the *Progress* continues:—

"Thursday, July 31, 1684.—His Grace the Duke of Beaufort left *Lloydyarth* and arrived at Powis Castle (vulgarly called *Red* Castle, being formed, founded, and hewn out of a high red rock in Montgomeryshire), where he was met by her Grace the Lady Duchess of Beaufort, the Marchioness of Worcester, and other noble ladys, his Grace's daughters, with four coaches of six horses and attendants suitable. Here were noble enterteinments repeated, and their Graces rested, the day following being August 1, 1684 "—(p. 85).

"Saterday, July 19.—His Grace lay that night at Powis Castle, from which the day folowing, being Sunday, he went, accompanied by the Earle of Worcester, Sir John Talbot, and a great number of knights, militia officers, and gentlemen, besides the officers of his family, &c., to the church of Welsh-pool, where divine service was read, and a loyall sermon preached by the Reverend . . . . the militia foot with their respective officers making a guard for his passing and returne through ye town, where the Magistracy also attended him in their formalities; after which his Grace the Earle of Worcester, *Lord Herbert of Cherbury*, Sir John Talbot, and most of the gentlemen of Montgomeryshire, were very nobly enterteined at Powis Castle, though neither the Earle of Powis nor his Countess were there.

> 'Discubuêre toris proceres : et corpora tosta,
> Carne replent ; vinoque levant curasque sitimque,' &c.—*Ovid*, '*Met.*' xii., 4.

"The fairest roome above staires is boarded in panes, and inlaid with different woods, representing a stone or marble pavement. It is roofed with a sort of fretwork ceileing, showing the Globe Cœlestiall, all the signes of the Zodiack in figures, ye planets, &c. It hath a large chimney-piece of the old fashion, supported on two columns, the figures in two bustys of Seneca and Aristotle. Over the fireplace is this in golden letters,—

> 'Deus primum honos proxime' [*sic*].

"Over the cornish, at the top of rich ancient tapistrey, are good paintings representing in severall tables, as big as the life,—An *Europa* upon a Bull ; a *Perseus* and *Andromeda* in two tables; one hath him assaulting of a dragon, in ye other is seen a Cupid unloosing Andromeda ; a *Neptune* in his Triton Shell drawn with two sea-horses ; an *Acteon* and *Diana* with Nymphs bathing. Over the chimney the God of the Rivers ; a *Venus*, in a sea-chariot drawn by a Dolphin ; *Hero* and *Leander*, the work of *Van Lemon*, a good master ; *Hercules*, his wife, and the Hippocentaur. Over the window are two weverns. . . . The folding

𝔥𝔢𝔯𝔟𝔢𝔯𝔱 𝔄𝔯𝔪𝔰, 1684—(*Beaufort Progress*).

arms in ye Garter in this room are seen quartered with Northumberland, viz., *gules*, 3 *lucies hauriant argent*. A Northumberland again impaled with it by a marriage with the Lady Elizabeth, second daughter to Henry Percy, Earle of Northumberland, viz., quarterly, the first, *or, a lion rampant azure;* on a second, *gules*, 3 *lucies haurient argent*, the third as the second, the last as the first."

"The gallery leads into the fairest Roomes, and is adorned among others with these pieces :—1. Of the Duke of Norfolk, lately dead. 2. The Lady Eleanor Percy, dau. of Henry, Earle of Northumberland, a piece at length superscribed, *Ætat.* 13, 1595, *Mort.* 1657. 3. William Herbert, Lord Powis, *Ætat.* 23, 1595, *Mort.* 1656. 4. Opposite to ye great Roome in the same Gallery, Sir Edward Herbert, Knight of the Bath, who was Embassador in France, sitting in his night-gown, and dictateing to his Secretary. Here are also three or four excellent pieces of great masters—*ideo quaere*." [These portraits are still in the Castle, chiefly in the Drawing Room.]

"At the end of this Gallery is a pleasant Bed-chamber, with alcove, wherein his Grace the Duke of Beaufort lay. The furniture is of Crimson velvet, fringed with gold; ye Ballastars are also richly guilded and deversify'd. The paintings are two Tables; one of the *Nativity*, the other of the *Resurrection*, by a good hand.

"In the Roome on ye left hand, the foot of ye great staircase, ye chimney-piece hath the history of *Sampson* and *Dalilah;* over the door *Parnassus*, whereon ye nine muses; *Perseus* and *Andromeda*.

"Dineing Room where his Grace was enterteined; over the entrance into it is y^e painting of a *Pan* and *Cyringa* turning into Reeds. The Anti-room to this hath for chimney-piece, ill done, a *Phaeton* overturning his Chariot.

"Within a mile of Montgomery and $\frac{4}{5}$ miles from Powis Castle is scituate in

LYMORE (*from a photo. by Mr. Owen*).

a Park of Red and Fallow Deer, the seat [*Lymore*] belonging to the learned Lord Herbert of Cherbury who wrote a Tract *De Veritate*, &c. Ann. Dom. 1624."

Lymore (*Llys-mawr*) has continued in the Powis family. It is kept in good preservation, and is one of the most interesting specimens remaining in these parts of the timbered mansions of the aristocracy. It is said to have been at first a Lodge in the Deer Park belonging to the mansion of the Herberts at *Blackhall*, on the destruction of which by fire Lymore was enlarged and converted into a substitute, about 1585.

To return to Powis Castle. The building as now standing is much reduced in dimensions from what it was in past times, dilapidated portions having been removed and the structure made more compact and somewhat modernised. When Leland visited it about 1540, the castle, according to his description, was more like two castles than one. "Walsch-pool, five miles from Montgomerik, the best market in Powisland," he says, "had two Lord Marchers castels within one wall, the Lord Powis named Grey, and the Lord Dudley named Sutton, but now the Lord Powis hathe bothe in his hand. The Walch Pole is in compas almoste as muche as a little town. The Lord Duddeley's part is almost fallen down. The Lord Powis's part is metely good." Respecting these "two castels," a remark in the "Additions" to *Camden* is worthy of attention. "What Mr. Camden, after Leland, says of the different proprietors of the two castles here seems to mean no more than that the Baron Dudley (of whom John, *temp.* Edward III., married Isabel, daughter of John de Charleton, Lord of Powis), had a tower or apartment here."

In the civil war the then Lord Powis declared for the king, but the castle was at last surrendered to the Parliamentary forces led by Sir Thomas Myddelton. The estates were then confiscated, but were compounded for, and restored.

In the ancient divisions of Upper Powys, of which we have said the Red Castle was for ages the centre and princely seat, this immediate part was situated in the *cantref* of Fyrnwy. That these divisions, as transmitted to us in the *Myvyrian Archaiology of Wales*, and purporting to be the work of Llewelyn, the last Prince of Wales (*d.* 1282), are really of a date even earlier than his time receives some confirmation from a casual remark in the introduction, where it is said that of the three provinces which existed in Wales, "the third was at Mathrafael in Powys"—language which must refer to a state of things prior to the age of Llewelyn, for in his time Mathrafael had long ceased to be the seat of the Powysian government, having been converted into a lordship of Robert de Vipont, and "Castell Coch" having become the seat of the line of Bleddyn ap Cynfyn.

The Principality of Upper Powys (or P. Wenwynwyn) was divided into five *cantrefs* and thirteen *comots*, as follows:—

Cantrefs.	Comots.
1. Y FYRNWY (from the river of that name) .	1. Mochnant Uwch Rhaiadr ["Mochnant, on the Upper Rhaiadr River"]. 2. Mechain Iscoed ["M. of the lower Forest"]. 3. Llanerch-hudol ["the charming district"].
2. CYNAN	1. Mawddwy. 2. Cyfeiliog.
3. LLYSWYNAF	1. Caereinion. 2. Mechain uwch Coed ["M. of the upper Forest"].
4. YSTLYG	1. Deuddwr "the two waters:" sit. at the junction of the Fyrnwy and Severn. Now corrupted into Deythur]. 2. Corddwr. 3. Ystrad Marchell ["The Vale of Marchell"].
5. ARWYSTLI	1. Uwch Coed ["of the upper Forest"]. 2. Iscoed ["of the lower Forest"]. 3. Gwrthrynion.

All these are included in the county of Montgomery, excepting the comot of *Mawddwy*, which belongs to Merioneth, and the comot of *Gwrthrynion*, which is in Radnor. They all belonged to the territory ruled by the princes of Upper Powis, although acquired at different times, and occasionally partly lost and again recovered. (See *Montgomeryshire Coll.*, 1867.)

The Red Castle demesne was included in the comot of *Llanerch-hudol*, "the charming or comely part," a description strictly appropriate to the nature of the landscape. From the swelling grounds of Powis Castle park, and from the turrets of the castle itself, the panorama of mountain, vale, and plain, is truly magnificent, and from the grounds of Llanerch-hudol Mansion the prospect is only slightly less enchanting.

The neighbourhood of Welshpool (a place which, from a mere "pool," grew into a fortress, and next into a flourishing borough) is one which would unfailingly become the resort of persons of taste and intelligence. Its grand traditions, historic deeds and associations, numerous memorials of long-past chivalry, and spots consecrated by the long-continued residence of influential households, give it a character of powerful fascination. Hence we find, within a narrow circle around the Red Castle, a large number of the *generosi* of the county assembled. For many ages this has been the case, but some of the

GUNLEY—THE RESIDENCE OF MRS. PRYCE (*from a photograph by Mr. Owen*).

older homes have been removed or converted to humbler uses, while others have bravely persisted against the mouldering effects of time, and some new mansions have sprung into being. Here we find *Llanerch-hudol*, the noble and delightfully situated residence of Lady Edwards; *Cyfronydd* (Rob. Davies Pryce, Esq.); *Garth* (Capt. D. H. Mytton); *Trelydan Hall* (General Ed. Scott); *Crosswood* (Major Heyward Heyward—see *Heyward of Cilbronnau*, Pemb.); *Derwen* (Capt. G. Jenkins—see *Jenkins of Pen'rallt*, Card.); *Leighton Hall* (John Naylor, Esq.); *Brooklands* (Mrs. Curling); *Dysserth* (J. Davies Corrie, Esq.); *Edderton House* (Richard Edmunds, Esq.); *Nantcribba Hall* (formerly *Llwyd*, afterwards Purcell, and then Devereux, Viscount Hereford); *Gunley*, the ancient home of the Pryce family (see *Pryce of Gunley*) Gunley is a modernized mansion, still containing parts of considerable antiquity, where an interesting series of family and other portraits are preserved. The pedigree of the Pryce family in the handwriting of *Lewys Dwnn* in 1608—

with his autograph attached—one of a very few existing, is also here. Gunley stands on the margin of the county, looking towards Corndon Hill and the rich lands of Salop.

Near Llanfair Caereinion are found *Dolarddyn Hall* (formerly Wynn, now E. Humphreys, Esq); *The Mount* (J. R. Pickmere, Esq.); *Bryn Peniarth* (E. T. Greves, Esq.); while further north we have *Dyffryn*, Meifod (J. Buckley Williames, Esq.); *Ystum-Colwyn* (formerly *Williams*); The Vicarage, Meifod (Rev. Canon R. Wynne Edwards); *Penylan* (E. S. R. Trevor, Esq.); *Llwyn*, Llanfyllin (John Dugdale, Esq.); *Bodfach*, Llanfyllin (formerly Kyffin, and Price, old fams., now T. O. Lomax, Esq.); *Bronheuddan* (R. S. Perrott, Esq.); *Llanfechain* (Rev. W. Maddock Williams); *Brynderwen* (Thos. Gill, Esq.); *Bodynfoel* (R. M. Bonnor Maurice, Esq.); *Bryn-Tanat* (Mrs. Perry). In this locality also, in the level lands between the Fyrnwy and the Severn, are *Rhysnant Hall* (formerly Penrhyn); *Penrhos Hall;* and east of the latter river *Llandrinio Hall*, *Criggion* (formerly Williams), and the ancient *Buttington*.

The *Abbey* of *Ystrad Marchell* in the township of Gungrog-fawr, three miles east of Welshpool, on the left bank of the Severn, has entirely disappeared. Nothing marks the spot to the common eye beyond some inequalities of the ground, too broken and effaced to show the plan of the foundations. Dugdale has called it "Valle Crucis" by mistake. Like most of the abbeys of Wales it belonged to the Cistercian order, and was an offshoot of *Alba Domus*, or Ty Gwyn ar Dâf, in Carmarthenshire.

Montgomery, that first slice of Powysian ground taken from the Cymry subsequently to the encroachments of Offa of Mercia and Egbert, must be considered as another centre of influence in this county, both in ancient and more modern times.

To its first builder, Baldwyn, and first lord, Roger de Montgomery—that bold warrior who commanded the central wing in William's army of invasion—allusion has already been made. The castle was several times destroyed and rebuilt. It was made a powerful fortress by Henry III., and was the scene of keen contention and ferocious barbarities during the wars of that king with Llewelyn the Great. That energetic prince took possession of it, put the garrison to the sword, and burnt the place. The Mortimers in the fourteenth century were lords of this castle. It became the property of the house of York; reverted to the Crown; and was finally obtained by the Herberts, ancestors of the celebrated Lord Herbert of Chirbury (see *Powis Castle*). It continued for some time the residence of the Herberts, Lords of Chirbury. *Lymore* is now the venerable memorial of it in that respect. In the civil war it was garrisoned for the hapless king, and capitulated to the Parliamentary General, Sir Thomas Myddelton, who for some time had been driven from his own castle of Chirk by Charles's army (see p. 369). Before final possession was secured, however, another and fierce battle took place which resulted in the total defeat of the king's forces. The castle was now by order of Parliament dismantled; at present but a small part of it crowns the rock—a crumbling fragment, at once a symbol and memorial of an iron system of feudal oppression for ever passed away.

The division of country, in which, in the earlier times, the site of Montgomery was situated, was the—

Cantref of Cedewain.

and belonged, not to Upper Powys but to the territory of Elystan Glodrydd, Prince of Ferlex, a princedom usually described as lying "between the Severn and the Wye." In later times, however, except at intervals of violent dispossession by the Princes of North or South Wales, or the English king, it formed part of Powys Wenwynwyn, which is described in the document "Parthau Cymru," in the *Myvyr. Archæol. of Wales*, but, in a manner by no means clear and free from contradiction. But it is to be kept in mind that ever since the Norman Conquest, ever since the seizure by De Montgomery of the Montgomery lordship, there existed a two-fold possession of all these parts—the King of England, as Suzerain, placed in the March lands whatever lord he chose; the princes of

VAYNOR PARK—THE SEAT OF MAJOR WILLIAM CORBETT (*from a photo. by Mr. Owen*).

Powis ruled as *reguli*, holding their lands by homage to the "King of London," and paying tribute in acknowledgment of their subjection. The Welsh historians very often speak of the Princes of Wales as independent princes long ages after they had been placed in the position of *reguli*, and even "lords," and as a rule ignore the fact that they paid tribute or had lost a shadow of their pristine dignity. A proud contempt of the invader, a brave but unreasoning love of nation and country, led them to attempt ignoring, in the face of irrefragable *fact*, the humiliation which might had ruthlessly imposed upon right. Powys, after the Conquest of Wales by Edward I., and under the triumphant and domineering rule of the Lords Marchers, whose great castles frowned down upon the helpless natives from Chester to the Bristol Channel—at Shrewsbury, Caurs, Mathrafal, Pool, Clun, Montgomery, Builth, &c., had almost passed out of mind, and Henry VIII., when framing his enactment constituting Montgomery a *county* (A.D. 1533), speaks of these parts as simply belonging to the "Marches."

MONTGOMERYSHIRE.

The vale of Severn near Montgomery may be termed luxuriant, attractive for its quiet retirement and pleasing variety of scene, rather than very beautiful or picturesque; but the demesne of *Vaynor Park* (see *Corbett-Winder of Vaynor*) is one of the most delightful in Powys—that land described by the ancient poet, *Llywarch Hên*, as—

Powys, paradwys Cymru,
"Powys, paradise of Wales."

and still entitled to no small portion of the poet's eulogium. The noble mansion of Vaynor, supposed to be originally *Y fan oer*, "the exposed (cold) place," is planted on lofty ground, now well wooded, and diversified by curious swellings of the surface, suggesting sand-bank formation under water. The park is remarkable not only for the wide and splendid prospect it commands, but for its tasteful ornamentation, and the unusually luxuriant

GLANSEVERN—THE RESIDENCE OF MRS. OWEN (*from a drawing by Gastineau*).

hawthorn and May trees which in great numbers adorn it. The mansion, in the Elizabethan style, is one of the most substantial and picturesquely planted in the county. The front and back are of almost similar design, with courtyard and massive entrance gateway to the latter. It once belonged to the Hereford family (see *Viscount Hereford*).

From Vaynor Park a pleasing view is obtained of the near valley of the Rhiw, deep and prettily wooded, in which stands *Rhiw-port* (A. Howell, Esq.), and further down, near the junction or *aber* of the Rhiw with the Severn, the hamlet of Berriew (a corruption of *Aber-Rhiw*), and the mansion of *Glansevern*, a large and substantial house standing in the sunny and fertile valley which is watered equally by the two rivers. Glansevern contains a number of valuable family and other portraits, and some interesting antiquities and curiosities. (See further, *Owen of Glansevern*.)

Rhiewport, now the seat of A. Howell, Esq., who purchased it in 1866 (see *Howell of Rhiewport*), was for several generations the property and residence of the ancient family of Jones, known as Jones of Trewythen, Pen'ralltgoch, and Rhiewport. They were seated at Trewythen (near Llanidloes) since about A.D. 1500, and possessed Rhiewport for above a century. For the genealogy of this family, now extinct in the direct male line, see *Jones of Trewythen*, also *Combe of Oaklands*, the latter its only surviving representative. Owing to family misfortunes, the failure of a bank, &c., the estates, consisting of about 4,000 acres, were sold to various purchasers in 1862 for about £70,000. The old mansion of Trewythen has been

RHIEWPORT, MONTGOMERYSHIRE.

modernized into a common red brick farmhouse, and the family town house at Llanidloes is converted into an inn, called the "Trewythen Arms." This family bore—"Quarterly: 1st and 2nd, or, a lion rampant gu.; 2nd and 3rd, sa., three nags' heads erased arg., two and one. *Crest*: a lion rampant, as in the arms. *Motto*: Heb Dduw heb ddim; Duw a digon." A more modern motto, "Frangas non flectes," was also adopted.

The view here given is engraved from an old coloured drawing, corrected by a photograph recently taken, but the house in the interval had undergone no alteration in plan.

The Mount, near Llanfair, is prettily situated on high ground above the river Vyrnwy, surrounded by charming scenery. The house consists partly of an older residence, tastefully modernized and much extended.

THE MOUNT.—The Seat of J. R. PICKMERE, Esq.

In the same immediate neighbourhood are located *Garthmyl* (late J. Arthur Johnes, Esq., now A. C. Humphreys, Esq.); *Caerhowel* (Rev. John Harrison); at *Montgomery* (Richard Smith Humphreys, Esq.); *Pennant* (Mrs. P. Buckley Williames); *Glanhafren* (Mrs. Buckley Williames); *Castell Forwyn* (Rev. John Lloyd); *Dolforwyn Hall* (Mrs. Devereux Pryce), all suspended on the fertilizing Severn like beads upon a silver string. Castell Forwyn ("the Maiden's Castle") derives its name from the association of the spot with the pretty legend of *Hafren*. The ruins of a castle (a fortress probably built by Llewelyn or Bleddyn ap Cynfyn) are on the eminence above the house, and the rock from which she was thrown into the river is shown in the vale below.

New Troy (so runs the legend in *Brut Tyssilio*, and in an improved form in *Geoffrey* of Monmouth) was built on the river Thames by Brutus, who had come to Britain from ancient Troy. Brutus dying, left his government in the hands of his three sons, of whom Locrinus, the eldest, possessed the middle part of the island. He was attacked by Humber, King of the Huns, but proved victorious, and the invader was driven in his flight into the river which ever since has borne his name, wherein he was drowned. In one of the enemy's hollow ships was found much treasure, which fell to the share of Locrinus, but chief of all were three virgins of celestial beauty, one of whom was the daughter of the "King of Germany," previously conquered and despoiled by the pirate Humber. She bore the name of Essyllt (in Geoffrey, "Estrildis"); her skin was fairer than the snow or lily, or the bone of the whale ("asgwrn morfil"), and Locrinus at the sight of her was smitten with overpowering love, and at once wished to make her his queen. But among his father's warriors was Corineus the Strong, whose daughter, Gwendolen, Locrinus had already espoused. "Is it thus, young man," cried the incensed Corineus, "thou rewardest my wounds and sufferings endured in thy father's wars with strange nations? Is it thus thou slightest my daughter in favour of a barbarian damsel? While these two arms have strength thou shalt not do thus with impunity;" and swaying his two-edged battle-axe, he threatened to strike him down. But friends interposed between the chieftains, and Locrinus was compelled to marry Gwendolen.

But his love for Essyllt did not cease. For seven years he concealed her underground in London (New Troy), in great halls he had excavated for the purpose, and there he visited her in secret under pretence of worshipping the gods. And it came to pass when Corineus was dead, that Locrinus abandoned Gwendolen, and brought Essyllt openly to his court as his queen. Now was the grief of Gwendolen great, and she went as far as Cornwall, and gathered a great army of youth, and fought against Locrinus. The two hosts met on the river Verram (in Geoffrey, the river "Sture"), where Locrinus was struck by an arrow in the forehead, and died. Then did Gwendolen assume the reins of government in the island of Britain, and she commanded that Essyllt and her daughter *Havren* should be taken and cast into the river; and from that time the river has been known through all Britain as "Havren" (Lat., *Sabrina*, whence *Severn*), and so it shall be called till the day of doom. The legend refers to a time about B.C. 1000.

According to Milton's fancy Hafren was not drowned, but became a virgin goddess, and ever since "with moist curb sways the smooth Severn stream, bestowing her care upon "ensnared chastity" in "hard-besetting need." When cruel Gwendolen commanded ".her fair innocence to the flood,"—

> "The water-nymphs, that in the bottom played,
> Held up their pearled wrists and took her in,
> Bearing her straight to aged Nereus' hall ;
> Who, piteous of her woes, reared her lank head,
> And gave her to his daughters to imbathe
> In nectared lavers, strewed with asphodel ;
> And through the porch and inlet of each sense
> Dropped in ambrosial oils, till she revived,
> And underwent a quick immortal change."—"*Comus.*"

A little higher up the river than Dolforwyn Castle is Aber-Bechan, the junction of the Bechan with the Severn. From the height on which the castle of Dolforwyn stands a fine prospect opens of the vale of the Severn, and the rising woodlands and cultured slopes on either side, with the added beauties of the smaller valleys of the Mule and the Bechan,

GREGYNOG—THE SEAT OF THE HON. H. HANBURY-TRACY (*from a photo. by Mr. Owen*).

both within the compass of the eye. The Mule, joining the Severn at Aber-Mule, flows from the neighbourhood of Kerry, the ancient comot of *Ceri*, in Maelienydd—where the Kerry hills form the watershed, directing the Mule to the west, to find the shortest course to the "Sandy Severn," and the Caebitra to the east, first to visit Church Stoke, and blend its waters with the Camlan, and then to proceed northward under the Corndon Hill, in front of Gunley, and here turn abruptly westward to meet the Severn about a mile below Aber-Rhiw (Berriew). On the banks of this stream, between Cherbury and its entrance into the Severn, several *tumuli* and *barrows* are noticed. The locality is redolent of historic associations, and is apparently marked by several *pre-historic* monuments, such as the barrows of *Hên Dommen, Maen Beuno*, &c. *Caer Flos*, on the Severn, is said to be a Roman camp.

The Bechan river comes down from the high and comparatively bleak region of Carno and Tregynon, passing the noble mansion of *Gregynog* (Hon. H. Hanbury Tracy ; see also

Sudeley, Lord, of Toddington and Gregynog), the ancient home of the Blayneys. Gregynog is situated on the breezy upper lands of Tregynon; the park sloping down towards the margin of the rapid Bechan ("the small"—in contrast with the larger Severn, to which it hastens), and judiciously planted with groves of various species of pine and other forest trees adapted to the ground. The mansion, of recent erection, though not built of timber is in imitation of the ancient timbered houses, and parts of the interior consist of portions of the older house, the wainscoting and mantel-pieces of one or two of the apartments exhibiting exquisite specimens of elaborate oak carvings, and some of the new parts in concrete work, made to imitate pannelled and moulded oak wainscoting.

Mr. Tracy, whose care and judgment are visible, not only in the planning and ornamentation of the mansion, but generally on the estate, has set to the landowners of Wales an example in *cottage-building*, which it is to be hoped will be extensively followed. He has adopted the method of building with *concrete* as a substitute for stone or brick, and has

COTTAGES ON THE GREGYNOG ESTATE, BUILT OF CONCRETE.

proved that the whole of a house, including the roof, mouldings and mullions of windows, doorways, &c., can be built of concrete, and at a cost little exceeding one-half that of the ordinary mode of building. But the economy of the first erection is but a small part of the merits of this method. The building, if well done, is almost imperishable. As a habitation it is warmer in winter and cooler in summer than if built of stone and covered with slate. The materials are not dependent on stone quarries, or brick-clay; the gravel from a river-bed, old bricks pounded into small fragments, or any stony rubbish, and cement, being all that is wanted. In many parts of the country, more especially in the alluvial plains of England, stone cannot be got at reasonable cost, and brick-making stuff is often poor and hard to get. The usual building materials of every kind are now high in price, and the cottages of the poor on many estates are more comfortless than the dog-kennels and stables. Mr. Tracy, in Montgomeryshire, has proved how easy it is for the landlord to study at once economy of management and beneficence towards the tenantry; and if a few gentlemen in each county would "go and do likewise," the advantage to the health, morals, and comfort of the people would soon be great beyond calculation. The rickety mud hovel with its pitted earth-floor and rotting, leaking roof, would be replaced by the neat and durable cottage with solid pavement and equally solid roof, requiring next to no repairs, making cleanliness easy, and inspiring the peasant with proper self-respect, mingled with gratitude to his landlord. A snug and handsome cottage suggests, and almost of necessity leads to neatness of dress, a neatly kept garden, and the culture of flowers—matters of "taste and refinement" within the province and reach of the poor, and no mean appendages to the acres of the wealthy.

Newtown, a name translated from the earlier Welsh *Y Dref-newydd*, was formerly known only as a parish church by the name of Llanfair yn Nghedewain, "The Church of Mary in (the cantref of) Cedewain;" and it is probable that when the place grew from a hamlet into a small town it was dignified with the present designation in allusion to the old Roman settlement of *Caersws*, which had fallen into decay. Here is *Newtown Hall*, for many generations the home of the *Price* family (see *Price of Newtown Hall*); and in the vicinity are *Glan-hafren* (Col. G. Edward Herbert); *Dolforgan Hall* (James Walton, Esq., formerly *Long*); *Aberhavesp* (formerly Morgan); *Glan-meheli* (formerly Price); *Dolfor* (formerly Evans); *Gwernygo* (formerly Lloyd)*;* *Kerry* (formerly Evans); *Fronfelen* (J. P. Davies, Esq.).

As we move towards Llanidloes, leaving to the right, at the distance of five or six miles from the high-road, the fatal field of *Carno*—the scene of one of the most bloody battles recorded in the annals of Wales, fought in 1077, when Gruffydd ap Cynan, rightful Prince of N. Wales defeated the usurper, Trahaearn ap Caradog, we pass *Llandinam Hall* (Capt. Crewe-Read, R.N.), an ancient timbered mansion of picturesque appearance and curious history; *Maesmawr* (formerly Blayney, and Davies); *Berth-ddu* (Thos. William Hare, Esq.); the ancient mansion of *Perth-lwyd* (long the residence of the Lloyds). In the close neighbourhood of Llanidloes is *Mount-Severn*, the delightfully situated residence of Col. Hunter, embosomed in richly wooded grounds, and looking down on the youthful Severn as it takes a sharp turn towards the famous valley which, from Llanidloes to the Salop border, it fills with beauty and fertility. Here also is *Dol-y-llys*, often written "Dollys" (formerly Owen); *Pen-y-Green* (John Jenkins, Esq.); at the *Vicarage* is Rev. J. Harris Jones, M.A., Vicar of Llanidloes. At no great distance from Llanidloes is *Clochfaen* (J. Yonde W. Lloyd, Esq.), an ancient place, and the home of one of the old families of Montgomeryshire, long resident also at *Plas Madoc*, Denbighshire.

Between Llanidloes and Machynlleth extend the ancient comots of—

Uwch-coed, cantref of *Arwystli*, and—
Cyfeiliog, cantref of *Cynan:*

Carno and Caersws being in the former, and Machynlleth, Penegos, Cemmaes, &c., in the latter. Few comots in Wales abound more in remains of sepulchral antiquity than that of

Uwch-Coed. Within its boundaries between Llanidloes, Carno and Caersws, are the cairns or barrows of Pen-y-Castell; Carn; Pen-y-Glyn; Pen-y-Castell; y Gaer; Cefn-Carnedd, near Llandinan Hall; Caersws; the *menhir* of Argoed; Castell Caer Noddfa; Carno (a real Roman fortress); Twr-Gwyn-mawr; Careg-hir, &c., a multitude of monuments, some historic, some pre-historic, sufficiently attesting the important transactions of this locality in early times. Under some of these tumuli repose the ashes of those stretched in death on the field of Carno eight hundred years ago. The frequent *caers* and entrenched camps were used in all ages from pre-Roman to post-Norman times. The *menhirs* may have kept watch over all the movements of contending mortals for 3,000 years; but for what other purpose set up no record or sign remains to tell.

In the churchyard of Carno are some venerable yews, which must have been sturdy trees when Gruffydd ap Cynan won the memorable battle of 1077. On the way towards Machynlleth

MOUNT-SEVERN—THE SEAT OF COL. WILLIAM HUNTER (*from a photo. by J. Owen.*)

we pass *Plas Llysin* (W. H. Adams, Esq.), and at Talerddig come not only to a parting of the roads, but to a high ground which forms a parting of the waters—turning the Carno river eastward to join the Severn, and another stream, rushing wildly for scenes more picturesque, westward towards the Dyfi. At *Tafolwern*, a remarkable locality for *tumuli*, *menhirs*, and *cairns*, this prattling stream is joined by two others from opposite sides, the one from the foot of Penllyman (Plinlimmon), the other from the direction of Mallwyd, their intersecting valleys crowding upon this spot a variety of landscape beauty, truly charming to the observant traveller. At some distance to the left is *Ceniarth* (Pritchard Pritchard, Esq.); on the left is *Rhiwsaeson*, the ancient abode of the Owens; and nearer Machynlleth the venerable *Mathafarn*, where lived the celebrated bard, Dafydd Llwyd, who entertained for the night Henry Tudor, Earl of Richmond, on his way in 1485 to Bosworth Field and the throne of England (see p. 686). The bards of those days were supposed to hold some converse with the occult powers, and to be able like the ancient seers to prognosticate events. It is said that the Earl of Richmond sought from Dafydd Llwyd some forecasting of his fortune. Sir Rhys ap Thomas, his friend in the south, we have seen, pursued a similar course (see p. 242). Dafydd Llwyd, not over-confident in his own prophetic power, took the wise course of consulting his wife, who with the instinctive wisdom of her sex promptly helped him out of his difficulty. Said she in effect, " Foretell success, to be sure! for if it prove true, your character is established; and if false, why, then the Earl of Richmond will not return to reproach you. As it turned out Henry was successful, and Dafydd Llwyd of Mathafarn gained a great accession to his fame.

Near Rhiwsaeson are two *tumuli* of some note, and on the top of the Cemmaes hill a *cairn* called Carnedd-Cerrig. To the south, near Darowen, are the two *menhirs* called *meini llwydion* ("the grey stones"), and the camp of *Fron-goch*.

Plas Machynlleth, the seat of the Earl Vane, adjoins the town of Machynlleth, whose chief monument of antiquity is the fragment that survives of the parliament-house of *Owen Glyndwr*. Here that intrepid chieftain in 1402, two years after he first unfurled the banner of insurrection against Henry IV., called together a parliament of Wales, and wore the title of Prince of Wales (see pp. 384, 386); and here poor impetuous Sir David Gam attempted a dastardly deed which only brought him grief and left his name under dishonour (see p. 91). *Llynlloedd*, the residence of the Owens in the sixteenth century (now Richard Gillart, Esq.) ; *Dolguog* (David Howell, Esq.), where tradition relates that Llywarch Hên, after the disastrous battle of Rhiwaedog, occupied a cell, and sought solace in the tones of his harp and the exercise of poetry ; *Morben* (formerly Owens), on the extreme western angle of the county ; *Llugwy, Talgarth Hall, Pant-lludw*, and *Glanwern*, already noticed under Merioneth, are the chief residences around Machynlleth.

Out of our view as we followed the course of the Severn, and marked the great estates and family abodes enlivening its margin, was the venerable *Llwydiarth*, a lordly and renowned place in the seventeenth century. (See *Vaughan of Llwydiarth*.) The great Duke of Beaufort, Charles II.'s Lieutenant and Lord President in Wales and the Marches, found, in 1684, that Llwydiarth and Powis Castle were the two places in Montgomeryshire suitable to entertain him and his numerous retinue. Mr. Dineley, his Grace's secretary, though ignorant of the name of the "county," and puzzled about the spelling of Llwydiarth, was evidently pleased with the reception given his master at that place.

From Rhiwlas "his Grace went on his progress to Mr. Vaughan of *Lloydyarth, Lloydwersht*, or *Lloyddwecht*. Thither from Bala you are directed by guides, by reason of dangerous bogges in the passage, after the precepitous ascents and descents near Bala.

"Wednesday, July 30, 1684.—His Grace the Duke of Beaufort, Lord President of Wales, &c., came to Lloydyarth, the seat of Vaughan, Esq., in the county of, ... attended with the Lord Worcester, Sir John Talbot, and several gentlemen of the county, where a noble enterteinement was provided, with good standing and provender for above ninety horse. Here his Grace made a stay all night, with all knights, gentlemen, &c., of his company and retinue. Having entered the court through the porch, over the entrance into the house are these arms cut in stone :—the first hath a wolf's head erased, and the shield beareth a chevron between 3 wolves' heads erased, by the name of Vaughan of Lloydyarth." [The second escutcheon was figured quarterly : 1st, a goat passant;] " The 2nd coat is a chevron between 3 cocks arg. armed, crested, jelloped, by the name of . . . ; the third is arg., a cross between four lyoncells rampant gules ; the fourth is gules, a lion rampant regardant or."—(*Beaufort Progress.*)

Section II.—GEOLOGY OF MONTGOMERYSHIRE.

The geology of this county exhibits a considerable variety of rocks of the primary series, commencing, in point of greatest age, in that part of the county between Machynlleth and Llanidloes, where the *Llandeilo* (Lower Silurian) formation almost alone prevails, and ending in the greatly more recent but still enormously old *Permian* group, on the east of the Briedden, and other spots near Welshpool.

A large extent of ground in the middle of Montgomeryshire, stretching between irregular lines from about Garthmyl to Garthbeibio and thence to Llangynog, belongs to the *Caradoc* group, and adjoining this, to the north-east, from the Kerry Hills by Newtown round by Llanfair Caereinion to Welshpool, the *Wenlock* group (Upper Silurian) bears almost exclusive control. In the valley of the Severn, from Montgomery to the junction with that river of the Vyrnwy, a narrow strip on either side the stream consists of the Llandeilo ; and the same formation obtains along the Vyrnwy from the neighbourhood of Dolgoed and Garthlwyd about the confluence of the Einion and the Banw, by Mathrafal, Meifod, Llanfyllin, and Llansantffraid to the Severn.

The most complex part of the geology of this county is found about Welshpool, and the Breidden and Corndon Hills, where the stratified rocks of the Silurian system have been shattered and pierced by eruptive masses of a truly volcanic character. Corndon Hill, as Professor Ramsey has shown in a section of the North Wales strata, has an enormous core, 1,700 feet high, of igneous materials. The sedimentary rocks of the Llandeilo series have been penetrated by large masses of eruptive trap in a state of fusion, and in the process been thrown into undulating and irregular forms all around. The eruptive rocks in and around the Corndon Mountain, and in the neighbouring mineral district of Shelve, are chiefly coarse-grained hornblendic greenstone and felspar, passing, as Murchison says, into basalt. The shale or schist in contact with the eruptive rock has been often cemented into a complete porcellanite, " with surfaces as smooth as the finest lithographic stone."

" The Breidden hills, including the picturesque Moel-y-Golfa," says Murchison, " also exhibit illustrations both of contemporaneously bedded trap, and of posterior or intrusive rocks which have broken out along the same line at different periods." From the terrace of Powis Castle the lower Silurian volcanic masses of the Breidden are seen distinctly on the left, separated by a small valley and the Shrewsbury high-road from the upper Silurian, or Ludlow non-volcanic mass of the Long Mountain on the right. Rodney's Pillar on the Breidden stands on a compact cone of volcanic rock. The site of Powis Castle is on the highly inclined edges of lower Silurian rocks, thrown into this position from the horizontal line of their deposition by the volcanic disturbance, and we are not without evidence that, after this disturbance took place, during long ages of tranquillity, a carboniferous deposit covered up the jagged edges of the lower Silurian, which deposit in its turn, along with a later stratum of *new red sandstone* (seen plainly on the road from Welshpool towards Caerynwch) was again broken up by another eruptive disturbance. The legend says that the pool at Welshpool has no bottom; it is highly probable, considering the violent agencies which geology shows at work in the district in the far past, that many pits, fiery, and all but bottomless, once existed hereabouts. Legends often carry with them echoes of truth more marvellous than themselves.

Section III.—OLD AND EXTINCT FAMILIES OF MONTGOMERYSHIRE.

As a Marcher district this county experienced a wholesale devastation of its old Cymric houses. During 800 years of an iron oppression, which had little mercy to show the natives either in goods or person, scores of households of gentle and even of princely blood melted away into a blank oblivion, only better than an existence subject to the ignominy of the Norman's rule. Their names are confided to the "Silences." Notwithstanding this, and the second hurricane of desolation which passed over the county in the Tudor period, when the hasty Cymric furor of the eighth Henry, and of Elizabeth in part, sought to regenerate Wales by extinguishing everything distinctively national in language, law, custom, a goodly number of families had survived who could trace their origin to an honourable, and many to a princely parentage. Add to these the new comers of alien blood but of patrician lineage, or of common lineage but happy fortune, who in time had come to like the land which gave them plenty, and identify themselves in feeling, language, religion, with the native population, and we have in the sixteenth and seventeenth centuries a host of households in Montgomeryshire of good consideration and competent means. But two hundred years have wrought havoc among them almost equal to the desolations of a conquest. An enormous proportion have given place to others. The manor-house has become a tenant farmer's abode; the moated castle has been covered by the greensward; the halls that echoed to the voices of generation after generation of the same lineage, have been inhabited by the casual and temporary tenant. At Newton Hall, Llwydiarth, Maesmawr, Dolarddyn, Trelydan, Abertanat, Aberbechan, Leighton, Vaynor, Nantcribba, Bodfach, Peniarth, Dolforgan, Aberhavesp, Blackhall, Dol-llys, Berth-lwyd, Llynllo, Dolguog, Morben, and many others, the hand of time has left its mark, and in many cases we inquire in vain for the old names, except at the sculptured marble in the parish church. Here and there the change has brought a benefit, but in many instances the reverse.

The following are a few of the chief old Montgomeryshire families now extinct, or surviving only in different collateral and female descents:—

Vaughan of Llwydiarth, descended from Uchtryd ap Aleth, Prince of Dyfed, and extinct through the marriage of Anne, heiress of Edward Vaughan, Esq. (see *Vaughan of Glan-llyn* and *Llwydiarth*), with the great-grandfather of the present Sir Watkin Williams Wynn of Wynnstay (who now in virtue of that marriage enjoys the estates of Llwydiarth and Llangedwyn); *Price of Newton*, from Tudor Trevor, founder of the tribe of the Marchers; *Pugh of Mathafarn*, from Gwyddno Garanhir, Lord of Merioneth, whose representative, John Pugh, was member for Montgomery till 1718, whose estates were sold in 1752 to the then possessor of Wynnstay; *Blayney of Tregynon* and *Gregynog*, from Brochwel Ysgythrog, Prince of Powys, and long settled at Gregynog, Aberbechan, and Maesmawr (Llandinam), &c. (see *Lewis Glyn Cothi*, p. 431); *Owen of Rhiwsaeson*, of the tribe of Tudor Trevor, not long extinct; *Tanat of Aber-Tanat* (a surname assumed from the river of that name), also settled at *Broniarth*, Guilsfield, of the line of Bleddyn ap Cynfyn, Prince of Powys, through his grandson Madoc, extinct in the male line with the death of Owen Tanat, Esq., of Abertanat, whose distant descendant, Mary Godolphin, conveyed the estates by marriage to the Owens of Porkington (Brogyntyn), in whose representative, Mr. Ormsby-Gore, they now vest (see *Ormsby-Gore of Glyn*, Mer.); *Kyffin of Bodfach*, Llanfyllin (thirteenth century), tracing from Einion Efell, great-grandson of Bleddyn ap Cynfyn, assumed the surname Cyffin from a place so called in Llangedwyn, and ended in an heiress, who married Adam Price, of Glanmiheli (Yorke, *Royal Tribes*); *Lloyd of Perth-lwyd*, Llanidloes, according to *Dwnn* descended from Tudor Trevor's tribe, but others say from Rhys Goch ap Llewelyn Aurdorchog, of Iâl, long extinct, and estates passed first to Lloyds of Pontruffydd, Flint, and thence to the Mostyns.

The descendants of *Brochwel Ysgythrog*, Prince of Powys, as late as the seventeenth century were numerous in Montgomeryshire, and owners of much territory; but at the present time there is not a single land-owning family of this lineage in the county. Of this clan were, besides the *Blayneys, of Gregynog*, already named—whose name now survives only in Ireland, in Lord Blayney of Castle Blayney, co. Monaghan,—*Wynn of Garth*, Guilsfield, passed into Myttons through marriage of Dorothy, the heiress (1718), to Richard Mytton, of Pont-is-Cowryd (see *Mytton of Garth*); *Lloyd of Moel-y-garth; Lloyd of Broniarth, Maesmawr,* and *Trawscoed* in Guilsfield; *Lloyd of Gwernygo; Penrhyn of Rhysnant,* from Gruffydd Deuddwr, descendant of Gwyn ap Gruffydd, Lord of Guilsfield,—pedigree taken in 1586 by *Dwnn; Williams of Willaston*, Alberbury, a prominent family, gave several sheriffs to Mont. (see *Sheriffs*, 1546, 1560, &c.); *Wynn of Dolarddyn*, Castle Caer Einion; *Lloyd of Morton*, in Chirbury; *Lloyd of Glan-havon; Price of Manafon; Lloyd of Hem*, or great Haim (Dwnn), in Forden; *Lloyd of Leighton; Jones of Welshpool; Lloyd of Gungrog-fawr*, and many others.

SECTION IV.—HIGH SHERIFFS OF MONTGOMERYSHIRE, FROM A.D. 1541 TO A.D. 1872.

In the attempt to ascertain who were men of consideration in the county at different periods during the last three hundred years, the roll of high sheriffs is of most valuable assistance. Here an authentic record nearly free from error, and distorted by no false colouring, is preserved of those who in the estimation of the sovereign and their compeers were most entitled to the honour and fittest for the duties of so important an office. In this roll is included a considerable number of heads of houses which have now no known representatives. Some have had a persistent vitality, and still continue in vigour.

In the valuable series of the Montgomeryshire Collections, vol. ii., p. 185 *et seq.*, is a list of the sheriffs of the co. of Montgomery up to 1626, by the Rev. W. V. Lloyd, M.A. It shows the result of careful research in the public records, and has been collated with an imperfect calendar of sheriffs published in the *Gwiliedydd*, 1828. This corrected list has been relied upon in drawing up the following roll. Morris C. Jones, Esq., F.S.A., has given his valuable aid with respect to sheriffs subsequent to 1828. It is regretted that from want of space the biographical and genealogical notices of the earlier sheriffs which Mr. Lloyd has supplied, and which are so interesting as illustrative of the old families of Montgomeryshire, cannot here be introduced.

HENRY VIII.

	A.D.
Humphrey Lloyd, Esq., of Leighton [was grandson of Sir Gruffydd Vaughan, Kt., Lord of Burgerdyn, Garth, &c. in Guilsfield]; descended from Brochwel Ysgythrog, and bore his reputed arms—*Sa., three nags' heads erased, 2 and 1 arg.*	1541
Sir Robert Acton, Kt., of Acton Hall, Wor. [was Lord of Dauddwr ("Deythur") in Mont. Arms: *Gu., a fesse and bordure engrailed ermine*]	1542
Lewis Jones, Esq. [or ap John, son of John = John's. Of him little is known]	1543
Gruffydd ap David ap John, Esq.	1544
Lewis Jones, Esq. [same as for 1543]	1545
Reginald Williams, Esq., of Willaston, Alberbury. [Arms of Brochwel Ysgythrog: *Sa., 3 nags' heads erased arg.*]	1546

EDWARD VI.

William Herbert, Esq., of Park, Llanwnog [3rd son of Sir Richard Herbert. Arms of Herbert: *Az. and gu., 3 lions rampant or*]	1547
Matthew Price, Esq., of Newtown [Quarterly: 1 and 4, *gu., a lion rampant regardant or*; 2 and 3, *arg., 3 boars' heads couped sa., langued gu., tusked or*]	1548
Robert Acton, Esq., Lord of Deythur (*Deuddwr*), [son probably of Sheriff for 1542. Same arms. The lordship of *Deu-ddwr*, "the two waters," was in the fork of the two meeting rivers, Vyrnwy and Severn]	1549
Sir Robert Acton, Kt. [the Sheriff for 1542]	1550
James Leeche, Esq. [probably of Newton]	1551
Edward Leighton, Esq., of Wattlesborough [knighted 1591. *Quarterly, per fesse indented or and gu.*]	1552
Nicholas Purcell, Esq. (prob. of Shrewsbury). [Of the line of Purcells of Marton, Salop. *Barry nebulée arg. and gu., over all a bend sa., 3 boars' heads couped of the first*]	1553

PHILIP AND MARY.

Richard Powell, Esq., of Ednop (Edenhope). (Arms from Elystan Glodrudd, same as those under 1548]	1554
Richard Powell, Esq., of Ednop (the same)	1555
Henry Acton, Esq., Lord of Deythur (Deuddwr). [Prob. resident at Acton Hall, *Wor.* See under 1542]	1556
Edward Herbert, Esq., of Blackhall, or Lymore. [4th son of Sir Richard Herbert of Mont-	

	A.D.
gomery (but his eldest son by his wife Anne), and grandfather of Lord Herbert of Chirbury. Was a successful soldier in France, &c., "acquired so much money that he was enabled to purchase the greater part of the estates which descended to the Lords Herbert of Chirbury." *L. Herb. of Chirb.*]	1557
Lewis Jones, Esq. [The Sheriff for 1543]	1558

ELIZABETH.

John Herbert, Esq. ("of Cemmaes"). [Brother of Sheriff for 1557. *Dwnn, Her. Visit.*, i., 312, describes him as "of Kemmes"].	1559
Thomas Williams, Esq., of Willaston. [Eldest son of Sheriff for 1546. Arms the same]	1560
Randolph Hanmer, Esq., of Penley, *Flint*. [Of the Hanmers of Hanmer. *Arg., two lions passant guardant az., armed and langued gu.*]	1561
John Price, Esq., of Eglwyseg-le, Llanfyllin. [From Iestyn ap Gwrgant, whose arms, *Gu., 3 chevronels arg.*, quartered with those of Alo ap Rhiwallon, *Or, 3 lions' heads erased gu. in a bordure engrailed az.*]	1562
Andrew Vavasour, Esq., of Newtown. [Of Norman origin. Mauger le Vavasour came to England with the Conqueror. He held office of king's "valvasour," a degree little inferior to that of baron—Camden. *Or, a fesse indented sa.*]	1563
George Beynon [ap Einion], Esq., residence uncertain	1564
Rhys ap Morris ap Owen, Esq., of Aberbechan. [Line of Brochwel Ysgythrog, prince of Powys. A cadet of the Mirlir Grug or Blayney branch of the tribe of Brochwel (Lloyd in *Montgom. Coll.*) *Sa., three nags' heads erased arg.*]	1565
John Price, Esq., of Newtown Hall. [Eldest son of Sheriff for 1548. Was M.P. for Mont. bor. 1558, 1562, 1567. See *Parl. Annals;* also Card. *Sheriffs*, 1568]	1566
Richard Salway, Esq. (residence uncertain). [Held office of Chief Steward to the Actons, Lords of Deythur. *Sa., a saltire engrailed or*]	1567
Edward Herbert, Esq., of Lymore (same as for 1557)	1568
William Herbert, Esq., of Park, Llanwnog. [Sheriff for 1547. Herbert *arms*]	1569
Thomas Tanat, Esq., of Aber-tanat. [See *Tanat of Aber-Tanat and Broniarth. Per*	

HIGH SHERIFFS OF MONTGOMERYSHIRE. 813

	A.D.
Jesse sa. and arg., a lion rampant counter-changed]	1570
Robert Lloyd, Esq., of Plas-is-Clawdd, Chirk. [From Tudor Trevor, *Per bend sinister ermine and ermines a lion rampant or*] .	1571
Robert Puleston, Esq., of Havod-y-Wern, Denb. [Of the Emral stock. *Sa., three mullets or*]	1572
John Trevor, Esq., of Trevalyn, or "Alington." [*M.* dau. of Sir John Bruges, Kt., of London ; *d.* 1589, bur. at St. Bride's, Fleet St. Of line of Tudor Trevor, and used his arms, as under 1571] . .	1573
David Lloyd ap Jenkin, Esq., of Perth-lwyd. Quart. : 1 and 4, *ermine, a lion rampant sa.* ; 2 and 3, *ermine and ermines, a lion rampant or*]	1574
John Herbert, Esq. (same as Sheriff 1559) .	1575
Richard Herbert, Esq., of Park, Llanwnog. [Eldest son of William Herbert, Sheriff for 1547]	1576
David Lloyd Blayney, Esq., of Gregynog. [From Brochwel Ysgythrog. See *p.* 110].	1577
Arthur Price, Esq., of Vaynor . . .	1578
Richard ap Morris, Esq.	1579
Thomas Jukes, Esq., of Buttington . .	1580
Griffith Lloyd, Esq., of Maesmawr . .	1581
Morgan Gwyn, Esq., of Llanidloes . .	1582
John Owen Vaughan, Esq., of Llwydiarth .	1583
Richard Herbert, Esq., of Park . . .	1584
David Lloyd Blayney, Esq. [See 1577]. .	1585
John Price, Esq.	1586
David Lloyd Jenkin, Esq. (prob. of Perth-lwyd	1587
Jenkin Lloyd, Esq., of Perth-lwyd . .	1588
William Williams, Esq.	1589
Morgan Meredith, Esq.	1590
Sir Richard Pryse, |Kt., [of Gogerddan, Card. He *m.* Gwenllian, d. and h. of Thomas ap Morys ap Owen ap Evan *Blaen* of Aber-bechan, Mont.]	1591
Sir Edward Leighton, Esq. . . .	1592
Thomas Lewis, Esq., of Harpton . .	1593
Reginald Williams, of Willaston . .	1594
Francis Newton, Esq., of Heightley . .	1595
William Williams, Esq., of Cowhitlans .	1596
Thomas Purcell, Esq. (prob. of Din-lle). [In Dwnn "Thomas Pursell of Dintle" is said to marry "Mary, dau. of Edward Herbert, Esq., of Montgomery"] . .	1597
Edward Hussey, Esq. [of Crugion ?] . .	1598
Richard Leighton, Esq. of Gwern-y-go' .	1599
Hugh Lloyd, Esq., of Bettws . . .	1600
Charles Lloyd, Esq., of Leighton. . .	1601
Thomas Jukes, Esq., of Buttington . .	1602

JAMES I.

	A.D.
Richard Price, Esq., of Aber-bechan . .	1603
William Penrhyn, Esq., of Rhysnant . .	1604
Sir Edward Herbert, Kt.	1605
Jenkin Lloyd, Esq., of Perth-lwyd . .	1606
Sir Richard Hussey, Kt., of Crugion . .	1607

	A.D.
Charles Herbert, Esq., of Aston . . .	1608
Rowland Pugh, Esq., of Mathafarn . .	1609
Lewis Gwynne, Esq., of Llanidloes . .	1610
Rowland Owen, Esq.	1611
Morris Owen, Esq., of Rhiw-saeson . .	1612
Sir William Herbert, Kt.	1613
Edward Price, Esq., of Kerry . . .	1614
Edward Price, Esq., of Newtown . . .	1615
Richard Lloyd, Esq., of Marrington . .	1616
Sir Edward Foxe, Kt.	1617
Thomas Kerry, Esq., of Binweston (probably)	1618
Robert Owen, Esq.	1619
Richard Rock, Esq., of Abbey Foregate .	1620
Thomas Jukes, Esq., of Buttington . .	1621
Sir Richard Pryse, Kt. [of Gogerddan ?] .	1622
Edward Kynaston, Esq., of Hordley . .	1623
Sir William Owen, Kt.	1624

CHARLES I.

	A.D.
Edward Purcell, Esq., of Wropton . .	1625
Rowland Pugh, Esq., of Mathafarn . .	1626
Richard Pughe, Esq.	1627
Evan Glynn, Esq., of Glyn	1628
Edward Lloyd, Esq.	1629
John Blayney, Esq. [of Gregynog ?]. . .	1630
William Washbourne, Esq.	1631
Jacob Phillips, Esq.	1632
John Heyward, Esq.	1633
Philip Eyton, Esq.	1634
Thomas Ireland, Esq.	1635
Meredith Morgan, Esq.	1636
Lloyd Piers, Esq.	1637
John Newton, Esq.	1638
Richard Price, Esq., of Gunley . . .	1639
Edward Morris, Esq.	1640
Roger Kynaston, Esq., of Hordley . .	1641
Thomas Nicholls, Esq.	1642
John Blaeney, Esq. [of Gregynog ?] . .	1643
Arthur Blaeney, Esq., of Gregynog . .	1644
No Sheriff appointed	1645
No Sheriff appointed	1646
Rowland Hunt, Esq.	1647
Matthew Morgan, Esq.	1648

THE COMMONWEALTH & PROTECTORATE.

Lloyd Piers, Esq.	1649
Evan Lloyd, Esq.	1650
Edward Ffoulkes, Esq.	1651
Richard Price, Esq.	1652
Richard Owen, Esq.	1653

OLIVER CROMWELL, LORD PROTECTOR.

Hugh Price, Esq.	1654
John Kynaston, Esq.	1655
Thomas Lloyd, Esq.	1656
Richard Herbert, Esq.	1657

RICHARD CROMWELL, LORD PROTECTOR.

George Devereux, Esq., of Nantcribba . .	1658
Sir Matthew Price, Bart.	1659

MONTGOMERYSHIRE.

CHARLES II.

	A.D.
Edward Whittingham, Esq.	1660
Roger Mostyn, Esq. [of Mostyn?]	1661
David Powell, Esq.	1662
Watkin Kyffin, Esq. [of Bodfach?]	1663
Rowland Nicholls, Esq.	1664
John Williams, Esq.	1665
Edward Kynaston, Esq., of Hordley	1666
Arthur Weaver, Esq.	1667
Evan Lloyd, Esq.	1668
Robert Owen, Esq.	1669
Sir Charles Lloyd, Bart.	1670
Thomas Ireland, Esq.	1671
Thomas Lloyd, Esq.	1672
George Devereux, Esq.	1673
Richard Mytton, Esq. [of Pont-is-Cowryd?]	1674
Evan Glynn, Esq.	1675
George Llewellin, Esq.	1676
David Maurice, Esq.	1677
John Kyffin, Esq.	1678
John Williams, Esq.	1679
Richard Ingram, Esq.	1680
John Thomas, Esq.	1681
Edward Lloyd, Esq., of Mathraval	1682
Walter Clopton, Esq.	1683
Edward Lloyd, Esq.	1684
John Lloyd, Esq., of Glanhafon; he dying was succeeded by his brother— Robert Lloyd, Esq.	1685

JAMES II.

David Maurice, Esq., of Penybont	1686
Gabriel Wynn, Esq., of Dolarddyn	1687
Edward Vaughan, Esq., of Llwydiarth	1688

WILLIAM AND MARY.

Richard Glynn, Esq., of Maesmawr	1689
Edward Lloyd, Esq., of Perth-lwyd	1690
Arthur Vaughan, Esq., of Tredderwen	1691
Philip Fyton, Esq.	1692
Humphrey Kynaston, Esq.	1693
Richard Owen, Esq., of Peniarth	1694
Humphrey Lloyd, Esq.	1695
John Read, Esq. [of Llandinam?]	1696
Thomas Severne, Esq., of Wallop	1697
Thomas Foulkes, Esq.	1698
John Cale, Esq., of London	1699
Sam. Atherton, Esq., Salop	1700
Piers Lloyd, Esq.	1701

QUEEN ANNE.

John Felton, Esq., Salop	1702
William Meredith, Esq., of London	1703
Henry Bigg, Esq., of Bentall	1704
Sir William Williams, Bart. [of Llanvorda?]	1705
Adam Price, Esq.	1706
Sir Charles Lloyd, Bart.	1707
Richard Lyster, Esq.	1708
Sir Vaughan Price, Bart.	1709

	A.D.
Francis Herbert, Esq., of Blomfield	1710
William Leighton, Esq., of Salop	1711
Evan Jones, Esq., of Llanllodian	1712
Jenkin Lloyd, Esq., of Clochfaen	1713

GEORGE I.

Thomas Owen, Esq., of Nantymeichied	1714
John Blayney, Esq., of Gregynog	1715
Thomas Lloyd, Esq., of Glanhafon	1716
John Herbert, Esq., of Kerry	1717
Francis Evans, Esq., of Oswestry; he died in July, and was succeeded by his son— John Evans, Esq.; he also dying in September was succeeded by— Humphrey Parry, Esq., as *deputy*	1718
Brochwell Griffiths, Esq., of Broniarth	1719
Edward Lloyd, Esq., of Aberbechan	1720
John Scott, Esq., of Shrewsbury	1721
George Ambler, Esq., of Salop	1722
Robert Phillips, Esq., of Shrewsbury	1723
Walter Warring, Esq., of Wolberry	1724
Methuselah Jones, Esq., of Under Hill	1725
Thomas Owen, Esq., of Llynllo, Machynlleth	1726

GEORGE II.

Athelstan Owen, Esq., of Rhiwsaeson	1727
Richard Price, Esq., of Trewylan	1728
Arthur Devereux, Esq., of Nantcribba	1729
Richard Mytton, Esq., of Garth	1730
Valentine Hughes, Esq., of Park	1731
Richard Jones, Esq., of Poole	1732
Roger Trevor, Esq., of Trevilock	1733
Edward Price, Esq., of Gunley	1734
Thomas Brown, Esq., of Mellington	1735
Edward Glynn, Esq., of Glynn	1736
Edward Rogers, Esq., of Burgedin	1737
Morgan Edwards, Esq., of Melingryg	1738
John Thomas, Esq., of Aston	1739
Edward Price, Esq., of Bodfach	1740
Corbet Owen, Esq., of Rhiwsaeson	1741
Henry Thomas, Esq., of Llechweddgarth	1742
Rees Lloyd, Esq., of Clochfaen	1743
Thomas Ffoulkes, Esq., of Penthryn	1744
Gabriel Wynn, Esq., of Dolarddyn	1745
Thomas Edwards, Esq., of Pentre	1746
William Mostyn, Esq., of Bryngwyn	1747
Thomas Lloyd, Esq., of Trefnant	1748
Thomas Lloyd, Esq. (the same)	1749
Bagot Read, Esq., of Llandinam	1750
Price Jones, Esq., of Glanhafren	1751
Edward Lloyd, Esq., of Domgay	1752
William Powell, Esq., of Poole	1753
William Humphreys, Esq., of Llwyn	1754
Jenkin Parry, Esq., of Maine	1755
Richard Powell, Esq., of Pool	1756
Jenkin Parry, Esq., of Maen	1757
John Lloyd, Esq., of Trawscoed	1758
George Mears, Esq., of Ty-nant	1759
Richard Owen, Esq., of Garth	1760

HIGH SHERIFFS OF MONTGOMERYSHIRE.

GEORGE III.

	A.D.
Richard Price, Esq., of Gunley	1761
Roger Wynn, Esq.	1762
Pryce Davies, Esq., of Maesmawr	1763
Arthur Blayney, Esq., of Gregynog	1764
John Amler, Esq.	1765
Owen Owens, Esq., of Tyn-y-coed	1766
William Pugh, Esq., of Cilrhiw	1767
Thomas Thomas, Esq., of Garth-celyn-fawr	1768
Henry Wynn, Esq., of Dolarddyn	1769
John Baxter, Esq., of Rock	1770
John Lloyd, Esq.	1771
Matthew Jones, Esq., of Cyfronydd	1772
William Wynn, Esq.	1773
Sir E. Lloyd, Bart., of Perth-lwyd	1774
Clopton Prys, Esq., of Llandrinio	1775
Henry Proctor, Esq., of Aberhavesp	1776
Sir J. D. King, Bart., of Aberhiraeth	1777
Henry Shales, Esq., of Carno	1778
Robert Corbet, Esq., of Layton	1779
R. H. Vaughan, Esq., of Ystym-colwyn	1780
Hugh Mears, Esq., of Llandinam	1781
Hon. Henry Tracy, of Llwyn-y-brain	1782
William Humphreys, Esq., of Llwyn	1783
Bell Lloyd, Esq., of Bodvach	1784
Samuel Yate, Esq.	1785
Richard Rocke, Esq., of Trefnanney	1786
Trevor Lloyd, Esq.	1787
R. John Harrison, Esq., of Gaer	1788
Francis Lloyd, Esq., of Domgay	1789
Maurice Stephens, Esq., of Berth-ddu	1790
John Moxon, Esq., of Vaynor	1791
Sir R. Clifton, Bart., of Aberbechan	1792
David Pugh, Esq., of Llanerchudol	1793
John James, Esq., of Sylfaen	1794
Lawton Parry, Esq., of Hem	1795
John Dickin, Esq., of Pool	1796
J. C. Clifton Jukes, Esq., of Trelydan	1797
W. W. Bowen, Esq., of Llandinam	1798
J. P. Chichester, Esq., of Gungrog	1799
Henry Proctor, Esq., of Aberhavesp	1800
Joseph Lyon, Esq., of Vaynor	1801
Thomas Jones, Esq., of Llanllodian	1802
John Winder, Esq., of Vaynor Park	1803
C. Hanbury Tracy, Esq., of Gregynog	1804
Bagot Read, Esq., of Llandinam Hall	1805
William Owen, Esq., of Bryngwyn	1806
D. E. Lewes Lloyd, Esq., of Farm	1807
Francis Lloyd, Esq., of Domgay	1808
John Mytton, Esq., of Penylan	1809
J. Owen Herbert, Esq., of Dolforgan	1810
Edward Heyward, Esq., of Crosswood	1811
George Mears, Esq., of Ty-nant	1812
William Pugh, Esq., of Caerhowel	1813
Arthur Davies Owen, Esq., of Glansevern	1814
Price Jones, Esq., of Cyfronydd	1815
John Arthur Lloyd, Esq., of Domgay	1816
Richard Price, Esq., of Gunley	1817
John Edwards, Esq., of Machynlleth	1818
John Davies, Esq., of Machynlleth	1819

GEORGE IV.

	A.D.
J. Buckley Williames, Esq., of Pennant	1820
Valentine Vickers, Esq., of Crugyn	1821
Joseph Hayes Lyon, Esq.	1822
David Pugh, Esq., of Llanerchudol	1823
S. A. Severne, Esq., of Wallop Hall	1824
Philip Morris, Esq., of Trehelyg	1825
John Hunter, Esq., of Glynhafren	1826
John Jones, Esq., of Maesmawr	1827
John James Turner, Esq., of Pentreheilin	1828
Wythen Jones, Esq., of Trewythen	1829

WILLIAM IV.

	A.D.
H. A. Proctor, Esq., of Aberhavesp Hall	1830
R. M. Bonnor Maurice, Esq., of Bodynfoel	1831
Sir Charles Thomas Jones, Kt., of Broadway	1832
John Jones, Esq., of Deythur	1833
H. D. Griffiths, Esq., of Llechweddgarth	1834
William Morris, Esq., of Pentre-nant	1835
J. P. Johnson, Esq., of Monksfield	1836

VICTORIA.

	A.D.
R. Phillips, Esq., of Hiroes	1837
Martin Williams, Esq., of Brongwyn	1838
David Hamer, Esq., of Glanrafon	1839
Thomas Evans, Esq., of Maenol	1840
J. Vaughan, Esq., of Rhos Brynbwa	1841
Sir J. Roger Kynaston, Bart. of Hardwick Hall	1842
Sir J. Conroy, Bart., of Plas-y-pennant	1843
John Dorset Owen, Esq., of Broadway	1844
J. W. Lyon Winder, Esq., of Vaynor Park	1845
John Ffoulkes, Esq., of Carno	1846
J. O. Crewe Read, Esq., of Llandinam Hall	1847
William Lutener, Esq., of Dolerw	1848
Robert Gardiner, Esq., of Plas-y-court	1849
John Davies Corrie, Esq., of Dyserth	1850
Charles Jones, Esq., of Garthmill	1851
E. S. R. Trevor, Esq., of Trawscoed	1852
John Naylor, Esq., of Leighton Hall	1853
J. Michael Severne, Esq., of Wallop	1854
E. Ethelston Peel, Esq., of Llandrinio	1855
R. Herbert Mytton, Esq., of Garth	1856
Maurice Jones, Esq., of Fronfraith	1857
R. P. Long, Esq., of Dolforgan	1858
Edward Morris, Esq., of Perthlwyd	1859
William Curling, Esq., of Maesmawr	1860
H. Heyward Heyward, Esq., of Crosswood	1861
John Lomax, Esq., of Bodfach	1862
John Dugdale, Esq., of Llwyn	1863
Major-General W. G. Gold, of Garthmill Hall	1864
R. Simcox Perrott, Esq., of Bronhyddon	1865
Edwin Hilton, Esq., of Rhiwhirieth	1866
Major Joseph Davies, of Brynglas	1867
William Fisher, Esq., of Maes-y-fron	1868
John Pryce Davies, Esq., of Fronfelen	1869

	A.D.		A.D.
Capt. Offley Malcolm Crewe-Read, R.N., of Llandinam Hall	1870	H. Bertie W. Watkin Williams Wynne, Esq., of Plas Nant-y-meichiad	1872
John Robinson Jones, Esq., of Brithdir Hall	1871		

Section V.—PARLIAMENTARY ANNALS OF MONTGOMERYSHIRE,
A.D. 1542—A.D. 1872.

In the representation of this county and its district of boroughs the prominence of the Herberts is most remarkable. It is an adumbration of the powerful position they had occupied as Lords of Montgomery and Powis Castle, as well as a proof of the fecundity of the family and their taste for public affairs. The Prices, Vaughans, Williams, and Pughs also stand high, but in no county in Wales or in the kingdom has there been a family that can compete with the Herberts in Montgomeryshire for the absorption of parliamentary representation; and it is to be noted that during the same periods, members of this noble house were foremost in public trust and influence in several other counties of Wales—such as Monmouth, Glamorgan, Carmarthen, Cardigan, and Pembroke.

The following details have been carefully compiled from Willis and others, and tested by reference to the Crown Office *docket-books*, and other public records; and several valuable facts and suggestions have been contributed by Mr. E. R. Morris, of Welshpool.

HENRY VIII.

	A.D.
Edward Leech, Esq. [one of the Leeches of Carden Hall, Cheshire], for the *Co.* William Herbert, Esq., of Park, Llanwnog, for the *Bor.*	1542
William Herbert, Esq., of Park, for the *Co.* No name given for the *Bor.*	1545

EDWARD VI.

	A.D.
William Herbert, Esq., of Park, for the *Co.* No name given for the *Bor.*	1547
Edward Herbert, Esq., of Montgomery Castle Richard Herbert, Esq. [? of Park], for the *Bor.*	1552-3

MARY.

	A.D.
Edward Herbert, Esq., of Montgomery Castle John ab Edmund, for the *Bor.*	1553
Lewis Owen, Esq. [the "Baron" of Dolgelley; or more prob. Edward Herbert, as above. See *Arch. Cambr.*, 1846, p. 359] Richard Lloyd [or prob. David Jennings. *Ibid.*]	1554

PHILIP AND MARY.

	A.D.
Edward Herbert, Esq., of Montgomery Castle No name given for the *Bor.*	1554
Edward Herbert, Esq. (the same), for the *Co.* No name given for the *Bor.*	1555
Edward Herbert, Esq. (the same), for the *Co.* William Herbert, sen., prob. of Park, for the *Bor.*	1557

ELIZABETH.

	A.D.
Edward Herbert, Esq., of Montgomery Castle, for the *Co.*	1558
John Price, Esq., of Newtown, for the *Bor.*	
Edward Herbert, Esq. (the same), for the *Co.* John Price, Esq. (the same), for the *Bor.*	1562-3
Edward Herbert, Esq. (the same), for the *Co.* Arthur Price, Esq., of Vaenor, for the *Bor.*	1571
John Price, Esq., of Newtown, for the *Co.* Rowland Pugh, Esq., of Mathafarn, for the *Bor.*	1572

Note.—In the vacations between the sessions of this Parliament several writs were issued and members elected. Richard Herbert was elected for the Montgomery borough *vice* Mr. Pugh, who was supposed to be "dead, but was only sick," and it was ordered by the House "That Richard Herbert, Esq., returned a burgess for this borough in the room and place of Rowland Pugh, Esq., supposed to be dead, but yet known to be in plain life, shall be forthwith removed from his place, and the said Rowland Pugh shall stand and continue for the same place."

	A.D.
Richard Herbert, Esq., for the *Co.* Richard Herbert, Esq., of Gray's Inn [father of Edward, Lord Herbert of Chirbury], for the *Bor.*	1585
Oliver Lloyd, Esq., of Leighton, for the *Co.* Matthew Herbert, Esq., of Dolguog, for the *Bor.*	1586
Edward Herbert, Esq., for the *Co.* Rowland Pugh, Esq., of Mathafarn, for the *Bor.*	1518

PARLIAMENTARY ANNALS OF MONTGOMERYSHIRE.

Reginald Williams, Esq. [of Willaston], for *Co.* } 1592
Richard Morgan, Esq., for the *Bor.* }
William Herbert, Esq. [probably Sir William Herbert K.B., cr. Baron Powis 1629], for the *Co.* . . . . . . } 1597 to 1598
William Jukes, Esq. [probably a brother of Thomas Jukes, of Buttington, Welshpool], for the *Bor.* . . . . . }
Edward Herbert, Esq., for the *Co.* . } 1601
John Harris, Esq., for the *Bor.* . . }

JAMES I.

Sir William Herbert, K.B. [the same as for the year 1597, for the *Co.*] . . . . } 1603
Edward Whittingham, Esq., for the *Bor.* }
Sir William Herbert (the same) for the *Co.* } 1614
Edward Herbert, Esq., for the *Bor.* . }
Sir William Herbert (the same) for the *Co.* } 1620
Edward Herbert, Esq. (the same), for the *Bor.* }
Sir William Herbert (the same), for the *Co.* } 1623
George Herbert, Esq. (the same), for the *Bor.* }

CHARLES I.

Sir William Herbert, K.B., for the *Co.* }
Sir Thomas Myddelton, Kt., of Chirk, *vice* Herbert, for *Co.* First Session . } 1625
Lewis Powell, Esq., for the *Bor.* . }
Sir William Herbert, K.B., for the *Co.* } 2nd Sess.,
Hugh Owen, Esq., for the *Bor.* . } 1625-6.
Sir William Herbert, K.B., for the *Co.* . } 1628
Sir Richard Lloyd, Kt., for the *Bor.* . }
Richard Herbert, Esq. [prob. of Dolguog], for the *Co.* . . . . . . } 1640
Sir Henry Lloyd, Kt., for the *Bor.* . }
Sir John Price, Bart., of Newtown, for the *Co.* }
Richard Herbert, Esq. [prob. of Dolguog], for the *Bor.* . . . . . } 1640
Edward Vaughan, Esq., of Llwydiarth [*vice* Price, who had joined the king at Oxford, and was disabled by Parliament ; was one of those who voted, Dec. 6th, 1648, "That the king's answer to the propositions of both Houses was a ground for peace ;" one of the Members imprisoned or secluded by the army], for the *Co.* . } 1646
George Devereux, Esq. [elected to fill the place of Herbert, who had joined the king's party at Oxford, and disabled by Parliament ; probably the son of Sir George Devereux, of Sheldon Hall, Warwickshire ; *m.* Bridget, dau. and heir of Arthur Price, of Vaynor, Mont.], for the *Bor.* . . . . }

COMMONWEALTH AND PROTECTORATE.

Wales returned to the "Little" or "Barebones" Parliament six Members ; for names, see p. 606 . . . . . } 1653

OLIVER CROMWELL, LORD PROTECTOR.

Sir John Price, Bart., of Newtown, for the *Co.* } 1654
Charles Lloyd, Esq., of Garth, for the *Bor.* . }

Hugh Price, Esq., of Gwern-y-go', Kerry, for the *Co.* . . . . } 1656
Charles Lloyd, Esq. (the same), for the *Bor.* . }

RICHARD CROMWELL, LORD PROTECTOR.

Edward Vaughan, Esq., of Llwydiarth, for the *Co.* . . . . . . } 1658
Charles Lloyd, Esq., of Garth, for the *Bor.* . } -9.

CHARLES II., "THE RESTORATION."

John Pursell, Esq. [prob. of Nantcribba], for *Co.* }
Sir Thomas Myddelton, Bart., of Chirk Castle, for the *Bor.* . . . . . } 1660
John Pursell (the same) for the *Co.* . } 1661
Edward Vaughan, of Llwydiarth, for the *Bor.* }
Edward Vaughan, Esq., of Llwydiarth, for the *Co.* . . . . . . } 1679
Matthew Price, Esq., of Park, for the *Bor.* . }
Edward Vaughan, Esq. (the same) for the *Co.* } 1681
Edward Lloyd, Esq. (the same) for the *Bor.* }

JAMES II.

Edward Vaughan, Esq. (the same), for the *Co.* }
William Williams, Esq. (who was removed, and *Charles Herbert* chosen in his place), for the *Bor.* . . . . . . } 1685
Edward Vaughan, Esq. (the same) for the *Co.* } 1688
Charles Herbert, Esq., for the *Bor.* . } -9

WILLIAM III. AND MARY.

Edward Vaughan, Esq. (the same) for the *Co.* }
Price Devereux, Esq., of Vaynor, for the *Bor.* } 1689
[Succ. as 9th Viscount Hereford in 1700] }
Edward Vaughan, Esq. (the same), for the *Co.* } 1695
Price Devereux, Esq. (the same), for the *Bor.* }
Edward Vaughan, Esq. (the same), for the *Co.* } 1698
Price Devereux, Esq. (the same), for the *Bor.* }
Edward Vaughan, Esq. (the same), for the *Co.* } 1701
John Vaughan, Esq., *vice* Devereux, for *Bor.* . }

ANNE.

Edward Vaughan, Esq. (the same), for the *Co.* } 1702
John Vaughan, Esq. (the same), for the *Bor.* }
Edward Vaughan, Esq. (the same), for the *Co.* }
Charles Mason, Esq., for the *Bor.* . . } 1705
Edward Vaughan, Esq. (the same), for the *Co.* } 1707
Charles Mason, Esq. (the same), for the *Bor.* }
Edward Vaughan, Esq. (the same), for the *Co.* } 1708
John Pugh, Esq., of Mathafarn, for the *Bor.* } -15

GEORGE I.

Edward Vaughan, Esq. (the same), for the *Co.* } 1715
John Pugh, Esq. (the same), for the *Bor.* . }
Edward Vaughan having died, a new writ was issued, Dec. 19, 1718, and—
Hon. Price, Devereux, Esq., *vice* Vaughan, *dec.*, [son of the 9th Viscount Hereford], for the *Co.* . . . . } 1718
John Pugh, Esq. (the same), for the *Bor.* . }

GEORGE II.

Hon. Price Devereux (the same), for the *Co.*
Robert Williams, Esq., of Erbistock, Denb., } 1728
for the *Bor.*
Hon. Price Devereux, Esq. (the same), for the *Co.*
William Corbett, Esq. [A double return, } 1734
Corbett seated]
Robert Williams, Esq., of Erbistock [*vice*
Devereux, succ. to the peerage], for the } 1740
Co.
William Corbett, Esq., for the *Bor.*
Robert Williams, Esq. (the same), for the *Co.*
Sir Watkin Williams Wynn. A double return. [Sir Watkin elected also for Denbighshire and made his choice to sit for it]. } 1741
James Cholmondeley, Esq., for the *Bor.*
Edward Kynaston, Esq., for the *Co.*
William Bodvel, Esq., for the *Bor.* } 1754
Richard Clive, Esq., of Styche [father of Robert Lord Clive, *vice* Bodvel *dec.*] for the *Bor.* 1759

GEORGE III.

Edward Kynaston, Esq. (the same), for the *Co.*
Richard Clive, Esq. (the same), for the *Bor.* } 1761
Thomas Cornwall, Capt. R.N. [*vice* Clive, *dec.*], for the *Bor.* 1771
Watkin Williams, Esq. [*vice* Edward Kynaston, *dec.*], for the *Co.* 1772
William Mostyn Owen, Esq., for the *Co.*
[Contest: Votes for Owen 700, for Watkin Williams 624]. } 1774
Whitshed Keene, Esq., for the *Bor.*
William Mostyn Owen, Esq. (the same), for the *Co.*
Whitshed Keene, Esq. (the same), for the *Bor.* } 1780
William Mostyn Owen, Esq. (the same), for the *Co.*
Whitshed Keene, Esq. [the same], for the *Bor.* } 1784
Francis Lloyd, Esq., for the *Co.*
Whitshed Keene, Esq. (the same), for the *Bor.* } 1795
Charles W. W. Wynn, Esq., of Pentrego', *vice* Francis Lloyd, *dec.* [Wynn continued to sit for fifty-one years], for the *Co.*
Whitshed Keene, Esq. (the same), [he continued to sit till 1818,] for the *Bor.* } 1799

Charles W. W. Wynn (the same), for the *Co.*
Henry Clive, Esq., *vice* Keene, for the *Bor.* } 1818

GEORGE IV.

Charles W. W. Wynn (the same), for the *Co.*
[Contest.—Votes for Wynn, 703; for Jos. H. Lyons, 302] } 1831
Henry Clive (the same) for the *Bor.*
Charles W. W. Wynn (the same), for the *Co.*
David Pugh, Esq., of Llanerchudol, for the *Bor.* } 1832
[Contest: Votes for Pugh 335, for Col. John Edwards 321.]
Charles W. W. Wynn (the same) for the *Co.*
Sir John Edwards, of Machynlleth [*vice* Pugh, unseated], for the *Bor.* } 1833

VICTORIA.

Right Hon. Charles W. W. Wynn (the same) for the *Co.*
Sir John Edwards (the same) for the *Bor.* } 1837
[Contest: Votes for Edwards 472, for Panton Corbett 443.]
Right. Hon. Charles Watkin W. Wynn, of Pentre-go', for the *Co.*
Hon. Hugh Cholmondeley for the *Bor.* } 1841
Charles Watkin W. Wynn (the same) for the *Co.*
David Pugh, Esq., of Llanerchydol, for the *Bor.* } 1847
Herbert W. W. Wynn [second son of the late Sir Watkin, of Wynnstay] for the *Co.* } 1851 to
David Pugh, Esq. (the same) for the *Bor.* } 1862
The same for the *Co.* } 1857 to 1859
David Pugh, Esq. (the same) for the *Bor.*
The same for the *Co.* } 1859 to 1863
David Pugh, Esq. (the same) for the *Bor.*
Charles W. W. Wynn, Esq., of Coed-y-Maen [eldest surviving son of the late Rt. Hon. Charles Watkin W. Wynn], for the *Co.* } 1863
Hon. C. D. R. Hanbury-Tracy for the *Bor.*
Chas. W. W. Wynn, Esq. (the same) for the *Co.* } 1868
Hon. C. D. R. Hanbury-Tracy (the same) for the *Bor.*

The Present Sitting Members, 1872.

Section VI.—COUNTY MAGISTRATES OF MONTGOMERYSHIRE, 1872.

(Corrected to Last Date.)

Sudeley, The Right Honourable Lord, of Toddington, *Lord Lieutenant and Custos Rotulorum.*
Adams, William Henry, Esq., of Plas Llyssin, Carno.
Bayard, John C., Esq., of Gwernydd, Berriew.
Beadnell, Col. George, 104, Belgrave Road, London.
Bonsall, John George William, Esq., of Fronfraith, *Card.*
Botfield, W. B. (*Clerk*), Decker Hill, Shiffnal.
Bowen, Thomas, Esq., of Welshpool.
Browne, Thomas Browne, Esq., of Mellington Hall.
Cleaton, Edmund, Esq., of Llanidloes.
Conroy, Sir John, Bart., Arborfield Hall, *Berks.*
Corbett, Major William, of Vaynor Park, Berriew.
Corrie, John Davies, Esq., of Dyserth.
Crewe-Read, Offley John, Esq., Llandinam Hall.
Crewe-Read, Captain Offley Malcolm, R.N., of Llandinam Hall.
Davies, John Pryce, Esq., of Fronfelen, Caersws.
Davies, Major Joseph, of Brynglas, Llanfair.
Davies, William Gabriel (*Clerk*), Rectory, Cemmaes.
Dugdale, John, Esq., of Llwyn, Llanfyllin.
Evans, John (*Clerk*), Llangurig, Llanidloes.
Fisher, William, Esq., of Maesfron, Welshpool.
Ford, John Randle Minshall, Esq., of Llwyngwern.
Frost, Sir Thomas Gibbons, Kt., Chester.
Gill, Thomas, Esq., of Brynderwen.
Gough, R. D., Esq., Aberhafesp Hall.
Griffith, Joseph William (*Clerk*).
Haines, Thomas William, Esq., Dolcorslwyn.
Hare, Thomas William, Esq., of Berth-ddu, Llandinam.
Hayhurst, Henry Hayhurst, Esq., Ystum-colwyn.
Herbert, Col. George Edward, of Glanhafren.
Herbert, Canon, (*Clerk*), of Glanhafren.
Heyward, Major John Heyward, of Crosswood.
Hilton, Edwin, Esq., 40, Spring Gardens, Manchester.
Humphreys, Richard Smith, Esq., of Montgomery.
Hunter, Col. Charles, Downe House Villa, Richmond, *Sur.*
Hunter, Col. William, of Mount Severn.
Johns, Jasper Wilson, Esq., 80, Seymour Street, W.
Jones, John Robinson, Esq., of Brithdir Hall.
Jones, Richard Edward, Esq., of Cefn Bryntalch.
Kirkham, John William (*Clerk*), Llanbrynmair.
Leighton, Sir Baldwyn, Bart., of Loton Park, Salop.
Lloyd, John (*Clerk*), of Castell Forwyn, Abermule.
Long, R. Penruddock, Esq., of Rood Ashton, Wilts.
More, Robert Jasper, Esq., of Linley Hall, Salop.
Morgan, William (*Clerk*), Kerry, Newtown.
Mytton, Capt. Devereux Herbert, of Garth.
Naylor, John, Esq., of Leighton Hall.
Nicholls, Henry, Esq.
Peel, Edmund Ethelston, Esq., of Brynypys, *Flint.*
Perrott, Robert S. Esq., of Bronheuddan.
Powell, Col. W. T. R., of Nanteos, *Card.*
Powis, The Right Hon. The Earl of, of Powis Castle.
Pryce, Robert Davies, Esq., of Cyfronydd.
Scott, Septimus, Esq.
Severne, John Edmund, Esq., of Wallop Hall, *Salop.*
Stephens, John, Esq., of Shelton, *Salop.*
Thruston, Charles Frederick, Esq., of Talgarth Hall, *Mer.*
Tracy, Hon. Charles D. R. Hanbury-, M.P.
Tracy, Hon. Henry Hanbury-, of Gregynog.
Trevor, Edward Sal. R., Esq., of Penylan, Meifod.
Turner, John James, Esq., of Pentreheilin.
Vane, The Right Hon. Earl, Plas Machynlleth.
Walton, William, Esq., of Dolforgan Hall.
Whalley, George Hammond, Esq., M.P., of Plasmadoc, *Denb.*
White, Robert More (*Clerk*), Churchstoke.
Williames, John Buckley, Esq., of Glyncogan, Manafon.
Williams, William Maddock (*Clerk*), Llanfechain.
Wingfield, Walter Clopton, Esq., of 112, Belgrave Road, London.
Woosnam, Richard, Esq., of Llanidloes.
Wynn, Charles Watkin Williams, Esq., M.P., 2, Lower Berkeley Street, London.
Wynn, Sir Watkin Williams, Baronet, M.P., of Wynnstay.
Wynne, William Robert Maurice, Esq., of Peniarth, *Mer.*

THE COUNTY FAMILIES OF MONTGOMERYSHIRE.

ADAMS, William Henry, Esq., of Plâs-Llysin, Montgomeryshire.

J. P. for the co. of Montgomery; Capt. R. M. Y. Cavalry; son of Thomas Adams, Esq., formerly Att. Gen. of Hong Kong; *b.* 1834; *m.* a dau. of Rev. D. James of Llanwnog, and has issue.

Residence: Plâs-Llysin, Carno, Mont.

BONNOR-MAURICE, Robert Maurice, Esq., of Bodynfoel, Montgomeryshire.

J. P. for counties of Montgomery and Denbigh; D. L. of Montgomeryshire; Sheriff for the latter county 1834; 2nd son of J. Bonnor, Esq., by Jane, dau. and h. of the Rev. Richard Maurice of Bryn-y-gwalie; *b.* 1805; *ed.* at Westminster and Chr. Ch., Oxford; *m.*, 1834, Judith, daughter of the late Rev. Henry Cripps, Vicar of Preston and Stonehouse, Gloucestershire; has issue 7 children; second branch of the Maurices of Bryn-y-gwalie, co. Denbigh (26th in descent from Bleddyn ap Cynfyn, A.D. 1068, Prince of Powys.

Heir: Henry Bonnor-Maurice, Lieut. H.M. 15th foot.
Residence: Bodynfoel, Llanfechain, Oswestry.

CORBETT-WINDER, Mrs., of Vaynor Park, Montgomeryshire.

Mary Anne Jane, widow of Uvedale Corbett, Judge of County Court of Shropshire; dau. of the late Joseph Lyon, Esq., of Ashfield Hall, Cheshire; *b.* at London, 30th August, 1792; *m.*, 8th December, 1817, Uvedale Corbett, Esq., Barrister-at-law (son of the Ven. Archdeacon Corbett, of Longnor Hall, Shropshire), who, in accordance with the will of Edmund Lyon Winder, Esq. (see *Note* below), assumed the name and arms of Winder in addition to those of Corbett June 2, 1869; *s.* 24th June, 1868; has issue seven sons and three daughters.

Heir: William Corbett, Major 58th Foot, retired; J. P. and D. L. for the co. of Montgomery.

Residences: Vaynor Park, Montgomeryshire; and Ashfield Hall, Cheshire.
Arms: The arms of *Winder* quartered with those of *Corbett*.
Crest: Buffalo's head ppr.—WINDER; or a raven ppr.—CORBETT.
Motto: Nulla pallescere culpa—*Winder;* and Deus pascit corvos—*Corbett.*

LINEAGE.

This family descends from John Winder of Helston, co. of Westmoreland, who *m.* a sister of Edmund Gibson, Bishop of London. Their son, Joseph Winder, Esq., of Helston, *m.*, 1790, Ann Moxon, dau. and heiress of John Moxon, Esq., inheritor of Vaynor on the death of his brother, Robert Moxon, Esq., in 1785, who had become its possessor by purchase. The dau. of Joseph Winder, Esq., and Ann Moxon,—

Elizabeth, *m.* Joseph Lyon, Esq., of Ashfield Hall, Cheshire, and had issue—

John Lyon Winder, Esq., who was succeeded in the Vaynor estate by his brother,—

Edmund Henry Lyon, Esq., and he by his sister,—

MARY ANNE JANE, who *m.* Uvedale Corbett, Esq. (as above).

Note.—For an *engraving* and notice of Vaynor Park, see p. 801.

CORRIE, John Davies, Esq., of Dysserth, Montgomeryshire.

J. P. for the co. of Montgomery since 1837; D. L. of the same co. since 1846; High Sheriff 1850; Capt. in Montgomeryshire Yeomanry for twenty-five years; son of the late John Corrie, Esq., of Vauxhall, Surrey, and Susanna, his wife, second dau. and co-heiress of John Davies, Esq., of Dysserth, Montgomeryshire; *b.* at Vauxhall, Surrey, 1798; *ed.* at Monmouth Grammar School; *m.*, 1st, Mary Anne, dau. of Joseph Meire, Esq., of Sutton, in the co. of Salop, and Ann, dau. and heiress of Richard Tandrell, Esq., of Church Pulverbatch, co. Salop; 2nd, Emma, relict of Rev. Edward Ward, Esq., and dau. of Rev. H. Crump, of Leighton, Salop; *s.* 1825; has issue three sons (deceased) and one dau. by first marriage.

Heir: His daughter.
Residence: Dysserth, near Welsh Pool.
Arms: Or, three mullets, 2 and 1; on a chief gu. three griffins' heads erased ppr.

THE COUNTY FAMILIES OF MONTGOMERYSHIRE.

Crest: A demi-griffin displayed.
Motto: Virtute et labore.

LINEAGE.

This family derives on the maternal side from Hugh Davies of Dysserth, and from the Corries of Dumfries on the paternal. John Davies, the grandfather of the present representative, was born at Dysserth in the year 1691; *m.*, in the year 1755 for his 2nd wife, Mary, niece of T. Harvey Thursby, Esq., at that time M.P. for the borough of Shrewsbury: his first wife was the dau. of Thomas Thomas, Esq., of Pentrinant, in the co. of Montgomery.

Among its distinguished members in past time may be named the Rev. Thomas Bray, D.D., of Marton, Salop, whose niece, Esther, *m.* Hugh Davies, Esq., of Dysserth. Dr. Bray was one of the earliest promoters of the Society for the Propagation of the Gospel and of the Christian Knowledge Society.

Note.—The date of the first building of *Dysserth* is unknown; the present house was enlarged 1825.

CREWE-READ, Offley Malcolm, Esq., of Llandinam Hall, Montgomeryshire.

Late Comm. R.N.; D. L. and J. P. for Montgomeryshire, and J. P. for Flintshire; High Sheriff for Montgomeryshire 1870; was first lieutenant of a ship during the Russian war, and was severely wounded; five years Inspecting Commander of Coastguard in South Wales; three years Commander of Steam Reserve in the Medway, and was in command of H.M.S. *Leander* for the purpose of saluting the Princess of Wales on her arrival at the Nore from Denmark in 1863; son of the late John Offley Crewe-Read, Esq., of Wern, co. of Flint, Llandinam Hall, Mont., and Laverton, Southampton (High Sheriff of Flintshire 1839, and of Mont. 1847), and Charlotte Prestwood, dau. of Admiral Sir W. T. Lake, K.C.B., &c.; *b.* at Almington Hall, near Market Drayton, Sept. 13th, 1821; *ed.* by private tutors and Royal Naval College; *m.*, Feb., 1848, Charlotte Lucy, dau of Thomas Marmaduke George, Esq, and his wife, *née* Anne Hereford of Herefordshire; *s.* Dec., 1862, on death of brother, Bagot Offley, *unm.;* has issue one son and two daughters.

Heir: Offley John, *b.* 1848.
Residence: Llandinam Hall, Montgomeryshire.
Town Address: United Service Club, Pall Pall; Brooks's Club, St. James's Street.
Arms: Quarterly: 1st and 4th, az., a griffin segreant or; 2nd and 3rd, az., a lion rampant arg.
Crest: 1st, an eagle displayed sa.; 2nd, out of a ducal coronet or, a lion's gamb arg. charged with a crescent.
Motto: Sola virtute salutem.

LINEAGE.

This family traces its lineage from Thomas de Crewe, of Crewe, Cheshire, *temp.* Henry III., and John Read, of Roch Castle, Carmarthenshire [see *Ryd or Reed of Castell Moel*, p. 266, and *Reads of Carmarthen*, p. 267], who settled in Montgomeryshire 1670, and who, according to an illuminated pedigree, derives descent from Peter de Rupibus, time of King John.

Among its distinguished members in past time may be named Lord Crewe, Bishop of Durham; Sir Randulph Crewe; Lord Chief Justice Sir Thomas Crewe, both latter Speakers of House of Commons; John Read (or Reade), Sheriff of Montgomeryshire 1696, and was Clerk of the Peace and held several important Court offices; Bagot Read, Sheriff in 1750; Bagot Read, 1805; J. O. Crewe-Read, 1847. (See *Sheriffs.*)

The *Crewes* are traced from Henry de Criwa to Sir Randulph Crewe, from an illuminated pedigree roll by Dugdale in the possession of Lord Crewe; thence to end of male line from Sir John Crewe of Utkinton's entries in his prayer-book copied in Cole's *Collections* in the Brit. Museum, and compared with monuments and entries in Coll. of Arms, we get down to Anne Crewe (co-heiress), who marries John Offley, of Madeley, Stafford, in 1670, has a son and heir, John Offley, who changed his name to Crewe, married Sarah Price, from whom, amongst others, came Doctor Randulph Crewe, LL.D., who married Anne *Read*, and had issue—

1. Offley Crewe, Rector of Barthomly Warmincham, Astbury, and Mucklestone, *m.* Harriet, dau. of Thomas Assheton-Smith, Esq., of Vaenol, Carnarvonshire, and had issue—
John Offley Crewe Read, who *m.* Charlotte Prestwood, and had with other issue—
OFFLEY MALCOLM CREWE-READ (as above);
Emma, *d. s. p.;* Frances, *m.* Rev. R. Wedgwood, and *d. s. p.;* Harriet, *m.* Sir Thomas Tancred, Bart; *d.*, leaving issue present Bart., &c.

2. Randulph, LL.B., Rector of Hawarden, *m.* Frances, dau. of Sir John Glynne, Bart., and had issue Charles, Vicar of Longdon, Worcestershire, Stephen, Randulph, Richard, and Selina, all died unmarried.

3. Charles, Rector of Lawton, *m.* Sarah, widow of R. Glynne, Esq., and *d. s. p.* Anne *d. unm;* and Mary *m.* Dr. Chorley, of Doncaster, and *d. s. p.*

The *Reads.*—From Peter de Rupibus (see also Lewys Dwnn's *Heraldic Visit. of Wales*, 1586 and 1613, by Sir S. Meyrick) comes John Read, Sheriff of Montgomeryshire in 1696, &c. He *m.* Anne Bagot, of Hargreaves, Salop; had issue Bagot, who *m.*, 1714, Margaret Jones, dau. of Humphrey Jones, Esq., High Sheriff of co. Flint in 1716; Letitia, *m.* Edward Thelwall, Esq., of Llanbedr (Denbigh); and Anne, *m.* R. Hughes, Esq., of Halkin, Flint. *Bagot* leaves issue Bagot, who *d. s. p.;* Margaret, who *m.* Edward Thornycroft, Esq., of Thornycroft, co. Cheshire; and Anne, who married (as already shown) *Dr. Randulph Crewe*, LL.D, in 1749. Bagot Read *d.* in 1816, and left his estates in Flintshire, Montgomeryshire, and in the city of Chester, to Mrs. Thornycroft, his sister, for life, and then to Rev. Offley Crewe and his heirs, on condition that they should assume the additional surname and arms of *Read* in conjunction with those of Crewe, which injunction was complied with on the death of Rev. Offley Crewe in Jan., 1836, by royal licence obtained 5th March, 1836, by petition of his only son, John Offley Crewe, who thereupon became John Offley Crewe-Read, the father of the present representative (as above).

Note.—The date of erection of *Llandinam Hall* is not known. It was purchased by John Read in 1688 from an old and influential family named Powell. Has been a farmhouse for many years. Rooms retained now for a temporary family residence. It has some good oak carving and timber twists.

DAVIES, John Pryce, Esq., of Fron-felen, Montgomeryshire.

J. P. for the co. of Montgomery; Sheriff for same co. 1869.

Residence: Fron-felen, near Caersws.

DAVIES, Major Joseph, of Bryn-glas, Montgomeryshire.

J. P. for the co. of Montgomery; High Sheriff for the same co. in the year 1867; a major retired from the army; served in the East Indies from 1826 to 1831; son of the late Joseph Davies, Esq., of Machynlleth; *b.* 1861; is *unm.*

Residence: Bryn-glas, Llanfair Caereinion.

DUGDALF, John, Esq., of Llwyn, Montgomeryshire.

J. P. for the co. of Montgomery; High Sheriff for same co. 1863; is *m.*

Residence: Llwyn, near Llanfyllin.

(*Further information not received.*)

EDWARDS, Lady Harriet, of Llanerchydol Hall, Montgomeryshire.

Widow of Sir John Edwards, Bart., of Garth and of Plas Machynlleth, for many years M.P. for Montgomery, and Lieut.-Col. of the Montgomeryshire Militia (*d.* 1850), her 2nd husband, whom she *m.* in 1825. Lady Edwards had previously been *m.* to John O. Herbert, Esq., of Dolforgan, Montgomeryshire (*d.* 1824); dau. of the Rev. Francis Johnson, M.A., Prebendary of Wells, and granddau. of the Rev. Dr. Willes, Archdeacon of Wells; has had issue, by first mar. a dau.,—

Avarina Brunetta, who *m.* Walter Long, Esq., and *d.* 1847; by second mar., Mary Cornelia, *m.* to the Right Hon. Earl Vane (see *Vane, Earl of, Plas Machynlleth*).

Residence: Llanerchydol Hall, near Welshpool.

Arms: Quarterly: gu. and or, a fesse between four lions passant guardant, all counterchanged— Edwards (quartering *Owen of Garth*).

Crest: A lion passant guardant per pale or and gu.

Motto: Y gwir yn erbyn y byd—"Truth against the world."

EDWARDS, Rev. Robert Wynne, M.A., of Meifod, Montgomeryshire.

Vicar of Meifod, Dio. of St. Asaph, 1860; Canon of St. Asaph; Chaplain to Bishop of St. Asaph; formerly Rector of Llanfihangel-yn-Gwynfa 1858—60; P. C. of Gwersyllt 1852—8; son of the Rev. Thomas Wynne Edwards, Vicar of Rhuddlan, co. of Flint; *ed.* at Brasenose Coll., Oxford; *grad.* B.A. 1846, M.A. 1849; *m.* to Elizabeth Anne, dau. of Ven. Archdeacon Wickham, M.A., Vicar of Gresford and Canon of St. Asaph, and has issue—

1. Alathea Mary Wynne.
2. Edith Anna Wynne.
3. Robert Wickham Wynne.
4. Edward Capner Wynne.
5. Emily Jane Wynne.
6. Charlotte Elizabeth Wynne.
7. Laura Wynne.

Residence: The Vicarage, Meifod, near Welshpool.

LINEAGE.

Trahaiarn Goch, Lord of Is-Cych, in the cantref of Emlyn, Dyfed, bore "arg., six bees, 3, 2, and 1, volant in arriére sa.," and claimed to have descended in the direct lineage of *Beli Mawr*. According to a genealogical table in the *Harl. MSS.*, Brit. Museum, No. 2,291, p. 71 (apparently written by Hugh Thomas),—

Tudyr ap Dafydd ap Ievan, of *Plas Nantglyn*, was fifteenth in descent from Trahaiarn Goch. He *m.* Anne, dau. of Robert Wynne, of Berain, and his gr. gr. grandson,—

Robert *Wynn* ap Ffouk, *m.* Jane, eldest dau. of Hugh Llwyd Rosindale (called of Segroit), Esq., Alderman of Denbigh 1631, and Sheriff of co. of Denbigh 1635 (see *Sheriffs, sub ann.* 1635, p. 399; and *Lloyd of Foxhall*, p. 393). The writer of the pedigree states that he found "this monument" —probably in the church of Whitchurch, near Denbigh, but he mentions no place:—"Here lyeth the bodyes of Robert Wynne, Esq., of Nantglan, and Jane, his wife, dau. to Hugh Llwyd Rossendale, Esq., of Segroit, by whom he had issue one son and five daughters; he died May the 3rd, 1698, aged 88 years. She died in the yeare 1651, aged 40 years."

The male line ended with his grandson, Meredydd Wynne, whose dau. Mary *m.*, as her second husband, Hugh Parry, Esq., of Deunant, and had a dau. Margaret, who *m.*—

Cadwaladr ap *Edward*, of Plasau Llangwm, Llansannan, and had issue Evan (*d.* 1796), who *m.* Margaret Roberts, of Llanasnnan, and left a son,—

Thomas Wynne, Clerk, Vicar of Rhuddlan, who by his wife, Eliza Gardner, dau. of John Copner Williams, Esq., Alderman of Denbigh, had issue—

Thomas Wynne Edwards, Clerk, now Vicar of Rhuddlan (see *Edwards of Rhuddlan*), who has, with other issue,—

Robert Wynne Edwards (as above).

FISHER, William, Esq., of Maes-y-fron, Montgomeryshire.

J. P. for the co. of Montgomery; Sheriff for same co. 1868.

Residence: Maes-y-fron, near Welshpool.

(*Further information not received.*)

FORD, John Randle Minshull, Esq., of Llwyngwern, Montgomeryshire.

Late Capt. 8th "The King's" Regt.; Magistrate for cos. of Montgomery and Merioneth; son of Francis J. Ford, Esq. (second son of the late Col. Ford of Abbeyfield, co. Chester); J. P. for the cos. of Cheshire, Montgomery, and Merioneth; *b.* at The Cottage, Sandbach, Cheshire, 24th January, 1842; *ed.* at Eton; *m.*, the 25th Nov., 1869, Florence Helen Oldham, eldest surviving dau. of Charles Oldham, Esq., second son of James Oldham Oldham, Esq., of Bellamour Hall, near Rugeley, Staffordshire; has issue two sons, Francis Charles Minshull Ford, and Hugh Lechmere Minshull Ford.

Residence: Llwyngwern, near Machynlleth.
Arms: Per fesse, or and ermine, a lion rampant az.
Crest: A lion's head erased az.

GILL, Thomas, Esq., of Bryn-derwen, Montgomeryshire.

J. P. for the co. of Montgomery; son of the late James Gill, Esq., of Bryngwyn, Montgomeryshire, and Frances, his wife, dau. of Thomas Lowndes, Esq.; *b.* at Bryngwyn, 28th June, 1811; *ed.* at Shrewsbury School, and Queen's Coll., Oxford; is *unm.*

Residence: Brynderwen, near Llanfyllin.
Arms: Lozengy or and vert, a lion rampant ppr.
Crest: A squirrel ppr.
Motto: In nemoris umbrâ.

GRIFFITH, Hugh Davies, Esq., of Llechweddgarth, Montgomeryshire.

Sheriff for Carnarvonshire 1825, for Anglesey 1826, and Montgomeryshire 1847; son of Rev. Hugh Davies Griffith of Caerhun, co. of Carnarvon, and Emma, his wife, sister of Sir John Williams, 1st Bart., of Bodelwyddan, Flintshire; *m.* Hester, only surviving child and heiress of T. Thomas, Esq., of Downing, Flintshire, and Llechwedd-garth, Montgomeryshire.

Heir: His son, Hugh Thomas Davies.
Residence: Llechwedd-garth, Montgomeryshire.

LINEAGE.

The Griffiths are the eldest branch of the family of that name long resident in Llanfechain, co. Montgomery. the first of whom was twenty-second in descent from Rhodri Mawr, King of Wales A.D. 877.

HARE, Thomas William, Esq, of Berth-ddu, Montgomeryshire.

J. P. for the county of Montgomery; son of the late James Hare, Esq., and Louisa his wife, daughter of Thomas Selleck Brome, Esq., of Colwich, Staffordshire, whose son, the Rev. Henry Selleck Brome, A.M., purchased the Berth-ddû property, and devised it to his nephew, the present proprietor.

Residence: Berth-ddû, near Llanidloes.
Arms: (*Not received*).

LINEAGE.

Mr. Hare's family, which came from Norfolk, has been for a long time connected with the Indian service. His grandfather, Joseph Hare, was chief of Patna under the East India Company. Many of his descendants have been in the military service of the Company; and one of his grandsons, George Hare, a captain in the Hyderabad Contingent, distinguished himself in the mutiny which broke out in 1857, to which he fell a victim.

HERBERT, Rev. John Arthur, of Glan-Hafren, Montgomeryshire.

Rector of Penstrowed; Rural Dean of Arwystli; Hon. Canon of Bangor; J. P. for the co. of Montgomery; son of George Arthur Herbert, Esq., of Glan-hafren, J. P. and D. L. for Montgomeryshire; *b.* at Glan-hafren 1807; *ed.* at Univ. Coll., Oxford; *grad.* B.A. 1830, M.A. 1834; *m.*, 1850, Ellen Mary, only child of Rev. Canon Philipps, Vicar of Pembroke; succ. on the death of his father in 1820; is patron of the living of Llanllugan, of which place he is Lord of the Manor.

Heir presumptive: His brother, Col. George Edward Herbert, *b.* 1809.
Residence: Glan-Hafren, near Newtown.
Arms: The *Herbert* arms:—Per pale az. and gu., three lions arg.
Crest: A wyvern vert.
Motto: Ung je serveray.

LINEAGE.

This family derives its descent from the *Herberts of Chirbury.*

HEYWARD, John Heyward, Esq., of Crosswood, Montgomeryshire, and Cilbronnau, Cardiganshire.

(See *Heyward of Cilbronnau, Cardiganshire,* p. 196, *ante.*)

MONTGOMERYSHIRE.

HUMPHREYS, Charles Jones, Esq., of Dolarddyn Hall, Montgomeryshire.

Son of Charles Milward Dovaston Humphreys, Esq., and grandson of the late Charles Humphreys, Esq., of Pennant, in the co. of Montgomery; *b.* Nov. 18, 1824; *m.*, Feb. 21, 1857, Harriet, third daughter of John Joce Strick, Esq., of Ynystanglws, Glamorganshire, Mayor of Swansea 1852; has issue Charles Martin Strick, William Frederick, Gertrude Susannah, Constance Margaretta, Charlotte Frederica, Alethea Maud.

Heir: Charles Martin Strick, *b.* 1858.
Residence: Dolarddyn Hall, near Welshpool.
Arms: Quarterly: 1st and 4th, or, a lion passant gu.; 2nd and 3rd, sa., three nags' heads ppr.
Crest: A nag's head erased ppr.
Motto: Honor vertutis præmium.

HUNTER, Col. William, of Mount-Severn, Montgomeryshire.

J. P. for the co. of Montgomery 1859; Lieut.-Col.; held in India the appointments of Political Agent in the Hilly Tracts of Mêwar, and also that of Commandant of the Mêwar Bheel Corps; was present at the siege of Bhurtpore with the army under the command of Lord Combermere in the years 1825-6, and received medal for services on that occasion (see further, *note* below); eldest son of the late Robert Hunter, Esq., of Kew, Surrey; *b.* in Cavendish Square, London, 1800; *ed.* at Harrow School, and afterwards in France and Germany; *m.*, 1854, Emily Jane, daughter of Robert Wood, Esq., of Bath; and has issue one son and one daughter; succ., 1854, as proprietor of the Mount-Severn estate; brother living, Col. Charles Hunter, also of Mount Severn.

Heir: William Charles Hunter.
Residence: Mount Severn, near Llanidloes.
Town House: 22, Lancaster Gate, Hyde Park.
Arms: Three greyhounds and three bugles.
Crest: A greyhound's head.
Motto: Free for a blast.

LINEAGE.

Col. Hunter derives his descent through Sir John Paulet, of Paulet and Gatehurst, Somerset, who died 1356, and who was sixth in descent from Hercules, Lord of Tournon, in Picardy, who came to England *temp.* Henry I., and settling in the lordship of Paulet, Hants, assumed the name of his residence.

His son, Sir John de Paulet, died in 1378, leaving a son, Sir John Paulet, Kt., who died 1429-30.

The great-grandson of the last Sir John Paulet was Sir William Paulet, Lord St. John of Basing 1538, Lord of Wiltshire 1550, and Marquess of Winchester 1551, K.G., Lord Treasurer of England *temp.* Edward VI., Mary, and Elizabeth.

The Marquess of Winchester's second son was Sir Thomas Paulet, of Cossington, Somerset, whose granddaughter, Frances, dau. of George Paulet, of Holborne, Dorset, *m.* Thomas Gollop, Esq., of Strode and North-Bowood. Their son Thomas Gollop, and his son, of the same name, also were of Strode and North Bowood.

The son of the latter, George Gollop, of Berwick, had a dau., Elizabeth, who *m.* — Hansford, Esq., whose granddaughter, Elizabeth, dau. of Capt. Hansford, R.N., *m.* Robert Hunter, Esq., of Kew, Surrey, whose eldest son is

Col. WILLIAM HUNTER (as above).

Note.—Col. Hunter during, and on account of, his long and arduous services in India, and especially owing to his firm and skilful but humane government of the Bheel tribes, and as Political Superintendent of the hilly tracts in Mêwar, received the frequent acknowledgments of his superiors and the thanks of the Indian Government, as, *ex. gr.*, on his report on the Bheel tribes in 1841, and on his successful efforts for their civilization, military training, and general government in 1843, 1844, 1846, and 1848. On this last occasion the Governor-General in council conveyed to Col. Hunter "the high sense entertained of his services, and the regret felt that he was about to leave the scene of his useful and beneficent exertions."

JENKINS, John, Esq., of Pen-y-green, Llanidloes, Montgomeryshire.

Town Clerk and Clerk to borough and co. sessions held at Llanidloes, Montgomeryshire, and Chief Registrar of the County Courts of Cardiganshire held at Aberystwyth, holding also judicial appointment in Bankruptcy over extended districts of Cardiganshire, Montgomeryshire, and Merionethshire; Author of "Observations on Law Reform," principally advocating the establishment of local courts in England and Wales (Sweet, Chancery Lane, London, 1845); and an "Essay on National Education" (Longmans, 1849); son of Mr. Edward Jenkins, of Llanidloes, manufacturer, deceased; *b.* at Llanidloes, November 26, 1821; *ed.* at Shrewsbury School; is *unm.*

Residence: Pen-y-green, Montgomeryshire.

Note.—The estate of *Pen-y-green* in ancient times belonged to the Hunter family, who held vast possessions on the Upper Severn, and intermarried with the Lloyds (Kenyon) of Gredington, Flintshire; and Mr. Jenkins holds among his title deeds a conveyance from the Right Honourable Lloyd, Lord Kenyon, then Chief Justice of his Majesty's Court of King's Bench.

The parish church of Llanidloes is one of the oldest (date unknown) and most interesting in Wales. It has magnificent pillars, upholding arches decorated with exquisite carved work. The walls have rich fresco paintings, and at the altar is a fine ancient screen. There is a National School, built in 1845, and a British School in 1865.

JONES, Richard Edward, Esq., of Cefn Bryntalch, Montgomeryshire.

J. P. for the co. of Montgomery; son of Richard Jones, Esq., The Rock, Newtown, Mont.; *m.* to Catharine, dau. of the late John Buckley Williames, Esq., of Glanhafren, Montgomeryshire, and has issue two sons and one dau.

Residence: Cefn Bryntalch, Abermule.

LLOYD, Jacob Youde William, Esq., of Clochfaen, Montgomeryshire.

(*Particulars not received*).

MYTTON, Devereux Herbert, Esq., of Garth, Montgomeryshire.

J. P. for the co. of Montgomery; late Captain 85th Light Infantry; eldest son of the late Richard Herbert Mytton, Esq., of Garth, and formerly of the Bengal Civil Service (*d.* 1869), by his wife Charlotte, third dau. of Lieut.-Gen. Paul Macgregor, Auditor-General of Bengal (she *d.* 1861); *b.* 9th September, 1832, in India; *ed.* at Eton; *s.* to estates 1869.

Residence: Garth, near Welshpool.
Arms: Quarterly: 1st and 4th, per pale az. and gu., an eagle displayed with two heads or, within a bordure engrailed of the last; 2nd and 3rd. arg., a cinquefoil az.
Crest: A ram's head couped arg., horned or.

LINEAGE.

In the present family of Garth are united the lines of Myttons of Pont-is-Cowyrd and the Wynns of Garth, both houses of influence in Salop and Montgomery for several generations. Richard Mytton, of Pont-is-Cowryd, Sheriff for co. of Montgomery in 1674 (see *Sheriffs*), by his wife Bridget, dau. of George Devereux, Esq., of Vaynor, left a son and heir,—

Richard Mytton, Esq., who *m.* Dorothy, dau. and h. of Brochwel *Wynn*, Esq., of Garth (of the line of *Brochwel Ysgythrog*, Prince of Powys), and had (besides a dau. Catherine, who *m.* Edward Devereux, Viscount Hereford) a son,—

Devereux Mytton, Esq., of Garth, whose son Richard died *vita patris*, leaving a son, Richard Mytton, clerk, who succeeded as heir to the estates on the demise of his grandfather in 1809. He *m.*, 1804, Charlotte, dau. of John Herbert, Esq., of Dolforgan, co. of Montgomery, and left a son,—
Richard Herbert Mytton, Esq., of Garth, father of the present representative,—
DEVEREUX HERBERT MYTTON, Esq. (as above)

NAYLOR, John, Esq., of Leighton Hall, Montgomeryshire.

J. P. and D. L. for the co. of Montgomery; Sheriff for same co. 1853; son of the late John Naylor, Esq., of Hartford Hill, Cheshire, by his wife Dorothy Bullin; *b.* 1813; *m.*, 1846, Georgiana dau. of John Edwards, Esq., of Ness Strange, Salop (see *Edwards of Dolserau*), and has issue three sons and seven daughters.

Heir: Christopher John, *b.* 1849.
Residence: Leighton Hall, Welshpool.
Arms: Per pale or and arg., a pale sa, fretty gold, between 2 lions rampant of the third.
Crest: A lion passant sa. charged on the body with two saltiers or.

OWEN, Mrs, of Glan-Severn, Montgomeryshire.

Anne Warburton Owen, widow of William Owen, Esq., J. P. and D. L. for the co. of Montgomery; Fellow of Trin. Coll., Cambridge; fifth wrangler and B.A. 1782, M.A. 1785; Commissioner of Bankrupts; King's Counsel, Bencher and Treasurer of Lincoln's Inn; son of Owen Owen, Esq., of Cefn Hafod, co. Montgomery, High Sheriff 1766, by Anne, his wife, dau. and heiress of Charles Davies, Esq., of Llifion, in the same co. Mr. Owen *s.* on the death of his elder brother, Sir Arthur Davies Owen, Knt.; *m* 1816; *d.* 1837. Mrs. Owen is dau. and only child of the late Capt. Thomas Slaughter, 16th, or Queen's Light Dragoons, only son of Thomas Slaughter, Esq. (High Sheriff for co. of Chester 1755), and Anne, his wife, dau. of Thomas Warburton, Esq., son of Sir Peter Warburton, of Arlay, co. of Chester, 2nd Bart.

Residence: Glan-Severn, near Montgomery.
Arms: Quarterly: 1st, sa., between three scaling-ladders a spear-head embrued arg.; on a chief ermine a tower triple-turreted ppr. (*Cadifor ap Dinawal*)—OWEN; 2nd, ermine, a lion rampant sa. in a bordure gu. semée of mullets arg.—for *Madoc Danwr*; 3rd, az., a lion rampant guardant or—for *Llewelyn Aurdorchog*; 4th, sa., three nags' heads erased arg.—for *Brochwel Ysgythrog*.
Crests: 1st, a wolf salient ppr.—*Owen*; 2nd, a stag trippant ppr., horned and hoofed or—Evans of Rhyd-y-Carn.

LINEAGE.

This family derives by male descent from Rhodri Mawr, King of N. Wales and Powis, and eventually of all Wales, and in the female line from Llewelyn Aurdorchog (through the Evanses of Rhyd-y-Carn), and from Brochwel Ysgythrog (through the Davieses of Llifion). Among distinguished members of this family in past time may be named Edward Owen (brother of Owen Owen above named), Rector of Warrington, co. Lancaster, Head Master of the Grammar School there, translator of Juvenal and Persius; Vice-Admiral Sir E. W. C. R. Owen, G.C.B., G.C.H., &c.

Note.—For a view of *Glan-Severn*, see p. 802. The mansion was erected by Sir A. D. Owen, Kt., above named, but was much enlarged and improved by its late possessor. The grounds are laid out with much taste, with an ornamental lake in sight of the house; and a fine view is obtained from the windows of the Corn-du and Montgomery hills. Among the works of art and objects of interest it contains are portraits of Admiral Sir E. W. C. R. Owen, G.C.B., by Pickersgill; William Owen, Esq., King's Counsel, commenced by an artist who died, and finished by Pickersgill; Mrs. Owen, by Sant; Sir A. D. Owen; his brother, Rev. David Owen, Fell. of Trin. Coll., Cambr., Senior Wrangler 1777.

Among chief *antiquities* on the estate (which lies for the most part in the parishes of Berriew and Llangurig) is a large British tumulus or earthwork on the bank of the Luggy Brook, about one hundred yards to the west side of the Newtown and Welshpool road. Between this tumulus and another on Hen-domen Hill, near Montgomery, is a line of monoliths, one of which, called *Maen Beuno*, is connected by tradition with St. Beuno, the patron saint of the church of Berriew. Several of these stones are on the Lower Luggy and Llwyn-y-Cruth farms, which are part of the Berriew estate.

PERROTT, Robert Simcocks, Esq., of Brynhyddon, Montgomeryshire.

J. P. for the co. of Montgomery (1857); Sheriff for same co. 1865; son of the late Robert Perrott, Esq., of Brynhyddon, formerly Capt. 4th or King's Own Regt., by Magdalene, dau. of Thomas Evans, Esq, of Glanbrogan; *m.*, Sept. 12, 1849. Elizabeth Ann, second dau. of the Rev. Griffith Owen, of Ymwlch, Rector of Dolbenmaen and Penmorfa, Carnarvonshire, and has issue; eldest son,—
Robert Owen Perrott, *b.* 10th July, 1850.

Residence: Brynhyddon, Oswestry.
Arms: (*Not sent*).

PICKMERE, John Richard, Esq., of The Mount, Montgomeryshire.

Son of John Pickmere, Esq, of The Grove, Warrington, Lancashire; *b.* at Warrington, 28th Dec., 1794; *ed.* at Dr. Fawcett's School, Chester; *m.*, 3rd May, 1823. Eliza, dau. of John Thornhill, Esq., of Buxton, and has issue three sons and three daus.; author of "Being, analytically described in its Chief Respects;" acquired the Mount estate, Llanfair-Caereinion, by purchase in 1853.

Eldest son: John R. *Pickmere*, Esq., late Major of the 9th Royal Lancashire Rifle Volunteers.
Residence; The Mount, Llanfair-Caereinion.
Arms: (as illustrated in the plates of arms in King's "Vale Royal of England," published in 1656): Ermine, three lions' jambes erased gu.

Crest: On a wreath, a demi-lion rampant gu., ducally crowned or.
Motto: Fide et amore.

LINEAGE.

This family derives its descent from the Pikemeres, formerly of Pikemere, a township (now and for very many years past spelt Pickmere) in Cheshire. Hugh Venables, Baron of Kinderton, having, *temp.* Henry III., granted to Hugh de Pikemere and his heirs a moiety of the village of Pikemere. This is recorded in Sir Peter Leycester's "Historical Antiquities of Cheshire," published in 1673.

Among its distinguished members may be named Sir William Pickmere, who, in Pennant's "Tour in Wales," 1784, is stated to have been appointed by Edward the First Governor of Beaumaris Castle, Anglesey, after its erection by that monarch, and the late Vice-Admiral Francis Pickmere, Governor of Newfoundland.

Note.—The Mount is a plain structure, chiefly modern, on a site commanding extensive views of the varied and beautiful scenery around Llanfair, watered by the river Vyrnwy.

POWIS, Edward James Herbert, Earl of, Powis Castle, Montgomeryshire.

Creations: Baron Powis, of Powis Castle, and Baron Herbert, of Chirbury, Viscount Clive, and Earl of Powis, peerage of United Kingdom, 1804; Baron in the Irish peerage, 1762; Baron Clive of Walcot, 1794.

Third Earl of Powis; High Steward of the University of Camb.; LL.D., D.C.L.; Lieut.-Col. Comm. S. Salop Yeom. Cavalry; J. P. and D. L. for the cos. of Montgomery and Salop; was M.P. for N. Salop 1843-8; is patron of fifteen livings; eldest son of Edward Herbert, second Earl of Powis, K.G., &c., by the Lady Lucy Graham, third dau. of James, third Duke of Montrose, K.G. (see *Lineage*); *b.* 1818; *ed.* at Eton and St. John's Coll. Cambridge; *grad.* M.A. and D.C.L. 1840 (Hon. D.C.L. of Oxford 1857).

Heir Presumptive: Right Hon. Sir Percy Egerton Herbert, K.C.B., M.P.
Residences: Powis Castle, Montgomeryshire; Walcot, Shropshire.
Town House: 45, Berkeley Square.
Arms: Per pale az. and gu., three lions rampant arg. (See Herbert, Shield of, 1684, p 796.)
Crest: A wyvern vert holding in the mouth a sinister hand, couped at the wrist gu.
Supporters: Dexter, an elephant arg.; *sinister*, a griffin wings elevated arg., ducally gorged gu., and charged with five mullets in saltire sa.
Motto: Ung je serviray.

LINEAGE.

The earlier stages in the genealogy of this noble house, in the *Herbert* line, are already given under *Powis Castle*, p. 794, and under *Raglan Castle* and *Llanarth*, co. Monmouth, pp. 718, 741, 776. For the earlier Barons of Powys, and details concerning various members of the influential and numerous clan of *Herbert*, see also "Nicolas's Peerage" and "Collins' Peerage."

The present noble owner of Powis Castle traces his lineage from the union of the *Herbert* line with that of *Clive* of Huxley, Cheshire, and Styche, Salop, and has among his more distinguished forefathers, in either line, the celebrated "Lord Herbert of Chirbury," and the distinguished soldier, Lord Clive, known for his brilliant career in India, in token of which he was created Baron Clive of Plassey. The eminent *George Herbert*, the poet, was brother of Lord Herbert of Chirbury.

Henry Arthur Herbert, Earl of Powis, and first Lord Herbert of Chirbury of the *third* creation, eighth in descent from Sir William ap Thomas ap Gwilym, of Raglan Castle, dying in 1772 without issue. was succeeded by his brother George, last Earl of Powis of the *Herbert* line, who *d. s. p.* 1801, when the title became extinct, and the estates devolved upon his niece, Henrietta Antonia Herbert, dau. of Henry Arthur Herbert, Earl of Powis aforesaid. She *m.* 1784.

Edward *Clive*, second Baron Clive of Plassey (son of the eminent Lord Clyde above named), who was created Baron Powis of Powis Castle, Baron Herbert of Cherbury, Viscount Clive, and Earl of Powis, in 1804. He left issue—

1. EDWARD, second Earl of Powis (of this creation), *b.* 1785, of whom hereafter.
2. Robert Henry, *b.* 1789; entered the army; *m.* Harriet, dau. of fifth Earl of Plymouth, and had issue.
3. Henrietta Antonia, *m.*, 1817, Sir Watkin Williams Wynn, Bart. (See *Williams Wynn of Wynnstay.*)
4. Charlotte Florentia, *m.*, 1817, Hugh Percy, third Duke of Northumberland.

EDWARD, second Earl of Powis, *m.*, 1818, Lucy, third dau. of James, third Duke of Montrose, K.G., and had issue—

1. EDWARD JAMES HERBERT, the present and third earl (as above).
2. Lucy Caroline, *b.* 1819; *m.*, 1865, Frederick Calvert, Esq., Q.C.
3. Charlotte Elizabeth, *b.* 1821; *m.*, 1846, Hugh Montgomery, Esq., of Grey Abbey, co. Down.
4. Right Hon. Sir Percy Egerton (heir presumptive), *b.* 1822; Major-Gen., C.B., P.P.; Treasurer of Her Majesty's Household 1867-8; M.P. for South Salop since 1865; *m.*, 1860, Lady Mary, dau. and only child of the late Earl of Kerry, eldest son of the third Marquess of Lansdowne, K.G., and has with other issue *George, b.* 1862. *Residence*: 43, Charles Street, Berkeley Square, W. *Clubs*: Carlton; United Service.
5. The Very Rev. George, Dean of Hereford; *b.* 1825; *m.*, 1863, Elizabeth Beatrice, fourth dau. of the late Sir Tatton Sykes, Bart., and has issue.
6. Robert Charles, *b.* 1827; a barrister; *m.*, 1854, Anna Maria, dau. and h. of the late Edward Cludde, Esq., of Orleton, Shropshire, and has issue.
7. Harriet Jane, *b.* 1831.
8. William Henry, *b.* 1834; Lieut.-Col. in the army.

Note.—For a notice of *Powis Castle*, with engravings and a history of the family, see pp. 792-8 *ante*.

PRITCHARD, David Pritchard, Esq., of Ceniarth, Montgomeryshire.

Son of Catharine, *née* Pritchard (only child of David Pritchard, Esq.) who *m.* David, third son of William Cobb Gilbertson, Esq., of Cefngwyn, Cardiganshire, nephew and heir of William Jones, Esq., of Dol-y-Clettwr, who served as High Sheriff for the co. of Cardigan 1766; *b.* at Western House, South Kensington, 13th Oct., 1849; *ed.* at Westminster School, and is now (1872) an undergraduate at Trinity Coll., Cambridge; *s.* to estates 13th Oct., 1870, on attaining his majority. (See *Lineage*).

Residence: Ceniarth, near Machynlleth.
Crest: A wild boar ppr.
Motto: Duw a'n bendithio.

LINEAGE.

The Pritchards of Ceniarth trace their lineage to a stock settled at an early period in the parish of Meifod, of whom "Y Llyr Craff o Feifod" was a prominent member. They have been known by the surname *Pritchard* from the time when surnames were first introduced into Wales (*temp*. Henry VIII.). Edward Pritchard, the owner of Ceniarth about eighty years ago, being, it is believed, the *ninth* possessor of the name.

Edward Pritchard (the sixth, *d.* 1698) *m.* a sister of William Pughe, of Mathafarn (*d.* Sept. 26, 1719); he was the son of Rowland, the sixth Ap Edward, &c., for twelve generations.

Rowland Pritchard (the seventh, *d.* 1709) *m.* Jane Owen, of Llynlloedd (*d.* 26th March, 1709).

Edward Pritchard (the seventh) *m.* Sarah, dau. of Morgan Lloyd (2nd son of Edward Lloyd of Clochfaen) of Caelan, Llanbrynmair, and sister of Lyttleton Lloyd, a part of whose will is copied into the Powysland Club papers, but not correctly. His father's name, Morgan Lloyd, is put instead of his own. His last will, dated 10th January, 1734, devises among other things "a small tenement in the parish of Trefeglwys and county of Montgomery, commonly called by the name of Cefn y Cloddiau, in the possession of one David Williams, towards the schooling of the poor of the parish of Llanbrynmair, to read, write, and casting up accounts as be fit and reasonable to their use," &c., and in default of the performance of such uses by the vicar and churchwardens, then to his "nephew, Rowland Pritchard, his heirs and assigns," &c.; he also devised the sum of ten pounds, the interest to be paid to the rector of Newtown "for preaching a sermon on Good Friday, and that every year as long as the Severn runs." (See *Lloyd of Clochfaen*.)

Rowland, the eighth (*b.* 1704, *d.* 1768), *m.* Jane, dau of Richard Edwards, Esq., of Gwern y Bere, Darowen, and left a son, Edward, the eighth, who *m.*, 1756, Jane, dau. of David Rees, Esq., of Maesypandy, Mer., and had a son, Edward, the ninth, who *m.*, 1803, Bridget, dau. of John Parry, Esq., of Aberystwyth, *d. s. p.* 1810, and his wife, *d.* 1811. The second son, David Pritchard, Esq., *m.*, 1794, Sarah, dau. of Thomas Newel, Esq., of Shrewsbury, and had issue—

David Pritchard, Esq. (*b.* 1797), who succ. to the estate on the decease of his uncle above named (1810); *m.*, 1819, Bridget, dau of Thomas James, Esq., of Aberystwyth; *d.* 30th Dec., 1859; Mrs. Pritchard *d.* 11th Jan., 1863, leaving an only child,—

CATHERINE PRITCHARD, *m.* David, 3rd son of

W. Cobb Gilbertson, Esq., J. P. of Cefn-gwyn, Card. (by his third wife, Elizabeth, dau. of the Rev. Isaac Williams, of Ystrad-teilo), and has with other issue a second eldest son,— DAVID PRITCHARD PRITCHARD, Esq., present representative (as above).

Note.—The old house of *Ceniarth* was erected more than 200 years ago, but a part was added about eighty years since by Edward Pritchard, above mentioned.

PRYCE, Mrs., of Gunley, Montgomeryshire.

Eliza Pryce, widow of the Rev. Richard Henry Mostyn Pryce, M.A., of Gunley (see the Gunley pedigree following); dau. and only child of John Williams, Esq., of Hêndydley Hall, Newtown; *m.* to the Rev. R. H. Mostyn Pryce in 1856; and *succ.* on his decease 1858.

Heir Presumptive : Edward Mostyn Harryman Price (see *Lineage*).
Residence : Gunley, Chirbury, Salop.
Arms : Arg. a lion passant sa. armed and langued gu. between three fleurs de lis two and one of the last.

LINEAGE.

The substance of this pedigree is taken direct from the family pedigree now at Gunley, and collated with *Lewys Dwnn's* autograph MS., also preserved at the same place.

Hugh of Gunley, living in the fifteenth century, was lineally descended from *Einion ap Seissyllt*, Lord of Meirionydd, (of the reputed line of Canedda Wledig, King of Britain). He *m.* Margaret, heiress of Gunley, living 1450, the dau. and heiress of David Lloyd, descended through Trahaiarn, Lord of Guilsfield, from Balliol, Lord of Guilsfield. The wife of David Lloyd was Sislie, dau. of John, Lord of Rossell, great-grandson of Sir. W. Rossell, and of Elinor, great-granddaughter of Sir Philip Thornes. The son of Hugh and Margaret of Gunley,—
Morris, *m.* Agnes, dau. of John Cliprie, Lord of Cliprie [Cleobury], by Jane, dau. of Sir William Newton, Kt. Their son,—
Rees, Lord of Marton, *m.* Margaret [Dwnn " Ales "], dau. of John Myddelton, descended from " Y Pothan Flaidd," great-grandson of Rhirid Flaidd, Lord of Penllyn. (See *Myddelton-Biddulph of Chirk Castle.*) Their son Richard was surnamed *ap Rhys* (Pryse), and his son—
Richard *Pryce*, of Gunley (the first so named), *m.* Jane, dau. and co-h. of Richard ap Owen, of direct descent through Lloyds of Tregynon from Bleddyn ap Cynfyn, prince of Powys, from Brochwel Ysgythrog. Their son,—
Edward Pryce, of Gunley, *m.* Bridget, dau. of John, one of Cromwell's captains, and granddau. of John Richard of Chirbury, in direct line fiom " John Warin o Mwythig," of the line of the Earl of Warren and Surrey, who *m.* Gundred, fifth dau. of William the Conqueror. Their son,—
Edward Pryce, of Pont-y-Porchill, had, by Sinah his wife, a numerous family, one of whom,—
Edmund Pryce, Esq., of Gunley, *m.* a dau. of J. Edwards, Esq., Rearington, and had issue—
Richard, Sheriff of Montgomeryshire, 1761, whose son John *m.* Mary, dau. of Maunsell Bransby, Esq., and had three children, one of whom,—
Richard Pryce, Esq., of Gunley, Sheriff of Mont. 1817, *m.* Eliza Constantia Edwards, dau. of Samuel D'Elboeuf Edwards, of Pentre, Esq., who was lineally descended from Baron D'Elboeuf, first cousin of William the Conqueror. They had twelve children, two sons and ten daughters, one of the latter of whom, Eliza Constantia, *m.* Capt. Robert Campbell, R.N. (1827), and had issue Lewis D'Elboeuf (*d.* 1828) Lewis and Robert; another, Charlotte Margaret, *m.*, 1842, the Rev. James Wilding, Vicar of Chirbury, Salop ; a third, Emma, *m.* Mathew Crosier, Esq. ; and a fourth, Harriotte, *m.* Robert Devereux Harrison, and had issue Sarah Harriotte, and George Devereux ; Constantia, Charlotte, and Robert. Their eldest son,—
RICHARD HENRY MOSTYN PRYCE (*d.* 1858), in holy orders, *m.*, 1856, *Eliza*, only child of John Williams, Esq., of Hêndydley Hall, near Newtown, now of Gunley (as above).
The second son, John Edward Harryman Pryce, (*d.* 1866), Capt. in the Army, and Col. of the Montgom. Rifles, *m.*, 1st., 1850, Eliza Martha, dau. of the late F. Burton, Esq., of the Twelfth Lancers (she *d.* 1866) ; 2ndly, 1862, Sarah Beatrice Hamilton, dau. of Major-Gen. Hamilton, and had from the former one son, *Edward Mostyn Harryman, ed.* at Chebenham College, now of the University of Cambridge, heir to the Gunley estates, and from the latter two sons. (See further *Pryce, Mrs., of Mont., &c.*

PRYCE, Mrs., of Montgomeryshire.

Sarah Beatrice, widow of Lieut.-Col. John Edward Harryman Pryce, (*d.* 1866), Capt. in the Army, and Lieut.-Col. of the Royal Montgomery Rifles. He was second son of Richard Pryce, Esq., of Gunley, co. of Montgomery (see *Pryce, Mrs. of Gunley); b.* 1818 ; *m.*, 29th July, 1862, Sarah Beatrice (now his widow), dau. of the late Major-Gen. Christopher Hamilton, C.B. (*d.* 1842, when in command of the South Western district of Ireland) ; youngest son of James Hamilton, Esq., of Sheephill (now Abbotstown), near Dublin ; for many years M.P. for the co. of Dublin, by the Hon. Sarah, second dau. of the second Baron Castlemaine of Moydrum Castle, co. Westmeath, and has left issue two sons :—
Richard, *b.* 14th May, 1864.
George Henry, *b.* 25th June, 1866.

Residence : (At present) Homburg, near Frankfort-on-the-Maine.

PRYCE, Robert Davies, Esq., of Cyfronydd, Montgomeryshire.

J. P. and D. L. for cos. Montgomery and Merioneth ; High Sheriff for former co. 1849 ; Captain Mont. Yeom. Cavalry ; eldest son of the late Pryce Jones, Esq., of Cyfronydd, by his wife, Jane, dau. of

John Davies, Esq., of Aberllefeny, co. of Merioneth ; *b.* at Cyfronydd, Dec. 25, 1819 ; *ed.* at Rugby and St. John's Coll., Cambridge; *grad.* B.A. 1842 ; *m.*, 1849, Jane Sophia, dau. of St. J. C. Charlton, Esq., of Apley Castle, Shropshire ; has issue four sons,—
1. *Athelstane Robert, b.* 16th Nov., 1850 ; Lieut. 13th Hussars.
2. Pryce Meyrick, *b.* 2nd April, 1851.
3. Arthur Hamilton, *b.* 12th June, 1864.
4. Walter Charlton, *b.* 16th Sept., 1865.

Heir : Athelstane Robert.
Residences : Cyfronydd, near Welshpool ; Aberllefeny, Merionethshire.
Arms : Quarterly : 1st and 4th, or, a lion rampant gu. ; 2nd and 3rd, arg., three bears' paws ppr.
Crest : A lion rampant gu.
Motto : Heb Dduw heb ddim ; Duw a digon.

Note.—*Cyfronydd* has been in the possession of this family for more than a century and a half. The present mansion is recently built.

SUDELEY, Sudeley Charles George Hanbury-Tracy, Baron of Gregynog, Montgomeryshire, and Toddington, Gloucestershire.

Creation 1838. Third Baron Sudeley of Toddington ; Lord Lieutenant and Custos Rotulorum of the co. of Montgomery ; late Capt. Grenadier Guards, retired 1863 ; eldest son of Thomas Charles, second Lord Sudeley (see *Lineage*); *b.* 1837 ; *ed.* at Harrow ; *succ.* 1863 ; is *unm.*

Heir Presumptive : His brother, Hon. Charles Douglas Pennant, M.P. for the Montgomery Boroughs since 1863 ; *b.* 1840 ; entered the Navy, served in the *Hecla* and *Blenheim* during the Crimean war ; resigned 1863 ; was called to the bar 1866 ; J. P. and D. L. for the co. of Mont. ; *m.*, 1868, Ada Maria, dau. of the Hon. Frederick J. Tollemache, and has issue.
Residences : Gregynog, near Newtown, Mont. ; Toddington, Gloucestershire.
Town Address : St. James's Club.
Arms : Quarterly : 1st and 4th, or, an escallop in the chief point sa. between two bendlets gu.— TRACY ; 2nd and 3rd, or, a bend engrailed vert plain cotised sa.—HANBURY.
Crests : 1. On a chapeau turned up ermine an escallop sa. between two wings or—*Tracy ;* 2. Out of a mural crown sa. a demi-lion rampant or, holding in the paws a battle-axe sa., helved gold —*Hanbury.*
Supporters : On either side a falcon, wings elevated ppr., beaked and belled or.
Motto : Memoria pii æterna.

LINEAGE.

The *Tracys* claim to be of Saxon descent, and trace their lineage, with possession of the demesne of Toddington, from times anterior to the Norman Conquest. The *Hanburys*, seated in Worcestershire before the fifteenth century, were afterwards of Pont-y-pool, co. Monmouth. (See *Capel Hanbury, of Pont-y-pool Park.*)
John Hanbury, Esq., of Pont-y-pool Park, *b.* 1744 (*d.* 1784), M.P. for the co. of Monmouth (see *Parl. Annals of Mon.*), by his wife Anne, dau. of Morgan Lewis, Esq., of St. Pierre, co. Monmouth, left, with other issue,—(the eldest son, John, *d. unm.,* the second son, *Capel,* inherited Pont-y-pool Park)—
Charles Hanbury, Esq., third son, *b.* 1777 ; *m.,* 1798, Henrietta Susannah *Tracy,* only child and h. of Henry, Eighth and last Viscount Tracy, peerage of Ireland, and assumed thereupon the additional surname and arms of *Tracy.* He was raised to the peerage 1838 as Baron Sudeley of Toddington, and dying in 1858, left by his wife, before named, who *d.* 1839, surviving issue :—
1. THOMAS CHARLES, second Baron Sudeley.
2. Henry, *b.* 1802. (See *Hanbury-Tracy of Gregynog.*)
3. William, *b.* 1810, late of the Civil Service of Madras.
4. Henrietta.
5. Laura Susannah.

THOMAS CHARLES HANBURY-TRACY, second Baron Sudeley, Lord Lieutenant of co. Montgomery, *b.* 1801 ; *m.,* 1831 (*d.* 1863), Emma Elizabeth Alicia, dau. of George Hay Dawkins Pennant, Esq., of Penrhyn Castle, co. of Carnarvon (see *Penrhyn, Lord, of Penrhyn Castle*), by whom he had issue six sons and six daus. :—
1. SUDELEY CHARLES GEORGE HANBURY-TRACY, present and third baron (as above).
2. *Charles Douglas Richard,* M.P. (as above).
3. Algernon Cornwallis Henry, *b.* 1844 ; *d.* 1845.
4. Alfred Francis Algernon, *b.* 1846 ; *m.,* 1868, Agnes Jane, dau. of the late H. J. Hoare, Esq., of Morden Lodge, Surrey.
5. Frederick Stephen Archibald, *b.* 1848.
6. Hubert George Edward, *b.* 1855.
1. Juliana Sophia Elizabeth.
2. Georgiana Henrietta Emma ; *m.* Charles H. Maude, Esq., in the Madras Military Service.
3. Adelaide Frances Isabella ; *m.,* 1859, the Rev. Frederick Peel, M.A.
4. Alice Augusta Gertrude ; *m.,* 1861, Charles Edmund Webber, Esq., Capt. Royal Engineers.
5. Madeline Emily Augusta ; *b.* 1852.
6. Gertrude Emily Rosamond ; *d.* an infant.

Note.—For a notice of *Gregynog,* with engraving of the mansion, &c., see p. 804, *ante.*

TRACY, Hon. Henry Hanbury-, of Gregynog, Montgomeryshire.

J. P. and D. L. for the co. of Montgomery ; formerly Lieut.-Col. of Royal Montgomery Militia ; second son of Charles, 1st Baron Sudeley, of Gregynog, Mont., and Toddington, co. of Gloucester (see *Sudeley, Baron, of Gregynog,* &c) ; *b.* 1802 ; *ed.* at Cambridge University ; *m.,* 1841, Rosamond Anne Myrtle Shirley, dau. of the late Lord Tamworth ; has issue one son and two daus.

Residence : Gregynog, near Newtown.
Arms : Quarterly : 1st and 4th, or, an escallop

in the chief point sa. between two bendlets gu.—TRACY; 2nd and 3rd, or, a bend engrailed vert plain cotised sa.—HANBURY.

Crests: 1. On a chapeau turned up ermine, an escallop sa. between two wings or—*Tracy;* 2. Out of a mural crown a demi-lion rampant or, holding in the paws a battle-axe sa., helved gold —*Hanbury.*

Motto : Memoria pii æterna.

LINEAGE.

For *lineage,* see *Sudeley, Baron, of Gregynog and Toddington.*

Note.—For an *engraving* and notice of Gregynog, see p. 804; and for the ancient family of *Blayney* of Gregynog, see notices at pp. 804, 810.

VANE, George Henry Robert Charles Vane Tempest, Earl, of Plas Machynlleth, Montgomeryshire.

Vide English peerage. Creation 1823. Second Earl Vane and Viscount Seaham of Wynward and Seaham, in the peerage of the United Kingdom; M.P. for North Durham from 1847 to 1854; Lieutenant 1st Life Guards 1843; retired 1848; Col. North Durham Militia; Lieut.-Col. Commandant 2nd Durham (Seaham) Artillery Volunteers; Major Montgomeryshire Yeomanry Cavalry; Knight Grand Cross of St. Alexander Newski of Russia; is patron of six livings—St. John's, Seaham Harbour; Seaham; New Seaham; St. Nicholas's, and St. Giles's, Durham; Corris, Merionethshire. Second son of Charles William, third Marquess of Londonderry, K.G., by his second wife, Frances Anne, dau. of Sir Henry Vane-Tempest, Bart. ; *b.* in Vienna, April 26, 1821; *ed.* at Eton Coll., and Balliol Coll., Oxford; *grad.* B.A. 1844, M.A. 1848; *m.,* August 3, 1846, Mary Cornelia, only child of Sir John Edwards, Bart., of Machynlleth (see *Edwards, Lady, of Llanerch-hudol Hall); succ.* to Earldom and Viscountcy 1854; has issue living—

1. CHARLES STEWART, Viscount Seaham, *b.* 1852; Major Durham, Vol. Corps, 1869.
2. Henry John, *b.* 1854.
3. Herbert Lionel Henry, *b.* 1862.
1. Frances Cornelia Harriet Emily, *b.* 1850.
2. Avarina Mary, *b.* 1857.
3. Alexandrina Louisa Maud, *b.* 1863.

Heir: Charles Viscount Seaham.
Residences: Plâs Machynlleth, Mont.; Wynyard Park, Stockton-on-Tees; Seaham Hall, Sunderland.
Town House: Holdernesse House, Park Lane, W.
Arms: Quarterly: 1st and 4th grand quarters, 1st and 4th, arg., a bend engrailed between six martlets, three and three, sa.; 2nd and 3rd, az., three sinister gauntlets, two and one, or—VANE; 2nd and 3rd grand quarters, or, a bend compony arg. and az. between two lions rampant gu.—STEWART.

Crests : 1st, an arm in armour holding a sword ppr., hilted and pommelled or—VANE; 2nd, a dragon statant or—STEWART.

Supporters : Dexter, a grey horse guardant caparisoned, thereon mounted an hussar of the 18th regiment, armed and accoutred, all ppr. ; *sinister,* a bay horse mounted as the dexter.

Mottoes : Metuenda corolla draconis ; Nec temere nec timide.

LINEAGE.

The lineage of Earl Vane belongs to the English peerage; that of the Countess Vane is indicated under the article *Lady Edwards of Llanerch-hudol.*

Charles William Vane Stewart, third Marquess of Londonderry, Earl of Londonderry, peerage of Ireland, Baron Stewart (1814) and Earl Vane (1823) in the peerage of the United Kingdom, K.C., G.C.B., by his first wife, Catherine, dau. of John, the third Earl of Darnley (she *d.* 1812), had an only son and heir, —

Frederick William Robert, the present Marquess of Londonderry.

His lordship *m.,* secondly, 1819, Frances Jane, only dau. of Sir Harry Vane Tempest, Bart. (she *d.* 1865), by Anne Catherine, late Countess of Antrim, and thereupon assumed the surname and arms of Vane. By this marriage the Marquess, who *d.* 1854, left issue surviving—

1. GEORGE HENRY ROBERT CHARLES, the present Earl Vane and Viscount Seaham (as above), heir presumptive to the Marquisate of Londonderry.
2. Adolphus Fred Charles William, *b.* 1825, an officer in the guards, *deceased.*
3. Ernest M'Donnell Vane-Tempest, *b.* 1836; was in Light Dragoons; *m.* Mary Townhend, dau. of Thomas Hutchinson, Esq.
4. Frances Anne Emily, *m.,* 1843, to the sixth Duke of Marlborough.
5. Alexandrina Octavia Maria, *m.,* 1847, to the third Earl of Portarlington.
6. Adelaide Emelina Caroline, *m.,* 1852, the Rev. Frederick H. Law, Rector of Croft, Yorkshire.

WILLIAMS, Martin, Esq., (late) of Bryngwyn, Llanfechain, Montgomeryshire.

Was J. P. and D. L. of Montgomeryshire, and Sheriff of same co. 1838; *ed.* at Eton, afterwards at Magdalen Coll., Oxford, and became Capt. 15th Hussars, and Aide-de-camp to the Duke of Cumberland; *m.* Mary, daughter of John Madocks, Esq., of Vron-iw, in the co. of Denbigh, and left 4 daughters, now co-heiresses.

Residence: Bryngwyn, Montgomeryshire.

LINEAGE.

Descended from a family of that name who emigrated to Jamaica with Col. Wayte in 1656, and had large allotments of land assigned to them in that island.

WILLIAMES, Mrs. Buckley, of Glan-Hafren, Montgomeryshire.

Catharine, widow of the late John Williames Buckley Williames, Esq. (*d.* 1866), of Pennant and Glan-Hafren, J. P. and D. L. for the co. of Montgomery, served the office of High Sheriff for same co. 1820, and was Major of the Montgomeryshire Yeomanry Cavalry, constituted so for life by King George on the occasion of the disbanding of the Yeomanry; also Receiver-General of Taxes for cos. of Montgomery, Radnor, and Brecon; dau. and heiress of Rice Pryce, Esq., of Glyn-Cogan (formerly "Tyddyn-Glyn Cogan"), Montgomeryshire, who was D. L. for his county; *m.* to Mr. Buckley Williames in 1800; had issue—

1. Rice Pryce Buckley Williames, Esq., of Pennant, who *d.* 1871 (see *Williames of Pennant*).
2. John Buckley Williames, J. P.
3. Catharine Buckley Williames.
4. Mary Buckley Williames.

Residence: Glan-Hafren, Abermule, Mont.
Arms: (See *Williames of Pennant*.)
Crest: A lion rampant.
Motto: Heb Dduw heb ddim; Duw a digon.

LINEAGE.

The descent of this family is from the Williamses of Ystum-Colwyn, the Prices of Newtown, and the Buckleys of Dolfor.

WILLIAMES, Mrs. Pryce Buckley, of Pennant, Montgomeryshire.

Anna Frances, widow of Rice Pryce Buckley Williames, Esq. (*d.* March 23, 1871), J. P. for the co. of Montgomery, formerly a major in the Yeomanry Militia. Mr. Williames had a chief hand in originating the *Cambrian Quarterly*, and for some years acted as its editor. He was son of John Williames Buckley Williames, Esq., of Pennant, who *d.* 1866; *b.* 1802; *ed.* at Shrewsbury School under Dr. Butler; *m.* 1854, to Anna Frances Parslow (now his widow), eldest dau. of Humphrey Rowlands Jones, Esq., of Garthmyl Hall, Montgomeryshire, and had issue an only child, a daughter, deceased.

Residence: Pennant, Abermule, Mont.
Crest: A Saxon's head as in the arms.
Arms: Gu. a chevron ermine between three Saxons' heads couped gory proper.—WILLIAMES (with many quarterings).
Mottoes: Heb Dduw heb ddim; Duw a digon.

LINEAGE.

This family derives its descent from the Williamses of Ystum-colwyn, Carnarvonshire, descended from Ednyfed Fychan, the Pryces of Newtown Hall, and the Buckleys of Dolfor.

William Williames, Esq., of Cochwillan, Carn.; Sheriff of co. Carnarvon 1542, of the line of *Edn yfed Fychan*, and the first of the Penrhyn Cochwillan sept to adopt the surname *Williams*, was grandfather of Arthur Williams, of Meillionydd, co. of Carnarvon, Precentor of Bangor Cathedral (*d.* 1621), from whom descended the Williamses of Meillionydd, and of Ystumcolwyn, co. Mont. The last and eldest Miss Williams of Ystumcolwyn *m.* the late—

Price *Buckley*, Esq., representative of Glan-Hafren and Dolfor, and had issue—

John Buckley Williames, Esq., late of Glan-Hafren (See *B. Williames of Glan-Hafren*), who *m.*, as there stated, and had, with other issue, an eldest son,—

RICE PRYCE BUCKLEY WILLIAMES (as above).

Mrs. Buckley Williames's family, *Jones of Garthmyl Hall*, have been of long standing in the co. of Montgomery, Humphrey Jones, the founder of the Garthmill Free Schools, being one of *fourteen* of the same name who in succession represented the house.

Note.—The old residence of *Garthmill Hall* was taken down and the present building erected by the late Humphrey R. Jones, Esq., about fifty-nine years ago. The place was sold in 1858 to Gen. Gold. An eastern window has recently been erected in Bettws Church in memory of J. Buckley Williames, Esq., of Glan-Hafren, and his grandchild, of Pennant, and a reredos in memory of the late Pryce Buckley Williames, Esq., of Pennant, both executed in excellent taste.

WILLIAMS, The Rev. William Maddock, of Llanfechain, Montgomeryshire.

M.A., Rector of Llanfechain, Montgomeryshire, 1851; formerly Incumbent successively of Flint and Halkin 1825 and 1839; J. P. for the counties of Flint, Denbigh, and Montgomery; son of the late Rev. William Williams, M.A, Rector of Ysceifiog, and Canon of St. Asaph; *b.* at Bronwylfa, St. Asaph, March, 1799; *ed.* at Shrewsbury School and Ball. Coll, Oxon; *grad.* B.A. 1821, M.A. 1827; *m.* Harriet Elizabeth, only dau. of Joseph Greaves, Esq., of Liverpool.

Residence: Llanfechain Rectory, Oswestry.
Arms: Quarterly: 1st and 4th, ar., a lion rampant arg., on a chief azure three stars or—WILLIAMS; 2nd, ermine, a lion rampant sa.; 3rd, arg., a chevron sa. between three castellated towers with flames issuing from top—MADDOCK.

Note.—The church of Llanfechain is small, but of great antiquity, date unknown, character Norman.

ANNALS, &c., OF WALES.

PEMBROKESHIRE

(SIR BENFRO).

THE county of Pembroke, though now and for many past ages in *speech* nearly as much English as Welsh, retains, in a form well-nigh unaltered, its ancient Welsh name. It may indeed be said that the English *Pembroke* preserves the ancient Cymric name with greater fidelity than does the modern Welsh *Penfro*, for the etymology of the word is Pen-bro-og (*pen*, head, extreme part; *bro*, region, district, tract, lowland; *og*, or *wg*, a terminal particle often applied in old Welsh to an inhabited region, as in Brycheini*og*, Rhyfoni*og*, Morgan*wg*, Essyll*wg*. The Middle-Age Latin of the chronicles—for example, the *Annales Cambriæ*— caught and perpetuated the right native articulation in " *Pembroc*" and " *Pembroch-ia*," and the modern W. *Pen-fro* drops an element of the old word for the sake of euphony or supposed accuracy. The name was doubtless first applied to the locality or the site of the town of Pembroke as situated at the " end " of the country, in later times to the division or *cantref*, and then to the "county" when this county palatine had its birth. The more ancient name *Dyfed*, by the Romans called *Dimetia*, will be hereafter noticed. (See *History and Antiq. of Pemb.*)

SECTION I.—PHYSICAL DESCRIPTION OF PEMBROKESHIRE.

Two-thirds of the margin of this county, S.W. and N.W., are washed by the sea; on the north it is bounded by the river *Teivi*, which separates it from Cardiganshire, and on the east by Carmarthenshire, from which it is in part divided by the Cych, a tributary of the Teivi, in part by the small " trout-bearing " river *Tâf*, in part by the Cleddeu, and in part by an arbitrary boundary crossing the hilly midland region to connect the roots of Tâf and Cych. From Strumble Head, in " Pencaer," to the Castle-Martin coast at St. Govan's Head, the county measures about thirty-one miles in length, and from St. Bride's Bay to the Carmarthenshire boundary about twenty-one miles in breadth. Its superficial contents may be estimated at 627 square miles, or 401,691 acres. As to the general form of the county, it can be compared to no geometrical figure known, and the only brief description of it possible is found in the term " irregular." Old George Owen, nearly three hundred years ago, was anxious to define its shape, and painfully floundered as follows:—"It is neither perfect square, long, nor round, but shaped with divers corners, some sharpe, some obtuse, in some places concave, in some convex, but in most places concave and bending inwarde, as doth the moone in her decreasing." The county being destitute of mining or manufacturing operations of importance, or other powerful stimulus for the creation of large towns, the population is sparse and nearly stationary. During the present century the following are the vital statistics :—

Total population of Pembrokeshire in	1801	...	...	...	...	56,280.
,,	,,	1831	...	...	...	...	80,900.
,,	,,	1841	...	...	...	...	88,044.
,,	,,	1851	...	...	...	...	94,140.
,,	,,	1861	...	...	...	...	96,278.
,,	,,	1871	...	...	...	...	91,936.

The last decade shows for the first time within the century a marked decline, owing perhaps to the reduction of troops at Pembroke Dock—a loss to the *trade*, a gain to the *morals* of the county. In density, the population is considerably below the average for all Wales, that average being 178 persons to the square mile. The population of Glamorganshire is close upon 500 persons to the square mile.

Pembrokeshire is essentially an agricultural county; much of its surface is hilly and even mountainous, but in the main presents a broken, undulating aspect; it has no plains or wide valleys, rivers of large volume, or mountains of great height ; but its springs and streamlets are multitudinous, combining with the almost perpetual mists or showers of the western sea to water abundantly the rather shallow and reluctant " lower Silurian " soil composing the main part of the county, and making it a tolerably good grazing and corn-producing region.

It is doubtful whether the inhabitants of Pembrokeshire feel any pride in their *mountains*, for with the exception of "*Precelly Top*" (1,754 feet above the sea level), situated in the background of the county, and the rocky heights of Trefgarn, or " Plumstone," and on the coast of St. David's and Pencaer, the elevations of the county are very moderate, and possess no striking character of boldness, wildness, or beauty. But for broken, indented, beetling cliffs, stormy headlands, rocky islands waging perpetual war with a chafing and often angry sea, no county in Britain, not excepting even the nearly related promontory of Cornwall, can compete with Pembrokeshire. In point of physical effect, the grandeur of this county can be chiefly seen in its magnificent coast-line, in the wide and varied prospect of a cultured country and an encompassing sea which opens to the beholder who may ascend Precelly mountain, and in the spacious and sheltered waters of its incomparable haven of Milford—a haven which, but for the law which the growth of Liverpool and its interests has imposed upon maritime commerce, should have become the great trysting-place between England and the trading powers of the world. Compared with Milford Haven, the Mersey, the Tyne, the Avon, and the Thames, are mere muddy and dangerous tidal inlets, and as points of arrival and departure confessedly inconvenient.

The locality of Milford Haven has always been the centre of Pembrokeshire life and influence. In its vicinity and along its shores are still situated the chief towns and a large proportion of the chief mansions of the county. The land is here richer, the scenery fairer than in other parts, and here naturally the principal people have settled. The foremost place must be assigned to *Picton Castle* (the Rev. J. H. A. Philipps, M.A.), a place of great antiquity and eventful history, planted on a pleasant slope, overlooking the waters of the haven near the point of junction of the two streams of East and West *Cleddau*. This spot has been famous since that early age when the Norman, Arnulph de Montgomery, *temp.* William Rufus, took possession of the district, and assigned this lordship to *William de Picton*, who built here a castle and called it after his own name. Around this castle have grown, in the long succession of ages, all the tokens of a venerable antiquity and true lordly grandeur. Injudicious restoration and alteration have marred the external form of the fabric, but parts still remain which are hoary and pitted over with age, and eloquent concerning times when the castle was a Norman fortress, defiant of attack and fearless of beleaguerment. Time, *currente calamo*, has writ upon the demesne the story of seven centuries—"ancestral woods," lichen-covered walls, which have witnessed the passing in and out of many succeeding proprietors, memorials of moat and drawbridge, outstanding watch-towers and camps, secret passages, the appointments of more recent and peaceful times, and the elegance and taste

PICTON CASTLE: THE SEAT OF THE REV J. H. A. PHILLIPS, M.A. (*from a photograph*).

of the present. This is one of the very few Norman castles in Britain which have never been dismantled or alienated, and the only one of the kind in Wales. Picton Castle has always been inhabited, has never been forfeited, and has continued in the same line of proprietors from the beginning. From the Pictons it passed by marriage of the heiress, Ivan, to the Wogans in the person of Sir John Wogan; from the Wogans it passed in like manner to the line of Donne of Cydweli by the marriage of Catherine, dau. and heiress of Sir John Wogan, to Owen Donne; and lastly, from the Donnes, by the marriage of Jane, dau. and heiress of Sir Henry Donne, of Picton, to Thomas ap Phylip, otherwise Sir Thomas Philips, Lord of Cilsant, time of Richard III., whose posterity, in direct or indirect line, has ever since remained in possession (see further *Philipps of Picton Castle*, and Fenton's *Pembrokeshire*).

Adjoining the manor of Picton Castle is *Slebech*, now called *Slebech Hall*, a name the origin of which is unknown (Baron de Rutzen), a place of great antiquity, remarkable as having been a commandery of the Knights Hospitallers of St. John of Jerusalem, and as such the resort of pilgrims, devotees, and mendicants for several ages. *Lewis Glyn Cothi*, the historic bard of the time of the Wars of the Roses, in a poem addressed to his friend Sir Thomas Philips, of Picton, aforesaid, whom he calls " Tomas ab Phylip o Bictwn," gives us to understand that he was himself of the number of such pilgrims, and bespeaks a resting-place at Picton, while in search, we suppose, of ghostly benefit. He says that at Slebech, as at the holy island of Bardsey, pardons and purification were to be obtained under St. John's auspices. In his greeting to Sir Thomas Philips and his lady he alludes to the latter as "descended from two Barons, Wogan the Fair and Owen Dwnn," calls her "the golden daughter of Harri Dwnn," and avers that in her old age she wore "a saintly face." (L. G. Cothi's *Works*, p. 301.)

Facing the other Cleddau, and within a short distance of Picton Castle park, is *Boulston*, formerly the residence of the Wogans, now of the Acklands (see *Ackland of Boulston*). The estate was purchased by R. G. Ackland, Esq., who built the present mansion on an elevated part of the grounds, on the lower skirts of which, near the river, are the ruins of the ancient abode of the Wogans, and the little church, a " peculiar " in the gift of the family, where there are some elaborate monuments to the Wogans One of these, to Sir John Wogan, Kt. enumerates six generations of the Wogans living at Boulston, from Sir John Wogan, Kt., of Wiston, downwards. The inscription states that Sir John died A.D. 1616, and yet that he "made and set up" the monument in 1617, which clearly implies error in one of the dates. Several memorial tablets to the Acklands also are here.

On a fine elevation further down the haven, and commanding extensive views both of the wooded country around and of the creeks of the estuary, is the castellated mansion of *Lawrenny Park* (Mrs. Lort Phillips), an imposing and conspicuous structure. *Cresselly*, the seat of H. S. Allen, Esq. (see *Allen of Cresselly*), is near, fronting Cresswell (Christ's Well) Creek and the haven. The name Cresselly is doubtless related to "Christ's Well," but of the well we have no information. There used to be a " Christ's Well Chapel" near the water's edge.

Across another branch of this sinuous and splendid haven, and near Carew Castle, is *Upton Castle*, formerly the abode of the ancient family of Maliphant, of Norman-French origin, and long extinct in these parts; and *Woodfield*, the residence of —— Wedgwood, Esq.; *Williamston*, the residence of J. H. Scourfield, Esq., M.P.; *Hayston* (J. H. Davies, Esq.); *Scoveston* (William Rees, Esq.); *Johnston* (Capt. Carron); *Hazel Hill* (late Robertson), are on the northern side of Milford Haven, and on the productive old red sandstone soil, for which the hundreds of Roose (Rhos) and Castlemartin are so celebrated as corn-bearing and grazing districts.

Between Milford Haven and St. Bride's Bay, besides *St. Botolph's* (Stokes); *Rickeston Hall* (George Harries, Esq.); *Butter-hill* (Roche); *Castle Hall* (late Greville); *Pierston; St. Bride's Hill; Orlandon* (the old abode of the Laugharnes), we find the important demesne of *Dale Castle* (J. A. P. Lloyd-Philipps, Esq.), situated near the creek where the Earl of Richmond landed, prior to the battle of Bosworth Field (see p. 242). From the high ground near Marloes the eye sweeps a glorious prospect of well-cultivated country of the red sandstone soil, a broken and precipitous coast-line, the rocky and wild islands of Skomer and Skokham—names which are memorials of the sea-roving and plundering Danes—

the fine crescent of St. Bride's Bay with its fringe of level sands, miles in length at Broad Haven and Newgale, and unsurpassed cliff scenery of the carboniferous Silurian series, terminating in St. David's Head and Ramsey Island, and then the noble sheet of the Haven waters as far as Pembroke and the Royal Dockyard of Pater, decked with the ponderous ironclads and guard-ships, with many smaller craft, and only wanting the tall India merchant, and the American cotton and Emigration ships to make it, in all respects, the grandest of known harbours.

On the other side of Milford Haven is situated the famous seat of *Orielton*, long associated with the name of Owen, now the seat of M. A. Saurin, Esq., near which is the ancient *Henllan*, the early abode of the Whites, and *Castleton*, once a manor of a De Castle, and on a creek, sheltered and woody, *Stackpool Court*, on the site of a castle founded by the Norman Elidur de Stackpole, eleventh century, formerly belonging to the Lorts, now to

UPTON CASTLE: THE SEAT OF CHARLES T. EVANS, ESQ. (*from a photo. by Allen*).

the Earl of Cawdor. (See *Cawdor of Stackpool Court.*) *Corston* (Henry Leach, Esq.); *Castlemartin* (Rev. Chancellor Allen, M.A.); *Bush* (T. Charlton Meyrick, Esq., M.P.); *Hollyland* (John Adams, Esq.); *Lamphey Court* (L. Matthias, Esq.); *Trewarren* (G. W. W. Davies, Esq.); *Milton House* (Capt. Bowen Summers) are all near. *Pater-Church*—the ancient abode of the Adams, now of Hollyland, has long been swept away by the dockyard—leaving behind a fragment only of its name. The chief natural features of this side of Milford Haven—a kind of promontory, or headland, stretching westwards from Tenby—the form of which, a very *pen-y-fro*, probably gave origin to the name of "Pem-broke," first applied to the tract, next to the settlement, or town, and lastly to the county, are the magnificent limestone cliffs which face the stormy seas, beating on its southern and south-western sides. These cliffs in places, by the long contention of the waves, have been worn into clefts and deep cavernous recesses of great extent; in places they have been entirely dissociated by abrasion from the main-land, and left standing in solitary grandeur in the distance, still defying the might of the sea. The precipitous and inaccessible character of these cliffs has recommended them as a summer settlement to innumerable tribes of sea birds, chiefly of the puffin kind (called by the country people "eligugs," probably from the cry of the bird), with colonies, occupying distinct territory, of razor-bills, herring-gulls, and others. The first mentioned, birds of passage, arrive in myriad flocks in the early summer, and by the end of August, when they begin to consult together and devise plans for emigration, have multiplied so enormously as literally to cover the rocks and fill the air far and wide.

Guide books, in perplexing number, speak of the attractions and merits of Tenby as a place for summer resort and renewal of health, and nothing of that kind is needed here.

Tenby—from the North.

Of the castle and old annals of Tenby, something must be related hereafter. More can be said for the position and sea-environment of this beautiful watering-place than for the country immediately behind it—which is merely a cold clayey tract of the coal-bearing formation. The site of Tenby is faultless—a rocky tongue of land reaching out boldly into the sea, and in the distant past doubtless continuing to St. Catherine's Rock, now seen on the extreme left of our view—an island rock, formerly one of the chief attractions of Tenby, but recently marred by the wasteful use of public money in the erection upon it of huge and needless fortifications. Caldy Island is seen in the distance.

Memorial to Albert, Prince Consort.
[Erected by the People of Wales.]

Upon the Castle Hill eminence, to the south of the town, the site of the ancient fortress, is erected a graceful and loyal tribute to the memory of the late lamented Prince Consort. It was actively promoted (with the co-operation of a large committee) by

George White, Esq., then and repeatedly Mayor of Tenby, who laid the foundation-stone December 14, 1864. This beautiful memorial to the Prince, designed and executed by the eminent sculptor, John Evan Thomas, Esq., of London, was inaugurated August 2, 1865, by H. R. H. Prince Arthur, who was accompanied on the occasion by the Right Hon. Lord Llanover, Bishop Thirlwall of St. David's, and other men of note in Wales. The majestic statue, eight feet nine inches high, on a limestone pedestal fifteen feet high, is of fine Sicilian marble. The prince is attired in Field Marshal's uniform, and wearing the mantle and collar of the Order of the Garter. The front tablet, one of four of Sicilian marble, bears the inscription—

ALBERT DDA, PRIOD EIN GORHOFFUS FRENHINES VICTORIA.
"*Albert the Good, Consort of our most beloved Queen Victoria.*"

This memorial was got up by subscriptions from all parts of Wales, and was designed to be a national tribute of the Welsh people to the personal and public worth of the Prince Consort:—

"A Prince indeed
Beyond all titles; and a household name
Hereafter through all time—ALBERT THE GOOD."
"*Idylls of the King.*"

Equally appropriate and even more beautiful are the utterances of a local muse,

> "Here by the likeness on our height
> Shall memories of a Life be fed,
> Which, generous as our daily light,
> Was simple as our daily bread;
> And lives, not kindled yet, be taught
> Pure hope, strong effort, noble thought."—M. B. S.

St. Gowan's Well, on this rugged shore, in the olden and dusky ages was a place of resort for invalids, seekers for a miraculous cure. A small spring of water not far above the level of the tide, was said to possess preternatural virtues for the healing of cripples—and it is indeed hard to imagine impotent folk tarrying long amid such scenes, inhaling the pure breath of the sea, and hobbling along the gravelly and sunny beach, without being somewhat benefited—a rustic "chapel" was built, with its congenial altar of rock, and its superfluous holy water stoup, and pilgrims were encouraged to arrive, bringing, of course, such coins and gifts as they could find. It is said that crutches soon became unnecessary and were hung up as memorials of curing in the chapel, the owners returning to their homes on their own legs. Somehow, although unfortunately cripples are not wanting in Pembrokeshire any more than in other counties, we hear in modern times of no cures at St. Gowan's Well; if not the usual virtues, the glory of the place has sadly departed, and the humble little chapel has only left its ruins to be a memento of past superstition. Mr. Fenton in his "*Pembrokeshire*" relates other marvels about this place. Pirates on one occasion stole the chapel bell; ever since, certain blocks of limestone rock on which it rested in transit have emitted when struck a musical tone. A cleft in the rock on the east side of the "oratory" is said to have "first opened to afford shelter to a saint closely pursued by his pagan persecutors, and after the chase was given up and the danger over, let him out again, never closing afterwards, and retaining a faint impression of the body it had once enfolded." He adds that ever since it is believed to be "of so accommodating a nature as to admit the largest as well as the smallest man, and that if you frame a wish while in it, and do not change your mind during the operation of turning about, you will certainly obtain it." It is said that the only pilgrims who visit St. Gowan's in our material and self-seeking age, are those who desire the accomplishment of soft and otherwise all but hopeless wishes formed not for the first time in this friendly cleft.

Nearer Tenby is *Elm Grove*, St. Florence (Nicholas J. Dunn, Esq.); *Ivy Tower* (John Leach, Esq.); *Begelly* (Child). At Tenby, the house of *Allen* is represented by Charles Allen, Esq., and that of *White* by George White, Esq., both ancient Pembrokeshire families. *Scotsborough*, the old residence of the Perrotts, and afterwards *ap Rhys*, from a natural son of Sir Rhys ap Thomas of Dinefawr (see *Rickeston*, Brawdy), is still standing and bearing marks of age and suffering.

The land between Tenby and Narberth is not of a kind to invite the settlement of prominent families. *Kilgetty*, formerly the residence of a family of the name of *Canon*, merged by marriage in the Picton estate, being the only place of note; but at Narberth the face of nature becomes more attractive, and the soil, nursed into fertility by a tributary of the Eastern Cleddeu, more productive. A little further west that river itself, in its passage by Egremont and Lawhaden on its way to the famous lands of Slebech and Picton Castle, is environed by a succession of beautiful spots. It passes *Talybont*, once a place of some note under "the rapacious Bishop Barlow," and *St. Kennox*, a residence of Rhys Prichard, the celebrated "Vicar." Here are *Robeston Wathen* (Ven. Geo. Clark, M.A.); *Ridgeway* (R. P. Davies, Esq.); *Sodston* (Ward); *North Sodston* (Rev. H. C. D. Chandler); and *Lam-*

HENLLAN: THE SEAT OF J. L. G. POYER LEWIS, ESQ. (*from a photo. by Allen*).

HENLLAN—SIDE VIEW.

peter House (J. R. Thomas, Esq.). Nearer the border of Carmarthenshire are *Trewern* (J. T. Beynon, Esq.), and *Henllan*, the beautiful residence of J. L. G. Poyer Lewis, Esq.; and just over the border, *Tegfynydd* (Howard Spear Morgan, Esq.), and *Clynderwen* (R. F. Gower, Esq.—see *Gower of Glandovan*).

Colby, west of Lawhaden, now wears a humble aspect, but at one time as part of the barony of Slebech, when the Barlows held sway, was invested with no small distinction. We are here also in the classic neighbourhood of *Wiston*—(W., *Cas'-Gwys*, the *ton* or settlement of *Wys*,)—the ruins of whose castle recall ages of warfare and feudal oppression. The remains of an ancient mansion remind us of the great and excellent family of the *Wogans*, now long extinct (see *Wogans of Wiston*, &c.). *Penty-park* (F. L. Lloyd Philipps, Esq.), long the residence of one or other branch of that ancient Welsh family, and *Haythog*, belonging to the same estate, are in this neighbourhood.

Haverford-west (the *ford* at the *aber* [of two streams], standing "west," called in Welsh *Hwlffordd* (*hewl-fford*, the passage, or way-ford), the county town, an ancient centre of warlike, monastic, and political activity, might be expected to be the cynosure of powerful

COTTESMOOR: THE SEAT OF E. T. MASSY, ESQ. (*from a photograph*).

houses; and so, to some considerable extent, it has been. But priory and castle have long sunk in the decrepitude of age; *Prendergast* has lost its Stepneys, *Haroldston* its Perrotts, and many a name of note gracing in past ages the rolls of sheriffs, commanders, mayors, have passed into oblivion. And yet around Haverfordwest we find even now a goodly number of mansions fit to environ a county town, and form the materials of a refined circle of society. Picton Castle and Boulston have already been mentioned. *Glanafon* (Xavier de C. R. Peel, Esq.), *Withybush* (William Owen, Esq.), *Cottesmoor* (Edw. T. Massy, Esq.), and *Scotchwells* (late Stokes) are in the near vicinity; while at various distances, besides some already specified, are *Sealyham*, the beautiful and ancient abode of the Tuckers and Edwardeses (see *Edwardes of Sealyham*), *Cuffern* (John Stokes, Esq.), *Camrose* (C. W. T. Webb Bowen, Esq.), *Hilton* (G. A. Harries, Esq.), *Scolton* (James Higgon, Esq.), *Leweston* (W. Fortune, Esq.), *Stonehall* (Peel), and others. *Poyston* was the abode of the Pictons, and the birthplace of **General** Sir

Thomas Picton. At *Rhôs-market* was the seat of the Walters, and the birth-place of Miss Williams, the blind poetess succoured by Johnson. *Roblinston* and *Wolf-dale* had their days of note under the Bowens; and *Nash* was the residence of a branch of the great race of the Corbetts. *Summerhill* was a seat of the Edwardeses; *Moat*, even to recent times, maintained its dignity as a mountain barony, and is still owned by the Scourfields; *Earwear* (Amroth Castle) was possessed by the Elliotts, and subsequently by the Nicholases; and at *Neeston* the Bowens dwelt. What difference does it make that the scythe has passed over the land, and so many of the old households have succumbed?—the new have filled the place of the old, as they had come in lieu of others; and so it will be in the coming time!

Under the rocky eminence of Trefgarn (the "rock settlement") was the Bishop of St. David's forest, where game was reared for the bishop's liberal table at St. David's; but here also was the house of *Little Trefgarn*, where lived *Thomas ap Llewelyn ap Owain* and the only survivor of his line, who married a granddaughter of the last Prince Llewelyn whose daughter Helen was mother of *Owen Glyndwr*. Owain, in right of his mother, claimed the throne of the Principality; and it is maintained by many that his birthplace was Little Trefgarn, his mother's early home (Thomas's *Memoirs of Glyndwr*, p. 48).

Quitting the ancient cantref of *Dau-gleddau*—the "two Cleddeu (rivers),"—now absurdly corrupted into "Dungleddy," and entering the *cantref* or hundred of *Pebydiog*, we pass out of what is called "little England beyond Wales" into unsophisticated Welsh territory. In Pebydiog there are at present but few seats of the leading gentry, but many with old and interesting memories:—*Llethr House* (formerly Jones), now occupied by John Thomas, Esq., has somewhat changed its residential character, but not its respectability; *Brawdy* (formerly Jones, a race long extinct), now occupied by the Gwythers in the third generation; *Lochmeilir* (now occupied by Harries), which is said to have had its origin many centuries ago in *Meilir* (of the line of Bleddyn ap Cynfyn, Prince of Powys), who "came to Pembrokeshire and built Llech Meilir," and founded there a family called in later times Bowen of *Llech-Meilir*, whose heiress eventually married a Scourfield of Moat, in whose house the property, we believe, still remains. *Rickeston* (now Griffiths) was once the residence of a scion of the house of Sir Rhys ap Thomas, Lord of Dinefawr, whose grandson married the heiress of Perrott, o$_f$ Scotsborough, near Tenby, and removed thither :—" I was told," says Fenton, " by some of the old inhabitants, who had heard it from their fathers, that in that court [of Rickeston] had often been seen three or four coaches-and-six at a time, and the family were known to attend the parish church of Brawdy in such an equipage,"—a glory which, with some others, has long departed from the said church! *Poyntz Castle* (now Griffiths), a name derived from *Castrum Pontii* (perhaps a Roman castelet, the mound of which still remains), was a grange belonging to the see of St. David's, where the grain of the district was granaried for the bishop's benefit, and his servants and cattle kept.

Beyond the picturesquely situated little town of *Solva*—a name corrupted from St. Elvis (W., St. Eilyw),—a rustic church hard by, is *Llanunwas* (Harries); and nearer St. David's, *Trevaccoon* (George Harries, Esq.; see also *Harries of Rickeston Hall*). *Cryg-glas* (now Thomas) was also a residence of a branch of the Harries family. The parish of St. David's, and parishes immediately adjoining, include an extensive tract of flat, stony land, shallow in soil, and to a proverb bare of trees, but eminently productive of corn, and settled upon by numerous opulent farmers, themselves often owners of the land they cultivate. *Cwmwdig*

(Howells); *Trenyfed,* properly Tre-Ednyfed (T. Nicholas, Esq.); *Llanrian* (Williams); *Longhouse* (Lloyd), may be mentioned. Tre-Ednyfed, recently rebuilt, has many indications of an ancient place; but who "Ednyfed" was who gave it his name is unknown.

Further to the north-east, on one of the small tributaries of the West Cleddeu, are *Llanstinan* (formerly Symmons, then Owen), *Heathfield* (J. H. Harries, Esq.), *Priskilly* (late Harries), *Letterston* (C. H. Allen, Esq.), *Trecwn* (Rev. C. H. Barham); and near the sea, in the old comot of Pencaer, *Tregwynt* (late Richard Llewellin, Esq.); *Manor-Owen* (Moses Griffith, Esq.); and *Trenewydd* (John James, Esq.); in the pretty valley of the Gwaen, *Glynamel* (J. Worthington, Esq.), the residence of the Fenton family, of which Richard Fenton, Esq., the topographic historian of Pembrokeshire, is the best known. Further up, under the shadow of Precelly mountain, lie the ancient mansion and estate of Cilcyffeth, otherwise called "Cilyceithed" (Fenton), and more anciently "Cilgynffydd" (*Dale Castle MS.*), now faded into obscurity, but at one time holding supreme sway in this district as the patrimony of the family of *Dafydd Ddu* (the black), described by Fenton as "kings of the mountains," which ended in three co-heiresses, between whom the estate fell and was divided, the Cilcyffeth portion going with one of them by marriage to the Barlows of Slebech, thence to the Hamiltons, and thence to the Grevilles. In the same sunny vale is *Pontfaen* (R. E. Arden, Esq.), formerly the residence of the Laugharnes, removed from Orlandon. *Morville* and *Gelli-gelynen* are mansions in the same district, turned for more than a century to common uses; and the same may be said of *Cronllwyn,* said by Fenton to have been a favourite spot of Sir William Martin, Lord of Cemmaes, who married a daughter of the "Lord Rhys" of the princely line of South Wales (see "*the Lord Rhys,*" and "*Barony of Cemmaes*").

If here we mount in imagination the summit of *Precellyu,* (*bre,* a hill, *selu,* to espy), Pembrokeshire, with scarcely an acre wanting, lies open to the astonished view. We are 1,754 feet above sea level, and all around, from Cardigan and the silvery winding thread of the Teivi to St. David's Head and Ramsey Island, the bay of St. Bride's, the jagged coast from Talbenny to St. Ann's, the Danish-named and Viking-looking isles of Skomer and Skokham, the branching and peerless *Hoven,* to Tenby and Caldy Island, like a map the whole county lies before you, as it were laid out on a table of sea. We saw it on an afternoon not to be forgotten, when the shadows of the setting sun were long, and the roseate sky shed its wondrous radiance over scores of miles of the placid channel, whose gentle play seemed to utter delight at the glory which covered its face.

Near Newport, where the Norman pitched his tent and built his castle, to overawe and possess the cantref of *Cemmaes,* are *Llwyngwair* (James B. Bowen, Esq.), and *Cwmgloyne* (M. W. Ll. Owen, Esq.). Nor is it possible here to omit the name of *Henllys* (now occupied by Mr. Harries), in the old mansion of which, long wholly disappeared, resided a long line of an honourable family (ancestors on one side of the Lloyds of Bronwydd, &c.), among whom is always mentioned with pleasure "*George Owen of Henllys, the antiquary.*" (See *Lloyd of Bronwydd; Owen of Henllys.*) Nearer Cardigan are *Pantsaison* (J. T. W James, Esq.), *Trevigin* (Major T. A. Jenkins), and *Pantirion* (R. D. Jenkins, Esq.). In the extreme north-east corner of the county, and in the fair and fertile lands of the Teivi basin we find an assemblage of mansions of the gentry, whose number in so small a space is quite remarkable, especially when we remember that the Cardigan side of the river is almost as thickly studded with similar seats. Here are *Clynfyw* (Major Henry Lewis), *Ffynonau* (John

Colby, Esq.), *Cilwendeg* (M. A. Saurin, Esq.), *Pant-y-deri* (Thomas Colby, Esq.), *Rhos-y-gilwen* (Colby), *Pentre* (A. H. S. Davies, Esq.), *Cil-rhiwiau* (Sir T. D. Lloyd, Bart.), *Castle Maelgwyn* (Mrs. Gower), and *Glandovan* (R. F. Gower, Esq.). The country around is truly beautiful, as is every part of the basin of the Teivi from Lampeter to the sea; the cultivation is almost everywhere unexceptionable, and an appearance of general comfort and competency prevails among the population.

The little valley of the Nevern, from *Eglwys-wrw* to the sea, is in its measure capable of competing with that of Teivi for its pretty scenery. The Nevern draws its waters from three tributaries, one coming from the Precelly hills, one from the direction of Llantwood, and the third from beyond Eglwys-wrw. In the space intervening between the two latter is situated the ancient forest of *Pencelli*, belonging to the lord of the sub-barony of Eglwys-wrw,—for we are to remember that though now a humble village merely, having no known distinction in

FFYNONE: THE SEAT OF JOHN COLBY, ESQ. (*from a photograph*).

modern times except having given birth to the late Rev. Caleb Morris, in ancient times Eglwys-wrw witnessed the pomp of the feudal baron and all the paraphernalia of developed chivalry. The seat of the Norman Lord of Cemmaes was Newport Castle, and Eglwys-wrw was constituted one of five sub-baronies, and conferred on David Martin, Bishop of St. David's, son of Sir William Martin, third successor of *Martin de Tours*, the Norman conqueror of Cemmaes. The manor-house was at *Court*, a place about half a mile from the village, now scarcely retaining a vestige to hint at its former greatness, but which in the time of George Owen of Henllys (*circa* 1591), still wore some of the tatters of its lordly drapery. "I have seen there," he says, "huge walls, and rounes of greate breadth, all environed with a strong and deepe moate, digged out of the main rock, fed with a fresh springe, rising in the same, and all the greens thereabout growne with chamomile." Within the manor, as already said, the lord of the place had a wood called "Pencelli Forest." This contained, in George Owen's time, about five hundred acres, enclosed in quickset hedge and paling of about four miles and three quarters in circumference. Oaks of two hundred years old were then growing there, with underwood, hazel thorns, and willows, and herbage that would "summer thirty breeding mares, and winter three hundred sheep and two hundred cattle well and sufficiently, besides swine which might be kept there." The forest contained "thirteen glades," which in Queen Elizabeth's time were valued at only *ten shillings!*" Pencelli Forest still exists, but in rather diminished dimensions, and certainly of greatly augmented value.

Section II.—THE GEOLOGY OF PEMBROKESHIRE.

Speaking generally, the two extreme western points of Wales, Pembrokeshire and Anglesey, assimilate to each other in geological structure more nearly than they do to any other of the thirteen counties. Pembrokeshire is like Glamorgan in possessing a large development of the coal measures and old red sandstone, but notably differs from it in possessing the Lower Silurian *Llandeilo* group, of which its main body is composed, with considerable intrusions of igneous rock, and in being wholly destitute of the Permian and new red sandstone. In all these points it agrees with Anglesey, and in most of them with Carnarvonshire. The same primitive features are encountered if a line is drawn northward, in Scotland, or westward at right angles with it, in the south of Ireland.

The three chief series of strata in Pembrokeshire are—1. The *Llandeilo rocks*, which compose nearly the whole of the county from the Teivi and the Carmarthenshire boundary westward to the river Cleddeu, and, with certain interruptions, to the channel, and southward as far as the line roughly marked by the positions of St. Clear's, Narberth, Haverfordwest, and Haroldston. 2. The *carboniferous* strata, generally indicated by the coal mining operations from Saundersfoot and Begelly in the east to Littlehaven and Newgale on the western coast, and commanding an irregular breadth averaging about three miles. 3. The *Ola rea sandstone*, composing nearly the whole of Castlemartin and Roose hundreds together with a large tract stretching from St. Clear's to the sea at Pendine, and elongated westward in diminishing breadth until it terminates at a branch of the Haven near Slebech. This is but a continuation of the great old red sandstone field of Herefordshire and Breconshire, which sinks into a trough of many thousand feet deep to contain the coal beds of Monmouthshire, Glamorganshire, and Carmarthenshire, and after serving the same office in Pembrokeshire proceeds across the Irish Channel, and reappears to form a large tract of country on the south of Ireland.

In addition to the above, Pembrokeshire contains a large development of carboniferous limestone, stratified *Cambrian* beds, and *igneous rocks*, stratified and eruptive. The carboniferous *limestone* associated stratigraphically with the coal beds, is now geographically in many parts widely separated from them, as on the southern coast of Castlemartin, where they form the lofty and precipitous cliffs of St. Gowan's, the Stack Rocks, and Linney Head, and in a band stretching east and west from Caldy Island to Pembroke and the mouth of the Haven; and another, parallel to it, from Tenby, where it forms the Castle Hill and basis of the town, to the Haven at Pater, and other places. This is the useful rock which yields lime to the agriculturist in the various ports of Pembrokeshire and other counties. The *Cambrian* group presents itself, irregularly mixed with purple beds, &c., along the coast from the creek of Cwm-mawr to Porthllisky, near St. David's. These purple beds are quarried at Trefgarn Owen and Troedyrhiw, and yield good building stone. They are also found near St. David's, and were much used in building the cathedral.

In the Precelly range, in the heights of Pencaer and St. David's, and in the Trefgarn and Plumstone and other rocks we encounter *igneous* stratified masses of great extent; and at St. David's Head, Ramsey Island, Skomer Island, Talbenny Cliffs, and in a strip several miles in length eastward from those cliffs, there occur *eruptive* igneous rocks, unstratified, of great thickness.

Section III.—HISTORY AND ANTIQUITIES OF PEMBROKESHIRE.

The annals of Pembrokeshire, though in a general sense divided into epochs corresponding with those of other parts of Wales, in a more specific sense have characters and periods of their own. Through British, Roman, and Saxon times, Pembrokeshire—*Dyfed*, as then mostly called—differed in little from the various districts of Western Britain, all populated by Cymric clans, divided into small sovereignties, and governed by their own hereditary princes. These princes were generally engaged in a pastime of war among themselves, busily reducing their own resources and power of resistance. In due course, accordingly, the independence which from time immemorial their forefathers had enjoyed was rudely disturbed, gradually exchanged for feudal subjection under the English kings Edgar, Alfred, and Athelstan, further curtailed under the Conqueror, Rufus, and the Henrys, and totally annihilated under Edward I. In all these phases Pembrokeshire shared, in the general sense mentioned, the like fate with all *Gwynedd, Deheubarth, Gwent,* and *Morganwg* or N. Wales, S. Wales, and the lands of Monmouth and Glamorgan; but from William Rufus to Henry VIII. it had a mixed history of its own, which assimilated, but still only in part, with the history of the Marcher lands of Glamorgan, Brecknock, and Montgomery.

Pembrokeshire *history*, scientifically partitioned, would have these three leading divisions:—1. The British Period. 2. The Norman Period. 3. The English Period

British Period.

For the British period the history of Pembrokeshire and all Wales is left very much at the mercy of legend and poetic fancy; but we have, even along this shadowy track, a few glimpses at bare and real history for at least 1,800 years. We know beyond doubt that the country was inhabited by the old Britons when the Romans subdued Britain. At that time Pembrokeshire, with parts of Cardigan and Carmarthen, went under the name *Dyfed*, which the Romans imitated in their *Dimetia*, at the same time calling the people *Dimetæ*. In later times this designation was applied to all three counties together, and still more recently to our county alone, as fortune, moulded by war or alliance of the princely houses, determined. We hear obscurely in the native records of Brochmael and other kings of Dyfed in Roman times. Asser of St. David's, a writer of authority (ninth cent.), informs us that when he was invited to the court of Alfred, Hemeid, King of Dyfed with all the region of Dimetia, forced by the violence of the six sons of Rhodri (the Great), had placed themselves under the protection—no doubt in the sense of a mild feudal subjection—of King Alfred. We also hear of Meurig, King of Dyfed. On the division of Wales by Rhodri the Great, Cadell, one of the "six sons," became ruler of *Deheubarth* (S. Wales), containing at least *Dyfed*, *Ceredigion* (Cardigan) and *Ystrad Tywi* (Carmarthenshire), and the country, eastward as far as the Tawe, in Glamorgan. Howel Dda, son of Cadell, in 907 succeeded to this same district and to Powys, both of which he ruled in the entire absence of war for many years. In 940 he became ruler of all Wales. Of his code of laws, &c., see at p. 229 *et seq.*

The tread of the *Roman* on Dimetian soil was, for so iron a heel, comparatively so light and harmless, that for Pembrokeshire we need not have a Roman "period." As Cæsar never saw or dealt with any part of Britain west of the Severn, the Roman conquest of Dyfed, if such superiority as was here exercised can be termed a conquest, was probably brought to pass between the subjugation of the Silures under Caractacus by Ostorius, A.D. 50 and the recall of Agricola, A.D. 85, but possibly at a much later date. Of Roman doings in Pembrokeshire we know extremely little. That they overran the county, and made roads across it from end to end, is witnessed by the *Itinerary* of Antoninus and by remains of their roads and stations here and there to this day observable. From Carmarthen (*Maridunum*), their chief city west of Caerleon (see *Caerleon*), they made a road direct to St. David's, having a station at *Ad Vicessimum*, near Ambleston; and to meet this at St David's they made another, known more recently by the misnomer *Via Flandrica*, coming from the *Via Occidentalis* (called *Sarn Helen* by the Welsh), which passed from Carmarthen for North Wales through the vale of the Upper Teivi, having a station at Llanio (*Loventium*), —see p. 254. This road travelled for St. David's, across Precelly mountain, by Cil-rhedyn, Priskilly, Croes-gôch, and Waun-y-beddau.

The *antiquities* of the British and pre-historic period are numerous in Pembrokeshire. Chief amongst them may be mentioned the great *cromlechs* of Pentre-Evan, near Felin-dre; Llech-y-dribedd, between Newport and Cardigan; one at Tre-llys, in Pencaer; one at Longhouse, near Mathry; another at Manor-bier, near Tenby. Cromlechs of lesser size are also found, if not destroyed, at Newton, Castlemartin; *Llech-faen* (now usually pronounced Lloch-faen), near Solva. At St. Dogmael is one of the finest *Ogham* stones in the Principality, a narrow slab of porphyritic greenstone such as is known in the Precelly Hills, semi-columnar in form, and seven feet long, tapering upwards from twelve to nine inches in width, and in average thickness about seven inches. Stones of this sort are prized by farmers for gate-posts, and two holes in its side show that to such service this ancient monument was at one time converted. It also served as a foot-bridge across a brook for generations. Afterwards it was removed into a wall, upon the pulling down of which it fell and was broken in two pieces. It was only then that its character became fully known. On one side it bears the inscription,—SAGRANI FILI CUNOTAMI, which had been noticed before by Camden; but on the edge, thanks to the hard and solid nature of the stone, remain still legible and even sharply defined the ancient "Ogham" indentations, which give the reading *Sagram ni maqi Cunatami, i. e.,* "Sagram, a warrior, son of Cunatamus." The only other Ogham stone in Pembrokeshire is at Bridell. An account of both may be seen in *Arch.*

Cambrensis, 3rd Ser. VI., pp. 128 and 314. (See on the *Ogham Alphabet* and *Stones*, p. 155, *ante*.)

The *caers* and *camps*, the *tumuli* and ancient *graves* of Pembrokeshire are very numerous. Of *ecclesiastical* antiquities, also, there are many, but these are all cast into shadow by the most ancient and best known of them, *St. David's Cathedral*, now in course of costly restoration. Of this historic pile, as venerable as ill-placed for the service of the diocese, it is impossible here to attempt an account; and this is the less necessary, as the valuable work of Messrs. Jones and Freeman is so generally known to readers of these pages.

Norman Period.

A new and distinctly marked period opens in Pembrokeshire with the coming of the Normans. We know the men who act, the posts they occupy, the castles they build, the families they found. The epoch is remarkable, full of incident, of social, political, and racial change. It annihilates the rule of the native princes and lords, fills half the county with a mixed but alien people (see *Flemings*, hereafter), treads to the dust the rightful owners of the soil, presents a long march of martial power, baronial magnificence, luxury, and proud contempt, and leaves behind it in the ruins of its mighty fortresses a symbol of power, and power fallen, such as have seldom been equalled. The story of these fortresses is in fact the story of Pembrokeshire for the space of four hundred years or more—from William the Red in 1090 to the 27th year of the eighth Henry, when Wales was completely united to England.

As the *ancient divisions* of Dyfed were settled anew by the last Llewelyn during the Norman period, and assist to illustrate the various settlements, they can here be fully noted. They consisted of seven *cantrefs*, each having three *comots*, and it will be seen that the cantrefs, in the main, are followed in the modern division into *hundreds*.

Ancient Cantrefs.	Ancient Comots.	Modern Hundreds.
CEMMAES	Is Never Uwch Never Trefdraeth	KEMES.
DAU-GLEDDEU	Amgoed Pennant Efelfre	DUNGLEDDY.
PEBYDIOG	Pebidiog Mynyw Pencaer	DEWSLAND (*Dewis-land*).
RHÔS	Hwlffordd Castell Gwalchmai Y Garn	ROOSE.
PEN-FRO	Penfro Coed-yr-hâf Maenor-Pyr	CASTLE-MARTIN.
AR-BERTH	Penrhyn-ar-glais Esger Olef Tal-lacharn	NARBERTH.
EMLYN	Uwch Cych Is Cych Llefether	CILGERRAN.

HISTORY AND ANTIQUITIES: PEMBROKE CASTLE.

It is scarcely necessary here to remark that the word *cantref* (*cant*, a hundred; *tref*, an abode, settlement) signified a district roughly estimated to contain one hundred houses or abodes,—in an enlarged sense a "settlement" grown into a village; and that *comot* (*cwmmwd*—*cyd*, together; *bod*, to be, dwell) meant, a "neighbourhood," probably not strictly defined, but small enough to admit of acquaintanceship and those mutual neighbourly amenities and services which go far to constitute a unity,—hence the word *cymmydog*, "a neighbour," one with whom we acknowledge a tie of neighbourly relationship, like the Latin *vicinus*—one living near, of the same *vicus* or village.

It is very observable in the history of the Norman domination in Pembrokeshire how carefully they kept their hands from violating *Pebydiog*—a land which had assumed a sacredness in their eyes, plunderers though they were, through its having been assigned for many ages to the tutelage of St. David. They called it emphatically "Dewi's-land" (David's-land), as the Welsh in later times called the cathedral church of St. David's, *Ty-Ddewi*—"David's abode." While *Cemmaes*, Rhôs, Penfro, nearly all Daugleddeu, and Arberth were overrun with fire and sword, and then possessed, not a finger was laid upon sacred Pebydiog, for it was the patrimony of David and the Church. This cantref, therefore, was not affronted with alien settlers, and its inhabitants to this day are a specimen of the *Cymric* breed as pure as any in Wales, and perhaps not even Brittany can produce a more unadulterated sample of the *Celtic* race. The three hundreds of Cemmaes, Cilgerran, and Dewsland, with some half-dozen parishes on the margins of Daugleddeu (Dungleddy) and Narberth are properly, and for 600 years have continued the "Welshery" of this county (*Pembrochia Wallicana*), the remaining parts being the "Englishery"—known since the age of Camden, who baptized it as *Anglia Transwalliana*, "Little England beyond Wales."

The first and chiefest place pounced upon by the fell Norman was Pembroke, and here he built one of his mightiest castles. The site of this stupendous pile, inferior only to Caerphilly (see *Frontispiece*, and pp. 533—39) and Caernarvon (see pp. 328, 329), and one or two others in the kingdom, is believed to have been a British stronghold prior to the arrival of Arnulph (otherwise Arnold) de Montgomery, but neither in the *Annales Cambriæ* nor other reliable chronicle do we find any definite account to that effect. The site is a limestone rock some forty feet in elevation, projecting into the water between two diminutive creeks, washed on three-fourths of its margin by the tide, and forming the end of the ridge upon which the town of Pembroke has been built. The plan displays all the arrangements of a mighty fortress, with projecting towers, bastions, portcullises and drawbridges, walls in many parts fourteen feet in thickness, and a circular tower or keep rising from the interior (seen the highest object in the view), of enormous strength and dimensions—the part which snugly encased the garrison which gave Cromwell so much trouble, and was only reduced at last by famine and thirst. If viewed from one of the neighbouring eminences, or better still from the water, and imagination builds the walls, towers, and turrets to their accustomed height, capping the circular keep (on the authority of old Leland, with a huge millstone for a roof—"the toppe wherof is kevered with a flat mille-stone"), the scene is grand and inspiring to a degree. But perhaps the effect is even greater if imagination, except to recall its story, leaves the region as it is, rearing its gigantic form, now broken and crumbling, in bold and defiant protest against the merciless devastations of time and storm. A sense of wonder creeps over the mind at the character of times and usages which required such artificial mountain fortresses to shelter and save from speedy vengeance "the legitimate owners of the soil," and at the hetacombs of men slain in attack and defence under such frowning battlements, and the scenes of fire and blood, the din of whizzing arrows, clashing swords, and strokes of heavy battle-axe on helmet and cuirass, and of cries of vengeance

PEMBROKE CASTLE.

and of suffering, which are wrapped up in the story of liberty grappling with tyrannic might at such a place!

Arnulph de Montgomery, son of that Roger de Montgomery whom we have seen ensconcing himself in a similar robber's nest at that town which afterwards bore his name (see p. 789) in 1090, or thereabouts, received a *carte blanche* from King Rufus to seize and possess himself of any district in Wales he might covet and was able to take. He was to hold it from the king during good behaviour. Arnulph had a discerning eye, which glistened as he looked out on that beauteous Milford Haven and the fat red sandstone lands which on either side, like a bordure of purple and gold, enfolded it. He fought for and won the land, and on this rock built his eyrie. But of the extent and strength of this first Norman fortress we have no information. To become what at last it became would require many years and successive possession; but it is believed that in the few years which Arnulph and his immediate successor, Gerald de Windsore, remained masters of Pembroke Castle, the fortress assumed much of the shape which it ever after presented. It is hard to believe that Arnulph only erected here "a slender fortress with stakes and turf," as is said by Giraldus Cambrensis—language that would rather apply to the earlier stronghold of the British possessor.

Gerald de Windsore, a younger son of the Saxon Walter, Castellan of Windsor, and ancestor of the Geralds and Fitzgeralds, succeeded to Pembroke Castle by gift of the king; having already been of service as sub-lieutenant under Arnulph, and having slain Owen, son of Cadwgan ap Bleddyn, chief Lord of Cardiganshire—then called *Ceredigion*. While master of this castle he greatly strengthened it. Giraldus Cambrensis relates (*Itin.*, xii.) that immediately on the death of *Rhys ap Tewdwr*, Prince of South Wales, and sworn foe of the Normans—an event which must have occurred in 1091 or 1092 (see pp. 232-4), Gerald had to sustain a terrible siege in this castle as lieutenant or steward to Arnulph, who had gone to England. On this occasion, however, he proved himself a man of sagacity and good mettle. One night during the siege, when his case had almost become desperate, the garrison from the length of the siege being reduced to the utmost want of provisions, the governor caused four hogs which yet remained to be cut into small pieces and thrown down to the enemy; and on the day following, having recourse to a still more subtle stratagem, he contrived that a letter, sealed with his own signet, should be found, apparently accidently dropped, before the house of Wilfred, Bishop of St. David's, then by chance in the neighbourhood, "stating that there would be no necessity of soliciting the aid of Earl Arnulph for the next four months to come." These things being made known to the besiegers, the siege was at once raised. Arnulph was dismissed after about a year's possession, and Gerald was appointed to the lieutenancy.

Soon after this, Gerald married the frail Nesta, dau. of the late Prince Rhys ap Tewdwr, (see account of Nesta, p. 146), and removed to the domain of Carew, her dowry, of which castle we shall treat hereafter.

The De Clares, Gilbert and Richard, Earls of Pembroke, entered this place under the high designation of *earls*, the former in 1138, the latter—the conqueror of a part of Ireland—in 1149, whose daughter and heiress, Isabel, married William Marshall, who in her right succeeded as Earl of Pembroke in 1189. His line continued till 1245, when it became extinct. There were after this Earls of Pembroke bearing the name of Valence for two generations, and Hastings for three generations, when the castle and lands fell to Humphrey Plantagenet, youngest son of Henry IV., summoned to Parliament as Earl of Pembroke and Duke of Gloucester in 1414—1446. Then came William de la Pool, whose estates were forfeited on his demise, 1450. Jasper Tudor, son of Owen Tudor, founder of the Tudor dynasty, obtained the earldom of Pembroke in 1452; and it was here, in 1456, that Henry, Earl of Richmond (son of Jasper's brother, Edmund Tudor), and afterwards Henry VII., was born. Jasper's attainder took place in 1461, when his estates were forfeited. The earldom was next conferred by Edward IV. upon William, Lord Herbert (see Lineage, *Herbert of Llanarth*), the first person of British blood who had held Pembroke Castle since the time of Rufus. William Herbert was beheaded at Banbury, 1469, and was succeeded by his son William, who died without an heir, and the earldom reverted to the Crown. Herberts again came into possession, 1551, by favour of Edward VI., who created Sir

William Herbert, K.G., of Ewias, Earl of Pembroke, and Baron Herbert of Cardiff (see *Bute, Marquess of*), but the former title carried no estates, the jurisdiction and ancient revenues and lands of the earldom being retained by the sovereign. The earldom still continues in the Herbert line, and is now vested in George Robert Charles, thirteenth Earl of Pembroke, of Wilton House, Salisbury, *b.* 1850.

During the wars between Charles I., and his Parliament, Pembroke Castle stood its last siege and burning, when it required all the energy and force of Cromwell to compass its subjugation. In June, 1648, the intrepid general, himself a Welshman by paternal descent (see p. 589), and not ill-acquainted with the martial qualities of the hot "Church-and-King Britons" whom he had now to quell, marched hastily from Chepstow for Pembroke, eager and resolved to bring Major-Gen. Laugharne, Col. Poyer, and Col. Powel to their senses, or to something worse. But implements for the battering of such a place are not at command. June 9th, he orders the blast-furnaces of Carmarthen to melt iron and make "shells for our mortar-pieces," with some "D cannon-shot and some culverins," to be sent with all possible speed. Hugh Peters, that useful man to Cromwell, goes across to Milford, and from the *Lion*, a Parliament ship riding there, gets "two drakes, two demi-culverins, and two whole culverins," and conveys them to the *Leaguer*. With these scanty machines an essay is made to batter and storm, but not with success. June 14, the general writes to Speaker Lenthall, " They begin to be in extreme want of provisions, so as in all probability they cannot live a fortnight without being starved;" "last night we got two little guns planted, which in twenty-four hours will take away their mills;" "last night we fired divers houses, which fire goes up the town still;" "confident I am we shall have it in fourteen days by starving," says the fell man. His calculations however, were rather hasty.

June 28, the castle not yet taken, but progress through hot energy making, Cromwell writes to General Fairfax, " The country since we sat down before this place has made two or three insurrections, and are ready to do it every day; so that what with looking to them," &c., things are bad enough. Not till July 11, 1648, is Oliver able to announce to Speaker Lenthall, " The town and castle of Pembroke were surrendered to me this day." Most of the garrison are allowed to surrender on terms, but the three leading men above-named are obliged to surrender at discretion. They are expressly "excepted" on these grounds:—
" They are such as have formerly served you [the Parliament] in a very good cause, but being now apostatised, I did rather make election of them than of those who had always been for the king, judging their iniquity double." The Parliament, however, decides upon sparing some two of them, and they have to draw lots for life. Three pieces of paper are supplied, on two of which is written, " Life given by God,"—the other is a blank. Poor Colonel Poyer—"drunken Poyer," as Carlyle calls him—draws the blank, and is shot in Covent Garden.

Carew Castle, which comes next in natural order in the Normanic history of Pembrokeshire, had its origin as a palace-fortress in the marriage of the above-mentioned Gerald de Windsore with Nest, daughter of Prince Rhys ap Tewdwr, of Dinefawr. This marriage was one of policy, as we are told marriages sometimes even in our own civilized and Christian times continue to be. Gerald knew his difficulties, and knew that Nest, though a concubine of Henry I., as the daughter of a Welsh prince would conciliate the Welsh to his person and rule, and as a large heiress would usefully add to his narrow fortune.

On a spot already called *Caerau*, "the fortified camps," he builds his castle, afterwards by helpless foreign tongues pronounced *Carew*. Caerau was one of the demesnes belonging to the princes of Dinefawr, and, as would seem, had along with other lands been given as her

CAREW CASTLE—FRONTING THE CREEK.

dowry to Nesta. The extent of the first erection is not known, but it is certain that additions were made to it at different periods. The character of the architecture in the superb front facing the creek pronounces it to be late—probably of the time of Sir Rhys ap Thomas's

CAREW CASTLE—INTERIOR.

possession. For more than 350 years the castle of Carew and its extensive lands remained in the direct descendants of Gerald de Windsore, who, however, as early as the third generation had assumed the surname "De Carew," from their estate. The last possessor of this name, Edmond Carew, sold or mortgaged it in the fifteenth century to the celebrated Sir Rhys ap Thomas, Kt. of Dinefawr (see *Rhys ap Thomas*), who was proprietor of the lordship of Dinefawr (attempted for a time to be called "Newton"), Carew, Llansadwrn, Cilsane, Emlyn, Cilcenin, Aberayron, Llanrhystyd, Narberth, Llangybi, and two or three others; but on the unjust and cruel attainder of his grandson, Rhys ap Gruffydd ap Rhys, who had married Catherine Howard, daughter of Thomas, Duke of Norfolk, his estates were forfeited to the Crown. Carew was leased for a term of years to Sir John Perrott, a court favourite, and to others, the remainder of whose leases, according to Fenton, were purchased by Sir John Carew, a remote descendant and heir of that Sir Edmond Carew who had mortgaged the castle to Sir Rhys ap Thomas. His great-grandson, Thomas Carew, who died 1774, left only two daughters, co-heiresses, one of whom having died unmarried, the survivor, Elizabeth, married James Bernard, Esq., after whose death Carew Castle reverted to the Carew line, formerly known as Carews of Crowcombe Court, Somerset, where they are still settled. The Carews are not known to have resided at Carew Castle since the time when the place was battered down by Cromwell in 1644 (when Sir John Carew had garrisoned it for the king), but the property still continues in the family.

It is not from its position, which is but a slightly raised rock on one of the arms of Milford Haven, that this magnificent ruin gains any of its charms. The scenery around is quiet, the ground slopes gently to the water, and the shore close under the walls is often muddy and forbidding. But the colossal size of the mouldering pile, and the elaborate character of the architecture are sufficient, without the accessories of beetling cliffs and mountain solitudes, to excite attention and wonderment. Our first engraving shows the powerful towers and bastions, tapering from their foundations and containing elegant chambers, and the long ranges of finely mullioned and traceried square windows (the work probably of the fifteenth century) which lighted the great state apartments; and the second engraving clearly defines some of the features of the interior in archway and oriel window, niche, doorway, and ascending steps. When Fenton figured this castle in 1810, the battlements along the whole front were nearly perfect; since then the central bastion and tower, with the great bay-windows they enclosed, have fallen, and several breaches made by time— the leisurely but most powerful of all agents of destruction—have assisted to change a great palatial façade into the appearance of an ancient but exquisite ruin.

Sir Rhys ap Thomas is said to have built the projecting bastions and great windows, and to have much enlarged and decorated the state apartments. A chimney-piece with finely wrought Corinthian columns is among the more recent decorations, and the interior in other parts displays a mixture with the Gothic of the classic style. The later additions, though strong, are not so colossal as the ancient parts, as if the builders were already conscious that the age of barbarism was passing away, and quieter times were approaching. The great banqueting-hall, 102 feet long, with proportional width, in decorated Gothic highly ornamented, must have been a superb apartment, for even the defaced and broken remains of it are still beautiful. Over the gateway are the arms of England, of the House of Lancaster, and of the Carews.

HISTORY AND ANTIQUITIES—SEAL OF RICHARD, PRINCE OF WALES.

It was in consequence of the conquest of Pembroke by Arnulph de Montgomery that the county of Pembroke was ultimately constituted a county *palatine*. As such it had a chancery and other courts of its own held in the lord's castle, and was thus of higher dignity than any other county in the kingdom except its palatine compeers of Lancaster, Chester and Durham. The palatinate character of Pembrokeshire was ultimately taken away; Henry VIII., when he created new counties for Wales, made them all of the same level, and fully united the thirteen counties to England (see p. 755). The princes of Wales of the Plantagenet line had their chancery for South Wales at Carmarthen. At pp. 244—246 an account is given of the chancery *seal* of South Wales; but the discovery of that seal, or a cast of it which was considered a great rarity, has been now succeeded by a still more interesting discovery, viz., the seal of Richard, Prince of Wales, son of the Black Prince. It was figured in 1684 in the *Progress* of the Duke of Beaufort already repeatedly referred to (see pp. 740-41), and is transferred to our pages by kind permission of his Grace the present Duke of Beaufort, who has recently privately printed the *Progress*. The workmanship, clearly too good for the fourteenth century, must be ascribed in part to the skill of the

SEAL OF RICHARD, PRINCE OF WALES, A.D., 1376.

modern artist; but the charges on the escutcheon—the arms of France and England quarterly, with the former "fleurs-de-lis semée" (not "three fleurs-de-lis," as in the later seal of Prince Henry, described at p. 245), the arms known to have been borne by Richard II. as well as by Edward III. and the Black Prince, are demonstrably correct. So is the label of three points. The inscription running round the seal—SIGILLUM RICARDI PRINCIPIS WALLIÆ, DUCIS CORNUBIE, COMITIS CESTRIE, PRO OFFICIO SUTH WALLIE, carries several marks of genuineness in the Latinity of the Plantagenet period, seen in the terminations "Cornub*ie*," "Cestr*ie*," "Wall*ie*," and the mongrel "Suth."

The account of the finding of it is thus given in the *Progress*:—" The procurement of the view of a seale of green wax of Richard, Prince of Wales, I ow to the civility of . . . Gent., Under Sheriff of this county [Carmarthen]. It was fastened to a deed with a silken labell woven of yellowe and red, bearing date thus,—' Kaermerdyn, 16 Aprilis, in the 7th year of his reign, annoque Domini 1376.'" It is further stated with respect to the other side of the seal:—" He is represented on the face side in armour, on horseback, with his sword chains in one hand and shield and bridle in the other, in his surtout, and his horse caparizon'd, which, with the shield, are all charged with quarterly France, semée of flower de luces, and England, a labell of three poynts " (comp. p. 245).

In the close vicinity of Carew Castle, as if erected by some of the early proprietors—but possibly existing long ages before *Caerau* became Carew,—is still standing an exquisite CROSS, formed of one piece of stone. No inscription is legible. It has a cross pattée in a circle at the top, and diminishes in breadth as it approaches the pedestal, which is simply powerful masonry enclosing the basis of the stone. The surface is divided into panels, all of which are wrought with interlaced devices similar to those of the ancient crosses so numerous in Ireland.

Ancient Cross at Carew.

Two great events took place at Carew Castle during its occupation by Sir Rhys ap Thomas—his entertainment there of the Earl of Richmond after his landing at Dale in 1485, and the tournament (the first exhibited in Wales) held there in honour of Sir Rhys's admission to the Order of the Garter after Richmond had become King Henry VII.

We have already (pp. 240—244) narrated the distinguished part taken by Sir Rhys ap Thomas in placing the Tudor on the throne. On his way from the place of landing, where he was allowed to "pass over Sir Rhys's body" to Bosworth Field, the Earl tarried a night at Carew Castle, and, losing no time, pushed on through the heart of the country, receiving everywhere accessions to his hosts of adherents of those brave men of South Wales who turned the tide of battle at Bosworth. The second night he was entertained by Dafydd ap Ieuan at Llwyn-Dafydd, Llandyssilio-Gogo, Cardiganshire, and so pleased was Richmond at his reception that on his accession he sent as a present to Dafydd ap Ieuan a *hirlas*, or drinking-horn, chased and mounted in silver, with heraldic devices of much beauty. Its supporters are the greyhound of the Llwyn-Dafydd arms and the dragon of Cadwaladr. It stands eight or nine inches high, and is about sixteen inches in length. Having become the property of the Earl of Carbery during the civil wars, it thus came to Golden Grove, where it still remains.

The engraving we give of this interesting relic is copied by permission of the Duke of Beaufort from the *Progress* of his ancestor, written in 1684, and must be taken as representing the *hirlas* as it then was and the workmanship of the period; but it differs slightly from the illustration supplied by the Earl of Cawdor to Dwnn's *Heraldic Visitations of Wales* (1846), —and which is exactly reproduced at p. 881—in having more silver chasing, armorial bearings, and a more elaborate stand, while it is less skilfully shown in perspective. When the Carmarthenshire part was printed this very beautiful illustration was not at command.

THE HIRLAS HORN OF HENRY VII. (*from the Beaufort "Progress"*).

Another memento of Henry VII. is in the possession of E. P. Lloyd, Esq., of Glansevin co. Carmarthen. It is a silver *flagon* presented by the king, in 1485, to Einion ap Dafydd Llwyd, an ancestor of Mr. Lloyd who dwelt at Wern-newydd, parish of Llanarth, Cardiganshire, near Llwyn-Dafydd already mentioned. Tradition relates that Richmond slept a night at Wern-newydd, and the room and bed he used are still shown there, with an inscription on the wall commemorating of the event. It is scarcely probable that under the circumstances the earl would have staid a night at two places so near each other.

When Henry was firmly seated on the throne, he added to the many distinctions he had already conferred on Sir Rhys ap Thomas the honour of the Garter, and Sir Rhys to celebrate the occasion held a grand tournament and "feate of armes" at Carew. The account of this event carries us back to strange times, customs, ideas, and reveals the men who in Wales were of chief consideration. In the *Memoir* of Sir Rhys, printed in the *Cambrian Register* (1796), is a long description of the celebrations, from which we learn that Sir Rhys ap Thomas made publication of a "solemn just and tournament," the fame of which being blown abroad, "manie worthie and valerouse gentlemen of his blood, some to do him honour and some to make triall of their abilities in feates of armes, came unto him from all partes of Wales." They flock in on their caparisoned chargers, Herberts, Perrotts, Wogans, Butlers, Gruffydds, Morgans, Dunns, Vaughans (of Tretwr), Jenkin Mansell, "the valiant" (of Oxwich); from North Wales, Griffith, son of Sir John Griffith, Lord of Llansadwrn, and young Wynn of Gwydir, "two hopefull gentlemen of good towardlinesse, and with them the lustie Robert Salisburie, a man noted for his greate strength of bodie, a fast friend and companion of Sir Rhys in many of his warlike adventures."

These men of "prime ranke" were all lodged within the castle. For some 500 more, "moste of them of goode ranke and qualitie," tents and pavilions were pitched in the castle park. This festival and "time of jollitie" continued through the space of five days. On St. George's Eve it began, when Sir Rhys took a view of all the company, choosing out 500 of the tallest and ablest of them, dividing them into five troops, and placing each troop under the direction of a captain. The second day was occupied in exercising the troops in the field "in all points as if they were suddenly to goe on some notable service." The third day the drummers beat up, the trumpets sound, and the whole host comes forth as in battle array, "well armed at all points." They march to the bishop's palace at *Lamphey* (now a ruin, whose owner has not the taste to show it decent respect), a mile or thereabouts distant from Carew, "bidd goode morrowe to the bishoppe in the language of souldiers with arquebusses, musketts, and callivers;" the bishop having with him the abbot of Talley [for a glimpse at the character of bishop and abbot, see p. 242] and the prior of Carmarthen, "all with rich capes," after some mock parley, "the business being so ordered aforehand," give entrance to Sir Rhys; the bishop ascends to the high altar, reads divine service, new hymns are sung "for the reste of St. George's soule, and his safe deliverance out of purgatorie."

On the return of the cavalcade to Carew a grand solemnity of dining takes place, bishop and abbot being of the company; the "sewer" for the time being the entertainer's son, Sir Griffith ap Rhys, "who had binn bredd up at coorte, and had some advantage of the others in point of curialitie and courtlinesse;" Sir William Herbert of Coldbrook is the carver, and "young Griffith of Penrhyn the pocillator or cupbearer." Music goes on; "hautboies and other wind instruments weare not silent;" the bishop says grace; the dinner begins; health of king, queen, and prince are "often drank;" bards and prydydds accompanied by the harp sing many a song; after the entertainment "they walke abroad and take the fresh aire of the parke," and lastly, in the chapel, "heare solemne service."

Next day, the real day of joust and tournament, Sir William Herbert's challenge to all comers, four to four, "for the honour of ladies" is presently accepted by Sir Griffith Rice, Sir Rhys "on a goodlie steed, in fine gilt armour, two pages on horseback before him with a herauld," &c., is judge of the jousts. The trumpets sound, and the knights present themselves for the conflict, each with his device and motto displayed. "The two first combattants putt their launces into their restes, and soe rann each theire six courses. In like sorte followed the reste," and the rest—to the end of the brilliant tournament. "Sound knockes you may be sure were receaved and returned on both sides, butt noe harme at all done."

At supper, Sir Griffith ap Rhys, in the presence of his father, makes challenge to Sir William Herbert, four to four at the ring next morning, for a supper which the losers should pay for at Carmarthen for their farewell at parting. The challenge was accepted, and the loser by his father, Sir Rhys's judgment, was Sir Griffith ap Rhys—a thing "agreed upon beforehand," as the careful narrator tells us, "that soe he might show his friendes the towne of Carmarthen before they went away." Carmarthen must have been a fine place in those days! After dinner Sir Rhys ap Thomas gives his guests a hunt in the park, where "they killed divers buckes" destined to be consumed at the Carmarthen supper.

This supper at Carmarthen—*where* there we should be glad to know—ended this memorable and unique tournament, a strange medley of healthful and knightly pastime, religious farce, and chivalric gallantry, wherein " one thinge " our conscientious chronicler declares, " is note-worthie, that for the space of five dayes, among a thousand people there was not one quarrell, crosse worde, or unkind looke that happened." Early in the morning before they parted, we should also observe, " the bishoppe bestowed a sermon upon them tending to all loyall admonitions, obedience to superiors, love and charitie one towards another." His text was out of Eccles. x. 20, " Curse not the king, no, not in thy thoughte, and curse not the rich in thy bedd-chamber,"—a text and subject fully explained by the political crisis referred to at p. 242 *ante*. Hugh Parry was Bishop of St. David's when this tournament took place, but as the date of his appointment is generally given as Sept. 19, 1485, he was possibly not the bishop of St. David's who figures in consultation with Sir Rhys ap Thomas about the duty of joining the Earl of Richmond, and it is difficult to say who was *de facto* bishop of St. David's in the early part of 1485.

MANORBIER CASTLE.—EXTERIOR (*from a photograph by Bedord*).

Manorbier Castle, the birthplace of Giraldus Cambrensis, and home and patrimony for some time of his family, though probably owing its origin to a Norman settler of the eleventh century, was not prominently associated with the sanguinary deeds of the Anglo-Norman conquest of Pembroke, as some of the other castles ; was never, as far as is known, subject to a siege ; and was not laid in the dust by violence. William de Barri, the father of Giraldus, was first possessor of his line of the manor. His father, a Norman or Anglo-Norman, had assumed the name from the little island of *Barry*, on the coast of Glamorganshire where he had first settled. William de Barri took up his abode at " Maenor-Pyr," as Giraldus spells it, in the reign of King Stephen, a few years only before the birth of Giraldus (1146). He married Angharad, daughter of Gerald de Windsore, of Carew Castle, already mentioned, by Nesta, his wife, daughter of Prince Rhys ap Tewdwr, by whom he had

Giraldus and other sons. The estate continued in this family till the time of Henry IV., who in his first year (1399) granted to John de Windsor, in fee, the manors of Manorbier, Penally, and Begelly, and all other lands held by David de Barry in Wales; so that the continuance of the De Barris at Manorbier was not much over two hundred and fifty years.

The best account of this interesting spot is that which has been left in the words of the enthusiastic archdeacon himself, whose native place it was, and whose exaggerative language touching its character may be pardoned. The present walls were not those within which he dwelt, but the magnificent scenery in earth and sea was the same then as now, with the difference in its favour that the castle, though humbler, was surrounded by park, orchards, gardens, and all the concomitants of a baronial hall of the secondary class, while at present

MANORBIER CASTLE.—INTERIOR.

the village has an impoverished look, the park, woodland, orchard, lake, and fishpond have disappeared, and a bald landscape capping magnificent rocks, and sloping down by the castle ruins to a lovely little cove, crescent-like and sandy, is all that remains.

Giraldus, writing in the year 1188, gives us a graphic account of "Maenor-Pyr," as it then was. Of his attempt at etymology we only need say that nothing is really known of the element "Pyr," or "Byr," in the name, while "Maenor" is plainly the same as Manor. "The Castle of Maenor Pyr, that is the mansion of Pyrrhus, who also possessed the island of Caldy, which the Welsh call Ynys Pyr, or the island of Pyrrhus, is distant about three miles [in modern measurement five miles] from Pen-broch. It is exceedingly well defended by turrets and bulwarks, and is situated on the summit of a hill extending on the western side towards the sea, having on the northern and southern sides a fine fishpond under its walls, as remarkable for its grand appearance as for the depth of its waters ; and a beautiful orchard on the same side, bounded on one part by a vineyard and on the other by a wood, remarkable for the projection of its rocks and the height of its hazel trees. On the right hand of the promontory between the castle and the church, near the site of a very large lake and mill, a rivulet of never-failing water flows through a valley, rendered sandy by the violence of the winds. Towards the west, the Severn sea, bending its course towards Ireland, enters a hollow bay at some distance ; and the southern rocks, if extended a little farther towards the north, would render it a most excellent harbour for shipping. From this point you will see almost all the ships from Great Britain, which the east wind drives upon the Irish coast, daringly brave the inconstant and raging waves. This country [Dimetia] is well supplied with corn, sea-fish, and imported wines; and what is preferable to every other advantage, from its vicinity to Ireland, it is tempered by a salubrious air. Dimetia, therefore, with its seven cantrefs, is the most beautiful as well as the most powerful district of Wales, Penbroch the finest part of the province of Dimetia, and the place I have just described the most delightful part of Penbroch. It is evident, therefore, that Maenor-Pyr is the pleasantest spot in Wales, and the author may be pardoned for having thus extolled his native soil, his genial territory, with a profusion of praise and admiration." Giraldus's logical demonstration, we fear, will not stand scrutiny, but this will not invalidate the fact that Manorbier Castle is a most picturesque ruin, and has an interesting if not a romantic history.

Giraldus Cambrensis himself, after all, constitutes the chief interest attached to Maenor-Pyr, although he was probably dead before the actual castle whose ruins we now depict was built. He was grandson of the puissant Prince Rhys ap Tewdwr, of Dinefawr, and had a strong attachment to Wales. Paternally he was descended from a foreign race, and often in ecclesiastical matters displayed a strong leaning antagonistic to Welsh ideas. He was strongly superstitious, active in habit, eloquent in speech ; travelled to Italy, and in Ireland ; traversed Wales north and south, in company with Archbishop Baldwin of Canterbury, anticipating modern Methodistic custom, " preaching the Cross," with the difference that preaching the Cross in Giraldus's case included, as a main element, inciting the youth of Wales to enlist as soldiers under the banners of the Crusades. He wrote, while Archdeacon of Brecon, works of considerable extent and of extreme value, couched in graphic style, full of fact and anecdote, in tolerable Latin, and only marred by occasional exaggeration and frequent displays of excessive credulity. His ambition to become Bishop of St. David's, thwarted long by King Henry, seemed at last destined to be gratified. In 1198 he was chosen a second time by the chapter of St. David's to be their bishop ; but the Archbishop of Canterbury—not his old crusading companion, Baldwin, who was now dead, but Hubert Walter—opposed the measure, on the ground that to appoint a Welshman to the metropolitan see of Wales would be fraught with danger to the supremacy of the English. Giraldus was set aside, and Geoffrey de Henelawe, a Norman, was appointed in 1203, after a stormy interregnum of four years, during which Kings Richard and John promised, temporized, and refused; the Pope listened to appeals and oracularized; and Giraldus uttered wrathful and biting words, which led to his being declared an enemy of the Crown, and to the seizure of his lands. He made his peace, however, with the king, and recovered his property, and on the death of Henelawe in 1215 the see of St. David's was again offered to him ; but he was now sixty-nine years of age, tired of care, toil, and controversy, and declined the post. He lived some eight years longer, but how employed, and how his strenuous and energetic life toned down to the final rest, is not known.

A little to the interior is St. Florence (old *Tre-goyr*), a decayed village prettily situated, once the resort of "Tenby merchants," when Tenby was "a great trading mart," and in earlier times having in its vicinity an extensive deer-park belonging to the Earls of Pembroke, some traces of the boundaries of which are still discernible. Leland, who passed here *circa* 1540, says, "Coming from Llanfeth [Lamphey ; *Llan-foi* = "St. Faith "] towards Tenby, I rode by a ruinouse walle of a parke sometime longing to Sir Rhyse [Sir Rhys ap Thomas, who, however, had died in 1527], now voide of deere." Further on towards Tenby is "Trefloyne" (old *Tre-llwyn*), formerly the home of a branch of the Ap Owens (Bowen—see *Bowen of Llwyn-gwair*) of Pentre-Evan, in Cemmaes. In the civil war it was garrisoned for the king, and formed the head-quarters of the Earl of Carbery, but being invested by the Parliamentarians, "after some battery and forcing of an outhouse," it surrendered, and "there were found there forty good horses ready saddled and bridled, and 150 men." *Scotsborough*, another historic house, has been already noticed.

TENBY—TOWER OF ANCIENT GATEWAY.

Tenby, now a jaunty and fashionable watering-place (already partly described), was better known to our forefathers as a trading and fishing port of no small importance, and "a metely waullid burg," with strong gates, defended on two sides of the promontory on which it picturesquely stands by precipitous cliffs meeting in a point at the Castle Hill (which cuts the sea and shelters a cove for the shipping), and connected landward by powerful walls running at right angles to each other and to the cliffs, thus forming a nearly rectangular site. The walls, greatly strengthened in the time of Elizabeth, and still partly remaining, were high and powerful, and from the description given of one of the gates by Leland, who wrote before Elizabeth's improvements, they must have been fitted for stubborn defence even before her time. He says of the "west gateway" that it was "the seemliest," as "circuled on the outside with an embattiled but open rofid tour,"—which exactly corresponds with the Gateway Tower in the *engraving* just given. An inscription commemorative of the Elizabethan restoration is still visible in the wall,—"A.D. 1588, E. R. 30."

As to the name *Tenby*—a bone of contention among etymologists,—the key to its explanation is the old Cymric *Dinbych* (probably *din*, a fortified hill, and *bach*, small), precisely the same as the Dinbych (Denbigh) of the North, and meant originally to mark the smaller rock of the Castle Hill as compared with the larger one of St. Catherine, which then may have been connected with the mainland. In the *Annales Cambriæ*, A.D. 1154, it is called *Dynbech* and *Tinebeth*.

TOWER—SOUTH PARADE.

Of the time of the first building of Tenby Castle, or whether it was the work of Flemings or Normans, or both, nothing is certainly known. It is clear that it existed in 1152, for it was taken in that year by the sons of Gruffydd ap Rhys, when one of them, Cadell, was severely wounded (*Annal. Cambr.*, *sub* 1154); and was reduced and destroyed by Maelgwyn, son of the Lord Rhys, in 1186. Nothing is more probable than that such a rock as the Castle Hill had been occupied as a place of strength by the Britons before Norman or Fleming, or even Saxon or Dane, had afflicted Dyfed; but beyond some mystic shadowings in a Welsh poem, *Mic Dinbych*, in the *Myvyr. Arch. of Wales*, we have no reference to it in such early literature of the country as has come down to our time.

During the Plantagenet and Tudor periods we hear not much of Tenby except as a place of trade; but in the troubles of Charles I. and his Parliament the town was a post of great importance. In March, 1644, "Col. Rowland Laugharne proceeded to attack Tenbigh, where Commissary Gwyn was governor, and made a resolute defence, but after three days' battery, a great part of the town being beaten down, it was taken by storm." In 1648, when Cromwell came to the siege of Pembroke, the reduction of Tenby was entrusted to Col. Reade, who succeeded in taking the place on the 2nd June. The resistance, however, had been stubborn, as may be supposed from Cromwell's letter of the 21st of May to Parliament:—" The reducement of Wales is more difficult than expected, the town and castles of Pembroke and Tenby being equal to any in England, and well provided of all things" (*Fenton*, p. 370). This is the last we hear of Tenby as a warlike fortress. It then became as distinguished as "Dinbych y Pysgod" (Fish-Tenby) as it is in our day as "Tenby the Delightful."

The limestone rock of these parts is famous for its caves, as those of Lydstep,—cool and romantic retreats for the Tenby summer visitants—but it is more to our purpose to notice here the *bone caves* of Caldy Island, wherein some years ago were discovered great quantities

NARBERTH CASTLE (*drawn by Birket Foster*).

of bones of animals of an early period, denizens too of a climate much warmer than our present climate, such as the *Elephas primigenius* (mammoth), rhinoceros, tiger (*Felis tigris*) the hyena, as well as the bear, the deer, the wolf, the fox, pig, sheep, &c., from which two conclusions are legitimate and obvious,—first, that all these animals were in past time natives of Britain ; and secondly, that Caldy Island, during the lifetime of such of those animals as lived only on dry land, was not an island, but was connected with the mainland. Little or no light, however, has been thrown by these explorations on the question of the "antiquity of man" in these parts. The remains of the *priory* on Caldy Island are a memorial of Robert de Tours, who in the time of Henry I. founded the establishment as a cell to St. Dogmael's.

At *Narberth* (W., *Ar-berth*, "above the wood," spelled Arberth in the *Annales Cambriæ* as early as A.D. 1116) was a castle of great antiquity, planted in a bold and picturesque situation, and commanding an attractive though limited prospect. It is related that on the descent of Arnulph de Montgomery upon Pembrokeshire in 1092, he gave a portion of the usurped territory around this spot to a knight in his train of the name of Stephen Perrott. This man is not said to have built a castle at Arberth, but to have provided for himself a temporary place of strength on an elevated spot between Arberth and Templeton, and in the midst of a deep forest. Of this place Fenton says that in his time some slight vestiges stil appeared. But there was a castle at Arberth in 1219, for Llewelyn the Great burned it (*Annal. Cambr.*). Stephen Perrott was fortunate in marrying Eleanor, daughter and heiress of Meirchion ap Rhys, of Iestynton (now Eastington, and popularly called *Isseson*), in Castle-martin, who was not "grandson," as Fenton says, but direct descendant in the *sixth* degree of Iestyn, Lord of Iestynton, grandson of Howel Dda, whereby he obtained a large accession to his lands, and the shortest means of conciliating the natives, having married into the princely line of Howel the Good. His son, Sir Andrew Perrott, was the builder of Narberth Castle *circa* 1246. He married in that year Janet, daughter of Ralph, Lord Mortimer, created Earl of March. The castle was afterwards the possession of the Mortimers, Earls of March, and from them passed to Richard, Duke of York. In time it fell to the Crown, and was in the eighth of Henry VIII. given to Sir Rhys ap Thomas, "in recompense for his good services in the wars, as well in England and Wales as beyond seas done." Not long after Sir Rhys's death Leland describes it as "a praty pile of old Sir Rhees's," and adds, "there is a poor village, and by it a littel forest." The castle was inhabited as late as 1657 by a gentleman of the name of Castell, an adherent, it is believed, of the Commonwealth for the castle had, as usual with the castles of Wales, sided with the king, been worsted by battery, and got into the hands of the parliamentary leaders. Capt. Castell had raised the ire of the men of Tenby, who petitioned the king (Charles II.) to the effect that he had "during the time of usurpation" set up a market at the "village" of Narberth, to the detriment of the "loyal town of Tenby." Narberth Castle and manor became the property of the Barlows of Slebech, and continued in that estate.

Lawhaden Castle.—This name has assumed various shapes, and it seems difficult to decide which is the best. Llewhaden, Lawhaden, Llanhawaden, Llanhuaden, have all been tried, with the result that modern choice has settled upon Lawhaden—furthest of all from the true etymology. The name of castle and village of course followed that of the church close by, so that the first syllable, *Llan*, is presumably settled. The church was said to be dedicated to *St. Aeddan*, and if so, Llan-Aeddan is the genuine and original form of the name. This would easily slip into Llan-aedan, or Llan-aden; but it required the aid of dark times and ingenuity of strange tongues to bring it into Llan-huadain, or Lawhaden. With the last form, however, we must for the present rest satisfied.

Lawhaden Castle, although a bastioned and moated place, was never in fact a military fortress, and was not destroyed by warlike attack. It was, on the contrary, a sumptuous episcopal palace, a place therefore of peace. But it was made strong by reason of the wealth it contained in days when the Bishop of St. David's was a territorial baron, living in great pomp and circumstance, when insurrection and conflict were frequent, and the abodes of the Norman chieftains and all their friends and supporters—which the Bishops of St. David's generally were—were subject to attack from the Welsh princes and people. The barony of Lawhaden had been given the Bishops of St. David's from an early time, and in virtue of this possession they were summoned to sit in parliament.

The castle stands on an elevation overlooking the wooded and pretty valley of the Cleddeu. It was built of hewn, closely jointed stone, with square-headed mullioned and labelled windows dressed with freestone, and was entered by a drawbridge and a great doorway surmounted by a magnificent semicircular arch, flanked by two powerful circular towers. The builder's name is not certainly known, but Bishop Thomas Beck (appointed in 1280),

LAWHADEN CASTLE.

who founded the *hospitium* whose ruins are close by, is thought to have begun it. The style of architecture of the front elevation betrays, however, a later date. Bishop Gower (1328), though a great builder, is not mentioned as having enlarged it; but Houghton (1361), who preferred it as a residence even to the magnificent palace at St. David's, added greatly to its buildings. Bishop John Gilbert (1389) resided and died here; Bishop Edward Vaughan (1509), a man of sumptuous taste, built the beautiful chapel of the place. It appears that with Vaughan ceased the addition of ornament and pride at Lawhaden Palace. In 1536 came Bishop William Barlow, who, in the plain language of Richard Fenton, "thought of nothing but translation to a better see, and enriching himself *per fas et nefas*, while he continued to wear the mitre of St. David, stripped the castle of Llewhaden and palace of St. David's of their leaden roofs, as well as all his other palaces of everything that could be converted into immediate profit, to furnish him by the dilapidations he himself had occasioned with a plea for removing the see to Carmarthen." Archbishop Abbott in 1616 authorized Bishop Milbourne to demolish Lawhaden Castle, and also " the hall, chapel, cellar, and bakehouse belonging to the palace of St. David's; in short, to perfect what Barlow had begun." But this entire demolition was prevented by the translation of Milbourne to Carlisle, and thus the fine walls of Lawhaden Castle have been left to cope as best they can with time, the elements, and the sacrilegious road-maker and hovel-builder; trees now grow in the courtyard, and spring from the rubbish-covered floors of saloon and boudoir ; the fine park which surrounded it is defaced and deforested, and the red deer park belonging to it at Llwydiarth, which existed as late as the time of Leland, is no longer known.

Whiston Castle (W., *Castell Gwys*) was the residence of a Norman settler of the name of Wiz, the daughter of whose grandson, Sir Philip Gwys, married the Welshman, *Gwgan* ap Bleddyn, from whom emanated the family of *Wogan* of Wiston, Picton, &c. Wiston was the head place of the Norman barony of *Dau-gleddeu*—a name already existing in that of the British *cantref* situated between the two rivers *Cleddeu*. Standing in the open country towards the mountains it was exposed to frequent attack during the raids of the Welsh princes into the territories of the Norman settlers. Cadell and his brother, sons of Gruffydd ap Rhys ap Tewdwr, assisted by Howel, son of Owain Gwynedd, demolished it in 1146— "Castellum Wiz destruxerunt" (see *Annal. Cambr.*, 1148); in 1193 Howel Sais, a son of " the Lord Rhys," surprised and captured Wiston, whereupon the Flandrenses and Franks of Pembroke attacked the town of *Llanwaden*, then in his hands, but failed in the attempt and returned in disgrace—" cum opprobrio" (*Annal. Cambr.*); but about two years later the " Flandrenses " succeeded in recapturing Wiston Castle (*ib.*, 1195); in 1220 Llewelyn the Great of North Wales, having made way against the Normans in North and South, and given peace to the Flemings or "Flandrenses" of Dyfed, on their swearing allegiance to him, when they violated the oath, razed the castle of Wiston to the ground, putting the garrison to the sword. After this Wiston Castle became an unimportant fortress, and gradually fell into decay. Gwgan about this time married the heiress, and as a Welshman, being at peace with the native princes, established at Wiston a family of great respectability and long continuance in Pembrokeshire. (See *Wogan of Wiston, Picton, Boulston.*)

Haverfordwest Castle, perched on a rock overlooking the western Cleddeu at its junction with a smaller stream, was a place of magnitude and great strengh. The spot, already a settlement of the Welsh, was seized upon by the Flemings on their introduction into the county (see *Flemings*), and made their chief post to defend the territory assigned them in Rhôs. It was well situated for the purpose right between that tract and the free mountains whence danger was to be apprehended, and also on the tidal river Cleddeu. The building of Haverfordwest Castle is attributed to Gilbert de Clare, first *Earl* of Pembroke, father of Richard (Strongbow) Earl of Pembroke, conqueror of Ireland. He is believed to have resided alternately here and at the castle of Pembroke. The date of the erection may be placed about the year 1112 or 1115. Giraldus Cambrensis tells us that in 1188 he and Archbishop Baldwin visited " Haverford" on their preaching tour, that " a sermon was preached by the archbishop," and " the word of God preached by the archdeacon," namely himself, —a distinction, we trust, without a difference,—and both the præternatural sensibility of the

Haverfordians and the eloquence of the archdeacon are by implication extolled in the assurance that, "wonderful and miraculous as it might appear, although the archdeacon addressed them both in the Latin and French tongues, those persons who understood neither of those languages were equally affected, and flocked in great numbers to the cross" (*Itin.*, xi.). At the castle a strange circumstance happened in those days: "A famous robber, confined in one of its towers, by stratagem, got three boys,—one the son of the Earl of Clare, another the son of the governor of the castle, into his hands in a bolted room, and threatening them with instant destruction, obtained indemnity and liberty on condition of sparing them."

The lordship and castle of Haverford were given by De Clare to his castellan, Richard Fitz-Tancred, whose son Robert was called Richard *de Hwlffordd*, a designation which shows

HAVERFORDWEST CASTLE.

that "Hwl-ffordd" was the old name of the place among the Welsh. The lordship was next vested in King John, who bestowed it on Walter Marshall (*circa* 1241), from whom it descended to the De Breoses, De Bohuns, &c., and was tossed from owner to owner for many years, until, like Pembroke, it came to Jasper Tudor, then to Henry, Duke of York, and finally to the Crown, where it has since continued.

Owen Glyndwr invested this castle, but had to retire without success. During the civil wars it had a garrison in defence of King Charles's cause, under command of Sir John Stepney; but they were half-hearted in the work, and evacuated the place. Cromwell having reduced Pembroke was not inclined to allow so strong a castle as that of Haverford to remain a danger behind him after his return. Nor was he inclined to go to the cost of bringing cannon from Pembroke to demolish it. The following letters under command of the general to the Mayor, &c., of Haverfordwest, and that functionary's replies, are historically interesting as well as full of character and suggestiveness. They are found in the Haverfordwest Archives. (See also, Carlyle's *Cromwell*, iii., 404.)

"*To the Mayor and Aldermen of Haverfordwest.*—We being authorized by Parliament to view and consider what garrisons and places of strength are fit to be demolished; and we finding that the Castle of Haverford is not tenable for the services of the State, and yet that it may be possessed by ill-affected persons, to the prejudice of the peace of these parts : These are to authorize you to summon in the hundred of Roose and the inhabitants of the Town and County of Haverfordwest ; and that they forthwith demolish the several walls and towers of the said Castle, so as that the said Castle may not be possessed by the enemy to the endangering of the peace of these parts. Given under our hands, this 12th of July, 1648 [the next day after the fall of Pembroke].

"ROGER LORT, JOHN LORT.
"SAMSON LORT, THOMAS BARLOWE."

"We expect an account of your proceedings, with effect, in this business, by Saturday, being the 15th of July instant."
[And the general himself, to prevent all parley, adds :—]
"If a speedy course be not taken to fulfil the commands of this warrant, I shall be necessitated to consider of settling a garrison.

"OLIVER CROMWELL."

The meekness of the following reply is remarkable, considering that the "castle" had hitherto been virtually Haverfordwest :—

"*For the Hon. Lieut.-Gen. Cromwell at Pembroke.*—Honoured Sir, we received an order from your Honour and the Committee for the demolishing of the Castle of Haverfordwest ; according to which we have this day set some workmen about it ; but we find the work so difficult to be brought about without powder to blow it up by, that it will exhaust an 'huge' sum of money, and will not in a long time be effected. Wherefore we become suitors of your Honour that there may a competent quantity of powder be spared out of the ships, for the speedy effecting the work, and the county paying for the same. And we likewise desire that your Honour and the Committee be pleased that the whole county may join with us in the work ; and that an order may be considered for the levying of a competent sum of money on the several hundreds of the county, for the paying for the powder and defraying the rest of the charge. Thus being over-bold to be troublesome to your Honour—desiring to know your Honour's resolves, we rest your Honour's humble servants,—

"JOHN PRYNNE, *Mayor.*
{ JENKIN HOWELL, WILLIAM WILLIAMS.
  WILLIAM BOWER, JOB DAVIES.
  ROGER BEVANS, ETHELDRED DAVIES."

"*To the Mayor, &c.*—Whereas upon view and consideration with Mr. Roger Lort, Mr. Samson Lort, and the Mayor and Aldermen of Haverfordwest, it is thought fit for the preserving of the peace of this county that the Castle of Haverfordwest should be speedily demolished : These are to authorize you to call unto your assistance in the performance of this exercise (?) the inhabitants of the hundreds of Dungleddy, Dewisland, Kemis, Roose, and Kilgerran ; who are hereby required to give you assistance. Given under our hands this 14th of July, 1648.

"OLIVER CROMWELL."

So fell quickly, by the aid of the inhabitants of five hundreds, the great castle of Haverfordwest. The keep, and certain other parts, however, were not demolished, and have since been of better service to the county as a county gaol.

The *Priory* at Haverfordwest, near the river-side below the town, of which there yet remain considerable ruins, was founded and liberally endowed by Robert de Hwlffordd, the second lord of Haverford Castle after the De Clares. It was a priory of Black Canons, dedicated to St. Mary and St. Thomas the Martyr, having endowments consisting of advowsons and tithes of several parishes in the barony. At the dissolution of "religious houses" in the time of Henry VIII., its annual revenue was £135 6s. 1d. (Speed), and was granted to Roger and Thomas Barlow of Slebech. The appearance of the site, with its mounds of ruins scattered over a wide extent of ground, gives evidence of the great dimensions and importance of the place when in its prime. The church was a spacious cruciform structure, 160 feet in length by 80 feet at the transepts, at the intersection of which there arose a massive tower supported by elegant pointed arches. It had an existence of about 350 years, when its tower bell resounded through the vale its matin and vesper call, and the slow monks went their measured rounds of devotion and meditation, and potation. It has had 330 years of rest, silence, and decay; and now only a small portion of its walls remains as a monument and a lesson. But all such spots are full of poetry and materials for the imagination. It may be too hard to say in the review—

> " O Monachi, vestri Stomachi
> Sunt amphora Bacchi;
> Vos estis, Deus est testis,
> Turpissima pestis;"

but it is true and charitable to say, with Thomson,—

> " Full oft by holy feet our ground was trod;
> Of clerks good plenty here you mote espy;"

and, taking it all and in all, the old church for its old time was not, perhaps, relatively less serviceable to humanity than is the modern church to the present time. But we cast off old garments, and choose the new.

On a crag in the open and slightly elevated country near the sea between Haverfordwest and St. David's—a district now remarkable for nothing except the poverty of its soil and the depressed and backward condition of its semi-Flemish population—stands the beautiful and romantic structure, *Roch Castle*, so called from the rock (Fr., *roche*) on which it is planted. Beyond doubt, it was built as a post of observation by the Flemish settlers. It sweeps far and wide the country of Pebydiog, then as Cymric and hostile as it could be, as far as the eye can reach, the ridge of Plumstone, and the bay of St. Bride's from the mouth of Milford Haven to St. David's Head. Its rocky site gave name to its earliest possessor known to history, Adam *de Rupe* ("Adam of the Rock"), founder also of Pill Priory, near Milford. The De la Roches in their earliest stages were of the first rank of Norman families, and of great possessions in Pembrokeshire. It appears probable that they had the province (now hundred) of Rhôs (Roose) committed to their care by Henry II., when it had been peopled with Flemings, for one of the family was styled "Comes Littoris," which office was hereditary, and the extent of its jurisdiction was marked by the two castles of Roch and Benton, the latter being on the haven, near Williamston, and nearly opposite Lawrenny. Roch Castle would be exactly suited for the residence of such an official, being in a commanding situation at the upper end of the Flemish province of Rhos, as Benton Castle was at the lower end. Fenton seems to think, from an "inquisitio post mortem" made after the demise of Thomas de la Roche, and mentioning the castle as being then deserted, that it was never since his time inhabited; and he intimates an opinion that Thomas de la Roche lived in the time of the Crusades. But we find from the pedigree of the family in *Dwnn* that there were in that family three of this name, the first and last living five generations apart—the first (probably the "Crusader") living *circa* 1250, for his daughter married William de Valence, for a short time Earl of Pembroke (*d*. 1296); the second about the year 1420. This man died without issue male, and probably was the Thomas meant by the "inquisitio." It is clear, at least, whether the De la Roches dwelt at Roch Castle or not, during these generations, that they continued in the county, and their intermarriages with the Carews, Malifants, Flemings, &c., are evidence of the standing they maintained. The name Roch still lives in Pembrokeshire, but is not traceable to this ancient Norman stock.

Roch Castle, during the civil wars, was put in a state of defence for King Charles I., under command of Capt. Francis Edwards, of Summerhill, but was as early as 1644 surrendered after a sharp siege and burning. The tradition, therefore, that Cromwell attacked it (Cromwell has been traditionally present wherever a castle has been destroyed !) is at fault, because Cromwell only came to this county in 1648, to the difficult task of reducing Pembroke Castle. The castle, never after restored, passed through various hands, and became at last the property of the Stokes family.

Beyond the peaceful region of Dewsland (*Pebydiog*), never desecrated by a Norman *Conquest*—although St. David's was "piously" visited by the great Conqueror himself, and also by his son Rufus, and many a raid was made upon the land by "Franci" and "black pagans,"—lies the old cantref of *Cemmaes*, where the Norman pitched his tent with full and

CILGERRAN CASTLE (*from a photograph*).

effective purpose, built his castles, and took full possession of the soil. Here the castle of Newport and the barony of Cemmaes are the abiding memorials of his presence, and of many dark and sanguinary deeds which that presence occasioned ; and on the margin of the barony the castle of Cilgerran serves the same purpose.

Cilgerran Castle, on the precipitous bank of the Teivi, more admirable for situation than any other castle in South Wales, not even excepting Pembroke or Llanstephan (see *engraving*,

p. 138) was begun, as reasonably conjectured by Roger de Montgomery, father of Arnulph, or Arnold, conqueror of Pembroke. This would probably be about the year 1092, after he had established himself at Montgomery (see *Montgomery Castle*)—but of definite statement on this subject the chronicles supply little or nothing. The position, on a lofty rock at the junction of a smaller stream with the Teivi, here dividing the Lord Marcher territory of Cemmaes from the unappropriated country, and commanding an extensive prospect on both sides the river, would commend itself to the warlike and ever-warring Britons from early times, and such castle-builders as the Normans would not be slow to see its value. Roger de Montgomery's raid into Ceredigion and Dyfed, however, would not detain him long, his territories in Montgomery and Salop were a sufficient care to him; and leaving some of his knights to try their fortune in Cardiganshire, he would be glad to leave a post like Cilgerran—from *his* point of view standing inconveniently beyond the Teivi, and exposed to constant attack from Dyfed. This was an exciting time in Dyfed, Ceredigion, Brecknock, and Glamorgan, as well as in North Wales. The Norman freebooting knights were everywhere busy on the borders, carving for themselves lordships out of the best spots in the lands of the Welsh, and building their castles to protect their ill-gotten gains. Already in Brecknock, Glamorgan, Cydweli, and Pembroke, in Montgomery, Chester, Shrewsbury, and Hereford, they were safely ensconced in their frowning fortresses, and treading on the neck of vassal natives.

The princes of the various provinces of Wales, not yet quite dislodged, but sitting on crumbling thrones of dominions more and more curtailed, sought each the increase of his own power by the destruction of that of the other; not unfrequently the diadem of the father was snatched from his brow by an ungrateful son, and that of brother by brother; or failing this, they plotted against the liberties and independence of their own country by basely aiding the common enemy. Henry I. was determined to perfect the work of Rufus by crushing the Welsh. It was only some three years before Roger de Montgomery's raid that the brave Rhys ap Tewdwr had won the bloody battle of Llechryd against the sons of Bleddyn ap Cynfyn (see pp. 145-6); but in 1092 Rhys ap Tewdwr succumbed to the Norman Newmarch, and before his mighty son, Gruffydd ap Rhys, had fully attained his manhood, South Wales south of the Teivi was at the mercy of the foreigner. In Ceredigion, the other side of that river, the proceedings of Cadwgan ap Bleddyn, lord of the territory, and his son Owain (see p. 146), raised the ire of "the King of London" (Henry I.) to the highest pitch, and now it was that the time for the building of Cilgerran Castle, begun by Roger de Montgomery, came about.

Henry having proscribed Cadwgan, and having no liking for a Welsh campaign himself, gave the lands of Cadwgan to Gilbert de Clare, at the time Earl of Striguil, in Gwent, in case he could conquer them. Gilbert succeeded in the enterprise, and built a castle at Aberystwyth on the northern, and another at Cilgerran (or as called in the Brut, *Din-geraint* —the strong hill of Geraint) on the southern limit of the territory, the spot "whereon Roger the Earl had aforetime founded a castle" (*Brut y Tywysog.*). In the year 1161 or 1162 King Henry in person invades these parts, but at Pencader (*Annal. Cambr.*, 1164) makes peace with the disturber, "the Lord Rhys," who had destroyed many castles. Two years later, however, he gathers a great army for a second invasion, "comes as far as Oswestry," vowing "the expulsion and destruction of all the Britons" (*Brut y Tywysog.*), and all North and South Wales arise in stern defiance. Owain Gwynedd, and Cadwaladr, his intrepid brother, are in the field, followed by all the hosts of Gwynedd; "the Lord Rhys,' and all the South with him; Owain Cyfeiliog and Iorwerth Gôch ap Meredydd, and the sons of Madoc ap Meredydd, and all Powys with them; they mustered at Corwen; Henry advanced on the Ceiriog, near to Chirk, where he had a most narrow escape of his life; and what with terrific storms and floods, constant harassment, difficulty of obtaining provisions and the troubles from A'Becket's proceedings at Canterbury, Henry felt that he had more than enough to do, relinquished the campaign, and sullenly returned "without honour to London" (*Brut y Tywysog.*). In that same year, according to the same authority, did the Lord Rhys bring down wholesale destruction upon the castles of the Normans, amongst others the castle of Aberteivi (Cardigan), which he entered and burnt, and the castle of *Cilgerran*, where he took Robert Fitz-Stephen prisoner (*ibid.*, and *Annal. Cambr.*, ann. 1166). The Lord Rhys held it for many years, and here and at Cardigan Castle, where in 1188 he entertained Archbishop Baldwin and Giraldus with great magnificence (see p. 148), he maintained, although deprived of the title of "prince," a state and splendour equal to those of a king. His death, however, which took place in 1196, again drew a veil of stormy clouds over the prospects of Dyfed and Cardigan, and we find the castle of Cilgerran possessed alternately by the contending native princes, and sometimes by the foreign usurper. Gruffydd, son of the Lord Rhys, inherited it after his father, but we are told, on the generally safe authority of the *Annales Cambriæ* (*ann.* 1201), that his brother, Maelgwyn, who had been disinherited, snatched it from him, and he again in turn was deprived of it by William Marshal, Earl of Pembroke, who allowed the garrison to depart, but "without their arms." In 1214 Prince Llewelyn ap Iorwerth, of North Wales, assisted by several other princes made a desolating raid into the south, overwhelming the Normans in their castles, and taking possession of many chief strongholds not then in their hands. Cardigan and Cilgerran Castles fell before them, as did also those of Cydweli, Llanstephan, and Carmarthen; but the two former they did not destroy (*Annal. Cambr.*).

Llewelyn for a time enjoyed an apparent triumph over the Plantagenets, and all their Lords of the Marches and Lieutenants in Wales (see p. 149). In 1216 he redistributed the princedoms or lordships of South Wales, and gave to Malgwyn, the turbulent and disinherited son of the Lord Rhys, Cilgerran Castle. William Marshal, the second Earl of Pembroke of that name, however, recovered possession in 1222 of this and the other castles which Llewelyn ap Iorwerth had conquered; and so great was the value he set upon this position that he immediately set to work to built a new castle at Cilgerran, on the same site, and probably incorporating parts of the old, and this is the castle whose remains now crown the rock.

From this time forth the castle of Cilgerran for ages remained in possession of the Earls of Pembroke for the time being. In 1258 a great army of Welsh under command of David ap Gruffydd, Meredydd ap Owain, and Rhys Fychan encamped near Cilgerran Castle, and fought a sanguinary battle with a host of English, Normans, and Welsh, under Rhys Gryg and Seneschal Patrick, when at length the Welsh, "Dei auxilio," got the better of the day, the English took to flight, leaving the dead and their caparisoned cavalry horses behind them, and with difficulty escaped into Cilgerran Castle (*Annal. Cambr.*). Lord (dominus) Patric Walter Malifant, the bold soldier of Pembroke, and several other distinguished knights recently come from England, were among the slain. There was no attempt to capture the castle on this occasion; indeed, so great was the strength of the fortress after its renewal by Marshal, and so reduced were the resources of the Welsh, that we hear of no further siege or investment of the place until the Parliament in the time of the civil war attacked and dismantled it. Several minute details concerning its subsequent transference from earl to earl, its lapses to the Crown, its bestowment on Jasper Tudor, Earl of Pembroke, &c., are found in Fenton's *Pembrokeshire*, and in Phillips's *Hist. of Cilgerran*, pp. 88—92, Henry VII. gave the Constableship of Cilgerran Castle to William Vaughan, of the Corsygedol stock (see *Vaughan of Corsygedol*), whose grandson, Rhys Vaughan, says Fenton, "styled of Cilgerran, laid the foundation of a respectable house in the vicinity, Glanddyvan, and married a daughter of Thomas Phaer, Doctor of Physic" (p. 505.) The present owner is Sir Pryse Pryse, Bart., of Gogerddan.

It is worthy of remark that Cilgerran Castle was properly and strictly a military post and fortress, and was in no sense the castle of a Lord Marcher or centre of territorial ownership. It conferred no baronial title, was not held on conditions of knightly service, nor had attached to it any court or jurisdiction. Had it been otherwise the already ennobled family of Gogerddan might one day wear the added dignity of Barons of Cilgerran.

A full description of this mighty ruin and its superb environment of river, rock, and woodland would require too much space, but a reference to the view of the castle given on p. 138, will fully justify the language of Sir Richard Colt Hoare, Bart., who has said, " I have never seen ruins more happily combined with rocks, woods, and water, a more pleasing composition, or a more captivating landscape; . . . a more striking assemblage of natural and artificial beauties can nowhere be met with."

> "Time was—and when the eve breeze whistled by,
> The flap of red-cross banner ye might hear,
> And sound of harp and voice, sweet minstrelsy!
> Like fountain murmur stole upon the ear.
> What floateth now beneath the clear blue sky?
> What music greets the lonely wanderer?
> The rank grass waving from yon hoary wall,
> The sigh of night-winds through deserted hall!"—*Blackwell.*

Newport Castle, though now a more obscure remain, commemorates a far more perfect development of the feudal system than Cilgerran, or even Cardigan and Aberystwyth Castles. Sir Thomas Lloyd of Bronwydd, lineal heir of the Barony of Cemmaes, represents a baronial itle of higher dignity in some respects than even the Palatinate Countship of Pembroke.

The conquest of *Cemmaes* was effected about 1094 by Martin de Tours, a knight who by his name is marked as having originally come from Tours in France. He had settled at first in Devonshire, and came thence to the conquest of this district (see *Baronia de Kemeys*, p. 8). Newport before that time was called only by the name which still clings to it in the Welsh—*Trefdraeth*, and received the new name of Novo-Burgus, since modified into Newport, from the new possessor (*ib.*, p. 10). Martin de Tours, on the conquest being effected, was invested with the usual attributes of a Lord Marcher; he and his successors were summoned to the sovereign's council as barons, holding *in capite* from the English or Plantagenet king; the territory was constituted a lordship marcher, having *jura regalia* and courts of its own, where all matters affecting life and property were tried; and the barons of Cemmaes continued to be "lordes of the Parliamente of England" up to the time when the lordship came by descent to the Audeleys, "whoe of themselves before were lordes of the Parliamente, and soe the place of Kemes was drowned in that respecte. But whiles it contynued in the names of the Martins, the first lordes thereof, and untill it came to the Lorde Audeley they were lordes of Parliament by the name of Lordes of Cemeis" (*Baronia de Kemeys*, p. 24). The third Lord of Cemmaes, Sir William Martin, married Angharad, daughter of the Lord Rhys, and thus the family became identified with the people of the country. Sir Thomas D. Lloyd Bart., a lineal descendant of the Martins, first Lords of Cemmaes, and as such himself lord of the lordship, is quite entitled to claim the name and rank of Baron of Cemmaes—the last Lord Marcher title now subsisting (see *Lloyd of Bronwydd*).

The lordship marcher of Cemmaes, as described by the antiquary, George Owen of Henllys, himself its inheritor, extended along the sea-coast from the mouth of the Teivi to Fishguard, and thence southward by a line nearly direct to St. Dogwell's, where it took an eastern direction, passing Castle Henry, Maenclochog, Monachlog-ddu, to Llanfyrnach, its extreme eastern point, and thence northward, west of *Frenni Fawr*, to the Teivi, below Cilgerran Castle.

The following charter, granted to the town of Newport by Nicholas Martin, fifth Lord of Cemmaes, and last of that name, is interesting as showing the condition of the people and the species of power exercised by a Lord Marcher in the time of King John. The date of the charter is 1215. The language is the dog-Latin of the period.

CHARTER OF THE TOWN OF NEWPORT, A.D. 1215.

"LET THOSE, present and to come, know that I, Nicholas, son of William son of Martin, Lord of Kemes, have given and granted, and by this my Charter have confirmed to my Burgessess of Newburgh all the Liberties and Customs underwritten, which William son of Martin, my Father, to the same did grant and give, that is to say—That they shall have Common of Pasture in my Land and Common, in the Water from the Fosse which encloses the Town Eastwards to the Sea, and Easement of Wood for their Houses and Buildings, and for Firing, by view of the Forester. Likewise, if a Burgess dies of what death soever, unless by Judgment for Felony he should lose his life, I will have nothing of his Chattels, but his Relief, to wit, Twelve Pence. Likewise if a Burgess delivers up any of his Cattle (in charge) to any one, and the same is judged guilty of Felony or Robbery, or shall lose his Cattle, the Burgess, by good and lawful men may prove his Cattle, and have them. Likewise, if a Burgess hath hired Land of any Free Man, and that Free Man infringe the compact, I ought to cause him to hold to the Agreement; in the same manner I ought to compel the debtors of Burgesses of whom they hold bail and witnesses, and make them render their Debts. Likewise, a Burgess accused of any Forfeiture may be repledged by his Neighbours. Likewise, they ought to have a Bailiff and a Common Council for me and them. Likewise, no Foreign Merchant may buy or sell outside (*extra*) of my Borough of Newburgh. Likewise, a Burgess accused of Felony, or Robbery, if he calls on me, I am to defend him, and take upon me to enable him to make a good defence. Likewise, the Burgesses shall not be bound to go in the Army, except as the Burgesses of Pembroke do. Likewise, with the aforesaid Liberties, I have granted to them all the Liberties and good Customs of Pembroke, all which said Liberties I have granted and confirmed to them and their Heirs to be holden and had of me, and of my Heirs, freely and entirely and peaceably; and that this my Donation and Grant and Confirmation may be firm and steadfast for ever, to this Charter and Confirmation I have put my Seal. These being Witnesses—John de Arundel; Jordan de Cantiton; Robert ap Owen; William ap Gwrwared, then Constable; David ap Owen; Henry Goit; William . . .; Howel ab Evan Meredith, Clerk; and many others."—(*Baronia de Kemeys*, p. 50.)

Newport Castle, said to have been founded by Martin de Tours, the conqueror of Cemmaes, is believed to have been completely built by his great-grandson, Sir William

Martin, son of the Sir William who married the daughter of the Lord Rhys, and in the time of King John. We are shut in to this later date by the language of Giraldus, who passed here in 1188, and informs us that at that time the principal castle of Cemmaes was that of Lan-Never (Nevern), which clearly implies that Newport Castle was not then built. The site is a knoll above the town, commanding seaward a wide marine prospect, and landward the magnificent mountainous scenery of Carn Ingli and Precelly. The building, when in its prime, must have been an imposing and powerful fortress-palace, of great extent and ornamentation. The grand entrance from the north was, as usual with Norman castles, between two massive circular towers. There was an inner gate with portcullis. The ground plan of the castle was nearly circular, fifty paces in diameter, and included at least four principal towers, in which were built the great residential apartments. The whole was surrounded with a deep moat, in communication with an abundant supply of water—the " fossato qui claudit villam " mentioned in the Charter—notwithstanding the elevated situation.

We have no details within reach of the vicissitudes through which the castle of Newport passed, nor the manner and occasion of its destruction. The Lords of Cemmaes were generally, since the alliance with the princely house of Dinefawr, on good terms with the natives, and we have no account of their coming into collision with the English king. In the fifteenth century, after the excitement of Owen Glyndwr's insurrection had passed, the Lords of Cemmaes made *Henllys* their principal manorial residence, and allowed Newport Castle to fall into decay; but even long before this time—as early as the time of the great-grandson of Nicholas Fitz-Martin, " Philip Fychan of Henllys," *circa* 1300—they were named after that place.

Nevern Castle, situated on the hill above the village and church of Nevern, formerly called Llan-nyfer, or, as in Giraldus, Llanhever, was of earlier origin than that of Newport. We learn in the *Annales Cambriæ* that in 1191 " Rhys, son of Gruffydd," that is, " the Lord Rhys," having expelled the French from the castle of Newer (Nevern), took possession of it; and the same authority states, under the year 1195, that Howel Sais (one of the sons of the Lord Rhys) demolished the castle and kept the lands in his own hands. The former transaction, or a similar transaction, may have taken place a few years earlier than stated by the *Annales*, for Giraldus in 1188 uses these terms:—" I shall not pass over in silence the circumstance which occurred in the principal castle of Cemmeis at Llanhever in our days. Rhys, son of Gruffydd, by the instigation of his son Gruffydd, a cunning and artful man, took away by force from William, son of Martin (de Tours), his son-in-law [a mistake: William was *grand*son of Martin], the castle of Llanhever, notwithstanding he had solemnly sworn by the most precious relics that his indemnity and security should be faithfully maintained " (*Itin.*, ii.). This castle was at that time, therefore, the residence of the Lords of Cemmaes, for William was the then lord, and it follows that Newport Castle was not yet built. The castle of Nevern was probably never thoroughly rebuilt after its destruction by Howel Sais in 1195.

Henllys, we have said above, had become the chief manor-house of the Lords of Cemmaes since about the year 1300. This was brought to pass by the marriage of the heir of the barony, Philip ap Richard, of Cemmaes, with Nest, daughter and co-heir of Llewelyn ap Rhydderch, of Henllys, from which time Henllys became the seat of the united family. In the days of Fenton the old mansion had already gone to ruin, and now not a trace of it remains. But in digging, the old foundations are sometimes come upon.

St. Dogmael's Priory, near Cardigan, an important institution between the thirteenth and fifteenth centuries, dedicated to St. Tegwel, or Dogfael, was indebted for its establishment to the Norman Lords of Cemmaes, although its first beginning was in British times, and at a place called Caerau, about a mile distant. No sooner had Martin de Tours completed his conquest than he devoted a portion of the wealth he had acquired to the founding of a new monastery, in place of the more humble one hitherto supported by the family of Gwynfardd Dyfed. He was followed in the work by his son Robert Fitz-Martin, who completed it. Martin de Tours and Robert are said to have been both buried in the choir of the abbey. Here it was that Archbishop Baldwin and Giraldus Cambrensis slept a night on their way from St. David's to Aberteivi, where they were to meet, and be entertained by the Lord Rhys (see p. 158). The abbey, on the dissolution of the monasteries by Henry, was given or sold to John Bradshaw, whose descendants for several generations resided there (see *Sheriffs of Pembroke*, 1571). The remains of this monastery and abbey, once so notable and extensive, are very insignificant.

Section IV.—Nationality and Language in Pembrokeshire.

About one-half of Pembrokeshire is occupied by a people of a mixed nationality, speaking a modified English, and usually considered to be of Flemish origin. Hence the name *Anglia Transwalliana*, which Camden somewhat aptly applied to the district, and which has since become current as "Little England beyond Wales." The account usually given of the Flemish immigration, and, as a supposed consequence, of the type of language found in Roose and Castle-martin, although scarcely sufficient to explain all the features of the case, may be taken as correct as far as it goes. In the reigns of Henry I. and his brother William Rufus, we are told, great numbers of Flemings were encouraged or allowed to settle in the north of England, and the reason given for such encouragement is the fact that Matilda, or Maud, wife of the conqueror and mother of Rufus and Henry, was daughter of Baldwin, Earl of Flanders, and that the immigrants had been driven in a state of destitution from their former homes by a great inundation of the sea. Having multiplied and become troublesome in the north, and the Norman settlers in Pembrokeshire at the same time being much molested by the Welsh, whom they had dispossessed of their lands, Henry hit upon the expedient both of relieving the northern districts of a nuisance, and protecting his kinsmen, the Normans in Wales, by transferring the Flemings bodily into Pembrokeshire, giving them a portion of the lands taken from the Welsh for their support, and the duty of "repressing the brutal temerity of the Welsh" as a pastime (*Will. Malmesb. Chron.*, ann. 1106).

But it is to be noted that before the first arrival of these particular Flemings in England, a considerable number of their countrymen had already come over in the miscellaneous multitude of the conqueror's army. William had sent his enticing proclamation to Flanders, as well as other neighbouring states, inviting all who wished for conquest and booty in England to rank themselves under his standards. And Malmesbury tells us that in Rufus's time such numbers of these people had come over that they appeared burdensome to the kingdom. The Flemings first settled in Rhôs, according to the *Annales Cambriæ*, our most reliable chronicle, in the year 1107; and according to *Brut y Tywysogion* (agreeing with Malmesbury), a year or two earlier. We have also intimation in the Welsh *Brut* of another settlement in the same parts in the year 1113; but this was probably only one of the many accessions which at different times before and after were made to the general body.

The notices given are so meagre and general that we can form no clear conception of the composition and organization of these new settlers. No hint is given as to their leaders, if they had any, of the mode of their transit, of the specific spots where they found shelter, or of the conflicts with the natives, whereby, with the aid of the Anglo-Normans, they must by degrees have fought for themselves a home. They were probably a horde of humble industrious people, having no persons of exceptional influence to act as guides or leaders, obeying the command of the king, as feudal discipline and necessity had taught them to do, and placed in their new homes under the military supervision and direction of Norman officials. As part of this arrangement the castle of Roch at one end of their territory, and of Benton at the other (see *Roch Castle*) would be well placed, and here we are told was stationed Adam de Rupe, in whose family was vested the hereditary office of *comes littoris*, "count of the shore," whose functions pertained to the government of the district lying on the sea from Newgale to Milford Haven. Haverford-west was the main centre for trade and defence of the Flemish territory. Giraldus Cambrensis, who flourished within fifty years of their settlement, and must have been well acquainted with their character and condition, describes them as "a people brave and robust; ever most hostile to the Welsh; well versed in commerce and woollen manufacture; anxious to seek gain by sea or land; a hardy race, equally well fitted for the plough or the sword." All this is likely enough to be true, but they seem to have lost some other qualities which, if Giraldus is correct, made them a still more extraordinary race. "These people," he says, "from the inspection of the right shoulder [bones] of rams, which have been stripped of their flesh, and not roasted but boiled, can discover future events, or those which have passed and remained long unknown. They know also what is transpiring at a distant place by a wonderful art and prophetic kind of spirit." Belief in fortune-telling and occult knowledge is still strong in Pembrokeshire.

The Language of the "Englishry."

The facts above given are sufficient to explain the character of the *language* of the Pembrokeshire "Englishry." How the Flemings, who used in their own homes a very different speech, came to speak English, is made clear by their previous sojourn and settlement in the north and other parts of England. How they cast their English into a peculiar mould, and made it a linsey-woolsey fabric of divers strange vocables and articulations, will be at once understood from the mixture of Normans, English, Welsh, and Flemish, which constituted their society. For even Welsh would in time settle among them; and that many English had been brought hither by the policy of Henry and his predecessors (as sagaciously conjectured by the antiquary, George Owen of Henllys) in order "to get rid of them" is not only highly probable, but almost satisfactorily proved by the physical characteristics, the names, and the mixed language of the district.

NATIONALITY AND LANGUAGE IN PEMBROKESHIRE.

"Pembrokeshire English" has peculiar words, peculiar inflexions, idioms, and articulations. It has no words, but "*o*ords;" is not pronounced, but "pron*aaw*nced." Mr. Purnell informs us (*Cambr. Journ.*, 1859), among other things, of a general habit of omitting the auxiliary verb, as "I written" for "I have written;" the vowel *o* is frequently ill-used, "cold" being pronounced "caauld," and "told" "taauld;" the terminal *ow* in "borrow" is sounded "bor*ra*," in "morrow" "mor*ra*;" to "mow" as to "maoo;" "going" is "gwain." The neuter gender is never recognised by the common people, but everything is either *he* or *she*, and the masculine objective is always *n*, "I told him" is "I taauld'n." "How" is universally used for "why." "How did you come" would here have no reference to the manner of coming, but solely to the reason for coming. For "I am not," "he is not," the common expression is "I arn't," "he arn't." A couple does not necessarily mean two of a kind, but most usually usurps the meaning "a few." When a person does a thing "leisurely" he does it "all by lejurs;" one person throwing a stone at another is said to "pile" him: "orra one" and "norra one" are used for "one" and "not one;" a cow addicted to pushing is said to "pilk;" a large piece of bread is a "culf;" a small cake baked is a "cook," boiled it is a "trolly;" an article of good substance is said to have a good "sump" in it; a boon companion is a "scud;" one of stunted growth is "cranted;" one of weak condition of body is "hash;" one whose intellect is impaired is "dotty;" to be stern is to be "dern;" an unworthy person is "a pelt;" to be showy is to be "filty," a woman over-dressed is "filty-fine;" oatmeal gruel is called "budram;" when a person discourses incoherently his address is a "rammas;" to fallow the land is to "velge" it; a furrow is a "voor;" any small meadow is "burgage;" to save water from running to waste is to "vang" it; to cover a fire so as to keep it over night is to "stum" it; to beg is to "kedge," "soul," or "hoggle," and the second means begging at All Soul's time; *man* is used very peculiarly under the form of "men," "no, my good fellow," is "no men;" "answer my lad" is "answer men;" a gap in a hedge is a "slop." Traces of *Welsh* are seen in "cowell," a kind of basket, W., *cawell;* "coppat," the thatch on a mow, or small stack of corn, W., *cap, coppa;* "to freeth," as in Devon, is to wattle, W., *ffridd*, a division, quickset; completely is "rottle," W., *trwyadl*, thorough; to pour is to "hild," W., *hidlo*, to pass through a sieve; a great eater is a "gorral," W., *gor*, much, extreme, and *bol*, belly.

The boundaries of the "Englishry" and "Welshery" in Pembrokeshire are about the same to-day that they were 650 years ago. Roose, Castlemartin, Narberth, and Dungleddy hundreds, a few parishes excepted, were the parts peopled by the strangers in the twelfth century, and those are the parts which constitute the "Englishry" of the county now. In this general sense there is scarcely a parish which can be pronounced to have been lost or won on either side. George Owen, 260 years ago, with perfect knowledge of the subject, writes thus:—"The shire is well neere divided into two partes between the English speeche and the Welshe, for the hundreds of Castlemartin, Rowse, and all Narberth, excepting the parishes of Llandewi and Lampeter, and all Dougledy, excepting the parishes of Lanvalteg, Langain, Landyssilio, Lanykeven, and Crynow doe speake the Englishe, and then the hundreds of Kemes, Kilgerran, and Dewisland speake all the Welsh tongue; so that above seventy-four parishes are inhabited by the Englishmen and sixty-four parishes more by the Welshe, and the rest, being about six, speake both languages, beginning at Cronwere by Carmarthenshire, and soe passeth up to Lanhaden, where both languages are spoken, and from thence between Bletherston and Lanykeven to New Mote, and soe betweene Castle Blythe and Ambleston, and so betweene Trefgarn and St. Dogwell's, and over the hills betweene Hayse Castle, and then turning down Newgall Moore, as the same river leadeth to the sea betweene Roche Castle and bridge, the southern parte of which Lansker speaketh all English, and the Norther side Welshe, well neere, as I sayde before, parting the shire in two equall halves betweene them." (*Camb. Reg.*, ii., 78.)

This description would apply to the present state of things, with this important qualification, viz., that the line of demarcation marks nowhere so distinctly and definitely the parting of languages as it did in George Owen's time. With the march of education the English diffuses itself everywhere throughout the Welsh parts, not to the exclusion of the vernacular but as a companion speech; and on the other hand, Welsh people in no inconsiderable numbers, drawn by trade and inclination, settle in different parts, especially the towns of Roose and Narberth hundreds, and so far carry their language with them as to require places of worship where the ministrations are in that tongue. This is not the only happy result of the—

"Toning power of time,
And evanescent march of memory."

The hostility of the two races, once so intense and bitter, has disappeared, leaving behind it at the worst only a faint residuum which can be designated as "something" that is chilly and unsympathetic. But generally the tone of feeling is free from a sense of estrangement. Intermarriages often take place, promoted by and promoting reciprocal settlement and race admixture on either side the border line. Long past is the time when George Owen's words in this application, were true, that the English "held themselves so close" as "to wonder at a Welshman coming among them, the one neighbour saying to the other, 'Look, there goeth a Welshman.'"

Names of places naturally follow race settlements. Names ending in *ton*, the Teutonic for "abode," are almost as common in Roose and Castlemartin, as those ending in the corresponding Cymric *tre* are in Dewsland. But through all time and circumstances, expulsion of race and hot furnace of bloody conflict, not a few of the ancient Welsh designations have come down to us almost unharmed and without disfigurement. Pembroke, Tenby, Narberth, and the various parish *Llans*, are conspicuous instances. With almost braver and more strenuous affection, like the little local shell-fish adhering to their native rock, the obscure hamlets, farmsteads, rills, and ridges cling to their early Cymric names, We have Tre-frân, Camrôs, Talbeny (*tal* and *pen*, by the way, meaning the same thing—a reduplication not uncommon in ancient twice-baptized local names, though here *tal* may be an adjective), Coedganlas, Pennar, and Pwll-y-crochan (Castlemartin), as well as Carew (*caer*), *Ben*ton (*pen*), and Begelly.

The question of local names brings into singular prominence the settlement in Pembrokeshire of another nationality—the *Danish*. In the ninth and tenth centuries, during the long struggle of the Danes to effect the conquest of England, the creeks and islands on the coast of Wales, and especially those of Pembrokeshire, were much infested with these strangers. They came in their ships in search of plunder. Sometimes their visits were hasty and brief, but at other times prolonged. Where they impressed their mark so deeply in the form of a local name in their own strange language as to send it down through all time, it must be presumed that they had formed a prolonged settlement, and in the case of individuals a permanent home. The words *gard*, or *garth* (a protection); *wick* (a creek); *thorpe*, or *drop* (a village); *by* (an abode); *holm, ey* an) island); *stack, stakr* (a columnar rock), are all Norse, and are all found in Pembrokeshire names:—

Fish*guard*.	Freys*trop*.	Steep*holm*.
Has*guard*.	Goul*trop*.	St. Bride's *Stack*.
Good*wick*.	Col*by*.	*Stack* Rocks.
Gellys*wick*.	Grass*holm*.	*Stack*pool.
Mussel*wick*.	Flat*holm*.	Cald*y*.
Wick Haven.	Skok*holm*.	Rams*ey*.

Then there are such obviously Scandinavian names as Skomer, Skerry-back Islands, Haroldston, Hubbaston, Strumble Head, Sker-las. The same result would be obtained from a minute examination of *personal* names, and the *physical characteristics*, such as complexion, hair-colour, stature, &c., of the people; all would tend to show that the county of Pembroke has in past times been largely visited by the North Sea vikings, and that they left here not only fragments of their language, but a slight tinge of their blood.

THE HIRLAS HORN AT GOLDEN GROVE.
(*As Engraved in Dunn's "Herald. Visitations of Wales"), see p. 857, ante*).

Section V.—HIGH SHERIFFS OF PEMBROKESHIRE FROM A.D. 1540 TO A.D. 1872.

As from absolute want of space the usual section on old and extinct families is unavoidably omitted, it is with the more gratification that we insert here a complete list of the Sheriffs of Pembrokeshire from the first appointment under the Act of Union in 1540 to the year 1872. This list contains representatives of almost every leading family in the county of Pembroke through that long period of time, with many historical and genealogical facts bearing upon their fortunes. It has had the advantage of revision by Jos. Joseph, Esq., F.S.A., of Brecon, and has been collated with a roll collected by the late Sir Thomas Phillipps, Bart., of Middlehill, which was very imperfect.

HENRY VIII.

	A.D.
Sir Thomas Jones, Kt., of Harroldston, [*m.* Mary, dau. and h. of James Berkeley, and widow of Thomas Perrott, Esq.]	1540
John Philips, Esq., of Picton Castle	1541
Sir John Wogan, Knt., of Wiston Castle	1542
John Vaughan, Esq., of Whitland	1543
Owen ap Owen, Esq., of Pentre Evan	1544
John Sutton, Esq., of Camrose	1545
Morgan Jones, Esq., of Milton	1546

EDWARD VI.

Henry Wyrriott, Esq., of Orielton [*m.* Margaret, dau. of Sir Rhys ap Thomas, Kt.]	1547
Thomas Philips, Esq., of Picton Castle	1548
John Wogan, Esq., of Wiston Castle	1549
John Perrott, Esq., of Scotsborough [*m.* Jane, dau. of John Lloyd, of Tenby, and had an only daughter, Katherine, who *m.* John ap Rhys. See *Rickeston*].	1550
Sir John Perrott, Knt., of Carew Castle [son of Sir Thomas, by Mary, dau. and h. of James, second son of Maurice, Lord Berkley ; *m.* Anne, daughter of Sir Thomas Cheney, K.G., and died in the Tower 3rd November, 1599]	1551
John Bowen, Esq., of Trefloyne (properly Trellwyn), near Tenby	1552

MARY.

John Bowen, Esq. (the same)	1553
Sir John Wogan, Knt., of Wiston Castle	1554
John Vaughan, Esq., of Whitland	1555
John Williams, Esq., of Panthowell	1556
William Rhys, Esq., of Sandyhaven [illegitimate son of Sir Rhys ap Thomas]	1557
Arnold Butler, Esq., of Johnstone [*m.* Ellen, dau. of Sir John Wogan. See also *Butler of Dunraven*]	1558

ELIZABETH.

Henry Wyrriott, Esq., of Orielton [*m.* Margaret, daughter of Sir Rhys ap Thomas, K.G.]	1559
John Bowen, Esq., of Trefloyne	1560
Griffith White, Esq., of Henllan, Castlemartin [son of James, by Margaret, dau. of John Herbert, of Laugharne ; *m.*, 1st, Margaret, dau. and h. of Thomas Watkins, had issue Henry and three other sons ; and 2nd, Mary, daughter of Sir Owen Perrott, by whom he had two daughters]	1561
John Barlow, Esq., of Slebech [son of Roger, by Julian, dau. and h. of Roger Dews, of Bristol]	1562
William Philips, Esq., of Picton Castle [eldest son of John Philips, by Elizabeth, dau. of Sir William Griffith, of Penryn (see 1541)]	1563
Rhys ap Owen, Esq., of Upton Castle	1564
Thomas Cadarn, Esq., of Prendergast Place	1565
Sir John Wogan, Knt., of Wiston Castle	1566
John Wogan, Esq., of Boulston	1567
Francis Laugharne, Esq., of St. Bride's	1568
Thomas Bowen, Esq., of Pentre Evan	1569
Griffith White, Esq., of Henllan	1570
John Bradshaw, Esq., of St. Dogmael's. [John Bradshaw, who, on suppression of monasteries, obtained the abbey of St. Dogmael's, *d.* 1588, and was succ. by his son John]	1571
John Wogan, Esq., of Wiston Castle	1572
Alban Stepney, Esq., of Prendergast (see 1605)	1573
John Wogan, Esq., of Wiston Castle [son of Richard, by Elizabeth, dau. of Sir Thomas Gamage]	1574
John Barlow, Esq., of Slebech (see 1562)	1575
Morgan Philips, Esq., of Picton Castle [2nd son of John and father of Sir John, cr. a Bart. 1621]	1576
George Wyrriott, Esq., of Orielton. [He *m.* Jane, dau. of John Philips ; his dau., Elizabeth, *m.* Sir Hugh Owen, of Bodowen, Angl. See *Angl. Sheriffs, ann.* 1608]	1577
Francis Laugharne, Esq., of St. Bride's	1578
Thomas Revell, Esq., of Forest	1579
George Devereux, Esq., of Lamphey	1580
Griffith White, Esq., of Henllan (see 1561)	1581
John ap Rhys, Esq., of Rickeston, Brawdy [gr. son of David, nat. son of Sir Rhys ap Thomas, *m.* dau. of John Perrott, of Scotsborough. See 1550.]	1582
Sir Hugh Owen, Knt., of Orielton (see 1577)	1583
Sir John Wogan, Knt., of Boulston	1584
John Elliot, Esq., of Narberth [*m.* Jane, dau. and h. of John Vaughan, of Narberth, son of John Vaughan, of Pembrey, and had issue Owen, &c.]	1585
Rowland Laugharne, Esq., of St. Bride's [son of Francis Laugharne, *m* Lettice, dau. of Sir John Perrott, and had issue John and Dorothy. His widow *m.* Walter Vaughan, of Golden Grove]	1586
George Owen, Esq., of Henllys [the well-known antiquary ; *m.*, 1591, Eliz., dau. and co-h. of William Philips, of Picton]	1587
Henry Adams, Esq., of Pater-church [son of John ; *m.* Anne, dau. of Richard Wogan, of Boulston, by Maud, dau. of Sir Thomas Philips ; was M.P. for Pembroke, 1st and 7th Edward VI. and 1st Mary]	1588
Thomas Jones, Esq. (same as for 1540), of Harroldston [afterwards knighted ; was of Abermarlais, co. Carm.]	1589

HIGH SHERIFFS OF PEMBROKESHIRE.

	A.D.
Alban Stepney, Esq., of Prendergast (see 1605)	1590
Edmund Winstanley, Esq., of St. Dogmael's	1591
Henry White, Esq., of Henllan, Castlemartin [son of Griffith (see 1561), *m.* Jane, daughter of Rich Fletcher, and had issue]	1592
John ap Rhys, Esq., of Rickeston (see 1582)	1593
Walter Vaughan, Esq., of St. Bride's [and of Golden Grove, *Carm.*,—see 1586]	1594
John Philips, Esq., of Picton Castle	1595
John Lloyd, Esq., of Kilkiffeth	1596
Thomas Parry, Esq., of St. Dogmael's	1597
John Wogan, Esq., of Boulston (see 1574)	1598
Hugh Butler, Esq., of Johnstone [*m.* Elizabeth, dau. of Sir John Perrott. See also 1588]	1599
John Scourfield, Esq., of New Moat	1600
Devereux Barrett, Esq., of Tenby [son of James, son of Harri Barrett of Pendine]	1601
George Owen, Esq., of Henllys (see 1587)	1602

JAMES I.

James Bowen, Esq., of Trefloyne (see 1552)	1603
Henry White, Esq., of Henllan (see 1592)	1604
Alban Stepney, Esq., of Prendergast [2nd son of Thomas Stepney ; *m.*, as wife, Mary, dau. and co-h. of William Philipps, of Picton, by whom alone he had issue, see *Cowell-Stepney of Llanelly*]	1605
Sir John Wogan, Knt., of Boulston	1606
Roger Lort, Esq., of Stackpool Court (see 1619)	1607
John Butler, Esq., of Coedcanlas (see 1558)	1608
Owen Elliott, Esq., of Narberth (see 1585)	1609
Thomas ap Rhys, Esq., of Scotsborough [son of Sheriff for 1593, see monument in Tenby Church]	1610
John Philipps, Esq., of Picton Castle (afterw. Knt. and Bart.)	1611
William Barlow, Esq., of Criswell [*Christ's Well*. He was of the *Slebech* family ; *m.* Eliz., dau. of John ap Rhys of Rickeston, —see 1593]	1612
Thomas Lloyd, Esq., of Kilkiffeth.	1613
John Stepney, Esq., of Prendergast [afterw. Bart. ; son of Alban Stepney, by his second wife, Mary (see 1605) ; *m.* Frances, dau. of Sir Francis Mansel, of Muddlescombe, *d.* 1637]	1614
Richard Cuny, Esq., of Lamphey	1615
Devereux Barrett, Esq., of Tenby (see 1601)	1616
William Scourfield, Esq., of New Moat [*m.* a dau. of Geo. Owen, of Henllys, see 1602]	1617
George Barlow, Esq., of Slebech	1618
Henry Lort, Esq., of Stackpool [son of Roger, —see 1607 ; *m.* Judith, dau. of Henry White (see 1604); father of Sir Roger, the first Bart. See 1651]	1619
Alban Philipps, Esq., of Nash [son of Morgan Philipps, of Picton ; he *m.* Janet, dau. and h. of Richard Nash, of Nash]	1620
	A.D.
John Philipps, Esq., of Pentre Park. [See *Philipps, Penty Park*]	1621
Sir John Carew, Knt. [see *Carew Castle*]	1622
James Bowen, Esq., of Llwyngwair. [See *Bowen, Llwyngwair*]	1623
John Lloyd, Esq., of Hendre	1624

CHARLES I.

John Laugharne, Esq., of Tenby	1625
Griffith White, Esq., of Henllan, Castlemartin	1626
George Bowen, Esq., of Trefloyne (see *Trefloyne* and *Trellwyn*)	1627
David Thomas Parry, Esq., of Noyadd Trefawr, *Card.*	1628
David Parry, his grandson (both in one year)	
Sir John Wogan, Knt., of Boulston [son of Sir John Wogan, by Jane, dau. of Richard Wogan, of Wiston. See *Boulston*]	1629
John Laugharne, Esq., of St. Bride's [son of Rowland, by Lettice, dau. of Sir John Perrott, of Haroldston ; *m.* Jane, dau. of Sir Hugh Owen, Knt.]	1630
George Bowen, Esq., of Llwyngwair [see *Llwyngwair*]	1631
Sir Richard Philipps, Bart., of Picton Castle [son of Sir John, 1st Bart., by Anne, dau. of Sir John Perrott, of Haroldston]	1632
Hugh Owen, Esq., of Orielton (afterw. Kt.)	1633
John Scourfield, Esq., of New Moat	1634
John Wogan, Esq., of Wiston Castle	1635
John Stepney, Esq., of Prendergast	1636
John Philipps, Esq., of Fynnon-gain	1637
Thomas Warren, Esq., of Trewern. [Par. of Nevern ; of the line of Gwrwared, son of William. Arms : *Az., a lion ramp. or—Dwnn*]	1638
George Carew, Esq., of Carew Castle [son of Sheriff 1622]	1639
Lewis Barlow, Esq., of Criswell [son of Sheriff 1612]	1640
James Lewis, Esq., of Kilkiffeth	1641
Alban Owen, Esq., of Henllys [son of Sheriff 1587]	1642
Thomas Butler, Esq., of Scoveston (for two years)	1643 / 1644
William Philipps, Esq., of Haythog	1645
John Lloyd, Esq., of Lanfyrnach	1646
Abraham Wogan, Esq., of Boulston [son of Morris, by Frances, dau. of Sir Hugh Owen, of Orielton ; *m.* Jane, dau. of Sir Lewis Mansel, of Margam]	1647

THE COMMONWEALTH AND CROMWELL.

Arnold Thomas, Esq., of Haverfordwest (for Llangwa*th*an)	1648
Sampson Lort, Esq., of East Meare	1649
James Philips, Esq., of Tref-gib, Carmarthenshire	1650
Roger Lort, Esq., of Stackpool Court. [Cr. a baronet 1662 ; *m.*, 1st, Hester, sister of	

884 PEMBROKESHIRE.

	A.D.
Arthur Annesley, Earl of Anglesey ; 2ndly, Anne, dau. of Humphrey Wyndham, Esq., of Dunraven. His gr. dau., Eliz., *m.* Sir Alex. Campbell, ancest. to the Earls of Cawdor]	1651
John Lort, Esq., of Prickeston [son of above]	1652
Sir Hugh Owen, Knt. and Bart., of Orielton	1653

OLIVER CROMWELL, LORD PROTECTOR.

	A.D.
James Price (*ap Rhys*), Esq., of Rickeston [son of John,—see 1593]	1654
Sir Erasmus Philipps, Bart., of Picton Castle [son of Sir Richard, second Bart., by Elizabeth, dau. of Sir Erasmus Dryden]	1655
Richard Walter, Esq., of Roch Castle [descended from an Essex family, intermarried with the Laugharnes and Warrens. The Walters are believed not to be extinct]	1656
Henry White, Esq., of Henllan, Castlemartin	1657

RICHARD CROMWELL, LORD PROTECTOR.

	A.D.
Henry White, Esq., of Henllan (the same)	1658
George Howard, Esq., of Fleather Hill	1659

CHARLES II.

	A.D.
George Howard, Esq., of Flether Hill	1660
James Lloyd, Esq., of Kilrhiwe	1661
David Morgan, Esq., of Coed Llwyd	1662
William Scourfield, Esq., of New Moat. Sir Hugh Owen, Bart., of Landshipping	1663
Griffith Davies, Esq., of Bangeston	1664
Sir Herbert Perrott, Kt., of Haroldston [son of James Perrott, by Dorothy, dau. and co-h. of Sir Thomas Perrott, by Lady Dorothy Devereux]	1665
Thomas Phillips, Esq., of Tre-Llewelyn	1666
Lewis Barlow, Esq., of Criswell	1667
James Lewis, Esq., of Coedmore, *Card.* [maternal grandson of John Wogan, Esq., of Wiston]	1668
Thomas Lloyd, Esq., of Morvil	1669
John Williams, Esq., of Gumfreston	1670
James Bowen, Esq., of Llwyngwair	1671
Lewis Wogan, Esq., of Boulston [son of Sheriff for 1647]	1672
William Meares, Esq., of Eastington (see *Iestynton*), Castlemartin	1673
William Warren, Esq., of Trewern, Nevern	1674
Nicholas Roch, Esq., of Richardson, in Roose	1675
Lewis John, Esq., of Lampeter Velfrey	1676
David Morris Griffith Beynon, of Manordivy	1677
Reynold Lewis, Esq. (see *Lewis of Henllan*) Francis Phillips, Esq., of Lampeter Velfrey	1678
Thomas Jones, Esq., of Wenallt, Newport	1679
Francis Phillips, Esq., of Waingron	1680
Sir John Barlow, Bart., of Minwear [son of George Barlow, by Joan, dau. and co-h. of David Lloyd, Esq., of Kilkiffeth]	1681
George Bowen, Esq., of Llwyngwair	1682

	A.D.
David Williams, Esq., of Hên Castle	1683
John Owen, Esq., of Trecwn	1684

JAMES II.

	A.D.
David Morgan, Esq., of Coed Llwyd	1685
John Barlow, Esq., of Criswell (*Christ's Well*)	1686
Charles Philipps, Esq., of Sandy Haven	1687
James ap Rhys, Esq., of Rickeston (son of Sheriff for 1654)	1688

WILLIAM AND MARY.

	A.D.
William Lewis, Esq., of Carew Castle	1689
Griffith Hawkwell, Esq., of Talybont	1690
Edward Philipps, Esq., of Picton Castle and Kilgetty [son of Sir Erasmus, by his second wife ; *m.* the heiress of Kilgetty, but *d. v. p.* and *s. p.*]	1691
George Meares, Esq., of Rhoscrowther	1692
William Allen, Esq., of Gelliswick (see *Allen of Cresselly*)	1693
David Parry, Esq., of Noyadd-trefawr, *Card.*	1694
Francis Meares, Esq., of Corston (*d.* in office)	1695

WILLIAM III.

	A.D.
George Lloyd, Esq., of Cwmgloyne	1696
Sir Thomas Stepney, of Prendergast (see *Cowell-Stepney* of Llanelly)	1697
Hugh Bowen, Esq., of Upton Castle	1698
William Scourfield, Esq., of New Moat	1699
Thomas Lewis, Esq., of Grove, Narberth	1700
Hugh Lloyd, Esq., of Ffoes-helig, *Card.* [for lands in Clydey and Narberth, in right of his wife]	1701

ANNE.

	A.D.
John Edwardes, Esq., of Tref-garn [son of Owen Edwardes, by Damaris, dau. of James Perrot (see *Edwardes of Sealyham*)]	1702
Julius Deedes, Esq., of Exeter, [for his lands in St. Dogmael's]	1703
Simon Willy, Esq., of Lampeter Velfrey	1704
John Barlow, Esq., of Lawrenny	1705
George Owen, Esq., of Priskilly	1706
Sir Arthur Owen, Bart., M.P. and Lord-Lieut., of Landshipping [of the Orielton line ; son of Sir Hugh, second Bart. ; *m.* Emma, dau. of Sir W. Williams, Speaker of House of Commons *temp.* Charles II.]	1707
Sir William Lewis, Kt., Bristol (see *Henllan*)	1708
Thomas Lloyd, Esq., of Grove, Pembroke	1709
John Vaughan, Esq., of Trecwn (see *Barham of Trecwn*)	1710
Morris Morris, Esq., of Manordivy	1711
John Warren, Esq., of Trewern, Nevern	1712
John Symmons, Esq., of Llanstinan	1713
Charles Owen, Esq., of Great Nash	1714

GEORGE I.

	A.D.
Thomas Davids, Esq., of Dyffryn, Cilgerran	1715
John Skyrme, Esq., of Llawhaden	1716

HIGH SHERIFFS OF PEMBROKESHIRE.

	A.D.
Lewis Vaughan, Esq., of Jordanston, Fishguard	1717
Thomas Parry, Esq., of Manorowen	1718
William Wheeler, Esq., of Haverfordwest	1719
Richard Lowe, Esq., of Linney	1720
Stephen Lewis, Esq., of Llangolman	1721
Lawrence Colby, Esq., of Bletherstone	1722
John Lort, Esq., of Prickeston	1723
William Wogan, Esq., of Wiston	1724
John Child, Esq., of Begelly	1725
David Lewis, Esq., of Vogart, or Llandewi	1726

GEORGE II.

	A.D.
Sir Richard Walter, Kt., of Rhos Market	1727
Robert Popkins, Esq., of Forest	1728
Nicholas Roch, Esq., of Paskeston	1729
James Lloyd, Esq., of Kilrhue	1730
John Laugharne, Esq., of Llanrythan	1731
John Allen, Esq., of Cresselly [see *Allen of Cresselly*]	1732
Nicholas Roch, Esq., of Prickeston	1733
James Philipps, Esq., of Pentrepark (now Pentypark)	1734
John Philipps, Esq., of Ford	1735
William Philipps, Esq., of Sandy Haven	1736
Thomas Davies, Esq., of Nash	1737
George Harries, Esq., of Tregwynt	1738
George Meare, Esq., of Pennar	1739
William Warren, Esq. of Longridge	1740
Matthew Bowen, Esq., of Westfield	1741
William Allen, Esq., of Gelliswick	1742
David Paynter, Esq., of Dale	1743
William Jones, Esq., of Llether	1744
John Wogan, Esq., of Wiston	1745
Morris Bowen, Esq., of Upton Castle	1746
Rowland Edwardes, Esq., of Tref-garn [son of Owen Edwardes; *m.* Anne, dau. of George Harries, of Priskilly, and had issue John, who *m.* the heiress of Sealyham,—see *Edwardes of Sealyham*]	1747
John Wogan, Esq., of Boulston	1748
Thomas Picton, Esq., of Poyston	1749
Sparks Martin, Esq., of Withy-Bush	1750
Hugh Meare, Esq., of Pearston	1751
John Owen, Esq., of Berllan	1752
George Barlow, Esq., of Slebech	1753
Essex Marychurch Meyrick, Esq., of Bush	1754
John Smith, Esq., of Jeffreyston	1755
John Hook, Esq., of Bangeston	1756
John Allen, Esq., of Dale (see *Allen-Philipps of Dale Castle*)	1757
John Adams, Esq., of Whitland	1758
Thomas Jones, Esq., of Brawdy	1759
Thomas Roch, Esq., of Butter Hill	1760

GEORGE III.

	A.D.
Rowland Philipps Laugharne, Esq., of Orlandon [son of Rowland Philipps, Esq., by Martha, dau. of John Edwardes, Esq.; *m.* Anne, dau. of the Rev. J. Laugharne, and assumed her nam]	1761
William Wheeler Bowen, Esq., of Lambston	1762
John Tucker, Esq., of Sealyham	1763
William Ford, Esq., of Stone Hall	1764
John Francis Meyrick, Esq., of Bush	1765
William Williams, Esq., of Ivy Tower	1766
Council Williams, Esq., of Hermon's Hill, Haverfordwest	1767
John Griffiths, Esq., of Clynderwen	1768
Thomas Skyrme, Esq., of Vaynor	1769
Thomas Colby, Esq., of Rhosygilwen	1770
Thomas Lloyd, Esq., of Cwmgloyne	1771
John Parry, Esq., of Portclew	1772
John Jones, Esq., of Brawdy	1773
Cæsar Mathias, Esq., of Hook	1774
John Lort, Esq., of Prickeston	1775
John Harries, Esq., of Cryg-glâs	1776
Nicholas Roch, Esq., of Paskeston	1777
Thomas Williams, Esq., of Trelethin	1778
John Griffiths, Esq., of Llancych	1779
Thomas Lloyd, Esq., of Kilrhue	1780
Henry Scourfield, Esq., of Robeston	1781
Vaughan Thomas, Esq., of Posty, Bletherston	1782
Thomas Wright, Esq., of Pope Hill	1783
John Protheroe, Esq., of Egremont	1784
John Lloyd, Esq., of Dale Castle [*m.*, 1776, Elinor, dau. and h. of John Allen, Esq., of Dale Castle; *d.* 1820]	1785
William Knox, Esq., of Slebech [bought Slebech from John Symmons (Llanstinan), who had *m.* the heiress of the Barlows]	1786
James Philipps, Esq., of Pentrepark (see *Philipps of Pentypark*)	1787
John Philipps Laugharne, of Orlandon (son of Sheriff for 1761)	1788
George Roch, Esq., of Clareston	1789
William Philipps, Esq., of St. Bride's	1790
William Wheeler Bowen, Esq., of Lambston	1791
John Mathias, Esq., of Llangwarren	1792
John Higgon, Esq., of Scolton	1793
John Phelps, Esq., of Withy-bush	1794
John Herbert Foley, Esq., of Ridgeway	1795
Nathaniel Philipps, Esq., of Slebech [bought Slebech from William Knox, Sheriff for 1786]	1796
Abraham Leach, Esq., of Corston	1797
John Tasker, Esq., of Upton Castle	1798
Gwynn Vaughan, Esq., of Jordanston	1799
John Meares, Esq., of Eastington	1800
Morgan Jones, Esq., of Cilwendeg	1801
Hugh Stokes, Esq., of Hubberston	1802
George Bowen, Esq., of Llwyngwair	1803
Sir Hugh Owen, Bart., of Orielton [6th Bart.; son of Sir Hugh, by Anne, dau. of John Colby, Esq.; *d.*, 1809, unmarried, leaving Orielton to J. Lord. See *Owen, of Orielton*]	1804
John Hill Harries, Esq., of Heathfield (see *Harries of Heathfield*)	1805
Hugh Webb Bowen, Esq., of Camrose	1806
John Colby, Esq., of Fynnone	1807
John Hensleigh Allen, Esq., of Cresselly	1808
Charles Allen Philipps, Esq., of St. Bride's	

	A.D.
Hill [third son of Joseph Allen, by Anne Philipps, of St. Bride's Hill,—see *Allen-Phillips of Dale Castle*). He assumed the name of Philipps on succeeding to the estate]	1809
John Mirehouse, Esq., of Brownslade [son of the Rev. Canon Thomas Mirehouse ; *m.* Mary, sister of Sir John Edwards, Bart., of Greenfields, Machynlleth, 1823]	1810
Lewis Mathias, Esq., of Llangwarren	1811
William Henry Scourfield, Esq., of Robeston Hall	1812
Gwynn Gill Vaughan, Esq., of Jordanston	1813
John Harcourt Powell, Esq., of Hook	1814
Morris Williams, Esq., of Cymgloyne	1815
Henry Mathias, Esq., of Fernhill (afterwards knighted)	1816
Charles Mathias, Esq., of Llangwarren	1817
Robert Innes Ackland, Esq., of Boulston, by purchase (see *Ackland of Boulston*)	1818
Henry Davies, Esq., of Mullock	1819

GEORGE IV.

Nathaniel Phillips, Esq., of Slebech [only son of Nathaniel Phillips, Sheriff 1796 ; *d. unm.*, and was succ. by his eldest sister, who *m.* Baron de Rutzen]	1820
Joseph Harries, Esq., of Llanunwas	1821
John Meares, Esq., of Eastington	1822
Owen Lewis, Esq., of Trewern, Nevern	1823
Orlando Harries Williams, Esq., of Ivy Tower. [He *m.*, in 1809, Maria, only dau. and h. of William Williams, of Ivy Tower ; in 1824 assumed her name ; *d.* in 1849, *s. p.*, his wife having predeceased]	1824
George Bowen, Esq., of Llwyngwair [see *Bowen of Llwyngwair*]	1825
Jonathan Haworth Peel, Esq., of Cottesmoor [see *Massy of Cottesmoor*]	1826
Anthony Innys Stokes, Esq., of St. Botolph's	1827
Thomas Meyrick, Esq., of Bush	1828
William Edwardes Tucker, Esq., of Sealyham [see *Edwardes of Sealyham*]	1829

WILLIAM IV.

George Clayton Roch, of Clareston	1830
Morgan Jones, Esq., of Cilwendeg	1831
David Davies, Esq., of Carnachenwen	1832
John Henry Philips, Esq., of Williamston (see *Scourfield of Williamston*)	1833
John Barham, Esq., of Trecwn (see *Barham of Trecwn*)	1834
Nicholas Roch, Esq., of Cosheston	1835
Charles Wheeler Townsend Webb Bowen, Esq., of Camrose	1836

VICTORIA.

John Adams, Esq., of Hollyland (see *Adams of Hollyland*)	1837
John Colby, Esq., of Fynnoné	1838
Gilbert William Warren Davis, Esq., of Mullock	1839
Richard Llewellyn, Esq., of Tregwynt [son of Richard Llewellyn, of Holme Wood, near Bristol, by Anne Maria Ames, sister of Lionel Lyde, of Ayott St. Lawrence, Herts]	1840
George Roch, Esq., of Butter Hill [son of George Roch, by Mary, daughter and coheiress of William Jones, of Llether]	1841
Robert Frederick Gower, Esq., of Glandovan	1842
George Lort Philipps, Esq., of Dumpledale [eldest son of John Lort Phillips ; *m.*, 1811, Isabella Georgiana, only dau. of John Hensleigh Allen, of Cresselly]	1843
William Charles Allen Philipps, Esq., of St. Bride's Hill	1844
Abel Lewis Gower, Esq., of Castlemalgwyn (see *Gower of Glandovan*)	1845
John Harding Harries, Esq., of Trevacoon	1846
William Henry Lewis, Esq., of Clynfyw	1847
Owen Owen, Esq., of Cwmgloyne	1848
Seymour Philipps Allen, Esq., of Cresselly	1849
William Richards, Esq., of Tenby	1850
John Harcourt Powell, Esq., of Hook	1851
Henry Leach, Esq., of Corston	1852
Adrian Nicholas J. Stokes, Esq., of St. Botolph's	1853
The Hon. R. Fulke Greville, of Castle Hall [son of Robert Fulke Greville, by Louisa, Countess of Mansfield. He *m.* Georgiana Cecilia, dau. of Charles Locke, and had issue ; succ. to the property of Sir William Hamilton, which the latter had enjoyed by his first marriage with Miss Barlow]	1854
John Leach, Esq., of Ivy Tower	1855
Lewis Mathias, Esq., of Lamphey Court	1856
Sir James John Hamilton, Bart.	1857
Nicholas John Dunn, Esq., of West Moor (see *Dunn of Elm Grove*)	1858
William Owen, Esq., of Poyston	1859
George Augustus Harries, Esq., of Hilton	1860
Edward Wilson, Esq., of Hên Castle	1861
James Bevan Bowen, Esq., of Llwyngwair	1862
William Rees, Esq., of Scovaston	1863
Thomas Harcourt Powell, Esq., of Hook	1864
Thomas Henry Davies, Esq., of Clareston	1865
William Walters, Esq., of Haverfordwest	1866
Mark Anthony Saurin, Esq., of Orielton	1867
George Richard G. Rees, Esq., of Penllwyn	1868
Robert Pavin Davies, Esq., of Ridgeway	1869
Morris William Lloyd Owen, Esq., of Cwmgloyne	1870
Baron F. De Rutzen, Slebech	1871
Richard Edward Arden, Esq., of Pontfaen	1872

Section VI.—THE PARLIAMENTARY ANNALS OF PEMBROKESHIRE, A.D. 1542—1872.

Like all the other counties, Pembrokeshire in its roll of parliamentary knights presents a faithful reflection of the most public-spirited and honoured of its patrician houses for the time being. The following lists cover a space of 330 years in the family history of Pembrokeshire, and a comparison of the names they contain with those in the roll of High Sheriffs, and in the preceding historical and antiquarian notes, will show that the great houses which have come down to us by tradition, and in some cases in their lineal representatives, were those to whose care were entrusted, by their fellow-citizens, the highest offices and most important trusts.

Whether to its credit or otherwise, Pembrokeshire has been pre-eminent for stubborn election contests, whose ruinous expenditure has told severely on the fortunes of more than one family. In 1831 the political tournament lasted *fifteen days*, and was renewed for another *fifteen days*. The time for such folly is past for ever. Landowners will have henceforth a better chance to retain their acres, and "independent voters" their senses. Perhaps education will also give the tenant-farmer and householder some conception of the meaning and reason of the franchise, and why this or that knight of the shire or burgess of a burgh should be sent up to "sit" at St. Stephen's.

1.—*Members of Parliament for the County.*

HENRY VIII.
	A.D.
Thomas Jones, Esq., of Haroldston	1542

EDWARD VI.
John Wogan, Esq., probably of Wiston Castle	1553

MARY.
Sir John Wogan, Kt., of Wiston Castle	1553
Arnold Butler, Esq., of Johnston	1554

PHILIP AND MARY.
Arnold Butler, Esq. (the same)	1554
Arnold Butler, Esq. (the same)	1555
Thomas Cathern, Esq., of Prendergast [otherwise *Cadern,*—see *Sheriffs* 1565]	1557

ELIZABETH.
William Philips, Esq., of Picton Castle	1558
Sir John Perrott, Kt., of Haroldston	1563
John Wogan, Esq., of Wiston Castle	1571
William Philips, Esq., of Picton Castle	1572
Thomas Revell, Esq., of Forest, Cilgerran	1585-6
George Devereux, Esq. (of Lamphey ?)	1588
[Bishop Barlow alienated the manor of Lamphey to Richard Devereux, of the *Essex* and *Hereford* line.]	
Sir Thomas Perrott, Kt., of Haroldston	1592
John Philips, Esq., of Picton Castle	1597
John Philips, Esq. (the same)	1601

JAMES I.
	A.D.
Alban Stepney, Esq., of Prendergast	1603
Sir James Perrott, Kt. [for H. West, 1620]	1614
John Wogan, Esq., of Wiston Castle	1620
Sir James Perrott, Kt. (same as for 1614)	1623

CHARLES I.
John Wogan, Esq., of Wiston Castle, 1st Sess. } Robert (?) Wogan, Esq., 2nd Sess. }	1625
John Wogan, Esq., of Wiston Castle	1628
John Wogan, sen., Esq., of Wiston Castle } Arthur Owen, Esq., *vice* Wogan }	1640

OLIVER CROMWELL, LORD PROTECTOR.
Sir Erasmus Philipps, Bart., of Picton Castle } Arthur Owen, Esq., of New Moat }	1554
James Phillips, Esq., of Tirgibby, *Card.* } Col. John Clarke, of Kensington, *Mid.* }	1656

RICHARD CROMWELL, LORD PROTECTOR.
Sir Erasmus Philipps, Bart., of Picton Castle	1658-9

CHARLES II.
Sir Erasmus Philipps, Bart., of Picton Castle (*d.* 1696)	1660
[*Members from* 1678—1714 *not found.*]	

888 PEMBROKESHIRE.

GEORGE I.

	A.D.
Sir Arthur Owen, Bart., of Landshipping [Seat contested by *John Barlow, Esq.*, of Lawrenny.]	1714
Sir Arthur Owen, Bart. (the same)	1722

GEORGE II.

John Campbell, Esq. [*jure matris*, of Stackpool. Seat contested by *Sir Arthur Owen, Bart.*]	1727
John Campbell, Esq. (the same) [Contested by John Symmons, Esq., of Llanstinan.]	1741
William Owen, Esq. [son of Sir Arthur Owen]	1747
Sir William Owen, Bart. [*succ.* on death of Sir Arthur, 1753]	1754

GEORGE III.

Sir John Philipps, Bart., of Picton Castle [*d.* 1764] [Contested by *Hugh Owen, Esq.*, son of Sir William.]	1761
Sir Richard Philipps, Bart., of Picton Castle [son of Sir John]	1765
Sir Richard Philipps, Bart. (the same) [Contested by *Hugh Owen, Esq.*, as before.]	1768
Hugh Owen, Esq. [*vice* Philipps, whose election was declared void ; *succ.* as Bart. 1781]	1770
Lord Milford [late Sir R. Philipps], of Picton Castle, *vice* Owen *dec.*]	1786
Lord Milford, of Picton Castle [Contest : votes for Lord Milford 1,195, for Sir Hugh Owen 1,102.]	1807

	A.D.
Sir John Owen, Bart., of Orielton. [Sir Hugh Owen *d. unm.* in 1809, and bequeathed his estates to his kinsman, John Lord, Esq., who assumed name of Owen, and was cr. a Bart. Contest : votes for Owen 1,529, for Hon. J. F. Campbell 1,344. Owen sat till 1831 unopposed]	1812

GEORGE IV.

Sir John Owen, Bart., of Orielton	1820

WILLIAM IV.

Sir John Owen, Bart., of Orielton	1830
Sir John Owen, Bart., of Orielton [Contest : Polling 15 days ; votes for Owen 1,949, Hon. R. Fulke Greville 1,850.]	1831
Sir John Owen, Bart., of Orielton [The former election of Owen being declared void, writ issued for new election in October, when Greville again contested the seat. Polling 15 days. Votes : for Owen 1,531, for Greville 1,423.]	1831

VICTORIA.

Sir John Owen, Bart., of Orielton	1837
Viscount Emlyn [now Earl Cawdor, *vice* Owen, who was returned for Pembroke district]	1841
George Lort Phillips, Esq., of Lawrenny Park	1860
James Bevan Bowen, Esq., of Llwyngwair	1866
John Henry Scourfield, Esq., of Williamston	1868

[*The present sitting Member,* 1872.]

2.—*Members of Parliament for the Pembroke District of Boroughs,* A.D. 1542 *to* A.D. 1872.

HENRY VIII.

John Adams *de Peterston* [Peter-Church—whence "Pater ;" also Patrick's-Church]	1542

EDWARD VI.

Henry Adams, Esq., of Peter-church	1547
Henry Adams, Esq. (the same)	1553

MARY.

Henry Adams, Esq. (the same)	1553
Henry Adams, Esq. (the same)	1554

PHILIP AND MARY.

John Garnons, Esq., "of the Middle Temple"	1554
William Watkyn, Gent.	1557

ELIZABETH.

No Member given	1558
William Revell, Esq. [of Forest ?]	1563

Robert Davyes, Esq.	1571
Robert Lougher, Esq., LL.D.	1572
John Vaughan, Esq.	1585-6
Nicholas Adams, Gent., of Pater-church	1588
Sir Conyers Clifford, Kt.	1592
John Lougher, Esq.	1601

JAMES I.

Richard Cuny, Gent. [see *Sheriffs*, ann. 1615]	1603
No name given	1614
Lewis Powell, Gent. [member for Haverfordwest 1614 to 1623].	1620
Sir Walter Devereux, Kt. [of Lamphey ?]	1623

CHARLES I.

Lewis Powell, Esq., 1st Session	} 1625
Sir Hugh Owen, Kt., of Orielton, 2nd Session	
Sir Hugh Owen, Kt., of Orielton (afterwards a Bart.)	1628

PARLIAMENTARY ANNALS OF PEMBROKESHIRE.

	A.D.
Sir John Stepney, 2nd Bart., of Prendergast— 1st Session	
Sir Hugh Owen, Kt., 2nd Session	1640
Six Members for all Wales,—see names at p. 606	1653

OLIVER CROMWELL, LORD PROTECTOR.

No name given 1654
No name given. Possibly the second Member given under the *County* was a Borough representative. 1656

RICHARD CROMWELL, LORD PROTECTOR.

Sampson Lort, Esq.. . . . .
Arthur Owen, Esq. (afterw. Bart.), Orielton } 1658—9

CHARLES II.

[*Members from the Restoration to* 1710 *not found.*]

ANNE.

Sir Arthur Owen, Bart., of Landshipping
But on petition, after a contest— } 1710
Lewis Wogan, Esq., of Boulston, *vice* Owen .

GEORGE I.

Thomas Ferrers, Esq. 1714
[Contested unsuccessfully by *Sir George Barlow*]
William Owen, Esq. (afterwards Bart.), of Orielton, *vice* Ferrers *dec.* . . . 1722

GEORGE II.

William Owen, Esq. (the same) . . . 1741
[Contested by *Rawleigh Mansel*, Esq., of Abercyfor, *Carm.*]
Hugh Barlow, Esq. (formerly *Owen*), of Lawrenny [*vice* Owen, who took the *County*] . 1747

GEORGE III.

Sir William Owen, Bart., of Orielton . . 1761

	A.D.
Hugh Owen, Esq. [son of last Member].	1774
Sir Hugh Owen, Bart. (the same), of Orielton	1780

[Contest: Votes for Owen, 1,089; for *Lord Milford*, 912.]
Hugh Barlow, Esq. (form. Owen), of Lawrenny 1790
Hugh Barlow, Esq. (the same) . . . 1796
Sir Hugh Owen, Bart., of Orielton [son of Member for 1780] 1809
Sir John Owen (formerly *Lord*), *vice* Owen *dec.*
[succ., on decease of Sir Hugh, to estates of Orielton, but not to title, and was created a baronet] 1809
Sir John Owen, Bart., of Orielton . . . 1812
[Contested by *John Hensleigh Allen*, Esq.]
Gen. Sir Thomas Picton, K.B., of Poyston,
[*vice* Owen, who took the *County*] . . 1813
John Jones, Esq. [*vice* Picton, killed at Waterloo] 1815
John Hensleigh Allen, Esq. 1818

GEORGE IV.

John Hensleigh Allen, Esq. (the same) . . 1820
Hugh Owen Owen, Esq. [now Sir Hugh, 2nd Bart.; sat till 1838 through five elections unopposed] 1826

WILLIAM IV.

Hugh Owen Owen, Esq. (the same) . . 1830

VICTORIA.

Sir James R. G. Graham, Bart., *vice* Owen resigned 1838
Sir John Owen, Bart., of Orielton . . . 1841
[Contest: Votes, Sir John 246; *Hugh O. Owen* (his son) 172; *James Mark Child* 84. Sir John sat till his decease in 1861.]
Sir Hugh Owen Owen, *vice* Owen *dec.* . . 1861
[Contest: Votes Owen 668, *Hardwick* 304].
Thomas Charlton-Meyrick, Esq., of Bush . 1868
[Contest: Votes for Charlton-Meyrick 1,419, Owen 1,049.]
[*The present sitting Member*, 1872.]

3.—*Members of Parliament for the Town and County of Haverfordwest, from A.D.* 1547 *to A.D.* 1872.

EDWARD VI.

Richard Howell, Gent. 1547
Richard Howell, Gent. (the same) . . . 1553

MARY.

Richard Tailour, Gent. 1553
Richard Howell, Gent. 1554

PHILIP AND MARY.

Richard Hordell (query Howell?), Gent. . 1554

John Button, Gent. 1555
Thomas ap Owen, Gent. [probably of *Pentre-Evan*] 1557

ELIZABETH.

Hugh Harries, Esq. of Haverfordwest [son of Sir Hugh Harris, Kt.] . . . 1558
Rhys Morgan, Esq. [perhaps of Iscoed, *Carm.*] 1563
John Garvans, Gent. 1571
Rhys Morgan, Esq. (same as for 1563) . . 1572

PEMBROKESHIRE.

	A.D.
Alban Stepney, Esq., of Prendergast [S. 1590]	1585-6
Sir John Perrott, Kt. [of Scotsborough?]	1588
Sir Nicholas Clifford, Kt.	1592
James Perrott, Esq. [prob. of Haroldston]	1597
John Canon, Gent. [Kilgetty family]	1601

JAMES I.

Sir James Perrott, Kt., of Haroldston	1603
Sir James Perrott, Kt. (the same)	1614
Sir James Perrott. Kt. (the same)	1620
Lewis Powell, Gent. [M.P. for Pembroke 1620. The Powells were afterwards of Greenhill]	1623

CHARLES I.

Sir Thomas Canon, Kt. [of Cilgetty]	1625
Sir James Perrott, Kt., of Haroldston	1628
Hugh Owen, Esq., of Orielton. 1st session	
Sir John Stepney, 2nd Bart. } 2nd session.	1640
Sir Robert Needham, Kt.	

COMMONWEALTH AND CROMWELL.

The "Barebones" Parliament. Six members summoned for all Wales, see p. 606] . 1653

OLIVER CROMWELL, LORD PROTECTOR.

John Upton, Esq. [place unknown]	1654
John Upton, Esq. (the same)	1656

RICHARD CROMWELL, LORD PROTECTOR.

John Upton, Esq. (the same) . . 1658-9

CHARLES II.

[*Members from the Restoration to 1715 not found.*]

GEORGE I.

John Laugharne, Esq. [probably of St. Bride's]	1714
Sir George Barlow, Bart., of Slebech [*vice* Laugharne, *dec.* Contest: Votes for George Barlow 222; for *John Barlow* 181. On petition the latter seated]	1715
Sir John Philipps, of Picton Castle, *vice* Barlow deceased	1718
Francis Edwardes [prob. of Trefgarn,—see *Sealyham*]	1722
Erasmus Philipps, Esq., of Picton Castle [son of Sir John, at whose decease in 1736 he *succ.* as 5th Bart.]	1726

	A.D
Erasmus Philipps, Esq. (the same) [Seat contested by *Wyrriot Owen.*]	1734

GEORGE II.

Sir Erasmus Philipps, Bart., of Picton Castle [Contest: Votes for Philipps 247, for *Hugh Barlow*, 207.]	1741
Sir George Barlow, Bart., of Slebech, *vice* Philipps *dec.*	1743
William Edwardes [son of M. for 1722; sat till 1784]	1747

GEORGE III.

William Edwardes (the same)	1760
William Edwardes, cr. Baron Kensington	1776
Lord Milford, *vice* Kensington	1784
Lord Kensington, *vice* Milford, who sat for co.	1786
William, 2nd Lord Kensington, *vice* his father, deceased	1802
Lord Kensington	1812
[Seat contested: Votes for Kensington 220; for *Nathaniel Phillips* 98.]	
William Henry Scourfield, Esq., of New Moat	1818

GEORGE IV.

Richard Bulkeley Philipps, Esq., Picton Castle 1826
[Assumed name Philipps for Grant; cr. a Bart. 1828, and succ. to Picton estates 1833; cr. Baron Milford 1847; *d.* 1857.]

WILLIAM IV.

Sir R. B. P. Philipps, Bart., of Picton Castle	1830
William Henry Scourfield, Esq., of Moat	1835
[Contest: Votes for Scourfield 251, for *S. H. Peel* 125.]	

VICTORIA.

Sir R. B. P. Philipps, Bart., of Picton Castle	1837
[Contest: Votes: Philipps 247; *Scourfield* 125.]	
Sir R. B. P. Philipps, Bart. (the same)	1841
J. H. Philipps, Esq., of Williamston	1852
Hon. William Edwardes, *viee* Scourfield, who took the Co.	1868
The same, as Lord Kensington	1871
[*The present sitting Member*, 1872.]	

SECTION VII.—COUNTY MAGISTRATES OF PEMBROKESHIRE, 1872.
(CORRECTED TO DATE BY THE CLERK OF THE PEACE.)

Cawdor, The Earl of, Stackpool Court, Pembroke.
Lord Kensington, 12, John Street, Berkeley Square, London.
Viscount Emlyn, Stackpool Court, Pembroke.
Sir Hugh Owen, Bart., Reform Club, London.
Hon. William Henry Yelverton, Whitland Abbey.

Sir James John Hamilton, Bart., Llanstephan, Carm.
Sir Thomas Davies Lloyd, Bart., of Bronwydd, Card.
Ackland, Robert Dudley, Esq., of Boulston.
Adams, John, Esq., of Hollyland, Pembroke.
Allen, Charles Hugh, Esq., of Letterston.
Allen, Charles, Esq., Tenby.

COUNTY MAGISTRATES OF PEMBROKESHIRE. 891

Allen, George Baugh, Esq., of Kilrhiw, Narberth.
Allen, Henry Seymour, Esq., of Cresselly, Pembroke.
Allen, James, *Chancellor*, Castlemartin.
Barham, Charles Henry, *Clerk*, of Trecwn, Fishguard.
Berrington, William Morgan Davies, *Clerk*, Druidston.
Beynon, John, Esq., the younger, Trewern, Narberth
Beynon, John Thomas, Esq., of Trewern, Narberth.
Bowen, Chas. W. Townsend Webb, Esq., of Camrose.
Bowen, James Bevan, Esq., of Llwyngwair, Newport, Pembr.
Bowen, James, Esq., of Haverfordwest.
Bowen, James, Esq., of Troedyraur, Cardigan.
Brenchley, Thomas Harman, Esq., of Glan-eirw, *Card.*
Brigstocke, William Owen, Esq., of Blaenpant, Newcastle Emlyn.
Bryant, James Robertson, Esq., of Pembroke.
Buck, William, Esq., Plasnewydd, N. Castle Emlyn.
Buckby, R. H., Esq., Begelly, Narberth.
Buckby, Richard, *Clerk*, of Begelly, Narberth.
Clark, Frederick Guy L'Estrange, Esq., Pembroke.
Colby, John, Esq., of Fynoné, Newcastle Emlyn.
Colby, Thomas, Esq., of Pant-y-deri, Eglwyswrw.
Davies, Arthur H. Saunders, Esq., of Pentre.
Davies, David, Esq., of Cardigan.
Davies, Gilbert William Warren, Esq., of Trewarren.
Davies, Owen Edmund, Esq., Haverfordwest.
Davies, Robert Pavin, Esq., Ridgeway, Narberth.
Davies, Thomas, Esq., Bank House, Cardigan.
Davies, Thomas Henry, Esq., of Hayston.
Douglas, Charles, *Clerk*, Pembroke.
Dunn, Nicholas John, Esq., of Elm Grove, Tenby.
Dunn, Thomas Higgon, *Clerk*, Tenby.
Dyster, Frederick Daniel, Esq., Tenby.
Edwardes, Owen Tucker, Esq., Trerhos, Haverford.
Evans, Benjamin, Esq., Kidigill, Cardigan.
Fitzwilliams, Edward C. Lloyd, Esq., Adpar, *Card.*
Griffith, Moses, Esq., of Manorowen, Fishguard.
Harford, Summers, Esq., of Clarbeston Grange.
Harries, Cecil Anscn, Esq., of Llanunwas.
Harries, George Augustus, Esq., of Hilton.
Harries, Hugh Lloyd, Esq., Cefendref, Fishguard.
Harries, John Henry, Esq., Heathfield, Letterston.
Hartley, Milham, Esq., Bridell, Cardigan.
Harvey, John, Esq., Haverfordwest.
Higgon, James, Esq., of Scolton.
Higgon, John, Esq., 14, Marlborough Hill, St. John's Wood, London.
Howell, Hugh, *Clerk*, Llanfirnach.
Hulm, William, Esq., Pembroke.
Jackson, Thomas Thompson, Esq., New Milford.
James, John, Esq., Trenewydd.
James, John T. William, Esq., of Pantsaison.
Jones, John Morgan, Esq., Llanllwch House, Carmarthen.
Jones, Richard Bowen, *Clerk*, Kilmaenllwyd, Narberth.
Jordan, George Bowen Price, Esq., of Pigeonsford.
Leach, Francis George, *Clerk*, St. Petrox, Pembroke.
Leach, Henry, Esq., of Corston, Pembroke.
Lewellin, Llewelyn, Dean of St. David's, Lampeter College.

Lewes, William Price, Esq., Llysynewydd, Llandysil.
Lewis, John Lennox Griffith Poyer, Esq., of Henllan, Narberth.
Lewis, William Henry, Esq., of Clynfyw, N.C., Emlyn.
Lloyd, J. F. Jones, Esq., Llancych, Llandyssil.
Lloyd, Thomas Davies, Esq., of Kilrhue, Cardigan.
Lloyd, William, *Clerk*, Manordivy, Cardigan.
Massy, Edward Taylor, Esq., of Cottesmoor.
Mathias, Lewis, Esq., of Lamphey Court, Pembroke.
Morgan, Howard Spear, Esq., Tegfynydd, Narberth.
Morison, Alexander John, Esq., Portclew, Pembroke.
Owen, Morris Williams Lloyd, Esq., of Cwmgloyne.
Owen, William, Esq., Withybush, Haverford West.
Owen, William Herbert Gwynne, Esq., Narberth.
Owen, William Stephenson, Esq., Haverfordwest.
Peel, Xavier de Castanos Royds, Esq., of Glanafon.
Phelps, John, *Clerk*, Carew, Pembroke.
Phelps, Peter, *Clerk*, Ambleston.
Philipps, Frederick L. Lloyd, Esq., of Panty-park.
Philipps, John Allen Lloyd, Esq., Mabus, Cardigan.
Philipps, John Allen Philipps Lloyd, Esq., of Dale Castle.
Powell, Walter Rice Howell, Esq., of Maesgwynne.
Price, Lloyd, Esq., of Castle Pigyn, Carmarthen.
Rees, George Richards Graham, Esq., of Penllwyn.
Rees, William, Esq., of Scoveston, Haverford West.
Richardson, William, *Clerk*, Canon of St. David s.
Roberts, John Davies, Esq., London.
Roberts, Thomas, Esq., of Milford.
Roch, Nicholas Adamson, Esq., of Pasketon, Pemb.
Rowe, George, Esq., Haverfordwest.
Sanders, Henry, Esq., Tenby.
Saunders, Samuel Walker, *Clerk*, St. Ishmael's.
Saurin, Mark Anthony, Esq., of Orielton, Pembroke.
Scourfield, John Henry, Esq., M.P., of Williamston, *Chairman of Quarter Sessions.*
Scourfield, Owen Henry Philipps, Esq., Williamstòn.
Skone, Thomas, Esq., Haroldston House.
Stanley, Edmund Stanley, *Clerk.*
Starbuck, Alfred Basset, Esq., Milford.
Stokes, John, Esq., of Cuffern, Haverford West.
Summers, James Bowlas, Esq., of Moor, H. West.
Summers, J. Bowen, Esq., Milton, Pembroke.
Sutton, John Maule, Esq., Landshipping.
Thomas, Theophilus Evan, Esq., Trehale, Mathry.
Thomas, Thomas Reece, Esq., of Lampeter House, Narberth.
Thomas, Richard James Harries, *Clerk*, Pembroke.
Thomas, William Beach, *Clerk*, Canon of St. David's, Steynton, Milford.
Tombs, Joseph, *Clerk*, Burton, Haverford West.
Walcott, Henry Lyons, Esq., St. David's.
Walters, William, Esq., Haverfordwest.
Ward, Robert, Esq., Sodson, Narberth.
Watkins, William, Esq., Pembroke.
Wells, Charles Cook, Esq., Penally, Tenby.
Williams, Ben Thomas, Esq., Merryvale, Narberth.
Williams, Samuel Propert, Esq., of Lamphey Park, Pembroke.
Worthington, John, Esq., Glynamel, Fishguard.

THE COUNTY FAMILIES OF PEMBROKESHIRE.

ACKLAND, Robert Dudley, Esq., of Boulston, Pembrokeshire.

J. P. of the co. of Pembroke; Freeman and J. P. of the co. of the town of Haverfordwest; formerly served in the Queen's 2nd Dragoon Guards (Bays); a Commissioner of Income Tax, &c.; son of the late Robert Innes Ackland, Esq., of Boulston, J. P. and D. L. of the co. of Pembroke, who also served in the 79th in seven general engagements in the Peninsular War (*d.* 22nd Nov., 1851); *b.* at Cottrell, Glamorganshire, 1820; *ed.* at Eton; *m.*, 1847, to Elizabeth Mary Lloyd, dau. of John Philipps Allen Lloyd-Philipps, Esq., of Dale Castle, co. of Pembroke, and of Mabus, co. of Cardigan, and has issue—
1. Dudley John Innes.
2. Robert.
3. Innes Baldwin.
4. Jane.
5. Emily Winifred.
6. Lillian Constance.

Heir: Dudley John Innes Ackland.
Residence: Boulston, near Haverfordwest.

LINEAGE.

From the monuments in the interesting little church of Boulston (among which are several to the great family of Wogan, formerly possessors of the estate, see *Wogans of Boulston, Picton, Wiston,* and *passim*) it is seen that Dudley Ackland, Esq., was born at Philadelphia, North America, in 1748, and descended from the family of Ackland of Trennington, in Devonshire, having attained the rank of Major in the 91st Regt. Foot, *m.*, 1783, Jane, dau. of Francis Innes, Esq., of Dublin, and after a residence of several years at Pembroke, purchased in 1797 the estate of Boulston, and erected the present mansion on a more elevated spot in the grounds than the site of the ancient house now in ruins. He *d.* Oct. 4, 1809. His son,—
Robert Innes Ackland, Esq., entered the army and rendered distinguished service under Wellington, *m.* Caroline, dau. of Admiral Sir Charles Tyler, G.C.B. (see *Tyler of Cottrell, Glam.*), and had issue the following sons :—
1. ROBERT DUDLEY, now of Boulston (as above).
2. Charles, *d.* Aug. 31, 1858, *æt.* 34.
3. Frederick, civil engineer, *d.* July 6, 1858, *æt.* 29.
4. Henry, Lieut. in R. Pembroke Art. Militia, *d.* May 31, 1860, *æt.* 29.
5. Robert Innes Ackland, Esq.; is in the Civil Service at Somerset House; *m.* Jane, elder dau. of Dr. Henry Brown, of Mortlake, Surrey.

Note.—The ruins of the old mansion of Boulston, formerly *Bul*ston, the residence of the ancient family of the Wogans, adjoin the grounds. The church of Boulston, rebuilt by Robert Innes Ackland, Esq., in 1843, is also in the grounds, and is a "peculiar" in the gift of the family. A *tumulus,* also in the grounds, is spoken of by Fenton in his *Pembrokeshire* (p. 237) as being 300 feet in circumference and twelve feet high at the apex; it was opened in his presence, and yielded near the surface "a small urn with its mouth up very unusually, covered with a thin flag, and nothing in it;" about three feet lower "a rude cist, lined with a sort of clay, containing 'half-calcined bones' mingled with charcoal, having in the midst a flint with a broad end, grown smooth evidently by attrition, as if it had long been in the habit of polishing some hard substance." Fenton was not aware that this was an implement or tool of the "neolithic age," *made* smooth and sharp on purpose for cutting. The approach of night and bad weather caused the explorers to stop their work with this discovery, and possibly the tumulus has never yet been thoroughly examined. Fenton adds that other but smaller barrows lay near the large one. See further under Boulston, at p. 834.

ADAMS, John, Esq., of Hollyland, Pembrokeshire.

J. P. and D. L. for the co. of Pembroke; Sheriff for the same county 1837; son of John Adams, Esq., of Hollyland, by Sophia, dau. of the late Ven. Archdeacon Holcombe, M.A.; *b.* at Market Harborough 1796; *ed.* at Brasenose College, Oxford; *m.*, July 25th 1828, Anne (*d.* 1864), dau. of Henry Gibbons, Esq., of Oswestry, co. Salop; *s.* to estates 1833; has surviving issue,—
1. John A. Philipps, Capt. R.A., *b.* 1831.
2. Henry Joseph, *b.* 1835.
3. Augusta Mary.
4. Frances Louisa.
5. Agnes Anne.

Heir: John Alexander Philipps Adams.
Residence: Hollyland, near Pembroke.
Arms: Quarterly, 1st and 4th arg., a cross gu., thereon five mullets or—(*De Paterchurch*); 2nd and 3rd, sa., a martlet arg., the ancient arms of ADAMS.
Crest: A martlet, as in the arms.
Motto: Certior in cœlo domus.

LINEAGE.

This family derives its descent from Nicholas Adams, of Buckspool, co. of Pembroke, *circa* 1370. We have two good authorities for the genealogy of this ancient family in Lewys Dwnn's *Visitations* and the *Dale Castle MS.* Though independent of each other, they agree in making John Adams (son of Nicholas aforesaid) to be the husband of Alson or Elen, dau. of David *Patrick-Church*, otherwise called De Patrick-Church, from the place or parish where he had lands—afterwards called Pater-Church, and now *Pater*. John was succ. by his son,—

William Adams, who *m.*, according to Dwnn, Alson (*D. Castle MS.*, Margaret), dau. of Sir William Herbert, of Troy, cr. afterwards Earl of Pembroke. Here we ascertain the *period*, for Sir William Herbert was made Earl of Pembroke in 8th Edward IV., or 1468 (see *Herbert of Llanarth*, p. 777), and falling into the hands of the Lancastrians after the battle of Danes' Moor, 26th July, 1469, was beheaded at Banbury the day following. A great grandson of William,—

Harri Adams, was in possession of Hollyland when Lewys Dwnn, as deputy herald, visited the place in 1591, and he signed the pedigree which Dwnn then made out, "Harry Adams." He was, as our deputy herald expresses it, "Dustus off the Pies in the kowntie of Pembrwck," and *m.* Ann, dau. of Richard Wogan, Esq., of Bovestone, by Maud, dau. of "Sir Thomas Ffylips," of Picton. His son Nicholas was succ. by William (1608), he by Nicholas (1650), whose grandson,—

William Adams, Esq., of Hollyland, was succ. by his son,—

William Adams, Esq., also of Hollyland, who *m.* Elizabeth, dau. of John Campbell, Esq., of Stackpool, and with other issue left an eldest son,—

John Philipps Adams, Esq., of Hollyland, father of—

John Adams, Esq., of Hollyland, who by his wife, Sophia Holcombe (*m.* 1795), left a son,—

JOHN ADAMS, ESQ., (as above).

Note.—The date of the erection of *Hollyland* is unknown, but the lands came into the possession of the Adams family in the year 1422. See further *Pater-Church*, p. 836.

ALLEN, Charles Hugh, Esq., of Priskilly Forest, Pembrokeshire.

J. P. for the co. of Pembroke; third, but only surviving son of the late Charles Bowen Allen, Esq., of Rickeston Hall, Pembrokeshire, by Elizabeth, dau. of John Bowen, Esq.; *b.* at Haverfordwest, 1831; *m.*, 1856, Mary, youngest dau. of Thomas Richard Sanders, Esq., of Clifton, Bristol; and has issue 3 sons and 1 dau.

Heir: Allen Charles Allen, *b.* 1857.
Residence; Priskilly Forest, Letterston, R.S.O.
Arms: Quarterly: 1st and 4th, a bend rompu gu. between six martlets sa.; 2nd, ermine, on a canton gu. an owl arg.; 3rd, az., a chevron between three plates, each charged with an ermine spot gu.
Crest: A dove with an olive branch.
Motto: Amicitia sine fraude.

ALLEN, Henry-Seymour, Esq., of Cresselly, Pembrokeshire.

D. L. and J. P. for the co. of Pembroke, formerly Cornet and Sub-Lieut. 1st Life Guards; Capt. Castlemartin, Yeomanry Cavalry; son of Seymour-Philipps Allen, Esq. (J. P. and D. L. for Pembrokeshire, and High Sheriff for the same, 1849), and the Lady Catherine, dau. of Newton, fourth Earl of Portsmouth; *b.* at Cresselly, 30th August, 1847; *ed.* at Harrow; *s.* to estates 1861.

Heir Presumptive: His brother, Frederick-Seymour, *b.* 1849, Lieut. 15th Foot.
Residence: Cresselly, co. of Pembroke.
Town Address: Brooks's, St. James's Street.
Arms: Per bend rompu arg. and sa., six martlets counterchanged.
Crest: A dove with olive branch ppr.
Motto: Amicitia sine fraude.

LINEAGE.

This honourable family derives descent from Thomas Allen, of Gelliswick, who is said to have served with Cromwell in Ireland. John [William?] Allen, fourth in descent from Thomas, and Sheriff of Pembrokeshire in 1732 (see *Sheriffs*, co. Pembr.), *m.* Joan Bartlett, heiress of Cresselly, 1723, ever since which time the family have resided at Cresselly.

They have intermarried with Hertford (Marquess of), Sismondi (the historian), Sir James Mackintosh, Drewe of Grange, co. of Devon, Bayning (Baron), &c.

Note.—The mansion of Cresselly stands on the margin of an arm of Milford Haven, and is surrounded on all sides by a landscape of great beauty. The house, originally built in 1770, was enlarged by the present owner in 1869.

ARDEN, Richard Edward, Esq., of Pontfaen, Pembrokeshire.

High Sheriff for the co. of Pembroke 1872; J. P. and D. L. for Middlesex; F.G.S.; F.R.G.S.; patron of three livings; second son of the late Joseph Arden, Esq., of Islington, Middlesex; *b.* 1804; *m.*, first, 1832, Fanny (*d.* 1836), dau. of John Whitsed, Esq., M.D.; secondly, 1839, Mary, dau. of John Finney, Esq., and has, besides other children, a son,—

Percy, *b.* 1840; *ed.* at Harrow and Brasenose Coll., Oxford; a barrister of the Inner Temple.

Residences: Pontfaen, near Fishguard; Sunbury Park, Middlesex.

BARHAM, Rev. Charles Henry, of Trecwn, Pembrokeshire.

Was once M.P. for Appleby; J. P. for Pembrokeshire and Westmoreland; son of Joseph Foster Barham, Esq., M.P. for Stockbridge, and Lady Caroline, 2nd dau. of Sackville, 8th Earl of Thanet; *b.* in London 1808; *ed.* at Ch. Ch., Oxford; *grad.* M.A.; *m.* 1st, in 1836, Elizabeth Maria, dau. of William Boyd Ince, Esq., of Ince, co. Lancaster; 2ndly, Ellen Catherine, dau. of E. T. Massy, Esq., of Cottsmoor, co. Pembroke, only son of the Hon. E. Massy. (See *Massy of Cottsmoor.*)

Residence: Trecwn, Haverfordwest.
Town Address: Arthur's Club, St. James's St.
Arms: Quarterly, Barham, Foster, and Tufton (as heir-at-law to the late Earl of Thanet).
Crests: A heron among bulrushes—BARHAM; an arm in armour embowed, holding the head of a broken spear—FOSTER; on a wreath a sea-lion sejant ppr.—TUFTON.
Mottoes: Tout bien ou rien. Si fractus fortis. Fiel pero Desdicado.

LINEAGE.

This family (whose name was *Foster*) derives its descent from the ancient family of Foster, or Forster, or Forester, a border clan of Northumberland A.D. 911, one of whose descendants, Joseph Foster, took the name of *Barham* in 1749 by act of parliament. His son, Joseph Foster Barham, *m.* Dorothea Vaughan, of *Trecwn*, Pembr., whose family came from an ancient race in Monmouthshire and Breconshire, and who settled in Pembrokeshire in the time of Henry VIII.

The Barhams are found in England soon after the Conquest at Barham Court and Barham Downs in Kent. One of them, Sir Randall Fitz Urse, was concerned in the murder of A'Becket in Canterbury Cathedral A.D. 1170, being one of the four king's knights, and in consequence fled the country. One of his relations took possession of his estate, and assumed the surname *Barham* from it, and from him it descended in unbroken line to Barth Barham, who did homage for it to Archbishop Wareham, *temp.* Henry VIII. In his posterity it continued till Thomas Barham, *temp.* James I. alienated it. His descendant, Dr. Barham, a learned and distinguished author, *b.* 1680, went to Jamaica and *m.* Elizabeth, widow of Thomas John *Foster*. His descendant,—

Joseph Foster Barham, Esq., inherited Trecwn, Pemb., from his aunt, Mrs. Martha Vaughan, the last of the ancient and honourable family of that name from Monmouthshire, above mentioned (see *Fenton's Pembrokeshire*). His son,—

Joseph Foster Barham, Esq., M.P. for Stockbridge for about fifty years, *m.* the Lady Caroline Tufton, dau. of Sackville Tufton, eighth Earl of Thanet, by whom he had five children.
1. Mary, *m.* Count Gaggiotti.
2. John Foster, *m.* Lady Catherine Grimston (who after her husband's death *m.* the Earl of Clarendon), was M.P. for Kendal, and *d. s. p.*
3. William, *d. s. p.*
4. CHARLES HENRY, now of Trecwn (as above).
5. Caroline Gertrude, *m.* the Rev. Saunderson Robins, and has issue.

BEYNON, John Thomas, Esq., of Trewern, Pembrokeshire.

J. P. for the co. of Pembroke; son of the late John Beynon, Esq., of Trewern; *b.* 1807; *m.*, 1829, Catherine, second dau. of the late Charles Allen Philipps, Esq., of St. Bride's Hill (of the Cresselly family, and assumed name Philipps), and has issue,—

John, *b.* 1829; J. P. for the co. of Pembroke.

Residence: Trewern, near Narberth.

BOWEN, Charles Wheeler Townsend Webb-Esq., of Camrose, Pembrokeshire.

J. P. for the co. of Pembroke; High Sheriff for the same co. 1836; eldest son of the late Hugh Webb-Bowen, Esq., of Camrose, who was son of George Webb, Esq., of Hasguard, in the same co. of Pembroke, by his wife, Anne Bowen, ultimate heiress of Camrose. Hugh Webb succ. to the estate in 1821, when he assumed the surname and arms of Bowen in addition to his own. He was twice *m.*, and left, with other issue, *Charles Wheeler Townsend*, as above, who is *unm.*

Residence: Camrose House, Haverfordwest.
Arms: Quarterly: 1st and 4th, arg., a lion rampant sa.—BOWEN; 2nd and 3rd, gu., a fesse between three owls or—WEBB.
Crest: A lion rampant as in the arms.

LINEAGE.

The *Bowens* of Camrose and Wolfsdale "were offsets" of the line of John Bowen of Llech-meilir (now often named Lochmeyler), and his wife Ivan, dau. and h. of William Roblyn, of Roblinston, co. of Pemb., about the time of Henry IV. (*Fenton*).

BOWEN, James Bevan, Esq., of Llwyngwair, Pembrokeshire.

M.P. for co. Pemb. 1866 to 1868; Vice-Chairman Pemb. Quarter Sessions (appointed 1870); was High Sheriff Pemb., 1862; Mayor of Newport, Pemb., 1870-71. J. P. for the cos. of Pemb. and Cardigan; and D. L. cos. Pemb. and Carmarthen; a member of the Inner Temple; son of the late George Bowen, Esq., of Llwyngwair, and Sarah his wife, dau. of J. Thomas, Esq., of Long-House, co. of Pemb.; *b.* at Llwyngwair, 21st May, 1828; *ed.* at King's Coll., London, and Worcester Coll., Oxford; *grad.* B.A. 1849, M.A. 1851; *s.* 1856; *m.*, 6th, May, 1857, Harriette, youngest dau. of the late Rev. John Standly, of Southoe, Hants; has issue—

1. George Bevan, b. 1858.
2. James Robert, b. 1860.
3. Blanche Harriette, b. 1864.

Heir: George Bevan Bowen.
Residence: Llwyngwair, near Newport, Pemb.
Town Address: United University Club, S.W.
Arms: Quarterly: 1st and 4th, az., a lion rampant or between eight bezants; 2nd, gu., a chevron or between two knots in chief, and a lion rampant or in base; 3rd, az., a hawk ppr.
Crest: A lion rampant or, holding in the paws a knot as in the arms.
Motto: Audaces fortuna juvat.

LINEAGE.

The *Bowens* of Llwyngwair, previous to the beginning of the sixteenth century seated at *Pentre-Evan*, in the same co. of Pemb., trace an unbroken descent from the poet-prince *Gwynfardd Dyfed* (living A.D. 1038), who was himself of the lineage of Meurig, an early King of Dyfed. A careful collation of the *Dale Castle* or *Mabws* MS. with Lewys Dwnn, the *Golden Grove MS.*, &c., results in the following reliable genealogy:—
Gwynfardd was *s*. by his son,—
Cyhylyn, Prince of Dyfed, who *m*. Gwrangen *Fein-droed* ("the slender-footed"), dau. and h. of Sir Tristram, Comes or Earl of Worcester. His son,—
Gwrwared of Cemmaes (corrupted "Kemeys"), *s*. about 1195.
The princely character was now lost, for Cemmaes had been made a Norman barony, and the native lords held under the foreigner. The historic reality and period of Cyhylyn and Gwrwared are clearly demonstrated by a charter of Nicholas (son of Sir William Martin), Lord of Cemmaes (*circa* 1220), granting and confirming to the heirs of Gwrwared and Llewelyn, sons of Cyhylyn, the lands of Precelly from the Via Flandrica, crossing the mountains at Bwlchgwynt, to Eglwyswen, Melinau, Cilgwyn, &c. ("Ego Nicholaus . . . confirmavi heredibus Gwrwared filii Cuhelyn, et hered. Lewelini filii Cuhelyn, totam terram meam in Presselewe, &c."—*Baronia de Kemeys*, p. 48).
He *m*. Gwenllian, dau. of Ednyfed Fychan, Councillor and General of Prince Llewelyn ap Iorwerth of North Wales (see *Ednyfed Fychan*). His son,—
Gwilym ap Gwrwared (*circa* 1227), *m*. Joan, dau. of Sir Leonard Stackpool of Stackpool, Pemb. [Some pedigrees repeat Gwrwared and Gwilym, which is an obvious mistake.]
Einon Vawr, "o'r Coed" ["of the Wood"], Esq., *m*. Dido, dau. of Cadwgan Dhu, Lord of Aberporth. [From this point the pedigree is more clear.]
Owen ap Einion. &c., Esq., *m*. Gwenllian, dau. of Sir William Cantington, Kt., of Trewilym.
Llewelin *ap Owen*, &c., Esq., *m*. Nest, dau. of Howell Fychan, Esq.
Evan *Bowen* Esq., of Pentre Evan, [the first to assume the surname Bowen—he built Pentre-Evan], *m*. Margaret, dau. of Arnold of Hubberston, Esq.
Gwilym Bowen, Esq., *m*. Agnes, dau. of James ap Einion, Esq., of Henllan [in Castlemartin. Here the Bowens of Trellwyn, near Tenby, branch off with Thomas, 3rd son.—*D. Castle MS.*].
Owen Bowen, Esq. [Sheriff of Pemb. 1544], *m*. Janett, dau. and h. of John ap Harry ap Llewelyn, Esq., of Gumfreyston.
Sir James Bowen, Kt., *m*. Mary, dau. of John Herle, Esq., of Brecknockshire,—her mother was [Margaret,] dau. of Thomas ap Gruffydd ap Nicolas, of Newton [Dinefawr,—comp. *Dwnn*, i., 169. In the 8th Henry VIII., A.D. 1516, Sir James Bowen was commissioned to be auditor and attorney for the barony of Cemmaes, to take fines of tenants, punish offenders, &c. He was prob. the same Sir James, and this was the period when the family became seated at Llwyngwair. See *Baronia de Kemeys*, p. 19].
Matthias Bowen, Esq., of *Llwyngwair*, *m*. Mary, dau. of John Philips, Esq., son of Sir Thomas Philips, Kt., of Picton.
James Bowen, of *Llwyngwair*, Esq. [Sheriff of Pemb. 1622; was at Llwyngwair when Dwnn visited it 1591], *m*. Elenor, dau. of John Griffith, Esq., of North Wales [son to Sir William Griffith, of Penrhyn, Kt., *Dwnn*, and *Golden Grove MS.* Dwnn gives the names of 17 children born to James Bowen, 10 sons and 7 daus.].
George Bowen, of Llwyngwair, Esq. [Sheriff of Pemb. 1632], *m*. Dorothy, dau. of John Scourfield, Esq., of Moat.
James Bowen, Esq. [of Llwyngwair], High Sheriff of Pemb. 1671, *m*. Elizabeth, dau. of John Owens, Esq., of Orielton. [He was living in 1705. *Dale Castle MS.*]
George Bowen, Esq., of Llwyngwair [Sheriff of Pemb. 1682], *m*. Dorothy, dau. of Essex Meyrick, Esq., of Bush, near Pembroke.
James Bowen, Esq., of Llwyngwair, *m*. Alice, dau. of Robert Rowe, Esq., of Luny.
George Bowen, of Llwyngwair, Esq. [Sheriff of Pemb. 1803], *m*. Easter, dau. of William Thomas, Esq., of Pentowyn.
James Bowen, Esq., of Llwyngwair, *m*. Martha, dau. of Evan Jenkins of Gloquely.
George Bowen, Esq., of Llwyngwair, Sheriff of Pemb. 1825, *m*. Sarah, dau. of J. Thomas, Esq., of Long-house, co. of Pemb., and was *s*. by his eldest son,—
JAMES BEVAN BOWEN, Esq., now of Llwyngwair (as above).

Note.—The mansion of *Llwyngwair*, beautifully situated, enrivoned by noble woods and rising grounds, near the historic Nevern and Newport, and a tidal river, has a name which is peculiarly agreeable to Pembrokeshire people, and indeed to the people of Wales generally, the particular reasons for which need not be here specified. It is sheltered from the keener winds, and commands in the milder direction a fine prospect, including in its features the boldly planted ruins of Newport Castle. Under the Norman conquest of Cemmaes it fell to the lot of one Cole, a knight in the service of the lord of the barony, and his descendants continued here, according to Fenton, till "about the middle of the fifteenth century."
A cluster of cistvaens with an overthrown cromlech are on the estate. In 1810 Mr. Fenton found in them charcoal, pieces of urns of rudest pottery, particles of bones, and black sea-pebbles (*Hist. of Pemb.*, pp. 554-5).

BOWEN, James William, Esq., of Tygwyn, Pembrokeshire.

Barrister-at-law in leading practice on the South Wales Circuit; D. L. for the co. of Pembroke, and J. P. for the cos. of Pembroke and Cardigan; Patron of the living of Llanfair-nant-Gwyn, co. of Pembroke; son of the late Thomas Bowen, Esq., of Pantyderi, in the co. of Pembroke, formerly a Captain in the 10th Royal Hussars; *ed.* at Shrewsbury School; *m.*, 1st, Charlotte Augusta, daughter of the late Edward Bearcroft, Esq., of Meer Hall, in the co. of Worcester; 2nd, Jane Eliza, youngest dau. of Francis Huntsman, Esq., of Loversall Hall, Doncaster; *s.* in right of his mother to estates of William Morgan Williams, Esq., of Trefach, in the co. of Pembroke; has issue one son and one daughter.

Residence: Tygwyn, Pembrokeshire.
Town Address: 10, Sussex Gardens, Hyde Park.

BOWEN, Rev. William Wheeler Webb-, of Camrose, Pembrokeshire.

M.A., Vicar of Camrose (*cam-rhos*), co. of Pembroke, since 1833; second son of the late Hugh Webb-Bowen, Esq. (see *Webb-Bowen of Camrose*); *b.* at Camrose House, November 7, 1803; *ed.* at the Grammar School, Bristol, under Dr. Goodenough, and *grad.* at Peterhouse, Cambridge, 1828; B.A. 1830, M.A. 1832; *m.*, 1st, June 29, 1830, Mary Grace Josephine Vonburr Fortune, dau. of Rev. Frederic Fortune, M.A., Rector of Moat, in the co. of Pemb. (she *d.* June 13, 1841); 2nd, October 14, 1845, Olivia Duffin, dau. of Charles Duffin, Capt. Bengal Cavalry, and has had issue by the two marriages ten sons living and two dead, and four daughters, two of whom are married.

Residence: The Vicarage, Camrose, Haverfordwest.
For *Arms.* see *Webb-Bowen of Camrose.*

BRYANT, James Robertson, Esq., of Pembroke.

J. P. and D. L. for co. of Pembroke; J. P. for the borough of Pembroke; M.R.C.S., London; Capt. Castlemartin Yeomanry Cavalry; son of the late James Bryant, Esq.; *b.* at Lynn Regis, Norfolk; *ed.* at Dr. Valpy's school at Reading; *m.*, 1st, 1836, Harriet, dau. of Lieut.-Col. Lascelles, late 66th Regt.; 2nd, 1855, Eliza Juliana, dau. of Rev. James D. Hastle, Rector of Euston, Suffolk, Fellow and Tutor of Trin. Coll., Cambridge; has issue three sons and three daughters.

Residence: Pembroke, South Wales.

CAREW, George Henry Warrington, Esq., of Carew Castle, Pemb., and Crowcombe Court, Som.

Descended maternally from the Carews of Carew Castle.

(*Particulars not received in time.*)

CAWDOR, John Frederick Vaughan Campbell, Earl of, of Stackpool Court, Pembrokeshire.

Creations—Baron Cawdor 1796, Earl of Cawdor 1827. Second Earl of Cawdor; Lord-Lieutenant and Custos Rotulorum of the co. of Carmarthen; J. P. and D. L. for Nairnshire, and J. P. for Pembrokeshire; was M.P. for co. Pemb. 1841—1859; President of Carmarthenshire Chamber of Agriculture; patron of 12 livings; eldest son of John Frederick Campbell, first Earl of Cawdor and third Baron Cawdor (see *Lineage*); *b.* 1817; *ed.* at Eton and Christ Church, Oxford; *grad.* B.A. 1838, M.A. 1840; *m.*, 1842, Sarah Mary, second dau. of the Hon. Henry Frederick Compton Cavendish, and has issue surviving—

1. *Frederick Archibald Vaughan Campbell, Viscount Emlyn, b.* 1847; *m.*, 1868, Edith, eldest dau. of C. Turnor, Esq., and Lady Turnor, of Stoke Rochford; J. P. and D. L. for the cos. of Pemb. and Carm.
2. Ronald George Elidor, *b.* 1848.
3. Alexander Francis Henry, *b.* 1855.
1. Victoria Alexandrina Elizabeth, *b.* 1843; *m.*, 1846, Lieut.-Col. F. Lambton, S. F. Guards.
2. Muriel Sarah, *b.* 1845.
3. Evelyn Caroline Louisa, *b.* 1851.
4. Rachel Anne Georgiana, *b.* 1853.

His lordship *s.* on the death of his father, 1860.

Heir: Frederick Archibald, Viscount Emlyn
Residences: Stackpool Court, near Pembroke; Golden Grove, Carmarthen; Cawdor Castle, N.B.
Town House: 74, South Audley Street, W.
Arms: Quarterly: 1st, or, a stag's head caboshed sa.—CALDER; 2nd, gyronny of eight or and sa.—CAMPBELL; 3rd, arg., a galley sa.—CAMPBELL; 4th, gu., a cross or—LORT.
Crest: A swan ppr.
Supporters: Dexter, a lion guardant gu.; *Sinister,* a stag ppr.
Motto: Be mindful.

LINEAGE.

This family is of the clan *Campbell,* and a junior branch of the house of Argyll in Scotland. Their first coming into Wales was through the marriage of Sir Alexander Campbell, Bart., of Cawdor Castle, Nairnshire, with Elizabeth, sister and only heir of Sir Gilbert Lort, Bart., of Stackpool Court. Their son,—

John Campbell, Esq., *m.* Mary, eldest dau. and co-h. of Lewis Pryse, Esq., of Gogerddan, *Card.;* and *d.* 1775, was succ. by his eldest son,—

Pryse Campbell, Esq., of Stackpool Court and Cawdor Castle, who *m.* Sarah, dau. of Sir Edmund Bacon, Bart., and had issue—
John Campbell, Esq., of Stackpool Court, &c.; created, 1796, Baron Cawdor; *m.*, 1789, Lady Caroline Howard, eldest dau. of the Earl of Carlisle ; *d.* 1821. His son,—
John Frederick, second Baron Cawdor, *b.* 1790 ; created Earl of Cawdor 1827 ; *m.*, 1842, Elizabeth, dau. of Thomas, second Marquess of Bath, and left, with other issue, at his decease in 1860, an eldest son,—
JOHN FREDERICK VAUGHAN, now Earl of Cawdor (as above).

Note.—The name *Stackpool* was at first the designation of the *inlet* near the *Stack,* a projecting rock at its mouth ; and the first Norman settler, Sir Elidur, called himself De Stackpool. The spelling Stack*pole* is incorrect and misleading.

CHANDLER, Rev. Henry Christian David, of Narberth, Pembrokeshire.

Rector of Narberth; Surrogate of St. David's; son of Thos. Chandler, Esq., late of Yardley Wood, Worcestershire ; *b.* at Yardley, Worcestershire, Jan. 19, 1837 ; *ed.* at College School, Bristol, and by private tuition; took B.A. (Ægrotat.), 1859, at Gonv. and Cai. Coll., Cambridge; *m.*, 23rd February, 1865, Harriet Mary, only dau. of General Robert Home, C.B., late H.M. Madras Army; has issue two daus. and one son.

Residence: North Sodstone House, near Narberth.

CLARK, The Venerable George, of Robeston Wathen, Pembrokeshire.

Archdeacon and Prebendary of St. David's ; Prebendary of Hereford ; M.A. of Oxford ; held Vicarage of Cantley, Yorkshire, 1845 ; Rectory of Tenby, Pembrokeshire, 1854 ; Prebend. of Hereford Cathedral 1849 ; Archdeaconry and Prebend of St. David's, 1864 ; Author of *Visitation Charges,* 1865 and 1867, and sundry *Sermons,* published at different times; *b.* in London, 1809 ; *ed.* at University Coll., Oxford ; *grad.* B.A. 1831, M.A. 1834 ; *m.*, 1837, a dau. of Rev. J. R. Senior; and has issue 1 son and 4 daus. ; *s.* to Robeston Wathen House by purchase 1867.

Residence: Robeston Wathen.
Town Address: United Clergy and Laity Club, Charles Street, St. James's.
Arms: Arg., a chevron gules charged with three cross crosslets between three martlets ppr. ; on a chief azure a lion passant or.
Crest: A demi-lion rampant or, holding in its dexter paw a trefoil.
Note.—Mansion erected about 1815.

COLBY, John, Esq., of Fynone, Pembrokeshire.

J. P. and D. L. for the cos. of Pembroke, Carmarthen, and Cardigan ; High Sheriff for Pembrokeshire in 1838 ; son of the late John Colby, Esq., of Fynone, and his wife, Cordelia Maria, dau. of Major Colby, of Rhosygilwen, co. Pembroke ; *b.* at Fynone on February 24th, 1816; *ed.* at Trinity Coll., Oxford ; *m.*, 1841, Frances Anna, eldest dau. of James Higgon, Esq., of Scolton, Pembrokeshire (see *Higgon of Scolton*); *s.* to estates in 1831.

Heir presumptive: His brother Robert, Rector of Ansford, Somerset.
Residences: Fynone, and Rhosygilwen, Pemb.
Town Address: University Club, Pall Mall.
Arms: Az., a chevron between three escallop shells or.
Crest: A broken dagger with four drops of blood.
Motto: Dum spiro spero.

LINEAGE.

The Colby family is one of considerable age, originally settled in Norfolk. One of its members was Sir John Colby of Swarston (fourteenth century). One branch came to Pembrokeshire to Blatherston, which place still belongs to Mr. Colby of Fynone. Laurence Colby was High Sheriff in 1722 ; Thomas Colby in 1770 ; John Colby in 1807, and in 1816 for Carmarthenshire. (See *Sheriffs.*)

The Colbys have been represented in the army and navy by several distinguished officers, four of whom of high rank were killed during the civil wars. Major-Gen. Colby, R.E., *b.* 1784, and Capt. Colby, R.N., are names well known. The Colbys entered *Rhosygilwen* through the marriage about 1715, of John Colby, Esq., brother of Laurence Colby, Esq., the sheriff above-mentioned, with Miss Jones, heiress of that place. (See further *Colby of Pant-y-deri.*)

John Colby, Esq., of Fynone, *m.* Cordelia Maria Colby of Rhos-y-gilwen (the late Mrs. Colby of Rhos-y-gilwen, a descendant of the above-named John Colby, Esq. and Miss Jones, whereby the two branches of the family were united, and left issue,—
1. JOHN COLBY, ESQ., of Fynone (as above).
2. Charles, Capt. 28th Regt., *d.* in India.
3. Edward, also an officer in the army, *dec.*
4. Robert, in Holy Orders, Rector of Ansford (as above), *m.* Miss Vaughan, of Brynog, Card., and has issue a son.
    1. Cordelia, *m.* Capt. McNeill Boyde, R.N. (*dec.*), and has issue, John McNeill Boyde, *b.* Sept. 2, 1841 ; Archibald Henry, *b.* April 1, 1851 ; Colin Edward, *b.* Jan. 1, 1853.
    2. Mary, *m.* Major Henry Lewis of Clynview.
    3. Eliza, *m.* Edward Bearcroft, Esq., of Meer Hall, Wor., and has issue Hugh Edward.

Note.—The mansion of *Fynone* (see *engraving,* p. 844) was erected about the year 1795, a little distance from the site of the old house. It is in the midst of fine trees, and grounds tastefully kept ; a waterfall about a mile from the house is especially an object of admiration.

COLBY, Thomas, Esq., of Pant-y-deri, Pembrokeshire.

Eldest son of Major-General Thomas Frederic Colby (*d.* 1852), by his wife, Elizabeth Hester Boyd, dau. of Archibald Boyd, Esq., Treasurer of Derry, Ireland, and sister of the Very Rev. Archibald Boyd, Dean of Exeter; son of Thomas Colby, Captain Royal Marines, son of Thomas Colby of Rhos-y-gilwen, son of John Colby of Cilgerran, son of Laurence Colby of Castle Deran; *b.* 1830; *ed.* at Bonn on the Rhine; *s.* 1852; is *unm.*

Residence: Pant-y-deri, Eglwys-wrw, Pemb.
Arms: Per pale, *dexter*—az., on a chevron between three camels' heads arg., two crescents and a star, gules; *sinister*—azure, a chevron between three escallop shells or.
Crest: An arm in armour, in the hand a dagger embrued.
Motto: Dum spiro spero.

LINEAGE.

The descent of this family is the same with that of Colby of Fynone, two lines of Colbys having been united in the latter. (See *Colby of Fynone.*)
Thomas Colby, Esq., of Rhos-y-gilwen (*b.* 1717, *d.* 1789), descended maternally through Anne Jones of Rhos-y-gilwen (like Colby of Fynone ultimately), from the Warrens of Trewern (ext.), by his wife, Esther Davies, of Gilfach, left a son, Thomas Colby, Capt. of Marines, who, besides other issue left a dau., Cordelia Maria, (who *m.* John Colby, Esq., of Fynone, and survived him as Mrs. Colby of Rhos-y-gilwen; *d.* 1869); and an eldest son and successor,—
Thomas Frederic Colby, Major-Gen., *b.* 1784, who *m.*, 1828, Hester Boyd (as above), who had issue—
Thomas Colby, Esq., now of Pant-y-deri (as above); William Henry; John; James; Anne; Cordelia; Maria.

Note.—The mansion of Pant-y-deri, which is of moderate size, contains parts which are of considerable age, although the time of its erection is unknown; several additions have been made, the last of which, about the year 1840, was the most considerable.

DAVIS, Gilbert William Warren, Esq., of Trewarren, Pembrokeshire.

Lord of the Manor of St. Ishmael's, Pembrokeshire; J. P. for the co. of Pembroke; High Sheriff for the same co. 1839; son of Henry Davis, Esq., of Mullock in the said co.; *b.* at Mullock, March 14, 1809; *ed.* at Dr. Butler's at Shrewsbury; *m.* Margaret, dau. of the Rev. T. S. Biddulph, of Amroth Castle, Pembroke; *s.* on his attaining his 25th year, March 14, 1834; has issue three sons and seven daughters.

Heir: Henry Warren Davis.
Residence: Trewarren, Milford Haven.

Note.—On the estate at Trellwyn-uchaf, near Fishguard, is a *cromlech* or so-called Druidic altar. The house of *Trewarren* was erected in 1872.

DE RUTZEN, Frederick Leopold, Baron, of Slebech Hall, Pembrokeshire.

A Baron of the (late) kingdom of Hanover; J. P. and D. L. for the co. of Pembroke; High Sheriff for same co. 1871; son of the late Franz, Baron de Rutzen, of Slebech Hall, by his wife Mary Dorothea, dau. and co-h. of the late Nathaniel Phillips, Esq., of Slebech Hall (See *Slebech*), and has issue—

Albert, *b.* 18—; Stipendiary Magistrate for Merthyr Tydfil 1872; *m.*, 1872, Horatia Augusta, eldest dau. of Alan James Gulston, Esq., of Dirleton, co. of Carm.

Residence: Slebech Hall, near Haverfordwest.

DUNN, Nicholas John, Esq., of Elm Grove, Pembrokeshire.

J. P. and D. L. for the co. of Pembroke; High Sheriff for same co. 1858; son of the late John Dunn, Esq., of Westmoor House, Pembrokeshire, who was in the Commission of the Peace (but never qualified) for Pembrokeshire, and was an officer in the Yeomanry Cavalry; *b.* at Westmoor House, 23rd July, 1820; *ed.* at Pembroke Coll., Oxford, and Middle Temple; *s.* on death of his father, October, 1834; *m.*, 1855, Emma, dau. of Major Hutchins, 30th B.N. Infantry, and has issue four sons and six daughters.

Heir: John Henry, *b.* 1857.
Residence: Elm Grove, St. Florence, Tenby.
Arms: Az., a wolf rampant arg., armed and langued gu.
Crest: A lion's paw erased, grasping a serpent.
Mottoes: Profuit hoc vincente capi. Industrioso otium pœna.

LINEAGE.

This family derives its descent from Sir Henry Dwnn, son of Owen Dwnn, Esq., of Muddlescombe. Owen Dwnn (*Picton Castle*), of the line of Dwnns of Abercyfor and Cydweli, *m.*, about 1460, Catherine, dau. and h. of Sir John Wogan of Picton, whose gr. grandfather, Sir John Wogan of Wiston, had *m.* Joan, or Ivan, dau. and h. of Sir William Picton, a Norman knight who had settled on the lands of Picton Castle (so called after his name), given him by Arnulph de Montgomery, *temp.* William Rufus. (See *Picton Castle* and *Pembroke Castle.*) We are informed in The *Heraldic Visitations of Wales* by Lewys Dwnn, who himself claimed to be of this venerable lineage, that the Dwnns of Cydweli traced direct to *Meurig*, King of Dyfed. The lineage paternal and maternal of the present family is thus of a very ancient description, the former being Cymric, the latter Norman.

THE COUNTY FAMILIES OF PEMBROKESHIRE. 899

The celebrated Dr. John Donne, Dean of St. Paul's, theologian and poet (*b*. 1573), whose biography, by quaint Izaac Walton, is one of the most delightful books of that age, was descended from a branch of this family.

Lewys Dwnn, the Deputy Herald, was by his mother (whose surname he assumed) grandson of Capt. Rhys Gôch Dwnn, gr. gr. grandson in a direct line of David Dwnn, brother of Owen Dwnn of Cydweli, Carm., above named. David removed to Montgomeryshire, being appointed steward to Edward Cherleton, Lord Powys, and by marriage became possessed of Cefn y Gwestyd, near Welshpool. Lewys was the only child of his parents, and was born in that neighbourhood. His labours in Welsh genealogy extended from about 1580 to 1614, and he is supposed to have died about 1620. The pedigrees he collected, published in 1846 under the editorship of Sir S. R. Meyrick, and entitled *Heraldic Visitations of Wales*, are of the greatest value in the investigation of the descent of Welsh families; but Lewys Dwnn was not only industrious and honest, but also credulous and uncritical, and his immense collection must be used with care and sifting discrimination.

EDWARDES, Mrs. Tucker-, of Sealyham, Pembrokeshire.

Anna Martha Tucker-Edwardes, widow of William Tucker-Edwardes, Esq., of Sealyham (who was *b*. 1873; *d*. 1825), is the second dau. of the late John George Philipps, Esq., of Cwmgwili, co. of Carm. (see *Philipps of Cwmgwili*, and of *Ystradwrallt*); was *m*. to Mr. Tucker-Edwardes in 1807, and has surviving issue—

John Owen, *b*. 1808; *m*., 1840, Anna Jane, dau. of W. Jones, Esq.
Owen John, *b*. 1815; *m*.; *residence*, Trerhos.
Thomas, *b*. 1816; *residence*, Cleddy Lodge, Haverfordwest.
Mary, *m*., 1845, Col. A. Borradaile.
Anna Martha, *m*. William Owen, Esq., Tan-y-gyrt, Denbighshire.
Emma Mary Anne Grace.

Residence: Sealyham, near Haverfordwest.
Arms: Quarterly: 1st and 4th, az., a chevron embattled and counter-embattled or between three sea-horses naiant arg.—TUCKER; 2nd and 3rd, ermine, a lion rampant sa.—EDWARDES.
Crest: A bear's paw holding a battle-axe arg.
Motto: Garde la foi.

LINEAGE.

This family represents the Tuckers of Sealyham, who claimed through female descent to be of the *Games* of Breconshire through Sir David Gam, Kt., and the *Edwardes* of Trefgarn, descended, according to the *Dale Castle MS.* and *Lewis Dwnn* (who visited Sealyham and drew out the family lineage in 1597, when *Richard Edwardes*, who signs the pedigree, was Chancellor of St. David's), from the line of *Tudor Trevor*, Lord of the Marches. The representative of the family at this time was *Thomas Edwardes*, Esq., of Trefgarn, who *m*. Sage, dau. of Thomas *Tucker*, Esq., of Sealyham. His son,—
Owen Edwardes, Esq. (living 1613), *m*. Elliw,

dau. of Morgan Foel, of Haverfordwest, and had a son, John, of Trefgarn, who by his wife Anne, dau. of Thomas Birt, left a son and heir,—
Owen Edwardes, Esq., of Trefgarn, who *m*. Damaris, dau. of James Perrott, Esq., and sister (*Dale Castle MS.*) of Sir Herbert Perrott, Kt., of Haroldston (see *Sheriffs*, 1665), and left a son,—
John Edwardes, Esq., of Trefgarn, who by his wife Frances (*m*. 1685), dau. and co-h. of William Philipps, Esq., of Haythog, had a son,—
Owen Edwardes, Esq., of Trefgarn, living 1720. He *m*. Jane, dau. and heiress of Rowland Mortimer, Esq., of Castell-llwyd, *Carm*. (see *Mortimer of Geneurglyn* and *Coedmore*), by Jane, dau. of Thomas Bowen, Esq., of Trellwyn (see *Trellwyn* and *Llwyngwair*). They had two sons, *Rowland* and Francis, from the latter of whom descended the Pembrokeshire Barons Kensington (see *Kensington*), and from the former—by his wife Anne, dau. of George Harries, Esq., of Priskilly—the family of Tucker-Edwardes of Sealyham. His son,—
John Owen, *m*., 1777, Catherine, dau. and co-h. of John Tucker, Esq., of Sealyham. His son was the late—
William Tucker *Edwardes*, Esq., of Sealyham (as above).

EVANS, Charles Tasker, Esq., of Upton Castle, Pembrokeshire.

Late Ensign 1st Batt. 10th Foot; is patron of the living of Nash, Diocese of St. David's; son of the late William Paynter Evans, Esq., of Upton Castle, and great-nephew of Pierce Evans, Esq., J. P., formerly of Upton Castle; *b*. at Upton Castle, 3rd December, 1844; *m*., 26th April, 1870, Mary Paynter, dau. of Joshua Paynter, Esq., Inspector-General of Hospitals.

Residence: Upton Castle, near Pembroke.
Crest: A boar's head.

LINEAGE.

The family of Evans, of Upton Castle, the ancient residence of the *Malefants* (extinct since fourteenth century), trace from the Rev. Mr. Evans, who *m*. a niece of Mr. Tasker, owner by purchase of Upton. On Mr. Tasker's decease, leaving no issue, she, along with her two sisters, co-heiresses, succeeded to the estate, which ultimately devolved upon Mr. Evans and his issue.

The Malefants, of Norman origin, were a prominent family also in Glamorganshire, which county they had entered from Pembrokeshire during its occupation by the Norman lords (see *Malefant of St. George's*). The original stock at Upton became extinct with Henry Malefant, whose dau. and co-heiress, Alice, *m*. Owen, son of Griffith ap Nicholas of Dinefawr, grandfather of *Sir Rhys ap Thomas*, of Dinefawr, Carew Castle, &c. Their issue took the surname Bowen (*ap Owen*), and continued at Upton Castle for many generations until the race ended in heiresses, the estate, about 1760, was sold, and the demesne of Upton became the property of Mr. Tasker, before named.

Note.—For a view of Upton Castle see p. 836. Of its condition about the commencement of the present century Mr. Fenton says:—"There is but little of the castle remaining besides the entrance between two bastions finely overgrown with ivy, giving it a picturesque appearance. The chapel is a simple plain building as it now appears, without doubt totally altered as to its external form, having modern windows and a common slated roof. It stands a little apart from the castellated remnant of the building, but was at one time, I am inclined to think, attached to and made a portion of it. Divine service is never performed there now, and it seems perfectly desecrated. The mother church, about a mile off, is called Nash."

FORTUNE, William, Esq., of Leweston House, Pembrokeshire.

D. L. and in the Commission of the Peace for the co. of Pembroke; son of the late William Fortune, Esq., J. P., of Leweston House, and formerly of Haverfordwest, by Catherine, dau. of John Savery, Esq., of Butcombe Court, Somerset, and Shilston House, Devon; *b.* at Haverfordwest, 21st of March, 1802; *ed.* at Eton; *m.*, 19th July, 1828, Thomasina Hannah Newtonia von Burr, youngest dau. of the Rev. Joseph Fortune, M.A., of New Moat, by Harriette Sophia, only dau. of Major Newton Barton Burr, whose father, Frederic Burr, Esq., *m.* Catherine Barton, only dau. of Lieut.-Col. Robert Barton, whose father, Robert Barton, Esq., of Brigstock, Northamptonshire, *m.*, 1677, Hannah Smith, one of the half-sisters of Sir Isaac Newton, Kt., the astronomer; *s.* to estates in 1826; has issue two daughters,—

1. Newtonia von Burr. 2. Marianne.

Heirs: His two daus., co-heiresses.
Residence: Leweston House, near Haverford.
Arms: Or, on a mount, in base vert, a female figure representing "Fortune," the dexter hand resting on a wheel, in her sinister a cornucopia; in chief gules a tower, on each side two swords in saltire proper.
Crest: A dexter arm in armour embowed, hand clenched, the wheel of Fortune suspended from the wrist.
Motto: Audaces fortuna juvat.

GOWER, Robert Frederic, Esq., of Glandovan, Pembrokeshire, and Clyn-Derwen, Carmarthenshire.

High Sheriff for co. Pembroke 1844; son of the late Robert Gower, Esq., of Glandovan; *b.* 31st December, 1794; *m.* Lillias Millar Stewart, dau. of the Rev. Dr. Stewart, of Kirkcowan, N.B.; *s.* 1837; has issue—

1. Capt. Erasmus Gower, *b.* 1833; was Capt. 12th Lancers, now of the Castlemartin Yeomanry; J. P. for co. Carmarthen.
2. Abel Anthony Gower, } both *d.* young.
3. Robert Lewes Gower, }
4. Grace Lillias Gower.
5. Sarah Amelia Georgiana Gower.

Heir: Erasmus Gower.
Residences: Glandovan, Cilgerran; Clyn Derwen, Narberth Road.
Town Address: Conservative Club.
Arms: Quarterly: 1st and 4th, az., a chevron between three wolves' heads or; 2nd, or, a cross patoncé az.; 3rd, gu., three snakes enowed ppr.
Crest: A wolf's head.
Motto: Frangas non flectes.

LINEAGE.

In addition to the article under *Clynderwen* (p. 285) the following particulars of lineage subsequently obtained are now supplied.

The Gowers of Glandovan are descended from the Gowers of Trentham, before they were created Dukes of Sutherland. William Gower, Esq., of Boughton St. John's, M.P. for Ludlow twenty-six successive years (his name appears as subscriber to fund for rebuilding St. Mary's Church, Cardigan, 1703), *m.* Jane Stedman, only dau. of James Stedman, Esq., of Strata Florida, and Margaret, dau. of Richard Owen, of Rhiwsaeson, Mont. Her grandfather, John Stedman, Esq., of Strata Florida, had *m.* Jane, dau. of Edward Vaughan, Esq., of Trawscoed, 1628 (see *Lisburne of Trawscoed*, and *Stedman of Strata Florida*), heiress of Glandovan, and on failure of male issue, heiress also of Strata Florida. William Gower was the son of Abel Gower, Esq., of Boughton St. John's (who was second cousin of Lord Gower, of Trentham); grandson of Abel; great-grandson of George, of Colemarsh, Worcestershire; and gr. gr. grandson of William Gower, Esq., of Colemarsh.

William Gower, Esq., by the above-named Jane Stedman, of Glandovan, had issue—

1. William Gower, Esq., Capt. in the East India Service; *m.* Bridget Ford, of Bury, and had issue 2 sons and 2 daus. All *d.* young but Anna Emma, who *m.* J. Fox, Esq.
2. James, *d.* unmarried.
3. *Abel Gower*, Esq., of whom again.
4. Martha, *d.* unmarried.
5. Jane, *m.* Capt. John Donkley, R.N., *d.* 1758.
6. Barbara, *m.* Captain Blarkeny, R.N.
7. Anna Emma, *d.* at Glandovan.
8. Margaret, *m.* John Clies, Esq., whose dau. Henrietta *m.* the celebrated first Lord Rodney.
9. Adeliza, *m.* Robert Gustard, Esq.
10. Catherine, *m.* Lieut. Owen, R.N.

Abel Gower, Esq., of Glandovan, *m.* Letitia, only dau. and h. of the Rev. Erasmus Lewes, of Lampeter-pont-Stephan, sixth son of John Lewes, Esq., of Gernos, Cardiganshire, and had issue 9 sons and 8 daus. The eldest son,—

Sir Erasmus Gower, Admiral of the White in 1792, received, with Admiral Lord Cornwallis, the thanks of both Houses of Parliament, and in 1794 the thanks of the East India Company for the safe convoy of thirteen of their ships from China to England; in 1798 he was sent to quell the mutiny at the Nore; commanded Lord Macartney's Embassy to China; and was Governor of Newfoundland; *d., unm.,* 1814.

Abel Anthony Gower, Esq., of Glandovan, Castle Malgwyn, Clyn Derwen, and Pontvane, *d. unm.* at Glandovan, 1837.

Robert Gower, Esq., *m.* Sarah, dau. of George Royal, Esq., had issue 4 sons and 3 daus. ROBERT FREDERIC GOWER, ESQ., now of Glandovan, &c. (as above).

Abel Lewes Gower, Esq., of Castle Malgwyn,

THE COUNTY FAMILIES OF PEMBROKESHIRE

m. Elizabeth, youngest dau. of James Logan, Esq., of Clarkeston, Stirlingshire; *d. s. p.* 1849, at Castle Malgwyn.
John Lewes Gower, } both *d.* young.
Erasmus William Gower, }
Georgiana Gower, *d.* unmarried.
Sarah Gower, *d.* unmarried.

Note.—Glandovan is at present let to Archdeacon North.

GRIFFITH, Moses, Esq., of Manor-Owen, Pembrokeshire.

J. P. and D. L. for the co. of Pembroke; on the roll of Sheriffs for 1871; formerly in the Medical Department of the Army; son of Samuel Griffith, Esq., of Poyntz Castle, Pembrokeshire; *b.* at Poyntz Castle, 30th April, 1789; *ed.* at the Grammar School, Haverfordwest; is *unm.*

Residence: Manor-Owen, near Fishguard.

HARRIES, George Esq., of Trevaccoon, Pembrokeshire.

Son of the late John Harding Harries, Esq., J. P. for the co. of Pemb., and Sheriff for the same 1846, and Martha, dau. of William Williams, Esq., of Llandygige, St. David's; *b.* at Solva, October 31, 1818; *ed.* at Elizabeth Coll., Guernsey; *m.*, 1855, Charlotte Frances Forster, dau. of Rev. Charles Manners Forster and Charlotte Frances Forster; *s.* to Trevaccoon estates 1869; and has issue one son, Charles Harding, and six daughters.

Heir: Charles Harding, *b.* 1859.
Residences: Trevaccoon, St. David's, and Rickeston Hall, Milford.
Crest: A rising eagle.

LINEAGE.

This family has long been settled in Pembrokeshire, possessing the estates of Cryglas and Trevaccoon, and has intermarried with the ancient family of Warenne of Trewern, Newport, now extinct (see Trewern), who are held to have originated in the marriage of one of the Conqueror's followers with a dau. of Gwynfardd, a regulus of Dyfed.
They were formerly known as Harries of Crygglâs, in the same co., a property still in their possession. The late Major Harries, grandfather of the present representative, was a gentleman on active military duty in the Cinque Ports Cavalry, but resided at Trevaccoon the latter part of his life. He *m.* Mary, dau of Thomas Williams, Esq., of Pope Hill, co. of Pembroke, by whom he had—
John Harding Harries, Esq., father of—
GEORGE HARRIES, Esq. (as above).

HARRIES, George Augustus, Esq., of Hilton, Pembrokeshire.

J. P. and D. L. for the co. of Pembroke; High Sheriff for same co. 1860 (see *Sheriffs*); younger son of the late Major Samuel Harries, of Trevaccoon (see *Harries of Trevaccoon*), by Mary, dau. of the late Thomas Williams, Esq., of Pope Hill, both in the co. of Pembroke; *m.*, 1845, Bridget, dau. of the late Thomas Perkins, Esq., of Haverfordwest, and has issue.

Residence: Hilton, near Haverfordwest.
Arms: See *Harries of Trevaccoon.*

HARRIES, John Henry, Esq., of Heathfield, Pembrokeshire.

J. P. for the co. of Pembroke; Lieut. Royal Pembroke Artillery Militia; son of the late George Jordan Harries, Esq., of Heathfield and Priskilly, co. Pemb., by his wife Susannah Caroline, dau. of Henry Skrine, Esq., of Warleigh, Somerset; *b.* at Heathfield, 2nd December, 1840; *m.*, 16th March, 1867, Ellen Eliza Florence, dau. of Lieut.-Col. James Florence Murray; and has issue two daus.,—Eliza Caroline, *b.* 1868, and Frances Maria, *b.* 1870; *s.* to estates on the death of his father in 1865.

Residence: Heathfield, Letterston, S. Wales.
Arms: Quarterly: 1st and 4th, az., three mullets pierced or; 2nd and 3rd, gu., a chevron ermine between three garbs or.
Crest: A mullet of five points pierced or.
Mottoes: Y gwir yn erbyn y byd. Integritas semper tutamen.

LINEAGE.

This family has been known as of Tregwynt, Tresissyllt, Priskilly, and Heathfield successively. They were settled at the first-named place about the year 1600, the then owner being Llewelyn Harries, Esq., whose son,—
Thomas Harries, Esq., *m.*, 1640. Anne Bowen, of Llwyngwair. His 2nd son, James, *m.* Ellen Griffiths, of Tresissyllt, and his son, John, *m.* Ursula Owen, of Priskilly. There followed George Harries, of Tresissyllt (*d.* 1766), who *m.* a Symmons, of Llanstinan; John, of Tresissyllt, who *m.* a dau. of the Rev Joseph Hill, of Colebrook, co. Carm.; and his son,—
George Harries, Esq., of Priskilly, who *m.*, 1781, a Bowen of Leweston. His eldest son, John Hill, was father of—
George Jordan Harries, Esq., of Priskilly and Heathfield, whose eldest son is—
JOHN HENRY HARRIES, Esq. (as above).

Note.—The well-preserved Cromlech at Trellys, near Fishguard, and a very fine old Roman encampment at Pwllcawrog (Pwll-*caerog*), St. David's parish, are on this estate.

HIGGON, James, Esq., of Scolton, Pembrokeshire.

J. P. for the co. of Pembroke; son of John Higgon, Esq., who was High Sheriff for Pembrokeshire 1793; *b.* at Haverfordwest 1793; *ed.* at Eton, and Brasenose Coll., Oxford; *m.*, 1818, Frances, dau. of Abel Walford Bellairs, Esq., of Uffington, co. Lincoln; *s.* to estates 1817; has issue two sons and two daus. The eldest dau. *m.* to John Colby, Esq. (see *Colby of Fynone*), the youngest *m.* to Rev. J. A. Clarke, of Welton Park, Northamptonshire.

Residence: Scolton, near Haverfordwest.
Arms: Arg., a lion rampant gu.
Crest: A lion rampant as in arms.
Motto: Mea gloria fides.

LINEAGE.

This family derives its descent from the ancient Welsh family of *Higgon*, one of whom served as High Sheriff for Carmarthenshire in 1551, and another in 1558 (see *Sheriffs, co. of Carm.*).

Note.—The old mansion of *Scolton* was destroyed by lightning about two centuries ago, when the family went to reside in Haverfordwest, and remained there till 1841, when they returned to their old and newly restored family place.

JAMES, John Taubman William, Esq., of Pantsaison, Pembrokeshire.

J. P. and D. L. co. of Pembroke, and J. P. co. of Cardigan; formerly an officer 83rd Regt.; son of the late Col. John James, of Pantsaison, and his wife, Margaret Christian Taubman, eldest dau. of Major Taubman, of the Nunnery, Isle of Man; *b.* at Haverfordwest, Oct. 31st, 1812; *s.* 1819; *m.*, Dec. 28th, 1836, Margaret Elizabeth, eldest dau. of Capt. Jones-Parry, R.N., of Llwyn-Onn, co. Denbigh (see *Jones-Parry of Llwyn-Onn*); has issue one son, Robert Lloyd James, and one dau., Margaret Ellen James.

Heir: Robert Lloyd James, *b.* 1854, *m.*, 29th Aug., 1872, Annie Sophia, eldest dau. of F. W. Docker, Esq., of Bangor, co. of Carnarvon.
Residence: Pantsaison, near Cardigan.
Arms: Sable, a dolphin naiant, embowed or, between three cross crosslets of the second—JAMES; quartering *Taubman, Bateman,* and *Vaughan.*
Crest: A demi-bull rampant, sable, horned and hoofed or.
Motto: Ffyddlon at y gorphen—"Faithful to the end."

LINEAGE.

This family has been resident at and in possession of Pantsaison beyond any record to the contrary. There is a tradition in the family that there were thirteen William Jameses in succession before the last two Johns; but it does not seem ever to have had very extensive possessions, or to have arrogated to itself a place among the chief families of the county. It has intermarried with families of higher pretensions for the last four generations, the Jones-Parrys of Llwyn-Onn, Madryn, &c., the Taubmans of the Isle of Man (through them from the Christians, Curwens, and other old families of Cumberland), the Batemans of Pembrokeshire, and Vaughan Thomas of Posté, Pembrokeshire, descended from the Vaughans of Brecknockshire.

William Jones, Esq., of Pantsaison, gr. gr. father of the present proprietor, *m.* Margaret, dau. and h. of Vaughan Thomas Esq., of Posté, co. of Pemb. His eldest son,—

William Jones, Esq., of Pantsaison, *m.* Rebecca Bateman, sister and sole heiress of John Bateman, Esq., of Robeston Wathen, and had a large family of sons and daughters, the eldest son being—

Col. John James, of Pantsaison (as above), who *d.* 1819, leaving two sons,—
 JOHN TAUBMAN WILLIAM, now of Pantsaison (as above), and—
 Rev. Mark Wilks W. James, M.A., who *m.*, 1846, Charlotte Ellen, dau. of Capt. Jones Parry, of Llwyn-Onn, co. of Denbigh, and had issue.

Note.—At the west end of Pantsaison there is a scarped earthwork, marked in the ordnance map as "Castell," locally, however, called *Castell-ion;* there is also on a farm belonging to the estate, called Waun-Whiod, a *tumulus,* called in the ordnance map "crug," whether originally a burial-place or beacon is not known; there is also a smaller one (not marked in the map) on an adjoining farm of the estate, called Bryncws.
The present house of *Pantsaison* is of the Italian villa style, and was built in the year 1836. Two or three (and probably more) successive houses have been standing on or near the same spot.

JENKINS, Richard David, Esq., of Pantirion, Pembrokeshire.

In the Commission of the Peace for the cos. of Pembroke and Cardigan, and J. P. for the borough of Cardigan; has been thirteen times Mayor of Cardigan; patron of the living of Llangoedmore, Card.; eldest son of the late Griffith Jenkins, Esq.; youngest son of Griffith Jenkins, Esq., of Cilbronnau, co. of Cardigan (see Lineage, *Heyward of Cilbronnau,* Card.), by Anne, his wife, dau. of Richard Jones, Esq., of Pantirion aforesaid; *b.* at Pantirion, August 1, 1815; *m.*, 1st, May 19, 1840, Elizabeth Anne, the only child of John Bowen, Esq., of Tredefaid, Pembrokeshire, and Mary, his wife, dau. of Thomas Davies, Esq., of the Bridge House, Cardigan; 2nd, February 1, 1855, Elizabeth, dau. of Thomas Lewis, Esq., surgeon R.N., and Jane, his wife, dau. of Hugh Davies, Esq., a banker at Machynlleth, Mont., and has surviving issue—

1. Richard Bowen, in holy orders.
2. Mary Anne.
3. Margaretta Elizabeth, *m.* to William Picton Evans, Esq., and has issue.
4. Laurence Hugh.
Heir: Rev. Richard Bowen Jenkins, M.A., Queen's Coll., Oxford.
Residence: Pantirion, Pembrokeshire.
Arms: Quarterly: 1st and 4th, arg., on a cross sa., five crescents. In the dexter canton a spearhead erect gu.—*Sir Griffith ap Elidur Goch;* 2nd and 3rd, quarterly: 1st and 4th, arg., three boars' heads caboshed sa., for *Cadwgan;* 2nd and 3rd, gu., a lion rampant regardant or—*Elystan Glodrydd*—JENKINS.
Crest: A naked arm holding an oak club.
Motto: Da yw ffon amddiffyniad.

LINEAGE.

The descent is from *Elystan Glodrydd* through Sir Griffith ap Elidur Goch, for the full particulars of which see the family pedigree under *Heyward of Cilbronnau*, Card.
Griffith Jenkins, Esq., above named, and Ann, his wife, had issue—
1. RICHARD DAVID JENKINS, as above.
2. Griffith John, *d. s. p.*
3. Elizabeth Mary, *m.* to Rev. D. P. Thomas, M.A., of Cwm-mawr, Carm., Rector of Llan-maes, Glam., and had issue John Griffith Stuart, *d. s. p.*, and Frances Anne.
4. Anne, *d. s. p.*
5. Mary, *m.* to Thomas Davies, Esq., of Park-y-prat, Pemb., and had issue Griffith Ormond and William Henry.

Note.—It is believed that an old monastery was erected in a field still called "Park Monachlog," on a slope not far from Pantirion House, overlooking the river Teivi prior to the erection by Martin de Tours of the abbey of *St. Dogmael's.* The last portion of the ruins were taken down about eighty years ago. *Trefasser*, in the par. of Llanwnda, Pemb., now belonging to Mr. Jenkins, is said to have been the birthplace of *Asser Menevensis*, the friend and biographer of King Alfred. See Fenton's *Pembrokeshire*, p. 26.

JENKINS, Thomas Askwith, Esq., of Trevigin, Pembrokeshire.

Major on the Retired List of the Madras Army, on the General Staff of which he served ten years, and latterly as Deputy Quarter master-General; in the Commission of the Peace for the cos. of Pembroke and Cardigan; eldest son of the late Capt. Thomas Jenkins of Pen'rallt, Cardiganshire (who was the third son of Griffith Jenkins, Esq., of Cilbronnau), by Jane, only dau. of Thomas Morris, Esq., of Trevigin and Bachhendre; *b.* at Trevigin, 10th July, 1809; *m.* at Madras, on the 15th May, 1841, Harriet, eldest dau. of Capt. Henry Hutchinson, H.E.I.C. Maritime Service, by his wife, Christian Wilkinson, only child of Henry Tripp, Esq.; *s.* to Trevigin, and to the lordship of the manor of Monnington on the demise of his uncle, Thomas Morris, Esq., in 1851; has issue—

1. Thomas Morris, Lieut. Madras Staff Corps.
2. John Henry.
3. Harriet Hannah Morris.
Residence: Trevigin, Pembrokeshire.
Arms: Quarterly: 1st and 4th, arg., on a cross sa. five crescents or; in the dexter canton a spear's head erect, gu.—*Sir Griffith ap Elidur Goch;* 2nd and 3rd, quarterly: 1st and 4th, arg., three boars' heads caboshed, sa.—*Cadwgan;* 2nd and 3rd, gu., a lion rampant or—*Elystan Glodrydd*, for JENKINS, and quartering, besides thirty-three others, the arms of MORRIS—Az., in an orle of roses, arg. a lion rampant or, charged on the shoulder with the escutcheon of Rhys ap Tewdwr; gu., a lion rampant within a bordure indented or, for *Jenkin Llwyd of Cemmaes*.
Crest: A dexter arm embowed, holding a club, all proper.
Motto: Da yw ffon amddiffyniad.

LINEAGE.

For full lineage of the Jenkins family see *Jenkins of Cilbronnau*, Card. The family of *Morris*, now extinct in the male line, is descended from Jenkin Llwyd of Cemmaes, of the tribe of *Gwynfardd Dyfed*, a powerful chieftain in his time. He *m.* Eva, the dau. and h. of Meredydd ap Thomas, of Trefgarn, ap Llewelyn the last Lord of South Wales, who *m.* the Lady Eleanor, gr. dau. of Edward I., King of England.
Morris ap Morris ap Owen of Pencelly, in Cenarth, ap Hywel ap Jenkin Llwyd, of Cemmaes, was in 1580 residing at Fynnonau, in the parish of Manordeivi, Pemb., and the family records further show that the third from him, Philip Morris, settled in 1650 at Bach-hendre, parish of Llanvihangel Penbedw, Pemb., and his gr. grandson, Thomas Morris, of that place, the father of the late Thomas Morris, Esq., removed to Trevigin in 1803.

KENSINGTON, William Edwardes, Baron,

Creation 1776. Fourth Baron Kensington in the peerage of Ireland; formerly in the Coldstream Guards; Lord Lieutenant of the co. of Pembroke; M.P. for Haverfordwest since 1868; eldest son of William, third Baron Kensington, by Laura Jane, dau. of Cuthbert Ellison, Esq., of Hepburn, co. of Durham; *b.* 1835; *ed.* at Eton; *m.*, 1867, Grace Elizabeth, eldest dau. of Robert Johnstone Douglas, Esq., of Lockerbie House, co. Dumfries, N.B.; *s.* as fourth Lord Kensington on the death of his father, 1871, but is not prevented by his title from retaining his seat in the Commons. Has brothers living—
Cuthbert Ellison, *b.* 1838.
Henry George, *b.* 1844.
Residence: 69, Grosvenor Street, W.
Arms: Quarterly: 1st and 4th, ermine, a lion rampant sa.—EDWARDES; 2nd and 3rd, gu., a chevron between three crosses bottony or—RICH.
Crest: On a mount vert, a wyvern, wings expanded arg.
Supporters: Two reindeer ppr. armed and unguled or.
Motto: Garde la foi.

LINEAGE.

The descent of Lord Kensington is from the house of *Edwardes of Sealyham*, co. of Pembroke, the grandfather of the late Lord Kensington, being Francis Edwardes, Esq., second son of Owen Edwardes, Esq., of Trefgarn, whose eldest son became progenitor of the Sealyham family. Francis Edwardes *m.* the Lady Elizabeth *Rich*, only dau. of Robert Rich, second Lord Holland, Earl of Warwick, and Baron Kensington. His only surviving son was *William*, second Baron Kensington, who inherited estates of Rich family on demise of his cousin, Edw. Henry Rich, seventh Earl Warwick, but not title, which went to Edward Rich, cousin and heir male. He was created Baron Kensington, peerage of Ireland, in 1776, the former barony having expired at the death of Edward, eighth Baron, *s. p. m.* (See further *Edwardes of Sealyham.*)

LEACH, Henry, Esq., of Corston, Pembrokeshire.

Late Capt. H.M. 45th Regiment; J. P. for co. of Pembroke; Sheriff for same co. 1852; Capt. Pembrokeshire Yeomanry Cavalry; eldest son of the late Henry Leach, Esq., D. L. and J. P. for co. of Pembroke, Major Commandant of Pembrokeshire Yeomanry Cavalry; *b.* at Ddol, Cardiganshire, 15th August, 1824; *ed.* at private schools; *m.*, 1867, Mary, second dau. of the late Francis Edwardes Lloyd, Esq., of Plas Cil-y-bebyll, Glamorganshire; J. P. for that co.; *s.* 1864.

Heir Presumptive: His brother, William, Major H. P., unattd.
Residence: Corston, near Pembroke.
Crest: A swan on a bugle.
Motto: Jubeo cavere.

LEACH, John, Esq., of Ivy Tower, Pembrokeshire.

J. P. for the co. of Pembroke; High Sheriff for same co. 1855; Major of Pembrokeshire Yeomanry Cavalry; son of the late John Leach, Esq., of Pembroke, by his wife, Charlotte, dau. of G. Elliot, Esq.; *b.* at Pembroke, Jan. 8th, 1826; *ed.* at Harrow, and University Coll., Oxford; *m.*, Sept., 1851, Mary Anne Agnes, dau. of the late Henry Skrine, Esq., of Warleigh Manor, Bath, Somerset, and Stubbings House, Berks; *s.* 1837.

Residence: Ivy Tower, near Tenby.
Town Address: Windham Club.
Arms: Gu.,a chevron arg.betw.three swans ppr.
Crest: A swan on a trumpet.
Motto: Jubeo cavere.

LEWIS, John Lennox Griffith Poyer, Esq., of Henllan, Pembrokeshire.

D. L. for the co. of Pembroke; J. P. for the cos. of Pembroke and Carmarthen; High Sheriff for the latter co. in 1867; son of the late John Lewis, Esq., of Henllan (see *Lineage*); *b.* 1819; *ed.* at Bromsgrove School, and St. John's Coll., Cambridge; called to the Bar at Lincoln's Inn 1848; *s.* 1834; *m.*, Feb., 1857, Katharine, dau. of Daniel Poyer Callen, Esq., of Molleston, co. of Pembroke.

Heir Presumptive: His brother, the Rev. Richard Lewis, Rector of Lampeter Velfrey, Pembrokeshire.
Residence: Henllan, Narberth, Pembrokeshire.
Town Address: Oxford and Cambridge Club.
Motto: Be wise as serpents.

LINEAGE.

The family of Lewis of Henllan trace a direct lineage from *Gwynfardd Dyfed*, a lord of Dyfed, or Pembrokeshire, and descendant of Meurig, an early King of Dyfed. Gwynfardd, a poet as well as a lord of territory, was a contemporary with Howel Dda (the Good), the Legislator of Wales (*d.* 948), and resided near Whitland, *Carm.* From the valuable MS., "*The Book of Golden Grove*," we learn that a descendant of Gwynfardd,—

Llewelyn *y Coed* ("of the wood"), son of Owen ap Robert, *m.*, 43 Edward III. (A.D. 1369) Nest, dau. of Howel Fychan (Vaughan), and had issue besides Rhys, ancestor of the Owens (extinct) of Trecwn, and Ievan, ancestor of the Bowens of Pentre-Ivan, Llwyngwair, and Trelloyne (see *Bowen of Llwyngwair*), and other children,—

Philip, of Pant-têg, who had a son Howel, and he a son,—

Lewis, of Panteg (in Velfre), who *m.* Gwenllian, dau. of Sir Thomas Philips, Kt., of Cilsant (15th cent.), (who became the founder of the great family of Picton Castle by his mar. with Jane, dau of Henry Donne of that place,—see Lewis Glyn Cothi, *Works*, p. 301,) and had issue a son,—

Davis *ap Lewis* (here the surname Lewis begins to be settled), who *m.* Dyddgu, dau. of Lewis ap Thomas ap John, of Cwmgwili (D., 860, p. 12) and had, with other issue, a second son,—

Lewis David, whose wife was Agnes, dau. of Jenkin Ievan Powell, who had a son David, who *m.*, and besides an eldest son,—

John David Lewis, of whom hereafter, and a youngest, Lodwick, had a second son,—

Gruffydd David Lewis. He *m.* Dorothy, dau. of Lewis Richard, and had a son and successor, Reynold Lewis, Esq., of Llanddewi (Velfrey), whose wife was dau. of John Philip Lewis Thomas of that place, by whom he had issue. Her mother was dau. of John Holland, jun.

John David Lewis, above named, eldest son of David, left a son, -

Lewis John (Sheriff of co. of Pemb. 1676?), who had four sons,—1. Sir William Lewis, Kt., Mayor of Bristol; 2. George, *m.* a dau. of Francis Phillips, of Waun-gron, Sheriff of co. of Pemb. 1680; 3. Reynold, *m.* Cissil, dau. of John Lloyd, of Cilgwyn, Card.; 4. Roger : and two daus.,—Mary, who *m.* Morris Davids, of Gilfach Simmons, near Llampeter Velfrey; Anne, who *m.* John Howell, of Glan-tâf, and a 4th son,—

Griffith Lewis, who *m.* Mary, dau. of Robert Prust, and left a son, Roger, whose son,—

Richard Lewis, Esq., *b.* May, 1727, *m.* Mary,

THE COUNTY FAMILIES OF PEMBROKESHIRE. 905

dau. of John Griffith, Esq., of Glan-yr-hydd, co. of Carm., and by her had five children—John, David, Catherine, Mary, and Margaret. Richard d. in 1770, and was s. by his son,—
John Lewis, Esq., who d. unm. in 1780, and was s. by his brother,—
David Lewis, Esq., who m., 1786, Elizabeth, dau. of Mr. Morgan Lewis, merchant of Carm., and had issue seven children, Mary, John Evan, Margaret, Elizabeth, Catherine, Elinor, and Owen. David d. in 1816, and was s. by his son,—
John Lewis, Esq., of Henllan, who m., 1st, 1817, Eliza, dau. of Charles Callen, Esq., of Grove, and had by her two sons,—
1. JOHN LENNOX GRIFFITH POYER LEWIS, Esq., now of Henllan (as above).
2. Richard, b. 1820, in Holy Orders, Rector of Lampeter Velfrey (1851), M.A. of Wor. Coll., Oxford 1846; m., 1847, Georgiana, dau. of Major Lewis, and has one son, Arthur Griffith Poyer Lewis, b. March, 1848.
Mr. Lewis m., 2ndly, in 1823, Elizabeth, dau. of William Humphreys, Esq., of Pembroke, and had by her surviving issue one son, Hubert, and one dau., Elizabeth. He d. 14th March, 1834, and was s. by his son, as above.

LEWIS, William Henry, Esq., of Clynfyw, Pembrokeshire.

J. P. and D. L. for the co. of Pembroke; in the Commission of the Peace for the cos. of Carmarthen and Cardigan; High Sheriff for co. of Pemb. 1847; Major of Royal Pemb. Art. Militia; son of the late Thomas Lewis, Esq., of Clynfyw, J. P. and D. L. for the co. of Pemb., by Elizabeth, dau. of William Lewis, Esq., of the Llwyn-y-grawys family; b. 1807; m., 1850, Mary, dau. of John Colby, Esq., of Ffynonau (Fynoné), Pembrokeshire; ed. at Harrow and Trin. Coll., Oxford.

Residence: Clynfyw, near New Castle-Emlyn.

LLOYD-PHILIPPS, Frederick Lewis, Esq., of Pentypark, Pembrokeshire.

J. P. for the cos. of Cardigan, Carmarthen, and Pembroke; D. L. for Cardiganshire; a Capt. Royal Carmarthen Artillery Militia; is patron of the living of Walton East, Pembrokeshire; son of Col. James Philipps Lloyd-Philipps (see *lineage*); b. at Mabws, Cardiganshire, 15th June, 1823; ed. at Brasenose College, Oxford; grad. B.A. 1848, M.A. 1851; m., 1851, Elizabeth Francis, dau. and co-heiress of John Walters-Philipps, Esq., of Aberglasney, co. Carmarthen; succ. brother, J. Beynon Lloyd-Philipps, Esq., 1865.

Heir presumptive: His Cousin, Harry Lloyd.
Residences: Penty Park, Haverfordwest; Hafodneddyn, Carmarthen.

Arms: Az., a wolf rampant argent—LLOYD; arg., a lion rampant sa, ducally gorged and chained or—PHILIPPS.
Crests: A wolf as in the arms. A lion as in the arms.
Mottoes: Ar Dduw y gyd. Ducit amor patriæ.

LINEAGE.

This family of Philipps of Penty Park (formerly generally written *Pentre-park*) has descended—as we learn from the pedigrees in *Lewys Dwnn* and in the *Dale Castle* and *Gilfach MSS.*—from a junction of the great houses of Thomas of Dinefawr, father of Sir Rhys ap Thomas, *Bowens* of Pentre-evan (see *Bowen of Llwyngwair*), *Philipps* of Picton, and *Lloyd* of Ffoes-y-bleiddiaid. (For full lineage see *Lloyd Philipps of Dale Castle*).
John Lloyd, Esq., of Ffoes-y-bleiddiaid, had a third son,—
Col. James Philipps Lloyd, of Pentypark, b. 1762, who m. Winifred, dau. of J. Thomas, Esq., and had issue two sons,—
James Beynon, who in 1837 succeeded his father at Pentypark, d. 1865, and
FREDERICK LEWIS, now of Pentypark (as above)

Note.—The old mansion of *Pentypark* having been destroyed by fire, the present one was built in 1710. See a reference to the situation of Pentypark, p. 841.

LLOYD-PHILIPPS, John Philipps Allen, Esq., of Dale Castle, Pembrokeshire, and Mabws, Cardiganshire.

J. P. and D. L. for cos. of Cardigan and Pembroke, and the county and town of Haverfordwest; High Sheriff for co. Cardigan 1844; Major of Royal Cardigan Militia; patron of the living of Dale, Pemb.; eldest son of the late John Allen Lloyd, Capt. Coldstream Guards, of Dale Castle, by Elizabeth, dau. of Col. Bishopp, of Storrington, Sussex, and assumed the surname Philipps in addition to his own of Lloyd, under direction of the will of James Philipps, Esq., of Pentypark (see *Lineage*); b. at Chichester June 26, 1802; ed. at Bury St. Edmund's School; succ. 1823 on death of his grandfather, John Lloyd, Esq. (see *lineage*); m., 1st, Dec. 9, 1823, Charlotte, youngest dau. of the late Capt. Bartlet, R. E., she d. 1863; 2ndly, June 20th, 1865, Elizabeth Anne, eldest dau. of Peel Stevenson, Esq., of Uffington, Linc.; has surviving issue from the first marriage one son and five daus. now living.

1. John Allen (see *Lloyd-Philipps of Mabws*).
2. Charlotte Maria, m. Henry Mathias, Esq., of Haverfordwest, and has issue.
3. Elizabeth Mary (see *Ackland of Boulston*).
4. Mary Frances, m. Capt. Cornes, R.E.

Heir: John Allen Lloyd-Philipps, late Capt. 82nd Regt., b. 1824.

Residences: Dale Castle, Haverfordwest, Pembrokeshire; and Mabws, Cardiganshire.
Arms: Arg., a lion rampant sa., ducally gorged and chained or.
Crest: A lion, as in the arms.
Motto: Ducit amor patriæ.

LINEAGE.

Rhodri Mawr, or Roderick the Great (*d.* A.D. 876), king, first of North Wales, then of all Wales, had six sons, between the three elder of whom he divided his dominion, and the youngest of whom was Idwal or *Tydwal Gloff*, who *m.* Helen, dau. of Aleth, ruler of *Dyfed*, which included Pembrokeshire (see p. 846).
From them, in the sixth generation (see *Gilfach and Dale Castle MSS.*, and Dwnn's *Herald. Visit. of Wales*), came the celebrated knight or Lord of Castell Hywel, *Cadivor ap Dinawal*, or Dyfnwal, who took the fortress of Cardigan from the Normans A.D. 1155 (p. 168), and *m.* Catharine, dau. of Lord Rhys, deprived by the Plantagenet king of his rightful title of "Prince of South Wales." See *Lloyd of Maesyfelin; Lloyd of Castell-Howel.*
His descendants in regular succession were— Rhydderch ap Cadivor, Rhys ap Rhydderch, Cadwgan Fawr ap Rhys, Cadwgan Vychan, Cadwgan Grach of Carrog, Llewelyn ap Cadwgan Vychan, Rhys Ddu ap Llewelyn, Evan ap Rhys, Meredydd ap Evan, Morgan ap Meredydd, David Llwyd ap Morgan, who *m.* a dau. of Gogerddan, and had a son,—
Oliver *Lloyd*, Esq., of Ffosybleiddiaid (the first mentioned as of Ffosybleiddiaid, a property still in the family). David Lloyd of Ffosybleiddiaid, his son, *m.* Gwladys, dau. of Richard Herbert, Esq., of Pencelli, and left a son,—
Oliver Lloyd, who *m.* a Lloyd of Llanllyr. His son, David Lloyd, had a son,—
John Lloyd, Esq., of Ffosybleiddiaid, who *m.* Mary, a dau. of James *Philipps*, Esq., of Pentypark, co. Pemb. (first mention of Pentypark, which still continues in the family). Their son,—
James Lloyd, Esq., *m.* Anna Maria, dau. and heiress of Richard Lloyd, Esq., of Ystradteilo and Mabws; *d.* June 6, 1800. The eldest son of James Lloyd, Esq., of Mabws, was—
John Lloyd Philipps, Esq., who *m.* Elinor, dau. and heir of John Allen, Esq., of Dale Castle, Pemb. He *d.* 1820, leaving an eldest son,—
John Allen Lloyd, Esq., of Dale Castle and Mabws, of the Coldstream Guards; *b.* 1777; *m.*, 1801, Elizabeth, dau. of Col. Bishopp, *d.* 1805, and was succ. by his eldest son,—
JOHN PHILIPPS ALLEN LLOYD-PHILIPPS, Esq., now of Dale Castle (as above).

MASSY, Edward Taylor, Esq., of Cottesmore, Pembrokeshire, and Dirreens, co. Limerick.

J. P. and D. L. of the co. of Pembroke; formerly a Capt. in the Royal Flintshire Militia; only son of the Hon. Edward Massy, second son of the second Lord Massy, by Catharine, only dau. of John Villiers Tuthill, Esq., of Kilmore, in the co. of Limerick (see *Lineage*); *b.* in the city of Chester on the 4th of July, 1807; *ed.* at Brasenose Coll., Oxford; B.A. 1830; *m.*, 8th October, 1835, Helen, only dau. of Jonathan Haworth Peel, Esq., of Cottesmore (formerly known by the name of "the Cotts") and Denant, in the co. of Pembroke, who was first cousin of the late Right Hon. Sir Robert Peel, second Bart., and has issue 6 sons, and 7 daus. one of whom is dead; *s.* to the co. Limerick estates January, 1836; to Cottesmore by purchase from J. H. Peel, Esq., 1839.

Residence: Cottesmore, near Haverfordwest.
Arms: Quarterly: 1st and 4th, arg., on a chevron between three lozenges sable a lion passant or—MASSY; 2nd and 3rd, sable, a lion passant arg—TAYLOR; and impaling PEEL,— three sheaves of as many arrows ppr., banded gu., on a chief az. a bee volant or.
Crest: Out of a ducal coronet or, a bull's head gu. armed sa.
Motto: Pro libertate patriæ.

LINEAGE.

Hamon de Massy came over from Normandy with William the Conqueror, and received large grants of land from Hugh Lupus, first Earl of Chester, who made him one of his eight barons under the title of "Baron de Dunham-Massy" in Cheshire. The title and lands of Dunham-Massy descended in direct succession to the sixth baron Hugh Massy of Sale, a descendant of Robert, second son of Hamon, the second baron, *m.* Margaret Percy, and went over to Ireland in 1641 holding a military command, and received some years afterwards, in reward for his services, the lands of Duntrileague, in the co. of Limerick.
Hugh, his eldest son, *m.* Amy, dau. of John Benson, Esq., and had issue 3 sons and 2 daus.; his 3rd son, Charles, Dean of Limerick, was father of Sir Hugh Dillon Massy, first baronet.
Col. Hugh, his eldest son, *m.* Elizabeth, dau. of the Rt. Hon. George Evans, father of the first Lord Carbery, and had issue 6 sons and 4 daus.; his sixth son, General Eyre Massy, in reward for his services, was created in 1800 Baron Clarina, of Elm Park, co. Limerick.
Hugh, eldest son of Col. Hugh Massy, created in 1776 Baron Massy of Duntrileague, in the co. of Limerick, *m.*, 1st, Mary, dau. and co-h. of Col. James Dawson, of Ballynacourty, co. Limerick, and had issue 3 sons and 2 daus.; his 2nd son, James, assumed the name of Dawson, from whom the family of Massy Dawson; 2ndly, Rebecca, dau. of Francis Dunlap, Esq., and had issue 3 sons and 3 daus.
Hugh, his eldest son, second baron, *b.* 1733, *d.* 1790, having *m.*, 1760, Catherine, eldest dau., and, with her sister, Sarah, Countess of Carrick, co-h. of Edward Taylor, Esq., of Ballyport, co. Limerick, had issue 4 sons and 4 daus.
The Hon. Edward Massy, his second son, *b.* 1766, *d.* 1836, having *m.* in 1795, Catherine, only dau. of John Villiers Tuthill, Esq., of Kilmore, co. Limerick, had issue, besides 4 daus., an only son,— EDWARD TAYLOR MASSY, Esq., now of Cottesmore, co. Pembroke (as above).
Note.—The present house, erected nearly on the site of the old house by the present proprietor, was completed in 1841. See *Engraving*, p. 841.

MATHIAS, Lewis, Esq., of Lamphey Court, Pembrokeshire.

J. P. of the co. of Pembroke; High Sheriff 1856; Guardian of the Poor of the parish of Lamphey; son of the late Charles Mathias, Esq., of the same place; *b.* 1813; *ed.* at Oxford; *m.*, 1845, Emily, dau. of Mr. J. B. Lawes, Roehamstead, Herts, and has issue.

Residence: Lamphey Court, Pembroke.

LINEAGE.

This family was formerly of Llangwarren, co. Pemb., and held a good position in the county.

Note.—Near Lamphey Court stand the ruins of *Lamphey Palace*, one of the several sumptuous residences of the Bishops of St. David's in the fourteenth and fifteenth centuries. It is one of the most venerable piles in a district abounding in memorials of the past. A good part of this splendid ruin is turned into a kitchen and fruit garden, and many of the finest architectural features are concealed or destroyed. Whether this arises from the want of thought, or from the misfortune of its having no owner to protect it, we know not, but it is impossible to witness the Vandalism without real regret. In spite of all, however, the place continues to present some beautiful features, among which are remains of an arcade similar in conception to those witnessed in the great palace of St. David's, and in the castle of Swansea, and in all cases owing their existence, it is believed, to that great builder, Bishop Gower.

MEYRICK, Thomas Charlton, Esq., of Bush, Pembrokeshire.

M.P. for Pembroke boroughs from 1868; patron of the living of Gumfreston, near Tenby; son of Sir John Chiverton Charlton, of Apley Castle, Shropshire, by his 1st wife, Sophia Jane, dau. and heiress of Thomas Meyrick, Esq., of Bush, Pembroke, whose surname he has assumed in addition to his own; *b.* at the Vineyard, Wellington, Shropshire, March 14th, 1837; *m.*, 10th of April, 1860, Mary Rhoda, 2nd dau. of Col. Frederick Hill, who is brother of the 2nd Viscount Hill, and has issue—
1. Frederick Charlton, *b.* July, 1862.
2. St. John Meyrick, *b.* August, 1866.
3. Rowland Francis, *b.* Sept., 1867.
4. Dora Rhoda, *b.* May, 1861.

Residence: Bush, near Pembroke.
Town Address: Windham Club, St. James's.
Arms: The Meyrick arms—Sa. on a chevron arg. between three brands erect raguly fired, ppr., a fleur-de-lis gu. between two Cornish choughs respecting each other ppr.
Crest: A tower arg., thereon a Cornish chough.
Motto: Heb Dduw heb ddim; Duw a digon.

MORGAN, Howard Spear, Esq., of Tegfynydd, Pembr., and Carmarthenshire.

J. P. for cos. of Carmarthen and Pembroke, and J. P. and D. L. for the bor. and co. of Haverfordwest; only son of the late John Lloyd Morgan, Esq, M.D, of Haverfordwest and Tegfynydd; *b.* at Haverfordwest, April 30th, 1824; *ed.* at Swansea and University of Edinburgh; *m.*, 27th Nov., 1856, Annie, dau. of Henry Lloyd, Esq.; *s.* to estates 1867: has issue—
1. Christopher Hird, *b.* 29th Nov., 1857.
2. Hugh Kenyon.
3. Edith Margaret.
4. Lloyd Spear.
5. Katherine Jane.

Heir: Christopher Hird Morgan.
Residence: Tegfynydd, near Narberth.
Crests: A stag's head couped at the shoulders; an armed arm embowed grasping a javelin.
Motto: Fortitudine et prudentia.

OWEN, Sir Hugh Hugh, Bart.

Baronetcy created 1813. Second Bart.; J. P. and D. L. for the co. of Pembroke; Lieut.-Col. Pemb. Militia; was M.P. for the Pembroke boroughs from 1826 to 1838, and afterwards from 1861 to 1868 (see *Parl. Annals*); eldest son of Sir John, first Bart., of Orielton; *b.* 1803; *s.* 1861; *m.*, first, 1825, Angelina Maria Cecilia, dau. of Sir C. G. Morgan, Bart., of Tredegar Park (she *d.* 1844); secondly, 1845, Henrietta, dau. of the Hon. Edward Rodney, Captain R.N., and has issue from both marriages; eldest son,—

Hugh Charles Owen, *b.* 1826.

Town Address: Reform Club.
Arms: Gu., a chevron between three lions rampant or.
Crest: A lion rampant, as in the arms.
Motto: Honesta optima politia.

LINEAGE.

Sir John Owen, the first Baronet, was maternally descended from the old house of Orielton, beginning in that line with Sir Hugh Owen, Knight, of Bodowen, Anglesey (see *Sheriffs*, 1577), who *m.* Jane, dau. and sole h. of George Wyrriott, possessor of Orielton. Paternally he was descended from the family of Lord, being the son of Joseph Lord, Esq., who *m.* Corbetta, dau. of Lieut.-Gen. John Owen; *s.* to the estates under the will of Sir Hugh Owen, sixth and last bart. of that line, and assumed the name and arms of Owen. He was created a Bart. in 1813; was Lord Lieutenant of Pembrokeshire, and Governor of Milford Haven; and represented successively for many years the boroughs of Pembroke and Haverfordwest (see *Parl. Annals*).

OWEN, William, Esq., of Withybush, Pembrokeshire.

J. P. and D. L. for the co. of Pembroke; High Sheriff for co. of Pembroke 1859, being then of Poyston in the same co.

Residence: Withybush, near Haverfordwest.

(*Further information in next edition.*)

PEEL, Xavier de Castanos Royds, Esq., of Glanafon, Pembrokeshire.

J. P. for the co. of Pembroke; Lieut.-Col. of the Rifle Volunteers; was in the Army; son of the late Jonathan Haworth Peel, Esq., of Glanafon; *b.* at Bury St. Edmund's, 13th of July, 1808; *m.*, April 17, 1838, Mary, dau. of Roger Eaton, Esq., of Parkglas, in the co. of Pembroke.

Residence: Glanafon, near Haverfordwest.

LINEAGE.

This family is from a younger branch of the Peels of Lancashire, of whom the Right Hon. Sir Robert Peel, Bart., was the most distinguished.

PHILIPPS, Rev. James Henry Alexander (late Gwyther), of Picton Castle, Pembrokeshire.

Clerk in Holy Orders; M.A., Trinity Coll., Cambridge; Vicar of St. Mary's, Haverfordwest; was for many years Vicar of Madeley, Salop; is patron of the livings of Morvil, Llanycefn, Mynachlog-ddu, Llysyfrân (alternately with J. W. Scourfield, Esq., M.P.), Begelly and East Williamston, Llandowror and Reynalton; author of various sermons, published separately and at different times; son of Rev. H. Gwyther, Vicar of Yardley, Worcestershire, and assumed the surname Philipps on succeeding his half-brother, Lord Milford, in 1857 (see *Lineage*); *b.* at Winkfield, Wilts, Aug. 26, 1814; *ed.* at Trinity Coll., Camb., where he *grad.* B.A. 1838, M.A. 1841; *m.*, Feb. 14, 1844, Mary Catherine, dau. of William Woolrych Lea, Esq., of Ludstone Claverley, Salop; *s.* to Picton Castle and the extensive estates thereto belonging in 1857; has had issue 2 sons (both deceased) and 6 daus, 2 living:—

1. Mary Philippa, *m.*, 1868, to Charles F. G. Fisher, Esq., and has issue.
2. Amy Octavia.

Residence: Picton Castle, Haverfordwest.

Town Address: 60, Princes Gate, Hyde Park.
Arms: Arg., a lion rampant sa., ducally gorged and chained or.
Crest: A lion, as in the arms.
Motto: Ducit amor patriæ.

LINEAGE.

The ancient house of Picton traces in unbroken line from Cadifor ap Collwyn, Lord of Dyfed, in Pembrokeshire, otherwise called Cadifor Vawr, or Cadivor the Great. It has intermarried at different periods of its more recent history with the Philippses of Cilsant; the Perrotts of Haroldston; the Wogans of Wiston; the Droydens of Northamptonshire; the Earl of Wicklow's family; the Leas of Ludstone, Shropshire, and of Hagley, Worcestershire. Among the distinguished men it has supplied in past time may be named Sir John Wogan, Chief Justice of Ireland, Sir Henry Donn, and Sir John Philipps (the Good).

Cadifor Fawr, Lord of Blaen-Cych, was father of Bledri, Lord of Cilsant (the place which became so celebrated as the cradle of the clan Philips, Philipps, and Phillipps, so widely spread in South Wales); and he of Rhys ap Bledri, whose son, Sir Aaron, fought in the Crusades under Richard I., and was made Knight of the Sepulchre.

Philip ap Meredith of Cilsant was *sixth* in direct line from Sir Aaron; and his son,—

Sir Thomas ap Philip, *m.* Jane, dau. of Sir Henry Donne, Kt., of *Picton*, who had inherited that place in right of his mother, Catherine, dau. and co-h. of Sir John Wogan of Picton, whose ancestor, Sir John Wogan, Kt., of Wiston, had entered Picton by marrying Joan, dau. and h. of Sir William *Picton*, the first and only Norman possessor of the place. (See further *Picton Castle*.)

John *Philips* of Picton, son of Sir Thomas, *m.* Elizabeth, dau. of Sir William Gruffydd of Penrhyn, co. of Carn., Chamberlain of North Wales. His grandson,—

Sir John Philips, was Lord of Picton when Lewys Dwnn, Deputy Herald, visited the place in Oct., 1591, and completed the pedigree of the family up to that date, and the document was signed by him as "John Phillipps," though Dwnn persists in spelling the name according to his own notion of phonography, "Ffylips, Esgwier, Dustus o'r Pies a'r Corwm." He was made a bart. in 1621, and *m.*, as first wife, Ann, dau. of Sir John Perrott, Kt., of Haroldston, and was *s.* by his eldest son,—

Sir Richard Philipps. Here the name first assumed this form, and has been followed by different branches of the clan; but the late Sir Thomas Phillipps, of Middlehill, preferred the form adopted by "John Phillipps" in Dwnn. Sir Richard was followed by Sir Erasmus (*d.* 1697), he by Sir John (*d.* 1736), and he by a second Sir Erasmus, fifth Bart., who dying *s. p.*, the title devolved on his brother,—

Sir John Philipps, sixth Bart. Of another brother, *Bulkeley Philipps*, hereafter. Sir John was *s.*, 1704, by his only son,—

Sir Richard Philipps, seventh Bart., of Picton Castle, cr. Lord Milford 1776, and *d. s. p.* 1823, when the title became extinct.

Bulkeley Philipps, above mentioned, of Abercover, left a dau., Mary Philippa, who *m.* James Child, Esq., of Begelly, and left an only child of the same name, who, by her first husband, *John Grant*, Esq., of Nolton, left a son,—

Richard Bulkeley Philipps Grant, who became in 1823 heir to the Picton estates under the will of

THE COUNTY FAMILIES OF PEMBROKESHIRE. 909

Lord Milford, assumed the name and arms of Philipps, was cr. a baronet in 1828, and Baron Milford in 1847. He *m.*, 1854, the Lady Anne Jane, dau. of the Earl of Wicklow, and *d. s. p.* 1857. His mother, Mrs. Grant, *m.*, secondly, the Rev. Henry Gwyther, M.A., of Yardley, Worcestershire, by whom she left, besides a dau., Maria Philippa, now *dec.*, a son,—
JAMES HENRY ALEXANDER, who, on the death of his half-brother, Lord Milford, became inheritor of the Picton estates, assumed the surname Philipps, and is now of Picton (as above).

Note.—For an account of *Picton Castle*, with an *engraving*, see p. 834. To the particulars there given it may be added that the castle is an oblong building, flanked with six large bastions, with a narrow projection, terminating in two bastions of smaller dimensions at the east end with handsome doorway —originally moated ,with drawbridge. The west end was materially added to, at a very large cost, by the first Lord Milford.

PHILLIPS, Mrs. LORT-, of Lawrenny Park, Pembrokeshire.

Isabella Georgiana, widow of George Lort Phillips, Esq., of Lawrenny Park, (M.P. for the co. of Pembroke from 1860 until his death in 1866; High Sheriff for the same co. 1843; J. P. and D. L.; who was son of John Lort Phillips, Esq., of Lawrenny, by Augusta, dau. of William Ilbert, Esq., of Bowrings Leigh, co. of Devon, *b.* July, 1811; *ed.* at Harrow and Trin. Coll., Cambridge; and *s.* to a portion of his estates on death of his father in 1840, and to the remainder on death of Sir Wm. Owen Barlow, Bart. to whom he was heir-at-law, in or about 1852); is the only dau. of John Hensleigh Allen, Esq., of Cresselly, in same co., by Gertrude, third dau. of Lord Robert Seymour, son of a Marquess of Hertford; she was *m.* to Mr. Lort Phillips in 1841, and *s.* at his decease *s. p.* 1866.

Heir: Her husband's nephew, a minor.
Residences: Lawrenny Park, Pembroke; and Ashdale, Haverfordwest
Arms: Arg., a lion rampant, sa., ducally gorged and chained or.
Crest: A lion rampant, as in the arms.
Motto: Animo et fide.

LINEAGE.

The family of *Lort Phillips* trace to George Phillips, Esq., M.D., and a junior branch of the *Lorts* of Stackpool, through the marriage of the said George Phillips with Eliza, dau. of John Lort, Esq., of Prickeston; and to the Barlows of Cresswell. The property of the Lorts of Stackpool (an ancient family now extinct) passed, through marriage of the heiress into the family of Campbell, now Earls of Cawdor. John Barlow, Esq. was High Sheriff for the co. 1562. The name is now extinct, the property having come through the female line to George Lort Phillips, Esq.

Note.—On the estate is *Creswell Priory*, originally a seat of the very ancient family of Barlow, now extinct. The names of Barlows of Slebech and Creswell are often seen in the roll of High Sheriffs for the co. in the reign of Queen Elizabeth.
Lawrenny Hall was pulled down after the death of the last resident, Hugh Barlow, Esq., M.P., who *d.* in 1809. The present handsome castellated building was erected on the ruins of the old house in 1852, by George Lort Phillips, Esq., M.P., who *s.* to the estates collaterally on the death of Sir William Owen, Bart.

ROBERTS, John Davies, Esq., of Rose Hill, Pembrokeshire.

J. P. for co. of Pembroke, appointed in 1860; second son of William and Margaret Roberts, of Milford; *b.* at Milford, February 20th, 1828; *ed.* at Bristol; *m.*, 1st January, 1857, Frances Maria Byrde, dau. of George Samuel and Charlotte Carpenter Byrde; has issue 2 sons and 5 daus.

Heir: George William Roberts.
Residence: Rose Hill, Pembrokeshire.
Town Address: Royal Crescent, Notting Hill.
Arms: See *Roberts, Thomas, of Milford.*

ROBERTS, Thomas, Esq., of Hamilton House, Milford, Pembrokeshire.

J. P. and D. L. for the co. of Pembroke; eldest son of the late William Roberts, Esq., by his wife Margaret, *née* Davies, of Newport; *b.* at Milford, August 6th, 1823; *s.* 1837; *m.*, 1848, Jane, dau. of John Ralph, Esq., then of Beaumaris, and has surviving issue 2 sons and 1 dau.

Heir: William Robert Roberts, *b.* 1856.
Residence: Hamilton House, Milford.
Arms: Erminois, a lion rampant guardant gu. in chief, two square castles towered and domed ppr., all within a bordure indented of the second.
Crest: A lion rampant guardant gu. gorged with a collar engrailed gold, holding in the dexter paw a dagger ppr., and resting the sinister paw upon a shield, or, charged with a bull's head caboshed between three mullets of six points gu.
Motto: Gwna ddaioni nid rhaid ofni.

LINEAGE.

This family is of Powysian and Dyvedian descent. William Roberts, father of the present representative, was an eminent shipowner and shipbuilder, whose father was originally from North Wales, and whose family, according to Lewys Dwnn's *Heraldic Visitations of Wales*, is entitled to direct descent from Celynyn of Llwydiarth in Powys, who was sixth in descent from Aleth, Lord of Dyved. The mother of the present Mr. Roberts was Margaret, dau. of John Davies, Esq., Newport, Pemb., paternally descended from the Havards of Moilgrove, who are stated by Theophilus Jones, in his history of Brecknockshire, to be lineally descended from Laurence Havard, Esq., of Cryngae, co. of Carm., an estate which comprised the Dolhaidd and Goytre properties at that time. The said Laurence Havard, *temp.* Elizabeth, resided at Cringae Castle, now in ruins. That part of the Priory Church at Brecon now called "The Vicar's Chapel" was erected by the Havards of Pontwilym, and the historian referred to states that it was called in the reign of Elizabeth "The Havard Chapel." In the wall of that chapel is the Havard crest, a bull's head cut in stone, with the motto underneath, "In Deo spes est." (See further *Evans of Nantyderry,* and *Havard of Pontwilym.*)

ROCH, Nicholas Adamson, Esq., of Paskeston, Pembrokeshire.

J. P. and D. L. for the co. of Pembroke; son of the late Rev. Dr. Roch of Paskeston, who was son of Nicholas Roch, Esq., of Paskeston, J. P. for the co. of Pembroke, and Sheriff for the same co. 1777.

Residence: Paskeston, near Pembroke.

ROCH, William Francis, Esq., of Butter Hill, Pembrokeshire.

Son of the late George Roch, Esq., of Butter Hill, who was son of George Roch, Esq., by Mary, dau. and co-h. of William Jones, Esq., of Llethr, Brawdy.

Residence: Butter Hill, near Haverfordwest.

SAURIN, Mark Anthony, Esq., of Orielton, Pembrokeshire.

(*Particulars not received.*)

SCOURFIELD, John Henry, Esq., of Williamston, Pembrokeshire.

M.P. for the co. of Pembroke since 1868; was M.P. for the bor. of Haverfordwest 1852—1868; J. P. and D. L. for the co. of Pembr.; High Sheriff for same co. (as Phillips) 1833; son of the late Owen Phillips, Esq., of Williamston, by Elizabeth, dau. of the late Henry Scourfield, Esq., of Moat, co. of Pemb.; *b.* 1808; *ed.* at Harrow and Oriel Coll., Oxford; *grad.* B.A. 1828, M.A. 1832; *m.*, 1845, Augusta, second dau. of the late John Lort Phillips, Esq., of Lawrenny and Haverfordwest; assumed in 1862, by royal license, the name of Scourfield on inheriting under the will of his maternal uncle, W. H. Scourfield, Esq., late of Moat; has, with other issue,—

Owen Henry Phillips, *b.* 1847.
Residence: Williamston, Haverfordwest.
Town Address: Boodle's, and Oxford and Cambridge Clubs.

Note.—The Scourfields of Moat were an ancient Pembrokeshire family, who intermarried with the Wogans of Wiston, Bowen of Llech-Meilir, Owen of Henllys, Owen of Orielton, &c.

THOMAS, Rev. Llewelyn Lloyd, of Newport, Pembrokeshire.

Rector of Newport and Morvil; Rural Dean of Upper Cemmaes, Pembrokeshire; appointed to Capel Cynon, Card., November 3rd, 1822, which was resigned for Newport, Pemb., September 3rd, 1824; appointed to Morvil August 7th, 1844; son of John Thomas, Esq., surgeon, &c., Aberdûar, Carmarthenshire; *b.* at Aberdûar, November 11th, 1798; *ed.* at Lampeter Pont Stephen; *m.*, 1st, February 23rd, 1820, Louisa Charlotta, dau. of Colonel Owen Lloyd, of Cardigan; 2ndly, May 2nd, 1839, Eliza Dickinson, of Guildhall, London; has had issue by the first marriage 4 sons and 10 daus.,—by the second 6 sons and 4 daus.

Residence: Newport Rectory, Pembrokeshire.

Note.—For a notice of *Newport Castle* see p. 874. There is a cromlech below the town, as well as at Pentre-Evan. The tower of Newport Church is considered very handsome. The school, supported until lately by Lady Bevan's charity, was established about the year 1820.

WALTERS, William, Esq., of Haverfordwest, Pembrokeshire.

J. P. and D. L. for the co. of Pembroke; High Sheriff for same co. 1866; a banker at Haverfordwest and other places.

(*Further information in next edition.*)

WHITE, George, Esq., of Tenby, Pembrokeshire.

J. P.; Mayor of Tenby for the seventh time in 1871; son of the late Robert Davis White, Esq. (see *lineage*); *b.* at St. Florence 1825; *m.*, 1st, Mary, dau. of Thomas Baldwin Dundridge, Esq., of the co. of Devon, by whom he had issue a son, George Dundridge, *b.* 1845, *deceased;* 2ndly, Letitia, dau. of David Hart, Esq., of Leytonstone Park, Essex, by whom he has issue,—

Arthur White, *b.* June 15, 1871.

Heir: Arthur White.
Residence: St. Mary's Hill, Tenby.
Town Residence: 23, York Terrace, Regent's Park.
Arms: (*Temp.* Henry III.). Sa., a chevron between three stags' heads caboshed or.
Crest: A peacock in its pride.
Motto: Stare super vias antiquas.

LINEAGE.

When this ancient Pembrokeshire family first settled at Tenby is not now to be ascertained. So early as the middle of the thirteenth century, however, the name of Jasper le White occurs. One of his descendants, John White, was bailiff of the town in 1415, and from that year we have no difficulty in tracing the pedigree to the existing representative. John White in 1420 filled the office of mayor, a post to which he was re-elected no fewer than seventeen times. His tomb exists at Tenby Church, but the date of his death is illegible.

Thomas White, as Mayor of Tenby, succoured and entertained Jasper, Earl of Pembroke, the Countess of Richmond, and her young son Henry (who was born at Pembroke Castle), on their flight to Brittany. He *d*. in 1482. His son,—

Jenkyn, or John, Mayor of Tenby in 1498, had issue by his second wife, Christina, co-heiress of John Eynon of *Henllan*, James White, whose eldest son,—

Griffith White, *m*., firstly, Mary, dau. of Sir Owen Perrott, and secondly, Margaret, dau. and co-heiress of Thomas Watkins, of Narberth, by whom he had a son,—

Henry White, who *m*. Jane, dau. of Richard Fletcher, of Bangor, whose eldest son,—

Griffith White, Esq., of Henllan, Castlemartin (Sheriff of Pembrokeshire 1626), *m*. a dau. of Richard Lort, Esq., of Stackpool, and had issue,— Roger, Thomas, John, Henry. Thomas and John *d*. unmarried. Henry, by his wife, Mary Bodely, left one son only, Griffith, who *m*. the dau. and heiress of Griffith Davies of Bangeston.

Roger White, Esq., the eldest, had three sons— Thomas, John, William, of whom the first died without issue. John's grandson,—

Francis White, Esq., born at Studdock, near Henllan, 1698, by his second marriage had three sons and several daus., the eldest being—

Henry White, Esq., of Hill, *b*. 1749, *m*. Jane, dau. of Robert Davies, Esq., of Prickeston, and had issue,—

Robert Davies White, Esq., *b*. 1787, *m*. Martha, dau. of William Palmer, of Couchyland, and had issue,—

GEORGE WHITE, ESQ. (as above).

Note.—It is noteworthy in the history of this patriotic family that one of its line should be mayor of the then important town of Tenby when Henry Tudor made his escape from Pembroke in 1472, and that the present representative, to whose exertions was mainly due the erection of the beautiful memorial to the Prince Consort (see p. 838), should in 1865 be the Mayor of Tenby to receive H.R.H. Prince Arthur, when commissioned by the Queen to inaugurate it. It is said that so sensible was Henry VII. when, after thirteen years of exile, he succeeded in gaining the throne, of the service and loyalty of the mayor of Tenby, that he granted to his family—for Thomas White had now been three years dead—a lease at a nominal rent of all the Crown lands about Tenby, and kept up at intervals a friendly correspondence with them. The roll of Pembrokeshire *Sheriffs* contains the names of members of this family not less than seven times between the years 1559 and 1657. (See *Sheriffs*, pp. 882—4).

WILLIAMS, Ben Thomas, Esq., of Merryvale, Pembrokeshire.

Barrister-at-Law (called January, 1859); Recorder of Carmarthen 1872; practises on the South Wales Circuit; J. P. for the co. of Pembroke; has written extensively for the legal press; author of several pamphlets, one of which on the "Jamaica Riots" attracted much attention; son of Rev. Thomas R. Williams, of Merryvale, in the co. of Pembroke, Independent Minister; *b*. at Merryvale, Nov. 19th, 1832; *ed*. at the University of Glasgow; *grad*. M.A. May, 1854; *m*., August 20th, 1857, Margaret, only surviving child of Thomas John, jun., of Dolemain, in the co. of Pembroke, gentleman, deceased, who, on decease of her grandfather, succeeded to estate of Dolemain, which has been for several centuries in the family; has issue two sons and one daughter.

Heir: Oliver John.
Residence: Merryvale, near Narberth.
Town Address: 1, Pump Court, Temple.
Arms: Argent, a lion rampant sable.
Crest: Out of a mural crown a demi-lion, as in the arms.
Motto: Heb Dduw heb ddim.

Note.—Mr. Williams's maternal grandfather, the late Mr. B. R. Thomas, of Narberth, was a gentleman of great ability, and an active promoter of education. The present holder, as his heir-at-law, has succeeded to Merryvale, a small estate comprising part of the ancient village of Templeton.

ANNALS, &c., OF WALES.

RADNORSHIRE.

(MAESYFED.)

1.—*The Name.*

THE Welsh name of this district took in early times the forms *Maes-hyfed* and *Maes-hyfaidd* —from *maes*, a field, and *Hyfaidd*, said by some to be the name of its ruler, a son of the rather fabulous Caradoc Freichfras; but as some explain it, "summer-like, fair" (*haf-aidd*). *Maeshyfed* is the name which occurs in Caradoc of Llancarfan's *Brut y Tywysogion*, written probably in the twelfth century, and in other *Bruts*, and in all cases seems to apply to a particular spot or fortress (either New or Old Radnor) rather than to a district or territory. The name *Radnor* presents no obvious etymons, but it may claim an antiquity almost equal to that of Maes-hyfed, for we find it mentioned in the *Annales Cambriæ* as early as A.D. 1196, where it is said that Rhys ap Gruffydd (the "Lord Rhys") led an army into Herefordshire, and burned it—" redenor combussit;" and under the year 1231 it records that Llewelyn the Great devastated Brecon, Hay, and the castle of *Radenor*. There was an ancient castle at ' Old Radnor " in early times, called *Pen-crug*, by Giraldus " Cruker" (*Crug-caer*, the fortress rock or eminence), as well as at the place called New Radnor, once a considerable town. To whichever of the two places the *Annales* refer, Giraldus evidently means by "Radnor" New Radnor, and by "Cruker" Old Radnor, for he states that they went from Radnor to Cruker, which stood at a distance of "two miles."

2 —*General Description and History of Radnorshire.*

Radnorshire, which by the 27th Henry VIII., cap. 26 (see p. 757), was made a county proper out of the " Lordships Marchers" formed by the Normans "within the countrey or dominion of Wales," in ancient times belonged principally to the kingdom of Powys, but partly to *Gwent* and partly to Feryllwg; it is bounded on the north by Montgomeryshire, on the south by Breconshire, on the east by Shropshire and Herefordshire, and on the west by Breconshire and Cardiganshire. The population for the last five decades has been as follows :—

Total population of Radnorshire—1831	...	...	...	...	24,651
,,	,,	1841	...	...	...	...	25,356
,,	,,	1851	...	...	...	...	24,957
,,	,,	1861	...	...	...	...	25,382
,,	,,	1871	...	...	...	...	25,428

Without any lofty mountains, Radnor must still be termed a mountainous county. A large proportion of its surface is covered by eminences too high to be correctly described as hills, but not sufficiently imposing to be classed with such mountains as those of Merioneth or Carnarvon; and although in places, as in the romantic valley—or rather, gorge—of the Elan, along the Wye at Rhayader, on the Ithon, and on the Edw (made for ever famous as the stream which watered the demesne and castle of Llewelyn), there are spots of great boldness and sublimity, the heights and depressions of Radnorshire generally offer quiet and rounded surfaces, and few features of striking grandeur. The hills are not arranged in chains

MAES-LLWCH CASTLE: THE SEAT OF WALTER DE WINTON, ESQ. (*from a photograph*).

or ridges, but are massive groups thrown confusedly, as it were, on the platform of the county, and left to settle their points of junction and rights of occupation as they best could. *Radnor Forest*, belonging to the Crown, and running nearly east and west (2,163 feet above sea-level) gives the highest elevation and the most connected range in the county. On the right of the road leading from Rhayader to Llanidlas arises to the height of 1,750 feet *Rhydd Hywel*: and *Bryn Maen* ("the Stone Hill"), in the parish of Llanfihangel-nant-Melan, is 1,700 feet; Camlo Hill, near Abbey Cwm-hir (1,650 feet); and Craig-y-Foel, near Nant-gwyllt, overhanging precipitously the Elan (1,550 feet), are the next chief eminences. The side of the county lying upon Herefordshire is generally level.

The *Wye*, its western boundary, is the chief river of Radnorshire. From Rhayader to Llyswen it pursues a course nearly due south, and through scenes of almost unsurpassable beauty. At Glasbury it takes a sharp turn eastward, forming an angle, on the slope above which, in full command of extremely rich and varied scenery, is planted one of the most imposing mansions in the county, *Maes-llwch Castle;* a little further down the river is Clyro Court (Thos. B. Baskerville, Esq.), and Clyro (Rev. R. L. Venables); and two or three miles up the stream is Boughrood Castle (Rev. Hugh Bold), and Boughrood Vicarage (Rev. Henry de Winton). In the neighbourhood of Builth, so famous for its scenery, are Llanelwedd Hall (H. G. Howell, Esq.); Wellfield (E. D. Thomas, Esq.); Pencerrig (Mrs. Thomas); Llwyn Madoc (Samuel Beavan, Esq.); and a few miles east, Glascwm Court, the property of the same gentleman, descended from the Beavans of Ty'n-y-cwm; Llysdinam Hall (G. Stovin Venables, Esq.), on the margin of the Wye above Penybont, is just within the limits of Breconshire. Near Rhayader are several mansions of the gentry, as Penlanoleu (Henry Lingen, Esq.); Y Dderw (Hugh P. Prickard, Esq.); Bryn-tirion (Sam. C. Evans Williams, Esq.); Nantgwyllt (Robert Lewis Lloyd, Esq.), situated in one of the most picturesque dells in Wales; Cwm Elan (Lady Otway); Doldowlod (James W. Gibson Watt, Esq.); Abbey Cwm-hir, on a tributary of the Ithon; and further north, Penithon (George Augustus Haig, Esq.). Passing Nantmel (Rev. Thos. James Thirlwall), and Llwyn-y-barried (E. M. Evans, Esq), the road for New Radnor eastwards, cutting the county nearly into two halves, brings us to the fertile district of Pen-y-bont, as remarkable for the abundance of its streams as Llandrindod, two or three miles southward, is for its bleakness and salubrity. The watersheds of the county pour into this favoured locality the Ithon, with its several tributaries of the Clywedog, the Aran, the Carnau, &c., making a pleasant land of streams and richly wooded valleys, well chosen by the monks of Abbey Cwm-hir for its productiveness and peaceful quiet, as well as for a landscape universally admired, as being, in places, of extreme picturesqueness and grandeur. The three churches of Nantmel, Llanybister, and Llangunllo, standing at small distances from the interesting remains of Abbey Cwm-hir, have the reputation of having been founded at a very early period of the British Church, the coming of Austin to convert the Saxons.

Between Penybont (J. C. Severn, Esq.), situated about the centre of the county, and Presteign, the chief county town, are Downton (Lady Cockburn), Harpton Court (Rev. Sir Gilbert F. Lewis, Bart.), the ancient abode of the Lewis family; Evancoed (R. B. R. Mynors, Esq); Newcastle Court (Lord Ormathwaite); Barland (T. B. Mynors, Esq.); New Radnor (Rev. T. C. Prickard. Both Old and New Radnor were in past times more eminent than at present; had warlike castles, good markets, and a large population—the position of the former being important from its natural strength as an elevated base of limestone rock, and of the latter as guarding one of the principal passes into the territory of the Welsh princes from hostile Mercia. Why two places of equal antiquity should bear the contrasting names of "Old" and "New" is not quite clear, and is made less so by the circumstance that New Radnor has been marked in recent times more by decay than growth. It was at New Radnor that Giraldus Cambrensis and Archbishop Baldwin in A.D. 1188 began their crusading tour through Wales. They were met here by Prince Rhys ap Gruffydd ("the Lord Rhys"), who seemed disposed to become a crusader himself, but afterwards failed—as the celibate archdeacon says, through the wicked dissuasion of his wife. Giraldus speaks of Old Radnor, which, as already said, he calls "Cruker," as simply a "castle." At Glascwm, he tells us (following his bent for marvels), that there was a "portable bell endowed with great virtues called Bangu" the bell carried by the sexton at funerals in all Catholic churches of that period], "and said to have belonged to St. David." A certain woman "secretly conveyed this bell to her husband, who was confined in the castle of Raiadr-gwy [Rhayader]—which Prince Rhys, son of Gruffydd, had lately [1178] built—for the purpose of his deliverance." The keepers of the castle "not only refused to liberate the man, but seized and detained the bell, and in the same night, by divine vengeance, the whole town except the wall on which the bell hung was consumed by fire."

The town of New Radnor had been destroyed by Meredydd ap Owain long before the visit of Giraldus. It again grew into some note, but *temp.* Henry IV. was burnt by Owen Glyndwr, and was never restored to its former state. On the creation of the county by 27th Henry VIII., New Radnor, still maintaining traditional repute, was appointed, alternately with Rhayader, as the place for holding the courts and assizes of the shire, but in after years Presteign, although on the extreme verge of the county, became the county town, and has continued so ever since. The chief mansions near Presteign are Boultibrook, the beautiful seat of Sir Harford J. J. Brydges, Bart., and Norton Manor (R. Green Price, Esq.).

In pre-Norman times, when the Briton enjoyed his own land, the great Cantref of *Maelienydd* in this region belonged to Powys, the remainder of Radnor was chiefly in *Feryllwg*, usually described as lying "between the Severn and the Wye," among whose princes Elystan (Athelstan) Glodrudd is the best known. He was godson of the English king Athelstan, of the lineage of Tudor Trevor, founder of the "tribe of the Marches," and died about A.D. 1000. The Romans had doubtless asserted a general dominion over this part after their conquest of the Silures (the inhabitants of this and adjoining districts), as evidenced by their roads and stations, as at Cwm, on the Ithon north-east of Llandrindod; but of their doings here we find no historic trace. The eighth century conflicts between the Welsh and the Mercians are commemorated for ever by the great earthwork of Offa's Dyke, which cuts off a corner of this county between Knighton and Old Radnor, leaving Presteign some four miles on the English side of the boundary. When the Norman Lords Marchers attacked Wales, and established head-quarters at Brecknock and Hereford, this district was absorbed into those great lordships, under the rule prominently of the Mortimer and De Breos families. The Lord Marcher government was of course only strengthened by the conquest of Wales by Edward I. It was brought to an end, Radnorshire made a county, and the equal laws of England established in it by Henry VIII. when the history of Wales merges in the general history of the empire.

3.—*High Sheriffs of Radnorshire from* A.D. 1544 *to* A.D. 1872.

The roll of sheriffs of this county with some few omissions as far as the year 1856, was published in Williams's "Hist. of Radnorshire." The following list has been collated with it, and brought down to the present time.

HENRY VIII.	A.D.		A.D.
		John Vaughan, Esq., of Hargest	1545
John Baker, Esq., of Presteign	1544	John Bradshaw, Esq., of Presteign	1546

RADNORSHIRE.

EDWARD VI.

	A.D.
Richard Bleck, Esq., of New Radnor	1547
Peter Lloyd, Esq., of Boultibrook	1548
Rhys Gwilim, Esq., of Aberedw	1549
Sir Adam Melton, Kt., of Salop	1550
Thomas Lewis, Esq., of Harpton	1551
James Price, Esq., of Monach-ty	1552

MARY.

Griffith Jones, Esq., of Trewern	1553
Francis Price, Esq., of Knighton	1554
Sir Adam Melton, of Salop	1555
John Bradshaw, Esq., of Presteign	1556
Peter Lloyd, Esq., of Boultibrook	1557

ELIZABETH.

John Bradshaw, Esq., of Presteign	1558
Stephen Price, Esq., of Pilleth	1559
Evan Lewis, Esq., of Gladestry	1560
John Knill, Esq., of Knill	1561
Sir Robert Whitney, Kt., of Whitney	1562
Morgan Meredydd, Esq., of Llyn-went	1563
John Price, Esq., of Monach-ty	1564
Evan Lewis, Esq., of Gladestry	1565
Robert Vaughan, Esq., of Winforton	1566
Griffith Jones, Esq., of Llowes	1567
John Bradshaw, Esq., of Presteign	1568
Edward Price, Esq., of Knighton	1569
Lewis Lloyd, Esq., of Boultibrook	1570
Robert Vaughan, Esq., of Presteign	1571
David Lloyd Meredith, Esq., of Nant-mel	1572
William Lewis, Esq., of Nash	1573
James Price, Esq., of Monach-ty	1574
Edward Price, Esq., of Knighton	1575
John Price, Esq., of Monach-ty	1576
John Price, Esq., of Pilleth	1577
Evan Lewis, Esq., of Gladestry	1578
Hugh Lloyd, Esq., of Bettws	1579
Roger Vaughan, Esq., of Clyro	1580
Lewis Lloyd, Esq., of Boultibrook	1581
Rhys Lewis, Esq., of Gladestry	1582
Thomas Wigmore, Esq., of Shobdon	1583
Evan Lewis, Esq., of Gladestry	1584
Morgan Meredith, Esq., of Llyn-Went	1585
Thomas Hankey, Esq., of Ludlow	1586
Lewis Lloyd, Esq., of Boultibrook	1587
John Weaver, Esq., of Stepleton	1588
John Bradshaw, Esq., of Presteign	1589
Edward Price, Esq., of Knighton	1590
Hugh Lloyd, Esq., of Bettws	1591
Evan Lewis, Esq., of Gladestry	1592
Peter Lloyd, Esq., of Stocking	1593
Thomas Price, Esq., of Knighton	1594
Humphrey Cornewall, Esq., of Stanage	1595
Edmund Vinsalley, Esq., of Presteign	1596
Clement Price, Esq., of Coed-gwgan	1597
Thomas Wigmore, Esq., of Shobdon	1598
James Price, Esq., of Monach-ty	1599
Richard Fowler, Esq., of Abbey Cwm-hir	1600

	A.D.
James Price, Esq., of Pilleth	1601
Lewis Lloyd, Esq., of Boultibrook	1602

JAMES I.

Edward Winston, Esq., of Presteign	1603
John Bradshaw, Esq., of Presteign	1604
Humphrey Cornewall, Esq., of Berrington	1605
Evan Vaughan, Esq., of Bugeil-dy	1606
John Townsend, Esq., of Ludlow	1607
—— Whitney, Esq., of Whitney	1608
Sir Robert Harley, Kt., of Brampton	1609
John Vaughan, Esq., of Kinnersley	1610
Hugh Lewis, Esq. [of Harpton]	1611
Thomas Powell, Esq., of Cwm-dauddwr	1612
James Price, Esq., of Pilleth	1613
John Lloyd, Esq., of Bettws	1614
Richard Fowler, Esq., of Abbey Cwm-hir	1615
Robert Whitney, Esq., of Whitney	1616
Richard Jones, Esq., of Tre-wern	1617
Ezekiel Beestone, Esq., of Walton	1618
Samuel Parker, Esq., of Ludlow	1619
Hugh Lewis, Esq., of Harpton	1620
Humphrey Cornewall, Esq., of Brampton	1621
Allen Currard, Esq., of Presteign	1622
Thomas Rhys, Esq., of Dysserth	1623
John Read, Esq., of Presteign	1624

CHARLES I.

Humphrey Walcot, Esq., of Walcot	1625
Richard Fowler, Esq. [of Abbey Cwm-hir]	1626
Evan Vaughan, Esq., of Bugeil-dy	1627
Robert Weaver, Esq., of Aylmstry	1628
Griffith. Jones, Esq., of Presteign	1629
William Vaughan, Esq., of Llowes	1630
John Maddocks, Esq.	1631
James Phillips, Esq., of Llan	1632
Roderic Gwynne, Esq., of Llanelwedd	1633
Richard Rodd, Esq., of Rodd	1634
Nicholas Meredith, Esq., of Presteign	1635
Morgan Vaughan, Esq., of Bugeil-dy	1636
Morris Lewis, Esq., of Stones	1637
Evan Davies, Esq., of Llanddewi	1638
Brian Crowther, Esq., of Knighton	1639
Robert Williams, Esq., of Caebalfa	1640
John Powell, Esq., of Stanage	1641
William Latchard, Esq., of Bettws	1642
Hugh Lloyd, Esq., of Caer-fagu	1643
Hugh Lloyd, Esq., of Caer-fagu (the same)	1644
Brian Crowther, Esq., of Knighton	1645
Thomas Weaver, Esq., of Aylemstry	1646
Robert Martin, Esq, of New Radnor	1647
Robert Martin, jun., Esq., ditto	1648

INTERREGNUM.

Henry Williams, Esq., of Caebalfa	1649
Nicholas Taylor, Esq., of Presteign	1650
John Dantzey, Esq., of Gladestry	1651
John Will, Esq., [imperfect]	1652

HIGH SHERIFFS OF RADNORSHIRE.

OLIVER CROMWELL, LORD PROTECTOR.

	A.D.
John Walsham, Esq., of Knill	1653
Samuel Powell, Esq., of Stanage	1654
Richard Fowler, Esq., of Abbey Cwm-hir	1655
John Davies, Esq., of Monach-ty	1656
James Price, Esq , of Pilleth	1657

RICHARD CROMWELL, LORD PROTECTOR.

Thomas Lewis, Esq., of Harpton	1658
Thomas Lewis, Esq., of Harpton (the same)	1659

CHARLES II.

Evan Davies, Esq., of Llanddewi	1660
John Walcot, Esq., of Walcot	1661
—— Lewis, Esq., of Hindwell	1662
Henry Williams, Esq., of Caebalfa	1663
Thomas Eaglestone, Esq., of Presteign	1664
Nicholas Taylor, Esq., of Heath	1665
Robert Martin, Esq., of New Radnor	1666
Andrew Philipps, Esq., of Llanddewi	1667
Ezekiel Beestone, Esq., of Walton	1668
Roger Stephens, Esq., of Knowle	1669
John Walsham, Esq., of Knill	1670
John Richards, Esq., of Evan-jobb	1671
Edward Davies, Esq., of Llanddewi	1672
James Lloyd, Esq., of Kington	1673
William Whitcombe, Esq., of London	1674
William Probert, Esq., of Llanddewi	1675
Robert Cutler, Esq., of Farington	1676
Richard Vaughan, Esq., of Monmouth	1677
Hugh Powell, Esq., of Cwm-Elan	1678
Thomas Vaughan, Esq., of Bugeil-dy	1679
Henry Probert, Esq., of Llowes	1680
Henry Mathews, Esq., of Llantwardine	1681
Evan Powell, Esq., of Llanbister	1682
Thomas Lewis, Esq., of Harpton	1683
John Davies, Esq., of Coed-gleison	1684

JAMES II.

Samuel Powell, Esq., of Stanage	1685
Henry Davies, Esq., of Graig	1686
William Taylor, Esq., of Norton	1687
Nicholas Taylor, Esq., of Heath	1688

WILLIAM III. AND MARY.

Richard Vaughan, Esq., of Clyro	1689
John Fowler, Esq., of Bron-y-dre	1690
William Probert, Esq., of Llanddewi	1691
Thomas Vaughan, Esq., of Bugeil-dy	1692
Hugh Lewis, Esq., of Hindwell	1693
Robert Cutler, Esq., of Street	1694
Thomas Lewis, Esq., of Nant-gwyllt	1695
William Fowler, Esq., of Grainge	1696
Thomas Lewis, Esq., of Harpton	1697
Thomas Williams, Esq., of Caebalfa	1698
Walter Davies, Esq., of Ludlow	1699
Edward Price, Esq., of Boultibrook	1700
John Waddeley, Esq., of Hereford	1701

ANNE.

	A.D.
John Read, Esq., of Montgomery	1702
—— Price, Esq., of Presteign	1703
Morgan Vaughan, Esq., of Bugeil-dy	1704
David Morgan, Esq., of Coed-gleison	1705
Edward Howarth, Esq., of Caebalfa	1706
Adam Price, Esq., of Boultibrook	1707
Hugh Gough, Esq., of Knighton	1708
William Chase, Esq., of London	1709
Charles Hanmer, Esq., of Llanddewi	1710
Charles Walcot, Esq., of Walcot	1711
James Stephens, Esq., of Bess-brook	1712
Robert Tonman, Esq., of Fron	1713

GEORGE I.

Walter Price, Esq., of Cefn-pwll	1714
Edward Fowler, Esq., of Abbey Cwm-hir	1715
John Clarke, Esq., of Blaidd-fa	1716
John Miles, Esq., of Evan-jobb	1717
Marmaduke Gwynne, Esq., of Garth	1718
Hugh Powell, Esq., of Cwm-Elan	1719
Fletcher Powell, Esq., of Downton	1720
Nicholas Taylor, Esq., of Heath	1721
Charles Hanmer, Esq., of Llanddewi	1722
Giles Whitehall, Esq., of Moor	1723
Hugh Morgan, Esq., of Bettws	1724
Folliot Powell, Esq., of Stanage	1725
Edward Burton, Esq., of Fron-lâs	1726
Edward Shipman, Esq., of Bugeil-dy	1727

GEORGE II.

Henry Williams, Esq., of Skyn-lâs	1728
Harford Jones, Esq., of Kington	1729
John Tyler, Esq., of Dilwyn	1730
Stephen Harris, Esq., of Bessbrook	1731
Thomas Holland, Esq., of Llangunllo	1732
Thomas Gronows [? Gronw], Esq., of London	1733
Matthew Davies, Esq., of Presteign	1734
John Clarke, Esq., of Blaidd-fa	1735
John Williams, Esq., of Skreen	1736
John Jones, Esq., of Tre-vannon	1737
Sir Robert Cornewall, Kt., of Berrington	1738
Henry Howarth, Esq., of Caebalfa	1739
Mansel Powell, Esq., of Eardisley	1740
Edward Price, Esq., of Boultibrook	1741
Thomas Hughes, Esq., of Gladestry	1742
Peter Rickards, Esq., of Evan-jobb	1743
William Wynter, Esq., of Brecon	1744
William Ball, Esq., of Kington	1745
Henry Williams, Esq., of Skyn-lâs	1746
John Patteshall, Esq., of Puddlestone	1747
John Warter, Esq., of Kington	1748
Morgan Evans, Esq , of Llanbarryd [? Llwyn-barried]	1749
Hugh Gough, Esq., of Knighton	1750
Francis Walker, Esq., of Verny-hall	1751
Thomas Vaughan, Esq., of Bugeil-dy	1752
Richard Lloyd, Esq., of Llanbadarn-fynydd	1753
John Bishop, Esq., of Gladestry	1754
William Go—, Esq., of Kingwood	1755

918 RADNORSHIRE.

	A.D.
John Lewis, Esq., of Presteign	1756
John Evans, Esq., of Cwm-dauddwr	1757
Daniel Davies, Esq., of Llanbadarn-fawr	1758
David Stephens, Esq., of Nant-mel	1759
John Daykins, Esq., of Llanbister	1760

GEORGE III.

	A.D.
John Evans, Esq., of Llanbarryd [? Llwyn-barried]	1761
Evan Vaughan, Esq., of Llwyn-madog	1762
James Williams, Esq., of Trawley	1763
James Broom, Esq., of Ewithington	1764
Sir Hans Fowler, Kt., of Abbey Cwm-hir	1765
Samuel Evans, Esq., of Newchurch	1766
Sir John Meredith, of Brecon	1767
John Trumper, Esq., of Michael-Church	1768
James Watkins, Esq, of Clifford	1769
Marmaduke Gwynne, Esq., of Garth	1770
Charles Gore, Esq., of Ty-'faenor	1771
William Whitcombe, of Clyro	1772
Bernard Holland, Esq., of Llanbister	1773
Walter Wilkins, Esq., of Maes-llwch	1774
John Griffiths, Esq., of Kington	1775
Richard Davies, Esq., of Llan-Stephen	1776
William Powell, Esq., of Llanwrthwl	1777
Harford Jones, Esq., of Presteign	1778
Jonathan Field, Esq., of Llanbadarn-fynydd	1779
Thomas Cook, Esq., of Ludlow	1780
Jonathan Bowen, Esq., of Knighton	1781
Thomas Bevan, Esq., of Skynlâs	1782
Thomas Price, Esq., of Glascwm	1783
Buthe Shelley, Esq., of Michael-Church	1784
James Price, Esq., of Clyro	1785
Bridgwater Meredith, Esq., of Clyro	1786
John Price, Esq., of Penybont	1787
Bell Lloyd, Esq., of Boultibrook	1788
Thomas Duppa, Esq., of Longueville	1789
Francis Garbett, Esq., of Knill	1790
Thomas Jones, Esq., of Pencerrig	1791
John Lewis, Esq., of Harpton	1792
William Symonds, M.D., Hereford	1793
Richard Price, Esq., of Knighton	1794
Francis Fowke, Esq., of Llanstephan	1795
John Pritchard, Esq., of Dolyfelin	1796
Percival Lewis, Esq., of Downton	1797
John Benn Walsh, Esq., of Cefn-llys	1798
John Bodenham, Esq., of Grove	1799
James Lloyd Harris, Esq., of Kington	1800
Hugh Powell Evans, Esq., of Noyadd	1801
John Sherburne, Esq., of Llandrindod	1802
Marmaduke Thomas Howell Gwynne, Esq., Llanelwedd	1803
Thomas Frankland Lewis, Esq., of Harpton	1804
Charles Rogers, Esq., of Stanage	1805
Thomas Stephens, Esq., of Kinnerton	1806
Thomas Burton, Esq., of Llanbister	1807
Thomas Thomas, Esq., of Pencerrig	1808
Thomas Whittaker, Esq., of Cascôb	1809
George Crawford Ricketts, Esq., of Cwm	1810

	A.D.
John Cheesement Severn, Esq., of Michael Church	1811
Thomas Grove, Esq., jun., of Cwm-Elan	1812
Daniel Reed, Esq., of Cornel	1813
Charles Humphreys Price, Esq., of Knighton	1814
William Davies, Esq., of Caebalfa	1815
Sir Harford Jones Brydges, Bart., of Boultibrook	1816
Penry Powell, Esq., of Penllan	1817
Hugh Stephens, Esq., of Cascôb	1818
Morgan John Evans, Esq., of Llwyn-barried	1819
James Crummer, Esq., of Howey Hall	1820
Robert Peel, Esq., of Cwm-Elan	1821
Peter Richard Mynors, Esq., of Evan-coed	1822
John Hugh Powell, Esq., of Clyro	1823
Hugh Vaughan, Esq., of Llwyn-Madoc	1824
Sir John Benn Walsh, Bart., of Cefn-llys	1825
James Watt, Esq., of Doldowlod [the eminent engineer]	1826
Samuel Beavan, Esq., of Glas-cwm	1827
David Thomas, Esq., of Well-field	1828
John Morris, Esq., of Kington	1829
Robert Bell Price, Esq., of Downfield	1830
Thomas Duppa, Esq., of Longueville	1831
Thomas Evans, Esq., of Llwyn-barried	1832
Walter Wilkins, Esq., of Maes-llwch	1833
Guy Parsons, Esq., of Presteign	1834
Thomas Williams, Esq., of Crossfoot	1835
James William Morgan, Esq., of Glasbury	1836
Hans Busk, Esq., of Nant-mel	1837
Sir John Dutton Colt, Bart., of Llanyre	1838
Henry Lingen, Esq., of Penlan-oleu	1839
Edward Rogers, Esq., of Stanage Park	1840
Edward Breese, Esq., of Knighton	1841
David Oliver, Esq., of Rhydoldog	1842
Edward David Thomas, Esq., of Wellfield	1843
David James, Esq., of Wonaston, Presteign	1844
James Davies, Esq., of Moor Court	1845
Thomas Prickard, Esq., of Dderw	1846
Henry Miles, Esq., of Downfield	1847
John Edwards, Esq., of Brampton Brian	1848
Edw. Myddleton Evans, Esq., of Llwyn-barried	1849
Edward Morgan Stephens, Esq., of Llananno	1850
Aspinall Phillips, Esq., of Abbey Cwm-hir	1851
Sir Harford James Jones Brydes, Bart., of Boultibrook	1852
Jonathan Field, Esq., of Esgair-drain-llwyn	1853
John Jones, Esq., of Cefn-faes	1854
John Abraham Whittaker, Esq., of Newcastle Court	1855
Robert Baskerville Mynors, Esq., of Evan-coed	1856
Francis Evelyn, Esq., of Corton	1857
Howel Gwynne Howell, Esq., of Llanelwedd	1858
James Watt Gibson Watt, Esq., of Doldowlod	1859
George Harry Philips, Esq., Abbey Cwm-hir	1860
George Greenwood, Esq., of Abernant	1861
Walter de Winton, Esq., of Maesllwch Castle	1862
Henry Thomas, Esq., of Pencerrig	1863
George Augustus Haig, Esq., of Pen-Ithon	1864
Thomas William Higgins, Esq., Cwm Llanyre	1865
Edward Coates, Esq., of Whitton	1866

	A.D.		A.D.
Charles Marsh Vialls, Esq., of Hendre . .	1867	Edward Jenkins, Esq., of The Grove . .	1870
Walter Thomas Mynors Baskerville, Esq., of Clyro Court	1868	Sir John James Walsham, Bart., of Knill Court	1871
		Robert Lewis Lloyd, Esq., of Nant-gwyllt .	1872
James Beavan, Esq., of Presteign . . .	1869	John Percy Severn, Esq., Penybout, *nom.* for 1873.	

4.—*Members of Parliament for Radnorshire and Radnor Boroughs from* A.D. 1542 *to* A.D. 1872.

HENRY VIII.

Sir John Baker, Kt., for *County* . . . 1542

EDWARD VI.

Rhys Lewis, Esq., for the *Borough* . . 1547

MARY.

Charles Vaughan, Esq., for the *Co.* . . . } 1553
Rhys Lewis, Esq., for the *Bor.* . . . }
John Bradshaw, jun., Esq., for the *Co.* . } 1554
Robert Vaughan, Gent., for the *Bor.* . . }

PHILIP AND MARY.

Charles Vaughan, Esq. (?), for the *Co.* . . } 1554
John Knill, Esq., for the *Bor.* . . . }
No name given for the *Co.* . . . } 1555
Stephen Price, Esq. (Presteigne), for the *Bor.* }
Jenner Lewis, Esq., for the *Co.* . . . } 1557
Rhys Lewis, Esq., for the *Bor.* . . . }

ELIZABETH.

Thomas Lewis, Esq., for the *Co.* . . . } 1559
Robert Vaughan, Esq., for the *Bor.* . . }
Thomas Lewis, Esq., for the *Co.* . . . } 1563
Morgan Price, Esq., for the *Bor.* . . }
Walter Price, Esq., for the *Co.* . . . } 1571
Rhys Lewis, Esq., for the *Bor.* . . }
Roger Vaughan, Esq., for the *Co.* . . } 1572
Watkin Vaughan, Gent., for the *Bor.* . }
Thomas Lewis, Esq., for the *Co.* . . . } 1585
Hugh Davies, Gent., for the *Bor.* . . }
The same for *Co.* and *Bor.* respectively . 1586
Evan Lewis, Esq., for the *Co.* . . . } 1588
James Walter, Esq., for the *Bor.* . . }
James Price, Esq., for the *Co.* . . . } 1592
Thomas Crompton, Esq., for the *Bor.* . }
James Price, Esq., for the *Co.* . . . } 1597
Stephen Price, (?), for the *Bor.* . . }

JAMES I.

James Price, Esq., for the *Co.* . . . } 1603
Sir Robert Harley, Kt., for the *Bor.* . . }
The same for *Co.* and *Bor.* respectively . 1614
James Price, Esq., for the *Co.* . . . } 1623
Charles Price, Gent., for the *Bor.* . . }
James Price, Esq., of Pilleth, for the *Co.* } 1626
Charles Price, Gent., for the *Bor.* . . }

Richard Jones, Esq., for the *Co.* . . } 1628
Charles Price, Gent., for the *Bor.* . . }
The same for *Co.* and *Bor.* respectively . . 1640
Charles Price, Esq., *succ.* by— } for the *Co.* } 1640
Arthur Annesley, Esq. . . } to
Philip Warwick, Esq., *succ.* by— } for the *Bor.* } 1653
Robert Harley, Esq. . . . }

THE COMMONWEALTH AND CROMWELL.

"Rump" or "Little" Parliament: Six
Members summoned for all Wales . . 1653

OLIVER CROMWELL, LORD PROTECTOR.

George Gwyn, Esq., for the *Co.* . . . } 1654
Henry Williams, Esq. [for the *Bor.* ?] . . }
The same 1656

RICHARD CROMWELL, LORD PROTECTOR.

Henry Williams, Esq., for the *Co.* . . } 1658
Robert Weaver, Esq., for the *Bor.* . . }

CHARLES II.

Sir Richard Lloyd, Kt., for the *Co.* . . } 1660
Member for *Bor.* not found . . . . }
Rowland Gwynne, Esq., for the *Co.* . . } 1678
Member for the *Bor.* not found . . . }

JAMES II.

Richard Williams, Esq., for the *Co.* . . } 1685
Member for *Bor.* not found . . . . }
Sir Rowland Gwynne, Kt., for the *Co.* . . } 1688
Member for *Bor.* not found . . . . }

WILLIAM III. AND MARY.

John Jefferies, Esq., for the *Co.* . . } 1690
Member for *Bor.* not found . . . . }
Thomas Harley, Esq., for the *Co.* . . } 1698
Member for *Bor.* not found . . . . }

ANNE.

Thomas Harley, Esq., for the *Co.* . . . 1702
Thomas Harley, Esq., for the *Co.* . . } 1707
Robert Harley, Esq., for the *Bor.* . . }
Thomas Harley, Esq., for the *Co.* . . } 1710
Lord Edward Harley for the *Bor.* . . }

GEORGE I.

	A.D.
Sir Richard Fowler, Bart., for *Co.*	} 1714
Lord Edward Harley for the *Bor.*	
Sir Richard Fowler, Bart., for *Co.*	} 1715
Thomas Lewis, Esq., for the *Bor.*	
Sir Humphrey Howarth, Kt., for the *Co.*	} 1722
Thomas Lewis, Esq., for the *Bor.*	

GEORGE II.

Sir Humphrey Howarth, Kt., for the *Co.* [sat till 1755] . . . . . } 1727
Thomas Lewis, Esq., for the *Bor.* [sat till 1768]
Howel Gwynne, jun., Esq., for the *Co.* . } 1755
Thomas Lewis, Esq., for the *Bor.* . .

GEORGE III.

Lord Carnarvon for the *Co.* . . . } 1761
Thomas Lewis, Esq., for the *Bor.* . .
[*Edward Lewis* also ret. for *Bor.*, but retired.]
Chase Price, Esq., of Harpton, for *Co.* . .
John Lewis, Esq., of Harpton } for *Bor.* . } 1768
Edward Lewis, Esq., of Downton
[Double return—Edward Lewis seated.]
Edward Lewis, Esq., of Downton. } for *Bor.* 1774
John Lewis, Esq., of Harpton
[On petition, Edward Lewis seated.]
Thomas Johnes, Esq. [of Llanfair-Clydogau, *Card.*, and of Croft Castle, *Heref.*], for the *Co.* 1777
Thomas Johnes, jun., Esq. [son of last; of Hafod, *Card.*, M.P. for Cardigan 1774], for the *Co.* . . . . . . } 1770
John Lewis, Esq., of Harpton } for the *Bor.*
Edward Lewis, Esq., of Downton
[Double return: on petition, John Lewis of Downton seated.]

	A.D.
David Murray, Esq. (brother to Lord Elibank), for the *Bor.*	1790
Viscount Malden, *vice* Murray *dec.*, for *Bor.*	1794
Walter Wilkins, Esq., for the *Co.*	} 1796
Richard Price, Esq., *vice* Malden, for *Bor.*	
Walter Wilkins, Esq., for the *Co.*	1802
[Contested by *John Macnamara.*]	
Richard Price, Esq., [sat till 1847] for the *Bor.*	1812
[Contested by *Percival Lewis.*]	

GEORGE IV.

Right Hon. Thomas Frankland Lewis, *vice* Wilkins *deceased*, for the *Co.* . . . 1828

WILLIAM IV.

Walter Wilkins, Esq., for the *Co.* . . . 1835

VICTORIA.

Walter Wilkins, Esq. (the same, *d.* 1840) . 1837
Sir John Benn Walsh, Bart., for the *Co.* 1840—1868
Right Hon. Sir Thomas Frankland Lewis, Bart., *vice* Price, for the *Bor.* . . . 1847
Sir George Cornewall Lewis, Bart., *vice* Lewis *dec.*, for the *Bor.* 1855
Richard Green Price, Esq., *vice* Lewis *dec.*, for the *Bor.* 1863
Hon. Arthur Walsh, *vice* Walsh raised to the peerage, for the *Co.* 1868
[*The present sitting Member*, 1872.]
Marquess of Hartingten, *vice* Price *retired*, for the *Bor.* 1869
[*The present sitting Member*, 1872.]

THE COUNTY FAMILIES OF RADNORSHIRE.

BASKERVILLE, Walter Thomas Mynors, Esq., of Clyro Court, Radnorshire.

J. P. and D. L. for the co. of Radnor; High Sheriff for same co. 1868; eldest son of the late Thomas B. Mynors Baskerville, Esq., of Clyro Court, J. P. and D. L., and sometime M.P. for Herefordshire, by his second wife, Elizabeth Mary, dau. of Rev. Powell Colchester Guise; *b.* 1839; *s.* on death of his father 1864.

Heir (presumptive): His brother, Henry Witherstone, *b.* 1841, an officer in the army.
Residence: Clyro Court, near Hay.
Arms: Arg., a chevron gu. between three hurts.
Crest: A wolf's head erased, arg., holding in the mouth a broken spear.
Motto: Spero ut fidelis.

LINEAGE.

The line of Baskerville is traceable to the age of the Conquest, and finds its first representative in England on the roll of Battle Abbey as *Baskervile*, and in Leland's *Collectanea*, as Baskville.

John Baskerville, Esq., of Aber-Edw, co. of Radnor (A. D. 1597), was son of Humphrey Baskerville, whose brother James was ancestor of the later Baskervilles of Erdisley, Heref., whose pedigree was recorded in the *Visitation* of Hereford in 1634 (see note on Dwnn's *Herald. Visit. of Wales*, i., 256). He *m.* Sarah, dau. of Thomas Lewis, Esq., of Harpton. Fifth in descent from John Baskerville was—

Thomas Baskerville, Esq., of Aber-Edw, whose line terminated in an heiress, whose dau., Meliora Powell, in 1787 *m*, Peter Rickards *Mynors*, Esq., of Treago, (Tre-iago) and had a second son,—

Thomas Baskerville Mynors, who on the death *s. p.* of Lieut.-Col. Baskerville, of Richardston, representative of the elder branch, inherited his estates and assumed the surname Baskerville in addition to his own of Mynors. His eldest son,—

WALTER THOMAS B. MYNORS BASKERVILLE, is now of Clyro Court (as above).

BEAVAN, Samuel, Esq., of Glascomb Court, Radnorshire.

J. P. and D. L. for the co. of Radnor; Sheriff for same co. 18—; only surviving son of Edward Beavan, Esq., of Kington, by his wife, Elizabeth Lewis; *b.* 1790, at Island House, Kington; *m.*, Firstly, Elizabeth, dau. and heiress of —— Lewis, Esq., 2ndly, Eliza, dau. and heiress of Dr. Gommery of Leominster; 3rdly, 1855, Eliza Ann (*d.* 1872), dau. of Hugh Vaughan, Esq., of Llwynmadock, Radnorshire, J. P. and D. L. of that co., and High Sheriff for the same 1825; and has issue.

Residence: Glascomb Court, Colwyn, near Builth.
Arms: Az., a dove arg. between three gem rings or.
Crest: On a mount vert an eagle rising, in its beak a gem ring, as in the arms.
Motto: Semper virtute constans.

LINEAGE.

This family derives maternally from the *Beavan of Ty'n-y-cwm*, Rad., and paternally from the *Bevan of Castle Cradock*, Carm., members of which family served the office of sheriff for the co. of Carmarthen on several occasions (see *Sheriffs*).

Francis *Beavan*, LL.D., of Ty'n-y-cwm, Radnorshire, had a grandson,—

John Beavan, *b.* 1609, whose only dau. and heiress *m.* John *Bevan* of Castle Cradock, Carmarthen, *b.* 1648, *d.* 1693. The Bevans of Castle Cradock originated in

Lewis Bevan, whose grandson, Lewis Bevan, Esq., of Pen-y-coed, High Sheriff for the co. of Carmarthen 1634, *m.* Miss Lewis of Carmarthen, and had with other issue,—

John Bevan, above mentioned.

John Bevan had issue by Miss Beavan of Ty'nycwm, Samuel, *b.* 1680 (*d.* 1721), *m.*, 1708, Hannah Beavan of Llwyn-gwilym, and had issue a son,—

Samuel Beavan (*b.* 1721), who adopted the surname (Beavan) of his maternal ancestors; *m.*, 1742, Fortune Williams, of Skreen, Radnor (she *d.* 1802), and had, with other issue,—

Samuel, Rector of Newchurch, *d. s. p.* 1820; John; and *Edward*.

John Beavan, *b.* 1748, Major Commandant of the Radnorshire Militia, *m.* Elizabeth, dau. of —— Trumper, Esq., of Michael Church, and had issue *Hannah* (who *m.* Rev. John Wall of Kington, *d.* 1826).

Samuel, of Ty'nycwm, J. P., Major of the Hereford Militia; *b.* 1783 (*d.* 1836), *m.*, 1808, Elizabeth, dau. of Nicholas Simmonds, Esq., of Dover, and had issue, Samuel (who *d.* young); *John*, *b.* 1793, *d.* 1849, Capt. in the 54th Regt., *Henry Augustus*, *d.* 1843, Surgeon Hereford Militia, and in practice at Hereford, and

Elizabeth Hexilrigge Curre, *b.* 1816; *m.*, 1836, Frederick Seekamp Dixon, Esq., son of Thomas Dixon, Surgeon Hereford Militia, and has issue,—

Rosa Theresa Mary Seekamp, *b.* 1837, *d.* **1840.**
Anne Maria Elizabeth Beavan, *b.* 1845.
Arthur Thomas Frederick Beavan, *b.* 1847.

Frederica Frances Mary Seekamp, b. 1849.
Hannah Rosina D'Olly Wall, b. 1851.
Edward Beavan, Esq., above named, b. 1761 (d. 1831), m. Mary Lewis, and had by her a family of twelve children, among whom were the following :—*Edward*, b. 1784, Lieut. in the 1st Royals, d. at Lisbon, *John*, b. 1787, d. s. p. *Henry* (d. 1838), m. Mary Nicholls, and had issue. He was paymaster of the Hereford Militia. *Fortune*, m. to Morris Sayce. *Theophilus*, d. s. p. *Thomas*, d. 1843 s. p; was Surgeon 7th Hussars, and— SAMUEL BEAVAN, Esq., now of Glascomb Court (as above).

BRYDGES, Sir Harford James Jones-, Bart., of Boultibrook, Radnorshire.

Baronetcy created 1807. Second Baronet; J. P. for cos. of Radnor and Hereford; High Sheriff for Radnor 1852; only son of the late Rt. Hon. Sir Harford Jones Brydges, Bart., K.C., LL.D., of Boultibrook, sometime ambassador in Persia; b. at The Whittern (Lyonshall Parish), Herefordshire, 1808; *grad.* at Merton Coll., Oxford, B.A. 1830, M.A. 1858; m., October 10, 1850, Mary Sarah, eldest dau. of the late Captain John Moberly, R.N., at Barrie, co. of Simcoe, Dominion of Canada; s. 1847.

Residence: Boultibrook, near Presteign.
Town Address: Athenæum Club, Piccadilly.
Arms: The arms of *Harford, Brydges, Moberly*, and *Jones*. The arms of Brydges and Jones are quartered thus: 1st and 4th, arg., a chief gu. over all a bend engrailed sa., charged on the chief point with a chaplet or—BRYDGES; 2nd and 3rd, arg., a chevron between three crows sa., in chief the star of the Order of the Crescent; on a chief of augmentation vert a lion couchant in front of the sun in splendour ppr., being the royal arms of Persia, granted to the first Bart. by Fateh Ali Shah, King of Persia—JONES.
Crests: 1. Two wings addorsed arg., charged with a bend engrailed sa.—*Brydges*; 2, on a cushion gu., garnished and tasselled or, a representation of the royal crown of Persia—*Jones*; 3, a crow sa., resting the dexter claw on the star of the Order of the Crescent.
Supporters: Dexter, a wyvern vert gorged with an eastern crown or; *sinister*, a lion ppr. gorged with an Eastern crown vert, granted by royal warrant with the arms of *Jones*, 1810.
Motto: Deus pascit corvos.

LINEAGE.

Lieut.-Col. James Jones, son of Griffith Jones, Esq., of Trewern, Radnorshire, distinguished himself in the battle of Blenheim, and received from the hand of Queen Anne a sword of honour, still preserved in the archives of the family. By his third wife, Mary, dau. and co-h. of B. Harford, Esq., of Bosbury, Heref., he left a son,—
Harford Jones, Esq., who m. Elizabeth, dau. of William Brydges, Esq., of Old Colwall, Heref. His only son,—
Harford Jones, Esq., of Presteign, Sheriff of co. Radnor 1778; d. 1798, leaving an only son,—
The Right. Hon. Sir Harford Jones Brydges, Bart., of Boultibrook, Minister Plenipotentiary in Persia, &c.; created a baronet 1807; m., 1796, Sarah, dau. of Sir Henry Gott, Kt., and widow of Robert Whitcomb, Esq., of Whittern, Herefordshire; assumed in 1826, by royal licence, the surname Brydges in addition to his own of Jones, and left, with other issue,—
HARFORD JAMES JONES-BRYDGES, the present Baronet, of Boultibrook (as above).

COCKBURN, Sir Robert, Bart., of Downton, Radnorshire.

Creation 1628.—Eighth Baronet, and a minor; son of Sir Edward Cludde Cockburn, seventh Bart., of Cockburn, Berwickshire, by his wife Mary Anne Frances, dau. of Robert Kerr Elliot, Esq., of Harwood and Clifton, Roxburghshire; b. 1861; has a brother, James Stanhope, b. 1867, and three sisters.

Residence: Downton, New Radnor.
Arms: Quarterly: 1st and 4th, gu., six mascles or, three, two, and one; 2nd and 3rd, arg., three cocks gu.; in the centre over all a heart gu.
Crest: A cock ppr.
Supporters: Two lions rampant gu.
Motto: Accendit cantu. Over Crest: Vigilans et audax.

DE WINTON, Rev. Henry, Boughrood, Radnorshire.

Rector of Boughrood 1849; Rural Dean; Proctor in Convocation for the diocese of St. David's; son of the late Rev. Walter de Winton, Vicar of Llanigon, Bronllys, and Boughrood, diocese of St. David's; b. at Hay 7th Nov., 1823; *ed.* at Shrewsbury School and Trin. Coll., Cambridge; *grad.* B.A. 1846, M.A. 1849; m., 7th Nov., 1848, Thomasine Septima, dau. of Rev. John Collinson, Rector of Boldon, Durham; has issue seven sons and seven daus. (including one dau. deceased).

Residence: Boughrood Rectory, Radnorshire.
Arms: Arg., a wyvern vert.
Crest: A wyvern's head erased vert.
Motto: Syn ar dy hyn (=Estote prudentes).

LINEAGE.

The descent is from Robert de Wintona, who came into Glamorganshire with Robert Fitzhamon soon after the Conquest. The pedigree of the family is given in Jones' *Hist. of Breconshire*. See also *De Winton of Maesllwch Castle*.

DE WINTON, Walter, Esq., of Maes-llwch Castle, Radnorshire.

J. P. for the cos. of Brecon and Radnor; High Sheriff for the latter co. 1862; eldest son of the late Walter Wilkins, Esq., of Maes-llwch Castle, sometime M.P. for the co. of Radnor (see *Parl. Annals*), who in 1839 assumed the surname De Winton, by Julia Cecilia, dau. of the Rev. R. J. Collinson, rector of Gateshead, Durham; *b*. 1832; *m*., 1867, Frances Jessie, dau. of the Hon. and Rev. Arthur Chetwynd Talbot, rector of Ingestrie and Church Eaton, Stafford.

Residence: Maes-llwch Castle, near Hay.
Town Address: Carlton Club.
Arms: Per pale or and arg., a wyvern vert between two spear-heads, sa.
Crest: 1. A wyvern's head erased vert, collared, arg.; 2. issuing from a mural crown a demi-lion rampant, holding in his paws a rose branch, all ppr.
Motto: Syn ar dy hun.

LINEAGE.

Thomas Wilkins, living 1700, prothonotary South Wales circuit, was son of Rev. Thomas Wilkins, rector of St. Mary Church, co. Glam., and Prebendary of Llandaff, who claimed descent from Robert *De Wintona*, said to have obtained lands near Cowbridge at the conquest by Robert Fitzhamon.

The Roll of Sheriffs and Parliamentary Annals of Radnorshire show the names of several members of the Wilkins family.

Note.—For an *engraving* of the noble castellated mansion of Maes-llwch, see p. 913.

EVANS, Edward Middleton, Esq., of Llwynbarried, Radnorshire.

J. P. for the co. of Radnor.

(*Full particulars not received in time*.)

HAIG, George Augustus, Esq., of Pen-ithon, Radnorshire.

J. P. for the co. of Radnor; High Sheriff for same co. 1864; son of the late Robert Haig, Esq., by Caroline, dau. of Sir William Wolseley, 7th Bart. of Wolseley, co. of Stafford; *m*., and has issue 5 sons and 5 daus., all living; settled at Pen Ithon 1858, which estate he acquired by purchase.

Heir: Charles Edwin Haig, educated at Shrewsbury and Exeter Coll., Oxford, B.A. 1870.
Residence: Pan Ithon, Radnorshire, via Newtown, North Wales.
Town Address: 7, Argyle Street.
Arms: Az., a saltire with a star in chief and base, and a crescent on each flank arg.
Crest: In a weir a rock ppr.
Motto: Tyde what may.

LINEAGE.

The descent of this family is from the Haigs of Bemerside, a house of great prominence in the Scottish wars of the fifteenth century.

HOWELL, Howel Gwynne, Esq., of Llanelwedd Hall, Radnorshire.

J. P. for Radnorshire and Brecknockshire; High Sheriff for Radnorshire in 1858 eldest son of the late Thomas Howell, Esq., surgeon 6th Dragoon Guards, by Anne Howell Gwynne, only dau. of Marmaduke H. T. Gwynne, Esq., of Garth, Brecknockshire, and Llanelwedd Hall, Radnorshire; *b*. 1820; *m*., 1860, Mary Henrietta, only dau. of the late Rev. T. K. Warren Harries, M.A., Rector of Mursley, Bucks, and second son of the late Major Harries, of Trevaccoon, Pembrokeshire; *s*. to the Llanelwedd estate 1849, on the death of his maternal uncle, Marmaduke Gwynne, Esq., without issue.

Residence: Llanelwedd Hall, Builth, Radnorshire.

LEWIS, Rev. Sir Gilbert Frankland, Bart, of Harpton Court, Radnorshire.

Creation 1846.—Third Baronet; Canon of Worcester 1856; was Rector of Gladestry, co. Radnor, 1832—1860, and of Monnington-on-Wye 1832—1864; Rural Dean; J. P. for the co. of Hereford; second son of the late Rt. Hon. Sir Thomas Frankland Lewis, P. C. M. P., first Bart., of Harpton Court, by his first wife, Harriet, dau. of Sir George Cornewall, Bart., of Moccas Court, Heref.; *b*. 1819; *ed*. at Eton and Magdalene Coll., Cambridge; B.A. 1830, M.A. 1833; *m*., 1843, Jane dau. of Sir Edmund Antrobus, second Bart.; *s*. his brother the late Sir George Cornewall Lewis, the distinguished writer and minister, 1863; has issue surviving,—

Herbert Edmund Frankland, *b*. 1846.
Mary Ann.
Elinor.

Heir: His son, Herbert Edmund Frankland.
Residence: Harpton Court, near Kington.
Arms: Arg., a cross double-parted sa. fretty or, in the first and fourth quarters an eagle displayed gu.; in the second and third a lion rampant of the second, ducally crowned or.
Crest: On a cap of maintenance an heraldic tiger statant or.
Motto: Expertus fidelem.

LINEAGE.

In the roll of *Sheriffs*, and in the *Parl. Annals* of the co. of Radnor, the names of Lewises of Harpton are seen frequently to occur since the middle of the sixteenth century. Sometimes they are of Harpton, sometimes of Downton in the same county.

John Lewis, Esq., of Harpton, fourth in descent

from Thomas, Sheriff for the co. in 1552; *m.*, 1778, Anne, dau. of Sir Thomas Frankland, Bart.; was father of—
Sir Thomas Frankland Lewis, first Bart., of Harpton Court. He followed out the traditions of his family by devoting his life to public affairs, and rose to distinction in the various offices of Secretary to the Treasury, Vice President of the Board of Trade, Commissioner of the Poor Law, &c., and was succeeded by his eldest son,—
Sir George Cornewall Lewis, second Bart.; *b.* 1806; *m.*, 1844, Lady Maria Theresa Villiers (sister of the late Earl of Clarendon), widow of Thomas H. Lister, Esq.; M.P. for Radnor; P. C.; successively Chancellor of the Exchequer, Secretary for the Home Department, and Secretary of War, and author of several important works on History and Politics. He *d. s. p.* in 1863, and was succeeded by his only brother,—
THE REV. SIR GILBERT FRANKLAND LEWIS, now of Harpton Court (as above).

LINGEN, Henry, Esq., of Penlanoleu, Radnorshire.

J. P. and D. L. for the co. of Radnor; High Sheriff for same co. 1840 (see *Sheriffs);* second son of the late William Lingen, Esq., of Burghill, Hereford, by his wife, Anne, dau. and h. of John Barrett, Esq., of Hollins Hill, Wor.; *b.* 1803; *m.*, 1837, Priscilla, dau. of Joseph Jones, Esq., of Aberystwyth, Card., and has issue surviving one son. Brother living, Charles Lingen, Esq., M.D., J. P. Hereford.

Heir: Rev. Charles Nelson, *b.* 1843; *ed.* at Pemb. Coll., Cambridge; B.A.; J. P. for the co. of Radnor.
Residence: Penlanoleu, near Rhayader.
Arms: Barry of six or and az.; on a bend gu. three roses arg.
Crest: Out of a ducal coronet or a garb vert.

LINEAGE.

The seat of this family was originally in the neighbouring co. of Hereford, where Sir John Lingen, of Stoke Edith, *temp.* Charles I., was prominent among its ancestors.

LLOYD, Robert Lewis, Esq., of Nantgwyllt, Radnorshire.

J. P. and D. L. for the co. of Radnor; called to the Bar at the Inner Temple; High Sheriff for Radnor 1872; son of the late Thomas Lewis Lloyd, Esq., J. P., D. L., of Nantgwyllt, High Sheriff for the co. of Cardigan 1822, by his wife Anna, dau. of the late E. Davies, Esq., of Treforgan, Card.; *b.* Jan. 9th, 1836; *ed.* at Eton, and Magdalen Coll., Cambridge; *grad.* M.A. 1862; *m.*, June 6th, 1865, Mary Anne Jane, eldest dau. of John Lewis, Esq., late of Llanllyr, co. of Cardigan; has issue 3 sons and 1 dau.

Heir: His son, Robert Wharton Lewis Lloyd.
Residence: Nantgwyllt, near Rhayader.
Crest: A wolf statant ppr.

LINEAGE.

The lineage of this family combines the two well-known houses of *Lewis* of Cwm-dauddwr ("the valley of two waters," a faithful description of the locality between the rivers Wye and Elan near their junction, often erroneously spelled "Cwmtoyddwr") and *Lloyd* of Nantgwyllt (*nant*, a dingle; *gwyllt*, wild, rugged).

The Lewises of Cwm-dauddwr had become allied with the old family of the Lloyds of Wern-newydd, Llanarth, Card. David Lloyd, of Wern-newydd (living 1690), had four sons—Watkin, Edward (who *m.* Anne, dau. of James Stedman, of Strata Florida, and *d.* 1754), David, and Richard, who all *d. s. p.*, leaving the race to be represented by two surviving daus.—Bridget, who *m.* Morgan Lloyd of Glansevin (see *Lloyd, Glansevin);* and *Posthuma*, who *m.* Robert Lewis, Esq., whose grandson,—

John Lewis, Esq., of Cwm-dauddwr, Rad., *m.* Elizabeth Lloyd, of Nantgwyllt, and had a son,— Thomas Lewis (Lloyd), Esq., who, in 1824, by sign-manual adopted his mother's surname in addition to his own of Lewis; and by his wife Anna, before-named, had, with other issue, a son,—
ROBERT LEWIS LLOYD, Esq., now of Nantgwyllt (as above).

MYNORS, Robert Baskerville, Esq., of Evancoed, Radnorshire.

J. P. and D. L. for cos. of Radnor and Hereford; High Sheriff for Radnor 1856; eldest son of the late Peter Rickards Mynors, Esq., of Tre-ago, co. Hereford and Evan-coed, Rad., by Mary, dau. of Edmund Trowbridge Halliday, of Chapel-Cleeve, Somerset; *b.* 1819; *ed.* at Christ Church, Oxford, and called to the Bar; *m.*, 1852, Ellen, dau. of Rev. Edward Higgins, of Bosbury, Hereford, and has issue.

Heir: His son, Willoughby Baskerville, *b.* 1854.
Residences: Evancoed, New Radnor; Tre-ago, near Ross.
Arms: Sa., an eagle displayed or, on a chief az., bordured arg., a chevron between two crescents in chief and a rose in base of the second.
Crest: A naked arm embowed, the hand grasping a bear's paw erased.
Motto: Spero ut fidelis.

LINEAGE.

The Mynors are said to have settled at Treago (Tre-iago) soon after the Conquest. The family combines by marriage the Prickards of Evancoed and Baskervilles of Aberedw (see *Baskerville of Clyro Court*).

MYNORS, Thomas Baskerville, Esq., of Barland, Radnorshire.

J. P. and D. L. for the co. of Radnor; youngest son of the late Peter Rickards

THE COUNTY FAMILIES OF RADNORSHIRE. 925

Mynors, Esq., of Evancoed, Rad., and Treago (Tre-iago), Heref. (see *Mynors of Evancoed*); *b.* 1834; *ed.* at Eton, and Christ Church, Oxford; *m.*, 1865, Constance, dau. of Green Price, Esq., of Norton, Presteign.

Residence: Barland, near New Radnor.
Arms: For *arms* and *lineage* see *Mynors of Evancoed*.

PHILIPS, George Henry, Esq., of Abbey Cwmhir, Radnorshire.

J. P. and D. L. for the co. of Radnor; High Sheriff for same co. 1860; second son of the late Francis Aspinall Philips, Esq., Bank Hall, Lancashire (the eldest son being Francis, now of Bank Hall); *b.* 1831; *ed.* at Chr. Ch., Oxford; *m.*, 1867, Anne, dau. of the Rev. Charles Kenrick Prescot, M.A., Rector of Stockport; is heir presumptive to his brother of Bank Hall.

Residence: Abbey Cwm-hir, Penybout, Rad.
Arms: Per pale az. and sa. within an orle of fleurs-de-lis arg., a lion rampant erminois ducally crowned and holding in the paws a mascle or, a canton ermine.
Crest: A demi-lion rampant erminois collared sa. ducally gorged or.
Motto: Simplex munditiis.

LINEAGE.

This family in its chief branches has been seated for several generations at Heath House, co. of Stafford, and Manchester, co. of Lancaster, but came originally from Wales. (See *Philips, Gwernvale, Brec.*) Several members of the family removed to America, where in Pennsylvania and New York they rose to eminence. The patriarch of the family removed from Wales in the reign of Edward VI., and settled at Heath House, Staffordshire, a property which has ever since continued in his descendants. From him in the third or fourth generation sprang Nathaniel Philips, Esq., of Manchester, *b.* 1693, ancestor in direct line of Mr. Philips of Abbey Cwm-hir (as above), R. N. Philips, Esq., M.P., of the Park, Manchester, &c. *Philips of Heath House*, co. Stafford, and *Philips of Wilcombe*, co. of Warwick, represent the elder branch.

PRICE, Richard Green, Esq., of Norton Manor, Radnorshire.

J. P. and D. L. for co. of Radnor; was M.P. for Radnor District of Boroughs 1863—1869; Lord of the Manor of Norton; eldest son of the late George Green, Esq., by Margaret, dau. of the late Richard Price, Esq., of Knighton, whose eldest son, Col. Richard Price, for many years M.P. for the Radnor boroughs (see *Parl. Annals*), *d. s. p.*, and left his estate to his nephew, Richard Green, who thereupon assumed the additional surname Price; *b.* 1803; *m.*, first, 1837, Frances Milborough, dau. of D. R. Dansey, Esq., of Easton Court, Heref.; secondly, Laura, dau. of Richard H. King, Esq., M.D., of Mortlake, Surrey, and has issue by both marriages.

Heir: Richard Dansey, *b.* 1838.
Residence: Norton Manor, near Presteign.
Town Address: Reform Club.

LINEAGE.

The Prices (from *Ap Rhys*) of Knighton are an ancient Welsh family, among whose most distinguished members may be mentioned *Chase Price*, Esq., M.P. for his co., and Col. Richard Price, his nephew, who represented the Radnor district of boroughs for the period of forty-eight years (see *Parl. Annals*).

PRICKARD, Mrs., of Dderw, Radnorshire.

Maria Maude Prickard, widow of Thomas Prickard, Esq, of Dderw, J. P. and D. L. for the co. of Radnor, who *d.* 1869, leaving, with other issue, an eldest son and heir,—

HUGH POWEL, Major commanding Royal Radnor Rifles.

Residence: Dderw, near Rhayader.
Arms: (Not sent.)

(*Further particulars in next edition.*)

PRICKARD, Rev, Thomas Charles, of New Radnor, Radnorshire.

Clerk in Holy Orders; Rector of New Radnor; J. P. for the co. of Radnor; son of the late Thomas Prickard, Esq., of Dderw, near Rhayader (see *Prickard of Dderw*); *b.* at Dderw, Aug. 19, 1831; *ed.* at Oxford; *grad.* B.A. 1854; *m.*, Aug., 1866, Emily Matilda, dau. of the Rev. Augustus James Sharp, Rector of Snailwell-cum-Chippenham, Cambridgeshire.

Residence: The Rectory, New Radnor.
Arms: See *Prickard of Dderw*.

THOMAS, Edward David, Esq., of Wellfield, Radnorshire.

J. P. and D. L. for cos. of Brecon and Radnor; eldest son of David Thomas, Esq., of Wellfield; *b.* at Wellfield on 1st March, 1808; *ed.* at Shrewsbury and Wadham Coll., Oxford; *grad.* B.A. in 1829, and subsequently M.A.; *m.*, 12th Sept., 1837, Arabella Emma, younger of the two daus. of John Samuel Gowland, Esq., of Cagebrook, co. Hereford; *s.* to estate in 1841; is patron of the living of Llanelwedd, co. Radnor; has issue three sons and two daus. living, eldest dau. *d.* Feb., 1858.

Heir: Edward David Thomas, *b.* Oct., 1839; *ed.* at Rugby and Univ. Coll., Oxford; *m.* to Caroline Louisa, eldest dau. of C. Greenly, Esq., of Titley Court, co. Hereford.
Residence: Wellfield, near Builth.
Arms: Per pale arg. and gu. on a chevron engrailed two griffins passant, combattant, counterchanged; on a chief wavy az. three cinquefoils arg.
Crest: Out of a mural crown arg. a demi seahorse gu.
Motto: I Dduw bo'r diolch.

LINEAGE.

This family is a younger branch of the ancient family of *Thomas of Llwyn-madoc*, co. of Brecon, and Pencerrig, co. of Radnor, and claim to be of the lineage of *Elystan Glodrudd*, Prince of Ferlex.

Note.—*Well-field*, sometimes incorrectly spelled Welfield, is beautifully situated on high ground above the Wye, near Builth. There is an ancient British or Danish camp on an elevated part of the grounds, a quarter of a mile eastward of the house.

VAUGHAN, James, Esq., of Builth, Breconshire.

J. P. for Radnorshire and Breconshire; Surgeon-Major retired, Indian Army (Bombay); F.R.C.S., F.R.G.S.; author of a pamphlet on "The Gums and other Products of Aden, Arabia Felix;" youngest son of the late Hugh Vaughan, Esq., of Llwynmadock, Llansaintffraed in Elvel, Radnorshire; *b.* at Llwynmadock, 18th June, 1818; *ed.* at private schools, Ludlow Grammar School, &c.; is *unm.*

Residence: Castle, Builth, Breconshire.
Town Address: East India United Service Club, 14, St. James's Square, S.W.

LINEAGE.

For lineage see *Vaughan of Llansantffraed, Rad.*

VAUGHAN, Rev. Hugh, of Llantsantffraed and Llwynmadock, Radnorshire.

M.A.; Vicar of Llansantffraed in Elvel, co. Radnor, 1838; Rural Dean 1852; eldest son of the late Hugh Vaughan, Esq., of Llwynmadock, co. of Radnor, J. P., D. L., High Sheriff for Radnor 1825; *b.* 1802; *ed.* at Jesus Coll., Oxford; B.A. 1825, M.A. 1828.

Residence: The Vicarage, Llansantffraed, Builth.
Arms: The pedigree of Vaughans of Glascwm gives no account of their arms.

LINEAGE.

Evan Vaughan (1679) lived at *Y Fedw*, Rad. His son Evan lived at *Disserth*, Rad., and afterwards at Cil-y--berllan, which became his property after the death of Hugh Evans in 1710. His son,—
Hugh Vaughan, *b.* 1722; Sheriff of Radnorshire 1762; *m.*, 1775, second wife (portion £280), Ann Williams of Llanybister, and had by her an only son,—
Hugh Vaughan, *b.* 1777 (*d.* 1851), *m.* Hannah Lewis, of Tanhouse, Builth, and had issue ten children, of whom the eldest is—
HUGH VAUGHAN, now Vicar of Llansantffraed (as above); and the youngest James Vaughan, Esq., now of Builth (see *Vaughan of Builth*).

VENABLES, George Stovin, Esq., Llysdinam Hall, Breconshire.

Barrister-at-Law; Queen's Counsel; J. P. for the cos. of Brecon and Radnor, and D. L. for Breconshire; second son of the late Ven. Richard Venables, Archdeacon of Carmarthen (see *Venables of Clyro*); *b.* June, 1810; *ed.* at Charterhouse and Jesus Coll., Cambridge; *grad.* M.A. 1835; is *unm,*

Residence: Llysdinam Hall, Breconshire.
Town Address: 2, Mitre Court, Temple, E.C. Athenæum, and Oxford and Cambridge Clubs.

VENABLES, Rev. Richard Lister, of Clyro, Radnorshire.

Vicar of Clyro, with Bettws Clyro, 1847; J. P. for cos. of Hereford, Brecon, and Radnor; D. L. for the co. of Radnor, and Chairman of Quarter Sessions; eldest son of the late Ven. Richard Venables, M.A., Archdeacon of Carmarthen, and Sophia, his wife, dau. of George Lister, Esq., of Grosby House, Lincolnshire; *b.* May, 1809; *ed.* at Charterhouse and Emmanuel Coll., Cambridge; *grad.* B.A. 1831, M.A. 1835; *m.*, 1st, 1834, Mary Augusta, widow of F. Adams, Esq. (she *d.* 1865); 2ndly, 1867, Agnes Minnie, dau. of the late Henry Shepherd Pearson, Esq.; has issue by second marriage one dau., Katharine Diana.

Residences: Clyro Vicarage, Radnorshire; Llysdinam Hall, Breconshire.
Town Address: Oxford and Cambridge Club.

WATT, James Watt Gibson, Esq., of Doldowlod House, Radnorshire.

J. P. and D. L. for the co. of Radnor; son of James Gibson, Esq,, M.D., late 13th Light Dragoons; *b.* at Edinburgh Aug. 4, 1831; *ed.* at Rugby and Magdalen Coll., Cambridge; assumed the surname Watt by letters patent in 1856 in addition to that of Gibson on succeeding to the estates of the late James Watt, Esq., his great uncle.

Residences: Doldowlod House, Radnorshire; Heathfield, Staffordshire.
Town Address: Carlton Club.
Arms: The arms of Gibson and Watt quartered.
Crests: An elephant and a pelican in her nest.
Motto: Pandite cœlestes portæ.

LINEAGE.

This family derives its descent from the celebrated mechanician, *James Watt*, of Greenock, D.C.L., F.R.S., Member of Royal Institute of France, &c., so well known for his inventions for the application of steam-power. He left a dau. who *m.*

James Miller, Esq., of Glasgow, and had issue two daus, Margaret and Agnes, the younger of whom *m.* in 1826,

James Gibson, Esq., M.D., 13th Light Dragoons, and had issue,—

1. Agnes Miller, *m.* Chilley Pine, Esq., 4th Dragoon Guards, *dec.*, and has issue a son, *Arthur*, *b.* 20th April, 1854.
2. JAMES WATT GIBSON, now of Doldowlod (as above).
3. Margaret Elizabeth, *m.*, 1864, to Henry B. Marsh, Esq., and has issue a dau., *b.* 29th May, 1870.

Note.—The mansion of Doldowlod in the Elizabethan style was erected in 1845. The date of Heathfield is about 1792.

WILLIAMS, Samuel Charles Evans, Esq., of Bryntirion, Radnorshire.

Bachelor of Arts, Oxon; Student of Law, Lincoln's Inn; J. P. for the co. of Radnor; County Magistrate; son of Rev. John Williams (late Censor of Christ Church, Oxford, afterwards Vicar of Spelsbury, Oxfordshire, now of Bryntirion Hall, Radnorshire) and Jane Patterson, of Devonshire; who *m.*, 1st, John Patterson, Esq., *b.* at Spelsbury, Oxfordshire; *ed.* at Westminster School and Christ Church, Oxford; *grad.* B.A. 1864; *m.*, Feb. 26th, 1867, Mary Caroline, 3rd dau. of the late Rev. Henry William Robinson *Luttman-Johnson*, formerly *Michell*, Fellow of Trin. Coll., Oxford; afterwards of Binderton House, Sussex, and has issue three daus.

Residence: Bryntirion Hall, near Rhayader.
Town Address: New University Club.
Arms: Party per cross; 1st and 4th, arg., three horses' heads sa.; 2nd, a chevron or between three boars' heads ppr.; 3rd, arg-, a lion rampant gu.
Crests: A boar's head ppr. and a lion rampant, as in the arms.
Motto: Deo fidelis et Regi.

LINEAGE.

This family derives its descent from David Williams of Rhayader, and Evan Evans of Noyadd, Cwmdauddwr, Radnorshire, whose descendants intermarried. Jonathan Williams, Author of the *History of Radnorshire*, was a member of this family.

Note.—The mansion of *Bryntirion Hall* is newly erected in an elegant style of architecture partaking of some of the features of the Swiss and French villa. It stands on a slope, and has command of much of the fine scenery of the Wye valley near Rhayader.

ADDENDA TO COUNTY FAMILIES.

All other particulars with which the Editor is favoured in time will be put in their proper places under their proper counties in the Second Edition.]

GRIFFITH, Boscawen Trevor, Esq., of Trevalyn Hall, Denbighshire.

Was an officer 23rd Welsh Fusiliers; J. P. and D. L. for the co. of Denbigh; High Sheriff for same co. 1864 (see *Sheriffs*); son of the late Thomas Griffith, Esq., of Trevalyn Hall, J. P. and D. L., High Sheriff for 1849 for the co. of Denbigh (*d.* 1856), by Elizabeth, dau. of William Boscawen, Esq.; *b.* 1835; *m.*, 1857, Ellen, dau. of V.-Admiral N. Duff, of Bath, and has issue.

Residence: Trevalyn Hall, near Wrexham.

HOPE, Samuel Pearce, Esq., of Marchwiel Hall, Denbighshire.

J. P. and D. L. for the co. of Denbigh; High Sheriff for the same co. 1871; son of the late Samuel Hope, Esq., by Rebecca, dau. of Thomas Bateman, Esq., of Middleton Hall, Derbyshire; *b.* 1823; *m.*, 1855, Amelia, dau. of John Prys Eyton, Esq., of Plas Llannerch-y-mor, Flintshire, and sister of Adam Eyton, Esq., and has issue.

Residence: Marchwiel Hall. near Wrexham.
Town Address: Carlton Club.

SAUNDERS, William Francis David, Esq., of Glanrhydw, Carmarthenshire.

Only surviving son of the late Francis David Saunders, Esq., of Tymawr, J. P. and D. L. for the co. of Cardigan, Capt. 16th Regt. Trichinopoli Light Infantry (*d.* Jan. 8, 1867, *æt.* seventy-nine), by Mary Jane, dau. of the Rev. George W. Green, of Court Henry, co of Carm., now residing, as do her daughters, at *Court Henry; b.* Sept. 7, 1851; is *unm.*

Residence: Glanrhydw, Llandeveilog, Carm.
Arms: (Not sent).

VAUGHAN, Henry Gwynne, Esq., of Cynghordy,

(Additional, see p. 305.)

J. P. and D. L. for the co. of Brecon, and J. P. for the co. of Carmarthen; Sheriff of former co. 1865; second son of the late Samuel Jones, Esq., of Llanvillo, Talgarth, by Jane, dau. of William Vaughan, Esq., of Penymaes (of the line of Vaughans of Merthyr), Llanvillo, by Isabella Gwynne, the last survivor of the line of Gwynnes of Cynghordy; *b.* 1812; *m.*, 1839, Anne, youngest dau. of the late David Pritchard, Esq., of Dolygaer, J. P. for the co. of Brecon, by Anne, dau. of Edward Thomas, Esq., of Llwynmadoc; assumed by royal licence in 1855 the surnames Gwynne Vaughan instead of his own of Jones; has issue ten children, the eldest son being Thomas, *b.* 1844; *ed.* at Shrewsbury School; a Capt. Royal Brecknock Militia.

Heir: Thomas Gwynne Vaughan.
Residence: Cynghordy, Llandovery.
Arms: Ermines, two chevronels arg. between three boys' heads affronté couped at the shoulders ppr., crined or, around the neck of each a snake nowed ppr., all within a bordure of the second.
Crest: In a wreath on a mount vert, in front of a boy's head, as in the arms, a snake, also as in the arms.
Motto: Asgre lan diogel ei pherchen.

LINEAGE.

The old family of *Gwyn*, otherwise *Gwynne*, of Cynghordy, had dwelt at that place for several generations prior to Thomas Gwynne, who *m.* Mary, dau. of Dr. Richard Baily, Chancellor of Hereford. His son,—
William Gwynne, Esq., of Cynghordy, *m.* Elizabeth, dau. of John Morgan, Esq., Braham Hall, Yorkshire, and had issue a dau. and h.,—
Isabella, who *m.* William Vaughan, Esq., of Penymaes, Llanvillo, co. of Brecon, and had a dau., Jane, who *m.*—
Samuel Jones, Esq., of Llanvillo, and had with other issue—
HENRY, now of Cynghordy, who adopted the surname *Gwynne-Vaughan* (as above shown).

YORKE, Simon, Esq., of Erddig Park, Denbighshire.

J. P. and D. L. for the co. of Denbigh; High Sheriff 1848; son of the late Simon Yorke, Esq., J. P. and D. L. of the same place; *b.* 6th April, 1811, at Erddig; *s.* 1833; *m.*, August 6, 1846, Victoria Mary Louisa, dau. of General the Hon. Sir Edward Cust, K.C.H., youngest son of Lord Brownlow, and has issue 2 sons and 2 daughters.

Heir: His eldest son, Philip, *b.* 1849.
Residence: Erddig Park, Wrexham.
Arms: Argent, on a saltier az. a bezant or, with a crescent for difference.
Crest: A lion's head erased proper, collared gu., thereon a bezant or.
Motto: Nec cupias, nec metuas.

LINEAGE.

The Yorkes have long resided at Erddig, and trace their descent from the Yorkes of Dover, of

ADDENDA TO COUNTY FAMILIES.

whom Philip, Earl of Hardwicke, in the Peerage of England, appointed Lord Chancellor of England in 1736, created Earl of Hardwicke 1754, represented the elder branch. Amongst the distinguished members of the Erddig house may be mentioned—
Philip Yorke, Esq., author of the *Royal Tribes of Wales*, published in 1799, which has now become very rare.
Simon Yorke, Esq., of Erddig (uncle of the distinguished Lord Chancellor Hardwicke), *m.* Anne, sister and *h.* of John Miller, Esq., Master in Chancery, of Erddig, who purchased that place, and enlarged the mansion in 1713, *d. s. p.* 1733, leaving his estate of Erddig to his sister's son, Simon.
Simon Yorke, Esq., of Erddig, *m.* Dorothea, dau. of M. Hutton, Esq., of Newnham, Herts, and *d.* 1768, leaving his property to his only son Philip.
Philip Yorke, Esq., of Erddig, author of *The Royal Tribes of Wales*, *m.*, 1770, Elizabeth, dau. of the Right Hon. Sir John Cust, Bart., Speaker of the House of Commons, and had by her a son, Simon, as below. He married, secondly, Diana, dau. and h. of Peirce Wynne, Esq. (see *Yorke of Dyffryn Aled*). He *d.* 1804, and was succ. by his eldest son,—
Simon Yorke, Esq., of Erddig, *b.* 1771, *m.*, 1807, Margaret, dau. of John Holland, Esq., and dying 1834, was succ. by his son, —
SIMON YORKE, Esq., now of Erddig, as above.

Note.—Erddig Park mansion was built in 1687 and in 1713 purchased and enlarged by John Miller, Esq., as shown above. Erddig is a large, solid, unpretending mansion, with suites of rooms furnished in the antique style, and enriched with objects of art and antiquity, arms of the royal tribes of Wales, &c. The situation of the house is highly picturesque.

CORRECTIONS, ETC. IN COUNTY FAMILIES.

ANWYL, Robert Charles, Esq., of Llugwy, p. 699; has five (not "six") sisters living.
ARENGO-CROSS, John William, Esq., of Iscoed, p. 280; *d.* at Biebrich on the Rhine, 25th Sept., 1872.
BULKELEY, Sir Richard B. Williams-, of Baron Hill; is tenth baronet, not tenth "baron." At p. 363, Edmund and Arthur Williams were fifth and seventh sons respectively of William Williams of Cochwillan, "called sometimes W. Wynn Williams."
CONWY, Capt. Conwy G. H. R., p. 444; Gwenydd Frances Conwy *m.* 1872, to Capt. Somerset.
COWELL-STEPNEY, Sir John S., Bart., p. 283. Eldest son, William Frederick, *d.* Nov. 1872.
GLYNNE, Sir Stephen R., Bart., p. 447. Rev. Henry Glynne, *d.* July 20, 1872.
GRIFFITH, Capt. David White, of Bryntêg; p. 43, *read* Emily, dau. of J. Keily (not Reily), Esq., and gr. dau. of the late John Keily, Esq., of Strancally Castle, co. Waterford.
GULSTON, Alan James, Esq., of Dirleton, p. 288. Horatia Augusta Stepney Gulston *m.*, 1872, Albert de Rutzen, Esq., Stipendiary Magistrate of Merthyr Tydfil.
HANMER, Sir John, of Bettisfield Park, p. 447; created Baron Hanmer of Hanmer, 1872.
HORTON, Isaac, Esq., of Ystrad; p. 290, *d.* June 23rd, 1872, *æt.* sixty-four.
JAMES, J. T. W., Esq., of Pantsaison, p. 902. Robert Lloyd James, Esq., *m.*, 29th Aug., 1872, Annie Sophia, eldest dau. of F. W. Docker, Esq., of Menai View, Bangor.
KNEESHAW, Richard, Esq., of Penmaenmawr; p. 356. The arms are—Gu., a *raven* volant arg.; Joshua Kneeshaw *m.* Lucy, dau. of John Dobby, not Dobling. William Kneeshaw, son of Joshua, was Lieut. R.A.; Louisa Domville *m.* Capt. Stratford Tuke; Mary *m.* Arnold Loxley, Esq., of Norcott Court.
LEWES, William Price, Esq., of Llysnewydd, p. 293. Capt. William Price Llewellyn Lewes *m.*, 1872, Sarah Cecilia, younger dau. of the late John Drane Drake, Esq., of Stokestown, co. Wexford.
LLOYD, Thomas Edward John, Esq., of Aberdunant, p. 357. Robert Lloyd Jones-Parry, Esq., of Aberdunant, was eldest son of Thomas Parry Jones-Parry, Esq., of Llwyn-Onn.
MORRIS, Thomas Charles, Esq., of Bryn-Myrddin, p. 297; *s.* to a moiety of the estates of his cousin (not "uncle"), the late David Morris, Esq.
MYDDELTON-BIDDULPH, Col. Robert, of Chirk Castle, p. 412; *d.* 1872.
PLATT, John, Esq., of Bryn-y-neuadd, p. 360, *d.* 1872.
POWELL, Lancelot, Esq., of Aberclydach House, p. 118. John Powell, Esq., of Brecon, *d.* 1809.
PROTHEROE, Mrs., of Dolwilim, p. 301, *d.* 20th May, 1872.
REES, John Van der Horst, Esq., of Kilymaenllwyd, p. 302; *dele* "*m.* dau. of B. Jones, Esq., of Llanelly, and has issue," an inadvertent error.
RICHARDSON, John Crow, Esq., p. 632, Amy Serocold *d.* 15th Aug., 1872.
ROBERTS, Gabriel, Esq., of Plas Gwyn, p. 415. Rev. Gabriel Lloyd Roberts, *d.* 7th May, 1872.
ROGERS, J. E., Esq., of Abermeurig, p. 210; was High Sheriff of co. Cardigan 1872.
WEST, W. Cornwallis, Esq., p. 416; appointed, 1872, Lord Lieutenant of the co. of Denbigh; *m.*, Oct. 5, 1872, Mary Fitz-patrick, dau. of Rev. Frederick and the Lady Olivia Fitz-patrick, of Cloone, co. Leitrim, and niece of the Marquess of Headford.
WILLIAMS-DRUMMOND, Sir James Hamlyn, of Edwinsford, p. 306. The Lady Mary Eleanor Williams-Drummond *d.* Aug. 18, 1872.
WILLIAMS, Edward, Esq., of Wrexham, p. 417. Heir, Joseph Llewelyn Williams, M.B., eldest son.
WILLIAMS, Richard, Esq., of Trosyrafon, p. 49; *d.* 1871.

HIGHER EDUCATION IN WALES.

To the leading families of a province the superior culture of its sons is an appropriate subject of thought and care.

Time was when the high schools of Britain—schools really high and distinguished for their period—were confined to this western region now called *Wales*. To the Germanic clans who conquered what is now named England, schools were unknown; and some centuries had passed before Alfred the Great—in large degree through the aid of the Welshman Asser, whom he summoned for the purpose from St. David's—succeeded in turning the minds of the Anglo-Britons (miscalled "Anglo-Saxons") from the barbaric pursuit of the sword to mental culture and semi-civilized manners. Great schools at this time existed at Llanilltyd-fawr (now Llantwit-major) in Glamorgan, Bangor-Iscoed near Wrexham, and other places, to which the youth of Wales, and even of foreign countries, resorted by thousands. The domestic feuds of the Welsh in the early Middle Ages, and the desolating wars of the various invasions and conquests of Wales by English and Normans, totally annihilated, even to their last remains, these seats of learning, while side by side with the growing power of the English people arose by steady progress a taste for knowledge and great institutions of learning. Thus was Wales made to change positions with England.

Time will again come when Wales shall possess her schools, and the genius of her sons shall have free scope and the stimulus of native culture. Education, by stealing marches, will create its own opportunities and deliverance. Statesmen will arise who, free from prejudice, and capable of rational judgment, will discern and recognise the claims of *thirteen counties of the realm*, with a population of over *a million and three hundred thousand souls*. Already a new life is being infused into the older grammar schools, which, mainly through the pious liberality of individuals, had since the Reformation been established; and in healthful competition with these, as population is increasing, middle-class schools of a superior kind, through the enterprise and ability of independent teachers, are arising. Under the new Education Act, with all its imperfections, a vast impulse is being imparted to *Elementary* Education; and more pressing demands will be felt for a *higher* education midway between the Common School and the University. The Cambridge University Local Examinations are doing a real work in this direction, and have, along with other movements within the last seven years, created a new educational period in Wales.

We accordingly already find, in addition to the excellent grammar schools of Monmouth, Cowbridge, Llandovery, Swansea, Ruthin, and Beaumaris, and some others, such vigorous Middle-class Schools as that of *Grove Park, Wrexham*, conducted by Mr. J. Pryce Jones, L.C.P., taking high rank in these examinations. The only private schools belonging to

Wales which are mentioned, *ex. gr.*, in the Schools Inquiry Commissioners' Report for 1868, are the Grove Park School and Thistleboon House School, Swansea. Both these are named on account of the number of pupils they have passed through the University and other School Examinations. *Grove Park School*, from its long standing (estab. 1823), its extensive and convenient premises, the number of its masters, and the success of its pupils in the various public examinations, may fairly rank as one of our most efficient Public Schools.

We have other good grammar schools at Aberystwyth (Mr. Edward Jones, B.A.), Swansea, Cardiff, Haverfordwest, Cardigan, Bangor (endowed), Bottwnog (endowed), &c.; and altogether, it may be said that Middle-class Education gives fair promise of keeping in advance of Elementary Education in the Principality. What we now want is *not* an institution to occupy the ground legitimately possessed by these schools, but one of a different order, to take the better class pupils prepared by these, and carry them on to higher studies.

The proposed University College of Wales.—It is generally known that an effort has for some years been making to establish a University College for Wales. The chief requisites were—a broad, unsectarian basis, and a scheme of thorough education, adapted in its working to the circumstances of the Principality. In 1862 a beginning was made and carried efficiently forward to establish such an institution; and after a large sum of money had been obtained, and popular interest evoked by the labours of one individual, a committee was formed, from whose *Minutes* (1864) this account of the origin of the Foundation is extracted:—

"The movement for the establishment of collegiate and university education in the principality of Wales originated in a series of letters to the public journals in the autumn of the year 1862, by the Rev. Dr. T. Nicholas, Professor of Theology, Philosophy, &c., at the Carmarthen College, which series of letters, at the request of several friends of education, afterwards appeared in the form of a pamphlet, entitled *Middle and High Schools and a University for Wales*. The question speedily won a good amount of public attention and favour, and a desire was generally felt for further action in the matter. Mr. W. Williams, M.P., on the 23rd October, 1863, announced to Dr. Nicholas his willingness to contribute £1,000 towards the object."

The founder of the enterprise acted as secretary until a subscribed fund of about £14,000 was secured, and the noble building, called the "Castle House," at Aberystwyth was purchased for £10,000. He then, in 1867, left the matter in the hands of a "Committee." At p. 140 a reference has been made to the state of the enterprise in the beginning of 1872; and now an effort is being made (Nov., 1872) to open a Boys' School as a "beginning." So much time and money, however, have been lost, that the success of the work has become problematical. The interests of the youth of a whole province have been made to wait upon an incompetent management. It is to be hoped that by and by the Government will rescue the enterprise from impending failure. Many persons have wrought earnestly and contributed largely towards this much-desired object, and they have a right to expect from those who have undertaken to expend the fund a reasonable account.

BOROUGH MAGISTRATES OF WALES.

[*Many names in this list are also included among the "County Families." The Borough Justices of Swansea and Cardiff are given under Glamorganshire.*]

ALEXANDER, William, Esq., Park Place, Cardiff; J. P. and Alderman for the bor. of Cardiff; Mayor of Cardiff 1859-60.

ALLEN, Charles, Esq., Norton, Tenby, Pemb.; J. P. for the bor. of Tenby, and for the co. of Pembroke.

BAGNALL, James, Esq., Carmarthen; J. P. for the bor. of Carmarthen.

BARRETT, Thomas Brettell, Esq., of Welshpool, Mont., M.R.C.S.L.; J. P. for the bor. of Welshpool; Alderman and late Mayor of Welshpool; Surg. to Welshpool Dispensary.

BATE, Edward, Esq., Kelsterton, Flint; J. P. and Ald. for the bor. of Flint.

BEYNON, Thomas, Esq., Newport, Mon.; J. P. for the bor. of Newport; Mayor of Newport 1870.

BIRD, George, Esq., Cardiff; J. P. for the bor. of Cardiff.

BOWEN, James, Esq., of Haverfordwest; J. P. for the town and co. of Haverfordwest.

BOWEN, Thomas, Welshpool; Banker; J. P. for the bor. of Welshpool; Mayor of do. 1871.

COCKS, James, Esq., Pembroke Dock; J. P. for the bor. of Pembroke.

CORDES, Thomas, Esq., of Bryn-glas, Mon.; J. P. for the bor. of Newport and for co. of Mon.

DAVID, Charles W., Esq., Cardiff; J. P. for the bor. of Cardiff; Mayor of Cardiff 1870-1.

DAVIES, Isaac, Esq., The Bulwark, Brecon; C.E.; J. P. for the bor. of Brecon.

DAVIES, John, Esq., Aberystwyth; J. P. and Alderman, and has been Mayor of Aberystwyth.

DAVIES, John, Esq., Glamorgan Street, Brecon; J. P. for the bor. of Brecon; *m.*, 1843, Elizabeth, dau. of W. Greathead, Esq., of Yarm, Yorkshire, and has issue 1 son and 4 daus.

DAVIES, John, Esq., M.D., Brecon; J. P. for the bor. of Brecon.

DAVIES, Thomas Henry, Esq., of Hayston, Pemb.; J. P. for the town and co. of Haverfordwest, and for the co. of Pembroke.

DAWKINS, Jonas, Esq., Pembroke; Alderman and J. P. for the bor. of Pembroke.

DAWKINS, William, Esq., Pembroke Dock; J. P. for the bor. of Pembroke.

DE WINTON, Henry, Esq., of Ty'nycae, Brecon; J. P. for the bor. and co. of Brecknock.

DE WINTON, J. Parry, Esq., Bangor Road, Carnarvon; J. P. for the bor. of Carnarvon; Mayor of same in 1872.

DE WINTON, William, Esq. See *De Winton of Maesderwen*.

DYSTER, Fred. D., Esq., Tenby, Pemb.; M.R.C.P.; L.S.A.; J. P. for the bor. of Tenby, and for the co. of Pembroke.

EDWARDES, Brown, Esq., Carmarthen; J. P. for the bor. of Carmarthen; Superintendent of Police for the same bor.

EDWARDS, William Thomas, Esq., of Cardiff, Glamorganshire; M.D.(Lond.); Fell. Univ. Coll., Lond.; M.R.C.S.; L.S.A.; J. P. for the bor. of Cardiff; *m.*, 1845, Mary Elizabeth, dau. of the late John Paine, Esq., of Stroud, co. of Gloucester.

EVANS, John, Esq., of the Old Bank, Brecon; J. P. for the bor., and also for the co. of Brecknock.

EVANS, John, Esq., Old Bank, Brecon; J. P. for the bor. and for the co. of Brecon.

EVANS, Thomas, Esq., of Tros-y-park, Denbigh; J. P. for the bor. of Denbigh; Lieut. 3rd County Denb. Rifle Volunteers; *m.*, 1865, Helen, dau. of Francis Burton, Esq., of Berksvill, co. of Warwick.

EVANS, William, Esq., of Newport, Mon.; J. P. for the bor. of Newport.

FORTUNE, William, Esq., of Leweston House, Pemb.; J. P. for the town and co. of Haverfordwest. See *Fortune of Leweston*.

GARDNER, Sankey, Esq., of Eaglesbush, Neath; four times Mayor of Neath; Alderman of Neath.

GEE, Thomas, Esq., Denbigh; Mayor of Denbigh 1871-2, and 1872-3.

GOODE, Harry Phelps, Esq., of Haverfordwest, Pemb.; J. P. for the town and co. of Haverfordwest; member of town Council, and has been Mayor of Haverfordwest.

GOSLING, Henry, Esq., Monmouth; J. P. for the bor. of Monmouth.

GRATREX, Thomas, Esq., of Farmwood, Newport, Mon.; J. P. for the bor. of Newport and for the co. of Mon.

BOROUGH MAGISTRATES OF WALES. 933

HARFORD, Summers, Esq., of Charleston Grange, Pemb.; J. P. for the town and co. of Haverfordwest, and for the co. of Pemb.; is member of Town Council, and has been Mayor of Haverfordwest.

HARRIES, William Bowen, Esq., of Haverfordwest, Pemb.; J. P. for the town and co. of Haverfordwest.

HARREY, David, Esq., Newport, Mon.; Mayor of Newport 1872, and J. P.

HARRISON, E. T. D., Esq., Welshpool, M.R.C.S., L.S.A.; J. P. for Welshpool.

HARVEY, John, Esq., of Picton Place, Haverfordwest; J. P. for the town and co. of Haverfordwest, and for the co. of Pemb.

HELLICAR, John, Esq., of Newport, Mon.; J. P. for the bor. of Newport.

HENLEY, John Bryant, Esq., of Haverfordwest; J. P. for the town and co. of Haverfordwest.

HIGGON, John, Esq., 28 Queen's Road, St. John's Wood, N.W.; J. P. for the town and co. of Haverfordwest.

HOMFRAY, Lorenzo Augustus, Esq., of Woodlands, Newport, Mon.; J. P. for the bor. of Newport, and for the co. of Mon.; Mayor of Newport 1871.

HOMFRAY, Samuel, Esq., of Glen Usk, Mon.; J. P. and Ald. for the bor. of Newport, and for the co. of Mon. See *Homfray of Glen Usk.*

HOWELL, Abraham, Esq., of Rhiewport, Mon.; Alderman and ex-Mayor of Welshpool.

HUGHES, Charles, Esq., Bryn-hyfryd, Wrexham; J. P. for the bor. of Wrexham; Commissioner of Property and Income Tax; *m.*, 1854, Catherine, dau. of T. Lewis, Esq., of Penucha, Caerwys.

HUGHES, David, Esq., of Lion Street, Brecon; Banker; J. P. for the bor. and also for the co. of Brecknock.

HUGHES, John, Esq., Carmarthen; F.R.C.S.; L.A.H.; J. P. and Coroner for the bor. of Carmarthen.

HUGHES, John George Parry, Esq., of Allt-boyd, Cardiganshire; J. P. for the co. of Cardigan, and for the bor. of Aberystwyth.

HULM, William, Esq., Pembroke; Banker; J. P. for the bor. of Pembroke, and for the co. of Pembroke.

HUSTLER, Spencer W., Esq., Pembroke; J. P. for the bor. of Pembroke.

INSOLE, James H., Esq., Ely Court, Cardiff; J. P. for the bor. of Cardiff and co. of Glamorgan.

JAMES, Thomas, Esq., Monmouth; J. P. and Ald. for the bor. of Monmouth.

JENKINS, John, Esq., Plas Issa, Ruthin, Denb.; J. P. for the bor. of Ruthin; Mayor of do. 1866.

JONES, Edward Bowen, Esq., Carmarthen; J. P. for the bor. of Carmarthen; has been Mayor of Carmarthen.

JONES, Griffith Thomas Picton, Esq., Yoke House, Pwllheli, Carn.; Mayor of Pwllheli for the fourth time; Under-Sheriff of co. Carn. 1867-70; Comm. Officer No. 5, Carn. Rifle Vol.; a Solicitor in practice; *m.*, 1859, Edith Anne, dau. of John Morgan, Esq., J. P. and D. L. for the co. of Carnarvon.

JONES, Thomas, Esq., Marine Terrace, Aberystwyth; J. P.; Mayor of Aberystwyth 1872, 1873. See *Jones of Aberystwyth.*

JONES, Thomes Eyton, Esq., The Priory, Wrexham; M.R.C.S. and L.S.A. (Lond.); Hon. Surgeon of the Wrexham Infirmary; Chairman of Sanitary Comm. of Wrexham 1865-70; Hon. Surg. D. Yeo. Cavalry; Pres. N. Wales Branch Brit. Medical Assoc. 1867-8; J. P. for the bor. of Wrexham, and Town Councillor; *m.*, 1860, Susannah, dau. of Mortimer Maurice, Esq., of Oak Lodge. The old seat of Mr. Jones's ancestors was Tir-llanerch, Corwen, still in the family; maternally he is descended from the Eytons of Craig-ddu, Llangollen.

JONES, Tubal C., Esq., Leeswood House, Wrexham; J. P. for the bor. of Wrexham.

JOSEPH, Jos., Esq., of Brecon. See *Joseph of Brecon.*

LEWIS, Thomas, Esq., Bryn Edwin, Flint; J. P. and Ald. for the bor. of Flint.

LEWIS, Thomas, Esq., Carmarthen: M.D. (Lond. Univ.); M.R.C.P. (Lond.); M.R.C.S. (Lond.); J. P. for the bor. of Carmarthen; Physician to Carmarthen Infirmary, &c.

LLOYD, John Williams, Esq., Brookhouse, Denbigh; J. P. for the bor. of Denbigh; Town Councillor; for many years Chairman and Vice-Chairman of Poor Law Guardians, Ruthin Union; *m.*, 1828, Alice, eldest dau. of Mr. Thomas Williams, of Plas Llanynys.

LYNE, Charles, Esq., Brynhyfryd, Newport, Mon.; Capt. R.N.; J. P. for the bor. of Newport.

MADOCKS, John, Esq., of Picton Place, Haverfordwest; J. P. for the town and co. of Haverfordwest; is member of the Town Council, and has been Mayor.

MAUGHAM, William, Esq., Carnarvon; M.D., M.R.C.S.; J. P. for the bor. of Carnarvon.

MORGAN, Howard Spear, Esq., of Haverfordwest; J. P., &c. See *Morgan of Tegfynydd.*

MORGAN, Will. Williams, Esq., M.D., Newport, Mon.; J. P. for the bor. of Newport.

MORRIS, Thomas Charles, Esq., of Bryn-Myrddin, Carmarthen; J. P. for the bor. of Carmarthen. See *Morris of Bryn-Myrddin.*

MORRIS, William, Esq., of Cwm, Carmarthen; J. P. and Ald. for the bor. of Carmarthen. See *Morris of Cwm.*

MUSPRATT, Frederick, Esq., Flint; J. P. for the bor. of Flint.

3 P

MUSPRATT, Richard T., Esq., Flint; J. P. and Ald. for the bor. of Flint.
NICHOLAS, Thomas Leach, Esq., Coleford, Glouc.; J. P. for the bor. of Monmouth.
NORTON, Henry, Esq., Greenhill, Carmarthen; ex-Mayor and Alderman, Mayor of Carmarthen 1872-3.
OWEN, Morris William Lloyd, Esq., High Street, Haverfordwest, and *Cwmgloyne*, Pemb.; J. P. for the town and co. of Haverfordwest, and for the co. of Pemb.
OWEN, Thomas Rule, Esq., Foley House, Haverfordwest; J. P. for the town and co. of Haverfordwest.
OWEN, William, Esq., of Withybush, Pemb.; J. P. for the town and co. of Haverfordwest. See *Owen of Withybush*.
OWEN, William Stephenson, Esq., Haverfordwest; J. P. for the town and co. of Haverfordwest, and for the co. of Pemb.
PARKER, William Thomas, Esq., of Traeth-llawn, Welshpool; J. P. for the bor. of Welshpool; Lieut. of 3rd Mont. Rifle Volunteers; only son of the late Griffith Parker, Esq., Alderman, Mayor of Welshpool 1869 70.
PHILIPPS, Griffith Grismond, Esq., Picton Terrace, Carmarthen; Capt. R.N.; J. P. for the bor. of Carmarthen.
PHILIPPS, Grismond. Esq., of Cwmgwili, Carmarthen; J. P. for the bor. of Carm. See *Philipps of Cwmgwili*.
PHILLIPS, Edward James, Esq., of Drayton Villa, Newport, Mon.; J. P. for the bor. of Newport and for the co. of Mon.
PHILLIPS, James, Esq., Haverfordwest; J. P. for the town and co. of Haverfordwest.
PHILLIPS, John Lewis, Esq., Bolahaul, Carmarthen; J. P. for the bor. of Carmarthen; Mayor of Carmarthen 1856-7; Chairman of Board of Guardians, Carmarthen Union.
PHILLIPS, John William, Esq., Haverfordwest, Pemb.; J. P. for the town and co. of Haverford.
PIERCE, Evan, Esq., Salusbury Place, Denbigh; M.D.; F.R.C.S. (Edin.); L.R.C.S. (Edin.); L.S.A. (Lond.); one of the Coroners for the co. of Denbigh; Mayor of Denbigh five years in succession; Alderman and J. P. for the bor. of Denbigh. Dr. Pierce is well known as a zealous promoter of the good of the town of Denbigh.
POWELL, Jonathan Roger, Esq., Haverfordwest; J. P. for the town and co. of Haverfordwest; Comm. to administer oaths; Town Clerk for bor. of Wiston; Steward of manors of Penally, Manorbier, &c.
POWELL, Samuel, Esq., Welshpool; J. P. of Welshpool.
PRIDE, James, Esq., Charles Street, Cardiff; J. P. for the bor. of Cardiff 1859; Alderman of Cardiff; Mayor of Cardiff 1864 5; Comm. of Income Tax.

PROTHERO, John, Esq., Sunny Bank, Brecon; J. P. for the bor. of Brecon; has filled office of Mayor of Brecon.
PRYCE-JONES, John, Esq., The Groves, Wrexham; Principal of Grove Park School; L.C.P., F.R.G.S. (Lond.); J. P. for the bor. of Wrexham. See p. 930, and *Price of Corsygarnedd*.
PUGH, Hugh, Esq., Minmanton Villa, Carnarvon, J. P. for the bor. and co. of Carnarvon and bor. of Pwllheli; has been Mayor of Pwllheli.
REES, James, Esq., Castle Street, Carnarvon; Mayor of Carnarvon 1872-3; Alderman, &c., of Carn.
REES, William, Esq., of Scoveston, Pemb.; J. P. for the town and co. of Haverfordwest; and for the co. of Pemb.
REID, Douglas Arthur, Esq., Pembroke, M.D. (Edin.); M.R.C.S. (Edin.); J. P. for the bor. of Pembroke.
ROBERTS, John, jun., Esq., North Parade, Aberystwyth; J. P. for the bor. of Aberystwyth.
ROBERTS, Richard, Esq., Bridge Street, Aberystwyth; J. P. and Alderman for the bor. of Aberystwyth; Mayor of Aberystwyth 1867 and 1868; *m.*, 1850, Sarah, dau. of Robert Davies, Esq., of Aberystwyth.
ROBERTS, Watkin W., Esq., Carnarvon, F.R.C.S., L.S.A.; J. P. for the bor. of Carnarvon.
ROWE, George, Esq., of Haverfordwest, Pemb., J. P. for the town and co. of Haverfordwest, and for the co. of Pembroke; *m.*, 1836, Frances, dau. of Henry Stokes, Esq., of Scotchwell.
ROWLAND, John Henry, Esq., Ffrwd Vale, Neath, J. P. and Ald. for the bor. of Neath, and J. P. for the co. of Glamorgan.
ROWLANDS, James, Esq., Carmarthen; F.R.C.S. (Lond.); Surgeon to Carmarthen Infirmary; Coroner for the Lordship of Cydweli; Alderman and J. P. for the bor. of Carmarthen; *m.*, 1835, Anne, dau. of the late John Brown, Solicitor, Brecon.
ROWLAND, Thomas, Esq., The Grove, Wrexham; Mayor of Wrexham 1869; Commissioner of Property and Income Tax; Guardian of the Poor 1868 70; Churchwarden 1868-70; *m.*, 1851, Anne Dorothy, dau. of James Barlow, Esq., Ironmaster, of Gwersyllt.
ROWLAND, William, Esq., Wrexham Fechan House, Wrexham; Mayor of Wrexham 1870; Alderman of Wrexham; descended maternally through the Bromfields of Bromfield, from Edwin, Lord of Tegeingl; *m.* Mary Ann Trandle, of Manor House, near Swaffham.
SANDERS, Henry, Esq., Tenby, Pemb.; J. P. for the bor. of Tenby, and for the co. of Pembroke.
SPILSBURY, Samuel, Esq., Croydon, Surrey; J. P. for the bor. of Monmouth.
THOMAS, John, Esq., Carmarthen; J. P. for the bor. of Carmarthen 1865; Alderman 1868; Mayor of Carmarthen 1859, 1860, 1872; Commissioner of Income and Assessed Taxes, &c., &c.

BOROUGH MAGISTRATES OF WALES.

TREWENT, William, Esq., Pembroke ; J. P. for the bor. of Pembroke ; memb. of Town Council ; has been Mayor of Pemb.

TURNER, Sir Llewelyn, Kt., Carnarvon ; J. P., &c. See *Turner of Parkia.*

TURNOUR, A. Edw., Esq., Denbigh ; M.D. (Edin.) ; M.R.C.S. ; J. P. for the bor. of Denbigh.

WARREN, W. de G., Esq., Picton Terrace, Carmarthen ; J. P. and Ald. for the bor. of Carmarthen ; second time Mayor of Carmarthen 1872-3 ; Capt. No. 6, Carm. Rifle Vol. ; Vice-Consul for Denmark in Carm.

WATKINS, Thomas, Esq., Monmouth ; J. P. and Ald. for the bor. of Monmouth.

WATKINS, W. Bradley, Esq., Cardiff ; J. P. and Ald. for the bor. of Cardiff ; has been Mayor of Cardiff.

WELLS, Charles Cook, Esq., of Penally, Tenby, Pemb. ; J. P. for the bor. of Tenby and for the co. of Pemb. ; Vice-Adml. of port of Milford ; was Comm. in Roy. Indian Navy.

WILLIAMS, James, Esq., of Honddu House, Brecon ; J. P. for the bor. of Brecon.

WILLIAMS, Philip, Esq., Aberbaiden, Mon. ; J. P. for the bor. of Monmouth.

WILLIAMS, R. Lloyd, Esq., Denbigh ; J. P. for the bor. of Denbigh ; Mayor of do. 1866.

WILLIAMS, Ven. Archd. D. A., Carmarthen ; J. P. for the bor. and co. of Carmarthen.

WILLIAMS, William, Esq., of Newport, Mon. ; J. P. for the bor. of Newport.

WILLIS, George, Esq., Monmouth ; M.D. ; L.R.C.S. (Edin.) ; L.S.A. ; J. P. for the bor. of Monmouth.

WOOLLETT, John M., Esq., Monmouth ; J. P. for the bor. of Monmouth.

WOOLLETT, Rob. Francis, Esq., the Mount, Newport, Mon. ; J. P. for the bor. of Newport.

ADDED SINCE 1872.

BURY, John, Esq , J. P. for the *bor.* of Wrexham.

DARBY, William Henry, Esq., Brymbo (see *Darby of Brymbo*), J. P. for the *bor.* of Wrexham.

DAVIES, Edward, M.D., F.R.C.S., &c., J. P. for the *bor.* of Wrexham.

DAVIES, Richard Morgan, Esq., King Street, Carmarthen, J. P. for the *bor.* of Carmarthen 1875.

EDWARDS, Alexander Wilson, Esq., J. P. for the *bor.* of Wrexham.

EVANS, Thomas Henry, Esq., J. P. for the *bor.* of Carnarvon.

FITZHUGH, Thomas Lloyd, Esq., of Plas Power (see *Fitzhugh, Plas Power*), J. P. for the *bor.* of Wrexham.

FOULKES, James Hassell, Esq., Llay Place, J. P. for the *bor.* of Wrexham.

FOULKES, William Langford, Esq., Rackery Hall, J. P. for the *bor.* of Wrexham.

GRIFFITH, Thomas Taylor, Esq., (see *Griffith of Wrexham*), J. P. for the *bor.* of Wrexham.

JONES-PARRY, Thomas Parry, Esq., Llwyn Onn, (see *Jones-Parry, of Llwyn Onn*), J. P. for the *bor.* of Wrexham.

LESTER, Robert, Esq., Furnace House, Carmarthen, J. P. for the *bor.* of Carmarthen 1875.

LEWIS, Lewis, Esq., Mayor of Carnarvon 1875.

LLOYD, Robert, Esq., Mayor of Wrexham 1875.

LOW, William, Esq., of Roseneath, J. P. for the *bor.* of Wrexham.

McCOY, Daniel, Esq., Wrexham, J P. for the *bor.* of Wrexham.

MEREDITH, Henry Warter, Esq., Pentrebychan.

MORGAN, Charles, Esq., Alltygôg, J. P. for the *bor.* of Carmarthen 1875 (never acted).

OVERTON, William, Esq., formerly Mayor of Wrexham, J. P. for the *bor.* of Wrexham.

OWEN, John, Esq., J. P. for the *bor.* of Carnarvon.

PAINTER, Thomas, Esq., J.P. for the *bor.* of Wrexham.

REES, Griffith Roberts, Esq., J.P. for the *bor.* of Carnarvon.

SPURRELL, William, Esq., King Street, Carmarthen, publisher, &c., J. P. for Carmarthen.

TENCH, Edward, Esq , of Maesgwyn, J. P. for the *bor.* of Wrexham.

TIMMINS, Joseph, Esq., Bath, J. P. for *bor.* of Carmarthen.

WHITE, George White, Esq., King-street, Carmarthen, J. P. for the *bor.* of Carmarthen 1875.

WILLIAMS, Edward, Esq., Clwy House, J. P. for the *bor.* of Wrexham.

WILLIAMS, John Lewis, Esq., Carmarthen, F.R.C.S., L.S.A., J. P. for Carmarthen 1875.

YORKE, Simon, Esq., Erddig Park (see *Yorke of Erddig*,) J. P. for the *bor.* of Wrexham.

SUPPLEMENT.

Vaughan of Golden Grove.

This family, long extinct, but in its time of high fame in Carmarthenshire, and, in the person of its most distinguished member, Richard Vaughan, Earl of Carbery (A.D. 1660—62), Lord Lieutenant of nearly all Wales, of still wider influence, was descended from Gwathfoed, prince of *Powys*, and not, as often represented, Gwaethfoed, prince of Ceredigion. The distinguished gr. grandson of Gwaethfoed, Bleddyn ap Cynfyn, was ancestor in the eleventh degree of *Hugh Fychan*, of Cydweli, who was father, by Jane, dau. of Morus ap Owain, of Llechdwni, of John Fychan, Esq., of Golden Grove, whose son and suc., Walter Fychan, *m.* Mary, dau. of Gruffydd ap Rhys, of Dinefawr, gr. grandson of Sir Rhys ap Thomas, and had by her John Fychan (Vaughan), his successor at Golden Grove, cr. 1st Earl of Carbery in Ireland, and by Margaret, dau. of Sir Gelly Meyrick, Kt., was father of Richard Vaughan, of Golden Grove, 2nd Earl of Carbery, cr. 1643, Baron Vaughan, of Emlyn, co. Carmarthen, Lord Lieutenant, as above, and Lord President of the Marches of Wales. His second son and suc., John, 3rd Earl of Carbery, *m.* but *d.* 1713 without male issue, and the title became extinct. The property afterwards passed to the heirs-at-law, descendants of Sir William Vaughan, Kt., of Terracoed, or Tyrycoed, and ultimately as a gift to an ancestor of the Earl of Cawdor, the present possessor.

Stedmans of Strata Florida.

In addition to the account already given of Strata Florida and of the Stedmans (see pp. 163—4, 168-9), the following particulars, and view of the mansion and abbey ruins, as existing *circa* 1740, when the last Richard Stedman was living, have been supplied by Mr. W. G. Stedman Thomas, himself a descendant and representative through junior and female lines of this house. The view given is taken from S. and N. Buck's *Castles and Abbeys of Wales*, and was dedicated by the authors to "Richard Stedman, Esq.," the last possessor of his line (see *lineage* hereafter), under the name of "Stratflour Abbey." The engraving given on p. 164, from a drawing made within recent years, contrasted with the one seen on the next page, shows what havoc the lapse of a little more than a century commits upon venerable structures when left in a neglected state. The arms borne by the Stedmans at this time, and for many generations preceding, were—" vert, a cross moline or; crest, a virgin holding in her dexter hand a cross as in the arms." In Buck's work, named above, the cross is

SUPPLEMENT.

incorrectly coloured. Motto, Nec temere nec timide. The direct line of the Stedmans proceeds thus :—

The Stedman already mentioned as first of the family in England (p, 168), by his wife Joan de Tateshale, had a son John, who *s.* to his mother's land in Kent, and is said to have *m.* Anne, dau. of James Forster (Forester), of Berkshire, by whom he left a son, also named John, who *m.* Anne, dau. of James Chetwynd, and had by her a son,—

William Stedman, who espoused Frances, dau. and *h.* of Sir John Mareschal, Kt., of York, a younger branch of the Mareschal Earls of Pembroke, and left by her a son, Thomas Stedman, Esq., of Berks, who had for wife, Eleanor, dau. of William, lord of Willie, co. Stafford, by whom he left a son, John Stedman, Esq., who *m.* Margaret, dau. of Sir William Stafford, Kt., leaving issue Henry Stedman, Esq., also of Staffordshire, who *m.* Margaret, dau. of Andrew Cotton, Esq., and left a son and heir,—

Humphrey Stedman, Esq., of Chebsey, in the same co., who by his wife Catherine, dau. and *co-h.* of William Hill, Esq., of Bletchley, became progenitor of the Stedmans of Berks, Stafford, and Shropshire. His second son, John Stedman, of Chebsey, *m.* Anne, dau. of Nicholas Beeston, or more probably Buxton, Esq.,

STRATA FLORIDA ABBEY (A.D. 1740).

and had a son and heir, John, also of Chebsey, who *m.* Joan, dau. of John Lewis, Esq. (called Lewis ap Philip), and is described as having become first proprietor, of this line, of Strata Florida Abbey, in the co. of Cardigan, soon after the dissolution of the monasteries (*temp.* Henry VIII.). His son,—

John Stedman, Esq., said to have been born at Strata Florida, where his father had built a house out of the out-buildings, &c., of that abbey, was twice Sheriff for Cardiganshire (1581 and 1589), and was known as John "Moel," or the bald ; *m.*, first, Anne, dau. of William Philipps, Esq., of Pentypark, 2nd son of Sir Thomas Philips, Kt., of Cilsant ; secondly, Elizabeth, widow of David Lloyd, Esq., of Porthycrwys and Towi in Brecknockshire, and dau. of Sir John Wogan, Kt., of Wiston, Pemb. By the former he had, besides a dau. Mary, and a second son Rowland, of Plas Cilcenin, an elder son and heir,—

John Gwyn Stedman, Esq., of Strata Florida, Sheriff for Cardiganshire 1595 and 1608 (in the latter year styled as of Ystradffin, co. Carmarthen), and in 1609 for Brecknockshire (styled also as of Ystradffin, in right of his wife as daughter of Elizabeth, sister and co-heiress of Thomas Williames, Esq., of Ystradffin (*d.* 1597). He *m.* Margaret, eldest of three daus., co-heiresses of David Lloyd, Esq., of Porthycrwys and Towi, Breck., by whom he had issue three sons and six daus. The daus. were Elizabeth, *m.* Rhys Gwyn, of Llwynywermwood ; Lettice, *m.* Edward Vaughan, of Trawscoed, whose 2nd son, Henry, became, by marriage, of *Plas Cilcennin ;* Dorothy, *m.* Thomas Vaughan, of Pencelly, Breck. ; Catherine, *m.* John Jones, of Tregaron ; Mary, *m.* Sir Marmaduke Lloyd, of Maesyfelin ; Anne, *m.* William Williams, of Cnwckyllo, Breck. The second son, John, of whom hereafter, became of *Dolygaer*. The eldest son,—

SUPPLEMENT.

James Stedman, Esq., of Strata Florida, Sheriff 1617, *m*. Catherine, fifth dau. of Sir Richard Pryse, of Gogarthan, by whom he had a son John, of Strata Florida, *m*. Jane, dau. of Edw. Vaughan, Esq., of Trawscoed, and sister of Lord Justice Sir John Vaughan (see *Lisburne of Trawscoed*), by whom he had two sons. Richard, the younger, was of Kerry, Mont.; and the elder,—

James Stedman, Esq., *s*. to Strata Florida, *m*. first Elizabeth, sister and ultimately heiress of Rhys Vaughan, Esq., of Glandovan, Cilgerran, and had a dau. Jane, who *m*. William Gower, Esq., of Ludlow, which family on the death of Mr. Stedman *s*. to the Glandovan estate. Mr. Stedman *m*. secondly, in 1663, Margaret, dau. of Richard Owen, Esq., of Rhiwsaeson, Mont., and was *s*. at Strata Florida by his second son (the eldest, John, having *d. s. p.*),—

Richard Stedman, Esq., Sheriff for his co. 1691; *m*., first, Joan, dau. of Rowland Gwynne, Esq., of Glanbrn, and by her had issue an only dau., Anne Stedman. He *m*. secondly Jane, dau. of Richard Stedman of Kerry aforesaid, and left, besides a dau. Malet, a son,—

Richard Stedman, Esq., the last owner, of his line, of Strata Florida, mentioned at p. 169 as having *m*. Anne, dau. of William Powell, Esq., of Nanteos. Having no surviving issue, he bequeathed the Strata Florida estate to his wife's family (in whose possession it still remains), and *d*. circa 1740.

We now return to the branch settled at *Dolygaer*. Arms: those of their ancestress Joan de Tateshale, "Chequy or and gu. a chief ermine."

John Stedman, Esq., second son of John Gwyn Stedman, aforesaid, of Strata Florida, by wife Margaret Lloyd, of Porthycrwys and Towi, Breck., inherited the old mansion-house of *Dolygaer*, where he resided; Sheriff for co. Carm. 1624, for co. Breck. 1630; *m*. Anne, dau. of James Lewis, Esq., of Harpton, Rad., tracing ultimately to Gruffydd ap Rhys ap Tewdwr, and had issue besides Henry, who was of the Priory, Brecon. and Jane, who *m*. Thomas Phillips, Esq., of Lletygariad, co. Carm.,

John Stedman, Esq., elder son and *h*. of Dolygaer, Sheriff of his co. of Breck. 1667, *m*. Margaret, dau. of William Phillips, Esq., of Lletygariad, and was *s*. by his elder son and *h*.,—

Miles Stedman, Esq., of Dolygaer (*d*. 1719), *m*. Mary dau. of Thomas Gwyn, Esq., of Cynghordy, and left issue, besides a dau. Jane, wife of the first Grismond Philipps, Esq., of Cwmgwili, a son and *h*.,—

Miles Stedman, Esq., of Dolygaer, (Sheriff 1725 *d*. 1744) who *m*. Mary, *elder* of the two daus. (the younger, Anne, *m*. Walter Lloyd, of Olmarch), co-*h*. of John Lloyd, Esq., of Glangwili, co. Carm. (*d*. 1684), by his wife Anne, dau. of James Jones, Esq., of Abermad, co. Card., and Dolaucothi, co. Carm., by his *second* wife, Mary Pryse, dau. of Sir John Pryse, of Gogarthan (see *Pryse of Gogerddan*, p. 209), and sister and *co-h*. of Sir Richard Pryse, Bart., of Gogarthan (cr. 1641), whose line male became extinct with his gr.-son, Sir Carbery Pryse, and was thenceforth represented by the descendants of his said sister, Mary Pryse); and had issue two daus., co-heiresses, Jane Stedman, the elder, who *m*. Richard Davies, Esq., and whose present representatives are the children and grandchildren of the late Rev. Thomas Evans of Llanstephan, and—

Dorothy Stedman, the younger (*d*. 1793), who *m*., first, (1737) Grismond Philipps, Esq., of Cwmgwili; and secondly (1740), the Rev. Thomas Prothero, B.A., Chr. Ch., Oxon, Vicar of Llywel, and had by him one son, Gwynne Prothero, Esq., of Dolygaer, and of Pantygof, co. Carm., *m*. but *d. s. p.* 1780; and four daus. co-*h*., the youngest of whom, Frances Prothero (*d*. 1790), inherited the Pantygof and other property, *m*. (1783) Richard Williams, Esq., of the co. of Devon (who bore, "arg., a stag lodged ppr., attired and unguled or, in his mouth an ivy branch ppr.), and had an only child and *h*.,—

Dorothy (*d*. 1832), who *m*. (1814) William Thomas, merchant, of Carmarthen, and had issue, besides two daus., Jane Stedman (who *m*. William Hulm, Esq., J. P. for co. of Pemb., and has issue four sons and two daus) and Mary Anne, two sons, the elder,—(for Thomas of Pantygof, see Burke's *Seats and Arms*, I. 45.)

R. F. J. H. Thomas, Clerk, B.D., C. C. Coll., Cambr., Rector of Hodgeston, co. Pemb., and J. P., *d. unm*. Nov. 12, 1873; the younger,—

William G. Stedman Thomas, Esq., of Pantygof, co. Carmarthen, who *m*., 18th Oct., 1853, at St. John's Episcopal Chapel, Edinburgh, Julia Elizabeth (*d*. 1867), eldest dau. of the Hon. J. Shafto Vaughan, third son of John, 3rd Earl of Lisburne, of Crosswood, co. Card., and his countess, Lucy Courtenay (see *Lisburne of Trawscoed*), by whom he has issue surviving three sons and three daus. The Hon. J. S. Vaughan *m*., 1826, Elizabeth, dau. of Mr. John Edwards, and cousin to the late Rev. John Edwards, rector of Newtown, Mont.

Note.—The Stedmans settled at *Dolygaer* and the *Priory*, in Brecknockshire, and became possessors of *Ystradffin*, in Carm., in virtue of the marriage mentioned above of John Gwyn Stedman, of Strata Florida, with Margaret Lloyd, dau. of David Lloyd, of Porthycrwys and of Elizabeth Williams, heiress of Ystradffin. The Lloyds traced back through Thomas Lloyd ap Meredydd (a great partisan of the Earl of Richmond, and after the battle of Bosworth Field, Lord Lieut. of Brecknock for forty years) paternally to Elystan Glodrudd, and maternally to Edward I. of England. The Stedmans of *Plas Cilcennin*, Card., originated in Rowland, third son of John Stedman "Moel," of Strata Florida (see above), who *m*. Jane, dau. of Hugh Lloyd of Llanllyr (Sheriff of Card. 1567), of the line of *Castell Howel* (see pp. 170-1).

SUPPLEMENT.

Sir Rhys ap Thomas.

(*See pp.* 240—244.)

Some documents of interest relating to this celebrated man still survive at. Dynevor Castle, and through the courtesy of Lord Dynevor and the Rev. J. G. Joyce, M.A., have been examined and placed at our service. The memoir of Syr Rhys written *temp.* James I., and published in the *Cambrian Register*, 1796 (see p. 243), informs us in too general a form of the honours and emoluments conferred by Henry VII. upon his devoted adherent, abstains too much from dates and distinctions of gifts, and renders it altogether uncertain whether Sir Rhys ap Thomas's immense wealth and extensive official rule in the counties of South Wales were not, for the most part, the result of Tudor favour. It must be confessed that the papers relating to Sir Rhys ap Thomas which have outlived the vicissitudes of the three and a half centuries elapsed since his death are, considering the height of his fame and influence during life, surprisingly few, and scanty in information. The sequestration to the Crown of the estates under Henry VIII., who in addition to this injustice caused Sir Rhys's grandson, Rhys ap Gruffydd (sometimes called Rice Griffith), to be beheaded under an unproved charge of treason, and the troubles that ensued, doubtless caused the dispersion and loss of many papers which would now be of great value in throwing light not only upon the domestic annals of Dynevor, but upon the political history of the time.

From the papers still surviving we gather the dates of various letters-patent in favour of Sir Rhys ap Thomas, nearly all in the early part of the reign of Henry VII. The papers, although of considerable antiquity, appear to be, not themselves original and contemporaneous State documents, but copies of such documents, and extracts from them, made in a lawyer's handwriting and probably for family purposes—possibly as materials for the petition presented to the sovereign by Griffith Rice, great-grandson of Sir Rhys ap Thomas, for the further restoration of property. The battle of Bosworth Field, which greatly through the aid of Sir Rhys ap Thomas placed Henry VII. on the throne, having occurred August 22, 1485, the bearing of the following grants is evident:—

Nov. 3rd, 1485. A grant by Henry VII., seventy-three days after his accession, conferring on Sir Rhys ap Thomas the offices of constable, lieutenant-governor, and seneschal of Brecknock.

Nov. 6th, 1485 (only three days later), letters-patent conferring on Sir Rhys ap Thomas the office of Chamberlain of South Wales in the counties of Carmarthen and Cardigan.

Nov. 7th, 1485 (next day after the last), letters-patent conferring the office of the king's Justiciary for South Wales.

Nov. 7th, 1485 (same day as last) letters patent, not yet fully made out, but believed to confer grants of certain lands.

March 9th, 1488. Grant by Henry VII., conferring an annuity of 100 marks per annum on Sir Rhys ap Thomas, payable out of the estates of the Duke of Buckingham.

May 6th, 1492. Grant by Henry VII., conferring on Sir Rhys ap Thomas the offices of seneschal, chancellor, and supervisor of the royal manors of "Haverford West and Rouze" (*Rhôs*, now *Roose*), " in the Welsh Marches."

In the reign of Henry VIII. letters-patent were issued, Sept. 25, 1514, *i.e.*, thirteen years prior to the death of Sir Rhys ap Thomas, granting to his son, Sir Gruffydd ap Rhys, Kt., the offices of seneschal and receiver of the royal demesnes of " Dynas (Dinas), in the Welsh Marches." Upon the margin of this document is the copy of an entry setting forth the resignation on the 15th of March preceding (the *year* not being given) of these letters, and the offices they conferred, by the personal appearance of Sir Gruffydd at Westminster, " litteras suas patentes . . tunc et ibidem puré, sponté, et absoluté restituit."

As the gift of receiver, &c., of the royal demesne of " Dynas " was made in 1514, as seen above, the *memoir* in the Cambrian Reg. errs in placing it in 1511. It falls into another inaccuracy (which the papers now quoted correct) in stating that the offices of seneschal, chancellor, &c., of " Haverfordwest and Rouze " were conferred on Sir Rhys by Henry VIII., whereas they were manifestly first the gifts of Henry VII.

The many and extensive manors and strong castles possessed by Sir Rhys ap Thomas, such as Dynevor, Carew, Abermarles, Newcastle in Emlyn, Narberth, &c., were all his property, Narberth alone excepted, before the accession of Henry VII. *Carew*, his favourite residence, restored, or rather, rebuilt in the style of magnificence which the surviving ruins continue to witness, was his property by purchase from the Carew family. Dynevor and Abermarles were his by inheritance. Carmarthen Castle became his official residence as chamberlain and justiciary of South Wales by gift of Henry VII.

The arms of Sir Rhys ap Thomas, still forming the first and fourth quarters in the shield of the noble family of Dynevor, were—*Arg. a chevron between three ravens sa.*

Gamage of Coity.
(See pp. 566—569.)

Joan Champernoun, mentioned in the last paragraph but one, p. 567, should be of Dartington, not of Darlington, Devon; and under *Gamage of Abergarw* (p. 568) it is to be noted that " John Thomas, parson of Coity," who married Sarah Gamage of Abergarw, was of the line of Thomas of Llanvihangel, near Cowbridge, probably from William Thomas of Llanvihangel, sergeant-at-law, whence descended the Thomases of Caldicot.

It has been the custom to say that the Gamages trace in a direct line from Regnovald, one of the nobles to whom Harold Harfager, the first Christian king and conqueror of Norway (*circ.* 850—934), granted fiefs for services rendered during his conquest of that country. Regnovald was father to Rollo the Dane, Duke of Normandy, ancestor of William the Conqueror, and also of Inczer, his companion in the conquest of that land. Charles the Simple, in 912, ceded the province of Neustia to Rollo, who now embraced Christianity, changed his name to Robert, and his duchy was called Normandy. Inczer was father to Herluin, Count of Ponthieu, whose paternal grandson, William, *m.* Alice, sister of Hugh Capet, King of France, 987. William and Alice had Barnard, Count of Guines, Lord of *Gamaches*, near Rouen, from which lordship or castle the family name is derived. Barnard de Gamaches became also Count of St. Valeri by marriage with its heiress. His son Gilbert, or Barnard, *m.* Papia, dau. of Richard II., Duke of Normandy. St. Valeri passed by an heiress to the Counts of Dreux, but the two male representatives of the family were Thomas and Godfrey de Gamaches, who served Henry II. with fifty knights and a thousand retainers. The Gamage arms—as described by Sir Robert Atkyns, and recently also discovered by Miss Charlotte Thomas of Caerleon, a descendent of the family, in a cottage wall built from the ruins of Coity Castle, were—" *Arg., five fusils in bend gu.; on a chief azure, three escallops or. Crest: a griffin segreant or. Motto : Pro aris et focis.*"

COUNTY FAMILIES.

JONES OF TREWYTHEN, PENYRALLT-GOCH, AND RHIEWPORT, MONTGOMERYSHIRE.

This ancient family—a junior branch, as may be seen from the genealogy of the eminent house of Nannau,—though no longer surviving in the direct male line, or retaining the extensive estates it once possessed in the co. of Montgomery, still exists in the next degrees to the last male representative in the persons of Mrs. Caroline Combe, widow of Boyce Combe, Esq., barrister-at-law, and her son, Boyce Harvey Combe, Esq., J.P., of Oaklands, Sussex, whose family and pedigree are given in full underneath. See a further notice of this family, and a view of Rhiewport, under *Rhiewport.*

COMBE, Boyce Harvey, Esq., of Oaklands, Battle, Sussex.

J.P. for the county of Sussex; Major Commanding 1st Battalion Cinque Ports Rifle Volunteers; was formerly an officer in the H.E.I.C. cavalry; eldest surviving son of the late Boyce Combe, Esq., Barrister-at-law, Bencher of Gray's Inn, and for upwards of thirty years one of the Metropolitan Police Magistrates (*d.* 1864); who was eldest son and heir-at-law of Harvey Christian Combe, of Cobham Park, Surrey, Esq., M.P. for the City of London, and Lord Mayor of London in 1799, by Caroline, dau. of the Rev. Evan Jones, (*d.* 16th July, 1827,) Rector of Aberhavesp, Mont., (see further in *Lineage*); *b.* 1816; *m.*, 1850, Ann Sarah, only dau. of Hercules Sharpe, Esq., of Oaklands, Westfield, Sussex, and niece of the late Sir William J. Brabazon, Bart., of Brabazon Park, co. Mayo, M.P. for that co.; has issue—

Harvey Trewythen Brabazon, *b.* 1852; *ed.* at Eton.
Herbert Wythen, *d.* an infant.
Mary Catherine.
William Edmond, *b.* 1864.
Heir: Harvey Trewythen Brabazon.
Residence: Oaklands, Battle, Sussex.
Town Address: Junior United Service Club, Charles Street, S.W.
Arms: Ermine, three lions passant arg. in pale.

Crest: An arm embowed in armour, the hand grasping a lance, all ppr.
Motto: Nil timere nec temere.

LINEAGE.

This pedigree of the Joneses of Trewythen, &c., in the co. of Montgomery, is taken in the main from a book containing the pedigrees of the ancient families of North Wales, once existing among the records of Hengwrt, now at Peniarth, Mer.

BLEDDYN AP CYNVYN, Prince of Powys, 1064, also under the patronage of Edward the Confessor appointed Prince of South Wales (*d.* 1073), by Agnes, dau. of Giffri ap Carwad, lord of Twrcelyn in Anglesey, had, with other issue, a son,—

Cadwgan ap Bleddyn, Prince of Powys, lord of Nannau, and ruler of South Wales, under William Rufus; *m.* Gwenlliam, dau. of Gruffydd ap Cynan, Prince of North Wales, and was *s.* by his son,—

Madoc, Prince of Powys, lord of Nannau, who *m.* Eva, dau. and *h.* of Madoc ap Philip ap Ychtryd ap Edwin, lord of Englefield, Flint., and left issue—

Rhiwallon, who *m.* Ales (Alice), dau. of Gwrgenau ap Howel ap Eva, Lord of Arwystli, in Mont., whose son—
Dolphin *m.* Alice, dau. of Cadwallon ap Madoc, lord of Kerry, Mont., by whom he had,—
Cynfelyn, lord of Manafon in Mont., whose wife was Gwenllian, dau. of Sir Roger Mortimer, Earl of March (first junction with the Normans), by whom he left a son,—
Einion, who *m.* Alice, dau. of Llewelyn ap Robert, lord of Cedewain, Mont., and had issue—
Meredydd Du, of Arwystli, Mont., who *m.* Jonet, dau. of Goronwy ap Einion ap Sissyllt, lord of Mathafarn, and had issue—
Gruffydd, who *m.* Ardden. dau. of Meurig Fychan, Esq., of Nannau, whose son,—
Gruffydd Fychan (Vaughan), *m.* Eva, dau. of Llewelyn Fychan, Lord of Tregynon, Mont., and had issue,—
Gruffydd Du, Esq., who by his wife Janet, dau. of Meurig Llwyd (Lloyd), of Nannau, Esq., left a son,—
Llewelyn, who *m.* Angahrad, dau. of Howel Iorwerth ap Gruffydd Fychan, of Neuaddwen, Llanerfyl, Mont., and had issue—
David Llwyd (Lloyd), Esq., who *m.* Jonet, dau. of Madoc Lloyd of Llwynmelyn in Tregynon, Mont., Esq., whose son,—
Jenkin, *m.* Margaret, dau. of John ap Evan ap Madoc ap Kyffin, Esq., by whom he had—
David, whose wife was Jane, dau. of David Lloyd ap Meredith, Esq.; he left a son,—
Evan Goch, Esq., who *m.* Gwenllian, dau. of Meredith ap Morgan of Maclonyd (Machynlleth?) Esq., and whose son,—
John, *m.* Angharad, dau. of Morris ap Ednyfed ap David Lloyd of Llandinam, Mont., Esq., and had issue—

Hugh ap John, or Jones (here the surname "Jones," begins), Esq., who *m.* Margaret, dau. of Sir Richard Herbert of Montgomery, son of Sir William Herbert, son of Sir Thomas Herbert, Kt. of Colebrook, Monmouthshire, and had issue—
Evan Jones, Esq., of Trewythen, who *m.* Dorothy, dau. of Sir Thomas Scrims, of Staffordshire. His son.—
Wythen Jones, Esq., of Trewythen, *m.* Judith, dau. of Edward (or Humphrey?) Lloyd, Esq., of Llanynis, Denb., and had a son,—
Wythen Jones, Esq., who *m.* Margaret, dau. of Thomas Johnes, Esq., of Dalaucothi, co. of Carmarthen, and had three sons, Hugh, Evan (of whom hereafter), and John. The eldest son,—
Hugh Jones, Esq., *m.* Elizabeth, dau. of Morris Lewis, Esq., of Dolaugwenith, Mont., and had issue—
Wythen Jones, Esq., who *m.* Jane, dau. of Edward Owen ap Bowen, Esq., of Pen'ralltgoch, Mont., and left a son,—
Evan Jones, Esq., of Trewythen, who *m.* Joan, dau. of Thomas Foulks, Esq., of Penthrin (Penrhyn?), and had issue two daus., Mary (1746), and Jane, the former of whom, the heiress, *m.*—
Bowen Jones, Esq., of Pen'ralltgoch (*b.* 1720), a descendant the junior line of the above-named Wythen Jones, the second of that name, and his wife, Margaret Johnes, of Dolaucothi. He was son of Wythen Jones, Esq. (*b.* 1695), who *m.* Mary, dau. and h. of Richard Bowen, Esq., of Pen'ralltgoch, and left issue besides Bowen, Jane, *b.* 1723; Valentine, *b.* 1724, a general officer, *d. unm.;* Bridget, *b.* 1727; Wythen, *b.* 1729; John, Judith, Elizabeth. Wythen Jones, *b.* 1695, was son of John Jones, of Crucklas (Crug-glas), co. Cardigan, by Sarah, dau. of John Jenkins, of Pentre, in the same co., and grandson of Evan Jones (by his wife Margaret, dau. of David Robert Clerk, Vicar of Llandinam, Mont.), who was son as before mentioned, of Wythen Jones, Esq. (the second of that name), of Trewythen. Thus the two lines became united by the marriage of Mary Jones, heiress of Trewythen, with Bowen Jones, heir of Pen'ralltgoch, both gr.-gr.-grandchildren of the last-named Wythen Jones. The issue of this marriage—besides the eldest son, Wythen (who *m.* Sarah, dau. of Nathaniel Williams, Esq., of Hendir, co. Cardigan, and *d. s. p.*); Jane, *m.* Wiliam Tilsey, Esq., of Llandinam, Mont., and left issue; Valentine, *d. unm.;* and Mary, *m.* John Williams, Esq., of Castle Hill, co. Cardigan, and left a son, John, who *d. s. p.*—was a second son,—
Evan Jones, Clerk, many years Rector of Aberhavesp, Mont. (*d.* 16th July, 1827); *m.* Charlotte, dau. of Harvey Combe, Esq., of Andover, Hants, and had issue besides *Caroline*, of whom hereafter,—
Charlotte, *b.* 1786, *m.* John Hunter, Esq., of Mount Severn, Mont., and *d. s. p.*
Wythen Jones, Esq., of Trewythen and Rhiewport, Mont., *b.* 1789; *m.* Mary, dau. of Rev. William Thomas, of Alderbury, Salop, and left a dau., Charlotte, who *d. s. p.* 1855.
Harvey Bowen Jones, Esq., of Trewythen and Rhiewport, Mont., last representative in the direct male line, *b.* 1797, *m.* Sophia, dau. of John Frederick Pieht, Esq., of Enfield, and *d. s. p.* 1864.
Caroline, above-named, the third child, *b.* 1793, and still surviving, *m.* as already stated, in 1815, Boyce Combe, Esq., of Cobham Park, Surrey, and has had issue—
BOYCE HARVEY COMBE, Esq., now of Oaklands, as above; Harvey Edmond, James, Matthew, Christian Evan, Alfred, Caroline Charlotte, Juliana, Mary Ann, Fanny.

DARBY, William Henry, Esq., of Brymbo, Denbighshire.

Is J. P. for Denbighshire; son of Richard Darby, Esq., of Coalbrookdale; *b.* at Coalbrookdale, 1819.
Residence: Brymbo, near Wrexham.

DAVID, Evan Edgar, Esq., of Fairwater House, Glamorganshire.

Eldest son of the late Evan Williams David, Esq., J. P. of Fairwater (who *d.* 1872), by his 2nd wife, Jessie, dau. of R. Herring, Esq., of Cromer, Norfolk; *b.* at Radyr Court, Cardiff, August 9, 1853; *ed.* at Caius College, Cambridge; is *unm.*
Residence: Fairwater House, Cardiff.
Arms: Az., a ship in full sail or, on a chief arg., a garb between two cinquefoils, all gu.
Crest: A dove and branch, all ppr.
Motto: Pax et copia.

DAVIES, John Pryce, Esq., of Bronfelen, Montgomeryshire.

J. P. for the co. of Montgomery; Sheriff of his co. in 1869; *b.* 1822; is *unm.*
Residence: Bronfelen, Montgomeryshire.
Arms: Quarterly: 1st, sa. a goat passant arg.; 2nd, or, a lion passant sa., in a bordure engrailed gu.; 3rd, az., three bugle-horns, two and one, stringed arg.; 4th, sa., three nags' heads erased arg.
Crest: A holly tree ppr. on a mount vert a he-goat arg., attired or, browsing on the tree, which he holds with his two fore-feet; over it the legend "Gwell angau na gwarth."
Motto: Comes invidia virtutis.

LINEAGE.

The following is in the main a copy of the family pedigree in the possession of Mr. John Piyce Davies, of Bronfelen, first compiled about 1653, and added to for the subsequent descents by members of the family at different periods.
The Davieses of Maesmawr, parish of Llandinam, co. Montgomery, deduce their lineage from ALETH, lord of Dyfed, 11th century. He *m.* Nest (Agnes), dau. of Llewelyn ap Gwrgant, prince of Morganwg and Glamorgan, (two synonymous names anciently applied to separate parts of that princedom), and whose son Uchdryd *m.* Maredd, dau. of Cadivor, Vawr, lord of Blaencych, Carmarthenshire, and was *s.* by his son, Gwrgeneu ap Uchdryd, who *m.* Ales, dau. of Gronwy ap Einion ap Llywarch ap Cynhaethwy, and had issue,—
Jerwerth ap Gwrgeneu, who *m.* Eve, dau. of Sir Aron ap Rhys ap Bledri ap Cadivor Vawr, and was succeeded by his son, Cynddelw ap Jerwerth, who *m.* Jane, dau. of Gorwared ap Cemmaes, Esq. His son, Rhirid ap Cynddelw, who *m.* Gwladus, dau. of Richard, lord of Dinas Certhin, was father of *Celynin* (sa., a goat arg., horns or), who is recognised as the common ancestor of the Davieses of Trewern, and the Vaughans of Llwydiarth, co. of Montgomery

(see in Dwnn's *Visitations*, i. 306, "Davies of Trewern"). Celynin, according to the family pedigree at Bronfelen, *m.* Gwen, dau. of Meredith ap Rhydderch, of the line of Tewdwr Mawr; but by Dwnn he is stated to have *m.* Alson, dau. of Cynvelyn ap Dolphwyn (i. p. 306), by Julian Mortimer. He was *s.* by his son,—

Einion, who *m.* Gwenllian, dau. of Adam Meyrick ap Pasgen ap Gwyn ap Griffith, lord of Guilsfield, whose son Llewelyn *m.* Lleucu (Lucy), dau of Ednyfed Llwyd ap Griffith ap Jevan of Maelor, otherwise Bromfield. Llewelyn had 2 sons: 1, Jenkin ap Llewelyn (ancestor of the Vaughans of Llwydiarth); and 2, Howell, who *m.* Annes (Agnes), dau. of Griffith ap Evan ap Madoc, of Hope Bach (now Buttington), and was *s* by his son,—

David ap Howell, who *m.* Joned, dau. of Madoc ap——? and was *s.* by a son, William ap David, who *m.* Margaret, dau. of David Lloyd of Deuddwr. Their son and *s.* was,—

Evan ap William, who *m.* Alson, dau. of John Hughes of Carstone, and had a son,—

David ap 'Evan, whose wife was Elinor, dau. and co-h. of John ap William ap John ap Griffith ap Evan ap Ririd ap Trahaearn (her mother was Christian, dau. of Roger Nunnerley, of Pontsbury), and by her had two sons,—1, Reynold Davis (of whom presently), 2, Edward.

Edward Davies, or ap David, 2nd son, a barrister-at-law, was on the Sheriffs' file for many years as chief steward of the manors of Nethergorther, Overgorther, Tirtref, and Bansley. His last year in this capacity is 31st Elizabeth (1588-9). He resided at Shrewsbury, and *d.* 9th March, 1589. (See further *Montg. Coll.*, vol. iii., pp. 330, 331.) He was *s.* by a son,—

Edward Davies (the surname becomes now settled), who settled at Trewern, co. Montgomery; and *m.*, 1596, Elizabeth, dau. of Richard Langley, Esq., of the Abbey, Shrewsbury. He had a son,— Edward, who *m.* a dau. of OwenGeorge, Gent., of Shrewsbury, and left issue.

Reynold Davies, the elder son, above-named, was of *Marsh*, in the co. of Salop; and *m* Eleanor, dau. of James Maurice ap Philip, of Cardigan; was *s.* by a son Edward, also of Marsh, who *m.* Frances, dau. of Robert Charlton, of Terne, in the co. of Salop, grandfather of Sir Job Charlton, an eminent lawyer; *b.* 1614; created sergeant immediately after the Restoration, July 4, 1660; appointed Chief Justice of Chester in 1662; promoted to be King's Sergeant, May 20, 1668; elected Speaker of the House of Commons, 1672; subsequently raised to be Judge in the Common Pleas, and knighted by King James, May 12, 1686. He subsequently removed to Maesmawr, parish of Llandinam, in the chancel of which church he was buried 1688; and was *s.* by his son,—

Robert Davies, Esq., of Maesmawr, who in 1653 *m.* Dorothy, dau. of Edward Sontley, Esq., of Sontley, co. of Denbigh (see Dwnn's *Visitations*, vol. ii., 358). They had, among other children, a son,— Edward Davies, also of Maesmawr, who *m.*, 1701, Jane, dau. of Thomas Morris, Esq., of Hurst, Salop; and dying 1733, was *s.* by his son, Robert Davies, Esq., *b.* 1704, at Maesmawr; *m.*, 1729, Elizabeth, dau. of Richard Pryce, Esq., of Trewylan Llansantffraid, Mont.; only son of Edmund Pryce, Esq., of Gunley, by his second wife, Catherine, only dau. of Edward Tanatt, of Trewylan; *s.* at Maesmawr by,—

Pryce Davies, Esq., *b.* 1731; Sheriff of his co. 1763; *m.*, 1768, Ann, dau. of John Rowland, of Llanfair-issa, Merioneth, by Margaret, his wife,

dau. of Robert Lloyd, of Dduallt, Merioneth, by Ann, dau. of — Vaughan, of Dolymelynllyn, same co.; eldest son of Robert Lloyd, of Dduallt, by Elizabeth, dau. of — Wynn, of Maesyneuadd, same co.; *d.* 1813, and was *s.* by his eldest son,— Edward Davies, Esq., *b.* 1769; was in the profession of the law; and had by Harriet, only dau. of Wm. Morris, Esq. of Argoed, younger son of Philip Morris, Esq., of Hurst, Salop, ten children; *d.* 1841. His brother,—

John Davies, second son, was in holy orders; *b.* 1770; *m.*, 1814, Jane, dau. and co-h. of Rice Pryce, Esq., of Manafon, Mont., by Catherine, eldest dau. of Humphrey Jones, Esq., of Garthmill Hall, same co.; and dying 1869, left surviving issue, besides a dau.,—

Jane Ann,—
John Pryce Davies, Esq., now of Maesmawr Hall and Bronfelen, as above.

Note.—Bronfelen, the present residence of the family, was built by the present proprietor's father, who had acquired a portion of the old family property, from his elder brother by purchase. Bronfelen, about four miles south-west of Newtown, is beautifully situated on a gentle elevation in the vale of the Severn, commanding extensive and charming scenery.

DAVIES, Mrs. Frances Saunders, of Pentre, Pembrokeshire.

Widow of Arthur Picton Saunders Davies, Esq., of Pentre, who *d.* June 8, 1873. He was the eldest son of the late D. A. Saunders Davies, Esq., M.P. for Carmarthenshire, Chairman of the Cardiganshire Quarter Sessions, &c., by his wife Elizabeth Maria, only dau. of Col. Owen Philipps, of Williamston, in the co. of Pembroke; *b.* April 22nd, 1832; *ed.* at Eton and Christ Church, Oxford; *s.* to estates in 1857; *m.* March 31, 1860, Frances (as above), 4th dau. of the late Grismond Philipps, Esq., of Cwmgwili, co. of Carmarthen, M.P. for the borough of Carmarthen, and had issue 5 sons and 2 daus.

Heir: The eldest son, Arthur Picton Saunders, *b.* July 26, 1862.
Residence: Pentre, Boncath, R. S. O., South Wales.
Arms: Quarterly: 1st and 4th, az., a wolf rampant arg.; 2nd and 3rd, on a field of the first, a chevron or between 3 eagles' heads erased of the second impaling quarterly. 1st and 4th, sa., a chevron ermine between 3 bulls' heads afronté, arg.; 2nd and 3rd, on a field of the first, 3 scaling-ladders arg., on a chief gu. a castle triple-towered of the second.
Crests: 1. A wolf rampant arg.; 2. A demi bull rampant of the same.
Motto: Solem ferre possum.

EVANS, Edward, Esq., of Bronwylfa, Denbighshire.

J. P. for Denbighshire; son of the late John Evans, Esq., of Leamington, formerly of London and Liverpool; *b.* at Worcester, 16th June, 1816; *ed.* at Radley School,

Berkshire; m., 2nd Aug., 1841, Margaret, 2nd surviving dau. of the late Robert Paterson, Esq., J. P. of Nunfield and Brocklehirst, Dumfriesshire; came into possession of the estate of Bronwylfa by purchase in 1871; has issue 5 sons and 4 daughters, as follows:—John James, Edward, William Paterson, Alfred Bickerton, Arthur Ernest, Margaret Rimmer, Hannah Rose, Edith Mary, Constance Elizabeth.

Heir: John James, eldest son.
Residence: Bronwylfa, Denbighshire.
Arms: Per pale arg. and gu., a lion passant reguardant armed az. between two fleurs-de-lis in chief, a bundle of rods banded in base, all counter-changed.
Crest: A lion passant reguardant arg., the body charged with three crosses moline gu., resting the dexter paw upon a bundle of rods banded, of the second.
Motto: Libertas.

EVANS, Thomas John, Esq., of Aberglasney, Carmarthenshire.

J. P. for cos. of Brecon and Glamorgan; High Sheriff for Breconshire, 1871; son of the late David Evans, Esq., Banker; b. at Merthyr Tydvil; m. first, 1861, Ida Rebekah Wood, dau. of Edward Morgan, Esq., of Merthyr, and secondly, Frances Sarah Griffith, dau. of Rev. John Griffith, M.A., Rector of Merthyr Tydvil; has issue 1 son and 2 daus., Edward David, b. 1864, Mary Ida, and Sybil Frances.

Residence: Aberglasney, Carmarthenshire.

EYTON, Peter Ellis, Esq., Rhyl, Flintshire.

M.P. for the Flintshire Boroughs, elected February, 1874; Town Clerk of Flint, 1856; author of "Trip to the Isle of Man;" son of the late Jas. Eyton, Esq., by Mary, dau. and heiress of the late David Parry, Esq., of Rhydycilgwyn Isa, in the county of Denbigh; born at Flint, 9th September, 1827; ed. at the High School, Liverpool Institute; is unm.; s. to estates, 1864.

Residences: 2, Kensington Gore, London; and Rhydycilgwyn Isa, Denbighshire.
Arms: Gu., on a bend arg., a lion passant sa.
Crest: A demi-lion rampant arg., holding in the paws a ducal coronet.
Motto: Hwy pery clod na golud.

LINEAGE.

This family is descended from the Eytons of Flintshire. As a branch of the Eytons of Leeswood they were settled at Maes y groes, in Cilcen, from early times, and their arms and crest, as shown upon monuments in Cilcen Church, are the same as those of Eytons, Leeswood, one of whom, Mr. Eyton's great-grandfather, lost the estates, which are now in the possession of Mr. Potts, of Glan-yr-afon. After this loss of ancestral property the family engaged in mercantile pursuits, and the late Mr. Thos. Eyton, Mr. Eyton's grandfather, opened collieries at Flint and Mostyn, besides becoming an extensive shipowner. (See also *Eyton of Llanerch y Mor.*)

GLADSTONE, Right Hon. William Ewart, of Hawarden Castle, Flintshire.

P.C.; M.P.; D.L.; D.C.L.; M.A., &c.; fourth son of the late Sir John Gladstone, 1st Bart. (cr. 1846), a Merchant of Liverpool, by his 2nd wife Anne, dau. of Andrew Robertson, Esq., Provost of Dingwall; b. Dec. 29th, 1809; ed. at Eton and Christ Church, Oxford; grad. B.A. double 1st Class, 1831, M.A., 1834, and became Hon. D.C.L., 1848; m., 1839, Catherine, dau. of the late Sir Stephen Richard Glynne, 8th Bart. of Hawarden Castle, Flintshire; to which estate he recently suc. *jure uxoris,* on the death, in 1874, of his wife's unm. brother, Sir Stephen Richard Glynne, Bart. (see p. 447), and has, with other issue, a son, William Henry.

Mr. Gladstone began his political career, in which he has gained so much distinction, as M.P. for Newark, 1832—45; he was M.P. for the University of Oxford, 1847—65; for South Lancashire, 1865—68; since the latter year he has sat for Greenwich. He was a Lord of the Treasury, 1834; Under Secretary for the Colonies, 1835: Vice-President of the Board of Trade, and Master of the Mint, 1841—43; President of the Board of Trade, 1843—45; Colonial Secretary, Dec., 1845—July, 1846; Chancellor of the Exchequer, 1852—55, and 1859—66; became Premier in Dec., 1868—Feb., 74, and from Aug., 1873 till the latter date performed, in addition, the duties of Chancellor of the Exchequer. Mr. Gladstone's numerous literary productions cover a wide and varied field of knowledge and scholarship; a large proportion, both of his earlier and later works, displaying familiar acquaintance with and taste for ecclesiastical studies. His chief works are "*The State in its relation with the Church,*" 1838, 4th Edition, 1841; "*Church Principles considered in their Results;*" "*Remarks on Recent Commercial Legislation,*" 1845; "*Studies on Homer and the Homeric Age,*" 1858; "*A Chapter of Autobiography,*" 1868; "*Juventus Mundi: The Gods and Men of the Heroic Age,* 1869;" "*The Vatican Decrees in their bearing on Civil Allegiance,*" 1874; "*Vaticanism: An Answer to Replies and Reproofs,*" 1875; and a large number of important contributions to high class periodical literature.

Heir: His son William Henry, b. 1840; ed. at Eton and Christ Church, Oxford, where he grad.

B. A. 1862 ; M.A. 1865 ; M.P. for Whitby, 1868 ; was M.P. for Chester, 1865—8 ; was a Lord of the Treasury, 1869—74.
Residence: Hawarden Castle, Flintshire.
Town Address: Reform Club ; United University Club.
Arms: Arg., a savage's head, affrontée, distilling drops of blood, about the temples a wreath of holly vert, within an orle fleury gu., all within eight martlets sa.
Crest: Issuant from a wreath of holly vert, a demi griffin sa., supporting between the claws a sword, the blade enfiled by a bonnet of holly and bay, also vert.
Motto: "Fide et virtute."

LINEAGE.

This family is of Scotch origin, the present head of it being Sir Thomas Gladstone, 2nd Bart., D.C.L., &c., of Fasque and Balfour, Kincardineshire, the ex-Premier's eldest brother. For the Hawarden genealogy and history, see *Glynne of Hawarden Castle*, p. 447.

GWYN, William Edward Bevan, Esq., of Plas Cwrt Hir, Carmarthenshire.

J. P. for the co. of Carmarthen ; Chairman of Joint Counties Asylum of Carmarthen, Pembroke, and Cardigan; son of tne late William Bevan Gwyn, Esq., of Pilroath, co. of Carmarthen; *b.* at Pilroath, 29th April, 1826; *m.* Ann, dau. of Mr. D. Charls of Waunmably in same county; *s.* 1852; has issue 5 sons and 6 daus.
Residence: Plas Cwrt Hir, near Carmarthen.
Arms: Per fesse: az and arg. in chief an arm in armour embowed, the hand grasping an arrow in pale of the second; in base five bendlets of the first. With several quarterings. (See *Lineage.*)
Crest: Out of a ducal crown an arm in armour as in the arms, the hand grasping a sword.
Motto: Fiat lux.

LINEAGE.

The Gwyns of Plas Cwrt Hir, formerly of Pilroath, co. Carmarthen, derive through the Gwyns of Gwempa, in the same county, from Meredydd ap David of Cilrhychen, Llandebie, eleventh in descent from Morgan Hên, prince of Glamorgan (for his period see pp. 486-7), who is said to have borne "arg., two lions passant reguardant in pale gu." The said—
Meredydd ap David, to whom the heralds give as arms "arg., a bull passant sa., armed and unguled or;" *m.* Efa, dau. of Howel ap Ievan ap Gwilym Ddu, and left a son,—
David ap Meredydd of Cilrhychen, who *m.* Margaret, dau. of Thomas ap David, descending from Cadwgan Fawr, by whom he had a son,—
Meredydd ap David, of Cilrhychen, whose wife was Ellen, dau. of Howel ap Ievan ap Rhys Gôch, of the line of Urien Rheged, by Gwerfil, dau. of "Syr Dafydd ap Walter, Parson Llanedi." Meredydd's grandson,—
Ievan (or Ivan) Gwyn, of Llanon, ap Ievan ap Meredydd, *m.* Margaret, dau. and h. of Morgan ap John of Bailyglâs (a descendant of Urien Rheged), bearing "arg., a chevron sa. inter three ravens ppr.," and had, with other issue, a son,—
John Gwyn, Esq, of Gwempa, Sheriff for the co. of Carmarthen 1622 (see *Sheriffs*), who *m.* Martha, 2nd dau. of Charles Vaughan, Esq , of Cwmgwili, 7th son of Walter Vaughan, Esq., of Pembre Court, of the line of Sir Roger Vaughan of Tretower (which see), and left a son and heir,—
Charles Gwyn, Esq., of Gwempa, Sheriff of his co. 1646, who *m.* Jane, dau. of David Evans, Esq , of Neath (see *Sheriffs of Glamorgan*, 1632), and was *s.* by his son,—
Richard Gwyn, Esq., of Gwempa, Sheriff of his co. 1671, who *m.* Rachel, 3rd dau. and co-h. of Thomas Gwyn, Esq., of Hay Castle, co. Brecknock, and had a son,—
Thomas Gwyn, Esq , Sheriff of his co. 1731, who *m.* Elizabeth, dau. and co-h. of Richard Middleton, Esq., of Middleton Hall, co. of Carmarthen, and is found (see MS. by Mr. W. G. Stedman Thomas) to have had four sons, viz., Thomas, Richard (who *s.* to Middleton Hall, and was Sheriff of his co. 1761), Francis Edward (a General, Equerry to George III., *m.* Mary, dau. of General Horneck, and *d. s. p.*), and Leonard Bilson, of Glyn Abbey (a receiver of taxes, *m.* an heiress, Miss Rogers, was Sheriff of his co. 1769, as of Gwempa, his paternal estate, which he is said to have purchased). The eldest son,—
Thomas Gwyn, styled "Capt.," succeeded to Gwempa, but subsequently disposed of his estates. He *m.* Katherine, dau. of Mr. Bevan of Pencoed, and left a son,—
William Bevan Gwyn, Esq., of Pilroath, *b.* 1776, *m.* Elizabeth, dau. of James Phillips, Esq., of Trebersed, near Carmarthen, and had issue *William Bevan*, Thomas Bevan, Mary Bevan, and James Bevan. The eldest,—
William Bevan Gwyn, Esq., of Pilroath, J. P. for the co. of Carmarthen, *m.* Margaret, 2nd dau. of John Thomas, Esq., of Longhouse, Pembrokeshire, and had issue, besides Elizabeth Mary, Margaret Ellen, John Thomas, Sarah Catherine, James Bevan, and Francis Bilson, an eldest son,—
William Edward Bevan Gwyn, Esq., now of Plas Cwrt Hir, as above.

HOWELL, Abraham, Esq., of Rhiewport, Montgomeryshire.

J. P. for the county of Montgomery; was formerly a solicitor in practice at Welshpool, and for many years County Treasurer; four times Mayor of Welshpool, and long an Alderman of that borough, an active sanitary reformer and promoter of local railways ; *b.* at Llanbrynmair, Mont., 4th April, 1810, of an old Welsh family long located in that co.; *m.*, 1840, Mary, dau. of Edward Purcell Jones, Esq., surgeon, of Welshpool, descended on the grandmother's side from the Purcells of Nantycriba, and has issue three sons and four daughters.
Residence: Rhiewport, Berriew, and Clive Place, Welshpool, Montgomeryshire.

Note.—For date of erection of *Rhiewport* (more correctly Rhiwport) see further notice, with an *engraving*, under that name. The mansion with part of the estate came to the present possessor by purchase in 1866. It is pleasantly situated on the left bank of the Rhiw, near its junction with the Severn, in the neighbourhood of Montgomery

HUNTER, William Charles, Esq., of Mount Severn, Montgomeryshire.

Son of the late Lieut.-Colonel William Hunter, of Mount Severn, by Emily Jane, dau. of Robert Wood, Esq., of Bath, Somerset; *b.* 1856; *ed.* at Harrow School; *s.* to Mount Severn estate on the death of his father, 1874.

Heir pres.: His sister, Emily Grace Hansford Hunter.

Residence: Mount Severn, near Llanidloes.

Note.—For *arms* and other particulars of this family see p. 824.

JONES, Morris Charles, Esq., of Gungrog, Montgomeryshire.

F. S. A. Lond. and Scot., and member of several other learned societies in England and America; author of "The Abbey of Valle Crucis, its Origin and Foundation Charter," 1866; "The Feudal Barons of Powys," 1868, and numerous genealogical and antiquarian articles contributed to archæological journals, and several privately printed pamphlets; only son of the late Morris Jones, Esq., of Gungrog, (*d.* 1843), the only surviving son of Morris Jones, of Eardiston, Salop; *b.* 9th May, 1819; *ed.* at Bruce Castle School, Tottenham, Middlesex; *m.*, 1844, Elizabeth, eldest dau. of Robert Paterson, Esq., J. P., of Nunfield, Dumfriesshire, and has issue 4 sons and 4 daughters, viz,—

1. Morris Paterson, 27, Edge Lane, Liverpool, a solicitor, *b.* 1847; *m.*, 1874, Clara, eldest dau. of John Vernon, Esq., of Tushingham House, Cheshire.
2. Robert James, *b.* 1849.
3. Thomas Simpson, *b.* 1853, of Trinity College, Cambridge, and Lincoln's Inn.
4. Charles William, *b.* 1857.
5. Elizabeth Grace Harriet.
6. Margaret Rimmer, *m.*, 1874, Adam William Black, Esq., J. P. of Edinburgh, youngest son of the late Adam Black, Esq., formerly M.P. for that city, and has issue a dau., Elizabeth Adelaide.
7. Clara Sophia. 8. Amy Gertrude.

Residences: Gungrog, near Welshpool; and 20, Abercromby Square, Liverpool.

Note.—Mr. Morris Charles Jones was brought up to the law, and has for many years practised as a solicitor in Liverpool. He is the originator and chief promoter of the "Powysland Club," and has throughout acted as the hon. secretary, and in this capacity has devoted much time to the illustration of the archæology and history of his native county. The transactions of the club, edited by the hon. sec., and entitled "*Collections Historical and Archæological relating to Montgomeryshire and its Borders*," now (1875) extend to eight volumes 8vo., and abound with the fruits of his zealous labours, and also afford evidence of his tact in eliciting latent archæological talent in many of his fellow-countrymen.

We have before remarked (p. 794) that many of "the papers in the *Montgomeryshire Collections* are among the most elaborate and useful contributions to local topography, biography, and history published in any part of the kingdom;" and may add that no county in Wales has materials for its history so complete and extensive as Montgomeryshire has in these collections.

In 1874, through the instrumentality of Mr. Morris C. Jones, the *Powysland Museum and Library* were established in connection with the Powysland Club, and give promise of being a most successful institution, and a lasting memorial of the Powysland Club.

His residence, Gungrog, which, with the small estate on which it stands, was purchased by his father in 1832, and to which he succeeded in 1843, is a building of Elizabethan character, of the early part of the eighteenth century. It has undergone considerable alterations within the last twelve years, and several of the rooms have been fitted with dark oak wainscoting. The dining-room has been decorated with finely carved panelling taken out of an ancient house in the city of London; and to preserve as far as possible the history of remains so interesting, a privately printed pamphlet, entitled "Reminiscences connected with old oak panelling now at Gungrog" (Welshpool, 1864), was written by the proprietor, and afterwards reproduced in several popular serials, *New Monthly Magazine*, *Leisure Hour*, *Chambers's Journal*, &c. The object of the pamphlet was principally to discover the artist who executed the carving, which is of the style and period of *Grinling Gibbons*; and although no certain information has hitherto been obtained, still many very plausible and ingenious arguments are therein adduced to show the strong probability that the work may be justly attributed to that celebrated carver.

We consider that the antiquarian and historical practical zeal of Mr. Jones of Gungrog is such as might be imitated with immense advantage to literature in the various counties of Wales. He has been fortunate in meeting with able coadjutors of kindred zeal and devotedness with his own, and we have little doubt but that similar bodies of educated men could be found in the other counties whose united labours might end in similar results.

LLOYD, Charles, Esq., of Brunant, Carmarthenshire.

J. P. for the co. of Carmarthen; formerly held commission in the Royal Carmarthen Rifles; third son of the late George Lloyd, Esq., J. P. of Brunant, by his wife Margaret Jane Martha, dau. of the late George Harries, Esq., of Priskilly, co. of Pembroke; *b.* at Haverfordwest, Pembrokeshire, 4th March, 1830; *ed.* at Bromsgrove School; *m.*, 10th April, 1862, Emma W. Webb-Bowen, eldest dau. of the Rev. Wm. W. Webb-Bowen, Vicar of Camrose, Pembrokeshire, and granddaughter of the late Hugh Webb-Bowen, Esq., J. P. of Camrose House, in same county; *s.* to estates September, 1861; has issue 1 son, George W. D. B. Lloyd, and 2 daughters, Emma Grace and Katharine M. Alice.

Heir: George W. D. B. Lloyd, *b.* November 6th, 1866.

Residence: Brunant, near Llandilo, Carmarthenshire.

Arms: Sa., a spear-head imbrued ppr., point upwards, between three scaling-ladders, 2 and 1,

arg.; on a chief gu., a castle triple-towered of the second ; impaling az. three mullets pierced or—for *Harries*.
Crests : 1. A lion rampant arg. 2. A lion couchant ppr.
Mottoes : Sic itur ad astra ; Dum spiro spero.

LINEAGE.

This family derives, in common with the numerous clan of *Lloyds* of Cardiganshire, from *Cadifor ap Dinawal*, lord of Castell-howel (son-in-law of the Lord Rhys of Dinefawr), who was rewarded for his bravery in capturing Cardigan Castle from the Normans under De Clare, *circ.* A.D., 1165, with the arms which are still borne by his descendants, and with an extensive territory in Cardiganshire. See further for the origin of the Lloyds, pp. 167, 170--5. Mr. Lloyd of Brunant traces, by a younger branch, through the Lloyds of Alltyrodyn and Blaendyffryn. His father, Charles Lloyd, Esq., suc. to Brunant after an uncle.

LLOYD, Henry, Esq., of Dolobran, Meifod, Montgomeryshire.

Lieut. in Montgomeryshire Yeomanry; 2nd son of Richard Herman Lloyd, Esq., banker, of London, and of Allesley, Warwickshire ; *b.* in the parish of Streatham, in Surrey, November 29, 1840 ; *ed.* at Marlborough College ; is *unm.*; *s.* in 1872, by re-purchase, to Dolobran-fach, and other portions of the Dolobran property.
Residence and Town Address : 43. Half-moon Street, Piccadilly ; St. James's and Oriental Clubs.
Arms : Quarterly : 1st and 4th, sa., a he-goat statant arg. ; 2nd and 3rd, az., three cocks, two and one, of the second.
Crest : A he-goat rampant arg., as in the arms.
Motto : Watch.

Note.—This family is descended from Ivan Têg, of Dolobran, 2nd son of Llewelyn of Llwydiarth, and had been seated at Dolobran from 1476 to 1780. The old mansion-house of Dolobran has been demolished.

LLOYD, Sampson Samuel, Esq., of Moor Hall, Warwickshire.

M.P. for Plymouth 1874; J. P. for the co. of Warwick, and the bor. of Birmingham ; son of George Braithwaite Lloyd, Esq., banker, of Birmingham ; *b.* at Birmingham, 10th Nov., 1820 ; *m.*, first, Emma, dau. of Samuel Reeves, Esq., of Leighton Buzzard, 14th Nov., 1844 (*d.* 9th March, 1863) ; and 2ndly, 1st Oct., 1865, Marie Wilhelmine Sophie Christiane, dau. of His Excellency Lieut.-General W. F. Menckhoff (Prussian Army). Has issue,
By first mar., Emma Mary, *b.* 1845 ; *m.*, 1872, to James Johnstone, Capt. 68th Bengal Nat. Inf.
Sampson Samuel, *b.* 1846, *m.*, 1868, Jane Emilia, dau. of Thomas Lloyd, Esq., of The Priory, Warwick, a D. L. for Warwickshire.
Mary Dearman, *b.* 1848.
George Herbert, *b.* 1850 ; *m.*, 1873, Anna Elizabeth, dau. of Thos. Colmore, Esq.
Rachel Louisa, *b.* 1851 ; *m.*, 1874, to Dearman Janson, Esq., of Chislehurst, Kent.
Priscilla Caroline, *b.* 1852.
Alice Elizabeth, *b.* 1854.
Arthur Llewellyn, *b.* 1855.
Adelaide Beatrice, *b.* 1857.
By second mar., Charles Frederick, *b.* 1866.
Walter Reginald, *b.* 1868.
Heir : Sampson Samuel, eldest son.
Residence : Moor Hall, Sutton Coldfield, Warwickshire.
Town Residence : *at present* 14, Queen's Gate Gardens S.W.
Arms : Azure, a chevron argent between three gamecocks of the same, langued, attired and unguled or.
Crest : He-goat rampant.
Motto : Esto vigilans.

LINEAGE.

Mr. Lloyd, of Moor Hall (which he occupies as a tenant), lineally represents an ancient family of Montgomeryshire, long seated at Dolobran in that co. (See further, *Lloyd of Dolobran*.)

LLOYD, Thomas Edward, Esq., of Coedmore, Cardiganshire.

M.P. for Cardiganshire, and J. P. for Cardigan and Carmarthenshire ; son of the late Thomas Lloyd, Esq., of Coedmore, Lord Lieutenant of Cardiganshire, and who died in 1857 ; *b.* at Coedmore, April 12, 1820 ; *ed.* at Rugby School ; *m.*, April 27, 1850, Clemena F. P. Daniel, daughter of the late Rev. David Daniel, M.A., Oxon., and Clemena his wife, daughter of Major Edward Lyons, who was on the staff of the late Duke of Kent when in Canada; *s.* to estates, 1857, and on the death of his mother, 1866 ; patron of the living of Llechryd, Cardiganshire ; has issue a dau., Edith, *b.* April 10, 1856.
Heiress : his daughter Edith.
Residence : Coedmore, Cardiganshire.
Town Address : 3, Edinburgh Mansions, London, S. W.
Arms : Gu., a lion rampant regardant or—
ELYSTAN GLODRUDD.
Crest : A lion rampant.
Motto : Fide et fortitudine.

Note.—At Coedmore are traces of the walls of an old castle called *Cefen*, in a part of the grounds overlooking the Teifi.

LINEAGE.

The Lloyds of Coedmore, formerly properly spelt *Coedmawr*, are of long standing in Cardiganshire and Carmarthenshire (see *Note*, p. 204). Paternally the descent is from Tudor Trevor, through his great-grandson Elystan Glodrudd (10th cent.), founder of one of the royal tribes of Wales, who is said by some to have borne " Gu., a lion rampant regardant or," and by others " Gu., a lion rampant arg., armed or."
From Elystan, in the fourth degree, was descended Elidyr Goch, lord of Llangathen, who *m.* a dau. of Trahaern of Rhydodyn ; and from him, also in the fourth degree, was Rhys ap Thomas ap David,

who *m.* a dau. and co-h. of Jenkin of Gilfachwen, whose descendant, sixth degree, Thomas *Lloyd*, the fourth who used that surname, *m.* Mary, dau. and co-h. of Rhys Lloyd of Cilgwyn. His grandson Thomas Lloyd (Capt.), living 1693, *m.* Jane, dau. of James Lewis, Esq., of Coedmawr, of the line of Lewis of Abernantbychan, whereby the Lloyds became possessors of the estate of Coedmawr. His lineal descendants five generations in succession, ending with the late— Thomas Lloyd, Esq., were of Coedmore, and were called also of Cilgwyn. He, by his wife Charlotte, dau. of the late C. Longcroft, Esq., had, with other issue, an eldest son, THOMAS EDWARD LLOYD, Esq., of Coedmore, now M.P. for Cardiganshire as above. See further *Lloyd of Coedmore*, p. 204.

LUCAS, The Rev. J. Ponsonby, of Uplands, Glamorganshire.

Rector of Rhossili, Vicar of Llangennith; son of the late Henry Lucas, Esq., of Uplands and Cheriton, J. P. for the co. Glamorgan (*d.* 1870), by his first wife, Caroline, dau. and co-h. of Ponsonby Tottenham, Esq., Sheriff for his co. 1842, and sometime M.P. for Fethard and New Ross, co. Wexford; *b.* 1823, at Fairy Hill, Reynoldston, Glamorgan; *ed.* at New Inn Hall, Oxford; *grad.* B.A., 1851; *m.*, 1857, Hannah Rebecca Dolbeare, youngest dau. of the late Rev. T. Mathews; *s.* his father, 1870; has issue—1.Charles Gardner Tottenham, *b.* 1859; 2. Loftus Tottenham; 3. Ponsonby Tottenham; 4. Henry Loftus Tottenham; 5. Caroline Tottenham; 6. Maria Louisa Tottenham.

Heir: His eldest son.
Residence: The Rectory, Rhossili, Reynoldston, Glamorgan.
Arms: Arg., a fesse between 6 annulets gu.
Crest: A wyvern surmounting a cap of maintenance.
Motto: Mynde the end.

LINEAGE.

Mr. Lucas is the head of the ancient family of Lucas of Stouthall, in the county of Glamorgan, the estates of which, by breaking the entail, became vested in Lt.-Col. John Nicholas Lucas, the elder brother of Mr. Lucas's father, who devised them by will to his daughter, Mary Catherine Lucas, wife of Lt.-Col. E. R. Wood, the cousin of Mr. Lucas.

This family, descending from Egidus Lucas, of *Domesday Book*, has been for several centuries settled in Glamorgan, the elder branch being seated in Essex, from whence, on the murder of Sir Charles Lucas, by Fairfax, and the flight abroad of his elder brother, Lord Lucas, of Shenfield, in Essex, the elder and younger branches became amalgamated by the marriage of Margaret Lucas, heiress of Stouthall, to her cousin, Henry Lucas, in the year 1654.

MARTEN, Thomas Arnold, Esq., of Fern Hill, Glamorganshire.

Son of the late Charles Marten, Esq., of Walworth, Surrey; *b.* at Camberwell, Surrey, 6th July, 1814; *m.* first, 20th Oct., 1837, Anne, dau. of Samuel Heineken, Esq., of Berkeley Square, Clifton; and secondly, 14th Oct., 1871, Georgiana Catherine Dixon, dau. of Major Richard Jeffreys, 53rd Regiment, of Pwllfadu, Glamorganshire, an old family originating in John Jeffreys, of Abercynrig, Breconshire, of which co. he was Sheriff in 1631, afterward seated at the Priory, Brecon, of which place was Jeffrey Jeffreys, Esq., Sheriff of his co. 1741; has issue,—

By first mar., Mary Worsley, Robert Humphrey, Henry Heineken, and Jessie Maria; by second mar., Arnoldine Georgiana and Arnold Jeffreys.

Heir: Robert Humphrey, eldest son, *m.*, 27th April, 1875, Blanche, dau. of Charles Anthony, Esq., of The Elms, Hereford.
Residence: Fern Hill, near Swansea, Glamorganshire.
Arms: Ermine, an eagle displayed or.
Crest: A griffin ppr.
Motto: Spes super sidera.

LINEAGE.

This family is lineally descended from Sir Henry Marten, of Longworth, Abingdon, Berks., a principal Judge of the Admiralty, twice Dean of the Arches, and in 1624 Judge of the Prerogative Court; known as a great favourite of James I. Sir Henry's son was the celebrated Henry Marten, Esq., M.P. for Berkshire, and one of the judges at the trial of King Charles I. (See an account of the long confinement of Henry Marten in Chepstow Castle, pp. 751—753.) Hunphrey Marten, Esq., great-uncle of the present representative of the family, was many years Governor of Albany and York Forts, Hudson's Bay, and was taken prisoner by the French in 1781. Mr. Snell, another great-uncle, was a friend of the Prince of Orange, afterwards William III., and assisted at his accession to the throne.

MIERS, Henry Nathaniel, Esq., of Ynyspenllwch, Glamorganshire.

J. P. for Glamorganshire, Chairman of the Rhyngdwyclydach School Board; son of Richard Hill Miers, Esq., of Ynyspenllwch, grandson of John Nathaniel Miers, Esq., of Ynyspenllwch, and Cadoxton Lodge, Neath; *b.* 6th Sept., 1848, at Ynyspenllwch, Swansea Valley; *ed.* at Westminster School; *m.* 12th Feb., 1870, Lydia Kate Probyn, dau. of John Miles Probyn, Esq.; *s.* 1869; patron of the Vicarage of Cadoxton-juxta-Neath; joint lord of the manors of Cadoxton, Neath Ultra and Kilybebyll, and Caegerwain; has issue 1 dau. and 2 sons, Sybil Hill, Richard Henry Probyn, and Harrold Gwyn Bonnor.

Heir: Richard Henry Probyn, eldest son, *b.* 12th June, 1873.
Residence: Ynyspenllwch, Swansea Valley.
Town Address: Junior Conservative Club

Arms: Gu., a fesse ermine between 3 water bougets arg., an annulet for difference—*Miers;* impaling ermine, on a fesse gu., a lion passant or—*Probyn.*
Crest: A plume of peacocks' feathers, encircled with a ring d'or.
Motto: Virtus est vitium fugere.

LINEAGE.

This family derives from the Meares, or Meeres, of Cumberland and Lincolnshire. The family arms and crest as above given were recorded in the Heralds' Visitation List of Lincolnshire in 1634, Thomas Meeres being then the head of the family.

Note.—The old house was, about 1831, pulled down, and the present one built.

MORTIMER, Rev. Mortimer Lloyd Jones, M.A., of Trewellwell, Pembrokeshire.

Vicar of Higher Tranmere, Cheshire; son of Rev. Thos. Wm. Jones, Vicar of Llanybri, Carmarthen, and Eleanor, dau. of the late Thomas Mortimer, of Trewellwell; *b.* 1828; *ed.* at Clifton and Corpus Christi Coll., Cambridge; *grad.* B.A. in 1856, M.A. 1861; *m.,* in 1860, Elizabeth Hooper, dau. of F. B. Hooper, Esq., M.D., of Reading, Berks; secondly, 1865, Eliza Walker, dau. of George Walker, Esq., of Walthamstow, Essex; *s.* to Trewellwell by purchase, 1874, assuming the family name of Mortimer; has issue 4 sons— Reginald, Francis, George, and Mansel.

Heir: Reginald Mortimer.
Residence: Trewellwell, Pembrokeshire, and Higher Tranmere, Cheshire.
Crest: Lion salient arg. on a wreath or and gu.
Motto: Kowir i Dduw a dyn.

This family derives its descent from the Mortimers of Trewellwell, where they have resided for 300 years, and is related by marriage to the Mansels of Glamorganshire. The house at Trewellwell was erected 1776.

NICHOLL, George Whitlock, Esq., of the Ham, Glamorganshire.

J. P. for the counties of Glamorgan and Monmouth; Recorder of Usk; Constable of the Castle of Llanblethian, and, as such, *ex officio* Mayor of Cowbridge; eldest surviving son of the late Iltyd Nicholl, Esq., J. P. of the Ham (*d.* 1871), by Eleanor, only child and *h.* of the late George Bond, Esq., of Newland, Gloucestershire, and Court Blethin, Mon.; *b.* at Usk, 2nd February, 1816; called to the bar, Middle Temple, 1840; *m.,* 12th October, 1853, Mary Lewisa, dau. and co-heiress of William Nicholl, Esq., M.D., of Ryde, Isle of Wight, and Pelline, Glamorganshire; *s.* to estate 1871; has issue—1, Iltyd Bond; 2, George Bleddyn Tyrrell; 3, Digby Seys Whitlock; 4, Edith Eleanor.

Heir: Iltyd Bond Nicholl, *b.* 1862.
Residence: The Ham, Cowbridge, Glamorgan; and Court Blethin, Monmouthshire.
Town Address: Athenæum Club.
Arms: Sa., three pheons arg.
Crest: On a tower a Cornish chough with wings expanded.
Motto: Duw a digon.

LINEAGE.

For the lineage of this family see under *Iltyd Nicholl, of the Ham,* p. 637.
Note.—The house at Ham was rebuilt 1861—3, on the site of the old house, which had become dilapidated.

PEACOCK, The Rev. Edward, of Stone Hall, Pembrokeshire.

Formerly Vicar of Road Hill, Wiltshire; J. P. for Wiltshire; B.A. 1843, M.A. 1846, in Mathematical Honours Senior Optime of Trin. Coll., Cambridge; eldest son of the late Rev. Edward Peacock, Vicar of Fifehead Magdalen, Dorsetshire, by Ann, dau. of William Lort Mansel, Bishop of Bristol; *b.* at Fifehead Magdalen, 6th June, 1820; *m.,* May, 1848, Eleanor, dau. of M. T. Hodding, Esq., of Fryern Court, Hants; and has issue 3 sons and 4 daughters, viz.,—

Edward Hodding. Eleanor.
Reginald. Lucy Williams.
Ferdinand Mansel. Augusta Caroline.
  Barbara Reade.

Heir: Edward Hodding Peacock.
Residence: Stone Hall, near Haverfordwest.
Arms: Gu., on a fesse engrailed arg., between 3 mascles, each within an annulet or, as many peacocks' heads erased ppr.
Crest: A peacock's head erased ppr., gorged with a mural crown or, holding in the beak a rose gu., leaved and slipped ppr.
Motto: Be just and fear not.

LINEAGE.

This family paternally belong to Lincolnshire, the present representative being Mildmay Willson, Esq., of South Ranceby (High Sheriff for his county for the present year, 1875), whose father, Anthony Willson, Esq., formerly High Sheriff and M.P. for the southern division of Lincolnshire, assumed by royal licence the surname of Willson, in lieu of his patronymic *Peacock.* Through his mother, who was a Mansel, the Rev. Edward Peacock, now of Stone Hall, is of Welsh descent, deriving through a long and honourable South Wales ancestry, the Mansels, Wogans, &c., his gr.-grandfather being William Wogan Mansel, Esq.

Note.—*Stone Hall,* parish of St. Lawrence, county of Pembroke, a very old mansion, was originally, with much more land than is now attached to it, the property of the ancient family of Wogan, from whom it passed to the families of Ford, Skyrme, Protheroe, Phillips, and Peel, and was purchased of John Entwistle Peel, Esq., in 1873, by the Reverend Edward Peacock, the present owner. Fenton, in his history of Pembrokeshire, gives a quotation from George

Owen, who wrote in 1595, in which Stone Hall is mentioned, but how old the house was at that time it is impossible to say. The great thickness of the walls in the old portion of the house probably prove great age.

The house would seem to have taken its name from a large *cromlech*, now partly fallen, in one of the adjoining fields.

The late Dr. Bowen, Bishop of Sierra Leone, was born at Stone Hall during the tenancy of his father, Thomas Bowen, Esq.

PELHAM, Pelham Thursby, Esq., of Ridgeway, Pembrokeshire, and Abermarles, Carmarthenshire.

J. P. for co. of Pembroke, late Capt. 30th Foot and late Major in Auxiliary Forces; 3rd surviving son of Rev. Henry Thursby-Pelham, of Cound Hall, Salop, by Elizabeth Mary, dau. of Thomas Papillon, Esq., of Crowther's Park, Sussex; *b.* 1840; *ed.* at Sandhurst; 1st commission obtained 1858; *m.*, 1872, to Emily Florence, dau. and sole *h.* of the late Henry Foley, Esq., of Ridgeway and Abermarles, by Anne, dau. of William Butler, Esq., of co. Tipperary; *s.* to estates, *jure uxoris*, 1872; patron of vicarage of Llansadwrn, Carm.

Residence: Ridgeway, Narberth, Pembrokeshire.

Town Address: Army and Navy Club.

Arms: Quarterly: 1st and 4th, az., three pelicans arg. vulning themselves ppr.—PELHAM; 2nd, arg., a chevron between 3 lions rampant, all sa.—THURSBY; 3rd, or, a chevron betw. 3 leopards' heads, all gu.—HARVEY. Differ from Harvey, of Ickwellbury, in not having trefoils on chevron.

Crests: A curlew with wings expanded ppr.—*Thursby*; a peacock in pride ppr.—*Pelham*.

Mottoes: In silentio fortitudo.—*Thursby*; Vincit amor patriæ—*Pelham*.

LINEAGE.

This family descends in direct male line from Robert Harvey, Esq., of Stockton and Grandborough, co. Warwick, 3rd son of Robert, ancestor of the family of Harvey, of Ickwellbury, co. Bedford, a junior branch of the present noble family of Bristol. The aforesaid Robert having married Mary, sole heir of the Thursbys, of Abington Abbey, co. Northampton, their only son John assumed his mother's name in addition to Harvey, early in the 18th century by royal licence.

The present Rev. H. Thursby-Pelham assumed the latter surname in 1852, by royal licence, as representative of the Cressett-Pelhams, of Upton Cressett, and of Cound, co. Salop, in right of his mother Frances, senior co-heir of that ancient family—(in addition to Thursby, and dropping Harvey).

The Foley family. The present Mrs. Thursby-Pelham claims to represent the senior branch of the Foleys of Ridgeway. The original deed of gift, bearing date 1383, from Adam de Hoton, Bishop of St. David's, to John Fauley and Elen his wife, "Constable of our castle Llawaden, and master of our board of works," exists. A trial before the "Star Chamber" confirmed this original deed, and the property has ever since remained, though much was confiscated by Cromwell to one Col. Skyrme, his follower.

Abermarles was bought by Admiral Sir Thos. Foley, K.C.B., from the Cornwallis family early in the present century. He pulled down the ancient seat in the Park (where formerly stood a large tilting yard), and erected the present mansion.

Ridgeway House, completed 1740—the ancient mansion having stood in the *now* stable yard.

PENRY, John Morgan, Esq., of Peterwell Court, Carmarthenshire.

J. P. for the county of Pembroke, and Commissioner of Taxes; an officer in the 2nd Somerset Militia; son of the late John Penry Jones, Esq., J. P. and D. L., of Sutton Lodge, Pembrokeshire, and Court-y-Ceidrym, Llanedi, by his wife Mary, dau. of the Rev. T. Brigstocke, Vicar of Llawhaden, Pemb.; *b.* 1836; *ed.* at Corpus Christi Coll., Camb., *grad.* B.A., 1857; is *unm*; *s.* 1872.

Residence: Peterwell Court, and Plas Court Ceidrym, Carmarthenshire.

Town Address: Raleigh Club, Waterloo Place.

Arms: Quarterly: 1st and 4th, az., a griffin segreant or; 2nd and 3rd, gu., three roaches in pale of the second; with several quarterings.

Crest: On an esquire's helmet, surmounted by a wreath az. and or, a martlet ppr.

Motto: Non vox sed votum.

LINEAGE.

Mr. Penry, of Peterwell Court, &c., now represents and is lineally descended from the ancient family of Penry of Plas Court Ceidrym, Llanedi, who derived in direct line from Gruffydd Gwyr, of Gower, son of Cadifor ap Gwrgan ap Bleddyn ap Maenarch, regulus of Brecknock, brother-in-law of Rhys ap Tewdwr, Prince of South Wales, and through descent is entitled to quarter the arms of the following:—*De Guise* of Wiston, co. Pembroke; Llewelyn Vychan ap Llewelyn ap Gwrgan of Gower, whose ensigns were—"argent, a stag lodged gu. attired or, having in his mouth an ivy branch ppr.; Cradock lord of Penycoed; David ap Jenkyn ap Dafydd of Margam, co. Glamorgan; Reade of Green Castle; Sir John Vaughan, of Whitland, co. Carmarthen.

PULESTON, John Henry, Esq., of Ffynogion, Denbighshire.

M.P. for Devonport, elected 1874; J.P.; is a banker in London; eldest son of the late John Puleston, Esq., of Plasnewydd, co. Denbigh, by Mary, dau. of J. Jones, Esq.; *b.* 1830; *ed.* at King's College, London; *m.*, 1857, Margaret, dau. of the late Rev. Edward Lloyd, of Llanfyllin; is proprietor of the estate of Ffynogion, with adjoining lands, in Denbighshire; has issue two daus., Mary Emily, and Alice Bruce.

Residence: Marden Park, Caterham; Ffynogion, Ruthin.

COUNTY FAMILIES OF WALES. 951

Town Address: Carlton Club, S.W.
Arms: Sa., three mullets of five points arg., two and one.
Crest: A stag statant or.
Note.—*Ffynogion* is an old place, once rather famous. The parish church has a chancel window of great beauty, to the memory of Mr. Puleston's father and mother.

RALSTON, William Crawshay, Esq., of Pontywall Hall, Breconshire.

Late Captain 21st Fusiliers; J. P. for Breconshire, and Captain Breconshire Volunteers; son of Gerald Ralston, Esq.; *b.* 1st March, 1840; *ed.* Royal Military College, Sandhurst; *m.*, 29th April, 1871, Henrietta Louise, second dau. of Robert Crawshay, Esq., Cyfarthfa Castle, co. of Glamorgan; has issue 2 sons, Wm. Robert Crawshay and Gerard Crawshay.

Heir: William Robert Crawshay.
Residence: Pont-y-wall Hall, Talgarth, Breconshire.
Town Address: Junior United Service Club, Charles Street, St. James's.
Arms: On a band az. 3 acorns in the seed, or.
Crest: A falcon, ppr. *Supporters:* Dexter, a man in armour; sinister, a horse rampant, both ppr.
Motto: Fide et marte.

LINEAGE.

This family is descended from the Ralstons of that ilk, co. Renfrew. Ralston, (Ralston, co. Renfrew) descended, according to Crawford, from a younger son of Macduff, thane of Fife, named Ralph, who, obtaining some lands in Renfrewshire called Ralphstown, originated the family surname. The Ralstons of that ilk are mentioned in charters so far back as 1272 and 1346, and early in the 15th century John de Ralstoune, or Ralphstown, was Lord High Treasurer and Bishop of Dunkeld.

REES, Rev. William, of Llanboidy, Carmarthenshire.

Vicar of Llanboidy, in *suc.* to the Ven. Archdeacon J. Evans, 1865; formerly Vicar of Bettws, in the same co.; ordained deacon, Feb., 1848; priest, 1850; *b.* Oct., 1823; *m.*, 1859, Charlotte, eldest dau. of the late William Thomas, Esq., of Penrhiwfelen, Llangyfelach, Glam., and has issue 2 sons, William Thomas and John Llewelyn.
Residence: Llanboidy Vicarage, Whitland R. S. O., S. Wales.
Arms: (Those of Rhys ap Cynan) or, a stag passant gu. attired and hoofed sa., in a bordure gu.; for addition, a crescent of the third in the field, for *Hopkin ap David.*
Crest: A stag passant, as in the arms.
Motto: Vim repellam non inferam.

LINEAGE.

Griffith Gethin, Esq., of *Ynys Tawe*, near Swansea, was son of Sir Madoc ap Rhys, Kt., and grand-nephew of the famous Griffith ap Cynan, Prince of North Wales. He *m.* a dau. of Sir Thomas de Avan, and widow of Cynfrig Fychan.
Hopkin ap Griffith Gethin, of Ynys Tawe, Esq., *m.* Maud, dau. of Howel ap Blethyn, of Sanghenydd (Caerphilly).
David ap Hopkin, of Ynys Tawe, Esq., *m.* Eva, dau. of Jenkin ap Leyson, of Avan, Esq.
Hopkin ap David ap Hopkin, of Ynys Tawe, Esq., *m.* Maud, dau. of Morgan David ap Howell, of Defynog, Esq.
David ap Hopkin, of Ynys Tawe, Esq., *m.* Margaret, dau. of Thomas Havard Hir, of Breconshire, Esq.
Hopkin David, of Ynys Tawe, Esq., *m.* Denis, dau. of William John ap Rhys, of Glyn Nedd, and had two sons: the younger, Hopkin, settled in Forest, and commenced the line of Hopkins of Forest.
David ap Hopkin, or Popkin, eldest son of Ynys Tawe, Esq., *m.* Jennet, dau. of Robert William, of Court Rhyd Hir, gent.
John David Popkin, of Ynys Tawe, Esq., *m.* Eva, dau. of Thomas Powell John Goch.
Hopkin John David Popkin, of Ynys Tawe, Esq., *m.* Lucy, dau. of Harry Rees ap Griffith ap Evan Melyn.
David Popkin, of Ynys Tawe, Esq., *m.* Jane, dau. of Thomas ap Morgan, of Cadwgan, gent. (See the genealogy to this point, and further, under *Popkin of Ynystawe, &c.*, p. 584.)
John David Popkin (second son) *m.* a dau. of Evan ab Howel, and left a son,—
Rees John David Popkin, of Maesgwernen, Llangyfelach, who *m.* and had a son,—
John Rees, of Brynbrodorion, Llangyfelach, *m.* Elizabeth Jenkins, of Brynybanal, near Llanon, and had a son—
David Rees, of Cadlé, Llangyfelach, who *m.* Anne, dau. of Thomas Rosser, of Penlanfawr. Their son,—
John Rees, *m.* Jennet, dau. of Llewelyn Davies, of Cadlé, Llangyfelach, and left a dau.,—
Anne Rees, who was *m.* to Matthew Rees, whose son is—
WILLIAM REES, Clerk, now Vicar of Llanboidy, as above.

RICHARDSON, Jeremiah Clarke, Esq., of Derwen Fawr, Glamorganshire.

J. P. for the co. of Glamorgan and for the borough of Swansea, was Mayor of Swansea 1863-4, and for some years Captain and Acting Commander of the 3rd. Glamorgan Rifle Volunteers. Fifth son of John Richardson, Esq., J. P., of Swansea, and brother to John Crow Richardson, Esq., of Pantygwydir, Swansea; *b.* at South Shields, co. Durham, 1822; *ed.* at Myrtle Hall School, Gloucestershire; *m.*, first, Margaret, dau. of Thos. Walters, Esq., of Picton House, Swansea, (who *d.* March 28, 1856,) and had issue 1 son and 2 daughters,—Arthur Henry, *b.* 31st Dec., 1854; Mary Clarke, *b.* 2nd Feb., 1850, *m.* G. Pearce Serocold, Esq., of Rodborough Lodge, Stroud, Gloucestershire; Jessie Margaret, *b.* 6th March, 1853; *m.*, secondly, Sophia Laugharn, second dau. and co-heiress of John Lucas Popkin, Esq. Her sister *m.* Charles Bath, Esq., Fynone House, Swansea (see p. 621). Has issue by second *m.*, Emily Livia, *b.* 1861; Frederick Lucas Popkin, *b.* 1864; Esther Sophia Clarke, *b.* 1866; Margaretta Clare, *b.* 1867; John Laugharn, *b.* 1872.

Residence: Derwen Fawr, near Swansea.
Arms: Sa. on a chief arg., three lions' heads erased ermines, langued gu.
Crest: On a mural crown or, a lion's head erased of the arms.
Motto: Pretio prudentia præstat.

ST. DAVID'S, The Right Rev. William Basil Jones, D.D., Bishop of.

Formerly Michel Fellow of Queen's, and Fellow and Tutor of University College, Oxford; Archdeacon of York (1867-74); Chancellor and Canon Residentiary of York Cathedral (1873-4); Prebendary of St. David's (1859-65); Examining Chaplain to the Archbishop of York (1861-74); a magistrate for Cardiganshire. For Dr. Jones's various publications see first edition, under the head "Jones of Gwynfryn." Son of William Tilsley Jones, Esq., of Gwynfryn; *b.* at Cheltenham, 1822; *ed.* at Shrewsbury School, and Trin. Coll., Oxford; Ireland University Scholar, 1842; *grad.* B.A. (2nd Class Lit. Hum.) 1844, M.A. 1847, D.D. 1874; *m.* Frances Charlotte, dau. of Rev. Samuel Holworthy, M.A., Vicar of Croxall, Derbyshire; *s.* to his father, 1861; *pat.* of all the dignities in St. David's Cathedral, and 132 livings, in right of the see.

Heir pres.: Everard Whiting Jones, Esq. (his brother).
Residences: Abergwili Palace, Carmarthen; Gwynfryn, Aberystwyth.
Town Address: Athenæum Club.
Arms of the See: Sa. on a cross or, five cinquefoils of the field.
Arms of the Family: Arg., a cross fleury sa. between 4 Cornish choughs ppr.

Note.—For the lineage of this family, see p. 199.

TENNANT, Charles Coombe, Esq., of Cadoxton Lodge, Glamorganshire.

Only son of the late Charles Tennant, Esq. (who *d* 1873), of Cadoxton Lodge, Neath, Glamorganshire, and of Gertrude, dau. of the late Admiral Collier; *b.* in London, 30th July, 1852; *ed.* at Harrow, and is now, (1875) at Balliol College, Oxford.

Heirs Pres.: His sisters.
Residence: Cadoxton Lodge, near Neath.

Town Address: 2, Richmond Terrace, Whitehall, S.W.
Arms: Ermine, on two bars sa., three bezants, two and one.
Crest: A winged heart gu., pierced with a dagger ppr. hilted or.
Motto: Tenax et fidelis.

Note.—The ruins of Neath Abbey are on the banks of the Tennant Canal.

THOMAS, Rev. Owen Davies, of Pengwern House, Glamorganshire.

Vicar of Llangorse, Breconshire; B.D. of St. David's College, Lampeter, 1873; formerly Phillips and Simonburn Scholar, Llandovery and Lampeter, 1853—1858; author of "Justice to Wales," "A University for Wales," 1863; son of William Thomas, Esq., Clase, Morriston, Swansea; *b.* at Clase, near Swansea, May 1st, 1834; *ed.* at Llandovery, under Archdeacon Williams, and at Swansea Grammar Schools; *grad.* at Lampeter College, June, 1873, B.D.; is *unm.*; *s.* his father at Llangyfelach, Swansea, 1856-9.

Residence: Pengwern House, Morriston, Glamorganshire.
Town Address: 129, Tufnell Park Road, N.
Arms: Or, a stag passant gu., attired and hoofed sa., in a bordure of the second; for addition a crescent of the third in the field, for *Hopkin ap David.*
Crest: A stag, as in the arms.
Motto: Vim repellam, non inferam.

LINEAGE.

For the preceding parts of this descent, which traces ultimately on the paternal side, through the Popkins of Forest, from Gruffydd ap Cynan, Prince of North Wales, a descendant of *Rhodri Mawr*) see "Lineage," under "Thomas of Lan," Glam., and "Rev. W. Rees of Llanboidy," Carm. Maternally this family derives from the Penrys of Breconshire, of which John Penry, "the martyr," was the most distinguished member. The Rev. O. D. Thomas's mother is gr.-granddau. of Mary Penry, wife of the Rev. Lewis Rees, and mother by him of Dr. Abraham Rees, editor of the well-known *Cyclopædia.*

John Matthew Thomas, maternally a grandson of Hopkin Popkin, Esq., of Forest, left a dau. Mary, who by her husband, William Thomas of Penrhiwfelen, Glam., had a son,—

John Thomas, who *m.* Charlotte, dau. of Wm. Evans, Llangyfelach; their son, William Thomas, *m.* Mary, dau. of David Jenkins, of Swansea, and had issue—

OWEN DAVIES THOMAS, Clerk, as above; also Charlotte, *m.* to Rev. W. Rees, Vicar of Llanboidy; Anne, *m.* to Rev. M. Hughes, Vicar of Bettws; Esther, *m.* to Rev. D. Davies, of Warboys; William, now of Pengwern House, near Swansea; John, now of Penrhiwfelen, and Elizabeth Frances, *m.* to Wm. Ling, Esq. (surgeon), of Brightlingsea.

THOMAS, William, Esq., of Lan House, Glamorganshire.

Some time Capt. 4th Glamorgan Volunteers; son of William Thomas, Esq., Lan, near Swansea, Glam. ; *b.* at Lan, January 23rd, 1816 ; *m.*, April 2nd, 1853, Jane, only dau. of Evan Williams, Esq., of Bronygader, Dolgelley.

Residence: Lan House, near Swansea.
Arms: Or, a stag passant gu., attired and hoofed sa., in a bordure of the second ; for addition, a crescent of the third in the field, for *Hopkin ap David.*
Crest: A stag, as in the arms.
Motto: Vim repellam, non inferam.

LINEAGE.

For the earlier part of the pedigree of this family see "*Lineage,*" under "Rev. William Rees of Llanboidy, Carm." The present family separates as a junior branch with Hopkin, 2nd son of Hopkin David, Esq., of Ynystawe, commencing the *Forest* line. Hopkin ap Hopkin David, of *Forest, m.* Jane, dau. of William Godwyn of Llantwit, near Neath, and had a son,—
David ap Hopkin, of *Forest,* who *m.* Catherine, dau. of Roger Jenkin, of Swansea, and had a son,—
John David Popkin, of Forest, who *m.* Catherine, dau. of Thomas ap Thomas ap Jenkin, of Veinwyllt, leaving a son,—
Hopkin Popkin, of Forest, who *m.* Catherine dau. of George Lewis, of Llystalybont, and besides a son, had a dau.,—
Mary Popkin, of Gwernfadog, Llangyfelach, who *m.* Matthew Thomas, and had with other issue a son,—
John Matthew Thomas, of Llanllianwen, who by his wife Rachel left a dau.,—
Mary Thomas, who *m.* William Thomas, of Penrhiwfelen, and had two sons, William and Thomas ; their son,—
William Thomas *m.* Mary, dau. of —Edwards, of Montgomeryshire, and left with other issue a son,—
William Thomas, Esq., now of Lan House, as above.

TRIPP, Rev. Henry, M.A., Winford Rectory, Somerset.

Rector of Winford, near Bristol, late Fellow of Worcester College, Oxford ; author of "Selections from Percy's Reliques," (Bell and Daldy, London) ; son of Rev. C. Tripp, D.D., Rector of Silverton, Devon ; *b.* April 6th, 1815, at Boneleigh, Devon ; *ed.* at Winchester College and Oxford ; *grad.* B.A. 1839, M.A. 1841 ; *m.* Annie, daughter of Rev. James Gould, M.A., of Luccombe, Somerset ; *succ.* to estates 1865. Mr. Tripp, owing to his descent on the female side from the Owens of Orielton, in 1853 laid claim to the extinct baronetcy. See *Petition* at end of pedigree. Patron of Sampford Brett, near Taunton ; has issue twelve children.

Heir : Owen Howard Tripp, *b.* in 1862.
Residence : Winford Rectory, near Bristol.
Arms : Gu., a scaling-ladder in bend between 6 cross crosslets fitchés, three and three, all or.
Crest : Upon a steel helmet, an eagle close ppr.
Motto : "Tripp."

LINEAGE.

This family derives, on the male side, from Lord Howard's fifth son, in the reign of Henry V. The arms now borne by the family were given by King Henry V. to the fifth son of the Lord Howard, after the storming of Boulogne. The king being there, asked, "how they took ye town and castle?" Howard answered, 'I tripped up ye walls.' Saith his Majesty, 'Tripp shall be thy name, and no longer Howard, and honored him with ye scaling-ladder for his Bend."—(From the old escutcheon.)

The descent on the female side is from the Owens of Orielton and Bodowen, the Rev. Charles Tripp, D.D., father of the above Rev. Henry Tripp, having married Frances Owen, daughter of Brigadier-General Owen, and last representative of the Owens of Orielton, as seen from the following Owen pedigree. From—

Hwva ap Cynddelw (A.D. 1137-69), founder of the first of the fifteen noble tribes of North Wales, and seated at Llys Llivon, and Presaddfed, Anglesey, through his descendants in direct line, and in the tenth degree, came—

Llewelyn ap Hwlcyn, whose son Meyrick (Meurig) ap Llewelyn had a son—
Owen ap Meyrick, who *m.* Ellen, dau. of Robert ap Meredith of Glynllivon, Carn., and had a son and heir—
Hugh ap Owen, who by Gwen, dau. of Morris ap John, left a son—
Owen up Hugh of Bodeon, Sheriff of Anglesey, 1580 (see *Sheriffs,* Anglesey), whose wife was Isabel, dau. of Sir William Griffith. Their son—
Sir Hugh Owen, Kt., barrister-at-law, of Bodowen, Anglesey, and, *jure uxoris,* of Orielton, Pembrokeshire, was Sheriff of Pembrokeshire 1583. He *m.* Elizabeth, dau. of George Wirriott, Esq., of Orielton, (see *Sheriffs,* Pemb., 1577), by whom (he *m.* 2ndly Lucy, dau. of Henry, 9th Earl of Northumberland) he had, with other issue, an eldest son and successor (the second son, William, succeeding to Bodowen)—
John Owen, Esq., of Orielton, who *m.* Dorothy, dau. of John Laugharne, Esq., of St. Bride's, co. Pemb.; by Lettice, dau. of Sir John Perrot, Kt. of Haroldston, M.P. for co. Pemb. 1563, and dying before 1636, was succ. by his eldest son—
Sir Hugh Owen of Orielton, cr. a baronet 11th August, 1641, M.P. for Pembroke 1625—1640 (see p. 888), *d.* 1670. He *m.* first Frances, dau. of Sir John Philipps, of Picton Castle, Pemb. (and had no surviving issue) ; secondly, Katherine, dau. of Evan Lloyd, Esq., of Yale, co. Denbigh, by whom he had, with other issue,—
Sir Hugh Owen, 2nd Bart, of Orielton, M.P. for co. Pemb. in four Parliaments. By his first wife, Anne, dau. and *h.* of Henry Owen, Esq., of Bodowen (by which mar. the estates were reunited), besides other children, he had an eldest son,—
Sir Arthur Owen, 3rd Bart. of Orielton and Bodowen, M.P. in several Parliaments, for Pembroke, and Lord Lieut. of the co., *d.* 1753. He *m.* Emma, dau. of Sir William Williams, Bart., son of the celebrated Sir William Williams, Kt. and Bart., called "Speaker Williams." His eldest son and successor Sir William Owen, 4th Bart., was succ. at Orielton and Bodowen by his eldest son, Sir Hugh Owen, 5th Bart., who (by his wife Ann, dau. of John Colby, Esq., of Bletherston) had a son and successor Sir Hugh Owen, 6th Bart. of Orielton and Bodowen, M.P. for Pembroke 1809, and *d.* in the same year *unm.* Hereupon, 1809, the title devolved upon his kinsman and next heir, Arthur Owen, as 7th Bart., Adjutant-General in the East Indies, *d . unm* 1817. He was son of—

John Owen, Esq., Col. and Lieut.-General 59th Foot (second son of Sir Arthur, 3rd Bart. aforesaid), who by his wife Anne, only dau. of his uncle, Charles Owen, Esq., of Nash, co. Pemb., had a large family, most of whom or their issue dying s. p., the representation devolved upon William Owen, third son (of whom hereafter), and Corbetta, second and younger dau., who m. Joseph Lord, Esq., of Pembroke, succ. to estates under the will of the 6th Bart, Sir Hugh Owen aforesaid, and left, with numerous other issue, a son, John Lord, Esq., barrister-at-law, who in 1809 assumed the name of Owen, became M.P. for Pembroke 1809, and for the co. 1812, was cr. a baronet 1813, and is succeeded in the title as second Bart. of the new creation by his son Sir Hugh Hugh Owen. Sir Arthur's third son,

William Owen aforesaid, Brigadier-General in the army (d. at Martinique, 1795), m. Anne, dau. of Rev. John Tripp,,D.D.,Rector of Spofforth,co.York, and had, with two daus., Emma and Frances, only one son, (sustaining the direct male line of Orielton),—

Sir William Owen, 8th Bart., barrister-at-law, of the Inner Temple, b. 1775, succ. to the baronetcy Jan., 1817, afterwards, 1844, assumed the additional surname Barlow on succeeding to the Lawrenny Estate, co. Pembroke (inherited from his great aunt Elizabeth, who m. Hugh Barlow, Esq., of Lawrenny), and d. unm. at Fig Tree Court, Temple, 25th Feb., 1851. With him the title of baronet, conferred on his ancestor Sir Hugh Owen in 1641, became extinct and the representation devolved upon his sisters above-named. The elder, Emma. m. Thomas Jones, Esq., of Esgair Evan Machynlleth, but has no issue. The younger,—

Frances Owen, m. 15th June 1814, her first cousin, the Rev. Charles Tripp, D.D., and had issue,—

HENRY TRIPP, clerk, eldest son, as above.

Frances, b. 22nd Oct., 1817 ; d. 25th Feb., 1818.

Frances Anne, b. 31st May, 1819 ; m., 8th Dec., 1850, Rev. I. H. Wise, of Hankerton, Wilts, and has issue.

John, in holy orders, b. 20th July, 1821.

Eliza, b. 14th March, 1823; m., 27th Aug., 1846, Capt. C. T. Bentley, 17th Highlanders, and has issue.

Charles, b. 30th April, 1825 ; d. 8th Aug., 1825.

Charles George, barrister-at-law, of Lincoln's Inn, now of Geraldine, Canterbury, New Zealand ; b. 1st July, 1826.

William Owen, clerk, b. 13th May, 1828.

Arthur Sampford, b. 1st Jan., 1831.

Howard, . 18th Aug., 1832.

PETITION FOR THE BARONETCY.

To the Queen's Most Excellent Majesty.

THE PETITION of HENRY TRIPP, M.A,, Clerk, Fellow of Worcester College, in the University of Oxford, eldest son and heir-apparent of Charles Tripp, D.D., Rector of Silverton, in the county of Devon, a Justice of the Peace for the counties of Devon and Somerset, by Frances Owen, his wife, sister and co-heir of Sir William Owen Barlow, Baronet, deceased.

HUMBLY SHEWETH,—That on the 11th August, A.D. 1641, a Patent of Baronetcy was conferred by your Majesty's royal predecessor, King Charles I., on Sir Hugh Owen, Knt., of Orielton, in the county of Pembroke, M.P., the representative of a very eminent and distinguished Welsh family, descended from Hwfa ap Kynthel, founder of the first noble tribe of North Wales, with limitation to the heirs male of the body of the grantee.

That the said Sir Hugh Owen, first Baronet of Orielton, was succeeded by his grandson, Sir Hugh Owen, second Baronet of Orielton, member in four parliaments for his native county of Pembroke, whose son and successor was Sir Arthur Owen, third Baronet of Orielton and Badowen.

That the said Sir Arthur Owen, third Baronet of Orielton, who served in several parliaments for the town and county of Pembroke, and was Lord Lieutenant and Custos Rotulorum, was enabled on one occasion to render signal service to the Royal House of Hanover, in the reign of your Majesty's predecessor Queen Anne, when, on a motion having been brought forward in the Commons House of Parliament for altering the succession from the Elector of Hanover to the son of King James II., he hastened to the House, and was fortunate enough, by his single vote, to equalize the numbers, which Sir Arthur's friend, Mr. Rice, M.P. for Carmarthenshire, who followed his example, increased to a majority.

That, for this important service, your Majesty's royal predecessor King George I. is stated to have proffered to the said Sir Arthur Owen the grant of an earldom.

That the said Sir Arthur Owen married Emma, daughter of the famous Sir William Williams, Bart., Speaker of the House of Commons, and Solicitor General at the period of the trial of the Seven Bishops, and by her had three sons,—William, his successor ; John, ancestor of your Majesty's petitioner ; and Arthur.

That the eldest of these sons, Sir William Owen, fourth Baronet of Orielton, was also member in several parliaments for the town and county of Pembroke, as well as Lord Lieutenant and Custos Rotulorum of the said county.

That the said Sir William Owen's son and successor, Sir Hugh Owen of Orielton, fifth Baronet, M.P., Lord Lieutenant and Custos Rotulorum of Pembrokeshire, died in the year 1786, and was succeeded by his only son, Sir Hugh Owen, sixth Baronet of Orielton, M.P. for Pembroke, who died unmarried 8th August, 1809.

That upon the decease of the said Sir Hugh Owen, sixth Baronet, unmarried, the title devolved on his kinsman and next heir, Arthur Owen, Esq., Adjutant-General in the East Indies, who likewise died unmarried 4th January, 1817, whereupon the baronetcy passed to his nephew, Sir William Owen, as eighth Baronet.

That the said Sir William Owen, eighth Baronet (who afterwards assumed the additional surname of Barlow on inheriting the Lawrenny estate), was Attorney-General for the Carmarthen Circuit, and a Bencher of the Middle Temple, died unmarried 25th February, 1851, when the title of Baronet, conferred on his ancestor, Sir Hugh Owen, in 1641, became extinct and the representation of the ancient, influential, and historic family of Owen of Orielton devolved on his sisters and co-heirs, Emma Anne, the wife of Thomas Jones, Esq., of Esgair Evan, and Frances, the wife of the Rev. Charles Tripp, D.D., Rector of Silverton, co. Devon.

That of these ladies, the elder, Emma Anne, has no issue ; and the younger, Frances, is mother of the Rev. Henry Tripp, your Majesty's petitioner.

That, for centuries, no family in the county of Pembroke held a more elevated position than that of Owen of Orielton ; distinguished alike for its extensive landed possessions, the great public services of its various members, the high official appointments held by them generation after generation, and the ancient and eminent families with which they formed alliances.

That of this distinguished race your Majesty's petitioner is the present heir, and is also the descendant paternally of the old and respectable Somersetshire family of Tripp, which traditionally deduces its origin from a scion of the illustrious house of Norfolk, whose arms they bear, in addition to the scaling-ladder which was substituted for their bend by Henry V., when their name was changed from Howard to Tripp, for the gallant services of their ancestor.

That of the family of Tripp it may be mentioned that your Majesty's petitioner's grandfather, the Rev. John Tripp, was Rector of Spofforth, Yorkshire, the intimate friend of George O'Brien, Earl of Egremont, whose friendship and regard he retained till the day of his death; and that the father of this Dr. Tripp was barrister-at-law, and Deputy Recorder of Taunton, under Charles, Earl of Egremont, us well as a magistrate in four western counties.

That in many similar instances, baronetcies, extinct in the male line, have been revived by the gracious favour of the Crown in favour of the next heirs, by female descent.

That, in confirmation of this statement, it will suffice to cite the recent re-creations of Pakington in the person of the Right Honourable Sir John Pakington, one of your Majesty's late Secretaries of State; of Mill, in the person of the Rev. Sir John Barker Mill, of Mottisfont, Hants; and of Douglas, in the person of the late General Sir Kenneth Mackenzie, of Glenbervie.

Wherefore your Majesty's petitioner humbly prays that your Majesty, taking into your gracious consideration the great eminence, antiquity, and public services of your petitioner's ancestors, the Owens of Orielton, and the many similar cases in which a like favour has been granted, will be graciously pleased to confer on your Majesty's petitioner, in consideration of his being the heir in blood of the ancient Baronets of Orielton, the style, title, and dignity of a Baronet of the United Kingdom of Great Britain and Ireland, with remainder to the heirs male of his body lawfully begotten.

And your Majesty's petitioner will ever pray.

HENRY TRIPP.

VAUGHAN, John Williams, Esq., of Velin-newydd, Brecknockshire.

J. P. and D. L. of the two counties of Brecknock and Radnor; High Sheriff for the former co. 1855; eldest son of the late Samuel Jones, Esq., by Jane, younger dau. of the late William Vaughan, Esq., of Penymaes, Llanvillo, and granddau. of the late William Gwynne, Esq., of Cynghordy, co. of Carmarthen; *b.* Dec., 1810; *m.* 1845, Elizabeth Fortune Mary, only child and *h.* of the late John Williams, Esq., of Skreen, co. of Radnor, and of Vilinnewydd, co. of Brecon (see second *Genealogy* below); assumed by royal licence in 1846 the arms and name of Vaughan in compliance with the will of his uncle, the late William Gwynne Vaughan, Esq., whom he succeeded in the Llanvillo property, and subsequently the additional name Williams; has issue one son, John Williams.

Heir: His son John Williams Vaughan, *b.* 1853; ed. at St. John's Coll., Cambridge; J. P. of the co. of Brecknock.

Residences: Velin-newydd House, near Brecon; Skreen, Radnorshire.

Arms: Quarterly: 1st, sa., a chevron arg. inter 3 boys' heads couped at the shoulders 2 and 1, ppr., around the neck of each a snake vert— *Vaughan*; 2nd, sa., a chevron inter 3 fleurs-de-lis 2 and 1, all or—*Hughes of Glasbury*; 3rd sa. a lion passant or—*Smith of Peterchurch*; 4th gu. a stag passant guardant arg. collared and chained or—*Williams*.

Crests: 1. A boy's head couped at the shoulders, as in the arms; 2. A stag's head couped, collared as in the arms.

Mottoes: Innocentes sicut pueri, sagaces sicut serpentes. Asgre lân diogel ei pherchen.

LINEAGE.

The genealogy of this ancient family in both lines of descent is now for the first time completely constructed from materials which exist in abundance but which hitherto had received a too careless handling. The descent is British, and is clearly traceable to the age of the conquest of Brecknock, (Garthmadryn) by the Normans under Bernard Newmarch, A.D. 1091. The sept is that of *Vaughan of Tretower* (see p. 94,).

Maenarch, prince of Brecknock (11th cent.) had, besides other issue, two sons, the eldest, Bleddyn, who *s.* him in the princedom, and succumbed to the Norman invader, and a second, *Drympenog*, lord of Cantref Selyf.

Drympenog ap Maenarch *m.* Gwenllian, dau. of Jestyn ap Gwrgant, prince of Glamorgan, whose power was usurped by the Norman, Robert Fitzhamon, and left a son,—

Moreiddig (surnamed Warwyn), born, as fabled, with a snake round his neck, and hence the arms adopted by his descendants,—sa., 3 boys' heads, full faced, couped at the shoulders, arg. their perukes, or. with a snake about their necks, ppr." He *m.* Elinor dau. of the Lord Rhys (see p. 148), and was *s.* by his son,—

Llewelyn, lord of Cantref Selyf, *m.* Joan. dau. of Cynhyllyn ap Rhys Goch, lord of Ystrad-wy. His son,—

Sissyllt, lord of Cantref Selyf, *m.* Lleuci (Lucy—sometimes named Lydia), dau. of Griffith ap Madoc ap Cadrod Einion, lord of St. Kenyth (otherwise, as afterwards called, *Senghenydd*, or Caerphili, co. Glam.), and was *s.* by his son,—

Howel, lord of Cantref Selyf, who *m.* Gwladys, dau. of Morgan Vychan lord of Avon, or Avan, in Glamorgan. His son—

Einion (or Yevan) *m.* Jennet, dau. of (Ievan ap) Rhys Grug, of Cwmdu, or Trertwr, ap Rhys ap Gruffydd, prince of South Wales, and left a son,—

Roger (otherwise Rosser) Fawr, of Llechryd, lord of Cantref Selyf, who by his wife, Joice, dau. of Sir William Walbeoffe of Llanhamlach (see p. 87), had a son, named—

Roger Fychan, and at times Roger Ivange, *i.e.* Roger, jun. lord of Cantref Selyf, who *m.* a dau. and sole heir of Sir Ralph Baskerville, Knight, of Llechryd. His son—

Gwallter, surnamed Sais, *m.* Florence, dau. of Sir Walter Bredwardine, and left a son,—

Roger *Hên*' or senior, of Bredwardine, who by his wife Margaret, dau. of Sir Walter Devereux, Lord Ferrers of Chartley, had a son called—

Sir Roger *Fychan*, or "jun," (the original of *Vaughan*), of Bredwardine and Trertwr (Tretower) who *m*. Gwladys dau. of Sir David Gam, Kt. He as well as his father-in-law was knighted and slain at Agincourt in 1415 (see pp. 91, 95). The next step in the descent is not through a natural son, Lewis Vaughan of Merthyr Tydfil, as represented by Jones (*Hist. Breck.*), but (Harl. MSS. Brit. Mus. No. 2289) through the eldest son—
Sir Roger Vaughan, Kt., of Tretower. Here the surname *Vaughan* becomes established. He *m*. Denis, dau. of Thomas Philip Vaughan, Esq., of Tyle-glas, beheaded at Chepstow, by order of Jasper, Earl of Pembroke, 1471, and leaving a son.—
Sir Thomas Vaughan of Tretower, Kt., beheaded by Richard III. for his good services to young King Edward V. His wife was Cecily, dau. of Morgan Jenkin Philip of Pencoed, Esq. (he *m*. secondly Jane, Lady Ferrers), by whom he left a son,—
Roger Vaughan, Esq., of Talgarth, who *m*. Jane, dau. of Sir Robert Whitney, Kt. of Whitney. His son,—
Matthew Vaughan, Esq., of Trephilip, *m*. Joan, dau. of Gwilym Fychan (Vaughan), of Peytyn Gwyn (Harl. MSS. *Ibid.*), and had a son,—
Roger Vaughan, Esq., of Merthyr-*Cynog*, who *m*. Margaret, dau. of Roger Thomas Hir ap Gwilym, of Eglwys Jeuan, or the Gaer, in Aberhonddu (*Ibid.*). His son,—
Watkin Vaughan, Esq., of Merthyr-Cynog, *m*. Margaret, a dau. of Thomas Powel Watkin, of Ponfaen, by whom he left, with other issue, a son,—
Roger Vaughan, Esq., who *m*. Sibyl, dau. of John Games, Esq., of Aberbrân, and had an eldest son,—
Watkin Vaughan, Esq., of Merthyr-Cynog, whose wife was Catherine, dau. of William Parry, of Trebarried (living 1625). A younger son,—
Thomas Vaughan, Esq., of Peytyn Glas (Harl. MSS., *ibid.*), and not the eldest son Roger, as in some MSS. (whose line is ext.), was father of—
William Vaughan, Esq., the first of Llanvillo, who by his wife Ann had a son,—
Walter Vaughan, Esq., who *m*. Elizabeth Hutchins, and had a son,—
William Vaughan, Esq., of Penymaes, the second of Llanvillo, who *m*. Hester, dau. and heir of William Gwynne, Esq., of Cynghordy, co. of Carmarthen, and had with other issue—
Jane Vaughan, who *m*. Samuel Jones, Esq., of Llanvillo, and had two sons, Henry the younger (see Gwynne-Vaughan of Cynghordy), and John the elder, now—
JOHN WILLIAMS VAUGHAN, Esq., of Velinnewydd and Skreen, as above.

The Genealogy of Williams of Skreen.

It is seen above that Mr. Williams Vaughan *m*. Elizabeth Fortune Williams Mary, of Skreen, who traced ultimately to a Norman ancestor, in the person of Sir Richard Bois, one of the assistants of Newmarch in the conquest of Brecknock. Of the descendants of Bois for several generations the mere names only are given in the pedigrees. The sixth in descent was—
John Bois, Esq., of Trebois, who bore a coat—"gu. a stag standing at gaze arg., attired unguled and gorged, with a collar and chain affixed reflexing over back or." He had a son Richard, and he a son Griffith, whose son—
John Bois married and left as next and successor,—
Richard Bois, Esq., of Llandevalle, whose wife was a dau. of John Vaughan, and who was *s*. by his son,—

Jenkin Bois, Esq., who *m*. Alice, dau. of David Jenkin *Hir* (the tall),—
William Bois, Esq., his son, *m*. a dau. of Roger Vaughan, Esq., of Trebarried, and had a son,—
Jenkin Bois, Esq., who *m*. a dau. of Gwilym Goch (William the "Red"), of Pantygored. His son—
William Bois, otherwise William ap Jenkin (here the surname *Bois* disappears), *m*. Joan, dau. of Jenkin Thomas of Velinnewydd, co. of Brecon, and had, besides a younger son John (of whom hereafter), an elder son,—
William ap William, or *Williams* (here the surname becomes settled), who *m*. a dau. of John Beavan of Gwenddwr (*d*. 1720), and had, besides a son Jenkin, who *m*., but *d. s. p.* 1754, a dau. *Gwenllian.*
John Williams, the younger son above mentioned, was of Skreen, or "Ynys-gryn," co. Radnor. He *m*. his cousin, Gwenllian Williams, just named, of Velinnewydd, who on the demise *s. p.* of her brother, Jenkin Williams (1754), became sole *h*. of the Skreen property as well as of that of Velinnewydd. Besides two daus.—Anne, who *m*. Howel Harris of Trevecca, and Fortune, who *m*. Samuel Beavan of Ty'nycwm—they left a son, an eldest child,—
Thomas Williams, of Velinnewydd, who *m*. a dau. of — Smith of Peterchurch, and besides Jenkin, who *m*. Elizabeth, dau. of Samuel Beavan of Tynycwm, and Bridget, who *m*. Marmaduke Gwynne, Esq., of Llanelwedd, had an elder son,—
Thomas Williams, Esq., of Velinnewydd, *m*. Elizabeth, dau. of Thomas Hughes, Esq., of Glasbury; and his elder son Thomas, dying *s. p.* in 1803, was *s*. by his younger son,—
John Williams, Esq., of Skreen, who by his wife Elizabeth, dau. of the late Thomas Williams, Esq., of Cwm, co. of Radnor, had a dau. and *h*.,—
Elizabeth Fortune Mary, who *m*. John Jones, Esq., now *John Williams-Vaughan, Esq.*, of Velinnewydd and Skreen, as above.

WILKINSON, Sir Gardner, of Brynfield House, Glamorganshire.

Knighted 1839; D.C.L.; F.R.S.; F.R.G.S.; F.R.S.L.; and is cor. member of the Imperial Academy of Vienna; cor. member of the Royal Society of Sciences, Turin; hon. member American Oriental Society; hon. member American Ethnological Society; hon. member Oriental Society of Paris; hon. member Egyptian Society, Cairo; hon. member of Egyptian Association, Cairo; hon. member of the Bombay branch of the Royal Asiatic Society; ordinary member of the Instituto di Cor. Archeologia di Roma; hon. member of the "Institute Egyptien," Alexandria; hon. member of the Oxford Architectural Society; hon. member R. I. Brit. Architects; Vice-President of the British Architectural Association; V.P. of the Cambrian Archæological Association; V.P. of the Lincoln Architectural Society; author of "Materia Hieroglyphica," 1827-8; "Extracts from some Hieroglyphical Subjects," 1830: (both these works were executed in lithography by himself, printed off by his Arab groom, and consecutively published at Malta in the year above mentioned); " Topography of Thebes," 1835; "Manners and Customs of the Ancient Egyptians," 1837; second series of the same, 1841; "Modern Egypt and Thebes," 1843; "Dalmatia and Montenegro," 1848; "Architecture of Ancient Egypt" (folio), 1850; "Turin Papyrus of Kings" (folio), 1851; "Popular Account of the Ancient Egyptians," 1854; "Egypt in the Time of the Pharaohs," 1857; "Handbook of Egypt," 1858; "Colour, and the Necessity of a General Diffusion of Taste among all Classes," 1858; together with a very large number of papers published by different societies; has also published out of the large mass of maps and plans made by him a small map of the Fyoom, and his large "Topography of Thebes" in six sheets. Sir Gardner Wilkinson is son of the Rev. John Wilkinson, of Hardendale, co. Westmoreland, by Mary Anne his wife, dau. of the Rev. Richard Gardner, and great-granddau. of Sir Salathiel Lovell, of Tichmarsh, co. Northampton; *b.* at Missenden, co. Berks, Oct. 1797; *ed.* at Harrow School and Exeter Coll., Oxford; *m.*, Oct., 1856, Caroline Catherine, eldest dau. of Henry Lucas, Esq., of Uplands and Cheriton, co. Glamorgan, by his first wife, Caroline, dau. and co-h. of Ponsonby Tottenham, sometime M.P. for Fethard and New Ross, Esq.; *s.* his father in the Hardendale Estate, co. Westmoreland, 1810, but subsequently sold it during his long residence abroad.

Residence: Brynfield House, Reynoldston, Glamorgan.
Town Address: Athenæum Club, Pall Mall, S.W.
Arms: Az., a chevron between three whelk shells or; impaling arg. a fesse between six annulets gu, for *Lucas*.
Motto: Pro patria.

WILLIAMS, The Rev. Herbert, of Brecknock.

M.A.; Curate of Steynton, Pembrokeshire, 1860—1862; Vicar of Brecon, 1864; Member of Board of Guardians and School Board; Surrogate, Brecon; son of the Very Rev. Thomas Williams, M.A., Dean of Llandaff, by his wife Elizabeth, dau. of Archdeacon Davies, of Brecon; *b.* at Llanvapley Parsonage, Mon., Feb. 15, 1836; *ed.* at Sherborne School, Dorsetshire, and Oriel College, Oxford; *grad.* M.A. 1862; *m.*, 1868, Catherine Frances, dau. of the late Col. Dickinson, of Glanhonddu, Brecon, and Col. of Brecon Militia; has issue 1 son and 3 daughters.

Heir: Douglas Herbert, *b.* Jan. 10, 1870.
Residence: Brecon.
Crest: A bull's head (as Williams of Abercamlais).
Motto: Fide et amore.

Note.—Mr. Williams derives from the well-known stock of Aberbran, Penpont, and Abercamlais.

WINWOOD, Thomas Henry Ricketts, Esq., of Tyglyn Ayron, Cardiganshire.

J. P. for the county of Cardigan, and Lieutenant in the Royal Cardiganshire Rifles; son of the late Thomas Henry Winwood, Esq. (*d.* 1857), J. P., High Sheriff in 1857, by his wife, Phœbe Ann Henderson, dau. of James Henderson, Esq., M.D.; *b.* at Tyglyn Ayron, 14th September, 1852; *ed.* at Winchester College and Exeter College, Oxford; is *unm.*

Residence: Tyglyn Ayron, Ciliau Ayron, Cardiganshire.
Town Address: 26, Leinster Square, Hyde Park, W.
Arms: Per pale, arg. and gu., on the dexter a cross patoncé sa., on sinister a lion rampant between three roses, two and one of the last.
Crest: From a crescent on its back, a cross patoncé, as in the arms.
Motto: Merere et confide.

LINEAGE.

This family derives its descent from Sir Ralph Winwood, Kt., Secretary of State and Ambassador to the court of Holland *temp.* Elizabeth and James I.

YORKE, Simon, Esq., of Erddig Park, Denbighshire.

J. P. and D. L. for the co. of Denbigh; High Sheriff 1848; son of the late Simon Yorke, Esq., J. P. and D. L. of the same place; *b.* 6th April, 1811, at Erddig; *s.* 1833; *m.*, August 6th, 1846, Victoria Mary Louisa, dau. of General the Hon. Sir Edward Cust, K.C.H., youngest son of Lord Brownlow, and has issue two sons and two daus.

Heir: His eldest son, Philip, *b.* 1849.
Residence: Erddig Park, Wrexham.
Arms: Argent, on a saltire az. a bezant or, with a crescent for difference.
Crest: A lion's head, erased, proper, collared gu., thereon a bezant or.
Motto: Nec cupias, nec metuas.

LINEAGE.

The Yorkes have long resided at Erddig, and trace their descent from the Yorkes of Dover, of whom Philip, Earl of Hardwicke, in the Peerage of England, appointed Lord Chancellor of England in 1736, created Earl of Hardwicke 1754, represented the elder branch. Amongst the distinguished members of the Erddig house may be mentioned —

Philip Yorke, Esq., author of *The Royal Tribes of Wales*, published in 1799, which has now become very rare.

Simon Yorke, Esq., of Erddig (uncle of the distinguished Lord Chancellor Hardwicke), *m*. Anne, sister and *h*. of John Miller, Esq., Master in Chancery, of Erddig, who purchased that place, and enlarged the mansion in 1713, *d. s. p.* 1733, leaving his estate of Erddig to his sister's son, Simon.

Simon Yorke, Esq., of Erddig, *m*. Dorothea, dau. of M. Hutton, Esq., of Newnham, Herts, and *d*. 1768, leaving his property to his only son Philip.

Philip Yorke, Esq., of Erddig, author of *The Royal Tribes of Wales*, *m*., 1770, Elizabeth, dau. of the Right Hon. Sir John Cust, Bart., Speaker of the House of Commons, and had by her a son, Simon, as below. He *m*., secondly, Diana, dau. and *h*. of Peirce Wynne, Esq. (see *Yorke of Dyffryn Aled*). He *d*. 1804, and was succ. by his eldest son,—

Simon Yorke, Esq.,'of Erddig, *b*. 1771 ; *m*., 1807, Margaret, dau. of John Holland, Esq., and dying 1834, was succ. by his son,—

SIMON YORKE, Esq., now of Erddig, as above.

Note.—Erddig Park mansion was built in 1687, and in 1713 purchased and enlarged by John Miller, Esq., as shown (p. 370). Erddig is a large, solid, unpretending house, with suites of rooms furnished in the antique style, and enriched with objects of art and antiquity, arms of the royal tribes of Wales, &c. The situation is highly picturesque.

Evans of Highmead, Maternal Lineage. See "C," *p*. 194.

C.—*Cadwgan*, Lord of Talyllyn, *m*. Margaret, dau. of the Lord Rhys, Prince of South Wales, who *d*. 1197 ; Rhydderch Ddu, Lord of Talyllyn, *m*. Lleucu, a dau. of Cadwgan ap Mordafrych, Lord of Cilycwm.

Owen *m*. a dau. of Sir Owen ap Bledri ; Arod ap Owen, second son, *m*. Maud, dau. of Meredith ap Rhydderch ap Bledri ; Rhys ap Arod, *m*. Joan, dau. of Gwilym ap Gwgan ; Griffith ap Rhys *m*. Margaret, dau. of Llewelyn Vaughan, of Sanghenydd, Glam. ; Llewelyn ddu ap Griffith *m*. Jenett, dau. of David ap Meurig Goch.

Gwilym ap Llywelyn, of Caio, *m*. Gwladys, dau. of Philip ap Elidr ; David ap Gwilym *m*. Margaret, dau. of Rhydderch ap Jenkin Llwyd ; Evan ap David *m*. Joan, dau. of William Llewelyn ddu.

William ap Evan, of Caio, *m*. Jenet, dau. of David ap Gwilym ; Evan ap William *m*. Jane, dau. of Rhys ap David, of Coedtren ; Llewelyn ap Evan *m*. a dau. of Howel ap Rhys ap Morgan ; William ap Llewelyn, of Llansawel, *m*. a dau. of Wm. Morris ap Einon of Rhydodyn.

John Williams, D.D., Dean of Bangor and Principal of Jesus Coll., Oxon., *m*. Joan, dau. of Sir Walter Price, of Newton, Mont. Kt. ; James Williams *m*. Jane, dau. and h. of George Jones, of Abercothy, Sheriff of co. Carm. 1664.

John Williams, Sheriff of co. Carm. 1681, *m*. Joyce, dau. of Richard Herbert, of Kerry, Mont. His heiress,—

HESTER WILLIAMS, *m*. 1712 (*d*. 1749, aged 74) *Thomas Evans*, Esq., of Acheth, as already shown. John, no issue ; George, *m*. Anne, dau. of Walter Jones,—their dau. *d. s. p.; James d. s. p.;* Herbert *d*. at siege of Namur ; Jonathan *d. s. p.* 1764 ; Jane *d. s. p.;* Joyce *d. s. p.*

ADDITIONS AND CORRECTIONS.

BASSET, William West, Esq., of Beaupré, p. 620 ; *d*. 1872, and is suc. by his son, William Richard Basset, a minor, *b*. 1863. See a further account of this ancient family, and a view of the curious and beautiful *porch* of old Beaupré Castle, pp. 528-9.

BOWEN, James, Esq., of Troedyraur, p. 191 ; *d*. 1873 ; William Rice Bowen, Esq., his son and successor, *d*. 3rd Feb., 1874.

BUCKLEY, James, Esq., of Penyfai, p. 281 ; J.P. for the co. of Carmarthen, and second on the roll of Sheriffs for same co. 1875

BULKELEY, Sir Richard B. W., Bart., of Baron Hill, p. 38 ; *d*. Aug. 28, 1875, and is suc. by his eldest son, Richard Lewis Mostyn Williams Bulkeley (see p. 41).

CHAMBRES, William, Esq., of Dolben, p. 405 ; is D. L. for co. of Denbigh ; High Sheriff for same co. 1875. Mr. Chambres is the *eldest* son of the late W. C. Chambres, Esq.

CLAY, Henry, Esq., of Piercefield Park, p. 773; *d*. Jan. 1874, and was suc. by his eldest son, Henry Clay, Esq., M.A., J.P., of St. Arvan's Park, Chepstow ; *b*. 1825 ; *m*., 1863, Mary Louisa, second dau. of the late H. Boden, Esq., and by her, who *d*. 1872, has issue, Henry Hastings, *b*. 1864. Mrs. Henry Clay, sen., continues to reside at Piercefield Park.

CLOUGH, Charles Butler, Esq., of Llwyn Offa, p. 444 ; dele, "and Llwyn Offa," and add after "Rugby," "inherited the Llwyn Offa Estate from his uncle, Charles Butler Clough, Dean St. Asaph." *Motto*: Sine maculâ macla.

COLBY, John, Esq., of Ffynone, p. 897 ; *d*. 6th June, 1874, aged 59 ; and was suc. by his heir pres., the Rev. Robert Colby, M.A., rector of Ansford, Somerset.

CORDES, Thomas, Esq., of Bryn Glâs, Monmouthshire, p. 774 ; M.P. for Monmouth 1874 ; J. P.,

COUNTY FAMILIES OF WALES.

D. L., for co. of Monmouth; Sheriff of same co. 1871; late commanding officer of the third Monmouthshire Rifle Volunteers; eldest son of the late James C. Cordes, Esq., J. P. for co. Monmouth (*d.* 1867), by Mary, dau. of J. Lucas, Esq., of Hatcham Grove, Surrey; *b.* 1826; is *unm. Residence:* Bryn Glâs, Newport, Mon. *Lineage:* The family of Cordes came to England with the Huguenots who left France at the revocation of the Edict of Nantes.

DAVIES, James, Esq., of Ffosrhydgaled, p. 191; *d.* Dec., 1874, and is suc. by his only son, Morris Davies, Esq., barrister-at-law.

DAVIES, Rees Edward, Esq., of Gwaelod-y-garth, p. 625.; *d.* July, 1873; and was suc. by his heir pres., his brother, Augustus Richard, an officer in the 22nd Foot.

EVANS, John, Esq., of Lovesgrove, p. 195; *d.* 28th Jan., 1874, and is suc. by his son, the Rev. John Pugh Evans, rector of Efenechtyd, near Ruthin.

FINCH, Charles Wynne, Esq., of Voelas, p. 407; *d.* 3rd March, 1874, and was suc. by his son, Capt. Charles Arthur Wynne, of the Scots Fusilier Guards.

FRANKLIN, James Franklin, Esq., of Llwyn-ynn, p. 414; *d.* 13th Nov., 1873, and left issue.

GLYNNE, Sir Stephen Richard, Bart., of Hawarden Castle, p. 447; *d.* 17th June, 1874 (his decease being preceded in 1872 by that of his brother and heir presumptive, the Rev. Henry Glynne, M.A., rector of Hawarden, who *d. s. p.*) He is now succeeded by the Right Hon. W. E. Gladstone in right of his wife Catherine, elder sister of the late baronet. (See further, *Gladstone of Hawarden.*)

HORMAN-FISHER, Samuel Sharpe, Esq., of Llwyn Derw, p. 627. The surname is properly expressed in this form, and not as given at the p. referred to.

HUGHES, J. W. M. Gwynne, Esq , of Tregilb, p. 290; *d.* 1875, leaving issue.

HUGHES, T. H. Forde, of Penbryn House, co. Cardigan. Mr. Hughes, who at p. 192 appears under the name *Davies*, has since adopted the surname *Hughes*, and changed his residence to Penbryn House, Rhydlewis, Cardiganshire. The date of his succession to the Nantgwilan Estate was 1867, not 1866. Mr. Hughes' father, the late Thomas Davies, Esq., of Nantgwilan, was son of the Rev. David Davies, vicar of Llanfihangel Is-Croyddyn, by his wife, a Miss Hughes, of Nantgwilan, heiress to the Faenog Estate. *London Address:* Conservative Club; and Junior Naval and Military Club.

HUMBERTSON, Capt. Philip Hugh, of Glanywern, Denbighshire; J. P. for co. Denbigh; *b.* 1841; *m.*, July 3, 1873, Edith Caroline, dau. of Major J. Jocelyn Foulkes, of Eriviatt. *Residence:* Glanywern, near Denbigh.

HUNTER, Col. William, of Mount Severn, p. 824; *d.* 11th Dec,. 1874, and was suc. by his only son, William Charles. See *Hunter of Mount Severn*, in "Supplementary Index." For the capture of Bhurtpoor fortress, 1825-6, deemed by the natives impregnable, the army in which Col. W. Hunter held command under Lord Combermere received the thanks of both Houses of Parliament.

JAMES, John Taubman William, Esq., of Pantsaison, p. 902. His son and heir, Robert Lloyd James, *m.*, 29th Aug., 1872, Annie Sophia, eldest dau. of F. W. Docker, Esq., of Menai View Terrace, Bangor, co. Carnarvon. In second paragraph, second col., after William, for *Jones*, read *James*, and likewise in the next paragraph following.

JENNINGS, Richard, Esq., of Gelli-dêg, p. 290. His wife Agnes *d.* 16th May, 1874.

JONES-BATEMAN, Mrs., of Pentremawr, p. 411. She *d.* 1875, and is suc. by her son, the Rev. B. J. Bateman, rector of Sheldon, and rural dean of Coleshill, co. Warwick; B.A., Cambridge, 1848, M.A. 1851; *b.* 1825; *m.*, 1852, Mary, only dau. of J. Jennens, Esq., of Aston, co. Warwick, and has issue nine children. *Residences:* Peutremawr, Abergele; Sheldon Rectory, Warwickshire.

JONES, Rev. Latimer Maurice, B.D., of Carmarthen, p. 292; elected 1874 a Proctor in Convocation for the Diocese of St. David's.

KNIGHT, Rev. Edward Doddridge, M.A., of Nottage Court, p. 633; *d.* 1872, leaving issue several daus.

LEWIS, Charles Edward, Esq., of St. Pierre, p. 779. For "by Mary," read, "by his cousin Mary;" and dele. "George Emerson," Esq., substituting "the Rev. Edward Lewis, rector of Portskewet (she *d.* 1846)."

LEWES, W. P., Esq., of Llysnewydd, p. 293. Capt. William Price Llewelyn, eldest son, *m.* at Whitchurch, co. Wexford, Sarah Cecilia, younger dau. of the late John Dean Drake, Esq., of Stokestown, co. Wexford.

LISBURNE, Ernest Augustine Vaughan, Earl of, p. 201; *d.* 8th Nov., 1873, and is suc. by his eldest son, Ernest Augustus Malet, as fifth Earl of Lisburne.

LLOYD, Rev. Francis Llewelyn, of Ty'n Rhyl, p. 449. In third paragraph of *lineage*, instead of " besides a dau.," read, " besides *other issue*, a dau.," and insert "and" before the words "a son " in the next line. The Rev. Robert Watkin Lloyd, father of the present Rev. Francis Llewelyn Lloyd, was the only survivor of four sons, and the only one who left issue.

LLOYD, John, Esq., of Plâs Issa, Corwen, p. 705; *d.* 5th Aug., 1875, and left issue, who inherit.

LLOYD, Capt., M.P. of Glansevin, *p.* 294, is D.L. for the co. of Carmarthen.

LLOYD, John Ellis, Esq., of Trallwyn, p. 357; *d.* 8th Dec., 1873, and was suc. by his eldest son.

MESHAM, Miss Margaret Elizabeth, of Pontruffydd, p. 412; *d.* 1873, and was under her will suc. in the Pontruffydd Estate by her nephew, Capt. Arthur Mesham, J. P. for Flintshire, and formerly Captain first R. Dragoons, eldest son of the late Rev. Arthur Bennett Mesham, of Ripple, and Wootton Rectory, Kent; *b.* 1837; *m.*, 1861, Elizabeth Emmeline, dau. of Major Burridge, of Barton Fields, Kent; and has issue Arthur Bennett, *b.* 1864. *Residence:* Pontruffydd, Rhyl.

MORGAN, Howard Spear, Esq., Tegfynydd, p. 907; High Sheriff for Carmarthenshire 1875.

NANNEY, Hugh J. Ellis, Esq., of Gwynfryn, p. 358; *m.*, 13th Jan., 1875, the Hon. Elizabeth Octavia Dillon, *b.* 1848, youngest dau. of Lord Clonbrook, of Clonbrook, co. Galway.

PROTHEROE, Mrs., of Dolwilim, p. 301, *d.* 1872, and was suc. by her eldest surviving son, Edward Schaw Protheroe, Esq., J.P. for Cos. Carm. and Pemb., *b.* 1823, *m.* as stated, and has, with other issue, John Baldwin Brydges, *b.* 1862.

PRYCE, John Bruce, Esq., of Dyffryn, p. 638; *d.* 1873, and was suc. by his grandson, Alan Cameron Bruce-Pryce, Esq. (who thereupon assumed his name), son of his eldest brother, John Wyndham Bruce, Esq., M.A., barrister-at-law, by Mary Ann, dau. of Lieut.-Col. Cameron; *b.* 1836; *m.* first, 1858, Louisa, dau. and h. of the late Col. Henry J. Slade (she *d.* 1868); secondly, 1873, Anna Mary, dau. of George Woods Mannsell, Esq., of Dublin; has issue by former mar. a son, John Henry, *b.* 1859.

REES, William, Esq., of Tonn, p. 303; *d.* 3rd July, 1873; and is suc. by his eldest son, George Arthur Rees, Esq.; *b.* 1843; *m.* 5th March, 1872, and has issue a dau., Sarah, *b.* 15th March, 1873, and a son, William, *b.* 9th Aug., 1874. *Tonn* continues to be the residence of the widow, Mrs. Rees. (See *engraving*, p. 215.)

RICHARDES, Capt. W. E., of Bryneithin, p. 210; *d.* 1874, and is suc. by his son, Hugh Stephen Richardes, Esq.

RICHARDSON, James Coxon, Esq., of Glan'rafon, p. 639; *d.* at Cairo, during his travels, 6th Jan., 1874, leaving issue as stated.

ROLLS, John Allan, Esq., of The Hendre, p. 784, has issue, in addition to his eldest son John Maclean, Henry Allan, *b.* 1871, and Eleanor Georgiana, *b.* 1872. *Town Address:* Carlton Club.

RICHARDS, Richard Meredith, Esq., of Caerynwch, p. 707; *d.* 1873, and is suc. by his son Richard Edwd. Lloyd Richards; a minor, *b.* 1865.

SMITH, Charles Henry, Esq., of Gwernllwynwith, p. 640; *m.* secondly, 2nd April, 1873, Miss G. M. Willis, of Tenby.

THOMAS, William, Esq., of Lan House, *p.* 952. His ancestor, Mary Popkin, was dau. not of Hopkin the elder son of John David Popkin of *Forest*, but of Robert, son of Thomas Popkin, a younger son of the same John David Popkin. Robert *m.* Jane, dau. of John Nicholl, of Newbridge, and had issue, besides two younger daus., Catherine and Anne, a son, Thomas Popkin, Sheriff of Glamorgan 1718, and Mary aforesaid, who *m.* Matthew Thomas, and so on.

TREDEGAR, Charles Morgan Robinson, Baron, of Tredegar Park, p. 785; *d.* April, 1875, and was suc. by his eldest son, Charles Godfrey, late M.P. for co. of Brecknock. See *Morgan of Ruperra Castle.*

TREVOR-ROPER, Charles Blayney, Esq., of Pâstêg, p. 456. His eldest son, Charles James Trevor-Roper, Esq., of Nantygaer, *m.*, 1873, Miss Kortright, of Clifton.

TURNER, Thomas, Esq., of Plâs Brereton, p. 361; *d.* 24th Dec., 1873; was *m.*, and left issue.

WALTERS, William, Esq., of Haverfordwest, p. 910, *d.* 1874, suc. by his son.

VANE, George Henry Robert Vane Tempest, Earl, of Plâs Machynlleth, p. 830; succ. 25th Nov., 1872, as fifth Marquess of Londonderry, on the death of his father, Frederick William Robert, fourth Marquess. His eldest son and heir, Charles Stewart, Viscount Seaham, also suc. as third Earl Vane. The Lady Frances Cornelia Harriet Emily, eldest dau., *d.* 1872; and her sister, Lady Avarina Mary, *d.* 1873.

WATKINS, The Rev. Thomas, of Lloegyr Fawr, p. 120; *d.* 17th Feb., 1875, and is suc. by his son, Thomas Chichele Bargrave Watkins, Esq.

WILLIAMS, Rev. Garnons, of Abercamlais, p. 121. His mother's name is Elizabeth (not "Martha") dau. of the Ven. Richard Davies, Archdeacon of Brecon.

WILLIAMS, Gwilym, Esq., of Miskin Manor, p. 647. His *crest* is—A goat's head erased. *Motto* Llafur orfu bobpeth.

WILLIAMS, Sir Hugh, Bart., of Bodelwyddan, p. 457; under *Heir*, for "Naval," read "*First* Life Guards;" and read "*Crests:* A fox's head erased; and, an eagle displayed or."

WILLIAMS, Morgan Stuart, Esq., of Aberpergwm, p. 647, *m.*, 22nd July, 1873, Josephine, dau. of William Herbert, Esq., of Clytha, co. of Monmouth.

WILLIAMS, Richard, Esq., of Trosyrafon, p. 49; *d.* 14th Nov., 1871. *Dele* the article.

HIGH SHERIFFS SINCE 1871.

Anglesey.

William Williams, Esq., of Tyddyn Mawr
William Duff Assheton Smith, Esq., of Vaenol } 1872
William Humphrey Owen, Esq., of Plas yn Penrhyn. 1873
Lord Clarence Paget, of Plas Llanfair . . 1874
David Morgan, Esq., of Bryngwyn Hall . 1875

Breconshire.

John Jayne, Esq., of Pantybaili . . . 1872
Oliver Morgan Bligh, Esq., of Cilmery . . 1873
William Rees, Esq., of Tirymryson . . 1874
James Vaughan, Esq., the Castle, Builth . 1875

Cardiganshire.

John Edwardes Rogers, Esq., of Aber-Meurig 1872
William Buck, Esq., of Stradmore. . . 1873
John Pughe Vaughan Pryse, Esq., of Bwlchbychan 1874
Matthew L. V. Davies, Esq., of Tanybwlch . 1875

Carmarthenshire.

John Davie Ferguson Davie, Esq., of Derllys Court 1873
David Pugh, Esq., of Manoravon . . . 1874
Howard Spear Morgan, Esq., of Tegfynydd . 1875

Carnarvonshire.

Thomas Turner, Esq., of Plâs Brereton . . 1873
Benjamin Thomas Ellis, Esq., of Rhyllech . 1874
Edward Griffith Powell, Esq., of Coedmawr . 1875

Denbighshire.

James Hassall Foulkes, Esq., of Llay Place . 1873
John Carstairs Jones, Esq., of Gelligynan . 1874
William Chambres, Esq., of Dolben . . 1875

Flintshire.

Thomas Griffies Dixon, Esq., of Nant . . 1873
William Keates, Esq., of Pickhill Hall . . 1874
John Churton, Esq., of Morannedd, Rhyl . 1875

Glamorganshire.

Francis Edmund Stacey, Esq., of Llandough . 1873
John Nicholl Carne, Esq., Dimlands Castle . 1874
Morgan Stuart Williams, Esq., Aberpergwm . 1875

Merionethshire.

Hon. Charles Henry Wynn, of Rhug . . 1873
William Edward Oakeley, Esq., of Tanybwlch 1874
Athelstan J. Soden Corbet, Esq., of Ynysymaengwyn 1875

Monmouthshire.

John Jefferies Stone, Esq., of Scyborwen . 1873
Crawshay Bailey, Esq., of Maendiff Court . 1874
John Allan Rolls, Esq., of The Hendre . . 1875

Montgomeryshire.

Devereux H. Mytton, Esq., of Garth . . 1873
Richard Smith Humphreys, Esq., Montgomery 1874
Richard Edward Jones, Esq., of Cefn Bryntalch 1875

Pembrokeshire.

Henry Seymour Allen, Esq., of Cresselly 1873
John Bowen Summers, Esq., of Milton . . 1874
John T. William James, Esq, of Pantsaison . 1875

Radnorshire.

John Percy Severn, Esq., of Penybont . . 1873
John Stephens, Esq., of Castle Vale . . 1874
Gen. John Ramsey Sladen, R.A., Rhydoldog. 1875

MEMBERS OF PARLIAMENT FOR WALES, 1875.

Anglesey.

Richard Davies, Esq., for co., first elected . 1868
Morgan Lloyd, Esq., for boroughs (vice Hon. W. O. Stanley, retired) 1874

Breconshire.

W. Fuller Maitland, Esq. (vice Hon. Godfrey C. Morgan, elevated to the Peerage as second Baron Tredegar), for co. . . 1875
J. P. W. Gwynne Holford, Esq., for borough, first elected July 19 . . . 1870

Cardiganshire.

Thomas Edward Lloyd, Esq. (vice Evan M. Richards), for co. 1874
David Davies, Esq. (vice Sir T. D. Lloyd, resigned), for Cardigan boroughs, Feb. . 1874

Carmarthenshire.

John Jones, Esq., first elected Nov. . . 1868
Viscount Emlyn (vice E. J. Sartoris), Feb. 1874
Charles W. Nevill (vice Sir J. Cowell Stepney, Bart., resigned), for the boroughs, Feb. . 1875

Carnarvonshire.

Hon. George Sholto Douglas Pennant (*vice* Love Jones-Parry, Esq.), for *co.*, Feb. . 1874
William Bulkeley Hughes, for *boroughs* . . 1868

Denbighshire.

Sir Watkin Williams Wynn, Bart., first elected for the *co.* 1841
G. Osborn Morgan, Esq., for *co.* . . . 1868
Watkin Williams, Esq., for *boroughs* . . 1868

Flintshire.

Right Hon. Lord Richard Grosvenor for *co.* . 1861
Peter Ellis Eyton, Esq. (*vice* Sir Robert A. Cunliffe, Bart.), for *boroughs*, Feb. . . 1874

Glamorganshire.

Christopher Rice Mansel Talbot, Esq., has sat for Glamorganshire since . . . 1830
Henry Hussey Vivian, Esq., for same . . 1857

Cardiff.

Col. J. F. D. Crichton Stuart, first elected . 1857

Swansea and Contributory Boroughs.

Lewis Llewelyn Dillwyn, Esq., first elected . 1855

Merthyr Tydfil.

Richard Fothergill, Esq., first elected . . 1868
Henry Richard, Esq., first elected. . . 1868

Merionethshire.

Samuel Holland, Esq., first elected . . 1870
(No borough representation in this co.)

Monmouthshire.

Rt. Hon. Lord Henry Charles Somerset . 1871
Hon. Frederick Courtenay Morgan . . 1874

Monmouth Boroughs.

Thomas Cordes, Esq., first elected. . . 1874

Montgomeryshire.

Charles Watkin Williams-Wynn, Esq., first elected 1862

Montgomery.

Hon. Chas. Rich. D. Hanbury Tracy, first elected for *co.* 1863

Pembrokeshire.

John Henry Scourfield, Esq., first elected for *co.* 1868

Haverfordwest.

William Edwardes, Baron Kensington (succ. to title as fourth baron 1872), first elected 1868

Pembroke.

Edward James Reed, Esq. (*vice* E. Charlton Meyrick), first elected Feb. . . . 1874

Radnorshire.

Hon. Arthur Walsh, first elected . . . 1868

Radnor Boroughs.

Rt. Hon. Marquis of Hartington, first elected. 1869

CORRIGENDA.

PAGE
15 4th par., *dele* "Rev. Hugh Prichard and."
35 In title bottom par., *dele* "HENRY VIII."
61 1st par., *for* "Langharn" *read* "Laugharn."
81 3rd par., *for* 68 *read* 72, 74; and 12th line from bottom *for* "Menthyr" *read* "Merthyr."
84 3rd par., *for* "Ystradwy" *read* "Ystradiyw," 2nd and 4th line from bottom, *for* "Gwrgan" *read* "Gwgan."
86 2nd par., *dele* last two lines from "himself."
88 Last line 2nd par., after "Chevron" *dele* "or."
90 2nd line last par. *for* "83" *read* "92."
95 2nd par., *for* "as Syr" *read* " ap Syr."
122 1st col., under *lineage*, for "Christian name" *read* "surname."
142 11 lines from bottom, *for* "fifth" *read* "fifth and sixth."
152 12 lines from bottom, *for* "is" *read* "are."
233 2nd line from bottom, *for* "inter" *read* "iter."
250 Last par., *for* "Robert of Normandy" *read* "Hamlet's father."

PAGE
282 2nd line from bottom, *for* "dau." *read* "granddau."
353 1st col., 2nd par., *for* "Bronderw" *read* "Brondanw."
366 7th line from bottom, after "Waterloo column" *read* "erected by his mother to the memory of the fourth Sir Watkin, who d. 1789, bearing," &c.
390 3rd par., before Ranulph *read* "the forces of."
400 After Sheriffs of 1718 and 1752, *for* "Llwyn-Ynn" *read* "Llwyn-Onn."
403 1st col., six lines from bottom, *for* "John" *read* "Thomas."
446 2nd col., six lines from bottom, *for* "nobille" *read* "nobile."
447 2nd col., sixth par., from top, *for* "345" *read* "435."
460 7 lines from bottom, *for* "Lundy" *read* "Sully."
493 21 lines from bottom, *for* "reddit" *read* "rediit."

COUNTY FAMILIES OF WALES. 963

PAGE	
499	13 lines from top, *for* "combustam" *read* "combustum."
505	13 from top, *for* "Anglica" *read* "Anglici."
553	11 lines from bottom, *for* "their" *read* "her."
561	10 lines from top, *for* "Edward" *read* "Thomas."
562	1st line, *for* "by" *read* "or."
575	9 lines from bottom, *for* "Caradog Freichfras" *read* "Princes of Dyfed;" and two lines lower *omit* "Caradog Freichfras."
587	6 lines from top, *for* "1656" *read* "1660."
590	15 lines from top, *for* "Oliver" *read* "Cromwell."
„ 16	„ „ "Henry" *read* "Oliver."
605	10 „ „ "1683" *read* "1653."
607	18 „ „ "1598" „ "1698."
632	25 „ „ "1849" „ "1649."
„ 31	„ „ "1854" „ "1654."
„ 32	„ „ "1665" „ "1655."
647	1st col., thirty lines from bottom, *for* "1752" *read* "1572."

PAGE	
672	20 lines from bottom, *for* "1782" *read* "1282."
701	2 lines from bottom, *for* "is" *read* "are."
738	5 lines from bottom, *for* "738" *read* "739."
740	16 lines from top, *for* "turbarum" *read* "tubarum."
828	2nd col., fourth par., *for* "Chebenham" *read* "Cheltenham."
843	1st line 2nd paragraph, *for* "Precellyu" *read* "Precelly."
843	6th line, *for* "Hoven read Haven."
847	2nd par., near end, *for* "254" *read* "154."
850	2nd line from top, *for* "hetacombs" *read* "hecatombs."
856	6 lines from top, *for* "diminishes" *read* "increases."
861	2nd par., third line, *for* "grandson" *read* "great grandson."
920	2nd col., three lines from bottom, *for* "Hartingten" *read* "Hartington."

[N.B.—*As this work is intended to be made as complete a record as possible of the families of the Principality, it is respectfully requested that all omissions or inaccuracies may be noted, and communicated to the* EDITOR *at the Publishers'.*

Many families were absent from the First Edition owing to the impossibility of obtaining authentic information in time. Some are still left out for a similar reason. The same remark applies to the illustrations. All mansions, photographs of which are supplied by the proprietors, will be engraved in the same manner as those already inserted, and it is hoped that the Third Edition will be much more complete than the present in this respect.]

September, 1875.

SUPPLEMENTARY INDEX.

Aberdyfi, corrupted "Aberdovey," 649.
Abermarles, 950.
Anarawd, prince of N. Wales, 321.
Annales Cambriæ 163, and quoted *passim*.

Basset of Beaupré, 952.
Beaupré Castle, *Porch*, with *engraving*, 528.
Borough Magistrates since 1872, 935.
Bowen of Troedyraur, 958.
Buckley of Penyfai, 948.
Bulkeley of Baron Hill, 958.

Cangi, Cangiani, 319.
Carbery, Earl, of Golden Grove, 108, 278, 936.
Cefn y Bryn, in Gower, 478.
Chambres of Dolben, 958.
Combe of Oaklands, 941.
Clay of Piercefield and St. Arvan's, 958.
Clough of Llwyn Offa, 959.
Cordes of Bryn Glâs, 958.

Darby of Brymbo, 942.
David of Fairwater, 942.
Davies of Bronfelen, 942.
Davies, Saunders, of Pentre, 943.
Deheubarth, meaning of, 847.
Demetia, a Roman name, 846.
Dinefawr, estates confiscated, 939.
Dolwilim *Cromlech*, 222.
Dyffryn, Neath, *engraving*, 529.

Edwinsford, with *engraving*, 215.
Erddig, Yorke of, 957.
Evans of Aberglasney, 944.
Evans of Bronwylfa, 943.
Evans of Highmead, 192—195, 958.
Eyton of Rhyl and Rhydycilgwyn, 944.

Fairwater, David of, 942.
Foley family, 950.

Gamage of Coity and Abergarw, 940.
Gladstone of Hawarden, 944.
Glanbrydan Park, *engraving*, 211.
Glynne of Hawarden, 447, 944, 959.
Gruffydd ap Cynan, 321.
Gwyn of Plâs Cwrt-hir, 945.

Henry VII.'s grants to Sir Rhys ap Thomas, 939.
Howell of Rhiewport, with *engraving*, 802, 945.
Hughes of Penbryn House, 959.
Humbertson of Glanywern, 959.
Hunter of Mount Severn, 824, 946.

Jones-Bateman of Pentremawr, 959.
Jones of Carmarthen, 959.
Jones of Gungrog, 946.
Jones of Trewythen and Rhiewport, 941.

Lewis Glyn Cothi, quoted, 516.
Lisburne, Earl of, 959.
Lloyd of Brunant, 946.
Lloyd of Coedmore, 947.
Lloyd of Dolobran, 947.
Lloyd of Moor Hall, 947.
Lloyd of Porthycrwys, 937, 938.
Londonderry, Marquess of, 960.
Lucas of Uplands, 948.

Magistrates of Boroughs since 1872, 935.
Malgwyn Gwynedd, Prince, 320.
Marten of Fern Hill, 948.
Marten, Henry, 752, 948.
Meirionydd, the name, 649.
Members of Parliament in 1875, 961.
Mesham of Pontruffydd, 960.
Miers of Ynyspenllwch, 948.
Mortimer of Trewellwell, 948.
Mount, The, Llanfair, *engraving*, 803.

Neuaddfawr, *engraving*, 214.
Nicholl, Whitlock, of the Ham, 949.

Orielton, the Owens of, 953.
Owen of Orielton, 953.

Parliamentary, 961.
Peacock of Stone Hall, 949.
Pelham, Thursby—of Ridgeway, 950.
Penry of Peterwell, 950.
Penry of Peterwell Court, 950.
Pentre, Saunders Davies of, 943.
Powys-land Club and Museum, 946.
Protheroe of Dolwilim, 960.
Puleston of Ffynogion and Marden Park, 950.

Ralston of Pontywall Hall, 951.
Rees of Tonn, 960.
Rees of Llanboidy, 951.
Rhieworth, with *engraving*, 802.
Rhys ap Gruffydd, attainted, 939.
Rhys ap Thomas, Sir, 240—244, 939.
Richardson of Derwen Fawr, 951.
Rolls of Hendre, 960.

Sheriffs of Wales since 1871, 961.
St. David's, Bishop Jones of, 198, 952.
Stedman of Dolygaer, 938.
Stedman of Strata Florida, *engraving*, 936.
Stone Hall, Peacock of, 949.
Strata Florida Abbey, 937.

Tennant of Cadoxton Lodge, 952.
Thomas of Lan House, 952.
Thomas of Pengwern House, 952.
Tonn, Rees of, with *engraving*, 215, 303, 960.
Tredegar, Lord, 960.
Trewythen, Jones of, 941.
Trewellwell, Mortimer of, 948.
Tripp of Winford, &c., 953.

Vane, the Earl, 960.
Vaughan, Gwynne, of Cynghordy, 956.
Vaughan of Golden Grove, 936.
Vaughan of Plâs-Cilcenin, 937, 938.
Vaughan of Trawscoed, 938.
Vaughan, Williams, of Velinnewydd (*engravings*), 955.
Velinnewydd, *engravings* of, 56.
Venedotia, 320

Walters of Haverfordwest, 960.
Williams of Aberpergwm, 960.
Williams of Brecknock, 957.
Williams of Skreen, 956.
Wilkinson, Sir Gardner, of Brynfield House, 956.
Winwood of Tyglyn Aeron, 957.

Ynyspenllwch, Miers of, 948.
Yorke of Erddig Park, 957.
Yorke's *Royal Tribes*, 654 *et passim*.

INDEX.

A.

Abadam of Middleton Hall, 280.
Abadam of Tymawr, 190.
Aberdare, valley of, and works, 473.
Aberffraw, Royal residence at, 13.
Abergavenny, and Castle of, 719, 735.
Aberglasney, 217.
Abergwili Palace, 219.
Abermarlais, Lloyd-Price of, 300.
Aberpergwm, with *engraving*, 475, 647.
Aberystwyth, 140.
Aberystwith, Castle of, *engraving* and history of, 156.
Aberystwith, proposed University College at, 140.
Ackland of Boulston, 892.
Ad Vicessimum, Roman station of, 847.
Adams of Hollyland, 836, 892.
Adams of Plas Llysin, 821.
Aeron, Vale of, 133.
Albert, Prince Consort, Memorial to, 838.
Alexander of Cardiff, 932.
Alfred, King, protector of Wales, 485.
Alfred, King, his power in Wales, 229.
Allen of Cresselly, 893.
Allen of Oakfield, 112.
Allen of Priskilly Forest, 893.
Allen of Tenby, 932.
Alltyferin, *engraving* of, 219.
Amphitheatre, Roman, at Caerleon, 730.
Anglesey, name of, 1.
,, description of, 3.
,, geology of, 6.
,, history of, 9—14.
,, antiquities of, 14—25.
,, old and Extinct Families of, 25—28.
,, high Sheriffs of, 31—43.
,, members of Parliament of, 43.
,, magistrates of, 36.
Antiquities of Glamorgan, 506—544.
Anwyl of Llugwy, 699.
Aran Fawddwy Mountain, 659.
Arberth (Narberth) Castle, 864-5.
Ardudwy, comot and hundred of, 661.
Arengo-Cross of Iscoed, 280.
Arenig Mountains, 650.
Arms, escutcheon of, of Jones-Parry, 364.
Arthur, King, and the Round Table, 731.
Arthur's Stone, with *engraving*, 507.
Artro, antiquities of, 673-4.
Artro, vale of, 661, 673.
Arwystli, cantref of, 798.
Asser, on the Condition of the Welsh, 228.
Asser Menevensis quoted, 847.
Assheton-Smith of Vaenol, 350.
Aveland, Baron, of Gwydir, 350.
Awbrey of Abercynrig, &c., 87.

B.

Bailey of Glan-Usk Park, 112.

Bailey of Maindiff Court, 770.
Bala Lake, 668.
Bala, neighbourhood of, 668.
Baldwin, Abp., preaching the Crusades, 861.
Bangor, Campbell, Lord Bishop of, 351.
Bankes of Soughton Hall, 444.
Bannium, or Old Brecon, 62, 79.
Bardsey Island, 316.
Barham of Trecwn (Trecoon), 894.
Barlow, Bp. of St. David's, 866.
Barnes of Brookside, 405.
Baron Hill, Anglesey, with *engraving*, 6.
Baronia de Kemeys, quoted, 874, 875, 895.
Baronies Marchers, 496.
Baron Owen of Dolgelly, 658.
Basingwerk Abbey, 433.
Baskerville of Clyro Court, 921.
Basset of Beaupre, 620.
Basset of Bonvilston, 620.
Bateman of Bertholeu, 770.
Bath of Alltyferin, 280.
Bath of Ffynone House, 621.
Battersby-Harford of Falcondale, 190.
Beacons, Breconshire, 55.
Beauchamps, Lords of Glamorgan, 554.
Beaufort, Duke of, of Troy House and Badminton, 770.
Beaufort *Progress*, the, quoted, 518.
Beaufort *Progress* quoted, 795, 808.
Beaufort *Progress*, 739.
Beaumaris Castle, *engraving* and account of, 21.
Beaupre, Basset of, 465, 528, 620.
Beaupre Castle, 528.
Beavan of Glascomb Court, 921.
Beddau Gwyr Ardudwy, 674.
Benton Castle, 870.
Beri, Castell y, 674.
Berkrolles of St. Athan's, 558.
Berriew (Aber-Rhiw), 802.
Berrington of Pant-y-goetre, 772.
Bethesda slate quarries, 311.
Bevan of Fosbury, 621.
Biddulph of Swansea, 622.
Biddulph—see *Myddelton-Biddulph*, 412.
Bishops of Llandaff, list of, 612.
"Black Book of Carmarthen," 653.
Blayneys of Gregynog, 805, 810, 811.
Bleddyn ap Cynfyn, Prince of Powys, 792.
Bligh of Cilmery, 112.
Blosse of Newcastle House, 622.
Bodrhyddan, 424.
Booker of Velindre, 623.
"Book of Aberpergwm," 489, 490.
Bone caves of Gower, 508.
Bonnor-Maurice of Bodynfoel, 821.
Bonsall of Fronfraith, 190.
Bonsall of Glan-rheidol, 190.
Bonville of Bonvilston, 573.
Borough Magistrates of Wales, 932.
Bosanquet of Dingestow Court, 772.
Boston, Lord, of Llanidan, 38
Bosworth Field, 240, 857.
Boulston House, 834, 892.

938   INDEX.

Bovium, Roman station of (Boverton), 484.
Bowen of Chancefield, 112.
Bowen of Llwyngwair, 894.
Bowen of Troed-yr-aur, 191.
Bowen of Tygwyn, 895.
Bowen, Webb-, of Camrose, 894.
Brawdy, Jones of, 842.
Brecon Castle, 67, 80.
Breconshire, name of, 53.
　　,,　antiquities of, 75—82.
　　,,　description of, 53—57.
　　,,　geology of, 57—61.
　　,,　high Sheriffs of, 103.
　　,,　historical Sketch of, 61—75.
　　,,　Lord Lieutenants of, 108.
　　,,　members of Parliament of, 108.
　　,,　old and Extinct Families of, 82.
　　,,　population of, 57.
Breese of Dolfriog, 351.
Brereton of Bersham, 397.
Bridge, Suspension, 4.
Bridgewater of Coity Mawr, 112.
Britannia, Lhwyd's, notes in 151.
"Britain," meaning of, in old Welsh writers, 488.
Britons, their feudal subjection, 228.
Brittany, *Menhirs* in, 18.
Brochmael stone, the, 389.
Bro Essyllt, 485.
Brogden of Coytrehen, 623.
Brogden of Tondu, 623.
Bromfield, Gruffydd Maelor, Lord of, 792.
Broughs of Dinas Mawddwy, 688.
Bruce of Dyffryn, 623.
Bryant of Pembroke, 896.
Brychan Brycheiniog, 64.
Brydges, Jones-, of Boultibrook, 922.
Brynmyrddin, seat of T. C. Morris, Esq., 219.
Buckley of Penyfai, 281.
Buckley of Plas Dinas Mawddwy, 700.
Bulkeley, Williams, of Baron Hill, 38.
Bunbury of Abergwynant, 700.
Burghill of Talgarth, 88.
Bute, Marquess of, 619.
Butler, Clifford-, of Llantilio Court, 773.
Butler of Dunraven, 569.
Byrde of Goetre House, 773.

C.

Cader Idris, 660.
Cadvan Stone at Towyn, 675.
Caer Bradwen, 653.
Caerau, *Tibia amnis* of the Romans, 484.
Caergwrle Castle, 436.
Caerleb, antiquities of, 17.
Caerleon, with a *view*, 722, 729—731.
Caerphilly Castle, with *engravings*, 533—538.
Caersws, Roman station at, 791.
Caerwent (*Venta Silurum*), 729.
Caldecot Castle, with *engraving*, 734.
Caldy Island, priory, fossil remains in, 864.
Campbell-Davys of Neuaddfawr, 281.
Cantref, Welsh, what, 849.
"Cantref y Gwaelod," 661, 676.
Capel Curig Lake, *view* of, 310.
Capel Garmon cromlech, 389.
Cardiff Castle, with *engravings*, 461—463, 539—543.
Cardiff Priories, 543.
Cardigan Castle, 1—579.
Cardiganshire made a county, 123.
　　,,　antiquities of, 151.

Cardiganshire, county Magistrates of, 188.
　　,,　description of, 123—140.
　　,,　geology and Mineralogy of, 141.
　　,,　high Sheriffs of, 180—184.
　　,,　historical Sketch of, 142—151.
　　,,　members of Parliament of, 184—189.
　　,,　name of, 123.
　　,,　norman settlements in, 145.
　　,,　old and Extinct Families of, 167—179.
Carew Castle, with *engraving*, 852.
Carew Cross, with *engraving*, 856.
Carews of Carew Castle, 854, 896.
Carmarthen Castle, 248.
Carmarthen, Chancery Seal of, 244, 855.
Carmarthen, the name, 211; origin of, 227.
Carmarthenshire made a county, 240.
　　,,　antiquities of, 246—263.
　　,,　description, of 212—223.
　　,,　geology of, 223—226.
　　,,　high Sheriffs of, 273—277.
　　,,　its History, 226.
　　,,　members of Parliament of, 277.
　　,,　old and Extinct Families of, 263—273.
　　,,　population of, 212.
Carnac, in Brittany, Monuments of, 18.
Carnarvon Castle, with *engravings*, 327—331.
Carnarvonshire made a county, 327.
　　,,　description of, 309—319.
　　,,　geology of, 318.
　　,,　high sheriffs of, 344—347.
　　,,　history and Antiquities of, 319—337.
　　,,　old and extinct families of, 339—344.
　　,,　parliamentary annals of, 347—349.
　　,,　population and extent of, 309.
Carnarvon, the name, 309.
Carne, Nicholl-, of St. Donat's Castle, 624.
Carreg Cennen Castle, *engraving*, 258.
Casgwent (Chepstow), 749.
"Castell Coch" (Powis Castle), 793.
Castell Coch, with *engraving*, 532.
Castell Crogen (Chirk Castle), 369.
"Castell Forwyn," 803.
Castle Green, Cardigan, 139.
Castle Pigyn, *engraving* of, 220.
Cawdor of Stackpool Court, 896.
Cedewain, cantref of, 653.
Cemmaes (Kemes), Barony of, 843, 871-877.
Ceredig, the Early prince, 142.
Cilcyffeth, 843.
Cilgerran Castle, *View* of, 138.
Cilgerran Castle, with *engraving*, 871.
Cilmin Droetu, founder of noble tribe, 338.
Chambers of Havod, 191.
Chambres of Dolben, 405.
Chambres of Llysmeirchion, 405.
Chandler of Narberth, 897.
Chepstow Castle, with *engravings*, 749—754.
Chepstow, town of, 749.
Cherletons, Lords of Powis Castle, 794.
Chirbury, Lord Herbert of, 795, 797, 827.
Chirk Castle, with *engraving*, 368.
Clark of Dowlais House, 625.
Clark of Robeston Wathen, 897.
Clark, G. T., Esq., cited, 559, 561.
Clay of Piercefield Park, 773.
Cleddeu rivers, 867.
Cliff scenery of Pembrokeshire (2), 835, 836.
Clough of Llwyn Offa, 444.
Clynnog, church of, 314.
Clynnog, cromlech at, 336.
Clytha House, Mon., 719.
Coal-basin of Glamorgan, 482.
Coal-beds of Carmarthenshire, 224.
Coal-field of South Wales, 481.

INDEX. 939

Coal, undiscovered, in vale of Glamorgan, 481.
Cochwillan, Williams of, 312, 341, 361.
Cockburn of Downton, 922.
Coity Castle, with *engraving*, 520.
Colby of Fynone, 897.
Colby of Pant-y-deri, 898.
Coldbrook Park, 719.
Collwyn ap Tangno, founder of noble tribe, 337.
Comots, Welsh, what, 849.
Conovium of the Romans, 320.
Conway Castle, with *engraving*, 331.
Conway-Griffith, of Carreglwyd, 37—41.
Conwy of Bodrhyddan, 444.
Cooke of Colomendy, 445.
Cooke of Gwasanau, 445.
Copper-smelting at Swansea, 545.
Copper-smoke, condensed, 547.
Coracles on the Towy, 215.
Corbet of Ynys-y-maengwyn, 701.
Corbett of Cogan Pill, 625.
Corbett-Winder of Vaynor, 821.
Cordes of Bryn-glas, 774.
Corrie of Dysserth, 821.
Cors-y-gedol, ancient mansion of, 661.
Corwen, victory of the Welsh at, 670.
Cottages built of concrete, 805.
Cottesmoor with *engraving*, 841.
Coulson of Cors-y-gedol, 701.
Cowell-Stepney of Llanelly, 282.
Cradock of Cheriton, 576.
Cradock of Long Ash, 586.
Cradock of Swansea, 575.
Craig y Dinas, a *caer* at, 672.
Crannoge of Llyn Savathan 77.
Crawshay of Cyfarthfa Castle, 625.
Crawshay of Danypark, 113.
Cresselly, Allen of, 893.
Cresswell (Christ's well), 834.
Crewe-Read of Llandinam Hall, 822.
Criccieth Castle, 335.
Crickhowel Castle, *View* of, 74.
Crickhowel, Gateway at, *View* of, 100.
Crime in Glamorgan, 548.
Cromlech in Anglesey, with *engraving*, 15.
Cromlech of Capel Garmon, 389.
Cromlech in Carnarvonshire, 336.
Cromlech at Dolwilym, 222.
Cromlech of " Llech-yr-ast," 153.
Cromlech of St. Nicholas, 529.
Cromlechs at Pentre-Evan, Llech-y-drybedd, Trellys, Longhouse, Manorbier.
Cromwell, a letter of, 754.
Cromwell family, the, 589.
Cromwell at Pembroke, 852.
Crynfryn, Lloyds of, 179.
Cunliffe of Acton Park, 406.
Curre of Itton Court, 774.
Curthose Tower, Cardiff Castle, 541.
Cwmgwili, *view* in, 221,
Cydweli Castle, *view* of, 250.
Cyfarthfa Castle, with *engraving*, 474.
Cymmer Abbey, 660.

D.

Dale Castle, Lloyd-Philipps of, 905.
Danes, the, in Anglesey, 10.
Danes in Glamorgan, 485, 510, 732.
Danes in Pembrokeshire, 880.
Davis of Maesyffynon, 626.
Davis of Trewarren, 898.
Davies of Abercery, 192.
Davies of Aberystwyth, 932.

Davies of Bank House, 191.
Davies of Brynglâs, 823.
Davies of Castle Green, 191.
Davies of Ffosrhydgaled, 191.
Davies of Fronfelen, 823.
Davies of Gwaelod-y-garth, 625.
Davies of Gwasanau, 441.
Davies of Hayston, 932.
Davies of Trawsmawr, 284.
Davies of Ty-Glyn, 192.
Davies of Upland, 284.
Dawkin of Kilvrough, 574.
De Barri of Manorbier Castle, 859.
Debeubarth, meaning of, 485.
De Breos family, the, 556.
De Breos, Reginald, 69.
De Breos, William, 69.
De Cardiff of Cardiff, 572.
De Clare, Gilbert (Strongbow), 748.
De Clares, the, the Lords of Glamorgan, 552.
De Granvilles, the, 557.
De Grey of Ruthin, 33-48.
De la Roche, 870.
De la Beche, or coal-field of S. Wales, 470.
De Londres, the, 557.
Denbigh Castle, with *engraving*, 382.
Denbigh, Earl, of Downing, 445.
Denbigh, etymology of name, 365.
Denbighshire created a county, 365.
„ description of, 365—380.
„ population 365.
„ geology, 380.
„ history and antiquities, 381—390.
„ old and extinct families of, 391—398.
„ high sheriffs of, 398—402.
„ parliamentary annals of, 402—404.
Derry-Ormond, *Engraving* of, 135.
Derry-Ormond, Inglis-Jones of, 197.
De Rupe, Adam, 870.
De Rutzen of Slebech Hall, 898.
Despencer family, the, 535, 538, 553.
De Winton of Boughrood, 922.
De Winton of Maesderwen, 113.
De Winton of Maesllwch, 922.
Deudraeth Castle, with *engraving*, 664.
Devil's Bridge, 125.
Diganwy Castle (Gannock), 322, 335.
Dillwyn of Hendrefoelan, 626.
Dinas Bran Castle, 385.
Dinas Mawddwy, 654.
Dinefawr Castle, 216, 255.
Dingeraint (Cilgerran) Castle, 872.
Dirleton, *engravings* of, 213-14.
Dirleton, Gulston of, 286.
Dod of Llanerch, 406.
Dodridge, Sir John, on the Marches of Wales, 493, 496.
Dolau-Cothi, Johnes of, 291.
Dolbadarn Castle, 335.
Dolforwyn Castle, 803.
Dolfriog, with *engravings*, 666.
Dolmelynllyn, Vaughans of, 684.
Dolmelynllyn, Williams of, 711.
Dolwilym, *engraving* of, 221.
Dolwyddelan Castle, 335.
Donne of Picton and Cydweli, 835.
Downing, Flintshire, 423.
Drummond, Williams-, of Edwinsford, 306.
Drws Ardudwy, 664.
Dryslwyn Castle, with *view*, 256.
Du Buisson of Glynhir, 284.
Dugdale of Llwyn, 823.
Dunn of Elm Grove, 898.
Dunraven Castle, 466, 487, 524, 569.

INDEX.

Dunraven, Lord, of Dunraven, 466, 626.
Dyer, the poet, his birthplace, 217.
Dyfed (*Dimetia*), 832, 846, 848.
Dynevor of Dynevor Castle, 285.
Dyserth Castle, 453.

E.

Earls of Glamorgan, 501, 551—556.
Edeirnion, vale of, 668.
Edisbury of Bersham, 397.
Ednowain ap Bradwen, noble tribe of, 678.
Ednowain Bendew, noble tribe of, 438.
Ednyfed Fychan, his castle of Tregarnedd, 23; arms of, 390.
Edwardes, Tucker-, of Sealyham, 899.
Edward I. conquers Wales, 325—327.
Edwards (Canon) of Meifod, 823.
Edwards of Carnarvon, 351.
Edwards of Dolserrau, 702.
Edwards (Lady) of Llanerchudol, 823.
Edwards of Nanhoron, 352.
Edwards of Prysg, 684.
Edwards of Rhuddlan, 446.
Edwards, "the bridge-builder," 472.
Edwin of Englefield, noble tribe of, 438.
Efnydd, or Eunydd, noble tribe of, 391.
Eglwys-wrw, lordship of, 844.
Einion ap Cadivor ap Collwyn, 490, 495.
Eleanor, Queen, at Carnarvon, 330.
Elfin, son of Gwyddno, 674.
Eliseg, pillar of, 388.
Ellis of Rhyllech, 352.
Ellis, Williams-, of Brondanw, 702.
,, ,, of Glasfryn, 352.
England, Kings of, their power in Wales before the Conquest by Edward I., 228-9.
Englefield, name of a district, 428.
English language in Pembrokeshire, 878.
"Englishry" of Pembrokeshire, 84, 870—880.
"Englishry" of Glamorgan, 496, 505.
Erddig, with *engraving*, 370.
Eryri (Snowdon), etymology of word, 510.
Essyllwg, Essyllwyr, 483.
Evans of Brecon, 932.
Evans of Broomhall, 353.
Evans of Crickhowel, 113.
Evans of Gnoll, 585.
Evans of Highmead, 192.
Evans of Llanllechid, 353.
Evans of Llwynbarried, 923.
Evans of Lovesgrove, 195.
Evans of Nantyderry, 774.
Evans of Peterwell, 174.
Evans, Rev. Theophilus, 180.
Evans, Thomas, the Cromwellite, 174.
Evans of Upton Castle, 899.
Ewenny Abbey, 466, 523.
Ewloe, battle and castle of, 428, 435.

F.

Falconer of Usk, 775.
Earre of Dolfriog, 702.
Fenton, quoted, 839, 866, *et passim*.
Festiniog, 666.
Feudal government in Glamorgan, 497—500, 502.
Ffoulkes of Eriviatt, 406.
Ffynone (Pemb.), with *engraving*, 844.
Finch, Wynne-, of Voelas, 407.
Fisher of Llwyn-derw, 627.

Fisher of Maes-y-fron, 824.
Fitzhamon, Robert, conqueror of Glamorgan, 488—494, 551.
Fitzhamon's "twelve knights," 494.
Fitzhugh of Plas Power, 407.
Fitz-Maurice, of Plas Llwynon, 42.
Fitz-Osberne, William, 750.
Fleming, Le, of Flemingston, 563.
Fleming of St. George, &c., 563.
Flemings, supposed, of Gower, 505.
Flemings, the, of Pembrokeshire, 877.
Fletcher of Nerquis Hall, 446.
Fluellin, not Sir David Gam, 92.
Flint, the name, 421.
Flint Castle, 435.
Flintshire created a county, 421.
,, ancient and modern divisions, 422.
,, described, 422—426.
,, geology, 426.
,, high sheriffs of, 442.
,, history and antiquities, 426—437.
,, old and extinct families of, 439—442.
,, parliamentary annals of, 442.
,, population, 425.
Fortune of Leweston House, 900.
Fothergill of Abernant House, 627.
Fowler of Gnoll, 627.
Fowler, J. C., Esq., on crime in Glamorgan, 548.
Foxwist, William, 605, 610, 692.
Francis, Col. G. Grant, F.S.A., 477, 515, 545.
Francis of Cae-Bailey, 628.
Franklen of Clementston, 628.
Fronfraith, Bonsall of, 190.

G.

Gamage of Coity Castle, &c., 522, 566—569.
Games of Newton, 90.
Gam, Sir David, 91.
Gee of Denbigh, 932.
"Gelert's Grave," legend of, 675.
Geoffrey of Monmouth, 425.
Geology of Glamorgan, 479.
Gibbon of Trecastle, 583.
Gill of Brynderwen, 824.
Giraldus Cambrensis cited, 494, 501, 531.
,, ,, birthplace of, 859.
,, ,, life and character, 861.
,, ,, on Bardsey Island, 315.
,, ,, on "Merionyth," 670.
,, ,, quoted, 36, 47, 134, 147, 158, 162, 163, 165, 6, 730, 867—878.
"Glamorgan and Morganok," 503.
Glamorgan, the name, 459, 485.
,, ancient divisions of, 595.
,, ancient limits and divisions of, 595.
,, ancient manors of, 591.
,, antiquities of, 506—544.
,, described, 459—478.
,, families, British, 575.
,, ,, Norman, 551.
,, geology and mineralogy of, 479.
,, government of, under Normans, 497.
,, history of, 482—506.
,, industry and crime in, 544, 548.
,, Lords-Lieutenants of, 612.
,, magistrates of, 614.
,, Norman conquest of, 488—497.
,, old and extinct families of, 550—590.
,, parliamentary annals of, 604—612.
,, population and extent of, 459.
,, rivers and watersheds of, 460.

INDEX.

Glamorgan, sheriffs and under-sheriffs of, 597—604.
,, the district of "the hills," 461, 473.
,, "vale" of, and its mansions, 463—467.
Glanbrân Park, 216.
Glangwili, Lloyd Price of, 299.
Glansevern, with *engraving*, 802.
Glewysig, 485.
Glynllifon, with *engraving*, 315.
Glynne of Hawarden, 447.
Gogerddan, *engraving* of, 126.
Gogerddan, Pryse of, 207.
Golden Grove, 217.
Goode of Haverfordwest, 932.
Goodman of Ruthin, 395.
Goodrich of Eyarth, 408.
Gore, Ormsby-, of Glyn Hall, 703, 811.
Gough of Ynyscedwin, 114.
Gower, Bp. of St. David's, 513, 866.
Gower, etymology of name, 506.
Gower, lordship of, 503.
Gower, Flemish settlers in, 505.
Gower, peninsula of, 477.
Gower of Clynderwen, 285.
Gower of Glandovan, 900.
Gratrex of Farmwood, 775.
Green Castle (Castle Moel), 260.
Green of Court Henry, 285.
Greenhow-Relph of Beech-hill, 775.
Gregynog, with *engraving*, 804.
Gregynog, concrete cottages at, with *engraving*, 805.
Grenfell of Maesteg House, 628.
Griffith of Bryntêg, 42.
Griffith of Cefn-coch, 353.
Griffith of Glyncelyn, 114.
Griffith of Llechweddgarth, 824.
Griffith of Manor-Owen, 901.
Griffith of Merthyr, 629.
Griffith of Tanybwlch, 686.
Griffith of Wrexham, 408.
Griffiths of Llandeilo, 286.
Griffiths of Neath, 629.
Griffiths of Tynewydd.
Griffith, Trevor-, of Trevalyn Hall, 928.
Grongar Hall, *view* of, 217.
Grosmont Castle, 736.
Grove Park School, Wrexham, 930.
Gruffydd ap Cynan.
Gruffydd ap Rhys, 234.
Gruffydd of Mynydd-hywel, 176.
Gulston of Dirleton, 286.
Gunley, with *engraving*, 749.
Gunter of Tregunter, 87.
Gwaenynog, Myddelton of, 377, 414.
Gwasanau, Cooke of, 441, 445.
Gwent and Gwentllwg, 483.
Gwenwynwyn, Prince of Powys, 791.
Gwgan ap Bleddyn, ancestor of the Wogans, 867.
"Gwilliaid Cochion Mawddwy," 656.
Gwrgant, King of Glamorgan, 487.
Gwydir, with *engraving*, 313, 458.
Gwynne-Holford of Buckland, 114.
Gwynne-Holford of Cilgwyn, 289.
Gwynne of Monachdy, 195.
Gwyn of Dyffryn, 629.
Gwyn of Moelifor, 176.

H.

Hafren (Severn), legend of, 803.
Haig of Pen-ithon, 923.
Hall, Benjamin, Esq., of Hensol, 471.
Hall, Dr., of Hensol, 464.
Hamilton of Hilston Park, 775.

Hampton-Lewis, of Henllys, 45.
Hanbury of Pontypool Park, 776.
Hanmer of Hanmer, 447.
Hare of Berth-ddû, 824.
Harford of Clarbeston Grange, 933.
Harlech Castle, 662.
Harlech Mountains, 650, 663.
Haroldstone, 841.
Harries of Aberglasney, 289.
Harries of Heathfield, 901.
Harries of Hilton, 901.
Harries of Llandingat House, 308.
Harries of Trevaccoon and Rickeston Hall, 901.
Harris, Howel, 101.
Harris of Tregunter, 101.
Harvey of Haverfordwest, 933.
Havard of Pontwilym, 89.
Haverfordwest Castle, with *engraving*, 868.
Haverfordwest Priory, 869.
Haverfordwest, the name, 841.
Havod, the estate of, 127—129, 178.
Havren, legend of, 483.
Hawarden Castle, 425, 435.
Heaton of Plas Heaton, 408.
Hedd Molwynog, noble tribe of, 390.
Hendre, The, with *engravings*, 725.
Henelawe, Bp. of St. David's, 861.
Hengwrt, old mansion of, 659
Henllan in Castlemartin,
Henllan, with *engravings*, 840.
Henllys, Anglesey, with *engraving* of, 5.
Henllys, manor of, 876.
Henllys, Owen of, 843, 875, 879, *et passim*.
Henry I. in Wales, 234, *et passim*.
Henry II. in Wales, 235. ,,
Henry III. in Wales, 236. ,,
Henry V. born at Monmouth, 738.
Henry VII., lands in Wales, 243.
Hensol Castle, with an *engraving*, 464.
Herbert of Clytha, 778.
Herbert of Glanhafren, 824.
Herbert of Hafod Ychtryd, 177.
Herbert of Llanarth, 776.
Herberts of Crickhowel, 99.
Herberts, Earls of Pembroke, 851.
Herberts, Lords of Glamorgan, 556.
Herberts of Powis Castle, 794.
Hereford of Tregoyd [Tre-coed], 115.
Heriri Mons (Tommen y Mur), 320.
Heyward of Cilbronnau, 196.
Higgon of Scolton, 902
Highmead, Evans of, 192.
Highmead, *view* of, 137.
Hill of Rookwood, 630.
Hill of The Brooks, 778.
Hill-Trevor of Brynkinallt, 415.
"Hills," the, district of Glamorgan, 461, 473.
"Hirlas" Horn of Henry VII. with *engraving*, 857, 881.
History of Glamorgan, 482—506.
Holford, Gwynne, of Buckland, 114.
Holland of Berw, Arms of, 37, 42.
Holland of Glan-William, 703.
Holland of Kinmel, 396.
Holt Castle, 386.
Holywell, the name, 433.
Homfray of Glen-Usk, 778.
Homfray of Penlline Castle, 630.
Homfray of Woodlands, 933.
Hope of Marchwiel Hall, 928.
Horton of Ystrad, 290.
Howard of Broughton Hall, 448.
Howard of Soughton, 448.
Howel Dda (the Good), 229, *et passim*.

INDEX.

Howel, James, the author, 102.
Howell of Llanelwedd, 923.
Howell of Llangattock, 116.
Howell of Rhiwport, 933.
Howel Selé, slain by Glyndwr, 659.
Howel y Fwyall, Sir, 336.
Hughes, Bishop of St. Asaph, 448.
Hughes of Carmarthen, 933.
Hughes of East Bergholt, 397.
Hughes of Gwerclas, 682.
Hughes of Kinmel, 409.
Hughes of Plas Coch, 43.
Hughes of Plas Llangoed, 43.
Hughes, Ralph, arms of, and of Kinmel, 458.
Hughes of Tregib, 290.
Hughes of Wrexham, 933.
Hughes of Ystrad, 410.
Humble of Gwersyllt Park, 410.
Humfreville of Penmark, 558.
Humfrey of Llanwenarth, 778.
Humphreys of Dolarddyn, 824.
Hunter of Mount-Severn, 825.
Huxley, Professor, on earliest *vertebratæ*, 225.
Hyfeidd, a Prince of Dyfed, 229.

I.

Iestyn ap Gwrgant, 232, 488, *et passim*.
Iestynton (Eastington), 865.
Iltutus, St., cross of, 527.
Illtyd, St., 465, 527.
Insole of Ely Court, 933.
Iolo Morganwg, 483, 527.
Iron ore district of Glamorgan, 480.
Isca Silurum, 483.
Ithel Ddu, King of Glamorgan, 487.
Ivor Bach, 501, 532, 540.

J.

James of Llangollen, 410.
James of Myrtle Grove, 778.
James of Pantsaison, 902.
James of Tynewydd, 778.
Jasper Tudor, Earl of Pembroke, 851.
Jeffreys, Judge, birthplace of, 371.
Jeffreys of Gelligron, 630.
Jenkin of Swansea, 631.
Jenkins of Aberdare, 631.
Jenkins of Hensol, 586.
Jenkins of Pantirion, 902.
Jenkins of Pen'rallt, 197.
Jenkins of Pen-y-green, 825.
Jenkins of Trevigin, 903.
Jenkins of Walterston, 631.
Jennings of Gelli-deg, 290.
Jesse of Llanbedr Hall, 411.
Johnes of Dolau-Cothi, 291.
Johnes of Havod, 128, 178.
John, King, 236.
John of Monmouth, *tomb* of, 739.
Johnys, Sir Hugh, 579.
Jones-Bateman of Pentremawr, 411.
Jones, Col. Philip, 589, 606, 632.
Jones of Aberystwyth, 198, 933.
Jones of Barmouth, 704.
Jones of Blaenôs, 292.
Jones of Carmarthen, 292.
Jones of Cefn-Bryntalch, 826.
Jones of Derry-Ormond, 197.
Jones of Fonmon Castle, 631.
Jones of Fron-dderw, 704.
Jones of Gelligynan, 449.

Jones of Glandenys, 198.
Jones of Glandwr, 704.
Jones of Gwynfryn, 198.
Jones of Heartsheath, 448.
Jones of Llwyn-y-groes, 198.
Jones of Llynon, 44.
Jones of Maesygarnedd, 688.
Jones of Neuadd, Brec., 98.
Jones of Pant-glas, 292.
Jones of Pwllheli, 933.
Jones of The Priory, Wrexham, 933
Jones of Tre-Iorwerth, 44.
Jones of Ynysfawr, 704.
Jones of Ynysgain, 353.
Jones of Ystrad, 292.
Jones-Parry, escutcheon of, 364.
Jones-Parry of Llwyn-Onn, 411.
Jones-Parry of Madryn Castle, 354.
Jones-Parry of Ty-llwyd, 199.
Jones, Theophilus, Historian of Breck., 102.
Jones, Thomas, or "Twm Shon Catti," 272.
Joseph of Brecon, 104, 116.
"Jura Regalia" of the Lords Marchers, 496.
Jurisdiction of the Lords Marchers, 496.

K.

Kelly of Bryn-coch, 449.
Kenfig Castle, 520.
Kennard of Crumlin Hall, 779.
Kensington, Lord, 903.
Kilgetty, 839.
Kilymaenllwyd, Rees of, 302.
King of Presaddfed, 44.
Kings of Glamorgan after Morgan Hên, 487.
Kings of Glamorgan, residence of, 487.
Kinmel, Hughes of, *escutcheon* of, 420.
Kneeshaw of Plas-Celyn, 356.
Knight of Nottage Court, 633.
Knight of Tythegston Court, 632.
Kyffin of Bodfach, 811.

L.

Lake of Llangors (Llyn Savathan), 55.
Lampeter College, 135.
Lamphey Palace, 858, 907.
Lascelles of Pencraig, 199.
Laugharn Castle (with *view*, 254.
Lawhaden Castle (with *engraving*), name and history, 865.
Lawrence of Crick House, 779.
Lawrenny Park, 834.
Laws of Howel Dda enacted, 229.
Leach of Corston, 904.
Leach of Ivy Tower, 904
Lee of Rheola, 633.
Le Sore of St. Fagan's, 565.
Lewes of Llanllyr, 200.
Lewes of Llysnewydd, 293.
Lewis Glyn Cothi quoted, 835.
Lewis, Hampton, of Henllys, 45.
Lewis Morganwg, 514.
Lewis of Carmarthen, 933.
Lewis of Clynfyw, 905.
Lewis of Greenmeadow, 633.
Lewis of Gwinfe, 293.
Lewis of Harpton Court, 923.
Lewis of Henllan, 904.
Lewis of Llanaeron, 200.
Lewis of Llwyncelyn, 293.
Lewis of St. Pierre, 779.

INDEX.

Leucarum (Loughor), Roman station, 844.
Lhwyd, Edward, the antiquarian, 180.
Lingen of Penlanoleu, 924.
Lisburne, Lord, of Trawscoed, 201.
Llanaeron, *engraving* of, 133.
Llanaeron, Lewis of, 200.
Llanarth, Herbert of, 717.
Llanbadarn Church, *engraving* of, 161.
Llanblethian Castle, 465.
Llancarvan, Caradoc of, 529.
Llancarfan monastery, 529.
Llandaff, Bishops of, 612.
Llandaff Cathedral, with *engravings*, 467—471, 530.
Llandaff, cross at, with *engraving*, 530.
Llandaff, Oliphant, Bishop of, 613, 634.
Llandaff, See of, 530.
Llanddewi-brefi, 165.
Llandough Castle, 465.
Llandovery Castle, 259.
Llandrindod, 914.
Llanerchudol, 798, 799.
Llanfechan (or Llanvaughan), *view* of, 137.
Llanfihangel Court, 721, 783.
Llanio (*Loventium*), 154.
Llanover (Lady) of Llanover, 779.
Llanover, with *engraving*, 716.
Llanrhaiadr Hall, with *engraving*, 375.
Llanstephan Castle, siege of, 253.
Llanstephan Castle, *view* of, 251.
Llantarnam Abbey, 721.
Llantony Abbey, 737.
Llantrisant Castle, 527.
Llantwit, Major, 465, 525.
Llantwit, ancient college of, 526.
Llantwit, proposed modern college at, 526.
" Llech y Filast " cromlech, 529.
Llech-y-gawres, *cromlech* of, 153.
Lleiniog Castle, 23.
Llethr House, Jones and Thomas of, 842.
Llewellyn of Baglan Hall, 635.
Llewellyn of Court Colman, 635.
Llewelyn ap Gruffydd called to rule, 323.
Llewelyn ap Gruffydd, Prince, Death of, 70.
Llewelyn ap Gruffydd, Prince, 149, 237.
Llewelyn ap Iorwerth at Cilgerran, 873.
Llewelyn ap Iorwerth, Prince, 148, 236.
Llewelyn Bren, 535, 563.
Llewelyn of Penlle'rgaer, 635.
Llewelyn of Ynysygerwn, 635.
Llewelyn, Prince, his letter to Henry III., 671.
Llewellyn, his energy and success, 234.
Lleyn, promontory of, 315.
Lloyd, Lewis-, of Nantgwyllt, 924.
Lloyd of Aberdunant, 357.
Lloyd of Alltyrodyn, 170.
Lloyd of Bronwydd, 202.
Lloyd of Brookhouse, 933.
Lloyd of Cefngellgwm, 705.
Lloyd of Cilcen Hall, 449.
Lloyd of Cilybebyll, 635.
Lloyd of Clochfaen, 826.
Lloyd of Coedmore, 204.
Lloyd of Dinas, 117.
Lloyd of Foxhall, 393.
Lloyd of Gilfachwen, 203.
Lloyd of Glansevin, 294.
Lloyd of Hafodunos, 397.
Lloyd of Huntingdon Court, 117.
Lloyd of Maesyfelin, 172.
Lloyd of Peterwell, 175.
Lloyd of Plas-issaf, 705.
Lloyd of Rhagatt, 705.
Lloyd of Trallwyn, 357.
Lloyd of Ty'n Rhyl, 449.

Lloyd of Waunifor, 203.
Lloyd-Philipps of Dale Castle, 905.
Lloyd-Philipps of Pentypark, 905.
Lloyd, Pryce- of Pengwern, 450.
Lloyds of Castell Howel, 170.
Lloyds of Dolygelynen, 686.
Lloyds of Nantymynach, 687.
Lloyds of Rhiwaedog, 682.
Lloyds of Rhiwgoch, 685.
Llwyd, Humphrey, the historian, 394.
Llwydiarth, the ancient, 808.
Llwynynn, with *engraving*, 374.
Llys Bradwen, 678.
Llysmeirchion, with *engraving*, 378.
Llysnewydd, *with engraving*, 223.
Llywarch ap Brân, 437.
Lochmeyler (Llech-Meiler), 842.
" Lord Rhys," the, 158, 875, *et passim*.
Lordships, the twelve, of Glamorgan, 495.
Lords Marchers, 234—237.
Lords Marchers in Cardiganshire, 145-6, 147, 150.
Lords Marchers, Law-making under, 73.
Lords of Glamorgan, 501, 551—556.
Loughor Castle, 513.
Lougher of Tythegston, 577.
Loxdale of Castle Hill, 204.
Luxmoore of Bryn Asaph, 450.
Lydstep Caves, 864.
Lyell, Sir Charles, 7, 225.
Lymore, with *engraving*, 797, 8.00

M.

Machynlleth, Owen Glyndwr at, 91, 808.
Mackworth of Glen-Usk, 782.
Mackworth of Gnoll, 585.
Madocks of Llanfrynach, 96.
Madog ap Meredydd, 792.
Madryn Castle, Jones-Parry of, 354.
Madryn Castle, with *engraving*, 317.
Maelog Crwm, founder of noble tribe, 338.
Maenhirs in Carnarvonshire, 337.
Maen Llythyrog, 544.
" Maen y Morwynion," 80.
Maesllwch Castle, 913.
Maesmynan, a seat of Prince Llewelyn, 323, 429.
Maesyfelin, legend of, 173.
Maesyneuadd, old family of, 683.
Maesypandy, old family of, 683.
Mainwaring of Galltfaenan, 412.
Malefant of St. George's, 574.
Mallwyd, 653.
Malpas Court, with *engraving*, 721.
Manoravon, Pugh of, 302.
Manorbier Castle, with *engravings*, 859-86.
Manors of Glamorgan, 591.
Mansel of Maesdeilo, 296.
Mansels of Penrice, Margam, &c., 509, 517—20.
Marchudd ap Cynan, noble tribe of, 390.
Marchweithian, noble tribe of, 391.
Margam Abbey, with *engravings*, 517.
Margam Abbey, Mansels of, tombs of, 519.
Maridunum, Carmarthen, 261.
Marloes, 834.
Marshall, W., Earl of Pembroke, 851, 873.
Marten, Henry, 752.
Martin de Tours, 874.
Martin, Sir William, 875.
Massy of Cottesmoor, 906.
Mathafarn, Henry VII. at, 807.
Mathew of Llandaff, &c., 578-9.
Mathew of Wern, 357.

INDEX.

Mathias of Lamphey, 907.
Mathrafael, royal seat, 79.
Maurice of Ruthin, 412.
Mawddach, estuary of, 660.
McDonnell of Plasnewydd, 782.
Mediolanum, Roman station of, 791.
Meirion, the cantref of, 651.
Menhirs in Anglesey, 18.
Merioneth, the name, 649.
,, created a county, 649.
,, description of, 649—669.
,, population of, 650.
,, history and antiquities of, 669—677.
,, magistrates of, 698.
,, geology of, 677.
,, old and extinct families of, 679.
,, high sheriffs of, 689—694.
,, lord lieutenants of, 694.
,, parliamentary annals of, 696.
Merlin, or Myrddin, 227.
Merthyr Tydfil, centre of "Black Country," 473.
Mesham of Pontryffydd, 450.
Meyrick of Bodorgan, 45.
Meyrick of Bush, 907.
Meyrick of Ucheldref, 684.
Meyrick, Rees, his *Morganiæ Archeogr.*, 539, 588.
Middleton Hall, Abadam of, 218, 280.
Milford Haven, 833, 836, 850.
Millar of Penrhos, 357.
Mining companies, early, in Glamorgan, 545.
Miskin Manor, 464.
Mitchell of Llanfrechfa Grange, 782.
Moat, lordship of, 842.
Mold Castle, 436.
Monachdy, *engraving* of, 132.
Monachdy, Gwynne of, 195.
Monmouth Bridge, with *engraving*, 738.
Monmouth, name of, 715.
Monmouthshire, ancient division, 715.
,, description of, 715—725.
,, population of, 715.
,, geology of, 727.
,, history and antiquities of, 728—754.
,, a part of Wales, 755—759.
,, high sheriffs of, 759—764.
,, parliamentary annals of, 764.
,, magistrates of, 767.
Môn, name of Anglesey, 1.
Montgomery, Arnulf de, 850.
Montgomery Castle, 789, 800.
Montgomery, the name, 789.
"Montgomeryshire Collections," 794.
Montgomeryshire made a county, 790, 801.
,, situation and extent of, 790.
,, population of, 790.
,, described, 790—809.
,, geological structure, 809.
,, old and extinct families, 810.
,, high sheriffs of, 811.
,, parliamentary annals, 816.
,, county magistrates of, 819.
,, watersheds and rivers of, 790.
,, ancient inhabitants, 791.
,, ancient divisions of, 798.
"Morfa Rhuddlan," 427.
Morgan Hên, 486.
Morgan Mwynfawr, 485.
Morgan of Aberystwyth, 205.
Morgan of Bolgoed, 117.
Morgan of Defynog, 97.
Morgan of Hengwrt-uchaf, 705.
Morgan of Llandudno, 358.
Morgan of Rhyl, 450.
Morgan of Ruperra Castle, 636.

Morgan of St. Helen's, 636.
Morgan of Taltreuddyn, 688.
Morgan of Tegfynydd, 907.
Morgan of The Friars, 782.
Morlais Castle, 539.
Morris of Blaenywern, 205.
Morris of Bryn-Myrddin, 297.
Morris of Cwm (or Coom), 297.
Morris of Sketty, 636.
Morris of Sketty Park, 637.
Mortimers of Coedmor and Geneu'rglyn, 169.
Mostyn, Baron, of Mostyn Hall, 451.
Mostyn, etymology of, 428.
Mostyn Hall, 423.
Mostyn of Talacré, 452.
Moulsdale of Bryndyffryn, 412.
Mount-Severn, with *engraving*, 807.
Murchison, Sir Roderick, 7, 480, 809,
Myddelton-Biddulph of Chirk Castle, 412.
Myddelton of Gwaenynog, 414.
Myddelton, Sir Hugh, 370.
Myddelton, Sir Thomas, 369.
Mynors of Barland, 924.
Mynors of Evancoed, 924.
Mytton of Dinas Mawddwy, 688,
Mytton of Garth, 826.
"Myvyrian Archaiology of Wales"—the division of Wales in, 596, 798, 801.

N.

Names of places in Pembrokeshire, 880.
Nannau, seat of the Vaughans, 659.
Nanney of Bronwylfa, 452.
Nanney of Gwynfryn, 358.
Nanneys of Cefndeuddwr, 685.
Nanneys of Nannau, 680.
Nanteos, *engraving* of, 130.
Nanteos, Powell of, 130, 206.
Nantyderry, with *engraving*, 719.
Narberth, castle and town, with *engraving*, 865.
Nationality and language in Pemb., 877.
Naylor of Leighton Hall, 826.
Neath Abbey, with *engravings*, 513.
Neath Castle, with *engraving*, 515.
Neath, Vale of, 474.
Neave of Llys-dulas, 46.
Nefydd Hardd, founder of noble tribe, 338.
Nerquis Hall, Fletcher of, 423, 446.
Nesta, princess, 146, 852.
Nevern, castle of, 876.
Nevern, vale of, 844.
Neville, Richard, his wealth and splendour, 555.
Nevill of Westfa, 297.
Nevilles, Lords of Glamorgan, 555.
Newborough, Baron, of Glynllifon, 358.
Newcastle Emlyn, the Castle, 137.
Newmarch, his Conquest of Brecknockshire, 66.
Newport Castle, with *engraving*, 732.
Newton, Games of, 90; *View* of, 91.
Newton Nottage, Knight of, 523.
Newtown Hall, 806.
Newtown, the name, 806.
Newport Castle (Pemb.), 874.
Newport (Pemb.), Norman charter to, 875.
Nicholas, Gruffydd ap, 240.
Nicholas, Lord of Cemmaes, 237.
Nicholas of Trenyfed, 843.
Nicholas, St., cromlech of, 529.
Nicholl of Ham, 637.
Nicholl of Merthyr Mawr, 638.
Nidum (Neath), Roman station of, 484.

INDEX.

Noble tribes of North Wales, 337, 390, 437, 678.
Norman conquest of Breconshire, 66.
Norman conquest of Glamorgan, 488—497.
Norman families in Glam., their total extinction, 550.
Normans in Anglesey, 12.
Norman policy in Wales, 491.
Norman rule in Breconshire, 72.
Normans, the, in Anglesey, 12; in Brecknock, 72; in Cardiganshire, 145; in Carmarthenshire, 232; Carnarvonshire, 321; in Denbighshire, 381; in Flintshire, 428; in Glamorgan, 488; in Merioneth, 670; in Monmouthshire, 733; in Pembrokeshire, 17, 847.
Normans, the, struggles of the Welsh against, 321.
Norris of Penlline, 573.

O.

Oakeley of Plas Tanybwlch, 668, 706.
Offa of Mercia invades Flintshire, 427.
Offa's Dyke in Denbighshire, 388.
Offa's Dyke in Flintshire, 437.
Offa's Dyke in Denbighshire, 388.
Offa's Dyke in Montgomeryshire, 791.
Ogham Stone near Crickhowel, 80.
Ogham Stone of Llanfechan, 155.
Ogham Stone of St. Dogmael's, 847.
Ogmore Castle, 522.
Oldfield of Ffarm, 414.
"Orinda," Catherine Philips, 180.
Orlandon, 835.
Owain Glyndwr at Carmarthen, 249.
Owain Gwynedd defeats Henry II., 13, 428.
Owen Brogyntyn, 668, 679.
Owen Brogyntyn, his lineage, 792.
Owen Cyfeiliog, his lineage, 792.
Owen (George) of Henllys, 60, 843, 875, 879.
Owen Glyndwr's alleged birthplace, 842.
Owen Glyndwr, 386-7, 669.
Owen of Dolgelley, 681.
Owen of Gadlys, 47.
Owen of Glansevern, 826.
Owen of Haulfre, 47.
Owen of Haverfordwest, 934.
Owen of Orielton, 907.
Owen of Rhiwsaeson, 811.
Owen of Rhyllon, 452.
Owen of Withybush, 908.
Owen Tudyr of Penmynydd, 29.
Oxwich Castle, 511.
Oystermouth Castle, 512.

P.

Paget of Plas Llanfair, 47.
Panton of Holyhead, 47.
Pantygwydir, with *engraving*, 476.
Parry of Llwynynn, *arms* of, &c., 374.
Parry of Nantgwynant, 3, 59.
Parry of Ruthin, 395.
Parys Mountain and mines, 8.
Pater-church, 836, 893.
Paxton Tower, 219.
Paynter of Maesllwyn, 47.
Pebydiog, 849.
Peel of Bryn-y-pys, 452.
Peel of Glanafon, 908.
Pemberton of Plas-issa, 453.
Pembroke Castle, with *engraving*, 849—852.
Pembroke, Earls of, 851.
Pembroke, etymology of name, 833, 836.
Pembrokeshire, situation and extent, 832.
  „   a county *palatine*, 855.
  „   ancient divisions of, 848.
  „   description of, 832—845.
Pembrokeshire, geology of, 845.
  „   high sheriffs of, 881.
  „   history and antiquities of, 846—877.
  „   population of, 833.
  „   nationality and language in, 877.
Pencelli Forest, 844.
Pencoed Castle, with *engraving*, 733.
Peniarth, with *engraving*, 651—653.
Penlline Castle, 465, 528.
Penllyn, cantref of, 668, 672.
Pennant of Brynbella, 453.
Pennard Castle, with *engraving*, 511.
Penrhyn, Baron, of Penrhyn Castle, 359.
Penrhyn Castle, with *engraving*, 311.
Penrhyn, Griffith of, 41, 311, 362.
Penrhys monastery, 538.
Penrice Castle, Mansel-Talbot of, 478, 510, 641.
Penrice Castle, with *engraving*, 509.
Penrice of Kilvrough, 638.
Penry, John, the Martyr, 102.
Pentremawr, with *engraving*, 379.
Pen-y-bont, Radnor, 914.
Perfedd-wlad, what, 381.
Perrott of Brynhyddon, 827.
Perrott, Stephen, Lord of Narberth, 865.
Philipps, Lloyd-, of Mabus, 206.
Philipps of Carmarthen, 934.
Philipps of Cwmgwili, 297.
Philipps of Dale Castle, 905.
Philipps of Penty Park, 905.
Philipps of Picton Castle, 908.
Philipps of Ystradwrallt, 298.
Philips of Abbey Cwm-hir, 925.
Philips, Catherine, "Orinda," 180.
Philips of Gwernvale, 117.
Philips of Hendrefechan, 688.
Philips of Rhual, 453.
Philips, Sir Thomas, de Picton, 835.
Phillpps, Sir Thomas, the late, cited, 534 *et passim*.
Phillips of Aberystwyth, 206.
Phillips' Hist. of Cilgerran, 874.
Phillips, Lort, of Lawrenny Park, 909.
Phillips of Bolahaul, 934.
Pickmere of The Mount, 826.
Picton Castle, with *engraving*, 834.
Pierce of Denbigh, 934.
Pilkington of Downing, &c., 453.
Plas Crug Castle, 159.
Plas Dinas Mawddwy, with *engravings*, 654—657.
Plas-newydd, Llangollen, 371.
Platt of Bryn-y-neuadd, 360.
Platt of Gorddinog, 360.
Plumstone Mountain, 833.
Pont Aberglaslyn, 666.
Pontryffydd, with *engraving*, 378.
Pontypridd Bridge, with *engraving*, 472.
Popkin of Ynystawe, 584.
Population of Glamorgan, 459.
Portmadoc, 664.
Potts of Glanrafon, 454.
Powel, Dr. David, the historian, 397.
Powell of Aberclydach, 118.
Powell of Haverfordwest, 934.
Powell of Llanharan, &c., 588.
Powell of Maesgwynne, 299.
Powell of Nanteos, 206.
Powis Castle, with *engravings*, 793—798.
Powis (Earl) of Powis Castle, 827.
Powys Fadog, 792.
Powys of Cymmer, 685.
Powys Wenwynwyn, 791.
Powys Wenwynwyn, ancient divisions of, 798.
Poyer, Col., 754.

Poyntz Castle, 842.
Poyston, Picton of, 841.
Precelly Top, 833, 843.
Pre-historic monuments of Ardudwy, 661.
Prendergast, 841.
Presaddfed, Lewis of, 28 ; King of, 44.
Preston of Llwyn-ynn, 414.
Price of Abermarlais Park, 300.
Price of Castle Madoc, 118.
Price of Castle Pigyn, 301.
Price of Corsygarnedd, 687.
Price of Esgaer-weddan, 686.
Price of Gellihir, 589.
Price of Glangwili, 299.
Price of Newton Hall, 810.
Price of Norton Manor, 925.
Price of Penlle'rgaer, 584.
Price of Rhiwlas, 706.
Price, Sir John, of Brecon, 111.
Pritchard of Ceniarth, 828.
Prichard of Crofta House, 638.
Prichard of Dinam, 48.
Prickard of Dderw, 925.
Prickard of New Radnor, 925.
Priories of Cardiff, 543.
Protheroe of Dolwilym, 301.
Prothero of Malpas Court, 782.
Pryce of Cyfronydd, 829.
Pryce of Dyffryn, 638.
Pryce of Gunley, 829.
Pryse of Bwlchbychan, 209.
Prys, Edmund, of Tyddyn-du, 689.
Pryse of Gogerddan, 207.
Pryse of Peithyll, 207.
Prysg, Edwards of, 684.
Pughe of Brynawel, 706.
Pugh of Abermaide, 210.
Pugh of Manoravon, 302.
Pugh of Mathavarn, 810.
Puleston of Emral, 454.

R.

Race admixture in Glamorgan,
Radir, old mansion of, 471, 485.
Radnor, the name, 912.
,, made a county, 912.
,, situation and population of, 912.
,, forest and hills of, 913.
,, the Romans in, 915.
,, high sheriffs of, 915.
,, parliamentary annals of, 919.
Radnor, " New and Old," 914, 915.
Raglan Castle, with *engravings*, 741—745.
Raglan of Carnllwyd, 572.
Raglan (Lord) of Cefn-tilla, 783.
Ramsay, Prof., on rocks of N. Wales, 318, 809.
Ravenscroft of Bretton, 440.
Rayle, De, of Wrinston, 573.
Rees of Carnarvon, 934.
Rees of Kilymaenllwyd, 302.
Rees of Scoveston, 934.
Rees of Tonn, 303.
Reveley of Bryn-y-gwin, 707.
Rhayader Castle, 915.
Rhianva, Lady Williams of, 50.
Rhirid Flaidd, 678.
Rhiwport, 802.
Rhiwsaeson, 807.
Rhodri the Great, 11, 143, 228.
Rhos-market, 842.
Rhuddlan Castle, with *engraving*, 430.
Rhuddlan Marsh, battle and air of, 427.

Rhuddlan Monastery, 432.
Rhûg, with *engraving*, 669.
Rhymney River, 726.
Rhys ap Gruffydd—" the Lord Rhys," 235.
Rhys ap Tewdwr, 232, 233.
Rhys ap Tewdwr and Glamorgan, 489-90.
Rhys ap Thomas, Sir, 240—244. 854, 857.
Rhys, Dr. John David, 539.
Rhys Prichard, " the Vicar,"
Rhys, the Lord, 148, *et passim.*
Richards of Brooklands, 639.
Richards of Caerynwch, 707.
Richardes of Bryneithin, 210.
Richardes of Penglais, 210.
Richardson of Corwen, 708.
Richardson of Glanrafon, 639.
Richardson of Pant-y-Gwydir, 639.
Richmond, Earl of, lands in Wales, 243.
Rickeston, Brawdy, 842.
Robert Curthose, his imprisonment, 541.
Robert of Gloucester, Lord of Glamorgan, 551.
Roberts of Aberystwyth, 934.
Roberts of Coed-du, 456.
Roberts of Milford, 909.
Roberts of Plas-Gwyn, 415.
Robertson of Crogen, or Palé, 708.
Roch Castle, 870.
Roch of Butterhill, 910.
Roch of Paskeston, 910.
Rodney of Llanfihangel Court, 783.
Rogers of Abermeurig, 210.
Rolls of Croft-y-Bwla, 785.
Rolls of The Hendre, 784.
Roman Conquest of Breconshire, 61, 79.
Roman Roads in Breconshire, 79.
Romans, the, in Anglesey, 9 ; in Breconshire, 61. 79 in Cardiganshire, 143, 154 ; in Carmarthenshire, 226, 248 ; in Carnarvonshire, 319, 336 ; in Denbighshire, 381 ; in Flintshire, 427 ; in Glamorgan, 483 ; in Merioneth, 670 ; in Monmouth, 674 ; in Montgomery, 791 ; in Pembrokeshire, 847.
Romilly of Porth-Kerry, 640.
Rosindale of Foxhall, 393.
Roskell of Stockyn, 456.
Rous of Courtyrala, 640.
Rowland of Wrexham, 934.
Rowlands of Carmarthen, 934.
Rowlands of The Grove, Wrexham, 934.
Royal Institution of South Wales, 477.
Ruck of Pant-lludw, 708.
Rudds of Castell Moel, 261.
Rufus not the conqueror of Glamorgan, 490.
Ruthin Castle, ancient, 383.
Ruthin Castle, modern, with *engravings*, 372.

S.

Sabrina, legend of, 803.
Salmon of Penlline Court, 640.
Salusburys of Lleweni, 392.
Samson, Archbishop of Dol, 527.
Sarn Badrig, 677.
Sarn Helen (*Via Maritima*), 675.
Sarn Helen, 79, 847.
Sartoris of Llangenech, 304.
Saunders of Glanrhydw, 928.
Saurin of Orielton, 910.
Saxon period in Glamorgan, 484.
Saxons in Anglesey, 10.
Scotsborough, 839, 862.
Scourfield of Williamston, 910.
Scurlage Castle, 513.
Severn, the river, 790, 803.

INDEX.

Severn, origin of name, 483.
Seal of Carmarthen, *Chancery*, 245, 855.
Sealyham, Tucker-Edwards, of, 899.
Segontium of the Romans, 309, 320, 336.
Senghennydd (Caerphilly), 495, 533—539.
Seys of Boverton, 581.
Sharpe of Glaslyn Court, 119.
Silures, the, of the Romans, 483, 575.
Sir Rhys ap Thomas's letter to the king, 241.
Sir Rhys ap Thomas, march to Bosworth Field, 243, 857.
Sir Rhys ap Thomas, tournament at Carew Castle, 857-9.
Skyrrid (Sugar-loaf) Mountain, 719, 784.
Slebech, 835.
Smith of Gwernllwynwith, 640.
Snowdon (Eryri), 310.
Squire of Swansea, 641.
Stackpool, 836.
Stack Rocks, 837.
Stanley, A. P., Dean of Westminster, 48.
Stanley of Penrhos, 48.
St. Asaph Cathedral, with *engraving*, 424.
St. Asaph, Hughes, Bishop of, 448.
St. David's Cathedral, 848.
St. David's, Thirlwall, Bishop of, 304.
St. Dogmael's Ogham Stone, 847.
St. Dogmael's Monastery, 877.
St. Donat's Castle, with *engraving*, 465, 524.
St. Florence, Pemb.
St. Gowan's Well, 839.
St. Hilary, Traherne of, 465.
St. John of Fonmon Castle, 558.
St. Quintin of Llanblethian, 564.
Stedmans of Strata Florida, 168.
Stephen Bauson, defeated, 238.
Sterry of Danycoed, 641.
Stones, inscribed, 154.
Stradlings, the, of St. Donat's, 559.
Strata Florida Abbey, 162—164.
Strongbow, Gilbert de, 748.
Stuart, Crichton-, of Cardiff, 641.
Sudeley (Baron) of Gregynog &c., 830.
Sugar-loaf (Skyrrid) Mountain, 719.
Swansea Castle, with *engraving*, 512.
Swansea, copper-smelting at, 545.
Swansea, early mining companies at, 545.
Swansea, common seal of, 618.
Swansea, mayors and portreeves of, 616.
Swansea, Cromwell's charter to, 618.
"Symond's Yat," 725.
Syward of Talyfan, 565.

T

Taff Vale, 467.
Tancred, or Tankard, Fitz, of Haverfordwest, 868.
Talbot of Hensol, 464.
Talbot, Mansel-, of Margam Park, 641.
Taliesin's Grave, 152.
Talley Monastery, 261.
Talybont, comot of, 651—653.
Talybont, seat of Prince Llewelyn at, 653, 671.
Taylor, Jeremy, at Golden Grove, 217.
Tegeingl, the old name, 421, 425, 428.
"Teilo and Dewi," 486.
Teivi, the river and vale of, 134, 138.
Tenby, with *engraving*, 837.
Tenby Castle and walls, with *engravings*, 862.
Tenby memorial to Prince Consort, *engraving*, 838.
Thelwalls of Plas-yn-Ward, 394.
Thirlwall, Lord Bishop of St. David's, 304.
Thomas of Carmarthen, 935.
Thomas of Coedhelen, 360.
Thomas of Court House, 642.
Thomas of Danygralg, 587.

Thomas of Gurrey, 304.
Thomas of Llanbradach, 586.
Thomas of Llanfihangel, 583.
Thomas of Llanon, 305.
Thomas of Llan-Thomas, 120.
Thomas of Llwyn-Madoc, 119.
Thomas of Llethr House, 842.
Thomas of Newport, 910.
Thomas of Pwllywrach, 642.
Thomas of Tregroes, 642.
Thomas of Trevor, 49.
Thomas of Wellfield, 925.
Thomas of Wenvoe Castle, 587.
Thruston of Pennal Tower, 710.
Thruston of Talgarth Hall, 709.
Tibia amnis (Caerau), Roman station, 484.
Tintern Abbey, with *engravings*, 746—749.
Tomb of Sir Rhys ap Thomas, 244.
Tommen y Mur (*Heriri Mons*), 320.
Tottenham of Plas Berwyn, 415.
Tournament at Carew Castle, 857.
Towy, river and vale of, 214.
Tracy, Hanbury —, of Gregynog, 830.
Traherne, Mrs., of St. Hilary, 643.
Traherne of St. Hilary, 643.
Trawscoed, or Crosswood, *view* of, 129.
Tredegar (Lord) of Tredegar Park, 785.
Tredegar Park, 722.
Trefgarn, 842.
Tregaian, Battle-field of, 37.
Tregaian, Lloyd of, 45.
Trelech cromlech, 745.
Trellwyn (Trefloyne) Ap Owen of, 862.
Trenyfed, Nicholas of, 843.
Tre-Owain, Mon., 718.
Trevor of Brynkinallt (see *Hill Trevor*), 415.
Trevor of Trevalyn, 393.
Trevor-Roper of Plas-teg, 457.
Trewent of Pembroke, 935.
Triley Court, with *engraving*, 720.
Troy House, with *engraving*, 723.
Tudyr of Berain, 393.
Tudors, origin of, in Anglesey, 29.
Turberville of Coity, 557.
Turbervill of Ewenny Abbey, 644.
Turner of Parkia, 361.
Turner of Plas Brereton, 361.
Twelve knights, the, settlements of, 494.
"Twm Shôn Catti," 272.
Ty-Glyn, *engraving* of, 131.
Tyler of Cottrell, 644.
Tyler of Llantrithyd, 644.
Tynte of Keven Mably, 645.
Tythegstone Court, 467.

U

Union of Wales with England, Act of, 111.
Union of Wales with England, 111, 327, 756.
University College for Wales, proposal, 140, 526, 931.
Upton Castle with, *engraving*, 836.
Usk Castle, 745.

V

Vale of Clwyd, 377.
Valle Crucis Abbey, 387.
Vane (Earl) of Plas Machynlleth, 831.
Van of Marcross, 582.
Vaughan, Henry, "Silurist," 102.
Vaughan (Lisburne), of Trawscoed, 201.
Vaughan of Brynog, 210.
Vaughan of Builth, 926.
Vaughan of Cynghordy, 305, 928.

Vaughan of Llansantffraed, 926.
Vaughan of Llwydiarth, 808, 810.
Vaughans of Cors-y-gedol, 680.
Vaughans of Nannau, 681, 710.
Vaughans of Llanuwchllyn, 684.
Vaughans of Trebarried, 95.
Vaughans of Tretower, 94.
Vaynor Park, with *engraving*, 801.
Venables of Clyro, 926.
Venables of Llysdinam Hall, 926.
Venat Silurum (Caerwent), 729.
Via Flandrica, the, 847.
Via Julia, 79.
Vivian of Clyné Castle, 646.
Vivian of Glanafon, 645.
Vivian of Park Wern, 646.
Vivian of Plas Gwyn, 49.
Vincent, Dean, of Bangor, 361.
Vipont, Robert de, 793.

W

Walbeoffe of Llanhamlach, 87.
Wales, higher education in, 930.
Wales in the ninth century, 229.
Wales, proposed University College for, 140, 526, 931.
Wales, union of, with England, 111, 327, 756.
Walter of Ffynone, 646.
Walker of Castleton, 786.
Walters of Haverfordwest, 910.
Walters of Rhos-market, 842.
Warren of Carmarthen, 935.
Warwick the "king-maker," 555.
Waters of Sarnau, 305.
Watkins of Lloegyr Fawr, 120.
Watkins of Llwynybrain, 305.
Watt, James, the great engineer, 927.
Watt of Doldowlod, 926.
Watt's Dyke, 388, 437.
Wayne of Cae-Nest, 710.
Wells of Penally, 935.
Welsh, distress of the, under Henry III., 323.
"Welsherie" and "Englisherie" in Glamorgan, 496·
"Welshery," 849, 878.
Welsh, their feudal subjection, 228.
West of Ruthin Castle, 416.
Whalley of Plas Madoc, 416.
White Castle, 737.
White of Tenby, 838, 910.
Whitland Abbey, 261.
"Will Goch" of Mawddwy, 688.
William de Londres, 249.
William Rufus and conquest of Glamorgan, 490, 492—494.
William the Conqueror at St. David's, 491.
Williames, Buckley —, of Pennant, 831.
Williames, Buckley —, of Glanhafren, 831.
Williams, Archd., 180, 935.
Williams-Bulkeley of Baron Hill, 361.
Williams-Drummond of Edwinsford, 306.
Williams, Hanbury-, of Nantoer, 786.
Williams, Lady, of Rhianva, 50.
Williams of Abercamlais, 120.
Williams of Aberpergwm, 647.
Williams of Aberyskir, 120.

Williams of Bassaleg, 786.
Williams of Bodelwyddan, 457.
Williams of Bryngwyn, 830.
Williams of Bryntirion, 927.
Williams of Carmarthen, 935.
Williams of Cefn, 364.
Williams of Craig-y-don, 50.
Williams of Denbigh, 935.
Williams of Deudraeth Castle, 711.
Williams of Dolmelynllyn, 711.
Williams of Dyffryn Ffrwd, 647.
Williams of Gellewig, 361.
Williams of Gwernyfed, 94.
Williams of Llandaff, 648.
Williams of Llanfaelog, 50.
Williams of Llanfechain, 831.
Williams of Llangibby Castle, 787.
Williams of Menai-fron, 51.
Williams of Merryvale, 911.
Williams of Miskin Manor, 647.
Williams of Penpont, 121.
Williams of the Friars, 364.
Williams of Treffos, 49.
Williams of Vronwnion, 711.
Williams of Wrexham, 417.
Williams, W., Esq., M.P. (the late), his legacy, 931.
Willis of Monmouth, 935.
Windsore, Gerald de, 851, 852.
Winifred's Well, 433.
Wiston Castle, 867.
Wogans of Boulston, 834.
Wogans of Picton, 833.
Wogans of Wiston, 867.
Wood of Stouthall, 648.
Woollett of Monmouth, 935.
Woollett of Newport, 935.
Worcester (Marquess), of Troy House, 787.
Wye, the river, 723, 725.
Wyn of Moel-iwrch, 396.
Wynne-Finch of Voelas, 407.
Wynne of Coed-coch, 418.
Wynne of Garthewin, 417.
Wynn of Garth, 811.
Wynn of Tower, 440.
Wynn, Sir John, of Gwydir, 313.
Wynn, Williams-, of Wynnstay, 418.
Weyriver, the, in Radnor, 913.
Wynne of Peniarth, 651, 689, 712.
Wynn of Bodtalog, 688.
Wynn of Pengwern, 686.
Wynn of Rhûg, 712.
Wynn of Glyn, 683.
Wynnstay, with *engravings*, 366, 367.

Y

Yale of Plas yn Yale, 419.
Yelverton of Whitland Abbey, 307.
Yorke of Brynllwyd, 51.
Yorke of Dyffryn Aled, 419.
Yorke of Erddig, 420, 928.
Ystrad-fflur, Abbey of, 162.
Ystrad Marchell Abbey, 800.
Ystrad Tywi, 847.
Ystwyth, valley of the, 127.